Songs
of the Theater

Songs of the Theater

RICHARD LEWINE AND ALFRED SIMON

THE H. W. WILSON COMPANY

NEW YORK   1984

Printed in the United States of America

Library of Congress Cataloging in Publication Data

Lewine, Richard.
    Songs of the theater.
    Includes indexes.
    1. Musical revues, comedies, etc.—Excerpts—
Bibliography. 2. Music, Popular (Songs, etc.)
United States—Bibliography.
I. Simon, Alfred, 1922-   . II. Title.
ML128.S3L55 1984   016.78281   84-13068

CONTENTS

PREFACE

THE THEATER SONG, that distinctly American institution, had its beginnings just before the turn of the century. There was no exact moment, or even year, of its birth; the arrival was gradual, an emergence from various roots: European operetta, English and American music hall songs, and those illustrious ancestors, Gilbert and Sullivan. As new rhythmic forms began to appear, with harmonies that were fresh, even daring, for popular songs, lyricists were finding topics that were more interesting and original to write about than the moon, girls' names and mother. George Gershwin, then twenty-three years old, was to write, on first hearing the music of Jerome Kern: "...it made me conscious that most popular music was of inferior quality and that musical comedy music was made of better material." Theater music and lyrics have come a very long way indeed since those early days, but clearly the way had been paved for a new and important American art form.

Logically enough, many of the composers in this new idiom were well-grounded musicians: John Philip Sousa, Victor Herbert and Jerome Kern among them. Especially prominent was Reginald De Koven, composer of *Robin Hood* in 1891, America's first successful and enduring theater piece. It is with this work that our listings begin, spanning the ninety-two years from then until Stephen Sondheim's *Sunday In the Park With George* at the end of 1983.

In the early period *Songs of the Theater* lists all the important shows and scores of the era, the balance of our musical stage at the time still being devoted to vaudeville and imported operetta. Beginning with the mid-teens the book includes the songs from virtually every theater piece seen on Broadway, "Broadway" being the term for New York's legitimate stage, and not an exact geographic area. Off-Broadway shows that ran for fifteen or more performances, or that are of unusual interest, are also listed as are film and television songs by theater composers and lyricists, songs we feel very much belong in this book.

Our earlier books on the subject were straightforward compilations of shows and their scores. *Encyclopedia of Theatre Music* covered the period through 1960 and included only songs which had been published; *Songs of the American Theater* went through 1971 and listed both published and unpublished songs. This volume is far more complete, going back to what we consider the beginnings of our musical theater. It also includes notes with further detail about the songs, the productions, and the authors, notes we hope will prove useful and interesting.

We wish especially to thank Stanley Green. His assistance to us was generous and invaluable.

Richard Lewine
Alfred Simon

EDITORIAL NOTE

SONGS OF THE THEATER is divided into two major sections: a Song section and a Show section.

The Song section contains some 17,000 titles. Each entry gives the names of the composer and lyricist, the name of the show in which the song was performed and the year the show opened on, or off, Broadway. The symbol OB indicates an Off-Broadway production, and the symbols F and TV indicate that the song was in a film or television production.

The Show section lists the stage productions with the opening date in New York, the composer, the lyricist and the songs in the score on opening night. The notes in the Show section relate only to the show as a whole and not to individual songs, but an asterisk beside a song title indicates that a note about that song can be found in the Song section. A record album of a score is indicated by RA, piano vocal scores by VS and vocal selections (paper-bound folios of a show's principal songs) by SEL. Shows that are essentially presentations of songs from another, earlier, show are not listed.

There are three other parts to the book: a Chronology of stage productions year by year in the order in which they opened; an Index of the film and television productions in which the songs in this book appeared; and an Index of Composers, Lyricists, and Authors of underlying works, and others mentioned in the book.

Songs

Songs

A-1 March
Music and lyrics by Stephen Sondheim
Anyone Can Whistle 1964

A la Viennese
Music by H. Maurice Jacquet
Lyrics by William Brady
The Silver Swan 1929

A Toujours
Music by Frederick Loewe
Lyrics by Alan Jay Lerner
Gigi (1957) F

A-B-C
Music by Elmer Bernstein
Lyrics by Carolyn Leigh
How Now, Dow Jones 1967

The A.B.C. Song
Music and lyrics by Leslie Bricusse
and Anthony Newley
Stop the World—I Want to Get Off 1962

A.B.C.'s
Music by Mark Bucci
Lyrics by David Rogers
New Faces of 1962

The ABC's of Success
Music by David Baker
Lyrics by Sheldon Harnick
Smiling, the Boy Fell Dead (OB) 1961

Abandon
Music and lyrics by Ida Hoyt Chamberlain
Enchanted Isle 1927

Abbondanza
Music and lyrics by Frank Loesser
The Most Happy Fella 1956

Abe Lincoln
Music and lyrics by Earl Robinson
and Alfred Hayes
Hellzapoppin 1938

Abie Baby
Music by Galt MacDermot
Lyrics by Gerome Ragni and James Rado
Hair 1968

Abou Ben Adhem
Music and lyrics by Ray Golden
Alive and Kicking 1950

About Face
Music by Gerald Marks
Lyrics by Sam Lerner
Hold It! 1948

Abracadabra
Music and lyrics by Cole Porter
Mexican Hayride 1944

Abraham
Music and lyrics by Irving Berlin
Holiday Inn (1942) F

Absinthe Frappé
Music by Victor Herbert
Lyrics by Glen MacDonough
It Happened in Nordland 1904

The Absolute Last Supper
Music by Scott Killian and Kim D. Sherman
Lyrics by Kenneth Robins, Scott Killian
and Kim D. Sherman
Lenny and the Heartbreakers (OB) 1983

Abuse
Music and lyrics by Scott Joplin
Treemonisha 1975

Written in 1909

1

Academic Fugue
Music and lyrics by Bob Merrill
Henry, Sweet Henry 1967

Ac-cent-tchu-ate the Positive
Music by Harold Arlen
Lyrics by Johnny Mercer
Here Come the Waves (1944) F

According to Dr. Holt
Music by Jerome Kern
Lyrics by Herbert Reynolds
Rock-a-Bye Baby 1918

According to Mr. Grimes
Music by George Gershwin
Lyrics by Ira Gershwin
Treasure Girl 1928

According to Plotnik
Music by Sol Berkowitz
Lyrics by James Lipton
Miss Emily Adam (OB) 1960

Ace in the Hole
Music and lyrics by Cole Porter
Let's Face It! 1941

Ace of Spades
Music and lyrics by Frank Marcus
and Bernard Maltin
Bamboola 1929

Aces Up
Music by William Heagney
Lyrics by William Heagney and Tom Connell
There You Are 1932

Acorn in the Meadow
Music and lyrics by Richard Adler
and Jerry Ross
John Murray Anderson's Almanac (1953)

Across the Sea
Music by George Gershwin
Lyrics by B.G. DeSylva and E. Ray Goetz
George White's Scandals (1922)

Act Like a Lady
Music by Robert Waldman
Lyrics by Alfred Uhry
Here's Where I Belong 1968

The Actress Hasn't Learned
Music by Andrew Lloyd Webber
Lyrics by Tim Rice
Evita 1979

The Ad
Music and lyrics by Earl Wilson, Jr.
Let My People Come (OB) 1974

Add a Little Wiggle
Music by Milton Ager
Lyrics by Jack Yellen
Rain or Shine 1928

Addie's at It Again
Music and lyrics by Jack Lawrence
and Stan Freeman
I Had a Ball 1964

The Ad-dressing of Cats
Music by Andrew Lloyd Webber
Lyrics by Trevor Nunn and Richard Stilgoe
Cats 1982

Lyrics based on T.S. Eliot's *Old Possum's Book of Practical Cats*

Adelaide
Music and lyrics by Frank Loesser
Guys and Dolls (film version, 1955)

Adelaide's Lament
Music and lyrics by Frank Loesser
Guys and Dolls 1950

Adios Barrio
Music and lyrics by John Clifton
El Bravo! (OB) 1981

Adolescents
Music and lyrics by Elizabeth Swados
Nightclub Cantata (OB) 1977

Adorable
Music and lyrics by Tom Ford and Ray Wynburn
Earl Carroll's Vanities (1926)

Adorable Julie
Music by Lewis E. Gensler
Lyrics by Owen Murphy and Robert A. Simon
The Gang's All Here 1931

Adorable You
Music by Karl Hajos (based on Chopin)
Lyrics by Harry B. Smith
White Lilacs 1928

Adrift
Music by John Addison
Lyrics by John Cranko
Cranks 1956

Adrift on a Star
Music by Jacques Offenbach (adapted by Robert DeCormier)
Lyrics by E.Y. Harburg
The Happiest Girl in the World 1961

Adultery
Music by Robert Kole
Lyrics by Sandi Merle
I Take These Women (OB) 1982

Advantages of Floating in the Middle of the Sea
Music and lyrics by Stephen Sondheim
Pacific Overtures 1976

Adventure
Music by Jule Styne
Lyrics by Betty Comden and Adolph Green
Do Re Mi 1960

Advertising
Music by Harry Ruby
Lyrics by Bert Kalmar
Helen of Troy, New York 1923

Advice to Husbands
Music by Erich Wolfgang Korngold (based on
Jacques Offenbach)
Lyrics by Herbert Baker
Helen Goes to Troy 1944

Aesthetic Dancing
Music by Karl Hoschna
Lyrics by Otto Harbach
Madame Sherry 1910

Affable, Balding Me
Music by Robert Emmett Dolan
Lyrics by Johnny Mercer
Texas, Li'l Darlin' 1949

Afferdytie
Music and lyrics by Jerry Herman
Madame Aphrodite (OB) 1961

The Affluent Society
Music and lyrics by Jack Lawrence and Stan
Freeman
I Had a Ball 1964

Afraid of Love
Music and lyrics by Alice Clark and David Morton
Vintage '60 (OB) 1960

Afraid to Fall in Love
Music by William Dyer
Lyrics by Don Parks and William Dyer
Jo (OB) 1964

Africa
Music by Emmerich Kálmán and Herbert Stothart
Lyrics by Otto Harbach and Oscar Hammerstein II
Golden Dawn 1927

Africa Speaks
Music by Bill Weeden
Lyrics by David Finkle
Hurry, Harry 1972

African Sequence
Music and lyrics by Voices, Inc.
The Believers (OB) 1968

African Shrieks
Music by Ned Lehak
Lyrics by Edward Eliscu
The Third Little Show 1931

African Whoopee
Music and lyrics by Frank Marcus
and Bernard Maltin
Bamboola 1929

The Africana Stomp
Music and lyrics by Donald Heywood
Africana 1927

Afro Blue
Music and lyrics by Oscar Brown, Jr.
and Mongo Santamaria
Joy (OB) 1970

After All, It's Spring
Music by Walter Kent
Lyrics by Kim Gannon
Seventeen 1951

After All, You're All I'm After
Music by Arthur Schwartz
Lyrics by Edward Heyman
She Loves Me Not 1933

After Graduation Day
Music by Sidney Lippman
Lyrics by Sylvia Dee
Barefoot Boy With Cheek 1947

After Hours
Music and lyrics by Charles Gaynor
Lend an Ear 1948

After Love
Music by Manos Hadjidakis
Lyrics by Joe Darion
Illya Darling 1967

After the Ball
Music and lyrics by Charles K. Harris

A popular song of the late nineteenth century
inserted by Jerome Kern in the score of *Show Boat*
(1927).

After Tonight
Music by Al Moss
Lyrics by Alfred Hayes
Tis of Thee 1940

After You
Music and lyrics by Cole Porter
Gay Divorce 1932

The Afternoon of a Phoney
Music by John Green
Lyrics by George Marion, Jr.
Beat the Band 1942

Age Is a State of Mind
Music and lyrics by Johnny Brandon
Love! Love! Love! (OB) 1977

The Age of Brass
Music by Keith Hermann
Lyrics by Charlotte Anker and Irene Rosenberg
Onward Victoria 1980

Age of Innocence
Music by Harold Levey
Lyrics by Zelda Sears
The Clinging Vine 1922

An Aged Aged Man
Music and lyrics by Elizabeth Swados
Alice in Concert (OB) 1980

Ages Ago
Music and lyrics by Vernon Duke
Time Remembered 1957

Aggie
Music by Leon Carr
Lyrics by Earl Shuman
The Secret Life of Walter Mitty (OB) 1964

Aggie, Oh Aggie
Music by Mitch Leigh
Lyrics by William Alfred and Phyllis Robinson
Cry for Us All 1970

The Aggie Song
Music and lyrics by Carol Hall
The Best Little Whorehouse in Texas 1978

Aggie's Sewing Machine Song
Music by Kurt Weill
Lyrics by Paul Green
Johnny Johnson 1936

Agnes and Me
Music by Baldwin Bergersen
Lyrics by William Archibald
The Crystal Heart (OB) 1960

Agua Sincopada Tango
Music and lyrics by Cole Porter
Wake Up and Dream 1929

Ah! Camminare
Music by Milton Schafer
Lyrics by Ronny Graham
Bravo Giovanni 1962

Ah, Hum; Oh, Hum
Music by Frank Fields
Lyrics by Armand Aulicino
The Shoemaker and the Peddler (OB) 1960

Ah Men
Music and lyrics by Alan Menken
Real Life Funnies (OB) 1981

Ah, Men
Music and lyrics by Paul Shyre
Ah, Men (OB) 1981

Ah, Miss
Music and lyrics by Stephen Sondheim
Sweeney Todd 1979

Ah, Paris!
Music and lyrics by Stephen Sondheim
Follies 1971

Ah Still Suits Me
Music by Jerome Kern
Lyrics by Oscar Hammerstein II
Show Boat (film version, 1936)

Ah! Sweet Mystery of Life
Music by Victor Herbert
Lyrics by Rida Johnson Young
Naughty Marietta 1910

A-Hunting We Will go
Music by George Gershwin
Lyrics by Ira Gershwin
Treasure Girl 1928

Dropped from production

Ai Yi Yi
Music by Manning Sherwin
Lyrics by Harold Purcell
Under the Counter 1947

Ain't Got No
Music by Galt MacDermot
Lyrics by Gerome Ragni and James Rado
Hair 1968

Ain't He a Joy?
Music by Michael Leonard
Lyrics by Herbert Martin
The Yearling 1965

Ain't it a Grand and a Glorious Feeling
Music by Jerome Kern
Lyrics by P.G. Wodehouse
Oh, Boy! 1917

Dropped from production

Ain't It a Shame
Music by Jack Urbont
Lyrics by Bruce Geller
Livin' the Life (OB) 1957

Ain't It Awful
Music and lyrics by George M. Cohan
Fifty Miles From Boston 1908

Ain't It Awful, the Heat?
Music by Kurt Weill
Lyrics by Langston Hughes
Street Scene 1947

Ain't It Funny What a Difference a Few Drinks Make?
Music by Jerome Kern
Lyrics by Gene Buck
Ziegfeld Follies of 1916

Ain't It Romantic
Music by George Gershwin
Lyrics by Ira Gershwin
Oh, Kay! 1926

Dropped from production

Ain't It the Truth
Music by Harold Arlen
Lyrics by E.Y. Harburg
Jamaica 1957

Ain't Love Grand
Music by Joseph Meyer and Philip Charig
Lyrics by Leo Robin
Just Fancy 1927

Ain't Love Grand
Music and lyrics by Melvin Van Peebles
Don't Play Us Cheap 1972

Ain't Love Wonderful?
Music by Lewis E. Gensler
Lyrics by B.G. DeSylva
Captain Jinks 1925

Ain't Misbehavin'
Music by Thomas (Fats) Waller
and Harry Brooks
Lyrics by Andy Razaf
Hot Chocolates 1929

Ain't No Party
Music by Henry Krieger
Lyrics by Tom Eyen
Dreamgirls 1981

Ain't No Place Like Home
Music and lyrics by Branch Nick
An Evening With Joan Crawford (OB) 1981

Ain't No Women There
Music by Scott MacLarty
Lyrics by Dorothy Chansky
The Brooklyn Bridge (OB) 1983

Ain't Puttin' Out Nothin'
Music and lyrics by J.C. Johnson
Change Your Luck 1930

Ain't We Got Love?
Music by Eubie Blake
Lyrics by J. Milton Reddie and Cecil Mack
Swing It 1937

Ain't You Ashamed?
Music by Sol Berkowitz
Lyrics by James Lipton
Nowhere to Go But Up 1962

Ain't You Never Been Afraid?
Music by Jerry Bock
Lyrics by Sheldon Harnick
Man in the Moon 1963

Ain'tcha Glad You Got Music?
Music and lyrics by Alexander Hill
Hummin' Sam 1933

Air
Music by Galt MacDermot
Lyrics by Gerome Ragni and James Rado
Hair 1968

Air Male
Music by Galt MacDermot
Lyrics by Gerome Ragni
Dude 1972

Air-Minded
Music by Ray Henderson
Lyrics by B.G. DeSylva and Lew Brown
Flying High 1930

Airship Joy Ride
Music by Raymond Hubbell
Lyrics by Glen MacDonough
The Jolly Bachelors 1910

A.J.
Music by Harry Archer
Lyrics by Will B. Johnstone
Entre-Nous (OB) 1935

Alabama Stomp
Music by James P. Johnson
Lyrics by Henry Creamer
Earl Carroll's Vanities (1926)

Aladdin
Music and lyrics by Cole Porter
Aladdin (1958) TV

Aladdin's Daughter
Music by Jimmy Van Heusen
Lyrics by Johnny Burke
Nellie Bly 1946

Alaiyo
Music by Judd Woldin
Lyrics by Robert Brittan
Raisin 1973

Alas for You
Music and lyrics by Stephen Schwartz
Godspell (OB) 1971

Alas, the Time Is Past
Music and lyrics by Noël Coward
Bitter Sweet 1929

Aldonza
Music by Mitch Leigh
Lyrics by Joe Darion
Man of La Mancha 1965

Ale, Ale
Music by Richard Rodgers
Lyrics by Lorenz Hart
Dearest Enemy 1925

Dropped from production

Ale House Song
Music by Robert Kessler
Lyrics by Lola Pergament
O Marry Me! (OB) 1961

Alessandro the Wise
Music by Kurt Weill
Lyrics by Ira Gershwin
The Firebrand of Florence 1945

Alexander's Ragtime Wedding Day
Music and lyrics by Porter Grainger
and Freddie Johnson
Lucky Sambo 1925

Alexius the Heroic
Music by Oscar Straus
Lyrics by Stanislaus Stange
The Chocolate Soldier 1909

Algy
Music by Victor Herbert
Lyrics by George V. Hobart
Old Dutch 1909

Alhambra Nights
Music by Howard Marren
Lyrics by Enid Futterman
Portrait of Jennie (OB) 1982

The Ali Baba Babies
Music by Jerome Kern
Lyrics by Anne Caldwell and Otto Harbach
Criss-Cross 1926

Alibi Baby
Music by Arthur Samuels
Lyrics by Howard Dietz
Poppy 1923

Alice Blue Gown
Music by Harry Tierney
Lyrics by Joseph McCarthy
Irene 1919

"Alice blue" was the name given to a special shade
of blue that was a favorite of President Theodore
Roosevelt's daughter Alice (Longworth).

Alice in Boogieland
Music by Sidney Lippman
Lyrics by Sylvia Dee
Barefoot Boy With Cheek 1947

Alice in Wonderland
Music and lyrics by Irving Berlin
The Century Girl 1916

Alien Song
Music and lyrics by Sam Shepard
Operation Sidewinder 1970

Alimony Blues
Music by Louis A. Hirsch
Lyrics by Rennold Wolf
The Rainbow Girl 1918

Alison Dear
Music by Paul Hoffert
Lyrics by David Secter
Get Thee to Canterbury (OB) 1969

Ali-Up
Music by Sigmund Romberg
Lyrics by Otto Harbach and Oscar Hammerstein II
The Desert Song 1926

Dropped from production

Alive and Kicking
Music by Hal Borne
Lyrics by Ray Golden and Sid Kuller
Alive and Kicking 1950

Alive and Kicking
Music and lyrics by Hugh Martin
and Ralph Blane
Best Foot Forward (1963 OB revival)

Alive and Well
Music and lyrics by Bob Ost
Everybody's Gettin' Into the Act (OB) 1981

All a Lie!
Music by Howard Talbot
Lyrics by Arthur Wimperis
The Arcadians 1910

All Aboard
Music by Sol Berkowitz
Lyrics by James Lipton
Miss Emily Adam (OB) 1960

All Aboard for Paris
Music by Edward Künneke
Lyrics by Harry B. Smith
The Love Song 1925

All Aboard for Times Square
Music by Dave Stamper
Lyrics by Gene Buck
Take the Air 1927

All About Me
Music and lyrics by Bruce Montgomery
The Amorous Flea (OB) 1964

All, All Alone
Music by Silvio Hein
Lyrics by George V. Hobart
The Yankee Girl 1910

All Alone
Music by Nancy Ford
Lyrics by Gretchen Cryer
Now Is the Time for All Good Men (OB) 1967

All Alone Monday
Music by Harry Ruby
Lyrics by Bert Kalmar
The Ramblers 1926

All American
Music by David Baker
Lyrics by Sheldon Harnick
Vintage '60 (OB) 1960

All American
Music and lyrics by Leslie Bricusse
and Anthony Newley
Stop the World—I Want to Get Off 1962

All American
Music and lyrics by Paul Nassau
and Oscar Brand
*The Education of H*y*m*a*n K*a*p*l*a*n* 1968

All American Male
Music by Harris Wheeler
Lyrics by Mary L. Fisher
Blue Plate Special (OB) 1983

All American Man
Music by Sammy Fain
Lyrics by George Marion, Jr.
Toplitzky of Notre Dame 1946

The All-American Two-Step
Music and lyrics by Will Holt
That 5 A.M. Jazz (OB) 1964

All Around the World
Music by Jimmy Van Heusen
Lyrics by Johnny Burke
Nellie Bly 1946

All Around the World
Music by David Baker
Lyrics by David Craig
Phoenix '55 (OB)

All at Once
Music by Richard Rodgers
Lyrics by Lorenz Hart
Babes in Arms 1937

All at Once
Music by Kurt Weill
Lyrics by Ira Gershwin
Where Do We Go From Here? (1945) F

All at Once You Love Her
Music by Richard Rodgers
Lyrics by Oscar Hammerstein II
Pipe Dream 1955

All by Yourself
Music and lyrics by Cliff Jones
Rockabye Hamlet 1976

All Choked Up
Music and lyrics by Jim Jacobs
and Warren Casey
Grease 1972

All Dark People
Music by Richard Rodgers
Lyrics by Lorenz Hart
Babes in Arms 1937

All Down Piccadilly
Music by Lionel Monckton
Lyrics by Arthur Wimperis and Lionel Monckton
The Arcadians 1910

All Dressed Up
Music by Ernest G. Schweikert
Lyrics by Frank Reardon
Rumple 1957

All er Nothin'
Music by Richard Rodgers
Lyrics by Oscar Hammerstein II
Oklahoma! 1943

All for Him
Music by Frederick Loewe
Lyrics by Alan Jay Lerner
Paint Your Wagon 1951

All for Love
Music by Allan Roberts
Lyrics by Lester Lee
All for Love 1949

All for One and One for All
Music by Rudolf Friml
Lyrics by P.G. Wodehouse and Clifford Grey
The Three Musketeers 1928

All for the Best
Music and lyrics by Stephen Schwartz
Godspell (OB) 1971

All for the Sake of a Girl
Music by Victor Herbert
Lyrics by Robert B. Smith
The Debutante 1914

All for You
Music by Victor Herbert
Lyrics by Henry Blossom
The Princess Pat 1915

All for You
Music by Lee Pockriss
Lyrics by Anne Croswell
Tovarich 1963

All Gall
Music by Donald Swann
Lyrics by Michael Flanders
At the Drop of Another Hat 1966

The All-Girl Band
Music by Morgan Lewis
Lyrics by Nancy Hamilton
Two for the Show 1940

All Good Gifts
Music and lyrics by Stephen Schwartz
Godspell (OB) 1971

All Hail the Empress
Music and lyrics by Robert Wright and George
Forrest (based on Rachmaninoff)
Anya 1965

All Hallowe'en
Music by Victor Herbert
Lyrics by James O'Dea
The Lady of the Slipper 1912

All I Can Do Is Cry
Music and lyrics by Sarah Weeks
and Michael Abbott
Upstairs at O'Neal's (OB) 1982

All I Care About
Music by John Kander
Lyrics by Fred Ebb
Chicago 1975

All I Got Is You
Music and lyrics by Jack Bussins
and Ellsworth Olin
Be Kind to People Week (OB) 1975

All I Need
Music and lyrics by Micki Grant
Don't Bother Me, I Can't Cope (OB) 1972

All I Need Is One Good Break
Music by John Kander
Lyrics by Fred Ebb
Flora, the Red Menace 1965

All I Need Is Someone Like You
Music by Harry Archer
Lyrics by Charles Tobias
Keep It Clean 1929

All I Need Is the Girl
Music by Jule Styne
Lyrics by Stephen Sondheim
Gypsy 1959

All I Owe Ioway
Music by Richard Rodgers
Lyrics by Oscar Hammerstein II
State Fair (1945) F

All I Want Is Love
Music by Hal Dyson
Lyrics by James Kendis
June Days 1925

All I Want Is My Black Baby Back
Music and lyrics by Buster Davis
Doctor Jazz 1975

All in Fun
Music by Jerome Kern
Lyrics by Oscar Hammerstein II
Very Warm for May 1939

All in Fun
Music and lyrics by Walter Marks
Golden Rainbow 1968

All in Love
Music by Jacques Urbont
Lyrics by Bruce Geller
All in Love (OB) 1961

All in the Cause of Economy
Music and lyrics by David Heneker
Half a Sixpence 1965

All in the Wearing
Music and lyrics by George M. Cohan
Little Nellie Kelly 1922

All Is Vanity
Music by Morris Hamilton
Lyrics by Grace Henry
Earl Carroll's Vanities (1926)

All Is Well in Larchmont
Music by Albert Hague
Lyrics by Allen Sherman
The Fig Leaves Are Falling 1969

All Is Well in the City
Music by Al Carmines
Lyrics by Maria Irene Fornes
Promenade (OB) 1969

All I've Got to Get Now Is My Man
Music and lyrics by Cole Porter
Panama Hattie 1940

All Kinds of Giants
Music by Sam Pottle
Lyrics by Tom Whedon
All Kinds of Giants (OB) 1961

All Kinds of People
Music by Richard Rodgers
Lyrics by Oscar Hammerstein II
Pipe Dream 1955

All Lanes Must Reach a Turning
Music by Jerome Kern
Lyrics by Howard Dietz
Dear Sir 1924

The melody later became the title song of the 1928
London musical *Blue Eyes*, sung by Evelyn Laye
and Geoffrey Gwyther.

All Love
Music by Stanley Silverman
Lyrics by Arthur Miller
Up From Paradise (OB) 1983

All My Days Till End of Time
Music by Frederic Norton
Lyrics by Oscar Asche
Chu Chin Chow 1917

All My Girls
Music by Karl Hoschna
Lyrics by Otto Harbach
Three Twins 1908

All My Good Mornings
Music by Galt MacDermot
Lyrics by Christopher Gore
Via Galactica 1972

All My Life
Music and lyrics by Cliff Jones
Rockabye Hamlet 1976

All Night Long
Music and lyrics by George M. Cohan
The Rise of Rosie O'Reilly 1923

All of 'Em Say
Music by Jack Urbont
Lyrics by Bruce Geller
Livin' the Life (OB) 1957

All of My Laughter
Music by Albert Hague
Lyrics by Allen Sherman
The Fig Leaves Are Falling 1969

All of My Life
Music by Jule Styne
Lyrics by Betty Comden and Adolph Green
Do Re Mi 1960

All of My Life
Music by Don Gohman
Lyrics by Hal Hackady
Ambassador 1972

All of That Made for Me
Music by Stanley Silverman
Lyrics by Arthur Miller
Up From Paradise (OB) 1983

All of Them Was Friends of Mine
Music by Lewis E. Gensler and Milton Schwarzwald
Lyrics by Marc Connelly and Ira Gershwin
Be Yourself 1924

All of These and More
Music by Jerry Bock
Lyrics by Sheldon Harnick
The Body Beautiful 1958

All of You
Music and lyrics by Cole Porter
Silk Stockings 1955

All-Out Bugle Call
Music and lyrics by Ann Ronell
Count Me In 1942

All Out for Freedom
Music by Harold Arlen
Lyrics by Ted Koehler
Up in Arms (1944) F

All Roads Lead to Hollywood
Music and lyrics by Beth Lawrence
and Norman Thalheimer
Marilyn 1983

All She Did Was This
Music by Vincent Youmans
Lyrics by Zelda Sears
Lollipop 1924

Dropped from production

All-Talking, All-Singing, All-Dancing
Music and lyrics by John Raniello
Movie Buff (OB) 1977

All That He Wants Me to Be
Music by Burton Lane
Lyrics by Alan Jay Lerner
Carmelina 1979

All That I Know
Music by Scott MacLarty
Lyrics by Dorothy Chansky
The Brooklyn Bridge (OB) 1983

All That Jazz
Music by John Kander
Lyrics by Fred Ebb
Chicago 1975

All the Comforts of Home
Music by Gary Geld
Lyrics by Peter Udell
Angel 1978

All the Dearly Beloved
Music by Harvey Schmidt
Lyrics by Tom Jones
I Do! I Do! 1966

All the Documents Must Be Signed
Music and lyrics by Gian-Carlo Menotti
The Consul 1950

All the Elks and Masons
Music by Harold Arlen
Lyrics by Ira Gershwin and E.Y. Harburg
Life Begins at 8:40 1934

All the Girls Were Pretty
Music and lyrics by Sandy Wilson
Valmouth (OB) 1960

All the King's Horses
Music and lyrics by Alec Wilder, Eddie Brandt
and Howard Dietz
Three's a Crowd 1930

All the Little Things in the World Are Waiting
Music by Lance Mulcahy
Lyrics by Paul Cherry
Park 1970

All the Livelong Day
Music and additional lyrics by Stephen Schwartz
Working 1978

Based on the poem "I Hear America Singing" by
Walt Whitman

All the Livelong Day (and the Livelong Night)
Music by George Gershwin
(Posthumous—from manuscript)
Lyrics by Ira Gershwin
Kiss Me, Stupid (1964) F

All the Pretty Little Horses
Music by Paul Klein
Lyrics by Fred Ebb
Morning Sun (OB) 1963

All the Same to Me
Music by Bert Keyes and Bob Larimer
Lyrics by Bob Larimer
But Never Jam Today 1979

All the Things You Are
Music by Jerome Kern
Lyrics by Oscar Hammerstein II
Very Warm for May 1939

This was the favorite song of both of its authors; and they were surprised and delighted at its great success, especially in view of its frequent changes of key.

All the Time
Music by Arthur Schwartz
Lyrics by Dorothy Fields
Stars in Your Eyes 1939

All the Time
Music and lyrics by Jay Livingston
and Ray Evans
Oh Captain! 1958

All the Time in the World
Music by Steve Jankowski
Lyrics by Kenny Morris
Francis (OB) 1982

All the Way Down
Music by Susan Hulsman Bingham
Lyrics by Myrna Lamb
Mod Donna (OB) 1970

All the World Is Swaying
Music by Jerome Kern
Lyrics by Edgar Allan Woolf
Head Over Heels 1918

All the World Loves a Lover
Music by Jean Gilbert
Lyrics by Harry B. and Robert B. Smith
Modest Suzanne 1912

All the World Loves a Lover
Music by Jean Gilbert
Lyrics by Harry Graham
Katja 1926

All the Wrongs You've Done to Me
Music and lyrics by Noble Sissle
and Eubie Blake
The Chocolate Dandies 1924

All the Young Men
Music and lyrics by Jay Thompson
Double Entry (OB) 1961

All Things Bright and Beautiful
Music and lyrics by Stephen Sondheim
Marry Me a Little (OB) 1981

Dropped from *Follies* (1971)

All Those Years
Music by Albert Hague
Lyrics by Marty Brill
Café Crown 1964

All Through the Day
Music by Jerome Kern
Lyrics by Oscar Hammerstein II
Centennial Summer (1946) F

All Through the Night
Music and lyrics by Cole Porter
Anything Goes 1934

All to Myself
Music by William Daly and Paul Lannin
Lyrics by Arthur Jackson
For Goodness Sake 1922

All Work and No Play
Music by Tom Johnstone
Lyrics by Phil Cook
When You Smile 1925

All Wrapped Up in You
Music by Harry Revel
Lyrics by Mack Gordon and Harold Adamson
Everybody's Welcome 1931

All Year Round
Music by Victor Herbert
Lyrics by Rida Johnson Young
The Dream Girl 1924

All You Have to Do Is Stand There
Music by Leo Edwards
Lyrics by Herman Timberg
You'll See Stars 1942

All You Need Is a Girl
Music by Jerome Kern
Lyrics by P. G. Wodehouse
Sitting Pretty 1924

All You Need Is a Quarter
Music by Jule Styne
Lyrics by Betty Comden and Adolph Green
Do Re Mi 1960

All You Need to Be a Star
Music by Richard Rodgers
Lyrics by Lorenz Hart
Poor Little Ritz Girl 1920

All Your Own Am I
Music by Victor Herbert
Lyrics by Harry B. Smith
The Enchantress 1911

Allaballa Goo-Goo
Music by Ivan Caryll
Lyrics by C.M.S. McLellan
Oh! Oh! Delphine 1912

Allah Be Praised
Music by Don Walker
Lyrics by George Marion, Jr.
Allah Be Praised! 1944

Allah's Holiday
Music by Rudolf Friml
Lyrics by Otto Harbach
Katinka 1915

Allegheny Al
Music by Jerome Kern
Lyrics by Oscar Hammerstein II
High, Wide and Handsome (1937) F

Allegro
Music by Richard Rodgers
Lyrics by Oscar Hammerstein II
Allegro 1947

Allez-Oop
Music by Richard Rodgers
Lyrics by Lorenz Hart
The Garrick Gaieties (2nd edition) 1926

Allez-Vous En
Music and lyrics by Cole Porter
Can-Can 1953

The Allied High Command
Music by Kurt Weill
Lyrics by Paul Green
Johnny Johnson 1936

Allies
Music by Victor Herbert
Lyrics by Henry Blossom
The Princess Pat 1915

Alligator Meat
Music by Mel Marvin
Lyrics by Robert Montgomery
Green Pond (OB) 1977

Allons
Music by Jerry Bock
Lyrics by Sheldon Harnick
The Rothschilds 1970

All's Fair in Love and War
Music by Jean Gilbert
Lyrics by Harry B. Smith
Marching By 1932

All's Well
Music by Arthur Schwartz
Lyrics by Howard Dietz
Flying Colors 1932

Alma Mater
Music and lyrics by Jim Jacobs
and Warren Casey
Grease 1972

The Almanac Covers
Music by Henry Sullivan
Lyrics by Edward Eliscu
John Murray Anderson's Almanac 1929

Almost
Music and lyrics by Jack Lawrence
and Stan Freeman
I Had a Ball 1964

Almost, but Not Quite
Music and lyrics by John Jennings
Riverwind (OB) 1962

Almost Like Being in Love
Music by Frederick Loewe
Lyrics by Alan Jay Lerner
Brigadoon 1947

Almost Maybes and Perhapses
Music and lyrics by Barbara Schottenfeld
I Can't Keep Running in Place (OB) 1981

Almost Too Good to Be True
Music by James Bredt
Lyrics by Edward Eager
The Happy Hypocrite (OB) 1968

Aloha
Music by Rudolf Friml
Lyrics by J. Keirn Brennan
Luana 1930

Aloha
Music and lyrics by Eaton Magoon, Jr.
Heathen 1972

Alone
Music by Giuseppe Verdi (adapted by Hans Spialek)
Lyrics by Charles Friedman
My Darlin' Aïda 1952

Alone
Music by Jacques Brel
English lyrics by Eric Blau and Mort Shuman
*Jacques Brel Is Alive and Well
and Living in Paris* (OB) 1968

Alone
Music and lyrics by David Langston Smyrl
On the Lock-In (OB) 1977

Alone at a Drive-In Movie
Music and lyrics by Jim Jacobs
and Warren Casey
Grease 1972

Alone at Last
Music by Jerome Kern
Lyrics by Harry B. Smith
Oh, I Say! 1913

Alone, at Last, Alone
Music and lyrics by Jill Williams
Rainbow Jones 1974

Alone (My Lover)
Music by Rudolf Friml
Lyrics by Brian Hooker
The White Eagle 1927

Alone Together
Music by Arthur Schwartz
Lyrics by Howard Dietz
Flying Colors 1932

Alone Too Long
Music by Arthur Schwartz
Lyrics by Dorothy Fields
By the Beautiful Sea 1954

Alone With You
Music by G. Romilli
Lyrics by Grace Henry and Jo Trent
Fioretta 1929

Along Came Another Little Girl
Music by Ivan Caryll
Lyrics by Benjamin Hapgood Burt
Jack O' Lantern 1917

Along Came Love
Music by Henry Tobias
Lyrics by Charles Tobias and Haven Gillespie
Earl Carroll's Vanities (1932)

Along the Winding Road
Music by Sigmund Romberg
Lyrics by Oscar Hammerstein II
Sunny River 1941

Along With Me
Music and lyrics by Harold Rome
Call Me Mister 1946

Alpha, Beta, Pi
Music by Jerome Kern
Lyrics by Otto Harbach
Roberta 1933

Alphabet
Music and lyrics by Elizabeth Swados
Alice in Concert (OB) 1980

Alphabet Song
Music and lyrics by Eaton Magoon, Jr.
13 Daughters 1961

The Alphabet Song
Music and lyrics by Rick Besoyan
Babes in the Wood (OB) 1964

The Alphabet Song
Music by Walt Smith
Lyrics by Leon Uris
Ari 1971

Alphagenesis
Music by Kenn Long and Jim Crozier
Lyrics by Kenn Long
Touch (OB) 1970

Always Always You
Music and lyrics by Bob Merrill
Carnival 1961

Always Another Girl
Music by Winthrop Cortelyou
Lyrics by Derick Wulff
Kiss Me 1927

Always Be a Gentleman
Music by Sigmund Romberg
Lyrics by Oscar Hammerstein II
May Wine 1935

Always Do as People Say You Should
Music by Victor Herbert
Lyrics by Harry B. Smith
The Fortune Teller 1898

Always in My Heart
Music and lyrics by Ralph Benatzky
Meet My Sister 1930

Always Keep a Fellow Guessing If You Want His Love
Music by Kerry Mills
Lyrics by S.M. Lewis
The Fascinating Widow 1911

Always Mademoiselle
Music by André Previn
Lyrics by Alan Jay Lerner
Coco 1969

Always on the Job
Music and lyrics by Porter Grainger
and Freddie Johnson
Lucky Sambo 1925

Always One Day More
Music by Philip Springer
Lyrics by Carolyn Leigh
Shoestring '57 (OB)

Always True to You in My Fashion
Music and lyrics by Cole Porter
Kiss Me, Kate 1948

For the title, Porter borrowed part of the line in
Ernest Dowson's poem which went: "I have been
faithful to thee, Cynara! in my fashion."

Always You
Music by Gerald Marks
Lyrics by Sam Lerner
Hold It! 1948

Am I?
Music by Harry Archer
Lyrics by Will B. Johnstone
Entre-Nous (OB) 1935

Am I a Man or a Mouse?
Music by David Raksin
Lyrics by June Carroll
If the Shoe Fits 1946

Am I Afraid?
Music and lyrics by Gian-Carlo Menotti
The Medium 1947

Am I Enchanted?
Music by Franz Steininger (adapted from
Tchaikovsky)
Lyrics by Forman Brown
Music in My Heart 1947

Amapu
Music by Melville Gideon
Lyrics by Edward Knoblock
The Optimists 1928

Amarillo
Music by Richard Rodgers
Lyrics by Lorenz Hart
They Met in Argentina (1941) F

Ambition
Music by Jule Styne
Lyrics by Betty Comden and Adolph Green
Do Re Mi 1960

Amen Corner
Music by Garry Sherman
Lyrics by Peter Udell
Amen Corner 1983

America
Music by Leonard Bernstein
Lyrics by Stephen Sondheim
West Side Story 1957

America
Music by Bob James
Lyrics by Jack O'Brien
The Selling of the President 1972

America Loves a Band
Music by John Green
Lyrics by George Marion, Jr.
Beat the Band 1942

An American Beauty Rose
Music by Rudolf Friml
Lyrics by Otto Harbach
The Firefly 1912

The Ameri-can-can
Music by Roger Wolfe Kahn
Lyrics by Irving Caesar
Americana 1928

American Cannes
Music by Jimmy McHugh
Lyrics by Harold Adamson
As the Girls Go 1947

American Couple
Music by Richard Rodgers
Lyrics by Lorenz Hart
I'd Rather Be Right 1937

Dropped after New York opening

American Dream
Music by David McHugh
Lyrics by Peter Copani
New York City Street Show (OB) 1977

The American Dream
Music and lyrics by Micki Grant
It's So Nice to Be Civilized 1980

American Eagles
Music and lyrics by Irving Berlin
This Is the Army 1942

The American Express
Music and lyrics by Cole Porter
Fifty Million Frenchmen 1929

American Family
Music and lyrics by Cole Porter
Panama Hattie 1940

American Family Plan
Music and lyrics by John Jennings
Riverwind (OB) 1962

The American Girl
Music by Gustav Luders
Lyrics by Frank Pixley
The Prince of Pilsen 1903

The American Girl
Music by John Philip Sousa
Lyrics by Leonard Liebling
The American Maid 1913

An American Heiress
Music by Victor Herbert
Lyrics by Harry B. Smith
Miss Dolly Dollars 1905

American Man on the Moon
Music and lyrics by John Phillips
Man on the Moon 1975

American Music ('Tis Better Than Old "Parsifal" to Me)
Music by Victor Herbert
Lyrics by Harry B. Smith
Miss Dolly Dollars 1905

American Plan
Music by Jay Gorney
Lyrics by Henry Myers
Meet the People 1940

American Primitive
Music by Jay Gorney
Lyrics by Jean and Walter Kerr
Touch and Go 1949

American Revue Girls
Music by Con Conrad
Lyrics by J.P. McEvoy
Americana 1926

The Americans Are Coming
Music by Sigmund Romberg
Lyrics by Oscar Hammerstein II
East Wind 1931

The Americans Are Here
Music by Ray Henderson
Lyrics by B.G. DeSylva
Three Cheers 1928

An Amishman
Music and lyrics by Howard Blankman
By Hex (OB) 1956

The Amoeba's Lament
Music by Arthur Schwartz
Lyrics by Agnes Morgan
The Grand Street Follies 1929

Among My Yesterdays
Music by John Kander
Lyrics by Fred Ebb
The Happy Time 1968

The Amorous Arrow
Music by James Bredt
Lyrics by Edward Eager
The Happy Hypocrite (OB) 1968

The Amorous Flea
Music and lyrics by Bruce Montgomery
The Amorous Flea (OB) 1964

Amsterdam
Music by Jacques Brel
English lyrics by Eric Blau and Mort Shuman
*Jacques Brel Is Alive and Well
and Living in Paris* (OB) 1968

Amy
Music by Roy Webb
Lyrics by F. Coulon
A Night in Paris 1926

Anatevka
Music by Jerry Bock
Lyrics by Sheldon Harnick
Fiddler on the Roof 1964

Anatole of Paris
Music and lyrics by Sylvia Fine
The Straw Hat Revue 1939

Ancestry
Music by Robert Hood Bowers
Lyrics by Francis DeWitt
Oh, Ernest! 1927

And
Music by Marvin Hamlisch
Lyrics by Edward Kleban
A Chorus Line 1975

And a Drop of Lavender Oil
Music and lyrics by Jerry Herman
Madame Aphrodite (OB) 1961

And Father Wanted Me to Learn a Trade
Music and lyrics by Irving Berlin
Stop! Look! Listen! 1915

And Furthermore
Music and lyrics by John Clifton
El Bravo! (OB) 1981

And He Flipped
Music and lyrics by John Rox
New Faces of 1956

And I Am All Alone
Music by Jerome Kern
Lyrics Jerome Kern and P.G. Wodehouse
Have a Heart 1917

And I Have You
Music by George Gershwin
Lyrics by Ira Gershwin
Girl Crazy 1930

Dropped from production

And I Love You
Music and lyrics by Melvin Van Peebles
Waltz of the Stork (OB) 1982

And I Was Beautiful
Music and lyrics by Jerry Herman
Dear World 1969

And I'm Telling You I'm Not Going
Music by Henry Krieger
Lyrics by Tom Eyen
Dreamgirls 1981

And I'm There!
Music and lyrics by Bob Ost
Everybody's Gettin' Into the Act (OB) 1981

And Love Was Born
Music by Jerome Kern
Lyrics by Oscar Hammerstein II
Music in the Air 1932

And Russia Is Her Name
Music by Jerome Kern
Lyrics by E.Y. Harburg
Song of Russia (1944) F

And She Loved Me
Music and lyrics by Earl Wilson, Jr.
Let My People Come (OB) 1974

And So He Died
Music by Mischa and Wesley Portnoff
Lyrics by Donagh MacDonagh
Happy as Larry 1950

And So Will You
Music by Frederick Loewe
Lyrics by Earle Crooker
Great Lady 1938

And That Little Girl Is You
Music by Victor Herbert
Lyrics by Harry B. Smith
The Enchantress 1911

And the Money Kept Rolling In
Music by Andrew Lloyd Webber
Lyrics by Tim Rice
Evita 1979

And the Mountains Sing Back
Music by John Morris
Lyrics by Gerald Freedman
A Time for Singing 1966

And They Call the Hatter Mad
Music by Bert Keyes and Bob Larimer
Lyrics by Bob Larimer
But Never Jam Today 1979

And This Is My Beloved
Music and lyrics by Robert Wright
and George Forrest
Kismet 1953

Based on Borodin's String Quartet in D

And What If We Had Loved Like That
Music by David Shire
Lyrics by Richard Maltby, Jr.
Baby 1983

And Why Not I?
Music by Morgan Lewis
Lyrics by Nancy Hamilton
Three to Make Ready 1946

Andiamo
Music by Harold Arlen
Lyrics by Dorothy Fields
Mr. Imperium (1951) F

Angel
Music by Peter de Rose
Lyrics by Mitchell Parrish
Earl Carroll's Vanities (1940)

Angel Theme
Music by Gary Geld
Lyrics by Peter Udell
Angel 1978

An Angel Without Wings
Music by Seymour Furth and Lee Edwards
Lyrics by R.F. Carroll
Bringing Up Father 1925

Angel Without Wings
Music by Richard Rodgers
Lyrics by Lorenz Hart
I Married an Angel 1938

Angela's Flight Dream
Music by Scott Killian and Kim D. Sherman
Lyrics by Kenneth Robins, Scott Killian
and Kim D. Sherman
Lenny and the Heartbreakers (OB) 1983

Angelette March
Music and lyrics by Carol Hall
The Best Little Whorehouse in Texas 1978

Angels On Your Pillow
Music by Paul Horner
Lyrics by Peggy Lee
Peg 1983

The Angelus
Music by Victor Herbert
Lyrics by Robert B. Smith
Sweethearts 1913

Animal Attraction
Music by Charles Strouse
Lyrics by Lee Adams
All American 1962

Animals Are Nice
Music by Lee Wainer
Lyrics by J.B. Rosenberg
New Faces of 1943

Ankle Up the Altar With Me
Music by Richard Myers
Lyrics by Edward Eliscu
The Garrick Gaieties (3rd edition) 1930

Anna
Music and lyrics by Frank Marcus
and Bernard Maltin
Bamboola 1929

Anna Lilla
Music and lyrics by Bob Merrill
New Girl in Town 1957

Anna Louise of Louisiana
Music by Will Irwin
Lyrics by Norman Zeno
Earl Carroll's Sketch Book (1935)

Anne of Green Gables
Music by Norman Campbell
Lyrics by Donald Harron and Norman Campbell
Anne of Green Gables (OB) 1971

Annette
Music by Walter Kollo
Lyrics by Harry B. Smith
Three Little Girls 1930

Annie
Music by Charles Strouse
Lyrics by Martin Charnin
Annie 1977

Annie's Lament
Music by Robert Kole
Lyrics by Sandi Merle
I Take These Women (OB) 1982

Another Autumn
Music by Frederick Loewe
Lyrics by Alan Jay Lerner
Paint Your Wagon 1951

Another Candle
Music and lyrics by Jerry Herman
Parade (OB) 1960

Another Case of the Blues
Music by Richard Myers
Lyrics by Johnny Mercer
Tattle Tales 1933

Another Day
Music by Henry Krieger
Lyrics by Robert Lorick
The Tap Dance Kid 1983

Another Hot Day
Music by Harvey Schmidt
Lyrics by Tom Jones
110 in the Shade 1963

Another Hundred People
Music and lyrics by Stephen Sondheim
Company 1970

Another Life
Music by Keith Hermann
Lyrics by Charlotte Anker and Irene Rosenberg
Onward Victoria 1980

Another Life
Music by Charles Strouse
Lyrics by Alan Jay Lerner
Dance a Little Closer 1983

Another Little Girl
Music by Jerome Kern
Lyrics by Herbert Reynolds
Nobody Home 1915

Another Memorable Meal
Music by Elizabeth Swados
Lyrics by Garry Trudeau
Doonesbury 1983

Another New Day
Music by Arthur Schwartz
Lyrics by Oscar Hammerstein II
American Jubilee 1940

Another One Gone Wrong
Music by Armand Vecsey
Lyrics by P.G. Wodehouse
The Nightingale 1927

Another Op'nin', Another Show
Music and lyrics by Cole Porter
Kiss Me, Kate 1948

Another Sleepless Night
Music and lyrics by William Finn
In Trousers (OB) 1981

Another Suitcase in Another Hall
Music by Andrew Lloyd Webber
Lyrics by Tim Rice
Evita 1979

Another Time, Another Place
Music and lyrics by Richard Adler
Kwamina 1961

The Answer Is No
Music and lyrics by Donald Heywood
Blackberries of 1932

Answer My Heart
Music and lyrics by Alexander Hill
Hummin' Sam 1933

The Anti-Cigarette Society
Music by Gustave Kerker
Lyrics by Hugh Morton
The Belle of New York 1897

Antioch Prison
Music by Harvey Schmidt
Lyrics by Tom Jones
Philemon (OB) 1975

The Antique Man
Music and lyrics by Jerry Herman
Parade (OB) 1960

Antiquity
Music and lyrics by Micki Grant
It's So Nice to Be Civilized 1980

Antoinette
Music by Victor Herbert
Lyrics by Henry Blossom
The Only Girl 1914

Any Afternoon About Five
Music and lyrics by William Roy
Maggie 1953

Any Day Now
Music and lyrics by Norman Dean
Autumn's Here (OB) 1966

Any Dream Will Do
Music by Andrew Lloyd Webber
Lyrics by Tim Rice
*Joseph and the Amazing
Technicolor Dreamcoat* 1982

Any Girl
Music by Jerome Kern
Lyrics by Edgar Allan Woolf
Head Over Heels 1918

Any Kind of Man
Music by Rudolf Friml
Lyrics by Rida Johnson Young
Sometime 1918

Any Little Fish
Music and lyrics by Noël Coward
The Third Little Show 1931

Dropped from production

Any Little Thing
Music by Harry Ruby
Lyrics by Bert Kalmar
The Five o'Clock Girl 1927

Any Little Tune
Music by Harry Ruby
Lyrics by Bert Kalmar
The Ramblers 1926

Any Moment Now
Music by Jerome Kern
Lyrics by E.Y. Harburg
Can't Help Singing (1944) F

Any Old Night
Music by Jerome Kern and Otto Motzan
Lyrics by Schuyler Green and Harry B. Smith
Nobody Home 1915

Any Old Place With You
Music by Richard Rodgers
Lyrics by Lorenz Hart
A Lonely Romeo 1919

Any Other Way
Music by John Clifton
Lyrics by John Clifton and Ben Tarver
Man With a Load of Mischief (OB) 1966

Any Place I Hang My Hat Is Home
Music by Harold Arlen
Lyrics by Johnny Mercer
St. Louis Woman 1946

Any Place the Old Flag Flies
Music and lyrics by George M. Cohan
The Little Millionaire 1911

Any Place Would Be Wonderful With You
Music and lyrics by Gene and Dave Stamper
Ziegfeld Follies of 1920

Any Step
Music by Maury Rubens
Lyrics by Clifford Grey
The Great Temptations 1926

Any Time
Music by Clarence Williams
Lyrics by Joe Jordan
Bottomland 1927

Any Time's Kissing Time
Music by Frederic Norton
Lyrics by Oscar Asche
Chu Chin Chow 1917

Any Way the Wind Blows
Music by Sam H. Stept
Lyrics by Bud Green
Shady Lady 1933

Anya
Music and lyrics by Robert Wright and George
Forrest (based on Rachmaninoff)
Anya 1965

Anybody's Man Will Be My Man
Music and lyrics by Porter Grainger
and Freddie Johnson
Lucky Sambo 1925

Anyone
Music and lyrics by Al Kasha
and Joel Hirschhorn
Copperfield 1981

Anyone Can Make a Mistake
Music and lyrics by Rick Besoyan
Babes in the Wood (OB) 1964

Anyone Can Whistle
Music and lyrics by Stephen Sondheim
Anyone Can Whistle 1964

Anyone Would Love You
Music and lyrics by Harold Rome
Destry Rides Again 1959

Anything Can Happen
Music by Ray Henderson
Lyrics by Jack Yellen and Ballard Macdonald
George White's Scandals (1936)

Anything Can Happen
Music by Jay Gorney
Lyrics by Barry Trivers
Heaven on Earth 1948

Anything Can Happen in New York
Music by Richard Lewine
Lyrics by Arnold B. Horwitt
Make Mine Manhattan 1948

Anything for You
Music by John Kander
Lyrics by James Goldman, John Kander

and William Goldman
A Family Affair 1962

Anything Goes
Music and lyrics by Cole Porter
Anything Goes 1934

Anything Is Possible
Music and lyrics by Paul Nassau and Oscar Brand
The Education of H*y*m*a*n K*a*p*l*a*n 1968

Anything May Happen Any Day
Music by Jerome Kern
Lyrics by Graham John
Ripples 1930

Dropped from production

Anything You Can Do
Music and lyrics by Irving Berlin
Annie Get Your Gun 1946

Anything You Want to Do Dear
Music by Louis A. Hirsch
Lyrics by Otto Harbach
Mary 1920

Anything Your Heart Desires
Music by Harry Archer
Lyrics by Walter O'Keefe
Just a Minute 1928

Anytime, Anywhere, Anyhow
Music by Richard Rodgers
Lyrics by Lorenz Hart
June Days 1925

Anyway, We've Had Fun
Music by Vincent Youmans
Lyrics by Ring Lardner
Smiles 1930

Anywhere I Wander
Music and lyrics by Frank Loesser
Hans Christian Andersen (1952) F

Anywhere the Wind Blows
Music and lyrics by Buster Davis
Doctor Jazz 1975

Aphrodite
Music by Walt Smith
Lyrics by Leon Uris
Ari 1971

Apology
Music and lyrics by Robert Wright
and George Forrest
Kean 1961

Appendectomy
Music and lyrics by Elizabeth Swados
Runaways 1978

Applause
Music by Charles Strouse
Lyrics by Lee Adams
Applause 1970

Applause! Applause!
Music by Burton Lane
Lyrics by Ira Gershwin
Give a Girl a Break (1953) F

Apple Blossom Victory
Music by Mel Marvin
Lyrics by Christopher Durang
A History of the American Film 1978

Apple Jack
Music by Jay Gorney
Lyrics by Barry Trivers
Heaven on Earth 1948

The Apple Stretching
Music and lyrics by Melvin Van Peebles
Waltz of the Stork (OB) 1982

The Apple Tree (Forbidden Fruit)
Music by Jerry Bock
Lyrics by Sheldon Harnick
The Apple Tree 1966

Apples, Bananas and You
Music by Walter L. Rosemont
Lyrics by Ballard MacDonald
Battling Buttler 1923

The Applicant
Music and lyrics by Elizabeth Swados
Nightclub Cantata (OB) 1977

Appointments
Music by Jerry Livingston
Lyrics by Mack David
Molly 1973

Après Vous I
Music by Al Carmines
Lyrics by Maria Irene Fornes
Promenade (OB) 1969

April Blossoms
Music by Herbert Stothart
Lyrics by Otto Harbach and Oscar Hammerstein II
Wildflower 1923

April Face
Music and lyrics by Ralph Blane
Three Wishes for Jamie 1952

April Fool
Music by Richard Rodgers
Lyrics by Lorenz Hart
The Garrick Gaieties (1st edition) 1925

April in Fairbanks
Music and lyrics by Murray Grand
New Faces of 1956

April in Harrisburg
Music by Baldwin Bergersen
Lyrics by Virginia Faulkner
All in Fun 1940

April in Paris
Music by Vernon Duke
Lyrics by E.Y. Harburg
Walk a Little Faster 1932

Written because the show's producer had an
expensive Parisian set that he insisted on using in
the show. Actually Harburg had never been to Paris
but Duke knew it well and between them the song
was written.

April in Wisconsin
Music by Monty Norman
Lyrics by Julian More
The Moony Shapiro Songbook 1981

April Showers
Music by Louis Silvers
Lyrics by B.G. DeSylva
Bombo 1921

April Snow
Music by Sigmund Romberg
Lyrics by Dorothy Fields
Up in Central Park 1945

April Song
Music by Richard Hill and John Hawkins
Lyrics by Nevill Coghill
Canterbury Tales 1969

Aqua Vitae
Music by Albert T. Viola
Lyrics by William S. Kilborne, Jr.
Head Over Heels 1981

Aquarius
Music by Galt MacDermot
Lyrics by Gerome Ragni and James Rado
Hair 1968

Arab Maid With Midnight Eyes
Music by Winthrop Cortelyou
Lyrics by Derick Wulff
Kiss Me 1927

Arabian for "Get Happy"
Music by Sammy Fain
Lyrics by E.Y. Harburg
Flahooley 1951

Arabian Moon
Music by Eubie Blake
Lyrics by Noble Sissle
Shuffle Along of 1933

Arabian Nights
Music by Maury Rubens and Sam Timberg
Lyrics by Moe Jaffe
Broadway Nights 1929

Araminto to Herself
Music and lyrics by Jack Lawrence
and Don Walker
Courtin' Time 1951

Arcady Is Ever Young
Music by Lionel Monckton
Lyrics by Arthur Wimperis
and Lionel Monckton
The Arcadians 1910

Are There Any More Rosie O'Gradys?
Music and lyrics by Robert Dahdah
Curley McDimple (OB) 1967

Are We Downhearted?
Music by Manning Sherwin
Lyrics by Arthur Herzog, Jr.
Bad Habits of 1926 (OB)

Are We Ready
Music and lyrics by Harry Chapin
Cotton Patch Gospel (OB) 1981

Are We Strong? (And Are We In?)
Music by Peter Link
Lyrics by Michael Cacoyannis
Lysistrata 1972

Are You a Man?
Music and lyrics by John Driver
Ride the Winds 1974

Are You Going to Dance?
Music by Franz Lehár
Lyrics by Basil Hood
The Count of Luxembourg 1912

Are You Havin' Any Fun?
Music by Sammy Fain
Lyrics by Jack Yellen
George White's Scandals (1939)

Are You Love?
Music by Sigmund Romberg
Lyrics by Oscar Hammerstein II
East Wind 1931

Are You My Love?
Music by Richard Rodgers
Lyrics by Lorenz Hart
Dancing Pirate (1936) F

Are You Ready, Gyp Watson?
Music and lyrics by Harold Rome
Destry Rides Again 1959

Are You Sure?
Music and lyrics by Meredith Willson
The Unsinkable Molly Brown 1960

Are You There?
Music by Harry Tierney
Lyrics by Joseph McCarthy
Rio Rita 1927

Are You With It?
Music by Harry Revel
Lyrics by Arnold B. Horwitt
Are You With It? 1945

Are You With Me?
Music and lyrics by Elizabeth Swados
Nightclub Cantata (OB) 1977

Aren't You Glad?
Music and lyrics by Frank Loesser
The Most Happy Fella 1956

Aren't You Kind of Glad We Did?
Music by George Gershwin
Lyrics by Ira Gershwin
The Shocking Miss Pilgrim (1947) F

Adapted by Kay Swift and Ira Gershwin from
manuscripts of George Gershwin.

Aren't You Warm?
Music by Richard B. Chodosh
Lyrics by Barry Alan Grael
The Streets of New York (OB) 1963

Argentina
Music by George Gershwin
Lyrics by B.G. DeSylva and E. Ray Goetz
George White's Scandals (1922)

Argentine
Music by Jean Schwartz
Lyrics by Alfred Bryan
A Night in Spain 1927

The Argument
Music by Milton Schafer
Lyrics by Ronny Graham
Bravo Giovanni 1962

Argument
Music by Steve Sterner
Lyrics by Peter del Valle
Lovers (OB) 1975

Aries
Music by Ron Steward and Neal Tate
Lyrics by Ron Steward
Sambo (OB) 1969

Ari's Promise
Music by Walt Smith
Lyrics by Leon Uris
Ari 1971

Arm in Arm
Music and lyrics by Meredith Willson
Here's Love 1963

Armadillo Idyll
Music by Donald Swann
Lyrics by Michael Flanders
At the Drop of Another Hat 1966

The Armorer's Song
Music by Reginald De Koven
Lyrics by Harry B. Smith
Robin Hood 1891

Arms for the Love of Me
Music by Richard B. Chodosh
Lyrics by Barry Alan Grael
The Streets of New York (OB) 1963

The Army Mule Song
Music and lyrics by Ralph Blane
Three Wishes for Jamie 1952

The Army of the Just
Music by Jerry Bock
Lyrics by Sheldon Harnick
Tenderloin 1960

Army Song
Music by Kurt Weill
Lyrics by Marc Blitzstein
The Threepenny Opera (OB) 1954

The Army's Made a Man Out of Me
Music and lyrics by Irving Berlin
This Is the Army 1942

Around the Town
Music and lyrics by Irving Berlin
Watch Your Step 1914

Around the World in Eighty Days
Music by Victor Young
Lyrics by Harold Adamson
Around the World in Eighty Days (1956) F

The Arrest
Music by Andrew Lloyd Webber
Lyrics by Tim Rice
Jesus Christ Superstar 1971

The Arrival
Music by Larry Grossman
Lyrics by Betty Comden and Adolph Green
A Doll's Life 1982

The Arrival of Society
Music and lyrics by George M. Cohan
The Rise of Rosie O'Reilly 1923

Arrival of Tourists
Music by Ralph Benatzky
Lyrics by Irving Caesar
White Horse Inn 1936

Art
Music by Frank Black
Lyrics by Gladys Shelley
The Duchess Misbehaves 1946

Art
Music and lyrics by Cole Porter
Silk Stockings 1955

Dropped from production

Art for Art's Sake
Music and lyrics by Marc Blitzstein
The Cradle Will Rock 1938

Art Is Calling Me (I Want to Be a Prima Donna)
Music by Victor Herbert
Lyrics by Harry B. Smith
The Enchantress 1911

The Art of Conversation
Music by Jerry Bock
Lyrics by Sheldon Harnick
The Body Beautiful 1958

The Art of the Possible
Music by Andrew Lloyd Webber
Lyrics by Tim Rice
Evita 1979

Art Song
Music and lyrics by Al Carmines
The Faggot (OB) 1973

Arthur in the Afternoon
Music by John Kander
Lyrics by Fred Ebb
The Act 1977

Arthur, Son of Martha
Music by John Addison
Lyrics by John Cranko
Cranks 1956

Artie
Music by Gustav Luders
Lyrics by Frank Pixley
The Prince of Pilsen 1903

Artificial Flowers
Music by Jerry Bock
Lyrics by Sheldon Harnick
Tenderloin 1960

Arty
Music by James Wise
Lyrics by David Bimonte
Put It in Writing (OB) 1963

Aryans Under the Skin
Music and lyrics by Irving Berlin
This Is the Army 1942

As a Troubador
Music by Milton Susskind
Lyrics by Paul Porter and Benjamin Hapgood Burt
Florida Girl 1925

As Adam
Music by Stan Harte, Jr.
Leaves of Grass (OB) 1971

As Busy as Anyone Can Be
Music by Gordon Duffy
Lyrics by Harry M. Haldane
Happy Town 1959

As Far as I'm Concerned
Music by Richard Rodgers
Lyrics by Martin Charnin
Two by Two 1970

As Good as Paradise
Music by Stanley Silverman
Lyrics by Arthur Miller
Up From Paradise (OB) 1983

As I Grow Older
Music and lyrics by Harry Chapin
The Night That Made America Famous 1975

As I Went Over
Music by Helen Miller
Lyrics by Eve Merriam
Inner City 1971

As If
Music by Albert T. Viola
Lyrics by William S. Kilborne, Jr.
Head Over Heels 1981

As I'm Growing Older
Music and lyrics by Al Carmines
Wanted (OB) 1972

As Long as He Needs Me
Music and lyrics by Lionel Bart
Oliver! 1963

As Long as I Have You
Music by Albert Von Tilzer
Lyrics by Neville Fleeson
The Gingham Girl 1922

As Long As I've Got My Mammy
Music by Joseph Meyer and James F. Hanley
Lyrics by B.G. DeSylva
Big Boy 1925

As Long as There's a Mother
Music by Glenn Paxton
Lyrics by Robert Goldman and George Weiss
First Impressions 1959

As Long as We're in Love
Music by Jimmy McHugh
Lyrics by Dorothy Fields
Hello Daddy 1928

As of Today
Music by Arthur Schwartz
Lyrics by Dorothy Fields
Stars in Your Eyes 1939

As On Through the Seasons We Sail
Music and lyrics by Cole Porter
Silk Stockings 1955

As Once I Loved You
Music by Richard Rodgers
Lyrics by Sheldon Harnick
Rex 1976

As Simple as That
Music and lyrics by Jerry Herman
Milk and Honey 1961

As the Girls Go
Music by Jimmy McHugh
Lyrics by Harold Adamson
As the Girls Go 1948

As Though You Were There
Music by Richard Rodgers
Lyrics by Lorenz Hart
Heads Up! 1929

Dropped from production

As Time Goes By
Music and lyrics by Herman Hupfeld
Everybody's Welcome 1931

Also in the film *Casablanca* (1942)

As We Leave the Years Behind
Music by Joseph Meyer
Lyrics by Ballard MacDonald
Battling Buttler 1923

Ascot Gavotte
Music by Frederick Loewe
Lyrics by Alan Jay Lerner
My Fair Lady 1956

Ashes and Fire
Music by Frank Harling
Lyrics by Laurence Stallings
Deep River 1926

Ask and You Shall Receive
Music by Ron Steward and Neal Tate
Lyrics by Ron Steward
Sambo (OB) 1969

Ask Dad
Music by Louis A. Hirsch
Lyrics by P.G. Wodehouse
Oh, My Dear! 1918

Ask Her While the Band Is Playing
Music by Victor Herbert
Lyrics by Glen MacDonough
Algeria 1908

Ask Me Again
Music by George Lessner
Lyrics by Miriam Battista and Russell Maloney
Sleepy Hollow 1948

Asking for You
Music by Jule Styne
Lyrics by Betty Comden and Adolph Green
Do Re Mi 1960

The Assyrians
Music by Galt MacDermot
Lyrics by William Dumaresq
The Human Comedy (OB) 1983

A-Stage
Music by Galt MacDermot
Lyrics by Gerome Ragni
Dude 1972

A-stairable Rag
Music and lyrics by Cole Porter
You'll Never Get Rich (1941) F

Dropped from film

Astoria Gloria
Music by Gary Geld
Lyrics by Peter Udell
Angel 1978

Astrociggy
Music by Susan Hulsman Bingham
Lyrics by Myrna Lamb
Mod Donna (OB) 1970

Astrology
Music by Ron Steward and Neal Tate
Lyrics by Ron Steward
Sambo (OB) 1969

At 0700 Tomorrow
Music and lyrics by Gene Curty, Nitra Scharfman
and Chuck Strand
The Lieutenant 1975

At Christmastime
Music and lyrics by Robert Wright and George
Forrest
Song of Norway 1944

Based on Grieg's song *Woodland Wanderings*

At Half Past Seven
Music by George Gershwin
Lyrics by B.G. DeSylva
Nifties of 1923

At Home With the Clinkers
Music and lyrics by Walter Marks
Broadway Follies 1981

At Last
Music by Henry Tobias
Lyrics by Charles Tobias and Sam Lewis
Earl Carroll's Sketch Book (1935)

At Last
Music by Larry Grossman
Lyrics by Betty Comden and Adolph Green
A Doll's Life 1982

At Last It's Love
Music by Morgan Lewis
Lyrics by Nancy Hamilton
Two for the Show 1940

At Long Last
Music by Lee Wainer
Lyrics by Robert Sour
Sing for Your Supper 1939

At Long Last Love
Music and lyrics by Cole Porter
You Never Know 1938

The lyric is a series of contrasts: "Is it the good turtle soup, or merely the mock?" There are three choruses and a fourth one which Porter never finished. The title itself is thought to have been suggested by the phrase, "at long last," with which King Edward VIII began his abdication speech in 1936.

At Longchamps Today
Music and lyrics by Cole Porter
Fifty Million Frenchmen 1929

At Lovetime
Music by H. Maurice Jacquet
Lyrics by Preston Sturges
The Well of Romance 1930

At Madame Regay's
Music and lyrics by George M. Cohan
The Rise of Rosie O'Reilly 1923

At Night She Comes Home to Me
Music by David Shire
Lyrics by Richard Maltby, Jr.
Baby 1983

At Our Tango Tea
Music by Bert Lee
Lyrics by Worton David
The Girl From Utah 1914

At Siesta Time
Music by Frederic Norton
Lyrics by Oscar Asche
Chu Chin Chow 1917

At That San Francisco Fair
Music by Jerome Kern, Ford Dabney
and James Europe
Lyrics by Schuyler Greene
Nobody Home 1915

Kern composed the verse, Dabney and Europe the chorus

At the Ball
Music by Sol Berkowitz
Lyrics by James Lipton
Miss Emily Adam (OB) 1960

At the Ballet
Music by Marvin Hamlisch
Lyrics by Edward Kleban
A Chorus Line 1975

At the Barbecue
Music by Dave Stamper and Harold Levey
Lyrics by Harry A. Steinberg and Eddie Ward
Lovely Lady 1927

At the Barbecue
Music and lyrics by Al Wilson, Charles Weinberg
and Ken Macomber
Yeah Man 1932

At the Bottom Lookin' Up
Music by Harris Wheeler
Lyrics by Mary L. Fisher
Blue Plate Special (OB) 1983

At the Check Apron Ball
Music and lyrics by Bob Merrill
New Girl in Town 1957

At the End of the Day
Music and lyrics by Johnny Brandon
Billy Noname (OB) 1970

At the Gate of Roses
Music and lyrics by Clarence Gaskill
Earl Carroll's Vanities (1925)

At the Mardi Gras
Music by Arthur Schwartz
Lyrics by Howard Dietz
Inside U.S.A. 1948

At the Matinee
Music by Frank Grey
Lyrics by McElbert Moore and Frank Grey
The Matinee Girl 1926

At the Music Hall
Music by Gerald Jay Markoe
Lyrics by Michael Colby
Charlotte Sweet (OB) 1982

At the Opera
Music and lyrics by Stephen Oliver
The Life and Times of Nicholas Nickleby 1981

At the Party
Music by Harry Ruby
Lyrics by Bert Kalmar
Sweetheart Time 1926

At the Playland Jamboree
Music and lyrics by Robert Dahdah
Curley McDimple (OB) 1967

At the Red Rose Cotillion
Music and lyrics by Frank Loesser
Where's Charley? 1948

At the Round Table
Music by Richard Rodgers
Lyrics by Lorenz Hart
A Connecticut Yankee 1927

At the Roxy Music Hall
Music by Richard Rodgers
Lyrics by Lorenz Hart
I Married an Angel 1938

At the Saskatchewan
Music by Richard Rodgers
Lyrics by Lorenz Hart
Betsy 1926

Dropped from production

At the Spotlight Canteen
Music by Philip Charig
Lyrics by Dan Shapiro and Milton Pascal
Follow the Girls 1944

At the Thé Dansant
Music by Jerome Kern
Lyrics by Edgar Allan Woolf
Head Over Heels 1918

At Twenty-Two
Music by Harvey Schmidt
Lyrics by Tom Jones
Shoestring '57 (OB)

At Ye Olde Coffee Shoppe in Cheyenne
Music and lyrics by Cole Porter
Red, Hot and Blue! 1936

At Your Service
Music by C. Luckey Roberts
Lyrics by Alex C. Rogers
My Magnolia 1926

At Ze Naughty Folies Bergères
Music by Gustave Kerker
Lyrics by Hugh Morton
The Belle of New York 1897

Athletic Prancing
Music by Karl Hoschna
Lyrics by Otto Harbach
Madame Sherry 1910

Atlanta
Music by Arthur Schwartz
Lyrics by Howard Dietz
Inside U.S.A. 1948

Dropped from production

The Atlantic City Girl
Music by Maury Rubens
Lyrics by Clifford Grey
The Great Temptations 1926

Au Revoir
Music by Joseph Meyer
Lyrics by William Moll
Jonica 1930

Au Revoir
Music by Laurence Rosenthal
Lyrics by James Lipton
Sherry! 1967

Au Revoir
Music and lyrics by Ann Harris
Sky High (OB) 1979

Au Revoir, Cher Baron
Music and lyrics by Cole Porter
You Never Know 1938

Au Revoir Poland—Hello New York
Music by Albert Hague
Lyrics by Marty Brill
Café Crown 1964

Au Revoir, Soldier
Music by Bronislaw Kaper (based on Chopin)
Lyrics by John Latouche
Polonaise 1945

Auctioneer's Song
Music by Reginald De Koven
Lyrics by Harry B. Smith
Robin Hood 1891

Auctions
Music by Leonard Bernstein
Lyrics by Alan Jay Lerner
1600 Pennsylvania Avenue 1976

Auf Wiedersehen
Music by Charles Strouse
Lyrics by Alan Jay Lerner
Dance a Little Closer 1983

Auf Wiedersehn!
Music by Sigmund Romberg
Lyrics by Herbert Reynolds
The Blue Paradise 1915

Aunt Dinah Has Blowed de Horn
Music and lyrics by Scott Joplin
Treemonisha 1975

Written in 1909

Aunt Jemima
Music and lyrics by Porter Grainger
and Freddie Johnson
Lucky Sambo 1925

Aurora Blushing Rosily
Music by Victor Herbert
Lyrics by David Stevens and Justin Huntly
McCarthy
The Madcap Duchess 1913

Aurory Bory Alice
Music by Lily Hyland
Lyrics by Agnes Morgan
The Grand Street Follies (1926) (OB)

Auto Da Fé—What a Day
Music by Leonard Bernstein
Lyrics by Stephen Sondheim and John Latouche
Candide (Added to 1973 revival)

Autograph Chant
Music by Jule Styne
Lyrics by Bob Hilliard
Hazel Flagg 1953

Autumn
Music by David Shire
Lyrics by Richard Maltby, Jr.
Starting Here, Starting Now (OB) 1977

Autumn Carol
Music by Michael J. Lewis
Lyrics by Anthony Burgess
Cyrano 1973

Autumn in New York
Music and lyrics by Vernon Duke
Thumbs Up! 1934

Autumn's Here
Music and lyrics by Norman Dean
Autumn's Here (OB) 1966

Aviator
Music by George Gershwin
Lyrics by Ira Gershwin
Funny Face 1927

Dropped from production

Avonlea, We Love Thee
Music by Norman Campbell
Lyrics by Donald Harron and Norman Campbell
Anne of Green Gables (OB) 1971

Away
Music by Giuseppe Verdi (adapted by Hans Spialek)
Lyrics by Charles Friedman
My Darlin' Aïda 1952

Away From You
Music by Richard Rodgers
Lyrics by Sheldon Harnick
Rex 1976

A-Weaving
Music by Gerald Jay Markoe
Lyrics by Michael Colby
Charlotte Sweet (OB) 1982

Awefull Battle of the Pekes and Pollicles
Music by Andrew Lloyd Webber
Cats 1982

Lyrics based on T.S. Eliot's *Old Possum*'s *Book of Practical Cats*

The Ayes of Texas
Music by Norman Martin
Lyrics by Fred Ebb
Put It in Writing (OB) 1963

B

The Babbitt and the Bromide
Music by George Gershwin
Lyrics by Ira Gershwin
Funny Face 1927

Written just before the show's Broadway opening, the song was sung and danced by Fred and Adele Astaire, playing two "sub-sti-an-tial" businessmen who meet from time to time over the years and always talk in the same dreary clichés—"How're You?...What's New?...How's the Wife?...That's Life!" After each chorus (including a final one inside the pearly gates) the Astaires did their famous run-around dance. It was also sung and danced by Fred Astaire and Gene Kelly in the film *Ziegfeld Follies of 1946*. Ira Gershwin's title combined the leading character of the Sinclair Lewis novel *Babbitt* (1922) with the word "bromide," from Gelett Burgess' *Are You a Bromide?* (1907).

Babbling Babette
Music by Jerome Kern
Lyrics by Anne Caldwell
Stepping Stones 1923

Babes in Arms
Music by Richard Rodgers
Lyrics by Lorenz Hart
Babes in Arms 1937

Babes in the Wood
Music by Jerome Kern
Lyrics by Jerome Kern and Schuyler Greene
Very Good Eddie 1915

Babes in the Wood
Music and lyrics by Rick Besoyan
Babes in the Wood (OB) 1964

Babette
Music by Cy Coleman
Lyrics by Betty Comden and Adolph Green
On the Twentieth Century 1978

Babette of Beaujolais
Music by Victor Herbert
Lyrics by David Stevens and Justin Huntly McCarthy
The Madcap Duchess 1913

Baby!
Music by George Gershwin
Lyrics by B.G. DeSylva and Ira Gershwin
Tell Me More 1925

Baby
Music by Percy Wenrich
Lyrics by Raymond Peck
Castles in the Air 1926

Baby!
Music by Jimmy McHugh
Lyrics by Dorothy Fields
Blackbirds of 1928

Dropped from production

A Baby
Music by George Fischoff
Lyrics by Carole Bayer
Georgy 1970

Baby, Baby
Music by Sol Berkowitz
Lyrics by James Lipton
Nowhere to Go But Up 1962

Baby! Baby!
Music and lyrics by Hal Hester and Danny Apolinar
Your Own Thing (OB) 1968

Baby, Baby, Baby
Music by David Shire
Lyrics by Richard Maltby, Jr.
Baby 1983

26

The Baby Blues
Music by George Gershwin
Lyrics by E. Ray Goetz
Snapshots of 1921

A Baby Bond
Music by Richard Rodgers
Lyrics by Lorenz Hart
I'd Rather Be Right 1937

Baby Boom Boogie Boy
Music by Elizabeth Swados
Lyrics by Garry Trudeau
Doonesbury 1983

Baby Breath
Music by Galt MacDermot
Lyrics by Gerome Ragni
Dude 1972

Baby Couldn't Dance
Music by Vernon Duke
Lyrics by Ogden Nash
Two's Company 1952

Baby Doll
Music by Rudolf Friml
Lyrics by Rida Johnson Young
Sometime 1918

Baby-Doll Dance
Music by Maury Rubens
and Phil Svigals
Lyrics by J. Keirn Brennan
and Moe Jaffe
Broadway Nights 1929

Baby Dolls
Music by George Gershwin
Lyrics by B.G. DeSylva and John Henry Mears
Morris Gest Midnight Whirl 1919

Baby, Don't Count on Me
Music by Clay Warnick
Lyrics by Edward Eager
Dream With Music 1944

Baby Dream Your Dream
Music by Cy Coleman
Lyrics by Dorothy Fields
Sweet Charity 1966

Baby Games
Music and lyrics by Cole Porter
Let's Face It! 1941

Baby, I Could Do It for You
Music and lyrics by Al Wilson, Charles Weinberg
and Ken Macomber
Yeah Man 1932

A Baby in Love
Music by Ralph Benatzky, adapted by Alfred
Goodman
Lyrics by Edward Delaney Dunn
The Last Waltz 1921

Baby, It's Cold Outside
Music and lyrics by Frank Loesser
Neptune's Daughter (1949) F

Academy Award winner

Baby Johann
Music by Galt MacDermot
Lyrics by Rochelle Owens
The Karl Marx Play (OB) 1973

Baby, Let's Face It
Music by Sammy Fain
Lyrics by George Marion, Jr.
Toplitzky of Notre Dame 1946

Baby Mine
Music by C. Luckey Roberts
Lyrics by Alex C. Rogers
My Magnolia 1926

Baby, Talk to Me
Music by Charles Strouse
Lyrics by Lee Adams
Bye Bye Birdie 1960

The Baby Vampire
Music by Jerome Kern
Lyrics by Harry B. Smith
Love o' Mike 1917

Baby Wanna Go Bye-Bye
Music by Lewis E. Gensler
Lyrics by Owen Murphy and Robert A.Simon
The Gang's All Here 1931

Baby Wants
Music by C. Luckey Roberts
Lyrics by Alex C. Rogers
My Magnolia 1926

Baby! What?
Music by Ray Henderson
Lyrics by B.G. DeSylva and Lew Brown
Good News 1927

Baby, You Bore Me
Music by Jeanne Bargy
Lyrics by Jeanne Bargy, Frank Gehrecke
and Herb Corey
Greenwich Village U.S.A. (OB) 1960

Baby, You Can Count on Me
Music by Charles Strouse
Lyrics by Lee Adams
Bring Back Birdie 1981

The Baby You Love
Music by Richard Rodgers
Lyrics by Oscar Hammerstein II
Me and Juliet 1953

Dropped from production

Babykins
Music by Oscar Levant
Lyrics by Irving Caesar and Graham John
Ripples 1930

Baby's Awake Now
Music by Richard Rodgers
Lyrics by Lorenz Hart
Spring Is Here 1929

Baby's Baby
Music by David Baker
Lyrics by David Craig
Copper and Brass 1957

Baby's Baby Grand
Music by Al Goodman and J. Fred Coots
Lyrics by Clifford Grey
Gay Paree 1925

A Baby's Best Friend
Music by Richard Rodgers
Lyrics by Lorenz Hart
She's My Baby 1928

Same music as "Lullaby," sung by Beatrice Lillie in
Andre Charlot's London revue *Please*! (1934).

Baby's Blue
Music and lyrics by Herman Hupfeld
A La Carte 1927

Bacchanale
Music by Don Elliott
Lyrics by James Costigan
The Beast in Me 1963

The Bachelor
Music by Jerome Kern
Lyrics by P.G. Wodehouse
Oh, Boy! 1917

Dropped from production

Bachelor Days
Music by Louis Hirsch
Lyrics by Gene Buck
Ziegfeld Follies of 1916

Bachelor Hoedown
Music by Jerry Bock
Lyrics by Larry Holofcener
Catch a Star! 1955

Bachelor's Dance
Music by Jacques Brel
English lyrics by Eric Blau and Mort Shuman
*Jacques Brel Is Alive and Well
and Living in Paris* (OB) 1968

Back at the Palace
Music by Clay Warnick
Lyrics by Mel Tolkin and Lucille Kallen
Tickets Please 1950

Back Bay Beat
Music by Jerry Livingston
Lyrics by Mack David
Bright Lights of 1944

The Back Bay Polka
Music by George Gershwin
Lyrics by Ira Gershwin
The Shocking Miss Pilgrim (1947) F

Adapted by Kay Swift and Ira Gershwin from
manuscripts of George Gershwin.

Back From Hollywood
Music by Ray Henderson
Lyrics by B.G. DeSylva and Lew Brown
George White's Scandals (1931)

Back in My Shell
Music by Jerome Kern
Lyrics by Dorothy Fields
One Night in the Tropics (1940) F

Back in Show Biz Again
Music by Charles Strouse
Lyrics by Lee Adams
Bring Back Birdie 1981

Back in the Days of Long Ago
Music by Alma Sanders
Lyrics by Monte Carlo
The Houseboat on the Styx 1928

Back in the Kitchen
Music by Jule Styne
Lyrics by Betty Comden and Adolph Green
Hallelujah, Baby! 1967

Back in the Street
Music by Ted Simons
Lyrics by Elinor Guggenheimer
Potholes (OB) 1979

Back in the World Now
Music and lyrics by Elizabeth Swados
Dispatches (OB) 1979

Back to Bundling
Music by Lee Wainer
Lyrics by Dorothy Sachs
New Faces of 1943

Back to Genesis
Music and lyrics by Peter Link
and C. C. Courtney
Salvation (OB) 1969

Back to the Boulevards
Music by Gustav Luders
Lyrics by Frank Pixley
The Prince of Pilsen 1903

Back to the Farm
Music and lyrics by Bud Burtson
Ziegfeld Follies (1943)

Back to Work
Music and lyrics by Harold Rome
Pins and Needles (OB) 1937

Added during run

Back With a Beat/Nothing But
Music by Gary William Friedman
Lyrics by Will Holt
Platinum 1978

Back Your Fancy!
Music by Lionel Monckton
Lyrics by Arthur Wimperis
The Arcadians 1910

Backstage Babble
Music by Charles Strouse
Lyrics by Lee Adams
Applause 1970

Backwards
Music by Hank Beebe
Lyrics by Bill Heyer
*Tuscaloosa's Calling Me
but I'm Not Going!* (OB) 1975

A Bad Boy and a Good Girl
Music by Lionel Monckton
Lyrics by Percy Greenbank
The Quaker Girl 1911

Bad Breath
Music and lyrics by Jill Williams
Rainbow Jones 1974

Bad but Good
Music and lyrics by Peter Copani
New York City Street Show (OB) 1977

Bad Companions
Music by Leroy Anderson
Lyrics by Joan Ford and Walter and Jean Kerr
Goldilocks 1958

The Bad, Bad Men
Music by George Gershwin
Lyrics by Ira Gershwin
Lady, Be Good! 1924

Dropped from production

Bad Girl
Music by Maurice Yvain
Lyrics by Max and Nathaniel Lief
Luckee Girl 1928

Bad If He Does, Worse If He Don't
Music by Ray Haney
Lyrics by Alfred Aiken
We're Civilized? (OB) 1962

The Bad in Every Man
Music by Richard Rodgers
Lyrics by Lorenz Hart
Manhattan Melodrama (1934) F

Same music as "Prayer" and "Blue Moon"

Bad Karma
Music and lyrics by Peter Stampfel and Antonia
Operation Sidewinder 1970

Bad Little Boy With Dancing Legs
Music by Mann Holiner
Lyrics by Alberta Nichols
Gay Paree 1926

Bad Luck, I'll Laugh at You
Music by Dave Stamper and Harold Levey
Lyrics by Cyrus Wood
Lovely Lady 1927

Bad Man Number
Music by Rudolf Friml
Lyrics by Brian Hooker
The White Eagle 1927

Bad Men
Music by Cole Porter
Lyrics by T. Lawrason Riggs and Cole Porter
See America First 1916

Bad Timing
Music by Morton Gould
Lyrics by Betty Comden and Adolph Green
Billion Dollar Baby 1945

Badaroma
Music by Albert Selden
Lyrics by Burt Shevelove
Small Wonder 1948

Baddest Mammyjammy
Music by Ron Steward and Neal Tate
Lyrics by Ron Steward
Sambo (OB) 1969

The Bag of Luck
Music and lyrics by Scott Joplin
Treemonisha 1975

Written in 1909

Bagdad
Music by Victor Herbert
Lyrics by James O'Dea
The Lady of the Slipper 1912

Bagdad
Music by Sigmund Romberg
Lyrics by Harold Atteridge
Sinbad (1918)

Bah! Bah!
Music by John Philip Sousa
Lyrics by Tom Frost and John Philip Sousa
El Capitan 1896

Bailar!
Music and lyrics by John Clifton
El Bravo! (OB) 1981

Bajour
Music and lyrics by Walter Marks
Bajour 1964

The Baker's Boy and the Chimney Sweep
Music by Victor Herbert
Lyrics by Robert B. Smith
The Debutante 1914

Bal Petit Bal
Music and lyrics by Francis Lemarque
New Faces of 1952

The Balalaika Serenade
Music by Franz Steininger (adapted from
Tchaikovsky)
Lyrics by Forman Brown
Music in My Heart 1947

Bali Ha'i
Music by Richard Rodgers
Lyrics by Oscar Hammerstein II
South Pacific 1949

Balinasia
Music and lyrics by Matt Dubey and Dean Fuller
Smith (OB) 1973

The Ball
Music by Mitch Leigh
Lyrics by Charles Burr and Forman Brown
Home Sweet Homer 1976

Ballad for a Firing Squad
Music by Edward Thomas
Lyrics by Martin Charnin
Ballad for a Firing Squad (OB) 1968

A Ballad for Americans
Music by Earl Robinson
Lyrics by John Latouche
Sing For Your Supper 1939

Ballad for Billionaires
Music by Albert Selden
Lyrics by Burt Shevelove
Small Wonder 1948

Ballad for Bimshire
Music and lyrics by Irving Burgie
Ballad for Bimshire (OB) 1963

Ballad Maker
Music and lyrics by Oscar Brand and Paul Nassau
A Joyful Noise 1966

Ballad of a Redneck
Music and lyrics by Don Tucker
Red, White and Maddox 1969

Ballad of Adam and Eve
Music by Joe Ercole
Lyrics by Bruce Kluger
Ka-Boom (OB) 1980

The Ballad of Cy and Beatrice
Music by Paul Trueblood
Lyrics by Jim Morgan
Upstairs at O'Neal's (OB) 1982

Ballad of Dependency
Music by Kurt Weill
Lyrics by Marc Blitzstein
The Threepenny Opera (OB) 1954

The Ballad of Johnny Pot
Music by Clinton Ballard
Lyrics by Carolyn Richter
The Ballad of Johnny Pot (OB) 1971

Ballad of Sir Topaz
Music by Paul Hoffert
Lyrics by David Secter
Get Thee to Canterbury (OB) 1969

The Ballad of Sweeney Todd
Music and lyrics by Stephen Sondheim
Sweeney Todd 1979

Ballad of Tancred
Music by Edward Earle
Lyrics by Yvonne Tarr
The Decameron (OB) 1961

Ballad of the Easy Life
Music by Kurt Weill
Lyrics by Marc Blitzstein
The Threepenny Opera (OB) 1954

Ballad of the Garment Trade
Music and lyrics by Harold Rome
I Can Get It for You Wholesale 1962

Ballad of the Gun
Music and lyrics by Harold Rome
Destry Rides Again 1959

Ballad of the Lily of Hell
Music by Kurt Weill
Lyrics by Bertolt Brecht (adapted by Michael
Feingold)
Happy End 1977

Ballad of the Robbers
Music by Kurt Weill
Lyrics by Maxwell Anderson
Knickerbocker Holiday 1938

The Ballad of the Sad Café
Music and lyrics by Elizabeth Swados
Nightclub Cantata (OB) 1977

The Ballad of the Sad Young Men
Music by Tommy Wolf
Lyrics by Fran Landesman
The Nervous Set 1959

Ballad of the Victim
Music and lyrics by Bob Ost
Everybody's Gettin' Into the Act (OB) 1981

Ballad to a Brute
Music by Moose Charlap
Lyrics by Eddie Lawrence
Kelly 1965

Ballade
Music and lyrics by Charles Gaynor
Lend an Ear 1948

The Ballerina's Story
Music by Franz Steininger (adapted from
Tchaikovsky)
Lyrics by Forman Brown
Music in My Heart 1947

Ballin'
Music and lyrics by Peter Link and C. C. Courtney
Salvation (OB) 1969

A Balloon Is Ascending
Music by Mark Sandrich, Jr.
Lyrics by Sidney Michaels
Ben Franklin in Paris 1964

Balloons
Music and lyrics by Jack Holmes
From A to Z 1960

Ballyhujah
Music by Lewis E. Gensler
Lyrics by E.Y. Harburg
Ballyhoo 1932

Baltimore Buzz
Music and lyrics by Noble Sissle
and Euble Blake
Shuffle Along 1921

Bambalina
Music by Vincent Youmans
Lyrics by Otto Harbach and
Oscar Hammerstein II
Wildflower 1923

Bambazoola
Music by Jean Schwartz
Lyrics by Alfred Bryan
A Night in Spain 1927

Bamboo Babies
Music by Joseph Meyer
and James F. Hanley
Lyrics by Ballard MacDonald
Gay Paree 1925

Bamboola
Music and lyrics by Frank Marcus
and Bernard Maltin
Bamboola 1929

The Band Started Swinging a Song
Music and lyrics by Cole Porter
Seven Lively Arts 1944

Added during run

Bandana Days
Music and lyrics by Noble Sissle
and Eubie Blake
Shuffle Along 1921

Bandanna Babies
Music by Jimmy McHugh
Lyrics by Dorothy Fields
Blackbirds of 1928

Bandanna Ball
Music and lyrics by Irving Berlin
Music Box Revue (4th edition) 1924

Bandanna Ways
Music by Eubie Blake
Lyrics by Noble Sissle
Shuffle Along of 1933

The Bane of Man
Music by Franz Lehár
Lyrics by Edward Eliscu
Frederika 1937

Bang!
Music and lyrics by Stephen Sondheim
Marry Me a Little (OB) 1981

Dropped from *A Little Night Music* (1973)

Bang, the Bell Rang!
Music by Irving Actman
Lyrics by Frank Loesser
The Illustrators' Show 1936

Banjo Eyes
Music by Vernon Duke
Lyrics by John Latouche
Banjo Eyes 1941

The Banjo That Man Joe Plays
Music and lyrics by Cole Porter
Wake Up and Dream 1929

Bankrupt Blues
Music by Stanley Silverman
Lyrics by Tom Hendry
Doctor Selavy's Magic Theatre (OB) 1972

Banks of the Wye
Music by Frank E. Tours
Lyrics by F. E. Wetherly
Miss Information 1915

The Banquet
Music by Max Ewing
Lyrics by Agnes Morgan
The Grand Street Follies (1927) (OB)

Barbara
Music by David Shire
Lyrics by Richard Maltby, Jr.
Starting Here, Starting Now (OB) 1977

Barbara Song
Music by Kurt Weill
Lyrics by Marc Blitzstein
The Threepenny Opera (OB) 1954

Barbary Coast
Music by George Gershwin
Lyrics by Ira Gershwin
Girl Crazy 1930

The Barber and His Wife
Music and lyrics by Stephen Sondheim
Sweeney Todd 1979

The Barber of Seville
Music by Maury Rubens
Lyrics by Clifford Grey
Sky High 1925

Barber's Song
Music by Mitch Leigh
Lyrics by Joe Darion
Man of La Mancha 1965

Barbizon
Music by Lionel Monckton
Lyrics by Adrian Ross
The Quaker Girl 1911

Barcelona
Music and lyrics by Stephen Sondheim
Company 1970

The Bard
Music by Alec Wilder
Lyrics by Arnold Sundgaard
Kittiwake Island (OB) 1960

Barefoot Boy
Music by James F. Hanley
Lyrics by Chris Taylor
Ziegfeld Follies (1934)

Barefoot Gal
Music and lyrics by Oscar Brand
and Paul Nassau
A Joyful Noise 1966

Barefoot Girl
Music by Oscar Levant
Lyrics by Irving Caesar and Graham John
Ripples 1930

Bargaining
Music by Richard Rodgers
Lyrics by Stephen Sondheim
Do I Hear a Waltz? 1965

A Barking Baby Never Bites
Music by Richard Rodgers
Lyrics by Lorenz Hart
Higher And Higher 1940

Barnabo
Music by Edward Earle
Lyrics by Yvonne Tarr
The Decameron (OB) 1961

Barnaby Beach
Music by Morgan Lewis
Lyrics by Nancy Hamilton
Three to Make Ready 1946

Barney O'Flynn
Music by Victor Herbert
Lyrics by Glen MacDonough
Babes in Toyland 1903

Barnum Had the Right Idea
Music and lyrics by George M. Cohan
The Little Millionaire 1911

The Barnyard
Music and lyrics by Walter Marks
Broadway Follies 1981

The Baron, the Duchess, and the Count
Music by Alberta Nichols
Lyrics by Mann Holiner
Angela 1928

Barrel of Beads
Music by Vernon Duke
Lyrics by Howard Dietz
Sadie Thompson 1944

Basic
Music and lyrics by Deed Meyer
She Shall Have Music (OB) 1959

Basket, Make a Basket
Music by Baldwin Bergersen
Lyrics by William Archibald
Carib Song 1945

The Basketball Song
Music and lyrics by Elizabeth Swados
Runaways 1978

Bathroom
Music and lyrics by James Rado
Rainbow (OB) 1972

The Battle at Eagle Rock
Music and lyrics by Mel Mandel
and Norman Sachs
My Old Friends (OB) 1979

Battle Cry
Music and lyrics by Eaton Magoon, Jr.
Heathen 1972

The Battle of Chicago
Music and lyrics by Johnny Brandon
Love! Love! Love! (OB) 1977

Battle of the Genie
Music by Clay Warnick
Lyrics by Edward Eager
Dream With Music 1944

Battleground Bummer
Music and lyrics by Harry Chapin
The Night That Made America Famous 1975

Baubles, Bangles and Beads
Music and lyrics by Robert Wright
and George Forrest
Kismet 1953

Based on Borodin's String Quartet in D

Bauer's House
Music by George Gershwin
Lyrics by Ira Gershwin
Pardon My English 1933

Dropped from production

Bazaar of the Caravans
Music and lyrics by Robert Wright
and George Forrest
Kismet 1953

Be a Clown
Music and lyrics by Cole Porter
The Pirate (1948) F

Be a Lion
Music and lyrics by Charlie Smalls
The Wiz 1975

Be a Little Lackadaisical
Music and lyrics by Herman Hupfeld
Hey Nonny Nonny! 1932

Be a Little Sunbeam
Music by Jerome Kern
Lyrics by P.G. Wodehouse
Oh, Boy! 1917

Dropped from production

Be a Lover
Music by Robert Kessler
Lyrics by Lola Pergament
O Marry Me! (OB) 1961

Be a Mess
Music by Jay Gorney
Lyrics by Jean and Walter Kerr
Touch and Go 1949

Be a Performer!
Music by Cy Coleman
Lyrics by Carolyn Leigh
Little Me 1962

Be a Pussycat
Music by George Kleinsinger
Lyrics by Joe Darion
Shinbone Alley 1957

Be a Santa
Music by Jule Styne
Lyrics by Betty Comden and Adolph Green
Subways Are for Sleeping 1961

Be Back Soon
Music and lyrics by Lionel Bart
Oliver! 1963

Be Black
Music by Ron Steward and Neal Tate
Lyrics by Ron Steward
Sambo (OB) 1969

Be Careful, It's My Heart
Music and lyrics by Irving Berlin
Holiday Inn (1942) F

Be Gentle
Music and lyrics by Hal Hester and Danny Apolinar
Your Own Thing (OB) 1968

Be Glad You're Alive
Music by Clay Warnick
Lyrics by Edward Eager
Dream With Music 1944

Be Good, Be Good, Be Good
Music and lyrics by James Shelton
Mrs. Patterson 1954

Be Good or Be Gone
Music and lyrics by Jim Swann
Pump Boys and Dinettes 1982

Be Good to Me
Music by Vincent Youmans
Lyrics by Ring Lardner
Smiles 1930

Be Grateful for What You've Got
Music and lyrics by Robert Dahdah
Curley McDimple (OB) 1967

Be Happy
Music by Larry Grossman
Lyrics by Hal Hackady
Minnie's Boys 1970

Be Happy
Music by Frederick Loewe
Lyrics by Alan Jay Lerner
The Little Prince (1975) F

Be Happy, Boys, Tonight
Music by Victor Herbert
Lyrics by Henry Blossom
The Only Girl 1914

Be Happy, Too
Music by Jerome Kern
Lyrics by Oscar Hammerstein II
Show Boat 1927

Dropped from production

Be Italian
Music and lyrics by Maury Yeston
Nine 1982

Be Kind to People Week
Music and lyrics by Jack Bussins
and Ellsworth Olin
Be Kind to People Week (OB) 1975

Be Kind to the Young
Music by Baldwin Bergersen
Lyrics by William Archibald
Rosa (OB) 1978

Be Kind to Your Parents
Music and lyrics by Harold Rome
Fanny 1954

Be Like the Bluebird
Music and lyrics by Cole Porter
Anything Goes 1934

Be My Guest
Music and lyrics by Johnny Mercer
Top Banana 1951

Be My Host
Music and lyrics by Richard Rodgers
No Strings 1962

Be Not Afraid
Music and lyrics by James Rado
Rainbow (OB) 1972

Be Oh So Careful, Ann
Music by H. Maurice Jacquet
Lyrics by Preston Sturges
The Well of Romance 1930

Be on Your Own
Music and lyrics by Maury Yeston
Nine 1982

Be Prepared
Music and lyrics by Tom Lehrer
Tomfoolery (OB) 1981

Be Sure It's Light
Music by Rudolf Friml
Lyrics by Otto Harbach and Edward Clark
You're In Love 1917

Be That Way
Music by Werner Janssen
Lyrics by Mann Holiner and J. Keirn Brennan
Boom-Boom 1929

Be the Life of the Crowd
Music by George Gershwin
Lyrics by B.G. DeSylva
Sweet Little Devil 1924

Dropped from production

Be Very Careful
Music by Ann Sternberg
Lyrics by Gertrude Stein
Gertrude Stein's First Reader (OB) 1969

Be Yourself
Music by Sam Pottle
Lyrics by Tom Whedon
All Kinds of Giants (OB) 1961

Beans, Beans, Beans
Music by Frederic Norton
Lyrics by Oscar Asche
Chu Chin Chow 1917

Bear Hunt
Music by Michael Leonard
Lyrics by Herbert Martin
The Yearling 1965

Bearing Silver Platters
Music by Alberta Nichols
Lyrics by Mann Holiner
Angela 1928

The Beast in You
Music by Leroy Anderson
Lyrics by Joan Ford and Walter and Jean Kerr
Goldilocks 1958

Beat, Little Pulse
Music and lyrics by Deed Meyer
'Toinette (OB) 1961

The Beat of a Heart
Music by Gordon Duffy
Lyrics by Harry M. Haldane
Happy Town 1959

The Beat of the City
Music by Mildred Kayden
Lyrics by Frank Gagliano
Paradise Gardens East (OB) 1969

Beat Out Dat Rhythm on a Drum
Music by Georges Bizet
Lyrics by Oscar Hammerstein II
Carmen Jones 1943

Beat the World
Music and lyrics by Jerry Herman
Madame Aphrodite (OB) 1961

Beatnik Love Affair
Music and lyrics by Noël Coward
Sail Away 1961

Beatrice Barefacts
Music by Victor Herbert
Lyrics by Glen MacDonough
Babes in Toyland 1903

Beatrice Lillie Ballad
Music by Randall Thompson
Lyrics by Agnes Morgan
The Grand Street Follies (1926) (OB)

Beautiful
Music and lyrics by Jerry Herman
Madame Aphrodite (OB) 1961

Beautiful
Music by John Kander
Lyrics by James Goldman, John Kander
and William Goldman
A Family Affair 1962

Beautiful
Music by David Shire
Lyrics by Richard Maltby, Jr.
Starting Here, Starting Now (OB) 1977

Beautiful
Music and lyrics by Stephen Sondheim
Sunday in the Park With George (OB) 1983

Beautiful Allelujah Days
Music and lyrics by Oscar Brown, Jr.
Buck White 1969

Beautiful Baby
Music by Con Conrad
Lyrics by William B. Friedlander
Mercenary Mary 1925

Beautiful Baby
Music by James F. Hanley
Lyrics by B.G. DeSylva
Queen High 1926

Beautiful, Beautiful Bed
Music by Dan Lipton
Lyrics by Lawrence Grossmith, C.W. Murphy
and Dan Lipton
Nobody Home 1915

Beautiful, Beautiful World
Music by Jerry Bock
Lyrics by Sheldon Harnick
The Apple Tree 1966

Beautiful Candy
Music and lyrics by Bob Merrill
Carnival 1961

Beautiful Children
Music and lyrics by Ronnie Britton
Gift of the Magi (OB) 1975

Beautiful for Once
Music and lyrics by Elizabeth Swados
Dispatches (OB) 1979

Beautiful Girls
Music by Joseph Meyer
Lyrics by William Moll
Jonica 1930

Beautiful Girls
Music and lyrics by Stephen Sondheim
Follies 1971

Beautiful Gypsy
Music by George Gershwin
Lyrics by Ira Gershwin
Rosalie 1928

Dropped from production

Beautiful Heaven
Music by Coleridge-Taylor Perkinson
Lyrics by Errol Hill
Man Better Man (OB) 1969

Beautiful Ladies of the Night
Music and lyrics by Clarence Gaskill
Earl Carroll's Vanities (1925)

Beautiful Lady, Tell Me
Music by Louis A. Hirsch
Lyrics by Rennold Wolf
The Rainbow Girl 1918

The Beautiful Land
Music and lyrics by Leslie Bricusse
and Anthony Newley
The Roar of the Greasepaint—The Smell of the Crowd 1965

Beautiful Man
Music by Susan Hulsman Bingham
Lyrics by Myrna Lamb
Mod Donna (OB) 1970

Beautiful Music
Music by Galt McDermot
Lyrics by William Dumaresq
The Human Comedy (OB) 1983

Beautiful Night
Music by Rudolf Friml
Lyrics by Rida Johnson Young
Sometime 1918

Beautiful Night
Music and lyrics by Ballard MacDonald,
Karl Stark and James F. Hanley
Thumbs Up! 1934

The Beautiful People
Music and lyrics by Tom Sankey
The Golden Screw (OB) 1967

Beautiful People of Denver
Music and lyrics by Meredith Willson
The Unsinkable Molly Brown 1960

The Beautiful Ship From Toyland
Music by Rudolf Friml
Lyrics by Otto Harbach
The Firefly 1912

Beautiful Soup
Music and lyrics by Elizabeth Swados
Alice in Concert (OB) 1980

Beautiful Through and Through
Music by Jule Styne
Lyrics by Bob Merrill
Sugar 1972

Beauty
Music by Ned Lehak
Lyrics by Allen Boretz
The Garrick Gaieties (3rd edition) 1930

Beauty
Music by Carl Millöcker (revised by Theo Mackeben)
Lyrics by Rowland Leigh
The Dubarry 1932

Beauty and the Beast
Music by Sigmund Romberg
Lyrics by Harold Atteridge
Sinbad (1918)

Beauty in the Movies
Music by Joseph Meyer and Roger Wolfe Kahn
Lyrics by Irving Caesar
Here's Howe 1928

Beauty Is Vanity
Music by Maury Rubens
Lyrics by Clifford Grey
The Great Temptations 1926

The Beauty of Bath
Music by Vivian Ellis
Lyrics by Graham John
By the Way 1925

Beauty School Dropout
Music and lyrics by Jim Jacobs
and Warren Casey
Grease 1972

The Beauty That Drives Me Mad
Music by Jule Styne
Lyrics by Bob Merrill
Sugar 1972

Because, Because
Music by George Gershwin
Lyrics by Ira Gershwin
Of Thee I Sing 1931

Because I'm a Woman
Music by Jimmy Horowitz
Lyrics by Leo Rost and Jimmy Horowitz
Marlowe 1981

Because You Love the Singer
Music by Jerome Kern
Lyrics by Anne Caldwell
Stepping Stones 1923

Because You're Beautiful
Music by Ray Henderson
Lyrics by B.G. DeSylva
Three Cheers 1928

Because You're Just You
Music by Jerome Kern
Lyrics by Gene Buck
Ziegfeld Follies of 1917

This melody, originally called "When Three Is Company" (lyric by M.E. Rourke), was interpolated in the 1913 show *The Doll Girl*. It was heard a third time in the Marilyn Miller version of *Peter Pan* (1924) as "The Sweetest Thing in Life" (lyrics by B.G. DeSylva).

Because You're You
Music by Victor Herbert
Lyrics by Henry Blossom
The Red Mill 1906

The Bed
Music by Galt MacDermot
Lyrics by Gerome Ragni and James Rado
Hair 1968

The Bedalumbo
Music by Sigmund Romberg
Lyrics by Harold Atteridge
Sinbad (1918)

A Bedtime Story
Music by Max Ewing
Lyrics by Agnes Morgan
The Grand Street Follies (1927) (OB)

Beecher's Defense
Music by Keith Hermann
Lyrics by Charlotte Anker and Irene Rosenberg
Onward Victoria 1980

Beecher's Processional
Music by Keith Hermann
Lyrics by Charlotte Anker and Irene Rosenberg
Onward Victoria 1980

Been a Long Day
Music and lyrics by Frank Loesser
How to Succeed in Business Without Really Trying 1961

Beer
Music and lyrics by Craig Carnelia
Is There Life After High School? 1982

Beer Is Best
Music by Richard Hill and John Hawkins
Lyrics by Nevill Coghill
Canterbury Tales 1969

The Beetle Race
Music by Harry Warren
Lyrics by Jerome Lawrence and Robert E. Lee
Shangri-La 1956

Before and After
Music by Victor Herbert
Lyrics by Glen MacDonough
Babes in Toyland 1903

Before and After
Music and lyrics by Billy Barnes
The Billy Barnes People 1961

Before I Gaze at You Again
Music by Frederick Loewe
Lyrics by Alan Jay Lerner
Camelot 1960

Before I Kiss the World Goodbye
Music by Arthur Schwartz
Lyrics by Howard Dietz
Jennie 1963

Before I Met You
Music by Jerome Kern
Lyrics by P.G. Wodehouse
Oh, Lady! Lady!! 1918

Before It's Too Late
Music by Baldwin Bergersen
Lyrics by William Archibald
Rosa (OB) 1978

Before the Parade Passes By
Music and lyrics by Jerry Herman
Hello, Dolly 1964

Before the World Was Made
Music by John Duffy
Lyrics by Rocco Bufano and John Duffy
Horseman, Pass By (OB) 1969

Before Your Very Eyes
Music and lyrics by Stephen Schwartz
The Magic Show 1974

Beg, Borrow or Steal
Music by Leon Pober
Lyrics by Bud Freeman
Beg, Borrow or Steal 1960

The Begat
Music by Burton Lane
Lyrics by E.Y. Harburg
Finian's Rainbow 1947

The Beggar Waltz (instrumental)
Music by Arthur Schwartz
Lyrics by Howard Dietz
The Band Wagon 1931

Subsequently set to words by Howard Dietz as "Is It All a Dream?," but not sung in the show.

Begging for Love
Music and lyrics by Irving Berlin
Shoot the Works 1931

Begin the Beguine
Music and lyrics by Cole Porter
Jubilee 1935

It wasn't until several years after the show closed that the song became popular. Then, helped considerably by an Artie Shaw recording, it was all but dinned to death. Porter himself grew so tired of hearing it that in the score for *Seven Lively Arts* he registered his own protest: "Dancing to a Jungle Drum (let's end the beguine!)." Noel Coward got In his whacks with the lyric of his song "Nina," from the London revue *Sigh No More* (1945): "...she declined to begin the beguine tho' they besought her to . . . she cursed Cole Porter too."

Beginner's Luck
Music by George Gershwin
Lyrics by Ira Gershwin
Shall We Dance (1937) F

The Beginning
Music by Wally Harper
Lyrics by Paul Zakrzewski
Sensations (OB) 1970

The Beginning
Music and lyrics by Charles Strouse
Six (OB) 1971

Beginning of Love
Music by Ray Henderson
Lyrics by B.G. DeSylva and Lew Brown
George White's Scandals (1931)

Beginning of the End
Music and lyrics by Harry Chapin
The Night That Made America Famous 1975

The Beguine
Music by Jim Wise
Lyrics by George Haimsohn and Robin Miller
Dames at Sea (OB) 1968

Behave Yourself
Music by Albert Hague
Lyrics by Dorothy Fields
Redhead 1959

Behind the Fan
Music and lyrics by Irving Berlin
Music Box Revue (1st edition) 1921

Behind the Mask
Music and lyrics by George M. Cohan
The Merry Malones 1927

Behold El Capitan
Music by John Philip Sousa
Lyrics by Tom Frost and Sousa
El Capitan 1896

Behold the Coming of the Sun
Music and lyrics by Ann Harris
Sky High (OB) 1979

Behold the King of Babylon
Music and lyrics by Gian-Carlo Menotti
The Medium 1947

Bein' a Kid
Music by Lance Mulcahy
Lyrics by Paul Cherry
Park 1970

Being Alive
Music by John Kander
Lyrics by Fred Ebb
The Happy Time 1968

Being Alive
Music and lyrics by Stephen Sondheim
Company 1970

Being Good Isn't Good Enough
Music by Jule Styne
Lyrics by Betty Comden and Adolph Green
Hallelujah, Baby! 1967

Being With You
Music and lyrics by Stan Daniels
So Long, 174th Street 1976

Believe
Music by John Kander
Lyrics by Fred Ebb
70, Girls, 70 1971

Believe in Me
Music by Arthur Schwartz
Lyrics by Harry B. Smith
The Red Robe 1928

Believe It or Not
Music by Percy Wenrich
Lyrics by Harry Clarke
Who Cares? 1930

Believe Me
Music by Rob Fremont
Lyrics by Doris Willens
Piano Bar (OB) 1978

Believe Us, Receive Us
Music by Joe Ercole
Lyrics by Bruce Kluger
Ka-Boom (OB) 1980

Believers' Chants
Music and lyrics by Voices, Inc.
The Believers (OB) 1968

Believers' Laments
Music and lyrics by Voices, Inc.
The Believers (OB) 1968

A Bell For Adano
Music by Arthur Schwartz
Lyrics by Howard Dietz
A Bell For Adano (1956) TV

Bella Donna
Music by Sigmund Romberg
Lyrics by Rowland Leigh
My Romance 1948

Bella Mia
Music by Jerome Kern
Lyrics by Herbert Reynolds
Rock-a-Bye Baby 1918

A Belle, a Beau and a Boutonnière
Music by Jean Schwartz
Lyrics by Clifford Grey and William Cary Duncan
Sunny Days 1928

Belle Plain
Music and lyrics by Irving Burgie
Ballad for Bimshire (OB) 1963

The Bellhops
Music and lyrics by Irving Berlin
The Cocoanuts 1925

Bells
Music and lyrics by Gary Portnoy and Judy Hart
Angelo
Preppies (OB) 1983

Bells
Music and lyrics by Irving Berlin
Ziegfeld Follies of 1920

Bells Are Ringing
Music by Jule Styne
Lyrics by Betty Comden and Adolph Green
Bells Are Ringing 1956

The Bells of St. Sebastian
Music and lyrics by Maury Yeston
Nine 1982

Belly Up to the Bar, Boys
Music and lyrics by Meredith Willson
The Unsinkable Molly Brown 1960

Belonging
Music and lyrics by Lionel Bart
La Strada 1969

Belt and Leather
Music by Steve Sterner
Lyrics by Peter del Valle
Lovers (OB) 1975

Ben Ali Haggin
Music by Rudolf Friml
Lyrics by Gene Buck
Ziegfeld Follies of 1923

Bench in the Park
Music by Jay Gorney
Lyrics by Barry Trivers
Heaven on Earth 1948

Benjamin Calypso
Music by Andrew Lloyd Webber
Lyrics by Tim Rice
*Joseph and the Amazing
Technicolor Dreamcoat* 1982

Benvenuta
Music and lyrics by Frank Loesser
The Most Happy Fella 1956

Bergerac
Music by Michael J. Lewis
Lyrics by Anthony Burgess
Cyrano 1973

Bertie and Gertie
Music and lyrics by Cole Porter
Red, Hot and Blue! 1936

Dropped from production

Beside the Star of Glory
Music by Karl Hajos (based on Tchaikovsky)
Lyrics by Harry B. Smith
Natja 1925

Bess, You Is My Woman Now
Music by George Gershwin
Lyrics by DuBose Heyward and Ira Gershwin
Porgy and Bess 1935

The Best Dance I've Had Tonight
Music by Vincent Youmans and Herbert Stothart
Lyrics by Otto Harbach and Oscar Hammerstein II
Wildflower 1923

The Best Dance of All
Music by Lehman Engel
Lyrics by Agnes Morgan
A Hero Is Born 1937

Best Gold
Music and lyrics by Jerry Herman
From A to Z 1960

The Best I Ever Get Is the Worst of It
Music by Rudolf Friml
Lyrics by Otto Harbach
The Blue Kitten 1922

The Best in the World
Music and lyrics by Jerry Herman
A Day in Hollywood, a Night in the Ukraine 1979

The Best Little Lover in Town
Music by Harry Tierney
Lyrics by Joseph McCarthy
Rio Rita 1927

Best Loved Girls
Music by David Baker
Lyrics by Sheldon Harnick
Shoestring '57 (OB)

The Best Man
Music and lyrics by Stephen H. Lemberg
Jazzbo Brown 1980

The Best Man
Music and lyrics by Jim Swann
Pump Boys and Dinettes 1982

The Best Night of My Life
Music by Charles Strouse
Lyrics by Lee Adams
Applause 1970

The Best of All Possible Worlds
Music by Leonard Bernstein
Lyrics by Richard Wilbur
Candide 1956

The Best of Everything
Music by George Gershwin
Lyrics by Arthur J. Jackson and B.G. DeSylva
La, La, Lucille 1919

The Best of Me
Music and lyrics by Beth Lawrence and Norman Thalheimer
Marilyn 1983

The Best of Times
Music and lyrics by Jerry Herman
La Cage aux Folles 1983

The Best of What the Country's Got
Music by Moose Charlap
Lyrics by Norman Gimbel
Whoop-Up 1958

The Best Songs of All
Music by Carlton Kelsey and Maury Rubens
Lyrics by Clifford Grey
Sky High 1925

The Best Thing for You
Music and lyrics by Irving Berlin
Call Me Madam 1950

The Best Things in Life Are Dirty
Music by André Previn
Lyrics by Alan Jay Lerner
Paint Your Wagon (film version, 1969)

The Best Things in Life Are Free
Music by Ray Henderson
Lyrics by B.G. DeSylva and Lew Brown
Good News 1927

The Best Time of Day
Music by Gordon Jenkins
Lyrics by Tom Adair
Along Fifth Avenue 1949

The Best Years of His Life
Music by Kurt Weill
Lyrics by Ira Gershwin
Lady in the Dark 1941

Bestiario
Music and lyrics by Elizabeth Swados
Nightclub Cantata (OB) 1977

Bet on the One You Fancy
Music by Harry Tierney
Lyrics by Joseph McCarthy
Kid Boots 1923

Betcha I Make Good
Music by Leo Edwards
Lyrics by Herman Timberg
You'll See Stars 1942

Betrayed
Music by Robert Kessler
Lyrics by Lola Pergament
O Marry Me! (OB) 1961

Better All the Time
Music by Sammy Fain
Lyrics by Marilyn and Alan Bergman
Something More 1964

Better Be Good to Me
Music by Richard Rodgers
Lyrics by Lorenz Hart
Chee-Chee 1928

Better Days
Music by Dov Seltzer
Lyrics by David Paulsen
To Live Another Summer 1971

Better Far
Music and lyrics by Oscar Brown, Jr.
Buck White 1969

Better Get Out of Here
Music and lyrics by Frank Loesser
Where's Charley? 1948

Better Luck Next Time
Music and lyrics by Irving Berlin
Easter Parade (1948) F

Better Not Try It
Music and lyrics by Michael H. Cleary,
Herb Magidson and Ned Washington
The Vanderbilt Revue 1930

Better Place to Be
Music and lyrics by Harry Chapin
The Night That Made America Famous 1975

Better Than Broadway
Music and lyrics by Tom Savage
Musical Chairs 1980

Better Times Are Coming
Music by Jimmie Steiger
Lyrics by Dolph Singer
White Lights 1927

Betty Lou
Music by Joe Jordan
Lyrics by Rosamond Johnson
Brown Buddies 1930

The Betty Song
Music by Cheryl Hardwick
Lyrics by Marilyn Suzanne Miller
Girls, Girls, Girls (OB) 1980

Between You and Me
Music and lyrics by Cole Porter
Broadway Melody of 1940 (1940) F

Bevo
Music and lyrics by Irving Berlin
Yip, Yip, Yaphank 1918

Also in *Ziegfeld Follies of 1919*

Beware As You Ride Through the Hollow
Music and lyrics by Norman Dean
Autumn's Here (OB) 1966

Beware of Lips That Say Chérie
Music by Alma Sanders
Lyrics by Monte Carlo
Louisiana Lady 1947

Beware of the Girl With the Fan
Music by Ray Henderson
Lyrics by B.G. DeSylva and Lew Brown
George White's Scandals (1925)

Bewitched, Bothered and Bewildered
Music by Richard Rodgers
Lyrics by Lorenz Hart
Pal Joey 1940

The lines "Couldn't sleep, and wouldn't sleep when love came and told me I shouldn't sleep" in the printed version of the song are substitutes for the original lines, which were considered salacious: "Couldn't sleep, and wouldn't sleep, unless I could sleep where I shouldn't sleep." Also deemed unprintable but used in the show were: "Romance—finis; your chance—finis; Those ants that invaded my pants—finis—."

Beyond My Wildest Dreams
Music by Elmer Bernstein
Lyrics by Don Black
Merlin 1983

B.G. Bigelow, Inc.
Music by Sammy Fain
Lyrics by E.Y. Harburg
Flahooley 1951

Bharatha Natyan
Music by Sammy Fain
Lyrics by Paul Francis Webster
Christine 1960

Bianca
Music and lyrics by Cole Porter
Kiss Me, Kate 1948

Bicentennial March
Music and lyrics by Ronnie Britton
Greenwich Village Follies (OB) 1976

The Bicycle Song
Music and lyrics by Hugh Martin
and Timothy Gray
High Spirits 1964

Bidding the World Farewell
Music by Steve Jankowski
Lyrics by Kenny Morris
Francis (OB) 1982

The Bide-a-Wee in Soho
Music by Kurt Weill
Lyrics by Marc Blitzstein
The Threepenny Opera (OB) 1954

Bidin' My Time
Music by George Gershwin
Lyrics by Ira Gershwin
Girl Crazy 1930

The Gershwins wrote this as a thirty-two bar song in the standard format of AABA. But as they played it through it seemed long to them and they eliminated the second eight bars, making the form ABA, a twenty-four bar song. (Ira had used the title fourteen years earlier in a piece for a humor magazine at college.)

Biff! Bang!
Music by Gustav Luders
Lyrics by Frank Pixley
The Prince of Pilsen 1903

The Big Back Yard
Music by Sigmund Romberg
Lyrics by Dorothy Fields
Up in Central Park 1945

The Big Beat
Music and lyrics by Richard M. Sherman
and Robert B. Sherman
Over Here! 1974

Big Best Shoes
Music and lyrics by Sandy Wilson
Valmouth (OB) 1960

Big Betty's Song
Music and lyrics by C. Jackson
and James Hatch
Fly Blackbird (OB) 1962

Big Bill
Music by George Kleinsinger
Lyrics by Joe Darion
Shinbone Alley 1957

Big Bird
Music by Ann Sternberg
Lyrics by Gertrude Stein
Gertrude Stein's First Reader (OB) 1969

The Big Black Giant
Music by Richard Rodgers
Lyrics by Oscar Hammerstein II
Me and Juliet 1953

Big Bottom Betty
Music by Richard Adler
Lyrics by Will Holt
Music Is 1976

The Big Bow-Wow
Music by Larry Grossman
Lyrics by Hal Hackady
Snoopy (OB) 1982

The Big Brass Band From Brazil
Music by Carl Sigman
Lyrics by Bob Hilliard
Angel in the Wings 1947

Big Brother
Music by Richard Rodgers
Lyrics by Lorenz Hart
The Boys From Syracuse 1938

The Big Clown Balloons
Music and lyrics by Meredith Willson
Here's Love 1963

Big 'D'
Music and lyrics by Frank Loesser
The Most Happy Fella 1956

Big Fish, Little Fish
Music by Gary Geld
Lyrics by Peter Udell
Purlie 1970

The Big Four
Music and lyrics by Peter Howard Weiss
All for Love 1949

Big Future
Music and lyrics by Melvin Van Peebles
Don't Play Us Cheap 1972

The Big Guitar
Music and lyrics by Oscar Brand
and Paul Nassau
A Joyful Noise 1966

Big Meeting Tonight
Music by Mary Rodgers
Lyrics by Martin Charnin
Hot Spot 1963

Big Mole
Music by Kurt Weill
Lyrics by Maxwell Anderson
Lost in the Stars 1949

The Big Movie Show in the Sky
Music by Robert Emmett Dolan
Lyrics by Johnny Mercer
Texas, Li'l Darlin' 1949

Big Old River
Music by Don Walker
Lyrics by Clay Warnick
Memphis Bound 1945

A Big One
Music by Gerard Calvi
Lyrics by Harold Rome
La Grosse Valise 1965

Big Papoose Is on the Loose
Music by Jimmy McHugh
Lyrics by Dorothy Fields
Lew Leslie's International Revue 1930

The Big Parade
Music and lyrics by Cole Porter
Seven Lively Arts 1944

The Big Show
Music by Jerome Kern
Lyrics by Edgar Allan Woolf
Head Over Heels 1918

Big Spender
Music by Cy Coleman
Lyrics by Dorothy Fields
Sweet Charity 1966

Big Time
Music and lyrics by Jerry Bock, George Weiss
and Larry Holofcener
Mr. Wonderful 1956

Big Time
Music and lyrics by Jerry Herman
Mack and Mabel 1974

Big Time Buck White Chant
Music and lyrics by Oscar Brown, Jr.
Buck White 1969

Big Town
Music and lyrics by Cole Porter
Seven Lively Arts 1944

Big Trouble
Music by Elmer Bernstein
Lyrics by Carolyn Leigh
How Now, Dow Jones 1967

Bigger and Better Than Ever
Music and lyrics by Cliff Friend
and George White
George White's Scandals (1929)

Bigger Isn't Better
Music by Cy Coleman
Lyrics by Michael Stewart
Barnum 1980

The Biggest Thing in My Life
Music by Frank Grey
Lyrics by McElbert Moore and Frank Grey
The Matinee Girl 1926

The Bilbao Song
Music by Kurt Weill
Lyrics by Bertolt Brecht (adapted by Michael
Feingold)
Happy End 1977

Bilbo's Song
Music by Donald Swann
Lyrics by Michael Flanders
At the Drop of Another Hat 1966

Bill
Music by Jerome Kern
Lyrics by P.G. Wodehouse
Show Boat 1927

Written for *Oh, Lady! Lady!!* in 1918, and to have
been sung by Vivienne Segal, the song was
dropped just before the opening. Two years later it
was put into the score of *Sally* for Marilyn Miller to
sing but again the song was cut. Finally, in 1927, it
emerged as Helen Morgan's famous top-of-the-
piano song in *Show Boat*. The original lyric had

been rewritten somewhat and although Oscar
Hammerstein II was *Show Boat's* lyricist, he was
always careful to point out that the lyric of "Bill"
was the work of P.G. Wodehouse. As a footnote
for collectors, a published copy of the song with
the original lyric and in the "Oh, Lady! Lady!!" cover
was sold at auction in late 1983 for over one
thousand dollars.

The Bill of Rights
Music by Jay Gorney
Lyrics by Henry Myers
Meet the People 1940

Billie
Music and lyrics by George M. Cohan
Billie 1928

Bill's Lament
Music and lyrics by Elizabeth Swados
Alice in Concert (OB) 1980

Billy
Music and lyrics by Ron Dante
and Gene Allan
Billy 1969

Billy Joe Ju
Music and lyrics by Don Tucker
Red, White and Maddox 1969

Billy Noname
Music and lyrics by Johnny Brandon
Billy Noname (OB) 1970

Bird Chorus
Music and lyrics by Elizabeth Swados
Nightclub Cantata (OB) 1977

Bird Lament
Music and lyrics by Elizabeth Swados
Nightclub Cantata (OB) 1977

A Bird of Passage
Music by Kurt Weill
Lyrics by Maxwell Anderson
Lost in the Stars 1949

Bird Song
Music and lyrics by Elizabeth Swados
Alice in Concert (OB) 1980

Bird Upon the Tree
Music and lyrics by Marc Blitzstein
Juno 1959

Bird Watcher's Song
Music by Jule Styne
Lyrics by Sammy Cahn
High Button Shoes 1947

Birdie Follies
Music and lyrics by Ann Harris
Sky High (OB) 1979

Birdies
Music by Maury Rubens
Lyrics by Clifford Grey
The Madcap 1928

Birdies
Music by Al Carmines
Lyrics by Rosalyn Drexler
Home Movies (OB) 1964

The Birds and the Bees
Music by Sigmund Romberg
Lyrics by Dorothy Fields
Up in Central Park 1945

The Birds in the Sky
Music by Galt McDermot
Lyrics by William Dumaresq
The Human Comedy (OB) 1983

Birds in the Spring
Music and lyrics by Ralph Benatzky
Meet My Sister 1930

The Birds in the Trees/A Lot of Men
Music by Galt McDermot
Lyrics by William Dumaresq
The Human Comedy (OB) 1983

Birds of a Feather
Music by Carmen Lombardo
Lyrics by Irving Caesar
George White's Music Hall Varieties 1932

Birds on High
Music by Richard Rodgers
Lyrics by Lorenz Hart
Betsy 1926

Birmingham
Music and lyrics by Randy Newman
Maybe I'm Doing It Wrong (1st edition) (OB) 1981

The Birth of Passion
Music by Karl Hoschna
Lyrics by Otto Harbach
Madame Sherry 1910

The Birth of the Blues
Music by Ray Henderson
Lyrics by B.G. DeSylva and Lew Brown
George White's Scandals (1926)

Birthday Party
Music by George Gershwin
Lyrics by Ira Gershwin
Funny Face 1927

Birthday Party
Music by Cy Coleman
Lyrics by Carolyn Leigh
Little Me 1962

Birthday Song
Music and lyrics by Harold Rome
Fanny 1954

Birthday Song
Music by Manos Hadjidakis
Lyrics by Joe Darion
Illya Darling 1967

A Bit of a Character
Music by Cyril Ornadel
Lyrics by Leslie Bricusse
Pickwick 1965

A Bit of Villainy
Music and lyrics by Stephen Schwartz
The Magic Show 1974

Bits and Pieces
Music by Larry Grossman
Lyrics by Hal Hackady
Goodtime Charley 1975

Bitten by Love
Music by Joseph Meyer
Lyrics by Floyd Huddleston
Shuffle Along of 1952

Bitter Harvest
Music by Raymond Scott
Lyrics by Bernard Hanighen
Lute Song 1946

Black
Music by Gary William Friedman
Lyrics by Will Holt
The Me Nobody Knows (OB) 1970

Black and Blue
Music by Thomas (Fats) Waller
and Harry Brooks
Lyrics by Andy Razaf
Hot Chocolates 1929

Black and Blue Pumps
Music by Mildred Kayden
Lyrics by Frank Gagliano
Paradise Gardens East (OB) 1969

Black and White
Music by Richard Rodgers
Lyrics by Lorenz Hart
The Garrick Gaieties (1st edition) 1925

Black and White
Music by George Gershwin
Lyrics by Gus Kahn and Ira Gershwin
Show Girl 1929

Black and White
Music by Cy Coleman
Lyrics by Michael Stewart
Barnum 1980

Black Balloons
Music and lyrics by Oscar Brown, Jr.
Buck White 1969

The Black-Black Song
Music by Coleridge-Taylor Perkinson
Lyrics by Ray McIver
God Is a (Guess What?) (OB) 1968

Black Bottom
Music by Ray Henderson
Lyrics by B.G. DeSylva and Lew Brown
George White's Scandals (1926)

Black Boy
Music and lyrics by Johnny Brandon
Billy Noname (OB) 1970

Black Boys
Music by Galt MacDermot
Lyrics by Gerome Ragni and James Rado
Hair 1968

Black Diamond
Music by Richard Rodgers
Lyrics by Lorenz Hart
Hollywood Party (1934) F

Dropped from film

Black Dog Rum
Music by Michael Valenti
Lyrics by John Lewin
Blood Red Roses 1970

Black Horse Tavern
Music by Frank D'Armond
Lyrics by Will Morrissey
Saluta 1934

Black Is Beautiful
Music and lyrics by Jack Bussins
and Ellsworth Olin
Be Kind to People Week (OB) 1975

Black Man
Music by Ron Steward and Neal Tate
Lyrics by Ron Steward
Sambo (OB) 1969

The Black Mask (Temptation)
Music by J. J. Shubert Jr.
Lyrics by Clifford Grey and McElbert Moore
A Night in Paris 1926

Black Pearls
Music and lyrics by Ed Tyler
Sweet Miani (OB) 1962

Black Rhythm
Music and lyrics by Donald Heywood
Black Rhythm 1936

Blackberries
Music and lyrics by Donald Heywood
Blackberries of 1932

The Blackberry Vine
Music by Ann Sternberg
Lyrics by Gertrude Stein
Gertrude Stein's First Reader (OB) 1969

Blacksheep
Music by Frank Grey
Lyrics by Earle Crooker and McElbert Moore
Happy 1927

Blade of Mine
Music by George Bagby
Lyrics by Grace Henry
Fioretta 1929

Blah, Blah, Blah
Music by George Gershwin
Lyrics by Ira Gershwin
Delicious (1931) F

First written under the title "Lady of the Moon" in 1928 for Ziegfeld's show *Ming Toy,* which was to have been a musical version of the play *East Is West.* It was to have starred Marilyn Miller, but was abandoned. A new lyric, "I Just Looked At You," was written for Ziegfeld's *Show Girl* in 1929, but the song was cut before the New York opening. It finally emerged in the film *Delicious* in 1931, and in the Broadway show *My One and Only* (1983).

Blah! but Not Blue
Music by Abel Baer
Lyrics by Sam Lewis and Joe Young
Lady Do 1927

Blame It All on Me
Music by Joseph Church
Lyrics by Joseph Church and Richard Schill
An Evening With Joan Crawford (OB) 1981

Blame It All on the Night
Music by Sigmund Romberg
Lyrics by Otto Harbach
Forbidden Melody 1936

Blame It on the Moon
Music and lyrics by Al Carmines
The Evangelist (OB) 1982

Blasé
Music by Berenice Kazounoff
Lyrics by John Latouche
Two for Tonight (OB) 1939

Bleecker Street
Music and lyrics by John Dooley
Hobo (OB) 1961

Bless the Lord
Music and lyrics by Stephen Schwartz
Godspell (OB) 1971

Bless This Land
Music by Jerry Bock
Lyrics by Sheldon Harnick
Tenderloin 1960

Bless You All
Music and lyrics by Harold Rome
Bless You All 1950

Bless Your Beautiful Hide
Music by Gene dePaul
Lyrics by Johnny Mercer
Seven Brides for Seven Brothers 1982

Blind Date
Music by Vernon Duke
Lyrics by Howard Dietz
Jackpot 1944

Blind Man's Buff
Music and lyrics by Deed Meyer
She Shall Have Music (OB) 1959

Blindman's Buff
Music by Richard Adler
Lyrics by Will Holt
Music Is 1976

Bliss
Music by Al Carmines
Lyrics by Maria Irene Fornes
Promenade (OB) 1969

Bloat
Music by Bob Brush
Lyrics by Martin Charnin
The First 1981

Blocks
Music and lyrics by Billy Barnes
The Billy Barnes Revue 1959

Blonde Blues
Music by Jerry Bock
Lyrics by Sheldon Harnick
The Body Beautiful 1958

Blood Red Roses
Music and lyrics by Michael Valenti
Lyrics by John Lewin
Blood Red Roses 1970

Bloody Mary
Music by Richard Rodgers
Lyrics by Oscar Hammerstein II
South Pacific 1949

The Bloom Is Off the Rose
Music by Arthur Schwartz
Lyrics by Howard Dietz
The Gay Life 1961

Blow a Balloon Up to the Moon
Music by Sammy Fain
Lyrics by Charles Tobias
Hellzapoppin 1938

Blow, Gabriel
Music by Henry Sullivan
Lyrics by Edward Eliscu
A Little Racketeer 1932

Blow, Gabriel, Blow
Music and lyrics by Cole Porter
Anything Goes 1934

Blow High, Blow Low
Music by Richard Rodgers
Lyrics by Oscar Hammerstein II
Carousel 1945

Blow Hot and Heavy
Music by Philip Charig and Richard Myers
Lyrics by Leo Robin
Allez-Oop 1927

Blow Hot—Blow Cold
Music by Louis Alter
Lyrics by Harry Ruskin and Leighton K. Brill
Ballyhoo 1930

Blow the Blues Away
Music by Werner Janssen
Lyrics by Mann Holiner and J. Keirn Brennan
Boom-Boom 1929

Blow Your Horn
Music and lyrics by Irving Berlin
Stop! Look! Listen! 1915

Blowin' the Blues Away
Music by Philip Charig
Lyrics by Ira Gershwin
Americana (1926)

Blowing the Top
Music by Philip Charig
Lyrics by Dan Shapiro and Milton Pascal
Artists and Models (1943)

Blue Again
Music by Jimmy McHugh
Lyrics by Dorothy Fields
The Vanderbilt Revue 1930

Blue and Troubled
Music and lyrics by Walter Cool
Mackey of Appalachia (OB) 1965

Blue, Blue, Blue
Music by George Gershwin
Lyrics by Ira Gershwin
Let 'Em Eat Cake 1933

A Blue Book of Girls
Music by Leo Fall
Lyrics by Harold Atteridge
The Rose of Stamboul 1922

Blue Danube Blues
Music by Jerome Kern
Lyrics by Anne Caldwell
Good Morning, Dearie 1921

Blue Day
Music by Abraham Ellstein
Lyrics by Walter Bullock
Great to Be Alive 1950

The Blue Devils of France
Music and lyrics by Irving Berlin
Ziegfeld Follies of 1918

Blue Eyes
Music by Robert Stolz
Lyrics by Irving Caesar
White Horse Inn 1936

Blue Grass
Music by Arthur Schwartz
Lyrics by Howard Dietz
Inside U.S.A. 1948

Blue Heaven
See "The Desert Song"

The Blue Kitten Blues (Me-Ow!)
Music by Rudolf Friml
Lyrics by Otto Harbach
The Blue Kitten 1922

Blue Monday
Music by Richard Rodgers
Lyrics by Lorenz Hart
Higher And Higher 1940

Blue Monday Blues
Music by George Gershwin
Lyrics by B.G. DeSylva and E. Ray Goetz
George White's Scandals (1922)

See note on show

Blue Moon
Music by Richard Rodgers
Lyrics by Lorenz Hart

Certainly the most rewritten lyric in all of Rodgers
and Hart, the song was first called "Prayer," to
have been sung by Jean Harlow in the film
Hollywood Party (1934). She was to have played a
telephone operator calling on the powers above to
help her become a star. However Harlow never
made the picture, and the lyric was scrapped and
rewritten as "Manhattan Melodrama" for a film of
that title. Again the song wasn't used and another
lyric was written. As "The Bad in Every Man" this
version was filmed, sung by Shirley Ross, but the
picture was not released. Finally publisher Jack
Robbins persuaded Hart to write a so-called
"commercial" lyric and it became "Blue Moon." One
of the few Rodgers and Hart songs not part of a
stage or film score, it is among their most
performed standards.

Blue Night
Music and lyrics by Bhumibol-Chakraband
and N. Tong Yai
Michael Todd's Peep Show 1950

Blue Ocean Blues
Music by Richard Rodgers
Lyrics by Lorenz Hart
Present Arms 1928

Originally written as "Atlantic Blues" for *Lido Lady*
(London,1926).

The Blue Pajama Song
Music by Arthur Schwartz
Lyrics by Lorenz Hart

See note on "I Guess I'll Have to Change My Plan."

Blue Plate Special
Music by Harris Wheeler
Lyrics by Mary L. Fisher
Blue Plate Special (OB) 1983

The Blue Room
Music by Richard Rodgers
Lyrics by Lorenz Hart
The Girl Friend 1926

Blue Shadows
Music by Louis Alter
Lyrics by Raymond Klages
Earl Carroll's Vanities (1928)

Blue Sierras
Music by Frederico Valerio
Lyrics by Elizabeth Miele
Hit the Trail 1954

Blue Skies
Music and lyrics by Irving Berlin
Betsy 1926

Blue Skies, Gray Skies
Music and lyrics by George M. Cohan
The Merry Malones 1927

The Bluebird
Music by Harry Archer
Lyrics by Harlan Thompson
Little Jessie James 1923

Bluebird
Music by Baldwin Bergersen
Lyrics by William Archibald
The Crystal Heart (OB) 1960

Blues
Music and lyrics by John Latouche
Two for Tonight (OB) 1939

Blues
Music and lyrics by Marc Blitzstein
Regina 1949

Blues In the Night
Music by Harold Arlen
Lyrics by Johnny Mercer
Blues In the Night (1941) F

Blues My Naughty Sweetie Gave to Me
Music and lyrics by Buster Davis
Doctor Jazz 1975

Bluff
Music and lyrics by George M. Cohan
Billie 1928

Blunderland
Music by Louis A. Hirsch
Lyrics by Gene Buck
Ziegfeld Follies of 1922

Bo Koo
Music by Vincent Youmans
Lyrics by Zelda Sears
Lollipop 1924

Boasting Song
Music by Al Carmines
Lyrics by Rosalyn Drexler
Home Movies (OB) 1964

A Boat Sails on Wednesday
Music by Jerome Kern
Lyrics by Adrian Ross and George Grossmith, Jr.
The Dollar Princess 1909

Bob About a Bit
Music by Harry Tierney
Lyrics by Joseph McCarthy
Up She Goes 1922

Bob White
Music by Jerome Kern
Lyrics by Anne Caldwell
The Night Boat 1920

Dropped from production

Bobbed-Haired Baby
Music by J. Fred Coots and Maury Rubens
Lyrics by McElbert Moore
A Night in Paris 1926

Bobby and Jackie and Jack
Music and lyrics by Stephen Sondheim
Merrily We Roll Along 1981

Bobby and Me
Music by Ray Henderson
Lyrics by B.G. DeSylva
Three Cheers 1928

Bobby's Songs
Music by Robert Mitchell
Lyrics by Elizabeth Perry
Bags (OB) 1982

Bobo's
Music by John Kander
Lyrics by Fred Ebb
The Act 1977

Body and Soul
Music by John Green
Lyrics by Edward Heyman, Robert Sour
and Frank Eyton
Three's a Crowd 1930

The Body Beautiful
Music by Jerry Bock
Lyrics by Sheldon Harnick
The Body Beautiful 1958

Boffola
Music by Philip Charig
Lyrics by Danny Shapiro, Milton Pascal
and Ray Golden
Catch a Star! 1955

Bohemia
Music by Franz Lehár
Lyrics by Basil Hood
The Count of Luxembourg 1912

Bojangles of Harlem
Music by Jerome Kern
lyrics by Dorothy Fields
Swing Time (1936) F

Bolero d'Amour
Music and lyrics by Stephen Sondheim
Follies 1971

Bolero on Rye
Music and lyrics by Stan Daniels
So Long, 174th Street 1976

The Bombay Bombashay
Music by Sigmund Romberg
Lyrics by Alex Gerber
Poor Little Ritz Girl 1920

Bon Jour
Music by Rudolf Friml
Lyrics by Johnny Burke
The Vagabond King (film version, 1956)

Bon Jour
Music and lyrics by Meredith Willson
The Unsinkable Molly Brown 1960

Bon Soir, Paris
Music by Heitor Villa-Lobos
Lyrics by Robert Wright and George Forrest
Magdalena 1948

Bon Vivant
Music and lyrics by Robert Wright
and George Forrest
Song of Norway 1944

Based on Grieg's song *Water Lily*

Bon Vivant
Music by Robert Emmett Dolan
Lyrics by Johnny Mercer
Foxy 1964

Bon Voyage
Music and lyrics by Cole Porter
Anything Goes 1934

Bon Voyage
Music by Jerome Moross
Lyrics by Kyle Crichton
Parade (1935)

Bon Voyage
Music by Leonard Bernstein
Lyrics by Richard Wilbur
Candide 1956

Bonds
Music by Jerry Bock
Lyrics by Sheldon Harnick
The Rothschilds 1970

Bone of Thy Bones
Music by Stanley Silverman
Lyrics by Arthur Miller
Up From Paradise (OB) 1983

Bonga Boo
Music by Owen Murphy
Lyrics by George S. Kaufman, Marc Connelly
and Ira Gershwin
Be Yourself 1924

Bongo on the Congo
Music by Jerome Kern
Lyrics by P.G. Wodehouse
Sitting Pretty 1924

Bongo-Boola
Music by Eubie Blake
Lyrics by Noble Sissle
Shuffle Along of 1952

Bonita
Music by Sigmund Romberg
Lyrics by Harry B. Smith
The Love Call 1927

Bonjour
Music and lyrics by Deed Meyer
'Toinette (OB) 1961

Bonne Nuit, Merci
Music and lyrics by Noël Coward
Bitter Sweet 1929

Bonnie Banks
Music by Lee Wainer
Lyrics by Robert Sour
Sing for Your Supper 1939

Bonnie Blue Flag
Music by Sigmund Romberg
Lyrics by Dorothy Donnelly
My Maryland 1927

Boo-Hoo, Tee-Hee, Ta-Ha
Music by Karl Hoschna
Lyrics by Otto Harbach
Three Twins 1908

Boogie Bacarolle
Music and lyrics by Cole Porter
You'll Never Get Rich (1941) F

The Book of Life
Music and lyrics by Melvin Van Peebles
Don't Play Us Cheap 1972

Book Report
Music and lyrics by Clark Gesner
You're a Good Man, Charlie Brown (OB) 1967

Boola Boo
Music by Rudolf Friml
Lyrics by Otto Harbach and Edward Clark
You're In Love 1917

Boom—Boom
Music by Cy Coleman
Lyrics by Carolyn Leigh
Little Me 1962

Boom Ditty Boom
Music by John Kander
Lyrics by Fred Ebb
70, Girls, 70 1971

The Boomerang
Music by Richard Rodgers
Lyrics by Lorenz Hart
Poor Little Ritz Girl 1920

In Boston production, but dropped before Broadway
opening

Boomerang
Music by Joe Jordan
Lyrics by Rosamond Johnson
Fast and Furious 1931

Boomps-a-Daisy
Music and lyrics by Annette Mills
Hellzapoppin 1938

Boondoggling
Music by Ray Henderson
Lyrics by Jack Yellen
George White's Scandals (1936)

The Boosters' Song of the Far North
Music by Randall Thompson
Lyrics by Agnes Morgan
The Grand Street Follies (1926) (OB)

Bootlegger's Chanty
Music by Richard Rodgers
Lyrics by Lorenz Hart
Heads Up! 1929

Dropped from production

Booze
Music by Judd Woldin
Lyrics by Robert Brittan
Raisin 1973

The Bop Will Never Die
Music by Diane Leslie
Lyrics by William Gleason
The Coolest Cat in Town (OB) 1978

Bored
Music by Harvey Schmidt
Lyrics by Tom Jones
Celebration 1969

Born Again
Music by Arthur Schwartz
Lyrics by Howard Dietz
Jennie 1963

Born Again
Music by Garry Sherman
Lyrics by Peter Udell
Comin' Uptown 1979

Born All Over Again
Music by Vernon Duke
Lyrics by Howard Dietz
Sadie Thompson 1944

Born and Bred in Brooklyn
Music and lyrics by George M. Cohan
The Rise of Rosie O'Reilly 1923

Born and Bred in Old Kentucky
Music by Joseph Meyer and James F. Hanley
Lyrics by B.G. DeSylva
Big Boy 1925

Born Lover
Music by Larry Grossman
Lyrics by Hal Hackady
Goodtime Charley 1975

Born to Hand-Jive
Music and lyrics by Jim Jacobs
and Warren Casey
Grease 1972

Born to Lose
Music and lyrics by David Langston Smyrl
On the Lock-In (OB) 1977

Born to Rock and Roll
Music by Diane Leslie
Lyrics by William Gleason
The Coolest Cat in Town (OB) 1978

Born to Sing
Music and lyrics by Stephen H. Lemberg
Jazzbo Brown 1980

Born Too Late
Music by Vernon Duke
Lyrics by Ogden Nash
The Littlest Revue (OB) 1956

Bosom Buddies
Music and lyrics by Jerry Herman
Mame 1966

Bosphorus
Music by Jerome Kern
Lyrics by Edward Madden
La Belle Paree 1911

Boss Tweed
Music by Sigmund Romberg
Lyrics by Dorothy Fields
Up in Central Park 1945

Boston
Music by James P. Johnson
Lyrics by Flournoy Miller
Sugar Hill 1931

Boston Beguine
Music and lyrics by Sheldon Harnick
New Faces of 1952

Boston in the Spring
Music by Richard Lewine
Lyrics by Ted Fetter
The Girl From Wyoming (OB) 1938

Boston Post Road
Music by Joseph Meyer
and Roger Wolfe Kahn
Lyrics by Irving Caesar
Here's Howe 1928

Both Ends Against the Middle
Music by Sol Kaplan
Lyrics by Edward Eliscu
The Banker's Daughter (OB) 1962

A Bottle and a Bird
Music and lyrics by Irving Caesar
George White's Music Hall Varieties 1932

Bottle Song
Music and lyrics by Al Kasha
and Joel Hirschhorn
Copperfield 1981

Bottleneck
Music and lyrics by Harold Rome
Destry Rides Again 1959

Bottom End of Bleecker Street
Music and lyrics by Tom Sankey
The Golden Screw (OB) 1967

Bottomland
Music by Clarence Williams
Lyrics by Jo Trent
Bottomland 1927

Bottoms Up
Music and lyrics by Cliff Friend and George White
George White's Scandals (1929)

Bottoms Up
Music by Richard Rodgers
Lyrics by Lorenz Hart
By Jupiter 1942

Bottom's Up
Music by Paul Hoffert
Lyrics by David Secter
Get Thee to Canterbury (OB) 1969

Boudoir Dolls
Music by Ned Lehak
Lyrics by Edward Eliscu
Nine-Fifteen Revue 1930

Bougainvillea
Music and lyrics by Elizabeth Swados
Dispatches (OB) 1979

The Bouilloux Girls
Music by Harvey Schmidt
Lyrics by Tom Jones
Colette (OB) 1970

Boukra Fill Mish Mish
Music by Jacques Belasco
Lyrics by Kay Twomey
The Girl From Nantucket 1945

The Boule' Miche'
Music by Victor Herbert
Lyrics by Glen MacDonough
Algeria 1908

Bounce Me
Music by Con Conrad
Lyrics by Gus Kahn
Kitty's Kisses 1926

Bound Away
Music and lyrics by Bland Simpson and Jim Wann
Hot Grog (OB) 1977

A Bouquet of Fond Memories
Music and lyrics by Maceo Pinkard
Pansy 1929

Bow Down, Sinners
Music and lyrics by Donald Heywood
Black Rhythm 1936

Bow-Legged Sal
Music by Sigmund Romberg
Lyrics by Oscar Hammerstein II
Sunny River 1941

Bowed With Tribulation
Music by John Philip Sousa
Lyrics by Tom Frost and Sousa
El Capitan 1896

The Bowery
Music by William Gaunt
Lyrics by Charles Hoyt
A Trip to Chinatown 1891

The Bowery
Music by Vincent Youmans
Lyrics by Harold Adamson and Clifford Grey
Smiles 1930

A Bowler Hat
Music and lyrics by Stephen Sondheim
Pacific Overtures 1976

Boy and Man
Music by Armando Trovaioli
Lyrics by Pietro Garinei and Sandro Giovannini
(Lyric translation by Edward Eager)
Rugantino 1964

Boy Blue
Music by Ron Steward and Neal Tate
Lyrics by Ron Steward
Sambo (OB) 1969

Boy, Do I Hate Horse Races
Music and lyrics by Norman Dean
Autumn's Here (OB) 1966

Boy, Do We Need It Now
Music and lyrics by Charles Strouse
Upstairs at O'Neal's (OB) 1982

Boy for Sale
Music and lyrics by Lionel Bart
Oliver! 1963

The Boy Friend
Music and lyrics by Sandy Wilson
The Boy Friend 1954

The Boy Friend Back Home
Music and lyrics by Cole Porter
Fifty Million Frenchmen 1929

Boy Friends
Music by Dave Stamper and Harold Levey
Lyrics by Cyrus Wood
Lovely Lady 1927

The Boy From
Music by Mary Rodgers
Lyrics by Stephen Sondheim
The Mad Show (OB) 1966

Boy, Girl, Moon
Music by Dave Stamper
Lyrics by Fred Herendeen
Orchids Preferred 1937

The Boy I Left Behind Me
Music by Richard Rodgers
Lyrics by Lorenz Hart
By Jupiter 1942

The Boy in the Blue Uniform
Music by Emil Gerstenberger and Carle Carlton
Lyrics by Howard Johnson
The Lace Petticoat 1927

A Boy Like That
Music by Leonard Bernstein
Lyrics by Stephen Sondheim
West Side Story 1957

A Boy Like You
Music by Kurt Weill
Lyrics by Langston Hughes
Street Scene 1947

Boy Meets Boy
Music and lyrics by Billy Solly
Boy Meets Boy (OB) 1975

Boy Meets Girl
Music and lyrics by Matt Dubey and Dean Fuller
Smith (OB) 1973

Boy Most Likely to Succeed
Music by Arthur Siegel
Lyrics by June Carroll
New Faces of 1956

A Boy Named Lem
Music by Sam Stept
Lyrics by Lew Brown and Charles Tobias
Yokel Boy 1939

The Boy Next Door
Music by Vincent Youmans
No, No, Nanette 1925

Dropped from production

The Boy Next Door
Music and lyrics by Hugh Martin and Ralph Blane
Meet Me in St. Louis (1944) F

Boy Oh Boy
Music and lyrics by Stan Daniels
So Long, 174th Street 1976

Boy Talk
Music by Michael Leonard
Lyrics by Herbert Martin
The Yearling 1965

Boy Wanted
Music by George Gershwin
Lyrics by Arthur Francis (Ira Gershwin)

The song was originally written for *A Dangerous Maid* (1921), which closed prior to Broadway. With revised lyrics by Ira Gershwin and Desmond Carter, it was included in the London hit *Primrose* (1924), and much later recorded by Ella Fitzgerald. Finally, sixty-two years after its creation, the song reached Broadway in the 1983 hit *My One and Only*.

Boy! What Love Has Done to Me!
Music by George Gershwin
Lyrics by Ira Gershwin
Girl Crazy 1930

The Boy With the Fiddle
Music by Alexander Argov
Lyrics by David Paulsen
To Live Another Summer 1971

Boychild
Music and lyrics by Johnny Brandon
Billy Noname (OB) 1970

Boys
Music by Franz Lehár
Lyrics by Basil Hood
The Count of Luxembourg 1912

Boys and Girls Come Out to Play
Music by Helen Miller
Lyrics by Eve Merriam
Inner City 1971

Boys and Girls Like You and Me
Music by Richard Rodgers
Lyrics by Oscar Hammerstein II
Oklahoma! 1943

Dropped from production, and added to stage version of *Cinderella*

Boys, Boys, Boys
Music and lyrics by Jack Lawrence
and Stan Freeman
I Had a Ball 1964

Boys From the South
Music and lyrics by John Phillips
Man on the Moon 1975

Boys in Blue
Music by Jerome Moross
Lyrics by Paul Peters and George Sklar
Parade (1935) 1935

Boys in Gray
Music by Sigmund Romberg
Lyrics by Dorothy Donnelly
My Maryland 1927

The Boys in the Back Room
Music by Frederick Hollander
Lyrics by Frank Loesser
Destry Rides Again (1939) F

Boys March
Music by Jerome Kern
Lyrics by Otto Harbach
Men of the Sky (1931) F

Boys Who Fight the Flames
Music and lyrics by George M. Cohan
Fifty Miles From Boston 1908

The Braggart Song
Music by Robert Kessler
Lyrics by Lola Pergament
O Marry Me! (OB) 1961

A Brand New Day
Music by Peter Link
Lyrics by Jacob Brackman
King of Hearts 1978

A Brand New Dress
Music by André Previn
Lyrics by Alan Jay Lerner
Coco 1969

Brandy in Your Champagne
Music by Don McAfee
Lyrics by Nancy Leeds
Great Scot! (OB) 1965

The Brave Deserve the Fair
Music by H. Maurice Jacquet
Lyrics by William Brady
The Silver Swan 1929

The Brave Old City of New York
Music by Helen Miller
Lyrics by Eve Merriam
Inner City 1971

Brave You
Music and lyrics by Ronnie Britton
Gift of the Magi (OB) 1975

Bravo, Bravo
Music by Emmerich Kálmán
Lyrics by Harry B. Smith
The Circus Princess 1927

Bravo, Bravo, Novelisto
Music by Sammy Fain
Lyrics by Marilyn and Alan Bergman
Something More 1964

Bravo, Giovanni
Music by Milton Schafer
Lyrics by Ronny Graham
Bravo Giovanni 1962

Brazilian Nuts
Music by Dorival Caymmi
Lyrics by Al Stillman
Star and Garter 1942

Breachy's Law
Music by Milton Schafer
Lyrics by Ronny Graham
Bravo Giovanni 1962

Bread and Butter
Music by Jerome Kern
Lyrics by Anne Caldwell and Otto Harbach
Criss-Cross 1926

Dropped from production

Bread and Butter and Sugar
Music by William B. Kernell
Lyrics by Dorothy Donnelly
Hello, Lola 1926

Break Into Your Heart
Music by Tom Johnstone
Lyrics by Will B. Johnstone
I'll Say She Is 1924

Break It Up
Music by John Green
Lyrics by George Marion, Jr.
Beat the Band 1942

Break It Up, Cinderella
Music by Hoagy Carmichael
Lyrics by Johnny Mercer
Walk With Music 1940

Break That Party
Music and lyrics by Melvin Van Peebles
Don't Play Us Cheap 1972

The Break-Me-Down
Music by Harry Archer
Lyrics by Walter O'Keefe
Just a Minute 1928

Breakfast Dance
Music by Ralph Rainger
Lyrics by Edward Eliscu
Nine-Fifteen Revue 1930

Breakfast in Bed
Music by Armand Vecsey
Lyrics by P.G. Wodehouse
The Nightingale 1927

Breakfast in Bed
Music by Dave Stamper and Harold Levey
Lyrics by Cyrus Wood
Lovely Lady 1927

A Breakfast Over Sugar
Music and lyrics by William Finn
In Trousers (OB) 1981

Breakfast With You
Music by Milton Ager
Lyrics by Jack Yellen
Rain or Shine 1928

Breakin' 'Em Down
Music and lyrics by Noble Sissle and Eubie Blake
The Chocolate Dandies 1924

Breakin' 'Em In
Music by Eubie Blake
Lyrics by Noble Sissle
Shuffle Along of 1933

Breakin' the Rhythm
Music and lyrics by Maceo Pinkard
Pansy 1929

Breathing In
Music and lyrics by Elizabeth Swados
Dispatches (OB) 1979

Breathing the Air
Music and lyrics by John Driver
Ride the Winds 1974

The Breeze Kissed Your Hair
Music by Jerome Kern
Lyrics by Otto Harbach
The Cat and the Fiddle 1931

Breezy
Music by Carl Sigman
Lyrics by Bob Hilliard
Angel in the Wings 1947

Brewing the Love Potion
Music by Ray Haney
Lyrics by Alfred Aiken
We're Civilized? (OB) 1962

The Bride
Music by Rudolf Friml
Lyrics by Otto Harbach
Katinka 1915

Bride and Groom
Music by George Gershwin
Lyrics by Ira Gershwin
Oh, Kay! 1926

The Bride Was Dressed in White
Music by Vincent Youmans
Lyrics by Oscar Hammerstein II
Rainbow 1928

The Bridge of Caulaincourt
Music by Marguerite Monnot
Lyrics by Julian More, David Heneker
and Monte Norman
Irma la Douce 1960

The Bridge to Nowhere
Music and lyrics by Ron Dante
and Gene Allan
Billy 1969

Bridge to the Future
Music by Scott MacLarty
Lyrics by Dorothy Chansky
The Brooklyn Bridge (OB) 1983

Brigadoon
Music by Frederick Loewe
Lyrics by Alan Jay Lerner
Brigadoon 1947

Bright and Black
Music by Leonard Bernstein
Lyrics by Alan Jay Lerner
1600 Pennsylvania Avenue 1976

Bright College Days
Music and lyrics by Harold Rome
Wish You Were Here 1952

Bright College Days
Music and lyrics by Tom Lehrer
Tomfoolery (OB) 1981

Bright Lights
Music and lyrics by Micki Grant
It's So Nice to Be Civilized 1980

Bright Lights
Music by Jerome Kern
Lyrics by P.G. Wodehouse
Have a Heart 1917

Bright Morning Star
Music and lyrics by Bland Simpson and Jim Wann
(Based on traditional folk music)
Diamond Studs (OB) 1975

Brighten Up and Be a Little Sunbeam
Music by Jimmy McHugh
Lyrics by Harold Adamson
As the Girls Go 1948

Bring All the Boys Back Home
Music by Galt MacDermot
Lyrics by John Guare
Two Gentlemen of Verona 1971

Bring Along the Camera
Music by Ivan Caryll
Lyrics by C.M.S. McLellan
The Pink Lady 1911

Bring Back Birdie
Music by Charles Strouse
Lyrics by Lee Adams
Bring Back Birdie 1981

Bring Back My Blushing Rose
Music by Rudolf Friml
Lyrics by Gene Buck
Ziegfeld Follies of 1921

Bring Back Swing
Music by Patrick Rose
Lyrics by Merv Campone and Richard Ouzounian
A Bistro Car on the CNR (OB) 1978

Bring Back Those Minstrel Days
Music by Martin Broones
Lyrics by Ballard MacDonald
Rufus Lemaire's Affairs 1927

Bring Back Tomorrow
Music by Monty Norman
Lyrics by Julian More
The Moony Shapiro Songbook 1981

Bring Back Your Love
Music by Jean Schwartz
Lyrics by Joseph W. Herbert and Harold Atteridge
The Honeymoon Express 1913

Bring 'Em Back
Music by Jerome Kern
Lyrics by Anne Caldwell
Hitchy-Koo 1920

Bring Him My Love Thoughts
Music by Oscar Straus
Lyrics by Edward Delaney Dunn
The Last Waltz 1921

Bring Me a Rose
Music by Lionel Monckton
Lyrics by Arthur Wimperis
The Arcadians 1910

Bring Me My Bride
Music and lyrics by Stephen Sondheim
*A Funny Thing Happened on the Way
to the Forum* 1962

Bring On the Concubines
Music by Erich Wolfgang Korngold (based on
Jacques Offenbach)
Lyrics by Herbert Baker
Helen Goes to Troy 1944

Bring On the Follies Girls
Music by Dave Stamper
Lyrics by Gene Buck
Ziegfeld Follies (1931)

Bring On the Girls
Music and lyrics by Gene Buck
and Dave Stamper
Ziegfeld Follies of 1922

Bring On the Girls
Music and lyrics by Richard Myers and Jack
Lawrence
Ziegfeld Follies (1957)

Bring On the Loot
Music and lyrics by Gary Portnoy
and Judy Hart Angelo
Preppies (OB) 1983

Bring On the Pepper
Music and lyrics by Irving Berlin
Music Box Revue (2nd edition) 1922

Bring Your Darling Daughter
Music by Arthur Schwartz
Lyrics by Howard Dietz
The Gay Life 1961

Bringing Up Daughter
Music by David Baker
Lyrics by David Craig
Copper and Brass 1957

The Briny Blues
Music by Serge Walter
Lyrics by Agnes Morgan
The Grand Street Follies (1928)

Briscoe, the Hero
Music by Coleridge-Taylor Perkinson
Lyrics by Errol Hill
Man Better Man (OB) 1969

Britain's Own Ambassadors
Music by Richard Rodgers
Lyrics by Lorenz Hart
A Connecticut Yankee 1927

Dropped from production

Britannia Rules the Waves
Music and lyrics by Noël Coward
This Year of Grace 1928

Britannia Waives the Rules
Music by Berenice Kazounoff
Lyrics by Arnold B. Horwitt and John Latouche
Pins and Needles (OB) 1937

Added during run

British Maidens
Music by Max Ewing
Lyrics by Agnes Morgan
The Grand Street Follies (1929)

The Broad Highway
Music by Sigmund Romberg
Lyrics by Rida Johnson Young
The Dream Girl 1924

Broadminded
Music by Frank Black
Lyrics by Gladys Shelley '
The Duchess Misbehaves 1946

Broads Ain't People
Music and lyrics by Jay Livingston and Ray Evans
Let It Ride 1961

Broads of Broadway
Music by Gitz Rice
Lyrics by Paul Porter
Nic-Nax of 1926

Broadway
Music by Ray Henderson
Lyrics by B.G. DeSylva and Lew Brown
Manhattan Mary 1927

Broadway
Music by Percy Wenrich
Lyrics by Harry Clarke
Who Cares? 1930

Broadway
Music by Jule Styne
Lyrics by Stephen Sondheim
Gypsy 1959

Broadway
Music and lyrics by Stephen H. Lemberg
Jazzbo Brown 1980

Broadway Baby
Music by Jim Wise
Lyrics by George Haimsohn and Robin Miller
Dames at Sea (OB) 1968

Broadway Baby
Music and lyrics by Stephen Sondheim
Follies 1971

Broadway Blossom
Music by Morton Gould
Lyrics by Betty Comden and Adolph Green
Billion Dollar Baby 1945

Broadway, Broadway
Music by Charles Strouse
Lyrics by Lee Adams
A Broadway Musical 1978

Broadway Follies
Music and lyrics by Walter Marks
Broadway Follies 1981

Broadway Indians
Music and lyrics by Gene Buck and Dave Stamper
Ziegfeld Follies of 1923

Broadway Love Song
Music by Jay Gorney
Lyrics by Jean and Walter Kerr
Touch and Go 1949

Broadway Mammy
Music and lyrics by Clarence Gaskill
and Jimmy Duffy
Keep It Clean 1929

A Broadway Musical
Music by Charles Strouse
Lyrics by Lee Adams
A Broadway Musical 1978

Broadway, My Street
Music by John Kander
Lyrics by Fred Ebb
70, Girls, 70 1971

Broadway New York
Music and lyrics by Ann Harris
Sky High (OB) 1979

The Broadway of My Heart
Music and lyrics by Skip Redwine
and Larry Frank
Frank Merriwell, or Honor Challenged 1971

Broadway Reverie
Music by Dave Stamper
Lyrics by Gene Buck
Ziegfeld Follies (1931)

Broadway to Madrid
Music by Morris Hamilton
Lyrics by Grace Henry
Earl Carroll's Vanities (1926)

The Broken Bus
Music by Heitor Villa-Lobos
Lyrics by Robert Wright and George Forrest
Magdalena 1948

The Broken Heart, or the Wages of Sin
Music by Mitch Leigh
Lyrics by William Alfred and Phyllis Robinson
Cry for Us All 1970

Broken-Hearted Romeo
Music by Maria Grever
Lyrics by Raymond Leveen
Viva O'Brien 1941

The Broken Kimona
Music by Robert Stringer
Lyrics by Richard Maury
New Faces of 1956

The Broken Pianolita
Music by Heitor Villa-Lobos
Lyrics by Robert Wright and George Forrest
Magdalena 1948

Broken Rhythm
Music by Mann Holiner
Lyrics by Alberta Nichols
Gay Paree 1926

Broken String Blues
Music by David Martin
Lyrics by Langston Hughes
Simply Heavenly 1957

Brom and Katrina
Music and lyrics by Norman Dean
Autumn's Here (OB) 1966

Broncho Busters
Music by George Gershwin
Lyrics by Ira Gershwin
Girl Crazy 1930

Brooklyn
Music by Scott MacLarty
Lyrics by Dorothy Chansky
The Brooklyn Bridge (OB) 1983

Brooklyn Cantata
Music by George Kleinsinger
Lyrics by Mike Stratton
Tis of Thee 1940

Also in *Of V We Sing* 1942

The Brooklyn Dodger Strike
Music by Bob Brush
Lyrics by Martin Charnin
The First 1981

Brother Blues
Music and lyrics by Al Carmines
The Evangelist (OB) 1982

Brother, Can You Spare a Dime?
Music by Jay Gorney
Lyrics by E.Y. Harburg
Americana (1932)

Brother, Give Yourself a Shove
Music by Kurt Weill
Lyrics by Bertolt Brecht (adapted by Michael
Feingold)
Happy End 1977

Brother to Brother
Music by Mel Marvin
Lyrics by Robert Montgomery
Green Pond (OB) 1977

Brother Trucker
Music and lyrics by James Taylor
Working 1978

Brother, Where Are You?
Music and lyrics by Oscar Brown, Jr.
Joy (OB) 1970

Brotherhood of Man
Music and lyrics by Frank Loesser
*How to Succeed in Business
Without Really Trying* 1961

Brothers
Music by Victor Jacobi
Lyrics by William LeBaron
Apple Blossoms 1919

The Brothers Come to Egypt
Music by Andrew Lloyd Webber
Lyrics by Tim Rice
*Joseph and the Amazing
Technicolor Dreamcoat* 1982

Brown
Music by Ford Dabney
Lyrics by Jo Trent
Rang-Tang 1927

Brown Baby
Music and lyrics by Oscar Brown, Jr.
Joy (OB) 1970

Brown-Eyed Girl
Music by Emmerich Kálmán
Lyrics by Harry B. Smith
Countess Maritza 1926

Brown Eyes
Music by Rudolf Friml
Lyrics by Otto Harbach and Oscar Hammerstein II
The Wild Rose 1926

Brown October Ale
Music by Reginald De Koven
Lyrics by Harry B. Smith
Robin Hood 1891

Brown Penny
Music by Duke Ellington
Lyrics by John Latouche
Beggar's Holiday 1946

Brown Penny
Music by John Duffy
Lyrics by Rocco Bufano and John Duffy
Horseman, Pass By (OB) 1969

Lyrics based on a poem by W.B. Yeats

Brown Sugar
Music and lyrics by Donald Heywood
Blackberries of 1932

Brush Up Your Shakespeare
Music and lyrics by Cole Porter
Kiss Me, Kate 1948

In his five choruses of lyric Porter manages to
mention, in one way or another, fourteen
Shakespeare plays and a sonnet or two.

Brussels
Music by Jacques Brel
English lyrics by Eric Blau and Mort Shuman
*Jacques Brel Is Alive and Well
and Living in Paris* (OB) 1968

The Bubble
Music by Rudolf Friml
Lyrics by Otto Harbach
High Jinks 1913

Bubbles
Music by Victor Herbert
Lyrics by Rida Johnson Young
The Dream Girl 1924

Bubbles in Me Bonnet
Music by Gerald Jay Markoe
Lyrics by Michael Colby
Charlotte Sweet (OB) 1982

Bubbles of Bliss
Music by Jerome Kern
Lyrics by Anne Caldwell
The City Chap 1925

Bucharest
Music by Sigmund Romberg
Lyrics by Otto Harbach
Forbidden Melody 1936

Buck in the Bank
Music by Gerald Marks
Lyrics by Sam Lerner
Hold It! 1948

Buck Up
Music by Rudolf Friml
Lyrics by Otto Harbach and Edward Clark
You're In Love 1917

Buckin' Barley
Music by Alfred Brooks
Lyrics by Ira J. Bilowit
Of Mice and Men (OB) 1958

Buckle Down, Winsocki
Music and lyrics by Hugh Martin and Ralph Blane
Best Foot Forward 1941

Buddy, Beware
Music and lyrics by Cole Porter
Anything Goes 1934

Buddy Rose
Music by Abel Baer
Lyrics by Sam Lewis and Joe Young
Lady Do 1927

Buds of May
Music and lyrics by Al Carmines
The Evangelist (OB) 1982

Buds Won't Bud
Music by Harold Arlen
Lyrics by E.Y. Harburg
Hooray for What! 1937

Dropped from production

Budweiser's a Friend of Mine
Music by Seymour Furth
Lyrics by Vincent Bryan
Follies of 1907

Buenos Aires
Music by Andrew Lloyd Webber
Lyrics by Tim Rice
Evita 1979

Buffalo Bill
Music and lyrics by Irving Berlin
Annie Get Your Gun 1946

Buggy Riding
Music by Jerome Kern
Lyrics by Anne Caldwell
Hitchy-Koo 1920

The Bugle
Music and lyrics by Meredith Willson
Here's Love 1963

Bugle Blow
Music by Richard Rodgers
Lyrics by Lorenz Hart
Betsy 1926

Builders of Dreams
Music by Henry Sullivan
Lyrics by John Murray Anderson
John Murray Anderson's Almanac (1929)

Building Up to a Let-Down
Music by Will Irwin
Lyrics by Norman Zeno and Lee Brody
Fools Rush In 1934

Bullfrog Patrol
Music by Jerome Kern
Lyrics by Anne Caldwell
She's a Good Fellow 1919

The Bulls
Music by Jacques Brel
English lyrics by Eric Blau and Mort Shuman
*Jacques Brel Is Alive and Well
and Living in Paris* (OB) 1968

The Bum Won
Music by Jerry Bock
Lyrics by Sheldon Harnick
Fiorello! 1959

The Bumble Bee
Music by Jerome Kern
Lyrics by Anne Caldwell
She's a Good Fellow 1919

Bump and Grind for God
Music by Joe Ercole
Lyrics by Bruce Kluger
Ka-Boom (OB) 1980

Bump, Bump, Bump
Music and lyrics by Stephen H. Lemberg
Jazzbo Brown 1980

Bumper Found a Grand
Music by Richard Rodgers
Lyrics by Lorenz Hart
Hallelujah, I'm a Bum (1933) F

Bumpity-Bump
Music by Monty Norman
Lyrics by Julian More
The Moony Shapiro Songbook 1981

Bums
Music by Bob Brush
Lyrics by Martin Charnin
The First 1981

Bums' Opera
Music by Richard Rodgers
Lyrics by Oscar Hammerstein II
Pipe Dream 1955

Bundle of Love
Music by Alberta Nichols
Lyrics by Mann Holiner
Angela 1928

Bundling
Music by Sigmund Romberg
Lyrics by Oscar Hammerstein II
Sunny River 1941

A Bungalow in Quogue
Music by Jerome Kern
Lyrics by P.G. Wodehouse
The Riviera Girl 1917

Bunk
Music and lyrics by Gene Lockhart
Bunk of 1926

Bunnies
Music by Larry Grossman
Lyrics by Hal Hackady
Snoopy (OB) 1982

Bunny, Bunny, Bunny
Music and lyrics by Harold Rome
Star and Garter 1942

Burlesque Modern Opera
Music by Victor Herbert
Lyrics by Robert B. Smith
The Debutante 1914

This song is an example of Herbert's little-known talent for satirizing grand opera.

Burma Moon
Music by Gitz Rice
Lyrics by Paul Porter
Nic-Nax of 1926

Burn, Baby, Burn
Music and lyrics by Johnny Brandon
Billy Noname (OB) 1970

Burn 'Em Up
Music by Edgar Fairchild
Lyrics by Henry Myers
The New Yorkers 1927

Burn On
Music and lyrics by Randy Newman
Maybe I'm Doing It Wrong (2nd edition) (OB) 1982

Burn This Town
Music and lyrics by Voices, Inc.
The Believers (OB) 1968

Burning
Music by Richard Rodgers
Lyrics by Lorenz Hart
Hollywood Party (1934) F

Dropped from film

Bus From Amarillo
Music and lyrics by Carol Hall
The Best Little Whorehouse in Texas 1978

A Bushel and a Peck
Music and lyrics by Frank Loesser
Guys and Dolls 1950

Business Is Bad
Music by Joseph Raposo
Lyrics by Erich Segal
Sing Muse! (OB) 1961

Business Is Business
Music and lyrics by Ida Hoyt Chamberlain
Enchanted Isle 1927

Bustopher Jones
Music by Andrew Lloyd Webber.
Cats 1982

Lyrics based on T.S. Eliot's *Old Possum's Book of Practical Cats*

The Busy Bees of DeVere's
Music and lyrics by George M. Cohan
Little Nellie Kelly 1922

A Busy Evening
Music by J. Fred Coots
Lyrics by Clifford Grey
June Days 1925

A Busy Little Center
Music and lyrics by George M. Cohan
The Merry Malones 1927

But
Music by Marguerite Monnot
Lyrics by Julian More, David Heneker and Monte Norman
Irma la Douce 1960

But Alive
Music by Charles Strouse
Lyrics by Lee Adams
Applause 1970

But if Something Leads to Good
Music by Stanley Silverman
Lyrics by Arthur Miller
Up From Paradise (OB) 1983

But in the Morning, No!
Music and lyrics by Cole Porter
Du Barry Was a Lady 1939

But, Mrs. Adams
Music and lyrics by Sherman Edwards
1776 1969

But Never Jam Today
Music by Bert Keyes and Bob Larimer
Lyrics by Bob Larimer
But Never Jam Today 1979

But Not for Me
Music by George Gershwin
Lyrics by Ira Gershwin
Girl Crazy 1930

Collectors of puns should take note of the end of the second chorus of Ira Gershwin's lyric: "...When ev'ry happy plot/ ends with the marriage knot,/ and there's no knot...for...me."

But That's the Way You Are
Music by André Previn
Lyrics by Alan Jay Lerner
Coco 1969

But Where Are You?
Music and lyrics by Irving Berlin
Follow the Fleet (1936) F

But Who Cares?
Music by Emmerich Kálmán
Lyrics by Harry B. Smith
The Circus Princess 1927

But Why Be Afraid?
Music and lyrics by Gian-Carlo Menotti
The Medium 1947

But Yours
Music and lyrics by Bob Merrill
Take Me Along 1959

Butcher, Baker, Candlestick-Maker
Music by Mana-Zucca
Lyrics by Benjamin M. Kaye
The Garrick Gaieties (1st edition) 1925

Butler in the Abbey
Music by Jule Styne
Lyrics by E.Y. Harburg
Darling of the Day 1968

Butler's Song
Music and lyrics by Stan Daniels
So Long, 174th Street 1976

Butter and Egg Baby
Music by Alma Sanders
Lyrics by Monte Carlo
Oh! Oh! Nurse 1925

The Butterflies and Bees
Music by Sigmund Romberg
Lyrics by Oscar Hammerstein II
Sunny River 1941

The Butterfly
Music by Karl Hoschna
Lyrics by Otto Harbach
Madame Sherry 1910

The Butterfly
Music by John Kander
Lyrics by Fred Ebb
Zorba 1968

The Butterfly Ballet (instrumental)
Music by Victor Herbert
Sally 1920

Button Up Your Heart
Music by Jimmy McHugh
Lyrics by Dorothy Fields
The Vanderbilt Revue 1930

Button Up Your Overcoat
Music by Ray Henderson
Lyrics by B.G. DeSylva and Lew Brown
Follow Thru 1929

Buy a Little Button From Us
Music by George Gershwin
Lyrics by Desmond Carter
Lady Be Good (London production, 1926)

Buy a Victory Bond
Music and lyrics by Richard M. Sherman
and Robert B. Sherman
Over Here! 1974

Buy an Extra
Music by Tom Johnstone
Lyrics by Phil Cook
When You Smile 1925

Buy Bonds, Buster, Buy Bonds
Music by Jack Holmes
Lyrics by Bill Conklin and Bob Miller
O Say Can You See! (OB) 1962

Buy Her a Box at the Opera
Music by Cole Porter
Lyrics by T. Lawrason Riggs and Cole Porter
See America First 1916

Buy My Pardons
Music by Paul Hoffert
Lyrics by David Secter
Get Thee to Canterbury (OB) 1969

Buy Your Way
Music by Maury Rubens
Lyrics by Clifford Grey
The Madcap 1928

Buy Yourself a Balloon
Music and lyrics by Herman Hupfeld
The Show Is On 1936

The Buzzard Song
Music by George Gershwin
Lyrics by DuBose Heyward
Porgy and Bess 1935

By and By
Music by George Gershwin
Lyrics by Brian Hooker
Our Nell 1922

By Candlelight
Music by Robert Katscher
Lyrics by Rowland Leigh
You Never Know 1938

By My Side
Music by Peggy Gordon
Lyrics by Jay Hamburger
Godspell (OB) 1971

By Myself
Music by Arthur Schwartz
Lyrics by Howard Dietz
Between the Devil 1937

**By Special Permission of the Copyright Owners,
I Love You**
Music by Lewis E. Gensler
Lyrics by Owen Murphy and Robert A.Simon
The Gang's All Here 1931

By Strauss
Music by George Gershwin
Lyrics by Ira Gershwin
The Show Is On 1936

By the Glenside
Music by Earl Robinson
Lyrics by Waldo Salt
Sandhog (OB) 1954

By the Mississinewah
Music and lyrics by Cole Porter
Something for the Boys 1943

By the Saskatchewan
Music by Ivan Caryll
Lyrics by C.M.S. McLellan
The Pink Lady 1911

By the Sea
Music and lyrics by Clark Gesner
New Faces of 1968

By the Sea
Music and lyrics by Stephen Sondheim
Sweeney Todd 1979

By the Side of the Mill
Music by Victor Herbert
Lyrics by Henry Blossom
The Red Mill 1906

By the Sweat of Your Brow
Music by Eubie Blake
Lyrics by J. Milton Reddie and Cecil Mack
Swing It 1937

By the Way
Music by Vivian Ellis
Lyrics by Graham John
By the Way 1925

By This Token
Music by Sigmund Romberg
Lyrics by Harry B. Smith
Princess Flavia 1925

By Threes
Music by Cy Coleman
Lyrics by Michael Stewart
I Love My Wife 1977

By Welawela
Music by Rudolf Friml
Lyrics by J. Keirn Brennan
Luana 1930

Bye and Bye
Music by Richard Rodgers
Lyrics by Lorenz Hart
Dearest Enemy 1925

Bye-Bye Babe
Music and lyrics by Leon DeCosta
The Blonde Sinner 1926

Bye Bye Baby
Music by Jule Styne
Lyrics by Leo Robin
Gentlemen Prefer Blondes 1949

Bye Bye, Bonnie
Music by Albert Von Tilzer
Lyrics by Neville Fleeson
Bye Bye, Bonnie 1927

Bye-Bye Butterfly Lover
Music by Arthur Schwartz
Lyrics by Howard Dietz
Between the Devil 1937

Bye, Bye, Dear Old Broadway
Music by Gus Edwards
Lyrics by Will Cobb
Follies of 1907

Ca C'est L'Amour
Music and lyrics by Cole Porter
Les Girls (1957) F

Ča, c'est Sixth Avenue
Music and lyrics by Lee Brady and Richard Jones
Fools Rush In 1934

Cab Song
Music by Emmerich Kálmán
Lyrics by George Marion, Jr.
Marinka 1945

Caballero
Music and lyrics by Noël Coward
This Year of Grace 1928

Cabaret
Music by John Kander
Lyrics by Fred Ebb
Cabaret 1966

Cabarets
Music by Richard Rodgers
Lyrics by Lorenz Hart
The Girl Friend 1926

The Cabby's Serenade
Music by Jimmy McHugh
Lyrics by Al Dubin
Keep Off the Grass 1940

Cabin Door
Music by Eubie Blake
Lyrics by Andy Razaf
Blackbirds of 1930

Cabin in the Cotton
Music by Harold Arlen
Lyrics by Irving Caesar and George White
George White's Music Hall Varieties 1932

Cabin in the Sky
Music by Vernon Duke
Lyrics by John Latouche
Cabin in the Sky 1940

Cacophony
Music and lyrics by James Rado
Rainbow (OB) 1972

Cadets of Gascony
Music by Victor Herbert
Lyrics by Harry B. Smith
Cyrano de Bergerac 1899

Cadillac Car
Music by Henry Krieger
Lyrics by Tom Eyen
Dreamgirls 1981

Caesar Is Wrong
Music and lyrics by Ervin Drake
Her First Roman 1968

Café Royale Rag Time
Music by Kenneth Jacobson
Lyrics by Rhoda Roberts
Show Me Where the Good Times Are (OB) 1970

Cahoots
Music by Jerry Livingston
Lyrics by Leonard Adelson
Molly 1973

Cake Walk Your Lady
Music by Harold Arlen
Lyrics by Johnny Mercer
St. Louis Woman 1946

Cakewalk Into Kansas City
Music and lyrics by Bland Simpson and Jim Wann
Diamond Studs (OB) 1975

Cal Gets By
Music by Robert Waldman
Lyrics by Alfred Uhry
Here's Where I Belong 1968

Calcutta
Music by Gerald Dolin
Lyrics by Edward J. Lambert
Smile at Me 1935

Californi-ay
Music by Jerome Kern
Lyrics by E.Y. Harburg
Can't Help Singing (1944) F

California
Music and lyrics by Ida Hoyt Chamberlain
Enchanted Isle 1927

California
Music by Richard B. Chodosh
Lyrics by Barry Alan Grael
The Streets of New York (OB) 1963

California Skies
Music by Harry Ruby
Lyrics by Bert Kalmar
The Ramblers 1926

The Calinda
Music and lyrics by Herman Hupfeld
A La Carte 1927

Call Around Again
Music by Victor Herbert
Lyrics by Robert B. Smith
The Debutante 1914

Call Back in the Morning
Music by Alan Menken
Lyrics by Howard Ashman
Little Shop of Horrors (OB) 1982

Call From the Grave
Music by Kurt Weill
Lyrics by Marc Blitzstein
The Threepenny Opera (OB) 1954

A Call From the Vatican
Music and lyrics by Maury Yeston
Nine 1982

Call In to Her
Music by Mitch Leigh
Lyrics by William Alfred and Phyllis Robinson
Cry for Us All 1970

Call It a Dream
Music by Sigmund Romberg
Lyrics by Oscar Hammerstein II
Sunny River 1941

Call It Applefritters
Music by Richard Stutz
Lyrics by Milton Pascal
Along Fifth Avenue 1949

Call It Love
Music by Abraham Ellstein
Lyrics by Walter Bullock
Great to Be Alive 1950

Call Me Babylove
Music by Claibe Richardson
Lyrics by Kenward Elmslie
The Grass Harp 1971

Call Me Back
Music and lyrics by Stan Freeman and Franklin
Underwood
Lovely Ladies, Kind Gentlemen 1970

Call Me Lucky
Music and lyrics by Johnny Brandon
Cindy (OB) 1964

Call Me Mister
Music and lyrics by Harold Rome
Call Me Mister 1946

Call Me Savage
Music by Jule Styne
Lyrics by Betty Comden and Adolph Green
Fade Out—Fade In 1964

Call Me Uncle
Music by Rudolf Friml
Lyrics by Otto Harbach
The Firefly 1912

The Call of Broadway
Music by Maury Rubens
Lyrics by Jack Osterman and Ted Lewis
Artists and Models (1927)

The Call of Life
Music and lyrics by Noël Coward
Bitter Sweet 1929

The Call of the Sea
Music by Vincent Youmans
Lyrics by Otto Harbach
No, No, Nanette 1925

The Call of the South
Music and lyrics by Irving Berlin
Music Box Revue (4th edition) 1924

Call of the Wild
Music by Berenice Kazounoff
Lyrics by Sylvia Marks
Two for Tonight (OB) 1939

Call the Doc
Music by Richard Rodgers
Lyrics by Lorenz Hart
Poor Little Ritz Girl 1920

Included in Boston production, but dropped before
Broadway opening

Call the Police
Music by David Baker
Lyrics by David Craig
Copper and Brass 1957

Calla Lily Lady
Music by Galt MacDermot
Lyrics by John Guare
Two Gentlemen of Verona 1971

Calling All Stars
Music by Harry Akst
Lyrics by Lew Brown
Calling All Stars 1934

Calling You My Own
Music by A. Baldwin Sloane
Lyrics by Harry Cort and George E. Stoddard
China Rose 1925

Calliope
Music and lyrics by Kay Swift
Paris '90 1952

Calypso Joe
Music by Morgan Lewis
Lyrics by Nancy Hamilton
Two for the Show 1940

Calypso Kitty
Music by Don Elliott
Lyrics by James Costigan
The Beast in Me 1963

Calypso Pete
Music and lyrics by Charles Gaynor
Show Girl 1961

Camelot
Music by Frederick Loewe
Lyrics by Alan Jay Lerner
Camelot 1960

The Camelot Samba
Music by Richard Rodgers
Lyrics by Lorenz Hart
A Connecticut Yankee (1943 revival)

Camera Shoot
Music by Richard Rodgers
Lyrics by Lorenz Hart
She's My Baby 1928

Camille, Colette, Fifi
Music by Victor Young
Lyrics by Stella Unger
Seventh Heaven 1955

Camp Karefree
Music and lyrics by Harold Rome
Wish You Were Here 1952

The Campaign
Music by Moose Charlap
Lyrics by Norman Gimbel
The Conquering Hero 1961

Campaign Song
Music and lyrics by Will Holt
That 5 A.M. Jazz (OB) 1964

Campus Walk
Music and lyrics by Maceo Pinkard
Pansy 1929

Can Anyone See?
Music by Robert Stolz
Lyrics by Robert Sour
Mr. Strauss Goes to Boston 1945

Can-Can
Music and lyrics by Cole Porter
Can-Can 1953

The Can-Canola
Music by J. Fred Coots
Lyrics by Arthur Swanstrom and Benny Davis
Sons o' Guns 1929

Can I Do It All?
Music by Scott MacLarty
Lyrics by Dorothy Chansky
The Brooklyn Bridge (OB) 1983

Can I Forget You?
Music by Jerome Kern
Lyrics by Oscar Hammerstein II
High, Wide and Handsome (1937) F

Can I Touch You?
Music and lyrics by Tom Sankey
The Golden Screw (OB) 1967

Can It Be Possible?
Music and lyrics by Jack Lawrence and Stan Freeman
I Had a Ball 1964

Can It Be That I'm in Love?
Music by Emmerich Kálmán
Lyrics by B.G. DeSylva
The Yankee Princess 1922

Can That Boy Foxtrot!
Music and lyrics by Stephen Sondheim
Marry Me a Little (OB) 1981

Dropped from *Follies* (1971)

Can the Can-Can
Music and lyrics by Dorcas Cochran
and Charles Rosoff
Earl Carroll's Vanities (1940)

Can This Be a Toe Print?
Music by Alec Wilder
Lyrics by Arnold Sundgaard
Kittiwake Island (OB) 1960

Can This Be Love?
Music by Kay Swift
Lyrics by Paul James
Fine and Dandy 1930

Can We E'er Forget?
Music by Ivan Caryll
Lyrics by C.M.S. McLellan
Oh! Oh! Delphine 1912

Can You Hear Me Now?
Music by Larry Grossman
Lyrics by Betty Comden and Adolph Green
A Doll's Life 1982

Can You Hear My Voice?
Music by Samuel Kraus
Lyrics by George Sherman
To Live Another Summer 1971

Can You See a Girl Like Me in the Role?
Music by William Howe
Lyrics by Max Showalter
Shoestring '57 (OB)

Can You Sing?
Music by Sigmund Romberg
Lyrics by Oscar Hammerstein II
Sunny River 1941

Can You Type?
Music by Ted Simons
Lyrics by Elinor Guggenheimer
Potholes (OB) 1979

Can You Use Any Money Today?
Music and lyrics by Irving Berlin
Call Me Madam 1950

Canajoharie
Music by Jerome Kern
Lyrics by Anne Caldwell
Hitchy-Koo 1920

Canary
Music by Stan Davis
Lyrics by Giles O'Connor
Wet Paint (OB) 1965

Cancun
Music and lyrics by John Forster
and Michael Leeds
Upstairs at O'Neal's (OB) 1982

Candy's Lament
Music by Alfred Brooks
Lyrics by Ira J. Bilowit
Of Mice and Men (OB) 1958

Canis Minor Bolero Waltz
Music and lyrics by John Phillips
Man on the Moon 1975

Can't Be Bothered Now
Music and lyrics by J.C. Johnson
Change Your Luck 1930

Can't Get Rid of Me
Music by Harry Revel
Lyrics by Mack Gordon
Smiling Faces 1932

Can't Help Lovin' Dat Man
Music by Jerome Kern
Lyrics by Oscar Hammerstein II
Show Boat 1927

Can't Help Singing
Music by Jerome Kern
Lyrics by E.Y. Harburg
Can't Help Singing (1944) F

Can't Leave Now
Music by Jimmy Horowitz
Lyrics by Leo Rost and Jimmy Horowitz
Marlowe 1981

Can't Stop the Sea
Music by Baldwin.Bergersen
Lyrics by William Archibald
Carib Song 1945

Can't We Be Friends?
Music by Kay Swift
Lyrics by Paul James
The Little Show (1st edition) 1929

Can't We Get Together
Music by Thomas (Fats) Waller
and Harry Brooks
Lyrics by Andy Razaf
Hot Chocolates 1929

Can't You Do a Friend a Favor?
Music by Richard Rodgers
Lyrics by Lorenz Hart
A Connecticut Yankee (1943 revival)

Can't You Hear Our Country Calling?
Music by Victor Herbert
Lyrics by Gene Buck
Ziegfeld Follies of 1917

Can't You Just See Yourself?
Music by Jule Styne
Lyrics by Sammy Cahn
High Button Shoes 1947

Can't You See I'm in Love
Music by Owen Murphy
Lyrics by George S. Kaufman, Marc Connelly
and Ira Gershwin
Be Yourself 1924

Can't You See It?
Music by Charles Strouse
Lyrics by Lee Adams
Golden Boy 1964

Cantata
Music by Gerald Alters
Lyrics by Herbert Hartig
Wet Paint (OB) 1965

Canteen Serenade
Music by Jack Holmes
Lyrics by Bill Conklin and Bob Miller
O Say Can You See! (OB) 1962

Canter Banter
Music by Paul Hoffert
Lyrics by David Secter
Get Thee to Canterbury (OB) 1969

Canterbury Day
Music by Richard Hill and John Hawkins
Lyrics by Nevill Coghill
Canterbury Tales 1969

Canticle of Pleasure
Music by Steve Jankowski
Lyrics by Kenny Morris
Francis (OB) 1982

Canticle to the Wind
Music and lyrics by Ed Tyler
Sweet Miani (OB) 1962

Capricious and Fickle
Music by Al Carmines
Lyrics by Maria Irene Fornes
Promenade (OB) 1969

Captain Henry St. James
Music and lyrics by Jay Livingston
and Ray Evans
Oh Captain! 1958

Captain Hook's Tango
Music by Mark Charlap
Lyrics by Carolyn Leigh
Peter Pan 1954

Captain Hook's Waltz
Music by Jule Styne
Lyrics by Betty Comden and Adolph Green
Peter Pan 1954

The Captain Lincoln March
Music by Victor Ziskin
Lyrics by Joan Javits
Young Abe Lincoln 1961

Captain, Mate and Crew
Music by Eubie Blake
Lyrics by J. Milton Reddie and Cecil Mack
Swing It 1937

Captain of the Ten-Day Boat
Music and lyrics by George M. Cohan
Little Johnny Jones 1904

Captain Terror
Music by Bob James
Lyrics by Jack O'Brien
The Selling of the President 1972

Captain Valentine's Tango
Music by Kurt Weill
Lyrics by Paul Green
Johnny Johnson 1936

Cardboard Madonna
Music and lyrics by Al Carmines
The Evangelist (OB) 1982

The Cardinal's Guard Are We
Music by Sigmund Romberg (developed by
Don Walker)
Lyrics by Leo Robin
The Girl in Pink Tights 1954

Career Guidance
Music by David Baker
Lyrics by David Craig
Copper and Brass 1957

Carefully Taught
Music by Richard Rodgers
Lyrics by Oscar Hammerstein II
South Pacific 1949

Careless Rhapsody
Music by Richard Rodgers
Lyrics by Lorenz Hart
By Jupiter 1942

Caress Me, Possess Me, Perfume
Music by Moose Charlap
Lyrics by Norman Gimbel
Whoop-Up 1958

Caribbeana
Music by Gerald Dolin
Lyrics by Edward J. Lambert
Smile at Me 1935

Carinito
Music by Maria Grever
Lyrics by Raymond Leveen
Viva O'Brien 1941

Carino Mio
Music by Frederick Loewe
Lyrics by Alan Jay Lerner
Paint Your Wagon 1951

The Carioca
Music by Vincent Youmans
Lyrics by Edward Ellscu and Gus Kahn
Flying Down to Rio (1933) F

Carissima
Music by G. Romilli
Lyrics by Grace Henry
Fioretta 1929

Carlotta
Music and lyrics by Cole Porter
Mexican Hayride 1944

Carmela
Music by Dave Stamper
Lyrics by Gene Buck
Take the Air 1927

Carmelina
Music by Burton Lane
Lyrics by Alan Jay Lerner
Carmelina 1979

Carmen Has Nothing on Me
Music by Dave Stamper
Lyrics by Gene Buck
Take the Air 1927

Carmen Jones Is Goin' to Jail
Music by Georges Bizet
Lyrics by Oscar Hammerstein II
Carmen Jones 1943

A Carnival for Life
Music by Franz Lehár
Lyrics by Basil Hood
The Count of Luxembourg 1912

Carnival in Court
Music by Jay Navarre
Lyrics by Ray Golden and I.A.L. Diamond
Catch a Star! 1955

The Carnival Song
Music by Jule Styne
Lyrics by Betty Comden and Adolph Green
Say, Darling 1958

Carnival Time
Music by George Gershwin
Lyrics by Ira Gershwin
Lady, Be Good! 1924

A Carol
Music by Clinton Ballard
Lyrics by Carolyn Richter
The Ballad of Johnny Pot (OB) 1971

Caroline
Music and lyrics by Cole Porter
High Society (1955) F

Dropped from film

Caroline
Music and lyrics by Randy Newman
Maybe I'm Doing It Wrong (1st edition) (OB) 1981

Carolita
Music by William Heagney
Lyrics by William Heagney and Tom Connell
There You Are 1932

Carousel
Music by Jacques Brel
English lyrics by Eric Blau and Mort Shuman
*Jacques Brel Is Alive and Well
and Living in Paris* (OB) 1968

Carousel in the Park
Music by Sigmund Romberg
Lyrics by Dorothy Fields
Up in Central Park 1945

Carousel Waltz (instrumental)
Music by Richard Rodgers
Carousel 1945

A Carriage for Alida
Music by Sol Kaplan
Lyrics by Edward Eliscu
The Banker's Daughter (OB) 1962

Carrie
Music and lyrics by Noël Coward
Charlot's Revue of 1926

Carry On
Music and lyrics by Cole Porter
Red, Hot and Blue! 1936

Carry On
Music and lyrics by James MacDonald, David Vos
and Robert Gerlach
Something's Afoot 1976

Carry On, Keep Smiling
Music by Vincent Youmans
Lyrics by Harold Adamson
Smiles 1930

Casamagordo, New Mexico
Music by Jule Styne
Lyrics by Sammy Cahn
Look to the Lilies 1970

Casanova
Music by Vernon Duke
Lyrics by Ted Fetter
The Show Is On 1936

A Case of Rape
Music by Robert Emmett Dolan
Lyrics by Johnny Mercer
Foxy 1964

Cash Politics
Music by Scott MacLarty
Lyrics by Dorothy Chansky
The Brooklyn Bridge (OB) 1983

Casimo
Music by Herbert Stothart
Lyrics by Otto Harbach and Oscar Hammerstein II
Wildflower 1923

Castle of Dreams
Music by Harry Tierney
Lyrics by Joseph McCarthy
Irene 1919

Castle of Love
Music by Karl Hajos (based on Chopin)
Lyrics by Harry B. Smith
White Lilacs 1928

Castles in the Air
Music by William Dyer
Lyrics by Don Parks and William Dyer
Jo (OB) 1964

Castles in the Sand
Music by Albert T. Viola
Lyrics by William S. Kilborne, Jr.
Head Over Heels 1981

Castles of the Loire
Music by Arthur B. Rubinstein
Lyrics by Hal Hackady
Goodtime Charley 1975

Catalina
Music by Michael Cleary
Lyrics by Arthur Swanstrom
Sea Legs 1937

Catch a Butterfly
Music by Jean Gilbert
Lyrics by Harry Graham and Cyrus Wood
The Lady in Ermine 1922

Catch a Star!
Music by Sammy Fain
Lyrics by Paul Webster
Catch a Star! 1955

Catch Hatch
Music by Kurt Weill
Lyrics by Ogden Nash
One Touch of Venus 1943

Catch Me
Music and lyrics by Sam Shepard
Operation Sidewinder 1970

Catch Me if You Can
Music by Kurt Weill
Lyrics by Langston Hughes
Street Scene 1947

Catch My Garter
Music by John Kander
Lyrics by Fred Ebb
The Happy Time 1968

Catch Our Act at the Met
Music by Jule Styne
Lyrics by Betty Comden and Adolph Green
Two on the Aisle 1951

Catch That on the Corner
Music and lyrics by Melvin Van Peebles
Ain't Supposed to Die a Natural Death 1971

Caterpillar's Advice
Music and lyrics by Elizabeth Swados
Alice in Concert (OB) 1980

Catfish
Music and lyrics by Jim Swann
Pump Boys and Dinettes 1982

The Cathedral of Clemenza
Music and lyrics by Sandy Wilson
Valmouth (OB) 1960

Catherine the Great
Music by Sam Stept
Lyrics by Lew Brown and Charles Tobias
Yokel Boy 1939

Cat's in the Cradle
Music and lyrics by Harry Chapin
The Night That Made America Famous 1975

Catskills, Hello
Music by Jerome Kern
Lyrics by Anne Caldwell
The Night Boat 1920

Caught in the Rain
Music by Henry Sullivan
Lyrics by Howard Dietz
The Little Show (1st edition) 1929

The Cause of the Situation
Music and lyrics by George M. Cohan
Billie 1928

'Cause We Got Cake
Music by Richard Rodgers
Lyrics by Lorenz Hart
Too Many Girls 1939

'Cause You Won't Play House
Music by Morgan Lewis
Lyrics by E.Y. Harburg
New Faces of 1934

Cavaliers
Music by Rudolf Friml
Lyrics by Rowland Leigh and John Shubert
Music Hath Charms 1934

Cavorting
Music and lyrics by Rick Besoyan
Babes in the Wood (OB) 1964

The Cecil in London Town
Music and lyrics by George M. Cohan
Little Johnny Jones 1904

Cecily
Music by Robert Hood Bowers
Lyrics by Francis DeWitt
Oh, Ernest! 1927

Celebration!
Music by Gordon Duffy
Lyrics by Harry M. Haldane
Happy Town 1959

Celebration
Music by Harvey Schmidt
Lyrics by Tom Jones
Celebration 1969

Celina Couldn't Say "No"
Music by Arthur Schwartz
Lyrics by Howard Dietz
Between the Devil 1937

Cell Block Tango
Music by John Kander
Lyrics by Fred Ebb
Chicago 1975

Cellini's Dream
Music by Alfred Goodman, Maury Rubens
and J. Fred Coots
Lyrics by Clifford Grey
Artists and Models (1925)

The Center of Your Mind
Music by Stanley Silverman
Lyrics by Arthur Miller
Up From Paradise (OB) 1983

Central Park on a Sunday Afternoon
Music by Hank Beebe
Lyrics by Bill Heyer
*Tuscaloosa's Calling Me
But I'm Not Going!* (OB) 1975

A Certain Girl
Music by John Kander
Lyrics by Fred Ebb
The Happy Time 1968

Certain Individuals
Music and lyrics by Harold Rome
Wish You Were Here 1952

Certainly, Lord
Music and lyrics by Marc Blitzstein
Regina 1949

Cesario's Party
Music and lyrics by Harold Rome
Fanny 1954

C'est Comme Ça
Music by Duke Ellington
Lyrics by Marshall Barer and Fred Tobias
Pousse-Café 1966

C'est Defendu
Music by Gerard Calvi
Lyrics by Harold Rome
La Grosse Valise 1965

C'est la Vie
Music by Harold Arlen
Lyrics by Ira Gershwin and E.Y. Harburg
Life Begins at 8:40 1934

C'est la Vie
Music by Victor Young
Lyrics by Stella Unger
Seventh Heaven 1955

C'est Magnifique
Music and lyrics by Cole Porter
Can-Can 1953

C'est Moi
Music by Frederick Loewe
Lyrics by Alan Jay Lerner
Camelot 1960

Chain Store Daisy
Music and lyrics by Harold Rome
Pins and Needles (OB) 1937

Champagne and Kisses
Music and lyrics by John Phillips
Man on the Moon 1975

Champagne Song
Music and lyrics by Ann Harris
Sky High (OB) 1979

The Championship of the World
Music by Victor Herbert
Lyrics by Gene Buck
Ziegfeld Follies of 1921

The Chance of a Lifetime
Music and lyrics by Gary Portnoy and Judy Hart
Angelo
Preppies (OB) 1983

Chances
Music and lyrics by Bob Goodman
Wild and Wonderful 1971

Change Partners
Music and lyrics by Irving Berlin
Carefree (1938) F

Change in Direction
Music and lyrics by Bland Simpson and Jim Wann
Hot Grog (OB) 1977

Change Your Luck
Music and lyrics by J.C. Johnson
Change Your Luck 1930

Change Your Mind About Me
Music and lyrics by Alexander Hill
Hummin' Sam 1933

Changes
Music by Keith Hermann
Lyrics by Charlotte Anker and Irene Rosenberg
Onward Victoria 1980

Changing
Music by Nancy Ford
Lyrics by Gretchen Cryer
Shelter 1973

Changing My Tune
Music by George Gershwin
Lyrics by Ira Gershwin
The Shocking Miss Pilgrim (1947) F

Adapted by Kay Swift and Ira Gershwin from
manuscripts of George Gershwin.

Changing of the Guard
Music and lyrics by Harry Chapin
The Night That Made America Famous 1975

Changing of the Guards
Music by Ben Oakland
Lyrics by Jack Murray and Barry Trivers
Ziegfeld Follies (1931)

A Chanson in the Prater
Music by Sigmund Romberg
Lyrics by Oscar Hammerstein II
May Wine 1935

Chansonette
Music by Rudolf Friml
Lyrics by Dailey Paskman, Sigmund Spaeth and
Irving Caesar
Ziegfeld Follies of 1923

Based on Friml's piece "Chanson," this was to
achieve wide popularity as "The Donkey Serenade."

Chant
Music and lyrics by Irving Burgie
Ballad for Bimshire (OB) 1963

Chant d'Amour
Music by Gordon Jenkins
Lyrics by Nat Hiken
Along Fifth Avenue 1949

Chanty
Music and lyrics by Ron Dante
and Gene Allan
Billy 1969

The Chaplin Walk
Music by Jerome Kern and Otto Motzan
Lyrics by Schuyler Greene
Nobody Home 1915

Chapter 54, Number 1909
Music by Cy Coleman
Lyrics by Dorothy Fields
Seesaw 1973

Charisma
Music and lyrics by Oscar Brand
How to Steal an Election (OB) 1968

Charity
Music by Nacio Herb Brown
and Richard Whiting
Lyrics by B.G. DeSylva
Take a Chance 1932

The Charity Class
Music by Jerome Kern
Lyrics by P. G. Wodehouse
Sitting Pretty 1924

Charity's Soliloquy
Music by Cy Coleman
Lyrics by Dorothy Fields
Sweet Charity 1966

Charles Atlas Song
Music and lyrics by Richard O'Brien
The Rocky Horror Show 1975

Charleston
Music and lyrics by James Johnson
and Cecil Mack
Runnin' Wild 1923

Charleston
Music by Morton Gould
Lyrics by Betty Comden and Adolph Green
Billion Dollar Baby 1945

Charleston Mad
Music by Con Conrad
Lyrics by William B. Friedlander
Mercenary Mary 1925

Charleston Rag
Music and lyrics by Buster Davis
Doctor Jazz 1975

Charley From That Charleston Dancin' School
Music and lyrics by Porter Grainger
and Freddie Johnson
Lucky Sambo 1925

Charlie
Music and lyrics by Fred Ebb and Norman Martin
From A to Z 1960

Charlie and Algernon
Music by Charles Strouse
Lyrics by David Rogers
Charlie and Algernon 1980

Charlie, I Really Loved You
Music by Charles Strouse
Lyrics by David Rogers
Charlie and Algernon 1980

Charlie, My Back Door Man
Music by Clarence Todd
Lyrics by Henry Creamer and Con Conrad
Keep Shufflin' 1928

Charlie Welch
Music and lyrics by Jerry Bock, George Weiss
and Larry Holofcener
Mr. Wonderful 1956

Charlie's Place
Music and lyrics by Richard M. Sherman
and Robert B. Sherman
Over Here! 1974

Charlie's Plaint
Music by Susan Hulsman Bingham
Lyrics by Myrna Lamb
Mod Donna (OB) 1970

Charlie's Songs
Music by Gary Geld
Lyrics by Peter Udell
Purlie 1970

Charlotte Sweet
Music by Gerald Jay Markoe
Lyrics by Michael Colby
Charlotte Sweet (OB) 1982

Charm
Music and lyrics by William Roy
Maggie 1953

Charmed Life
Music by David Shire
Lyrics by Richard Maltby, Jr.
The Sap of Life (OB) 1961

The Charmin' Son-of-a-Bitch
Music and lyrics by Bill and Patti Jacob
Jimmy 1969

Charming
Music and lyrics by George M. Cohan
The Merry Malones 1927

Charming
Music by Edward A. Horan
Lyrics by Frederick Herendeen
All the King's Horses 1934

Charming
Music and lyrics by Dorcas Cochran
and Charles Rosoff
Earl Carroll's Vanities (1940)

Charming, Charming
Music by Richard Rodgers
Lyrics by Lorenz Hart
Peggy-Ann 1926

Charming, Charming
Music and lyrics by Noël Coward
Conversation Piece 1934

Charming Ladies
Music by Oscar Straus
Lyrics by Edward Delaney Dunn
The Last Waltz 1921

Charming Weather
Music by Lionel Monckton
Lyrics by Arthur Wimperis
The Arcadians 1910

Charming Women
Music by J. Fred Coots
Lyrics by Clifford Grey
June Days 1925

Charmin's Lament
Music and lyrics by Stephen Schwartz
The Magic Show 1974

Charms Are Fairest When They're Hidden
Music by Rudolf Friml
Lyrics by Otto Harbach
Katinka 1915

The Chase
Music by Frederick Loewe
Lyrics by Alan Jay Lerner
Brigadoon 1947

The Chase
Music by Richard Rodgers
Lyrics by Sheldon Harnick
Rex 1976

The Chase of the Fox
Music by Vincent Youmans
No, No, Nanette 1925

Dropped from production

Chasing Henry
Music by Michael Cleary
Lyrics by Arthur Swanstrom
Sea Legs 1937

Chaste Woman
Music by Con Conrad
Lyrics by William B. Friedlander
Mercenary Mary 1925

Chatter
Music and lyrics by Gene Lockhart
Bunk of 1926

Chatter Chatter
Music and lyrics by Irving Berlin
Watch Your Step 1914

The Chatterbox
Music by Sam Morrison
Lyrics by Dolph Singer
Summer Wives 1936

Chauve Souris
Music and lyrics by Noël Coward
This Year of Grace 1928

Chaya
Music and lyrics by Stan Freeman
and Franklin Underwood
Lovely Ladies, Kind Gentlemen 1970

Check Your Troubles
Music by Frank Grey
Lyrics by Earle Crooker and McElbert Moore
Happy 1927

Cheek to Cheek
Music and lyrics by Irving Berlin
Top Hat (1935) F

Cheer for Simplicitas!
Music by Lionel Monckton
Lyrics by Arthur Wimperis
The Arcadians 1910

Cheer Up
Music by John Philip Sousa
Lyrics by Leonard Liebling
The American Maid 1913

Cheer Up
Music by Jerome Kern
Lyrics by Oscar Hammerstein II
Show Boat 1927

Dropped from production; rewritten as "I Might Fall
Back on You."

Cheer Up!
Music by Victor Ziskin
Lyrics by Joan Javits
Young Abe Lincoln 1961

Cheerful Little Earful
Music by Harry Warren
Lyrics by Ira Gershwin and Billy Rose
Sweet and Low 1930

Cheerio
Music by Richard Rodgers
Lyrics by Lorenz Hart
Dearest Enemy 1925

Cheerio
Music by Jesse Greer
Lyrics by James J. Walker
Say When 1928

This song was written when Walker was mayor of
New York City.

Cheers for the Hero
Music by Jacques Offenbach (adapted by Robert
DeCormier)
Lyrics by E.Y. Harburg
The Happiest Girl in the World 1961

Cheese Nips
Music by Alan Menken
Lyrics by Howard Ashman
God Bless You, Mr. Rosewater (OB) 1979

Cherchez la Femme
Music by Con Conrad
Lyrics by William B. Friedlander
Mercenary Mary 1925

Cherokee Rose
Music by Frank Harling
Lyrics by Laurence Stallings
Deep River 1926

Cherry Pies Ought to Be You
Music and lyrics by Cole Porter
Out of This World 1950

Cheshire Puss
Music and lyrics by Elizabeth Swados
Alice in Concert (OB) 1980

Chess and Checkers
Music and lyrics by Bob Merrill
New Girl in Town 1957

Chess Game
Music and lyrics by William Finn
March of the Falsettos (OB) 1981

The Chevalier of the Highway
Music by Maury Rubens
Lyrics by Clifford Grey
The Great Temptations 1926

Chewska
Music by Leo Fall
Lyrics by George Grossmith
The Dollar Princess 1909

Chi-Chi
Music by Rudolf Friml
Lyrics by Otto Harbach
High Jinks 1913

Chi-Chi
Music by Irvin Graham
Lyrics by June Sillman
New Faces of 1936

Chicago
Music by Richard Rodgers
Lyrics by Lorenz Hart
Pal Joey 1940

Chicago After Midnight
Music by John Kander
Lyrics by Fred Ebb
Chicago 1975

Chick! Chick! Chick!
Music by Jerome Kern
Lyrics by Anne Caldwell
Hitchy-Koo 1920

Dropped from production

Chick-a-Pen
Music and lyrics by Meredith Willson
The Unsinkable Molly Brown 1960

Chicken Is He
Music by Al Carmines
Lyrics by Maria Irene Fornes
Promenade (OB) 1969

Chicken's a Popular Bird
Music and lyrics by Irving Burgie
Ballad for Bimshire (OB) 1963

Chickens Come Home to Roost
Music by Eubie Blake
Lyrics by Noble Sissle
Shuffle Along of 1933

Chico-Chico Chico-Layo
Music by Jack Holmes
Lyrics by Bill Conklin and Bob Miller
O Say Can You See! (OB) 1962

Chief of Love
Music by Jule Styne
Lyrics by Betty Comden and Adolph Green
Say, Darling 1958

Chiffon
Music by Maurice Yvain
Lyrics by Max and Nathaniel Lief
Luckee Girl 1928

Child of Erin
Music by Franklin Hauser
Lyrics by Russell Janney
The O'Flynn 1934

Child of Pure Unclouded Brow
Music and lyrics by Elizabeth Swados
Alice in Concert (OB) 1980

Child You Are
Music by Michael Leonard
Lyrics by Herbert Martin
How to Be a Jewish Mother 1967

Childhood Days
Music by Louis A. Hirsch
Lyrics by P.G. Wodehouse
Oh, My Dear! 1918

Childhood Lullaby
Music by Frank Fields
Lyrics by Armand Aulicino
The Shoemaker and the Peddler (OB) 1960

Childhood's Days
Music by Jean Gilbert
Lyrics by Harry Graham and Cyrus Wood
The Lady in Ermine 1922

Children and Art
Music and lyrics by Stephen Sondheim
Sunday in the Park With George (OB) 1983

Children Are for Loving
Music and lyrics by Glory Van Scott
Miss Truth (OB) 1979

Children Have It Easy
Music by David Shire
Lyrics by Richard Maltby, Jr.
The Sap of Life (OB) 1961

Children of the Ritz
Music and lyrics by Noël Coward
Set to Music 1939

Children of the Sun
Music by Galt MacDermot
Lyrics by Christopher Gore
Via Galactica 1972

Children's Games
Music and lyrics by Voices, Inc.
The Believers (OB) 1968

Children's Lament
Music by Walt Smith
Lyrics by Leon Uris
Ari 1971

Children's Rhymes
Music and lyrics by Micki Grant
Don't Bother Me, I Can't Cope (OB) 1972

The Child's Song
Music by Alex Fry
Lyrics by Lyon Phelps
Do You Know the Milky Way? 1961

Chime In!
Music and lyrics by Robert Wright
and George Forrest
Kean 1961

Chin Up, Ladies
Music and lyrics by Jerry Herman
Milk and Honey 1961

Chin-Chin
Music by Ivan Caryll
Lyrics by Anne Caldwell and James O'Dea
Chin-Chin 1914

China Bogie Man
Music by A. Baldwin Sloane
Lyrics by Harry Cort and George E. Stoddard
China Rose 1925

China Chaps
Music by Ivan Caryll
Lyrics by Anne Caldwell and James O'Dea
Chin-Chin 1914

China Rose
Music by A. Baldwin Sloane
Lyrics by Harry Cort and George E. Stoddard
China Rose 1925

Chinese Firecrackers
Music and lyrics by Irving Berlin
Ziegfeld Follies of 1920

The Chinese Honeymoon
Music by Ivan Caryll
Lyrics by Anne Caldwell and James O'Dea
Chin-Chin 1914

The Chinese Idol
Music and lyrics by Berton Braley, M. de Jari
and Alex James
Earl Carroll's Vanities (1926)

Chinese Lantern Man
Music by A. Baldwin Sloane
Lyrics by Harry Cort and George E. Stoddard
China Rose 1925

Chinese Lullaby
Music and lyrics by Robert Hood Bowers
East Is West 1918

Chinese Market Place
Music by Raymond Scott
Lyrics by Bernard Hanighen
Lute Song 1946

Chinese Melody
Music by Franz Lehár
Lyrics by Harry Graham
Yours Is My Heart 1946

Chinese Potentate
Music by A. Baldwin Sloane
Lyrics by Harry Cort and George E. Stoddard
China Rose 1925

Chingo-Pingo
Music by Franz Lehár
Lyrics by Harry Graham
Yours Is My Heart 1946

Chinky China Charleston
Music by Milton Susskind
Lyrics by Paul Porter and Benjamin Hapgood Burt
Florida Girl 1925

Chinky Pin
Music and lyrics by Marc Blitzstein
Regina 1949

Chinquapin Bush
Music by Harold Arlen
Lyrics by Johnny Mercer
St. Louis Woman 1946

Chipper
Music by Ivan Caryll
Lyrics by Anne Caldwell and James O'Dea
Chin-Chin 1914

Chiquita Bonita
Music and lyrics by John Clifton
El Bravo! (OB) 1981

Chiquitin Trio
Music by Robert Stolz
Lyrics by Rowland Leigh
Night of Love 1941

Chiromancy
Music by John Addison
Lyrics by John Cranko
Cranks 1956

Chocolate Bar
Music by "Fats" Waller
Lyrics by Andy Razaf
Keep Shufflin' 1928

Chocolate Dandies
Music and lyrics by Noble Sissle
and Eubie Blake
The Chocolate Dandies 1924

Chocolate Pas de Trois
Music and lyrics by Robert Wright
and George Forrest
Song of Norway 1944

Based on Grieg's *Monte Pincio* and *Rigaudon*

Chocolate Turkey
Music by Al Carmines
Lyrics by Rosalyn Drexler
Home Movies (OB) 1964

The Choice Is Yours
Music by Edward Thomas
Lyrics by Martin Charnin
Ballad for a Firing Squad (OB) 1968

Choir Practice
Music and lyrics by Earl Wilson, Jr.
Let My People Come (OB) 1974

Choo-Choo Honeymoon
Music by Jim Wise
Lyrics by George Haimsohn and Robin Miller
Dames at Sea (OB) 1968

Choo Choo Love
Music by Con Conrad
Lyrics by Gus Kahn
Kitty's Kisses 1926

Choose a Partner Please
Music by Stephen Jones and Arthur Samuels
Lyrics by Dorothy Donnelly
Poppy 1923

Choose Your Flowers
Music by Lucien Denni
Lyrics by Helena Evans
Happy Go Lucky 1926

Chop Suey
Music by Richard Rodgers
Lyrics by Oscar Hammerstein II
Flower Drum Song 1958

Chorus Girl Blues
Music by Manning Sherwin
Lyrics by Arthur Herzog, Jr.
Bad Habits of 1926 (OB)

The Chow Mein Girls
Music and lyrics by Clarence Gaskill
Earl Carroll's Vanities (1925)

Christianity
Music and lyrics by Eaton Magoon, Jr.
Heathen 1972

Christine
Music by Sammy Fain
Lyrics by Paul Francis Webster
Christine 1960

Christmas at Hampton Court
Music by Richard Rodgers
Lyrics by Sheldon Harnick
Rex 1976

A Christmas Buche
Music by Gerald Jay Markoe
Lyrics by Michael Colby
Charlotte Sweet (OB) 1982

Christmas Carol
Music by Richard B. Chodosh
Lyrics by Barry Alan Grael
The Streets of New York (OB) 1963

Christmas Child
Music by Marguerite Monnot
Lyrics by Julian More, David Heneker
and Monte Norman
Irma la Douce 1960

Christmas Eve Broadcast
Music by Laurence Rosenthal
Lyrics by James Lipton
Sherry! 1967

Christmas Is Comin' Uptown
Music by Garry Sherman
Lyrics by Peter Udell
Comin' Uptown 1979

Christmas Is Coming
Music by Helen Miller
Lyrics by Eve Merriam
Inner City 1971

Christopher
Music by Jimmy Horowitz
Lyrics by Leo Rost and Jimmy Horowitz
Marlowe 1981

Christopher Street
Music by Leonard Bernstein
Lyrics by Betty Comden and Adolph Green
Wonderful Town 1953

Chromolume #7
Music and lyrics by Stephen Sondheim
Sunday in the Park With George (OB) 1983

Chrysanthemum Tea
Music and lyrics by Stephen Sondheim
Pacific Overtures 1976

Chuck It!
Music by Richard Rodgers
Lyrics by Lorenz Hart
Peggy-Ann 1926

The Church Around the Corner
Music by Walter G. Samuels
Lyrics by Morrie Ryskind
Ned Wayburn's Gambols 1929

Church Doors
Music and lyrics by Beth Lawrence
and Norman Thalheimer
Marilyn 1983

Church of My Choice
Music by Sammy Fain
Lyrics by Marilyn and Alan Bergman
Something More 1964

The Church 'round the Corner
Music by Jerome Kern
Lyrics by P.G. Wodehouse and Clifford Grey
Sally 1920

C.I.A. Man
Music and lyrics by Tuli Kupferberg,
Peter Stampfel and Antonia
Operation Sidewinder 1970

Cider Ella
Music by Henry Souvaine and Jay Gorney
Lyrics by Morrie Ryskind and Howard Dietz
Merry-Go-Round 1927

Cigarette
Music by H. Maurice Jacquet
Lyrics by William Brady
The Silver Swan 1929

Cigarette
Music by Ray Henderson
Lyrics by Jack Yellen
George White's Scandals (1936)

Cigarette Song
Music by Sigmund Romberg
Lyrics by Harry B. Smith
Cherry Blossoms 1927

The Cigarette Song
Music by Al Carmines
Lyrics by Maria Irene Fornes
Promenade (OB) 1969

Cigarettes
Music by Harry Ruby
Lyrics by Bert Kalmar
High Kickers 1941

Cigarettes, Cigars!
Music by Harry Revel
Lyrics by Mack Gordon
Ziegfeld Follies (1931)

Cinderelatives
Music by George Gershwin
Lyrics by B.G. DeSylva
George White's Scandals (1922)

Cinderella
Music by Charles Rosoff
Lyrics by Leo Robin
Judy 1927

Cinderella Brown
Music by Jimmy McHugh
Lyrics by Dorothy Fields
Lew Leslie's International Revue 1930

Cinderella, Darling
Music and lyrics by Frank Loesser
*How to Succeed in Business
Without Really Trying* 1961

Cinderella Girl
Music by Jerome Kern
Lyrics by Anne Caldwell and Otto Harbach
Criss-Cross 1926

Cinderella March (instrumental)
Music by Richard Rodgers
Cinderella (1957) TV

Cinderella of Our Block
Music by Manning Sherwin
Lyrics by Arthur Herzog, Jr.
Bad Habits of 1926 (OB)

Cinderella Sue
Music by Jerome Kern
Lyrics by Leo Robin
Centennial Summer (1946) F

Cinderella's Ride
Music by Jerome Kern
Lyrics by Anne Caldwell and Otto Harbach
Criss-Cross 1926

Cindy
Music and lyrics by John Dooley
Hobo (OB) 1961

Cindy
Music and lyrics by Johnny Brandon
Cindy (OB) 1964

Cinema Blues
Music and lyrics by Arthur Brander
The Seventh Heart 1927

Cinema Lorelei
Music by Ned Lehak
Lyrics by Edward Eliscu
The Third Little Show 1931

Cingalese Girls
Music by Harry Ruby
Lyrics by Bert Kalmar and Otto Harbach
Lucky 1927

Circe, Circe
Music by Jerome Moross
Lyrics by John Latouche
The Golden Apple 1954

The Circle Waltz
Music and lyrics by Al Kasha
and Joel Hirschhorn
Copperfield 1981

Circumstances
Music and lyrics by David Langston Smyrl
On the Lock-In (OB) 1977

Circus Days
Music by Milton Ager
Lyrics by Jack Yellen
Rain or Shine 1928

The Circus Is on Parade
Music by Richard Rodgers
Lyrics by Lorenz Hart
Jumbo 1935

Circus of Jade
Music by Tom Mandel
Lyrics by John Braswell
The Bar That Never Closes (OB) 1972

The Circus of Voices
Music by Gerald Jay Markoe
Lyrics by Michael Colby
Charlotte Sweet (OB) 1982

The Circus Wedding
Music by Richard Rodgers
Lyrics by Lorenz Hart
Jumbo 1935

The Citation
Music by Ernest Gold
Lyrics by Anne Croswell
I'm Solomon 1968

City Blues
Music and lyrics by Voices, Inc.
The Believers (OB) 1968

City Called Heaven
Music by Eubie Blake
Lyrics by Noble Sissle
Shuffle Along of 1952

The City Chap
Music by Jerome Kern
Lyrics by Anne Caldwell
The City Chap 1925

City Life
Music and lyrics by Don Tucker
Red, White and Maddox 1969

City Life
Music by Helen Miller
Lyrics by Eve Merriam
Inner City 1971

City Lights
Music by John Kander
Lyrics by Fred Ebb
The Act 1977

City Mouse, Country Mouse
Music by Albert Hague
Lyrics by Arnold B. Horwitt
Plain and Fancy 1955

City of the Angels
Music and lyrics by Billy Barnes
The Billy Barnes Revue 1959

City on Fire!
Music and lyrics by Stephen Sondheim
Sweeney Todd 1979

City Song
Music by Kenn Long and Jim Crozier
Lyrics by Kenn Long
Touch (OB) 1970

Ciumachella
Music by Armando Trovaioli
Lyrics by Pietro Garinei and Sandro Giovannini
(Lyric translation by Edward Eager)
Rugantino 1964

Civil War Ballet
Music by Harold Arlen
Lyrics by E.Y. Harburg
Bloomer Girl 1944

Civilization
Music by Monte Carlo and Alma Sanders
Lyrics by Howard Johnson
Tangerine 1921

Civilization
Music by Carl Sigman
Lyrics by Bob Hilliard
Angel in the Wings 1947

The Civilized People
Music by Heitor Villa-Lobos
Lyrics by Robert Wright and George Forrest
Magdalena 1948

Civilized People
Music and lyrics by Robert Wright
and George Forrest
Kean 1961

Clandestine
Music by Robert Kessler
Lyrics by Martin Charnin
Fallout (OB) 1959

Clang Dang the Bell
Music and lyrics by Frank Loesser
Greenwillow 1960

Clap Yo' Hands
Music by George Gershwin
Lyrics by Ira Gershwin
Oh, Kay! 1926

The lyric of the verse was written by Howard Dietz, filling in for Ira Gershwin, who had written words to the chorus (and the rest of the score), but who was briefly hospitalized as the score was being completed.

Clara
Music by Leon Pober
Lyrics by Bud Freeman
Beg, Borrow or Steal 1960

Clara, Don't You Be Downhearted
Music by George Gershwin
Lyrics by DuBose Heyward
Porgy and Bess 1935

Clarence and Mildred
Music and lyrics by Robert Dennis, Peter Schickele
and Stanley Walden
Oh! Calcutta! 1969

Clarence's Turn
Music and lyrics by Billy Solly
Boy Meets Boy (OB) 1975

Class
Music by John Kander
Lyrics by Fred Ebb
Chicago 1975

Class Act
Music by Henry Krieger
Lyrics by Robert Lorick
The Tap Dance Kid 1983

Clay and Frelinghuysen
Music and lyrics by Oscar Brand
How to Steal an Election (OB) 1968

The Clean Ones
Music by Robert Mitchell
Lyrics by Elizabeth Perry
Bags (OB) 1982

Clean Out the Corner
Music by Alma Sanders
Lyrics by Monte Carlo
Mystery Moon 1930

Clean Up Your Own Backyard
Music by Norman Curtis
Lyrics by Patricia Taylor Curtis
Walk Down Mah Street! (OB) 1968

Cleanin' Women
Music and lyrics by Micki Grant
Working 1978

Clear Out of This World
Music by Jimmy McHugh
Lyrics by Al Dubin
Keep Off the Grass 1940

Cleopatra
Music by Alma Sanders
Lyrics by Monte Carlo
Oh! Oh! Nurse 1925

Cleopatra
Music by Julian Slade
Lyrics by Dorothy Reynolds and Julian Slade
Salad Days (OB) 1958

Cleopatra Had a Jazz Band
Music and lyrics by Buster Davis
Doctor Jazz 1975

Cleopatra, We're Fond of You
Music by Alma Sanders
Lyrics by Monte Carlo
The Houseboat on the Styx 1928

Cleopatra's Nile
Music by Frederic Norton
Lyrics by Oscar Asche
Chu Chin Chow 1917

Cleopatterer
Music by Jerome Kern
Lyrics by P.G. Wodehouse
Leave It to Jane 1917

Clever, These Chinese
Music by Vincent Youmans
Lyrics by Harold Adamson and Clifford Grey
Smiles 1930

Clickety-Clack
Music by Kurt Weill
Lyrics by Maxwell Anderson
Knickerbocker Holiday 1938

Climb Ev'ry Mountain
Music by Richard Rodgers
Lyrics by Oscar Hammerstein II
The Sound of Music 1959

Climb Up the Mountain
Music and lyrics by Cole Porter
Out of This World 1950

Climb Up the Social Ladder
Music by George Gershwin
Lyrics by Ira Gershwin
Let 'Em Eat Cake 1933

Climbin'
Music by Monty Norman
Lyrics by Julian More
The Moony Shapiro Songbook 1981

Climbing the Scale
Music and lyrics by Irving Berlin
Music Box Revue (3rd edition) 1923

Climbing Up the Ladder of Love
Music by Jesse Greer
Lyrics by Raymond Klages
Earl Carroll's Vanities (1926)

Clinging to the Rock
Music and lyrics by Al Carmines
The Evangelist (OB) 1982

Clinging Vine
Music by Percy Wenrich
Lyrics by Otto Harbach
The Fascinating Widow 1911

The Clinging Vine
Music by Harold Levey
Lyrics by Zelda Sears
The Clinging Vine 1922

Clog and Grog
Music by Jimmy Van Heusen
Lyrics by Sammy Cahn
Walking Happy 1966

Cloistered From the Noisy City
Music by George Gershwin
Lyrics by Ira Gershwin
Let 'Em Eat Cake 1933

Clorinda
Music and lyrics by Donald Heywood
Africana 1927

Close
Music and lyrics by Cole Porter
Rosalie (1937) F

Close as Pages in a Book
Music by Sigmund Romberg
Lyrics by Dorothy Fields
Up in Central Park 1945

Close Every Door
Music by Andrew Lloyd Webber
Lyrics by Tim Rice
*Joseph and the Amazing
Technicolor Dreamcoat* 1982

Close Harmony
Music by Jule Styne
Lyrics by Betty Comden and Adolph Green
Fade Out—Fade In 1964

Close in Your Arms
Music and lyrics by Ida Hoyt Chamberlain
Enchanted Isle 1927

Close Upon the Hour
Music by Peter Link
Lyrics by Jacob Brackman
King of Hearts 1978

Close Your Eyes
Music by Alfred Nathan
Lyrics by George Oppenhelmer
The Manhatters 1927

Close Your Eyes
Music by Richard B. Chodosh
Lyrics by Barry Alan Grael
The Streets of New York (OB) 1963

Closed for Renovations
Music by Alan Menken
Lyrics by Howard Ashman
Little Shop of Horrors (OB) 1982

Closeness Begets Closeness
Music and lyrics by Bruce Montgomery
The Amorous Flea (OB) 1964

Closer and Closer and Closer
Music by Frederick Loewe
Lyrics by Alan Jay Lerner
The Little Prince (1975) F

Closing Time
Music and lyrics by Jim Swann
Pump Boys and Dinettes 1982

The Clothes Make the Man
Music by Al Carmines
Lyrics by Maria Irene Fornes
Promenade (OB) 1969

Clouds
Music by Larry Grossman
Lyrics by Hal Hackady
Snoopy (OB) 1982

Clown of London
Music and lyrics by Robert Wright
and George Forrest
Kean 1961

Clown Song
Music and lyrics by Ann Harris
Sky High (OB) 1979

Club Song
Music by Alma Sanders
Lyrics by Monte Carlo
The Houseboat on the Styx 1928

Clutching at Shadows
Music by Alexander Fogarty
Lyrics by Seymour Morris
Cape Cod Follies 1929

C.N.R.
Music by Patrick Rose
Lyrics by Merv Campone and Richard Ouzounian
A Bistro Car on the CNR (OB) 1978

Coaching
Music by Jerome Kern
Lyrics by P.G. Wodehouse
Sitting Pretty 1924

Dropped from production

Coal Oil
Music and lyrics by Porter Grainger
and Freddie Johnson
Lucky Sambo 1925

Coax Me
Music by Ernest G. Schweikert
Lyrics by Frank Reardon
Rumple 1957

The Cobbler's Song
Music by Frederic Norton
Lyrics by Oscar Asche
Chu Chin Chow 1917

Cockeyed John
Music and lyrics by Harry Chapin
The Night That Made America Famous 1975

A Cockeyed Optimist
Music by Richard Rodgers
Lyrics by Oscar Hammerstein II
South Pacific 1949

See note on "I'm in Love With a Wonderful Guy"

Cocktail Counterpoint
Music and lyrics by Jerry Herman
La Cage aux Folles 1983

Cocktail Melody
Music by Walter Donaldson
Lyrics by Ballard MacDonald
Sweetheart Time 1926

Coco
Music by André Previn
Lyrics by Alan Jay Lerner
Coco 1969

The Cocoa Bean Song
Music and lyrics by Richard Adler
Kwamina 1961

Cocoanut Cream Pie
Music by Galt MacDermot
Lyrics by William Dumaresq
The Human Comedy 1983

Cocoanut Sweet
Music by Harold Arlen
Lyrics by E.Y. Harburg
Jamaica 1957

The Coconut Girl
Music and lyrics by Noël Coward
The Girl Who Came to Supper 1963

The Code
Music by Sammy Fain
Lyrics by Dan Shapiro
Ankles Aweigh 1955

Code of the Licensed Pilot
Music and lyrics by Ed Tyler
Sweet Miani (OB) 1962

Coffee Break
Music and lyrics by Frank Loesser
*How to Succeed in Business
Without Really Trying* 1961

Coffee in a Cardboard Cup
Music by John Kander
Lyrics by Fred Ebb
70, Girls, 70 1971

Cold Cash
Music by Hank Beebe
Lyrics by Bill Heyer
*Tuscaloosa's Calling Me
but I'm Not Going!* (OB) 1975

Cold Clear World
Music and lyrics by Marian Grudeff
and Raymond Jessel
Baker Street 1965

Cold, Cold Room
Music and lyrics by Harold Rome
The Zulu and the Zayda 1965

Cold Comfort
Music by John Addison
Lyrics by John Cranko
Cranks 1956

Cold Cream Jar Song
Music and lyrics by Harold Rome
Fanny 1954

Cold Hard Cash
Music by Wally Harper
Lyrics by David Zippel
Marilyn 1983

Colie Gone
Music by Coleridge-Taylor Perkinson
Lyrics by Errol Hill
Man Better Man (OB) 1969

Collective Beauty
Music by William Roy
Lyrics by Michael McWhinney
New Faces of 1962 1962

College Days
Music by Mann Holiner
Lyrics by Alberta Nichols
Gay Paree 1926

The Colonel and the Major
Music by Rudolf Friml
Lyrics by P.G. Wodehouse and Clifford Grey
The Three Musketeers 1928

Color and Light
Music and lyrics by Stephen Sondheim
Sunday in the Park With George (OB) 1983

Color Blind
Music by Henry Sullivan
Lyrics by Earle Crooker
Thumbs Up! 1934

Color Me White
Music and lyrics by Johnny Brandon
Billy Noname (OB) 1970

The Color of Her Eyes
Music by Richard Rodgers
Lyrics by Lorenz Hart
Spring Is Here 1929

Dropped from production, and later included
in the score of *Ever Green* (London 1930)

Colorado Love Call
Music and lyrics by Rick Besoyan
Little Mary Sunshine (OB) 1959

Colored Spade
Music by Galt MacDermot
Lyrics by Gerome Ragni and James Rado
Hair 1968

Colorful
Music by Charles Strouse
Lyrics by Lee Adams
Golden Boy 1964

The Colors of My Life
Music by Cy Coleman
Lyrics by Michael Stewart
Barnum 1980

The Combat
Music by Mitch Leigh
Lyrics by Joe Darion
Man of La Mancha 1965

Come a Little Closer
Music and lyrics by Bob Goodman
Wild and Wonderful 1971

Come Along
Music by Louis Bellson and Will Irwin
Lyrics by Richard Ney
Portofino 1958

Come Along, Boys
Music by Jerome Moross
Lyrics by John Latouche
The Golden Apple 1954

Come Along, Come Along, Come Along
Music and lyrics by Irving Berlin
Yip, Yip, Yaphank 1918

Come Along Sextette
Music and lyrics by Irving Berlin
Ziegfeld Follies of 1920

Come Along, Sunshine
Music by Harry Tierney
Lyrics by Joseph McCarthy
Cross My Heart 1928

Come Along With Alice (Alice in Wonderland)
Music and lyrics by Irving Berlin
Music Box Revue (4th edition) 1924

Come Along With Me
Music and lyrics by Cole Porter
Can-Can 1953

Come and Be Married
Music by Earl Robinson
Lyrics by Waldo Salt
Sandhog (OB) 1954

Come and Bring Your Instruments
Music by David Raksin
Lyrics by June Carroll
If the Shoe Fits 1946

Come and Have a Swing With Me
Music by Ivan Caryll
Lyrics by Anne Caldwell
Jack O'Lantern 1917

Come and See Our Island
Music by Leslie Stuart
Lyrics by Ernest Boyd-Jones and Paul Rubens
Florodora 1900

Come and Tell Me
Music by Richard Rodgers
Lyrics by Lorenz Hart

Dropped during rehearsal from *Peggy Ann,* which
opened December 27, 1926, and from *Betsy,* which
opened the following night.

Come as a Carrier Dove
Music by Franz Lehár
Lyrics by Harry B. and Robert B. Smith
Gypsy Love 1911

Come A-Wandering With Me
Music by Arthur Schwartz
Lyrics by Howard Dietz
The Gay Life 1961

Come Away, Death
Music and lyrics by Hal Hester and Danny Apolinar
Your Own Thing (OB) 1968

Lyrics adapted from Clown's song in *Twelfth Night*
(Act 2, Scene 4)

Come Back to Me
Music by Louis A. Hirsch
Lyrics by Harold Atteridge
The Whirl of Society 1912

Come Back to Me
Music by Burton Lane
Lyrics by Alan Jay Lerner
On a Clear Day You Can See Forever 1965

Come, Boys
Music by Sigmund Romberg
Lyrics by Dorothy Donnelly
The Student Prince 1924

Come Down
Music by Earl Robinson
Lyrics by Waldo Salt
Sandhog (OB) 1954

Come Dream So Bright
Music by Reginald De Koven
Lyrics by Harry B. Smith
Robin Hood 1891

Come Follow the Band
Music by Cy Coleman
Lyrics by Michael Stewart
Barnum 1980

Come Hit Your Baby
Music by Maury Rubens and Sam Timberg
Lyrics by Moe Jaffe
Broadway Nights 1929

Come Home
Music by Richard Rodgers
Lyrics by Oscar Hammerstein II
Allegro 1947

Come, Little Fishes
Music by Victor Herbert
Lyrics by Harry B. Smith
The Enchantress 1911

Come, Oh Come (to Pittsburgh)
Music by Arthur Schwartz
Lyrics by Howard Dietz
Inside U.S.A. 1948

Come On
Music by Harry Archer
Lyrics by Harlan Thompson
Little Jessie James 1923

Come On Along
Music by Con Conrad
Lyrics by William B. Friedlander
Mercenary Mary 1925

Come On and Make Whoopee
Music by Werner Janssen
Lyrics by Mann Holiner
Luckee Girl 1928

Come On and Marry Me Honey
Music by Richard Hill and John Hawkins
Lyrics by Nevill Coghill
Canterbury Tales 1969

Come On and Pet Me
Music by Vincent Youmans
Lyrics by Oscar Hammerstein II and William Cary
Duncan
Mary Jane McKane 1923

Dropped from production. Rewritten as
"Sometimes I'm Happy" with lyrics by Irving Caesar
for *Hit the Deck* (1927)

Come On and Play
Music by Joseph Meyer and James F. Hanley
Lyrics by B.G. DeSylva
Big Boy 1925

Come On Down to the Sea
Music and lyrics by Bland Simpson and Jim Wann
Hot Grog (OB) 1977

Come On Feet, Do Your Thing
Music and lyrics by Melvin Van Peebles
Ain't Supposed to Die a Natural Death 1971

Come On Home
Music and lyrics by Donald Heywood
Bottomland 1927

Come On Home
Music by Ron Steward and Neal Tate
Lyrics by Ron Steward
Sambo (OB) 1969

Come On In
Music and lyrics by Cole Porter
Du Barry Was a Lady 1939

Come On In
Music and lyrics by Johnny Brandon
Love! Love! Love! (OB) 1977

Come On, Joan
Music and lyrics by Al Carmines
Joan (OB) 1972

Come On, L'il Augie
Music by Harold Arlen
Lyrics by Johnny Mercer
St. Louis Woman 1946

Come On Outside and Get Some Air
Music and lyrics by Deed Meyer
'Toinette (OB) 1961

Come On Strong
Music by Jimmy Van Heusen
Lyrics by Sammy Cahn
Come On Strong 1962

Come Play Wiz Me
Music and lyrics by Stephen Sondheim
Anyone Can Whistle 1964

Come Rain or Come Shine
Music by Harold Arlen
Lyrics by Johnny Mercer
St. Louis Woman 1946

Come Raise Your Cup
Music by Lee Pockriss
Lyrics by Anne Croswell
Ernest in Love (OB) 1960

Come Raising Your Leg on Me
Music and lyrics by Melvin Van Peebles
Ain't Supposed to Die a Natural Death 1971

Come, Said My Soul
Music by Stan Harte, Jr.
Leaves of Grass (OB) 1971

Comé Sta
Music by Sammy Fain
Lyrics by Marilyn and Alan Bergman
Something More 1964

Come Summer
Music by David Baker
Lyrics by Will Holt
Come Summer 1969

Come, Sweet Love
Music by Edward Earle
Lyrics by Yvonne Tarr
The Decameron (OB) 1961

Come the Gallants of the Court
Music by Victor Herbert
Lyrics by Harry B. Smith
Cyrano de Bergerac 1899

Come Tiny Goldfish to Me
Music by Harry Marlow
Lyrics by Jerome Kern
Our Miss Gibbs 1910

This is one of the very few songs for which
Kern wrote only the lyrics.

Come to Africa
Music by Ford Dabney
Lyrics by Jo Trent
Rang-Tang 1927

Come to Colombia
Music by Heitor Villa-Lobos
Lyrics by Robert Wright and George Forrest
Magdalena 1948

Come to Florence
Music by Kurt Weill
Lyrics by Ira Gershwin
The Firebrand of Florence 1945

At the end of the show the song was reprised as
"Come to Paris."

Come to Harlem
Music and lyrics by Al Wilson, Charles Weinberg
and Ken Macomber
Yeah Man 1932

Come to Lower Falls
Music by Harold Orlob
Lyrics by Irving Caesar
Talk About Girls 1927

Come to Me
Music and lyrics by Noël Coward
Sail Away 1961

Come to Me, Bend to Me
Music by Frederick Loewe
Lyrics by Alan Jay Lerner
Brigadoon 1947

Come to Mee-ow
Music by George Kleinsinger
Lyrics by Joe Darion
Shinbone Alley 1957

Come to Paris
Music by Kurt Weill
Lyrics by Ira Gershwin
The Firebrand of Florence 1945

See note on "Come to Florence"

Come to St. Thomas'
Music and lyrics by George M. Cohan
Billie 1928

Come to Sunny Spain
Music by Victor Herbert
Lyrics by Harry B. Smith
The Enchantress 1911

Come to the Ball
Music by Lionel Monckton
Lyrics by Adrian Ross
The Quaker Girl 1911

Come to the Ball
Music by Frederick Loewe
Lyrics by Alan Jay Lerner
My Fair Lady 1956

Dropped from production

Come to the Moon
Music by George Gershwin
Lyrics by Lou Paley and Ned Wayburn
Capitol Theatre Revue 1919

Come to the Road
Music by Kenn Long and Jim Crozier
Lyrics by Kenn Long
Touch (OB) 1970

Come to the Sacrifice
Music by Erich Wolfgang Korngold (based on
Jacques Offenbach)
Lyrics by Herbert Baker
Helen Goes to Troy 1944

Come to the Supermarket
Music and lyrics by Cole Porter
Aladdin (1958) TV

Come Up and Have a Cup of Coffee
Music by Ray Henderson
Lyrics by Jack Yellen
Ziegfeld Follies (1943)

Come Up to My Place
Music by Leonard Bernstein
Lyrics by Betty Comden and Adolph Green
On the Town 1944

Come West, Little Girl, Come West
Music by Walter Donaldson
Lyrics by Gus Kahn
Whoopee 1928

Come Where Nature Calls
Music by Louis A. Hirsch
Lyrics by P.G. Wodehouse
Oh, My Dear! 1918

Come With Me
Music by Richard Rodgers
Lyrics by Lorenz Hart
The Boys From Syracuse 1938

Come With Me
Music by Clay Warnick
Lyrics by Edward Eager
Dream With Music 1944

Come With Me
Music by Erich Wolfgang Korngold (based on
Jacques Offenbach)
Lyrics by Herbert Baker
Helen Goes to Troy 1944

Come With Me
Music by Jim Steinman
Lyrics by Michael Weller and Jim Steinman
More Than You Deserve (OB) 1973

Come You Men
Music by John Morris
Lyrics by Gerald Freedman
A Time for Singing 1966

Come-Along-a-Me, Babe
Music and lyrics by Johnny Brandon
Who's Who, Baby? (OB) 1968

Come-on-a-Good Life
Music by Bob James
Lyrics by Jack O'Brien
The Selling of the President 1972

Comedy Tonight
Music and lyrics by Stephen Sondheim
*A Funny Thing Happened on the Way
to the Forum* 1962

Comes Love
Music by Sam Stept
Lyrics by Lew Brown and Charles Tobias
Yokel Boy 1939

Comes Once in a Lifetime
Music by Jule Styne
Lyrics by Betty Comden and Adolph Green
Subways Are for Sleeping 1961

Comes the Revolution
Music by George Gershwin
Lyrics by Ira Gershwin
Let 'Em Eat Cake 1933

Comes the Revolution
Music by Galt MacDermot
Lyrics by Rochelle Owens
The Karl Marx Play (OB) 1973

Coming Attractions
Music and lyrics by Charles Strouse
Six (OB) 1971

Coming Attractions
Music and lyrics by John Raniello
Movie Buff (OB) 1977

Coming Out of the Garden
Music by Harry Archer
Lyrics by Walter O'Keefe
Just a Minute 1928

Coming Through the Rye
Music by Vincent Youmans
Lyrics by Oscar Hammerstein II
Rainbow 1928

Dropped from production

Command to Love
Music by Serge Walter
Lyrics by Agnes Morgan
The Grand Street Follies (1928)

Command to Love
Music by Henry Sullivan
Lyrics by Jack Scholl
Keep Moving 1934

Comme çi, Comme ça
Music by Philip Charig
Lyrics by Irving Caesar
Polly 1929

A Common Little Girl
Music by Paul A. Rubens
Lyrics by Paul A. Rubens and Arthur Wimperis
The Sunshine Girl 1913

Common Sense
Music by Sammy Fain
Lyrics by George Marion, Jr.
Toplitzky of Notre Dame 1946

Common Sense
Music by Robert Kole
Lyrics by Sandi Merle
I Take These Women (OB) 1982

The Commuters' Song
Music by Baldwin Bergersen
Lyrics by Phyllis McGinley
Small Wonder 1948

The Compact
Music by Victor Herbert
Lyrics by Henry Blossom
The Only Girl 1914

Company
Music and lyrics by Stephen Sondheim
Company 1970

Company Manners
Music by Will Morrisey
Lyrics by Edmund Joseph
Polly of Hollywood 1927

The Company Way
Music and lyrics by Frank Loesser
*How to Succeed in Business
Without Really Trying* 1961

Complicated Man
Music by Elizabeth Swados
Lyrics by Garry Trudeau
Doonesbury 1983

Complications
Music by Ronald Melrose
Lyrics by Bill Russell
Fourtune (OB) 1980

Compromise
Music by Lance Mulcahy
Lyrics by Paul Cherry
Park 1970

Comrade Alonzo
Music and lyrics by Cole Porter
Leave It to Me 1938

Comrade, You Have a Chance Here
Music by Karl Hajos (based on Tchaikovsky)
Lyrics by Harry B. Smith
Natja 1925

The Concert
Music by Cy Coleman
Lyrics by Dorothy Fields
Seesaw 1973

Concert Encore
Music and lyrics by Sheldon Harnick
Wet Paint (OB) 1965

Conchita
Music by Ray Henderson
Lyrics by Lew Brown
Hot-Cha! 1932

Coney by the Sea
Music by Richard Lewine
Lyrics by Ted Fetter
Naughty-Naught (OB) 1937

Coney Island
Music by Richard Rodgers
Lyrics by Lorenz Hart
Simple Simon 1930

Coney Island Boat
Music by Arthur Schwartz
Lyrics by Dorothy Fields
By the Beautiful Sea 1954

Coney Island, U.S.A.
Music and lyrics by Jack Lawrence
and Stan Freeman
I Had a Ball 1964

Confession
Music by Arthur Schwartz
Lyrics by Howard Dietz
The Band Wagon 1931

**Confession to a Park Avenue Mother (I'm in Love
With a West Side Girl)**
Music and lyrics by Jerry Herman
Parade (OB) 1960

The Confessional
Music by Mitch Leigh
Lyrics by William Alfred and Phyllis Robinson
Cry for Us All 1970

Confessional
Music by Larry Grossman
Lyrics by Hal Hackady
Goodtime Charley 1975

Confidence
Music by Jean Gilbert
Lyrics by Harry B. and Robert B. Smith
Modest Suzanne 1912

Confidence
Music by Leon Carr
Lyrics by Earl Shuman
The Secret Life of Walter Mitty (OB) 1964

The Confrontation
Music by Harvey Schmidt
Lyrics by Tom Jones
Philemon (OB) 1975

Confrontation Song
Music by Kenn Long and Jim Crozier
Lyrics by Kenn Long
Touch (OB) 1970

Confusion
Music and lyrics by Scott Joplin
Treemonisha 1975

Written in 1909

Conga!
Music by Leonard Bernstein
Lyrics by Betty Comden and Adolph Green
Wonderful Town 1953

Congratulations
Music by Jean Gilbert
Lyrics by Harry Graham
Katja 1926

Congratulations
Music by Rob Fremont
Lyrics by Doris Willens
Piano Bar (OB) 1978

Congratulations!
Music and lyrics by John Clifton
El Bravo! (OB) 1981

Conjuror's Forgiven
Music and lyrics by Scott Joplin
Treemonisha 1975

Written in 1909

Connubial Bliss
Music by Victor Herbert
Lyrics by Henry Blossom
The Only Girl 1914

The Conscience of a Nation
Music and lyrics by Gene Curty, Nitra Scharfman
and Chuck Strand
The Lieutenant 1975

Consenting Adults
Music and lyrics by Johnny Brandon
Love! Love! Love! (OB) 1977

Consider the Rain
Music and lyrics by Marc Blitzstein
Regina 1949

Consider Yourself
Music and lyrics by Lionel Bart
Oliver! 1963

Consolation
Music by Emmerich Kálmán and Herbert Stothart
Lyrics by Otto Harbach and Oscar Hammerstein II
Golden Dawn 1927

Consolation
Music by John Duffy
Lyrics by Rocco Bufano and John Duffy
Horseman, Pass By (OB) 1969

Constant Lover
Music by Herman Finck
Lyrics by Arthur Wimperis
Miss Information 1915

Contagious Rhythm
Music by Harold Arlen
Lyrics by Ted Koehler
Earl Carroll's Vanities (1930)

The Contest
Music by Mitch Leigh
Lyrics by Charles Burr and Forman Brown
Home Sweet Homer 1976

The Continental
Music by Con Conrad
Lyrics by Herb Magidson
The Gay Divorcee 1934 (film version of *Gay Divorce*)

Academy Award winner

Continental Honeymoon
Music by James F. Hanley
Lyrics by Ballard MacDonald and James F. Hanley
Thumbs Up! 1934

The Contract
Music by Frederick Loewe
Lyrics by Alan Jay Lerner
Gigi (stage version, 1973)

Convent
Music and lyrics by John Phillips
Man on the Moon 1975

Convent Bells Are Ringing
Music by Sigmund Romberg
Lyrics by Harry B. Smith
Princess Flavia 1925

The Convention
Music by Richard Rodgers
Lyrics by Lorenz Hart
The Phantom President (1932) F

Convention Bound
Music and lyrics by Ronny Graham
New Faces of 1952

Conversation Piece
Music by Leonard Bernstein
Lyrics by Betty Comden and Adolph Green
Wonderful Town 1953

The Conversation Step
Music by Louis A. Hirsch
Lyrics by Otto Harbach
The O'Brien Girl 1921

Coo-Coo
Music by Joseph Meyer and Philip Charig
Lyrics by Leo Robin
Just Fancy 1927

Coo Coo
Music and lyrics by Rick Besoyan
Little Mary Sunshine (OB) 1959

Cookie Cutters
Music and lyrics by James Quinn and Alaric Jans
Do Patent Leather Shoes Really Reflect Up? 1982

Cookies and Bookies
Music by Joseph Meyer and James F. Hanley
Lyrics by B.G. DeSylva
Big Boy 1925

Cool
Music by Leonard Bernstein
Lyrics by Stephen Sondheim
West Side Story 1957

Cool Combo Mambo
Music by David Baker
Lyrics by David Craig
Copper and Brass 1957

Cool, Cool, Considerate Men
Music and lyrics by Sherman Edwards
1776 1969

Cool Credo
Music by David Baker
Lyrics by David Craig
Copper and Brass 1957

Cool 'Em Off
Music by Morris Hamilton
Lyrics by Grace Henry
Earl Carroll's Vanities (1926)

Cool Off
Music by Harry Ruby
Lyrics by Bert Kalmar
Animal Crackers 1928

The Coolest Cat in Town
Music by Diane Leslie
Lyrics by William Gleason
The Coolest Cat in Town (OB) 1978

Coolest Place in Town
Music and lyrics by Melvin Van Peebles
Ain't Supposed to Die a Natural Death 1971

The Cooney Country Fair
Music by George Gershwin
Lyrics by Brian Hooker
Our Nell 1922

Copperfield
Music and lyrics by Al Kasha and Joel Hirschhorn
Copperfield 1981

Corduroy Road
Music by Cy Coleman
Lyrics by Carolyn Leigh
Wildcat 1960

The Corn-Huskers
Music and lyrics by Scott Joplin
Treemonisha 1975

Written in 1909

Corner of the Sky
Music and lyrics by Stephen Schwartz
Pippin 1972

Cornet Man
Music by Jule Styne
Lyrics by Bob Merrill
Funny Girl 1964

The Coronation
Music by Rudolf Friml
Lyrics by Otto Harbach and Oscar Hammerstein II
The Wild Rose 1926

Coronation
Music by Larry Grossman
Lyrics by Hal Hackady
Goodtime Charley 1975

Coronation Chorale
Music and lyrics by Noël Coward
The Girl Who Came to Supper 1963

Coronation Song
Music by George Fischoff
Lyrics by Verna Tomasson
The Prince and the Pauper (OB) 1963

Corraline
Music by Frederic Norton
Lyrics by Oscar Asche
Chu Chin Chow 1917

Correct
Music by Ivan Caryll
Lyrics by Adrian Ross
Our Miss Gibbs 1910

The Correspondence School
Music by Jerome Kern
Lyrics by Paul West
The Red Petticoat 1912

Corruption
Music and lyrics by Peter Copani
New York City Street Show (OB) 1977

Cossack Love Song (Don't Forget Me)
Music by George Gershwin and Herbert Stothart
Lyrics by Otto Harbach and Oscar Hammerstein II
Song of the Flame 1925

Cottage in the Country
Music by Richard Rodgers
Lyrics by Lorenz Hart
Simple Simon 1930

Cottage in the Country
Music by Walter Kollo
Lyrics by Harry B. Smith
Three Little Girls 1930

Cotton Blossom
Music by Jerome Kern
Lyrics by Oscar Hammerstein II
Show Boat 1927

Could Be
Music and lyrics by Harold Rome
Wish You Were Here 1952

Could He Be You?
Music by Albert T. Viola
Lyrics by William S. Kilborne, Jr.
Head Over Heels 1981

Could I Forget?
Music and lyrics by Ida Hoyt Chamberlain
Enchanted Isle 1927

Could I Leave You?
Music and lyrics by Stephen Sondheim
Follies 1971

Could It Be You?
Music and lyrics by Cole Porter
Something for the Boys 1943

Could She Be the One?
Music by Jim Steinman
Lyrics by Michael Weller and Jim Steinman
More Than You Deserve (OB) 1973

Could That Be?
Music and lyrics by Gian-Carlo Menotti
The Medium 1947

Could We Start Again, Please?
Music by Andrew Lloyd Webber
Lyrics by Tim Rice
Jesus Christ Superstar 1971

Could You Use a New Friend?
Music and lyrics by Eugene and Ralph Berton
Two for Tonight (OB) 1939

Could You Use Me?
Music by George Gershwin
Lyrics by Ira Gershwin
Girl Crazy 1930

Couldn't Be
Music and lyrics by Cole Porter
Something to Shout About (1943) F

Dropped from film

Couldn't Be More in Love
Music by Frank Black
Lyrics by Gladys Shelley
The Duchess Misbehaves 1946

Couldn't We?
Music and lyrics by C. Jackson and James Hatch
Fly Blackbird (OB) 1962

Could've Been a Ring
Music and lyrics by Frank Loesser
Greenwillow 1960

Count Your Blessings
Music and lyrics by Cole Porter
Mexican Hayride 1944

Count Your Blessings
Music by Baldwin Bergersen
Lyrics by Phyllis McGinley
Small Wonder 1948

Countermelody
Music by Mary Rodgers and Jay Thompson
Lyrics by Marshall Barer
From A to Z 1960

Countess Dubinsky
Music by Joseph Meyer
Lyrics by Billy Rose
Ziegfeld Follies (1934)

Countin' Our Chickens
Music by Harold Arlen
Lyrics by Johnny Mercer
Saratoga 1959

A Country Gentleman
Music by Tommy Wolf
Lyrics by Fran Landesman
The Nervous Set 1959

The Country Needs a Man
Music by Richard Rodgers
Lyrics by Lorenz Hart
The Phantom President (1932) F

A Country of the Mind
Music and lyrics by Al Carmines
Joan (OB) 1972

The Country's in the Very Best of Hands
Music by Gene de Paul
Lyrics by Johnny Mercer
Li'l Abner 1956

A Couple of Senseless Censors
Music and lyrics by Irving Berlin
Music Box Revue (4th edition) 1924

A Couple of Song and Dance Men
Music and lyrics by Irving Berlin
Blue Skies (1946) F

A Couple of Swells
Music and lyrics by Irving Berlin
Easter Parade (1948) F

Course I Will
Music by Vincent Youmans
Lyrics by Otto Harbach and Oscar Hammerstein II
Wildflower 1923

Cousins of the Czar
Music by Franz Lehár
Lyrics by Basil Hood
The Count of Luxembourg 1912

The Covenant
Music by Richard Rodgers
Lyrics by Martin Charnin
Two by Two 1970

Cover Girl
Music by Jerome Kern
Lyrics by Ira Gershwin
Cover Girl (1944) F

Cover Girls
Music by Seth Friedman
Lyrics by David L. Crane, Seth Friedman
and Marta Kauffman
Upstairs at O'Neal's (OB) 1982

A Cow and a Plough and a Frau
Music by Morton Gould
Lyrics by Dorothy Fields
Arms and the Girl 1950

The Cow Jumped Over the Moon
Music by Helen Miller
Lyrics by Eve Merriam
Inner City 1971

Cowboy Potentate
Music and lyrics by Ida Hoyt Chamberlain
Enchanted Isle 1927

Cowboy Song (Oh, the Rio Grande)
Music by Kurt Weill
Lyrics by Paul Green
Johnny Johnson 1936

Cradle of the Deep
Music by Richard Rodgers
Lyrics by Lorenz Hart
Betsy 1926

Cradle Song
Music by Charles M. Schwab
Lyrics by Henry Myers
Bare Facts of 1926

The Cradle Will Rock
Music and lyrics by Marc Blitzstein
The Cradle Will Rock 1938

Crap Game Fugue
Music by George Gershwin
Lyrics by DuBose Heyward
Porgy and Bess 1935

Crashing the Golden Gate
Music by Jay Gorney and Phil Cohan
Lyrics by E.Y. Harburg
Earl Carroll's Sketch Book (1929)

Crashing Thru
Music and lyrics by Sylvia Fine
The Straw Hat Revue 1939

Crazy
Music by Clinton Ballard
Lyrics by Carolyn Richter
The Ballad of Johnny Pot (OB) 1971

Crazy
Music and lyrics by Elizabeth Swados
Dispatches (OB) 1979

Crazy as a Loon
Music by Jimmy McHugh
Lyrics by Al Dubin
Keep off the Grass 1940

Crazy Elbows
Music by Richard Rodgers
Lyrics by Lorenz Hart
Present Arms 1928

Crazy Idea of Love
Music and lyrics by Al Wilson, Charles Weinberg
and Ken Macomber
Yeah Man 1932

Crazy Jane on the Day of Judgment
Music by John Duffy
Lyrics by Rocco Bufano and John Duffy
Horseman, Pass By (OB) 1969

Crazy Quilt
Music by Harry Warren
Lyrics by Bud Green
Crazy Quilt 1931

Crazy Rhythm
Music by Joseph Meyer and Roger Wolfe Kahn
Lyrics by Irving Caesar
Here's Howe 1928

Crazy With the Heat
Music by Rudi Revil
Lyrics by Irvin Graham
Crazy With the Heat 1941

Cream in My Coffee
Music by Ed Scott
Lyrics by Anne Croswell
Wet Paint (OB) 1965

The Cream of English Youth
Music by Michael Valenti
Lyrics by John Lewin
Blood Red Roses 1970

Creation (instrumental)
Music by Victor Herbert
Ziegfeld Follies of 1920

Credit Card
Music by Cheryl Hardwick
Lyrics by Marilyn Suzanne Miller
Girls, Girls, Girls (OB) 1980

The Credit's Due to Me
Music by Leslie Stuart
Lyrics by Ernest Boyd-Jones
Florodora 1900

Credo
Music by Elmer Bernstein
Lyrics by Carolyn Leigh
How Now, Dow Jones 1967

Creole Crooning Song
Music by Richard Rodgers
Lyrics by Lorenz Hart
The Girl Friend 1926

Creon
Music by Susan Hulsman Bingham
Lyrics by Myrna Lamb
Mod Donna (OB) 1970

Crescent Moon
Music by Walter G. Samuels
Lyrics by Morrie Ryskind
Ned Wayburn's Gambols 1929

The Cricket on the Hearth
Music by Victor Herbert
Lyrics by Robert B. Smith
Sweethearts 1913

The Crickets Are Calling
Music by Jerome Kern
Lyrics by P. G. Wodehouse
Leave It to Jane 1917

Crime
Music by Harry Archer
Lyrics by Harlan Thompson
Twinkle Twinkle 1926

Criminal
Music and lyrics by John Clifton
El Bravo! (OB) 1981

Crinoline Days
Music and lyrics by Irving Berlin
Music Box Revue (2nd edition) 1922

Criss Cross
Music by Jerome Kern
Lyrics by Anne Caldwell and Otto Harbach
Criss-Cross 1926

Dropped from production

The Critic
Music and lyrics by Charles Strouse
Six (OB) 1971

Critics
Music and lyrics by Robert Swerdlow
Love Me, Love My Children (OB) 1971

Crocodile Wife
Music and lyrics by Harold Rome
The Zulu and the Zayda 1965

Croon-Spoon
Music and lyrics by Marc Blitzstein
The Cradle Will Rock 1938

Cross On Over
Music by Galt MacDermot
Lyrics by Christopher Gore
Via Galactica 1972

Cross Word Puzzles
Music by Muriel Pollock
Lyrics by Max and Nathaniel Lief
and Harold Atteridge
Pleasure Bound 1929

Cross Your Fingers
Music by J. Fred Coots
Lyrics by Arthur Swanstrom and Benny Davis
Sons o' Guns 1929

Cross Your Heart
Music by Lewis E. Gensler
Lyrics by B. G. DeSylva
Queen High 1926

Crosstown
Music by Henry Krieger
Lyrics by Robert Lorick
The Tap Dance Kid 1983

Crossword Puzzle
Music by David Shire
Lyrics by Richard Maltby, Jr.
Starting Here, Starting Now (OB) 1977

Croupier
Music by Baldwin Bergersen
Lyrics by June Sillman
Who's Who 1938

The Crow
Music by John Kander
Lyrics by Fred Ebb
Zorba 1968

Crown Me
Music by Al Carmines
Lyrics by Maria Irene Fornes
Promenade (OB) 1969

The Crucifixion
Music by Andrew Lloyd Webber
Lyrics by Tim Rice
Jesus Christ Superstar 1971

Cruel Chief
Music by Jean Gilbert
Lyrics by Harry Graham
Katja 1926

The Cruelty Man
Music by Mitch Leigh
Lyrics by William Alfred and Phyllis Robinson
Cry for Us All 1970

Cry Baby
Music by Harry Ruby
Lyrics by Bert Kalmar
Helen of Troy, New York 1923

Cry, Baby, Cry
Music and lyrics by Harold Rome
Alive and Kicking 1950

Cry for Us All
Music by Mitch Leigh
Lyrics by William Alfred and Phyllis Robinson
Cry for Us All 1970

Cry Like the Wind
Music by Jule Styne
Lyrics by Betty Comden and Adolph Green
Do Re Mi 1960

Cry of the Peacock
Music and lyrics by Sandy Wilson
Valmouth (OB) 1960

Cry, the Beloved Country
Music by Kurt Weill
Lyrics by Maxwell Anderson
Lost in the Stars 1949

The Crystal Lute
Music by John Philip Sousa
Lyrics by Leonard Liebling
The American Maid 1913

The Cubist Opera
Music by Victor Herbert
Lyrics by Robert B. Smith
The Debutante 1914

This song, like "Burlesque Modern Opera," is an example of Hebert's little-known talent for satirizing grand opera.

Cuchifrito Restaurant
Music and lyrics by John Clifton
El Bravo! (OB) 1981

Cuckold's Delight
Music by Edward Earle
Lyrics by Yvonne Tarr
The Decameron (OB) 1961

The Cuckoo-Cheena
Music by Alma Sanders
Lyrics by Monte Carlo
Louisiana Lady 1947

Cuddle Up
Music and lyrics by Gene Lockhart
Bunk of 1926

Cuddle Up a Little Closer, Lovey Mine
Music by Karl Hoschna
Lyrics by Otto Harbach
Three Twins 1908

Cultural Pursuits
Music and lyrics by Doug Frank
Marilyn 1983

A Cup of China Tea
Music by Franz Lehár
Lyrics by Harry Graham
Yours Is My Heart 1946

A Cup of Coffee
Music and lyrics by Robert Dahdah
Curley McDimple (OB) 1967

A Cup of Coffee, a Sandwich and You
Music by Joseph Meyer
Lyrics by Billy Rose and Al Dubin
Charlot's Revue of 1926

A Cup of Tea
Music by Richard Rodgers
Lyrics by Lorenz Hart
Spring Is Here 1929

Dropped from production

A Cup of Tea
Music by Mischa and Wesley Portnoff
Lyrics by Donagh MacDonagh
Happy as Larry 1950

Cupid
Music by Harold Levey
Lyrics by Zelda Sears
The Clinging Vine 1922

Cupid at the Plaza
Music by Paul Rubens
Lyrics by Percy Greenbank
Nobody Home 1915

Cupid, the Cunnin' Paudeen
Music by Victor Herbert
Lyrics by Henry Blossom
Eileen 1917

Dropped from production

Cupid's College
Music by Robert Hood Bowers
Lyrics by Francis DeWitt
Oh, Ernest! 1927

The Cure
Music by Harold Arlen
Lyrics by Johnny Mercer
Saratoga 1959

The Cure
Music by Heinrich Reinhardt
Lyrics by Robert B. Smith
The Spring Maid 1910

The Curfew Shall Not Ring Tonight
Music by Charles Rosoff
Lyrics by Leo Robin
Judy 1927

The Curfew Walk
Music by Jean Schwartz
Lyrics by Alfred Bryan
A Night in Spain 1927

Curiosity
Music by Keith Hermann
Lyrics by Charlotte Anker and Irene Rosenberg
Onward Victoria 1980

Curiouser and Curiouser
Music by Bert Keyes and Bob Larimer
Lyrics by Bob Larimer
But Never Jam Today 1979

Curley McDimple
Music and lyrics by Robert Dahdah
Curley McDimple (OB) 1967

Curley's Wife
Music by Alfred Brooks
Lyrics by Ira J. Bilowit
Of Mice and Men (OB) 1958

Currier and Ives
Music by Sigmund Romberg
Lyrics by Dorothy Fields
Up in Central Park 1945

Curses
Music by Stanley Silverman
Lyrics by Arthur Miller
Up From Paradise (OB) 1983

Curt, Clear and Concise
Music and lyrics by Noël Coward
The Girl Who Came to Supper 1963

The Custody of the Child
Music by George Gershwin
Lyrics by Brian Hooker
Our Nell 1922

Dropped from production

Cut In
Music by Jimmy McHugh
Lyrics by Dorothy Fields
The Vanderbilt Revue 1930

Cute In My Bathing Suit
Music by Percy Wenrich
Lyrics by Julian Eltinge and Jack Mahoney
The Fascinating Widow 1911

Cute Soldier Boy
Music by Anatol Friedland
Lyrics by Berton Braley
Toot-Toot! 1918

Cutie
Music by Rudolf Friml
Lyrics by Otto Harbach
The Blue Kitten 1922

Cutting the Cane
Music by Richard Rodgers
Lyrics by Lorenz Hart
They Met in Argentina (1941) F

Cymbals and Tambourines
Music and lyrics by Arthur Siegel
New Faces of 1968

Cyrano's Nose
Music by Michael J. Lewis
Lyrics by Anthony Burgess
Cyrano 1973

Czardas
Music by Al Carmines
Lyrics by Maria Irene Fornes
Promenade (OB) 1969

D

Daarlin' Man
Music and lyrics by Marc Blitzstein
Juno 1959

Daddy Blues
Music and lyrics by Paul Shyre
Ah, Men (OB) 1981

Daddy, Daddy
Music and lyrics by Michael Brown
Different Times 1972

Daddy Has a Sweetheart (and Mother Is Her Name)
Music by Dave Stamper
Lyrics by Gene Buck
Ziegfeld Follies of 1912

Daddy Was a Railroad Man
Music by Paul Horner
Lyrics by Peggy Lee
Peg 1983

Daddy Will Not Come Walking Through the Door
Music by Galt MacDermot
Lyrics by William Dumaresq
The Human Comedy (OB) 1983

Daddy, Won't You Please Come Home?
Music and lyrics by Noble Sissle and Eubie Blake
Shuffle Along 1921

Da-Doo
Music by Alan Menken
Lyrics by Howard Ashman
Little Shop of Horrors (OB) 1982

Daedalus
Music and lyrics by Peter Link and C.C. Courtney
Salvation (OB) 1969

Daily Buzz
Music and lyrics by Voices, Inc.
The Believers (OB) 1968

Daily Dozen
Music by Richard Myers
Lyrics by Leo Robin
Hello, Yourself! 1928

Daisies
Music by Al Carmines
Lyrics by Rosalyn Drexler
Home Movies (OB) 1964

Daisy
Music by Jerome Kern
Lyrics by P.G. Wodehouse
Have a Heart 1917

Daisy
Music and lyrics by G. Wood
Put It in Writing (OB) 1963

The Daisy and the Lark
Music by Richard Rodgers
Lyrics by Lorenz Hart
Poor Little Ritz Girl 1920

Daisy Hill
Music by Larry Grossman
Lyrics by Hal Hackady
Snoopy (OB) 1982

Damages
Music by Cyril Ornadel
Lyrics by Leslie Bricusse
Pickwick 1965

Dames at Sea
Music by Jim Wise
Lyrics by George Haimsohn and Robin Miller
Dames at Sea (OB) 1968

Damn-Alot
Music and lyrics by Billy Barnes
The Billy Barnes People 1961

91

Damned for All Time
Music by Andrew Lloyd Webber
Lyrics by Tim Rice
Jesus Christ Superstar 1971

Damned No Matter How He Turned
Music and lyrics by Gene Curty, Nitra Scharfman
and Chuck Strand
The Lieutenant 1975

Damsel, Damsel
Music by Cole Porter
Lyrics by T. Lawrason Riggs and Cole Porter
See America First 1916

The Damsel Who Done All the Dirt
Music by Richard Rodgers
Lyrics by Lorenz Hart
The Girl Friend 1926

The Dance
Music and lyrics by Elizabeth Swados
Nightclub Cantata (OB) 1977

Dance a Little Closer
Music by Charles Strouse
Lyrics by Alan Jay Lerner
Dance a Little Closer 1983

Dance Alone With You
Music by George Gershwin
Lyrics by Ira Gershwin
Funny Face 1927

Dropped from production; rewritten as "Ev'rybody
Knows I Love Somebody" for *Rosalie* (1928).

Dance Away the Night
Music by Jerome Kern
Lyrics by Oscar Hammerstein II
Show Boat (London production, 1928)

Dance, Dance, Dance
Music by Jerome Kern
Lyrics by Paul West
The Red Petticoat 1912

Dance, Dance, Dance
Music by Rudolf Friml
Lyrics by Brian Hooker
The White Eagle 1927

Dance for Six
Music by Richard Adler
Lyrics by Will Holt
Music Is 1976

Dance for the Gentlemen
Music by Carl Millöcker (revised by Theo
Mackeben)
Lyrics by Rowland Leigh
The Dubarry 1932

The Dance From Down Yonder
Music by Joseph Meyer and James F. Hanley
Lyrics by B.G. DeSylva
Big Boy 1925

Dance if It Makes You Happy
Music by Henry Krieger
Lyrics by Robert Lorick
The Tap Dance Kid 1983

Dance, Little Lady
Music and lyrics by Noël Coward
This Year of Grace 1928

Dance Me a Song
Music and lyrics by James Shelton
Dance Me a Song 1950

Dance, My Darlings
Music by Sigmund Romberg
Lyrics by Oscar Hammerstein II
May Wine 1935

Dance of Distraction
Music by Clinton Ballard
Lyrics by Carolyn Richter
The Ballad of Johnny Pot (OB) 1971

Dance of the Fan
Music by Percy Wenrich
Lyrics by Harry Clarke
Who Cares? 1930

Dance of the Marionettes
Music by Victor Herbert
Lyrics by Rida Johnson Young
Naughty Marietta 1910

Dance Only With Me
Music by Jule Styne
Lyrics by Betty Comden and Adolph Green
Say, Darling 1958

Dance the Dark Away
Music by Galt MacDermot
Lyrics by Christopher Gore
Via Galactica 1972

Dance With Me
Music by Sigmund Romberg
Lyrics by Harry B. Smith
Princess Flavia 1925

Dance With You
Music by Jean Gilbert
Lyrics by Harry Graham
Katja 1926

Dance Your Troubles Away
Music and lyrics by Irving Berlin
Music Box Revue (2nd edition) 1922

Dancin' Shoes
Music and lyrics by Stephen H. Lemberg
Jazzbo Brown 1980

Dancin' to a Jungle Drum
Music and lyrics by Cole Porter
Seven Lively Arts 1944

Dancin' 'Way Your Sin
Music and lyrics by J.C. Johnson
Brown Buddies 1930

Dancing
Music and lyrics by Jerry Herman
Hello, Dolly 1964

Dancing Alone
Music and lyrics by Ralph and Eugene Berton
Two for Tonight (OB) 1939

Dancing, and I Mean Dancing
Music and lyrics by Alexander Hill
Hummin' Sam 1933

Dancing by Moonlight
Music by Martin Broones
Lyrics by Ballard MacDonald
Rufus Lemaire's Affairs 1927

The Dancing Detective
Music and lyrics by George M. Cohan
Little Nellie Kelly 1922

The Dancing Fiddler
Music by A. Baldwin Sloane
Lyrics by E. Ray Goetz
The Hen Pecks 1911

Dancing Fool
Music and lyrics by Al Wilson, Charles Weinberg and Ken Macomber
Yeah Man 1932

Dancing Girl
Music by Clarence Williams
Lyrics by Spencer Williams
Bottomland 1927

Dancing Honeymoon
Music and lyrics by Irving Berlin
Music Box Revue (2nd edition) 1922

Dancing Honeymoon
Music and lyrics by Philip Braham
Battling Buttler 1923

Dancing Hour
Music by George Gershwin
Lyrics by Ira Gershwin
Tip-Toes 1925

Dropped from production. Later dropped from *Funny Face* (1927).

Dancing in the Dark
Music by Arthur Schwartz
Lyrics by Howard Dietz
The Band Wagon 1931

Dancing in the Rain
Music and lyrics by Robert Dahdah
Curley McDimple (OB) 1967

Dancing in the Streets
Music by George Gershwin
Lyrics by Ira Gershwin
Pardon My English 1933

Dancing Is Everything
Music by Henry Krieger
Lyrics by Robert Lorick
The Tap Dance Kid 1983

Dancing Jim
Music by Marc Anthony
Lyrics by Donovan Parsons
The Merry World 1926

A Dancing Lesson
Music by Lionel Monckton
Lyrics by Adrian Ross
The Quaker Girl 1911

The Dancing Lesson
Music by Victor Herbert
Lyrics by Robert B. Smith
The Debutante 1914

The Dancing Lesson
Music by John Egan
Lyrics by Dorothy Donnelly
Poppy 1923

A Dancing M.D.
Music by Jerome Kern
Lyrics by P.G. Wodehouse
Miss 1917

Dancing My Worries Away
Music and lyrics by George M. Cohan
Little Nellie Kelly 1922

Dancing on a Rainbow
Music by Leo Edwards
Lyrics by Herman Timberg
You'll See Stars 1942

Dancing on the Ceiling
Music by Richard Rodgers
Lyrics by Lorenz Hart
Simple Simon 1930

Written for *Simple Simon*, but dropped from the score at the insistence of the producer, Florenz Ziegfeld. Rodgers and Hart then put it into the English film *Ever Green* which was released later in the same year; the song became a hit in England before it was known in America. Later the song was in an otherwise non-Rodgers and Hart score for a London revue *Happy Returns* (1938) where it was sung by Constance Carpenter.

Dancing Round
Music by Victor Herbert
Lyrics by Rida Johnson Young
The Dream Girl 1924

The Dancing Teacher
Music and lyrics by Irving Berlin
Watch Your Step 1914

Dancing the Devil Away
Music by Harry Ruby
Lyrics by Bert Kalmar and Otto Harbach
Lucky 1927

Dancing the Seasons Away
Music and lyrics by Irving Berlin
Music Box Revue (1st edition) 1921

Dancing Time
Music by Jerome Kern
Lyrics by Howard Dietz
Dear Sir 1924

Dancing to Our Score
Music by Vernon Duke
Lyrics by Ira Gershwin and Billy Rose
Ziegfeld Follies (1936)

Dancing to the Rhythm of the Raindrops
Music by Ruth Cleary Patterson
Lyrics by Gladys Shelley
Russell Patterson's Sketch Book (OB) 1960

Dancing Toes
Music and lyrics by Leon DeCosta
Kosher Kitty Kelly 1925

Dancing Town
Music by Maury Rubens
Lyrics by Clifford Grey
The Great Temptations 1926

The Dancing Wedding
Music and lyrics by George M. Cohan
The Little Millionaire 1911

Dancing Wedding
Music by Vincent Youmans
Lyrics by Harold Adamson and Clifford Grey
Smiles 1930

Dancing Will Keep You Young
Music by Sigmund Romberg
Lyrics by Rida Johnson Young
Maytime 1917

Dancing With Alice
Music by Milton Schafer
Lyrics by Ira Levin
Drat! The Cat! 1965

Dancing With Tears in Their Eyes
Music by Will Irwin
Lyrics by Billy Rose and Mort Dixon
Sweet and Low 1930

Dandy Dan
Music and lyrics by Porter Grainger
and Freddie Johnson
Lucky Sambo 1925

Danger If I Love You
Music by Henry Sullivan
Lyrics by Edward Eliscu
A Little Racketeer 1932

Danger in the Dark
Music by Jimmy McHugh
Lyrics by Al Dubin
The Streets of Paris 1939

The Danger of Peace Is Over
Music by Menachem Zur
Lyrics by Herbert Appleman
Unfair to Goliath (OB) 1970

The Dangerous Age
Music by Jule Styne
Lyrics by Betty Comden and Adolph Green
Fade Out—Fade In 1964

The Dangerous Age
Music and lyrics by Ervin Drake
Her First Roman 1968

Danube So Blue
Music by Johann Strauss
Lyrics by Desmond Carter
The Great Waltz 1934

Daphne
Music by Milton Susskind
Lyrics by Paul Porter and Benjamin Hapgood Burt
Florida Girl 1925

The Daring Gibson Girl
Music by Ray Henderson
Lyrics by B.G. DeSylva and Lew Brown
Follow Thru 1929

Dark New England Night
Music and lyrics by Norman Dean
Autumn's Here (OB) 1966

A Dark Stranger
Music by Michael Cleary
Lyrics by Arthur Swanstrom
Sea Legs 1937

The Darkies Song
Music by Coleridge-Taylor Perkinson
Lyrics by Ray McIver
God Is a (Guess What?) (OB) 1968

Darkness Song
Music by Al Carmines
Lyrics by Rosalyn Drexler
Home Movies (OB) 1964

Darky Rhythm
Music by Peter Tinturin
Lyrics by Joe Young
Brown Buddies 1930

The Darlin' of New York
Music and lyrics by Bill and Patti Jacob
Jimmy 1969

Darling
Music by Arthur Siegel
Lyrics by Mae Richard
Tallulah (OB) 1983

Darling, Let Me Teach You How to Kiss
Music by Richard Hill and John Hawkins
Lyrics by Nevill Coghill
Canterbury Tales 1969

Darn it, Baby, That's Love
Music and lyrics by Joan Edwards
and Lyn Duddy
Tickets Please 1950

A Darn Nice Campus
Music by Richard Rodgers
Lyrics by Oscar Hammerstein II
Allegro 1947

Darn That Dream
Music by Jimmy Van Heusen
Lyrics by Eddie De Lange
Swingin' the Dream 1939

Das Chicago Song
Music by Michael Cohen
Lyrics by Tony Geiss
New Faces of 1968

Dat Ol' Boy
Music by Georges Bizet
Lyrics by Oscar Hammerstein II
Carmen Jones 1943

Dat's Love
Music by Georges Bizet
Lyrics by Oscar Hammerstein II
Carmen Jones 1943

Dat's Our Man
Music by Georges Bizet
Lyrics by Oscar Hammerstein II
Carmen Jones 1943

Daughter
Music by Mel Marvin
Lyrics by Robert Montgomery
Green Pond (OB) 1977

A Daughter of Valentine's Day
Music by Gerald Jay Markoe
Lyrics by Michael Colby
Charlotte Sweet (OB) 1982

David and Bathsheba
Music by Ernest Gold
Lyrics by Anne Croswell
I'm Solomon 1968

David and Lenore
Music by Ray Henderson
Lyrics by B.G. DeSylva and Lew Brown
George White's Scandals (1926)

David Kolowitz, the Actor
Music and lyrics by Stan Daniels
So Long, 174th Street 1976

Davy the Fat Boy
Music and lyrics by Randy Newman
Maybe I'm Doing It Wrong (1st edition) (OB) 1981

Dawn
Music by Ray Henderson
Lyrics by B.G. DeSylva and Lew Brown
Manhattan Mary 1927

Dawn
Music by Robert Stolz and Herbert Stothart
Lyrics by Otto Harbach and Oscar Hammerstein II
Golden Dawn 1927

A Dawn
Music by Galt MacDermot
Lyrics by Gerome Ragni
Dude 1972

Dawn of Dreams
Music by Raymond Hubbell
Lyrics by Anne Caldwell
Yours Truly 1927

Day After Day
Music by Arthur Schwartz
Lyrics by Howard Dietz
Flying Colors 1932

Day After Day
Music by Meyer Kupferman
Lyrics by Paul Goodman
Jonah (OB) 1966

Day After Day
Music and lyrics by Ronnie Britton
Gift of the Magi (OB) 1975

A Day at the Club
Music by Harry Tierney
Lyrics by Joseph McCarthy
Kid Boots 1923

The Day Before Spring
Music by Frederick Loewe
Lyrics by Alan Jay Lerner
The Day Before Spring 1945

A Day Borrowed From Heaven
Music and lyrics by Frank Loesser
Greenwillow 1960

Day by Day
Music by Stephen Schwartz
Words by St. Richard of Chichester
Godspell (OB) 1971

Based on an old Episcopal hymn

Day Dreams
Music by Heinrich Reinhardt
Lyrics by Robert B. Smith
The Spring Maid 1910

Day Dreams
Music by Jacques Urbont
Lyrics by Bruce Geller
All in Love (OB) 1961

The Day I Met Your Father
Music and lyrics by Paul Nassau and Oscar Brand
*The Education of H*y*m*a*n K*a*p*l*a*n* 1968

The Day I Rode Half Fare
Music by Joseph Meyer and James F. Hanley
Lyrics by B.G. DeSylva
Big Boy 1925

Day of Judgement
Music by Paul Hoffert
Lyrics by David Secter
Get Thee to Canterbury (OB) 1969

The Day Off
Music and lyrics by Stephen Sondheim
Sunday in the Park with George (OB) 1983

The Day the Snow Is Meltin'
Music and lyrics by Johnny Burke
Donnybrook! 1961

Daydreams
Music by David Baker
Lyrics by Sheldon Harnick
Smiling, the Boy Fell Dead (OB) 1961

Days Gone By
Music by Jerome Kern
Lyrics by P. G. Wodehouse
Sitting Pretty 1924

Days Gone By
Music by Jerry Bock
Lyrics by Sheldon Harnick
She Loves Me 1963

The Days of Dancing
Music and lyrics by Frederick Silver
Gay Company (OB) 1974

The Days of Old
Music by Oscar Straus
Lyrics by Clare Kummer
Three Waltzes 1937

The Days of This Life
Music by Galt MacDermot
Lyrics by Gerome Ragni
Dude 1972

Dayton Ohio 1903
Music and lyrics by Randy Newman
Maybe I'm Doing It Wrong (1st edition) (OB) 1981

De Cards Don't Lie
Music by Georges Bizet
Lyrics by Oscar Hammerstein II
Carmen Jones 1943

De-dum-dum
Music by Jean Schwartz
Lyrics by Alfred Bryan
A Night in Spain 1927

De Goblin's Glide
Music by Jerome Kern
Lyrics by Frederick Day
La Belle Paree 1911

De Old Clay Road
Music by Frank Harling
Lyrics by Laurence Stallings
Deep River 1926

De Trop
Music by Rudolf Friml
Lyrics by Otto Harbach
The Firefly 1912

Dead Men Tell No Tales
Music by George Gershwin
Lyrics by Ira Gershwin
Treasure Girl 1928

Dropped from production

The Deal
Music by Susan Hulsman Bingham
Lyrics by Myrna Lamb
Mod Donna (OB) 1970

The Dealer
Music by Helen Miller
Lyrics by Eve Merriam
Inner City 1971

Dear, Dear
Music by Richard Rodgers
Lyrics by Lorenz Hart
Evergreen (1934) F

Dear Dear
Music and lyrics by Tom Mandel
The Bar That Never Closes (OB) 1972

Dear, Dear Departed
Music by Emil Gerstenberger and Carle Carlton
Lyrics by Howard Johnson
The Lace Petticoat 1927

Dear Eyes That Haunt Me
Music by Emmerich Kálmán
Lyrics by Harry B. Smith
The Circus Princess 1927

Dear Friend
Music by Jerry Bock
Lyrics by Sheldon Harnick
Tenderloin 1960

Dear Friend
Music by Jerry Bock
Lyrics by Sheldon Harnick
She Loves Me 1963

Dear Friend
Music by Baldwin Bergersen
Lyrics by William Archibald
Rosa (OB) 1978

Dear Girls, Goodbye
Music by Sigmund Romberg
Lyrics by Dorothy Donnelly
My Princess 1927

Dear Home of Mine, Goodbye
Music by Emmerich Kálmán
Lyrics by Harry B. Smith
Countess Maritza 1926

Dear Jane
Music by Richard Rodgers
Lyrics by Sheldon Harnick
Rex 1976

Dropped from production

Dear Jane
Music and lyrics by Mel Mandel and Norman Sachs
My Old Friends (OB) 1979

Dear June (Postcard Song)
Music by Richard Rodgers
Lyrics by Lorenz Hart
Hallelujah, I'm a Bum (1933) F

Dear Little Café
Music and lyrics by Noël Coward
Bitter Sweet 1929

Dear Little Girl
Music by George Gershwin
Lyrics by Ira Gershwin
Oh, Kay! 1926

The Dear Little Girl Who Is Good
Music by Victor Herbert
Lyrics by Henry Blossom
Mlle. Modiste 1905

Dear Little Peter Pan
Music by Jerome Kern
Lyrics by Anne Caldwell
Stepping Stones 1923

Dear Little Soldiers
Music and lyrics by Noël Coward
Conversation Piece 1934

Dear Lord
Music by Jonathan Holtzman
Lyrics by Susan Cooper and Jonathan Holtzman
Foxfire 1982

Dear Lord Chesterfield
Music by Don Pippin
Lyrics by Steve Brown
The Contrast (OB) 1972

Dear Love
Music by John Kander
Lyrics by Fred Ebb
Flora, the Red Menace 1965

Dear Madame Scarlatina
Music and lyrics by Jay Thompson
Double Entry (OB) 1961

Dear Me
Music by Richard Rodgers
Lyrics by Lorenz Hart
Dearest Enemy 1925

Dropped from production

Dear Mom
Music by Sol Berkowitz
Lyrics by James Lipton
Nowhere to Go But Up 1962

Dear Mr. Schubert
Music by Manos Hadjidakis
Lyrics by Joe Darion
Illya Darling 1967

Dear, Oh Dear
Music by Richard Rodgers
Lyrics by Lorenz Hart
Chee-Chee 1928

Dear Old Crinoline Days
Music and lyrics by Irving Berlin
Face the Music 1932

Dear Old Dad
Music by David Baker
Lyrics by Sheldon Harnick
Smiling, the Boy Fell Dead (OB) 1961

Dear Old Friend
Music by Sol Berkowitz
Lyrics by James Lipton
Miss Emily Adam (OB) 1960

Dear Old Land o'Mine
Music by Jean Gilbert
Lyrics by Harry Graham and Cyrus Wood
The Lady in Ermine 1922

Dear Old Syracuse
Music by Richard Rodgers
Lyrics by Lorenz Hart
The Boys From Syracuse 1938

Dear Ophelia
Music by Alan Menken
Lyrics by Dennis Green
God Bless You, Mr. Rosewater (OB) 1979

Dear Tom
Music by Nancy Ford
Lyrics by Gretchen Cryer
I'm Getting My Act Together and Taking It on the Road 1978

Dear World
Music and lyrics by Jerry Herman
Dear World 1969

Dearest Man
Music by Stanley Silverman
Lyrics by Tom Hendry
Doctor Selavy's Magic Theatre (OB) 1972

Dearly Beloved
Music by Jerome Kern
Lyrics by Johnny Mercer
You Were Never Lovelier (1942) F

Death Beware
Music by Paul Hoffert
Lyrics by David Secter
Get Thee to Canterbury (OB) 1969

Death Message
Music by Kurt Weill
Lyrics by Marc Blitzstein
The Threepenny Opera (OB) 1954

The Death of Me
Music by Richard Rodgers
Lyrics by Martin Charnin
Two by Two 1970

Dropped from production

Death's Frontiers Are Open
Music and lyrics by Gian-Carlo Menotti
The Consul 1950

Deauville
Music and lyrics by Herman Hupfeld
The Merry World 1926

Debutante
Music by Sigmund Romberg
Lyrics by Rowland Leigh
My Romance 1948

The Debutante's Ball
Music and lyrics by Randy Newman
Maybe I'm Doing It Wrong (1st edition) (OB) 1981

Deceive Me
Music by Edward Earle
Lyrics by Yvonne Tarr
The Decameron (OB) 1961

Deceiving Blue Bird
Music by J. Fred Coots
Lyrics by Al Dubin
White Lights 1927

The Decent Thing to Do
Music by Lewis E. Gensler and Milton Schwarzwald
Lyrics by George S. Kaufman, Marc Connelly and Ira Gershwin
Be Yourself 1924

Declaration
Music by Kenn Long and Jim Crozier
Lyrics by Kenn Long
Touch (OB) 1970

Declaration Day
Music by Ray Henderson
Lyrics by Ted Koehler
Say When 1934

A Dedicated Teacher
Music and lyrics by Paul Nassau and Oscar Brand
*The Education of H*y*m*a*n K*a*p*l*a*n* 1968

Dee-lightful Is the Word
Music and lyrics by Johnny Burke
Donnybrook! 1961

Deedle-Doodle
Music and lyrics by Marc Blitzstein
Regina 1949

Deep Down Inside
Music by Cy Coleman
Lyrics by Carolyn Leigh
Little Me 1962

Deep Harlem
Music by Joe Jordan
Lyrics by Homer Tutt and Henry Creamer
Deep Harlem 1929

Deep in Me
Music by James Bredt
Lyrics by Edward Eager
The Happy Hypocrite (OB) 1968

Deep in My Heart
Music by Vincent Youmans
Lyrics by Zelda Sears
Lollipop 1924

Deep in My Heart
Music and lyrics by Irving Burgie
Ballad for Bimshire (OB) 1963

Deep in My Heart, Dear
Music by Sigmund Romberg
Lyrics by Dorothy Donnelly
The Student Prince 1924

Deep in the Bosom of the Family
Music by William Dyer
Lyrics by Don Parks and William Dyer
Jo (OB) 1964

Deep in the Dark
Music and lyrics by James Rado
Rainbow (OB) 1972

Deep in the Night
Music by Helen Miller
Lyrics by Eve Merriam
Inner City 1971

Deep in Your Heart
Music by Milton Schafer
Lyrics by Ira Levin
Drat! The Cat! 1965

Deep Paradise
Music by Russell Tarbox
Lyrics by Charles O. Locke
Hello, Paris 1930

Deeper
Music by Louis A. Hirsch
Lyrics by Otto Harbach
Mary 1920

Deeper in the Woods
Music by Robert Waldman
Lyrics by Alfred Uhry
The Robber Bridegroom 1975

Déjà Vu
Music by Peter Link
Lyrics by Jacob Brackman
King of Hearts 1978

Delicatessen
Music by Hank Beebe
Lyrics by Bill Heyer
*Tuscaloosa's Calling Me
But I'm Not Going!* (OB) 1975

Delilah Done Me Wrong
Music by Gerard Calvi
Lyrics by Harold Rome
La Grosse Valise 1965

Delishious
Music by George Gershwin
Lyrics by Ira Gershwin
Delicious (1931) F

Deliver
Music by Joe Jordan
Lyrics by Homer Tutt and Henry Creamer
Deep Harlem 1929

Della's Desire
Music and lyrics by Ronnie Britton
Gift of the Magi (OB) 1975

Democracy's Call
Music by Kurt Weill
Lyrics by Paul Green
Johnny Johnson 1936

Demon Rum
Music by George Gershwin
Lyrics by Ira Gershwin
The Shocking Miss Pilgrim (1947) F

Adapted by Kay Swift and Ira Gershwin from
manuscripts of George Gershwin.

Den of Iniquity
Music by Richard Rodgers
Lyrics by Lorenz Hart
Pal Joey 1940

Denmark Is Still
Music and lyrics by Cliff Jones
Rockabye Hamlet 1976

Dentists!
Music by Alan Menken
Lyrics by Howard Ashman
Little Shop of Horrors (OB) 1982

The Denver Police
Music and lyrics by Meredith Willson
The Unsinkable Molly Brown 1960

The Departure
Music by Mitch Leigh
Lyrics by Charles Burr and Forman Brown
Home Sweet Homer 1976

The Departure
Music by Larry Grossman
Lyrics by Betty Comden and Adolph Green
A Doll's Life 1982

Deprogramming Song
Music and lyrics by Elizabeth Swados
Lullabye and Goodnight 1982

Dere's a Café on de Corner
Music by Georges Bizet
Lyrics by Oscar Hammerstein II
Carmen Jones 1943

The Desert Flame
Music and lyrics by Harold Rome
Bless You All 1950

Desert Moon
Music and lyrics by Walter Marks
Golden Rainbow 1968

Design for Living
Music by Donald Swann
Lyrics by Michael Flanders
At the Drop of a Hat 1959

Desire
Music by Sigmund Romberg
Lyrics by Rowland Leigh
My Romance 1948

Desmond's Dilemma
Music and lyrics by Bob Goodman
Wild and Wonderful 1971

Despair
Music and lyrics by Al Carmines
Joan (OB) 1972

Desperate
Music by Baldwin Bergersen
Lyrics by William Archibald
The Crystal Heart (OB) 1960

Desperate Ones
Music by Jacques Brel
English lyrics by Eric Blau and Mort Shuman
*Jacques Brel Is Alive and Well
and Living in Paris* (OB) 1968

Desperation
Music and lyrics by Al Carmines
The Faggot (OB) 1973

Destiny
Music by Gary William Friedman
Lyrics by Will Holt
Platinum 1978

The Deuce, Young Man
Music by Victor Herbert
Lyrics by David Stevens and Justin Huntly
McCarthy
The Madcap Duchess 1913

Deuteronomy 17, Verse 2
Music and lyrics by Peter Link and C.C. Courtney
Salvation (OB) 1969

Devil Man
Music and lyrics by Ann Harris
Sky High (OB) 1979

The Devil May Care
Music and lyrics by Ralph Benatzky
Meet My Sister 1930

The Devil's Song
Music and lyrics by Nick Branch
An Evening With Joan Crawford (OB) 1981

The Dew Was on the Rose
Music by Arthur Schwartz
Lyrics by Ira Gershwin
Park Avenue 1946

Dewey and Sal
Music by Patrick Rose
Lyrics by Merv Campone and Richard Ouzounian
A Bistro Car on the CNR (OB) 1978

Di Medici Cha Cha
Music by Scott Killian and Kim D. Sherman
Lyrics by Kenneth Robins, Scott Killian
and Kim D. Sherman
Lenny and the Heartbreakers (OB) 1983

The Diagnostician
Music and lyrics by William Roy
The Penny Friend (OB) 1966

Dialogue on Dalliance
Music and lyrics by Bruce Montgomery
The Amorous Flea (OB) 1964

Diamond Horseshoe
Music and lyrics by Irving Berlin
Music Box Revue (2nd edition) 1922

Diamond in the Rough
Music by Vincent Youmans
Lyrics by Oscar Hammerstein II
Rainbow 1928

Diamonds Are a Girl's Best Friend
Music by Jule Styne
Lyrics by Leo Robin
Gentlemen Prefer Blondes 1949

Diana
Music by Galt MacDermot
Lyrics by William Dumaresq
The Human Comedy (OB) 1983

Diane Is
Music by Mark Sandrich, Jr.
Lyrics by Sidney Michaels
Ben Franklin in Paris 1964

Dianna Lee
Music by Eubie Blake
Lyrics by Andy Razaf
Blackbirds of 1930

Diary of a Homecoming Queen
Music and lyrics by Craig Carnelia
Is There Life After High School? 1982

Diavolo
Music by Richard Rodgers
Lyrics by Lorenz Hart
Jumbo 1935

Dibarti
Music and lyrics by Elizabeth Swados
Nightclub Cantata (OB) 1977

Dice Are Rolling
Music by Andrew Lloyd Webber
Lyrics by Tim Rice
Evita 1979

Dickie
Music and lyrics by Jerry Herman
Dear World 1969

Dicky Birds
Music by Rudolf Friml
Lyrics by Otto Harbach
High Jinks 1913

Did He Really Think?
Music by Mitch Leigh
Lyrics by Charles Burr and Forman Brown
Home Sweet Homer 1976

Did I Ever Really Live?
Music by Albert Hague
Lyrics by Allen Sherman
The Fig Leaves Are Falling 1969

Did You Close Your Eyes?
Music and lyrics by Bob Merrill
New Girl in Town 1957

Did You Ever Get Stung?
Music by Richard Rodgers
Lyrics by Lorenz Hart
I Married an Angel 1938

Did You Ever Hear the Blues?
Music by David Martin
Lyrics by Langston Hughes
Simply Heavenly 1957

Did You Hear?
Music by Norman Campbell
Lyrics by Donald Harron and Norman Campbell
Anne of Green Gables (OB) 1971

Did You Hear That?
Music and lyrics by Richard Adler
Kwamina 1961

Diddle Diddle Dumpling
Music by Helen Miller
Lyrics by Eve Merriam
Inner City 1971

Didn't It
Music by Cliff Friend
Lyrics by Lew Brown
Piggy 1927

Didn't She Do It for Love?
Music and lyrics by Cliff Jones
Rockabye Hamlet 1976

Didn't You Believe?
Music by Jerome Kern
Lyrics by Anne Caldwell
Good Morning, Dearie 1921

Didn't Your Mother Tell You Nothing?
Music by Harry Ruby
Lyrics by Bert Kalmar
High Kickers 1941

Didoes
Music by Robert Hood Bowers
Lyrics by Francis DeWitt
Oh, Ernest! 1927

Die Zusammenfugung
Music by Sam Pottle
Lyrics by David Axelrod
New Faces of 1968

The Difference Is Me
Music and lyrics by Bland Simpson and Jim Wann
Hot Grog (OB) 1977

Different
Music by Galt MacDermot
Lyrics by Christopher Gore
Via Galactica 1972

A Different Drummer
Music and lyrics by Johnny Brandon
Billy Noname (OB) 1970

A Different Kind of World
Music and lyrics by Bob Goodman
Wild and Wonderful 1971

Different Times
Music and lyrics by Michael Brown
Different Times 1972

Dig, Dig, Dig
Music by Al Carmines
Lyrics by Maria Irene Fornes
Promenade (OB) 1969

Digga Digga Do
Music by Jimmy McHugh
Lyrics by Dorothy Fields
Blackbirds of 1928

Dime a Dozen
Music by Larry Grossman
Lyrics by Hal Hackady
Snoopy (OB) 1982

A Dime Ain't Worth a Nickel
Music by Gary Geld
Lyrics by Peter Udell
Angel 1978

The Dimple on My Knee
Music by George Gershwin
Lyrics by Ira Gershwin
Of Thee I Sing 1931

Dimples
Music by Cy Coleman
Lyrics by Carolyn Leigh
Little Me 1962

Ding Dong
Music and lyrics by Irving Berlin
Yip, Yip, Yaphank 1918

Ding Dong Bell
Music by Helen Miller
Lyrics by Eve Merriam
Inner City 1971

Ding Dong Dell
Music by George Gershwin
Lyrics by Ira Gershwin
Oh, Kay! 1926

Dropped from production

Ding, Dong, Dell
Music by Cliff Friend
Lyrics by Lew Brown
Piggy 1927

Ding Dong! The Witch Is Dead
Music by Harold Arlen
Lyrics by E.Y. Harburg
The Wizard of Oz (1939) F

Ding-a-Ling
Music by Leo Fall
Lyrics by Harold Atteridge
The Rose of Stamboul 1922

Ding-Dong, It's Kissing Time
Music by Jerome Kern
Lyrics by Anne Caldwell
Hitchy-Koo 1920

Dinghy
Music and lyrics by James MacDonald,
David Vos and Robert Gerlach
Something's Afoot 1976

Dinner at the Mirklines
Music by Rob Fremont
Lyrics by Doris Willens
Piano Bar (OB) 1978

The Dinner Pail
Music by John Philip Sousa
Lyrics by Leonard Liebling
The American Maid 1913

Dior, Dior
Music and lyrics by Jerry Herman
I Feel Wonderful (OB) 1954

Diplomacy
Music by Victor Herbert
Lyrics by Harry B. Smith
Cyrano de Bergerac 1899

Direct From Vienna
Music and lyrics by Bob Merrill
Carnival 1961

Dirge
Music by John Addison
Lyrics by John Cranko
Cranks 1956

Dirge for a Soldier
Music by Kurt Weill
Lyrics by Maxwell Anderson
Knickerbocker Holiday 1938

Dirge for Two Veterans
Music by Stan Harte, Jr.
Leaves of Grass (OB) 1971

The Dirty Dog
Music by Mischa and Wesley Portnoff
Lyrics by Donagh MacDonagh
Happy as Larry 1950

Dirty Words
Music and lyrics by Earl Wilson, Jr.
Let My People Come (OB) 1974

Dis Flower
Music by Georges Bizet
Lyrics by Oscar Hammerstein II
Carmen Jones 1943

Dis Is de Day
Music by Frank Harling
Lyrics by Laurence Stallings
Deep River 1926

Discarded Blues
Music by Clinton Ballard
Lyrics by Carolyn Richter
The Ballad of Johnny Pot (OB) 1971

Disco Destiny
Music by Gary William Friedman
Lyrics by Will Holt
Platinum 1978

Disco Rag
Music by Diane Leslie
Lyrics by William Gleason
The Coolest Cat in Town (OB) 1978

The Discontented Bandits
Music by Lily Hyland
Lyrics by Agnes Morgan
The Grand Street Follies (1926) (OB)

Dis-donc, Dis-donc
Music by Marguerite Monnot
Lyrics by Julian More, David Heneker
and Monte Norman
Irma la Douce 1960

Disgustingly Rich
Music by Richard Rodgers
Lyrics by Lorenz Hart
Higher And Higher 1940

Dissection Section
Music by Scott Killian and Kim D. Sherman
Lyrics by Kenneth Robins, Scott Killian
and Kim D. Sherman
Lenny and the Heartbreakers (OB) 1983

Dissertation on the State of Bliss
Music by Harold Arlen
Lyrics by Ira Gershwin
The Country Girl (1954) F

Distant Melody
Music by Jule Styne
Lyrics by Betty Comden and Adolph Green
Peter Pan 1954

Dites-Moi Pourquoi
Music by Richard Rodgers
Lyrics by Oscar Hammerstein II
South Pacific 1949

Ditty of the Drill
Music by John Philip Sousa
Lyrics by Tom Frost and John Philip Sousa
El Capitan 1896

Divorce
Music by Cheryl Hardwick
Lyrics by Marilyn Suzanne Miller
Girls, Girls, Girls (OB) 1980

Divorce Has Brought Us Together
Music and lyrics by Alan Menken
Real Life Funnies (OB) 1981

Dixie
Music by Jimmy McHugh
lyrics by Dorothy Fields
Blackbirds of 1928

Dixie Cinderella
Music by Thomas (Fats) Waller and Harry Brooks
Lyrics by Andy Razaf
Hot Chocolates 1929

Dixie Moon
Music and Lyrics by Noble Sissle and Eubie Blake
The Chocolate Dandies 1924

Dixie Vagabond
Music and lyrics by Frank Marcus
and Bernard Maltin
Bamboola 1929

Dixieland
Music by Percy Wenrich
Lyrics by Harry Clarke
Who Cares? 1930

Dizzily, Busily
Music by Kurt Weill
Lyrics by Ira Gershwin
The Firebrand of Florence 1945

Dizzy Feet
Music by Harry Ruby
Lyrics by Bert Kalmar
Top Speed 1929

Do a Revue
Music and lyrics by Billy Barnes
The Billy Barnes Revue 1959

Do Do Do
Music by George Gershwin
Lyrics by Ira Gershwin
Oh, Kay! 1926

Do I Dear, I Do
Music and lyrics by McElbert Moore
The Matinee Girl 1926

Do I Do It Through God?
Music and lyrics by Al Carmines
The Evangelist (OB) 1982

Do I Hear a Waltz?
Music by Richard Rodgers
Lyrics by Stephen Sondheim
Do I Hear a Waltz? 1965

Do I Hear You Saying "I Love You"?
Music by Richard Rodgers
Lyrics by Lorenz Hart
Present Arms 1928

Do I Love You?
Music by Henri Christine and E. Ray Goetz
Lyrics by E. Ray Goetz
Naughty Cinderella 1925

Do I Love You?
Music and lyrics by Cole Porter
Du Barry Was a Lady 1939

Do I Love You Because You're Beautiful?
Music by Richard Rodgers
Lyrics by Oscar Hammerstein II
Cinderella (1957) TV

Do It
Music by Tom Johnstone
Lyrics by Will B. Johnstone
I'll Say She Is 1924

Do It
Music by Tom Mandel
Lyrics by John Braswell
The Bar That Never Closes (OB) 1972

Do It Again!
Music by George Gershwin
Lyrics by B.G. DeSylva
The French Doll 1922

Do It for Me
Music by Louis A. Hirsch
Lyrics by Otto Harbach
Going Up 1917

Do It Girl
Music and lyrics by Peter Stampfel and Antonia
Operation Sidewinder 1970

Do It in Two
Music and lyrics by Jack Wilson and Alan Jeffreys
Vintage '60 (OB) 1960

Do It Now
Music by Jerome Kern
Lyrics by P.G. Wodehouse
Oh, Lady! Lady!! 1918

Do It Now
Music by Lewis E. Gensler and Milton Schwarzwald
Lyrics by George S. Kaufman, Marc Connelly and
Ira Gershwin
Be Yourself 1924

Do It the Hard Way
Music by Richard Rodgers
Lyrics by Lorenz Hart
Pal Joey 1940

Do It Yourself
Music and lyrics by Ann Harris
Sky High (OB) 1979

Do Look at Him
Music by Jerome Kern
Lyrics by P.G. Wodehouse
Oh, Lady! Lady!! 1918

Do My Eyes Deceive Me?
Music by Richard Lewine
Lyrics by Ted Fetter
The Fireman's Flame (OB) 1937

Do Not Bruise the Fruit
Music by Al Carmines
Lyrics by Rosalyn Drexler
Home Movies (OB) 1964

Do, Re, Do
Music by Leonard Bernstein
Lyrics by Betty Comden and Adolph Green
On the Town 1944

Do-Re-Mi
Music by Richard Rodgers
Lyrics by Oscar Hammerstein II
The Sound of Music 1959

Do Tell
Music by Charles M. Schwab
Lyrics by Henry Myers
The Garrick Gaieties (3rd edition) 1930

Do That Doo-Da
Music by Maury Rubens
Lyrics by J. Keirn Brennan
Gay Paree 1926

Do the Least You Can
Music and lyrics by Robert Swerdlow
Love Me, Love My Children (OB) 1971

Do the New York
Music by Ben Oakland
Lyrics by Jack Murray and Barry Trivers
Ziegfeld Follies (1931)

Do This, Do That
Music by George Fischoff
Lyrics by Verna Tomasson
The Prince and the Pauper (OB) 1963

Do Unto Others
Music and lyrics by Jill Williams
Rainbow Jones 1974

Do We?
Music by John Kander
Lyrics by Fred Ebb
70, Girls, 70 1971

Do What You Do!
Music by George Gershwin
Lyrics by Gus Kahn and Ira Gershwin
Show Girl 1929

Do What You Like
Music by Philip Charig
Lyrics by Leo Robin
Shoot the Works 1931

Do What You Wanna Do
Music by Vernon Duke
Lyrics by John Latouche
Cabin in the Sky 1940

Do You?
Music by Robert Russell Bennett
Lyrics by Owen Murphy and Robert A. Simon
Hold Your Horses 1933

Do You Care Too Much?
Music by Ron Steward and Neal Tate
Lyrics by Ron Steward
Sambo (OB) 1969

Do You Do the Charleston?
Music and lyrics by Gene Lockhart
Bunk of 1926

Do You Ever Dream of Vienna?
Music and lyrics by Rick Besoyan
Little Mary Sunshine (OB) 1959

Do You Ever Go to Boston?
Music and lyrics by Bob Merrill
Henry, Sweet Henry 1967

Do You Know?
Music by Victor Herbert
Lyrics by David Stevens and Justin Huntly
McCarthy
The Madcap Duchess 1913

Do You Know a Better Way to Make a Living?
Music and lyrics by Harold Rome
Bless You All 1950

Do You Know the Milky Way?
Music by Alex Fry
Lyrics by Lyon Phelps
Do You Know the Milky Way? 1961

Do You Love as I Love?
Music by Joseph Meyer
Lyrics by Irving Caesar
Yes, Yes, Yvette 1927

Do You Love Me?
Music by Richard Rodgers
Lyrics by Lorenz Hart
The Garrick Gaieties (1st edition) 1925

Do You Love Me?
Music by Jerry Bock
Lyrics by Sheldon Harnick
Fiddler on the Roof 1964

Do You Recall?
Music by Johann Strauss I, adapted by Oscar
Straus
Lyrics by Clare Kummer
Three Waltzes 1937

Do You Remember?
Music by Gary William Friedman
Lyrics by Will Holt
Taking My Turn (OB) 1983

Do You Suppose
Music by Stan Harte, Jr.
Leaves of Grass (OB) 1971

Do You Think I'm Pretty?
Music and lyrics by Norman Dean
Autumn's Here (OB) 1966

Do You Want to See Paris?
Music and lyrics by Cole Porter
Fifty Million Frenchmen 1929

Do Your Own Thing
Music and lyrics by Hal Hester
and Danny Apolinar
Your Own Thing (OB) 1968

Do Your Thing, Miss Truth
Music and lyrics by Glory Van Scott
Miss Truth (OB) 1979

Doatsey Mae
Music and lyrics by Carol Hall
The Best Little Whorehouse in Texas 1978

Doctor and Ella
Music and lyrics by Marc Blitzstein
The Cradle Will Rock 1938

A Doctor's Soliloquy
Music by Sammy Fain
Lyrics by Paul Francis Webster
Christine 1960

Does Anybody Love You?
Music and lyrics by Billy Solly
Boy Meets Boy (OB) 1975

Does It Pay to Be a Lady?
Music by Vincent Youmans
Lyrics by Billy Rose and Edward Eliscu
Great Day! 1929

Does It Really Matter?
Music by Jule Styne
Lyrics by Sammy Cahn
Look to the Lilies 1970

Doesn't Anybody Love Anymore?
Music and lyrics by Earl Wilson, Jr.
Let My People Come (OB) 1974

Doesn't It Bug You?
Music by Stanley Silverman
Lyrics by Tom Hendry
Doctor Selavy's Magic Theatre (OB) 1972

D-o-g
Music by Baldwin Bergersen
Lyrics by William Archibald
The Crystal Heart (OB) 1960

A Dog
Music by Ann Sternberg
Lyrics by Gertrude Stein
Gertrude Stein's First Reader (OB) 1969

Dog Eat Dog
Music by Harold Arlen
Lyrics by Johnny Mercer
Saratoga 1959

A Dog Is a Man's Best Friend
Music and lyrics by Johnny Mercer
Top Banana 1951

Dog Walker
Music by Ted Simons
Lyrics by Elinor Guggenheimer
Potholes (OB) 1979

Dogface Jive
Music by Jack Holmes
Lyrics by Bill Conklin and Bob Miller
O Say Can You See! (OB) 1962

Dog-Gone That Chilly Man
Music and lyrics by Irving Berlin
Ziegfeld Follies of 1911

Doggone
Music by Harry Archer
Lyrics by Walter O'Keefe
Just a Minute 1928

Doin' the Chamberlain
Music by Jimmy McHugh
Lyrics by Al Dubin
The Streets of Paris 1939

Doin' the Gorilla
Music by Philip Charig and Richard Myers
Lyrics by Leo Robin
Allez-Oop 1927

Doin' the Hot-cha-cha
Music and lyrics by Lester Lee
Keep It Clean 1929

Doin' the New Low-Down
Music by Jimmy McHugh
Lyrics by Dorothy Fields
Blackbirds of 1928

Doin' the Old Yahoo Step
Music and lyrics by Charles Gaynor
Lend an Ear 1948

Also in *Show Girl* (1961)

Doin' the Reactionary
Music and lyrics by Harold Rome
Pins and Needles (OB) 1937

Doin' the Shim Sham
Music by Alberta Nichols
Lyrics by Mann Holiner
Blackbirds of 1934

Doin' the Toledo
Music and lyrics by Donald Heywood
Black Rhythm 1936

Doin' the Waltz
Music by Richard Lewine
Lyrics by Ted Fetter
The Fireman's Flame (OB) 1937

Doin' What Comes Natur'lly
Music and lyrics by Irving Berlin
Annie Get Your Gun 1946

Doing Good
Music by Charles Strouse
Lyrics by Lee Adams
It's a Bird, It's a Plane, It's Superman 1966

Doing the Dumbbell
Music by Harry Revel
Lyrics by Mack Gordon
Fast and Furious 1931

Dolce Far Niente
Music and lyrics by Meredith Willson
The Unsinkable Molly Brown 1960

A Doll Fantasy
Music by Sigmund Romberg
Lyrics by Oscar Hammerstein II
May Wine 1935

Doll Song
Music by Walter Kollo
Lyrics by Harry B. Smith
Three Little Girls 1930

The Dollar Princesses
Music by Leo Fall
Lyrics by George Grossmith
The Dollar Princess 1909

Dolls
Music and lyrics by Billy Barnes
The Billy Barnes People 1961

A Doll's House
Music by Arthur Siegel
Lyrics by June Carroll
New Faces of 1956

Dolly
Music by Vincent Youmans
Lyrics by Arthur Francis and Schuyler Greene
Two Little Girls in Blue 1921

Dolly Dollars
Music by Victor Herbert
Lyrics by Harry B. Smith
Miss Dolly Dollars 1905

Dolly From the Follies Bergères
Music by Victor Young
Lyrics by Edward Heyman
Pardon Our French 1950

Domesticity
Music and lyrics by Robert Wright
and George Forrest
Kean 1961

Don José O'Brien
Music by Maria Grever
Lyrics by Raymond Leveen
Viva O'Brien 1941

Don José of Far Rockaway
Music and lyrics by Harold Rome
Wish You Were Here 1952

Don Medigua, All for Thy Coming Wait
Music by John Philip Sousa
Lyrics by Tom Frost and John Philip Sousa
El Capitan 1896

Don Medigua, Here's Your Wife
Music by John Philip Sousa
Lyrics by Tom Frost and John Philip Sousa
El Capitan 1896

Don' Shake My Tree
Music by Raymond Hubbell
Lyrics by Anne Caldwell
Yours Truly 1927

The Donkey Serenade
Music by Rudolf Friml (adapted by Herbert Stothart)
Lyrics by Robert Wright and George Forrest
The Firefly (film version, 1937)

See note on "Chansonette"

Donna
Music by Galt MacDermot
Lyrics by Gerome Ragni and James Rado
Hair 1968

Donny Didn't, Donny Did
Music by Ivan Caryll
Lyrics by C.M.S. McLellan
The Pink Lady 1911

Donnybrook
Music and lyrics by Johnny Burke
Donnybrook! 1961

The Dons' Chorus
Music by Julian Slade
Lyrics by Dorothy Reynolds and Julian Slade
Salad Days (OB) 1958

Don't Ask!
Music by George Gershwin
Lyrics by Ira Gershwin
Oh, Kay! 1926

Don't Ask Her Another
Music by Max Ewing
Lyrics by Agnes Morgan
The Grand Street Follies (1927) (OB)

Don't Ask Me
Music by Jacques Urbont
Lyrics by Bruce Geller
All in Love (OB) 1961

Don't Ask Me Not to Sing
Music by Jerome Kern
Lyrics by Otto Harbach
The Cat and the Fiddle 1931

Dropped from production. Later used in *Roberta* (1933).

Don't Be a Miracle
Music and lyrics by Robert Swerdlow
Love Me, Love My Children (OB) 1971

Don't Be a Woman if You Can
Music by Arthur Schwartz
Lyrics by Ira Gershwin
Park Avenue 1946

Don't Be Afraid
Music by Arthur Schwartz
Lyrics by Dorothy Fields
A Tree Grows in Brooklyn 1951

Don't Be Afraid
Music by Kurt Weill
Lyrics by Bertolt Brecht (adapted by Michael Feingold)
Happy End 1977

Don't Be Afraid of an Animal
Music and lyrics by Richard Rodgers
Androcles and the Lion (1967) TV

Don't Be Afraid of Romance
Music and lyrics by Irving Berlin
Mr. President 1962

Don't Be Anything Less than Everything You Can Be
Music by Larry Grossman
Lyrics by Hal Hackady
Snoopy (OB) 1982

Don't Betray His Love
Music by Steve Sterner
Lyrics by Peter del Valle
Lovers (OB) 1975

Don't Bother
Music and lyrics by Billy Barnes
The Billy Barnes People 1961

Don't Bother Me, I Can't Cope
Music and lyrics by Micki Grant
Don't Bother Me, I Can't Cope (OB) 1972

Don't Cry
Music and lyrics by Frank Loesser
The Most Happy Fella 1956

Don't Cry for Me Argentina
Music by Andrew Lloyd Webber
Lyrics by Tim Rice
Evita 1979

Don't Destroy the World
Music by Dov Seltzer
Lyrics by David Paulsen
To Live Another Summer 1971

Don't Do It
Music by Arthur Schwartz
Lyrics by Agnes Morgan
The Grand Street Follies (1929)

Don't Do the Charleston
Music by James F. Hanley
Lyrics by Gene Buck
No Foolin' 1926

Don't Eat It
Music by Al Carmines
Lyrics by Maria Irene Fornes
Promenade (OB) 1969

Don't Ever Book a Trip on the IRT
Music by Arthur Siegel
Lyrics by Mae Richard
Tallulah (OB) 1983

Don't Ever Leave Me
Music by Jerome Kern
Lyrics by Oscar Hammerstein II
Sweet Adeline 1929

Don't Fall Asleep
Music and lyrics by Ronny Graham
New Faces of 1952

Don't Fall in Love With Me
Music and lyrics by Herman Hupfeld
The Merry World 1926

Don't Fall Till You've Seen Them All
Music by Louis A. Hirsch
Lyrics by Otto Harbach
Mary 1920

Don't Feed the Plants
Music by Alan Menken
Lyrics by Howard Ashman
Little Shop of Horrors (OB) 1982

Don't Fence Me In
Music and lyrics by Cole Porter
Hollywood Canteen (1944) F

Written in early 1935 (and published in 1944) for a
projected film entitled *Adios, Argentina*, which was
abandoned. The film's producer had urged Porter
to use the title "Don't Fence Me In," the name of a
song that had been submitted to him by an amateur
songwriter. More to please the producer than
anything else, Porter agreed, wrote the song and
made an agreement with the other songwriter
providing for an initial payment and, later, a share
of the song's royalty. Porter used the title and
some isolated lines, but not a note of its music.
Gossip persisted nevertheless that Porter had
either "stolen" the song or purchased it outright, all
most unjust. In view of Porter's prolific and brilliant
output, it would hardly seem necessary for him to
purchase, or "borrow," a song.

Don't Forget
Music by James F. Hanley
Lyrics by B.G. DeSylva
Queen High 1926

Don't Forget
Music by Leon Carr
Lyrics by Earl Shuman
The Secret Life of Walter Mitty (OB) 1964

Don't Forget Bandanna Days
Music and lyrics by Porter Grainger
and Freddie Johnson
Lucky Sambo 1925

Don't Forget 127th Street
Music by Charles Strouse
Lyrics by Lee Adams
Golden Boy 1964

Don't Forget the Beau You Left Behind
Music by A. Baldwin Sloane
Lyrics by E. Ray Goetz
The Hen Pecks 1911

Don't Forget the Girl From Punxsutawney
Music by Jerry Livingston
Lyrics by Mack David
Bright Lights of 1944

Don't Forget the Lilac Bush
Music by Kurt Weill
Lyrics by Langston Hughes
Street Scene 1947

Don't Forget to Dream
Music by Jay Gorney
Lyrics by Barry Trivers
Heaven on Earth 1948

Don't Forget Your Etiquette
Music by Alberta Nichols
Lyrics by Mann Holiner
Angela 1928

Don't Give Up the Hunt, Dr. Puffin
Music by Alec Wilder
Lyrics by Arnold Sundgaard
Kittiwake Island (OB) 1960

Don't Go Away, Monsieur
Music by Arthur Schwartz
Lyrics by Howard Dietz
Between the Devil 1937

Don't Hang Up the Telephone
Music and lyrics by Jeanne Napoli
and Gary Portnoy
Marilyn 1983

Don't Hang Your Dreams on a Rainbow
Music by Arnold Johnson
Lyrics by Irving Kahal
Earl Carroll's Sketch Book (1929)

Don't Have a Song to Sing
Music and lyrics by Robert Dennis, Peter Schickele,
and Stanley Walden
Oh! Calcutta! 1969

Don't Have the Baby
Music by Galt MacDermot
Lyrics by John Guare
Two Gentlemen of Verona 1971

Don't Have to Take It Any More
Music by Norman Curtis
Lyrics by Patricia Taylor Curtis
Walk Down Mah Street! (OB) 1968

Don't Hold Everything
Music by Ray Henderson
Lyrics by B.G. DeSylva and Lew Brown
Hold Everything! 1928

Don't I Know You?
Music and lyrics by Bob Ost
Everybody's Gettin' Into the Act (OB) 1981

Don't It Go to Show Ya Never Know
Music by Alan Menken
Lyrics by Howard Ashman
Little Shop of Horrors (OB) 1982

Don't Kiki Me
Music by Harvey Schmidt
Lyrics by Tom Jones
Philemon (OB) 1975

Don't Laugh
Music by Mary Rodgers
Lyrics by Martin Charnin
Hot Spot 1963

Don't Leave Me
Music and lyrics by Hal Hester and Danny Apolinar
Your Own Thing (OB) 1968

Don't Leave Me Dangling in the Dust
Music and lyrics by Robin Remaily
Operation Sidewinder 1970

Don't Leave Your Little Blackbird Blue
Music and lyrics by Joe Jordan, Porter Grainger
and Sheldon Brooks
Brown Buddies 1930

Don't Let Him Know You
Music by John Addison
Lyrics by John Cranko
Cranks 1956

Don't Let It Get You Down
Music and lyrics by Cole Porter
You Never Know 1938

Don't Let It Get You Down
Music by Burton Lane
Lyrics by E.Y. Harburg
Hold On to Your Hats 1940

Don't Like Goodbyes
Music by Harold Arlen
Lyrics by Harold Arlen and Truman Capote
House of Flowers 1954

Don't Listen to Your Heart
Music by Bradford Greene
Lyrics by Marianne Brown Waters
Right This Way 1938

Don't Look at Me
Music and lyrics by Stephen Sondhelm
Follies 1971

Don't Look at Me That Way
Music and lyrics by Cole Porter
Paris 1928

Don't Look Back
Music and lyrics by Steve Allen
Sophie 1963

Don't Look Now
Music by David Baker
Lyrics by David Craig
Copper and Brass 1957

Don't Make a Move
Music by Sammy Fain
Lyrics by Marilyn and Alan Bergman
Something More 1964

Don't Marry Me
Music by Richard Rodgers
Lyrics by Oscar Hammerstein II
Flower Drum Song 1958

Don't Play That Lovesong Anymore
Music by Monty Norman
Lyrics by Julian More
The Moony Shapiro Songbook 1981

Don't P-P-Point Them Guns at Me
Music by Victor Ziskin
Lyrics by Joan Javits
Young Abe Lincoln 1961

Don't Put It Down
Music by Galt MacDermot
Lyrics by Gerome Ragni and James Rado
Hair 1968

Don't Rain on My Parade
Music by Jule Styne
Lyrics by Bob Merrill
Funny Girl 1964

Don't Say Shoo-Be-DoBop
Music by Diane Leslie
Lyrics by William Gleason
The Coolest Cat in Town (OB) 1978

Don't Say Yes if You Want to Say No
Music and lyrics by Barbara Schottenfeld
I Can't Keep Running in Place (OB) 1981

Don't Say You Like Tchaikowsky
Music by Claibe Richardson
Lyrics by Paul Rosner
Shoestring '57 (OB)

Don't Scold
Music by Robert Hood Bowers
Lyrics by Francis DeWitt
Oh, Ernest! 1927

Don't Sell the Night Short
Music and lyrics by Hugh Martin and Ralph Blane
Best Foot Forward 1941

Don't Send Me Back
Music and lyrics by Irving Berlin
Music Box Revue (4th edition) 1924

Don't Shoot the Hooey to Me, Louie
Music and lyrics by Richard M. Sherman
and Robert B. Sherman
Over Here! 1974

Don't Sing Solo
Music by George Kleinsinger
Lyrics by Roslyn Harvey
Of V We Sing 1942

Don't Stand Too Close to the Picture
Music by Leon Pober
Lyrics by Bud Freeman
Beg, Borrow or Steal 1960

Don't Stop
Music by William B. Kernell
Lyrics by Dorothy Donnelly
Hello, Lola 1926

Don't Take Our Charlie for the Army
Music and lyrics by Noël Coward
The Girl Who Came to Supper 1963

Don't Take Sides
Music by James Bredt
Lyrics by Edward Eager
The Happy Hypocrite (OB) 1968

Don't Take Your Beau to the Seashore
Music by Irving Berlin
Lyrics by E. Ray Goetz
The Fascinating Widow 1911

Don't Talk
Music by Morton Gould
Lyrics by Dorothy Fields
Arms and the Girl 1950

Don't Talk About God
Music by Jule Styne
Lyrics by Sammy Cahn
Look to the Lilies 1970

Don't Tamper With My Sister
Music by Burton Lane
Lyrics by Alan Jay Lerner
On a Clear Day You Can See Forever 1965

Don't Tear Up the Horse Slips
Music and lyrics by Robert Larimer
King of the Whole Damn World (OB) 1962

Don't Tell Mama
Music by John Kander
Lyrics by Fred Ebb
Cabaret 1966

Don't Tell Me
Music by Harold Karr
Lyrics by Matt Dubey
Happy Hunting 1956

Don't Tell Me
Music by Jack Urbont
Lyrics by Bruce Geller
Livin' the Life (OB) 1957

Don't Tell Me
Music by Charles Strouse
Lyrics by Lee Adams
A Broadway Musical 1978

Don't Tell Me
Music by Galt MacDermot
Lyrics by William Dumaresq
The Human Comedy (OB) 1983

Don't Tell Me It's Bad
Music by Ray Henderson
Lyrics by Ted Koehler
Say When 1934

Don't Tell Me It's Forever
Music by Nancy Ford
Lyrics by Gretchen Cryer
Shelter 1973

Don't Tell Your Folks
Music by Richard Rodgers
Lyrics by Lorenz Hart
Simple Simon 1930

Don't Tempt Me
Music by Jerome Kern
Lyrics by Harry B. Smith
Love o' Mike 1917

Don't Tempt Me
Music by Emmerich Kálmán
Lyrics by Harry B. Smith
Countess Maritza 1926

Don't Throw Me Down
Music by J. Fred Coots
Lyrics by Al Dubin
White Lights 1927

Don't Turn Away From Love
Music and lyrics by Noël Coward
Sail Away 1961

Don't Turn His Picture to the Wall
Music and lyrics by Skip Redwine and Larry Frank
Frank Merriwell, or Honor Challenged 1971

Don't Turn Us Out of the House
Music by Richard Lewine
Lyrics by John Latouche
Murder in the Old Red Barn (OB) 1936

Don't Twist My Mind
Music and lyrics by Robert Swerdlow
Love Me, Love My Children (OB) 1971

Don't Unmask Your Beauty to the Moon
Music and lyrics by Cliff Jones
Rockabye Hamlet 1976

Don't Wait Till It's Too Late to See Paris
Music by Arthur Siegel
Lyrics by June Carroll
New Faces of 1956

Don't Wake Them Up Too Soon
Music by Fred Spielman and Arthur Gershwin
Lyrics by Stanley Adams
A Lady Says Yes 1945

Don't Wanna Write About the South
Music and lyrics by Harold Rome
Bless You All 1950

Don't Worry
Music by Jimmy Van Heusen
Lyrics by Sammy Cahn
Skyscraper 1965

Don't You Cheat
Music and lyrics by Leon DeCosta
The Blonde Sinner 1926

Don't You Ever Give It All Away
Music and lyrics by Elizabeth Swados
Lullabye and Goodnight 1982

Don't You Make a Noise
Music by Kerry Mills
Lyrics by S.M. Lewis
The Fascinating Widow 1911

Don't You Think It's Very Nice?
Music and lyrics by Hugo Peretti, Luigi Creatore
and George David Weiss
Maggie Flynn 1968

Don't You Want to Take Me?
Music by Jerome Kern
Lyrics by Anne Caldwell
The Night Boat 1920

Doo-Dab
Music by Harry Ruby
Lyrics by Bert Kalmar
Puzzles of 1925

Doo-Waa Doo-Wee
Music and lyrics by James Quinn and Alaric Jans
Do Patent Leather Shoes Really Reflect Up? 1982

Doodly, Doodly, Are You Happy?
Music and lyrics by Gian-Carlo Menotti
The Medium 1947

Doomed, Doomed, Doomed
Music by Jerome Moross
Lyrics by John Latouche
The Golden Apple 1954

The Door of My Dreams
Music by Rudolf Friml
Lyrics by Oscar Hammerstein II and Otto Harbach
Rose Marie 1924

Dorothy
Music and lyrics by Clarence Gaskill
Earl Carroll's Vanities (1925)

Dorrie's Wish
Music and lyrics by Frank Loesser
Greenwillow 1960

Dou, Dou
Music by Henry Sullivan
Lyrics by Edward Eliscu
A Little Racketeer 1932

Double Dummy Drill
Music by George Gershwin
Lyrics by Ira Gershwin
Let 'Em Eat Cake 1933

Double Murder, Double Death
Music by Mischa and Wesley Portnoff
Lyrics by Donagh MacDonagh
Happy as Larry 1950

Double Soliloquy
Music by Jule Styne
Lyrics by E.Y. Harburg
Darling of the Day 1968

The Double Standard
Music by Arthur Schwartz
Lyrics by Agnes Morgan
The Grand Street Follies (1929)

Double Standard
Music and lyrics by Jay Livingston and Ray Evans
Oh Captain! 1958

Doughnuts
Music by George Gershwin
Lyrics by B.G. Desylva and John Henry Mears
Morris Gest Midnight Whirl 1919

Doughnuts and Coffee
Music by Sammy Fain
Lyrics by Irving Kahal
Right This Way 1938

Doughnuts for Defense
Music by Jack Holmes
Lyrics by Bill Conklin and Bob Miller
O Say Can You See! (OB) 1962

Dover
Music by Gerald Jay Markoe
Lyrics by Michael Colby
Charlotte Sweet (OB) 1982

Dov's Nightmare
Music by Walt Smith
Lyrics by Leon Uris
Ari 1971

Down Among the Grass Roots
Music and lyrics by Oscar Brand
How to Steal an Election (OB) 1968

Down at the Gaiety Burlesque
Music and lyrics by Arthur Malvin
Sugar Babies 1979

Down at the Village
Music by Ray Perkins
Lyrics by Max and Nathaniel Lief
The Greenwich Village Follies (1928)

Down by the Erie Canal
Music and lyrics by George M. Cohan
Hello, Broadway (1914)

Down by the River
Music by Richard Rodgers
Lyrics by Lorenz Hart
Mississippi (1935) F

Down by the Sea
Music by Richard Rodgers
Lyrics by Lorenz Hart
Present Arms 1928

Down Down Down
Music and lyrics by Elizabeth Swados
Alice in Concert (OB) 1980

The Down East Flapper
Music by Albert Von Tilzer
Lyrics by Neville Fleeson
The Gingham Girl 1922

Down Greenwich Village Way
Music by Albert Von Tilzer
Lyrics by Neville Fleeson
The Gingham Girl 1922

Down Home
Music by Gary Geld
Lyrics by Peter Udell
Purlie 1970

Down in the Depths, on the 90th Floor
Music and lyrics by Cole Porter
Red, Hot and Blue! 1936

Down in the Land of Dancing Pickaninnies
Music and lyrics by Noble Sissle and Eubie Blake
The Chocolate Dandies 1924

Down in the Streets
Music and lyrics by Tommy Garlock and Alan Jeffreys
Vintage '60 (OB) 1960

Down in the Valley
Music by Robert Emmett Dolan
Lyrics by Johnny Mercer
Texas, Li'l Darlin' 1949

Down on MacConnachy Square
Music by Frederick Loewe
Lyrics by Alan Jay Lerner
Brigadoon 1947

Down on the Dude Ranch
Music by Burton Lane
Lyrics by E.Y. Harburg
Hold On to Your Hats 1940

Down 'Round the 19th Hole
Music by Harry Tierney
Lyrics by Joseph McCarthy
Kid Boots 1923

Down the Well
Music by Gerald Marks
Lyrics by Sam Lerner
Hold It! 1948

Down Through the Agents
Music by John Green
Lyrics by George Marion, Jr.
Beat the Band 1942

Down to the Sea
Music and lyrics by Ida Hoyt Chamberlain
Enchanted Isle 1927

Down to the Sea
Music by David Baker
Lyrics by David Craig
Phoenix '55 (OB)

Down! Up! Left! Right!
Music by Louis A. Hirsch
Lyrics by Otto Harbach
Going Up 1917

Down Where the Jack O'Lanterns Grow
Music by Irving Berlin
Lyrics by George M. Cohan
The Cohan Revue of 1918

Down Where the East River Flows
Music by Vincent Youmans
Lyrics by Harold Adamson and Clifford Grey
Smiles 1930

Dropped from production

Down Where the Mortgages Grow
Music by Vincent Youmans and Herbert Stothart
Lyrics by Oscar Hammerstein II
and William Cary Duncan
Mary Jane McKane 1923

Down With Everybody But Us
Music and lyrics by Cole Porter
Fifty Million Frenchmen 1929

Dropped from production

Down With Love
Music by Harold Arlen
Lyrics by E.Y. Harburg
Hooray for What! 1937

Down With Sin
Music by Robert Stolz
Lyrics by Robert Sour
Mr. Strauss Goes to Boston 1945

Down Your Tea
Music and lyrics by Robert Wright
and George Forrest
Song of Norway 1944

Based on Grieg's song *Springtide*

The Dozens
Music and lyrics by Melvin Van Peebles
Ain't Supposed to Die a Natural Death 1971

Dr. Brock
Music by Jerry Bock
Lyrics by Sheldon Harnick
Tenderloin 1960

Dr. Crippen
Music by Kurt Weill
Lyrics by Ogden Nash
One Touch of Venus 1943

Dr. Iatro
Music and lyrics by Deed Meyer
'Toinette (OB) 1961

Dr. Jazz
Music and lyrics by Buster Davis
Doctor Jazz 1975

Dr. Lucy (The Doctor Is In)
Music and lyrics by Clark Gesner
You're a Good Man, Charlie Brown (OB) 1967

Drat! The Cat!
Music by Milton Schafer
Lyrics by Ira Levin
Drat! The Cat! 1965

The Dream
Music and lyrics by Johnny Brandon
Billy Noname (OB) 1970

The Dream
Music and lyrics by Charles Strouse
Six (OB) 1971

Dream a Dream
Music by Jerome Kern
Lyrics by Otto Harbach and Oscar Hammerstein II
Sunny 1925

Dropped from production

Dream Babies
Music by Gary William Friedman
Lyrics by Will Holt
The Me Nobody Knows (OB) 1970

Dream Boat
Music and lyrics by Ida Hoyt Chamberlain
Enchanted Isle 1927

Dream Boat
Music by George Bagby
Lyrics by Grace Henry and Jo Trent
Fioretta 1929

Dream Dancing
Music and lyrics by Cole Porter
You'll Never Get Rich (1941) F

Dream Drummin'
Music and lyrics by Richard M. Sherman
and Robert B. Sherman
Over Here! 1974

A Dream for Angela
Music by Louis Bellson and Will Irwin
Lyrics by Richard Ney
Portofino 1958

Dream Girl
Music and lyrics by Ida Hoyt Chamberlain
Enchanted Isle 1927

Dream Kingdom
Music by Harden Church
Lyrics by Edward Heyman
Caviar 1934

Dream of Dreams
Music by H. Maurice Jacquet
Lyrics by Preston Sturges
The Well of Romance 1930

A Dream of Orange Blossoms
Music by Victor Herbert
Lyrics by B.G. DeSylva
Orange Blossoms 1922

Dream On, Little Soldier Boy
Music and lyrics by Irving Berlin
Yip, Yip, Yaphank 1918

Dream Safe With Me
Music by Charles Strouse
Lyrics by David Rogers
Charlie and Algernon 1980

Dream Sweetheart
Music by Harry Tierney
Lyrics by Joseph McCarthy
Cross My Heart 1928

Dreamboat From Dreamland
Music by Jack Holmes
Lyrics by Bill Conklin and Bob Miller
O Say Can You See! (OB) 1962

The Dreamer
Music by Arthur Schwartz
Lyrics by Frank Loesser
Thank Your Lucky Stars (1943) F

Dreamer With a Penny
Music by Allan Roberts
Lyrics by Lester Lee
All for Love 1949

Dreamgirls
Music by Henry Krieger
Lyrics by Tom Eyen
Dreamgirls 1981

Dreaming
Music by Con Conrad and Henry Souvaine
Lyrics by J.P. McEvoy
Americana (1926)

Dreaming Princess
Music by Victor Herbert
Lyrics by Harry B. Smith
The Enchantress 1911

Dreams
Music by Harold Levey
Lyrics by Owen Murphy
Rainbow Rose 1926

Dreams
Music by Rudolf Friml
Lyrics by P.G. Wodehouse and Clifford Grey
The Three Musketeers 1928

Dreams
Music by Paul Hoffert
Lyrics by David Secter
Get Thee to Canterbury (OB) 1969

Dreams
Music by Billy Goldenberg
Lyrics by Alan and Marilyn Bergman
Ballroom 1978

Dreams Ago
Music by Abraham Ellstein
Lyrics by Walter Bullock
Great to Be Alive 1950

Dreams Come True
Music by Morton Gould
Lyrics by Betty Comden and Adolph Green
Billion Dollar Baby 1945

Dreams for Sale
Music by James F. Hanley
Lyrics by Eddie Dowling
Honeymoon Lane 1926

Dreamy Montmartre
Music by Abel Baer
Lyrics by Sam Lewis and Joe Young
Lady Do 1927

Dreary, Dreary, Rainy Days
Music and lyrics by Porter Grainger
and Freddie Johnson
Lucky Sambo 1925

The Dresden Northwest Mounted
Music by George Gershwin
Lyrics by Ira Gershwin
Pardon My English 1933

Dressed Up for Your Sunday Beau
Music by Joseph Meyer and Philip Charig
Lyrics by Leo Robin
Just Fancy 1927

Drift With Me
Music by Jerome Kern
Lyrics by Harry B. Smith
Love o' Mike 1917

Drifting
Music by Gary Geld
Lyrics by Peter Udell
Angel 1978

Drifting Along With the Tide
Music by George Gershwin
Lyrics by Arthur Jackson
George White's Scandals (1921)

Drill of the Seventh
Music and lyrics by George M. Cohan
The Little Millionaire 1911

Drink
Music and lyrics by Cole Porter
Seven Lively Arts 1944

Drink Me
Music and lyrics by Elizabeth Swados
Alice in Concert (OB) 1980

Drinkin' Shoes
Music and lyrics by Mark Hardwick, Cass Morgan
and Debra Monk
Pump Boys and Dinettes 1982

Drinking Fool
Music and lyrics by Bland Simpson and Jim Wann
Hot Grog (OB) 1977

Drinking Song
Music by Sigmund Romberg
Lyrics by Dorothy Donnelly
The Student Prince 1924

Drinking Song
Music by Rudolf Friml
Lyrics by Brian Hooker
The Vagabond King 1925

Drinking Song
Music and lyrics by Irving Berlin
Face the Music 1932

Drinking Song
Music and lyrics by Cole Porter
Les Girls (1957) F

Dropped from film

The Drinking Song
Music and lyrics by Rick Besoyan
The Student Gypsy (OB) 1963

Drip, Drop, Tapoketa
Music by Leon Carr
Lyrics by Earl Shuman
The Secret Life of Walter Mitty (OB) 1964

Drop Me a Line
Music by Efrem Zimbalist
Lyrics by Joseph W. Herbert
Honeydew 1920

Drop That Name
Music by Jule Styne
Lyrics by Betty Comden and Adolph Green
Bells Are Ringing 1956

Drop Your Kerchief
Music and lyrics by Cliff Friend and George White
George White's Scandals (1929)

Dropsy Cure Weather
Music by Claibe Richardson
Lyrics by Kenward Elmslie
The Grass Harp 1971

The Drug Store Song
Music and lyrics by Harold Rome
Call Me Mister 1946

Drugstore Scene
Music and lyrics by Marc Blitzstein
The Cradle Will Rock 1938

Drums
Music and lyrics by Johnny Brandon
Who's Who, Baby? (OB) 1968

Drums in My Heart
Music by Vincent Youmans
Lyrics by Edward Heyman
Through the Years 1932

Drums of Kane
Music by Rudolf Friml
Lyrics by J. Keirn Brennan
Luana 1930

Dry Mouth With No Water
Music and lyrics by David Langston Smyrl
On the Lock-In (OB) 1977

Du Barry Was a Lady
Music and lyrics by Cole Porter
Du Barry Was a Lady 1939

The Dubarry
Music by Carl Millöcker (revised by Theo
Mackeben)
Lyrics by Rowland Leigh
The Dubarry 1932

Dublin Town
Music and lyrics by Fred Ebb, Paul Klein
and Lee Goldsmith
Vintage '60 (OB) 1960

Dudin' Up
Music by Alfred Brooks
Lyrics by Ira J. Bilowit
Of Mice and Men (OB) 1958

The Duel
Music by Ivan Caryll
Lyrics by C.M.S. McLellan
The Pink Lady 1911

The Duel
Music by Jerome Kern
Lyrics by Edward Madden
La Belle Paree 1911

The Duel
Music by Richard Adler
Lyrics by Will Holt
Music Is 1976

The Duello
Music by Sigmund Romberg
Lyrics by Oscar Hammerstein II
Sunny River 1941

Duet for One (The First Lady of the Land)
Music by Leonard Bernstein
Lyrics by Alan Jay Lerner
1600 Pennsylvania Avenue 1976

Dulcinea
Music by Mitch Leigh
Lyrics by Joe Darion
Man of La Mancha 1965

Dull and Gay
Music by Richard Rodgers
Lyrics by Lorenz Hart
Simple Simon 1930

Dumb Girl
Music by Lewis E. Gensler
Lyrics by Owen Murphy and Robert A. Simon
The Gang's All Here 1931

Dumb Luck
Music and lyrics by Noble Sissle and Eubie Blake
The Chocolate Dandies 1924

Dusky Debutante
Music by Baldwin Bergersen
Lyrics by June Sillman
Who's Who 1938

Dusky Love
Music by Will Vodery
Lyrics by Henry Creamer
Keep Shufflin' 1928

Dusky Shadows
Music by Stanley Silverman
Lyrics by Tom Hendry
Doctor Selavy's Magic Theatre (OB) 1972

Dust in Your Eyes
Music and lyrics by Irving and Lionel Newman
Murder at the Vanities 1933

Dusting Around
Music by Eubie Blake
Lyrics by Noble Sissle
Shuffle Along of 1933

Dutch Country Table
Music and lyrics by Norman Dean
Autumn's Here (OB) 1966

A Dutiful Wife
Music by Franz Lehár
Lyrics by Adrian Ross
The Merry Widow 1907

Dwarf's Song
Music and lyrics by Robert Dahdah
Curley McDimple (OB) 1967

D'Ye Love Me?
Music by Jerome Kern
Lyrics by Otto Harbach and Oscar Hammerstein II
Sunny 1925

Dying Child
Music by Galt MacDermot
Lyrics by Rochelle Owens
The Karl Marx Play (OB) 1973

The Dying Cowboy
Music by Richard Lewine
Lyrics by Ted Fetter
The Girl From Wyoming (OB) 1938

The Dying Swan
Music by Dave Stamper
Lyrics by Fred Herendeen
Orchids Preferred 1937

Dynamic
Music by Frederico Valerio
Lyrics by Elizabeth Miele
Hit the Trail 1954

E

Each Pearl a Thought
Music by Jerome Kern
Lyrics by Harry B. Smith
Oh, I Say! 1913

Each Tomorrow Morning
Music and lyrics by Jerry Herman
Dear World 1969

Eadie Was a Lady
Music by Nacio Herb Brown and Richard Whiting
Lyrics by B.G. DeSylva
Take a Chance 1932

Eager Beaver
Music and lyrics by Richard Rodgers
No Strings 1962

The Eagle and Me
Music by Harold Arlen
Lyrics by E.Y. Harburg
Bloomer Girl 1944

Earl Is Crazy
Music by Peter Link
Lyrics by C.C. Courtney and Ragan Courtney
Earl of Ruston 1971

Earl Was Ahead
Music by Peter Link
Lyrics by C.C. Courtney and Ragan Courtney
Earl of Ruston 1971

Early in the Morning
Music by Con Conrad
Lyrics by Gus Kahn
Kitty's Kisses 1926

Early One Morning Blues
Music and lyrics by Voices, Inc.
The Believers (OB) 1968

Early to Bed
Music by Thomas (Fats) Waller
Lyrics by George Marion, Jr.
Early to Bed 1943

The Earth
Music by Galt MacDermot
Lyrics by Gerome Ragni
Dude 1972

The Earth and Other Minor Things
Music by Frederick Loewe
Lyrics by Alan Jay Lerner
Gigi (stage version, 1973)

The Earth and the Sky
Music and lyrics by John Rox
John Murray Anderson's Almanac (1953)

Earth Dance
Music by Susan Hulsman Bingham
Lyrics by Myrna Lamb
Mod Donna (OB) 1970

Earthly Paradise
Music by Harvey Schmidt
Lyrics by Tom Jones
Colette (OB) 1970

Earthworms
Music by Susan Hulsman Bingham
Lyrics by Myrna Lamb
Mod Donna (OB) 1970

Ease On Down the Road
Music and lyrics by Charlie Smalls
The Wiz 1975

Easier to Love
Music by David Shire
Lyrics by Richard Maltby, Jr.
Baby 1983

East River Rhapsody
Music by Monty Norman
Lyrics by Julian More
The Moony Shapiro Songbook 1981

East Wind
Music by Sigmund Romberg
Lyrics by Oscar Hammerstein II
East Wind 1931

Easter Parade
Music and lyrics by Irving Berlin
As Thousands Cheer 1933

Berlin first used this music for his song "Smile and Show Your Dimple" in 1917.

The Easter Sunday Parade
Music and lyrics by George M. Cohan
The Merry Malones 1927

Easy Come, Easy Go
Music by Richard Rodgers
Lyrics by Raymond Jessel
I Remember Mama 1979

Easy Does It
Music by Jay Gorney
Lyrics by Jean and Walter Kerr
Touch and Go 1949

Easy Pickin's
Music by Jerome Kern
Lyrics by Anne Caldwell
Good Morning, Dearie 1921

Easy Street
Music by Charles Strouse
Lyrics by Martin Charnin
Annie 1977

Easy to Be Hard
Music by Galt MacDermot
Lyrics by Gerome Ragni and James Rado
Hair 1968

Easy to Be Lonely
Music by Peter Link
Lyrics by C.C. Courtney and Ragan Courtney
Earl of Ruston 1971

Easy to Love
Music and lyrics by Cole Porter
Born to Dance (1936) F

Porter wrote this for the show *Anything Goes*, to have been sung by William Gaxton. Gaxton didn't care for the song, however, and Porter wrote "All Through the Night" in its place. With a somewhat changed lyric, "Easy to Love" became part of the score of the film *Born to Dance*.

Easy to Remember

See "It's Easy to Remember"

Easy to Take
Music by Duke Ellington
Lyrics by Marshall Barer and Fred Tobias
Pousse-Café 1966

Eat a Little Something
Music and lyrics by Harold Rome
I Can Get It for You Wholesale 1962

Eat It
Music by Galt MacDermot
Lyrics by Gerome Ragni
Dude 1972

Eat Your Breakfast
Music by Don Elliott
Lyrics by James Costigan
The Beast in Me 1963

Eat Your Nice Lily, Unicorn
Music by Don Elliott
Lyrics by James Costigan
The Beast in Me 1963

Eating Mushrooms
Music and lyrics by Elizabeth Swados
Alice in Concert (OB) 1980

Ebenezer McAfee III
Music by Robert Emmett Dolan
Lyrics by Johnny Mercer
Foxy 1964

Eccch
Music by Mary Rodgers
Lyrics by Marshall Barer
The Mad Show (OB) 1966

Eccentricity
Music by Alberta Nichols
Lyrics by Mann Holiner
Rhapsody in Black 1931

The Echo of a Song
Music by Dave Stamper
Lyrics by Fred Herendeen
Orchids Preferred 1937

The Echo Song
Music and lyrics by Stephen Sondheim
A Funny Thing Happened on the Way to the Forum 1962

Dropped from production

Echo Song
Music by James Bredt
Lyrics by Edward Eager
The Happy Hypocrite (OB) 1968

The Echo Waltz
Music by Jim Wise
Lyrics by George Haimsohn
Dames at Sea (OB) 1968

Ecology
Music and lyrics by Jack Bussins
and Ellsworth Olin
Be Kind to People Week (OB) 1975

The Economic Situation
Music by Vernon Duke
Lyrics by Ira Gershwin
Ziegfeld Follies (1936)

Economics
Music by Kurt Weill
Lyrics by Alan Jay Lerner
Love Life 1948

Economics I
Music and lyrics by Harold Rome
Pins and Needles (OB) 1937

Eddie's Teddy
Music and lyrics by Richard O'Brien
The Rocky Horror Show 1975

Eddy-Mac
Music by Dave Stamper
Lyrics by Fred Herendeen
Orchids Preferred 1937

Edelweiss
Music by Sigmund Romberg
Lyrics by Clifford Grey
Louie the 14th 1925

Edelweiss
Music by Richard Rodgers
Lyrics by Oscar Hammerstein II
The Sound of Music 1959

This is the last song Rodgers and Hammerstein
wrote together.

Edgar Allan Poe
Music by Larry Grossman
Lyrics by Hal Hackady
Snoopy (OB) 1982

The Edinburgh Wriggle
Music by Jerome Kern
Lyrics by M. E. Rourke
La Belle Paree 1911

Educate Your Feet
Music by Milton Ager
Lyrics by Jack Yellen
John Murray Anderson's Almanac (1929)

An Educated Fool
Music by Victor Herbert
Lyrics by Harry B. Smith
Miss Dolly Dollars 1905

Eels Are a Girl's Best Friend
Music by Peter Link
Lyrics by Michael Cacoyannis
Lysistrata 1972

Eenie, Meenie, Minee, Mo
Music by Vernon Duke
Lyrics by John Latouche
The Lady Comes Across 1942

The Egg
Music and lyrics by Sherman Edwards
1776 1969

Eglamour
Music by Galt MacDermot
Lyrics by John Guare
Two Gentlemen of Verona 1971

Eight Day Week
Music and lyrics by Melvin Van Peebles
Don't Play Us Cheap 1972

Eight Little Gringos
Music by Harry Tierney
Lyrics by Joseph McCarthy
Rio Rita 1927

18 Days Ago
Music and lyrics by B.G. DeSylva, Cliff Friend
and George White
George White's Scandals (1929)

1898
Music by Sigmund Romberg
Lyrics by Rowland Leigh
My Romance 1948

Eighth Day
Music and lyrics by Eaton Magoon, Jr.
Heathen 1972

Eileen, Alanna Asthore
Music by Victor Herbert
Lyrics by Henry Blossom
Eileen 1917

Eileen Avourneen
Music by Henry Sullivan
Lyrics by John Murray Anderson
Thumbs Up! 1934

El Bravo
Music and lyrics by John Clifton
El Bravo! (OB) 1981

El Matador Terrifico
Music by Maria Grever
Lyrics by Raymond Leveen
Viva O'Brien 1941

El Sombrero
Music by Cy Coleman
Lyrics by Carolyn Leigh
Wildcat 1960

Elbow Room
Music by Jerome Kern
Lyrics by E.Y. Harburg
Can't Help Singing (1944) F

Eldorado
Music by Leonard Bernstein
Lyrics by Lillian Hellman
Candide 1956

Election Day
Music and lyrics by Noble Sissle and Eubie Blake
Shuffle Along 1921

Electric Blues
Music by Galt MacDermot
Lyrics by Gerome Ragni and James Rado
Hair 1968

Electric Prophet
Music by Galt MacDermot
Lyrics by Gerome Ragni
Dude 1972

Elegance
Music and lyrics by Jerry Herman
Hello, Dolly 1964

An Element of Doubt
Music by Sammy Fain
Lyrics by Howard Dietz
Ziegfeld Follies (1957)

The Elements
Music and lyrics by Tom Lehrer
Tomfoolery (OB) 1981

The Elements
Music by Elmer Bernstein
Lyrics by Don Black
Merlin 1983

Elena
Music and lyrics by Robert Wright
and George Forrest
Kean 1961

The Elephant Song
Music by John Kander
Lyrics by Fred Ebb
70, Girls, 70 1971

Elevator Song
Music and lyrics by Johnny Mercer
Top Banana 1951

Eleven Levee Street
Music by Sigmund Romberg
Lyrics by Oscar Hammerstein II
Sunny River 1941

Dropped from production

Eleven o'Clock Song
Music by Sammy Fain
Lyrics by Dan Shapiro
Ankles Aweigh 1955

The Eleventh Commandment
Music by Duke Ellington
Lyrics by Marshall Barer and Fred Tobias
Pousse-Café 1966

Eliot . . . Sylvia
Music by Alan Menken
Lyrics by Howard Ashman
God Bless You, Mr. Rosewater (OB) 1979

Elizabeth
Music by Robert Katscher
Lyrics by Irving Caesar
The Wonder Bar 1931

Elizabeth
Music by Lance Mulcahy
Lyrics by Paul Cherry
Park 1970

Elizabeth
Music by Richard Rodgers
Lyrics by Sheldon Harnick
Rex 1976

Elizabeth's Song
Music and lyrics by Clark Gesner
The Utter Glory of Morrissey Hall 1979

Ellen Roe
Music and lyrics by Johnny Burke
Donnybrook! 1961

The Eltinge Moorish Dance
Music by Kerry Mills
The Fascinating Widow 1911

Emaline
Music and lyrics by Donald Heywood
Black Rhythm 1936

Embassy Waltz
Music by Frederick Loewe
My Fair Lady 1956

Embrace Me
Music by Sigmund Romberg
Lyrics by Oscar Hammerstein II
East Wind 1931

Embraceable You
Music by George Gershwin
Lyrics by Ira Gershwin
Girl Crazy 1930

Written in 1928 for Ziegfeld's *Ming Toy*, a musical version of the play *East Is West*, which was to have starred Marilyn Miller but was abandoned. In the score of *Girl Crazy* two years later it was sung by (then unknown) Ginger Rogers.

Emelia
Music by Jimmy Horowitz
Lyrics by Leo Rost and Jimmy Horowitz
Marlowe 1981

The Emerald
Music by Heitor Villa-Lobos
Lyrics by Robert Wright and George Forrest
Magdalena 1948

Emmy Lou
Music by Norman Martin
Lyrics by Fred Ebb
Put It in Writing (OB) 1963

The Emperor Me
Music and lyrics by John Driver
Ride the Winds 1974

The Emperor's Thumb
Music and lyrics by Richard Rodgers
Androcles and the Lion (1967) TV

Empty Pockets Filled With Love
Music and lyrics by Irving Berlin
Mr. President 1962

Empty Spaces
Music and lyrics by Johnny Brandon
Love! Love! Love! (OB) 1977

En Route
Music by Harry Tierney
Lyrics by Joseph McCarthy
Kid Boots 1923

Enchanted Castle
Music and lyrics by Ida Hoyt Chamberlain
Enchanted Isle 1927

Enchanted Isle
Music and lyrics by Ida Hoyt Chamberlain
Enchanted Isle 1927

The Enchanted Train
Music by Jerome Kern
Lyrics by P.G. Wodehouse
Sitting Pretty 1924

The End?
Music and lyrics by Billy Barnes
The Billy Barnes People 1961

End of a Perfect Night
Music by Vernon Duke
Lyrics by E.Y. Harburg
Walk a Little Faster 1932

The End of a String
Music by George Gershwin
Lyrics by Ira Gershwin
Lady, Be Good! 1924

The End of My Race
Music by Mitch Leigh
Lyrics by William Alfred and Phyllis Robinson
Cry for Us All 1970

The Ends Justify the Means
Music by Jimmy Horowitz
Lyrics by Leo Rost and Jimmy Horowitz
Marlowe 1981

Engagement Ring
Music by Emil Gerstenberger and Carle Carlton
Lyrics by Howard Johnson
The Lace Petticoat 1927

An English Gentleman
Music by Lionel Monckton
Lyrics by Percy Greenbank
Our Miss Gibbs 1910

English Lesson
Music and lyrics by Noël Coward
Conversation Piece 1934

English Lido
Music and lyrics by Noël Coward
This Year of Grace 1928

English Rose
Music and lyrics by Billy Solly
Boy Meets Boy (OB) 1975

An English Teacher
Music by Charles Strouse
Lyrics by Lee Adams
Bye Bye Birdie 1960

The Englishman's Head
Music by George Lessner
Lyrics by Miriam Battista and Russell Maloney
Sleepy Hollow 1948

Enough
Music by Stan Harte, Jr.
Leaves of Grass (OB) 1971

Entire History of the World in Two Minutes and Thirty-Two Seconds
Music by Charles Strouse
Lyrics by Mike Stewart
Shoestring Revue (1955) (OB)

Entrance of Lucy James
Music and lyrics by Cole Porter
Born to Dance (1936) F

Entrance of "Montana"
Music and lyrics by Cole Porter
Mexican Hayride 1944

Entrance of Robin Hood
Music by Reginald De Koven
Lyrics by Harry B. Smith
Robin Hood 1891

Entrance of the Wedding Guests
Music by Victor Herbert
Lyrics by Henry Blossom
The Red Mill 1906

Entre-Nous
Music by Richard Lewine
Lyrics by Will B. Johnstone
Entre-Nous (OB) 1935

Entre-Nous
Music and lyrics by Harold Rome
Sing Out the News 1938

Ephraham Played Upon the Piano
Music and lyrics by Irving Berlin
Ziegfeld Follies of 1911

Epilogue
Music by Vernon Duke
Lyrics by Ted Fetter
The Show Is On 1936

Epilogue
Music by Jerry Bock
Lyrics by Sheldon Harnick
Fiddler on the Roof 1964

Epiphany
Music and lyrics by Stephen Sondheim
Sweeney Todd 1979

Equal Rights
Music by Victor Herbert
Lyrics by Henry Blossom
The Only Girl 1914

Equipment Song
Music by Al Carmines
Lyrics by Rosalyn Drexler
Home Movies (OB) 1964

'Erbie Fitch's Twitch
Music by Albert Hague
Lyrics by Dorothy Fields
Redhead 1959

Esmerelda
Music and lyrics by Cole Porter
Hands Up (1915)

This was Porter's first song in a Broadway show.
The unusual spelling of the title is deliberate to
rhyme with "Griselda."

Esther
Music by Vernon Duke
Lyrics by Sammy Cahn
Two's Company 1952

The Eternal Virgin
Music by Ron Steward and Neal Tate
Lyrics by Ron Steward
Sambo (OB) 1969

Ethel, Baby
Music and lyrics by Jerry Bock, George Weiss
and Larry Holofcener
Mr. Wonderful 1956

Eulogy
Music and lyrics by Gene Curty, Nitra Scharfman
and Chuck Strand
The Lieutenant 1975

Euphemism
Music by Mel Marvin
Lyrics by Christopher Durang
A History of the American Film 1978

Euphoria
Music and lyrics by Robin Remaily
Operation Sidewinder 1970

Eureka
Music by Jacques Offenbach (adapted by Robert
DeCormier)
Lyrics by E.Y. Harburg
The Happiest Girl in the World 1961

Eva, Beware of the City
Music by Andrew Lloyd Webber
Lyrics by Tim Rice
Evita 1979

Eve
Music by Jerry Bock
Lyrics by Sheldon Harnick
The Apple Tree 1966

Evelina
Music by Harold Arlen
Lyrics by E.Y. Harburg
Bloomer Girl 1944

Evelyn, What Do You Say?
Music by Richard Rodgers
Lyrics by Lorenz Hart
A Connecticut Yankee 1927

Even a Doctor Can Make a Mistake
Music and lyrics by Deed Meyer
'Toinette (OB) 1961

Even As You and I
Music by Ray Henderson
Lyrics by B.G. DeSylva and Lew Brown
George White's Scandals (1925)

Even As You and I
Music by Sammy Fain
Lyrics by Irving Kahal
Everybody's Welcome 1931

Even If I Say It Myself
Music by Hoagy Carmichael
Lyrics by Johnny Mercer
Walk With Music 1940

Evenin'
Music and lyrics by Frank Marcus
and Bernard Maltin
Bamboola 1929

Evening
Music by Michael Dansicker
Lyrics by Sarah Schlesinger
On The Swing Shift (OB) 1983

Evening Star
Music by George Gershwin
Lyrics by Ira Gershwin
Lady, Be Good! 1924

Dropped from production

Evening Star
Music by Edward A. Horan
Lyrics by Frederick Herendeen
All the King's Horses 1934

Ever and Ever Yours
Music by Cole Porter
Lyrics by T. Lawrason Riggs and Cole Porter
See America First 1916

Everlasting
Music by Jule Styne
Lyrics by Betty Comden and Adolph Green
Two on the Aisle 1951

Everlasting
Music by Galt MacDermot
Lyrics by William Dumaresq
The Human Comedy (OB) 1983

Evermore and a Day
Music and lyrics by Noël Coward
Bitter Sweet 1929

Every Animal Has Its Mate
Music by Alfred Nathan
Lyrics by George Oppenheimer
The Manhatters 1927

Every Bee Has a Bud of Its Own
Music by Harold Levey
Lyrics by Edgar Allan Woolf
Head Over Heels 1918

Every Bit of You
Music and lyrics by Kenneth Friede
and Adrian Samish
Hello, Paris 1930

Every Day
Music by William Daly
Lyrics by Arthur Jackson
For Goodness Sake 1922

Every Day
Music and lyrics by John Driver
Ride the Winds 1974

Every Day a Little Death
Music and lyrics by Stephen Sondheim
A Little Night Music 1973

Every Day Another Tune
Music and lyrics by Arthur Malvin
Sugar Babies 1979

Every Day for Four Years
Music by Scott MacLarty
Lyrics by Dorothy Chansky
The Brooklyn Bridge (OB) 1983

Every Day in Every Way
Music by Jerome Kern
Lyrics by Anne Caldwell
The Bunch and Judy 1922

Every Day Is a Holiday
Music by Fred Stamer
Lyrics by Gen Genovese
Buttrio Square 1952

Every Day Is Ladies' Day With Me
Music by Victor Herbert
Lyrics by Henry Blossom
The Red Mill 1906

Every Eve
Music by David Raksin
Lyrics by June Carroll
If the Shoe Fits 1946

Every Girl
Music by Jerome Kern
Lyrics by Anne Caldwell
Good Morning, Dearie 1921

Every Girl in All America
Music by Jerome Kern
Lyrics by Berton Braley
Toot-Toot! 1918

Every Girl in Venice
Music and lyrics by Maury Yeston
Nine 1982

Every Girl Must Have a Little Bull
Music by Al Goodman and J. Fred Coots
Lyrics by Clifford Grey
Gay Paree 1925

Every Girl Wants to Get Married
Music by John Kander
Lyrics by James Goldman, John Kander
and William Goldman
A Family Affair 1962

Every Little Movement (Has a Meaning All Its Own)
Music by Karl Hoschna
Lyrics by Otto Harbach
Madame Sherry 1910

Every Little Note
Music by Harry Archer
Lyrics by Harlan Thompson
Merry-Merry 1925

Every Little Nothing
Music and lyrics by Rick Besoyan
Little Mary Sunshine (OB) 1959

Every Little Thing You Do
Music by James F. Hanley
Lyrics by Gene Buck
No Foolin' 1926

Every Little While
Music by Jerome Kern
Lyrics by Otto Harbach
Men of the Sky (1931) F

Every Lover Must Meet His Fate
Music by Victor Herbert
Lyrics by Robert B. Smith
Sweethearts 1913

Every Man Is a Stupid Man
Music and lyrics by Cole Porter
Can-Can 1953

Every Night at Seven
See "Ev'ry Night at Seven"

Every Now and Then
Music and lyrics by Elizabeth Swados
Runaways 1978

Every Once in a While
Music and lyrics by Harold Rome
Destry Rides Again 1959

Every Street's a Boulevard in Old New York
Music by Jule Styne
Lyrics by Bob Hilliard
Hazel Flagg 1953

Every Thursday Night
Music and lyrics by Alan Menken
Real Life Funnies (OB) 1981

Every Time I Hear a Band Play
Music by Rudolf Friml
Lyrics by Gene Buck
Ziegfeld Follies of 1921

Every Time the Music Starts
Music and lyrics by Tom Savage
Musical Chairs 1980

Every Time You Danced With Me
Music by Harry Warren
Lyrics by Jerome Lawrence and Robert E. Lee
Shangri-La 1956

Everybod-ee Who's Anybod-ee
Music and lyrics by Cole Porter
Jubilee 1935

Everybody Calls Me by My Name
Music by Michael Valenti
Lyrics by Donald Driver
Oh, Brother 1981

Everybody Gets It in the End
Music by Paul Hoffert
Lyrics by David Secter
Get Thee to Canterbury (OB) 1969

Everybody Has a Right to Be Wrong
Music by Jimmy Van Heusen
Lyrics by Sammy Cahn
Skyscraper 1965

Everybody Leaves You
Music and lyrics by Buster Davis
Doctor Jazz 1975

Everybody Likes a College Girl
Music by Kerry Mills
Lyrics by S.M. Lewis
The Fascinating Widow 1911

Everybody Likes You
Music and lyrics by Bob Merrill
Carnival 1961

Everybody Loves a Tree
Music and lyrics by Walter Cool
Mackey of Appalachia (OB) 1965

Everybody Loves Leona
Music by Richard Rodgers
Lyrics by Stephen Sondheim
Do I Hear a Waltz? 1965
Dropped from production

Everybody Loves Louis
Music and lyrics by Stephen Sondheim
Sunday in the Park With George (OB) 1983

Everybody Loves Somebody
Music and lyrics by Harold Rome
Wish You Were Here 1952

Everybody Loves to Take a Bow
Music by Jule Styne
Lyrics by Bob Hilliard
Hazel Flagg 1953

Everybody Must Sometime Love Somebody
Music by Dave Stamper
Lyrics by Gene Buck
Ziegfeld Follies of 1914

Everybody Ought to Have a Maid
Music and lyrics by Stephen Sondheim
*A Funny Thing Happened on the Way
to the Forum* 1962

Everybody Rejoice
Music and lyrics by Charlie Smalls
The Wiz 1975

Everybody Says Don't
Music and lyrics by Stephen Sondheim
Anyone Can Whistle 1964

Everybody Shout
Music by Ford Dabney
Lyrics by Jo Trent
Rang-Tang 1927

Everybody Step
Music and lyrics by Irving Berlin
Music Box Revue (1st edition) 1921

Everybody Swat the Profiteer
Music by George Gershwin
Lyrics by Arthur Jackson
George White's Scandals (1920)

Everybody Today Is Turning On
Music by Cy Coleman
Lyrics by Michael Stewart
I Love My Wife 1977

Everybody Wants to Be in Show Business
Music and lyrics by Ray Golden, Bud Burtson
and Philip Charig
Catch a Star! 1955

Everybody's Gettin' Into the Act
Music and lyrics by Bob Ost
Everybody's Gettin' Into the Act (OB) 1981

Everybody's Happy in Jimtown
Music by Waller
Lyrics by Andy Razaf
Keep Shufflin' 1928

Everyday I Do a Little Something for the Lord
Music by Keith Hermann
Lyrics by Charlotte Anker and Irene Rosenberg
Onward Victoria 1980

Everyone Has Something to Hide
Music by Edward Thomas
Lyrics by Martin Charnin
Ballad for a Firing Squad (OB) 1968

Everyone Here Loves Kelly
Music by Moose Charlap
Lyrics by Eddie Lawrence
Kelly 1965

Everyone Who's Who's Who
Music by Harold Karr
Lyrics by Matt Dubey
Happy Hunting 1956

Everything
Music by Jerry Bock
Lyrics by Sheldon Harnick
The Rothschilds 1970

Everything Beautiful
Music and lyrics by Jay Livingston
and Ray Evans
Let It Ride 1961

Everything Beautiful
Music by Michael Leonard
Lyrics by Herbert Martin
The Yearling 1965

Everything Beautiful Happens at Night
Music by Harvey Schmidt
Lyrics by Tom Jones
110 in the Shade 1963

Everything But My Man
Music and lyrics by Serge Walter
Shady Lady 1933

Everything Comes to Those Who Wait
Music and lyrics by C. Jackson and James Hatch
Fly Blackbird (OB) 1962

Everything God Does Is Perfect
Music and lyrics by Al Carmines
The Evangelist (OB) 1982

Everything Happens to Me
Music by Hoagy Carmichael
Lyrics by Johnny Mercer
Walk With Music 1940

Everything I Have Is Yours
Music by Burton Lane
Lyrics by Harold Adamson
Dancing Lady (1933) F

Everything in America Is Ragtime
Music and lyrics by Irving Berlin
Stop! Look! Listen! 1915

Everything in the World Has a Place
Music and lyrics by Michael Brown
Different Times 1972

Everything in the World I Love
Music by Michael Leonard
Lyrics by Herbert Martin
The Yearling 1965

Everything Is All Right
Music by Vincent Youmans and Herbert Stothart
Lyrics by Otto Harbach and Oscar Hammerstein II
Wildflower 1923

Dropped from production

Everything Is Changed
Music by Galt MacDermot
Lyrics by William Dumaresq (OB)
The Human Comedy 1983

Everything Is High Yellow Now
Music by Gitz Rice
Lyrics by Paul Porter
Nic-Nax of 1926

Everything Is Possible in Life
Music by Murray Rumshinsky
Lyrics by Jacob Jacobs
The President's Daughter 1970

Everything Is Wonderful
Music by Ray Haney
Lyrics by Alfred Aiken
We're Civilized? (OB) 1962

Everything Leads Right Back to Love
Music by Sidney Lippman
Lyrics by Sylvia Dee
Barefoot Boy With Cheek 1947

Everything Needs Something
Music by Eliot Lawrence
Lyrics by Martin Charnin
La Strada 1969

Everything Reminds Me of You
Music and lyrics by Noble Sissle
and Eubie Blake
Shuffle Along 1921

Everything That's Gonna Be Has Been
Music by Richard Rodgers
Lyrics by Martin Charnin
Two by Two 1970

Dropped from production

Everything Was Perfect
Music by Charles Strouse
Lyrics by David Rogers
Charlie and Algernon 1980

Everything Will Happen for the Best
Music by Lewis E. Gensler
Lyrics by B.G. DeSylva
Queen High 1926

Everything You Hate Is Right Here
Music by Hank Beebe
Lyrics by Bill Heyer
*Tuscaloosa's Calling Me
But I'm Not Going!* (OB) 1975

Everything's Alright
Music by Andrew Lloyd Webber
Lyrics by Tim Rice
Jesus Christ Superstar 1971

Everything's at Home Except Your Wife
Music by Ivan Caryll
Lyrics by C.M.S. McLellan
Oh! Oh! Delphine 1912

Everything's Coming Up Roses
Music by Jule Styne
Lyrics by Stephen Sondheim
Gypsy 1959

First written, but never used, as "I'm Betwixt and
Between," with lyrics by Sammy Cahn for *High
Button Shoes* (1947).

Everything's Easy When You Know How
Music by Charles Strouse
Lyrics by Lee Adams
It's a Bird, It's a Plane, It's Superman 1966

Everything's Going to Be All Right
Music by Con Conrad
Lyrics by William B. Friedlander
Mercenary Mary 1925

Everything's Great
Music by Charles Strouse
Lyrics by Lee Adams
Golden Boy 1964

Everytime I Meet a Lady
Music by Louis A. Hirsch
Lyrics by Otto Harbach
Mary 1920

Everytime We Call It Quits
Music by Garry Sherman
Lyrics by Peter Udell
Amen Corner 1983

Everywhere
Music by Manning Sherwin
Lyrics by Harold Purcell
Under the Counter 1947

Everywhere I Go
Music by Rob Fremont
Lyrics by Doris Willens
Piano Bar (OB) 1978

Evil
Music and lyrics by Sydney Shaw
New Faces of 1968

Eviva
Music by Sigmund Romberg
Lyrics by Dorothy Donnelly
My Princess 1927

Evocation
Music by Meyer Kupferman
Lyrics by Paul Goodman
Jonah (OB) 1966

Evolution Papa
Music and lyrics by Buster Davis
Doctor Jazz 1975

Ev'ry Boy in Town's My Sweetheart
Music and lyrics by George M. Cohan
Billie 1928

Ev'ry Day a Holiday
Music and lyrics by Cole Porter
Du Barry Was a Lady 1939

Ev'ry Day (Comes Something Beautiful)
Music by Richard Rodgers
Lyrics by Martin Charnin
I Remember Mama 1979

Ev'ry Little While
Music by Rudolf Friml
Lyrics by P.G. Wodehouse and Clifford Grey
The Three Musketeers 1928

Ev'ry Night at Seven
Music by Burton Lane
Lyrics by Alan Jay Lerner
Royal Wedding (1951) F

Ev'ry Other Heartbeat
Music by John Green
Lyrics by George Marion, Jr.
Beat the Band 1942

Ev'ry Sunday Afternoon
Music by Richard Rodgers
Lyrics by Lorenz Hart
Higher And Higher 1940

Ev'ry Time
Music and lyrics by Hugh Martin and Ralph Blane
Best Foot Forward 1941

Ev'ry Time We Say Goodbye
Music and lyrics by Cole Porter
Seven Lively Arts 1944

Ev'rybody Knows I Love Somebody
Music by George Gershwin
Lyrics by Ira Gershwin
Rosalie 1928

Originally written as "Dance Alone With You"
for *Funny Face* (1927)

Ev'rybody Loves You
Music by Richard Rodgers
Lyrics by Lorenz Hart
I'd Rather Be Right 1937

Dropped from production

Ev'rybody Needs Somebody to Love
Music by George Fischoff
Lyrics by Verna Tomasson
The Prince and the Pauper (OB) 1963

Ev'rybody's Got a Home but Me
Music by Richard Rodgers
Lyrics by Oscar Hammerstein II
Pipe Dream 1955

Ev'rything I Love
Music and lyrics by Cole Porter
Let's Face It! 1941

Ev'rything I've Got
Music by Richard Rodgers
Lyrics by Lorenz Hart
By Jupiter 1942

Exactly Like You
Music by Jimmy McHugh
Lyrics by Dorothy Fields
Lew Leslie's International Revue 1930

The Examination
Music and lyrics by Elizabeth Swados
Alice in Concert (OB) 1980

Excelsior
Music by Stan Harte, Jr.
Leaves of Grass (OB) 1971

Exchange for Lovers
Music by Bronislaw Kaper (based on Chopin)
Lyrics by John Latouche
Polonaise 1945

Exchanges of Information
Music and lyrics by Robert Dennis, Peter Schickele
and Stanley Walden
Oh! Calcutta! 1969

Excuse for Song and Dance
Music by Harry Warren
Lyrics by Mort Dixon and Joe Young
The Laugh Parade 1931

Ex-Gigolo
Music by Mario Braggiotti
Lyrics by E. Y. Harburg
The Vanderbilt Revue 1930

The Exodus
Music by Walt Smith
Lyrics by Leon Uris
Ari 1971

The Exorcism
Music and lyrics by Hugh Martin and Timothy Gray
High Spirits 1964

Expect Things to Happen
Music and lyrics by Meredith Willson
Here's Love 1963

Experience
Music by Arthur Schwartz
Lyrics by Howard Dietz
Between the Devil 1937

The Exposé
Music and lyrics by Ronnie Britton
Greenwich Village Follies (OB) 1976

Express Yourself
Music by John Kander
Lyrics by Fred Ebb
Flora, the Red Menace 1965

Exquisite Moment
Music by Rudolf Friml
Lyrics by Rowland Leigh and John Shubert
Music Hath Charms 1934

Extra! Extra!
Music by Erich Wolfgang Korngold (based on
Jacques Offenbach)
Lyrics by Herbert Baker
Helen Goes to Troy 1944

Extra, Extra!
Music and lyrics by Irving Berlin
Miss Liberty 1949

Extraordinary
Music and lyrics by Stephen Schwartz
Pippin 1972

Eyeful of You
Music by J. Fred Coots
Lyrics by Al Dubin
White Lights 1927

The Eyes of Egypt
Music by Mel Marvin
Lyrics by Robert Montgomery
Green Pond (OB) 1977

Eyes So Dark and Luring
Music by Emmerich Kálmán
Lyrics by B.G. DeSylva
The Yankee Princess 1922

Eyes That Haunt Me
Music by Karl Hajos (based on Tchaikovsky)
Lyrics by Harry B. Smith
Natja 1925

Eyes That Love
Music by Sigmund Romberg
Lyrics by Harry B. Smith
The Love Call 1927

F

Fabulous Feet
Music by Henry Krieger
Lyrics by Robert Lorick
The Tap Dance Kid 1983

The Face Behind the Mask
Music by Victor Herbert
Lyrics by Robert B. Smith
The Debutante 1914

A Face in the Crowd
Music by Victor Young
Lyrics by Edward Heyman
Pardon Our French 1950

The Face of Love
Music by James Bredt
Lyrics by Edward Eager
The Happy Hypocrite (OB) 1968

The Face on the Dime
Music and lyrics by Harold Rome
Call Me Mister 1946

Face to Face
Music and lyrics by Robert Swerdlow
Love Me, Love My Children (OB) 1971

A Fact Can Be a Beautiful Thing
Music by Burt Bacharach
Lyrics by Hal David
Promises, Promises 1968

The Facts
Music by Norman Campbell
Lyrics by Donald Harron and Norman Campbell
Anne of Green Gables (OB) 1971

Facts of Life
Music by Maurice Yvain
Lyrics by Max and Nathaniel Lief
Luckee Girl 1928

Fade Out—Fade In
Music by Jule Styne
Lyrics by Betty Comden and Adolph Green
Fade Out—Fade In 1964

A Faded Rose
Music by Vincent Youmans
Lyrics by Oscar Hammerstein II
Rainbow 1928

Dropped from production

Fag Hag
Music and lyrics by Al Carmines
The Faggot (OB) 1973

Fair Land of Dreaming
Music by Edward Künneke
Lyrics by Harry B. Smith
The Love Song 1925

Fair Trade
Music by Richard Rodgers
Lyrics by Martin Charnin
I Remember Mama 1979

Fair Warning
Music by Jerry Bock
Lyrics by Sheldon Harnick
The Body Beautiful 1958

Fair Warning
Music and lyrics by Harold Rome
Destry Rides Again 1959

Fair Weather
Music and lyrics by Edward Pola
and Eddie Brandt
Woof, Woof 1929

Fair Weather Friends
Music by Frank Black
Lyrics by Gladys Shelley
The Duchess Misbehaves 1946

Fairy Tales
Music and lyrics by John Clifton
El Bravo! (OB) 1981

Fairy Tales
Music and lyrics by Gary Portnoy
and Judy Hart Angelo
Preppies (OB) 1983

Faith
Music and lyrics by Jack Lawrence
and Stan Freeman
I Had a Ball 1964

Faith, Hope and Charity
Music by Jerome Kern
Lyrics by Anne Caldwell
She's a Good Fellow 1919

Faith Is Such a Simple Thing
Music and lyrics by Al Carmines
Joan (OB) 1972

Faithless
Music by Morton Gould
Lyrics by Betty Comden and Adolph Green
Billion Dollar Baby 1945

Fake Your Way to the Top
Music by Henry Krieger
Lyrics by Tom Eyen
Dreamgirls 1981

Fall In!
Music by Gustav Luders
Lyrics by Frank Pixley
The Prince of Pilsen 1903

The Fall of Man
Music by Emmerich Kálmán
Lyrics by P.G. Wodehouse
The Riviera Girl 1917

Fallen Angels
Music and lyrics by Bob Goodman
Wild and Wonderful 1971

Fallin'
Music by Marvin Hamlisch
Lyrics by Carole Bayer Sager
They're Playing Our Song 1979

The Fallin'-Out-of-Love Rag
Music and lyrics by Skip Redwine and Larry Frank
Frank Merriwell, or Honor Challenged 1971

Falling
Music by Eubie Blake
Lyrics by Noble Sissle
Shuffle Along of 1952

Falling in Love
Music by Oscar Straus
Lyrics by Stanislaus Stange
The Chocolate Soldier 1909

Falling in Love
Music by Henry Sullivan
Lyrics by Earle Crooker
The Third Little Show 1931

Falling in Love
Music by Eubie Blake
Lyrics by Noble Sissle
Shuffle Along of 1933

Falling in Love With Love
Music by Richard Rodgers
Lyrics by Lorenz Hart
The Boys From Syracuse 1938

Also in the London revue *Up and Doing* (1940)
sung by Binnie Hale.

Falling Leaves
Ballet Music by Victor Herbert
Miss 1917

Falling off the Wagon
Music by Lewis E. Gensler
Lyrics by E.Y. Harburg
Ballyhoo 1932

Falling Out of Love Can Be Fun
Music and lyrics by Irving Berlin
Miss Liberty 1949

Falling Star
Music by Milton Ager
Lyrics by Jack Yellen
Rain or Shine 1928

Fame!
Music by Joseph Raposo
Lyrics by Erich Segal
Sing Muse! (OB) 1961

Fame
Music by Baldwin Bergersen
Lyrics by William Archibald
Rosa (OB) 1978

Fame Is a Phoney
Music by Edward A. Horan
Lyrics by Frederick Herendeen
All the King's Horses 1934

Family
Music by Henry Krieger
Lyrics by Tom Eyen
Dreamgirls 1981

Family Fugue
Music and lyrics by Leslie Bricusse
and Anthony Newley
Stop the World—I Want to Get Off 1962

Family of Man
Music and lyrics by John Phillips
Man on the Moon 1975

Family Reputation
Music and lyrics by Irving Berlin
The Cocoanuts 1925

The Family Tree
Music by Harry Tierney
Lyrics by Joseph McCarthy
Irene 1919

Family Trouble
Music by Leopold Antelme
Lyrics by Anthony Chalmers
Shoestring '57 (OB)

The Family Way
Music and lyrics by Harold Rome
I Can Get It for You Wholesale 1962

The Family's Ancient Tree
Music by Oscar Straus
Lyrics by Joseph W. Herbert
A Waltz Dream 1908

A Fam'ly We Will Be
Music by Richard Rodgers
Lyrics by Martin Charnin
I Remember Mama 1979

Dropped from production

The Famous Rabbi
Music by Menachem Zur
Lyrics by Herbert Appleman
Unfair to Goliath (OB) 1970

Fan Club Chant
Music by James Mundy
Lyrics by John Latouche
The Vamp 1955

Fan Tan Fannie
Music by Richard Rodgers
Lyrics by Oscar Hammerstein II
Flower Drum Song 1958

Fan the Flame
Music by Leon Carr
Lyrics by Earl Shuman
The Secret Life of Walter Mitty (OB) 1964

Fancy, Fancy
Music by Vernon Duke
Lyrics by Ira Gershwin
Ziegfeld Follies (1936)

Fancy Forgetting
Music and lyrics by Sandy Wilson
The Boy Friend 1954

Fancy Free
Music by Harold Arlen
Lyrics by Johnny Mercer
The Petty Girl (1950) F

Fancy Our Meeting
Music by Joseph Meyer and Philip Charig
Lyrics by Douglas Furber
Wake Up and Dream 1929

Fannette
Music by Jacques Brel
English lyrics by Eric Blau and Mort Shuman
*Jacques Brel Is Alive and Well
and Living in Paris* (OB) 1968

Fanny
Music and lyrics by Harold Rome
Fanny 1954

Fantasy
Music by Ronald Melrose
Lyrics by Bill Russell
Fourtune (OB) 1980

Far Away
Music by George Gershwin and Herbert Stothart
Lyrics by Otto Harbach and Oscar Hammerstein II
Song of the Flame 1925

Far Away and Long Ago
Music by Karl Hajos (based on Chopin)
Lyrics by Harry B. Smith
White Lilacs 1928

Far Away Island
Music and lyrics by Ed Tyler
Sweet Miani (OB) 1962

Far Far Away
Music and lyrics by Cole Porter
Leave It to Me 1938

A Far, Far Better Way
Music by Mary Rodgers
Lyrics by Martin Charnin
Hot Spot 1963

Far From Home
Music by John Morris
Lyrics by Gerald Freedman
A Time for Singing 1966

Far From the Home I Love
Music by Jerry Bock
Lyrics by Sheldon Harnick
Fiddler on the Roof 1964

Far Rockaway
Music and lyrics by Robert Larimer
King of the Whole Damn World (OB) 1962

Far Up the Hill
Music by Victor Herbert
Lyrics by David Stevens and Justin Huntly
McCarthy
The Madcap Duchess 1913

Faraway Boy
Music and lyrics by Frank Loesser
Greenwillow 1960

Fare Thee Well
Music by H. Maurice Jacquet
Lyrics by Preston Sturges
The Well of Romance 1930

Farewell
Music by Sigmund Romberg
Lyrics by Otto Harbach and Oscar Hammerstein II
The Desert Song 1926

Farewell
Music and lyrics by Stephen Sondheim
*A Funny Thing Happened on the Way
to the Forum* (1972 revival)

Farewell, Amanda
Music and lyrics by Cole Porter
Adam's Rib (1949) F

 This melody is the same as that for "So Long,
Samoa," a song Porter had written in 1940 during a
South Seas cruise.

Farewell, Family
Music by David Shire
Lyrics by Richard Maltby, Jr.
The Sap of Life (OB) 1961

Farewell, Farewell
Music by Jule Styne
Lyrics by Betty Comden and Adolph Green
Hallelujah, Baby! 1967

Farewell, My Lovely
Music by Arthur Schwartz
Lyrics by Howard Dietz
At Home Abroad 1935

Farewell to Auld Lang Syne
Music by Gerald Jay Markoe
Lyrics by Michael Colby
Charlotte Sweet (OB) 1982

Farewell With Love
Music by Eubie Blake
Lyrics by Noble Sissle
Shuffle Along of 1952

The Farmer and the Cowman
Music by Richard Rodgers
Lyrics by Oscar Hammerstein II
Oklahoma! 1943

Farmer Jacob Lay a-Snoring
Music by Sigmund Romberg
Lyrics by Dorothy Donnelly
The Student Prince 1924

Farmer Tan
Music and lyrics by Jim Swann
Pump Boys and Dinettes 1982

Farmer's Daughter
Music by Harold Arlen
Lyrics by E.Y. Harburg
Bloomer Girl 1944

A Farmer's Life
Music by Edward Künneke
Lyrics by Harry B. Smith
The Love Song 1925

Farming
Music and lyrics by Cole Porter
Let's Face It! 1941

The Farrell Girl
Music by Allan Roberts
Lyrics by Lester Lee
All for Love 1949

Fascinating Rhythm
Music by George Gershwin
Lyrics by Ira Gershwin
Lady, Be Good! 1924

The Fascinating Widow Waltz
Music by Kerry Mills
The Fascinating Widow 1911

Fascinating You
Music and lyrics by Benee Russell, Vincent Rose
and Charles and Harry Tobias
Earl Carroll's Sketch Book (1929)

A Fashion Girl
Music by Harold Arlen
Lyrics by E.Y. Harburg
Hooray for What! 1937

Fashions
Music by Robert Kessler
Lyrics by Lola Pergament
O Marry Me! (OB) 1961

Fast and Furious
Music by Harry Revel
Lyrics by Mack Gordon
Fast and Furious 1931

Fast Cars and Fightin' Women
Music and lyrics by Steve Allen
Sophie 1963

Fast Food
Music by Ted Simons
Lyrics by Elinor Guggenheimer
Potholes (OB) 1979

Fasten Your Seat Belts
Music by Charles Strouse
Lyrics by Lee Adams
Applause 1970

Faster than Sound
Music and lyrics by Hugh Martin
and Timothy Gray
High Spirits 1964

Fat City
Music and lyrics by Robert Swerdlow
Love Me, Love My Children (OB) 1971

Fatal Fascination
Music by Arthur Schwartz
Lyrics by Howard Dietz
Flying Colors 1932

Fate
Music and lyrics by Cole Porter
Gay Divorce 1932

Dropped from production. Has the same music as the refrain of "Salt Air"

Fate
Music and lyrics by Robert Wright
and George Forrest
Kismet 1953

Based on a theme from Borodin's Symphony No. 2 in B minor

Fate
Music by Victor Herbert
Lyrics by Robert B. Smith
The Debutante 1914

Fated to Be Mated
Music and lyrics by Cole Porter
Silk Stockings (film version, 1957)

Father and Son
Music by Jean Gilbert
Lyrics by Harry B. and Robert B. Smith
Modest Suzanne 1912

The Father of the Bride
Music by Harvey Schmidt
Lyrics by Tom Jones
I Do! I Do! 1966

Father of the Queen of Comic Opera
Music by Gustave Kerker
Lyrics by Hugh Morton
The Belle of New York 1897

A Father Speaks
Music and lyrics by Deed Meyer
'Toinette (OB) 1961

Father to Son
Music and lyrics by William Finn
March of the Falsettos (OB) 1981

Fatherhood Blues
Music by David Shire
Lyrics by Richard Maltby, Jr.
Baby 1983

Fatherland, Mother of the Band
Music by George Gershwin
Lyrics by Ira Gershwin
Pardon My English 1933

Dropped from production

Fathers and Mothers (and You and Me)
Music by Galt MacDermot
Lyrics by William Dumaresq
The Human Comedy (OB) 1983

Fathers and Sons
Music and lyrics by Stephen Schwartz
Working 1978

Father's Daughter
Music by Sol Kaplan
Lyrics by Edward Eliscu
The Banker's Daughter (OB) 1962

Father's Day
Music by Jimmy McHugh
Lyrics by Harold Adamson
As the Girls Go 1948

Fatty
Music by Gary Geld
Lyrics by Peter Udell
Angel 1978

Faucett Falls Fancy
Music by David Baker
Lyrics by Will Holt
Come Summer 1969

F.D.R. Jones
Music and lyrics by Harold Rome
Sing Out the News 1938

Also in the London revue *The Little Dog Laughed* (1939).

Fear
Music by Kurt Weill
Lyrics by Maxwell Anderson
Lost in the Stars 1949

Fear
Music by Jule Styne
Lyrics by Betty Comden and Adolph Green
Fade Out—Fade In 1964

Fear in My Heart
Music by Jerome Moross
Lyrics by Paul Peters and George Sklar
Parade (1935)

Feast of the Lanterns
Music by Sigmund Romberg
Lyrics by Harry B. Smith
Cherry Blossoms 1927

Feast on Me
Music and lyrics by Melvin Van Peebles
Don't Play Us Cheap 1972

Feather in a Breeze
Music by Sammy Fain
Lyrics by Irving Kahal
Everybody's Welcome 1931

Feather in My Shoe
Music by David Baker
Lyrics by Will Holt
Come Summer 1969

Feather Your Nest
Music by Harold Orlob
Lyrics by Harry L. Cort and George E. Stoddard
Listen, Lester 1918

February
Music and lyrics by Danny Shapiro, Jerry Seelen
and Lester Lee
The Lady Comes Across 1942

Fee Fi Fo Fum
Music by Helen Miller
Lyrics by Eve Merriam
Inner City 1971

Fee-Fie-Fo-Fum
Music by Arthur Schwartz
Lyrics by Albert Stillman
Virginia 1937

Feed Me (Git It)
Music by Alan Menken
Lyrics by Howard Ashman
Little Shop of Horrors (OB) 1982

Feel the Love
Music by Nancy Ford
Lyrics by Gretchen Cryer
*I'm Getting My Act Together and Taking It
on the Road* 1978

Feelin' Good
Music by Owen Murphy
Lyrics by Jack Yellen
Rain or Shine 1928

Feelin' Loved
Music by Gary Geld
Lyrics by Peter Udell
Angel 1978

Feeling Good
Music and lyrics by Leslie Bricusse
and Anthony Newley
*The Roar of the Greasepaint—The Smell
of the Crowd* 1965

Feeling I'm Falling
Music by George Gershwin
Lyrics by Ira Gershwin
Treasure Girl 1928

A Feeling in Your Heart
Music and lyrics by George M. Cohan
The Merry Malones 1927

Feeling Sentimental
Music by George Gershwin
Lyrics by Gus Kahn and Ira Gershwin
Show Girl 1929

Dropped from production

The Feeling We Once Had
Music and lyrics by Charlie Smalls
The Wiz 1975

Feelings
Music by Jerry Bock
Lyrics by Sheldon Harnick
The Apple Tree 1966

Feet
Music and lyrics by William Roy
The Penny Friend (OB) 1966

The Feet
Music by Seth Friedman
Lyrics by David L. Crane, Seth Friedman
and Marta Kauffman
Upstairs at O'Neal's (OB) 1982

Feet Do Yo' Stuff
Music by Jule Styne
Lyrics by Betty Comden and Adolph Green
Hallelujah, Baby! 1967

Feet on the Sidewalk (Head in the Sky)
Music and lyrics by Sam Lerner and Gerald Marks
My Dear Public 1943

A Fella With an Umbrella
Music and lyrics by Irving Berlin
Easter Parade (1948) F

Fellatio 101
Music and lyrics by Earl Wilson, Jr.
Let My People Come (OB) 1974

A Fellow and a Girl
Music by Jay Gorney
Lyrics by Edward Eliscu
Meet the People 1940

A Fellow Needs a Girl
Music by Richard Rodgers
Lyrics by Oscar Hammerstein II
Allegro 1947

The Fellow Who Might
Music by Leslie Stuart
Lyrics by J. Hickory Wood
Florodora 1900

Feminine-inity
Music and lyrics by Johnny Brandon
Who's Who, Baby? (OB) 1968

Femininity
Music and lyrics by Jay Livingston and Ray Evans
Oh Captain! 1958

Femme du Monde
Music by Harvey Schmidt
Lyrics by Tom Jones
Colette (OB) 1970

Fergus' Dilemma
Music by Elmer Bernstein
Lyrics by Don Black
Merlin 1983

Ferhuddled and Ferhexed
Music and lyrics by Howard Blankman
By Hex (OB) 1956

Fetish
Music and lyrics by Richard Adler
Kwamina 1961

Feudin' and Fightin'
Music by Burton Lane
Lyrics by Al Dubin and Lane
Laffing Room Only 1944

A Few Get Through
Music by Joe Ercole
Lyrics by Bruce Kluger
Ka-Boom (OB) 1980

Fiasco
Music by André Previn
Lyrics by Alan Jay Lerner
Coco 1969

Fickle Finger of Fate
Music and lyrics by Jack Lawrence
and Stan Freeman
I Had a Ball 1964

Fiddle Dee Dee
Music by Lehman Engel
Lyrics by Agnes Morgan
A Hero Is Born 1937

The Fiddler and the Fighter
Music by Jule Styne
Lyrics by Betty Comden and Adolph Green
Fade Out—Fade In 1964

The Fiddlers' Green
Music and lyrics by Ron Dante and Gene Allan
Billy 1969

Fidgety Feet
Music by George Gershwin
Lyrics by Ira Gershwin
Oh, Kay! 1926

Fie on Goodness
Music by Frederick Loewe
Lyrics by Alan Jay Lerner
Camelot 1960

The Field and Forest
Music by Gustav Luders
Lyrics by Frank Pixley
The Prince of Pilsen 1903

The Field of Cloth of Gold
Music by Richard Rodgers
Lyrics by Sheldon Harnick
Rex 1976

Fiesta
Music by Sigmund Romberg
Lyrics by Harry B. Smith
The Love Call 1927

Fiesta
Music by Ray Henderson
Lyrics by Lew Brown
Hot-Cha! 1932

Fiesta in Madrid
Music by Gerald Dolin
Lyrics by Edward J. Lambert
Smile at Me 1935

Fifteen Minutes a Day
Music and lyrics by Alexander Hill
Hummin' Sam 1933

Fifth Avenue
Music by Gordon Jenkins
Lyrics by Tom Adair
Along Fifth Avenue 1949

Fifty Million Years Ago
Music by Harvey Schmidt
Lyrics by Tom Jones
Celebration 1969

Fifty Percent
Music by Billy Goldenberg
Lyrics by Alan and Marilyn Bergman
Ballroom 1978

The Fig Leaves Are Falling
Music by Albert Hague
Lyrics by Allen Sherman
The Fig Leaves Are Falling 1969

The Fight
Music by Charles Strouse
Lyrics by Lee Adams
Golden Boy 1964

Fight Fiercely, Harvard
Music and lyrics by Tom Lehrer
Tomfoolery (OB) 1981

Fight Over Me
Music by Vincent Youmans
Lyrics by Otto Harbach
No, No, Nanette 1925

The Fight Song
Music by Charles Strouse
Lyrics by Lee Adams
All American 1962

Fighting for Pharaoh
Music and lyrics by Micki Grant
Don't Bother Me, I Can't Cope (OB) 1972

Fill In the Words
Music by Marvin Hamlisch
Lyrics by Carole Bayer Sager
They're Playing Our Song 1979

Fill Up Your Life With Sunshine
Music by David Shire
Lyrics by Richard Maltby, Jr.
The Sap of Life (OB) 1961

Filth
Music by Charles Strouse
Lyrics by Lee Adams
Bring Back Birdie 1981

Final Report
Music and lyrics by Gene Curty, Nitra Scharfman
and Chuck Strand
The Lieutenant 1975

Finally
Music and lyrics by Beth Lawrence
and Norman Thalheimer
Marilyn 1983

Find a Good Time
Music by Carlton Kelsey and Maury Rubens
Lyrics by Clifford Grey
Sky High 1925

Find Me a Hero
Music and lyrics by Elizabeth Swados
Runaways 1978

Find Me a Primitive Man
Music and lyrics by Cole Porter
Fifty Million Frenchmen 1929

Find My Way Alone
Music by Clinton Ballard
Lyrics by Carolyn Richter
The Ballad of Johnny Pot (OB) 1971

Find Someone to Love
Music and lyrics by Johnny Brandon
Love! Love! Love! (OB) 1977

Find Your Own Cricket
Music and lyrics by Stan Freeman
and Franklin Underwood
Lovely Ladies, Kind Gentlemen 1970

Find Yourself a Man
Music by Jule Styne
Lyrics by Bob Merrill
Funny Girl 1964

Find Yourself Something to Do
Music by Julian Slade
Lyrics by Dorothy Reynolds and Julian Slade
Salad Days (OB) 1958

Finding Words for Spring
Music and lyrics by Marian Grudeff
and Raymond Jessel
Baker Street 1965

Fine and Dandy
Music by Kay Swift
Lyrics by Paul James
Fine and Dandy 1930

Fine Feathers
Music by Mann Holiner
Lyrics by Alberta Nichols
Gay Paree 1926

Fine for the Shape I'm In
Music by Gary William Friedman
Lyrics by Will Holt
Taking My Turn (OB) 1983

A Fine Romance
Music by Jerome Kern
Lyrics by Dorothy Fields
Swing Time (1936) F

Fine, Thank You, Fine
Music by David Baker
Lyrics by Will Holt
Come Summer 1969

Fine Words and Fancy Phrases
Music and lyrics by Norman Dean
Autumn's Here (OB) 1966

A Fine Young Man
Music and lyrics by Richard Rodgers
Androcles and the Lion (1967) TV

The Finger Song
Music by Al Carmines
Lyrics by Maria Irene Fornes
Promenade (OB) 1969

Fingers and Toes
Music by Gary Geld
Lyrics by Peter Udell
Angel 1978

Fini
Music and lyrics by Richard Adler and Jerry Ross
John Murray Anderson's Almanac (1953)

Finishing the Hat
Music and lyrics by Stephen Sondheim
Sunday in the Park With George (OB) 1983

Fioretta
Music and lyrics by G.Romilli
Fioretta 1929

Fire Belles' Gallop
Music by Richard Lewine
The Fireman's Flame (OB) 1937

The Fire in My Heart
Music by Steve Jankowski
Lyrics by Kenny Morris
Francis (OB) 1982

Fireflies
Music by Baldwin Bergersen
Lyrics by William Archibald
The Crystal Heart (OB) 1960

The Fireman's Bride
Music by Sigmund Romberg
Lyrics by Dorothy Fields
Up in Central Park 1945

The Fireman's Flame
Music by Richard Lewine
Lyrics by Ted Fetter
The Fireman's Flame (OB) 1937

Fireman's Song
Music by Stanley Silverman
Lyrics by Tom Hendry
Doctor Selavy's Magic Theatre (OB) 1972

A Firestorm Consuming Indianapolis
Music by Alan Menken
Lyrics by Howard Ashman
God Bless You, Mr. Rosewater (OB) 1979

Fireworks
Music by Harry Ruby
Lyrics by Bert Kalmar
Top Speed 1929

Fireworks
Music by Jule Styne
Lyrics by Betty Comden and Adolph Green
Do Re Mi 1960

Firing of Jimmy
Music by Henry Krieger
Lyrics by Tom Eyen
Dreamgirls 1981

The First
Music by Bob Brush
Lyrics by Martin Charnin
The First 1981

First Act Crisis
Music by Susan Hulsman Bingham
Lyrics by Myrna Lamb
Mod Donna (OB) 1970

First Campaign Song
Music and lyrics by Don Tucker
Red, White and Maddox 1969

First Class Number One Bum
Music by Jule Styne
Lyrics by Sammy Cahn
Look to the Lilies 1970

The First Day of May
Music by Jerome Kern
Lyrics by P.G. Wodehouse
Oh, Boy! 1917

First Impression
Music by Harold Rome
Lyrics by Charles Friedman and Harold Rome
Pins and Needles (OB) 1937

The First Lady
Music and lyrics by Irving Berlin
Mr. President 1962

First Lady and First Gent
Music by George Gershwin
Lyrics by Ira Gershwin
Let 'Em Eat Cake 1933

Dropped from production

The First Lady of the Land
Music by Michael H. Cleary
Lyrics by Max and Nathaniel Lief
Shoot the Works 1931

First, Last, and Only
Music by Harold Levey
Lyrics by Owen Murphy
Rainbow Rose 1926

The First Last Supper
Music by Scott Killian and Kim D. Sherman
Lyrics by Kenneth Robins, Scott Killian
and Kim D. Sherman
Lenny and the Heartbreakers (OB) 1983

The First Man I Kiss
Music by Sigmund Romberg
Lyrics by Oscar Hammerstein II
The New Moon 1928

Dropped from production

First Mate Martin
Music by Jerome Kern
Lyrics by Oscar Hammerstein II
Sweet Adeline 1929

First Prize at the Fair
Music by Arthur Schwartz
Lyrics by Howard Dietz
Inside U.S.A. 1948

The First Rose of Summer
Music by Jerome Kern
Lyrics by Anne Caldwell
She's a Good Fellow 1919

The First Spring Day
Music by Howard Jackson
Lyrics by Edward Eliscu
Tattle Tales 1933

First Thing in the Morning
Music and lyrics by Donald Heywood
Blackberries of 1932

First Thing Monday Mornin'
Music by Gary Geld
Lyrics by Peter Udell
Purlie 1970

The First Thing You Know
Music by André Previn
Lyrics by Alan Jay Lerner
Paint Your Wagon (film version, 1969)

The First Time
Music by John Kander
Lyrics by Fred Ebb
Zorba 1968

The First Time for Me
Music by Ray Henderson
Lyrics by B.G. DeSylva and Lew Brown
Flying High 1930

First Time I Saw You
Music and lyrics by Stephen H. Lemberg
Jazzbo Brown 1980

The First Time I Spoke of You
Music by Ernest G. Schweikert
Lyrics by Frank Reardon
Rumple 1957

Fish
Music by Arthur Schwartz
Lyrics by Howard Dietz
A Bell For Adano (1956) TV

Fish Song
Music by Frank Fields
Lyrics by Armand Aulicino
The Shoemaker and the Peddler (OB) 1960

Fish Soup Song
Music by Baldwin Bergersen
Lyrics by William Archibald
Rosa (OB) 1978

Fisherman's Prayer
Music and lyrics by Jim Swann
Pump Boys and Dinettes 1982

Fisherman's Wharf
Music by Vernon Duke
Lyrics by Howard Dietz
Sadie Thompson 1944

Five A.M.
Music by Vernon Duke
Lyrics by Ira Gershwin
Ziegfeld Follies (1936)

Five Daughters
Music by Glenn Paxton
Lyrics by Robert Goldman and George Weiss
First Impressions 1959

Five-Foot-Two
Music by William B. Kernell
Lyrics by Dorothy Donnelly
Hello, Lola 1926

Five Growing Boys
Music by Larry Grossman
Lyrics by Hal Hackady
Minnie's Boys 1970

Five Hundred Million
Music and lyrics by Cole Porter
Red, Hot and Blue! 1936

Five Lovely Ladies
Music and lyrics by Bill and Patti Jacob
Jimmy 1969

Five Minutes of Spring
Music by Jay Gorney
Lyrics by E.Y. Harburg
Americana (1932)

Five Minutes of Spring
Music by Jacques Offenbach (adapted by Robert
DeCormier)
Lyrics by E.Y. Harburg
The Happiest Girl in the World 1961

Five More Minutes in Bed
Music by Harry Revel
Lyrics by Arnold B. Horwitt
Are You With It? 1945

Five O'Clock
Music by Arthur Schwartz
Lyrics by Howard Dietz
Between the Devil 1937

Five O'Clock
Music by Bernie Wayne
Lyrics by Ben Raleigh
Two for Tonight (OB) 1939

Five O'Clock Tea
Music and lyrics by Irving Berlin
The Cocoanuts 1925

Five Shots of Whiskey
Music by Moose Charlap
Lyrics by Norman Gimbel
The Conquering Hero 1961

The Five-Step
Music by Ray Henderson
Lyrics by B.G. DeSylva and Lew Brown
Manhattan Mary 1927

Five Thousand Francs
Music and lyrics by Ralph Benatzky
Meet My Sister 1930

Five Zeros
Music by Cy Coleman
Lyrics by Betty Comden and Adolph Green
On the Twentieth Century 1978

Fixed for Life
Music by Randall Thompson
Lyrics by Agnes Morgan
The Grand Street Follies (1926) (OB)

Fixin' for a Long Cold Winter
Music and lyrics by Jack Lawrence and Don Walker
Courtin' Time 1951

Fizkin and Pickwick
Music by Cyril Ornadel
Lyrics by Leslie Bricusse
Pickwick 1965

The Flag That Flies Above Us
Music by Sigmund Romberg
Lyrics by Dorothy Donnelly
The Student Prince 1924

Flahooley
Music by Sammy Fain
Lyrics by E.Y. Harburg
Flahooley 1951

Flair
Music by David Shire
Lyrics by Richard Maltby, Jr.
Starting Here, Starting Now (OB) 1977

The Flame
Music by John Kander
Lyrics by Fred Ebb
Flora, the Red Menace 1965

Flamenco
Music by Arthur Schwartz
Lyrics by Howard Dietz
Revenge With Music 1934

Flamenco
Music by Henry Sullivan
Lyrics by Earle Crooker
Thumbs Up! 1934

Flaming Agnes
Music by Harvey Schmidt
Lyrics by Tom Jones
I Do! I Do! 1966

Flaming Youth
Music by Ray Henderson
Lyrics by B.G. DeSylva and Lew Brown
Good News 1927

Flaming Youth
Music by Albert Selden
Lyrics by Burt Shevelove
Small Wonder 1948

Flannel Petticoat Gal
Music by Vincent Youmans and Herbert Stothart
Lyrics by Oscar Hammerstein II and William Cary Duncan
Mary Jane McKane 1923

Flap-a-Doodle
Music by Jerome Kern
Lyrics by Anne Caldwell and Otto Harbach
Criss-Cross 1926

A Flapper Too
Music by Lewis E. Gensler and Milton Schwarzwald
Lyrics by George S. Kaufman, Marc Connelly and Ira Gershwin
Be Yourself 1924

Flash Bang Wallop
Music and lyrics by David Heneker
Half a Sixpence 1965

A Flat in Montmartre
Music by Maurice Yvain
Lyrics by Max and Nathaniel Lief
Luckee Girl 1928

Flattery
Music and lyrics by Harold Rome
Wish You Were Here 1952

Flattery
Music by Moose Charlap
Lyrics by Norman Gimbel
Whoop-Up 1958

The Flatulent Ballad
Music by Mischa and Wesley Portnoff
Lyrics by Donagh MacDonagh
Happy as Larry 1950

The Flesh Failures
Music by Galt MacDermot
Lyrics by Gerome Ragni and James Rado
Hair 1968

Fletcher's American Chocolate Choral Society
Music by George Gershwin
Lyrics by Ira Gershwin
Strike Up the Band (1930)

Flexatone
Music by Alfred Goodman, Maury Rubens and J. Fred Coots
Lyrics by Clifford Grey
Artists and Models (1925)

The Flickers
Music by James Mundy
Lyrics by John Latouche
The Vamp 1955

Flim Flam Flooey
Music by Jack Holmes
Lyrics by Bill Conklin and Bob Miller
O Say Can You See! (OB) 1962

Flings
Music and lyrics by Bob Merrill
New Girl in Town 1957

Flip Religion
Music and lyrics by Elizabeth Swados
Dispatches (OB) 1979

Flippin' Out
Music and lyrics by Tom Sankey
The Golden Screw (OB) 1967

Flirting
Music by Victor Herbert
Lyrics by Henry Blossom
The Princess Pat 1915

Float Me Down Your Pipeline
Music and lyrics by Antonia
Operation Sidewinder 1970

Floating Along
Music by Vincent Youmans
Lyrics by Anne Caldwell
Oh, Please! 1926

Dropped from production

Floating Thru the Air
Music by Arthur Schwartz
Lyrics by Henry Myers
The New Yorkers 1927

Floozies
Music by Claibe Richardson
Lyrics by Kenward Elmslie
The Grass Harp 1971

Floretta
Music by Victor Herbert
Lyrics by Glen MacDonough
Babes in Toyland 1903

Florida by the Sea
Music and lyrics by Irving Berlin
The Cocoanuts 1925

Florida, the Moon and You
Music by Rudolf Friml
Lyrics by Gene Buck
No Foolin' 1926

Florrie Was a Flapper
Music by Herman Finck
Lyrics by Arthur Wimperis
The Girl From Utah 1914

Flotsam and Jetsam
Music by George Kleinsinger
Lyrics by Joe Darion
Shinbone Alley 1957

A Flower
Music by Al Carmines
Lyrics by Maria Irene Fornes
Promenade (OB) 1969

Flower Child
Music by Norman Curtis
Lyrics by Patricia Taylor Curtis
Walk Down Mah Street! (OB) 1968

The Flower Garden of My Heart
Music by Richard Rodgers
Lyrics by Lorenz Hart
Pal Joey 1940

The Flower Song
Music by Victor Young
Lyrics by Edward Heyman
Pardon Our French 1950

Flower Song
Music and lyrics by John Driver
Ride the Winds 1974

The Flowers
Music and lyrics by Hal Hester
and Danny Apolinar
Your Own Thing (OB) 1968

Flowers A-Blooming So Gay
Music by Leslie Stuart
Lyrics by Ernest Boyd-Jones
Florodora 1900

Flowing to the Sea
Music and lyrics by Oscar Brown, Jr.
Joy (OB) 1970

Flubby Dub, the Cave Man
Music by Jerome Kern
Lyrics by P.G. Wodehouse
Oh, Boy! 1917

Flutterby Baby
Music by Morris Hamilton
Lyrics by Grace Henry
Earl Carroll's Vanities (1928)

Fly Away
Music and lyrics by Deed Meyer
'Toinette (OB) 1961

Fly Away
Music and lyrics by Ann Harris
Sky High (OB) 1979

Fly Blackbird
Music and lyrics by C. Jackson and James Hatch
Fly Blackbird (OB) 1962

Fly, Butterfly
Music by Ray Henderson
Lyrics by B.G. DeSylva and Lew Brown
George White's Scandals (1925)

Fly by Night
Music by Arthur Schwartz
Lyrics by Howard Dietz
Between the Devil 1937

Fly, Little Heart
Music by Jerry Bock
Lyrics by Larry Holofcener
Catch a Star! 1955

Fly Now, Pay Later
Music by Vernon Duke
Lyrics by Ogden Nash
The Littlest Revue (OB) 1956

Flying Down to Rio
Music by Vincent Youmans
Lyrics by Edward Eliscu and Gus Kahn
Flying Down to Rio (1933) F

Flying High
Music by Ray Henderson
Lyrics by B.G. DeSylva and Lew Brown
Flying High 1930

Flying Milk and Runaway Plates
Music by Gary William Friedman
Lyrics by Will Holt
The Me Nobody Knows (OB) 1970

The Fog and the Grog
Music and lyrics by Robert Wright
and George Forrest
Kean 1961

Fogarty the Great
Music by Jimmy Van Heusen
Lyrics by Johnny Burke
Nellie Bly 1946

A Foggy Day (in London Town)
Music by George Gershwin
Lyrics by Ira Gershwin
A Damsel in Distress (1937) F

Fol de Rol
Music by Louis A. Hirsch
Lyrics by Harold Atteridge
The Whirl of Society 1912

Folies Bergeres
Music and lyrics by Maury Yeston
Nine 1982

The Folk Song Army
Music and lyrics by Tom Lehrer
Tomfoolery (OB) 1981

Folk Songs
Music by Heinrich Reinhardt
Lyrics by Robert B. Smith
The Spring Maid 1910

The Folks Who Live on the Hill
Music by Jerome Kern
Lyrics by Oscar Hammerstein II
High, Wide and Handsome (1937) F

The Follies Salad
Music and lyrics by Gene Buck
and Dave Stamper
Ziegfeld Follies of 1919

Follow Him
Music by Paul Klein
Lyrics by Fred Ebb
Morning Sun (OB) 1963

Follow in our Footsteps
Music and lyrics by Richard Rodgers
Androcles and the Lion (1967) TV

Follow Master
Music by Joseph Meyer
Lyrics by Edward Eliscu
Lady Fingers 1929

Follow Me
Music by Emmerich Kálmán
Lyrics by C.C S. Cushing and E.P. Heath
Sari 1914

Follow Me
Music by Frederick Loewe
Lyrics by Alan Jay Lerner
Camelot 1960

Follow Me up the Stairs
Music by Duke Ellington
Lyrics by Marshall Barer and Fred Tobias
Pousse-Café 1966

Follow On
Music by Richard Rodgers
Lyrics by Lorenz Hart
Betsy 1926

Follow the Drum
Music by George Gershwin
Lyrics by Ira Gershwin
Rosalie 1928

Added to show during Broadway run

Follow the Fold
Music and lyrics by Frank Loesser
Guys and Dolls 1950

Follow the Girls
Music by Philip Charig
Lyrics by Dan Shapiro and Milton Pascal
Follow the Girls 1944

Follow the Girls Around
Music by Ivan Caryll
Lyrics by Anne Caldwell
Jack O' Lantern 1917

Follow the Guide
Music by Raymond Hubbell
Lyrics by Anne Caldwell
Yours Truly 1927

Follow the Lamb
Music by Jule Styne
Lyrics by Sammy Cahn
Look to the Lilies 1970

Follow the Leader Jig
Music and lyrics by Irving Berlin
Miss Liberty 1949

Follow the Leader Septet
Music by Sol Berkowitz
Lyrics by James Lipton
Nowhere to Go But Up 1962

Follow the Minstrel Band
Music by George Gershwin
Lyrics by Gus Kahn and Ira Gershwin
Show Girl 1929

Follow the Rainbow
Music by Galt MacDermot
Lyrics by John Guare
Two Gentlemen of Verona 1971

Follow the Rajah
Music by Sigmund Romberg
Lyrics by Arthur Wimperis
Louie the 14th 1925

Follow the Sun to the South
Music by Sigmund Romberg
Lyrics by Dorothy Donnelly
My Princess 1927

Follow the Yellow Brick Road
Music by Harold Arlen
Lyrics by E. Y. Harburg
The Wizard of Oz (1939) F

Follow Thru
Music by Ray Henderson
Lyrics by B.G. DeSylva and Lew Brown
Follow Thru 1929

Follow Your Heart
Music by Albert Hague
Lyrics by Arnold B. Horwitt
Plain and Fancy 1955

Follow Your Heart
Music by Kenneth Jacobson
Lyrics by Rhoda Roberts
Show Me Where the Good Times Are (OB) 1970

Follow Your Star
Music by Alfred Goodman, Maury Rubens
and J. Fred Coots
Lyrics by Clifford Grey
Artists and Models (1925)

Following in Father's Footsteps
Music by Harry Ruby
Lyrics by Bert Kalmar
The Five o'Clock Girl 1927

Following the Sun Around
Music by Harry Tierney
Lyrics by Joseph McCarthy
Rio Rita 1927

Fond of the Ladies
Music by Victor Herbert
Lyrics by James O'Dea
The Lady of the Slipper 1912

Fond of You
Music by Lewis E. Gensler
Lyrics by B.G. DeSylva
Captain Jinks 1925

Food for Scandal
Music by Richard Rodgers
Lyrics by Lorenz Hart
Fools for Scandal (1938) F

Food for Thought
Music by Heitor Villa-Lobos
Lyrics by Robert Wright and George Forrest
Magdalena 1948

Food for Thought
Music by Donald Swann
Lyrics by Michael Flanders
At the Drop of Another Hat 1966

Food, Glorious Food
Music and lyrics by Lionel Bart
Oliver! 1963

Food Is Love
Music by Susan Hulsman Bingham
Lyrics by Myrna Lamb
Mod Donna (OB) 1970

Fool for Luck
Music by Morgan Lewis
Lyrics by Nancy Hamilton
Two for the Show 1940

Fool Meets Fool
Music by Richard Rodgers
Lyrics by Lorenz Hart
By Jupiter 1942

Dropped from production

A Fool There Was
Music and lyrics by Cole Porter
Rosalie (1937) F

Dropped from film

Foolin' Ourselves
Music and lyrics by Billy Barnes
The Billy Barnes Revue 1959

Fooling Around With Love
Music by James P. Johnson
Lyrics by Flournoy Miller
Sugar Hill 1931

Foolish Face
Music by Arthur Schwartz
Lyrics by Howard Dietz
The Second Little Show 1930

The Foolish Gardener
Music by Victor Herbert
Lyrics by Glen MacDonough
Algeria 1908

Foolish Heart
Music by Kurt Weill
Lyrics by Ogden Nash
One Touch of Venus 1943

Foolish Wives
Music by Edward Künneke
Lyrics by Clifford Grey
Mayflowers 1925

Foolishness
Music by Jerome Kern
Lyrics by Harry B. Smith
Ninety in the Shade 1915

Fools Fall in Love
Music and lyrics by Irving Berlin
Louisiana Purchase 1940

Fool's Gold
Music and lyrics by Oscar Brand and Paul Nassau
A Joyful Noise 1966

Footlight Walk
Music and lyrics by Harry Denny
Footlights 1927

Footloose Youth and Fancy Free
Music and lyrics by Peter Link and C.C. Courtney
Salvation (OB) 1969

Footwork
Music by Ray Henderson
Lyrics by B.G. DeSylva and Lew Brown
Hold Everything! 1928

For a Girl Like You
Music by Harold Orlob
Lyrics by Harry L. Cort and George E. Stoddard
Listen, Lester 1918

For a Girl Like You
Music by Gitz Rice
Lyrics by Joe Goodwin
Nic-Nax of 1926

For a Quarter
Music by Lester Lee
Lyrics by Jerry Seelen
Star and Garter 1942

For Better or for Worse
Music by Victor Herbert
Lyrics by Henry Blossom
The Princess Pat 1915

For Better or Worse
Music by Arthur Schwartz
Lyrics by Howard Dietz
Jennie 1963

For Critics Only
Music by Shelley Mowell
Lyrics by Mike Stewart
Shoestring '57 (OB)

For Ever
Music and lyrics by Peter Link
and C.C. Courtney
Salvation (OB) 1969

For Every Fish
Music by Harold Arlen
Lyrics by E.Y. Harburg
Jamaica 1957

For Every Man There's a Woman
Music by Harold Arlen
Lyrics by Leo Robin
Casbah (1948) F

For Four Hundred Years
Music by Norman Curtis
Lyrics by Patricia Taylor Curtis
Walk Down Mah Street! (OB) 1968

For I'm in Love
Music and lyrics by Arthur Brander
The Seventh Heart 1927

For I'm in Love Again
Music by Mischa Spoliansky
Lyrics by Billy Rose and Mort Dixon
Sweet and Low 1930

For in the Field
Music by Gustave Kerker
Lyrics by Hugh Morton
The Belle of New York 1897

For Jupiter and Greece
Music by Richard Rodgers
Lyrics by Lorenz Hart
By Jupiter 1942

For Love
Music and lyrics by Marc Blitzstein
Juno 1959

For Love or Money
Music by Harold Karr
Lyrics by Matt Dubey
Happy Hunting 1956

For My Own
Music and lyrics by Johnny Burke
Donnybrook! 1961

For No Rhyme or Reason
Music and lyrics by Cole Porter
You Never Know 1938

For Once in My Life
Music by Paul Klein
Lyrics by Fred Ebb
Morning Sun (OB) 1963

For Once in Your Life
Music and lyrics by Walter Marks
Golden Rainbow 1968

For Our Sake
Music by Albert Hague
Lyrics by Allen Sherman
The Fig Leaves Are Falling 1969

For Poland
Music and lyrics by Jerry Herman
The Grand Tour 1979

For Someone I Love
Music by Ted Snyder
Lyrics by Benny Davis
Earl Carroll's Sketch Book (1929)

For Sweet Charity
Music and lyrics by Bob Merrill
Take Me Along 1959

For Sweet Charity's Sake
Music by Ray Henderson
Lyrics by B.G. DeSylva and Lew Brown
Hold Everything! 1928

For the First Time
Music by Arthur Schwartz
Lyrics by Howard Dietz
The Gay Life 1961

For the Good of Brotherhood
Music by Steve Jankowski
Lyrics by Kenny Morris
Francis (OB) 1982

For the Harvest Safely Gathered
Music and lyrics by Norman Dean
Autumn's Here (OB) 1966

For the Life of Me
Music by Arthur Schwartz
Lyrics by Ira Gershwin
Park Avenue 1946

For the Papa
Music by Emile Berté and Maury Rubens
Lyrics by J. Keirn Brennan
Music in May 1929

For the Rest of My Life
Music by Albert Hague
Lyrics by Allen Sherman
The Fig Leaves Are Falling 1969

For the Sake of Art
Music by Robert Stolz
Lyrics by Robert Sour
Mr. Strauss Goes to Boston 1945

For the Sake of Lexington
Music by Sam Stept
Lyrics by Lew Brown and Charles Tobias
Yokel Boy 1939

For the Twentieth Time We'll Drink
Music by Gustave Kerker
Lyrics by Hugh Morton
The Belle of New York 1897

For Them
Music and lyrics by Craig Carnelia
Is There Life After High School? 1982

For Two Minutes
Music and lyrics by Mel Mandel
and Norman Sachs
My Old Friends (OB) 1979

For We Love You Still
Music by Johann Strauss
Lyrics by Desmond Carter
The Great Waltz 1934

For You
Music by Gerard Calvi
Lyrics by Harold Rome
La Grosse Valise 1965

For You and for Me
Music by H. Maurice Jacquet
Lyrics by Preston Sturges
The Well of Romance 1930

For You, Brother
Music and lyrics by Eaton Magoon, Jr.
Heathen 1972

For You, for Me, for Evermore
Music by George Gershwin
Lyrics by Ira Gershwin
The Shocking Miss Pilgrim (1947) F

Adapted by Kay Swift and Ira Gershwin from
manuscripts of George Gershwin.

Forbidden Fruit
Music by Emmerich Kálmán
Lyrics by B.G. DeSylva
The Yankee Princess 1922

Forbidden Love (in Gaul)
Music by Jerry Bock
Lyrics by Sheldon Harnick
The Apple Tree 1966

The Forbidden Orchid
Music by Heitor Villa-Lobos
Lyrics by Robert Wright and George Forrest
Magdalena 1948

Fore Day Noon in the Mornin'
Music and lyrics by Irving Burgie
Ballad for Bimshire (OB) 1963

Foreign Cars
Music and lyrics by Norman Martin
Catch a Star! 1955

Foresight
Music by Stanley Lebowsky
Lyrics by Fred Tobias
Gantry 1970

The Forest Rangers
Music and lyrics by Rick Besoyan
Little Mary Sunshine (OB) 1959

Forever
Music and lyrics by Bob Merrill
Henry, Sweet Henry 1967

Forever
Music by Gerald Jay Markoe
Lyrics by Michael Colby
Charlotte Sweet (OB) 1982

Forever and a Day
Music and lyrics by Hugh Martin and Timothy Gray
High Spirits 1964

Forever and Always
Music and lyrics by Ed Tyler
Sweet Miani (OB) 1962

Forever and Ever
Music by Milton Ager
Lyrics by Jack Yellen
Rain or Shine 1928

Forget
Music by John Clifton
Lyrics by John Clifton and Ben Tarver
Man With a Load of Mischief (OB) 1966

Forget All Your Books
Music by Burton Lane
Lyrics by Howard Dietz
Three's a Crowd 1930

Forget Me
Music by David Baker
Lyrics by Sheldon Harnick
Vintage '60 (OB) 1960

Forsaken
Music by Richard Myers
Lyrics by Edward Heyman
Earl Carroll's Vanities (1932)

The Fortune
Music and lyrics by Jay Thompson
Double Entry (OB) 1961

Fortune
Music by Ronald Melrose
Lyrics by Bill Russell
Fourtune (OB) 1980

Fortune Telling
Music by Stephen Jones and Arthur Samuels
Lyrics by Dorothy Donnelly
Poppy 1923

Forty Acres and a Mule
Music by Leonard Bernstein
Lyrics by Alan Jay Lerner
1600 Pennsylvania Avenue 1976

Forty Days
Music by Meyer Kupferman
Lyrics by Paul Goodman
Jonah (OB) 1966

Forty Nights
Music by Richard Rodgers
Lyrics by Martin Charnin
Two by Two 1970

Dropped from production

45th Street and Broadway
Music and lyrics by Gene Buck and Dave Stamper
Ziegfeld Follies of 1922

Forty-Five Minutes From Broadway
Music and lyrics by George M. Cohan
Forty-Five Minutes From Broadway 1906

Forty-Niner and His Clementine
Music by Vincent Youmans
Lyrics by Oscar Hammerstein II
Rainbow 1928

Dropped from production

Forty-Second Street
Music by Harry Warren
Lyrics by Al Dubin
Forty-Second Street (1933) F

The 42nd Street and Broadway Strut
Music by Albert Von Tilzer
Lyrics by Neville Fleeson
The Gingham Girl 1922

42nd Street Blues
Music and lyrics by David Langston Smyrl
On the Lock-In (OB) 1977

Forward Into Tomorrow
Music and lyrics by Michael Brown
Different Times 1972

The Fountain Fay
Music by Heinrich Reinhardt
Lyrics by Robert B. Smith
The Spring Maid 1910

The Fountain Fay Protective Institution, Limited
Music by Heinrich Reinhardt
Lyrics by Robert B. Smith
The Spring Maid 1910

The Fountain of Youth
Music by Jerome Kern
Lyrics by Anne Caldwell
The City Chap 1925

The Fountain of Youth
Music by Alma Sanders
Lyrics by Monte Carlo
The Houseboat on the Styx 1928

Four
Music by Al Carmines
Lyrics by Maria Irene Fornes
Promenade (OB) 1969

Four Black Dragons
Music and lyrics by Stephen Sondheim
Pacific Overtures 1976

Four for the Road
Music by Paul Klein
Lyrics by Lee Goldsmith and Fred Ebb
From A to Z 1960

The Four Freedoms—Calypso
Music by John Green
Lyrics by George Marion, Jr.
Beat the Band 1942

Four Hundred Girls Ago
Music by Galt MacDermot
Lyrics by Christopher Gore
Via Galactica 1972

Four Jews in a Room Bitching
Music and lyrics by William Finn
March of the Falsettos (OB) 1981

Four Little Angels of Peace
Music and lyrics by Harold Rome
Pins and Needles (OB) 1937

Four Little Girls With a Future and Four Little Girls with a Past
Music by Rudolf Friml
Lyrics by B.G. DeSylva
Ziegfeld Follies of 1921

Four Little Misfits
Music by James Mundy
Lyrics by John Latouche
The Vamp 1955

Four Little Song Pluggers
Music by Richard Rodgers
Lyrics by Lorenz Hart
The Garrick Gaieties (2nd edition) 1926

Four Nightingales
Music by Larry Grossman
Lyrics by Hal Hackady
Minnie's Boys 1970

Four o'Clock Tea
Music by Louis A. Hirsch
Lyrics by Harold Atteridge
The Whirl of Society 1912

Four-Part Harmony
Music by Ronald Melrose
Lyrics by Bill Russell
Fourtune (OB) 1980

Four-Part Invention
Music by Patrick Rose
Lyrics by Merv Campone and Richard Ouzounian
A Bistro Car on the CNR (OB) 1978

Four Strikes Against Me
Music by Henry Krieger
Lyrics by Robert Lorick
The Tap Dance Kid 1983

Four Young People
Music and lyrics by James Shelton
The Straw Hat Revue 1939

The Fourth Light Dragoons
Music by Michael Valenti
Lyrics by John Lewin
Blood Red Roses 1970

The Fox Has Left His Lair
Music by Peggy Connor
Lyrics by Douglas Furber
Charlot's Revue of 1926

The Fox Hunt
Music and lyrics by Jerry Herman
Mame 1966

Fragrant Flower
Music by Glenn Paxton
Lyrics by Robert Goldman and George Weiss
First Impressions 1959

Frahngee-Pahnee
Music and lyrics by Cole Porter
Seven Lively Arts 1944

Fran and Jane
Music and lyrics by Craig Carnelia
Is There Life After High School? 1982

France Will Not Forget
Music and lyrics by Geoffrey O'Hara
and Gordon Johnstone
Half a Widow 1927

Frances' Ballad
Music by Cheryl Hardwick
Lyrics by Marilyn Suzanne Miller
Girls, Girls, Girls (OB) 1980

Francis
Music by Steve Jankowski
Lyrics by Kenny Morris
Francis (OB) 1982

Frank, Frank, Frank
Music and lyrics by Skip Redwine and Larry Frank
Frank Merriwell, or Honor Challenged 1971

Frank Mills
Music by Galt MacDermot
Lyrics by Gerome Ragni and James Rado
Hair 1968

Franklin Shepard, Inf.
Music and lyrics by Stephen Sondheim
Merrily We Roll Along 1981

Freddy and His Fiddle
Music and lyrics by Robert Wright and George Forrest
Song of Norway 1944

Based on Grieg's *Norwegian Dance* No. 2

Freddy Liked to Fugue
Music and lyrics by Frederick Silver
Gay Company (OB) 1974

Freddy, My Love
Music and lyrics by Jim Jacobs
and Warren Casey
Grease 1972

Free
Music and lyrics by Stephen Sondheim
*A Funny Thing Happened on the Way
to the Forum* 1962

Free and Easy
Music and lyrics by Jill Williams
Rainbow Jones 1974

Free and Easy
Music and lyrics by Buster Davis
Doctor Jazz 1975

Free as the Air
Music by Franz Lehár
Lyrics by Harry Graham
Yours Is My Heart 1946

Free, Cute and Size Fourteen
Music by John Green
Lyrics by George Marion, Jr.
Beat the Band 1942

Free for All
Music by Richard A. Whiting
Lyrics by Oscar Hammerstein II
Free for All 1931

Free, Free, Free
Music by Lucien Denni
Lyrics by Helena Evans
Happy Go Lucky 1926

Free to Be Free
Music by Rudolf Friml
Lyrics by Paul Francis Webster
Rose Marie (film version, 1954)

Free Trade and a Misty Moon
Music by Victor Herbert
Lyrics by Henry Blossom
Eileen 1917

Freedom
Music by Heitor Villa-Lobos
Lyrics by Robert Wright and George Forrest
Magdalena 1948

Freedom
Music by Gary Geld
Lyrics by Peter Udell
Shenandoah 1975

Freedom Can Be a Most Uncomfortable Thing
Music by Sammy Fain
Lyrics by Paul Francis Webster
Christine 1960

The Freedom Choo Choo Is Leaving Today
Music by Jack Holmes
Lyrics by Bill Conklin and Bob Miller
O Say Can You See! (OB) 1962

Freedom Diet
Music and lyrics by Glory Van Scott
Miss Truth (OB) 1979

The Freedom of the Press
Music and lyrics by Marc Blitzstein
The Cradle Will Rock 1938

Freedom Road
Music by Toby Sacher
Lyrics by Lewis Allen
Of V We Sing 1942

The Freedom Song
Music by Robert Mitchell
Lyrics by Elizabeth Perry
Bags (OB) 1982

Freedomland
Music and lyrics by Jack Holmes
New Faces of 1962

Freezing and Burning
Music and lyrics by Elizabeth Swados
Dispatches (OB) 1979

The French Have a Word for It
Music and lyrics by Harold Rome
The Streets of Paris 1939

The French Lesson
Music by Roger Edens
Lyrics by Betty Comden and Adolph Green
Good News (film version, 1947)

French Military Marching Song
Music by Sigmund Romberg
Lyrics by Otto Harbach and Oscar Hammerstein II
The Desert Song 1926

The French Pastry Walk
Music by William Daly and Paul Lannin
Lyrics by Arthur Jackson and Arthur Francis (Ira
Gershwin)
For Goodness Sake 1922

French With Tears
Music and lyrics by Harold Rome
Alive and Kicking 1950

Fresh as a Daisy
Music and lyrics by Cole Porter
Panama Hattie 1940

Freshie, O Freshie
Music by Raymond Hubbell
Lyrics by Glen MacDonough
The Jolly Bachelors 1910

Fresno Beauties (Cold and Dead)
Music and lyrics by Frank Loesser
The Most Happy Fella 1956

Freud
Music and lyrics by Jack Lawrence
and Stan Freeman
I Had a Ball 1964

Freud and Jung and Adler
Music by George Gershwin
Lyrics by Ira Gershwin
Pardon My English 1933

Dropped from production

Freud Is a Fraud
Music and lyrics by Jack Bussins
and Ellsworth Olin
Be Kind to People Week (OB) 1975

Friar's Tune
Music by Wally Harper
Lyrics by Paul Zakrzewski
Sensations (OB) 1970

Friday Dancing Class
Music and lyrics by Charles Gaynor
Lend an Ear 1948

A Friend Like You
Music by John Clifton
Lyrics by John Clifton and Ben Tarver
Man With a Load of Mischief (OB) 1966

Friend of the Family
Music by Hoagy Carmichael
Lyrics by Johnny Mercer
Walk With Music 1940

The Friendliest Thing
Music and lyrics by Ervin Drake
What Makes Sammy Run? 1964

Friendly Enemy
Music by Gerald Marks
Lyrics by Sam Lerner
Hold It! 1948

Friends
Music and lyrics by George M. Cohan
Billie 1928

Friends
Music by Sam Pottle
Lyrics by Tom Whedon
All Kinds of Giants (OB) 1961

Friends
Music by Jerry Bock
Lyrics by Sheldon Harnick
The Apple Tree 1966

Friends and Lovers
Music by Maurice Yvain
Lyrics by Max and Nathaniel Lief
Luckee Girl 1928

Friends the Best Of
Music and lyrics by James Quinn and Alaric Jans
Do Patent Leather Shoes Really Reflect Up? 1982

Friends to the End
Music by Frederick Loewe
Lyrics by Alan Jay Lerner
The Day Before Spring 1945

Friends Who Understand
Music by Vincent Youmans and Herbert Stothart
Lyrics by Otto Harbach and Oscar Hammerstein II
Wildflower 1923

Dropped from production

Friendship
Music by Emmerich Kálmán
Lyrics by B.G. DeSylva
The Yankee Princess 1922

Friendship
Music and lyrics by Ralph Benatzky
Meet My Sister 1930

Friendship
Music and lyrics by Cole Porter
Du Barry Was a Lady 1939

Frisco Fanny
Music by Henry Sullivan
Lyrics by Earl Crooker
Walk a Little Faster 1932

Fritzie
Music by Edward Thomas
Lyrics by Martin Charnin
Ballad for a Firing Squad (OB) 1968

From a Prison Cell
Music by Marguerite Monnot
Lyrics by Julian More, David Heneker
and Monte Norman
Irma la Douce 1960

From A to Z
Music by Albert Selden
Lyrics by Burt Shevelove
Small Wonder 1948

From Afar
Music by Richard Rodgers
Lyrics by Sheldon Harnick
Rex 1976

From Alpha to Omega
Music and lyrics by Cole Porter
You Never Know 1938

From Another World
Music by Richard Rodgers
Lyrics by Lorenz Hart
Higher And Higher 1940

From Broadway to Main Street
Music by Harry Archer
Lyrics by Harlan Thompson
Little Jessie James 1923

From Cairo, Bagdad
Music by Frederic Norton
Lyrics by Oscar Asche
Chu Chin Chow 1917

From Maine to Oregon
Music by John Philip Sousa
Lyrics by Leonard Liebling
The American Maid 1913

From Morning Till Night
Music by Jacques Belasco
Lyrics by Kay Twomey
The Girl From Nantucket 1945

From Now On
Music by George Gershwin
Lyrics by Arthur J. Jackson and B.G. DeSylva
La, La, Lucille 1919

From Now On
Music by Richard Myers
Lyrics by Edward Eliscu
The Street Singer 1929

From Now On
Music and lyrics by Cole Porter
Leave It to Me 1938

From Now Onward
Music by Sigmund Romberg
Lyrics by Rowland Leigh
My Romance 1948

From Now Till Forever
Music by Michael J. Lewis
Lyrics by Anthony Burgess
Cyrano 1973

From Our Bestiary
Music by Donald Swann
Lyrics by Michael Flanders
At the Drop of Another Hat 1966

From Peru's Majestic Mountains
Music by John Philip Sousa
Lyrics by Tom Frost and John Philip Sousa
El Capitan 1896

From the Bottom of the Sea
Music by Baldwin Bergersen
Lyrics by William Archibald
Rosa (OB) 1978

From the Chimney to the Cellar
Music by Frederick Loewe
Lyrics by Alan Jay Lerner
What's Up? 1943

From the Moment
Music and lyrics by John Dooley
Hobo (OB) 1961

From the U.S.A. to the U.S.S.R.
Music and lyrics by Cole Porter
Leave It to Me 1938

From This Day On
Music by Frederick Loewe
Lyrics by Alan Jay Lerner
Brigadoon 1947

From This Day On
Music by Abraham Ellstein
Lyrics by Walter Bullock
Great to Be Alive 1950

From This Moment On
Music and lyrics by Cole Porter
Out of This World 1950

One of Porter's most enduring hits, the song was dropped from the show *Out of This World* during the pre-Broadway tryout because the director, George Abbott, felt it would "help the book." Porter said later that his two best songs in the score (the other was "You Don't Remind Me") were cut for the same reason. The surgery didn't help, however; the show ran less than six months. Later (1953) the song was added to the score of the film version of *Kiss Me, Kate.*

Front Page News
Music by Arthur Schwartz
Lyrics by Howard Dietz
Between the Devil 1937

Frontier Politics
Music by Victor Ziskin
Lyrics by Joan Javits
Young Abe Lincoln 1961

Frowns
Music by Harry Revel
Lyrics by Mack Gordon
Fast and Furious 1931

Fruits and Vegetables
Music and lyrics by James Rado
Rainbow (OB) 1972

Fuddle-Dee-Duddle
Music by Sammy Fain
Lyrics by Charles Tobias
Hellzapoppin 1938

A Fugitive From Esquire
Music by Jimmy McHugh
Lyrics by Howard Dietz
Keep Off the Grass 1940

The Fugitive From Fifth Avenue
Music by Richard Stutz
Lyrics by Nat Hiken
Along Fifth Avenue 1949

Fugue for Four Girls
Music by Gary William Friedman
Lyrics by Will Holt
The Me Nobody Knows (OB) 1970

Fugue for Tinhorns
Music and lyrics by Frank Loesser
Guys and Dolls 1950

First called "Three Cornered Tune" and performed at a slower tempo, it was dropped during the pre-Broadway tour and rewritten in a brighter tempo for the three gamblers as the show's opening number.

Fugue on a Hot Afternoon in a Small Flat
Music by Earl Robinson
Lyrics by Waldo Salt
Sandhog (OB) 1954

Full Blown Roses
Music by Richard Rodgers
Lyrics by Lorenz Hart
Dearest Enemy 1925

Fun
Music by Sol Berkowitz
Lyrics by James Lipton
Miss Emily Adam (OB) 1960

Fun in the Country
Music and lyrics by William Roy
Maggie 1953

Fun Life
Music by Tommy Wolf
Lyrics by Fran Landesman
The Nervous Set 1959

Fun to Be Fooled
Music by Harold Arlen
Lyrics by Ira Gershwin and E.Y. Harburg
Life Begins at 8:40 1934

Fundamental Character
Music by Gerald Marks
Lyrics by Sam Lerner
Hold It! 1948

The Funeral Dirge
Music by Jimmy Horowitz
Lyrics by Leo Rost and Jimmy Horowitz
Marlowe 1981

Funeral of Charleston
Music by Manning Sherwin
Lyrics by Arthur Herzog, Jr.
Bad Habits of 1926 (OB)

Funeral Sequence
Music and lyrics by Stephen Sondheim
A Funny Thing Happened on the Way to the Forum 1962

Funeral Tango
Music by Jacques Brel
English lyrics by Eric Blau and Mort Shuman
Jacques Brel Is Alive and Well and Living in Paris (OB) 1968

Funky Bessie
Music and lyrics by Stephen H. Lemberg
Jazzbo Brown 1980

Funky Girl on Motherless Broadway
Music and lyrics by Melvin Van Peebles
Ain't Supposed to Die a Natural Death 1971

Funky Love
Music by Ronald Melrose
Lyrics by Bill Russell
Fourtune (OB) 1980

Funky Monkeys
Music and lyrics by Charlie Smalls
The Wiz 1975

Funky World
Music and lyrics by Oscar Brown, Jr.
Joy (OB) 1970

The Funnies
Music and lyrics by Irving Berlin
As Thousands Cheer 1933

Funny Face
Music by George Gershwin
Lyrics by Ira Gershwin
Funny Face 1927

Funny Feelin'
Music and lyrics by Oscar Brown, Jr.
and Luis Henrique
Joy (OB) 1970

Funny Funeral
Music and lyrics by Leslie Bricusse
and Anthony Newley
The Roar of the Greasepaint—The Smell of the Crowd 1965

Funny Girl
Music by Jule Styne
Lyrics by Bob Merrill
Funny Girl (film version, 1968)

A Funny Heart
Music by David Baker
Lyrics by David Craig
Phoenix '55 (OB)

Funny Honey
Music by John Kander
Lyrics by Fred Ebb
Chicago 1975

Funny Little Sailor Man
Music by Sigmund Romberg
Lyrics by Oscar Hammerstein II
The New Moon 1928

Funny Little Something
Music by Jerome Kern
Lyrics by Edgar Allan Woolf
Head Over Heels 1918

A Funny Thing Happened
Music and lyrics by Harold Rome
I Can Get It for You Wholesale 1962

The Future
Music by Mitch Leigh
Lyrics by Charles Burr and Forman Brown
Home Sweet Homer 1976

Future for Sale
Music by Stanley Silverman
Lyrics by Tom Hendry
Doctor Selavy's Magic Theatre (OB) 1972

Future Stars
Music by Leo Edwards
Lyrics by Herman Timberg
You'll See Stars 1942

Futuristic Rhythm
Music by Jimmy McHugh
Lyrics by Dorothy Fields
Hello Daddy 1928

G

Gabie
Music by Mary Rodgers
Lyrics by Martin Charnin
Hot Spot 1963

Gabriel
Music by Henry Souvaine and Jay Gorney
Lyrics by Morrie Ryskind and Howard Dietz
Merry-Go-Round 1927

Gabrielle
Music by André Previn
Lyrics by Alan Jay Lerner
Coco 1969

Gaby Glide
Music by Louis A. Hirsch
Lyrics by Harold Atteridge
The Whirl of Society 1912

Ga-Ga!
Music by Joseph Meyer
Lyrics by Edward Eliscu
Lady Fingers 1929

Ga-Ga
Music by Carl Millöcker (revised by Theo Mackeben)
Lyrics by Rowland Leigh
The Dubarry 1932

The Gainsboro Glide
Music by Seymour Furth and Lee Edwards
Lyrics by R.F. Carroll
Bringing Up Father 1925

A Gal in Calico
Music by Arthur Schwartz
Lyrics by Leo Robin
The Time, the Place and the Girl (1946) F

Gallivantin' Around
Music by Jerome Kern
Lyrics by Oscar Hammerstein II
Show Boat (film version, 1936)

Gallopin' Dominoes
Music by C. Luckey Roberts
Lyrics by Alex C. Rogers
My Magnolia 1926

Galloping
Music by Leslie Stuart
Lyrics by Ernest Boyd-Jones
Florodora 1900

Galloping Through the Park
Music by Robert Russell Bennett
Lyrics by Owen Murphy and Robert A. Simon
Hold Your Horses 1933

The Gambler of the West
Music by George Gershwin
Lyrics by Ira Gershwin
Girl Crazy 1930

Dropped from production

The Gamblers
Music by Harold Arlen
Lyrics by Johnny Mercer
Saratoga 1959

The Game
Music and lyrics by Richard Adler and Jerry Ross
Damn Yankees 1955

The Game of Love
Music by Victor Herbert
Lyrics by Robert B. Smith
Sweethearts 1913

The Game of Love
Music by Harold Karr
Lyrics by Matt Dubey
Happy Hunting 1956

The Game of Morra
Music by Armando Trovaioli
Lyrics by Pietro Garinei and Sandro Giovannini

(Lyric translation by Edward Eager)
Rugantino 1964

A Game of Poker
Music by Harold Arlen
Lyrics by Johnny Mercer
Saratoga 1959

The Games I Play
Music and lyrics by William Finn
March of the Falsettos (OB) 1981

The Gang's All Here
Music by Lewis E. Gensler
Lyrics by Owen Murphy and Robert A.Simon
The Gang's All Here 1931

Gant's Waltz
Music by Gary Geld
Lyrics by Peter Udell
Angel 1978

Garbage
Music and lyrics by Sheldon Harnick
Shoestring Revue (1955) (OB)

Garbage
Music and lyrics by Jerry Herman
Dear World 1969

Garbage Court Round
Music by George Fischoff
Lyrics by Verna Tomasson
The Prince and the Pauper (OB) 1963

Garbage-Ella
Music and lyrics by Ronnie Britton
Greenwich Village Follies (OB) 1976

Garçon, s'il Vous Plait
Music by George Gershwin
Lyrics by Ira Gershwin
Of Thee I Sing 1931

The Garden
Music and lyrics by Charles Strouse
Six (OB) 1971

A Garden for Two
Music and lyrics by James Rado
Rainbow (OB) 1972

Garden Guaracha
Music and lyrics by Stan Freeman
and Franklin Underwood
Lovely Ladies, Kind Gentlemen 1970

Garden in the Sky
Music by Vernon Duke
Lyrics by Howard Dietz
Sadie Thompson 1944

A Garden in the Sun
Music by Michael Valenti
Lyrics by John Lewin
Blood Red Roses 1970

Garden of Love
Music by George Gershwin
Lyrics by B.G. DeSylva, E. Ray Goetz
and Ballard MacDonald
George White's Scandals (1923)

A Garden of Memories
Music by Maury Rubens
Lyrics by Clifford Grey
The Great Temptations 1926

Garden Song
Music by Kenn Long and Jim Crozier
Lyrics by Kenn Long
Touch (OB) 1970

Garland Is My Man
Music and lyrics by Al Carmines
The Evangelist (OB) 1982

Gary, Indiana
Music and lyrics by Meredith Wilson
The Music Man 1957

The Gas Man Cometh
Music by Donald Swann
Lyrics by Michael Flanders
At the Drop of Another Hat 1966

Gascony
Music by Rudolf Friml
Lyrics by P.G. Wodehouse and Clifford Grey
The Three Musketeers 1928

The Gateway of the Temple of Minerva
Music by Richard Rodgers
Lyrics by Lorenz Hart
By Jupiter 1942

Gather Roses While You May
Music by Vivian Ellis
Lyrics by Graham John
By the Way 1925

Gather the Rose
Music by Rudolf Friml
Lyrics by Brian Hooker
The White Eagle 1927

Gather Ye Autographs While Ye May
Music and lyrics by Cole Porter
Jubilee 1935

Gather Ye Rosebuds
Music by George Gershwin
Lyrics by Ira Gershwin
Tip-Toes 1925

Dropped from production

The Gatsby Bridge March
Music by David Baker
Lyrics by Sheldon Harnick
Smiling, the Boy Fell Dead (OB) 1961

A Gaucho Love Song
Music by Sigmund Romberg
Lyrics by Irving Caesar
Nina Rosa 1930

Gavotte
Music by Richard Rodgers
Lyrics by Lorenz Hart
Dearest Enemy 1925

Gavotte
Music by Leonard Bernstein
Lyrics by Dorothy Parker
Candide 1956

Gavotte
Music by Richard Rodgers
Cinderella (1957) TV

A Gay Bar Cantata
Music and lyrics by Al Carmines
The Faggot (OB) 1973

Gay Little Wives
Music and lyrics by Cole Porter
Jubilee 1935

The Gazooka
Music by Vernon Duke
Lyrics by Ira Gershwin
Ziegfeld Follies (1936)

G'bye
Music and lyrics by Matt Dubey and Dean Fuller
Smith (OB) 1973

Gee, but I'd Like to Be Bad
Music by James F. Hanley
Lyrics by Eddie Dowling
Honeymoon Lane 1926

Gee, but It's Good to Be Here
Music by Harold Karr
Lyrics by Matt Dubey
Happy Hunting 1956

Gee Chee
Music by C. Luckey Roberts
Lyrics by Alex C. Rogers
My Magnolia 1926

Gee, I'm Glad I'm No One Else But Me
Music by Norman Campbell
Lyrics by Donald Harron and Norman Campbell
Anne of Green Gables (OB) 1971

Gee, It's Great to Be Alive
Music by Ray Henderson
Lyrics by B.G. DeSylva
Three Cheers 1928

Gee It's So Good, It's Too Bad
Music by Harold Arlen
Lyrics by Ted Koehler
Nine-Fifteen Revue 1930

Gee, Officer Krupke!
Music by Leonard Bernstein
Lyrics by Stephen Sondheim
West Side Story 1957

Gee, We Get Along
Music by Tom Johnstone
Lyrics by Phil Cook
When You Smile 1925

Geisha
Music and lyrics by Stan Freeman
and Franklin Underwood
Lovely Ladies, Kind Gentlemen 1970

Geisha Girl
Music by Manning Sherwin
Lyrics by Arthur Herzog, Jr.
Bad Habits of 1926 (OB)

The Gendarme
Music by Arthur Schwartz
Lyrics by Howard Dietz
Between the Devil 1937

Gendarme
Music by Robert Katscher
Lyrics by Rowland Leigh
You Never Know 1938

Genealogy
Music by Ray Henderson
Lyrics by B.G. DeSylva and Lew Brown
Hold Everything! 1928

General Store
Music by Norman Campbell
Lyrics by Donald Harron and Norman Campbell
Anne of Green Gables (OB) 1971

Generalonely
Music and lyrics by Steve Weber
Operation Sidewinder 1970

The General's Song
Music by Vernon Duke
Lyrics by John Latouche
Cabin in the Sky 1940

The General's Song
Music and lyrics by Don Tucker
Red, White and Maddox 1969

Genius Burns
Music by William Dyer
Lyrics by Don Parks and William Dyer
Jo (OB) 1964

Genteel
Music by Sol Kaplan
Lyrics by Edward Eliscu
The Banker's Daughter (OB) 1962

The Gentle Buffoon
Music and lyrics by John Driver
Ride the Winds 1974

Gentle Lover
Music and lyrics by Cliff Jones
Rockabye Hamlet 1976

Gentleman Friend
Music by Richard Lewine
Lyrics by Arnold B. Horwitt
Make Mine Manhattan 1948

The Gentleman Is a Dope
Music by Richard Rodgers
Lyrics by Oscar Hammerstein II
Allegro 1947

Gentleman Jimmy
Music by Jerry Bock
Lyrics by Sheldon Harnick
Fiorello! 1959

A Gentleman Never Falls Wildly in Love
Music by Glenn Paxton
Lyrics by Robert Goldman and George Weiss
First Impressions 1959

A Gentleman's Gentleman
Music by Cyril Ornadel
Lyrics by Leslie Bricusse
Pickwick 1965

A Gentleman's Gentleman
Music by Jule Styne
Lyrics by E.Y. Harburg
Darling of the Day 1968

Gentlemen of Leisure
Music and lyrics by Elizabeth Swados
Lullabye and Goodnight 1982

Gentlemen of the Press
Music and lyrics by George M. Cohan
Forty-Five Minutes From Broadway 1906

Gentlemen of the Press
Music by Oscar Levant
Lyrics by Irving Caesar and Graham John
Ripples 1930

Gentlemen of the Press
Music by Ernest G. Schweikert
Lyrics by Frank Reardon
Rumple 1957

Gentlemen Prefer Blondes
Music by Lewis E. Gensler
Lyrics by B.G. DeSylva
Queen High 1926

Gentlemen Prefer Blondes
Music by Jule Styne
Lyrics by Leo Robin
Gentlemen Prefer Blondes 1949

Gentlemen's Understanding
Music by Sol Kaplan
Lyrics by Edward Eliscu
The Banker's Daughter (OB) 1962

A Genuine Feminine Girl
Music and lyrics by Johnny Brandon
Cindy (OB) 1964

Genuine Grade A Canadian Superstar
Music by Patrick Rose
Lyrics by Merv Campone and Richard Ouzounian
A Bistro Car on the CNR (OB) 1978

Genuine Plastic
Music and lyrics by Michael Brown
Different Times 1972

George L.
Music by Jerry Bock
Lyrics by Sheldon Harnick
The Apple Tree 1966

Georgia Shows 'Em How
Music and lyrics by Buster Davis
Doctor Jazz 1975

Georgy
Music by George Fischoff
Lyrics by Carole Bayer
Georgy 1970

Geraniums in the Winder
Music by Richard Rodgers
Lyrics by Oscar Hammerstein II
Carousel 1945

The Germans at the Spa
Music and lyrics by Maury Yeston
Nine 1982

Gertie the Stool Pigeon's Daughter
Music by Ned Lehak
Lyrics by Joe Darion
Of V We Sing 1942

Gesticulate
Music and lyrics by Robert Wright
and George Forrest
Kismet 1953

Get a Horse, Get a Mule
Music by Vincent Youmans
Lyrics by Oscar Hammerstein II
Rainbow 1928

Dropped from production

Get a Load of That
Music by Kurt Weill
Lyrics by Langston Hughes
Street Scene 1947

Get a Load of This
Music by Harry Archer
Lyrics by Harlan Thompson
Twinkle Twinkle 1926

Get a Move on
Music by Paul A. Rubens
Lyrics by Paul A. Rubens and Arthur Wimperis
The Sunshine Girl 1913

Get an Education
Music by Ron Steward and Neal Tate
Lyrics by Ron Steward
Sambo (OB) 1969

Get Away for a Day in the Country
Music by Jule Styne
Lyrics by Sammy Cahn
High Button Shoes 1947

Get Away From It All
Music by Arthur Schwartz
Lyrics by Howard Dietz
At Home Abroad 1935

Get Away From That Window
Music by Jimmy Johnson
Lyrics by Perry Bradford
Messin' Around 1929

Get Away, Young Man
Music by Thomas (Fats) Waller
Lyrics by George Marion, Jr.
Early to Bed 1943

Get Down
Music and lyrics by Oscar Brown, Jr.
Buck White 1969

Get Down, Brother, Get Down
Music by Garry Sherman
Lyrics by Peter Udell
Comin' Uptown 1979

Get Happy
Music by Harold Arlen
Lyrics by Ted Koehler
Nine-Fifteen Revue 1930

Arlen was filling in as a rehearsal pianist for Vincent Youmans' "Great Day," (he was actually one of the show's orchestrators). He became bored with the obligatory "pickup," or vamp, the two bars the pianist plays preceding an actual start to set tempo, and began improvising his own two bars. The result was the opening strain of "Get Happy." After *The Nine-Fifteen Revue* it was sung by Judy Garland in the film *Summer Stock* (1950).

Get Hot Foot
Music by Sam H. Stept
Lyrics by Bud Green
Shady Lady 1933

Get in Line
Music by Jacques Urbont
Lyrics by David Newburger
Stag Movie (OB) 1971

Get Me Out
Music by Fred Stamer
Lyrics by Gen Genovese
Buttrio Square 1952

Get Me to the Church on Time
Music by Frederick Loewe
Lyrics by Alan Jay Lerner
My Fair Lady 1956

Get on the Raft With Taft
Music and lyrics by Oscar Brand
How to Steal an Election (OB) 1968

Get Out of Town
Music and lyrics by Cole Porter
Leave It to Me 1938

Get Out the Vote
Music and lyrics by Oscar Brand
How to Steal an Election (OB) 1968

Get Ready Eddie
Music and lyrics by James Quinn and Alaric Jans
Do Patent Leather Shoes Really Reflect Up? 1982

Get That Sun Into You
Music by Richard Myers
Lyrics by E.Y. Harburg
Americana (1932)

Get the Answer Now
Music and lyrics by Barbara Schottenfeld
I Can't Keep Running in Place (OB) 1981

Get Thee Behind Me Satan
Music and lyrics by Irving Berlin
Follow the Fleet (1936) F

Get Thee to Canterbury
Music by Paul Hoffert
Lyrics by David Secter
Get Thee to Canterbury (OB) 1969

Get Together
Music by Elizabeth Swados
Lyrics by Garry Trudeau
Doonesbury 1983

Get Up on a New Routine
Music by Arthur Schwartz
Lyrics by Howard Dietz
The Little Show (1st edition) 1929

Get Yer Program for de Big Fight
Music by Georges Bizet
Lyrics by Oscar Hammerstein II
Carmen Jones 1943

Get Your Act Together
Music by Garry Sherman
Lyrics by Peter Udell
Comin' Uptown 1979

Get Your Man
Music by Ray Perkins
Lyrics by Max and Nathaniel Lief
The Greenwich Village Follies (1928)

Get Your Rocks Off Rock
Music by Jacques Urbont
Lyrics by David Newburger
Stag Movie (OB) 1971

Get Your Slice of Cake
Music and lyrics by Johnny Brandon
Billy Noname (OB) 1970

Get Yourself a Geisha
Music by Arthur Schwartz
Lyrics by Howard Dietz
At Home Abroad 1935

Get Yourself a Girl
Music and lyrics by Cole Porter
Let's Face It! 1941

Gethsemane
Music by Andrew Lloyd Webber
Lyrics by Tim Rice
Jesus Christ Superstar 1971

Gettin' a Man
Music and lyrics by Johnny Mercer
Saratoga 1959

Gettin' Back to Me
Music by George Fischoff
Lyrics by Carole Bayer
Georgy 1970

Gettin' Together
Music and lyrics by Maceo Pinkard
Pansy 1929

Getting From Day to Day
Music and lyrics by Elizabeth Swados
Lullabye and Goodnight 1982

Getting Into the Talkies
Music by Milton Ager
Lyrics by Jack Yellen
John Murray Anderson's Almanac (1929)

Getting Married to a Person
Music by Richard Rodgers
Lyrics by Martin Charnin
Two by Two 1970

Dropped from production

Getting Married Today
Music and lyrics by Stephen Sondheim
Company 1970

Getting Oriental Over You
Music by Don Walker and
Lyrics by George Marion, Jr.
Allah Be Praised! 1944

Getting Tall
Music and lyrics by Maury Yeston
Nine 1982

Getting the Beautiful Girls
Music by Michael Cleary
Lyrics by Ned Washington
Earl Carroll's Vanities (1928)

Getting to Know You
Music by Richard Rodgers
Lyrics by Oscar Hammerstein II
The King and I 1951

The original version of the song was called
"Suddenly Lucky." It was written for, but dropped
from, *South Pacific* (1949).

Ghetto Life
Music and lyrics by Micki Grant
Don't Bother Me, I Can't Cope (OB) 1972

The Ghost of Little Egypt
Music by Philip Charig
Lyrics by James Dyrenforth
Nikki 1931

The Ghost of Old Black Joe
Music and lyrics by Vincent Valentini
Parisiana 1928

Ghost Town
Music by Will Irwin
Lyrics by Norman Zeno
Fools Rush In 1934

Giannina Mia
Music by Rudolf Friml
Lyrics by Otto Harbach
The Firefly 1912

Giant
Music by Ted Simons
Lyrics by Elinor Guggenheimer
Potholes (OB) 1979

The Gibson Bathing Girls
Music by Alfred Solomon
Lyrics by Paul West
Follies of 1907

Giddyup
Music and lyrics by Ann Harris
Sky High (OB) 1979

Gideon Briggs, I Love You
Music and lyrics by Frank Loesser
Greenwillow 1960

The Gift
Music and lyrics by Ronnie Britton
Gift of the Magi (OB) 1975

Gift Number
Music by Jay Gorney
Lyrics by Barry Trivers
Heaven on Earth 1948

The Gift of Maggie (and Others)
Music by Mary Rodgers
Lyrics by Marshall Barer
The Mad Show (OB) 1966

A Gift Today
Music and lyrics by Harold Rome
I Can Get It for You Wholesale 1962

Gigi
Music by Frederick Loewe
Lyrics by Alan Jay Lerner
Gigi (1958) F

Academy Award winner. Also in stage version
(1973)

Gigolette
Music by Franz Lehár
Lyrics by Irving Caesar
Charlot's Revue of 1926

Gigolo
Music by Richard Rodgers
Lyrics by Lorenz Hart
The Garrick Gaieties (2nd edition) 1926

Gigolo
Music by Sigmund Romberg
Lyrics by Dorothy Donnelly
My Princess 1927

Gilbert the Filbert
Music by Herman Finck
Lyrics by Arthur Wimperis
The Girl From Utah 1914

Gilding the Guild
Music by Richard Rodgers
Lyrics by Lorenz Hart
The Garrick Gaieties (1st edition) 1925

Gimme-a-Break Heartbreak
Music by Scott Killian and Kim D. Sherman
Lyrics by Kenneth Robins, Scott Killian
and Kim D. Sherman
Lenny and the Heartbreakers (OB) 1983

Gimme a "G"
Music by Joe Ercole
Lyrics by Bruce Kluger
Ka-Boom (OB) 1980

Gimme a Good Digestion
Music by Harvey Schmidt
Lyrics by Tom Jones
Philemon (OB) 1975

Gimme Some
Music by Charles Strouse
Lyrics by Lee Adams
Golden Boy 1964

Gimme the Shimmy
Music and lyrics by Harold Rome
Michael Todd's Peep Show 1950

Gina
Music and lyrics by Peter Link and C.C. Courtney
Salvation (OB) 1969

Ginette
Music by Jean Schwartz
Lyrics by Clifford Grey and William Cary Duncan
Sunny Days 1928

Gingerbread Girl
Music and lyrics by Robert Swerdlow
Love Me, Love My Children (OB) 1971

Gingerbrown
Music and lyrics by James Johnson
and Cecil Mack
Runnin' Wild 1923

Gip-Gip
Music and lyrics by George M. Cohan
The Merry Malones 1927

A Girl, a Man, a Night, a Dance
Music by Fritz Kreisler
Lyrics by William LeBaron
Apple Blossoms 1919

Based on Kreisler's violin piece "Tambourin
Chinois."

A Girl for Each Month of the Year
Music by Louis A. Hirsch
Lyrics by Channing Pollock and Rennold Wolf
Ziegfeld Follies of 1915

The Girl Friend
Music by Richard Rodgers
Lyrics by Lorenz Hart
The Girl Friend 1926

A Girl I Know
Music and lyrics by George M. Cohan
Little Johnny Jones 1904

The Girl I Might Have Been
Music and lyrics by Max Ewing
The Grand Street Follies (1929)

The Girl in His Arms
Music by Moose Charlap
Lyrics by Norman Gimbel
Whoop-Up 1958

Girl in the Coffee
Music by Coleridge-Taylor Perkinson
Lyrics by Errol Hill
Man Better Man (OB) 1969

The Girl in the Mirror
Music by Fred Hellerman
Lyrics by Fran Minkoff
New Faces of 1968

The Girl in the Show
Music and lyrics by Charles Gaynor
Show Girl 1961

The Girl in the Window
Music by Monty Norman
Lyrics by Julian More
The Moony Shapiro Songbook 1981

A Girl in Your Arms
Music by Jay Gorney
Lyrics by Irving Caesar
Sweetheart Time 1926

A Girl Is Like a Book
Music by Frederick Loewe
Lyrics by Alan Jay Lerner
What's Up? 1943

The Girl Is You and the Boy Is Me
Music by Ray Henderson
Lyrics by B.G. DeSylva and Lew Brown
George White's Scandals (1926)

The Girl I've Never Met
Music by Stephen Jones and Arthur Samuels
Lyrics by Dorothy Donnelly
Poppy 1923

A Girl Like You
Music and lyrics by Edward Pola
and Eddie Brandt
Woof, Woof 1929

The Girl Next Door
Music by Richard A. Whiting
Lyrics by Oscar Hammerstein II
Free for All 1931

The Girl of the Minute
Music by David Shire
Lyrics by Richard Maltby, Jr.
New Faces of 1968

The Girl of the Minute
Music by David Shire
Lyrics by Richard Maltby, Jr.
Starting Here, Starting Now (OB) 1977

Girl of the Moment
Music by Kurt Weill
Lyrics by Ira Gershwin
Lady in the Dark 1941

A Girl of the Pi Beta Phi
Music by Ray Henderson
Lyrics by B.G. DeSylva and Lew Brown
Good News 1927

The Girl of Tomorrow
Music by Ray Henderson
Lyrics by B.G. DeSylva and Lew Brown
George White's Scandals (1925)

The Girl on the Magazine Cover
Music and lyrics by Irving Berlin
Stop! Look! Listen! 1915

Girl on the Police Gazette
Music and lyrics by Irving Berlin
On the Avenue (1937) F

The Girl on the Prow
Music by Sigmund Romberg
Lyrics by Oscar Hammerstein II
The New Moon 1928

A Girl She Can't Remain
Music by Baldwin Bergersen
Lyrics by William Archibald
Carib Song 1945

The Girl That I Adore
Music by Emil Gerstenberger
Lyrics by Carle Carlton
The Lace Petticoat 1927

The Girl That I Court in My Mind
Music and lyrics by Ralph Blane
Three Wishes for Jamie 1952

The Girl That I Marry
Music and lyrics by Irving Berlin
Annie Get Your Gun 1946

The Girl That I'll Adore
Music by Niclas Kempner
Lyrics by Graham John
The Street Singer 1929

A Girl Who Doesn't Ripple When She Bends
Music by Thomas (Fats) Waller
Lyrics by George Marion, Jr.
Early to Bed 1943

The Girl Who Lived in Montparnasse
Music and lyrics by Charles Gaynor
Show Girl 1961

The Girl With a Brogue
Music by Lionel Monckton
Lyrics by Arthur Wimperis
The Arcadians 1910

A Girl With a Flame
Music by Morton Gould
Lyrics by Dorothy Fields
Arms and the Girl 1950

A Girl With a Ribbon
Music by Baldwin Bergersen
Lyrics by William Archibald
The Crystal Heart (OB) 1960

The Girl With the Paint on Her Face
Music and lyrics by Irvin Graham
Who's Who 1938

A Girl You Should Know
Music by David Shire
Lyrics by Richard Maltby, Jr.
Starting Here, Starting Now (OB) 1977

Girl, You're a Woman
Music and lyrics by Carol Hall
The Best Little Whorehouse in Texas 1978

Girlie
Music by Jerome Kern
Lyrics by Berton Braley
Toot-Toot! 1918

Girlies You've Kissed in Dreams
Music by Karl Hoschna
Lyrics by Otto Harbach
The Fascinating Widow 1911

The Girls
Music by Harry Ruby
Lyrics by Bert Kalmar
High Kickers 1941

Girls
Music and lyrics by Cole Porter
Mexican Hayride 1944

Girls
Music and lyrics by John Phillips
Man on the Moon 1975

The Girls Against the Boys
Music by Richard Lewine
Lyrics by Arnold B. Horwitt
The Girls Against the Boys 1959

Girls and Boys
Music by Richard Lewine
Lyrics by Arnold B. Horwitt
The Girls Against the Boys 1959

Girls and Dogs
Music by Jacques Brel
English lyrics by Eric Blau and Mort Shuman
*Jacques Brel Is Alive and Well
and Living in Paris* (OB) 1968

Girls and the Gimmies
Music by Percy Wenrich
Lyrics by Raymond Peck
Castles in the Air 1926

Girls Are Like a Rainbow
Music by Jerome Kern
Lyrics by Anne Caldwell
The Night Boat 1920

The Girls at Maxim's (Can-Can)
Music by Franz Lehár
Lyrics by Adrian Ross
The Merry Widow 1907

Girls Dream of One Thing
Music by J. Fred Coots
Lyrics by Clifford Grey
June Days 1925

Girls From DeVere's
Music and lyrics by George M. Cohan
Little Nellie Kelly 1922

Girls From the U.S.A.
Music and lyrics by George M. Cohan
Little Johnny Jones 1904

Girls! Girls!
Music by Moose Charlap
Lyrics by Norman Gimbel
The Conquering Hero 1961

Girls, I Am True to All of You
Music by Emmerich Kálmán
Lyrics by Harry B. Smith
The Circus Princess 1927

Girls in My Life
Music and lyrics by Randy Newman
Maybe I'm Doing It Wrong (2nd edition)
(OB) 1982

Girls in the Sea
Music by Jerome Kern
Lyrics by Anne Caldwell
Hitchy-Koo 1920

Dropped from production

Girls I've Met
Music by Ivan Caryll
Lyrics by Louis Harrison
Jack O' Lantern 1917

Girls Like Me
Music by Jule Styne
Lyrics by Betty Comden and Adolph Green
Subways Are for Sleeping 1961

Girls 'n Girls 'n Girls
Music and lyrics by Irvin Graham
New Faces of 1956

Girls of Long Ago
Music by Oscar Levant
Lyrics by Irving Caesar and Graham John
Ripples 1930

The Girls of My Dreams
Music and lyrics by Irving Berlin
Ziegfeld Follies of 1920

The Girls of New York
Music by Seymour Furth and Lee Edwards
Lyrics by R.F. Carroll
Bringing Up Father 1925

The Girls of Summer
Music and lyrics by Stephen Sondheim
Marry Me a Little (OB) 1981

Written for and first performed in the play *Girls of Summer* (1956).

The Girls of the Old Brigade
Music by Vincent Youmans
Lyrics by Anne Caldwell
Oh, Please! 1926

Girls Want a Hero
Music by Duke Ellington
Lyrics by John Latouche
Beggar's Holiday 1946

The Girls Who Sit and Wait
Music and lyrics by Jerry Herman
Madame Aphrodite (OB) 1961

The Gitka's Song
Music by Richard Rodgers
Lyrics by Martin Charnin
Two by Two 1970

Give a Girl a Break
Music by Burton Lane
Lyrics by Ira Gershwin
Give a Girl a Break (1953) F

Give a Little, Get a Little
Music by Jule Styne
Lyrics by Betty Comden and Adolph Green
Two on the Aisle 1951

Give a Little Whistle
Music by Cy Coleman
Lyrics by Carolyn Leigh
Wildcat 1960

Give a Man a Job
Music by Richard Rodgers
Lyrics by Lorenz Hart
Hollywood Party (1934) F

Dropped from film

Give 'Em a Kiss
Music and lyrics by G. Wood
Put It in Writing (OB) 1963

Give 'Em Hell
Music by Joseph Church
Lyrics by Kristine Zbornik
An Evening With Joan Crawford (OB) 1981

Give England Strength
Music by Jerry Bock
Lyrics by Sheldon Harnick
The Rothschilds 1970

Give, Give, Give
Music by Louis A. Hirsch
Lyrics by Otto Harbach
The O'Brien Girl 1921

Give Her a Kiss
Music by Richard Rodgers
Lyrics by Lorenz Hart
The Phantom President (1932) F

Give Him the Oo-La-La
Music and lyrics by Cole Porter
Du Barry Was a Lady 1939

Give It All You Got
Music and lyrics by Jay Livingston and Ray Evans
Oh Captain! 1958

Give It Back to the Indians
Music by Richard Rodgers
Lyrics by Lorenz Hart
Too Many Girls 1939

Give It Love
Music by Joseph Meyer
Lyrics by Floyd Huddleston
Shuffle Along of 1952

Give It to Me
Music and lyrics by Earl Wilson, Jr.
Let My People Come (OB) 1974

Give Me
Music by Stan Harte, Jr.
Leaves of Grass (OB) 1971

Give Me a Cause
Music by Albert Hague
Lyrics by Allen Sherman
The Fig Leaves Are Falling 1969

Give Me a Cause
Music and lyrics by Harry Chapin
The Night That Made America Famous 1975

Give Me a Man Like That
Music and lyrics by George A. Little
and Art Sizemore
Brown Buddies 1930

Give Me a Night
Music and lyrics by Frank E. Harling
Say When 1928

Give Me a Road
Music and lyrics by Harry Chapin
The Night That Made America Famous 1975

Give Me a Roll on a Drum
Music by Sigmund Romberg
Lyrics by Irving Caesar
Melody 1933

Give Me a Star
Music by David Krivoshei
Lyrics by David Paulsen
To Live Another Summer 1971

Give Me a Thrill
Music by Tom Johnstone
Lyrics by Will B. Johnstone
I'll Say She Is 1924

Give Me a Wall
Music and lyrics by Harry Chapin
The Night That Made America Famous 1975

Give Me More
Music and lyrics by Stephen H. Lemberg
Jazzbo Brown 1980

Give Me One Good Reason
Music by Walt Smith
Lyrics by Leon Uris
Ari 1971

Give Me One Hour
Music by Rudolf Friml
Lyrics by Brian Hooker
The White Eagle 1927

Give Me Someone
Music by Robert Hood Bowers
Lyrics by Francis DeWitt
Oh, Ernest! 1927

Give Me That Key
Music and lyrics by Clark Gesner
The Utter Glory of Morrissey Hall 1979

Give Me the Rain
Music by Maury Rubens
Lyrics by Lester Allen and Henry Creamer
Gay Paree 1925

Give Me the Simple Life
Music by Jim Steinman
Lyrics by Michael Weller and Jim Steinman
More Than You Deserve (OB) 1973

Give Me the Sunshine
Music by Jimmy Johnson
Lyrics by Henry Creamer and Con Conrad
Keep Shufflin' 1928

Give Me the Wild Trumpets
Music by Irving Actman
Lyrics by Frank Loesser
The Illustrators' Show 1936

Give Me Your Love
Music and lyrics by Al Wilson, Charles Weinberg
and Ken Macomber
Yeah Man 1932

Give Me Your Tired, Your Poor
Music by Irving Berlin
Lyrics by Emma Lazarus
Miss Liberty 1949

The lyrics are taken from Emma Lazarus' poem
inscribed on the Statue of Liberty.

Give My Regards to Broadway
Music and lyrics by George M. Cohan
Little Johnny Jones 1904

Give Our Child a Name
Music and lyrics by Ring Lardner
June Moon 1929   .

In the play, which is about Tin Pan Alley and "pop"
songs, an especially untalented songwriter submits
his latest to the publisher:
  Should a father's carnal sins
  Blight the life of babykins?
  All I ask is give our child a name
  I mean a last name.

Give Shalom and Sabbath to Jerusalem
Music by Dov Seltzer
Lyrics by David Paulsen
To Live Another Summer 1971

Give, Sinbad, Give
Music by Clay Warnick
Lyrics by Edward Eager
Dream With Music 1944

Give the Doctor the Best in the House
Music by Mischa and Wesley Portnoff
Lyrics by Donagh MacDonagh
Happy as Larry 1950

Give the Little Lady a Great Big Hand
Music by Leroy Anderson
Lyrics by Joan Ford and Walter and Jean Kerr
Goldilocks 1958

Give This Little Girl a Hand
Music by Richard Rodgers
Lyrics by Lorenz Hart
Peggy-Ann 1926

Give Trouble the Air
Music by Louis Alter
Lyrics by Leo Robin
A La Carte 1927

Give Us a Chance
Music and lyrics by Irving Berlin
Stop! Look! Listen! 1915

Give Us the Charleston
Music by Ray Henderson
Lyrics by B.G. DeSylva and Lew Brown
George White's Scandals (1925)

Give Your Heart a Chance to Sing
Music and lyrics by Charles Gaynor
Lend an Ear 1948

Give Your Heart in June-Time
Music by Victor Herbert
Lyrics by Clifford Grey and Harold Atteridge
Sky High 1925

Give Your Heart to Jesus
Music and lyrics by James Rado
Rainbow (OB) 1972

Givers and Getters
Music and lyrics by Don Tucker
Red, White and Maddox 1969

Giving It Up for Love
Music and lyrics by Billy Solly
Boy Meets Boy (OB) 1975

Giving Life
Music and lyrics by Earl Wilson, Jr.
Let My People Come (OB) 1974

Glad that You Were Born
Music and lyrics by Al Kasha and Joel Hirschorn
Seven Brides for Seven Brothers 1982

Glad Tidings
Music by Milton Ager
Lyrics by Jack Yellen
Rain or Shine 1928

Glad to Be Back
Music by Richard Lewine
Lyrics by Arnold B. Horwitt
Make Mine Manhattan 1948

Glad to Be Home
Music and lyrics by Irving Berlin
Mr. President 1962

Glad to Be Unhappy
Music by Richard Rodgers
Lyrics by Lorenz Hart
On Your Toes 1936

The Glamorous Life
Music and lyrics by Stephen Sondheim
A Little Night Music 1973

Glenda's Place
Music by Moose Charlap
Lyrics by Norman Gimbel
Whoop-Up 1958

Gliding Through My Memoree
Music by Richard Rodgers
Lyrics by Oscar Hammerstein II
Flower Drum Song 1958

Glimpse of Love
Music and lyrics by Harold Rome
Wish You Were Here 1952

Dropped from production

Glitter and Be Gay
Music by Leonard Bernstein
Lyrics by Richard Wilbur
Candide 1956

Globligated
Music and lyrics by James Rado
Rainbow (OB) 1972

Gloria
Music by Jerry Bock
Lyrics by Sheldon Harnick
The Body Beautiful 1958

Glorifying the Girls
Music and lyrics by Gene Buck and Dave Stamper
Ziegfeld Follies of 1923

Glorious Cheese
Music by Don Elliott
Lyrics by James Costigan
The Beast in Me 1963

Glorious Russian
Music and lyrics by Leslie Bricusse
and Anthony Newley
Stop the World—I Want to Get Off 1962

Glory
Music and lyrics by Stephen Schwartz
Pippin 1972

The Glory of Spring
Music by Emile Berté and Maury Rubens
Lyrics by J. Keirn Brennan
Music in May 1929

The Glory That Is Greece
Music by Jacques Offenbach (adapted by Robert
De Cormier)
Lyrics by E.Y. Harburg
The Happiest Girl in the World 1961

A Gnu
Music by Donald Swann
Lyrics by Michael Flanders
At the Drop of a Hat 1959

Go Away, Girls
Music by Sigmund Romberg
Lyrics by Rida Johnson Young
Maytime 1917

Go Back
Music and lyrics by Al Carmines
Joan (OB) 1972

Go Down to Boston Harbor
Music and lyrics by Burton Lane
Laffing Room Only 1944

Go Down to the River (Washer Woman)
Music by Baldwin Bergersen
Lyrics by William Archibald
Carib Song 1945

Go Gar Sig Gong-Jue
Music by Ivan Caryll
Lyrics by Anne Caldwell and James O'Dea
Chin-Chin 1914

Go Get 'Im
Music by Walter Donaldson
Lyrics by Gus Kahn
Whoopee 1928

The Go-Getter
Music by Jerome Kern
Lyrics by Anne Caldwell
The City Chap 1925

Go, Go, Go
Music by Don Elliott
Lyrics by James Costigan
The Beast in Me 1963

Go, Go, Go Guerillas
Music by Jim Steinman
Lyrics by Michael Weller and Jim Steinman
More Than You Deserve (OB) 1973

Go, Go, Joseph
Music by Andrew Lloyd Webber
Lyrics by Tim Rice
*Joseph and the Amazing
Technicolor Dreamcoat* 1982

Go, Holy Ghost
Music by Galt MacDermot
Lyrics by Gerome Ragni
Dude 1972

Go Home Ev'ry Once in a While
Music and lyrics by George M. Cohan
Billie 1928

Go Home Train
Music by Jule Styne
Lyrics by Betty Comden and Adolph Green
Fade Out—Fade In 1964

Go in the Best of Health
Music by Jerry Livingston
Lyrics by Mack David
Molly 1973

Go Into Your Dance
Music and lyrics by Cole Porter
The New Yorkers 1930

Go Into Your Trance
Music and lyrics by Hugh Martin
and Timothy Gray
High Spirits 1964

Go, Little Boat
Music by Jerome Kern
Lyrics by P.G. Wodehouse
Miss 1917

Dropped during run and interpolated into score of
Oh, My Dear! (1918)

Go Places and Do Things
Music by Harry Ruby
Lyrics by Bert Kalmar
Animal Crackers 1928

Go Sit by the Body
Music by Baldwin Bergersen
Lyrics by William Archibald
Carib Song 1945

Go Slow, Johnny
Music and lyrics by Noël Coward
Sail Away 1961

Go South
Music by Richard Myers
Lyrics by Owen Murphy
The Greenwich Village Follies (1925)

Go to Sleep
Music by Burton Lane
Lyrics by Alan Jay Lerner
On a Clear Day You Can See Forever
(film version, 1969)

Go to Sleep, Slumber Deep
Music by Victor Herbert
Lyrics by Glen MacDonough
Babes in Toyland 1903

Go to Sleep Whatever You Are
Music by Jerry Bock
Lyrics by Sheldon Harnick
The Apple Tree 1966

Go Up to the Mountain
Music and lyrics by Walter Cool
Mackey of Appalachia (OB) 1965

Go Visit
Music by John Kander
Lyrics by Fred Ebb
70, Girls, 70 1971

Go While the Goin' Is Good
Music by Victor Herbert
Lyrics by Henry Blossom
The Red Mill 1906

God Bless the Human Elbow
Music by Mark Sandrich, Jr.
Lyrics by Sidney Michaels
Ben Franklin in Paris 1964

God Bless the Women
Music and lyrics by Cole Porter
Panama Hattie 1940

God Could Give Me Anything
Music by Bert Keyes and Bob Larimer
Lyrics by Bob Larimer
But Never Jam Today 1979

God Gave Me Eyes
Music by Richard Rodgers
Lyrics by Lorenz Hart
America's Sweetheart 1931

Dropped from production

God Help Us
Music and lyrics by Micki Grant
It's So Nice to Be Civilized 1980

God Is an American
Music and lyrics by Don Tucker
Red, White and Maddox 1969

God Is Good to the Irish
Music and lyrics by George M. Cohan
The Merry Malones 1927

God Is in the People
Music and lyrics by Peter Copani
New York City Street Show (OB) 1977

God, That's Good
Music and lyrics by Stephen Sondheim
Sweeney Todd 1979

The God-Why-Don't-You-Love-Me Blues
Music and lyrics by Stephen Sondheim
Follies 1971

God Will Take Care
Music by Coleridge-Taylor Perkinson
Lyrics by Ray McIver
God Is a (Guess What?) (OB) 1968

Goddess of Mine
Music by Victor Herbert
Lyrics by David Stevens and Justin Huntly
McCarthy
The Madcap Duchess 1913

Goddess of Rain
Music by Thomas (Fats) Waller and Harry Brooks
Lyrics by Andy Razaf
Hot Chocolates 1929

God's Country
Music by Harold Arlen
Lyrics by E.Y. Harburg
Hooray for What! 1937

God's Green World
Music by Frederick Loewe
Lyrics by Alan Jay Lerner
The Day before Spring 1945

God's Song (That's Why I Love Mankind)
Music and lyrics by Randy Newman
Maybe I'm Doing It Wrong (1st edition) (OB) 1981

Goin' Back to New Orleans
Music and lyrics by Arthur Malvin
Sugar Babies 1979

Goin' Courting
Music by Gene dePaul
Lyrics by Johnny Mercer
Seven Brides for Seven Brothers 1982

Goin' Gone
Music by Garry Sherman
Lyrics by Peter Udell
Comin' Uptown 1979

Goin' Home Train
Music and lyrics by Harold Rome
Call Me Mister 1946

Goin' on a Hayride
Music and lyrics by Ralph Blane
Three Wishes for Jamie 1952

Going Back Home
Music by Robert Stolz
Lyrics by Robert Sour
Mr. Strauss Goes to Boston 1945

Going Down
Music by Galt MacDermot
Lyrics by Gerome Ragni and James Rado
Hair 1968

Going, Going, Gone!
Music by Henry Sullivan
Lyrics by Edward Eliscu
The Third Little Show 1931

Going Home
Music and lyrics by Scott Joplin
Treemonisha 1975

Written in 1909

Going Home Tomorrow
Music by Peter Link
Lyrics by Jacob Brackman
King of Hearts 1978

Going Home With My Children
Music by Nancy Ford
Lyrics by Gretchen Cryer
Shelter 1973

Going Native
Music and lyrics by Ed Tyler
Sweet Miani (OB) 1962

Going Over the Bumps
Music by Harold Levey
Lyrics by Owen Murphy
Rainbow Rose 1926

Going Rowing
Music by Vincent Youmans
Lyrics by Zelda Sears
Lollipop 1924

Going-Staying
Music by Lawrence Hurwit
Lyrics by Lee Goldsmith
Sextet 1974

Going to Town With Me
Music by Burton Lane
Lyrics by Harold Adamson
Earl Carroll's Vanities (1931)

Going Up
Music by Louis A. Hirsch
Lyrics by Otto Harbach
Going Up 1917

Going Up
Music by Jay Gorney
Lyrics by E.Y. Harburg
Earl Carroll's Vanities (1930)

Gol-Durn!
Music by George Gershwin
Lyrics by Brian Hooker
Our Nell 1922

Gold Cannot Buy
Music by Frederico Valerio
Lyrics by Elizabeth Miele
Hit the Trail 1954

Gold Fever
Music by André Previn
Lyrics by Alan Jay Lerner
Paint Your Wagon (film version, 1969)

Gold, Women and Laughter
Music by Alma Sanders
Lyrics by Monte Carlo
Louisiana Lady 1947

The Golden Age
Music by Victor Herbert
Lyrics by Robert B. Smith
The Debutante 1914

Golden Boy
Music by Charles Strouse
Lyrics by Lee Adams
Golden Boy 1964

Golden Days
Music by Sigmund Romberg
Lyrics by Dorothy Donnelly
The Student Prince 1924

The Golden Dream
Music and lyrics by Beth Lawrence
and Norman Thalheimer
Marilyn 1983

Golden Gate
Music by Ray Perkins
Lyrics by Max and Nathaniel Lief
The Greenwich Village Follies (1928)

Golden Gates of Happiness
Music by J. Fred Coots
Lyrics by Clifford Grey
The Merry World 1926

Golden Goblet
Music by Edward Earle
Lyrics by Yvonne Tarr
The Decameron (OB) 1961

Golden Helmet
Music by Mitch Leigh
Lyrics by Joe Darion
Man of La Mancha 1965

Golden Land
Music by Manos Hadjidakis
Lyrics by Joe Darion
Illya Darling 1967

Golden Moment
Music and lyrics by Jack Lawrence
and Don Walker
Courtin' Time 1951

Golden Oldie
Music by Monty Norman
Lyrics by Julian More
The Moony Shapiro Songbook 1981

Golden Rainbow
Music and lyrics by Walter Marks
Golden Rainbow 1968

The Golden Ram
Music by Richard Rodgers
Lyrics by Martin Charnin
Two by Two 1970

The Golden Rule Song
Music by Coleridge-Taylor Perkinson
Lyrics by Ray McIver
God Is a (Guess What?) (OB) 1968

The Goldfarb Variations
Music and lyrics by Stephen Schwartz
The Magic Show 1974

Goldfish Glide
Music by James F. Hanley
Lyrics by Eddie Dowling
Sidewalks of New York 1927

Golliwog
Music and lyrics by Vincent Valentini
Parisiana 1928

Gondolier Song
Music by Rudolf Friml
Lyrics by Rowland Leigh and John Shubert
Music Hath Charms 1934

Gone Away Blues
Music by Manning Sherwin
Lyrics by Arthur Herzog, Jr.
Bad Habits of 1926 (OB)

Gone, Gone, Gone!
Music by George Gershwin
Lyrics by DuBose Heyward
Porgy and Bess 1935

Gone in Sorrow
Music by John Morris
Lyrics by Gerald Freedman
A Time for Singing 1966

The Gong Song
Music and lyrics by C. Jackson and James Hatch
Fly Blackbird (OB) 1962

Gonna Build a Mountain
Music and lyrics by Leslie Bricusse
and Anthony Newley
Stop the World—I Want to Get Off 1962

Gonna Get a Woman
Music and lyrics by Will Holt
That 5 A.M. Jazz (OB) 1964

Gonna Run
Music and lyrics by Gary Portnoy
and Judy Hart Angelo
Preppies (OB) 1983

Gooch's Song
Music and lyrics by Jerry Herman
Mame 1966

Good Advice
Music and lyrics by Scott Joplin
Treemonisha 1975

Written in 1909

Good and Lucky
Music by Arthur Schwartz
Lyrics by Albert Stillman
Virginia 1937

Good as Anybody
Music by Paul Klein
Lyrics by Fred Ebb
Morning Sun (OB) 1963

Good Boy
Music and lyrics by Herbert Stothart,
Bert Kalmar and Harry Ruby
Good Boy 1928

Good Boy
Music by Robert Waldman
Lyrics by Alfred Uhry
Here's Where I Belong 1968

Good Boy Wedding March
Music and lyrics by Herbert Stothart,
Bert Kalmar and Harry Ruby
Good Boy 1928

Good Clean Fun
Music by Jerry Bock
Lyrics by Sheldon Harnick
Tenderloin 1960

Good Clean Sport
Music by Arthur Schwartz
Lyrics by Howard Dietz
The Second Little Show 1930

Good Evening, Friends
Music by Robert Katscher
Lyrics by Irving Caesar
The Wonder Bar 1931

Good Evening, Madame Flora
Music and lyrics by Gian-Carlo Menotti
The Medium 1947

Good Evening, Mr. Man in the Moon
Music by Robert Russell Bennett
Lyrics by Owen Murphy and Robert A. Simon
Hold Your Horses 1933

Good Evening, Princess
Music and lyrics by Cole Porter
You Never Know 1938

Good Fellow, Mine
Music by Richard Rodgers
Lyrics by Lorenz Hart
The Girl Friend 1926

Good for Nothing
Music and lyrics by John Dooley
Hobo (OB) 1961

Good for You—Bad for Me
Music by Ray Henderson
Lyrics by B.G. DeSylva and Lew Brown
Flying High 1930

Good Friends
Music by Charles Strouse
Lyrics by Lee Adams
Applause 1970

Good Friends Surround Me
Music by Sigmund Romberg
Lyrics by Irving Caesar
Melody 1933

Good Girls Love Bad Men
Music by Louis Alter
Lyrics by Harry Ruskin and Leighton K. Brill
Ballyhoo 1930

A Good Hand Organ and a Sidewalk
Music by Lewis E. Gensler and Milton Schwarzwald
Lyrics by George S. Kaufman, Marc Connelly
and Ira Gershwin
Be Yourself 1924

Good Little Boy
Music by Wally Harper
Lyrics by Paul Zakrzewski
Sensations (OB) 1970

Good Little Girls
Music by Vernon Duke
Lyrics by Sammy Cahn
The Littlest Revue (OB) 1956

Good Luck
Music by Georges Bizet
Lyrics by Oscar Hammerstein II
Carmen Jones 1943

Good Luck to You
Music by Gary William Friedman
Lyrics by Will Holt
Taking My Turn (OB) 1983

Good Morning
Music by David Shire
Lyrics by Richard Maltby, Jr.
The Sap of Life (OB) 1961

Good Morning, All
Music by Rudolf Friml
Lyrics by Bide Dudley and Otto Harbach
The Little Whopper 1919

Good Morning, Dearie
Music by Jerome Kern
Lyrics by Anne Caldwell
Good Morning, Dearie 1921

Good Morning, Dr. Puffin
Music by Alec Wilder
Lyrics by Arnold Sundgaard
Kittiwake Island (OB) 1960

Good Morning, Good Day
Music by Jerry Bock
Lyrics by Sheldon Harnick
She Loves Me 1963

Good Morning, Miss Standing
Music and lyrics by Cole Porter
Jubilee 1935

Good Morning Starshine
Music by Galt MacDermot
Lyrics by Gerome Ragni and James Rado
Hair 1968

Good News
Music by Ray Henderson
Lyrics by B.G. DeSylva and Lew Brown
Good News 1927

Good Night
Music by George Lessner
Lyrics by Miriam Battista and Russell Maloney
Sleepy Hollow 1948

Good Night
Music by Harvey Schmidt
Lyrics by Tom Jones
I Do! I Do! 1966

Good Night Boat
Music by Jerome Kern
Lyrics by Anne Caldwell
The Night Boat 1920

Good Night, Good Neighbor
Music by Arthur Schwartz
Lyrics by Frank Loesser
Thank Your Lucky Stars (1943) F

Good Night Hymn
Music by Richard Hill and John Hawkins
Lyrics by Nevill Coghill
Canterbury Tales 1969

Good Night Ladies
Music by Edward Künneke
Lyrics by Clifford Grey
Mayflowers 1925

Good Night, My Beautiful
Music by Sammy Fain
Lyrics by Jack Yellen
George White's Scandals (1939)

Good Night, Sweetheart, Good Night
Music by Karl Hoschna
Lyrics by Otto Harbach
Three Twins 1908

The Good Old American Way
Music by Don Pippin
Lyrics by Steve Brown
Fashion (OB) 1974

A Good Old Burlesque Show
Music by Jimmy McHugh
Lyrics by Arthur Malvin
Sugar Babies 1979

Good Old California
Music and lyrics by George M. Cohan
Little Johnny Jones 1904

The Good Old Days
Music by Ray Henderson
Lyrics by B.G. DeSylva and Lew Brown
George White's Scandals (1931)

The Good Old Days
Music by Richard Lewine
Lyrics by Arnold B. Horwitt and Ted Fetter
Make Mine Manhattan 1948

Good Old Days
Music by Earl Robinson
Lyrics by Waldo Salt
Sandhog (OB) 1954

The Good Old Days
Music by Duke Ellington
Lyrics by Marshall Barer and Fred Tobias
Pousse-Café 1966

A Good Old Egg
Music by Maurice Yvain
Lyrics by Max and Nathaniel Lief
Luckee Girl 1928

Good Old Girl
Music by David Martin
Lyrics by Langston Hughes
Simply Heavenly 1957

Good Old Girls
Music and lyrics by Carol Hall
The Best Little Whorehouse in Texas 1978

The Good Old Ways
Music by Jacques Urbont
Lyrics by Bruce Geller
All in Love (OB) 1961

Good Pals
Music by Sigmund Romberg
Lyrics by Harry B. Smith
The Love Call 1927

Good Thing Going
Music and lyrics by Stephen Sondheim
Merrily We Roll Along 1981

Good Things Come
Music by Gerald Jay Markoe
Lyrics by Michael Colby
Charlotte Sweet (OB) 1982

Good Time Charlie
Music by Arthur Schwartz
Lyrics by Dorothy Fields
By the Beautiful Sea 1954

Good Time Charlie
Music by David Baker
Lyrics by Will Holt
Come Summer 1969

Good-Time Flat Blues
Music and lyrics by Buster Davis
Doctor Jazz 1975

The Good-Time Girl
Music and lyrics by Richard M. Sherman
and Robert B. Sherman
Over Here! 1974

Good Times Are Here to Stay
Music by Jim Wise
Lyrics by George Haimsohn
Dames at Sea (OB) 1968

Good to Be Alive
Music and lyrics by Harold Rome
The Zulu and the Zayda 1965

Good Vibrations
Music and lyrics by Micki Grant
Don't Bother Me, I Can't Cope (OB) 1972

The Good-Will Movement
Music and lyrics by Cole Porter
Mexican Hayride 1944

Goodbye
Music by Bill Weeden
Lyrics by David Finkle
Hurry, Harry 1972

Goodbye
Music and lyrics by Al Carmines
The Evangelist (OB) 1982

Goodbye, au Revoir, auf Wiedersehn
Music by Eric Coates
Lyrics by Irving Caesar
White Horse Inn 1936

Adapted from Coates' *Knightsbridge March*

Goodbye, Becky Cohen
Music and lyrics by Irving Berlin
Ziegfeld Follies of 1910

Goodbye, Bohemia
Music by Victor Herbert
Lyrics by Glen MacDonough
Algeria 1908

Goodbye, Canavaro
Music by John Kander
Lyrics by Fred Ebb
Zorba 1968

Goodbye Charlie
Music by Duke Ellington
Lyrics by Marshall Barer and Fred Tobias
Pousse-Café 1966

Goodbye, Darlin'
Music and lyrics by Frank Loesser
The Most Happy Fella 1956

Goodbye, Dear Friend
Music and lyrics by Jack Lawrence and Don Walker
Courtin' Time 1951

Goodbye, Failure, Goodbye
Music by Elmer Bernstein
Lyrics by Carolyn Leigh
How Now, Dow Jones 1967

Goodbye Feet
Music and lyrics by Elizabeth Swados
Alice in Concert (OB) 1980

Goodbye, Flo
Music and lyrics by George M. Cohan
Little Johnny Jones 1904

Goodbye, Georg
Music by Jerry Bock
Lyrics by Sheldon Harnick
She Loves Me 1963

Goodbye Girls, Hello Yale
Music by Richard Lewine
Lyrics by Ted Fetter
Naughty-Naught (OB) 1937

Good-Bye Girls, I'm Through
Music by Ivan Caryll
Lyrics John Golden
Chin-Chin 1914

Goodbye, Jonah
Music by Arthur Schwartz
Lyrics by Albert Stillman
Virginia 1937

Good-bye, Lenny!
Music by Richard Rodgers
Lyrics by Lorenz Hart
The Girl Friend 1926

Goodbye, Little Dream, Goodbye
Music and lyrics by Cole Porter
Red, Hot and Blue! 1936

Dropped from production

Goodbye, Little Rosebud
Music by Herbert Stothart
Lyrics by Otto Harbach and Oscar Hammerstein II
Wildflower 1923

Goodbye, My Bachelor
Music by David Baker
Lyrics by Will Holt
Come Summer 1969

Goodbye, My City
Music by Frank Fields
Lyrics by Armand Aulicino
The Shoemaker and the Peddler (OB) 1960

Goodbye, My Fancy
Music by Stan Harte, Jr.
Leaves of Grass (OB) 1971

Goodbye, My Lady Love
Music and lyrics by Joseph E. Howard

A popular song written in 1904 and inserted in the score of *Show Boat* (1927) by Jerome Kern.

Goodbye, My Love
Music by Sigmund Romberg
Lyrics by Oscar Hammerstein II
Viennese Nights (1930) F

Goodbye, My Sweet
Music by John Clifton
Lyrics by John Clifton and Ben Tarver
Man With a Load of Mischief (OB) 1966

Goodbye, Old Girl
Music and lyrics by Richard Adler
and Jerry Ross
Damn Yankees 1955

Goodbye, Paree
Music by Franz Lehár
Lyrics by Harry Graham
Yours Is My Heart 1946

Goodbye Salome
Music by Robert Waldman
Lyrics by Alfred Uhry
The Robber Bridegroom 1975

Goodbye to All That
Music by Arthur Schwartz
Lyrics by Ira Gershwin
Park Avenue 1946

Goodbye to Flirtation
Music by Paul A. Rubens
Lyrics by Paul A. Rubens and Arthur Wimperis
The Sunshine Girl 1913

Goodbye to the Old Love, Hello to the New
Music by George Gershwin
Lyrics by Ira Gershwin
Treasure Girl 1928

Dropped from production

Goodbyes
Music by Kenn Long and Jim Crozier
Lyrics by Kenn Long
Touch (OB) 1970

Goodbyes
Music by Galt MacDermot
Lyrics by Gerome Ragni
Dude 1972

Goodness Gracious
Music by Harry Ruby
Lyrics by Bert Kalmar
Top Speed 1929

Goodnight
Music by John Addison
Lyrics by John Cranko
Cranks 1956

Goodnight
Music and lyrics by William Finn
In Trousers (OB) 1981

Goodnight and Thank You
Music by Andrew Lloyd Webber
Lyrics by Tim Rice
Evita 1979

Goodnight Is Not Goodbye
Music by Billy Goldenberg
Lyrics by Alan and Marilyn Bergman
Ballroom 1978

Goodnight, My Someone
Music and lyrics by Meredith Willson
The Music Man 1957

The music is the same as that of the song that followed it in the show, "Seventy-Six Trombones"; the tempo is changed from a slow romantic ballad in 3/4 to a rousing march in 6/8.

Goodtime Charley
Music by Larry Grossman
Lyrics by Hal Hackady
Goodtime Charley 1975

Goona Goona
Music by Gerald Dolin
Lyrics by Edward J. Lambert
Smile at Me 1935

Goona-Goona
Music by Jerome Moross
Lyrics by John Latouche
The Golden Apple 1954

Goose Never Be a Peacock
Music by Harold Arlen
Lyrics by Johnny Mercer
Saratoga 1959

Gorgeous
Music by Jerry Bock
Lyrics by Sheldon Harnick
The Apple Tree 1966

Gorgeous Alexander
Music by Sigmund Romberg
Lyrics by Oscar Hammerstein II
The New Moon 1928

Gospel: Great Day
Music by Vernon Duke
Lyrics by John Latouche
Cabin in the Sky (1964 OB revival)

The Gospel of Gabriel Finn
Music by Galt MacDermot
Lyrics by Christopher Gore
Via Galactica 1972

The Gospel of No Name City
Music by André Previn
Lyrics by Alan Jay Lerner
Paint Your Wagon (film version, 1969)

Gossip
Music by Franz Steininger (adapted from
Tchaikovsky)
Lyrics by Forman Brown
Music in My Heart 1947

Gossip
Music by Don Gohman
Lyrics by Hal Hackady
Ambassador 1972

Gossip
Music and lyrics by Stephen Sondheim
Sunday in the Park With George (OB) 1983

The Gossip Song
Music by Harold Arlen
Lyrics by Johnny Mercer
Saratoga 1959

The Gossip Song
Music and lyrics by Rick Besoyan
Babes in the Wood (OB) 1964

The Gossips
Music and lyrics by Frank Loesser
Where's Charley? 1948

Got a Bran' New Suit
Music by Arthur Schwartz
Lyrics by Howard Dietz
At Home Abroad 1935

Got a Notion
Music and lyrics by Bland Simpson
and Jim Wann
Hot Grog (OB) 1977

Got a Rainbow
Music by George Gershwin
Lyrics by Ira Gershwin
Treasure Girl 1928

Got That Good Time Feelin'
Music and lyrics by Burton Lane
Laffing Room Only 1944

Got the World in the Palm of My Hand
Music and lyrics by Johnny Brandon
Cindy (OB) 1964

Got to Go to Town
Music by Harry Warren
Lyrics by Mort Dixon and Joe Young
The Laugh Parade 1931

Got to Have More
Music by Harry Tierney
Lyrics by Joseph McCarthy
Kid Boots 1923

Got What It Takes
Music by Sammy Stept
Lyrics by Dan Shapiro
Michael Todd's Peep Show 1950

Gott Iss Gut
Music by Jule Styne
Lyrics by Sammy Cahn
Look to the Lilies 1970

Gotta Dance
Music and lyrics by Hugh Martin
Look Ma, I'm Dancin'! 1948

Gotta Find a Way to Do It
Music by Roger Wolfe Kahn
Lyrics by Paul James
Nine-Fifteen Revue 1930

Gotta Get de Boat Loaded
Music and lyrics by Al Wilson, Charles Weinberg
and Ken Macomber
Yeah Man 1932

Gotta Get Joy
Music by Burton Lane
Lyrics by Al Dubin and Burton Lane
Laffing Room Only 1944

Gotta Get Out
Music and lyrics by John Clifton
El Bravo! (OB) 1981

Gotta Have Hips Now
Music by Russell Tarbox
Lyrics by Charles O. Locke
Hello, Paris 1930

Gotta Have Me Go With You
Music by Harold Arlen
Lyrics by Ira Gershwin
A Star Is Born (1954) F

Gotta Live Free
Music by Giuseppe Verdi (adapted by Hans Spialek)
Lyrics by Charles Friedman
My Darlin' Aïda 1952

Gotta Pay
Music and lyrics by Walter Cool
Mackey of Appalachia (OB) 1965

The Gown Is Mightier Than the Sword
Music by Richard Rodgers
Lyrics by Lorenz Hart
Poor Little Ritz Girl 1920

Included in Boston production, but dropped before Broadway opening.

Grab a Girl
Music by Jerome Kern
Lyrics by Howard Dietz
Dear Sir 1924

Grade Polonaise
Music by Lee Pockriss
Lyrics by Anne Croswell
Tovarich 1963

Graduation
Music by Elizabeth Swados
Lyrics by Garry Trudeau
Doonesbury 1983

Grafitti
Music by Hank Beebe
Lyrics by Bill Heyer
Tuscaloosa's Calling Me But I'm Not Going! (OB) 1975

The Grand and Glorious Fourth
Music by Robert Stolz
Lyrics by Robert Sour
Mr. Strauss Goes to Boston 1945

The Grand Cafe
Music by Larry Grossman
Lyrics by Betty Comden and Adolph Green
A Doll's Life 1982

The Grand Canal
Music and lyrics by Maury Yeston
Nine 1982

Grand Imperial Cirque de Paris
Music and lyrics by Bob Merrill
Carnival 1961

Grand Jury Jump
Music by Paul Klein
Lyrics by Fred Ebb
From A to Z 1960

Grand Knowing You
Music by Jerry Bock
Lyrics by Sheldon Harnick
She Loves Me 1963

Grand Old Ivy
Music and lyrics by Frank Loesser
How to Succeed in Business Without Really Trying 1961

The Grand Parade
Music and lyrics by William Roy
The Penny Friend (OB) 1966

Grand Parade
Music and lyrics by Walter Marks
Broadway Follies 1981

The Grand Prix of Portofino
Music by Louis Bellson and Will Irwin
Lyrics by Richard Ney
Portofino 1958

Grandma
Music by Harold Levey
Lyrics by Zelda Sears
The Clinging Vine 1922

Grandma's Song
Music by Jerome Kern
Lyrics by Oscar Hammerstein II
High, Wide and Handsome (1937) F

Dropped from film

Grandpapa
Music by John Kander
Lyrics by Fred Ebb
Zorba 1968

Grant
Music and lyrics by Oscar Brand
How to Steal an Election (OB) 1968

Grant Avenue
Music by Richard Rodgers
Lyrics by Oscar Hammerstein II
Flower Drum Song 1958

The Grass Grows Green
Music and lyrics by Richard M. Sherman and Robert B. Sherman
Over Here! 1974

The Grass Is Always Greener
Music by John Kander
Lyrics by Fred Ebb
Woman of the Year 1981

Grasshop Song
Music and lyrics by Robert Larimer
King of the Whole Damn World (OB) 1962

The Gray Goose
Music by George Lessner
Lyrics by Miriam Battista and Russell Maloney
Sleepy Hollow 1948

Grazie per Niente
Music by Sammy Fain
Lyrics by Marilyn and Alan Bergman
Something More 1964

Greased Lightnin'
Music and lyrics by Jim Jacobs and Warren Casey
Grease 1972

The Great All American Power Driven Engine
Music and lyrics by Johnny Brandon
Love! Love! Love! (OB) 1977

Great Big Bear
Music by Herbert Stothart
Lyrics by Otto Harbach and Oscar Hammerstein II
Song of the Flame 1925

The Great Chandelier
Music and lyrics by Sylvia Fine
The Straw Hat Revue 1939

Great Day!
Music by Vincent Youmans
Lyrics by Billy Rose and Edward Eliscu
Great Day! 1929

The Great Dictator and Me
Music by Frank D'Armond
Lyrics by Will Morrissey
Saluta 1934

Great Divide
Music and lyrics by Harry Chapin
The Night That Made America Famous 1975

The Great Forever Wagon
Music by Galt MacDermot
Lyrics by Christopher Gore
Via Galactica 1972

The Great If
Music by Helen Miller
Lyrics by Eve Merriam
Inner City 1971

The Great Indoors
Music and lyrics by Cole Porter
The New Yorkers 1930

Great Little Guy
Music by Lewis E. Gensler
Lyrics by Robert A. Simon
Ups-a-Daisy 1928

The Great Lover Tango
Music by Otis Clements
Lyrics by Charles Gaynor
Irene (1973 revival)

The Great New York Police
Music and lyrics by George M. Cohan
Little Nellie Kelly 1922

Great Scot!
Music by Don McAfee
Lyrics by Nancy Leeds
Great Scot! (OB) 1965

The Great Unknown
Music and lyrics by William Roy
The Penny Friend (OB) 1966

The Great White Easiest Way
Music by Victor Herbert
Lyrics by Glen MacDonough
Algeria 1908

Great White Father
Music by Gary Geld
Lyrics by Peter Udell
Purlie 1970

Great White Way in China
Music by A. Baldwin Sloane
Lyrics by Harry Cort and George E. Stoddard
China Rose 1925

Great Workers for the Cause
Music by Norman Campbell
Lyrics by Donald Harron and Norman Campbell
Anne of Green Gables (OB) 1971

The Great Writer
Music by Larry Grossman
Lyrics by Hal Hackady
Snoopy (OB) 1982

The Great Zampano
Music and lyrics by Lionel Bart
La Strada 1969

The Greatest Gift
Music and lyrics by James Quinn and Alaric Jans
Do Patent Leather Shoes Really Reflect Up? 1982

The Greatest Invention
Music and lyrics by Matt Dubey, Harold Karr
and Sid Silvers
New Faces of 1956

The Greatest Show on Earth
Music by Kurt Weill
Lyrics by Ira Gershwin
Lady in the Dark 1941

The Greatest Team of All
Music by William Daly and Paul Lannin
Lyrics by Arthur Jackson
For Goodness Sake 1922

Greathead Shield
Music by Earl Robinson
Lyrics by Waldo Salt
Sandhog (OB) 1954

The Grecian Bend
Music by Edward Künneke
Lyrics by Clifford Grey
Mayflowers 1925

Greedy Girl
Music and lyrics by Marc Blitzstein
Regina 1949

The Greek Marine
Music by Jacques Offenbach (adapted by Robert DeCormier)
Lyrics by E.Y. Harburg
The Happiest Girl in the World 1961

The Greeks Have No Word for It
Music by Richard Rodgers
Lyrics by Lorenz Hart
The Boys From Syracuse (film version, 1940)

Green and Blue
Music by Eubie Blake
Lyrics by J. Milton Reddie and Cecil Mack
Swing It 1937

Green Carnations
Music and lyrics by Noël Coward
Bitter Sweet 1929

Green Finch and Linnet Bird
Music and lyrics by Stephen Sondheim
Sweeney Todd 1979

Green Pastures
Music by Eubie Blake
Lyrics by Will Morrissey and Andy Razaf
Blackbirds of 1930

A Green Place
Music by Howard Marren
Lyrics by Enid Futterman
Portrait of Jennie (OB) 1982

Green Pond
Music by Mel Marvin
Lyrics by Robert Montgomery
Green Pond (OB) 1977

Green River Glide
Music by Jerome Kern
Lyrics by Anne Caldwell
Good Morning, Dearie 1921

Dropped from production

Green-Up Time
Music by Kurt Weill
Lyrics by Alan Jay Lerner
Love Life 1948

Greenspons
Music by Rob Fremont
Lyrics by Doris Willens
Piano Bar (OB) 1978

Greenwich Village
Music by Jerome Kern
Lyrics by P.G. Wodehouse
Oh, Lady! Lady!! 1918

Greenwich Village Follies
Music and lyrics by Ronnie Britton
Greenwich Village Follies (OB) 1976

Greenwich Village U.S.A.
Music by Jeanne Bargy
Lyrics by Jeanne Bargy, Frank Gehrecke and Herb Corey
Greenwich Village U.S.A. (OB) 1960

Greenwillow Christmas
Music and lyrics by Frank Loesser
Greenwillow 1960

Greeting
Music by Heitor Villa-Lobos
Lyrics by Robert Wright and George Forrest
Magdalena 1948

The Greeting Cards
Music by Vernon Duke
Lyrics by John Latouche
Banjo Eyes 1941

Greetings
Music and lyrics by Rick Besoyan
The Student Gypsy (OB) 1963

Greetings, Gates
Music by Hoagy Carmichael
Lyrics by Johnny Mercer
Walk With Music 1940

The Grenadiers' Marching Song
Music and lyrics by Rick Besoyan
The Student Gypsy (OB) 1963

The Grey Dove
Music by Ivan Caryll
Lyrics by Anne Caldwell and James O'Dea
Chin-Chin 1914

Gringola
Music and lyrics by Charles Tobias, Charles Newman and Murray Mencher
Earl Carroll's Sketch Book (1935)

Grizabella, the Glamour Cat
Music by Andrew Lloyd Webber
Cats 1982

Lyrics based on T.S. Eliot's *Old Possum's Book of Practical Cats*

Grocery Boy
Music by Jacques Urbont
Lyrics by David Newburger
Stag Movie (OB) 1971

Groovy Green Man Groovy
Music and lyrics by James Rado
Rainbow (OB) 1972

The Ground Was Always in Play
Music and lyrics by Elizabeth Swados
Dispatches (OB) 1979

The Grove of Eucalyptus
Music by Naomi Shemer
Lyrics by George Sherman
To Live Another Summer 1971

Grovel, Grovel
Music by Andrew Lloyd Webber
Lyrics by Tim Rice
*Joseph and the Amazing
Technicolor Dreamcoat* 1982

Grow for Me
Music by Alan Menken
Lyrics by Howard Ashman
Little Shop of Horrors (OB) 1982

Growing Pains
Music by Don Walker
Lyrics by Clay Warnick
Memphis Bound 1945

Growing Pains
Music by Arthur Schwartz
Lyrics by Dorothy Fields
A Tree Grows in Brooklyn 1951

Growltiger's Last Stand
Music by Andrew Lloyd Webber
Cats 1982

Lyrics based on T.S. Eliot's *Old Possum's
Book of Practical Cats*

Gruntled
Music and lyrics by Ray Golden, Sy Kleinman
and Philip Charig
Catch a Star! 1955

Guarantee
Music and lyrics by Walter Marks
Bajour 1964

Guarded
Music by Emmerich Kálmán
Lyrics by Harry B. Smith
The Circus Princess 1927

The Guards of Fantasy
Music by Maury Rubens
Lyrics by Clifford Grey
The Great Temptations 1926

Guenevere
Music by Frederick Loewe
Lyrics by Alan Jay Lerner
Camelot 1960

Guess Who I Saw Today?
Music by Murray Grand
Lyrics by Elisse Boyd
New Faces of 1952

The Guests
Music and lyrics by Irving Berlin
The Cocoanuts 1925

Guido's Song
Music and lyrics by Maury Yeston
Nine 1982

Guilty!
Music by Frank Fields
Lyrics by Armand Aulicino
The Shoemaker and the Peddler (OB) 1960

Guilty
Music by Elizabeth Swados
Lyrics by Garry Trudeau
Doonesbury 1983

Guinea Pig
Music and lyrics by James Rado
Rainbow (OB) 1972

Guiness, Woman
Music by Kenn Long and Jim Crozier
Lyrics by Kenn Long
Touch (OB) 1970

Guitar Song
Music by Peter Link
Lyrics by C.C. Courtney and Ragan Courtney
Earl of Ruston 1971

The Gunman
Music by Raymond Hubbell
Lyrics by Anne Caldwell
Yours Truly 1927

Guns Are Fun
Music and lyrics by Al Carmines
Wanted (OB) 1972

Gus and Sadie Love Song
Music and lyrics by Marc Blitzstein
The Cradle Will Rock 1938

Gus: The Theatre Cat
Music by Andrew Lloyd Webber
Cats 1982

Lyrics based on T.S. Eliot's *Old Possum's
Book of Practical Cats*

Gussy and the Beautiful People
Music by Mildred Kayden
Lyrics by Frank Gagliano
Paradise Gardens East (OB) 1969

Gut Rocks
Music and lyrics by Ann Harris
Sky High (OB) 1979

The Gutter Song
Music and lyrics by James Shelton
New Faces of 1934

A Guy, A Guy, A Guy
Music by Alfred Brooks
Lyrics by Ira J. Bilowit
Of Mice and Men (OB) 1958

The Guy Who Brought Me
Music and lyrics by Hugh Martin and Ralph Blane
Best Foot Forward 1941

Guys and Dolls
Music and lyrics by Frank Loesser
Guys and Dolls 1950

Gypsy
Music by Harden Church
Lyrics by Edward Heyman
Caviar 1934

Gypsy Blues
Music and lyrics by Noble Sissle and Eubie Blake
Shuffle Along 1921

A great admirer of Victor Herbert, Eubie Blake
wrote this song as an obligato to the refrain of the
"Gypsy Love Song" from Herbert's *The Fortune
Teller.*

Gypsy, Bring Your Fiddle
Music by Emmerich Kálmán
Lyrics by P.G. Wodehouse
The Riviera Girl 1917

Gypsy Days
Music by Arthur Schwartz
Lyrics by Morrie Ryskind
Ned Wayburn's Gambols 1929

The Gypsy in Me
Music and lyrics by Cole Porter
Anything Goes 1934

Gypsy Jan
Music by Victor Herbert
Lyrics by Harry B. Smith
The Fortune Teller 1898

Gypsy Joe
Music by Walter Donaldson
Lyrics by Gus Kahn
Whoopee 1928

Gypsy Life
Music by Victor Herbert
Lyrics by Rida Johnson Young
The Dream Girl 1924

The Gypsy Life
Music and lyrics by Rick Besoyan
The Student Gypsy (OB) 1963

Gypsy Love
Music by Franz Lehár
Lyrics by Harry B. and Robert B. Smith
Gypsy Love 1911

Gypsy Love
Music by Jimmy McHugh
Lyrics by Dorothy Fields
Lew Leslie's International Revue 1930

Gypsy Love Song
Music by Victor Herbert
Lyrics by Harry B. Smith
The Fortune Teller 1898

Gypsy of Love
Music and lyrics by Rick Besoyan
The Student Gypsy (OB) 1963

Gypsy Rose
Music by Lewis E. Gensler
Lyrics by Owen Murphy and Robert A. Simon
The Gang's All Here 1931

Gypsy Song
Music by Sigmund Romberg
Lyrics by Rida Johnson Young
Maytime 1917

Gypsy Sweetheart
Music and lyrics by Irving Kahal, Francis Wheeler
and Ted Snyder
Footlights 1927

The Gypsy Trail
Music by Vincent Youmans and Paul Lannin
Lyrics by Arthur Francis
Two Little Girls in Blue 1921

Ha! Cha! Cha!
Music by Jerome Kern
Lyrics by Otto Harbach
The Cat and the Fiddle 1931

Also titled " Hh! Cha! Cha!"

Ha, Ha, Ha
Music and lyrics by Cole Porter
You Never Know 1938

Dropped from production

Ha! Ha! Ha! That's Interesting
Music by Franz Lehár
Lyrics by Harry B. and Robert B. Smith
Gypsy Love 1911

Hacienda Garden
Music and lyrics by Ida Hoyt Chamberlain
Enchanted Isle 1927

Hack 'Em
Music and lyrics by Bland Simpson and Jim Wann
Hot Grog (OB) 1977

Hackney-Blue Eyes
Music by Scott Killian
and Kim D. Sherman
Lyrics by Kenneth Robins, Scott Killian
and Kim D. Sherman
Lenny and the Heartbreakers (OB) 1983

Hail, Bibinski
Music and lyrics by Cole Porter
Silk Stockings 1955

Hail Britannia
Music and lyrics by Irving Burgie
Ballad for Bimshire (OB) 1963

Hail, Hail
Music and lyrics by Peter Copani
New York City Street Show (OB) 1977

Hail, Hail, Hail
Music and lyrics by Cole Porter
Out of This World 1950

Hail Sphinx
Music and lyrics by Ervin Drake
Her First Roman 1968

Hail Stonewall Jackson
Music by Sigmund Romberg
Lyrics by Dorothy Donnelly
My Maryland 1927

Hail the Bridegroom
Music by A. Baldwin Sloane
Lyrics by Harry Cort and George E. Stoddard
China Rose 1925

Hail, the Conquering Hero!
Music by Moose Charlap
Lyrics by Norman Gimbel
The Conquering Hero 1961

Hail the Happy Couple
Music by George Gershwin
Lyrics by Ira Gershwin
Pardon My English 1933

Hail the King
Music by H. Maurice Jacquet
Lyrics by Preston Sturges
The Well of Romance 1930

Hail, the Mythic Smew
Music by Alec Wilder
Lyrics by Arnold Sundgaard
Kittiwake Island (OB) 1960

Hail the Son of David
Music by Ernest Gold
Lyrics by Anne Croswell
I'm Solomon 1968

Hail to Christmas
Music by Victor Herbert
Lyrics by Glen MacDonough
Babes in Toyland 1903

Hail to MacCracken's
Music and lyrics by Johnny Mercer
Top Banana 1951

Hail to Our General
Music by Oscar Straus
Lyrics by Edward Delaney Dunn
The Last Waltz 1921

Hail to Our Noble Guest
Music by Gustav Luders
Lyrics by Frank Pixley
The Prince of Pilsen 1903

Hail to the Bride
Music by A. Baldwin Sloane
Lyrics by E. Ray Goetz
The Hen Pecks 1911

Hair
Music by Galt MacDermot
Lyrics by Gerome Ragni and James Rado
Hair 1968

The Hair of the Heir
Music by Edward A. Horan
Lyrics by Frederick Herendeen
All the King's Horses 1934

Hairpin Harmony
Music and lyrics by Harold Orlob
Hairpin Harmony 1943

Half a Married Man
Music by Emmerich Kálmán
Lyrics by P.G. Wodehouse
The Riviera Girl 1917

Half a Moon
Music by James F. Hanley
Lyrics by Eddie Dowling and Herbert Reynolds
Honeymoon Lane 1926

Half a Sixpence
Music and lyrics by David Heneker
Half a Sixpence 1965

Half Alive
Music by Helen Miller
Lyrics by Eve Merriam
Inner City 1971

Half as Big as Life
Music by Burt Bacharach
Lyrics by Hal David
Promises, Promises 1968

Half-Caste Woman
Music and lyrics by Noël Coward
Ziegfeld Follies (1931)

Half of a Couple
Music by Charles Strouse
Lyrics by Lee Adams
Bring Back Birdie 1981

The Half of It, Dearie, Blues
Music by George Gershwin
Lyrics by Ira Gershwin
Lady, Be Good! 1924

Half of Me
Music by George Fischoff
Lyrics by Carole Bayer
Georgy 1970

Half-Past Two
Music by Howard Talbot
Lyrics by Percy Greenbank and Arthur Wimperis
The Arcadians 1910

Half the Battle
Music by Mark Sandrich, Jr.
Lyrics by Sidney Michaels
Ben Franklin in Paris 1964

Half Way to Heaven
Music by Mario Braggiotti
Lyrics by David Sidney
The Vanderbilt Revue 1930

Halfway to Heaven
Music by Harris Wheeler
Lyrics by Mary L. Fisher
Blue Plate Special (OB) 1983

Hallelujah!
Music by Vincent Youmans
Lyrics by Leo Robin and Clifford Grey
Hit the Deck 1927

While serving at the Great Lakes Naval Training Station near Chicago during World War I, Youmans wrote this tune as a march to be performed by the U.S. Navy Band. The bandmaster was so impressed that he showed the score to John Philip Sousa, who liked it and conducted it at several concerts.

Hallelujah
Music by Don Elliott
Lyrics by James Costigan
The Beast in Me 1963

Hallelujah
Music by Stanley Silverman
Lyrics by Arthur Miller
Up From Paradise (OB) 1983

Hallelujah, Baby
Music by Jule Styne
Lyrics by Betty Comden and Adolph Green
Hallelujah, Baby! 1967

Hallelujah, I'm a Bum
Music by Richard Rodgers
Lyrics by Lorenz Hart
Hallelujah, I'm a Bum (1933) F

There were two songs in the film with this title,
each of them sung by Al Jolson. Both Richard
Rodgers and Lorenz Hart played bit parts in the
film; Rodgers was a photographer's assistant (non-
speaking), and Hart played a bank teller (speaking
briefly).

Halloween Hayride
Music by Nancy Ford
Lyrics by Gretchen Cryer
Now Is the Time for All Good Men (OB) 1967

Hallowe'en Whoopee Ball
Music by Walter Donaldson
Lyrics by Gus Kahn
Whoopee 1928

Ham and Eggs in the Morning
Music by Con Conrad and Abner Silver
Lyrics by Al Dubin
Take the Air 1927

Hamburg Waltz
Music by Gerard Calvi
Lyrics by Harold Rome
La Grosse Valise 1965

Hammerstein's Music Hall
Music by Howard Marren
Lyrics by Enid Futterman
Portrait of Jennie (OB) 1982

Hammock in the Blue
Music by Jacques Belasco
Lyrics by Kay Twomey
The Girl From Nantucket 1945

Hand in Hand
Music and lyrics by Robert Wright and George
Forrest (based on Rachmaninoff)
Anya 1965

The Hand-me-Down Blues
Music by Vincent Youmans
Lyrics by Zelda Sears
Lollipop 1924

Dropped from production

Hand Me Down That Can o' Beans
Music by Frederick Loewe
Lyrics by Alan Jay Lerner
Paint Your Wagon 1951

The Hand of Fate
Music by Galt MacDermot
Lyrics by Rochelle Owens
The Karl Marx Play (OB) 1973

A Handbag Is Not a Proper Mother
Music by Lee Pockriss
Lyrics by Anne Croswell
Ernest in Love (OB) 1960

Handle Me With Care
Music by Jean Schwartz
Lyrics by William Jerome
Follies of 1907

Handsome Husbands
Music by Baldwin Bergersen
Lyrics by William Archibald
The Crystal Heart (OB) 1960

Handsome Stranger
Music and lyrics by Frederick Silver
Gay Company (OB) 1974

The Handsomest Man
Music by Galt MacDermot
Lyrics by Gerome Ragni
Dude 1972

Hang a Little Moolah on the Washline
Music by Claibe Richardson
Lyrics by Kenward Elmslie
The Grass Harp 1971

Hang on to Me
Music by George Gershwin
Lyrics by Ira Gershwin
Lady, Be Good! 1924

Hang Up!
Music by Arthur Schwartz
Lyrics by Dorothy Fields
By the Beautiful Sea 1954

Hang Up Your Hat on Broadway
Music by Bernard Grossman
Lyrics by Dave Sylvester
Tattle Tales 1933

Hang Your Hat on the Moon
Music by Jean Schwartz
Lyrics by Clifford Grey and William Cary Duncan
Sunny Days 1928

Hang Your Sorrows in the Sun
Music by John Egan
Lyrics by Dorothy Donnelly
Poppy 1923

Hangin' Around With You
Music by George Gershwin
Lyrics by Ira Gershwin
Strike Up the Band 1930

Hanging Around Yo' Door
Music by James P. Johnson
Lyrics by Flournoy Miller
Sugar Hill 1931

Hanging Out
Music and lyrics by Peter Copani
New York City Street Show (OB) 1977

Hanging Throttlebottom in the Morning
Music by George Gershwin
Lyrics by Ira Gershwin
Let 'Em Eat Cake 1933

Happiest Day of My Life
Music by Burton Lane
Lyrics by Alan Jay Lerner
Royal Wedding (1951) F

The Happiest Girl in the World
Music by Jacques Offenbach (adapted by Robert
DeCormier)
Lyrics by E.Y. Harburg
The Happiest Girl in the World 1961

The Happiest House on the Block
Music by Richard Rodgers
Lyrics by Oscar Hammerstein II
Pipe Dream 1955

Happily Ever After
Music by Mary Rodgers
Lyrics by Marshall Barer
Once Upon a Mattress 1959

Happily Ever After
Music and lyrics by Stephen Sondheim
Marry Me a Little (OB) 1981

Dropped from *Company* (1970)

Happiness
Music by Marie Gordon
Lyrics by David Rogers
New Faces of 1962

Happiness
Music and lyrics by Clark Gesner
You're a Good Man, Charlie Brown (OB) 1967

Happiness and Joy to the King
Music by Albert Sirmay and Arthur Schwartz
Lyrics by Arthur Swanstrom
Princess Charming 1930

Happiness Is a Thing Called Joe
Music by Harold Arlen
Lyrics by E.Y. Harburg
Cabin in the Sky (film version, 1943)

Happy
Music and lyrics by Porter Grainger and Freddie
Johnson
Lucky Sambo 1925

Happy
Music by Frank Grey
Lyrics by Earle Crooker and McElbert Moore
Happy 1927

Happy
Music and lyrics by George M. Cohan
Billie 1928

Happy
Music by Nat Reed
Lyrics by Bob Joffe
Brown Buddies 1930

Happy Anniversary
Music by Galt MacDermot
Lyrics by William Dumaresq
The Human Comedy (OB) 1983

Happy Because I'm in Love
Music by Vincent Youmans
Lyrics by Billy Rose and Edward Eliscu
Great Day! 1929

Happy Birthday
Music by George Gershwin
Lyrics by Gus Kahn and Ira Gershwin
Show Girl 1929

Happy Birthday
Music by Frederico Valerio
Lyrics by Elizabeth Miele
Hit the Trail 1954

Happy Birthday
Music and lyrics by Jay Livingston and Ray Evans
Let It Ride 1961

Happy Birthday
Music by John Kander
Lyrics by Fred Ebb
Zorba 1968

Happy Birthday
Music by Nancy Ford
Lyrics by Gretchen Cryer
*I'm Getting My Act Together and Taking It
on the Road* 1978

Happy Birthday
Music by Galt MacDermot
Lyrics by William Dumaresq
The Human Comedy (OB) 1983

Happy Birthday, Mrs. J. J. Brown
Music and lyrics by Meredith Willson
The Unsinkable Molly Brown 1960

Happy Bride
Music by A. Baldwin Sloane
Lyrics by Harry Cort and George E. Stoddard
China Rose 1925

Happy Christmas, Little Friend
Music by Richard Rodgers
Lyrics by Oscar Hammerstein II
Written for *Life* magazine in 1952

Happy Days
Music by Ray Henderson
Lyrics by B.G. DeSylva and Lew Brown
Good News 1927

The Happy Daze Saloon
Music and lyrics by Will Holt
That 5 A.M. Jazz (OB) 1964

Happy Easter
Music and lyrics by Irving Berlin
Easter Parade (1948) F

The Happy End
Music by Kurt Weill
Lyrics by Bertolt Brecht (adapted by Michael
Feingold)
Happy End 1977

Happy Ending
Music by Harvey Schmidt
Lyrics by Tom Jones
The Fantasticks (OB) 1960

Happy Go Lucky
Music by Lucien Denni
Lyrics by Helena Evans
Happy Go Lucky 1926

Happy Go Lucky
Music by Harry Ruby
Lyrics by Bert Kalmar
The Five o'Clock Girl 1927

Happy Guy
Music by Jeanne Bargy
Lyrics by Jeanne Bargy, Frank Gehrecke
and Herb Corey
Greenwich Village U.S.A. (OB) 1960

Happy Habit
Music by Arthur Schwartz
Lyrics by Dorothy Fields
By the Beautiful Sea 1954

Happy, Happy New Year
Music by Charles Strouse
Lyrics by Alan Jay Lerner
Dance a Little Closer 1983

The Happy Heaven of Harlem
Music and lyrics by Cole Porter
Fifty Million Frenchmen 1929

Happy Hickory
Music by Monty Norman
Lyrics by Julian More
The Moony Shapiro Songbook 1981

Happy Hoboes
Music by Ray Henderson
Lyrics by B.G. DeSylva
Three Cheers 1928

Happy Holiday
Music and lyrics by Irving Berlin
Holiday Inn (1942) F

Happy Hunting
Music by Sammy Fain
Lyrics by E.Y. Harburg
Flahooley 1951

Happy Hunting
Music by Harold Karr
Lyrics by Matt Dubey
Happy Hunting 1956

Happy Hunting Horn
Music by Richard Rodgers
Lyrics by Lorenz Hart
Pal Joey 1940

Happy in Love
Music by Sammy Fain
Lyrics by Jack Yellen
Sons o' Fun 1941

Happy in the Morning
Music by John Kander
Lyrics by Fred Ebb
Woman of the Year 1981

Happy Landing
Music by Ray Henderson
Lyrics by B.G. DeSylva and Lew Brown
Flying High 1930

Happy Little Crook
Music by Victor Young
Lyrics by Stella Unger
Seventh Heaven 1955

Happy Little Jeanne
Music by Carl Millöcker (revised by Theo
Mackeben)
Lyrics by Rowland Leigh
The Dubarry 1932

Happy Little Weekend
Music by Robert Russell Bennett
Lyrics by Owen Murphy and Robert A. Simon
Hold Your Horses 1933

Happy Man
Music by Don Gohman
Lyrics by Hal Hackady
Ambassador 1972

Happy Melody
Music by Lucien Denni
Lyrics by Helena Evans
Happy Go Lucky 1926

Happy New Year
Music by Don McAfee
Lyrics by Nancy Leeds
Great Scot! (OB) 1965

Happy Rickshaw Man
Music by Sigmund Romberg
Lyrics by Harry B. Smith
Cherry Blossoms 1927

A Happy Song
Music by Donald Swann
Lyrics by Michael Flanders
At the Drop of a Hat 1959

Happy Song
Music by Gerard Calvi
Lyrics by Harold Rome
La Grosse Valise 1965

Happy Talk
Music by Richard Rodgers
Lyrics by Oscar Hammerstein II
South Pacific 1949

Happy the Day
Music by Jack Waller and Joseph Tunbridge
Lyrics by R.P. Weston and Bert Lee
Tell Her the Truth 1932

The Happy Time
Music by John Kander
Lyrics by Fred Ebb
The Happy Time 1968

Happy to Keep His Dinner Warm
Music and lyrics by Frank Loesser
*How to Succeed in Business
Without Really Trying* 1961

Happy to Make Your Acquaintance
Music and lyrics by Frank Loesser
The Most Happy Fella 1956

A Happy Wedding Day
Music by Jerome Kern
Lyrics by Anne Caldwell
She's a Good Fellow 1919

The Happy Wedding Day
Music by Victor Jacobi
Lyrics by William LeBaron
Apple Blossoms 1919

Harbor of Dreams
Music by George Gershwin
Lyrics by Ira Gershwin
Tip-Toes 1925

Dropped from production

The Harbor of My Heart
Music by Vincent Youmans
Lyrics by Leo Robin and Clifford Grey
Hit the Deck 1927

Hard-Boiled Herman
Music by Herbert Stothart
Lyrics by Oscar Hammerstein II
and Otto Harbach
Rose Marie 1924

Hard Candy Christmas
Music and lyrics by Carol Hall
The Best Little Whorehouse in Texas 1978

Hard Hat Stetsons
Music by Clinton Ballard
Lyrics by Carolyn Richter
The Ballad of Johnny Pot (OB) 1971

Hard Times
Music by C. Luckey Roberts
Lyrics by Alex C. Rogers
My Magnolia 1926

Hard to Get Along With
Music by Charles Rosoff
Lyrics by Leo Robin
Judy 1927

Hard to Love
Music by Mel Marvin
Lyrics by Robert Montgomery
Green Pond (OB) 1977

Hard to Say Goodbye, My Love
Music by Henry Krieger
Lyrics by Tom Eyen
Dreamgirls 1981

The Harder They Fall
Music by Gary Geld
Lyrics by Peter Udell
Purlie 1970

Hare Krishna
Music by Galt MacDermot
Lyrics by Gerome Ragni and James Rado
Hair 1968

The Harem
Music and lyrics by Irving Gordon, Alan Roberts
and Jerome Brainin
Star and Garter 1942

Harem Life
Music and lyrics by Irving Berlin
Ziegfeld Follies of 1919

Hari Krishna
Music and lyrics by Al Carmines
The Faggot (OB) 1973

Hark to the Song of the Night
Music and lyrics by Cole Porter
Out of This World 1950

Harlem
Music by Ford Dabney
Lyrics by Jo Trent
Rang-Tang 1927

Harlem Dan
Music and lyrics by Alexander Hill
Hummin' Sam 1933

Harlem Follies
Music and lyrics by Stephen H. Lemberg
Jazzbo Brown 1980

Harlem Lullaby
Music and lyrics by Willard Robinson
Tattle Tales 1933

Harlem Mania
Music and lyrics by Donald Heywood
Blackberries of 1932

Harlem Moon
Music by Alberta Nichols
Lyrics by Mann Holiner
Rhapsody in Black 1931

Harlem on My Mind
Music and lyrics by Irving Berlin
As Thousands Cheer 1933

Harlem River Chanty
Music by George Gershwin
Lyrics by Ira Gershwin
Tip-Toes 1925

Dropped from production

Harlem Serenade
Music by George Gershwin
Lyrics by Gus Kahn and Ira Gershwin
Show Girl 1929

Harlem Streets
Music and lyrics by Micki Grant
Don't Bother Me, I Can't Cope (OB) 1972

Harlem Town
Music by Jimmy Johnson
Lyrics by Perry Bradford
Messin' Around 1929

Harlequinade
Music and lyrics by Richard Adler and Jerry Ross
John Murray Anderson's Almanac (1953)

Harmony
Music by Jimmy Van Heusen
Lyrics by Johnny Burke
Nellie Bly 1946

Harmony
Music by John Kander
Lyrics by James Goldman, John Kander
and William Goldman
A Family Affair 1962

Harmony
Music by Mildred Kayden
Lyrics by Frank Gagliano
Paradise Gardens East (OB) 1969

Harmony, Mass.
Music by William Dyer
Lyrics by Don Parks and William Dyer
Jo (OB) 1964

Harriet Sedley
Music by Laurence Rosenthal
Lyrics by James Lipton
Sherry! 1967

Harrigan
Music and lyrics by George M. Cohan
Fifty Miles From Boston 1908

Has Anybody Here Seen Kelly?
Music by Raymond Hubbell
Lyrics by Glen MacDonough
The Jolly Bachelors 1910

From the show's theater program: "This song (Has Anybody Here Seen Kelly?) was originally introduced in this piece and has been widely pirated."

Has Anybody Seen Our Ship?
Music and lyrics by Noël Coward
Tonight at 8:30 ("Red Peppers") 1936

Has Anyone Seen My Joe?
Music by George Gershwin
Lyrics by B.G. DeSylva and E. Ray Goetz
George White's Scandals (1922)

See note on show

Has I Let You Down?
Music by Harold Arlen
Lyrics by Harold Arlen and Truman Capote
House of Flowers 1954

Hashish
Music by Galt MacDermot
Lyrics by Gerome Ragni and James Rado
Hair 1968

Hasseltown
Music by Kenn Long and Jim Crozier
Lyrics by Kenn Long
Touch (OB) 1970

Hasta Luego
Music and lyrics by Cole Porter
Something to Shout About (1943) F

The Hat
Music by Lee Pockriss
Lyrics by Anne Croswell
Ernest in Love (OB) 1960

Hate Song
Music by Mary Rodgers
Lyrics by and Steven Vinaver
The Mad Show (OB) 1966

Hate to Say Goodbye to You
Music by Richard Adler
Lyrics by Will Holt
Music Is 1976

Hathor
Music and lyrics by Peter Stampfel
Operation Sidewinder 1970

Hats
Music by Ivan Caryll
Lyrics by Adrian Ross
Our Miss Gibbs 1910

Hats and Mice and Fish
Music by Larry Grossman
Lyrics by Betty Comden and Adolph Green
A Doll's Life 1982

Hats Make the Woman
Music by Victor Herbert
Lyrics by Henry Blossom
Mlle. Modiste 1905

Hats Off
Music by Richard Lewine
Lyrics by Ted Fetter
The Girl From Wyoming (OB) 1938

Haunted Heart
Music by Arthur Schwartz
Lyrics by Howard Dietz
Inside U.S.A. 1948

Haunted Hot Spot
Music by Vernon Duke
Lyrics by Ogden Nash
Two's Company 1952

Haunting Refrain
Music by William Heagney
Lyrics by William Heagney and Tom Connell
There You Are 1932

Haute Couture
Music by Jimmy Van Heusen
Lyrics by Sammy Cahn
Skyscraper 1965

Havana
Music by Richard Rodgers
Lyrics by Lorenz Hart
Peggy-Ann 1926

Havanola Roll
Music by Frank Grey
Lyrics by McElbert Moore and Frank Grey
The Matinee Girl 1926

Have a Dream
Music by Charles Strouse
Lyrics by Lee Adams
All American 1962

Have a Good Time Everybody
Music and lyrics by Noble Sissle
and Eubie Blake
The Chocolate Dandies 1924

Have a Heart
Music by Jerome Kern
Lyrics by Gene Buck
Ziegfeld Follies of 1916

This song is entirely different from the title number
in the Kern-Wodehouse show *Have a Heart* (1917).

Have a Heart
Music by Jerome Kern
Lyrics by P.G. Wodehouse
Have a Heart 1917

Have a Heart
Music by Burton Lane
Lyrics by Harold Adamson
Earl Carroll's Vanities (1931)

Have I Finally Found My Heart?
Music by Garry Sherman
Lyrics by Peter Udell
Comin' Uptown 1979

Have I Got a Girl for You
Music and lyrics by Stephen Sondheim
Company 1970

Have I Got a Girl for You
Music and lyrics by Cliff Jones
Rockabye Hamlet 1976

Have I the Right?
Music by Charles Strouse
Lyrics by David Rogers
Charlie and Algernon 1980

Have I Told You Lately?
Music and lyrics by Harold Rome
I Can Get It for You Wholesale 1962

Have Some Pot
Music by Clinton Ballard
Lyrics by Carolyn Richter
The Ballad of Johnny Pot (OB) 1971

Have You Ever Been Alone With a King Before?
Music by Bill Weeden
Lyrics by David Finkle
I'm Solomon 1968

Have You Ever Seen a Prettier Little Congress?
Music by Jerry Bock
Lyrics by Sheldon Harnick
The Rothschilds 1970

Have You Forgotten?
Music by Emil Gerstenberger and Carle Carlton
Lyrics by Howard Johnson
The Lace Petticoat 1927

"Have You Forgotten Me" Blues
Music by Jerome Kern
Lyrics by Anne Caldwell
The Bunch and Judy 1922

Have You Got Charm?
Music and lyrics by Irving Burgie
Ballad for Bimshire (OB) 1963

Have You Heard?
Music by Ernest Gold
Lyrics by Anne Croswell
I'm Solomon 1968

Have You Heard the News?
Music by Glenn Paxton
Lyrics by Robert Goldman and George Weiss
First Impressions 1959

Have You Met Delilah?
Music by James Mundy
Lyrics by John Latouche
The Vamp 1955

Have You Met Miss Jones?
Music by Richard Rodgers
Lyrics by Lorenz Hart
I'd Rather Be Right 1937

Have You Seen the Countess Cindy?
Music by David Raksin
Lyrics by June Carroll
If the Shoe Fits 1946

Have You Used Soft Soap?
Music by Albert Von Tilzer
Lyrics by Neville Fleeson
Bye Bye, Bonnie 1927

Have Yourself a Merry Little Christmas
Music and lyrics by Hugh Martin and Ralph Blane
Meet Me in St. Louis (1944) F

Haven't We Met Before?
Music by Jerry Livingston
Lyrics by Mack David
Bright Lights of 1944

Havin' a Time
Music by Morton Gould
Lyrics by Betty Comden and Adolph Green
Billion Dollar Baby 1945

Havin' a Wonderful Time
Music and lyrics by Porter Grainger
and Freddie Johnson
Lucky Sambo 1925

Hawaii
Music by Richard Rodgers
Lyrics by Lorenz Hart
Present Arms 1928

Hawaii
Music by Gerard Calvi
Lyrics by Harold Rome
La Grosse Valise 1965

Hay, Hay, Hay
Music by Bronislaw Kaper (based on Chopin)
Lyrics by John Latouche
Polonaise 1945

Hay! Straw!
Music by Vincent Youmans
Lyrics by Oscar Hammerstein II
Rainbow 1928

Haywire
Music and lyrics by Edward Heyman
Caviar 1934

Ha-Za-Zaa
Music by Emmerich Kálmán
Lyrics by C.C.S. Cushing and E.P. Heath
Sari 1914

He Ain't Got Rhythm
Music and lyrics by Irving Berlin
On the Avenue (1937) F

He Always Comes Home to Me
Music by Charles Strouse
Lyrics by Alan Jay Lerner
Dance a Little Closer 1983

He and She
Music by Richard Rodgers
Lyrics by Lorenz Hart
The Boys From Syracuse 1938

He Can Dance
Music by Sammy Fain
Lyrics by Irving Kahal
Right This Way 1938

He Can Do It
Music by Gary Geld
Lyrics by Peter Udell
Purlie 1970

He Can Not, Must Not, Shall Not
Music by John Philip Sousa
Lyrics by Tom Frost and John Philip Sousa
El Capitan 1896

He Come Down This Morning
Music by Judd Woldin
Lyrics by Robert Brittan
Raisin 1973

He Could Show Me
Music by Nancy Ford
Lyrics by Gretchen Cryer
Now Is the Time for All Good Men (OB) 1967

He Did It, She Did It
Music and lyrics by Ronnie Britton
Gift of the Magi (OB) 1975

He Didn't Know Exactly What to Do
Music by Gustav Luders
Lyrics by Frank Pixley
The Prince of Pilsen 1903

He Died Good
Music and lyrics by Frank Loesser
Greenwillow 1960

He Eats
Music by Galt MacDermot
Lyrics by Rochelle Owens
The Karl Marx Play (OB) 1973

He Follows Me Around
Music by Frederick Loewe
Lyrics by Alan Jay Lerner
The Day Before Spring 1945

He Follws Me Around
Music by Buster Davis
Lyrics by Steven Vinaver
Diversions (OB) 1958

The "He" for Me
Music by Rudolf Frimi
Lyrics by P.G. Wodehouse and Clifford Grey
The Three Musketeers 1928

He Got It in the Ear
Music and lyrics by Cliff Jones
Rockabye Hamlet 1976

He Had Refinement
Music by Arthur Schwartz
Lyrics by Dorothy Fields
A Tree Grows in Brooklyn 1951

He Had the Callin'
Music and lyrics by Stephen H. Lemberg
Jazzbo Brown 1980

He Hasn't a Thing Except Me
Music by Vernon Duke
Lyrics by Ira Gershwin
Ziegfeld Follies (1936)

He Is My Bag
Music by Bill Weeden
Lyrics by David Finkle
Hurry, Harry 1972

He Is the Type
Music by Jerome Kern
Lyrics by Anne Caldwell
The City Chap 1925

He Just Beats a Tom-Tom
Music by Harry Akst
Lyrics by Lew Brown
Calling All Stars 1934

He Knows Where the Rose Is in Bloom
Music by Robert Hood Bowers
Lyrics by Francis DeWitt
Oh, Ernest! 1927

He Knows Where to Find Me
Music by Don McAfee
Lyrics by Nancy Leeds
Great Scot! (OB) 1965

He Looks So Good to Me
Music by Richard Rodgers
Lyrics by Lorenz Hart
The Hot Heiress (1931) F

Dropped from film

He Loves and She Loves
Music by George Gershwin
Lyrics by Ira Gershwin
Funny Face 1927

He Loves, He Loves Me Not
Music by Leslie Stuart
Lyrics by Ernest Boyd-Jones
Florodora 1900

He Loves Her
Music by Sammy Fain
Lyrics by Paul Francis Webster
Christine 1960

He Loves Me
Music by Cliff Allen
Lyrics by Nancy Hamilton
New Faces of 1934

He Makes Me Feel I'm Lovely
Music and lyrics by Johnny Burke
Donnybrook! 1961

The He-Man
Music by George Gershwin
Lyrics by B.G. DeSylva and Ira Gershwin
Tell Me More 1925

Dropped from production

He Man
Music by Richard Myers
Lyrics by Leo Robin
Hello, Yourself! 1928

He Needs Me Now
Music and lyrics by Walter Marks
Golden Rainbow 1968

He Needs You
Music and lyrics by Jay Livingston
and Ray Evans
Let It Ride 1961

He Plays the Violin
Music and lyrics by Sherman Edwards
1776 1969

He Sang Songs
Music by Mitch Leigh
Lyrics by Charles Burr and Forman Brown
Home Sweet Homer 1976

He Says
Music and lyrics by John Clifton
El Bravo! (OB) 1981

He Says "Yes," She Says "No"
Music by Rudolf Friml
Lyrics by Otto Harbach
The Firefly 1912

He Smiles
Music and lyrics by Michael Brown
Different Times 1972

He Takes Me Off His Income Tax
Music by Arthur Siegel
Lyrics by June Carroll
New Faces of 1952

He Talks to Me
Music by Lance Mulcahy
Lyrics by Paul Cherry
Park 1970

He Tossed a Coin
Music by Jerry Bock
Lyrics by Sheldon Harnick
The Rothschilds 1970

He Tried to Make a Dollar
Music by Jule Styne
Lyrics by Sammy Cahn
High Button Shoes 1947

He Wants to Put the Army in Jail
Music and lyrics by Gene Curty, Nitra Scharfman
and Chuck Strand
The Lieutenant 1975

He Was There
Music by Stanley Lebowsky
Lyrics by Fred Tobias
Gantry 1970

He Was Too Good to Me
Music by Richard Rodgers
Lyrics by Lorenz Hart
Simple Simon 1930

Dropped from production

He Who Knows the Way
Music by Elmer Bernstein
Lyrics by Don Black
Merlin 1983

He Who Loves and Runs Away
Music by Rudolf Friml
Lyrics by Gus Kahn
The Firefly (film version, 1937)

He Will Come Home Again
Music by Mitch Leigh
Lyrics by Charles Burr and Forman Brown
Home Sweet Homer 1976

He Will Tonight
Music by Morton Gould
Lyrics by Dorothy Fields
Arms and the Girl 1950

He Will Understand
Music by Rudolf Friml
Lyrics by Otto Harbach and Edward Clark
You're In Love 1917

He Won't Be Happy Till He Gets It
Music by Victor Herbert
Lyrics by Glen MacDonough
Babes in Toyland 1903

He Wore a Star
Music by Jerome Kern
Lyrics by Oscar Hammerstein II
High, Wide and Handsome (1937) F

Head Down the Road
Music by Clinton Ballard
Lyrics by Carolyn Richter
The Ballad of Johnny Pot (OB) 1971

Head in the Stars
Music by Sol Kaplan
Lyrics by Edward Eliscu
The Banker's Daughter (OB) 1962

Head Over Heels
Music by Jerome Kern
Lyrics by Edgar Allan Woolf
Head Over Heels 1918

Head Over Heels in Love
Music by James F. Hanley
Lyrics by Eddie Dowling
Honeymoon Lane 1926

The Head Song
Music and lyrics by Bland Simpson
and Jim Wann
Hot Grog (OB) 1977

A Headache and a Heartache
Music by Walter Kent
Lyrics by Kim Gannon
Seventeen 1951

Headin' for a Weddin'
Music by Abraham Ellstein
Lyrics by Walter Bullock
Great to Be Alive 1950

Headin' for Harlem
Music by James F. Hanley
Lyrics by Eddie Dowling
Sidewalks of New York 1927

Headin' for the Bottom
Music by Sammy Fain
Lyrics by Dan Shapiro
Ankles Aweigh 1955

Headin' South
Music by C. Luckey Roberts
Lyrics by Alex C. Rogers
My Magnolia 1926

Headlines
Music by Frank Fields
Lyrics by Armand Aulicino
The Shoemaker and the Peddler (OB) 1960

The Headsman and I
Music by Armando Trovaioli
Lyrics by Pietro Garinei and Sandro Giovannini
(Lyric translation by Edward Eager)
Rugantino 1964

Hear O Israel
Music by Joseph Rumshinsky
Lyrics by L. Wolfe Gilbert
The Singing Rabbi 1931

Hear the Bell
Music by Ivan Caryll
Lyrics by Anne Caldwell
Jack O' Lantern 1917

Hear the Gypsies Playing
Music by Sigmund Romberg
Lyrics by Otto Harbach
Forbidden Melody 1936

Hear the Trumpet Call
Music by Sigmund Romberg
Lyrics by Harry B. Smith
The Love Call 1927

A Heart for Sale
Music by Jerome Kern
Lyrics by Anne Caldwell
The Night Boat 1920

The Heart Has Won the Game
Music by Glenn Paxton
Lyrics by Robert Goldman and George Weiss
First Impressions 1959

Heart in Hand
Music and lyrics by Jack Lawrence
and Don Walker
Courtin' Time 1951

The Heart Is Free
Music by Emil Gerstenberger and Carle Carlton
Lyrics by Howard Johnson
The Lace Petticoat 1927

The Heart Is Quicker Than the Eye
Music by Richard Rodgers
Lyrics by Lorenz Hart
On Your Toes 1936

Heart of a Rose
Music by Maury Rubens and Sam Timberg
Lyrics by Moe Jaffe
Broadway Nights 1929

Heart of Mine
Music by Rudolf Friml
Lyrics by P.G. Wodehouse and Clifford Grey
The Three Musketeers 1928

Heart of Stone
Music by Leroy Anderson
Lyrics by Joan Ford and Walter and Jean Kerr
Goldilocks 1958

Hearts and Flowers
Music and lyrics by Noël Coward
Tonight at 8:30 ("Family Album") 1936

Heat Sensation
Music by Garry Sherman
Lyrics by Peter Udell
Amen Corner 1983

Heat Wave
Music and lyrics by Irving Berlin
As Thousands Cheer 1933

Heathen
Music and lyrics by Eaton Magoon, Jr.
Heathen 1972

The Heather on the Hill
Music by Frederick Loewe
Lyrics by Alan Jay Lerner
Brigadoon 1947

Heaven Hop
Music and lyrics by Cole Porter
Paris 1928

Heaven in My Arms (Music in My Heart)
Music by Jerome Kern
Lyrics by Oscar Hammerstein II
Very Warm for May 1939

Heaven Must Have Been Smiling
Music and lyrics by Bland Simpson
and Jim Wann
Hot Grog (OB) 1977

Heaven on Earth
Music by George Gershwin
Lyrics by Ira Gershwin and Howard Dietz
Oh, Kay! 1926

Heaven on Earth
Music by Jay Gorney
Lyrics by Barry Trivers
Heaven on Earth 1948

Heaven on Their Minds
Music by Andrew Lloyd Webber
Lyrics by Tim Rice
Jesus Christ Superstar 1971

Heaven Protect Me!
Music by Gordon Duffy
Lyrics by Harry M. Haldane
Happy Town 1959

Heaven Sent
Music by Gerald Marks
Lyrics by Sam Lerner
Hold It! 1948

A Heavenly Party
Music by Jerome Kern
Lyrics by Dorothy Fields
The Joy of Living (1938) F

Heavyweight Champ of the World
Music by Moose Charlap
Lyrics by Eddie Lawrence
Kelly 1965

Heel and Toe
Music by Philip Charig
Lyrics by Irving Caesar
Polly 1929

Heh Heh Good Mornin' Sunshine
Music and lyrics by Melvin Van Peebles
Ain't Supposed to Die a Natural Death 1971

Heidelberg Stein Song
Music by Gustav Luders
Lyrics by Frank Pixley
The Prince of Pilsen 1903

Heigh-Ho Cheerio
Music by Harry Archer
Lyrics by Walter O'Keefe
Just a Minute 1928

Heigh-Ho, Lackaday!
Music by Richard Rodgers
Lyrics by Lorenz Hart
Dearest Enemy 1925

Heigh Ho, the Gang's All Here
Music by Burton Lane
Lyrics by Harold Adamson
Earl Carroll's Vanities (1931)

Helen Is Always Willing
Music by Jerome Moross
Lyrics by John Latouche
The Golden Apple 1954

Helen of Troy
Music by Galt MacDermot
Lyrics by Christopher Gore
Via Galactica 1972

Helen of Troy, New York
Music by Harry Ruby
Lyrics by Bert Kalmar
Helen of Troy, New York 1923

Helen Quit Your Yellin'
Music by Joseph Raposo
Lyrics by Erich Segal
Sing Muse! (OB) 1961

Helena
Music and lyrics by Rick Besoyan
Babes in the Wood (OB) 1964

Helena's Solution
Music and lyrics by Rick Besoyan
Babes in the Wood (OB) 1964

Helicopter, Helicopter
Music and lyrics by Elizabeth Swados
Dispatches (OB) 1979

Heliopolis
Music and lyrics by James Rado
Rainbow (OB) 1972

He'll Come to Me Crawling
Music by Richard B. Chodosh
Lyrics by Barry Alan Grael
The Streets of New York (OB) 1963

Hell Hath No Fury
Music by James Bredt
Lyrics by Edward Eager
The Happy Hypocrite (OB) 1968

He'll Make Me Believe He's Mine
Music by Paul Horner
Lyrics by Peggy Lee
Peg 1983

He'll Never Be Mine
Music by Walt Smith
Lyrics by Leon Uris
Ari 1971

A Hell of a Hole
Music by George Gershwin
Lyrics by Ira Gershwin
Let 'Em Eat Cake 1933

Hello
Music by Richard Rodgers
Lyrics by Lorenz Hart
Peggy-Ann 1926

Hello
Music by Richard Rodgers
Lyrics by Lorenz Hart
Hollywood Party (1934) F

Hello, Cousin Lola
Music by William B. Kernell
Lyrics by Dorothy Donnelly
Hello, Lola 1926

Hello, Dolly!
Music and lyrics by Jerry Herman
Hello, Dolly 1964

The writer, Jerry Herman, was sued by Mack David, a well-known songwriter, who claimed that the main melodic line of "Hello, Dolly!" was identical with that of his earlier song "Sunflower." In an out-of-court settlement David was awarded $250,000.

Hello, Frisco!
Music by Louis A. Hirsch
Lyrics by Gene Buck
Ziegfeld Follies of 1915

Hello, Good Morning
Music by George Gershwin
Lyrics by Ira Gershwin
Of Thee I Sing 1931

Hello, Hazel
Music by Jule Styne
Lyrics by Bob Hilliard
Hazel Flagg 1953

Hello, Hello
Music by Galt MacDermot
Lyrics by Rochelle Owens
The Karl Marx Play (OB) 1973

Hello-Hello
Music and lyrics by Cliff Jones
Rockabye Hamlet 1976

Hello, Hello, Hello
Music and lyrics by Irving Berlin
Yip, Yip, Yaphank 1918

Hello, Hello There
Music by Jule Styne
Lyrics by Betty Comden and Adolph Green
Bells Are Ringing 1956

Hello, Hello Tokio!
Music and lyrics by Ring Lardner
June Moon 1929

Hello, I Love You, Goodbye
Music by Leon Carr
Lyrics by Earl Shuman
The Secret Life of Walter Mitty (OB) 1964

Hello Is the Way Things Begin
Music by Lance Mulcahy
Lyrics by Paul Cherry
Park 1970

Hello, Ma
Music by Michael H. Cleary
Lyrics by Max and Nathaniel Lief
The Illustrators' Show 1936

Hello, My Lover, Goodbye
Music by John Green
Lyrics by Edward Heyman
Here Goes the Bride 1931

Hello, New York
Music and lyrics by Ronnie Britton
Greenwich Village Follies (OB) 1976

Hello, the Little Birds Have Flown
Music by Carlton Kelsey and Maury Rubens
Lyrics by Clifford Grey
Sky High 1925

Hello, Tucky
Music by Joseph Meyer and James F. Hanley
Lyrics by B.G. DeSylva
Big Boy 1925

Hello Twelve, Hello Thirteen, Hello Love
Music by Marvin Hamlisch
Lyrics by Edward Kleban
A Chorus Line 1975

Hello, Waves
Music by John Kander
Lyrics by Fred Ebb
Flora, the Red Menace 1965

Hello World
Music and lyrics by Johnny Brandon
Billy Noname (OB) 1970

Hello Yank
Music by Edward Thomas
Lyrics by Martin Charnin
Ballad for a Firing Squad (OB) 1968

Hello, Young Lovers
Music by Richard Rodgers
Lyrics by Oscar Hammerstein II
The King and I 1951

Hello, Yourself
Music by Richard Myers
Lyrics by Leo Robin
Hello, Yourself! 1928

Hell's Finest
Music by Alma Sanders
Lyrics by Monte Carlo
The Houseboat on the Styx 1928

A Helluva Day
Music and lyrics by William Finn
In Trousers (OB) 1981

Hellzapoppin'
Music by Sammy Fain
Lyrics by Charles Tobias
Hellzapoppin 1938

Help the Seamen
Music by Frank D'Armond
Lyrics by Will Morrissey
Saluta 1934

Help Us Tonight
Music by Vincent Youmans
Lyrics by Billy Rose and Edward Eliscu
Great Day! 1929

Dropped from production

Help Yourself to Happiness
Music by Harry Revel
Lyrics by Harry Richman and Mack Gordon
Ziegfeld Follies (1931)

Hence It Don't Make Sense
Music and lyrics by Cole Porter
Seven Lively Arts 1944

Henry Street
Music by Jule Styne
Lyrics by Bob Merrill
Funny Girl 1964

Henry, Sweet Henry
Music and lyrics by Bob Merrill
Henry, Sweet Henry 1967

Her Anxiety
Music by John Duffy
Lyrics by Rocco Bufano and John Duffy
Horseman, Pass By (OB) 1969

Her Face
Music and lyrics by Bob Merrill
Carnival 1961

Her First Roman
Music and lyrics by Ervin Drake
Her First Roman 1968

Her Glove
Music by Franz Lehár
Lyrics by Basil Hood
The Count of Luxembourg 1912

Her Is
Music and lyrics by Richard Adler
and Jerry Ross
The Pajama Game 1954

Her Love Is Always the Same
Music by Rudolf Friml
Lyrics by Otto Harbach
The Blue Kitten 1922

Her Name Is Leona
Music and lyrics by Jill Williams
Rainbow Jones 1974

Her Pop's a Cop
Music by Ned Lehak
Lyrics by Irving Crane and Phil Conwit
Sing for Your Supper 1939

The Herb Song
Music by Baldwin Bergersen
Lyrics by William Archibald
Rosa (OB) 1978

Here Am I
Music by Jerome Kern
Lyrics by Oscar Hammerstein II
Sweet Adeline 1929

Here Am I—Broken Hearted
Music by Ray Henderson
Lyrics by B.G. DeSylva and Lew Brown
Artists and Models (1927)

Here and Now
Music by George Lessner
Lyrics by Miriam Battista and Russell Maloney
Sleepy Hollow 1948

Here and Now
Music and lyrics by Noël Coward
The Girl Who Came to Supper 1963

Here and There
Music by Gerald Dolin
Lyrics by Edward J. Lambert
Smile at Me 1935

Here Be Oysters Stewed in Honey
Music by Frederic Norton
Lyrics by Oscar Asche
Chu Chin Chow 1917

Here Come Your Men
Music by John Morris
Lyrics by Gerald Freedman
A Time for Singing 1966

Here Comes My Blackbird
Music by Jimmy McHugh
Lyrics by Dorothy Fields
Blackbirds of 1928

Here Comes the Ballad
Music by Buster Davis
Lyrics by Steven Vinaver
Diversions (OB) 1958

Here Comes the Bandwagon
Music and lyrics by Cole Porter
The Battle of Paris (1929) F

Here Comes the Prince of Wales
Music by Arthur Schwartz
Lyrics by Henry Myers
The New Yorkers 1927

Here I Am
Music and lyrics by Bob Merrill
Henry, Sweet Henry 1967

Here I Am Again
Music by Patrick Rose
Lyrics by Merv Campone and Richard Ouzounian
A Bistro Car on the CNR (OB) 1978

Here I Come
Music by Louis Bellson and Will Irwin
Lyrics by Richard Ney
Portofino 1958

Here I Go Again
Music by Harry Revel
Lyrics by Arnold B. Horwitt
Are You With It? 1945

Here I'll Stay
Music by Kurt Weill
Lyrics by Alan Jay Lerner
Love Life 1948

Here in Eden
Music by Jerry Bock
Lyrics by Sheldon Harnick
The Apple Tree 1966

Here in My Arms
Music by Richard Rodgers
Lyrics by Lorenz Hart
Dearest Enemy 1925

Also in Rodgers' and Hart's London score for
Lido Lady (1926)

Here in My Heart
Music by Joseph Meyer
Lyrics by William Moll
Jonica 1930

Here in the Dark
Music by Emmerich Kálmán and Herbert Stothart
Lyrics by Otto Harbach and Oscar Hammerstein II
Golden Dawn 1927

Here It Is
Music by Ray Henderson
Lyrics by B.G. DeSylva and Lew Brown
George White's Scandals (1931)

Here She Comes
Music by Richard Rodgers
Lyrics by Lorenz Hart
She's My Baby 1928

Here She Comes Now
Music by Jule Styne
Lyrics by Betty Comden and Adolph Green
Two on the Aisle 1951

Here, Steward
Music by Vincent Youmans and Paul Lannin
Lyrics by Arthur Francis
Two Little Girls in Blue 1921

Here They Come Now
Music by Al Carmines
Lyrics by Rosalyn Drexler
Home Movies (OB) 1964

Here 'Tis
Music by Eubie Blake
Lyrics by Noble Sissle
Shuffle Along of 1933

Here 'Tis
Music and lyrics by Donald Heywood
Black Rhythm 1936

Here Tonight, Tomorrow Where?
Music and lyrics by Robert Wright and George
Forrest (based on Rachmaninoff)
Anya 1965

Here We Are
Music by Sam Pottle
Lyrics by Tom Whedon
All Kinds of Giants (OB) 1961

Here We Are Again
Music by Richard Rodgers
Lyrics by Stephen Sondheim
Do I Hear a Waltz? 1965

Here We Are in Love
Music by Ben Oakland
Lyrics by Jack Murray and Barry Trivers
Ziegfeld Follies (1931)

Here We Are in Love
Music by Jean Gilbert
Lyrics by Harry B. Smith
Marching By 1932

Hereafter
Music and lyrics by Cole Porter
Mexican Hayride 1944

Dropped from production

Heredity—Environment
Music by David Baker
Lyrics by Sheldon Harnick
Smiling, the Boy Fell Dead (OB) 1961

Here's a Book
Music and lyrics by Al Kasha
and Joel Hirschhorn
Copperfield 1981

Here's a Cheer for Dear Old Ciro's
Music and lyrics by Cole Porter
Mexican Hayride 1944

Dropped from production

Here's a Day to Be Happy
Music by Vincent Youmans
Lyrics by Harold Adamson and Clifford Grey
Smiles 1930

Here's a Hand
Music by Richard Rodgers
Lyrics by Lorenz Hart
By Jupiter 1942

Here's a Kiss
Music by Richard Rodgers
Lyrics by Lorenz Hart
Dearest Enemy 1925

Here's a Kiss for Cinderella
Music by George Gershwin
Lyrics by Ira Gershwin
Of Thee I Sing 1931

Here's a Toast
Music and lyrics by Noël Coward
Tonight at 8:30 ("Family Album") 1936

Here's How
Music by Victor Herbert
Lyrics by Henry Blossom
The Only Girl 1914

Here's How
Music by Sigmund Romberg
Lyrics by Dorothy Donnelly
My Princess 1927

Here's Howe
Music by Joseph Meyer and Roger Wolfe Kahn
Lyrics by Irving Caesar
Here's Howe 1928

Here's Love
Music and lyrics by Meredith Willson
Here's Love 1963

Here's Momma
Music and lyrics by Michael Brown
Different Times 1972

Here's That Rainy Day
Music by Jimmy Van Heusen
Lyrics by Johnny Burke
Carnival in Flanders 1953

Here's to Dear Old Us
Music by Sammy Fain
Lyrics by Dan Shapiro
Ankles Aweigh 1955

Here's to Love
Music by Paul A. Rubens
Lyrics by Paul A. Rubens and Arthur Wimperis
The Sunshine Girl 1913

Here's to Night
Music by Henry Sullivan
Lyrics by Edward Eliscu
A Little Racketeer 1932

Here's to Panama Hattie
Music and lyrics by Cole Porter
Panama Hattie 1940

Dropped from production

Here's to the Girl of My Heart
Music by Walter Donaldson
Lyrics by Gus Kahn
Whoopee 1928

Here's to the Land We Love, Boys
Music by Victor Herbert
Lyrics by Henry Blossom
The Only Girl 1914

Here's to the Two of You
Music by Louis A. Hirsch
Lyrics by Otto Harbach
Going Up 1917

Here's to Us
Music by Cy Coleman
Lyrics by Carolyn Leigh
Little Me 1962

Here's to You
Music by Harden Church
Lyrics by Edward Heyman
Caviar 1934

Here's to You, Jack
Music by Frank Grey
Lyrics by Earle Crooker and McElbert Moore
Happy 1927

Here's to You, My Sparkling Wine
Music by Leo Edwards
Lyrics by Blanche Merrill
The Blue Paradise 1915

Here's to Your Illusions
Music by Sammy Fain
Lyrics by E.Y. Harburg
Flahooley 1951

Here's What a Mistress Ought to Be
Music and lyrics by Deed Meyer
She Shall Have Music (OB) 1959

Here's What I'm Here For
Music by Harold Arlen
Lyrics by Ira Gershwin
A Star Is Born (1954) F

Here's Where I Belong
Music by Robert Waldman
Lyrics by Alfred Uhry
Here's Where I Belong 1968

The Hermits
Music by Richard Rodgers
Lyrics by Lorenz Hart
Dearest Enemy 1925

Hernando's Hideaway
Music and lyrics by Richard Adler
and Jerry Ross
The Pajama Game 1954

Heroes in the Fall
Music by Richard Rodgers
Lyrics by Lorenz Hart
Too Many Girls 1939

A Hero's Love
Music by David Shire
Lyrics by Richard Maltby, Jr.
The Sap of Life (OB) 1961

He's a Bold Rogue
Music by Mischa and Wesley Portnoff
Lyrics by Donagh MacDonagh
Happy as Larry 1950

He's a Fool
Music by Nancy Ford
Lyrics by Gretchen Cryer
Shelter 1973

He's a Genius
Music by Jule Styne
Lyrics by E.Y. Harburg
Darling of the Day 1968

He's a Ladies' Man
Music by Ray Henderson
Lyrics by B.G. DeSylva and Lew Brown
Good News 1927

He's a Man
Music by Bob James
Lyrics by Jack O'Brien
The Selling of the President 1972

He's a Man's Man
Music by Ray Henderson
Lyrics by B.G. DeSylva and Lew Brown
Follow Thru 1929

He's a Right Guy
Music and lyrics by Cole Porter
Something for the Boys 1943

He's a Winner
Music by Richard Rodgers
Lyrics by Lorenz Hart
The Girl Friend 1926

He's Back
Music by John Kander
Lyrics by Fred Ebb
The Happy Time 1968

He's Coming
Music by Harvey Schmidt
Lyrics by Tom Jones
Philemon (OB) 1975

He's Goin' Home
Music by Arthur Schwartz
Lyrics by Dorothy Fields
Stars in Your Eyes 1939

He's Good for Me
Music by Cy Coleman
Lyrics by Dorothy Fields
Seesaw 1973

He's Good for Nothing but Me
Music by Vernon Duke
Lyrics by Howard Dietz
Jackpot 1944

He's Here!
Music by Elmer Bernstein
Lyrics by Carolyn Leigh
How Now, Dow Jones 1967

He's in Love!
Music and lyrics by Robert Wright
and George Forrest
Kismet 1953

Based on Alexander Borodin's *Polovetsian Dances*

He's Just My Ideal
Music by Werner Janssen
Lyrics by Mann Holiner and J. Keirn Brennan
Boom-Boom 1929

He's Never Too Busy
Music by Stanley Lebowsky
Lyrics by Fred Tobias
Gantry 1970

He's Not for Me
Music by Don McAfee
Lyrics by Nancy Leeds
Great Scot! (OB) 1965

He's Not Himself
Music by George Gershwin
Lyrics by Ira Gershwin
Pardon My English 1933

He's Only Wonderful
Music by Sammy Fain
Lyrics by E.Y. Harburg
Flahooley 1951

He's the Man
Music and lyrics by William Roy
Maggie 1953

He's the Wizard
Music and lyrics by Charlie Smalls
The Wiz 1975

He's the Wonder for Them All
Music by A. Baldwin Sloane
Lyrics by E. Ray Goetz
The Hen Pecks 1911

He's With My Johnny
Music by Mischa and Wesley Portnoff
Lyrics by Donagh MacDonagh
Happy as Larry 1950

He's Wonderful
Music by Kenneth Jacobson
Lyrics by Rhoda Roberts
Show Me Where the Good Times Are (OB) 1970

Hey!
Music and lyrics by Cliff Jones
Rockabye Hamlet 1976

Hey Babe Hey
Music and lyrics by Cole Porter
Born to Dance (1936) F

Hey Boy
Music by Ron Steward and Neal Tate
Lyrics by Ron Steward
Sambo (OB) 1969

Hey Chico!
Music and lyrics by John Clifton
El Bravo! (OB) 1981

Hey, Feller!
Music by Jerome Kern
Lyrics by Oscar Hammerstein II
Show Boat 1927

Hey, Gal!
Music by Will Irwin
Lyrics by June Carroll
New Faces of 1943

Hey, Girlie
Music by Richard Rodgers
Lyrics by Martin Charnin
Two by Two 1970

Hey, Good-Lookin'
Music and lyrics by Cole Porter
Something for the Boys 1943

Hey! Hey!
Music by Richard Rodgers
Lyrics by Lorenz Hart
The Girl Friend 1926

Hey! Hey! Let 'er Go!
Music by George Gershwin
Lyrics by B.G. DeSylva
Sweet Little Devil 1924

Hey, Jimmy, Joe, John, Jim, Jack
Music and lyrics by Jay Livingston
and Ray Evans
Let It Ride 1961

Hey Joe
Music by Earl Robinson
Lyrics by Waldo Salt
Sandhog (OB) 1954

Hey, Look at Me
Music by Charles Strouse
Lyrics by David Rogers
Charlie and Algernon 1980

Hey, Look at Me, Mrs. Draba
Music by Peter Link
Lyrics by Jacob Brackman
King of Hearts 1978

Hey, Look Me Over
Music by Cy Coleman
Lyrics by Carolyn Leigh
Wildcat 1960

Hey, Love
Music by Mary Rodgers
Lyrics by Martin Charnin
Hot Spot 1963

Hey, Madame
Music and lyrics by Jay Livingston
and Ray Evans
Oh Captain! 1958

Hey, Nonny, Hey
Music by Max Ewing
Lyrics by Agnes Morgan
The Grand Street Follies (1928)

Hey Nonny Nonny
Music by Will Irwin
Lyrics by Ogden Nash
Hey Nonny Nonny! 1932

Hey, Rube
Music by Milton Ager
Lyrics by Jack Yellen
Rain or Shine 1928

Hey, There
Music and lyrics by Richard Adler
and Jerry Ross
The Pajama Game 1954

Hey There, Fans
Music by David Shire
Lyrics by Richard Maltby, Jr.
Starting Here, Starting Now (OB) 1977

Hey There, Good Times
Music by Cy Coleman
Lyrics by Michael Stewart
I Love My Wife 1977

Hey, What's This?
Music by Meyer Kupferman
Lyrics by Paul Goodman
Jonah (OB) 1966

Hey, Why Not!
Music by Jule Styne
Lyrics by Bob Merrill
Sugar 1972

Hey Yvette
Music and lyrics by Richard M. Sherman
and Robert B. Sherman
Over Here! 1974

Hi
Music by Lawrence Hurwit
Lyrics by Lee Goldsmith
Sextet 1974

Hi de hi de hi, hi de hi de ho
Music and lyrics by Robert Dahdah
Curley McDimple (OB) 1967

Hi-Ho!
Music by George Gershwin
Lyrics by Ira Gershwin
Shall We Dance 1937 F

Dropped from film

Hi Ya Kid
Music by Galt MacDermot
Lyrics by William Dumaresq
The Human Comedy (OB) 1983

Hic Haec Hoc
Music by Mark Sandrich, Jr.
Lyrics by Sidney Michaels
Ben Franklin in Paris 1964

Hickety, Pickety
Music by Helen Miller
Lyrics by Eve Merriam
Inner City 1971

Hide and Seek
Music by Ivan Caryll
Lyrics by C.M.S. McLellan
The Pink Lady 1911

High Air
Music by Earl Robinson
Lyrics by Waldo Salt
Sandhog (OB) 1954

High and Low
Music by Arthur Schwartz
Lyrics by Howard Dietz
The Band Wagon 1931

High Class Ladies and Elegant Gentlemen
Music by Jerry Livingston
Lyrics by Leonard Adelson
Molly 1973

High Flyin' Wings on My Shoes
Music and lyrics by Cole Porter
Les Girls (1957) F

High Flying Adored
Music by Andrew Lloyd Webber
Lyrics by Tim Rice
Evita 1979

High Hat
Music by George Gershwin
Lyrics by Ira Gershwin
Funny Face 1927

High, High, High
Music by Emile Berté and Maury Rubens
Lyrics by J. Keirn Brennan
Music in May 1929

High, High Up in the Clouds
Music by Maury Rubens
Lyrics by Max and Nathaniel Lief
The Greenwich Village Follies (1928)

High in the Hills
Music by Lewis E. Gensler and Milton Schwarzwald
Lyrics by George S. Kaufman, Marc Connelly and Ira Gershwin
Be Yourself 1924

High Is Better Than Low
Music by Arthur Schwartz
Lyrics by Howard Dietz
Jennie 1963

High Jinks
Music by Rudolf Friml
Lyrics by Otto Harbach
High Jinks 1913

High School
Music by Cheryl Hardwick
Lyrics by Marilyn Suzanne Miller
Girls, Girls, Girls (OB) 1980

High School All Over Again
Music and lyrics by Craig Carnelia
Is There Life After High School? 1982

High Shoes
Music by Robert Russell Bennett
Lyrics by Owen Murphy and Robert A. Simon
Hold Your Horses 1933

High Society Calypso
Music and lyrics by Cole Porter
High Society (1956) F

High Street, Africa
Music by Vivian Ellis
Lyrics by Graham John
By the Way 1925

High Up in Harlem
Music by Jerome Kern
Lyrics by Oscar Hammerstein II
Very Warm for May 1939

Dropped from production

High Up on the Hills
Music by Ralph Benatzky
Lyrics by Irving Caesar
White Horse Inn 1936

High, Wide and Handsome
Music by Jerome Kern
Lyrics by Oscar Hammerstein II
High, Wide and Handsome (1937) F

Highbrow, Lowbrow
Music by Jay Gorney
Lyrics by Jean and Walter Kerr
Touch and Go 1949

Higher Than High
Music by Jimmy Horowitz
Lyrics by Leo Rost and Jimmy Horowitz
Marlowe 1981

The Highest Judge of All
Music by Richard Rodgers
Lyrics by Oscar Hammerstein II
Carousel 1945

Highway 57
Music and lyrics by Jim Swann
Pump Boys and Dinettes 1982

The Highway's Call
Music by Will Ortman
Lyrics by Gus Kahn and Raymond B. Egan
Holka-Polka 1925

Hiiaka
Music and lyrics by Eaton Magoon, Jr.
13 Daughters 1961

Hill of Dreams
Music and lyrics by Robert Wright and George
Forrest
Song of Norway 1944

Based on Grieg's Piano Concerto in A minor

The Hills of Ixopo
Music by Kurt Weill
Lyrics by Maxwell Anderson
Lost in the Stars 1949

The Hills of Tomorrow
Music and lyrics by Stephen Sondheim
Merrily We Roll Along 1981

Himmlisher Vater
Music by Jule Styne
Lyrics by Sammy Cahn
Look to the Lilies 1970

Hindu
Music by Percy Wenrich
Lyrics by Jack Mahoney
The Fascinating Widow 1911

Hindu Serenade
Music by Ray Henderson
Lyrics by Jack Yellen
Ziegfeld Follies (1943)

Hip, Hip, Hurrah!
Music by Leo Fall
Lyrics by George Grossmith
The Dollar Princess 1909

Hip-Hoorray for Washington
Music and lyrics by Don Tucker
Red, White and Maddox 1969

The Hippopotamus
Music by Donald Swann
Lyrics by Michael Flanders
At the Drop of a Hat 1959

Hire a Guy
Music by Mary Rodgers
Lyrics by Marshall Barer
From A to Z 1960

His and Hers
Music by Sammy Fain
Lyrics by Dan Shapiro
Ankles Aweigh 1955

His Love Makes Me Beautiful
Music by Jule Styne
Lyrics by Bob Merrill
Funny Girl 1964

His Old Man
Music and lyrics by Harold Rome
Call Me Mister 1946

His Own Little Island
Music and lyrics by Jay Livingston
and Ray Evans
Let It Ride 1961

His Spanish Guitar
Music by Frank Grey
Lyrics by McElbert Moore and Frank Grey
The Matinee Girl 1926

History
Music by Larry Grossman
Lyrics by Hal Hackady
Goodtime Charley 1975

History Is Made at Night
Music and lyrics by Harold Rome
The Streets of Paris 1939

The History of Three Generations of Chorus Girls
Music by Oscar Straus
Lyrics by Clare Kummer
Three Waltzes 1937

Hit It, Lorraine
Music by John Kander
Lyrics by Fred Ebb
70, Girls, 70 1971

Hit the Ladies
Music and lyrics by Tom Savage
Musical Chairs 1980

Hit the Ramp
Music by Vernon Duke
Lyrics by John Latouche
The Lady Comes Across 1942

Hit the Road to Dreamland
Music by Harold Arlen
Lyrics by Johnny Mercer
Star Spangled Rhythm (1942) Г

Hitch Your Wagon to a Star
Music by Richard Lewine
Lyrics by Ted Fetter
Broadway Sho-window 1936

Hittin' the Bottle
Music by Harold Arlen
Lyrics by Ted Koehler
Earl Carroll's Vanities (1930)

Hitting on High
Music by Frank Grey
Lyrics by Earle Crooker and McElbert Moore
Happy 1927

Hiya Sucker
Music by Jesse Greer
Lyrics by Stanley Adams
Shady Lady 1933

H.N.I.C.
Music and lyrics by Oscar Brown, Jr.
Buck White 1969

Ho, Billy O!
Music by Kurt Weill
Lyrics by Alan Jay Lerner
Love Life 1948

Ho! Ye Townsmen
Music by Victor Herbert
Lyrics by Harry B. Smith
The Fortune Teller 1898

Hobbies
Music by Harry Tierney
Lyrics by Joseph McCarthy
Irene 1919

Hobohemia
Music by Charles Rosoff
Lyrics by Leo Robin
Judy 1927

Hoch, Caroline!
Music by Jack Waller and Joseph Tunbridge
Lyrics by R.P. Weston and Bert Lee
Tell Her the Truth 1932

Hoe Down
Music and lyrics by Don Tucker
Red, White and Maddox 1969

Hoedown!
Music by Gordon Duffy
Lyrics by Harry M. Haldane
Happy Town 1959

The Hog Beneath the Skin
Music by Donald Swann
Lyrics by Michael Flanders
At the Drop of a Hat 1959

Hogan's Alley
Music by Henry Souvaine and Jay Gorney
Lyrics by Morrie Ryskind and Howard Dietz
Merry-Go-Round 1927

Hoku Loa
Music by Rudolf Friml
Lyrics by J. Keirn Brennan
Luana 1930

Hola, Follow, Follow Me
Music by Emmerich Kálmán
Lyrics by Harry B. Smith
Countess Maritza 1926

Hold It!
Music by Gerald Marks
Lyrics by Sam Lerner
Hold It! 1948

Hold Me Closer
Music and lyrics by Max Rich, Frank Littau
and Jack Scholl
George White's Music Hall Varieties 1932

Hold Me—Hold Me—Hold Me
Music by Jule Styne
Lyrics by Betty Comden and Adolph Green
Two on the Aisle 1951

Hold Me in Your Loving Arms
Music by Louis A. Hirsch
Lyrics by Gene Buck
Ziegfeld Follies of 1915

Hold On to Your Hats
Music by Burton Lane
Lyrics by E.Y. Harburg
Hold On to Your Hats 1940

Hold On to Your Hats
Music and lyrics by Steve Allen
Sophie 1963

Hold That Smile
Music by Ray Henderson
Lyrics by Jack Yellen
Ziegfeld Follies (1943)

Hold Your Horses
Music by Robert Russell Bennett
Lyrics by Owen Murphy and Robert A. Simon
Hold Your Horses 1933

Hold Your Man
Music by Maurice Yvain
Lyrics by Max and Nathaniel Lief
Luckee Girl 1928

Holding Hands
Music by Frank Grey
Lyrics by McElbert Moore and Frank Grey
The Matinee Girl 1926

Holiday in the Country
Music by Jimmy McHugh
Lyrics by Harold Adamson
As the Girls Go 1948

Holka-Polka
Music by Will Ortman
Lyrics by Gus Kahn and Raymond B. Egan
Holka-Polka 1925

Holler Blue Murder
Music by Carl Sigman
Lyrics by Bob Hilliard
Angel in the Wings 1947

Hollow
Music by Susan Hulsman Bingham
Lyrics by Myrna Lamb
Mod Donna (OB) 1970

Hollywood and Vine
Music by Sam Stept
Lyrics by Lew Brown and Charles Tobias
Yokel Boy 1939

Hollywood and Vine
Music and lyrics by Stephen Sondheim
Twigs 1971

Hollywood, California
Music by John Kander
Lyrics by Fred Ebb
The Act 1977

Hollywood Lullabye
Music and lyrics by Joseph Church
An Evening With Joan Crawford (OB) 1981

Hollywood, Park Avenue and Broadway
Music by Ray Henderson
Lyrics by Lew Brown
Strike Me Pink 1933

Hollywood Party
Music by Richard Rodgers
Lyrics by Lorenz Hart
Hollywood Party (1934) F

Hollywood Story
Music and lyrics by Hugh Martin and Ralph Blane
Best Foot Forward (1963 OB revival)

Holmes and Watson
Music by Milton Schafer
Lyrics by Ira Levin
Drat! The Cat! 1965

Holy Ghost Ride
Music and lyrics by Al Carmines
The Evangelist (OB) 1982

Holy Mystery
Music by Galt MacDermot
Lyrics by Rochelle Owens
The Karl Marx Play (OB) 1973

Home
Music by Franz Lehár
Lyrics by Adrian Ross
The Merry Widow 1907

Home
Music by A. Baldwin Sloane
Lyrics by Harry Cort and George E. Stoddard
China Rose 1925

Home
Music by Sol Berkowitz
Lyrics by James Lipton
Miss Emily Adam (OB) 1960

Home
Music by John Kander
Lyrics by Fred Ebb
70, Girls, 70 1971

Home
Music and lyrics by Charlie Smalls
The Wiz 1975

Home
Music and lyrics by Al Carmines
The Evangelist (OB) 1982

Home Again
Music by Jerry Bock
Lyrics by Sheldon Harnick
Fiorello! 1959

Home Blues
Music by George Gershwin
Lyrics by Gus Kahn and Ira Gershwin
Show Girl 1929

Based on the slow theme from *An American in Paris* (1928)

A Home for You
Music by Rudolf Friml
Lyrics by Brian Hooker
The White Eagle 1927

Home Free All
Music by Mitch Leigh
Lyrics by William Alfred and Phyllis Robinson
Cry for Us All 1970

Home in Your Arms
Music by Ben Oakland
Lyrics by Oscar Hammerstein II
The Lady Objects (1938) F

Home Is Where the Heart Is
Music by Jay Gorney
Lyrics by Barry Trivers
Heaven on Earth 1948

Home Is Where You Hang Your Hat
Music by Berenice Kazounoff
Lyrics by John Latouche
Two for Tonight (OB) 1939

Home o' Mine
Music by Jean Gilbert
Lyrics by Harry B. Smith
The Red Robe 1928

Home of My Heart
Music by Will Ortman
Lyrics by Gus Kahn and Raymond B. Egan
Holka-Polka 1925

A Home of Our Own
Music and lyrics by Harold Rome
Call Me Mister 1946

Home Sweet Heaven
Music and lyrics by Hugh Martin
and Timothy Gray
High Spirits 1964

Home Sweet Home
Music by Arthur Siegel
Lyrics by Mae Richard
Tallulah (OB) 1983

Home Sweet Homer
Music by Mitch Leigh
Lyrics by Charles Burr and Forman Brown
Home Sweet Homer 1976

Home to Harlem
Music by Ray Henderson
Lyrics by Lew Brown
Strike Me Pink 1933

Home Town
Music by Harold Orlob
Lyrics by Irving Caesar
Talk About Girls 1927

Homecoming
Music by Giuseppe Verdi (adapted by Hans Spialek)
Lyrics by Charles Friedman
My Darlin' Aida 1952

Homeland
Music by Sigmund Romberg
Lyrics by Arthur Wimperis
Louie the 14th 1925

Homeland
Music by Armand Vecsey
Lyrics by P.G. Wodehouse
The Nightingale 1927

Homely but Clean
Music by Vincent Youmans
Lyrics by Anne Caldwell
Oh, Please! 1926

Homemade Happiness
Music by Harold Levey
Lyrics by Zelda Sears
The Clinging Vine 1922

Homesick
Music by Charles Strouse
Lyrics by Alan Jay Lerner
Dance a Little Closer 1983

Homesick Blues
Music by Jule Styne
Lyrics by Leo Robin
Gentlemen Prefer Blondes 1949

Homesick in Our Hearts
Music and lyrics by Ed Tyler
Sweet Miani (OB) 1962

The Homestead Must Be Sold
Music by Vincent Youmans
Lyrics by Billy Rose and Edward Eliscu
Great Day! 1929

Dropped from production

Homeward
Music by Sol Berkowitz
Lyrics by James Lipton
Miss Emily Adam (OB) 1960

Homeward
Music and lyrics by Robert Wright and George Forrest (based on Rachmaninoff)
Anya 1965

Homeward Bound
Music and lyrics by Irving Berlin
Watch Your Step 1914

Homework
Music and lyrics by Irving Berlin
Miss Liberty 1949

A Homogeneous Cabinet
Music by Richard Rodgers
Lyrics by Lorenz Hart
I'd Rather Be Right 1937

Honest Confession Is Good for the Soul
Music and lyrics by Peter Link and C.C. Courtney
Salvation (OB) 1969

Honest Honore
Music and lyrics by Deed Meyer
'Toinette (OB) 1961

Honest John's Game
Music and lyrics by John Clifton
El Bravo! (OB) 1981

Honest Man
Music and lyrics by Walter Marks
Bajour 1964

Honestly Sincere
Music by Charles Strouse
Lyrics by Lee Adams
Bye Bye Birdie 1960

Honesty
Music and lyrics by J.C. Johnson
Change Your Luck 1930

Honey, Be Mine
Music by James F. Hanley
Lyrics by Gene Buck
No Foolin' 1926

Honey, Be My Honey-Bee
Music by Maury Rubens and J. Fred Coots
Lyrics by Clifford Grey
The Madcap 1928

Honey-Bun
Music by Vincent Youmans
Lyrics by Zelda Sears
Lollipop 1924

Honey Bun
Music by Richard Rodgers
Lyrics by Oscar Hammerstein II
South Pacific 1949

Honey Gal o' Mine
Music by Georges Bizet
Lyrics by Oscar Hammerstein II
Carmen Jones 1943

Honey, I'm in Love With You
Music by Con Conrad
Lyrics by William B. Friedlander
Mercenary Mary 1925

Honey in the Honeycomb
Music by Vernon Duke
Lyrics by John Latouche
Cabin in the Sky 1940

Honey Man Song
Music and lyrics by Oscar Brown, Jr.
Buck White 1969

A Honey to Love
Music and lyrics by Ed Tyler
Sweet Miani (OB) 1962

Honeymoon
Music by Paul Lannin
Lyrics by Arthur Francis
Two Little Girls in Blue 1921

Honeymoon
Music by Sammy Fain
Lyrics by Dan Shapiro
Ankles Aweigh 1955

Honeymoon Inn
Music by Jerome Kern
Lyrics by P.G. Wodehouse
Have a Heart 1917

The Honeymoon Is Over
Music by Frank Black
Lyrics by Gladys Shelley
The Duchess Misbehaves 1946

The Honeymoon Is Over
Music by Jerry Bock
Lyrics by Sheldon Harnick
The Body Beautiful 1958

The Honeymoon Is Over
Music by Harvey Schmidt
Lyrics by Tom Jones
I Do! I Do! 1966

Honeymoon Lane
Music by Jerome Kern
Lyrics by Herbert Reynolds
The Sunshine Girl 1913

Honeymooning Blues
Music by Maury Rubens
Lyrics by Clifford Grey
The Madcap 1928

Honky Jewish Boy
Music by Robert Mitchell
Lyrics by Elizabeth Perry
Bags (OB) 1982

Honky Tonk Queens
Music by Harris Wheeler
Lyrics by Mary L. Fisher
Blue Plate Special (OB) 1983

Honolulu
Music and lyrics by Marc Blitzstein
The Cradle Will Rock 1938

Honor and Glory
Music by Karl Hajos (based on Tchaikovsky)
Lyrics by Harry B. Smith
Natja 1925

Honor of the Family
Music and lyrics by George M. Cohan
The Merry Malones 1927

Honor the Brave
Music by Victor Herbert
Lyrics by George V. Hobart
Old Dutch 1909

Honorable Mambo
Music by Dean Fuller
Lyrics by Marshall Barer
Ziegfeld Follies (1957)

The Honorable Profession of the Fourth Estate
Music and lyrics by Irving Berlin
Miss Liberty 1949

Dropped from production

Honour
Music by Jacques Urbont
Lyrics by Bruce Geller
All in Love (OB) 1961

Hoof, Hoof
Music by Philip Charig and Richard Myers
Lyrics by Leo Robin
Allez-Oop 1927

The Hooker
Music by Helen Miller
Lyrics by Eve Merriam
Inner City 1971

Hoomalimali
Music and lyrics by Eaton Magoon, Jr.
13 Daughters 1961

Hoop-de-Dingle
Music and lyrics by Harold Rome
Destry Rides Again 1959

Hoops
Music by Arthur Schwartz
Lyrics by Howard Dietz
The Band Wagon 1931

Hooray for Anywhere
Music and lyrics by Burton Lane
Laffing Room Only 1944

Hooray for Captain Spalding!
Music by Harry Ruby
Lyrics by Bert Kalmar
Animal Crackers 1928

Hooray for George the Third
Music by Arthur Schwartz
Lyrics by Dorothy Fields
By the Beautiful Sea 1954

Hooray for Love
Music by Harold Arlen
Lyrics by Leo Robin
Casbah (1948) F

Hooray for the U.S.A.!
Music by George Gershwin
Lyrics by B.G. DeSylva
Sweet Little Devil 1924

Hooray for What!
Music by Harold Arlen
Lyrics by E.Y. Harburg
Hooray for What! 1937

Hoosier Way
Music by Walter Kent
Lyrics by Kim Gannon
Seventeen 1951

Hoot Mon
Music by Jerome Kern
Lyrics by Harry B. Smith
Love o' Mike 1917

Hootin' Owl Trail
Music by Robert Emmett Dolan
Lyrics by Johnny Mercer
Texas, Li'l Darlin' 1949

A Hop, a Skip, a Jump, a Look
Music by Fred Spielman and Arthur Gershwin
Lyrics by Stanley Adams
A Lady Says Yes 1945

Hope for the Best
Music by Arthur Schwartz
Lyrics by Ira Gershwin
Park Avenue 1946

Hope You Come Back
Music and lyrics by Richard Adler
and Jerry Ross
John Murray Anderson's Almanac (1953)

Horoscope
Music by Donald Swann
Lyrics by Michael Flanders
At the Drop of Another Hat 1966

Horrible, Horrible Love
Music and lyrics by Hugh Martin
Look Ma, I'm Dancin'! 1948

Horrortorio
Music by Jack Waller and Joseph Tunbridge
Lyrics by R.P. Weston and Bert Lee
Tell Her the Truth 1932

Hors d'Oeuvres
Music and lyrics by Herman Hupfeld
A La Carte 1927

The Horse
Music by Gary William Friedman
Lyrics by Will Holt
The Me Nobody Knows (OB) 1970

Horseshoes Are Lucky
Music by Robert Emmett Dolan
Lyrics by Johnny Mercer
Texas, Li'l Darlin' 1949

Hosanna
Music by Andrew Lloyd Webber
Lyrics by Tim Rice
Jesus Christ Superstar 1971

Hosanna
Music by Mitch Leigh
Lyrics by N. Richard Nash
Saravá 1979

Hose Boys
Music by Richard Lewine
Lyrics by Ted Fetter
The Fireman's Flame (OB) 1937

Hostess With the Mostes' on the Ball
Music and lyrics by Irving Berlin
Call Me Madam 1950

Hot
Music by Lewis E. Gensler
Lyrics by Robert A. Simon
Ups-a-Daisy 1928

Hot and Bothered
Music by Harry Ruby
Lyrics by Bert Kalmar
Top Speed 1929

Hot and Cold
Music by Sigmund Romberg
Lyrics by Oscar Hammerstein II
The New Moon 1928

Dropped from production

Hot as Hades
Music and lyrics by Ann Harris
Sky High (OB) 1979

Hot-Cha Chiquita
Music by Max Rich
Lyrics by Jack Scholl
Keep Moving 1934

Hot Dog
Music by Jerome Kern
Lyrics by Anne Caldwell
The Bunch and Judy 1922

Dropped from production

Hot Enough for You?
Music by John Kander
Lyrics by Fred Ebb
The Act 1977

Hot Feet
Music by Harry Revel
Lyrics by Mack Gordon
Fast and Furious 1931

Hot Grog
Music and lyrics by Bland Simpson
and Jim Wann
Hot Grog (OB) 1977

Hot Harlem
Music by James P. Johnson
Lyrics by Flournoy Miller
Sugar Hill 1931

Hot Heels
Music by Lee David
Lyrics by Billy Rose and Ballard MacDonald
Padlocks of 1927

Hot, Hot Honey
Music by Jean Schwartz
Lyrics by Alfred Bryan
A Night in Spain 1927

Hot, Hot Mama
Music and lyrics by Porter Grainger
Fast and Furious 1931

Hot Lover
Music by Galt MacDermot
Lyrics by John Guare
Two Gentlemen of Verona 1971

Hot Moonlight
Music by Jay Gorney
Lyrics by E.Y. Harburg
Shoot the Works 1931

Hot Pants
Music by Roger Wolfe Kahn
Lyrics by Irving Caesar
Americana (1928)

Hot Patootie Wedding Night
Music and lyrics by Frank Marcus
and Bernard Maltin
Bamboola 1929

Hot Rhythm
Music by Porter Grainger
Lyrics by Donald Heywood
Hot Rhythm 1930

Hot Rhythm
Music by James P. Johnson
Lyrics by Flournoy Miller
Sugar Hill 1931

Hot Sands
Music by Harry Tierney
Lyrics by Joseph McCarthy
Cross My Heart 1928

Hot Spot
Music by Jerome Kern
Lyrics by Otto Harbach
Roberta 1933

Hotcha Ma Chotch
Music by Vincent Youmans
Lyrics by Harold Adamson and Clifford Grey
Smiles 1930

Hotsy Totsy Hats
Music by Maury Rubens and Sam Timberg
Lyrics by Moe Jaffe
Broadway Nights 1929

Hottentot Potentate
Music by Arthur Schwartz
Lyrics by Howard Dietz
At Home Abroad 1935

Houp-La
Music by Jerome Kern
Lyrics by Edgar Allan Woolf
Head Over Heels 1918

A House Full of People
Music by Don Pippin
Lyrics by Steve Brown
The Contrast (OB) 1972

A House in Town
Music by Glenn Paxton
Lyrics by Robert Goldman and George Weiss
First Impressions 1959

A House Is Not the Same Without a Woman
Music by Armando Trovaioli
Lyrics by Pietro Garinei and Sandro Giovannini
(Lyric translation by Edward Eager)
Rugantino 1964

House of Flowers
Music by Harold Arlen
Lyrics by Harold Arlen and Truman Capote
House of Flowers 1954

House of Grass
Music and lyrics by Eaton Magoon, Jr.
Heathen 1972

The House of Marcus Lycus
Music and lyrics by Stephen Sondheim
*A Funny Thing Happened on the Way
to the Forum* 1962

House on the Hill
Music and lyrics by Eaton Magoon, Jr.
13 Daughters 1961

A House With a Little Red Barn
Music by Morgan Lewis
Lyrics by Nancy Hamilton
Two for the Show 1940

The Houseboat on the Styx
Music by Alma Sanders
Lyrics by Monte Carlo
The Houseboat on the Styx 1928

How About a Ball?
Music and lyrics by Hugo Peretti, Luigi Creatore
and George David Weiss
Maggie Flynn 1968

How About a Boy Like Me?
Music by George Gershwin
Lyrics by Ira Gershwin
Strike Up the Band 1930

How About a Cheer for the Navy
Music and lyrics by Irving Berlin
This Is the Army 1942

How About a Date?
Music by Jimmy Van Heusen
Lyrics by Johnny Burke
Nellie Bly 1946

How About It?
Music by Jesse Greer
Lyrics by Raymond Klages
Say When 1928

How About It?
Music by Richard Rodgers
Lyrics by Lorenz Hart
America's Sweetheart 1931

How About You
Music by Burton Lane
Lyrics by Ralph Freed
Babes on Broadway (1941) F

How America Got It's Name
Music and lyrics by William Finn
In Trousers (OB) 1981

How Are Things in Glocca Morra?
Music by Burton Lane
Lyrics by E.Y. Harburg
Finian's Rainbow 1947

How Are You, Lady Love?
Music by Lucien Denni
Lyrics by Helena Evans
Happy Go Lucky 1926

How Are You Since?
Music by Mitch Leigh
Lyrics by William Alfred and Phyllis Robinson
Cry for Us All 1970

How Beautiful It Was
Music and lyrics by Matt Dubey
and Dean Fuller
Smith (OB) 1973

How Beautiful the Days
Music and lyrics by Frank Loesser
The Most Happy Fella 1956

How Can Anyone So Sweet
Music by Jeanne Bargy
Lyrics by Jeanne Bargy, Frank Gehrecke
and Herb Corey
Greenwich Village U.S.A. (OB) 1960

How Can I Ever Be Alone?
Music by Arthur Schwartz
Lyrics by Oscar Hammerstein II
American Jubilee 1940

How Can I Get Rid of Those Blues?
Music by Lewis E. Gensler
Lyrics by Owen Murphy and Robert A. Simon
The Gang's All Here 1931

How Can I Wait?
Music by Frederick Loewe
Lyrics by Alan Jay Lerner
Paint Your Wagon 1951

How Can I Win You Now?
Music by George Gershwin
Lyrics by B.G. DeSylva and Ira Gershwin
Tell Me More 1925

How Can Love Survive?
Music by Richard Rodgers
Lyrics by Oscar Hammerstein II
The Sound of Music 1959

How Can the Night Be Good?
Music by Michael H. Cleary
Lyrics by Max and Nathaniel Lief
Shoot the Works 1931

How Can We Swing It?
Music by Lee Wainer
Lyrics by Robert Sour
Sing for Your Supper 1939

How Can You Describe a Face?
Music by Jule Styne
Lyrics by Betty Comden and Adolph Green
Subways Are for Sleeping 1961

How Can You Forget?
Music by Richard Rodgers
Lyrics by Lorenz Hart
Fools for Scandal (1938) F

How Can You Keep Your Mind on Business?
Music by Rudolf Friml
Lyrics by Otto Harbach and Oscar Hammerstein II
The Wild Rose 1926

Dropped from production

How Can You Kiss Those Times Goodbye?
Music by Laurence Rosenthal
Lyrics by James Lipton
Sherry! 1967

How Can You Tell?
Music by H. Maurice Jacquet
Lyrics by Preston Sturges
The Well of Romance 1930

How Can You Tell an American?
Music by Kurt Weill
Lyrics by Maxwell Anderson
Knickerbocker Holiday 1938

How Could a Fellow Want More?
Music by Sigmund Romberg
Lyrics by Otto Harbach
Forbidden Melody 1936

How Could I Be So Wrong
Music and lyrics by Walter Marks
Golden Rainbow 1968

How Could I Dare to Dream?
Music by Mitch Leigh
Lyrics by Charles Burr and Forman Brown
Home Sweet Homer 1976

How Could I Forget?
Music by George Gershwin
Lyrics by Gus Kahn and Ira Gershwin
Show Girl 1929

How Could You Believe Me When I Said I Love You When You Know I've Been a Liar All My Life
Music by Burton Lane
Lyrics by Alan Jay Lerner
Royal Wedding (1951) F

How Dear Is Our Day
Music by Frederic Norton
Lyrics by Oscar Asche
Chu Chin Chow 1917

How Did It Get So Late So Early?
Music by Will Irwin
Lyrics by June Sillman
All in Fun 1940

How Do I Feel?
Music by Kenneth Jacobson
Lyrics by Rhoda Roberts
Show Me Where the Good Times Are (OB) 1970

How Do They Ever Grow Up?
Music and lyrics by Robert Larimer
King of the Whole Damn World (OB) 1962

How Do You Do?
Music by Edward Künneke
Lyrics by Clifford Grey
Mayflowers 1925

How Do You Do?
Music and lyrics by Rick Besoyan
Little Mary Sunshine (OB) 1959

How Do You Do It?
Music by Lewis E. Gensler
Lyrics by E.Y. Harburg
Ballyhoo 1932

How Do You Do, Katinka?
Music by Jerome Kern
Lyrics by Anne Caldwell
The Bunch and Judy 1922

How Do You Do, Middle Age?
Music and lyrics by Noël Coward
The Girl Who Came to Supper 1963

How Do You Do, Miss Pratt?
Music by Walter Kent
Lyrics by Kim Gannon
Seventeen 1951

How Do You Do, Miss Ragtime?
Music by Louis A. Hirsch
Lyrics by Harold Atteridge
The Whirl of Society 1912

How Do You Doodle Do?
Music by J. Fred Coots
Lyrics by Clifford Grey
June Days 1925

How Do You Find the Words?
Music by Lee Pockriss
Lyrics by Anne Croswell
Ernest in Love (OB) 1960

How Do You Keep Out of Love?
Music by Albert T. Viola
Lyrics by William S. Kilborne, Jr.
Head Over Heels 1981

How Do You Know?
Music by Louis A. Hirsch
Lyrics by Harold Atteridge
The Whirl of Society 1912

How Do You Like Your Love?
Music by Tommy Wolf
Lyrics by Fran Landesman
The Nervous Set 1959

How Do You Raise a Barn?
Music by Albert Hague
Lyrics by Arnold B. Horwitt
Plain and Fancy 1955

How Do You Say Goodbye?
Music by Ernest G. Schweikert
Lyrics by Frank Reardon
Rumple 1957

How Do You Say Goodbye?
Music by Gary Geld
Lyrics by Peter Udell
Angel 1978

How Do You Speak to an Angel?
Music by Jule Styne
Lyrics by Bob Hilliard
Hazel Flagg 1953

How Do You Spell Ambassador?
Music and lyrics by Cole Porter
Leave It to Me 1938

How Do You Stop Loving Someone?
Music and lyrics by Johnny Brandon
Who's Who, Baby? (OB) 1968

How Do You Want Me?
Music by Michael Valenti
Lyrics by Donald Driver
Oh, Brother 1981

How Does It Start?
Music by Lawrence Hurwit
Lyrics by Lee Goldsmith
Sextet 1974

How Doth the Apple Butterfly
Music and lyrics by William Roy
The Penny Friend (OB) 1966

How Dreamlike
Music and lyrics by James Rado
Rainbow (OB) 1972

How D'ya Talk to a Girl?
Music by Jimmy Van Heusen
Lyrics by Sammy Cahn
Walking Happy 1966

How D'You Do?
Music by Philip Braham
Lyrics by Eric Blore and Dion Titheradge
Charlot's Revue of 1926

How Far Can a Lady Go?
Music by Jimmy Van Heusen
Lyrics by Johnny Burke
Carnival in Flanders 1953

How Far Is Too Far?
Music and lyrics by James Quinn and Alaric Jans
Do Patent Leather Shoes Really Reflect Up? 1982

How Fiercely You Dance
Music by Jean Gilbert
Lyrics by Harry Graham and Cyrus Wood
The Lady in Ermine 1922

How Fine It Is
Music by Stanley Silverman
Lyrics by Arthur Miller
Up From Paradise (OB) 1983

How Fly Times
Music by Frederick Loewe
Lyrics by Alan Jay Lerner
What's Up? 1943

How Fucked Up Things Are
Music by Michael Valenti
Lyrics by John Lewin
Blood Red Roses 1970

How Green Was My Valley
Music by John Morris
Lyrics by Gerald Freedman
A Time for Singing 1966

How Happy Is the Bride
Music by Vincent Youmans
Lyrics by Edward Heyman
Through the Years 1932

How High the Moon
Music by Morgan Lewis
Lyrics by Nancy Hamilton
Two for the Show 1940

How I Could Go for You
Music by Louis Alter
Lyrics by Harry Ruskin and Leighton K. Brill
Ballyhoo 1930

How I Feel
Music by Gary William Friedman
Lyrics by Will Holt
The Me Nobody Knows (OB) 1970

How I Love a Pretty Face
Music by Heinrich Reinhardt
Lyrics by Robert B. Smith
The Spring Maid 1910

How I Love Your Thingamajig
Music by Galt MacDermot
Lyrics by William Dumaresq
The Human Comedy (OB) 1983

How Jazz Was Born
Music by "Fats" Waller
Lyrics by Andy Razaf
Keep Shufflin' 1928

How Laughable It Is
Music by Mark Sandrich, Jr.
Lyrics by Sidney Michaels
Ben Franklin in Paris 1964

How Little We Know
Music by Hoagy Carmichael
Lyrics by Johnny Mercer
To Have and Have Not (1944) F

How Long?
Music by Maria Grever
Lyrics by Raymond Leveen
Viva O'Brien 1941

How Long?
Music by Richard Rodgers
Lyrics by Oscar Hammerstein II
Pipe Dream 1955

How Long Can Love Keep Laughing?
Music and lyrics by Harold Rome
Sing Out the News 1938

How Long Has This Been Going On?
Music by George Gershwin
Lyrics by Ira Gershwin
Funny Face 1927

Dropped from production and later used in *Rosalie* (1928)

How Lovely Is Eve
Music by Stanley Silverman
Lyrics by Arthur Miller
Up From Paradise (OB) 1983

How Lovely to Be a Woman
Music by Charles Strouse
Lyrics by Lee Adams
Bye Bye Birdie 1960

How Marvin Eats His Breakfast
Music and lyrics by William Finn
In Trousers (OB) 1981

How Much I Love You
Music by Kurt Weill
Lyrics by Ogden Nash
One Touch of Venus 1943

How Nice for Me
Music by Hoagy Carmichael
Lyrics by Johnny Mercer
Walk With Music 1940

How Sad
Music and lyrics by Richard Rodgers
No Strings 1962

How Solemn
Music by Stan Harte, Jr.
Leaves of Grass (OB) 1971

How Soon, Oh Moon?
Music by Jacques Offenbach (adapted by Robert DeCormier)
Lyrics by E.Y. Harburg
The Happiest Girl in the World 1961

How Strange the Silence
Music by Baldwin Bergersen
Lyrics by William Archibald
The Crystal Heart (OB) 1960

How Sweet You Are
Music by Arthur Schwartz
Lyrics by Frank Loesser
Thank Your Lucky Stars (1943) F

How Sweetly Friendship Binds
Music by Kurt Weill
Lyrics by Paul Green
Johnny Johnson 1936

How the First Song Was Born
Music and lyrics by Alexander Hill
Hummin' Sam 1933

How the Girls Adore Me
Music by Jean Gilbert
Lyrics by Harry B. Smith
The Red Robe 1928

How the Money Changes Hands
Music by Jerry Bock
Lyrics by Sheldon Harnick
Tenderloin 1960

How They Do, Do
Music by Ann Sternberg
Lyrics by Gertrude Stein
Gertrude Stein's First Reader (OB) 1969

How To
Music and lyrics by Frank Loesser
How to Succeed in Business Without Really Trying 1961

How to Handle a Woman
Music by Frederick Loewe
Lyrics by Alan Jay Lerner
Camelot 1960

How to Pick a Man a Wife
Music by Sammy Fain
Lyrics by Paul Francis Webster
Christine 1960

How to Steal an Election
Music and lyrics by Oscar Brand
How to Steal an Election (OB) 1968

How to Survive
Music by Kurt Weill
Lyrics by Marc Blitzstein
The Threepenny Opera (OB) 1954

How to Win a Man
Music by Vincent Youmans
Lyrics by Oscar Hammerstein II
Rainbow 1928

Dropped from production

How to Win Friends and Influence People
Music by Richard Rodgers
Lyrics by Lorenz Hart
I Married an Angel 1938

How Very Long Ago
Music and lyrics by Gene Lockhart
Bunk of 1926

How Was I to Know?
Music by Jerome Kern
Lyrics by Harry B. Smith
Love o' Mike 1917

How Was I to Know?
Music by Richard Rodgers
Lyrics by Lorenz Hart
She's My Baby 1928

Dropped from production, rewritten as "Why Do You Suppose?" for *Heads Up* (1929).

How We Get Down
Music by Mel Marvin
Lyrics by Robert Montgomery
Green Pond (OB) 1977

How We Would Like Our Man
Music and lyrics by Walter Cool
Mackey of Appalachia (OB) 1965

How Will He Know?
Music by Jule Styne
Lyrics by Betty Comden and Adolph Green
Two on the Aisle 1951

How Wonderful It Is
Music by Clinton Ballard
Lyrics by Carolyn Richter
The Ballad of Johnny Pot (OB) 1971

How Would a City Girl Know?
Music by Kay Swift
Lyrics by Paul James
Nine-Fifteen Revue 1930

How Young You Were Tonight
Music by Edward Thomas
Lyrics by Martin Charnin
Ballad for a Firing Squad (OB) 1968

How'd You Like To
Music by Stephen Jones
Lyrics by Irving Caesar
Yes, Yes, Yvette 1927

How'd You Like to Spoon With Me?
Music by Jerome Kern
Lyrics by Edward Laska
The Earl and the Girl 1905

Howdjadoo
Music by George Fischoff
Lyrics by Carole Bayer
Georgy 1970

Howdy Broadway
Music by Richard Rodgers
Lyrics by Lorenz Hart
Peggy-Ann 1926

Howdy, Mr. Sunshine
Music and lyrics by Skip Redwine and Larry Frank
Frank Merriwell, or Honor Challenged 1971

How'ja Like to Take Me Home
Music by Philip Charig
Lyrics by Dan Shapiro and Milton Pascal
Artists and Models (1943)

How's Chances?
Music and lyrics by Irving Berlin
As Thousands Cheer 1933

How's Your Health
Music by Richard Rodgers
Lyrics by Lorenz Hart
Higher And Higher 1940

How's Your Romance?
Music and lyrics by Cole Porter
Gay Divorce 1932

How's Your Uncle?
Music by Jimmy McHugh
Lyrics by Dorothy Fields
Shoot the Works 1931

The Hudson Belle
Music by Ivan Caryll
Lyrics by C.M.S. McLellan
The Pink Lady 1911

Hudson Duster
Music by Ray Henderson
Lyrics by B.G. DeSylva and Lew Brown
Manhattan Mary 1927

Huggin' and Muggin'
Music by Eubie Blake
Lyrics by J. Milton Reddie and Cecil Mack
Swing It 1937

Hugs and Kisses
Music by Louis Alter
Lyrics by Raymond Klages
Earl Carroll's Vanities (1926)

Huguette Waltz
Music by Rudolf Friml
Lyrics by Brian Hooker
The Vagabond King 1925

The Hula Girl
Music by John Green
Lyrics by George Marion, Jr.
Beat the Band 1942

Hula Hoop
Music by Diane Leslie
Lyrics by William Gleason
The Coolest Cat in Town (OB) 1978

Hullabaloo at Thebes
Music and lyrics by Ronny Graham
New Faces of 1968

Hulla-Baloo-Balay
Music by John Clifton
Lyrics by John Clifton and Ben Tarver
Man With a Load of Mischief (OB) 1966

Hum a Little Tune
Music by Vivian Ellis
Lyrics by Graham John
By the Way 1925

The Human Brush
Music by Jerome Kern
Lyrics by Edward Madden
La Belle Paree 1911

Human Nature
Music by Jerome Kern
Lyrics by Harry B. Smith
Ninety in the Shade 1915

Humble Pie
Music by Norman Campbell
Lyrics by Donald Harron and Norman Campbell
Anne of Green Gables (OB) 1971

Humdrum Life
Music by Galt MacDermot
Lyrics by Gerome Ragni
Dude 1972

Humming
Music and lyrics by Bob Merrill
Carnival 1961

Humpty-Dumpty
Music by Joseph Meyer and Philip Charig
Lyrics by Leo Robin
Just Fancy 1927

Humpty Dumpty
Music and lyrics by Elizabeth Swados
Alice in Concert (OB) 1980

Hunca Munca
Music and lyrics by Hal Hester
and Danny Apolinar
Your Own Thing (OB) 1968

A Hundred Million Miracles
Music by Richard Rodgers
Lyrics by Oscar Hammerstein II
Flower Drum Song 1958

A Hundred Thousand Ways
Music by Don Pippin
Lyrics by Steve Brown
The Contrast (OB) 1972

A Hundred Years From Today
Music by Victor Young
Lyrics by Joseph Young and Ned Washington
Blackbirds of 1934

Hundreds of Girls
Music and lyrics by Jerry Herman
Mack and Mabel 1974

Hung
Music by Galt MacDermot
Lyrics by Gerome Ragni and James Rado
Hair 1968

Hungaria
Music by Heinrich Reinhardt
Lyrics by Robert B. Smith
The Spring Maid 1910

Hungaria's Hussars
Music by Victor Herbert
Lyrics by Harry B. Smith
The Fortune Teller 1898

Hungry
Music and lyrics by Murray Grand
New Faces of 1968

Hungry Men
Music by Harvey Schmidt
Lyrics by Tom Jones
110 in the Shade 1963

The Hunt
Music by Percy Wenrich
Lyrics by Harry Clarke
Who Cares? 1930

The Hunted
Music by Duke Ellington
Lyrics by John Latouche
Beggar's Holiday 1946

Hunting
Music by Rudolf Friml
Lyrics by Brian Hooker
The Vagabond King 1925

Hunting Song
Music and lyrics by Tom Lehrer
Tomfoolery (OB) 1981

Hunting the Fox
Music by Richard Rodgers
Lyrics by Lorenz Hart
Simple Simon 1930

Hurray for Life
Music by Lehman Engel
Lyrics by Agnes Morgan
A Hero Is Born 1937

Hurricane
Music by Mel Marvin
Lyrics by Robert Montgomery
Green Pond (OB) 1977

Hurry
Music by Murray Grand
Lyrics by Murray Grand and Elisse Boyd
New Faces of 1956

Hurry Back
Music by Charles Strouse
Lyrics by Lee Adams
Applause 1970

Hurry, Harry
Music by Bill Weeden
Lyrics by David Finkle
Hurry, Harry 1972

Hurry Home
Music by William Dyer
Lyrics by Don Parks and William Dyer
Jo (OB) 1964

Hurry! It's Lovely up Here
Music by Burton Lane
Lyrics by Alan Jay Lerner
On a Clear Day You Can See Forever 1965

Hurry Now
Music by Jerome Kern
Lyrics by Herbert Reynolds
Rock-a-Bye Baby 1918

Hurry Up, Face
Music by Larry Grossman
Lyrics by Hal Hackady
Snoopy (OB) 1982

Husband, Lover, and Wife
Music by Lewis E. Gensler
Lyrics by Owen Murphy and Robert A.Simon
The Gang's All Here l931

A Husband's Love
Music by Oscar Straus
Lyrics by Joseph W. Herbert
A Waltz Dream 1908

A Husband's Only a Husband
Music by Emmerich Kálmán
Lyrics by B.G. DeSylva
The Yankee Princess 1922

Hush
Music by Galt MacDermot
Lyrics by Christopher Gore
Via Galactica 1972

Hush-Hush
Music by Julian Slade
Lyrics by Dorothy Reynolds and Julian Slade
Salad Days (OB) 1958

Hush! Hush! Hush!
Music by Ivan Caryll
Lyrics by C.M.S. McLellan
Oh! Oh! Delphine 1912

Hushabye Baby
Music by Helen Miller
Lyrics by Eve Merriam
Inner City 1971

The Husking Bee
Music by Jule Styne
Lyrics by Betty Comden and Adolph Green
Say, Darling 1958

Husky, Dusky Annabelle
Music by Max Ewing
Lyrics by Agnes Morgan
The Grand Street Follies (1928)

Hussars March
Music by Sigmund Romberg
Lyrics by P.G. Wodehouse
Rosalie 1928

The Hussars' Song
Music by Emmerich Kálmán
Lyrics by Harry B. Smith
The Circus Princess 1927

Hustle, Bustle
Music by Harry Archer
Lyrics by Harlan Thompson
Twinkle Twinkle 1926

The Hustler
Music and lyrics by Al Carmines
The Faggot (OB) 1973

Huxley
Music by Kurt Weill
Lyrics by Ira Gershwin
Lady in the Dark 1941

Hymen, Hymen
Music by Richard Hill and John Hawkins
Lyrics by Nevill Coghill
Canterbury Tales 1969

Hymn
Music by Steve Sterner
Lyrics by Peter del Valle
Lovers (OB) 1975

Hymn for a Sunday Evening
Music by Charles Strouse
Lyrics by Lee Adams
Bye Bye Birdie 1960

Hymn of Betrothal
Music and lyrics by Robert Wright and George Forrest
Song of Norway 1944

Based on Grieg's song *To Spring*

A Hymn to Him
Music by Frederick Loewe
Lyrics by Alan Jay Lerner
My Fair Lady 1956

Hymn to Hymen
Music and lyrics by Cole Porter
Red, Hot and Blue! 1936

Hymn to Hymie
Music and lyrics by Jerry Herman
Milk and Honey 1961

Hymn to Peace
Music by Kurt Weill
Lyrics by Paul Green
Johnny Johnson 1936

Hymns From the Darkness
Music and lyrics by Al Carmines
The Evangelist (OB) 1982

The Hypnotic Kiss
Music by Karl Hoschna
Lyrics by Otto Harbach
Three Twins 1908

Hypnotizing Rag
Music by Silvio Hein
Lyrics by George V. Hobart
The Yankee Girl 1910

I

I Accuse
Music by Monty Norman
Lyrics by Julian More
The Moony Shapiro Songbook 1981

I Admire You Very Much, Mr. Schmidt
Music by Jule Styne
Lyrics by Sammy Cahn
Look to the Lilies 1970

I Admit
Music by Emmerich Kálmán
Lyrics by George Marion, Jr.
Marinka 1945

I Adore You
Music and lyrics by Ballard MacDonald,
Sam Coslow and René Mercier
Footlights 1927

I Adore You
Music and lyrics by Cole Porter
Aladdin (1958) TV

I Ain't Down Yet
Music and lyrics by Meredith Willson
The Unsinkable Molly Brown 1960

I Ain't Looking Back
Music by Harris Wheeler
Lyrics by Mary L. Fisher
Blue Plate Special (OB) 1983

I Always Knew
Music and lyrics by Cole Porter
Something to Shout About (1943) F

I Am
Music by Niclas Kempner
Lyrics by Graham John
The Street Singer 1929

I Am a Cloud
Music and lyrics by James Rado
Rainbow (OB) 1972

I Am a Court Coquette
Music by Victor Herbert
Lyrics by Harry B. Smith
Cyrano de Bergerac 1899

I Am a Dumbbell
Music and lyrics by Irving Berlin
Music Box Revue (1st edition) 1921

I Am a Little Worm
Music by Meyer Kupferman
Lyrics by Paul Goodman
Jonah (OB) 1966

I Am a Preacher of the Lord
Music and lyrics by Al Carmines
The Evangelist (OB) 1982

I Am a Travelling Poet
Music by Joseph Raposo
Lyrics by Erich Segal
Sing Muse! (OB) 1961

I Am a Witch
Music by Richard Rodgers
Lyrics by Oscar Hammerstein II
Pipe Dream 1955

I Am All A-Blaze
Music by Richard Hill and John Hawkins
Lyrics by Nevill Coghill
Canterbury Tales 1969

I Am an Evangelist
Music and lyrics by Al Carmines
The Evangelist (OB) 1982

I Am Ashamed That Women Are So Simple
Music and lyrics by Cole Porter
Kiss Me, Kate 1948

The lyric is adapted, with only minor alteration,
from Katharina's speech in Shakespeare's *Taming
of the Shrew* (Act V, Scene 2).

212

I Am Captured
Music by Sigmund Romberg
Lyrics by Harry B. Smith
The Love Call 1927

I Am Changing
Music by Henry Krieger
Lyrics by Tom Eyen
Dreamgirls 1981

I Am Child
Music by Ron Steward and Neal Tate
Lyrics by Ron Steward
Sambo (OB) 1969

I Am Chu Chin Chow of China
Music by Frederic Norton
Lyrics by Oscar Asche
Chu Chin Chow 1917

I Am Daguerre
Music by Jerome Kern
Lyrics by Anne Caldwell
Hitchy-Koo 1920

I Am Easily Assimilated
Music and lyrics by Leonard Bernstein
Candide 1956

I Am Free
Music by John Kander
Lyrics by Fred Ebb
Zorba 1968

I Am Gaston
Music and lyrics by Cole Porter
You Never Know 1938

I Am Going to Dance
Music and lyrics by William Roy
The Penny Friend (OB) 1966

I Am Going to Like It Here
Music by Richard Rodgers
Lyrics by Oscar Hammerstein II
Flower Drum Song 1958

I Am Going to Love (The Man You're Going to Be)
Music by Larry Grossman
Lyrics by Hal Hackady
Goodtime Charley 1975

I Am Happy Here
Music by Kurt Weill
Lyrics by Ira Gershwin
The Firebrand of Florence 1945

I Am in Love
Music by Franz Lehár
Lyrics by Basil Hood
The Count of Luxembourg 1912

I Am in Love
Music by Fritz Kreisler
Lyrics by William LeBaron
Apple Blossoms 1919

I Am in Love
Music and lyrics by Cole Porter
Can-Can 1953

I Am It
Music by Richard Adler
Lyrics by Will Holt
Music Is 1976

I Am Loved
Music and lyrics by Cole Porter
Out of This World 1950

I Am Not Free
Music and lyrics by James Rado
Rainbow (OB) 1972

I Am Not Interested in Love
Music by Galt MacDermot
Lyrics by John Guare
Two Gentlemen of Verona 1971

I Am Not Old
Music by Gary William Friedman
Lyrics by Will Holt
Taking My Turn (OB) 1983

I Am Only Human After All
Music by Vernon Duke
Lyrics by Ira Gershwin and E.Y. Harburg
The Garrick Gaieties (3rd edition) 1930

I Am Royal
Music by Baldwin Bergersen
Lyrics by William Archibald
Rosa (OB) 1978

I Am Sick of Love
Music and lyrics by Elizabeth Swados
Lullabye and Goodnight 1982

I Am So Eager
Music by Jerome Kern
Lyrics by Oscar Hammerstein II
Music in the Air 1932

I Am the Light
Music by Gary William Friedman
Lyrics by Will Holt
Platinum 1978

I Am the Man
Music and lyrics by Al Carmines
Wanted (OB) 1972

I Am the River
Music by Stanley Silverman
Lyrics by Arthur Miller
Up From Paradise (OB) 1983

I Am the Sheriff of Nottingham
Music by Reginald De Koven
Lyrics by Harry B. Smith
Robin Hood 1891

I Am Wearing a Hat
Music and lyrics by William Finn
In Trousers (OB) 1981

I Am What I Am!
Music by Gordon Duffy
Lyrics by Harry M. Haldane
Happy Town 1959

I Am What I Am
Music and lyrics by Jerry Herman
La Cage aux Folles 1983

I Am You
Music and lyrics by Johnny Brandon
Love! Love! Love! (OB) 1977

I Am Yours
Music by Robert Kole
Lyrics by Sandi Merle
I Take These Women (OB) 1982

I Asked My Heart
Music by Franz Lehár
Lyrics by Edward Eliscu
Frederika 1937

I Beg Your Pardon
Music by Richard Rodgers
Lyrics by Lorenz Hart
Dearest Enemy 1925

I Believe
Music and lyrics by Ron Eliran
Don't Step on My Olive Branch (OB) 1976

I Believe in Love
Music by Galt MacDermot
Lyrics by Gerome Ragni and James Rado
Hair 1968

I Believe in Signs
Music by Jerome Kern
Lyrics by Anne Caldwell
She's a Good Fellow 1919

Dropped from production

I Believe in Takin' a Chance
Music by Arthur Schwartz
Lyrics by Howard Dietz
Jennie 1963

I Believe in You
Music and lyrics by Frank Loesser
*How to Succeed in Business
Without Really Trying* 1961

I Believe My Body
Music and lyrics by Earl Wilson, Jr.
Let My People Come (OB) 1974

I Believed All She Said
Music by Jerome Kern
Lyrics by Herbert Reynolds
Rock-a-Bye Baby 1918

I Belong Here
Music and lyrics by Jerry Herman
The Grand Tour 1979

I Blush
Music by Richard Rodgers
Lyrics by Lorenz Hart
A Connecticut Yankee 1927

Dropped from production

I Bought a Bicycle
Music and lyrics by Mel Mandel
and Norman Sachs
My Old Friends (OB) 1979

I Bring a Love Song
Music by Sigmund Romberg
Lyrics by Oscar Hammerstein II
Viennese Nights (1930) F

I Bring Him Seashells
Music by Nancy Ford
Lyrics by Gretchen Cryer
Shelter 1973

I Bring My Girls Along
Music by Walter G. Samuels
Lyrics by Morrie Ryskind
Ned Wayburn's Gambols 1929

I Brought You a Gift
Music by Richard Rodgers
Lyrics by Sheldon Harnick
Rex 1976

Dropped from production

I Built a Dream One Day
Music by Sigmund Romberg
Lyrics by Oscar Hammerstein II
May Wine 1935

I Cain't Say No
Music by Richard Rodgers
Lyrics by Oscar Hammerstein II
Oklahoma! 1943

I Came Here
Music by Lewis E. Gensler
Lyrics by George S. Kaufman, Marc Connelly
and Ira Gershwin
Be Yourself 1924

I Came to Life
Music by Jay Gorney
Lyrics by E.Y. Harburg
Earl Carroll's Vanities (1930)

I Came to Tan
Music by Elizabeth Swados
Lyrics by Garry Trudeau
Doonesbury 1983

I Came to Your Room
Music by Richard Addinsell
Lyrics by Clemence Dane
Come of Age 1934

I Can
Music and lyrics by Walter Marks
Bajour 1964

**I Can Always Find a Little Sunshine
in the Y.M.C.A.**
Music and lyrics by Irving Berlin
Yip, Yip, Yaphank 1918

I Can Be Like Grandpa
Music and lyrics by Harold Orlob
Hairpin Harmony 1943

I Can Carry a Tune
Music by Galt MacDermot
Lyrics by William Dumaresq
The Human Comedy (OB) 1983

I Can Cook Too
Music by Leonard Bernstein
Lyrics by Leonard Bernstein, Betty Comden
and Adolph Green
On the Town 1944

I Can Count on You
Music and lyrics by Barbara Schottenfeld
I Can't Keep Running in Place (OB) 1981

I Can Do That
Music by Marvin Hamlisch
Lyrics by Edward Kleban
A Chorus Line 1975

I Can Do Without Tea in My Teapot
Music and lyrics by Cole Porter
Something to Shout About (1943) F

Dropped from film

I Can Do Wonders With You
Music by Richard Rodgers
Lyrics by Lorenz Hart
Heads Up! 1929

Dropped from production. Used in *Simple Simon*
(1930)

I Can Dream, Can't I?
Music by Sammy Fain
Lyrics by Irving Kahal
Right This Way 1938

I Can Have It All
Music by Elizabeth Swados
Lyrics by Garry Trudeau
Doonesbury 1983

I Can Hear It Now
Music and lyrics by Harold Rome
Bless You All 1950

I Can Learn
Music and lyrics by Howard Blankman
By Hex (OB) 1956

I Can Make It Happen
Music by Elmer Bernstein
Lyrics by Don Black
Merlin 1983

I Can See
Music by Lance Mulcahy
Lyrics by Paul Cherry
Park 1970

I Can See Him Clearly
Music by Arthur Siegel
Lyrics by Mae Richard
Tallulah (OB) 1983

I Can See It
Music by Harvey Schmidt
Lyrics by Tom Jones
The Fantasticks (OB) 1960

I Can Speak Espagnol
Music by Harry Tierney
Lyrics by Joseph McCarthy
Rio. Rita 1927

I Can Teach Them
Music by Charles Strouse
Lyrics by Lee Adams
All American 1962

I Can Tell by the Way that You Dance, Dear
Music by Rudolf Friml
Lyrics by Otto Harbach
Katinka 1915

I Can Trust Myself with a Lot of Girls
Music by Jerome Kern
Lyrics by Herbert Reynolds
Rock-a-Bye Baby 1918

I Cannot Live Without Your Love
Music by Ralph Benatzky
Lyrics by Irving Caesar
White Horse Inn 1936

I Cannot Make Him Jealous
Music and lyrics by Ervin Drake
Her First Roman 1968

I Cannot Tell Her So
Music and lyrics by John Jennings
Riverwind (OB) 1962

I Cannot Wait
Music by Wally Harper
Lyrics by Paul Zakrzewski
Sensations (OB) 1970

I Can't Afford to Dream
Music by Sam Stept
Lyrics by Lew Brown and Charles Tobias
Yokel Boy 1939

I Can't Argue With You
Music by Victor Herbert
Lyrics by B.G. DeSylva
Orange Blossoms 1922

I Can't Be Bothered Now
Music by George Gershwin
Lyrics by Ira Gershwin
A Damsel in Distress (1937) F

I Can't Be Happy
Music by Vincent Youmans
Lyrics by Anne Caldwell
Oh, Please! 1926

I Can't Be in Love
Music by Leroy Anderson
Lyrics by Joan Ford and Walter and Jean Kerr
Goldilocks 1958

I Can't Believe It's True
Music by Alberta Nichols
Lyrics by Mann Holiner
Angela 1928

I Can't Believe It's True
Music by Lewis E. Gensler
Lyrics by Robert A. Simon
Ups-a-Daisy 1928

Dropped from production

I Can't Believe It's You
Music by Gary Geld
Lyrics by Peter Udell
Angel 1978

I Can't Complain
Music by Richard Rodgers
Lyrics by Martin Charnin
Two by Two 1970

Dropped from production

I Can't Do It Alone
Music by John Kander
Lyrics by Fred Ebb
Chicago 1975

I Can't Do That Sum
Music by Victor Herbert
Lyrics by Glen MacDonough
Babes in Toyland 1903

I Can't Forget Your Eyes
Music by Jerome Kern
Lyrics by Harry B. Smith
Oh, I Say! 1913

This music re-appeared as "Sunshine" (lyrics by Harbach and Hammerstein) in *Sunny* (1925). Before *Sunny* closed, Kern's next show *Criss Cross* opened with the same melody, this time as "In Araby With You" (lyrics by Anne Caldwell). Thus, for two whole months the same tune was being sung in two concurrent Broadway shows.

I Can't Get 'Em Up
Music by John Philip Sousa
Lyrics by Leonard Liebling
The American Maid 1913

I Can't Get Into the Quota
Music by Arthur Schwartz
Lyrics by Henry Myers
The New Yorkers 1927

I Can't Get Over a Girl Like You
Music by Martin Broones
Lyrics by Harry Ruskin
Rufus Lemaire's Affairs 1927

I Can't Get Started
Music by Vernon Duke
Lyrics by Ira Gershwin
Ziegfeld Follies (1936)

Vernon Duke's first title for the song was "Face the Music with Me." With Ira Gershwin's new lyric it became a witty and sophisticated "list" song, sung in a bright jaunty tempo by Bob Hope (to Eve Arden) in the *Ziegfeld Follies* (1936). It was all but forgotten until Bunny Berigan recorded it years later, turning it into a slow bluesy number, which is how it is performed today.

I Can't Give You Anything But Love
Music by Jimmy McHugh
Lyrics by Dorothy Fields
Blackbirds of 1928

Previously dropped from *Harry Delmar's Revels* (1927)

I Can't Keep Running in Place
Music and lyrics by Barbara Schottenfeld
I Can't Keep Running in Place (OB) 1981

I Can't Make It Anymore
Music and lyrics by Tom Sankey
The Golden Screw (OB) 1967

I Can't Make This Movie
Music and lyrics by Maury Yeston
Nine 1982

I Can't Remember
Music and lyrics by Tom Sankey
The Golden Screw (OB) 1967

I Can't Remember the Words
Music by Milton Ager and Henry Cabot Lodge
Lyrics by Jack Yellen
John Murray Anderson's Almanac (1929)

I Can't Sleep
Music and lyrics by William Finn
In Trousers (OB) 1981

I Can't Stop Talking
Music by Leon Pober
Lyrics by Bud Freeman
Beg, Borrow or Steal 1960

**I Can't Tell Where They're From
When They Dance**
Music by George Gershwin
Lyrics by B.G. DeSylva and E. Ray Goetz
George White's Scandals (1922)

I Can't Tell You
Music by Charles Strouse
Lyrics by David Rogers
Charlie and Algernon 1980

I Chose Right
Music by David Shire
Lyrics by Richard Maltby, Jr.
Baby 1983

I Come From Gascony
Music by Victor Herbert
Lyrics by Harry B. Smith
Cyrano de Bergerac 1899

I Come Out of a Dream
Music by Richard Addinsell
Lyrics by Clemence Dane
Come of Age 1934

I Concentrate on You
Music and lyrics by Cole Porter
Broadway Melody of 1940 (1940) F

I Could Be Happy With You
Music and lyrics by Sandy Wilson
The Boy Friend 1954

I Could Dig You
Music by Ron Steward and Neal Tate
Lyrics by Ron Steward
Sambo (OB) 1969

I Could Do a Lot for You
Music by Rudolf Friml
Lyrics by Otto Harbach
The Blue Kitten 1922

I Could Get Married Today
Music by Walter Kent
Lyrics by Kim Gannon
Seventeen 1951

I Could Get Used to Him
Music by Henry Krieger
Lyrics by Robert Lorick
The Tap Dance Kid 1983

I Could Give Up Anything but You
Music by Ray Henderson
Lyrics by B.G. DeSylva and Lew Brown
Follow Thru 1929

I Could Go on Singing
Music by Harold Arlen
Lyrics by E. Y. Harburg
I Could Go on Singing (1963) F

I Could Have Danced All Night
Music by Frederick Loewe
Lyrics by Alan Jay Lerner
My Fair Lady 1956

I Could Kick Myself
Music and lyrics by Cole Porter
Les Girls (1957) F

Dropped from film

I Could Write a Book
Music by Richard Rodgers
Lyrics by Lorenz Hart
Pal Joey 1940

I Couldn't Have Done It Alone
Music by Charles Strouse
Lyrics by Lee Adams
All American 1962

I Couldn't Hold My Man
Music by Harold Arlen
Lyrics by Ira Gershwin and E.Y. Harburg
Life Begins at 8:40 1934

I Cried for My Troubles
Music by Meyer Kupferman
Lyrics by Paul Goodman
Jonah (OB) 1966

I Dance Alone
Music and lyrics by James Shelton
Who's Who 1938

I Danced With You One Night
Music by Leo Fall
Lyrics by George Grossmith
The Dollar Princess 1909

I Dare Not Love You
Music by Sigmund Romberg
Lyrics by Harry B. Smith
Princess Flavia 1925

I Dare to Dream
Music by Michael Grace and Carl Tucker
Lyrics by Sammy Gallup
John Murray Anderson's Almanac (1953)

I Dare to Speak of Love to You
Music by Emmerich Kálmán
Lyrics by Harry B. Smith
The Circus Princess 1927

I Delight in the Sight of My Lydia
Music by Alec Wilder
Lyrics by Arnold Sundgaard
Kittiwake Island (OB) 1960

I Depend on You
Music by Keith Hermann
Lyrics by Charlotte Anker and Irene Rosenberg
Onward Victoria 1980

I Did It
Music and lyrics by Harry Chapin
Cotton Patch Gospel (OB) 1981

I Did Not Sleep Last Night
Music by Edward Thomas
Lyrics by Martin Charnin
Ballad for a Firing Squad (OB) 1968

I Didn't Know That It Was Loaded
Music by Michael H. Cleary
Lyrics by Max and Nathaniel Lief
Hey Nonny Nonny! 1932

I Didn't Know What Time It Was
Music by Richard Rodgers
Lyrics by Lorenz Hart
Too Many Girls 1939

I Dig Myself
Music by Hank Beebe
Lyrics by Bill Heyer
*Tuscaloosa's Calling Me
But I'm Not Going!* (OB) 1975

I Disremember Quite Well
Music and lyrics by Antonia
Operation Sidewinder 1970

I Do
Music by Lewis E. Gensler
Lyrics by B.G. DeSylva
Captain Jinks 1925

I Do! He Doesn't!
Music and lyrics by Jack Lawrence
and Don Walker
Courtin' Time 1951

I Do! I Do!
Music by Harvey Schmidt
Lyrics by Tom Jones
I Do! I Do! 1966

I Do Not Know a Day I Did Not Love You
Music by Richard Rodgers
Lyrics by Martin Charnin
Two by Two 1970

I Do, So There!
Music by Gustave Kerker
Lyrics by Hugh Morton
The Belle of New York 1897

I Do the Best I Can
Music by Al Carmines
Lyrics by Al Carmines and David Epstein
Wanted (OB) 1972

I Don't Believe It
Music by David Shire
Lyrics by Richard Maltby, Jr.
Starting Here, Starting Now (OB) 1977

I Don't Blame 'Em
Music by Percy Wenrich
Lyrics by Raymond Peck
Castles in the Air 1926

I Don't Care
Music by Kenn Long and Jim Crozier
Lyrics by Kenn Long
Touch (OB) 1970

I Don't Care
Music and lyrics by Gary Portnoy
and Judy Hart Angelo
Preppies (OB) 1983

I Don't Care What They Say About Me
Music by Fred Spielman and Arthur Gershwin
Lyrics by Stanley Adams
A Lady Says Yes 1945

I Don't Get It
Music by Doris Tauber
Lyrics by Sis Wilner
Star and Garter 1942

I Don't Hope for Great Things
Music and lyrics by James Rado
Rainbow (OB) 1972

I Don't Know
Music by Philip Braham
Lyrics by Ronald Jeans
Charlot's Revue 1924

I Don't Know
Music by Charles Strouse
Lyrics by Alan Jay Lerner
Dance a Little Closer 1983

I Don't Know Her Name
Music by Richard Lewine
Lyrics by Arnold B. Horwitt
Make Mine Manhattan 1948

I Don't Know His Name
Music by Jerry Bock
Lyrics by Sheldon Harnick
She Loves Me 1963

I Don't Know How
Music by Richard Rodgers
Lyrics by Raymond Jessel
I Remember Mama 1979

Dropped from production

I Don't Know How I Do It, But I Do
Music by Victor Herbert
Lyrics by Robert B. Smith
Sweethearts 1913

I Don't Know How to Love Him
Music by Andrew Lloyd Webber
Lyrics by Tim Rice
Jesus Christ Superstar 1971

I Don't Know What Is Happening to Me
Music by Stanley Silverman
Lyrics by Arthur Miller
Up From Paradise (OB) 1983

I Don't Know Where She Got It
Music by Jule Styne
Lyrics by Betty Comden and Adolph Green
Hallelujah, Baby! 1967

I Don't Know Why I Trust You (But I Do)
Music and lyrics by James MacDonald, David Vos
and Robert Gerlach
Something's Afoot 1976

I Don't Like This Dame
Music and lyrics by Frank Loesser
The Most Happy Fella 1956

I Don't Like You
Music and lyrics by Lionel Bart
La Strada 1969

I Don't Live Anywhere Anymore
Music by Patrick Rose
Lyrics by Merv Campone and Richard Ouzounian
A Bistro Car on the CNR (OB) 1978

I Don't Love Nobody But You
Music by Jimmy Johnson
Lyrics by Perry Bradford
Messin' Around 1929

I Don't Mind
Music and lyrics by Jerry Herman
Madame Aphrodite (OB) 1961

I Don't Need a Man to Know I'm Good
Music and lyrics by Bland Simpson and Jim Wann
Diamond Studs (OB) 1975

I Don't Need Anything but You
Music by Charles Strouse
Lyrics by Martin Charnin
Annie 1977

I Don't Remember Christmas
Music by David Shire
Lyrics by Richard Maltby, Jr.
Starting Here, Starting Now (OB) 1977

I Don't Remember You
Music by John Kander
Lyrics by Fred Ebb
The Happy Time 1968

I Don't See Him Very Much Anymore
Music by Edward Thomas
Lyrics by Martin Charnin
Ballad for a Firing Squad (OB) 1968

I Don't Think I'll End It All Today
Music by Harold Arlen
Lyrics by E.Y. Harburg
Jamaica 1957

I Don't Think I'll Ever Love You
Music by Tom Mandel
Lyrics by John Braswell
The Bar That Never Closes (OB) 1972

I Don't Think I'll Fall in Love Today
Music by George Gershwin
Lyrics by Ira Gershwin
Treasure Girl 1928

I Don't Think I'm in Love
Music by Jimmy Van Heusen
Lyrics by Sammy Cahn
Walking Happy 1966

I Don't Wanna Rock
Music by Colin Romoff
Lyrics by David Rogers
Ziegfeld Follies (1957)

I Don't Want a Boy
Music and lyrics by Al Kasha and Joel Hirschhorn
Copperfield 1981

I Don't Want a Girlie
Music by Vincent Youmans
Lyrics by B.G. DeSylva
No, No, Nanette 1925

Dropped from production

I Don't Want a Song at Twilight
Music by Alfred Nathan
Lyrics by George Oppenheimer
The Manhatters 1927

I Don't Want Him
Music by Con Conrad
Lyrics by Gus Kahn
Kitty's Kisses 1926

I Don't Want to Be Married
Music and lyrics by Irving Berlin
Face the Music 1932

I Don't Want to Be President
Music by Harry Akst
Lyrics by Lew Brown
Calling All Stars 1934

I Don't Want to Go Over to Vietnam
Music and lyrics by Gene Curty, Nitra Scharfman
and Chuck Strand
The Lieutenant 1975

I Don't Want to Know
Music and lyrics by Jerry Herman
Dear World 1969

I Don't Want to Watch TV
Music by Steve Sterner
Lyrics by Peter del Valle
Lovers (OB) 1975

I Don't Want You
Music by Giuseppe Verdi (adapted by Hans Spialek)
Lyrics by Charles Friedman
My Darlin' Aïda 1952

I Dream of a Girl in a Shawl
Music and lyrics by Cole Porter
Wake Up and Dream 1929

I Dream Too Much
Music by Jerome Kern
Lyrics by Dorothy Fields
I Dream Too Much (1935) F

I Dreamed About Roses
Music and lyrics by Michael Brown
Different Times 1972

I, Eliot Rosewater
Music by Alan Menken
Lyrics by Howard Ashman
Additional lyrics by Dennis Green
God Bless You, Mr. Rosewater (OB) 1979

I Enjoy Being a Girl
Music by Richard Rodgers
Lyrics by Oscar Hammerstein II
Flower Drum Song 1958

I Feel a Song Comin' On
Music by Jimmy McHugh
Lyrics by Dorothy Fields
and George Oppenheimer
Every Night at Eight (1935) F

I Feel at Home With You
Music by Richard Rodgers
Lyrics by Lorenz Hart
A Connecticut Yankee 1927

I Feel Grand
Music and lyrics by Michael Brown
Different Times 1972

I Feel Humble
Music and lyrics by Ervin Drake
What Makes Sammy Run? 1964

I Feel Like a Brother to You
Music by Gordon Duffy
Lyrics by Harry M. Haldane
Happy Town 1959

I Feel Like I'm Gonna Live Forever
Music by Jule Styne
Lyrics by Bob Hilliard
Hazel Flagg 1953

I Feel Like I'm Not Out of Bed Yet
Music by Leonard Bernstein
Lyrics by Betty Comden and Adolph Green
On the Town 1944

I Feel Like New Year's Eve
Music by Sammy Fain
Lyrics by Marilyn and Alan Bergman
Something More 1964

I Feel My Luck Comin' Down
Music by Harold Arlen
Lyrics by Johnny Mercer
St. Louis Woman 1946

I Feel Pretty
Music by Leonard Bernstein
Lyrics by Stephen Sondheim
West Side Story 1957

I Feel Sorry for the Girl
Music by Glenn Paxton
Lyrics by Robert Goldman and George Weiss
First Impressions 1959

I Feel Sorta—
Music by Harden Church
Lyrics by Edward Heyman
Caviar 1934

I Feel Wonderful
Music and lyrics by Jerry Herman
I Feel Wonderful (OB) 1954

I Fell Head Over Heels in Love
Music by Jean Gilbert
Lyrics by Harry Graham
Katja 1926

I Fell Head Over Heels in Love
Music by Pat Thayer
Lyrics by Donovan Parsons
The Merry World 1926

I Fell in Love With You
Music by Richard Lewine
Lyrics by Arnold B. Horwitt
Make Mine Manhattan 1948

I Forget What I Started to Say
Music by George Gershwin
Lyrics by Ira Gershwin
Rosalie 1928

Dropped from production

I Fought Every Step of the Way
Music and lyrics by Johnny Mercer
Top Banana 1951

I Found a Bud Among the Roses
Music by Rudolf Friml
Lyrics by Otto Harbach
The Blue Kitten 1922

I Found a Four-Leaf Clover
Music by George Gershwin
Lyrics by B.G. DeSylva
George White's Scandals (1922)

I Found a Friend
Music by Emile Berté and Maury Rubens
Lyrics by J. Keirn Brennan
Music in May 1929

I Found a Million Dollar Baby
Music by Harry Warren
Lyrics by Billy Rose and Mort Dixon
Crazy Quilt 1931

I Found a Song
Music by Edward A. Horan
Lyrics by Frederick Herendeen
All the King's Horses 1934

I Found Him
Music by Jacques Urbont
Lyrics by Bruce Geller
All in Love (OB) 1961

I Found Love
Music by Monty Norman
Lyrics by Julian More
The Moony Shapiro Songbook 1981

I Furnished My One Room Apartment
Music by Stephen Hoffman
Lyrics by Michael Mooney
Upstairs at O'Neal's (OB) 1982

I Get a Kick Out of You
Music and lyrics by Cole Porter
Anything Goes 1934

The line "I get no kick from cocaine" was changed
because of censor problems to "Some like the
perfumes from Spain." In another part of the song
Porter had written "I wouldn't care/ For those
nights in the air/ That the fair/ Mrs. Lindbergh went
through..." During the rehearsal period the
Lindbergh kidnapping occurred and Porter changed
the lines to "Flying too high/ with some guy in the
sky/ is my i-dea of nothing to do."

I Get Carried Away
Music by Leonard Bernstein
Lyrics by Betty Comden and Adolph Green
On the Town 1944

I Get Embarrassed
Msic and lyrics by Bob Merrill
Take Me Along 1959

I Give My Heart
Music by Carl Millöcker (revised by Theo
Mackeben)
Lyrics by Rowland Leigh
The Dubarry 1932

I Give Myself Away
Music by Jacques Fray
Lyrics by Edward Eliscu
The Vanderbilt Revue 1930

I Go to Bed
Music by Lee Pockriss
Lyrics by Anne Croswell
Tovarich 1963

I Got a Dream to Sleep On
Music by Gary Geld
Lyrics by Peter Udell
Angel 1978

I Got a Friend
Music by Charles Strouse
Lyrics by David Rogers
Charlie and Algernon 1980

I Got a Marble and a Star
Music by Kurt Weill
Lyrics by Langston Hughes
Street Scene 1947

I Got a New Girl
Music by Charles Strouse
Lyrics by Alan Jay Lerner
Dance a Little Closer 1983

I Got a Song
Music by Harold Arlen
Lyrics by E.Y. Harburg
Bloomer Girl 1944

I Got Beauty
Music and lyrics by Cole Porter
Out of This World 1950

I Got Everything I Want
Music and lyrics by Jack Lawrence
and Stan Freeman
I Had a Ball 1964

I Got It From Agnes
Music and lyrics by Tom Lehrer
Tomfoolery (OB) 1981

I Got Life
Music by Galt MacDermot
Lyrics by Gerome Ragni and James Rado
Hair 1968

I Got Lost in His Arms
Music and lyrics by Irving Berlin
Annie Get Your Gun 1946

I Got Love
Music by Jerome Kern
Lyrics by Dorothy Fields
I Dream Too Much (1935) F

I Got Love
Music by Gary Geld
Lyrics by Peter Udell
Purlie 1970

I Got Lucky in the Rain
Music by Jimmy McHugh
Lyrics by Harold Adamson
As the Girls Go 1948

I Got Plenty o' Nuttin'
Music by George Gershwin
Lyrics by DuBose Heyward and Ira Gershwin
Porgy and Bess 1935

I Got Religion
Music by Vincent Youmans
Lyrics by B.G. DeSylva
Take a Chance 1932

I Got Rhythm
Music by George Gershwin
Lyrics by Ira Gershwin
Girl Crazy 1930

It was with this song that, on the opening night of
Girl Crazy, Ethel Merman became an overnight star.
It was her first appearance on any stage. She
recalled later that after singing for George
Gershwin for the first time he said he had only one
piece of advice for her: "Never take lessons."

I Got the Blood
Music and lyrics by Melvin Van Peebles
Ain't Supposed to Die a Natural Death 1971

I Got the Sun in the Morning
Music and lyrics by Irving Berlin
Annie Get Your Gun 1946

I Gotta Be
Music by George Kleinsinger
Lyrics by Joe Darion
Shinbone Alley 1957

I Gotta Get Back to New York
Music by Richard Rodgers
Lyrics by Lorenz Hart
Hallelujah, I'm a Bum (1933) F

I Gotta Have My Moments
Music and lyrics by Ralph Benatzky
Meet My Sister 1930

I Gotta Have You
Music by Richard Lewine
Lyrics by Arnold B. Horwitt
The Girls Against the Boys 1959

I Gotta Keep Movin'
Music and lyrics by Micki Grant
Don't Bother Me, I Can't Cope (OB) 1972

I Guess I Love You
Music by Robert Russell Bennett
Lyrics by Owen Murphy and Robert A. Simon
Hold Your Horses 1933

I Guess I'll Have to Change My Plan
Music by Arthur Schwartz
Lyrics by Howard Dietz
The Little Show (1st edition) 1929

The song, also known as "The Blue Pajama Song,"
began life as a summer camp song with Arthur
Schwartz's music and lyrics by a fellow camp

counselor Lorenz Hart:
  I love to lie awake in bed
  Right after taps I pull the flaps
  Above my head . . .

I Had a Ball
Music and lyrics by Jack Lawrence
and Stan Freeman
I Had a Ball 1964

I Had a Dog
Music by Leo Edwards
Lyrics by Herbert Reynolds
The Blue Paradise 1915

I Had a Little Teevee
Music by Helen Miller
Lyrics by Eve Merriam
Inner City 1971

I Had Myself a True Love
Music by Harold Arlen
Lyrics by Johnny Mercer
St. Louis Woman 1946

I Had Twins
Music by Richard Rodgers
Lyrics by Lorenz Hart
The Boys From Syracuse 1938

I Had Two Dregs
Music by Mary Rodgers
Lyrics by Martin Charnin
Hot Spot 1963

I Hail From Cairo
Music by Sigmund Romberg
Lyrics by Harold Atteridge
Sinbad (1918)

I Happen to Be in Love
Music and lyrics by Cole Porter
Broadway Melody of 1940 F

Dropped from film

I Happen to Like New York
Music and lyrics by Cole Porter
The New Yorkers 1930

I Hate a Parade
Music and lyrics by Harold Rome
Michael Todd's Peep Show 1950

I Hate Him
Music and lyrics by Harold Rome
Destry Rides Again 1959

I Hate Him
Music and lyrics by Bob Merrill
Carnival 1961

I Hate Men
Music and lyrics by Cole Porter
Kiss Me, Kate 1948

I Hate Myself (for Falling in Love With You)
Music and lyrics by Abner Silver
and Dave Oppenheim
Brown Buddies 1930

I Hate Myself in the Morning
Music by Frank Black
Lyrics by Gladys Shelley
The Duchess Misbehaves 1946

I Hate to Talk About Myself
Music by Harry Archer
Lyrics by Harlan Thompson
Twinkle Twinkle 1926

I Hate to Think That You'll Grow Old, Baby
Music by Ray Henderson
Lyrics by Lew Brown
Strike Me Pink 1933

I Hate You
Music by Maurice Yvain
Lyrics by Max and Nathaniel Lief
Luckee Girl 1928

I Hate You
Music and lyrics by John Dooley
Hobo (OB) 1961

I Hate You, Darling
Music and lyrics by Cole Porter
Let's Face It! 1941

I Have a Date
Music by Rudolf Friml
Lyrics by Bide Dudley and Otto Harbach
The Little Whopper 1919

I Have a Friend at the Chase Manhattan Bank
Music and lyrics by Jack Bussins
and Ellsworth Olin
Be Kind to People Week (OB) 1975

I Have a Love
Music by Leonard Bernstein
Lyrics by Stephen Sondheim
West Side Story 1957

I Have a Noble Cock
Music by Richard Hill and John Hawkins
Lyrics by Nevill Coghill
Canterbury Tales 1969

I Have a Run in My Stocking
Music by Henry Sullivan
Lyrics by Edward Eliscu
A Little Racketeer 1932

I Have Been About a Bit
Music by Jerome Kern
Lyrics by Harry B. Smith
Ninety in the Shade 1915

I Have Confidence in Me
Music and lyrics by Richard Rodgers
The Sound of Music (film version, 1965)

I Have Dreamed
Music by Richard Rodgers
Lyrics by Oscar Hammerstein II
The King and I 1951

I Have Forgotten You Almost
Music by Gitz Rice
Lyrics by Anna Fitziu
Nic-Nax of 1926

I Have Lived
Music and lyrics by Howard Blankman
By Hex (OB) 1956

I Have My Moments
Music and lyrics by Herbert Stothart, Bert Kalmar
and Harry Ruby
Good Boy 1928

I Have My Own Way
Music and lyrics by Johnny Burke
Donnybrook! 1961

I Have Room in My Heart
Music by Frederick Loewe
Lyrics by Earle Crooker
Great Lady 1938

I Have Something Nice for You
Music by Winthrop Cortelyou
Lyrics by Derick Wulff
Kiss Me 1927

I Have the Love
Music by Rudolf Friml
Lyrics by Paul Francis Webster
Rose Marie (film version, 1954)

I Have the Room Above
Music by Jerome Kern
Lyrics by Oscar Hammerstein II
Show Boat (film version, 1936)

I Have to Tell You
Music and lyrics by Harold Rome
Fanny 1954

I Have What You Want!
Music by Murray Rumshinsky
Lyrics by Jacob Jacobs
The President's Daughter 1970

I Haven't Got a Worry in the World
Music by Richard Rodgers
Lyrics by Oscar Hammerstein II
Happy Birthday 1946

I Hear
Music by Cy Coleman
Lyrics by Carolyn Leigh
Wildcat 1960

I Hear a Song
Music and lyrics by Ron Eliran
Don't Step on My Olive Branch (OB) 1976

I Hear America Singing
Music by Stan Harte, Jr.
Leaves of Grass (OB) 1971

I Hear Bells
Music by David Shire
Lyrics by Richard Maltby, Jr.
Starting Here, Starting Now (OB) 1977

I Hear Love Call Me
Music by Karl Hajos (based on Tchaikovsky)
Lyrics by Harry B. Smith
Natja 1925

I Heard My Mother Crying
Music and lyrics by Tom Sankey
The Golden Screw (OB) 1967

I Hold Your Hand in Mine
Music and lyrics by Tom Lehrer
Tomfoolery (OB) 1981

I Hope I Get It
Music by Marvin Hamlisch
Lyrics by Edward Kleban
A Chorus Line 1975

I Hope You're Happy
Music by Norman Martin
Lyrics by Fred Ebb
Put It in Writing (OB) 1963

I Hurry Home to You
Music by Charles Strouse
Lyrics by Lee Adams
A Broadway Musical 1978

I Invented Myself
Music by Mark Sandrich, Jr.
Lyrics by Sidney Michaels
Ben Franklin in Paris 1964

I Jupiter, I Rex
Music and lyrics by Cole Porter
Out of This World 1950

I Just Can't Wait
Music by Jule Styne
Lyrics by Betty Comden and Adolph Green
Subways Are for Sleeping 1961

I Just Couldn't Take It, Baby
Music by Alberta Nichols
Lyrics by Mann Holiner
Blackbirds of 1934

I Just Got in the City
Music and lyrics by Voices, Inc.
The Believers (OB) 1968

I Just Heard
Music by Jerry Bock
Lyrics by Sheldon Harnick
Fiddler on the Roof 1964

I Just Looked At You
Music by George Gershwin
Lyrics by Gus Kahn and Ira Gershwin
Show Girl 1929

Dropped from production. *See* note on
"Blah-Blah-Blah."

I Keep Telling Myself
Music by Arthur Jones
Lyrics by Gen Genovese
Buttrio Square 1952

I Kiss Your Hand, Madame
Music by Ralph Erwin
Lyrics by Samuel Lewis
and Joseph Young
Lady Fingers 1929

I Kissed My Girl Goodbye
Music by Vernon Duke
Lyrics by Howard Dietz
Jackpot 1944

I Knew Him Before He Was Spanish
Music by Dana Suesse
Lyrics by Billy Rose and Ballard MacDonald
Sweet and Low 1930

I Knew I'd Know
Music by Sidney Lippman
Lyrics by Sylvia Dee
Barefoot Boy With Cheek 1947

I Know a Foul Ball
Music by George Gershwin
Lyrics by Ira Gershwin
Let 'Em Eat Cake 1933

I Know a Girl
Music by John Kander
Lyrics by Fred Ebb
Chicago 1975

I Know About Love
Music by Jule Styne
Lyrics by Betty Comden and Adolph Green
Do Re Mi 1960

I Know He Wants Us to Praise His Mornings
Music by Stanley Silverman
Lyrics by Arthur Miller
Up From Paradise (OB) 1983

I Know He'll Understand
Music and lyrics by Johnny Myers
Wet Paint (OB) 1965

I Know How It Is
Music and lyrics by Frank Loesser
The Most Happy Fella 1956

I Know, I Know
Music by Edward Earle
Lyrics by Yvonne Tarr
The Decameron (OB) 1961

I Know I'm Nobody
Music by Sam Stept
Lyrics by Lew Brown and Charles Tobias
Yokel Boy 1939

I Know It Can Happen Again
Music by Richard Rodgers
Lyrics by Oscar Hammerstein II
Allegro 1947

I Know It's Not Meant for Me
Music and lyrics by Cole Porter
Rosalie (1937) F

Dropped from film

I Know My Love
Music and lyrics by Howard Blankman
By Hex (OB) 1956

I Know Now!
Music and lyrics by Gian-Carlo Menotti
The Medium 1947

I Know Now
Music by Larry Grossman
Lyrics by Hal Hackady
Snoopy (OB) 1982

I Know Someone Loves Me
Music by Vivian Ellis
Lyrics by Graham John
By the Way 1925

I Know Something
Music by William B. Kernell
Lyrics by Dorothy Donnelly
Hello, Lola 1926

I Know That I Love You
Music by Harry Ruby
Lyrics by Bert Kalmar
Sweetheart Time 1926

I Know That You Know
Music by Vincent Youmans
Lyrics by Anne Caldwell
Oh, Please! 1926

I Know the Feeling
Music by Lee Pockriss
Lyrics by Anne Croswell
Tovarich 1963

I Know the Man
Music by Don Gohman
Lyrics by Hal Hackady
Ambassador 1972

I Know What I Am
Music and lyrics by David Heneker
Half a Sixpence 1965

I Know Where There's a Cozy Nook
Music by Kurt Weill
Lyrics by Ira Gershwin
The Firebrand of Florence 1945

I Know You by Heart
Music and lyrics by Hugh Martin
and Ralph Blane
Best Foot Forward 1941

I Know You Sell It
Music by Al Carmines
Lyrics by Rosalyn Drexler
Home Movies (OB) 1964

I Know Your Heart
Music and lyrics by Hugh Martin
and Timothy Gray
High Spirits 1964

I Know Your Kind
Music and lyrics by Harold Rome
Destry Rides Again 1959

I Leave the World
Music by Larry Grossman
Lyrics by Hal Hackady
Goodtime Charley 1975

I Left a Dream Somewhere
Music by Don McAfee
Lyrics by Nancy Leeds
Great Scot! (OB) 1965

I Left My Hat in Haiti
Music by Burton Lane
Lyrics by Alan Jay Lerner
Royal Wedding (1951) F

I Left My Heart at the Stage Door Canteen
Music and lyrics by Irving Berlin
This Is the Army 1942

I Like
Music by Ray Haney
Lyrics by Alfred Aiken
We're Civilized? (OB) 1962

I Like
Music by William Dyer
Lyrics by Don Parks and William Dyer
Jo (OB) 1964

I Like a Big Town
Music by Harry Ruby
Lyrics by Bert Kalmar
Helen of Troy, New York 1923

I Like Everybody
Music and lyrics by Frank Loesser
The Most Happy Fella 1956

I Like Her
Music by Robert Kole
Lyrics by Sandi Merle
I Take These Women (OB) 1982

I Like Him
Music by Milton Schafer
Lyrics by Ira Levin
Drat! The Cat! 1965

I Like It
Music by Ivan Caryll
Lyrics by C.M.S. McLellan
The Pink Lady 1911

I Like It
Music and lyrics by Edward Pola and Eddie Brandt
Woof, Woof 1929

I Like It
Music by Albert Hague
Lyrics by Allen Sherman
The Fig Leaves Are Falling 1969

I Like It
Music by Gary William Friedman
Lyrics by Will Holt
Taking My Turn (OB) 1983

I Like It Here
Music by Morton Gould
Lyrics by Dorothy Fields
Arms and the Girl 1950

I Like It With Music
Music by Ray Henderson
Lyrics by Jack Yellen
George White's Scandals (1936)

I Like London
Music by Howard Talbot
Lyrics by Arthur Wimperis
The Arcadians 1910

I Like the Boys
Music by Emmerich Kálmán
Lyrics by Harry B. Smith
The Circus Princess 1927

I Like the Company of Men
Music by Cyril Ornadel
Lyrics by Leslie Bricusse
Pickwick 1965

I Like the Girls
Music by A. Baldwin Sloane
Lyrics by Harry Cort and George E. Stoddard
China Rose 1925

I Like the Likes of You
Music by Vernon Duke
Lyrics by E.Y. Harburg
Ziegfeld Follies (1934)

I Like the Look
Music and lyrics by Robert Dennis, Peter Schickele
and Stanley Walden
Oh! Calcutta! 1969

I Like the Military Man
Music by H. Maurice Jacquet
Lyrics by William Brady
The Silver Swan 1929

I Like the Nose on Your Face
Music by Richard Lewine
Lyrics by Ted Fetter
The Fireman's Flame (OB) 1937

I Like to Be Liked
Music by Harry Ruby
Lyrics by Bert Kalmar
Top Speed 1929

I Like to Look My Best
Music and lyrics by Oscar Brand and Paul Nassau
A Joyful Noise 1966

I Like to Make It Cozy
Music by Albert Von Tilzer
Lyrics by Neville Fleeson
Bye Bye, Bonnie 1927

I Like to Recognize the Tune
Music by Richard Rodgers
Lyrics by Lorenz Hart
Too Many Girls 1939

I Like to Win
Music by Bert Keyes and Bob Larimer
Lyrics by Bob Larimer
But Never Jam Today 1979

I Like What I Do
Music by Charles Strouse
Lyrics by Lee Adams
Bring Back Birdie 1981

I Like What You Like
Music by Vincent Youmans
Lyrics by Billy Rose and Edward Eliscu
Great Day! 1929

I Like You
Music and lyrics by Ralph Benatzky
Meet My Sister 1930

I Like You
Music and lyrics by Harold Rome
Fanny 1954

I Like You
Music and lyrics by Billy Barnes
The Billy Barnes People 1961

I Like You as You Are
Music by Vincent Youmans
Lyrics by Oscar Hammerstein II
Rainbow 1928

I Like Your Style
Music by Cy Coleman
Lyrics by Michael Stewart
Barnum 1980

I Live a Little
Music and lyrics by Al Carmines
Joan (OB) 1972

I Live Alone
Music by Mel Marvin
Lyrics by Robert Montgomery
Green Pond (OB) 1977

I Live Alone
Music and lyrics by Barbara Schottenfeld
I Can't Keep Running in Place (OB) 1981

I Live by My Wits
Music by Stanley Silverman
Lyrics by Tom Hendry
Doctor Selavy's Magic Theatre (OB) 1972

I Live, I Die for You
Music by Sigmund Romberg
Lyrics by Harry B. Smith
The Love Call 1927

I Live to Love
Music and lyrics by Deed Meyer
She Shall Have Music (OB) 1959

I Look for Love
Music by Vincent Youmans
Lyrics by Oscar Hammerstein II
Rainbow 1928

Dropped from production

I Lost It
Music by Mitch Leigh
Lyrics by William Alfred and Phyllis Robinson
Cry for Us All 1970

I Lost the Rhythm
Music and lyrics by Charles Strouse
The Littlest Revue (OB) 1956

I Love a Cop
Music by Jerry Bock
Lyrics by Sheldon Harnick
Fiorello! 1959

I Love a Film Cliché
Music by Trevor Lyttleton
Lyrics by Dick Vosburgh
A Day in Hollywood, a Night in the Ukraine 1979

I Love a Fool
Music by Jacques Urbont
Lyrics by Bruce Geller
All in Love (OB) 1961

I Love a Man in Uniform
Music by Jimmy Monaco
Lyrics by Billy Rose and Ballard MacDonald
Harry Delmar's Revels 1927

I Love a Piano
Music and lyrics by Irving Berlin
Stop! Look! Listen! 1915

I Love a Polka So
Music by Berenice Kazounoff
Lyrics by Carl Randall
The Illustrators' Show 1936

I Love and the World Is Mine
Music by Oscar Straus
Lyrics by Joseph W. Herbert
A Waltz Dream 1908

I Love Everything That's Old
Music by Robert Kessler
Lyrics by Lola Pergament
O Marry Me! (OB) 1961

I Love Him
Music and lyrics by Frank Loesser
The Most Happy Fella 1956

I Love Him
Music by Sammy Fain
Lyrics by Paul Francis Webster
Christine 1960

I Love Him, the Rat
Music by Richard A. Whiting
Lyrics by Oscar Hammerstein II
Free for All 1931

I Love His Face
Music by Harvey Schmidt
Lyrics by Tom Jones
Philemon (OB) 1975

I Love It
Music and lyrics by Buster Davis
Doctor Jazz 1975

I Love Louisa
Music by Arthur Schwartz
Lyrics by Howard Dietz
The Band Wagon 1931

I Love Love
Music by Karl Hajos (based on Chopin)
Lyrics by Harry B. Smith
White Lilacs 1928

I Love Love
Music by Robert Emmett Dolan
Lyrics by Walter O'Keefe
Princess Charming 1930

I Love Love in New York
Music by Gordon Jenkins
Lyrics by Tom Adair
Along Fifth Avenue 1949

I Love My Boo Boo
Music by Galt MacDermot
Lyrics by Gerome Ragni
Dude 1972

I Love My Father
Music by Galt MacDermot
Lyrics by John Guare
Two Gentlemen of Verona 1971

I Love My Wife
Music by Harvey Schmidt
Lyrics by Tom Jones
I Do! I Do! 1966

I Love My Wife
Music by Leonard Bernstein
Lyrics by Alan Jay Lerner
1600 Pennsylvania Avenue 1976

I Love My Wife
Music by Cy Coleman
Lyrics by Michael Stewart
I Love My Wife 1977

I Love Nashville
Music and lyrics by Oscar Brand and Paul Nassau
A Joyful Noise 1966

I Love Order
Music by Harvey Schmidt
Lyrics by Tom Jones
Philemon (OB) 1975

I Love Paris
Music and lyrics by Cole Porter
Can-Can 1953

I Love Petite Belle
Music by Coleridge-Taylor Perkinson
Lyrics by Errol Hill
Man Better Man (OB) 1969

I Love That Boy
Music by Jacques Belasco
Lyrics by Kay Twomey
The Girl From Nantucket 1945

I Love the Ladies
Music by Mark Sandrich, Jr.
Lyrics by Sidney Michaels
Ben Franklin in Paris 1964

I Love the Lassies
Music by Jerome Kern
Lyrics by Anne Caldwell
The Night Boat 1920

I Love the Way We Fell in Love
Music by Sammy Fain
Lyrics by Irving Kahal
Right This Way 1938

I Love the Woods
Music by Richard Rodgers
Lyrics by Lorenz Hart
Simple Simon 1930

I Love Them All
Music by Sigmund Romberg
Lyrics by Harry B. Smith
Princess Flavia 1925

I Love This Land
Music by Leonard Bernstein
Lyrics by Alan Jay Lerner
1600 Pennsylvania Avenue 1976

I Love to Cry at Weddings
Music by Cy Coleman
Lyrics by Dorothy Fields
Sweet Charity 1966

I Love to Dance
Music and lyrics by Irving Berlin
Stop! Look! Listen! 1915

I Love to Dance
Music by Con Conrad
Lyrics by Gus Kahn
Kitty's Kisses 1926

I Love to Dance
Music by Billy Goldenberg
Lyrics by Alan and Marilyn Bergman
Ballroom 1978

Written for the television production *Queen of the Stardust Ballroom* (CBS, 1975), the song was then called "I Love to Dance Like They Used to Dance". The stage show *Ballroom* was based on the television show.

I Love to Flutter
Music by Gerald Dolin
Lyrics by Edward J. Lambert
Smile at Me 1935

I Love to Have the Boys Around Me
Music and lyrics by Irving Berlin
Watch Your Step 1914

I Love to Rhyme
Music by George Gershwin
Lyrics by Ira Gershwin
Goldwyn Follies (1938) F

I Love to Say Hello to the Girls
Music by Sigmund Romberg
Lyrics by Alex Gerber
Poor Little Ritz Girl 1920

I Love to Sing the Words
Music by Irving Caesar
Lyrics by Gerald Marks and Sam Lerner
My Dear Public 1943

I Love What I'm Doing
Music by Jule Styne
Lyrics by Leo Robin
Gentlemen Prefer Blondes 1949

I Love What the Girls Have
Music by Gary William Friedman
Lyrics by Will Holt
The Me Nobody Knows (OB) 1970

I Love You
Music by George Gershwin
Lyrics by Arthur Jackson
George White's Scandals (1921)

I Love You
Music by Harry Archer
Lyrics by Harlan Thompson
Little Jessie James 1923

I Love You
Music and lyrics by Cole Porter
Mexican Hayride 1944

I Love You
Music by Edvard Grieg
Lyrics by Robert Wright and George Forrest
Song of Norway 1944

I Love You
Music by Cy Coleman
Lyrics by Carolyn Leigh
Little Me 1962

I Love You
Music and lyrics by Al Carmines
The Evangelist (OB) 1982

I Love You
Music by Howard Marren
Lyrics by Enid Futterman
Portrait of Jennie (OB) 1982

I Love You All the Time
Music by Lawrence Hurwit
Lyrics by Lee Goldsmith
Sextet 1974

I Love You and I Adore You
Music by Karl Hajos (based on Chopin)
Lyrics by Harry B. Smith
White Lilacs 1928

I Love You and I Like You
Music by Arthur Schwartz
Lyrics by Max and Nathaniel Lief
The Grand Street Follies (1929)

I Love You for That
Music by Sol Berkowitz
Lyrics by James Lipton
Nowhere to Go But Up 1962

I Love You, Honey
Music by James P. Johnson
Lyrics by Flournoy Miller
Sugar Hill 1931

I Love You, I Adore You
Music by H. Maurice Jacquet
Lyrics by William Brady
The Silver Swan 1929

I Love You! I Love You! I Love You!
Music by Vincent Youmans
Lyrics by Otto Harbach and Oscar Hammerstein II
Wildflower 1923

I Love You More than Yesterday
Music by Richard Rodgers
Lyrics by Lorenz Hart
Lady Fingers 1929

I Love You, My Darling
Music by George Gershwin
Lyrics by B.G. DeSylva
George White's Scandals (1924)

I Love You, My Darling
Music by Jean Gilbert
Lyrics by George Hirst and Edward Eliscu
Marching By 1932

I Love You, Samantha
Music and lyrics by Cole Porter
High Society (1956) F

Porter recalled that before writing this he asked the film's producer, Sol Siegel, whether the heroine's name "Samantha" would actually be used in the film; otherwise, Porter felt, the song would make no sense. Siegel assured him that it would be, and often, and Porter wrote the song. In the final edited version of the film the name isn't mentioned once.

I Love You So
Music by Franz Lehár
Lyrics by Adrian Ross
The Merry Widow 1907

This is the familiar melody often referred to as "The Merry Widow Waltz".

I Love You So
Music by Maurice Yvain
Lyrics by Max and Nathaniel Lief
Luckee Girl 1928

I Love You So Much
Music by Harry Ruby
Lyrics by Bert Kalmar
The Cuckoos (1930) F

I Love You This Morning
Music by Frederick Loewe
Lyrics by Alan Jay Lerner
The Day Before Spring 1945

I Love You Today
Music and lyrics by Steve Allen
Sophie 1963

I Love Your Brains
Music and lyrics by Alan Menken
Real Life Funnies (OB) 1981

I Love ze Parisienne
Music by Victor Herbert
Lyrics by George V. Hobart
Old Dutch 1909

I Loved
Music by Jacques Brel
English lyrics by Eric Blau and Mort Shuman
*Jacques Brel Is Alive and Well
and Living in Paris* (OB) 1968

I Loved a Man
Music and lyrics by Sandy Wilson
Valmouth (OB) 1960

I Loved Her, Too
Music by Kurt Weill
Lyrics by Langston Hughes
Street Scene 1947

I Loved Him But He Didn't Love Me
Music and lyrics by Cole Porter
Wake Up and Dream 1929

I Loved You Once in Silence
Music by Frederick Loewe
Lyrics by Alan Jay Lerner
Camelot 1960

I Loves You, Porgy
Music by George Gershwin
Lyrics by DuBose Heyward and Ira Gershwin
Porgy and Bess 1935

I Made a Fist
Music and lyrics by Frank Loesser
The Most Happy Fella 1956

I Make Up for That in Other Ways
Music by Ray Henderson
Lyrics by Lew Brown
Hot-Cha! 1932

I Married an Angel
Music by Richard Rodgers
Lyrics by Lorenz Hart
I Married an Angel 1938

I May
Music by Maury Rubens and Kendall Burgess
Lyrics by Harry B. Smith
Naughty Riquette 1926

I May Be Wrong (But I Think You're Wonderful)
Music by Henry Sullivan
Lyrics by Harry Ruskin
John Murray Anderson's Almanac (1929)

I Mean to Say
Music by George Gershwin
Lyrics by Ira Gershwin
Strike Up the Band 1930

I Mean to Say I Love You
Music by Erich Wolfgang Korngold
Lyrics by Oscar Hammerstein II
Give Us This Night (1936) F

I Mean What I Say
Music and lyrics by Edward Pola
and Eddie Brandt
Woof, Woof 1929

I Meant You No Harm
Music by Henry Krieger
Lyrics by Tom Eyen
Dreamgirls 1981

I Met a Girl
Music by Jule Styne
Lyrics by Betty Comden and Adolph Green
Bells Are Ringing 1956

I Met My Love
Music and lyrics by Frederick Silver
Gay Company (OB) 1974

I Might
Music by Philip Braham
Lyrics by Ronald Jeans
Charlot's Revue 1924

I Might Be Your Once-in-a-While
Music by Victor Herbert
Lyrics by Robert B. Smith
Angel Face 1919

I Might Fall Back on You
Music by Jerome Kern
Lyrics by Oscar Hammerstein II
Show Boat 1927

First written as "Cheer Up"

I Miss Him
Music and lyrics by Michael Brown
Different Times 1972

I Miss My Man
Music by Peter Link
Lyrics by Michael Cacoyannis
Lysistrata 1972

I Miss You Old Friend
Music by Henry Krieger
Lyrics by Tom Eyen
Dreamgirls 1981

I Missed You
Music by Victor Herbert
Lyrics by B.G. DeSylva
Orange Blossoms 1922

I Must Be Home by Twelve o'Clock
Music by George Gershwin
Lyrics by Gus Kahn and Ira Gershwin
Show Girl 1929

I Must Be in Love
Music and lyrics by James Quinn and Alaric Jans
Do Patent Leather Shoes Really Reflect Up? 1982

I Must Devise a Plan
Music by Don Pippin
Lyrics by Steve Brown
Fashion (OB) 1974

I Must Have a Dinner Coat
Music and lyrics by James Shelton
Who's Who 1938

I Must Have Her
Music by Burton Lane
Lyrics by Alan Jay Lerner
Carmelina 1979

I Must Love You
Music by Richard Rodgers
Lyrics by Lorenz Hart
Chee-Chee 1928

Rewritten as "Send for Me" in *Simple Simon* (1930)

I Must Marry a Handsome Man
Music by Victor Herbert
Lyrics by Harry B. Smith
Cyrano de Bergerac 1899

I Must Paint
Music by Baldwin Bergersen
Lyrics by William Archibald
The Crystal Heart (OB) 1960

I Must Smile
Music by James Bredt
Lyrics by Edward Eager
The Happy Hypocrite (OB) 1968

I Must Waltz
Music by Baldwin Bergersen
Lyrics by Irvin Graham
Who's Who 1938

I Need a Garden
Music by George Gershwin
Lyrics by B.G. DeSylva
George White's Scandals (1924)

I Need a Little Bit, You Need a Little Bit
Music by Cliff Friend
Lyrics by Lew Brown
Piggy 1927

I Need Air
Music by Frederick Loewe
Lyrics by Alan Jay Lerner
The Little Prince (1975) F

I Need All the Help I Can Get
Music by David Baker
Lyrics by David Craig
Copper and Brass 1957

I Need Some Cooling Off
Music by Richard Rodgers
Lyrics by Lorenz Hart
She's My Baby 1928

I Need You
Music by Jimmy Johnson
Lyrics by Perry Bradford
Messin' Around 1929

I Need You
Music and lyrics by Jack Bussins
and Ellsworth Olin
Be Kind to People Week (OB) 1975

I Need You So
Music by Arthur Schwartz
Lyrics by Agnes Morgan
The Grand Street Follies (1929)

I Never Felt Better in My Life
Music and lyrics by Paul Nassau and Oscar Brand
*The Education of H*y*m*a*n K*a*p*l*a*n* 1968

I Never Had a Chance
Music by Arthur Schwartz
Lyrics by Howard Dietz
The Gay Life 1961

I Never Has Seen Snow
Music by Harold Arlen
Lyrics by Harold Arlen and Truman Capote
House of Flowers 1954

I Never Imagined Goodbye
Music by Mitch Leigh
Lyrics by Charles Burr and Forman Brown
Home Sweet Homer 1976

I Never Knew
Music by Galt MacDermot
Lyrics by Gerome Ragni
Dude 1972

I Never Know When
Music by Leroy Anderson
Lyrics by Joan Ford and Walter and Jean Kerr
Goldilocks 1958

I Never Laughed in My Life
Music and lyrics by William Roy
Maggie 1953

I Never Loved You
Music by Michael J. Lewis
Lyrics by Anthony Burgess
Cyrano 1973

I Never Made Money From Music
Music by Gary William Friedman
Lyrics by Will Holt
Taking My Turn (OB) 1983

I Never Meant to Fall in Love
Music by Sammy Fain
Lyrics by Paul Francis Webster
Christine 1960

I Never Met a Rose
Music by Frederick Loewe
Lyrics by Alan Jay Lerner
The Little Prince (1975) F

I Never Realized
Music and lyrics by Cole Porter
Buddies 1919

I Never Saw a King Before
Music by Frederick Loewe
Lyrics by Earle Crooker
Great Lady 1938

I Never Thought
Music by Jerome Kern
Lyrics by Herbert Reynolds
Rock-a-Bye Baby 1918

I Never Want to Go Home Again
Music by Frederick Loewe
Lyrics by Alan Jay Lerner
Gigi (stage version, 1973)

I Never Want to See You Again
Music by Charles Strouse
Lyrics by Alan Jay Lerner
Dance a Little Closer 1983

I Never Wanted to Love You
Music and lyrics by William Finn
March of the Falsettos (OB) 1981

I Never Was Born
Music by Harold Arlen
Lyrics by E.Y. Harburg
Bloomer Girl 1944

I Only Know
Music by Morgan Lewis
Lyrics by Nancy Hamilton
One for the Money 1939

I Only Wanna Laugh
Music and lyrics by Bill and Patti Jacob
Jimmy 1969

I Ought to Know More About You
Music by Victor Young
Lyrics by Edward Heyman
Pardon Our French 1950

I Owe It All
Music and lyrics by James MacDonald, David Vos
and Robert Gerlach
Something's Afoot 1976

I Owe Ohio
Music by Don Elliott
Lyrics by James Costigan
The Beast in Me 1963

I Plead, Dear Heart
Music by Jean Gilbert
Lyrics by Harry B. Smith
The Red Robe 1928

I Poured My Heart into a Song
Music and lyrics by Irving Berlin
Second Fiddle (1939) F

I Promise I'll Be Practically True to You
Music by Melville Gideon
Lyrics by Clifford Grey
The Optimists 1928

I Promise You
Music by Harold Arlen
Lyrics by Johnny Mercer
Here Come the Waves (1944) F

I Promise You a Happy Ending
Music and lyrics by Jerry Herman
Mack and Mabel 1974

I Promised Their Mothers
Music by Sigmund Romberg (developed by
Don Walker)
Lyrics by Leo Robin
The Girl in Pink Tights 1954

I Put My Hand In
Music and lyrics by Jerry Herman
Hello, Dolly 1964

I Quite Forgot Arcadia
Music by Lionel Monckton
Lyrics by Arthur Wimperis
The Arcadians 1910

I Really Like Him
Music by Mitch Leigh
Lyrics by Joe Darion
Man of La Mancha 1965

I Remember
Music and lyrics by Stephen Sondheim
Evening Primrose (1966) TV

I Remember Her
Music by Mischa and Wesley Portnoff
Lyrics by Donagh MacDonagh
Happy as Larry 1950

I Remember How It Was
Music by Henry Krieger
Lyrics by Robert Lorick
The Tap Dance Kid 1983

I Remember It Well
Music by Kurt Weill
Lyrics by Alan Jay Lerner
Love Life 1948

I Remember It Well
Music by Frederick Loewe
Lyrics by Alan Jay Lerner
Gigi (1958) F

Also in stage version (1973)

I Remember Mama
Music by Richard Rodgers
Lyrics by Martin Charnin
I Remember Mama 1979

I Resolve
Music by Jerry Bock
Lyrics by Sheldon Harnick
She Loves Me 1963

I Rise Again
Music by Cy Coleman
Lyrics by Betty Comden and Adolph Green
On the Twentieth Century 1978

I Said It and I'm Glad
Music by Jule Styne
Lyrics by Betty Comden and Adolph Green
Subways Are for Sleeping 1961

I Said, Oh No
Music by Galt MacDermot
Lyrics by William Dumaresq
The Human Comedy (OB) 1983

I Said to Love
Music by Paul Klein
Lyrics by Fred Ebb
From A to Z 1960

I Saw a Man
Music by Al Carmines
Lyrics by Maria Irene Fornes
Promenade (OB) 1969

I Saw Your Eyes
Music by Sigmund Romberg
Lyrics by Oscar Hammerstein II
East Wind 1931

I Say Hello
Music and lyrics by Harold Rome
Destry Rides Again 1959

I Say It's Spinach
Music and lyrics by Irving Berlin
Face the Music 1932

I Say Yes
Music and lyrics by Oscar Brand and Paul Nassau
A Joyful Noise 1966

I See a Man
Music by Jerry Livingston
Lyrics by Leonard Adelson
Molly 1973

I See a Road
Music and lyrics by Elizabeth Swados
Dispatches (OB) 1979

I See Something
Music and lyrics by Ervin Drake
What Makes Sammy Run? 1964

I See What I Choose to See
Music by Walt Smith
Lyrics by Leon Uris
Ari 1971

I See You But What Do You See in Me?
Music and lyrics by Lester Lee
Keep It Clean 1929

I See Your Face Before Me
Music by Arthur Schwartz
Lyrics by Howard Dietz
Between the Devil 1937

I Seen It With My Very Own Eyes
Music by Paul Klein
Lyrics by Fred Ebb
Morning Sun (OB) 1963

I Shall Be All Right Now
Music by Louis A. Hirsch
Lyrics by P.G. Wodehouse
Oh, My Dear! 1918

I Shall Love You
Music by Joe Jordan
Lyrics by Homer Tutt and Henry Creamer
Deep Harlem 1929

I Shall Miss You
Music and lyrics by Marian Grudeff
and Raymond Jessel
Baker Street 1965

I Shall Scream
Music and lyrics by Lionel Bart
Oliver! 1963

I Shiver and Shake With Fear
Music by Frederic Norton
Lyrics by Oscar Asche
Chu Chin Chow 1917

I Shot the Works
Music by Manning Sherwin
Lyrics by Arthur Lippmann and Milton Pascal
Everybody's Welcome 1931

I Sing of Love
Music and lyrics by Cole Porter
Kiss Me, Kate 1948

I Sing the Rainbow
Music and lyrics by Glory Van Scott
Miss Truth (OB) 1979

I Sit in the Sun
Music by Julian Slade
Lyrics by Dorothy Reynolds and Julian Slade
Salad Days (OB) 1958

I Sleep Easier Now
Music and lyrics by Cole Porter
Out of This World 1950

I Sometimes Wonder
Music by Oscar Straus
Lyrics by Clare Kummer
Three Waltzes 1937

I Spy
Music and lyrics by Bob Goodman
Wild and Wonderful 1971

I Started on a Shoestring
Music by Arthur Schwartz
Lyrics by Howard Dietz
The Second Little Show 1930

I Still Believe in Love
Music by Marvin Hamlisch
Lyrics by Carole Bayer Sager
They're Playing Our Song 1979

I Still Believe in You
Music by Richard Rodgers
Lyrics by Lorenz Hart
Simple Simon 1930

Written originally as "Singing a Love Song" in
Chee-Chee (1928)

I Still Can Dream
Music by Emmerich Kálmán
Lyrics by B.G. DeSylva
The Yankee Princess 1922

I Still Get Jealous
Music by Jule Styne
Lyrics by Sammy Cahn
High Button Shoes 1947

I Still Have to Learn
Music by George Lessner
Lyrics by Miriam Battista and Russell Maloney
Sleepy Hollow 1948

I Still Look at You That Way
Music by Arthur Schwartz
Lyrics by Howard Dietz
Jennie 1963

I Still Love the Red, White and Blue
Music and lyrics by Cole Porter
Gay Divorce 1932

I Still See Elisa
Music by Frederick Loewe
Lyrics by Alan Jay Lerner
Paint Your Wagon 1951

I Stumbled Over You
Music by Maury Rubens
Lyrics by Henry Dagand
Hello, Paris 1930

I Stumbled Over You and Fell in Love
Music by Harry Revel
Lyrics by Mack Gordon
Smiling Faces 1932

I Suddenly Find It Agreeable
Music by Glenn Paxton
Lyrics by Robert Goldman and George Weiss
First Impressions 1959

I Surrender
Music by Richard Rodgers
Lyrics by Lorenz Hart
Poor Little Ritz Girl 1920

Included in Boston production but dropped before
Broadway opening.

I Swear I Won't Ever Again
Music and lyrics by William Finn
In Trousers (OB) 1981

I Take After Rip
Music by Oscar Levant
Lyrics by Irving Caesar and Graham John
Ripples 1930

I Talk to the Trees
Music by Frederick Loewe
Lyrics by Alan Jay Lerner
Paint Your Wagon 1951

I Thank You
Music and lyrics by Clarence Gaskill
Earl Carroll's Vanities (1925)

I Think I May Want to Remember Today
Music by David Shire
Lyrics by Richard Maltby, Jr.
Starting Here, Starting Now (OB) 1977

I Think I Oughtn't Auto Any More
Music by E. Ray Goetz
Lyrics by Vincent Bryan
Follies of 1907

I Think, I Think
Music and lyrics by Jerry Herman
The Grand Tour 1979

I Think I'd Like to Fall in Love
Music and lyrics by Martin Charnin
Fallout (OB) 1959

I Think I'm Gonna Like It Here
Music by Charles Strouse
Lyrics by Martin Charnin
Annie 1977

I Think It's Going to Rain Today
Music and lyrics by Randy Newman
Maybe I'm Doing It Wrong (2nd edition)
(OB) 1982

I Think She Needs Me
Music by Manos Hadjidakis
Lyrics by Joe Darion
Illya Darling 1967

I Think the Kid Will Do
Music by Galt MacDermot
Lyrics by William Dumaresq
The Human Comedy (OB) 1983

I Think the World of You
Music by Mary Rodgers
Lyrics by Martin Charnin
Hot Spot 1963

I to the World
Music by Michael Valenti
Lyrics by Donald Driver
Oh, Brother 1981

I Told You So
Music by John Kander
Lyrics by Fred Ebb
Woman of the Year 1981

I Took Another Look
Music by David Raksin
Lyrics by June Carroll
If the Shoe Fits 1946

I Took These Women
Music by Robert Kole
Lyrics by Sandi Merle
I Take These Women (OB) 1982

I Try
Music and lyrics by Robert Dahdah
Curley McDimple (OB) 1967

I Used to Be Color Blind
Music and lyrics by Irving Berlin
Carefree (1938) F

I Walk With Music
Music by Hoagy Carmichael
Lyrics by Johnny Mercer
Walk With Music 1940

I Wanna Be Bad
Music by Duke Ellington
Lyrics by John Latouche
Beggar's Holiday 1946

I Wanna Be Good'n Bad
Music and lyrics by Hugh Martin
Make a Wish 1951

I Wanna Be Loved by You
Music and lyrics by Herbert Stothart, Bert Kalmar
and Harry Ruby
Good Boy 1928

I Wanna Get Married
Music by Philip Charig
Lyrics by Dan Shapiro and Milton Pascal
Follow the Girls 1944

I Wanna Go Back to Dixie
Music and lyrics by Tom Lehrer
Tomfoolery (OB) 1981

I Wanna Go to City College
Music by Sammy Fain
Lyrics by George Marion, Jr.
Toplitzky of Notre Dame 1946

I Wanna Go Voom Voom
Music by Cliff Friend
Lyrics by Lew Brown
Piggy 1927

I Wanna Make the World Laugh
Music and lyrics by Jerry Herman
Mack and Mabel 1974

I Want a Boy
Music by Louis A. Hirsch
Lyrics by Otto Harbach
Going Up 1917

I Want a Kiss
Music by Sigmund Romberg
Lyrics by Otto Harbach and Oscar Hammerstein II
The Desert Song 1926

I Want a Lovable Baby
Music by Ray Henderson
Lyrics by B.G. DeSylva and Lew Brown
George White's Scandals (1925)

I Want a Man
Music by Vincent Youmans
Lyrics by Oscar Hammerstein II
Rainbow 1928

I Want a Man
Music by Richard Rodgers
Lyrics by Lorenz Hart
America's Sweetheart 1931

I Want a Man to Love Me
Music by Victor Herbert
Lyrics by George V. Hobart
Old Dutch 1909

I Want a Pal
Music by Raymond Hubbell
Lyrics by Anne Caldwell
Yours Truly 1927

I Want a Surprise
Music and lyrics by John Jennings
Riverwind (OB) 1962

I Want a Toy Soldier Man
Music by Jean Schwartz
Lyrics by Joseph W. Herbert and Harold Atteridge
The Honeymoon Express 1913

I Want All the World to Know
Music by Rudolf Friml
Lyrics by Otto Harbach
Katinka 1915

I Want Another Portion of That
Music by Ray Henderson
Lyrics by Lew Brown
Hot-Cha! 1932

I Want It
Music and lyrics by Robert Dennis, Peter Schickele
and Stanley Walden
Oh! Calcutta! 1969

I Want It All
Music by David Shire
Lyrics by Richard Maltby, Jr.
Baby 1983

I Want It Just to Happen
Music by Lance Mulcahy
Lyrics by Paul Cherry
Park 1970

I Want More Out of Life Than This
Music by Jacques Urbont
Lyrics by David Newburger
Stag Movie (OB) 1971

I Want My Little Gob
Music by Jerome Kern
Lyrics by Anne Caldwell
She's a Good Fellow 1919

I Want My Mama
Music by Jararaca and Vincent Paiva
Lyrics by Al Stillman
Earl Carroll's Vanities (1940)

I Want Plenty of You
Music by Jimmy McHugh
Lyrics by Dorothy Fields
Hello Daddy 1928

I Want Someone
Music and lyrics by William B. Friedlander
Jonica 1930

I Want Something New to Play With
Music by Louis A. Hirsch
Lyrics by Harold Atteridge
The Whirl of Society 1912

I Want the Kind of a Fella
Music and lyrics by Steve Allen
Sophie 1963

I Want the Strolling Good
Music by Jean Schwartz
Lyrics by Joseph W. Herbert and Harold Atteridge
The Honeymoon Express 1913

I Want the World to Know
Music by Richard Myers
Lyrics by Leo Robin
Hello, Yourself! 1928

I Want to Be a Ballet Dancer
Music and lyrics by Irving Berlin
Music Box Revue (4th edition) 1924

I Want to Be a Little Frog in a Little Pond
Music by Victor Ziskin
Lyrics by Joan Javits
Young Abe Lincoln 1961

I Want to Be a Military Man
Music by Leslie Stuart
Lyrics by Frank A. Clement
Florodora 1900

I Want to Be a Popular Millionaire
Music and lyrics by George M. Cohan
Forty-Five Minutes From Broadway 1906

I Want to Be a War Bride
Music by George Gershwin
Lyrics by Ira Gershwin
Strike Up the Band 1930

Dropped during New York run

I Want to Be Bad
Music by Ray Henderson
Lyrics by B.G. DeSylva and Lew Brown
Follow Thru 1929

I Want to Be Happy
Music by Vincent Youmans
Lyrics by Irving Caesar
No, No, Nanette 1925

I Want to Be Raided by You
Music and lyrics by Cole Porter
Wake Up and Dream 1929

I Want to Be Rich
Music and lyrics by Leslie Bricusse
and Anthony Newley
Stop the World—I Want to Get Off 1962

I Want to Be Seen With You Tonight
Music by Jule Styne
Lyrics by Bob Merrill
Funny Girl 1964

I Want to Be There
Music by Jerome Kern
Lyrics by Howard Dietz
Dear Sir 1924

I Want to Be There
Music by Sigmund Romberg
Lyrics by Harry B. Smith
Cherry Blossoms 1927

I Want to Be With You
Music by Vincent Youmans
Lyrics by B.G. DeSylva
Take a Chance 1932

Dropped from production

I Want to Be With You
Music by Charles Strouse
Lyrics by Lee Adams
Golden Boy 1964

I Want to Blow Up the World
Music and lyrics by Al Carmines
Wanted (OB) 1972

I Want to Chisel In on Your Heart
Music by Michael H. Cleary
Lyrics by Max and Nathaniel Lief
Shoot the Works 1931

I Want to Dance
Music by Will Irwin
Lyrics by Norman Zeno
Fools Rush In 1934

I Want to Dance With You
Music and lyrics by Leon DeCosta
Kosher Kitty Kelly 1925

I Want to Do a Number With the Boys
Music by Roland Wilson
Lyrics by Ned Wever
Crazy Quilt 1931

I Want to Go Back to the Bottom of the Garden
Music by David Raksin
Lyrics by June Carroll
If the Shoe Fits 1946

I Want to Go Home
Music by Victor Herbert
Lyrics by Rida Johnson Young
The Dream Girl 1924

I Want to Go Home
Music and lyrics by Cole Porter
Leave It to Me 1938

I Want to Jazz Dance
Music by Dave Stamper
Lyrics by Gene Buck
Ziegfeld Follies of 1918

I Want to Live
Music by Sammy Fain
Lyrics by Jack Yellen
Boys and Girls Together 1940

I Want to Live
Music and lyrics by Johnny Brandon
Billy Noname (OB) 1970

I Want to Live—I Want to Love
Music by Alma Sanders
Lyrics by Monte Carlo
Louisiana Lady 1947

I Want to Make You Cry
Music and lyrics by James Rado
Rainbow (OB) 1972

I Want to Marry
Music by Jerome Kern
Lyrics by Anne Caldwell
Hitchy-Koo 1920

I Want to Marry a Male Quartet
Music by Rudolf Friml
Lyrics by Otto Harbach
Katinka 1915

I Want to Marry a Man, I Do
Music by Leslie Stuart
Lyrics by Paul Rubens
Florodora 1900

I Want to Marry a Marionette
Music by George Gershwin
Lyrics by Ira Gershwin
Treasure Girl 1928

Dropped from production

I Want to Play With the Girls
Music by Edgar Fairchild
Lyrics by Milton Pascal
The Illustrators' Show 1936

I Want to Pray
Music by Giuseppe Verdi (adapted by Hans Spialek)
Lyrics by Charles Friedman
My Darlin' Aïda 1952

I Want to Ride With You
Music Al Carmines
Lyrics by Al Carmines and David Epstein
Wanted (OB) 1972

I Want to See More of You
Music by Jacques Belasco
Lyrics by Kay Twomey
The Girl From Nantucket 1945

I Want to See My Child
Music and lyrics by Scott Joplin
Treemonisha 1975

Written in 1909

I Want to Share It With You
Music by Jerry Livingston
Lyrics by Leonard Adelson
Molly 1973

I Want to Take 'Em Off for Norman Rockwell
Music by Ruth Cleary Patterson
Lyrics by Les Kramer
Russell Patterson's Sketch Book (OB) 1960

I Want to Walk to San Francisco
Music by Nancy Ford
Lyrics by Gretchen Cryer
The Last Sweet Days of Isaac (OB) 1970

I Want What I Want When I Want It
Music by Victor Herbert
Lyrics by Henry Blossom
Mlle. Modiste 1905

I Want You All to Myself
Music by Joseph Meyer
Lyrics by Edward Eliscu
Lady Fingers 1929

I Want You to Be the First to Know
Music by Arthur Siegel
Lyrics by June Carroll
New Faces of 1962

I Want You to Marry Me
Music by Victor Herbert
Lyrics by Henry Blossom
The Red Mill 1906

I Wanted to Change Him
Music by Jule Styne
Lyrics by Betty Comden and Adolph Green
Hallelujah, Baby! 1967

I Wanted to See the World
Music by Baldwin Bergersen
Lyrics by William Archibald
The Crystal Heart (OB) 1960

I Was a Black Sheep
Music and lyrics by Al Carmines
The Evangelist (OB) 1982

I Was a Florodora Baby
Music and lyrics by Ballard MacDonald
and Harry Carroll
Ziegfeld Follies of 1920

I Was a Shoo-In
Music by Jule Styne
Lyrics by Betty Comden and Adolph Green
Subways Are for Sleeping 1961

I Was Alone
Music by Jerome Kern
Lyrics by Otto Harbach and Oscar Hammerstein II
Sunny (film version, 1930)

I Was Beautiful
Music by Robert Mitchell
Lyrics by Elizabeth Perry
Bags (OB) 1982

I Was Blue
Music by Harry Archer
Lyrics by Harlan Thompson
Merry-Merry 1925

I Was Born on the Day Before Yesterday
Music and lyrics by Charlie Smalls
The Wiz 1975

I Was Doing All Right
Music by George Gershwin
Lyrics by Ira Gershwin
Goldwyn Follies (1938) F

I Was in the Closet
Music by Don Pippin
Lyrics by Steve Brown
The Contrast (OB) 1972

I Was Lonely
Music by Jerome Kern
Lyrics by Edgar Allan Woolf
Head Over Heels 1918

I Was Meant for Someone
Music by James F. Hanley
Lyrics by Ballard MacDonald
Gay Paree 1925

I Was So Young (You Were So Beautiful)
Music by George Gershwin
Lyrics by Irving Caesar and Al Bryan
Good Morning, Judge 1919

I Was the Most Beautiful Blossom
Music by George Gershwin
Lyrics by Ira Gershwin
Of Thee I Sing 1931

I Was Wrong
Music by Mitch Leigh
Lyrics by Charles Burr and Forman Brown
Home Sweet Homer 1976

I Wash My Hands
Music by Moose Charlap
Lyrics by Norman Gimbel
Whoop-Up 1958

I Watch the Love Parade
Music by Jerome Kern
Lyrics by Otto Harbach
The Cat and the Fiddle 1931

I Went to a Marvelous Party
Music and lyrics by Noël Coward
Set to Music 1939

According to Coward, the song was inspired by a beach party in the south of France, a wild evening apparently, at which the hostess, Elsa Maxwell, without warning them in advance, fully expected Coward, Beatrice Lillie and Grace Moore to provide free entertainment for her guests.

I Whistle a Happy Tune
Music by Richard Rodgers
Lyrics by Oscar Hammerstein II
The King and I 1951

I Will Follow You
Music and lyrics by Jerry Herman
Milk and Honey 1961

I Will Give Him Love
Music and lyrics by Jack Bussins
and Ellsworth Olin
Be Kind to People Week (OB) 1975

I Will Give You All for Love
Music by Franz Lehár
Lyrics by Harry B. and Robert B. Smith
Gypsy Love 1911

I Will Make Things Happen
Music and lyrics by Gene Curty, Nitra Scharfman
and Chuck Strand
The Lieutenant 1975

I Will Miss You
Music and lyrics by Sandy Wilson
Valmouth (OB) 1960

I Wish
Music by David Raksin
Lyrics by June Carroll
If the Shoe Fits 1946

I Wish He Knew
Music and lyrics by Al Kasha and Joel Hirschhorn
Copperfield 1981

I Wish I Didn't Love Him
Music and lyrics by Michael Brown
Different Times 1972

I Wish I Was a Bumble Bee
Music and lyrics by James Shelton
Mrs. Patterson 1954

I Wish I Was an Island in an Ocean of Girls
Music by Victor Herbert
Lyrics by Henry Blossom
The Princess Pat 1915

I Wish I Were a Man
Music by Galt MacDermot
Lyrics by William Dumaresq
The Human Comedy (OB) 1983

I Wish I Were in Love Again
Music by Richard Rodgers
Lyrics by Lorenz Hart
Babes in Arms 1937

I Wish It So
Music and lyrics by Marc Blitzstein
Juno 1959

I Wish You a Waltz
Music by Billy Goldenberg
Lyrics by Alan and Marilyn Bergman
Ballroom 1978

I Wonder
Music by Victor Herbert
Lyrics by Harry B. Smith
Cyrano de Bergerac 1899

I Wonder
Music by Jerome Kern
Lyrics by Paul West
The Red Petticoat 1912

I Wonder
Music by Louis A. Hirsch
Lyrics by Rennold Wolf
The Rainbow Girl 1918

I Wonder
Music by Lawrence Hurwit
Lyrics by Lee Goldsmith
Sextet 1974

I Wonder
Music and lyrics by Harry Chapin
Cotton Patch Gospel (OB) 1981

I Wonder as I Wander
Music by Bronislaw Kaper (based on Chopin)
Lyrics by John Latouche
Polonaise 1945

I Wonder How I Ever Passed You By
Music by Louis A. Hirsch
Lyrics by Otto Harbach
The O'Brien Girl 1921

I Wonder How It Is to Dance With a Boy
Music and lyrics by Bob Merrill
Henry, Sweet Henry 1967

I Wonder How They Got That Way
Music and lyrics by Gene Buck and Dave Stamper
Ziegfeld Follies of 1923

I Wonder If
Music by John Morris
Lyrics by Gerald Freedman
A Time for Singing 1966

I Wonder if Love Is a Dream
Music and lyrics by Arthur Brander
The Seventh Heart 1927

I Wonder if She Will Remember
Music by Shep Camp
Lyrics by Frank DuPree and Harry B. Smith
Half a Widow 1927

I Wonder What Became of Me
Music by Harold Arlen
Lyrics by Johnny Mercer
St. Louis Woman 1946

Dropped from production

I Wonder What It's Like
Music by Jerry Bock
Lyrics by Sheldon Harnick
Tenderloin 1960

Dropped from production

I Wonder What the King Is Doing Tonight
Music by Frederick Loewe
Lyrics by Alan Jay Lerner
Camelot 1960

I Wonder Whether
Music by Louis A. Hirsch
Lyrics by P.G. Wodehouse
Oh, My Dear! 1918

I Wonder Why
Music by Jerome Kern
Lyrics by Harry B. Smith
Love o' Mike 1917

I Wonder Why
Music by Sigmund Romberg
Lyrics by Dorothy Donnelly
My Princess 1927

I Wonder Why
Music and lyrics by Walter Cool
Mackey of Appalachia (OB) 1965

I Wonder Why You Wander
Music by Fred Spielman and Arthur Gershwin
Lyrics by Stanley Adams
A Lady Says Yes 1945

I Won't Dance
Music by Jerome Kern
Lyrics by Otto Harbach, Dorothy Fields, Oscar
Hammerstein II and Jimmy McHugh
Roberta (film version, 1935)

The first version of the song, with Oscar
Hammerstein's lyrics and a somewhat different
melody, was in the London production *Three
Sisters* in 1934. For the film *Roberta* (1935) Dorothy
Fields rewrote the lyric, keeping the Oscar
Hammerstein title and some of his lines. Otto
Harbach is also credited as a writer of the words
because he had been the lyricist of the stage
musical on which the film was based.

I Won't Grow Up
Music by Mark Charlap
Lyrics by Carolyn Leigh
Peter Pan 1954

I Won't Let It Happen Again
Music and lyrics by Hugo Peretti, Luigi Creatore
and George David Weiss
Maggie Flynn 1968

I Won't Let You Get Away
Music by Jule Styne
Lyrics by Betty Comden and Adolph Green
Lorelei 1974

I Won't Say I Will, But I Won't Say I Won't
Music by George Gershwin
Lyrics by B.G. DeSylva and Arthur Francis
(Ira Gershwin)
Little Miss Bluebeard 1923

I Won't Send Roses
Music and lyrics by Jerry Herman
Mack and Mabel 1974

I Work With Wood
Music and lyrics by Mel Mandel
and Norman Sachs
My Old Friends (OB) 1979

I Worship You
Music and lyrics by Cole Porter
Fifty Million Frenchmen 1929

Dropped from production

I Would Die
Music and lyrics by Bob Merrill
Take Me Along 1959

I Would Like to Fondle You
Music by Percy Wenrich
Lyrics by Raymond Peck
Castles in the Air 1926

I Would Like to Play a Lover's Part
Music by Jerome Kern
Lyrics by Oscar Hammerstein II
Show Boat 1927

Dropped from production

I Would Love to Have You Love Me
Music by Irving Caesar, Sammy Lerner
and Gerald Marks
Lyrics by Irving Caesar
White Horse Inn 1936

I Wouldn't Bet One Penny
Music and lyrics by Johnny Burke
Donnybrook! 1961

I Wouldn't Have Had To
Music and lyrics by Jay Livingston
and Ray Evans
Let It Ride 1961

I Wouldn't Have You Any Other Way
Music and lyrics by Hugo Peretti, Luigi Creatore
and George David Weiss
Maggie Flynn 1968

I Wouldn't Marry You
Music by Arthur Schwartz
Lyrics by Howard Dietz
The Gay Life 1961

I Wrote a Song for You
Music by Sam Morrison
Lyrics by Dolph Singer and William Dunham
Summer Wives 1936

I Wrote the Book
Music by John Kander
Lyrics by Fred Ebb
Woman of the Year 1981

I, Yes Me, That's Who
Music by Jule Styne
Lyrics by Sammy Cahn
Look to the Lilies 1970

Ice Cold Katy
Music by Arthur Schwartz
Lyrics by Frank Loesser
Thank Your Lucky Stars (1943) F

Ice Cream
Music by Kurt Weill
Lyrics by Langston Hughes
Street Scene 1947

Ice Cream
Music by Jerry Bock
Lyrics by Sheldon Harnick
She Loves Me 1963

Ice Cream
Music by Norman Campbell
Lyrics by Donald Harron and Norman Campbell
Anne of Green Gables (OB) 1971

Ichabod
Music by George Lessner
Lyrics by Miriam Battista and Russell Maloney
Sleepy Hollow 1948

I'd Ask No More
Music by Louis A. Hirsch
Lyrics by P.G. Wodehouse
Oh, My Dear! 1918

I'd Be a Fool
Music by Sigmund Romberg
Lyrics by Oscar Hammerstein II
East Wind 1931

I'd Be Crazy to Be Crazy Over You
Music and lyrics by Skip Redwine and Larry Frank
Frank Merriwell, or Honor Challenged 1971

I'd Be Happy
Music and lyrics by Maceo Pinkard
Pansy 1929

I'd Be Surprisingly Good for You
Music by Andrew Lloyd Webber
Lyrics by Tim Rice
Evita 1979

I'd Do Almost Anything to Get Out of Here and Go Home
Music by Harvey Schmidt
Lyrics by Tom Jones
Philemon (OB) 1975

I'd Do Anything
Music and lyrics by Lionel Bart
Oliver! 1963

I'd Do It Again
Music by Richard Rodgers
Lyrics by Lorenz Hart
Hallelujah, I'm a Bum (1933) F

I'd Do It Again
Music and lyrics by Marian Grudeff
and Raymond Jessel
Baker Street 1965

I'd Forgotten How Beautiful She Could Be
Music and lyrics by John Jennings
Riverwind (OB) 1962

I'd Gladly Trade
Music and lyrics by Hugh Martin and Ralph Blane
Best Foot Forward 1941

I'd Gladly Walk to Alaska
Music by Alec Wilder
Lyrics by Arnold Sundgaard
Kittiwake Island (OB) 1960

I'd Know It
Music and lyrics by Steve Allen
Sophie 1963

I'd Like a Lighthouse
Music by Jerome Kern
Lyrics by Anne Caldwell
The Night Boat 1920

I'd Like My Picture Took
Music and lyrics by Irving Berlin
Miss Liberty 1949

I'd Like to Be a Quitter
Music by Victor Herbert
Lyrics by Henry Blossom
The Princess Pat 1915

I'd Like to Be a Rose
Music by Galt MacDermot
Lyrics by John Guare
Two Gentlemen of Verona 1971

I'd Like to Dunk You in My Coffee
Music by Harry Akst
Lyrics by Lew Brown
Calling All Stars 1934

I'd Like to Have a Million in the Bank
Music by Jerome Kern
Lyrics by Herbert Reynolds and John E. Hazzard
Very Good Eddie 1915

I'd Like to Hide It
Music by Richard Rodgers
Lyrics by Lorenz Hart
Dearest Enemy 1925

I'd Like to Know You Better
Music and lyrics by Jill Williams
Rainbow Jones 1974

I'd Like to Love Them All
Music by Emile Berté and Maury Rubens
Lyrics by J. Keirn Brennan
Music in May 1929

I'd Like to Take You Home
Music by Richard Rodgers
Lyrics by Lorenz Hart
The Girl Friend 1926

I'd Like to Take You Home to Meet My Mother
Music by Robert Russell Bennett
Lyrics by Owen Murphy and Robert A. Simon
Hold Your Horses 1933

I'd Like to Talk About the Weather
Music by Vernon Duke
Lyrics by John Latouche
The Lady Comes Across 1942

Dropped from production

I'd Love To
Music by Harold Orlob
Lyrics by Harry L. Cort and George E. Stoddard
Listen, Lester 1918

I'd Love to Waltz Through Life With You
Music by Victor Herbert
Lyrics by Gene Buck
Ziegfeld Follies of 1923

I'd Marry You Again
Music by Lance Mulcahy
Lyrics by Paul Cherry
Park 1970

I'd Rather Be a Fairy Than a Troll
Music by Ronald Melrose
Lyrics by Bill Russell
Fourtune (OB) 1980

I'd Rather Be Right
Music by Richard Rodgers
Lyrics by Lorenz Hart
I'd Rather Be Right 1937

Two songs were written with this title. The first, a ballad, was dropped during the pre-Broadway tour, and replaced by this more rhythmic tune. Hart wrote a new lyric for the first version with the title "Now That I Know You," for a summer revue "Two Weeks With Pay" (1940).

I'd Rather Charleston!
Music by George Gershwin
Lyrics by Desmond Carter
Lady, Be Good! (London production, 1926)

I'd Rather Dance Here Than Hereafter
Music by Joseph Meyer and Roger Wolfe Kahn
Lyrics by Irving Caesar
Here's Howe 1928

I'd Rather Lead a Band
Music and lyrics by Irving Berlin
Follow the Fleet (1936) F

I'd Rather See a Minstrel Show
Music and lyrics by Irving Berlin
Ziegfeld Follies of 1919

I'd Rather Stay at Home
Music by Jerome Kern
Lyrics by C. H. Bovill
A Waltz Dream 1908

I'd Rather Wake Up by Myself
Music by Arthur Schwartz
Lyrics by Dorothy Fields
By the Beautiful Sea 1954

I'd Steal a Star
Music by Vincent Youmans
Lyrics by Anne Caldwell
Oh, Please! 1926

I'd Sure Like to Give It a Shot
Music by Jule Styne
Lyrics by Sammy Cahn
Look to the Lilies 1970

I'd Write a Song
Music by Sigmund Romberg
Lyrics by Irving Caesar
Melody 1933

Idle Dreams
Music by George Gershwin
Lyrics by Arthur Jackson
George White's Scandals (1920)

Idles of the King
Music by Richard Rodgers
Lyrics by Lorenz Hart
The Garrick Gaieties (2nd edition) 1926

If
Music by George Lessner
Lyrics by Miriam Battista and Russell Maloney
Sleepy Hollow 1948

If a Girl Isn't Pretty
Music by Jule Styne
Lyrics by Bob Merrill
Funny Girl 1964

If Eve Had Left the Apple on the Bough
Music by Victor Herbert
Lyrics by Henry Blossom
Eileen 1917

If Ever I Would Leave You
Music by Frederick Loewe
Lyrics by Alan Jay Lerner
Camelot 1960

If Ever Married I'm
Music and lyrics by Cole Porter
Kiss Me, Kate 1948

Dropped from production

If Every Day Was Sunday
Music by Adorjan Otvos
Lyrics by Ballard MacDonald
Battling Buttler 1923

If Every Month Were June
Music by Henry Sullivan
Lyrics by John Murray Anderson
John Murray Anderson's Almanac (1953)

If Everyone Got What They Wanted
Music by Jerry Livingston
Lyrics by Leonard Adelson
Molly 1973

If Flutterby Wins
Music and lyrics by Jay Livingston and Ray Evans
Let It Ride 1961

If He Really Knew Me
Music by Marvin Hamlisch
Lyrics by Carole Bayer Sager
They're Playing Our Song 1979

If He Really Loves Me
Music by Harold Arlen
Lyrics by Jack Yellen
You Said It 1931

If He Walked Into My Life
Music and lyrics by Jerry Herman
Mame 1966

If He'd Only Be Gentle
Music and lyrics by Frederick Silver
Gay Company (OB) 1974

If He'll Come Back to Me
Music by Vincent Youmans
Lyrics by Leo Robin and Clifford Grey
Hit the Deck 1927

If I Am Dreaming
Music by Carl Millöcker (revised by Theo Mackeben)
Lyrics by Rowland Leigh
The Dubarry 1932

If I Am to Marry You
Music and lyrics by Deed Meyer
She Shall Have Music (OB) 1959

If I Be Your Best Chance
Music by Jimmy Van Heusen
Lyrics by Sammy Cahn
Walking Happy 1966

If I Became the President
Music by George Gershwin
Lyrics by Ira Gershwin
Strike Up the Band 1930

If I Could Be Beautiful
Music and lyrics by Tom Savage
Musical Chairs 1980

If I Could've Been
Music and lyrics by Micki Grant
Working 1978

If I Didn't Have You
Music and lyrics by Alexander Hill
Hummin' Sam 1933

If I Ever Loved Him
Music by Gary Geld
Lyrics by Peter Udell
Angel 1978

If I Felt Any Younger Today
Music by David Baker
Lyrics by Sheldon Harnick
Smiling, the Boy Fell Dead (OB) 1961

If I Find the Girl
Music by Jerome Kern
Lyrics by John E. Hazzard and Herbert Reynolds
Very Good Eddie 1915

If I Gave You
Music and lyrics by Hugh Martin
and Timothy Gray
High Spirits 1964

If I Gave You a Rose
Music by Melville Gideon
Lyrics by Granville English
The Optimists 1928

If I Give in to You
Music by Richard Rodgers
Lyrics by Lorenz Hart
Evergreen (1934) F

If I Had a Lover
Music by Henry Tobias
Lyrics by Billy Rose and Ballard MacDonald
Padlocks of 1927

If I Had a Million Dollars
Music by Gary William Friedman
Lyrics by Will Holt
The Me Nobody Knows (OB) 1970

If I Had a Talking Picture of You
Music and lyrics by B.G. DeSylva, Lew Brown
and Ray Henderson
Sunny Side Up (1929) F

If I Had My Druthers
Music by Gene de Paul
Lyrics by Johnny Mercer
Li'l Abner 1956

If I Knew
Music and lyrics by Meredith Willson
The Unsinkable Molly Brown 1960

If I Liken Thy Shape
Music by Frederic Norton
Lyrics by Oscar Asche
Chu Chin Chow 1917

If I Love Again
Music by Ben Oakland
Lyrics by J.P. Murray
Hold Your Horses 1933

If I Loved You
Music by Richard Rodgers
Lyrics by Oscar Hammerstein II
Carousel 1945

The title is part of a speech in Ferenc Molnar's *Liliom,* the play from which *Carousel* was adapted. Liliom asks Julie, "But you wouldn't marry a rough guy like me—that is—eh—if you loved me." Julie replies, "Yes, I would—if I loved you."

If I May
Music by Richard B. Chodosh
Lyrics by Barry Alan Grael
The Streets of New York (OB) 1963

If I Never See You Again
Music by Harry Ruby
Lyrics by Bert Kalmar
Helen of Troy, New York 1923

If I Never Waltz Again
Music by Emmerich Kálmán
Lyrics by George Marion, Jr.
Marinka 1945

If I Only Had
Music and lyrics by Oscar Brown, Jr.
Joy (OB) 1970

If I Only Had a Brain (A Heart) (The Nerve)
Music by Harold Arlen
Lyrics by E.Y. Harburg
The Wizard of Oz (1939) F

If I Ruled the World
Music by Cyril Ornadel
Lyrics by Leslie Bricusse
Pickwick 1965

If I Told You
Music by Vincent Youmans
Lyrics by Otto Harbach and Oscar Hammerstein II
Wildflower 1923

Although dropped from the show *Wildflower,* the melody of "If I Told You" (entirely by Youmans) was in three subsequent Broadway productions, each time with different lyrics. In *Rainbow* (1928) it was called "Virginia," in *Great Day!* (1929) the title was "Sweet as Sugar Cane," and in *Through the Years* (1932) it was "The Road to Home."

If I Was a Boy
Music and lyrics by James Shelton
Mrs. Patterson 1954

If I Was a Dove
Music by Leonard Bernstein
Lyrics by Alan Jay Lerner
1600 Pennsylvania Avenue 1976

If I Were a Bell
Music and lyrics by Frank Loesser
Guys and Dolls 1950

If I Were a Rich Man
Music by Jerry Bock
Lyrics by Sheldon Harnick
Fiddler on the Roof 1964

If I Were Anybody Else but Me
Music by Victor Herbert
Lyrics by Rida Johnson Young
Naughty Marietta 1910

If I Were King
Music and lyrics by Newell Chase, Leo Robin and Sam Coslow
The Vagabond King (film version, 1930)

If I Were on the Stage
Music by Victor Herbert
Lyrics by Henry Blossom
Mlle. Modiste 1905

This is a sequence in which the French stage-struck heroine proves her versatility in three types of songs. First, as a country girl she sings a gavotte. Then as a lady of history, she sings a polonaise. Finally, to show off her romantic side she sings a waltz—one of Herbert's most enduring—"Kiss Me Again." (*See* note on that song.)

If I Were Only Someone
Music by Sam Pottle
Lyrics by Tom Whedon
All Kinds of Giants (OB) 1961

If I Were the King of the Forest
Music by Harold Arlen
Lyrics by E. Y. Harburg
The Wizard of Oz (1939) F

If I Were the Man
Music by Milton Schafer
Lyrics by Ronny Graham
Bravo Giovanni 1962

If I Were You
Music by Richard Rodgers
Lyrics by Lorenz Hart
Betsy 1926

Later added to *She's My Baby* (1928) during the run

If I Were You
Music by Louis Alter
Lyrics by Harry Ruskin and Leighton K. Brill
Ballyhoo 1930

If I Were You
Music by Charles Strouse
Lyrics by Lee Adams
All American 1962

If I Were You, Love
Music by Vincent Youmans
Lyrics by Ring Lardner
Smiles 1930

If It Hadn't Been for Me
Music by Norman Campbell
Lyrics by Donald Harron and Norman Campbell
Anne of Green Gables (OB) 1971

If It Wasn't for People
Music and lyrics by Billy Barnes
The Billy Barnes People 1961

If It Were Easy to Do
Music by Carl Sigman
Lyrics by Bob Hilliard
Angel in the Wings 1947

If It's a Dream
Music by Victor Young
Lyrics by Stella Unger
Seventh Heaven 1955

If It's Any News to You
Music by Eubie Blake
Lyrics by Noble Sissle
Shuffle Along of 1933

If It's Good Enough for Lady Astor
Music and lyrics by Stan Freeman
and Franklin Underwood
Lovely Ladies, Kind Gentlemen 1970

If It's Love
Music by Harry Akst
Lyrics by Lew Brown
Calling All Stars 1934

If It's Love
Music by Morgan Lewis
Lyrics by Nancy Hamilton
Three to Make Ready 1946

If It's Love
Music and lyrics by Johnny Brandon
Cindy (OB) 1964

If Jesus Walked
Music and lyrics by Peter Copani
New York City Street Show (OB) 1977

If Love Should Come to Me
Music by Henry Souvaine and Jay Gorney
Lyrics by Morrie Ryskind and Howard Dietz
Merry-Go-Round 1927

If Love Were All
Music and lyrics by Noël Coward
Bitter Sweet 1929

If Love's Like a Lark
Music by Alec Wilder
Lyrics by Arnold Sundgaard
Kittiwake Island (OB) 1960

If Menelaus Only Knew It
Music by Erich Wolfgang Korngold (based on
Jacques Offenbach)
Lyrics by Herbert Baker
Helen Goes to Troy 1944

If Momma Was Married
Music by Jule Styne
Lyrics by Stephen Sondheim
Gypsy 1959

If Mr. Boston Lawson Had His Way
Music and lyrics by George M. Cohan
Little Johnny Jones 1904

If My Friends Could See Me Now
Music by Cy Coleman
Lyrics by Dorothy Fields
Sweet Charity 1966

If My Morning Begins
Music and lyrics by Cliff Jones
Rockabye Hamlet 1976

If Not to You
Music and lyrics by Cliff Jones
Rockabye Hamlet 1976

If Only
Music by Sigmund Romberg
Lyrics by Rowland Leigh
My Romance 1948

If Only
Music by Jim Steinman
Lyrics by Michael Weller and Jim Steinman
More Than You Deserve (OB) 1973

If Only He Were a Woman
Music by Arthur Siegel
Lyrics by Mae Richard
Tallulah (OB) 1983

If Only I Could Be a Kid Again
Music by Murray Rumshinsky
Lyrics by Jacob Jacobs
The President's Daughter 1970

If Only Mrs. Applejohn Were Here
Music and lyrics by Noël Coward
The Girl Who Came to Supper 1963

Dropped from production

If Only Someone Would Teach Me
Music by Karl Hoschna
Lyrics by Otto Harbach
The Fascinating Widow 1911

If She Has Never Loved Before
Music by Richard Hill and John Hawkins
Lyrics by Nevill Coghill
Canterbury Tales 1969

If That Was Love
Music and lyrics by Bob Merrill
New Girl in Town 1957

If That's What You Want
Music by Sigmund Romberg
Lyrics by Harry B. Smith
The Love Call 1927

If the Blues Don't Get You
Music and lyrics by Maceo Pinkard
Pansy 1929

If the Rain's Got to Fall
Music and lyrics by David Heneker
Half a Sixpence 1965

If the Shoe Fits
Music by David Raksin
Lyrics by June Carroll
If the Shoe Fits 1946

If There Is Someone Lovelier Than You
Music by Arthur Schwartz
Lyrics by Howard Dietz
Revenge With Music 1934

If There's Love Enough
Music by Claibe Richardson
Lyrics by Kenward Elmslie
The Grass Harp 1971

If They Ever Parted Me From You
Music by Louis A. Hirsch
Lyrics by P.G. Wodehouse
Oh, My Dear! 1918

If This Is Glamour!
Music by Richard Stutz
Lyrics by Rick French
Along Fifth Avenue 1949

If This Is Goodbye
Music and lyrics by Robert Wright and George
Forrest (based on Rachmaninoff)
Anya 1965

If This Isn't Love
Music by Burton Lane
Lyrics by E.Y. Harburg
Finian's Rainbow 1947

If We Only Could Stop the Old Town Clock
Music by Walter Kent
Lyrics by Kim Gannon
Seventeen 1951

If We Only Have Love
Music by Jacques Brel
English lyrics by Eric Blau and Mort Shuman

*Jacques Brel Is Alive and Well
and Living in Paris* (OB) 1968

If Wishes Were Horses
Music by Helen Miller
Lyrics by Eve Merriam
Inner City 1971

If You Are as Good as You Look
Music by Jerome Kern
Lyrics by Anne Caldwell
The City Chap 1925

If You Are in Love With a Girl
Music by Percy Wenrich
Lyrics by Raymond Peck
Castles in the Air 1926

If You Believe
Music and lyrics by Charlie Smalls
The Wiz 1975

If You Can Find a True Love
Music by William Dyer
Lyrics by Don Parks and William Dyer
Jo (OB) 1964

If You Can't Be as Happy as You'd Like to Be
Music by Victor Herbert
Lyrics by Harry B. Smith
The Enchantress 1911

If You Can't Bring It, You've Got to Send It
Music and lyrics by Porter Grainger
and Freddie Johnson
Lucky Sambo 1925

If You Cared
Music by Jean Gilbert
Lyrics by Harry Graham
Katja 1926

If You Could Care
Music by Herman Darewski
Lyrics by Arthur Wimperis
As You Were 1920

If You Could Only Come With Me
Music and lyrics by Noël Coward
Bitter Sweet 1929

If You Could See Her
Music by John Kander
Lyrics by Fred Ebb
Cabaret 1966

If You Examine Human Kind
Music by John Philip Sousa
Lyrics by Tom Frost and John Philip Sousa
El Capitan 1896

If You Go, I'll Die
Music by Rudolf Friml
Lyrics by Bide Dudley and Otto Harbach
The Little Whopper 1919

If You Got Music
Music by Colin Romoff
Lyrics by David Rogers
Ziegfeld Follies (1957)

If You Hadn't, But You Did
Music by Jule Styne
Lyrics by Betty Comden and Adolph Green
Two on the Aisle 1951

If You Have Troubles Laugh Them Away
Music and lyrics by Lester Lee
Harry Delmar's Revels 1927

If You Haven't Got a Sweetheart
Music by Arthur Schwartz
Lyrics by Dorothy Fields
A Tree Grows in Brooklyn 1951

If You Haven't Got "It"
Music by Max Ewing
Lyrics by Agnes Morgan
The Grand Street Follies (1927) (OB)

If You Knew Time
Music and lyrics by Elizabeth Swados
Alice in Concert (OB) 1980

If You Know What I Mean
Music by Arthur Schwartz
Lyrics by Theodore Goodwin and Albert Carroll
The Grand Street Follies (1926) (OB)

If You Know What I Think
Music by Sigmund Romberg
Lyrics by Harry B. Smith
Cherry Blossoms 1927

**If You Let Me Make Love to You
Then Why Can't I Touch You?**
Music and lyrics by Peter Link and C.C. Courtney
Salvation (OB) 1969

If You Like People
Music by Bob James
Lyrics by Jack O'Brien
The Selling of the President 1972

If You Look in Her Eyes
Music by Louis A. Hirsch
Lyrics by Otto Harbach
Going Up 1917

If You Love But Me
Music by Victor Herbert
Lyrics by Henry Blossom
The Red Mill 1906

If You Loved Me Truly
Music and lyrics by Cole Porter
Can-Can 1953

If You Only Cared Enough
Music by Jerome Kern
Lyrics by Berton Braley
Toot-Toot! 1918

If You Said What You Thought
Music and lyrics by Leon DeCosta
The Blonde Sinner 1926

If You Smile at Me
Music and lyrics by Cole Porter
Around the World 1946

If You Think It's Love You're Right
Music by Jerome Kern
Lyrics by Howard Dietz
Dear Sir 1924

If You Want to Break My Father's Heart
Music and lyrics by Stan Daniels
So Long, 174th Street 1976

If You Want to Get Ahead
Music by Norman Curtis
Lyrics by Patricia Taylor Curtis
Walk Down Mah Street! (OB) 1968

If You Want to Win a Girl
Music by Heinrich Reinhardt
Lyrics by Robert B. Smith
The Spring Maid 1910

If You Were Someone Else
Music by Harold Levey
Lyrics by Owen Murphy
Rainbow Rose 1926

If You Were Someone Else
Music by Arthur Schwartz
Lyrics by Albert Stillman
Virginia 1937

If You Were the Apple
Music by Joseph Meyer
Lyrics by William Moll
Jonica 1930

If You Wind Me Up
Music by Larry Grossman
Lyrics by Hal Hackady
Minnie's Boys 1970

If You Would Only Come Away
Music by Georges Bizet
Lyrics by Oscar Hammerstein II
Carmen Jones 1943

If You'd Be Happy, Don't Fall in Love
Music by Maurice Yvain
Lyrics by Max and Nathaniel Lief
Luckee Girl 1928

If You'll Always Say Yes
Music by Winthrop Cortelyou
Lyrics by Derick Wulff
Kiss Me 1927

If You'll Be Mine
Music and lyrics by Hugh Martin
Look Ma, I'm Dancin'! 1948

If You'll Put Up With Me
Music by Frank Grey
Lyrics by Earle Crooker and McElbert Moore
Happy 1927

If You're in Love, You'll Waltz
Music by Harry Tierney
Lyrics by Joseph McCarthy
Rio Rita 1927

If You've Got It, You've Got It
Music and lyrics by Johnny Brandon
Cindy (OB) 1964

If You've Never Been Vamped by a Brownskin
Music and lyrics by Noble Sissle and Eubie Blake
Shuffle Along 1921

If'n
Music by Harold Karr
Lyrics by Matt Dubey
Happy Hunting 1956

I'll Admit
Music by Maury Rubens
Lyrics by Henry Dagand
Hello, Paris 1930

I'll Always Be in Love
Music by Claibe Richardson
Lyrics by Kenward Elmslie
The Grass Harp 1971

I'll Always Love You
Music by Galt MacDermot
Lyrics by William Dumaresq
The Human Comedy (OB) 1983

I'll Applaud You With My Feet
Music by Jimmy McHugh
Lyrics by Al Dubin
Keep Off the Grass 1940

I'll Ballyhoo You
Music by Dimitri Tiomkin
Lyrics by Edward Eliscu
A Little Racketeer 1932

I'll Be a Buoyant Girl
Music by Sigmund Romberg
Lyrics by Otto Harbach and Oscar Hammerstein II
The Desert Song 1926

I'll Be Coming Home With a Skate On
Music and lyrics by Irving Berlin
Stop! Look! Listen! 1915

I'll Be Hard to Handle
Music by Jerome Kern
Lyrics by Bernard Dougall
Roberta 1933

I'll Be Here Tomorrow
Music and lyrics by Jerry Herman
The Grand Tour 1979

I'll Be Home
Music and lyrics by Randy Newman
Maybe I'm Doing It Wrong (1st edition) (OB) 1981

I'll Be Respectable
Music by Harold Arlen
Lyrics by Johnny Mercer
Saratoga 1959

I'll Be Seeing You
Music by Sammy Fain
Lyrics by Irving Kahal
Right This Way 1938

I'll Be Sittin' in de Lap o' de Lord
Music by Arthur Schwartz
Lyrics by Albert Stillman
Virginia 1937

I'll Be Smiling
Music by Jean Schwartz
Lyrics by Clifford Grey and William Cary Duncan
Sunny Days 1928

I'll Be There
Music by Albert Sirmay and Arthur Schwartz
Lyrics by Arthur Swanstrom
Princess Charming 1930

I'll Be True, but I'll Be Blue
Music and lyrics by Alexander Hill
Hummin' Sam 1933

I'll Be True to You
Music by Victor Jacobi
Lyrics by William LeBaron
Apple Blossoms 1919

I'll Be True to You
Music and lyrics by Charles Gaynor
Lend an Ear 1948

I'll Be Waiting
Music by Emmerich Kálmán
Lyrics by Harry B. Smith
The Circus Princess 1927

I'll Bet You
Music by Louis A. Hirsch
Lyrics by Otto Harbach
Going Up 1917

I'll Bet You're a Cat Girl
Music by Mildred Kayden
Lyrics by Frank Gagliano
Paradise Gardens East (OB) 1969

I'll Betcha That I'll Getcha
Music by Jesse Greer
Lyrics by Stanley Adams
Shady Lady 1933

I'll Black His Eyes
Music and lyrics by Cole Porter
You Never Know 1938

Dropped from production

I'll Build a Stairway to Paradise
Music by George Gershwin
Lyrics by B.G. DeSylva and Arthur Francis
George White's Scandals (1922)

The Gershwins (Ira was still using the pen name "Arthur Francis," his brother's and sister's first names) wrote a song called "A New Step Every Day," the last lines of which were "I'll build a staircase to paradise, with a new step every day." B.G. DeSylva felt the idea could be used for a large-scale production number and, joining Ira as co-lyricist, the song was entirely rewritten. It became the first act finale of *George White's Scandals of 1922* and was one of their first big hits.

I'll Build for You a Little Nest
Music by Karl Hoschna
Lyrics by Otto Harbach
Madame Sherry 1910

I'll Buy It
Music by Burton Lane
Lyrics by Dorothy Fields
Junior Miss (1957) TV

I'll Buy You a Star
Music by Arthur Schwartz
Lyrics by Dorothy Fields
A Tree Grows in Brooklyn 1951

I'll Can-Can All Day
Music by Johann Strauss II, adapted by Oscar Straus
Lyrics by Clare Kummer
Three Waltzes 1937

I'll Carry You an Inch
Music by Meyer Kupferman
Lyrics by Paul Goodman
Jonah (OB) 1966

I'll Collaborate With You
Music by Vincent Youmans and Herbert Stothart
Lyrics by Otto Harbach and Oscar Hammerstein II
Wildflower 1923

I'll Come Back to You
Music by Vincent Youmans
Lyrics by Edward Heyman
Through the Years 1932

I'll Cuddle Up to You
Music and lyrics by Leon DeCosta
Kosher Kitty Kelly 1925

I'll Dance My Way Into Your Heart
Music by Emmerich Kálmán
Lyrics by B.G. DeSylva
The Yankee Princess 1922

I'll Find a Dream Somewhere
Music by Don McAfee
Lyrics by Nancy Leeds
Great Scot! (OB) 1965

I'll Find My Love in D–I–X–I–E
Music and lyrics by Noble Sissle and Eubie Blake
The Chocolate Dandies 1924

I'll Follow My Secret Heart
Music and lyrics by Noël Coward
Conversation Piece 1934

Coward recalled that, after weeks of trying, he was unable to write the main waltz for "Conversation Piece" and was about to postpone the entire project. One evening, thoroughly discouraged, he had a few drinks and retired. Realizing that he had left a light burning—the piano light—he returned to the piano, sat down and found himself playing the entire melody of "I'll Follow My Secret Heart," and in the key of G flat, a key he had never played in before. He remembered also that he was, in his words, "fried as a coot" at the time.

I'll Follow You to Zanzibar
Music by Jean Gilbert
Lyrics by Harry Graham and Cyrus Wood
The Lady in Ermine 1922

I'll Get My Man
Music by Ray Henderson
Lyrics by B.G. DeSylva and Lew Brown
Flying High 1930

I'll Give My Love a Ring
Music by Richard Hill and John Hawkins
Lyrics by Nevill Coghill
Canterbury Tales 1969

I'll Give the World to You
Music by Alma Sanders
Lyrics by Monte Carlo
Oh! Oh! Nurse 1925

I'll Go Home With Bonnie Jean
Music by Frederick Loewe
Lyrics by Alan Jay Lerner
Brigadoon 1947

I'll Go the Route for You
Music and lyrics by George M. Cohan
The Man Who Owns Broadway 1909

I'll Hit a New High
Music by Kay Swift
Lyrics by Paul James
Fine and Dandy 1930

I'll Keep On Dreaming
Music by Emmerich Kálmán
Lyrics by Harry B. Smith
Countess Maritza 1926

I'll Keep On Dreaming of You
Music by J. Fred Coots
Lyrics by Al Dubin
White Lights 1927

I'll Know
Music and lyrics by Frank Loesser
Guys and Dolls 1950

I'll Know and She'll Know
Music by Harry Ruby
Lyrics by Bert Kalmar
Top Speed 1929

I'll Know Him
Music by Ray Henderson
Lyrics by B.G. DeSylva and Lew Brown
Flying High 1930

I'll Learn Ya
Music and lyrics by Jay Livingston
and Ray Evans
Let It Ride 1961

I'll Love Them All to Death
Music by Jean Gilbert
Lyrics by Harry B. Smith
The Red Robe 1928

I'll Make a Man of the Man
Music by Jimmy Van Heusen
Lyrics by Sammy Cahn
Walking Happy 1966

I'll Make a Ring Around Rosie
Music by Silvio Hein
Lyrics by George V. Hobart
The Yankee Girl 1910

I'll Miss You
Music by Richard Rodgers
Lyrics by Sheldon Harnick
Rex 1976

Dropped from production

I'll Never Be Jealous Again
Music and lyrics by Richard Adler
and Jerry Ross
The Pajama Game 1954

I'll Never Be Lonely Again
Music by Cyril Ornadel
Lyrics by Leslie Bricusse
Pickwick 1965

I'll Never Complain
Music by H. Maurice Jacquet
Lyrics by Preston Sturges
The Well of Romance 1930

I'll Never Fall in Love Again
Music by Burt Bacharach
Lyrics by Hal David
Promises, Promises 1968

I'll Never Forget
Music by Max Ewing
Lyrics by Albert Carroll
The Grand Street Follies (1929)

I'll Never Lay Down Any More
Music by Manos Hadjidakis
Lyrics by Joe Darion
Illya Darling 1967

I'll Never Learn
Music by Morton Gould
Lyrics by Dorothy Fields
Arms and the Girl 1950

I'll Never Leave You
Music by Albert Sirmay and Arthur Schwartz
Lyrics by Arthur Swanstrom
Princess Charming 1930

I'll Never Make a Frenchman out of You
Music and lyrics by Hugh Martin
Make a Wish 1951

I'll Never Say No
Music and lyrics by Meredith Willson
The Unsinkable Molly Brown 1960

I'll Only Miss Her When I Think of Her
Music by Jimmy Van Heusen
Lyrics by Sammy Cahn
Skyscraper 1965

I'll Pay the Check
Music by Arthur Schwartz
Lyrics by Dorothy Fields
Stars in Your Eyes 1939

I'll Peek-a-Boo You
Music by Sigmund Romberg
Lyrics by Harry B. Smith
Cherry Blossoms 1927

I'll Produce for You
Music by Frank D'Armond
Lyrics by Will Morrissey
Saluta 1934

I'll Putcha Pitcha in the Paper
Music by Michael H. Cleary
Lyrics by Max and Nathaniel Lief
The Third Little Show 1931

I'll Remember Her
Music and lyrics by Noël Coward
The Girl Who Came to Supper 1963

I'll See You Again
Music and lyrics by Noël Coward
Bitter Sweet 1929

About this song Coward wrote: "'I'll See You Again' (The Bitter Sweet Waltz) came to me whole and complete in a taxi in New York. My taxi got stuck in traffic, klaxons were honking, cops were shouting and suddenly in the general din there was the melody, clear and unmistakable." It was Coward's most successful song.

I'll See You Home
Music by Harry Archer
Lyrics by Will B. Johnstone
Entre-Nous (OB) 1935

I'll Share It All With You
Music and lyrics by Irving Berlin
Annie Get Your Gun 1946

I'll Show Him!
Music by Albert Hague
Lyrics by Arnold B. Horwitt
Plain and Fancy 1955

I'll Show Him
Music by Norman Campbell
Lyrics by Donald Harron and Norman Campbell
Anne of Green Gables (OB) 1971

I'll Show Them All
Music and lyrics by Steve Allen
Sophie 1963

I'll Show You a Wonderful World
Music by George Gershwin
Lyrics by B.G. DeSylva and John Henry Mears
Morris Gest Midnight Whirl 1919

I'll Sing You a Song
Music and lyrics by Ralph Blane
Three Wishes for Jamie 1952

I'll Stay, I'll Go
Music by Wally Harper
Lyrics by Paul Zakrzewski
Sensations (OB) 1970

I'll Still Love Jean
Music by Don McAfee
Lyrics by Nancy Leeds
Great Scot! (OB) 1965

I'll Take an Option on You
Music by Ralph Rainger
Lyrics by Leo Robin
Tattle Tales 1933

I'll Take Care of You
Music and lyrics by Edward Pola
and Eddie Brandt
Woof, Woof 1929

I'll Take My Fantasy
Music and lyrics by Al Carmines
The Faggot (OB) 1973

I'll Take Romance
Music by Ben Oakland
Lyrics by Oscar Hammerstein II
I'll Take Romance (1937) F

I'll Take the City
Music by Vernon Duke
Lyrics by John Latouche
Banjo Eyes 1941

I'll Take the Solo
Music by Clay Warnick
Lyrics by Edward Eager
Dream With Music 1944

I'll Take You Back to Italy
Music and lyrics by Irving Berlin
Jack O' Lantern 1917

I'll Take You to the Country
Music by Maurice Yvain
Lyrics by Max and Nathaniel Lief
Luckee Girl 1928

I'll Tell the Man in the Street
Music by Richard Rodgers
Lyrics by Lorenz Hart
I Married an Angel 1938

I'll Tell The World
Music by Sigmund Romberg
Lyrics by Harold Atteridge
Sinbad (1918)

I'll Tell the World
Music by Fred Stamer
Lyrics by Gen Genovese
Buttrio Square 1952

I'll Tell You
Music by Walter Kollo
Lyrics by Harry B. Smith
Three Little Girls 1930

I'll Tell You a Truth
Music by Jerry Bock
Lyrics by Sheldon Harnick
The Apple Tree 1966

I'll Tell You About My Family
Music by Galt MacDermot
Lyrics by William Dumaresq
The Human Comedy (OB) 1983

I'll Tell You All Someday
Music and lyrics by Ben Schwartz
Tales of Rigo 1927

I'll Think of You
Music by Louis A. Hirsch
Lyrics by Rennold Wolf
The Rainbow Girl 1918

I'll Treat You Just Like a Sister
Music by Louis A. Hirsch
Lyrics by Otto Harbach
The O'Brien Girl 1921

I'll Try
Music by Albert Hague
Lyrics by Dorothy Fields
Redhead 1959

I'll Try It Your Way
Music by Ronald Melrose
Lyrics by Bill Russell
Fourtune (OB) 1980

I'll Turn a Little Cog
Music by Sidney Lippman
Lyrics by Sylvia Dee
Barefoot Boy With Cheek 1947

The Ill-Tempered Clavichord
Music by Frederick Loewe
Lyrics by Alan Jay Lerner
What's Up? 1943

I'll Walk Alone
Music by Jule Styne
Lyrics by Sammy Cahn
Follow the Boys (1944) F

Ill Wind
Music by Donald Swann
Lyrics by Michael Flanders
At the Drop of Another Hat 1966

The Illegitimate Daughter
Music by George Gershwin
Lyrics by Ira Gershwin
Of Thee I Sing 1931

Illusions
Music and lyrics by Paul Shyre
Ah, Men (OB) 1981

Illya Darling
Music by Manos Hadjidakis
Lyrics by Joe Darion
Illya Darling 1967

Ilmar's Tomb
Music by Galt MacDermot
Lyrics by Christopher Gore
Via Galactica 1972

Ilona
Music by Jerry Bock
Lyrics by Sheldon Harnick
She Loves Me 1963

I'm a Bad, Bad Man
Music and lyrics by Irving Berlin
Annie Get Your Gun 1946

I'm a Bad Character
Music and lyrics by Melvin Van Peebles
Don't Play Us Cheap 1972

I'm a Brass Band
Music by Cy Coleman
Lyrics by Dorothy Fields
Sweet Charity 1966

I'm a Butter Hoarder
Music and lyrics by Harold Orlob
Hairpin Harmony 1943

I'm a Dandy
Music and lyrics by Irving Burgie
Ballad for Bimshire (OB) 1963

I'm a Dreamer (Aren't We All?)
Music and lyrics by B.G. DeSylva, Lew Brown
and Ray Henderson
Sunny Side Up (1929) F

I'm a Fan
Music and lyrics by Beth Lawrence
and Norman Thalheimer
Marilyn 1983

I'm a Fool, Little One
Music by Richard Rodgers
Lyrics by Lorenz Hart
Present Arms 1928

I'm a Funny Dame
Music by Harold Karr
Lyrics by Matt Dubey
Happy Hunting 1956

I'm a Gigolo
Music and lyrics by Cole Porter
Wake Up and Dream 1929

I'm a Highway Gentleman
Music by Joseph Meyer and Philip Charig
Lyrics by Leo Robin
Just Fancy 1927

I'm a Little Bit Fonder of You
Music and lyrics by Irving Caesar
Ripples 1930

I'm a One-Girl Man
Music and lyrics by George M. Cohan
Billie 1928

I'm a Poached Egg
Music by George Gershwin
(posthumous—from manuscript)
Lyrics by Ira Gershwin
Kiss Me, Stupid (1964) F

I'm a Queen in My Own Domain
Music by Richard Rodgers
Lyrics by Lorenz Hart
Hollywood Party (1934) F

Dropped from film

I'm a Rocket Tonight
Music by Scott Killian and Kim D. Sherman
Lyrics by Kenneth Robins, Scott Killian
and Kim D. Sherman
Lenny and the Heartbreakers (OB) 1983

I'm a Stranger Here Myself
Music by Kurt Weill
Lyrics by Ogden Nash
One Touch of Venus 1943

I'm a Vamp From East Broadway
Music and lyrics by Irving Berlin, Bert Kalmar
and Harry Ruby
Ziegfeld Follies of 1920

I'm a Woman
Music by Burton Lane
Lyrics by Alan Jay Lerner
Carmelina 1979

I'm a Wonderfully Wicked Woman
Music and lyrics by Harry Chapin
The Night That Made America Famous 1975

I'm About to Be a Mother (Who Could Ask for Anything More?)
Music by George Gershwin
Lyrics by Ira Gershwin
Of Thee I Sing 1931

I'm Afraid
Music by Albert Sirmay
Lyrics by Irving Caesar and Graham John
Ripples 1930

I'm Afraid
Music by Richard Rodgers
Lyrics by Lorenz Hart
Higher And Higher 1940

I'm Afraid I'm in Love
Music by Clay Warnick
Lyrics by Edward Eager
Dream With Music 1944

I'm Afraid of the Dark
Music by Richard Addinsell
Lyrics by Clemence Dane
Come of Age 1934

I'm Afraid, Sweetheart, I Love You
Music and lyrics by Cole Porter
Kiss Me, Kate 1948

Dropped from production

I'm Against Rhythm
Music by Arthur Schwartz
Lyrics by Howard Dietz
Between the Devil 1937

I'm Alive
Music by David Kriovshei
Lyrics by David Paulsen
To Live Another Summer 1971

I'm All Alone
Music by A. Baldwin Sloane
Lyrics by Harry Cort and George E. Stoddard
China Rose 1925

I'm All I've Got
Music by Milton Schafer
Lyrics by Ronny Graham
Bravo Giovanni 1962

I'm All O.K. With K. and E.
Music and lyrics by George M. Cohan
The Man Who Owns Broadway 1909

I'm All Right
Music by Karl Hoschna
Lyrics by Otto Harbach
Madame Sherry 1910

I'm All Smiles
Music by Michael Leonard
Lyrics by Herbert Martin
The Yearling 1965

I'm All Yours
Music by Leo Schumer
Lyrics by Mike Stuart
Alive and Kicking 1950

I'm Alone
Music by Jerome Kern
Lyrics by Oscar Hammerstein II
Music In the Air 1932

The music for this song (with no lyrics) was included among the manuscripts of *The Cat and the Fiddle* with the notation along the side "Save this."

I'm Already Gone
Music by Garry Sherman
Lyrics by Peter Udell
Amen Corner 1983

I'm Always Chasing Rainbows
Music by Harry Carroll
Lyrics by Joseph McCarthy
Oh, Look! 1918

Melodically an adaptation of the middle section of Chopin's Fantaisie Impromptu in C-sharp minor, Op. 66. In 1973 it was interpolated into the score of the Broadway revival of *Irene* and sung by Jane Powell.

I'm Always Happy When I'm in Your Arms
Music and lyrics by Al Wilson, Charles Weinberg and Ken Macomber
Yeah Man 1932

I'm Always Wrong
Music by John Morris
Lyrics by Gerald Freedman
A Time for Singing 1966

I'm an Actor
Music and lyrics by Robert Dennis, Peter Schickele and Stanley Walden
Oh! Calcutta! 1969

I'm an Indian
Music by Leo Edwards
Lyrics by Blanche Merrill
Ziegfeld Follies of 1920

I'm an Indian Too
Music and lyrics by Irving Berlin
Annie Get Your Gun 1946

I'm an International Orphan
Music by Jerome Moross
Lyrics by Paul Peters and George Sklar
Parade (1935)

I'm an Ordinary Man
Music by Frederick Loewe
Lyrics by Alan Jay Lerner
My Fair Lady 1956

I'm a'Tingle, I'm a'Glow
Music by Jule Styne
Lyrics by Leo Robin
Gentlemen Prefer Blondes 1949

I'm Available
Music and lyrics by Bob Ost
Everybody's Gettin' Into the Act (OB) 1981

I'm Back in Circulation
Music by Albert Hague
Lyrics by Dorothy Fields
Redhead 1959

I'm Back in Circulation Again
Music by Michael H. Cleary and Burton Lane
Lyrics by Max and Nathaniel Lief
Earl Carroll's Vanities (1931)

I'm Beautiful
Music by Moose Charlap
Lyrics by Norman Gimbel
The Conquering Hero 1961

I'm Bettin' on You
Music and lyrics by Stephen H. Lemberg
Jazzbo Brown 1980

I'm Betting on You
Music and lyrics by Ann Harris
Sky High (OB) 1979

I'm Blue
Music by Leonard Bernstein
Lyrics by Betty Comden and Adolph Green
On the Town 1944

I'm Blue Too
Music and lyrics by Bob Merrill
Henry, Sweet Henry 1967

I'm Breaking Down
Music and lyrics by William Finn
In Trousers (OB) 1981

I'm Bringing a Red, Red Rose
Music by Walter Donaldson
Lyrics by Gus Kahn
Whoopee 1928

I'm Bugs Over You
Music and lyrics by Gene Buck and Dave Stamper
Ziegfeld Follies of 1923

I'm Calm
Music and lyrics by Stephen Sondheim
*A Funny Thing Happened on the Way
to the Forum* 1962

I'm Comin' Round to Your Point of View
Music by Jimmy Horowitz
Lyrics by Leo Rost and Jimmy Horowitz
Marlowe 1981

I'm Comin', Virginia
Music by Donald Heywood
Lyrics by Will Marion Cook and Donald Heywood
Africana 1927

I'm Coming Home
Music by Jerome Kern
Lyrics by Oscar Hammerstein II
Music in the Air 1932

I'm Craving for That Kind of Love
Music and lyrics by Noble Sissle and Eubie Blake
Shuffle Along 1921

I'm Dreaming
Music by Jerome Kern
Lyrics by Oscar Hammerstein II
Sweet Adeline 1929

Dropped from production

I'm Dreaming of a Wonderful Night
Music by Edmund Eysler
Lyrics by Herbert Reynolds
The Blue Paradise 1915

I'm Dreaming While We're Dancing
Music by Gerald Dolin
Lyrics by Edward J. Lambert
Smile at Me 1935

I'm Everybody's Baby
Music by James Mundy
Lyrics by John Latouche
The Vamp 1955

I'm Falling in Love
Music by Robert Katscher
Lyrics by Irving Caesar
The Wonder Bar 1931

I'm Falling in Love With Some One
Music by Victor Herbert
Lyrics by Rida Johnson Young
Naughty Marietta 1910

I'm Fascinating
Music by Charles Strouse
Lyrics by Lee Adams
All American 1962

I'm Flyin' High
Music and lyrics by Abner Silver, Jack Le Soir
and Roy Doll
Earl Carroll's Vanities (1928)

I'm Flying
Music by Mark Charlap
Lyrics by Carolyn Leigh
Peter Pan 1954

I'm for You
Music by Lee David
Lyrics by J. Keirn Brennan
A Night in Venice 1929

I'm From Chicago
Music by Sigmund Romberg
Lyrics by Herbert Reynolds
The Blue Paradise 1915

I'm From Granada
Music by Mario Braggiotti
Lyrics by David Sidney
The Vanderbilt Revue 1930

I'm Gay
Music and lyrics by Earl Wilson, Jr.
Let My People Come (OB) 1974

I'm Getting Myself Ready for You
Music and lyrics by Cole Porter
The New Yorkers 1930

I'm Getting Tired So I Can Sleep
Music and lyrics by Irving Berlin
This Is the Army 1942

I'm Glad I Waited
Music by Vincent Youmans
Lyrics by Harold Adamson and Clifford Grey
Smiles 1930

I'm Glad I'm Here
Music and lyrics by Barbara Schottenfeld
I Can't Keep Running in Place (OB) 1981

I'm Glad I'm Leaving
Music by Jule Styne
Lyrics by Bob Hilliard
Hazel Flagg 1953

I'm Glad I'm Not a Man
Music by Vernon Duke
Lyrics by Ogden Nash
The Littlest Revue (OB) 1956

I'm Glad I'm Not Young Any More
Music by Frederick Loewe
Lyrics by Alan Jay Lerner
Gigi (1958) F

Also in stage version (1973)

I'm Glad I'm Single
Music by Arthur Schwartz
Lyrics by Howard Dietz
The Gay Life 1961

I'm Glad to See You've Got What You Want
Music by Harvey Schmidt
Lyrics by Tom Jones
Celebration 1969

I'm Glad You Didn't Know Me
Music and lyrics by Craig Carnelia
Is There Life After High School? 1982

I'm Going Back
Music by George Gershwin
Lyrics by B.G. DeSylva
George White's Scandals (1924)

I'm Going Back
Music by Jule Styne
Lyrics by Betty Comden and Adolph Green
Bells Are Ringing 1956

I'm Going Home
Music and lyrics by Gene Curty, Nitra Scharfman
and Chuck Strand
The Lieutenant 1975

I'm Going to Find a Girl
Music by Jerome Kern
Lyrics by P. G. Wodehouse
Leave It to Jane 1917

I'm Gonna
Music by Bill Weeden
Lyrics by David Finkle
Hurry, Harry 1972

I'm Gonna Be a Pop
Music by Fred Stamer
Lyrics by Gen Genovese
Buttrio Square 1952

I'm Gonna Be John Henry
Music by David Martin
Lyrics by Langston Hughes
Simply Heavenly 1957

I'm Gonna Do My Things
Music and lyrics by Voices, Inc.
The Believers (OB) 1968

I'm Gonna Get Him
Music and lyrics by Irving Berlin
Mr. President 1962

I'm Gonna Hang My Hat
Music by Philip Charig
Lyrics by Dan Shapiro and Milton Pascal
Follow the Girls 1944

I'm Gonna Have a Baby
Music by Don McAfee
Lyrics by Nancy Leeds
Great Scot! (OB) 1965

I'm Gonna Leave Off Wearing My Shoes
Music by Harold Arlen
Lyrics by Harold Arlen and Truman Capote
House of Flowers 1954

I'm Gonna Make a Fool out of April
Music by Victor Young
Lyrics by Edward Heyman
Pardon Our French 1950

I'm Gonna Miss Those Tennessee Nights
Music by Harris Wheeler
Lyrics by Mary L. Fisher
Blue Plate Special (OB) 1983

I'm Gonna Move
Music by Albert Hague
Lyrics by Marty Brill
Café Crown 1964

I'm Gonna Pin a Medal on the Girl I Left Behind
Music and lyrics by Irving Berlin
Ziegfeld Follies of 1918

I'm Gonna See My Mother
Music by George Gershwin
Lyrics by B.G. DeSylva and E. Ray Goetz
George White's Scandals (1922)

See note on show

I'm Gonna Take Her Home to Momma
Music by Monty Norman
Lyrics by Julian More
The Moony Shapiro Songbook 1981

I'm Gonna Walk Right up to Her
Music by Moose Charlap
Lyrics by Eddie Lawrence
Kelly 1965

I'm Gonna Wash That Man Right Outa My Hair
Music by Richard Rodgers
Lyrics by Oscar Hammerstein II
South Pacific 1949

I'm Grover
Music by Vernon Duke
Lyrics by Newman Levy
The Garrick Gaieties (3rd edition) 1930

I'm Gwine Lie Down
Music by Al Carmines
Lyrics by Rosalyn Drexler
Home Movies (OB) 1964

I'm Hans Christian Andersen
Music and lyrics by Frank Loesser
Hans Christian Andersen (1952) F

I'm Happy
Music by Armando Trovaioli
Lyrics by Pietro Garinei and Sandro Giovannini
(Lyric translation by Edward Eager)
Rugantino 1964

I'm Harold, I'm Harold
Music by Sigmund Romberg
Lyrics by Arthur Wimperis
Louie the 14th 1925

I'm Here
Music and lyrics by Stephen Sondheim
Evening Primrose (1966) TV

I'm Here, Little Girls, I'm Here
Music by Jerome Kern
Lyrics by P.G. Wodehouse
Have a Heart 1917

I'm High, I'm Low
Music by A. Baldwin Sloane
Lyrics by Harry Cort and George E. Stoddard
China Rose 1925

I'm Home
Music by Galt MacDermot
Lyrics by William Dumaresq
The Human Comedy (OB) 1983

I'm Honest
Music and lyrics by J.C. Johnson
Change Your Luck 1930

I'm in League With the Devil
Music by Louis Bellson and Will Irwin
Lyrics by Richard Ney
Portofino 1958

I'm in Like With You
Music and lyrics by Jack Bussins
and Ellsworth Olin
Be Kind to People Week (OB) 1975

I'm in London Again
Music and lyrics by Marian Grudeff
and Raymond Jessel
Baker Street 1965

I'm in Love
Music by Con Conrad
Lyrics by Gus Kahn and Otto Harbach
Kitty's Kisses 1926

I'm in Love
Music and lyrics by Cole Porter
Fifty Million Frenchmen 1929

I'm in Love
Music by Emile Berté and Maury Rubens
Lyrics by J. Keirn Brennan
Music in May 1929

I'm in Love
Music by Albert T. Viola
Lyrics by William S. Kilborne, Jr.
Head Over Heels 1981

I'm in Love Again
Music and lyrics by Cole Porter
Greenwich Village Follies 1924

I'm in Love! I'm in Love!
Music by Jerry Bock
Lyrics by Sheldon Harnick
The Rothschilds 1970

I'm in Love With a Soldier Boy
Music and lyrics by Cole Porter
Something for the Boys 1943

I'm in Love With a Wonderful Guy
Music by Richard Rodgers
Lyrics by Oscar Hammerstein II
South Pacific 1949

This lyric ("High as the flag on the Fourth of July")
and that of "A Cockeyed Optimist" ("I'm stuck like a
dope with a thing called hope") express eloquently
Hammerstein's outlook on life. In contrast,
Rodgers' former collaborator Lorenz Hart wrote in
the verse of "I Didn't Know What Time It Was,"
"Once I was young, but never was naive," surely as
autobiographical a line as he ever wrote.

I'm in Love With Miss Logan
Music and lyrics by Ronny Graham
New Faces of 1952

I'm in Love With One of the Stars
Music and lyrics by George M. Cohan
The Man Who Owns Broadway 1909

I'm in My Glory
Music by Harry Tierney
Lyrics by Joseph McCarthy
Kid Boots 1923

I'm in the Mood for Love
Music by Jimmy McHugh
Lyrics by Dorothy Fields
Every Night at Eight (1935) F

I'm Just a Little Sparrow
Music by Sammy Fain
Lyrics by Paul Francis Webster
Christine 1960

I'm Just a Little Bit Confused
Music by Harry Warren
Lyrics by Jerome Lawrence and Robert E. Lee
Shangri-La 1956

I'm Just a Sentimental Fool
Music by Sigmund Romberg
Lyrics by Oscar Hammerstein II
The New Moon 1928

Dropped from production

I'm Just a Statistic
Music by Norman Curtis
Lyrics by Patricia Taylor Curtis
Walk Down Mah Street! (OB) 1968

I'm Just Simply Full of Jazz
Music and lyrics by Noble Sissle and Eubie Blake
Shuffle Along 1921

I'm Just Taking My Time
Music by Jule Styne
Lyrics by Betty Comden and Adolph Green
Subways Are for Sleeping 1961

I'm Just Wild About Harry
Music and lyrics by Noble Sissle and Eubie Blake
Shuffle Along 1921

Eubie Blake, who loved to write and play waltzes,
composed this song in 3/4 time. In the show,
however, it was performed in 2/4 time. Although
well-known, it achieved a new lease on life as a
campaign song for Harry S. Truman in his race
against Thomas E. Dewey in the 1948 presidential
campaign.

I'm Keeping Myself Available for You
Music by Jimmy McHugh
Lyrics by Arthur Malvin
Sugar Babies 1979

I'm Lazy
Music and lyrics by Ann Harris
Sky High (OB) 1979

I'm Leaving the Bad Girls for Good
Music by Dave Stamper
Lyrics by Fred Herendeen
Orchids Preferred 1937

I'm Like a New Broom
Music by Arthur Schwartz
Lyrics by Dorothy Fields
A Tree Grows in Brooklyn 1951

I'm Like the Bluebird
Music and lyrics by Stephen Sondheim
Anyone Can Whistle 1964

I'm Lonely
Music by Sigmund Romberg
Lyrics by Oscar Hammerstein II
Viennese Nights (1930) F

I'm Lonely When I'm Alone
Music by Rudolf Friml
Lyrics by Bide Dudley and Otto Harbach
The Little Whopper 1919

I'm Looking for a Daddy Long Legs
Music and lyrics by Irving Berlin
Music Box Revue (2nd edition) 1922

I'm Looking for a Man
Music by Mitch Leigh
Lyrics by N. Richard Nash
Saravá 1979

I'm Lost
Music by George Lessner
Lyrics by Ruth Aarons
Sleepy Hollow 1948

I'm Madame Margaret, the Therapist
Music and lyrics by Al Carmines
Joan (OB) 1972

I'm Me
Music by Glenn Paxton
Lyrics by Robert Goldman and George Weiss
First Impressions 1959

I'm Me! (I'm Not Afraid)
Music and lyrics by Hal Hester and Danny Apolinar
Your Own Thing (OB) 1968

I'm Me, We're Us
Music by Stanley Silverman
Lyrics by Arthur Miller
Up From Paradise (OB) 1983

I'm Mother Nature of You All
Music and lyrics by Ann Harris
Sky High (OB) 1979

I'm Ninety-Eight Pounds of Sweetness
Music by Harry Archer
Lyrics by Walter O'Keefe
Just a Minute 1928

I'm No Butterfly
Music by A. Baldwin Sloane
Lyrics by Harry Cort and George E. Stoddard
China Rose 1925

I'm Not a Well Man
Music and lyrics by Harold Rome
I Can Get It for You Wholesale 1962

I'm Not at All in Love
Music and lyrics by Richard Adler
and Jerry Ross
The Pajama Game 1954

I'm Not Finished Yet
Music by Charles Strouse
Lyrics by Lee Adams
It's a Bird, It's a Plane, It's Superman 1966

I'm Not for You
Music and lyrics by Rick Besoyan
Babes in the Wood (OB) 1964

I'm Not Getting Any Younger
Music by Kenneth Jacobson
Lyrics by Rhoda Roberts
Show Me Where the Good Times Are (OB) 1970

I'm Not in Love
Music and lyrics by Charles Gaynor
Lend an Ear 1948

I'm Not Myself Tonight
Music by David Raksin
Lyrics by June Carroll
If the Shoe Fits 1946

I'm Not Old
Music and lyrics by Mel Mandel
and Norman Sachs
My Old Friends (OB) 1979

I'm Not So Bright
Music and lyrics by Hugh Martin
Look Ma, I'm Dancin'! 1948

I'm Not Through
Music and lyrics by Michael Brown
Different Times 1972

I'm Old Fashioned
Music by Jerome Kern
Lyrics by Johnny Mercer
You Were Never Lovelier (1942) F

Johnny Mercer's lyrics ranged the entire spectrum of popular music. There are out-and-out popular hits such as "Jeepers Creepers" and "I'm An Old Cowhand" (for which he also wrote the music) and the more thoughtful "Moon River" and "My Shining Hour." Of all of them—and he left us at least fifty of what the industry calls "standard songs"—he felt that "I'm Old Fashioned" came closest to expressing his own outlook on life.

I'm on My Own
Music and lyrics by Barbara Schottenfeld
I Can't Keep Running in Place (OB) 1981

I'm on My Way
Music by George Gershwin
Lyrics by DuBose Heyward
Porgy and Bess 1935

I'm on My Way
Music by Frederick Loewe
Lyrics by Alan Jay Lerner
Paint Your Wagon 1951

I'm on My Way to the Top
Music and lyrics by Hal Hester and Danny Apolinar
Your Own Thing (OB) 1968

I'm on the Crest of a Wave
Music by Ray Henderson
Lyrics by B.G. DeSylva and Lew Brown
George White's Scandals (1928)

I'm on the Lookout
Music and lyrics by Charles Gaynor
Lend an Ear 1948

I'm on Your Side
Music by Frederick Loewe
Lyrics by Alan Jay Lerner
The Little Prince (1975) F

I'm One Little Party
Music by Harry Ruby
Lyrics by Bert Kalmar
The Five o'Clock Girl 1927

I'm One of God's Children
Music by Louis Alter
Lyrics by Oscar Hammerstein II and Harry Ruskin
Ballyhoo 1930

I'm One of the Boys
Music by Richard Rodgers
Lyrics by Lorenz Hart
Hollywood Party (1934) F

Dropped from production

I'm One of Your Admirers
Music by Jimmy Van Heusen
Lyrics by Johnny Burke
Carnival in Flanders 1953

I'm Only a Fair Sun Bather
Music by Kerry Mills
Lyrics by S. M. Lewis
The Fascinating Widow 1911

I'm Only Dreaming
Music by Rudolf Friml
Lyrics by Otto Harbach and Edward Clark
You're In Love 1917

I'm Only Thinking of Him
Music by Mitch Leigh
Lyrics by Joe Darion
Man of La Mancha 1965

I'm Part of You
Music by Arthur Schwartz
Lyrics by Howard Dietz
A Bell For Adano (1956) TV

I'm Physical, You're Cultured
Music by John Green
Lyrics by George Marion, Jr.
Beat the Band 1942

I'm Putting All My Eggs in One Basket
Music and lyrics by Irving Berlin
Follow the Fleet (1936) F

I'm Ready
Music and lyrics by Oscar Brand
and Paul Nassau
A Joyful Noise 1966

I'm Ready Now!
Music by Steve Jankowski
Lyrics by Kenny Morris
Francis (OB) 1982

I'm Really Not That Way
Music by Will Irwin
Lyrics by Malcolm McComb
Hey Nonny Nonny! 1932

I'm Ridin' for a Fall
Music by Arthur Schwartz
Lyrics by Frank Loesser
Thank Your Lucky Stars (1943) F

I'm Saving My Kisses
Music by Louis A. Hirsch
Lyrics by Harold Atteridge
The Whirl of Society 1912

I'm Saving Myself for a Soldier
Music by Edward Thomas
Lyrics by Martin Charnin
Ballad for a Firing Squad (OB) 1968

I'm Sick of the Whole Damn Problem
Music and lyrics by C. Jackson and James Hatch
Fly Blackbird (OB) 1962

I'm Single for Six Weeks More
Music by Ivan Caryll
Lyrics by C.M.S. McLellan
The Pink Lady 1911

I'm Small
Music by Galt MacDermot
Lyrics by Gerome Ragni
Dude 1972

I'm So Busy
Music by Jerome Kern
Lyrics by P.G. Wodehouse
Have a Heart 1917

I'm So Excited
Music by Louis A. Hirsch
Lyrics by Otto Harbach
The O'Brien Girl 1921

I'm So Humble
Music by Richard Rodgers
Lyrics by Lorenz Hart
Peggy-Ann 1926

I'm So in Love
Music by Will Irwin
Lyrics by Norman Zeno
Fools Rush In 1934

I'm So in Love With You
Music and lyrics by Cole Porter
Broadway Melody of 1940 F

Dropped from film

I'm So Weary of It All
Music and lyrics by Noël Coward
Set to Music 1939

I'm Someone Now
Music by Michael Dansicker
Lyrics by Sarah Schlesinger
On the Swing Shift (OB) 1983

I'm Something on Avenue A
Music by George Gershwin
Lyrics by B.G. DeSylva and Ira Gershwin
Tell Me More 1925

Dropped from production

I'm Sorry Says the Machine
Music by Helen Miller
Lyrics by Eve Merriam
Inner City 1971

I'm Stepping Out of the Picture
Music by Harry Akst
Lyrics by Lew Brown
Calling All Stars 1934

I'm Still Here
Music and lyrics by Stephen Sondheim
Follies 1971

I'm Stuck With Love
Music by Gordon Duffy
Lyrics by Harry M. Haldane
Happy Town 1959

I'm Sure of Your Love
Music by Morton Gould
Lyrics by Betty Comden and Adolph Green
Billion Dollar Baby 1945

I'm Taking the Steps to Russia
Music and lyrics by Cole Porter
Leave It to Me 1938

I'm Talking to My Pal
Music by Richard Rodgers
Lyrics by Lorenz Hart
Pal Joey 1940

Dropped from production

I'm Telling You, Louie
Music by Jerome Moross
Lyrics by Paul Peters and George Sklar
Parade (1935)

I'm That Way Over You
Music by J. Fred Coots
Lyrics by Arthur Swanstrom and Benny Davis
Sons o' Guns 1929

I'm the Boy You Should Say "Yes" To
Music by John Addison
Lyrics by John Cranko
Cranks 1956

I'm the Bravest Individual
Music by Cy Coleman
Lyrics by Dorothy Fields
Sweet Charity 1966

I'm the Echo (You're the Song that I Sing)
Music by Jerome Kern
Lyrics by Dorothy Fields
I Dream Too Much (1935) F

I'm the Extra Man
Music by Rudolf Friml
Lyrics by Otto Harbach and Oscar Hammerstein II
The Wild Rose 1926

Dropped from production

I'm the Fellow Who Loves You
Music by Ray Henderson
Lyrics by Jack Yellen
George White's Scandals (1936)

I'm the First Girl
Music and lyrics by Hugh Martin
Look Ma, I'm Dancin'! 1948

I'm the Girl
Music and lyrics by James Shelton
Dance Me a Song 1950

I'm the Greatest Star
Music by Jule Styne
Lyrics by Bob Merrill
Funny Girl 1964

I'm the Guy Who Guards the Harem
Music and lyrics by Irving Berlin
Ziegfeld Follies of 1919

I'm the Woman You Wanted
Music by Arthur Siegel
Lyrics by Mae Richard
Tallulah (OB) 1983

I'm Thinking of Love
Music by Robert Stolz
Lyrics by Rowland Leigh
Night of Love 1941

I'm Through With War
Music by Shep Camp
Lyrics by Frank DuPree and Harry B. Smith
Half a Widow 1927

I'm Throwing a Ball Tonight
Music and lyrics by Cole Porter
Panama Hattie 1940

I'm Tickled Pink
Music and lyrics by Harold Orlob
Hairpin Harmony 1943

I'm Tickled Silly
Music by Vincent Youmans and Paul Lannin
Lyrics by Arthur Francis
Two Little Girls in Blue 1921

I'm Tired of Texas
Music and lyrics by Hugh Martin
Look Ma, I'm Dancin'! 1948

I'm To Be a Blushing Bride
Music by Kerry Mills
Lyrics by S.M. Lewis
The Fascinating Widow 1911

I'm to Blame
Music by Joseph Raposo
Lyrics by Erich Segal
Sing Muse! (OB) 1961

I'm Unlucky at Gambling
Music and lyrics by Cole Porter
Fifty Million Frenchmen 1929

I'm Waiting for a Wonderful Girl
Music by Vincent Youmans
Lyrics by Anne Caldwell
Oh, Please! 1926

I'm Waiting for You
See Waiting for You

I'm Walkin' the Chalk Line
Music by Alberta Nichols
Lyrics by Mann Holiner
Blackbirds of 1934

I'm Way Ahead
Music by Cy Coleman
Lyrics by Dorothy Fields
Seesaw 1973

I'm Way Ahead of the Game
Music by Robert Emmett Dolan
Lyrics by Johnny Mercer
Foxy 1964

I'm With You
Music by Jule Styne
Lyrics by Betty Comden and Adolph Green
Fade Out—Fade In 1964

I'm Worse Than Anybody
Music by John Kander
Lyrics by James Goldman, John Kander
and William Goldman
A Family Affair 1962

I'm You
Music by Irving Actman
Lyrics by Frank Loesser
The Illustrators' Show 1936

I'm Your Girl
Music by Richard Rodgers
Lyrics by Oscar Hammerstein II
Me and Juliet 1953

I'm Your Man
Music by Kurt Weill
Lyrics by Alan Jay Lerner
Love Life 1948

I'm Your Valentine
Music by Sol Berkowitz
Lyrics by James Lipton
Miss Emily Adam (OB) 1960

I'm Yours
Music and lyrics by Cole Porter
You Never Know 1938

Dropped from production

The Image of Me
Music by Burton Lane
Lyrics by Alan Jay Lerner
Carmelina 1979

Imagination
Music by Joseph Meyer and Roger Wolfe Kahn
Lyrics by Irving Caesar
Here's Howe 1928

Imagine
Music by Richard Rodgers
Lyrics by Lorenz Hart
Babes in Arms 1937

Imagine My Finding You Here
Music by Ned Lehak
Lyrics by Robert Sour
Sing for Your Supper 1939

Imagine That
Music by Laurence Rosenthal
Lyrics by James Lipton
Sherry! 1967

Immigration Rose
Music by Jimmy McHugh
Lyrics by Eugene West and Irwin Dash
Sugar Babies 1979

The Impeachment Waltz
Music and lyrics by Don Tucker
Red, White and Maddox 1969

An Imperial Conference
Music by Bronislaw Kaper (based on Chopin)
Lyrics by John Latouche
Polonaise 1945

Impossible
Music by Richard Rodgers
Lyrics by Oscar Hammerstein II
Cinderella (1957) TV

Impossible
Music and lyrics by Stephen Sondheim
*A Funny Thing Happened on the Way
to the Forum* 1962

The Impossible Dream (The Quest)
Music by Mitch Leigh
Lyrics by Joe Darion
Man of La Mancha 1965

The Impossible She
Music by James Mundy
Lyrics by John Latouche
The Vamp 1955

In a Brownstone Mansion
Music by Sol Kaplan
Lyrics by Edward Eliscu
The Banker's Daughter (OB) 1962

In a Cozy Little Kitchenette Apartment
Music and lyrics by Irving Berlin
Music Box Revue (1st edition) 1921

In a Garden
Music by Ann Sternberg
Lyrics by Gertrude Stein
Gertrude Stein's First Reader (OB) 1969

In a Gondola With You
Music and lyrics by Vincent Valentini
Parisiana 1928

In a Great Big Way
Music by Jimmy McHugh
Lyrics by Dorothy Fields
Hello Daddy 1928

In a Hurry
Music by Rudolf Friml
Lyrics by Otto Harbach
Katinka 1915

In a Kingdom of Our Own
Music and lyrics by George M. Cohan
The Royal Vagabond 1919

In a Little Stucco in the Sticks
Music by Harry Revel
Lyrics by Mack Gordon
Smiling Faces 1932

In a Little Swiss Chalet
Music by Will Irwin
Lyrics by Norman Zeno
White Horse Inn 1936

In a Little Town in California
Music by Galt MacDermot
Lyrics by William Dumaresq
The Human Comedy (OB) 1983

In a Little While
Music by Will Ortman
Lyrics by Gus Kahn and Raymond B. Egan
Holka-Polka 1925

In a Little While
Music by Mary Rodgers
Lyrics by Marshall Barer
Once Upon a Mattress 1959

In a Little World for Two
Music by Victor Herbert
Lyrics by Henry Blossom
The Princess Pat 1915

In a Month or Two
Music by Louis A. Hirsch
Lyrics by Rennold Wolf
The Rainbow Girl 1918

In a Pretty Little White House of Our Own
Music by Leo Edwards
Lyrics by Blanche Merrill
Ziegfeld Follies of 1912

In a Simple Way I Love You
Music by Nancy Ford

Lyrics by Gretchen Cryer
*I'm Getting My Act Together and Taking It
on the Road* 1978

In a Story Book
Music by George Fischoff
Lyrics by Verna Tomasson
The Prince and the Pauper (OB) 1963

In an Oriental Way
Music by Ivan Caryll
Lyrics by Anne Caldwell and James O'Dea
Chin-Chin 1914

In April
Music by Gary William Friedman
Lyrics by Will Holt
Taking My Turn (OB) 1983

In Araby With You
Music by Jerome Kern
Lyrics by Anne Caldwell and Otto Harbach
Criss-Cross 1926

See note on "I Can't Forget Your Eyes"

In Arcady
Music by Jerome Kern
Lyrics by Herbert Reynolds
Nobody Home 1915

In Armenia
Music by Oscar Straus
Lyrics by Harry B. Smith
Naughty Riquette 1926

In Between
Music by Frederick Loewe
Lyrics by Alan Jay Lerner
Paint Your Wagon 1951

In Between
Music and lyrics by Peter Link and C.C. Courtney
Salvation (OB) 1969

In Buddy's Eyes
Music and lyrics by Stephen Sondheim
Follies 1971

In Cahoots
Music and lyrics by Kelly Hamilton
Trixie True Teen Detective (OB) 1980

In Californ-i-a
Music by Richard Rodgers
Lyrics by Lorenz Hart
America's Sweetheart 1931

In Central Park
Music by Harold Orlob
Lyrics by Irving Caesar
Talk About Girls 1927

In Chichicastenango
Music by Jay Gorney
Lyrics by Henry Myers
Meet the People 1940

In Chinatown in Frisco
Music by Maurice Yvain
Lyrics by Clifford Grey and McElbert Moore
A Night in Paris 1926

In Dahomey
Music by Jerome Kern
Lyrics by Oscar Hammerstein II
Show Boat 1927

In Dreams Begin Responsibilities
Music and lyrics by Elizabeth Swados
Nightclub Cantata (OB) 1977

In Egern on the Tegern See
Music by Jerome Kern
Lyrics by Oscar Hammerstein II
Music in the Air 1932

In Endless Waiting Rooms
Music and lyrics by Gian-Carlo Menotti
The Consul 1950

In Erin's Isle
Music by Victor Herbert
Lyrics by Henry Blossom
Eileen 1917

In Florida Among the Palms
Music and lyrics by Irving Berlin
Ziegfeld Follies of 1916

In Heidelberg Fair
Music by Sigmund Romberg
Lyrics by Dorothy Donnelly
The Student Prince 1924

In Hennequeville
Music by Victor Herbert
Lyrics by B.G. DeSylva
Orange Blossoms 1922

In His Arms
Music by Richard Rodgers
Lyrics by Lorenz Hart
Peggy-Ann 1926

In His Own Good Time
Music by Garry Sherman
Lyrics by Peter Udell
Amen Corner 1983

In Honeysuckle Time
Music and lyrics by Noble Sissle and Eubie Blake
Shuffle Along 1921

In Izzenschnooken on the Lovely Essenzook Zee
Music and lyrics by Rick Besoyan
Little Mary Sunshine (OB) 1959

In Jail
Music by Jean Gilbert
Lyrics by Harry Graham
Katja 1926

In Louisiana
Music by Jimmy McHugh
Lyrics by Arthur Malvin
Sugar Babies 1979

In Love in Vain
Music by Jerome Kern
Lyrics by Leo Robin
Centennial Summer (1946) F

In Love With a Fool
Music by Ernest Gold
Lyrics by Anne Croswell
I'm Solomon 1968

In Love With Love
Music by Jerome Kern
Lyrics by Anne Caldwell
Stepping Stones 1923

In Love With Romance
Music by Sigmund Romberg
Lyrics by Rowland Leigh
My Romance 1948

In Loving Memory
Music by Robert Emmett Dolan
Lyrics by Johnny Mercer
Foxy 1964

In Marsovia
Music by Franz Lehár
Lyrics by Adrian Ross
The Merry Widow 1907

In My Arms Again
Music by Albert Von Tilzer
Lyrics by Neville Fleeson
Bye Bye, Bonnie 1927

In My Castle in Sorrento
Music by Abel Baer
Lyrics by Sam Lewis and Joe Young
Lady Do 1927

In My Garden
Music by Sigmund Romberg
Lyrics by Irving Caesar
Melody 1933

In My Love Boat
Music by Ray Perkins
Lyrics by Max and Nathaniel Lief
Say When 1928

In My Own Lifetime
Music by Jerry Bock
Lyrics by Sheldon Harnick
The Rothschilds 1970

In My Own Little Corner
Music by Richard Rodgers
Lyrics by Oscar Hammerstein II
Cinderella (1957) TV

In My Silent Universe
Music and lyrics by Al Carmines
Joan (OB) 1972

In No Time at All
Music by Sammy Fain
Lyrics by Marilyn and Alan Bergman
Something More 1964

In Nomine Dei
Music by Wally Harper
Lyrics by Paul Zakrzewski
Sensations (OB) 1970

In Old Mexico
Music and lyrics by Tom Lehrer
Tomfoolery (OB) 1981

In Old New York

See The Streets of New York

In Other Words, Seventeen
Music by Jerome Kern
Lyrics by Oscar Hammerstein II
Very Warm for May 1939

In Our Childhood's Bright Endeavor
Music by Kurt Weill
Lyrics by Bertolt Brecht (adapted by Michael
Feingold)
Happy End 1977

In Our Cozy Little Cottage of Tomorrow
Music by Harry Revel
Lyrics by Arnold B. Horwitt
Are You With It? 1945

In Our Hide-Away
Music and lyrics by Irving Berlin
Mr. President 1962

In Our Little Home, Sweet Home
Music by Sigmund Romberg
Lyrics by Rida Johnson Young
Maytime 1917

In Our Mountain Bower
Music by Monte Carlo and Alma Sanders
Lyrics by Howard Johnson
Tangerine 1921

In Our Own Little Salon
Music by Joseph Raposo
Lyrics by Erich Segal
Sing Muse! (OB) 1961

In Our Parlor on the Third Floor Back
Music by Richard Rodgers
Lyrics by Lorenz Hart
Betsy 1926

In Our Teeny Little Weeny Nest for Two
Music and lyrics by Charles Gaynor
Lend an Ear 1948

Later used in *Show Girl* 1961

In Our United State
Music by Burton Lane
Lyrics by Ira Gershwin
Give a Girl a Break (1953) F

In Paris and in Love
Music by Sigmund Romberg (developed by
Don Walker)
Lyrics by Leo Robin
The Girl in Pink Tights 1954

In Praise of Women
Music and lyrics by Stephen Sondheim
A Little Night Music 1973

In Real Life
Music and lyrics by Skip Redwine and Larry Frank
Frank Merriwell, or Honor Challenged 1971

In Romany
Music and lyrics by Ben Schwartz
Tales of Rigo 1927

In Ruritania
Music by Sigmund Romberg
Lyrics by Harry B. Smith
Princess Flavia 1925

In Sardinia
Music by George Gershwin
Lyrics by B.G. DeSylva and Ira Gershwin
Tell Me More 1925

In Society
Music by Franz Lehár
Lyrics by Basil Hood
The Count of Luxembourg 1912

In Some Little World
Music and lyrics by Bob Merrill
Henry, Sweet Henry 1967

In Someone Else's Sandals
Music by Ernest Gold
Lyrics by Anne Croswell
I'm Solomon 1968

In the Arms of a Stranger
Music and lyrics by Ron Dante
and Gene Allan
Billy 1969

In the Back of a Hack
Music by Jay Gorney
Lyrics by Barry Trivers
Heaven on Earth 1948

In the Bath
Music by Donald Swann
Lyrics by Michael Flanders
At the Drop of a Hat 1959

In the Beautiful Garden of Girls
Music by Raymond Hubbell
Lyrics by Dave Stamper
Ziegfeld Follies of 1917

In the Carefree Realm of Fancy
Music by Frederick Loewe
Lyrics by Earle Crooker
Great Lady 1938

In the Clouds
Music by Rudolf Friml
Lyrics by J. Keirn Brennan
Luana 1930

In the Convent They Never Taught Me That
Music by Victor Herbert
Lyrics by Robert B. Smith
Sweethearts 1913

In the Country Where I Come From
Music by Michael Valenti
Lyrics by John Lewin
Blood Red Roses 1970

In the Dark
Music by William B. Kernell
Lyrics by Dorothy Donnelly
Hello, Lola 1926

In the Days Gone By
Music by Emmerich Kálmán
Lyrics by Harry B. Smith
Countess Maritza 1926

In the Days Gone By
Music by Walter G. Samuels
Lyrics by Morrie Ryskind
Ned Wayburn's Gambols 1929

In the Days of Wild Romance
Music by William Daly and Paul Lannin
Lyrics by Arthur Jackson
For Goodness Sake 1922

In the Desert
Music by Donald Swann
Lyrics by Michael Flanders
At the Drop of Another Hat 1966

In the Gardens of Noor-Ed-Deen
Music by Harry Tierney
Lyrics by Joseph McCarthy
Cross My Heart 1928

In the Heart of Spain
Music by Philip Charig and Richard Myers
Lyrics by Leo Robin
Allez-Oop 1927

In the Heart of the Dark
Music by Jerome Kern
Lyrics by Oscar Hammerstein II
Very Warm for May 1939

In the House
Music by Gary William Friedman
Lyrics by Will Holt
Taking My Turn (OB) 1983

In the Land of Sunny Sunflowers
Music by Eubie Blake
Lyrics by Noble Sissle
Shuffle Along of 1933

In the Land of Yesterday
Music by Sigmund Romberg
Lyrics by Alex Gerber
Poor Little Ritz Girl 1920

In the Life
Music and lyrics by Elizabeth Swados
Lullabye and Goodnight 1982

In the Lobby
Music by Gordon Jenkins
Lyrics by Tom Adair
Along Fifth Avenue 1949

In the Long Run
Music by Abel Baer
Lyrics by Sam Lewis and Joe Young
Lady Do 1927

In the Meantime
Music by Ray Henderson
Lyrics by B.G. DeSylva and Lew Brown
Good News 1927

In the Merry Month of Maybe
Music by Harry Warren
Lyrics by Ira Gershwin and Billy Rose
Crazy Quilt 1931

In the Middle of the Night
Music by Arthur Schwartz
Lyrics by Howard Dietz
Revenge With Music 1934

In the Morning
Music by David Raksin
Lyrics by June Carroll
If the Shoe Fits 1946

In the Morning
Music and lyrics by Ronny Graham
New Faces of 1962

In the Noonday Sun
Music by Arthur Schwartz
Lyrics by Howard Dietz
Revenge With Music 1934

In the Prison
Music by Stan Harte, Jr.
Leaves of Grass (OB) 1971

In the Real World
Music by Garry Sherman
Lyrics by Peter Udell
Amen Corner 1983

In the Reign of Chaim
Music by Menachem Zur
Lyrics by Herbert Appleman
Unfair to Goliath (OB) 1970

In the Rough
Music by Harry Tierney
Lyrics by Joseph McCarthy
Kid Boots 1923

In the Same Way I Love You
Music by H. M. Tennent
Lyrics by Eric Little
By the Way 1925

In the Shade of a Sheltering Tree
Music and lyrics by Irving Berlin
Music Box Revue (4th edition) 1924

In the Shade of the New Apple Tree
Music by Harold Arlen
Lyrics by E.Y. Harburg
Hooray for What! 1937

In the Slums of the Town
Music and lyrics by George M. Cohan
The Rise of Rosie O'Reilly 1923

In the Spring
Music by Adorjan Otvos
Lyrics by Ballard MacDonald
Battling Buttler 1923

In the Starlight
Music by Emmerich Kálmán
Lyrics by B.G. DeSylva
The Yankee Princess 1922

In the Still of the Night
Music and lyrics by Cole Porter
Rosalie (1937) F

In the Stretch
Music and lyrics by Alexander Hill
Hummin' Sam 1933

In the Summer
Music by Harry Ruby
Lyrics by Bert Kalmar
Top Speed 1929

In the Swim
Music by Harry Tierney
Lyrics by Joseph McCarthy
Kid Boots 1923

In the Swim
Music by George Gershwin
Lyrics by Ira Gershwin
Funny Face 1927

In the Very Next Moment
Music by Laurence Rosenthal
Lyrics by James Lipton
Sherry! 1967

In the Waldorf Halls
Music and lyrics by George M. Cohan
The Man Who Owns Broadway 1909

In This Wide Wide World
Music by Frederick Loewe
Lyrics by Alan Jay Lerner
Gigi (stage version, 1973)

In Those Good Old Horsecar Days
Music by Will Irwin
Lyrics by Malcolm McComb
Hey Nonny Nonny! 1932

In Time
Music by Leon Pober
Lyrics by Bud Freeman
Beg, Borrow or Steal 1960

In Time
Music by Richard Rodgers
Lyrics by Sheldon Harnick
Rex 1976

In Times Like These
Music by Ernest G. Schweikert
Lyrics by Frank Reardon
Rumple 1957

In Times of Tumult and War
Music by Kurt Weill
Lyrics by Paul Green
Johnny Johnson 1936

In Tune
Music by Cy Coleman
Lyrics by Dorothy Fields
Seesaw 1973

In Twos
Music by Harold Orlob
Lyrics by Irving Caesar
Talk About Girls 1927

In Variety
Music by Richard Rodgers
Lyrics by Lorenz Hart
Betsy 1926

Dropped from production

In Vaudeville
Music by Lucien Denni
Lyrics by Helena Evans
Happy Go Lucky 1926

In Vino Veritas
Music and lyrics by Ervin Drake
Her First Roman 1968

In Waikiki
Music by Sammy Fain
Lyrics by Jack Yellen
George White's Scandals (1939)

In Yorkshire
Music by Lionel Monckton
Lyrics by Lionel Monckton and Ralph Roberts
Our Miss Gibbs 1910

In Your Chapeau
Music by Richard Rodgers
Lyrics by Lorenz Hart
Simple Simon 1930

In Your Defense
Music by Paul A. Rubens
Lyrics by Paul A. Rubens and Arthur Wimperis
The Sunshine Girl 1913

In Your Eyes
Music by Jerry Livingston
Lyrics by Leonard Adelson
Molly 1973

Incantation
Music by Susan Hulsman Bingham
Lyrics by Myrna Lamb
Mod Donna (OB) 1970

Inchworm
Music and lyrics by Frank Loesser
Hans Christian Andersen (1952) F

The Incinerator Hour
Music by Mildred Kayden
Lyrics by Frank Gagliano
Paradise Gardens East (OB) 1969

Incompatibility
Music by Harold Arlen
Lyrics by E.Y. Harburg
Jamaica 1957

Incomprehensible
Music by Robert Kole
Lyrics by Sandi Merle
I Take These Women (OB) 1982

The Incorporation
Music by Susan Hulsman Bingham
Lyrics by Myrna Lamb
Mod Donna (OB) 1970

Indecision
Music and lyrics by Elizabeth Swados
Nightclub Cantata (OB) 1977

Independence Day Hora
Music and lyrics by Jerry Herman
Milk and Honey 1961

Independent
Music by Jule Styne
Lyrics by Betty Comden and Adolph Green
Bells Are Ringing 1956

The Indian Benefit Ball
Music and lyrics by Al Carmines
Wanted (OB) 1972

Indian Blues
Music by Claibe Richardson
Lyrics by Kenward Elmslie
The Grass Harp 1971

Indian Fox Trot
Music by Jerome Kern
Lyrics by Berton Braley
Toot-Toot! 1918

Indian Love Call
Music by Rudolf Friml
Lyrics by Oscar Hammerstein II and Otto Harbach
Rose Marie 1924

When *Rose Marie* was first produced in London, this now famous song was as yet unknown. Oscar Hammerstein reported that at an understudy audition for the leading lady, one young soprano looked at the sheet music which read "When I'm Calling You-oo-oo-oo-oo-oo-oo" and sweetly warbled "When I'm Calling You—Double-oh, double-oh!"

Indian Lullaby
Music by Rudolf Friml
Lyrics by Brian Hooker
The White Eagle 1927

Indians
Music by Mark Charlap
Lyrics by Carolyn Leigh
Peter Pan 1954

The Indictment
Music and lyrics by Gene Curty, Nitra Scharfman and Chuck Strand
The Lieutenant 1975

Individuals
Music by Jerry Alters
Lyrics by Herb Hartig
Fallout (OB) 1959

Inevitably Me
Music and lyrics by Ken Welch
Shoestring Revue (1955) (OB)

Infatuation
Music by Michael Cleary
Lyrics by Arthur Swanstrom
Sea Legs 1937

Initials
Music by Galt MacDermot
Lyrics by Gerome Ragni and James Rado
Hair 1968

Inner Peace
Music by Charles Strouse
Lyrics by Lee Adams
Bring Back Birdie 1981

Inner Thoughts
Music by Charles Strouse
Lyrics by Lee Adams
Applause 1970

Innocent Chorus Girls of Yesterday
Music by Richard Rodgers
Lyrics by Lorenz Hart
America's Sweetheart 1931

Innocent Ingenue Baby
Music by George Gershwin
Lyrics by Brian Hooker
Our Nell 1922

Insane Poontang
Music and lyrics by C.C. Courtney
and Ragan Courtney
Earl of Ruston 1971

The Inside Story
Music by John Green
Lyrics by Edward Heyman
Here Goes the Bride 1931

Inside U.S.A
Music by Arthur Schwartz
Lyrics by Howard Dietz
Inside U.S.A. 1948

Inspection
Music by Leo Fall
Lyrics by George Grossmith
The Dollar Princess 1909

Instead-of Song
Music by Kurt Weill
Lyrics by Marc Blitzstein
The Threepenny Opera (OB) 1954

Interesting Use of Space
Music by Scott Killian and Kim D. Sherman
Lyrics by Kenneth Robins, Scott Killian
and Kim D. Sherman
Lenny and the Heartbreakers (OB) 1983

Intermission Talk
Music by Richard Rodgers
Lyrics by Oscar Hammerstein II
Me and Juliet 1953

International Rhythm
Music by Jimmy McHugh
Lyrics by Dorothy Fields
Lew Leslie's International Revue 1930

International Vamp
Music by Jean Schwartz
Lyrics by Alfred Bryan
A Night in Spain 1927

An Interrupted Love Song
Music by Sigmund Romberg
Lyrics by Oscar Hammerstein II
The New Moon 1928

Into Society
Music by Milton Susskind
Lyrics by Paul Porter and Benjamin Hapgood Burt
Florida Girl 1925

Into the Night
Music by Robert Stolz
Lyrics by Robert Sour
Mr. Strauss Goes to Boston 1945

Intoxication
Music by Dean Fuller
Lyrics by Marshall Barer
Ziegfeld Follies (1957)

The Intriguers
Music by Ivan Caryll
Lyrics by C.M.S. McLellan
The Pink Lady 1911

Introducin' Mr. Paris
Music by Jerome Moross
Lyrics by John Latouche
The Golden Apple 1954

The Invisible Man
Music and lyrics by Charles Strouse
Six (OB) 1971

An Invitation
Music by Vincent Youmans
Lyrics by Edward Heyman
Through the Years 1932

Invitation
Music by Susan Hulsman Bingham
Lyrics by Myrna Lamb
Mod Donna (OB) 1970

The Invitation to the Jellicle Ball
Music by Andrew Lloyd Webber
Cats 1982

Lyrics based on T.S. Eliot's *Old Possum's Book of Practical Cats*

Inza
Music and lyrics by Skip Redwine and Larry Frank
Frank Merriwell, or Honor Challenged 1971

Iowa Stubborn
Music and lyrics by Meredith Willson
The Music Man 1957

Ira, My Dope Fiend
Music and lyrics by Al Carmines
Joan (OB) 1972

An Irate Pirate Am I
Music by Alma Sanders
Lyrics by Monte Carlo
The Houseboat on the Styx 1928

Ireland Was Never Like This
Music by Sammy Fain
Lyrics by Paul Francis Webster
Christine 1960

Irene
Music by Harry Tierney
Lyrics by Joseph McCarthy
Irene 1919

Irish Ballad
Music and lyrics by Tom Lehrer
Tomfoolery (OB) 1981

An Irish Girl
Music by Otis Clements
Lyrics by Charles Gaynor
Irene (1973 revival)

The Irish Have a Great Day Tonight
Music by Victor Herbert
Lyrics by Henry Blossom
Eileen 1917

Irma la Douce
Music by Marguerite Monnot
Lyrics by Julian More, David Heneker
and Monte Norman
Irma la Douce 1960

Iron! Iron! Iron!
Music by Victor Herbert
Lyrics by Robert B. Smith
Sweethearts 1913

Irresistible You
Music by Jimmy Monaco
Lyrics by Billy Rose and Ballard MacDonald
Harry Delmar's Revels 1927

Is Anybody There?
Music and lyrics by Sherman Edwards
1776 1969

Is Everybody Happy Now?
Music by Maury Rubens
Lyrics by Jack Osterman and Ted Lewis
Artists and Models (1927)

Is He the Only Man in the World?
Music and lyrics by Irving Berlin
Mr. President 1962

Is It a Crime?
Music by Jule Styne
Lyrics by Betty Comden and Adolph Green
Bells Are Ringing 1956

Is It a Dream?
Music by Erich Wolfgang Korngold (based on
Jacques Offenbach)
Lyrics by Herbert Baker
Helen Goes to Troy 1944

Is It Any Wonder?
Music by Alma Sanders
Lyrics by Monte Carlo
Oh! Oh! Nurse 1925

Is It Art?
Music and lyrics by Alan Menken
Real Life Funnies (OB) 1981

Is It Him or Is It Me?
Music by Kurt Weill
Lyrics by Alan Jay Lerner
Love Life 1948

Is It Joy?
Music and lyrics by Cole Porter
Les Girls (1957) F

Dropped from film

Is It Love?
Music by Oscar Levant
Lyrics by Irving Caesar and Graham John
Ripples 1930

Is It Possible?
Music by Jimmy McHugh
Lyrics by Al Dubin
The Streets of Paris 1939

Is It Really Me?
Music by Harvey Schmidt
Lyrics by Tom Jones
110 in the Shade 1963

Is It the Girl?
Music and lyrics by Cole Porter
Seven Lively Arts 1944

Is It the Uniform?
Music by Richard Rodgers
Lyrics by Lorenz Hart
Present Arms 1928

Is Izzy Azzy Woz?
Music and lyrics by Cliff Friend and George White
George White's Scandals (1929)

Is My Girl Refined?
Music by Richard Rodgers
Lyrics by Lorenz Hart
Betsy 1926

Dropped from production

Is Rhythm Necessary?
Music by Sammy Fain
Lyrics by Irving Kahal
Everybody's Welcome 1931

Is That My Prince?
Music by Arthur Schwartz
Lyrics by Dorothy Fields
A Tree Grows in Brooklyn 1951

Is There Some Place for Me?
Music by Alfred Brooks
Lyrics by Ira J. Bilowit
Of Mice and Men (OB) 1958

Is There Something to What He Said?
Music and lyrics by Johnny Brandon
Cindy (OB) 1964

Is This a Fact?
Music by Edward Thomas
Lyrics by Martin Charnin
Ballad for a Firing Squad (OB) 1968

Is This My Town?
Music and lyrics by Bob Goodman
Wild and Wonderful 1971

Is This Not a Lovely Spot?
Music by Jerome Kern
Lyrics by P. G. Wodehouse
Sitting Pretty 1924

Is This the Way?
Music by Frank Fields
Lyrics by Armand Aulicino
The Shoemaker and the Peddler (OB) 1960

Is This Year Next Year?
Music by Bob Brush
Lyrics by Martin Charnin
The First 1981

Isaac's Equation
Music by Galt MacDermot
Lyrics by Christopher Gore
Via Galactica 1972

Isabella
Music and lyrics by Elizabeth Swados
Nightclub Cantata (OB) 1977

Island in the West Indies
Music by Vernon Duke
Lyrics by Ira Gershwin
Ziegfeld Follies (1936)

Island of Happiness
Music and lyrics by Johnny Brandon
Who's Who, Baby? (OB) 1968

The Island of Love
Music by Ivan Caryll
Lyrics by Aubrey Hopwood
Florodora 1900

Island Ritual
Music and lyrics by Matt Dubey and Dean Fuller
Smith (OB) 1973

Isle d'Amour
Music by Leo Edwards
Lyrics by Earl Carroll
Ziegfeld Follies of 1913

The Isle of Our Dreams
Music by Victor Herbert
Lyrics by Henry Blossom
The Red Mill 1906

Isle of Tangerine
Music by Monte Carlo and Alma Sanders
Lyrics by Howard Johnson
Tangerine 1921

Isn't It a Funny Thing?
Music by Max Rich
Lyrics by Jack Scholl
Keep Moving 1934

Isn't It a Lovely View?
Music by Jacques Belasco
Lyrics by Kay Twomey
The Girl From Nantucket 1945

Isn't It a Pity?
Music by George Gershwin
Lyrics by Ira Gershwin
Pardon My English 1933

Isn't It Fun to Be in the Movies
Music by Mel Marvin
Lyrics by Christopher Durang
A History of the American Film 1978

Isn't It Great to be Married
Music by Jerome Kern
Schuyler Green
Very Good Eddie 1915

Isn't It June?
Music by Ray Henderson
Lyrics by Ted Koehler
Say When 1934

Isn't It Kinda Fun?
Music by Richard Rodgers
Lyrics by Oscar Hammerstein II
State Fair (1945) F

Isn't It Remarkable?
Music by Jesse Greer
Lyrics by Stanley Adams
Shady Lady 1933

Isn't It Romantic?
Music by Richard Rodgers
Lyrics by Lorenz Hart
Love Me Tonight (1932) F

Isn't It Swell to Dream
Music by Sam H. Stept
Lyrics by Bud Green
Shady Lady 1933

Isn't It Wonderful?
Music by Louis Bellson and Will Irwin
Lyrics by Richard Ney
Portofino 1958

Isn't She Lovely?
Music by Dean Fuller
Lyrics by Marshall Barer
New Faces of 1956

Isn't That Clear?
Music by Al Carmines
Lyrics by Maria Irene Fornes
Promenade (OB) 1969

Isn't This a Lovely Day
Music and Lyrics by Irving Berlin
Top Hat (1935) F

"It"
Music by Sigmund Romberg
Lyrics by Otto Harbach and Oscar Hammerstein II
The Desert Song 1926

It Ain't Etiquette
Music and lyrics by Cole Porter
Du Barry Was a Lady 1939

It Ain't Gonna Work
Music by Bob Brush
Lyrics by Martin Charnin
The First 1981

It Ain't Necessarily So
Music by George Gershwin
Lyrics by Ira Gershwin
Porgy and Bess 1935

Ira Gershwin was persuaded to write another
quatrain of lyric as an encore. It is almost never
used. He supplied:
    Way back in 5000 B.C.
    Ole' Adam and Eve had to flee
    Sure, dey did dat deed in
    De garden of Eden
    But why chasterize you an' me?

It Ain't Us Who Make the Wars
Music and lyrics by Ron Dante and Gene Allan
Billy 1969

It All Belongs to Me
Music and lyrics by Irving Berlin
Ziegfeld Follies (1927)

It All Comes Out of the Piano
Music by Frank Lazarus
Lyrics by Dick Vosburgh and Frank Lazarus
A Day in Hollywood, a Night in the Ukraine 1979

It All Depends On You
Music by Ray Henderson
Lyrics by B.G. DeSylva and Lew Brown
Big Boy 1925

Interpolated into the score as a song for Al Jolson,
it was the team's first collaboration. Later it was
added to the score of *Lido Lady* (1926) in London.

It Always Seems to Rain
Music and lyrics by Bob Ost
Everybody's Gettin' Into the Act (OB) 1981

It Always Takes Two
Music by Lewis E. Gensler
Lyrics by Owen Murphy and Robert A.Simon
The Gang's All Here 1931

It Better Be Good
Music by Arthur Schwartz
Lyrics by Howard Dietz
The Band Wagon 1931

It Can Happen to Anyone
Music by Sigmund Romberg
Lyrics by Oscar Hammerstein II
Sunny River 1941

It Can't Be Wrong
Music by Rudolf Friml
Lyrics by Bide Dudley and Otto Harbach
The Little Whopper 1919

It Comes to Me
Music by Stanley Silverman
Lyrics by Arthur Miller
Up From Paradise (OB) 1983

It Could Only Happen in the Movies
Music by Vernon Duke
Lyrics by Harold Adamson
Banjo Eyes 1941

It Could Only Happen in the Theatre
Music by Gerald Jay Markoe
Lyrics by Michael Colby
Charlotte Sweet (OB) 1982

It Couldn't Be Done (But We Did It)
Music by Sidney Lippman
Lyrics by Sylvia Dee
Barefoot Boy With Cheek 1947

It Couldn't Please Me More
Music by John Kander
Lyrics by Fred Ebb
Cabaret 1966

It Depends on How You Look at Things
Music by Arthur Siegel
Lyrics by June Carroll
New Faces of 1962

It Depends on What You Pay
Music by Harvey Schmidt
Lyrics by Tom Jones
The Fantasticks (OB) 1960

It Depends on What You're At
Music by Richard Hill and John Hawkins
Lyrics by Nevill Coghill
Canterbury Tales 1969

It Doesn't Cost You Anything to Dream
Music by Sigmund Romberg
Lyrics by Dorothy Fields
Up in Central Park 1945

It Doesn't Look Deserted
Music by Alec Wilder
Lyrics by Arnold Sundgaard
Kittiwake Island (OB) 1960

It Feels Good
Music by Richard Rodgers
Lyrics by Oscar Hammerstein II
Me and Juliet 1953

It Gets Lonely in the White House
Music and lyrics by Irving Berlin
Mr. President 1962

It Happened
Music by Rudolf Friml
Lyrics by Rowland Leigh and John Shubert
Music Hath Charms 1934

It Happens Every Time
Music by Burton Lane
Lyrics by Ira Gershwin
Give a Girl a Break (1953) F

It Is Done
Music and lyrics by Cliff Jones
Rockabye Hamlet 1976

It Isn't Done
Music and lyrics by Cole Porter
Fifty Million Frenchmen 1929

It Isn't Easy
Music by Gordon Duffy
Lyrics by Harry M. Haldane
Happy Town 1959

It Isn't Easy
Music and lyrics by Harry Chapin
Cotton Patch Gospel (OB) 1981

It Isn't Enough
Music and lyrics by Leslie Bricusse
and Anthony Newley
*The Roar of the Greasepaint—The Smell
of the Crowd* 1965

It Isn't Working
Music by John Kander
Lyrics by Fred Ebb
Woman of the Year 1981

It Just Had to Happen
Music by Cliff Friend
Lyrics by Lew Brown
Piggy 1927

It Just Occurred to Me
Music by Vernon Duke
Lyrics by Sammy Cahn
Two's Company 1952

It Makes a Fellow Sort of Stop and Think
Music by Louis A. Hirsch
Lyrics by P.G. Wodehouse
Oh, My Dear! 1918

It Makes No Difference
Music and lyrics by Melvin Van Peebles
Don't Play Us Cheap 1972

It May Be a Good Idea
Music by Richard Rodgers
Lyrics by Oscar Hammerstein II
Allegro 1947

It Means So Little to You
Music by Richard Myers
Lyrics by Edward Heyman
Here Goes the Bride 1931

It Might as Well Be Her
Music by Jimmy Van Heusen
Lyrics by Sammy Cahn
Walking Happy 1966

It Might as Well Be Spring
Music by Richard Rodgers
Lyrics by Oscar Hammerstein II
State Fair (1945) F

Academy Award winner

It Might Be Love
Music by Louis Bellson and Will Irwin
Lyrics by Richard Ney
Portofino 1958

It Might Have Been
Music and lyrics by Gus Arnheim, George Waggner
and Neil Moret
Marching By 1932

It Might Have Been
Music and lyrics by Cole Porter
Something to Shout About (1943) F

Dropped from film

It Must Be Fun To Be You
Music and lyrics by Cole Porter
Mexican Hayride 1944

Dropped from production

It Must Be Heaven
Music by Richard Rodgers
Lyrics by Lorenz Hart
Heads Up! 1929

It Must Be Love
Music by Vincent Youmans
Lyrics by Zelda Sears
Lollipop 1924

Dropped from production

It Must Be Love
Music by Harry Archer
Lyrics by Harlan Thompson
Merry-Merry 1925

It Must Be Love
Music and lyrics by Matt Dubey and Dean Fuller
Smith (OB) 1973

It Must Be Me
Music by Leonard Bernstein
Lyrics by Richard Wilbur
Candide 1956

It Must Be So
Music by Leonard Bernstein
Lyrics by Richard Wilbur
Candide 1956

Same music as "O Miserere."

It Must Be Spring
Music and lyrics by Ralph Blane
Three Wishes for Jamie 1952

It Must Have Been the Night
Music by Ray Henderson
Lyrics by Ted Koehler
Say When 1934

It Never Entered My Mind
Music by Richard Rodgers
Lyrics by Lorenz Hart
Higher And Higher 1940

It Never, Never Can Be Love
Music by Victor Herbert
Lyrics by Rida Johnson Young
Naughty Marietta 1910

It Never Was You
Music by Kurt Weill
Lyrics by Maxwell Anderson
Knickerbocker Holiday 1938

It Never Would've Worked
Music by Charles Strouse
Lyrics by Alan Jay Lerner
Dance a Little Closer 1983

It Only Happens When I Dance With You
Music and lyrics by Irving Berlin
Easter Parade (1948) F

It Only Takes a Moment
Music and lyrics by Jerry Herman
Hello, Dolly 1964

It Pays to Advertise
Music by Lewis E. Gensler
Lyrics by B. G. DeSylva
Queen High 1926

It Says Here
Music by David Baker
Lyrics by David Craig
Phoenix '55 (OB)

It Still Isn't Over
Music by Gary William Friedman
Lyrics by Will Holt
Taking My Turn (OB) 1983

It Take a Long Pull to Get There
Music by George Gershwin
Lyrics by DuBose Heyward
Porgy and Bess 1935

It Takes a Whole Lot of Human Feeling
Music and lyrics by Micki Grant
Don't Bother Me, I Can't Cope (OB) 1972

It Takes a Woman
Music and lyrics by Jerry Herman
Hello, Dolly 1964

It Takes a Woman to Take a Man
Music by Jimmy McHugh
Lyrics by Harold Adamson
As the Girls Go 1948

It Takes Nine Tailors to Make a Man
Music by Reginald De Koven
Lyrics by Harry B. Smith
Robin Hood 1891

It Takes Time
Music and lyrics by Howard Blankman
By Hex (OB) 1956

It Took Them
Music by Baldwin Bergersen
Lyrics by William Archibald
The Crystal Heart (OB) 1960

It Used to Be
Music by Lee Pockriss
Lyrics by Anne Croswell
Tovarich 1963

It Was a Glad Adventure
Music by Jerome Moross
Lyrics by John Latouche
The Golden Apple 1954

It Was Destiny
Music by Frederico Valerio
Lyrics by Elizabeth Miele
Hit the Trail 1954

It Was Fate
Music by Rudolf Friml
Lyrics by Otto Harbach and Oscar Hammerstein II
The Wild Rose 1926

It Was for Fashion's Sake
Music by Don Pippin
Lyrics by Steve Brown
Fashion (OB) 1974

It Was Good Enough for Grandma
Music by Harold Arlen
Lyrics by E.Y. Harburg
Bloomer Girl 1944

It Was Good Enough for Grandpa
Music by Nancy Ford
Lyrics by Gretchen Cryer
Now Is the Time for All Good Men (OB) 1967

It Was Great Fun the First Time
Music and lyrics by Cole Porter
Kiss Me, Kate 1948

Dropped from production

It Was Great When It All Began
Music and lyrics by Richard O'Brien
The Rocky Horror Show 1975

It Was Long Ago
Music by Harold Arlen
Lyrics by Ira Gershwin and E.Y. Harburg
Life Begins at 8:40 1934

It Was Meant to Be
Music by Harry Ruby
Lyrics by Bert Kalmar
Helen of Troy, New York 1923

It Was Never Like This
Music by Arthur Schwartz
Lyrics by Howard Dietz
Flying Colors 1932

It Was Nice Knowing You
Music by Vernon Duke
Lyrics by Howard Dietz
Jackpot 1944

It Was So Nice Having You
Music by Gerald Marks
Lyrics by Sam Lerner
Hold It! 1948

It Was So Peaceful Before There Was Man
Music by Stanley Silverman
Lyrics by Arthur Miller
Up From Paradise (OB) 1983

It Was Worth It
Music and lyrics by Ron Eliran
Don't Step on My Olive Branch (OB) 1976

It Was Written in the Stars
Music and lyrics by Cole Porter
Du Barry Was a Lady 1939

It Was Written in the Stars
Music by Harold Arlen
Lyrics by Leo Robin
Casbah (1948) F

It Wasn't Meant to Happen
Music and lyrics by Stephen Sondheim
Marry Me a Little (OB) 1981

Dropped from *Follies* (1971)

It Wasn't Your Fault
Music by Jerome Kern
Lyrics by Herbert Reynolds
Love o' Mike 1917

It Wonders Me
Music by Albert Hague
Lyrics by Arnold B. Horwitt
Plain and Fancy 1955

It Won't Be Long
Music by Garry Sherman
Lyrics by Peter Udell
Comin' Uptown 1979

It Won't Be Long Now
Music by Ray Henderson
Lyrics by B.G. DeSylva and Lew Brown
Manhattan Mary 1927

It Won't Mean a Thing
Music by Jerome Kern
Lyrics by Otto Harbach and Oscar Hammerstein II
Sunny 1925

Dropped from production

It Would Have Been Wonderful
Music and lyrics by Stephen Sondheim
A Little Night Music 1973

Italian Street Song
Music by Victor Herbert
Lyrics by Rida Johnson Young
Naughty Marietta 1910

The Italian Whirlwind
Music and lyrics by George M. Cohan
The Rise of Rosie O'Reilly 1923

Italy
Music by Sammy Fain
Lyrics by Dan Shapiro
Ankles Aweigh 1955

Itch to Be Rich
Music by Jerry Bock
Lyrics by Sheldon Harnick
Man in the Moon 1963

It'd Be Nice
Music by Lawrence Hurwit
Lyrics by Lee Goldsmith
Sextet 1974

It'll Be All Right in a Hundred Years
Music by Jay Gorney
Lyrics by Jean and Walter Kerr
Touch and Go 1949

It's a Beautiful Day Today
Music by Walter Donaldson
Lyrics by Gus Kahn
Whoopee 1928

It's a Beginning
Music by Bob Brush
Lyrics by Martin Charnin
The First 1981

It's a Big, Wide, Wonderful World
Music and lyrics by John Rox
All in Fun 1940

It's a Bore
Music by Frederick Loewe
Lyrics by Alan Jay Lerner
Gigi (1958) F

Also in stage version (1973)

It's a Boy
Music by Gary Geld
Lyrics by Peter Udell
Shenandoah 1975

It's a Boy's Life
Music and lyrics by Billy Solly
Boy Meets Boy (OB) 1975

It's a Chemical Reaction
Music and lyrics by Cole Porter
Silk Stockings 1955

It's a Deal
Music by Judd Woldin
Lyrics by Robert Brittan
Raisin 1973

It's a Dolly
Music and lyrics by Billy Solly
Boy Meets Boy (OB) 1975

It's a Fine Life
Music and lyrics by Lionel Bart
Oliver! 1963

It's a Fine Old Institution
Music by Jimmy Van Heusen
Lyrics by Johnny Burke
Carnival in Flanders 1953

It's a Fish
Music by Jerry Bock
Lyrics by Sheldon Harnick
The Apple Tree 1966

It's a Grand Night for Singing
Music by Richard Rodgers
Lyrics by Oscar Hammerstein II
State Fair (1945) F

It's a Great Life
Music and lyrics by Cole Porter
Red, Hot and Blue! 1936

It's a Great Little World
Music by George Gershwin
Lyrics by Ira Gershwin
Tip-Toes 1925

It's a Great Sport
Music by Ray Henderson
Lyrics by B.G. DeSylva and Lew Brown
Follow Thru 1929

It's a Hard World for a Man
Music by Jerome Kern
Lyrics by P.G. Wodehouse
Oh, Lady! Lady!! 1918

It's a Hat
Music by Frederick Loewe
Lyrics by Alan Jay Lerner
The Little Prince (1975) F

It's a Helluva Way to Run a Love Affair
Music by Albert Hague
Lyrics by Arnold B. Horwitt
Plain and Fancy 1955

It's a Hit
Music by Arthur Siegel
Lyrics by Mae Richard
Tallulah (OB) 1983

It's a Law
Music by Kurt Weill
Lyrics by Maxwell Anderson
Knickerbocker Holiday 1938

It's a Lie
Music by Paul Klein
Lyrics by Fred Ebb
Morning Sun (OB) 1963

It's a Living
Music by Allan Roberts
Lyrics by Lester Lee
All for Love 1949

It's a Long Road Home
Music and lyrics by Norman Dean
Autumn's Here (OB) 1966

It's a Long Time Till Tomorrow
Music by Abraham Ellstein
Lyrics by Walter Bullock
Great to Be Alive 1950

It's a Lovely Day Today
Music and lyrics by Irving Berlin
Call Me Madam 1950

It's a Lovely Day Tomorrow
Music and lyrics by Irving Berlin
Louisiana Purchase 1940

It's a Lovely Night on the Hudson River
Music by Richard Lewine
Lyrics by Ted Fetter
The Fireman's Flame (OB) 1937

It's a Mighty Fine Country We Have Here
Music by Sammy Fain
Lyrics by Jack Yellen
Sons o' Fun 1941

It's a Most Unusual Day
Music by Jimmy McHugh
Lyrics by Harold Adamson
A Date With Judy (1948) F

It's a New Kind of Thing
Music by Sammy Fain
Lyrics by Jack Yellen
Sons o' Fun 1941

It's a New World
Music by Harold Arlen
Lyrics by Ira Gershwim
A Star Is Born (1954) F

It's a Nice Cold Morning
Music and lyrics by Hugo Peretti, Luigi Creatore
and George David Weiss
Maggie Flynn 1968

It's a Nice Face
Music by Cy Coleman
Lyrics by Dorothy Fields
Sweet Charity (film version, 1970)

It's a Nice Night for It
Music by Morgan Lewis
Lyrics by Nancy Hamilton
Three to Make Ready 1946

It's a Nice Place to Visit
Music and lyrics by Bill and Patti Jacob
Jimmy 1969

It's a Perfect Relationship
Music by Jule Styne
Lyrics by Betty Comden and Adolph Green
Bells Are Ringing 1956

It's a Premiere Night
Music and lyrics by Beth Lawrence
and Norman Thalheimer
Marilyn 1983

It's a Scandal! It's a Outrage!
Music by Richard Rodgers
Lyrics by Oscar Hammerstein II
Oklahoma! 1943

It's a Simple Little System
Music by Jule Styne
Lyrics by Betty Comden and Adolph Green
Bells Are Ringing 1956

It's a Stretchy Day
Music and lyrics by Bruce Montgomery
The Amorous Flea (OB) 1964

It's a Sure, Sure Sign
Music by Jerome Kern
Lyrics by P.G. Wodehouse
Have a Heart 1917

It's a Typical Day
Music by Gene de Paul
Lyrics by Johnny Mercer
Li'l Abner 1956

It's a Windy Day on the Battery
Music by Sigmund Romberg
Lyrics by Rida Johnson Young
Maytime 1917

It's a Wishing World
Music and lyrics by Ralph Blane
Three Wishes for Jamie 1952

It's a Wonderful Day to Do Nothing
Music and lyrics by Rick Besoyan
The Student Gypsy (OB) 1963

It's a Wonderful Thing for a King
Music by Albert Sirmay and Arthur Schwartz
Lyrics by Arthur Swanstrom
Princess Charming 1930

It's a Wonderful World
Music by Sigmund Romberg
Lyrics by Oscar Hammerstein II
East Wind 1931

It's About Magic
Music by Elmer Bernstein
Lyrics by Don Black
Merlin 1983

It's All in Fun
Music by Baldwin Bergersen
Lyrics by S.K. Russel
All in Fun 1940

It's All in the Book, You Know
Music by Victor Herbert
Lyrics by Harry B. Smith
Miss Dolly Dollars 1905

It's All in Your Mind
Music by Leon Pober
Lyrics by Bud Freeman
Beg, Borrow or Steal 1960

It's All O.K.
Music by Alma Sanders
Lyrics by Monte Carlo
Mystery Moon 1930

It's All Over But the Shoutin'
Music by Ray Henderson
Lyrics by B.G. DeSylva and Lew Brown
Hold Everything! 1928

It's All Over But the Shouting
Music and lyrics by Cole Porter
Rosalie (1937) F

It's All Right With Me
Music and lyrics by Cole Porter
Can-Can 1953

It's All the Same
Music by Mitch Leigh
Lyrics by Joe Darion
Man of La Mancha 1965

It's All Yours
Music by Arthur Schwartz
Lyrics by Dorothy Fields
Stars in Your Eyes 1939

It's Always Love
Music by Jule Styne
Lyrics by Bob Merrill
Sugar 1972

It's Always the Way
Music by Emmerich Kálmán and Herbert Stothart
Lyrics by Otto Harbach and Oscar Hammerstein II
Golden Dawn 1927

It's an Art
Music and lyrics by Stephen Schwartz
Working 1978

It's an Old Spanish Custom
Music by Ray Henderson
Lyrics by B.G. DeSylva
Three Cheers 1928

It's an Old Spanish Custom
Music by Jimmy Van Heusen
Lyrics by Johnny Burke
Carnival in Flanders 1953

It's Better With a Union Man
Music and lyrics by Harold Rome
Pins and Needles (OB) 1937

Added during run

It's Christmas Today
Music and lyrics by Jerry Herman
I Feel Wonderful (OB) 1954

It's Coming Back to Me
Music by Rob Fremont
Lyrics by Doris Willens
Piano Bar (OB) 1978

It's Commencement Day
Music and lyrics by Maceo Pinkard
Pansy 1929

It's Delightful Down in Chile
Music by Jule Styne
Lyrics by Leo Robin
Gentlemen Prefer Blondes 1949

It's Delightful to Be Married
Music by Vincent Scotto
Lyrics by Anna Held
The Parisian Model 1906

It's De-Lovely
Music and lyrics by Cole Porter
Red, Hot and Blue! 1936

It's Different With Me
Music by Harold Arlen
Lyrics by Jack Yellen
You Said It 1931

It's Doom
Music by Jule Styne
Lyrics by Betty Comden and Adolph Green
Say, Darling 1958

It's Easy for Her
Music by Keith Hermann
Lyrics by Charlotte Anker and Irene Rosenberg
Onward Victoria 1980

It's Easy to Remember
Music by Richard Rodgers
Lyrics by Lorenz Hart
Mississippi (1935) F

It's Easy to Say Hello
Music by Cliff Friend
Lyrics by Lew Brown
Piggy 1927

It's Easy to Sing
Music by Julian Slade
Lyrics by Dorothy Reynolds and Julian Slade
Salad Days (OB) 1958

It's Easy When You Know How
Music by Robert Emmett Dolan
Lyrics by Johnny Mercer
Foxy 1964

It's Enough to Make a Lady Fall in Love
Music by Jule Styne
Lyrics by E.Y. Harburg
Darling of the Day 1968

It's Every Girl's Ambition
Music by Vincent Youmans
Lyrics by Edward Heyman
Through the Years 1932

It's Fun to Think
Music by Charles Strouse
Lyrics by Lee Adams
All American 1962

It's Getting Dark on Old Broadway
Music and lyrics by Gene Buck and Dave Stamper
Ziegfeld Follies of 1922

It's Getting Hotter In the North
Music by Jerome Kern
Lyrics by Oscar Hammerstein II
Show Boat 1927

Dropped from production

It's Going to Be Good to Be Gone
Music by Richard Rodgers
Lyrics by Martin Charnin
I Remember Mama 1979

It's Good to Be Alive
Music and lyrics by Bob Merrill
New Girl in Town 1957

It's Good to Be Back Home
Music by Jule Styne
Lyrics by Betty Comden and Adolph Green
Fade Out—Fade In 1964

It's Got to Be Love
Music by Richard Rodgers
Lyrics by Lorenz Hart
On Your Toes 1936

It's Great to Be a Doughboy
Music by Shep Camp
Lyrics by Frank DuPree
Half a Widow 1927

It's Great to Be Alive
Music by Ray Henderson
Lyrics by Lew Brown
Strike Me Pink 1933

It's Great to Be Alive
Music by Robert Emmett Dolan
Lyrics by Johnny Mercer
Texas, Li'l Darlin' 1949

It's Great to Be Home Again
Music by Sammy Fain
Lyrics by Irving Kahal
Right This Way 1938

It's Great to Be in Love
Music by George Gershwin
Lyrics by Arthur J. Jackson and B.G. DeSylva
La, La, Lucille 1919

It's Great to Be in Love
Music and lyrics by Cliff Friend
Earl Carroll's Vanities (1931)

It's Great to Be Married
Music by Rudolf Friml
Lyrics by Bide Dudley and Otto Harbach
The Little Whopper 1919

It's Great to Be Married
Music by Monte Carlo and Alma Sanders
Lyrics by Howard Johnson
Tangerine 1921

It's Greek to Me
Music by Jerome Kern
Lyrics by Berton Braley
Toot-Toot! 1918

It's Hard to Care
Music by Nancy Ford
Lyrics by Gretchen Cryer
Shelter 1973

It's Hard to Tell
Music by George Gershwin
Lyrics by Arthur J. Jackson and B.G. DeSylva
La, La, Lucille 1919

It's High Time
Music by Jule Styne
Lyrics by Leo Robin
Gentlemen Prefer Blondes 1949

It's Hot Up There
Music and lyrics by Stephen Sondheim
Sunday in the Park With George (OB) 1983

It's Immaterial to Me
Music by Jerome Kern
Lyrics by Berton Braley
Toot-Toot! 1918

It's In, It's Out
Music by Lucien Denni
Lyrics by Helena Evans
Happy Go Lucky 1926

It's in the Stars
Music by Michael H. Cleary
Lyrics by Max and Nathaniel Lief
Shoot the Works 1931

It's Just Like I Was You
Music by Stanley Silverman
Lyrics by Arthur Miller
Up From Paradise (OB) 1983

It's Legitimate
Music by Jule Styne
Lyrics by Betty Comden and Adolph Green
Do Re Mi 1960

It's Like
Music and lyrics by Stan Daniels
So Long, 174th Street 1976

It's Like a Beautiful Woman
Music by Harold Karr
Lyrics by Matt Dubey
Happy Hunting 1956

It's Love
Music by Leonard Bernstein
Lyrics by Betty Comden and Adolph Green
Wonderful Town 1953

It's Love
Music and lyrics by Al Carmines
Wanted (OB) 1972

It's Magic
Music by Jule Styne
Lyrics by Sammy Cahn
Romance on the High Seas (1948) F

It's Mardi Gras
Music by Alma Sanders
Lyrics by Monte Carlo
Louisiana Lady 1947

It's Me
Music by Richard Rodgers
Lyrics by Oscar Hammerstein II
Me and Juliet 1953

It's Me Again
Music by Sam Stept
Lyrics by Lew Brown and Charles Tobias
Yokel Boy 1939

It's Me They Talk About
Music by Galt MacDermot
Lyrics by Rochelle Owens
The Karl Marx Play (OB) 1973

It's Mine
Music by Robert Mitchell
Lyrics by Elizabeth Perry
Bags (OB) 1982

It's Mine, It's Yours
Music by Harold Arlen
Lyrics by Ira Gershwin
The Country Girl (1954) F

It's Money–It's Fame–It's Love
Music and lyrics by Ralph Benatzky
Meet My Sister 1930

It's Money That I Love
Music and lyrics by Randy Newman
Maybe I'm Doing It Wrong (1st edition) (OB) 1981

It's More Fun Than a Picnic
Music by Jimmy McHugh
Lyrics by Harold Adamson
As the Girls Go 1948

It's My Belief
Music by Helen Miller
Lyrics by Eve Merriam
Inner City 1971

It's My Day
Music and lyrics by Harry Chapin
The Night That Made America Famous 1975

It's My Nature
Music by John Green
Lyrics by Edward Heyman
Here Goes the Bride 1931

It's Never Quite the Same
Music and lyrics by Jay Livingston
and Ray Evans
Oh Captain! 1958

It's Never Too Late to Fall in Love
Music and lyrics by Sandy Wilson
The Boy Friend 1954

It's Never Too Late to Mendelssohn
Music by Kurt Weill
Lyrics by Ira Gershwin
Lady in the Dark 1941

Dropped from production

It's Not Cricket to Picket
Music and lyrics by Harold Rome
Pins and Needles (OB) 1937

It's Not Easy
Music and lyrics by Billy Barnes
The Billy Barnes People 1961

It's Not Irish
Music and lyrics by Marc Blitzstein
Juno 1959

It's Not the End of the World
Music by Richard Rodgers
Lyrics by Martin Charnin
I Remember Mama 1979

It's Not the Trick Itself, But It's the Tricky Way It's Done
Music by A. Baldwin Sloane
Lyrics by E. Ray Goetz
The Hen Pecks 1911

It's Not Where You Start
Music by Cy Coleman
Lyrics by Dorothy Fields
Seesaw 1973

It's Only a Paper Moon
Music by Harold Arlen
Lyrics by Billy Rose and E.Y. Harburg
The Great Magoo 1932

Also in the film *Take a Chance* (1933)

It's Only a Show
Music by Monty Norman
Lyrics by Julian More
The Moony Shapiro Songbook 1981

It's Only Thirty Years
Music and lyrics by William Roy
Maggie 1953

It's Our Duty to the King
Music by Arthur Schwartz
Lyrics by Albert Stillman
Virginia 1937

It's Our Time Now
Music and lyrics by Johnny Brandon
Billy Noname (OB) 1970

It's Pleasant and Delightful
Music by Mischa and Wesley Portnoff
Lyrics by Donagh MacDonagh
Happy as Larry 1950

It's Positively You
Music by Sol Berkowitz
Lyrics by James Lipton
Miss Emily Adam (OB) 1960

It's Pretty in the City
Music by Richard Rodgers
Lyrics by Lorenz Hart
Higher And Higher 1940

Dropped before Broadway opening

It's Pretty Soft for Simon
Music by Victor Herbert
Lyrics by Rida Johnson Young
Naughty Marietta 1910

It's Quick and Easy
Music by Armando Trovaioli
Lyrics by Pietro Garinei and Sandro Giovannini
(Lyric translation by Edward Eager)
Rugantino 1964

It's Raining on Prom Night
Music and lyrics by Jim Jacobs
and Warren Casey
Grease 1972

It's Sad to Be Lonesome
Music and lyrics by Walter Cool
Mackey of Appalachia (OB) 1965

It's She and It's Me
Music by Michael J. Lewis
Lyrics by Anthony Burgess
Cyrano 1973

It's So Easy to Say
Music by Alec Wilder
Lyrics by Arnold Sundgaard
Kittiwake Island (OB) 1960

It's So Good
Music by Jacques Urbont
Lyrics by David Newburger
Stag Movie (OB) 1971

It's So Heart-Warming
Music by Sol Kaplan
Lyrics by Edward Eliscu
The Banker's Daughter (OB) 1962

It's So Nice
Music and lyrics by Al Carmines
Joan (OB) 1972

It's So Nice
Music and lyrics by Jill Williams
Rainbow Jones 1974

It's So Nice to Be Civilized
Music and lyrics by Micki Grant
It's So Nice to Be Civilized 1980

It's So Simple
Music and lyrics by Marian Grudeff
and Raymond Jessel
Baker Street 1965

It's Super Nice
Music by Charles Strouse
Lyrics by Lee Adams
It's a Bird, It's a Plane, It's Superman 1966

It's Superman
Music by Charles Strouse
Lyrics by Lee Adams
It's a Bird, It's a Plane, It's Superman 1966

It's the Darndest Thing
Music by Jimmy McHugh
Lyrics by Dorothy Fields
Singin' the Blues 1931

It's the Girl Everytime, It's the Girl
Music by Fred Spielman and Arthur Gershwin
Lyrics by Stanley Adams
A Lady Says Yes 1945

It's the Going Home Together
Music by Jerome Moross
Lyrics by John Latouche
The Golden Apple 1954

**It's the Gown That Makes the Gal
That Makes the Guy**
Music by Eubie Blake
Lyrics by Joan Javits
Shuffle Along of 1952

It's the Hard-knock Life
Music by Charles Strouse
Lyrics by Martin Charnin
Annie 1977

It's the Little Things in Texas
Music and lyrics by Richard Rodgers
State Fair (Re-make, 1962) F

It's the Nuns
Music and lyrics by James Quinn and Alaric Jans
Do Patent Leather Shoes Really Reflect Up? 1982

It's the Right Time to Be Rich
Music by Elizabeth Swados
Lyrics by Garry Trudeau
Doonesbury 1983

It's the Second Time You Meet That Matters
Music by Jule Styne
Lyrics by Betty Comden and Adolph Green
Say, Darling 1958

It's the Skirt
Music by A. Baldwin Sloane
Lyrics by E. Ray Goetz
The Hen Pecks 1911

It's the Strangest Thing
Music by John Kander
Lyrics by Fred Ebb
The Act 1977

It's the Weather
Music and lyrics by James Shelton
Dance Me a Song 1950

It's the Youth in Me
Music by Eubie Blake
Lyrics by J. Milton Reddie and Cecil Mack
Swing It 1937

It's Three o'Clock
Music by Rudolf Friml
Lyrics by Rowland Leigh and John Shubert
Music Hath Charms 1934

It's Time for a Cheer-Up Song
Music by Charles Strouse
Lyrics by Lee Adams
A Broadway Musical 1978

It's Time for a Love Song
Music by Burton Lane
Lyrics by Alan Jay Lerner
Carmelina 1979

It's Time to Say "Aloha"
Music by Sammy Fain
Lyrics by Charles Tobias
Hellzapoppin 1938

It's Today
Music and lyrics by Jerry Herman
Mame 1966

It's Too Much
Music by Don Pippin
Lyrics by Steve Brown
The Contrast (OB) 1972

It's Up to Me
Music by Charles Strouse
Lyrics by Lee Adams
All American 1962

It's Up to the Band
Music and lyrics by Irving Berlin
Ziegfeld Follies (1927)

It's Wonderful
Music by Sigmund Romberg
Lyrics by Harold Atteridge
Sinbad (1918)

It's Wonderful
Music by Lucien Denni
Lyrics by Helena Evans
Happy Go Lucky 1926

It's You
Music and lyrics by Meredith Willson
The Music Man 1957

It's You
Music by Jim Wise
Lyrics by George Haimsohn and Robin Miller
Dames at Sea (OB) 1968

It's You Again
Music and lyrics by Walter Marks
Golden Rainbow 1968

It's You for Me
Music by Ernest G. Schweikert
Lyrics by Frank Reardon
Rumple 1957

It's You I Love
Music by J. Fred Coots
Lyrics by Arthur Swanstrom and Benny Davis
Sons o' Guns 1929

It's You I Want
Music by Paul McGrane
Lyrics by Al Stillman
Who's Who 1938

It's You I Want to Love Tonight
Music by Rudolf Friml
Lyrics by Rowland Leigh and John Shubert
Music Hath Charms 1934

It's You Who Makes Me Young
Music by Harvey Schmidt
Lyrics by Tom Jones
Celebration 1969

It's Your Carriage That Counts
Music by Monte Carlo and Alma Sanders
Lyrics by Howard Johnson
Tangerine 1921

It's Your Fault
Music by Milton Schafer
Lyrics by Ira Levin
Drat! The Cat! 1965

I've a Most Decided Notion
Music by John Philip Sousa
Lyrics by Tom Frost and John Philip Sousa
El Capitan 1896

I've a Shooting-Box in Scotland
Music by Cole Porter
Lyrics by T. Lawrason Riggs and Cole Porter
See America First 1916

I've a Strange New Rhythm in My Heart
Music and lyrics by Cole Porter
Rosalie (1937) F

I've Always Been a Good Old Sport
Music and lyrics by George M. Cohan
The Man Who Owns Broadway 1909

I've Always Loved You
Music by James Mundy
Lyrics by John Latouche
The Vamp 1955

I've An Inkling
Music and lyrics by Paul Rubens
Florodora 1900

I've A'ready Started In
Music and lyrics by Meredith Willson
The Unsinkable Molly Brown 1960

I've Been a-Begging
Music by George Fischoff
Lyrics by Verna Tomasson
The Prince and the Pauper (OB) 1963

I've Been Decorated
Music by Victor Herbert
Lyrics by Glen MacDonough
Algeria 1908

I've Been in Love
Music and lyrics by Ronnie Britton
Greenwich Village Follies (OB) 1976

I've Been Invited to a Party
Music and lyrics by Noël Coward
The Girl Who Came to Supper 1963

I've Been Looking for a Perfect Man
Music by Victor Herbert
Lyrics by Harry B. Smith
The Enchantress 1911

I've Been Sent Back to the First Grade
Music by C.C. Courtney
Lyrics by C.C. Courtney and Ragan Courtney
Earl of Ruston 1971

I've Been There and I'm Back
Music and lyrics by Jay Livingston and Ray Evans
Oh Captain! 1958

I've Been to America
Music by Paul A. Rubens
Lyrics by Paul A. Rubens and Arthur Wimperis
The Sunshine Girl 1913

I've Been Too Busy
Music and lyrics by Jerry Bock, George Weiss
and Larry Holofcener
Mr. Wonderful 1956

I've Been Waiting All My Life
Music by Billy Goldenberg
Lyrics by Alan and Marilyn Bergman
Ballroom 1978

I've Been Waiting for You All the Time
Music by Jerome Kern
Lyrics by Anne Caldwell
She's a Good Fellow 1919

I've Come to Wive It Wealthily in Padua
Music and lyrics by Cole Porter
Kiss Me, Kate 1948

The title is taken from a speech by Petruchio in *The Taming of the Shrew:* "I come to wive it wealthily in Padua; If wealthily, then happily in Padua." Elsewhere in Shakespeare's play are the lines "Where is the life that late I led?" and, also spoken by Petruchio, "First kiss me, Kate" and "Come on, and kiss me, Kate."

I've Confessed to the Breeze
Music by Vincent Youmans
Lyrics by Otto Harbach
No, No, Nanette 1925

I've Fallen Out of Love
Music by Harry Revel
Lyrics by Mack Gordon
Smiling Faces 1932

I've Gone Nuts Over You
Music by Edward A. Horan
Lyrics by Frederick Herendeen
All the King's Horses 1934

I've Gone Romantic on You
Music by Harold Arlen
Lyrics by E.Y. Harburg
Hooray for What! 1937

I've Got a Baby
Music by Lewis E. Gensler
Lyrics by Robert A. Simon
Ups-a-Daisy 1928

I've Got a Cookie Jar but No Cookies
Music by Harry Archer
Lyrics by Walter O'Keefe
Just a Minute 1928

I've Got a Crush on You
Music by George Gershwin
Lyrics by Ira Gershwin
Treasure Girl 1928

In both shows in which the song appeared, *Strike Up the Band* (1930) and *Treasure Girl* (1928), it was sung and danced in a lively tempo. Gershwin's instruction was *Allegretto giocoso* (gaily). After Lee Wiley recorded it as a slow sentimental ballad, the song underwent a seemingly permanent change of tempo.

I've Got a Little Secret
Music and lyrics by Robert Dahdah
Curley McDimple (OB) 1967

I've Got a Lot to Learn About Life
Music by Tommy Wolf
Lyrics by Fran Landesman
The Nervous Set 1959

I've Got a Molly
Music by Jerry Livingston
Lyrics by Mack David
Molly 1973

I've Got a New Idea
Music by Jerome Kern
Lyrics by Oscar Hammerstein II
Sweet Adeline 1929

Dropped from production

I've Got a One Track Mind
Music by Vernon Duke
Lyrics by Howard Dietz
Jackpot 1944

I've Got a Rainbow Working for Me
Music by Jule Styne
Lyrics by E.Y. Harburg
Darling of the Day 1968

I've Got a Right to Sing the Blues
Music by Harold Arlen
Lyrics by Ted Koehler
Earl Carroll's Vanities (1932)

I've Got a Wonderful Future
Music by David Baker
Lyrics by Sheldon Harnick
Smiling, the Boy Fell Dead (OB) 1961

I've Got a Yes Girl
Music by Henry Souvaine and Jay Gorney
Lyrics by Morrie Ryskind and Howard Dietz
Merry-Go-Round 1927

I've Got an Awful Lot to Learn
Music by Cole Porter
Lyrics by T. Lawrason Riggs and Cole Porter
See America First 1916

I've Got Elgin Watch Movements in My Hips
Music and lyrics by Buster Davis
Doctor Jazz 1975

I've Got 'Em Standing in Line
Music and lyrics by Steve Allen
Sophie 1963

I've Got Five Dollars
Music by Richard Rodgers
Lyrics by Lorenz Hart
America's Sweetheart 1931

I've Got It
Music by Alberta Nichols
Lyrics by Mann Holiner
The Red Robe 1928

I've Got It Again
Music by Ned Lehak
Lyrics by Allen Boretz
The Garrick Gaieties (3rd edition) 1930

I've Got it All
Music by Cy Coleman
Lyrics by Betty Comden and Adolph Green
On the Twentieth Century 1978

I've Got Me
Music by Duke Ellington
Lyrics by John Latouche
Beggar's Holiday 1946

I've Got Me
Music by Jerome Moross
Lyrics by John Latouche
Ballet Ballads 1948

I've Got My Eyes on You
Music and lyrics by Cole Porter
Broadway Melody of 1940 F

Also in the film *Andy Hardy's Private Secretary* (1941) sung by Kathryn Grayson.

I've Got My Love to Keep Me Warm
Music and lyrics by Irving Berlin
On the Avenue (1937) F

I've Got My Orders
Music by Bert Keyes and Bob Larimer
Lyrics by Bob Larimer
But Never Jam Today 1979

I've Got Nothin' to Do
Music by Sammy Fain
Lyrics by Marilyn and Alan Bergman
Something More 1964

I've Got Rings on My Fingers
Music by Maurice Scott
Lyrics by F.J. Barnes and R.P. Weston
The Yankee Girl 1910

I've Got Some Unfinished Business With You
Music and lyrics by Cole Porter
Let's Face It! 1941

I've Got Something
Music by Harry Ruby
Lyrics by Bert Kalmar
High Kickers 1941

I've Got Something Better
Music and lyrics by Ronnie Britton
Gift of the Magi (OB) 1975

I've Got the Nerve to Be in Love
Music and lyrics by Harold Rome
Pins and Needles (OB) 1937

Added during run

I've Got the President's Ear
Music by Jimmy McHugh
Lyrics by Harold Adamson
As the Girls Go 1948

I've Got to Be Around
Music and lyrics by Irving Berlin
Mr. President 1962

I've Got to Be Good
Music by Jean Schwartz
Lyrics by Clifford Grey and William Cary Duncan
Sunny Days 1928

I've Got to Be Me
Music and lyrics by Walter Marks
Golden Rainbow 1968

I've Got to Be There
Music by George Gershwin
Lyrics by Ira Gershwin
Pardon My English 1933

I've Got to Dance
Music by Jerome Kern
Lyrics by Schuyler Greene
Very Good Eddie 1915

Although included in the vocal score, this song was unaccountably dropped from the original New York production. However, it was restored with great success in the show's 1975 revival.

I've Got to Find a Reason
Music and lyrics by Bob Merrill
Carnival 1961

I've Got to Get Hot
Music by Ray Henderson
Lyrics by Jack Yellen
George White's Scandals (1936)

I've Got to Hand It to You
Music by Vernon Duke
Lyrics by John Latouche
Banjo Eyes 1941

I've Got to Leave You
Music by Rudolf Friml
Lyrics by Bide Dudley and Otto Harbach
The Little Whopper 1919

I've Got to Trust You
Music by Bob James
Lyrics by Jack O'Brien
The Selling of the President 1972

I've Got to Try Everything Once
Music by Arthur Siegel
Lyrics by Mae Richard
Tallulah (OB) 1983

I've Got What It Takes
Music and lyrics by Al Wilson, Charles Weinberg
and Ken Macomber
Yeah Man 1932

I've Got What You Want
Music by Jerry Bock
Lyrics by Sheldon Harnick
The Apple Tree 1966

I've Got You on My Mind
Music and lyrics by Max Ewing
The Grand Street Follies (1929)

I've Got You on My Mind
Music and lyrics by Cole Porter
Gay Divorce 1932

I've Got You to Lean On
Music and lyrics by Stephen Sondheim
Anyone Can Whistle 1964

I've Got You Under My Skin
Music and lyrics by Cole Porter
Born to Dance (1936) F

I've Got Your Number
Music by Cy Coleman
Lyrics by Carolyn Leigh
Little Me 1962

I've Gotta Crow
Music by Mark Charlap
Lyrics by Carolyn Leigh
Peter Pan 1954

I've Gotta Keep My Eye on You
Music by Harry Revel
Lyrics by Mack Gordon
Marching By 1932

I've Gotta See a Man About His Daughter
Music and Lyrics by Jean Herbert, Karl Stark
and James F. Hanley
Thumbs Up! 1934

I've Grown Accustomed to Her Face
Music by Frederick Loewe
Lyrics by Alan Jay Lerner
My Fair Lady 1956

I've Heard It All Before
Music by Gary Geld
Lyrics by Peter Udell
Shenandoah 1975

I've Just Been to a Wedding
Music and lyrics by Frederick Silver
Gay Company (OB) 1974

I've Just Seen Her
Music by Charles Strouse
Lyrics by Lee Adams
All American 1962

I've Known a Lot of Guys
Music by Galt MacDermot
Lyrics by William Dumaresq
The Human Comedy (OB) 1983

I've Lost My Girl
Music by Raymond Hubbell
Lyrics by Glen MacDonough
The Jolly Bachelors 1910

I've Lost My Heart
Music by Morris Hamilton
Lyrics by Grace Henry
The Third Little Show 1931

I've Made a Habit of You
Music by Arthur Schwartz
Lyrics by Howard Dietz
The Little Show (1st edition) 1929

I've Made Up My Mind
Music by Arthur Schwartz
Lyrics by Howard Dietz
Between the Devil 1937

I've Never Been in Love Before
Music and lyrics by Frank Loesser
Guys and Dolls 1950

I've Never Said I Love You
Music and lyrics by Jerry Herman
Dear World 1969

I've Nothing to Offer
Music by Harry Akst
Lyrics by Lew Brown
Calling All Stars 1934

I've Still Got My Bite
Music and lyrics by Micki Grant
It's So Nice to Be Civilized 1980

I've Still Got My Health
Music and lyrics by Cole Porter
Panama Hattie 1940

I've Told Every Little Star
Music by Jerome Kern
Lyrics by Oscar Hammerstein II
Music in the Air 1932

Jerome Kern said that he had heard a bird singing a simple seven-note melody over and over and he became intrigued by it. It became the first two bars of this song.

I've Walked in the Moonlight
Music by Edgar Fairchild
Lyrics by Milton Pascal
The Illustrators' Show 1936

The Ivy and the Oak
Music by Victor Herbert
Lyrics by Robert B. Smith
Sweethearts 1913

Dropped from production

Jabberwocky
Music and lyrics by Elizabeth Swados
Alice in Concert (OB) 1980

Jack and Jill
Music and lyrics by George M. Cohan
Fifty Miles From Boston 1908

Jack and Jill
Music and lyrics by Robert Dennis, Peter Schickele
and Stanley Walden
Oh! Calcutta! 1969

Jack Be Nimble
Music by Helen Miller
Lyrics by Eve Merriam
Inner City 1971

Jack O'Lantern Moon
Music by Percy Wenrich
Lyrics by Julian Eltinge
The Fascinating Widow 1911

Jack Roosevelt Robinson
Music by Bob Brush
Lyrics by Martin Charnin
The First 1981

Jackie
Music by Jacques Brel
English lyrics by Eric Blau and Mort Shuman
*Jacques Brel Is Alive and Well
and Living in Paris* (OB) 1968

Jacques D'Iraq
Music and lyrics by Jerry Bock, George Weiss
and Larry Holofcener
Mr. Wonderful 1956

Jaded, Degraded Am I
Music by Sammy Fain
Lyrics by Marilyn and Alan Bergman
Something More 1964

J'ai
Music by Don Elliott
Lyrics by James Costigan
The Beast in Me 1963

J'ai Deux Amants
Music by Andre Messager
Lyrics by Sacha Guitry
Naughty Cinderella 1925

Jail-Life Walk
Music by Gary William Friedman
Lyrics by Will Holt
The Me Nobody Knows (OB) 1970

Jailer, Jailer
Music by Larry Grossman
Lyrics by Betty Comden and Adolph Green
A Doll's Life 1982

Jailhouse Blues
Music and lyrics by Jerry Herman
I Feel Wonderful (OB) 1954

Jailhouse Blues
Music and lyrics by Al Carmines
Wanted (OB) 1972

Jamie
Music by Lance Mulcahy
Lyrics by Paul Cherry
Park 1970

Jane
Music by Victor Herbert
Lyrics by Glen MacDonough
Babes in Toyland 1903

Janet Get Up
Music by Gary William Friedman
Lyrics by Will Holt
Taking My Turn (OB) 1983

Japanese Moon
Music by Dave Stamper
Lyrics by Gene Buck
Take the Air 1927

Japanese Serenade
Music by Sigmund Romberg
Lyrics by Harry B. Smith
Cherry Blossoms 1927

Jasbo Brown Blues
Music by George Gershwin
Porgy and Bess 1935

Onstage piano solo following overture

Jassamine Lane
Music and lyrics by Noble Sissle and Eubie Blake
The Chocolate Dandies 1924

Jazz
Music by Jerome Kern
Lyrics by Anne Caldwell
The Night Boat 1920

Dropped from production

Jazz
Music and lyrics by Ida Hoyt Chamberlain
Enchanted Isle 1927

Jazz City
Music by Henry Souvaine
Lyrics by J.P. McEvoy
Americana (1928)

Jazz Your Troubles Away
Music and lyrics by James Johnson
and Cecil Mack
Runnin' Wild 1923

Jazzbo Brown
Music and lyrics by Stephen H. Lemberg
Jazzbo Brown 1980

Jazztime Baby
Music and lyrics by Noble Sissle and Eubie Blake
The Chocolate Dandies 1924

J.B. Pictures, Inc.
Music by Ray Haney
Lyrics by Alfred Aiken
We're Civilized? (OB) 1962

Je t'Aime
Music by Arthur Schwartz
Lyrics by Howard Dietz
Three's a Crowd 1930

"Je t'Aime" Means I Love You
Music and lyrics by Powers Gouraud
Gay Paree 1926

Je Vous Aime
Music and lyrics by Arthur L. Beiner
Puzzles of 1925

Je Vous Aime
Music by Monty Norman
Lyrics by Julian More
The Moony Shapiro Songbook 1981

Jealous
Music by Harold Levey
Lyrics by Owen Murphy
Rainbow Rose 1926

Jealousy Begins at Home
Music by Franz Lehár
Lyrics by Edward Eliscu
Frederika 1937

Jealousy Duet
Music by Kurt Weill
Lyrics by Marc Blitzstein
The Threepenny Opera (OB) 1954

Jeannette and Her Little Wooden Shoes
Music by Victor Herbert
Lyrics by Robert B. Smith
Sweethearts 1913

Jeannie's Packin' Up
Music by Frederick Loewe
Lyrics by Alan Jay Lerner
Brigadoon 1947

Jeff's Plaints
Music by Susan Hulsman Bingham
Lyrics by Myrna Lamb
Mod Donna (OB) 1970

The Jellicle Ball
Music by Andrew Lloyd Webber
Cats 1982

Lyrics based on T.S. Eliot's *Old Possum's Book of Practical Cats*

Jellicle Songs for Jellicle Cats
Music by Andrew Lloyd Webber
Lyrics by Trevor Nunn and Richard Stilgoe
Cats 1982

Lyrics based on T.S. Eliot's *Old Possom's Books of Practical Cats*

Jelly Donuts and Chocolate Cake
Music by Charles Strouse
Lyrics by David Rogers
Charlie and Algernon 1980

Jenny
Music by Ann Sternberg
Lyrics by Gertrude Stein
Gertrude Stein's First Reader (OB) 1969

Jenny
Music and lyrics by Bob Goodman
Wild and Wonderful 1971

Jenny Is Like an Angel
Music by Galt MacDermot
Lyrics by Rochelle Owens
The Karl Marx Play (OB) 1973

Jenny Lind
Music by Arthur Schwartz
Lyrics by Oscar Hammerstein II
American Jubilee 1940

Jenny (The Saga of)
Music by Kurt Weill
Lyrics by Ira Gershwin
Lady in the Dark 1941

Jenny Westphalen
Music by Galt MacDermot
Lyrics by Rochelle Owens
The Karl Marx Play (OB) 1973

Jeremiah Obadiah
Music by Helen Miller
Lyrics by Eve Merriam
Inner City 1971

Jericho
Music by Richard Myers
Lyrics by Leo Robin
Hello, Yourself! 1928

Jerry, My Soldier Boy
Music and lyrics by Cole Porter
Let's Face It! 1941

Jersey Walk
Music by James F. Hanley
Lyrics by Eddie Dowling
Honeymoon Lane 1926

Jerusalem
Music and lyrics by Ron Eliran
Don't Step on My Olive Branch (OB) 1976

Jesse James Robbed This Train
Music and lyrics by Bland Simpson
and Jim Wann
Diamond Studs (OB) 1975

The Jester and I
Music by Mary Rodgers
Lyrics by Marshall Barer
Once Upon a Mattress 1959

Jesus Come Down
Music and lyrics by Tom Sankey
The Golden Screw (OB) 1967

Jesus Hi
Music by Galt MacDermot
Lyrics by Gerome Ragni
Dude 1972

Jet Song
Music by Leonard Bernstein
Lyrics by Stephen Sondheim
West Side Story 1957

A Jewel of a Duel
Music by John Mundy
Lyrics by Edward Eager
The Liar 1950

Jewelry
Music and lyrics by Marian Grudeff
and Raymond Jessel
Baker Street 1965

The Jig
Music by Arthur Schwartz
Lyrics by Howard Dietz
Jennie 1963

The Jig Hop
Music by Kay Swift
Lyrics by Paul James
Fine and Dandy 1930

Jig Saw Jamboree
Music by Eddie Bienbryer
Lyrics by William Walsh
Tattle Tales 1933

Jiggle Your Feet
Music by Abel Baer
Lyrics by Sam Lewis and Joe Young
Lady Do 1927

The Jijibo
Music by George Gershwin
Lyrics by B.G. DeSylva
Sweet Little Devil 1924

Jilted
Music by George Gershwin
Lyrics by Ira Gershwin
Of Thee I Sing 1931

Jim
Music by Rudolf Friml
Lyrics by Otto Harbach
High Jinks 1913

Jim Dandy
Music by Will Irwin
Lyrics by Norman Zeno
Fools Rush In 1934

Jimmy
Music and lyrics by Irving Berlin
Ziegfeld Follies (1927)

Jimmy
Music and lyrics by Bill and Patti Jacob
Jimmy 1969

Jimmy, Jimmy
Music and lyrics by Jeanne Napoli
and Doug Frank
Marilyn 1983

The Jitterbug
Music by Harold Arlen
Lyrics by E.Y. Harburg
The Wizard of Oz (1939) F

Jitters
Music and lyrics by Alexander Hill
Hummin' Sam 1933

Jockey on the Carousel
Music by Jerome Kern
Lyrics by Dorothy Fields
I Dream Too Much (1935) F

Jockey's Life for Mine
Music and lyrics by Noble Sissle and Eubie Blake
The Chocolate Dandies 1924

Joe
Music and lyrics by Craig Carnelia
Working 1978

Joe Worker
Music and lyrics by Marc Blitzstein
The Cradle Will Rock 1938

Joey, Joey, Joey
Music and lyrics by Frank Loesser
The Most Happy Fella 1956

Johanna
Music and lyrics by Stephen Sondheim
Sweeney Todd 1979

John Barleycorn
Music by Arthur Schwartz
Lyrics by Maxwell Anderson
High Tor 1956 TV

John 19:41
Music by Andrew Lloyd Webber
Lyrics by Tim Rice
Jesus Christ Superstar 1971

John Paul Jones
Music by Philip Charig
Lyrics by Dan Shapiro and Milton Pascal
Follow the Girls 1944

Johnny
Music and lyrics by Marc Blitzstein
Juno 1959

Johnny Mishuga
Music by Mark Bucci
Lyrics by David Rogers and Mark Bucci
New Faces of 1962

Johnny O
Music by Earl Robinson
Lyrics by Waldo Salt
Sandhog (OB) 1954

Johnny One Note
Music by Richard Rodgers
Lyrics by Lorenz Hart
Babes in Arms 1937

Johnny Ride the Sky
Music and lyrics by Jack Lawrence
and Don Walker
Courtin' Time 1951

Johnny Wanamaker
Music by Kay Swift
Lyrics by Paul James
The Garrick Gaieties (3rd edition) 1930

Johnny's Arrest and Homecoming
Music by Kurt Weill
Lyrics by Paul Green
Johnny Johnson 1936

Johnny's Creed
Music by Clinton Ballard
Lyrics by Carolyn Richter
The Ballad of Johnny Pot (OB) 1971

Johnny's Cursing Song
Music by Earl Robinson
Lyrics by Waldo Salt
Sandhog (OB) 1954

Johnny's Melody
Music by Kurt Weill
Lyrics by Paul Green
Johnny Johnson 1936

Johnny's Song (Listen to My Song)
Music by Kurt Weill
Lyrics by Paul Green
Johnny Johnson 1936

Later published as "To Love You and to Lose You"
with lyrics by Edward Heyman.

Join It Right Away
Music and lyrics by Cole Porter
Panama Hattie 1940

Join Our Ranks
Music by Jerome Moross
Lyrics by Paul Peters and George Sklar
Parade (1935)

Join the Army
Music and lyrics by Gene Curty, Nitra Scharfman
and Chuck Strand
The Lieutenant 1975

Join the Circus
Music by Cy Coleman
Lyrics by Michael Stewart
Barnum 1980

Join the Navy
Music by Vincent Youmans
Lyrics by Leo Robin and Clifford Grey
Hit the Deck 1927

Join Us in a Cup of Tea
Music and lyrics by Charles Gaynor
Lend an Ear 1948

Later used in *Show Girl* (1961)

Joke a Cola
Music and lyrics by James Rado
Rainbow (OB) 1972

The Joker
Music and lyrics by Leslie Bricusse
and Anthony Newley
*The Roar of the Greasepaint—The Smell
of the Crowd* 1965

Jolly Coppers on Parade
Music and lyrics by Randy Newman
Maybe I'm Doing It Wrong (1st edition) (OB) 1981

Jolly Good Fellow
Music by Jerome Kern
Lyrics by Clare Kummer
Ninety in the Shade 1915

Jolly Tar and the Milkmaid
Music by George Gershwin
Lyrics by Ira Gershwin
A Damsel in Distress (1937) F

Jolly Theatrical Season
Music and lyrics by Jerry Herman
Parade (OB) 1960

Jonah's Melodrama
Music by Meyer Kupferman
Lyrics by Paul Goodman
Jonah (OB) 1966

Jonah's Wail
Music and lyrics by John Dooley
Hobo (OB) 1961

The Jones' Family Friends
Music and lyrics by George M. Cohan
Billie 1928

José, Can't You See!
Music by Ray Henderson
Lyrics by Lew Brown
Hot-Cha! 1932

Joseph Taylor, Jr.
Music by Richard Rodgers
Lyrics by Oscar Hammerstein II
Allegro 1947

Josephine
Music by Paul A. Rubens
Lyrics by Paul A. Rubens and Arthur Wimperis
The Sunshine Girl 1913

Josephine
Music by Armand Vecsey
Lyrics by Clifford Grey
The Nightingale 1927

Josephine
Music and lyrics by Cole Porter
Silk Stockings 1955

Josephine Waters
Music by Harold Arlen
Lyrics by E.Y. Harburg
The Show Is On 1936

Joseph's Coat (The Coat of Many Colors)
Music by Andrew Lloyd Webber
Lyrics by Tim Rice
*Joseph and the Amazing
Technicolor Dreamcoat* 1982

Joseph's Dreams
Music by Andrew Lloyd Webber
Lyrics by Tim Rice
*Joseph and the Amazing
Technicolor Dreamcoat* 1982

Joshua
Music by Frederick Loewe
Lyrics by Alan Jay Lerner
What's Up? 1943

The Journey
Music by Paul Hoffert
Lyrics by David Secter
Get Thee to Canterbury (OB) 1969

Journey Home
Music and lyrics by Robert Swerdlow
Love Me, Love My Children (OB) 1971

Journey to Portsmouth
Music and lyrics by Stephen Oliver
The Life and Times of Nicholas Nickleby 1981

The Journey to the Heaviside Layer
Music by Andrew Lloyd Webber.
Cats 1982

Lyrics based on T.S. Eliot's *Old Possum's
Book of Practical Cats*

Journey's End
Music by Harry Tierney
Lyrics by Joseph McCarthy
Up She Goes 1922

Journey's End
Music by Jerome Kern
Lyrics by P.G. Wodehouse
The City Chap 1925

The Jousts
Music by Frederick Loewe
Lyrics by Alan Jay Lerner
Camelot 1960

Joy Bells
Music by Emmerich Kálmán
Lyrics by Harry B. Smith
The Circus Princess 1927

The Joy of Life
Music by Howard Talbot
Lyrics by Arthur Wimperis
The Arcadians 1910

The Joy of That Kiss
Music by Jerome Kern
Lyrics by Paul West
The Red Petticoat 1912

Joy or Strife
Music by Jean Gilbert
Lyrics by Harry B. Smith
The Red Robe 1928

Joy Ride
Music and lyrics by McElbert Moore
and Frank Grey
The Matinee Girl 1926

The Joy Spreader (musical scene)
Music by Richard Rodgers
Lyrics by Lorenz Hart
The Garrick Gaieties (1st edition) 1925

A Joyful Noise
Music and lyrics by Oscar Brand and Paul Nassau
A Joyful Noise 1966

A Joyful Thing
Music by Jimmy Van Heusen
Lyrics by Sammy Cahn
Walking Happy 1966

Juanita
Music by George Gershwin
Lyrics by Ira Gershwin
Lady, Be Good! 1924

Juba Dance
Music and lyrics by Buster Davis
Doctor Jazz 1975

Jubilation
Music and lyrics by Harry Chapin
Cotton Patch Gospel (OB) 1981

Jubilation T. Cornpone
Music by Gene de Paul
Lyrics by Johnny Mercer
Li'l Abner 1956

Jubilee
Music and lyrics by Alexander Hill
Hummin' Sam 1933

Jubilee Joe
Music and lyrics by Don Tucker
Red, White and Maddox 1969

Jubilo
Music by Jerome Kern
Lyrics by Anne Caldwell
She's a Good Fellow 1919

Based on *Kingdom Comin'* by Henry C. Work

Judas' Death
Music by Andrew Lloyd Webber
Lyrics by Tim Rice
Jesus Christ Superstar 1971

Jude's Holler
Music by David Baker
Lyrics by Will Holt
Come Summer 1969

Judgement Day
Music by Joe Ercole
Lyrics by Bruce Kluger
Ka-Boom (OB) 1980

The Judgement of Paris
Music by Erich Wolfgang Korngold (based on
Jacques Offenbach)
Lyrics by Herbert Baker
Helen Goes to Troy 1944

Judgement of Paris
Music by Donald Swann
Lyrics by Michael Flanders
At the Drop of a Hat 1959

Judging Song
Music and lyrics by Walter Cool
Mackey of Appalachia (OB) 1965

Judy, Who D'Ya Love?
Music by Charles Rosoff
Lyrics by Leo Robin
Judy 1927

A Jug of Wine
Music by Frederick Loewe
Lyrics by Alan Jay Lerner
The Day before Spring 1945

Juke Box
Music by Alex North
Lyrics by Alfred Hayes
Of V We Sing 1942

The Juke Box Hop
Music by Jule Styne
Lyrics by Betty Comden and Adolph Green
Do Re Mi 1960

Julianne
Music and lyrics by Ida Hoyt Chamberlain
Enchanted Isle 1927

Julie
Music and lyrics by John Dooley
Hobo (OB) 1961

Julius Caesar
Music and lyrics by Paul Nassau and Oscar Brand
*The Education of H*y*m*a*n K*a*p*l*a*n* 1968

Jump In
Music by Milton Schafer
Lyrics by Ronny Graham
Bravo Giovanni 1962

Jump, Jim Crow
Music by Sigmund Romberg
Lyrics by Rida Johnson Young
Maytime 1917

Jump, Little Chillun
Music by Sammy Fain
Lyrics by E.Y. Harburg
Flahooley 1951

Jump Steady
Music and lyrics by Noble Sissle and Eubie Blake
The Chocolate Dandies 1924

Jumping From Rock to Rock
Music by Bert Keyes and Bob Larimer
Lyrics by Bob Larimer
But Never Jam Today 1979

Jumping Jack
Music by Frank Grey
Lyrics by McElbert Moore and Frank Grey
The Matinee Girl 1926

June
Music by A. Baldwin Sloane
Lyrics by E. Ray Goetz
The Hen Pecks 1911

June
Music by Tom Johnstone
Lyrics by Phil Cook
When You Smile 1925

June
Music and lyrics by Porter Grainger
and Freddie Johnson
Lucky Sambo 1925

June Days
Music by Stephen Jones
Lyrics by Clifford Grey and Cyrus Wood
June Days 1925

June Is Bustin' Out All Over
Music by Richard Rodgers
Lyrics by Oscar Hammerstein II
Carousel 1945

June Moon
Music and lyrics by Ring Lardner
June Moon 1929

Jungle Jingle
Music and lyrics by Irving Berlin
Ziegfeld Follies (1927)

Jungle Rose
Music by Ford Dabney
Lyrics by Jo Trent
Rang-Tang 1927

Jungle Shadows
Music by Emmerich Kálmán and Herbert Stothart
Lyrics by Otto Harbach and Oscar Hammerstein II
Golden Dawn 1927

Junior Miss
Music by Burton Lane
Lyrics by Dorothy Fields
Junior Miss (1957) TV

Jupiter Forbid
Music by Richard Rodgers
Lyrics by Lorenz Hart
By Jupiter 1942

Just a Big-Hearted Man
Music by Werner Janssen
Lyrics by Mann Holiner and J. Keirn Brennan
Boom-Boom 1929

Just a Bit Naïve
Music by Alma Sanders
Lyrics by Monte Carlo
Louisiana Lady 1947

Just a House
Music by Elizabeth Swados
Lyrics by Garry Trudeau
Doonesbury 1983

Just a Housewife
Music and lyrics by Craig Carnelia
Working 1978

Just a Kiss
Music by A. Baldwin Sloane
Lyrics by Harry Cort and George E. Stoddard
China Rose 1925

Just a Kiss Apart
Music by Jule Styne
Lyrics by Leo Robin
Gentlemen Prefer Blondes 1949

Just a Little Bit More
Music by Arthur Schwartz
Lyrics by Dorothy Fields
Stars in Your Eyes 1939

Just a Little Blue for You
Music and lyrics by James F. Hanley
Keep It Clean 1929

Just a Little Joint With a Juke Box
Music and lyrics by Hugh Martin and Ralph Blane
Best Foot Forward 1941

Just a Little Line
Music by Jerome Kern
Lyrics by Anne Caldwell
She's a Good Fellow 1919

Just a Little Love Song
Music and lyrics by Max Ewing
The Grand Street Follies (1928)

Just a Little Penthouse and You
Music by William Heagney
Lyrics by William Heagney and Tom Connell
There You Are 1932

Just a Little Smile From You
Music by James F. Hanley
Lyrics by Eddie Dowling
Sidewalks of New York 1927

Just a Minute
Music by Harry Archer
Lyrics by Walter O'Keefe
Just a Minute 1928

Just a Pretty Widow
Music by Edmund Eysler
Lyrics by Herbert Reynolds
The Blue Paradise 1915

Just a Sentimental Tune
Music by Louis Alter
Lyrics by Max and Nathaniel Lief
Tattle Tales 1933

Just a Sister
Music and lyrics by Thomas McKnight
The Garrick Gaieties (3rd edition) 1930

Just a Voice to Call Me, Dear
Music by Emmerich Kálmán
Lyrics by P.G. Wodehouse
The Riviera Girl 1917

Just a Wonderful Time
Music by Frederico Valerio
Lyrics by Elizabeth Miele
Hit the Trail 1954

Just Across the River
Music by David Shire
Lyrics by Richard Maltby, Jr.
Starting Here, Starting Now (OB) 1977

Just Act Natural
Music and lyrics by George M. Cohan
The Rise of Rosie O'Reilly 1923

Just an Honest Mistake
Music and lyrics by Jay Livingston
and Ray Evans
Let It Ride 1961

Just an Ordinary Guy
Music by Albert Selden
Lyrics by Phyllis McGinley and Burt Shevelove
Small Wonder 1948

Just Another Guy
Music by Harold Karr
Lyrics by Matt Dubey
Happy Hunting 1956

Just Another Rhumba
Music by George Gershwin
Lyrics by Ira Gershwin
Goldwyn Follies (1938)

Dropped from film

Just as Father Used to Do
Music by Lionel Monckton
Lyrics by Percy Greenbank
The Quaker Girl 1911

Just Beyond the Rainbow
Music by Harry Revel
Lyrics by Arnold B. Horwitt
Are You With It? 1945

Just Cross the River From Queens
Music by Albert Von Tilzer
Lyrics by Neville Fleeson
Bye Bye, Bonnie 1927

Just Don't Make No Sense
Music and lyrics by Melvin Van Peebles
Ain't Supposed to Die a Natural Death 1971

Just Eighteen
Music by Richard A. Whiting
Lyrics by Oscar Hammerstein II
Free for All 1931

Just for Once
Music by Albert Hague
Lyrics by Dorothy Fields
Redhead 1959

Just for the Ride
Music by George Fischoff
Lyrics by Carole Bayer
Georgy 1970

Just for Today
Music and lyrics by Ervin Drake
Her First Roman 1968

Just for Tonight
Music by Maury Rubens
Lyrics by Clifford Grey
Katja 1926

Just for Tonight
Music and lyrics by Charlotte Kent
The Illustrators' Show 1936

Just for Tonight
Music by Bronislaw Kaper (based on Chopin)
Lyrics by John Latouche
Polonaise 1945

Just for Tonight
Music by Marvin Hamlisch
Lyrics by Carole Bayer Sager
They're Playing Our Song 1979

Just for You
Music by Herbert Stothart
Lyrics by Gus Kahn
Rose Marie (film version,1936)

Just Get Out and Walk
Music by Victor Herbert
Lyrics by Harry B. Smith
Miss Dolly Dollars 1905

Just Go to the Movies
Music and lyrics by Jerry Herman
A Day in Hollywood, a Night in the Ukraine 1979

Just Hello
Music by Sigmund Romberg
Lyrics by Otto Harbach
Forbidden Melody 1936

Just Him
Music by David Baker
Lyrics by David Craig
Phoenix '55 (OB)

Just Imagine
Music by Ray Henderson
Lyrics by B.G. DeSylva and Lew Brown
Good News 1927

Just in Case
Music by Kurt Weill
Lyrics by Ira Gershwin
The Firebrand of Florence 1945

Just in Time
Music by Jule Styne
Lyrics by Betty Comden and Adolph Green
Bells Are Ringing 1956

Just Let Me Look at You
Music by Jerome Kern
Lyrics by Dorothy Fields
The Joy of Living (1938) F

Just Like a Man
Music by Vernon Duke
Lyrics by Ogden Nash
Two's Company 1952

Just Like That
Music by Victor Herbert
Lyrics by B.G. DeSylva
Orange Blossoms 1922

Just Like You
Music by Paul Lannin
Lyrics by Arthur Francis
Two Little Girls in Blue 1921

Just Look!
Music by Armando Trovaioli
Lyrics by Pietro Garinei and Sandro Giovannini
(Lyric translation by Edward Eager)
Rugantino 1964

Just Mention Joe
Music by Harry Akst
Lyrics by Lew Brown
Calling All Stars 1934

Just Missed the Opening Chorus
Music by George Gershwin
Lyrics by B.G. DeSylva
George White's Scandals (1924)

Just My Luck
Music by Jimmy Van Heusen
Lyrics by Johnny Burke
Nellie Bly 1946

Just My Luck
Music by Jerry Bock
Lyrics by Sheldon Harnick
The Body Beautiful 1958

Just My Luck
Music and lyrics by Billy Solly
Boy Meets Boy (OB) 1975

Just Once Around the Clock
Music by Sigmund Romberg
Lyrics by Oscar Hammerstein II
May Wine 1935

Just Once More
Music and lyrics by Sandy Wilson
Valmouth (OB) 1960

Just One Kiss
Music by Harry Ruby
Lyrics by Bert Kalmar
The Ramblers 1926

Just One More Time
Music by Norman Curtis
Lyrics by Patricia Taylor Curtis
Walk Down Mah Street! (OB) 1968

Just One Night
Music by Elizabeth Swados
Lyrics by Garry Trudeau
Doonesbury 1983

Just One of Those Things
Music and lyrics by Cole Porter
The New Yorkers 1930

Dropped from production; title re-used for a completely new song in *Jubilee* (1935)

Just One of Those Things
Music and lyrics by Cole Porter
Jubilee 1935

Because it was fashionable in the mid-1930s to ascribe any and all witty remarks to Dorothy Parker, Porter began the verse to this: "As Dorothy Parker once said to her boy friend, 'Fare Thee Well.'"

Just One Person
Music by Larry Grossman
Lyrics by Hal Hackady
Snoopy (OB) 1982

Just One Step Ahead of Love
Music and lyrics by Cole Porter
You Never Know 1938

Dropped from production

Just One Way to Say I Love You
Music and lyrics by Irving Berlin
Miss Liberty 1949

Just Plain Folks
Music and lyrics by Jerry Herman
Parade (OB) 1960

Just Say the Word
Music by Frank D'Armond
Lyrics by Milton Berle
Saluta 1934

Just Sit Back
Music by Ted Simons
Lyrics by Elinor Guggenheimer
Potholes (OB) 1979

Just Sit Back and Relax
Music and lyrics by Ed Tyler
Sweet Miani (OB) 1962

Just Someone to Talk To
Music by Alfred Brooks
Lyrics by Ira J. Bilowit
Of Mice and Men (OB) 1958

Just Stay Alive
Music by Armando Trovaioli
Lyrics by Pietro Garinei and Sandro Giovannini
(Lyric translation by Edward Eager)
Rugantino 1964

Just Suppose
Music by Phil Baker and Maury Rubens
Lyrics by Sid Silvers and Moe Jaffe
Pleasure Bound 1929

Just Supposing
Music by George Gershwin
Lyrics by B.G. DeSylva
Sweet Little Devil 1924

Just Tell Me With Your Eyes
Music by A. Baldwin Sloane
Lyrics by E. Ray Goetz
The Hen Pecks 1911

Just the Crust
Music by Jimmy Van Heusen
Lyrics by Sammy Cahn
Skyscraper 1965

Just the Way You Are
Music by Jack Holmes
Lyrics by Bill Conklin and Bob Miller
O Say Can You See! (OB) 1962

Just Wait
Music by Jerome Kern
Lyrics by P.G. Wodehouse
Sitting Pretty 1924

Dropped from production

Just We Two
Music by Sigmund Romberg
Lyrics by Dorothy Donnelly
The Student Prince 1924

Just When I Thought I Had You All to Myself
Music and lyrics by Harry Denny
and Joe Fletcher
Footlights 1927

Just You Alone
Music by Louis A. Hirsch
Lyrics by Rennold Wolf
The Rainbow Girl 1918

Just You and I and the Baby
Music by Con Conrad
Lyrics by William B. Friedlander
Mercenary Mary 1925

Just You and I and the Moon
Music by Dave Stamper
Lyrics by Gene Buck
Ziegfeld Follies of 1914

Just You Wait
Music by Frederick Loewe
Lyrics by Alan Jay Lerner
My Fair Lady 1956

Just You Watch My Step
Music by Jerome Kern
Lyrics by P. G. Wodehouse
Leave It to Jane 1917

Just Your Old Friend
Music by Peter Link
Lyrics by C.C. Courtney and Ragan Courtney
Earl of Ruston 1971

Justice Triumphant
Music by Milton Schafer
Lyrics by Ira Levin
Drat! The Cat! 1965

Juvenile Fiction
Music and lyrics by Kelly Hamilton
Trixie True Teen Detective (OB) 1980

K

Ka Wahine Akamai
Music and lyrics by Eaton Magoon, Jr.
13 Daughters 1961

Kaleidoscope
Music by Tom Mandel
Lyrics by Louisa Rose
The Bar That Never Closes (OB) 1972

Kalialani
Music and lyrics by Eaton Magoon, Jr.
Heathen 1972

Kalidah Battle
Music and lyrics by Charlie Smalls
The Wiz 1975

Kalimera
Music by Peter Link
Lyrics by Michael Cacoyannis
Lysistrata 1972

Ka-lu-a
Music by Jerome Kern
Lyrics by Anne Caldwell
Good Morning, Dearie 1921

Kalua Bay
Music by John Kander
Lyrics by James Goldman, John Kander
and William Goldman
A Family Affair 1962

Kan the Kaiser
Music by Jerome Kern
Lyrics by Berton Braley
Toot-Toot! 1918

Kandahar Isle
Music by Mann Holiner
Lyrics by Alberta Nichols
Gay Paree 1926

Kangaroo
Music by James P. Johnson
Lyrics by Henry Creamer
A La Carte 1927

The Kangaroo
Music by Milton Schafer
Lyrics by Ronny Graham
Bravo Giovanni 1962

Kangaroo Court
Music by Richard Rodgers
Lyrics by Lorenz Hart
Hallelujah, I'm a Bum (1933) F

Kansas City
Music by Richard Rodgers
Lyrics by Oscar Hammerstein II
Oklahoma! 1943

Karen's Lullaby
Music by Walt Smith
Lyrics by Leon Uris
Ari 1971

Kathakali
Music by Sammy Fain
Lyrics by Paul Francis Webster
Christine 1960

Kathleen, Mine
Music by Vincent Youmans
Lyrics by Edward Heyman
Through the Years 1932

Katie Did in Madrid
Music by Frank Black
Lyrics by Gladys Shelley
The Duchess Misbehaves 1946

Katie Jonas
Music by Stanley Lebowsky
Lyrics by Fred Tobias
Gantry 1970

Katie O'Sullivan
Music by Earl Robinson
Lyrics by Waldo Salt
Sandhog (OB) 1954

Katie Went to Haiti
Music and lyrics by Cole Porter
Du Barry Was a Lady 1939

Katinka
Music by Rudolf Friml
Lyrics by Otto Harbach
Katinka 1915

Katinka
Music by George Gershwin
Lyrics by B.G. DeSylva, E. Ray Goetz
and Ballard MacDonald
George White's Scandals (1923)

Katinka/The Darkness
Music by Gerald Jay Markoe
Lyrics by Michael Colby
Charlotte Sweet (OB) 1982

Katinka to Eva to Frances
Music by Don Walker
Lyrics by George Marion, Jr.
Allah Be Praised! 1944

Katinkitschka
Music by George Gershwin
Lyrics by Ira Gershwin
Delicious (1931) F

Katy-Did
Music by Jerome Kern
Lyrics by Harry B. Smith
Oh, I Say! 1913

A Katzenjammer Kinda Song
Music and lyrics by Kelly Hamilton
Trixie True Teen Detective (OB) 1980

Kava Ceremony
Music and lyrics by Eaton Magoon, Jr.
Heathen 1972

K.C. Line
Music and lyrics by Bland Simpson and Jim Wann
(Based on traditional folk music)
Diamond Studs (OB) 1975

Keep a-Countin' Eight
Music and lyrics by George M. Cohan
The Rise of Rosie O'Reilly 1923

Keep A-Diggin'
Music and lyrics by Porter Grainger
and Freddie Johnson
Lucky Sambo 1925

Keep-a-Hoppin'
Music and lyrics by Meredith Willson
The Unsinkable Molly Brown 1960

Keep a Kiss for Me
Music by Alma Sanders
Lyrics by Monte Carlo
Oh! Oh! Nurse 1925

Keep Away From the Moonlight
Music by Richard Rodgers
Lyrics by Lorenz Hart
Hollywood Party (1934) F

Dropped from film

Keep Building Your Castles
Music by Tom Johnstone
Lyrics by Phil Cook
When You Smile 1925

Keep 'Em Busy, Keep 'Em Quiet
Music by Nancy Ford
Lyrics by Gretchen Cryer
Now Is the Time for All Good Men (OB) 1967

Keep It Casual
Music by John Green
Lyrics by George Marion, Jr.
Beat the Band 1942

Keep It Dark
Music by Gustav Luders
Lyrics by Frank Pixley
The Prince of Pilsen 1903

Keep It Dark
Music by Sigmund Romberg
Lyrics by Dorothy Donnelly
Blossom Time 1921

Keep It Gay
Music by Richard Rodgers
Lyrics by Oscar Hammerstein II
Me and Juliet 1953

Keep It Hot
Music by John Kander
Lyrics by Fred Ebb
Chicago 1975

Keep It Low
Music by Gerald Jay Markoe
Lyrics by Michael Colby
Charlotte Sweet (OB) 1982

Keep It Simple
Music and lyrics by Jay Livingston
and Ray Evans
Oh Captain! 1958

Keep It Under Your Hat
Music and lyrics by Vincent Valentini
Parisiana 1928

Keep It Up
Music by William B. Kernell
Lyrics by Dorothy Donnelly
Hello, Lola 1926

Keep Me Out of the Caisson
Music by Scott MacLarty
Lyrics by Dorothy Chansky
The Brooklyn Bridge (OB) 1983

Keep Off the Grass
Music by Rudolf Friml
Lyrics by Otto Harbach and Edward Clark
You're In Love 1917

Keep On Dancing
Music and lyrics by Vincent Valentini
Parisiana 1928

Keep On Dancing
Music by Lawrence Hurwit
Lyrics by Lee Goldsmith
Sextet 1974

Keep On Smiling
Music by Rudolf Friml
Lyrics by Rida Johnson Young
Sometime 1918

Keep Shufflin'
Music by Thomas (Fats) Waller
Lyrics by Andy Razaf
Keep Shufflin' 1928

Keep Them Guessing
Music by Tom Johnstone
Lyrics by Phil Cook
When You Smile 1925

Keep Working
Music and lyrics by Elizabeth Swados
Lullabye and Goodnight 1982

Keep Your Chin Up
Music by Eubie Blake
Lyrics by Noble Sissle
Shuffle Along of 1933

Keep Your Eye on the Ball
Music by Harry Tierney
Lyrics by Joseph McCarthy
Kid Boots 1923

Keep Your Eye on the Red
Music and lyrics by Micki Grant
It's So Nice to Be Civilized 1980

Keep Your Hand on Your Heart
Music by Frederick Loewe
Lyrics by Earle Crooker
Great Lady 1938

Keep Your Little Eye Upon the Main Chance, Mary
Music by Don Pippin
Lyrics by Steve Brown
The Contrast (OB) 1972

Keep Your Nose to the Grindstone
Music by James Mundy
Lyrics by John Latouche
The Vamp 1955

Keep Your Shirt On
Music by Manning Sherwin
Lyrics by Arthur Herzog, Jr.
Bad Habits of 1926 (OB)

Keep Your Undershirt On
Music by Harry Ruby
Lyrics by Bert Kalmar
Top Speed 1929

Keepin' It Together
Music and lyrics by Bob Ost
Everybody's Gettin' Into the Act (OB) 1981

Keepin' Myself for You
Music by Vincent Youmans
Lyrics by Sidney Clare
Hit the Deck (film version, 1929)

Keeping Cool With Coolidge
Music by Jule Styne
Lyrics by Leo Robin
Gentlemen Prefer Blondes 1949

Keeping Prigio Company
Music by Lehman Engel
Lyrics by Agnes Morgan
A Hero Is Born 1937

Kenosha Canoe
Music by Morgan Lewis
Lyrics by Nancy Hamilton
Three to Make Ready 1946

Kentucky
Music by Joe Jordan
Lyrics by Homer Tutt and Henry Creamer
Deep Harlem 1929

The Keokuk Culture Club
Music by Victor Herbert
Lyrics by Henry Blossom
Mlle. Modiste 1905

Kept in Suspense
Music by Carroll Gibbons
Lyrics by Billy Rose and James Dyrenforth
Crazy Quilt 1931

Ker-choo!
Music by Sigmund Romberg
Lyrics by Dorothy Donnelly
My Maryland 1927

A Kettle Is Singing
Music by Jerome Kern
Lyrics by Herbert Reynolds
Rock-a-Bye Baby 1918

The Key to My Heart
Music by Lou Alter
Lyrics by Ira Gershwin
The Social Register 1931

Keys to Heaven
Music by Richard Rodgers
Lyrics by Lorenz Hart
The Garrick Gaieties (2nd edition) 1926

Keys to Your Heart
Music by Jimmy McHugh
Lyrics by Dorothy Fields
Lew Leslie's International Revue 1930

Kick in the Pants
Music by Harry Archer
Lyrics by Will B. Johnstone
Entre-Nous (OB) 1935

Kickin' the Clouds Away
Music by George Gershwin
Lyrics by B.G. DeSylva and Ira Gershwin
Tell Me More 1925

Kickin' the Corn Around
Music by Richard Lewine
Lyrics by Ted Fetter
The Girl From Wyoming (OB) 1938

Kid
Music and lyrics by Walter Marks
Golden Rainbow 1968

The Kid Inside
Music and lyrics by Craig Carnelia
Is There Life After High School? 1982

Kidnapped
Music by Galt MacDermot
Lyrics by John Guare
Two Gentlemen of Verona 1971

Kids
Music by Charles Strouse
Lyrics by Lee Adams
Bye Bye Birdie 1960

Kids Are Out
Music and lyrics by Ronnie Britton
Gift of the Magi (OB) 1975

Kiki
Music by Lewis E. Gensler
Lyrics by B.G. DeSylva
Captain Jinks 1925

The Kill
Music by Wally Harper
Lyrics by Paul Zakrzewski
Sensations (OB) 1970

Kill
Music and lyrics by Gene Curty, Nitra Scharfman
and Chuck Strand
The Lieutenant 1975

Killing Time
Music by Michael Dansicker
Lyrics by Sarah Schlesinger
On The Swing Shift (OB) 1983

The Kind of Man
Music by Robert Kessler
Lyrics by Lola Pergament
O Marry Me! (OB) 1961

The Kind of Man a Woman Needs
Music by Michael Leonard
Lyrics by Herbert Martin
The Yearling 1965

Kind of Woman
Music and lyrics by Stephen Schwartz
Pippin 1972

Kind Old Gentleman
Music and lyrics by Ervin Drake
Her First Roman 1968

Kinda Cute
Music by Jay Gorney
Lyrics by E.Y. Harburg
Earl Carroll's Sketch Book (1929)

Kinda Like You
Music by Vincent Youmans
Lyrics by Edward Heyman
Through the Years 1932

Kinda Sorta Doin' Nothing
Music and lyrics by Jay Thompson
Double Entry (OB) 1961

Kindness
Music by Helen Miller
Lyrics by Eve Merriam
Inner City 1971

Kindred Spirits
Music by Norman Campbell
Lyrics by Donald Harron and Norman Campbell
Anne of Green Gables (OB) 1971

King Cole
Music and lyrics by Bland Simpson and Jim Wann
(Based on traditonal folk music)
Diamond Studs (OB) 1975

King Cotton
Music by Giuseppe Verdi (adapted by
Hans Spialek)
Lyrics by Charles Friedman
My Darlin' Aïda 1952

King Foo-Foo the First
Music by George Fischoff
Lyrics by Verna Tomasson
The Prince and the Pauper (OB) 1963

King Herod's Song
Music by Andrew Lloyd Webber
Lyrics by Tim Rice
Jesus Christ Superstar 1971

King Joe
Music and lyrics by Johnny Brandon
Billy Noname (OB) 1970

King of Hearts
Music by Peter Link
Lyrics by Jacob Brackman
King of Hearts 1978

King of London
Music and lyrics by Robert Wright
and George Forrest
Kean 1961

King of the Sword
Music by Robert Stolz and Maury Rubens
Lyrics by J. Keirn Brennan
The Red Robe 1928

King of the World
Music and lyrics by Robert Larimer
King of the Whole Damn World (OB) 1962

Kings and Queens
Music by Arthur Siegel
Lyrics by June Carroll
Shoestring Revue (1955) (OB)

The King's Musketeers
Music by Victor Herbert
Lyrics by Harry B. Smith
Cyrano de Bergerac 1899

The King's New Clothes
Music and lyrics by Frank Loesser
Hans Christian Andersen (1952) F

The King's Song
Music by Richard Rodgers
Lyrics by Oscar Hammerstein II
The King and I 1951

The Kinkajou
Music by Harry Tierney
Lyrics by Joseph McCarthy
Rio Rita 1927

The Kiss
Music by Rudolf Friml
Lyrics by Bide Dudley and Otto Harbach
The Little Whopper 1919

Kiss a Four Leaf Clover
Music by Jerome Kern
Lyrics by Anne Caldwell and Otto Harbach
Criss-Cross 1926

Dropped from production

A Kiss Before I Go
Music by Rudolf Friml
Lyrics by P.G. Wodehouse and Clifford Grey
The Three Musketeers 1928

A Kiss for Cinderella
Music by Richard Rodgers
Lyrics by Lorenz Hart
Present Arms 1928

Kiss Her Now
Music and lyrics by Jerry Herman
Dear World 1969

A Kiss I Must Refuse You
Music by Sigmund Romberg
Lyrics by Irving Caesar
Nina Rosa 1930

A Kiss in the Dark
Music by Victor Herbert
Lyrics by B.G. DeSylva
Orange Blossoms 1922

A Kiss in the Moonlight
Music and lyrics by Clarence Gaskill
Earl Carroll's Vanities (1925)

Kiss Me
Music by Louis A. Hirsch
Lyrics by Otto Harbach
Going Up 1917

Kiss Me
Music by Winthrop Cortelyou
Lyrics by Derick Wulff
Kiss Me 1927

Kiss Me
Music and lyrics by Noël Coward
Bitter Sweet 1929

Kiss Me
Music and lyrics by Rick Besoyan
The Student Gypsy (OB) 1963

Kiss Me
Music and lyrics by Stephen Sondheim
Sweeney Todd 1979

Kiss Me Again
Music by Victor Herbert
Lyrics by Henry Blossom
Mlle. Modiste 1905

Fritzi Scheff, the opera star for whom Herbert composed *Mlle. Modiste,* at first refused to sing this song, complaining that the opening notes were too low. Lyricist Blossom took her side, but Herbert won out, and Miss Scheff was still singing "Kiss Me Again" into the 1940s.

Kiss Me and Kill Me With Love
Music by Sammy Fain
Lyrics by Dan Shapiro
Ankles Aweigh 1955

Kiss Me, and 'Tis Day
Music by Rudolf Friml
Lyrics by Otto Harbach
The Firefly 1912

Kiss Me and We'll Both Go Home
Music by Morgan Lewis
Lyrics by Nancy Hamilton
One for the Money 1939

Kiss Me, Kate
Music and lyrics by Cole Porter
Kiss Me, Kate 1948

Kiss Me No Kisses
Music and lyrics by Ervin Drake
What Makes Sammy Run? 1964

A Kiss to Remind You
Music by Franz Lehár
Lyrics by Edward Eliscu
Frederika 1937

The Kiss Waltz
Music by Ivan Caryll
Lyrics by C.M.S. McLellan
The Pink Lady 1911

A Kiss With a Kick
Music by Philip Charig and Richard Myers
Lyrics by Leo Robin
Allez-Oop 1927

Kissing Time
Music by Oscar Straus
Lyrics by Joseph W. Herbert
A Waltz Dream 1908

Kitchen Police
Music and lyrics by Irving Berlin
Yip, Yip, Yaphank 1918

Kitchen Range
Music by Paul A. Rubens
Lyrics by Paul A. Rubens and Arthur Wimperis
The Sunshine Girl 1913

Kite
Music and lyrics by Clark Gesner
You're a Good Man, Charlie Brown (OB) 1967

The Kite
Music by Gary William Friedman
Lyrics by Will Holt
Taking My Turn (OB) 1983

Kitty Kat Song
Music and lyrics by Ann Harris
Sky High (OB) 1979

Kitty's Kisses
Music by Con Conrad
Lyrics by Gus Kahn
Kitty's Kisses 1926

The Kitzel Engagement
Music by Richard Rodgers
Lyrics by Lorenz Hart
Betsy 1926

The Kling-Kling Bird on the Divi-Divi Tree
Music and lyrics by Cole Porter
Jubilee 1935

Knee Deep in June
Music by Jay Gorney
Lyrics by E.Y. Harburg
Earl Carroll's Vanities (1930)

Knees
Music by Richard Rodgers
Lyrics by Lorenz Hart
Heads Up! 1929

The Knight of the Mirrors
Music by Mitch Leigh
Lyrics by Joe Darion
Man of La Mancha 1965

Knight of the Woeful Countenance
Music by Mitch Leigh
Lyrics by Joe Darion
Man of La Mancha 1965

Knights of the White Cross
Music by Giuseppe Verdi (adapted by Hans Spialek)
Lyrics by Charles Friedman
My Darlin' Aïda 1952

Knit, Knit, Knit
Music by Ivan Caryll
Lyrics by Anne Caldwell
Jack O' Lantern 1917

Knock, Knock
Music by John Kander
Lyrics by Fred Ebb
Flora, the Red Menace 1965

Knock on Wood
Music by Richard Myers
Lyrics by Edward Eliscu
Nine-Fifteen Revue 1930

The Knocking Bookworms
Music by Harry Archer
Lyrics by Harlan Thompson
Little Jessie James 1923

Knocking on Wood
Music by Niclas Kempner
Lyrics by Graham John
The Street Singer 1929

Know When to Smile
Music by Karl Hajos (based on Chopin)
Lyrics by Harry B. Smith
White Lilacs 1928

Know Your Business
Music and lyrics by Melvin Van Peebles
Don't Play Us Cheap 1972

Knowing When to Leave
Music by Burt Bacharach
Lyrics by Hal David
Promises, Promises 1968

Kohala, Welcome
Music by Richard Rodgers
Lyrics by Lorenz Hart
Present Arms 1928

Kokoraki
Music by Donald Swann
Lyrics by Michael Flanders
At the Drop of a Hat 1959

Kongo Kate
Music by George Gershwin
Lyrics by B.G. DeSylva
George White's Scandals (1924)

Koo-La-Loo
Music by Jerome Kern
Lyrics by P.G. Wodehouse
Oh, Boy! 1917

Kosher Kitty Kelly
Music and lyrics by Leon DeCosta
Kosher Kitty Kelly 1925

Kosher Kleagle
Music by Philp Charig
Lyrics by J.P. McEvoy
Americana (1926)

K-ra-zy for You
Music by George Gershwin
Lyrics by Ira Gershwin
Treasure Girl 1928

Kukla Katusha
Music by Lee Pockriss
Lyrics by Anne Croswell
Tovarich 1963

Kuli Kuli
Music and lyrics by Eaton Magoon, Jr.
13 Daughters 1961

Kung Fu
Music and lyrics by Peter Copani
New York City Street Show (OB) 1977

Kyrie Eleison
Music by Don Gohman
Lyrics by Hal Hackady
Ambassador 1972

L

La Belle Parisienne
Music by Gustave Kerker
Lyrics by Hugh Morton
The Belle of New York 1897

La Belle Province
Music by Patrick Rose
Lyrics by Merv Campone and Richard Ouzounian
A Bistro Car on the CNR (OB) 1978

La Cage aux Folles
Music and lyrics by Jerry Herman
La Cage aux Folles 1983

La Calinda
Music by Ruth Cleary Patterson
Lyrics by Gladys Shelley
Russell Patterson's Sketch Book (OB) 1960

La Fiesta
Music by Sammy Fain
Lyrics by Dan Shapiro
Ankles Aweigh 1955

La France, la France
Music by Michael J. Lewis
Lyrics by Anthony Burgess
Cyrano 1973

La Grosse Valise
Music by Gerard Calvi
Lyrics by Harold Rome
La Grosse Valise 1965

La Java
Music by Gerard Calvi
Lyrics by Harold Rome
La Grosse Valise 1965

La La La
Music and lyrics by Richard Rodgers
No Strings 1962

La Marseilles
Music by Vincent Youmans
Lyrics by Harold Adamson and Clifford Grey
Smiles 1930

La Princesse Zenobia (ballet)
Music by Richard Rodgers
On Your Toes 1936

La Prisonnière
Music by Max Ewing
Lyrics by Albert Carroll
The Grand Street Follies (1927) (OB)

The Label on the Bottle
Music by Arthur Schwartz
Lyrics by Howard Dietz
The Gay Life 1961

Labor Day Parade
Music by Clarence Todd
Lyrics by Andy Razaf
Keep Shufflin' 1928

Labor Day Parade
Music by Eubie Blake
Lyrics by Noble Sissle
Shuffle Along of 1933

Labor Is the Thing
Music by Richard Rodgers
Lyrics by Lorenz Hart
I'd Rather Be Right 1937

Lack-a-Day
Music by John Mundy
Lyrics by Edward Eager
The Liar 1950

Lackawanna
Music by Joseph Meyer and James F. Hanley
Lyrics by B.G. DeSylva
Big Boy 1925

Ladies
Music by Paul A. Rubens
Lyrics by Paul A. Rubens and Arthur Wimperis
The Sunshine Girl 1913

Ladies
Music and lyrics by Harold Rome
Destry Rides Again 1959

Ladies and Gentlemen, That's Love
Music by Ray Henderson
Lyrics by B.G. DeSylva and Lew Brown
George White's Scandals (1931)

Ladies Are Present
Music by Jerome Kern
Lyrics by P.G. Wodehouse
Sitting Pretty 1924

Dropped from production

Ladies, Beware
Music by Rudolf Friml
Lyrics by Rowland Leigh and John Shubert
Music Hath Charms 1934

Ladies' Choice!
Music by Franz Lehár
Lyrics by Adrian Ross
The Merry Widow 1907

Ladies' Choice
Music by Oscar Straus
Lyrics by Edward Delaney Dunn
The Last Waltz 1921

The Ladies From the Cultured West
Music by Leo Fall
Lyrics by Harold Atteridge
The Rose of Stamboul 1922

Ladies, Have a Care!
Music by Jerome Kern
Lyrics by Edgar Allan Woolf
Head Over Heels 1918

A Ladies' Home Companion
Music by Richard Rodgers
Lyrics by Lorenz Hart
A Connecticut Yankee 1927

Written for *Betsy* (1926) but dropped from
production

Ladies in Their Sensitivities
Music and lyrics by Stephen Sondheim
Sweeney Todd 1979

Ladies in Waiting
Music and lyrics by Cole Porter
Les Girls (1957) F

Ladies in Waiting
Music by Robert Colby
Lyrics by Robert Clay and Nita Jonas
Half-Past Wednesday (OB) 1962

Ladies, Look at Yourselves
Music and lyrics by Elizabeth Swados
Lullabye and Goodnight 1982

Ladies of the Box Office
Music by Richard Rodgers
Lyrics by Lorenz Hart
The Garrick Gaieties (1st edition) 1925

Ladies of the Evening
Music by Richard Rodgers
Lyrics by Lorenz Hart
The Boys From Syracuse 1938

Ladies of the Jury
Music by Sigmund Romberg
Lyrics by Oscar Hammerstein II
The New Moon 1928

Ladies of the Town
Music and lyrics by Noël Coward
Bitter Sweet 1929

The Ladies' Opinion
Music by John Mundy
Lyrics by Edward Eager
The Liar 1950

Ladies Room
Music by Alex Fogarty
Lyrics by Edwin Gilbert
You Never Know 1938

The Ladies Singin' Their Song
Music by David Shire
Lyrics by Richard Maltby, Jr.
Baby 1983

The Ladies Who Lunch
Music and lyrics by Stephen Sondheim
Company 1970

The Ladies Who Sing With a Band
Music by Thomas (Fats) Waller
Lyrics by George Marion, Jr.
Early to Bed 1943

The Lady
Music by Elsie Peters
Lyrics by Alfred Hayes
Tis of Thee 1940

Lady
Music by Vernon Duke
Lyrics by John Latouche
The Lady Comes Across 1942

Dropped from production

A Lady Bred in the Purple
Music by Seymour Furth and Lee Edwards
Lyrics by R.F. Carroll
Bringing Up Father 1925

The Lady Bug Song
Music by George Kleinsinger
Lyrics by Joe Darion
Shinbone Alley 1957

Lady Do
Music by Abel Baer
Lyrics by Sam Lewis and Joe Young
Lady Do 1927

Lady Fair
Music by Ray Henderson
Lyrics by B.G. DeSylva and Lew Brown
George White's Scandals (1926)

The Lady From the Bayou
Music by Vincent Youmans
Lyrics by Leo Robin
Hit the Deck (film version, 1954)

The Lady Has Oomph
Music and lyrics by Dorcas Cochran
and Charles Rosoff
Earl Carroll's Vanities (1940)

Lady in Ermine
Music by Jean Gilbert
Lyrics by Harry Graham and Cyrus Wood
The Lady in Ermine 1922

Lady in the Window
Music by Sigmund Romberg
Lyrics by Otto Harbach
Forbidden Melody 1936

Lady in Waiting
Music by Alberta Nichols
Lyrics by Mann Holiner
Hey Nonny Nonny! 1932

Lady in Waiting
Music by Leroy Anderson
Lyrics by Joan Ford,
Walter Kerr and Jean Kerr
Goldilocks 1958

The Lady Is a Tramp
Music by Richard Rodgers
Lyrics by Lorenz Hart
Babes in Arms 1937

The Lady Isn't Looking
Music by Galt MacDermot
Lyrics by Christopher Gore
Via Galactica 1972

The Lady I've Vowed to Wed
Music by Cole Porter
Lyrics by T. Lawrason Riggs and Cole Porter
See America First 1916

Lady Luck
Music by Harold Levey
Lyrics by Zelda Sears
The Clinging Vine 1922

Lady Luck
Music by George Gershwin
Lyrics by Ira Gershwin
Tip-Toes 1925

Lady Luck
Music by Ray Henderson
Lyrics by B.G. DeSylva
Three Cheers 1928

Lady Luck, Smile on Me
Music by Harry Tierney
Lyrics by Joseph McCarthy
Up She Goes 1922

A Lady Must Live
Music by Richard Rodgers
Lyrics by Lorenz Hart
America's Sweetheart 1931

A Lady Needs a Change
Music by Arthur Schwartz
Lyrics by Dorothy Fields
Stars in Your Eyes 1939

A Lady Needs a Rest
Music and lyrics by Cole Porter
Let's Face It! 1941

Lady of My Heart
Music by Milton Susskind
Lyrics by Paul Porter and Benjamin Hapgood Burt
Florida Girl 1925

Lady of the Evening
Music and lyrics by Irving Berlin
Music Box Revue (2nd edition) 1922

Lady of the Manor
Music and lyrics by Sandy Wilson
Valmouth (OB) 1960

Lady of the Rose
Music by Rudolf Friml
Lyrics by Otto Harbach and Oscar Hammerstein II
The Wild Rose 1926

The Lady of the Slipper
Music by Victor Herbert
Lyrics by James O'Dea
The Lady of the Slipper 1912

The Lady of the Snow
Music by Harold Levey
Lyrics by Owen Murphy
The Greenwich Village Follies (1925)

Lady Raffles
Music by Richard Rodgers
Lyrics by Lorenz Hart
Poor Little Ritz Girl 1920

Included in Boston production but dropped before
Broadway opening

Lady Wake Up
Music by Robert Mitchell
Lyrics by Elizabeth Perry
Bags (OB) 1982

The Lady Was Made to Be Loved
Music by Jacques Urbont
Lyrics by Bruce Geller
All in Love (OB) 1961

Lady Whippoorwill
Music by Harry Tierney
Lyrics by Joseph McCarthy
Cross My Heart 1928

The Lady Who Loved to Sing
Music by Patrick Rose
Lyrics by Merv Campone and Richard Ouzounian
A Bistro Car on the CNR (OB) 1978

The Lady With the Tap
Music by Arthur Schwartz
Lyrics by Howard Dietz
At Home Abroad 1935

Lady's Choice
Music by Richard Adler
Lyrics by Will Holt
Music Is 1976

The Lady's in Love With You
Music by Burton Lane
Lyrics by Frank Loesser
Some Like It Hot (1939) F

Laertes Coercion
Music and lyrics by Cliff Jones
Rockabye Hamlet 1976

Lak Jeem
Music by Rudolf Friml
Lyrics by Oscar Hammerstein II and Otto Harbach
Rose Marie 1924

Lambert's Quandary
Music by Don Gohman
Lyrics by Hal Hackady
Ambassador 1972

Lament
Music and lyrics by Frederick Silver
Gay Company (OB) 1974

Lament
Music by Andrew Lloyd Webber
Lyrics by Tim Rice
Evita 1979

The Lament of Shakespeare
Music by Morris Hamilton
Lyrics by Grace Henry
Earl Carroll's Vanities (1926)

Lament on Fifth Avenue
Music by Claibe Richardson
Lyrics by Paul Rosner
Shoestring '57 (OB)

Lamplight
Music and lyrics by James Shelton
New Faces of 1934

Land of Betrayal
Music by Galt MacDermot
Lyrics by John Guare
Two Gentlemen of Verona 1971

Land of Broken Dreams
Music by Martin Broones
Lyrics by Ballard MacDonald
Rufus Lemaire's Affairs 1927

The Land of Going to Be
Music and lyrics by E. Ray Goetz
and Walter Kollo
Paris 1928

The Land of Let's Pretend
Music by Jerome Kern
Lyrics by Harry B. Smith
The Girl From Utah 1914

Land of Mine
Music by Giuseppe Verdi (adapted by Hans
Spialek)
Lyrics by Charles Friedman
My Darlin' Aida 1952

The Land of Opportunitee
Music by Arthur Schwartz
Lyrics by Ira Gershwin
Park Avenue 1946

Land of Rockefellera
Music by Lee Wainer
Lyrics by John Lund
New Faces of 1943

Land of Romance
Music by Percy Wenrich
Lyrics by Raymond Peck
Castles in the Air 1926

Land of the Gay Caballero
Music by George Gershwin
Lyrics by Ira Gershwin
Girl Crazy 1930

The Land Where the Good Songs Go
Music by Jerome Kern
Lyrics by P.G. Wodehouse
Miss 1917

Langenstein in Spring
Music by Edward A. Horan
Lyrics by Frederick Herendeen
All the King's Horses 1934

The Language of Flowers
Music by Cole Porter
Lyrics by T. Lawrason Riggs and Cole Porter
See America First 1916

Lantern Night
Music by Armando Trovaioli
Lyrics by Pietro Garinei and Sandro Giovannini
(Lyric translation by Edward Eager)
Rugantino 1964

Lantern of Love
Music by Percy Wenrich
Lyrics by Raymond Peck
Castles in the Air 1926

L'Apres-Midi d'un Boeuf
Music and lyrics by Cole Porter
Du Barry Was a Lady 1939

Larceny and Love
Music by Robert Emmett Dolan
Lyrics by Johnny Mercer
Foxy 1964

The Lark
Music by Sigmund Romberg
Lyrics by Harry B. Smith
The Love Call 1927

Lars, Lars
Music by Richard Rodgers
Lyrics by Martin Charnin
I Remember Mama 1979

Las Vegas
Music and lyrics by Ray Golden, Sy Kleinman
and Lee Adams
Catch a Star! 1955

Las Vegas
Music and lyrics by Billy Barnes
The Billy Barnes Revue 1959

The Lass Who Loved a Sailor
Music by Richard Rodgers
Lyrics by Lorenz Hart
Heads Up! 1929

Lasses Who Live in Glass Houses
Music by A. Baldwin Sloane
Lyrics by E. Ray Goetz
The Hen Pecks 1911

The Last Blues
Music and lyrics by Cliff Jones
Rockabye Hamlet 1976

Last Confession
Music by John Duffy
Lyrics by Rocco Bufano and John Duffy
Horseman, Pass By (OB) 1969

The Last Dance
Music and lyrics by Noël Coward
Bitter Sweet 1929

The Last Long Mile
Music and lyrics by Emil Breiterfeld
Toot-Toot! 1918

The marching song of the U.S. Army Training
Station at Plattsburg, N.Y. during World War I.

The Last Long Mile
Music by Vernon Duke
Lyrics by Howard Dietz
Jackpot 1944

Last Night When We Were Young
Music by Harold Arlen
Lyrics by E.Y. Harburg

Written for Lawrence Tibbett and cut, successively,
from three forgettable films, the song was
nevertheless taken up not only by Tibbett, but also
by Judy Garland and Frank Sinatra.

The Last Minute Waltz
Music and lyrics by Paul Shyre
Ah, Men (OB) 1981

The Last Part of Ev'ry Party
Music by Harry Tierney
Lyrics by Joseph McCarthy
Irene 1919

The Last Supper
Music by Andrew Lloyd Webber
Lyrics by Tim Rice
Jesus Christ Superstar 1971

The Last Sweet Days of Isaac
Music by Nancy Ford
Lyrics by Gretchen Cryer
The Last Sweet Days of Isaac (OB) 1970

The Last Time I Saw Paris
Music by Jerome Kern
Lyrics by Oscar Hammerstein II
Lady, Be Good (1941) F

Academy Award winner

Although the song was not actually written for the
film it won the Academy Award. Kern and
Hammerstein felt strongly that the award should
have gone to Harold Arlen and Johnny Mercer for
"Blues in the Night." They were responsible for a
change in the Academy rules, and since 1942 a
song must have been written specifically for a film
in order to be eligible for the award.

The Last Waltz
Music by Oscar Straus
Lyrics by Edward Delaney Dunn
The Last Waltz 1921

The Last Word
Music by Lehman Engel
Lyrics by Agnes Morgan
A Hero Is Born 1937

Latavia
Music by Percy Wenrich
Lyrics by Raymond Peck
Castles in the Air 1926

The Latavian Chant
Music by Percy Wenrich
Lyrics by Raymond Peck
Castles in the Air 1926

Late Bloomer
Music and lyrics by James Quinn and Alaric Jans
Do Patent Leather Shoes Really Reflect Up? 1982

The Late, Late Show
Music by Jule Styne
Lyrics by Betty Comden and Adolph Green
Do Re Mi 1960

Late Love
Music by Jack Urbont
Lyrics by Bruce Geller
Livin' the Life (OB) 1957

Lately I've Been Feeling So Strange
Music and lyrics by Irving Burgie
Ballad for Bimshire (OB) 1963

Later
Music and lyrics by Stephen Sondheim
A Little Night Music 1973

Later than Spring
Music and lyrics by Noël Coward
Sail Away 1961

The Latest Thing From Paris
Music by Rudolf Friml
Lyrics by Otto Harbach
The Firefly 1912

Latigo
Music by Sigmund Romberg
Lyrics by Irving Caesar
Nina Rosa 1930

The Latin in Me
Music by Sammy Fain
Lyrics by Irving Kahal and Jack Yellen
Boys and Girls Together 1940

A Latin Tune, a Manhattan Moon and You
Music by Jimmy McHugh
Lyrics by Al Dubin
Keep Off the Grass 1940

Latins Know How
Music and lyrics by Irving Berlin
Louisiana Purchase 1940

Laugh
Music by Richard Rodgers
Lyrics by Lorenz Hart
Jumbo 1935

Laugh a Little
Music by Michael Leonard
Lyrics by Herbert Martin
How to Be a Jewish Mother 1967

Laugh After Laugh
Music by Richard B. Chodosh
Lyrics by Barry Alan Grael
The Streets of New York (OB) 1963

Laugh at Life
Music by Maury Rubens
Lyrics by J. Delany Dunn
The Red Robe 1928

Laugh, I Thought I'd Die
Music by Tommy Wolf
Lyrics by Fran Landesman
The Nervous Set 1959

Laugh It Off
Music by Vincent Youmans and Herbert Stothart
Lyrics by Oscar Hammerstein II
and William Cary Duncan
Mary Jane McKane 1923

Laugh It Up
Music and lyrics by Irving Berlin
Mr. President 1962

Laugh It Up
Music and lyrics by Johnny Brandon
Cindy (OB) 1964

The Laugh Parade
Music by Harry Warren
Lyrics by Mort Dixon and Joe Young
The Laugh Parade 1931

Laugh Your Blues Away
Music by C. Luckey Roberts
Lyrics by Alex C. Rogers
My Magnolia 1926

Laugh Your Cares Away
Music by George Gershwin
Lyrics by B.G. DeSylva, E. Ray Goetz
and Ballard MacDonald
George White's Scandals (1923)

Laughing Bells
Music by Bronislaw Kaper (based on Chopin)
Lyrics by John Latouche
Polonaise 1945

Laughing Face
Music and lyrics by John Jennings
Riverwind (OB) 1962

The Laughing Song
Music by Al Carmines
Lyrics by Maria Irene Fornes
Promenade (OB) 1969

Laughing Waltz
Music by Robert Stolz
Lyrics by Robert Sour
Mr. Strauss Goes to Boston 1945

An adaptation of a Johann Strauss melody

Laughter in the Air
Music by Erich Korngold
Lyrics by Oscar Hammerstein II
Give Us This Night (1936) F

Laura De Maupassant
Music by Jule Styne
Lyrics by Bob Hilliard
Hazel Flagg 1953

Law and Order
Music and lyrics by Oscar Brand
How to Steal an Election (OB) 1968

Law and Order
Music by Helen Miller
Lyrics by Eve Merriam
Inner City 1971

Law and Order
Music and lyrics by Johnny Brandon
Love! Love! Love! (OB) 1977

The Law Must Be Obeyed
Music and lyrics by Irving Berlin
Stop! Look! Listen! 1915

Lawyers
Music by Charles Strouse
Lyrics by Lee Adams
A Broadway Musical 1978

Lay Your Bets
Music and lyrics by Edward Pola
and Eddie Brandt
Woof, Woof 1929

Layers of Underwear
Music by Gerald Jay Markoe
Lyrics by Michael Colby
Charlotte Sweet (OB) 1982

Laying the Cornerstone
Music by Richard Rodgers
Lyrics by Lorenz Hart
Hallelujah, I'm a Bum (1933) F

Lazy Afternoon
Music by Jerome Moross
Lyrics by John Latouche
The Golden Apple 1954

Lazy Levee Loungers
Music and lyrics by Willard Robison
The Garrick Gaieties (3rd edition) 1930

Lazy Moon
Music by Leroy Anderson
Lyrics by Joan Ford and Walter and Jean Kerr
Goldilocks 1958

L'Chayim
Music and lyrics by Harold Rome
The Zulu and the Zayda 1965

Le Five o'Clock
Music by Will Irwin
Lyrics by Carl Randall
The Third Little Show 1931

Le Grand Cirque de Provence
Music by Peter Link
Lyrics by Jacob Brackman
King of Hearts 1978

Le Grand Rape
Music and lyrics by Ronnie Britton
Greenwich Village Follies (OB) 1976

Le Grisbi Is le Root of le Evil in Man
Music by Marguerite Monnot
Lyrics by Julian More, David Heneker
and Monte Norman
Irma la Douce 1960

Le Sport American
Music by Jerome Kern
Lyrics by Anne Caldwell
Good Morning, Dearie 1921

Lead 'Em On
Music by Joseph Meyer and James F. Hanley
Lyrics by B.G. DeSylva
Big Boy 1925

Lead Me to Love
Music and lyrics by Irving Berlin
Watch Your Step 1914

The Leader of a Big-Time Band
Music and lyrics by Cole Porter
Something for the Boys 1943

Leaf in the Wind
Music by Baldwin Bergersen
Lyrics by George Marion, Jr.
Allah Be Praised! 1944

Leaflets
Music and lyrics by Marc Blitzstein
The Cradle Will Rock 1938

The League of Nations
Music by George Gershwin
Lyrics by B.G. DeSylva and John Henry Mears
Morris Gest Midnight Whirl 1919

Leander
Music by Jean Gilbert
Lyrics by Harry Graham
Katja 1926

Leanin' on the Lord
Music by Garry Sherman
Lyrics by Peter Udell
Amen Corner 1983

Leaning on a Shovel
Music by Lee Wainer
Lyrics by John Latouche
Sing for Your Supper 1939

Learn How to Laugh
Music and lyrics by Hugo Peretti, Luigi Creatore
and George David Weiss
Maggie Flynn 1968

Learn to Be Lonely
Music by Larry Grossman
Lyrics by Betty Comden and Adolph Green
A Doll's Life 1982

Learn to Croon
Music by Harold Arlen
Lyrics by Jack Yellen
You Said It 1931

Learn to Do the Strut
Music and lyrics by Irving Berlin
Music Box Revue (3rd edition) 1923

Learn to Love
Music and lyrics by Voices, Inc.
The Believers (OB) 1968

Learn to Sing a Love Song
Music and lyrics by Irving Berlin
Ziegfeld Follies (1927)

Learn to Smile
Music by Louis A. Hirsch
Lyrics by Otto Harbach
The O'Brien Girl 1921

Learn Your Lessons Well
Music and lyrics by Stephen Schwartz
Godspell (OB) 1971

Learning Love
Music and lyrics by Bruce Montgomery
The Amorous Flea (OB) 1964

Least That's My Opinion
Music by Harold Arlen
Lyrics by Johnny Mercer
St. Louis Woman 1946

Leave It All to Your Faithful Ambassador
Music by Albert Sirmay and Arthur Schwartz
Lyrics by Arthur Swanstrom
Princess Charming 1930

Leave It to Jane
Music by Jerome Kern
Lyrics by P. G. Wodehouse
Leave It to Jane 1917

Leave It to Katarina
Music by Jara Benes
Lyrics by Irving Caesar
White Horse Inn 1936

Leave It to Levy
Music and lyrics by Irving Caesar
Betsy 1926

Leave It to Love
Music by George Gershwin
Lyrics by Ira Gershwin
Lady, Be Good! 1924

Leave It to Us, Gov
Music and lyrics by Marian Grudeff
and Raymond Jessel
Baker Street 1965

Leave the Atom Alone
Music by Harold Arlen
Lyrics by E.Y. Harburg
Jamaica 1957

Leave the World Behind
Music and lyrics by Robert Swerdlow
Love Me, Love My Children (OB) 1971

Leave Well Enough Alone
Music by Jerry Bock
Lyrics by Sheldon Harnick
The Body Beautiful 1958

Leavin' fo' de Promis' Lan'
Music by George Gershwin
Lyrics by DuBose Heyward
Porgy and Bess 1935

Leavin' Time
Music by Harold Arlen
Lyrics by Johnny Mercer
St. Louis Woman 1946

Leben Sie Wohl
Music and lyrics by Robert Wright and George
Forrest (based on Rachmaninoff)
Anya 1965

The Lees of Old Virginia
Music and lyrics by Sherman Edwards
1776 1969

Left All Alone Again Blues
Music by Jerome Kern
Lyrics by Anne Caldwell
The Night Boat 1920

Leg It
Music by Todd
Lyrics by Henry Creamer and Con Conrad
Keep Shufflin' 1928

The Leg of Nations
Music and lyrics by Irving Berlin
Ziegfeld Follies of 1920

The Leg of the Duck
Music by Mitch Leigh
Lyrics by William Alfred and Phyllis Robinson
Cry for Us All 1970

The Legacy
Music by Cy Coleman
Lyrics by Betty Comden and Adolph Green
On the Twentieth Century 1978

The Legal Heir
Music and lyrics by James MacDonald, David Vos
and Robert Gerlach
Something's Afoot 1976

Legalize My Name
Music by Harold Arlen
Lyrics by Johnny Mercer
St. Louis Woman 1946

The Legend
Music and lyrics by Robert Wright and George
Forrest
Song of Norway 1944

Based on Grieg's Piano Concerto in A minor

The Legend of Black-Eyed Susan Grey
Music by Gordon Duffy
Lyrics by Harry M. Haldane
Happy Town 1959

The Legend of King Arthur
Music by Steve Jankowski
Lyrics by Kenny Morris
Francis (OB) 1982

The Legend of Old Rufino
Music by Steve Jankowski
Lyrics by Kenny Morris
Francis (OB) 1982

The Legend of the Chimes
Music by Reginald De Koven
Lyrics by Harry B. Smith
Robin Hood 1891

The Legend of the Cyclamen Tree
Music by Victor Herbert
Lyrics by Gene Buck
Ziegfeld Follies of 1921

Legend of the Islands
Music and lyrics by Ed Tyler
Sweet Miani (OB) 1962

The Legend of the Mill
Music by Victor Herbert
Lyrics by Henry Blossom
The Red Mill 1906

Legend of the Mission Bells
Music by William Heagney
Lyrics by William Heagney and Tom Connell
There You Are 1932

The Legend of the Pearls
Music and lyrics by Irving Berlin
Music Box Revue (1st edition) 1921

Legend Song
Music by Sigmund Romberg
Lyrics by Harry B. Smith
Cherry Blossoms 1927

The Legendary Eino Fflliikkiinnenn
Music by Sidney Lippman
Lyrics by Sylvia Dee
Barefoot Boy With Cheek 1947

Legends of the Drums
Music by Victor Herbert
Lyrics by Gene Buck
Ziegfeld Follies of 1923

Legitimate
Music by Lee Wainer
Lyrics by John Latouche
Sing for Your Supper 1939

Legs, Legs, Legs
Music by Jay Gorney
Lyrics by E.Y. Harburg
Earl Carroll's Sketch Book (1929)

Lemme Tell Ya
Music by Alfred Brooks
Lyrics by Ira J. Bilowit
Of Mice and Men (OB) 1958

Lend Me a Bob Till Monday
Music and lyrics by Kay Swift
Paris '90 1952

Lenny and the Heartbreakers
Music by Scott Killian and Kim D. Sherman
Lyrics by Kenneth Robins, Scott Killian
and Kim D. Sherman
Lenny and the Heartbreakers (OB) 1983

Les Girls
Music and lyrics by Cole Porter
Les Girls (1957) F

Les Halles
Music by Monty Norman
Lyrics by Julian More
The Moony Shapiro Songbook 1981

Les Sylphides Avec la Bumpe
Music and lyrics by Irving Gordon, Alan Roberts
and Jerome Brainin
Star and Garter 1942

The Lesson
Music by Manos Hadjidakis
Lyrics by Joe Darion
Illya Darling 1967

Lesson in Love
Music by Oscar Straus
Lyrics by Joseph W. Herbert
A Waltz Dream 1908

A Lesson in Yiddish
Music by Murray Rumshinsky
Lyrics by Jacob Jacobs
The President's Daughter 1970

Lesson #8
Music and lyrics by Stephen Sondheim
Sunday in the Park With George (OB) 1983

Lessons in Love
Music by Franz Lehár
Lyrics by Harry B. and Robert B. Smith
Gypsy Love 1911

Lessons on Life
Music and lyrics by Bruce Montgomery
The Amorous Flea (OB) 1964

Let-a-Go Your Heart
Music and lyrics by Eaton Magoon, Jr.
13 Daughters 1961

Let Antipholus In
Music by Richard Rodgers
Lyrics by Lorenz Hart
The Boys From Syracuse 1938

Let Doctor Schmet Vet Your Pet
Music and lyrics by Cole Porter
Something to Shout About (1943) F

Dropped from film

Let Cutie Cut Your Cuticle
Music by George Gershwin
Lyrics by B.G. DeSylva and John Henry Mears
Morris Gest Midnight Whirl 1919

Let 'Em Eat Cake
Music by George Gershwin
Lyrics by Ira Gershwin
Let 'Em Eat Cake 1933

Let 'Em Eat Caviar
Music by George Gershwin
Lyrics by Ira Gershwin
Let 'Em Eat Cake 1933

Let Fate Decide
Music by Maury Rubens
Lyrics by Harry B. Smith
Marching By 1932

Let Him Kick Up His Heels
Music by Michael Leonard
Lyrics by Herbert Martin
The Yearling 1965

Let It Be Soon
Music by Rudolf Friml
Lyrics by Bide Dudley and Otto Harbach
The Little Whopper 1919

Let It Rain
Music and lyrics by James Kendis
and Hal Dyson
Sky High 1925

Let It Ride!
Music and lyrics by Jay Livingston
and Ray Evans
Let It Ride 1961

Let Love Go
Music by Sigmund Romberg
Lyrics by Otto Harbach and Oscar Hammerstein II
The Desert Song 1926

Let Me Awake
Music by Sigmund Romberg
Lyrics by Dorothy Donnelly
Blossom Time 1921

Let Me Be
Music by David Baker
Lyrics by Will Holt
Come Summer 1969

Let Me Be a Friend to You
Music by George Gershwin
Lyrics by Ira Gershwin
Rosalie 1928

Let Me Be a Kid
Music and lyrics by Elizabeth Swados
Runaways 1978

Let Me Be Born Again
Music by Victor Young
Lyrics by Joseph Young and Ned Washington
Blackbirds of 1934

Let Me Be Free
Music by Rudolf Friml
Lyrics by Rowland Leigh and John Shubert
Music Hath Charms 1934

Let Me Be Myself
Music by Manning Sherwin
Lyrics by Arthur Herzog, Jr.
Bad Habits of 1926 (OB)

Let Me Be Your Sugar Baby
Music and lyrics by Arthur Malvin
Sugar Babies 1979

Let Me Believe in Me
Music by Joe Ercole
Lyrics by Bruce Kluger
Ka-Boom (OB) 1980

Let Me Come In
Music by Gary William Friedman
Lyrics by Will Holt
The Me Nobody Knows (OB) 1970

Let Me Dance
Music by Alfred Goodman, Maury Rubens and J.
Fred Coots
Lyrics by Clifford Grey
Artists and Models (1925)

Let Me Down Walking in the World
Music and lyrics by Robert Swerdlow
Love Me, Love My Children (OB) 1971

Let Me Drink in Your Eyes
Music by Richard Rodgers
Lyrics by Lorenz Hart
Poor Little Ritz Girl 1920

In Boston production but dropped before Broadway
opening

Let Me Entertain You
Music by Jule Styne
Lyrics by Stephen Sondheim
Gypsy 1959

Let Me Give All My Love to Thee
Music by Vincent Youmans
Lyrics by Oscar Hammerstein II
Rainbow 1928

Let Me Hold You in My Arms
Music and lyrics by Clarence Gaskill
Keep It Clean 1929

Let Me Live Today
Music by Sigmund Romberg
Lyrics by Oscar Hammerstein II
Sunny River 1941

Let Me Look at You
Music by Harold Arlen
Lyrics by Dorothy Fields
Mr. Imperium (1951) F

Let Me Love You
Music by John Morris
Lyrics by Gerald Freedman
A Time for Singing 1966

Let Me Match My Private Life With Yours
Music by Vernon Duke
Lyrics by E.Y. Harburg
Americana (1932)

Let Me Sing!
Music and lyrics by Ronnie Britton
Greenwich Village Follies (OB) 1976

Let Me Sing My Song
Music by Charles Strouse
Lyrics by Lee Adams
A Broadway Musical 1978

Let Me Take You for a Ride
Music by David Martin
Lyrics by Langston Hughes
Simply Heavenly 1957

Let Me Tell You a Little Story
Music by Peter Link
Lyrics by Michael Cacoyannis
Lysistrata 1972

Let Me Weep on Your Shoulder
Music by Joseph Meyer
Lyrics by Edward Eliscu
Lady Fingers 1929

Let My People Come
Music and lyrics by Earl Wilson, Jr.
Let My People Come (OB) 1974

Let the Day Perish When I Was Born
Music and lyrics by Elizabeth Swados
Lullabye and Goodnight 1982

Let the Man Who Makes the Gun
Music by Gerald Marks
Lyrics by Raymond B. Egan
Earl Carroll's Sketch Book (1935)

Let the Moment Slip By
Music and lyrics by Peter Link
and C.C. Courtney
Salvation (OB) 1969

Let the Show Go On!
Music by Joe Ercole
Lyrics by Bruce Kluger
Ka-Boom (OB) 1980

Let the Sun of Thine Eyes
Music by Victor Herbert
Lyrics by Harry B. Smith
Cyrano de Bergerac 1899

Let Things Be Like They Always Was
Music by Kurt Weill
Lyrics by Langston Hughes
Street Scene 1947

Let Us Charm Each Other
Music by Baldwin Bergersen
Lyrics by William Archibald
Rosa (OB) 1978

Let Us Gather at the Goal Line
Music by Sammy Fain
Lyrics by George Marion, Jr.
Toplitzky of Notre Dame 1946

Let Us Sing a Song
Music by Sigmund Romberg
Lyrics by Dorothy Donnelly
The Student Prince 1924

Let Your Hair Down With a Bang
Music by Baldwin Bergersen
Lyrics by June Sillman
Who's Who 1938

Let Yourself Go
Music and lyrics by Irving Berlin
Follow the Fleet (1936) F

Let's
Music by Duke Ellington
Lyrics by Marshall Barer and Fred Tobias
Pousse-Café 1966

Let's All Be Exactly and Precisely What We Are
Music by Robert Kessler
Lyrics by Lola Pergament
O Marry Me! (OB) 1961

Let's All Go Raving Mad
Music by Philip Braham
Lyrics by Hugh E. Wright
Charlot's Revue of 1926

Let's All Sing the Lard Song
Music by Leslie Sarony
Lyrics by Anne Caldwell
Three Cheers 1928

Let's Ball Awhile
Music by David Martin
Lyrics by Langston Hughes
Simply Heavenly 1957

Let's Be Buddies
Music and lyrics by Cole Porter
Panama Hattie 1940

Let's Be Elegant or Die!
Music by William Dyer
Lyrics by Don Parks and William Dyer
Jo (OB) 1964

Let's Be Happy Now
Music by Henry Souvaine and Jay Gorney
Lyrics by Morrie Ryskind and Howard Dietz
Merry-Go-Round 1927

Let's Be Lonesome Together
Music by George Gershwin
Lyrics by B.G. DeSylva and E. Ray Goetz
George White's Scandals (1923)

Let's Be Strangers Again
Music by Leon Pober
Lyrics by Bud Freeman
Beg, Borrow or Steal 1960

Let's Begin
Music by Jerome Kern
Lyrics by Otto Harbach
Roberta 1933

Let's Believe in the Captain
Music and lyrics by Gene Curty, Nitra Scharfman
and Chuck Strand
The Lieutenant 1975

Let's Burn the Cornfield
Music and lyrics by Randy Newman
Maybe I'm Doing It Wrong (2nd edition)
(OB) 1982

Let's Call It a Day
Music by Ray Henderson
Lyrics by Lew Brown
Strike Me Pink 1933

Let's Call the Whole Thing Off
Music by George Gershwin
Lyrics by Ira Gershwin
Shall We Dance (1937) F

Let's Comb Beaches
Music by John Green
Lyrics by George Marion, Jr.
Beat the Band 1942

Let's Dance
Music and lyrics by Billy Solly
Boy Meets Boy (OB) 1975

Let's Dance and Make Up
Music by Tom Johnstone
Lyrics by Phil Cook
When You Smile 1925

Let's Do and Say We Didn't
Music by Harry Tierney
Lyrics by Joseph McCarthy
Kid Boots 1923

Let's Do and Say We Didn't
Music and lyrics by Hughie Prince
and Dick Rogers
The Girl From Nantucket 1945

Let's Do It, Let's Fall in Love
Music and lyrics by Cole Porter
Paris 1928

One of Porter's first major hits, the song
recommends falling in love. To prove the
universality of the practice, the lyric cites various
nationalities in the first chorus, denizens of the
deep for two more choruses, insects and then the
animal world in the fourth and fifth choruses. The
lyrics have been widely parodied, including two
Noël Coward versions, one written for his nightclub
act and another, more censorable, version.

Let's Evolve
Music by David Baker
Lyrics by Sheldon Harnick
Smiling, the Boy Fell Dead (OB) 1961

Let's Face It
Music and lyrics by Cole Porter
Let's Face It! 1941

Let's Face the Music and Dance
Music and lyrics by Irving Berlin
Follow the Fleet (1936) F

Let's Fall in Love
Music by Harold Arlen
Lyrics by Ted Koehler
Let's Fall in Love (1934) F

Let's Fetch the Carriage
Music by Glenn Paxton
Lyrics by Robert Goldman and George Weiss
First Impressions 1959

Let's Fly Away
Music and lyrics by Cole Porter
The New Yorkers 1930

Let's Get Back to Glamour
Music by Manning Sherwin
Lyrics by Harold Purcell
Under the Counter 1947

Let's Get Drunk
Music and lyrics by Billy Barnes
The Billy Barnes People 1961

Let's Get Lost in Now
Music and lyrics by Peter Link
and C.C. Courtney
Salvation (OB) 1969

Let's Get Married or Something
Music by Richard Lewine
Lyrics by Ted Fetter
Entre-Nous (OB) 1935

Let's Go
Music by Jerome Kern
Lyrics by Berton Braley
Toot-Toot! 1918

Let's Go
Music by Milton Schafer
Lyrics by Ira Levin
Drat! The Cat! 1965

Let's Go Back to the Waltz
Music and lyrics by Irving Berlin
Mr. President 1962

Let's Go Down
Music by Ron Steward and Neal Tate
Lyrics by Ron Steward
Sambo (OB) 1969

Let's Go Down to the Shop
Music by Louis A. Hirsch
Lyrics by Rennold Wolf
The Rainbow Girl 1918

Let's Go Eat Worms in the Garden
Music by Kay Swift
Lyrics by Paul James
Fine and Dandy 1930

Let's Go High Hat
Music by Richard Lewine
Lyrics by Will B. Johnstone
Entre-Nous (OB) 1935

Let's Go Home
Music by André Previn
Lyrics by Alan Jay Lerner
Coco 1969

Let's Go Lovin'
Music and lyrics by Herman Hupfeld
Hey Nonny Nonny! 1932

Let's Go Out in the Open Air
Music and lyrics by Ann Ronell
Shoot the Works 1931

Let's Go to the Dogs
Music and lyrics by Ann Harris
Sky High (OB) 1979

Let's Go Too Far
Music by Don Walker
Lyrics by George Marion, Jr.
Allah Be Praised! 1944

Let's Have a Good Time
Music by Tom Johnstone
Lyrics by Phil Cook
When You Smile 1925

Let's Have a Love Affair
Music by Sigmund Romberg
Lyrics by Otto Harbach and Oscar Hammerstein II
The Desert Song 1926

Let's Have a Simple Wedding
Music by Jim Wise
Lyrics by George Haimsohn and Robin Miller
Dames at Sea (OB) 1968

Let's Have Another Cup of Coffee
Music and lyrics by Irving Berlin
Face the Music 1932

Let's Hear It for Daddy Moola
Music by Stanley Silverman
Lyrics by Tom Hendry
Doctor Selavy's Magic Theatre (OB) 1972

Let's Hold Hands
Music by Richard Lewine
Lyrics by June Sillman
Fools Rush In 1934

Let's Improvise
Music and lyrics by Robert Wright
and George Forrest
Kean 1961

Let's Kiss and Make Up
Music by Harry Tierney
Lyrics by Joseph McCarthy
Up She Goes 1922

Let's Kiss and Make Up
Music by George Gershwin
Lyrics by Ira Gershwin
Funny Face 1927

Let's Laugh and Be Merry
Music by Shep Camp
Lyrics by Frank DuPree and Harry B. Smith
Half a Widow 1927

Let's Live It Over Again
Music by Diane Leslie
Lyrics by William Gleason
The Coolest Cat in Town (OB) 1978

Let's Make a Night of It
Music by Jerome Kern
Lyrics by P.G. Wodehouse
Oh, Boy! 1917

Let's Make It Christmas All Year Round
Music by Burton Lane
Lyrics by Dorothy Fields
Junior Miss (1957) TV

Let's Make It Forever
Music by Fred Stamer
Lyrics by Gen Genovese
Buttrio Square 1952

Let's Make Memories Tonight
Music by Sam Stept
Lyrics by Lew Brown and Charles Tobias
Yokel Boy 1939

Let's Merge
Music by J. Fred Coots
Lyrics by Arthur Swanstrom and Benny Davis
Sons o' Guns 1929

Let's Misbehave
Music and lyrics by Cole Porter
Paris 1928

Dropped from production

Let's Not Get Married
Music by Victor Herbert
Lyrics by B.G. DeSylva
Orange Blossoms 1922

Let's Not Get Married
Music by Ruth Cleary Patterson
Lyrics by George Blake and Les Kramer
Russell Patterson's Sketch Book (OB) 1960

Let's Not Talk About Love
Music and lyrics by Cole Porter
Let's Face It! 1941

Let's Not Waste a Moment
Music and lyrics by Jerry Herman
Milk and Honey 1961

Let's Play a Tune on the Music Box
Music and lyrics by Noël Coward
Tonight at 8:30 ("Family Album") 1936

Let's Pretend
Music by Robert Hood Bowers
Lyrics by Francis DeWitt
Oh, Ernest! 1927

Let's Pretend
Music and lyrics by Johnny Brandon
Cindy (OB) 1964

Let's Put It to Music
Music by Alex Fogarty
Lyrics by Edwin Gilbert
You Never Know 1938

Let's Put Out the Lights and Go to Sleep
Music and lyrics by Herman Hupfeld
George White's Music Hall Varieties 1932

Originally called "Let's Put Out the Lights and Go to
Bed". The final word was changed to "Sleep" in
order to placate radio censors of 1932.

Let's Raise Hell
Music and lyrics by Porter Grainger
Fast and Furious 1931

Let's Run Away and Get Married
Music by Harold Levey
Lyrics by Owen Murphy
Rainbow Rose 1926

Let's Say Good Night Till It's Morning
Music by Jerome Kern
Lyrics by Otto Harbach and Oscar Hammerstein II
Sunny 1925

Let's Say Goodnight With a Dance
Music by Sammy Fain
Lyrics by Jack Yellen
Sons o' Fun 1941

Let's See What Happens
Music by Jule Styne
Lyrics by E.Y. Harburg
Darling of the Day 1968

Let's Sit and Talk About You
Music by Jimmy McHugh
Lyrics by Dorothy Fields
Hello Daddy 1928

Let's Steal a Tune From Offenbach
Music by Jay Gorney
Lyrics by Henry Myers
Meet the People 1940

Let's Step Out
Music and lyrics by Cole Porter
Fifty Million Frenchmen 1929

Let's Stroll Along and Sing a Song of Love
Music by Cliff Friend
Lyrics by Lew Brown
Piggy 1927

Let's Swing It
Music and lyrics by Charles Tobias, Charles Newman and Murray Mencher
Earl Carroll's Sketch Book (1935)

Let's Take a Stroll Through London
Music by Julian Slade
Lyrics by Dorothy Reynolds and Julian Slade
Salad Days (OB) 1958

Let's Take a Walk Around the Block
Music by Harold Arlen
Lyrics by Ira Gershwin and E.Y. Harburg
Life Begins at 8:40 1934

Let's Take Advantage of Now
Music by Ray Henderson
Lyrics by Ted Koehler
Say When 1934

Let's Take an Old-Fashioned Walk
Music and lyrics by Irving Berlin
Miss Liberty 1949

Let's Take the Long Way Home
Music by Harold Arlen
Lyrics by Johnny Mercer
Here Come the Waves (1944) F

Let's Talk About the Weather
Music and lyrics by Charlotte Kent
The Illustrators' Show 1936

Let's You and I Just Say Goodbye
Music and lyrics by George M. Cohan
The Rise of Rosie O'Reilly 1923

Let's Vocalize
Music and lyrics by Cole Porter
High Society (1955) F

Dropped from film

The Letter
Music by Jay Gorney
Lyrics by Barry Trivers
Heaven on Earth 1948

The Letter
Music and lyrics by Frank Loesser
The Most Happy Fella 1956

The Letter
Music by Frank Fields
Lyrics by Armand Aulicino
The Shoemaker and the Peddler (OB) 1960

The Letter
Music by Clinton Ballard
Lyrics by Carolyn Richter
The Ballad of Johnny Pot (OB) 1971

The Letter
Music and lyrics by Clark Gesner
The Utter Glory of Morrissey Hall 1979

The Letter
Music by Gerald Jay Markoe
Lyrics by Michael Colby
Charlotte Sweet (OB) 1982

Letter From Klemnacht
Music by Larry Grossman
Lyrics by Betty Comden and Adolph Green
A Doll's Life 1982

The Letter (Me Charlotte Dear)
Music by Gerald Jay Markoe
Lyrics by Michael Colby
Charlotte Sweet (OB) 1982

The Letter Song
Music by Oscar Straus
Lyrics by Stanislaus Stange
The Chocolate Soldier 1909

The Letter Song
Music by Fritz Kreisler
Lyrics by William LeBaron
Apple Blossoms 1919

The Letter Song
Music by Carlton Kelsey and Maury Rubens
Lyrics by Clifford Grey
Sky High 1925

Letter Song
Music by Walter Kollo
Lyrics by Harry B. Smith
Three Little Girls 1930

The Letter Song (1932)
Music by Richard Rodgers
Lyrics by Lorenz Hart

See The Man for Me

Letter to the Children
Music by Larry Grossman
Lyrics by Betty Comden and Adolph Green
A Doll's Life 1982

Letters
Music and lyrics by Marian Grudeff
and Raymond Jessel
Baker Street 1965

Leviathan
Music by Meyer Kupferman
Lyrics by Paul Goodman
Jonah (OB) 1966

Liable to Catch On
Music by Sammy Fain
Lyrics by Irving Kahal and Jack Yellen
Boys and Girls Together 1940

Liaisons
Music and lyrics by Stephen Sondheim
A Little Night Music 1973

The Liar's Song
Music by John Mundy
Lyrics by Edward Eager
The Liar 1950

Libby
Music by Albert Von Tilzer
Lyrics by Neville Fleeson
The Gingham Girl 1922

Liberia
Music by Susan Hulsman Bingham
Lyrics by Myrna Lamb
Mod Donna (OB) 1970

Lichtenburg
Music and lyrics by Irving Berlin
Call Me Madam 1950

A Lick, and a Riff, and a Slow Bounce
Music by Jerry Livingston
Lyrics by Mack David
Bright Lights of 1944

Lida Rose
Music and lyrics by Meredith Willson
The Music Man 1957

The Lido Beach
Music and lyrics by Noël Coward
This Year of Grace 1928

Lieben Dich
Music and lyrics by Paul Nassau and Oscar Brand
*The Education of H*y*m*a*n K*a*p*l*a*n* 1968

Lies, Lies, Lies
Music and lyrics by Elizabeth Swados
Lullabye and Goodnight 1982

Lieutenants of the Lord
Music by Kurt Weill
Lyrics by Bertolt Brecht (adapted by Michael Feingold)
Happy End 1977

Lif' 'Em Up and Put 'Em Down
Music by Georges Bizet
Lyrics by Oscar Hammerstein II
Carmen Jones 1943

Life
Music by Bill Weeden
Lyrics by David Finkle
Hurry, Harry 1972

Life as a Twosome
Music by Joseph Meyer and Roger Wolfe Kahn
Lyrics by Irving Caesar
Americana (1928) and *Here's Howe* (1928)

Life Begins at Sweet Sixteen
Music by Ray Henderson
Lyrics by Jack Yellen
George White's Scandals (1936)

Life Can Be Beautiful
Music by Moose Charlap
Lyrics by Eddie Lawrence
Kelly 1965

Life Could Be So Beautiful
Music by Jerome Moross
Lyrics by Paul Peters and George Sklar
Parade (1935)

Life Does a Man a Favor
Music and lyrics by Jay Livingston
and Ray Evans
Oh Captain! 1958

Life in the Morning
Music and lyrics by Noël Coward
Bitter Sweet 1929

Life in Town
Music by Lewis E. Gensler and Milton Schwarzwald
Lyrics by George S. Kaufman, Marc Connelly
and Ira Gershwin
Be Yourself 1924

Life Is
Music by John Kander
Lyrics by Fred Ebb
Zorba 1968

Life Is a Game
Music and lyrics by Ring Lardner
June Moon 1929

Life Is a One-Way Street
Music and lyrics by Bill and Patti Jacob
Jimmy 1969

Life Is Happiness Indeed
Music by Leonard Bernstein
Lyrics by Stephen Sondheim
Candide (Added to 1973 revival)

Life Is Just a Bowl of Cherries
Music by Ray Henderson
Lyrics by B.G. DeSylva and Lew Brown
George White's Scandals (1931)

Life Is Like a Toy Balloon
Music by Harold Levey
Lyrics by Owen Murphy
The Greenwich Village Follies (1925)

Life Is Like a Train
Music by Cy Coleman
Lyrics by Betty Comden and Adolph Green
On the Twentieth Century 1978

Life Is Love
Music by Philip Charig
Lyrics by Irving Caesar
Polly 1929

Life Is Love and Laughter
Music by Oscar Straus
Lyrics by Joseph W. Herbert
A Waltz Dream 1908

Life Is Too Short
Music by Sammy Fain
Lyrics by Marilyn and Alan Bergman
Something More 1964

The Life of a Woman
Music and lyrics by Michael Brown
Different Times 1972

The Life of the Party
Music by Richard Myers
Lyrics by Harry Ruskin
The Greenwich Village Follies (1925)

The Life of the Party
Music by Nacio Herb Brown and Richard Whiting
Lyrics by B.G. DeSylva
Take a Chance 1932

The Life of the Party
Music by John Kander
Lyrics by Fred Ebb
The Happy Time 1968

Life on the Inside
Music by Stanley Silverman
Lyrics by Tom Hendry
Doctor Selavy's Magic Theatre (OB) 1972

The Life That I Planned for Him
Music and lyrics by Johnny Brandon
Cindy (OB) 1964

Life Upon the Wicked Stage
Music by Jerome Kern
Lyrics by Oscar Hammerstein II
Show Boat 1927

The chorus of this song (with no lyrics) was discovered among the manuscripts of *Lucky*, merely titled "Ruby Keeler's Dance."

Life Was Monotonous
Music by Richard Rodgers
Lyrics by Lorenz Hart
By Jupiter 1942

Dropped from production

Life Was Pie for the Pioneer
Music by Burton Lane
Lyrics by E.Y. Harburg
Hold On to Your Hats 1940

Life Wins
Music by Galt MacDermot
Lyrics by Christopher Gore
Via Galactica 1972

Life With Father
Music by Richard Rodgers
Lyrics by Lorenz Hart
By Jupiter 1942

A Life With Rocky
Music by Morton Gould
Lyrics by Betty Comden and Adolph Green
Billion Dollar Baby 1945

Life Without Her
Music by Don Pippin
Lyrics by Steve Brown
Fashion (OB) 1974

The Lifeguards
Music by Manning Sherwin
Lyrics by Arthur Herzog, Jr.
Bad Habits of 1926 (OB)

Lifeline
Music by Garry Sherman
Lyrics by Peter Udell
Comin' Uptown 1979

Life's a Dance
Music by Jerome Kern
Lyrics by Harry B. Smith
Love o' Mike 1917

Life's a Dance
Music by Harold Arlen
Lyrics by E.Y. Harburg
Hooray for What! 1937

Life's a Funny Present From Someone
Music by Vernon Duke
Lyrics by Howard Dietz
Sadie Thompson 1944

Life's a Game at Best
Music by Victor Herbert
Lyrics by Henry Blossom
Eileen 1917

Life's a Holiday
Music by George Fischoff
Lyrics by Carole Bayer
Georgy 1970

Life's a Masquerade
Music by Victor Herbert
Lyrics by Harry B. Smith
Miss Dolly Dollars 1905

Life's a Tale
Music by Emmerich Kálmán
Lyrics by P.G. Wodehouse
The Riviera Girl 1917

Life's Too Short to Be Blue
Music by George Gershwin
Lyrics by Ira Gershwin
Tip-Toes 1925

Dropped from production

A Lifetime Love
Music by Albert Hague
Lyrics by Marty Brill
Café Crown 1964

The Liffey Waltz
Music and lyrics by Marc Blitzstein
Juno 1959

Lift Every Voice and Sing
Music and lyrics by Glory Van Scott
Miss Truth (OB) 1979

Lifted
Music and lyrics by Alan Menken
Real Life Funnies (OB) 1981

The Light
Music and lyrics by Al Carmines
The Evangelist (OB) 1982

The Light Around the Corner
Music by Joe Ercole
Lyrics by Bruce Kluger
Ka-Boom (OB) 1980

Light of the World
Music and lyrics by Stephen Schwartz
Godspell (OB) 1971

Light One Candle
Music by Albert Hague
Lyrics by Allen Sherman
The Fig Leaves Are Falling 1969

Light Sings
Music by Gary William Friedman
Lyrics by Will Holt
The Me Nobody Knows (OB) 1970

A Light Thing
Music by Scott Killian
and Kim D. Sherman
Lyrics by Kenneth Robins, Scott Killian
and Kim D. Sherman
Lenny and the Heartbreakers (OB) 1983

The Lightning Bug Song
Music by George Kleinsinger
Lyrics by Joe Darion
Shinbone Alley 1957

The Lights of London
Music and lyrics by Al Kasha and Joel Hirschhorn
Copperfield 1981

Like a God
Music by Richard Rodgers
Lyrics by Oscar Hammerstein II
Flower Drum Song 1958

Like a Lady
Music and lyrics by Micki Grant
It's So Nice to Be Civilized 1980

Like a Little Ladylike Lady Like You
Music and lyrics by George M. Cohan
The Merry Malones 1927

Like-a-Me, Like-a-You
Music and lyrics by McElbert Moore
and Frank Grey
The Matinee Girl 1926

Like a Star in the Sky
Music by Johann Strauss
Lyrics by Desmond Carter
The Great Waltz 1934

Like a Woman Loves a Man
Music and lyrics by Frank Loesser
The Most Happy Fella 1956

Like a Young Man
Music and lyrics by Jerry Herman
Milk and Honey 1961

Like He Loves Me
Music by Vincent Youmans
Lyrics by Anne Caldwell
Oh, Please! 1926

Like Him
Music by Henry Krieger
Lyrics by Robert Lorick
The Tap Dance Kid 1983

Like It
Music by Clinton Ballard
Lyrics by Carolyn Richter
The Ballad of Johnny Pot (OB) 1971

Like It Was
Music and lyrics by Stephen Sondheim
Merrily We Roll Along 1981

Like Me Less, Love Me More
Music by Jay Gorney
Lyrics by E.Y. Harburg
Earl Carroll's Sketch Book (1929)

Like Ordinary People Do
Music by Richard Rodgers
Lyrics by Lorenz Hart
The Hot Heiress (1931) F

Like the Breeze Blows
Music and lyrics by Harold Rome
The Zulu and the Zayda 1965

Like the Eagles Fly
Music by Gary Geld
Lyrics by Peter Udell
Angel 1978

Like the Nymphs of Spring
Music by Jerome Kern
Lyrics by Anne Caldwell
The City Chap 1925

Like the Wandering Minstrel
Music and lyrics by George M. Cohan
The Merry Malones 1927

Like You
Music by Emmerich Kálmán
Lyrics by Harry B. Smith
The Circus Princess 1927

Like You Do
Music by Harry Ruby
Lyrics by Bert Kalmar
The Ramblers 1926

Like Yours
Music by Albert Hague
Lyrics by Allen Sherman
The Fig Leaves Are Falling 1969

L'il Augie Is a Natural Man
Music by Harold Arlen
Lyrics by Johnny Mercer
St. Louis Woman 1946

Lil' Ole Bitty Pissant Country Place
Music and lyrics by Carol Hall
The Best Little Whorehouse in Texas 1978

Lila Tremaine
Music by Jule Styne
Lyrics by Betty Comden and Adolph Green
Fade Out—Fade In 1964

Lilac Tree
Music and lyrics by C. Jackson and James Hatch
Fly Blackbird (OB) 1962

Lilac Wine
Music and lyrics by James Shelton
Dance Me a Song 1950

Lilas
Music by Don Gohman
Lyrics by Hal Hackady
Ambassador 1972

Lilies of the Field
Music by Vincent Youmans
Lyrics by Otto Harbach
No, No, Nanette 1925

Dropped from production

Lillian
Music by Albert Hague
Lyrics by Allen Sherman
The Fig Leaves Are Falling 1969

The Lily and the Nightingale
Music by Victor Herbert
Lyrics by Harry B. Smith
The Fortune Teller 1898

Lily Belle May June
Music by Henry Sullivan
Lyrics by Earle Crooker
Thumbs Up! 1934

**Lily Has Done the Zampoughi Every Time
I Pulled Her Coattail**
Music and lyrics by Melvin Van Peebles
Ain't Supposed to Die a Natural Death 1971

Lily of the Valley
Music by Vincent Youmans
Lyrics by Anne Caldwell
Oh, Please! 1926

Dropped from production

Lily, Oscar
Music by Cy Coleman
Lyrics by Betty Comden and Adolph Green
On the Twentieth Century 1978

Lima
Music by Cole Porter
Lyrics by T. Lawrason Riggs and Cole Porter
See America First 1916

Limehouse Blues
Music by Philip Braham
Lyrics by Douglas Furber
Charlot's Revue 1924

Sung by Gertrude Lawrence in her American stage debut

Limehouse Nights
Music by George Gershwin
Lyrics by B.G. DeSylva and John Henry Mears
Morris Gest Midnight Whirl 1919

Lincoln and Liberty
Music and lyrics by Oscar Brand
How to Steal an Election (OB) 1968

Lincoln and Soda
Music and lyrics by Oscar Brand
How to Steal an Election (OB) 1968

Linda, Georgina, Marilyn and Me
Music and lyrics by Earl Wilson, Jr.
Let My People Come (OB) 1974

Linger in the Lobby
Music by George Gershwin
Lyrics by Ira Gershwin
Lady Be Good! 1924

Lingerie
Music by Dave Stamper and Harold Levey
Lyrics by Cyrus Wood
Lovely Lady 1927

The Lion and the Lamb
Music by Clay Warnick
Lyrics by Edward Eager
Dream With Music 1944

The Lion and the Unicorn
Music and lyrics by Elizabeth Swados
Alice in Concert (OB) 1980

Lion Tamer
Music and lyrics by Stephen Schwartz
The Magic Show 1974

Lionnet
Music and lyrics by Marc Blitzstein
Regina 1949

The Lion's Queen
Music by Richard Fall
Lyrics by George Grossmith
The Dollar Princess 1909

Lips
Music and lyrics by Leon DeCosta
The Blonde Sinner 1926

Lips That Laugh at Love
Music by Emile Berté and Maury Rubens
Lyrics by J. Keirn Brennan
Music in May 1929

The Liquor Dealer's Dream
Music by Kurt Weill
Lyrics by Bertolt Brecht (adapted by Michael
Feingold)
Happy End 1977

Lisbon Sequence
Music and lyrics by Leonard Bernstein
Candide 1956

Listen, Cosette
Music by Laurence Rosenthal
Lyrics by James Lipton
Sherry! 1967

Listen, I Feel
Music by Al Carmines
Lyrics by Maria Irene Fornes
Promenade (OB) 1969

Listen to Me
Music by Monte Carlo and Alma Sanders
Lyrics by Howard Johnson
Tangerine 1921

Listen to the Beat!
Music and lyrics by Billy Barnes
The Billy Barnes Revue 1959

Listening
Music and lyrics by Irving Berlin
Music Box Revue (4th edition) 1924

Literary Cocktail Party
Music and lyrics by Bud McCreery
Put It in Writing (OB) 1963

Lites—Camera—Platitude
Music and lyrics by Ervin Drake
What Makes Sammy Run? 1964

Little Angel Cake
Music by Jerome Kern
Lyrics by Anne Caldwell
Stepping Stones 1923

Little Bird, Little Bird
Music by Mitch Leigh
Lyrics by Joe Darion
Man of La Mancha 1965

Little Bird of Paradise
Music by Victor Herbert
Lyrics by Glen MacDonough
Algeria 1908

A Little Birdie Told Me So
Music by Richard Rodgers
Lyrics by Lorenz Hart
Peggy-Ann 1926

Little Birds
Music and lyrics by John Dooley
Hobo (OB) 1961

Little Biscuit
Music by Harold Arlen
Lyrics by E.Y. Harburg
Jamaica 1957

A Little Bit Delighted With the Weather
Music by Morgan Lewis
Lyrics by Nancy Hamilton
One for the Money 1939

A Little Bit in Love
Music by Leonard Bernstein
Lyrics by Betty Comden and Adolph Green
Wonderful Town 1953

A Little Bit More
Music by Richard Rodgers
Lyrics by Raymond Jessel
I Remember Mama 1979

A Little Bit o' Glitter
Music by Joe Ercole
Lyrics by Bruce Kluger
Ka-Boom (OB) 1980

A Little Bit o' Jazz
Music by Harry Ruby
Lyrics by Bert Kalmar
Helen of Troy, New York 1923

A Little Bit of Blarney
Music by Raymond Hubbell
Lyrics by Glen MacDonough
The Jolly Bachelors 1910

A Little Bit of Constitutional Fun
Music by Richard Rodgers
Lyrics by Lorenz Hart
I'd Rather Be Right 1937

A Little Bit of Every Nationality
Music by Sigmund Romberg
Lyrics by Harold Atteridge
Sinbad (1918)

A Little Bit of Good
Music by John Kander
Lyrics by Fred Ebb
Chicago 1975

A Little Bit of Me in You
Music and lyrics by Jill Williams
Rainbow Jones 1974

A Little Bit of Paint
Music by Harold Levey
Lyrics by Zelda Sears
The Clinging Vine 1922

A Little Bit of Quicksilver
Music and lyrics by Alexander Hill
Hummin' Sam 1933

A Little Bit of Ribbon
Music by Jerome Kern
Lyrics by P.G. Wodehouse
Oh, Boy! 1917

A Little Bit of Spanish
Music by Frank Grey
Lyrics by McElbert Moore and Frank Grey
The Matinee Girl 1926

Little Bit of This
Music by Lewis E. Gensler and Milton Schwarzwald
Lyrics by George S. Kaufman, Marc Connelly
and Ira Gershwin
Be Yourself 1924

A Little Bit Off
Music by David Shire
Lyrics by Richard Maltby, Jr.
Starting Here, Starting Now (OB) 1977

The Little Blue Pig
Music by Sigmund Romberg
Lyrics by Arthur Wimperis
Louie the 14th 1925

Little Bo-Peep
Music by Philip Charig
Lyrics by Irving Caesar
Polly 1929

Little Boy
Music by Jean Gilbert
Lyrics by Harry Graham and Cyrus Wood
The Lady in Ermine 1922

Little Boy Blue
Music by William B. Kernell
Lyrics by Dorothy Donnelly
Hello, Lola 1926

The Little Boy Blues
Music and lyrics by Hugh Martin
Look Ma, I'm Dancin'! 1948

A Little Brains—a Little Talent
Music and lyrics by Richard Adler and Jerry Ross
Damn Yankees 1955

Little Bum
Music by James F. Hanley
Lyrics by Eddie Dowling
Sidewalks of New York 1927

A Little Bungalow
Music and lyrics by Irving Berlin
The Cocoanuts 1925

Little Butterfly
Music and lyrics by Irving Berlin
Music Box Revue (3rd edition) 1923

A Little Change of Atmosphere
Music by Cliff Friend
Lyrics by Lew Brown
Piggy 1927

A Little Chat
Music by Erich Wolfgang Korngold (based on
Jacques Offenbach)
Lyrics by Herbert Baker
Helen Goes to Troy 1944

Little Children on the Grass
Music and lyrics by Al Carmines
The Evangelist (OB) 1982

The Little Corporal
Music by Frederick Loewe
Lyrics by Earle Crooker
Great Lady 1938

Little Dance
Music by Rudolf Friml
Lyrics by Rida Johnson Young
Sometime 1918

Little Do They Know
Music by John Kander
Lyrics by Fred Ebb
The Act 1977

Little Dog Blue
Music and lyrics by Robert Larimer
King of the Whole Damn World (OB) 1962

Little Dream That's Coming True
Music by Walter G. Samuels
Lyrics by Morrie Ryskind
Ned Wayburn's Gambols 1929

Little Drops of Rain
Music by Harold Arlen
Lyrics by E.Y. Harburg
Gay Purr-ee (1962) F

Little Emmaline
Music by Sigmund Romberg
Lyrics by Rowland Leigh
My Romance 1948

Little Fat Girls
Music and lyrics by James Quinn and Alaric Jans
Do Patent Leather Shoes Really Reflect Up? 1982

A Little Fish in a Big Pond
Music and lyrics by Irving Berlin
Miss Liberty 1949

Little Fool
Music by Al Carmines
Lyrics by Maria Irene Fornes
Promenade (OB) 1969

A Little Game of Tennis
Music and lyrics by Charles Gaynor
Lend an Ear 1948

Little Geezer
Music by Michael H. Cleary
Lyrics by Max and Nathaniel Lief
and Dave Oppenheim
The Third Little Show 1931

Little Girl
Music by Harry Archer
Lyrics by Harlan Thompson
Merry-Merry 1925

Little Girl at Home
Music by Victor Herbert
Lyrics by James O'Dea
The Lady of the Slipper 1912

Little Girl Baby
Music and lyrics by Sandy Wilson
Valmouth (OB) 1960

Little Girl Blue
Music by Richard Rodgers
Lyrics by Lorenz Hart
Jumbo 1935

A Little Girl From Little Rock
Music by Jule Styne
Lyrics by Leo Robin
Gentlemen Prefer Blondes 1949

Little Girl, Mind How You Go
Music by Paul A. Rubens
Lyrics by Paul A. Rubens and Arthur Wimperis
The Sunshine Girl 1913

The Little Girl Up There
Music by Karl Hoschna
Lyrics by Otto Harbach
Three Twins 1908

Little Girls
Music by Charles Strouse
Lyrics by Martin Charnin
Annie 1977

Little Girls, Goodbye
Music by Victor Jacobi
Lyrics by William LeBaron
Apple Blossoms 1919

Little Golden Maid
Music by Jerome Kern
Lyrics by Paul West
The Red Petticoat 1912

A Little Gossip
Music by Mitch Leigh
Lyrics by Joe Darion
Man of La Mancha 1965

The Little Gray House
Music by Kurt Weill
Lyrics by Maxwell Anderson
Lost in the Stars 1949

Little Green Snake
Music and lyrics by Bob Merrill
Take Me Along 1959

Little Gypsy Lady
Music by Jerome Kern
Lyrics by Anne Caldwell
Stepping Stones 1923

Dropped from production

Little Hands
Music and lyrics by Robert Wright and George Forrest (based on Rachmaninoff)
Anya 1965

A Little House in Soho
Music by Richard Rodgers
Lyrics by Lorenz Hart
She's My Baby 1928

A Little Hut in Hoboken
Music and lyrics by Herman Hupfeld
The Little Show (1st edition) 1929

Little Igloo for Two
Music by Arthur Schwartz
Lyrics by Agnes Morgan
The Grand Street Follies (1926) (OB)

A Little Investigation
Music by Elmer Bernstein
Lyrics by Carolyn Leigh
How Now, Dow Jones 1967

Little Italy
Music by A. Baldwin Sloane
Lyrics by E. Ray Goetz
The Hen Pecks 1911

Married Couple Seeks Married Couple
Music by Cy Coleman
Lyrics by Michael Stewart
I Love My Wife 1977

Married Life
Music by Victor Herbert
Lyrics by Robert B. Smith
The Debutante 1914

Married Life
Music by Rudolf Friml
Lyrics by Otto Harbach and Edward Clark
You're In Love 1917

A Married Man
Music and lyrics by Marian Grudeff
and Raymond Jessel
Baker Street 1965

Married Men and Single Men
Music by Ray Henderson
Lyrics by B.G. DeSylva and Lew Brown
Follow Thru 1929

Marry an American
Music and lyrics by Billy Solly
Boy Meets Boy (OB) 1975

Marry Me
Music by Emmerich Kálmán
Lyrics by C.C.S. Cushing and E.P. Heath
Sari 1914

Marry Me a Little
Music and lyrics by Stephen Sondheim
Marry Me a Little (OB) 1981

Dropped from *Company* (1970)

Marry the Family
Music by Jerome Moross
Lyrics by Michael Blankfort
Parade (1935)

Marry the Girl Myself
Music by Laurence Rosenthal
Lyrics by James Lipton
Sherry! 1967

Marry the Man Today
Music and lyrics by Frank Loesser
Guys and Dolls 1950

Marry With Me
Music by Claibe Richardson
Lyrics by Kenward Elmslie
The Grass Harp 1971

Marrying for Love
Music and lyrics by Irving Berlin
Call Me Madam 1950

Martinique
Music and lyrics by Cole Porter
The Pirate (1948) F

Dropped from film

A Marvelous Weekend
Music and lyrics by James MacDonald, David Vos
and Robert Gerlach
Something's Afoot 1976

Marvin at the Psychiatrist
Music and lyrics by William Finn
March of the Falsettos (OB) 1981

Marvin Hits Trina
Music and lyrics by William Finn
March of the Falsettos (OB) 1981

Marvin Takes a Victory Shower
Music and lyrics by William Finn
In Trousers (OB) 1981

Marvin's Giddy Seizures
Music and lyrics by William Finn
In Trousers (OB) 1981

Mary
Music by Lionel Monckton
Lyrics by Adrian Ross
Our Miss Gibbs 1910

Mary
Music by Louis A. Hirsch
Lyrics by Otto Harbach
Mary 1920

Mary and Doug
Music and lyrics by Gene Buck and Dave Stamper
Ziegfeld Follies of 1920

Mary Dear
Music by James F. Hanley
Lyrics by Eddie Dowling
Honeymoon Lane 1926

Mary Has a Little Fair
Music by Raymond Hubbell
Lyrics by Anne Caldwell
Yours Truly 1927

Mary Jane McKane
Music by Vincent Youmans and Herbert Stothart
Lyrics by Oscar Hammerstein II
and William Cary Duncan
Mary Jane McKane 1923

Mary Make Believe
Music and lyrics by Noël Coward
This Year of Grace 1928

Mary Margaret's House in the Country
Music by Nancy Ford
Lyrics by Gretchen Cryer
Shelter 1973

Mary, Mary
Music by Helen Miller
Lyrics by Eve Merriam
Inner City 1971

Mary, Queen of Scots
Music by Richard Rodgers
Lyrics by Herbert Fields
Poor Little Ritz Girl 1920

Mary's a Grand Old Name
Music and lyrics by George M. Cohan
Forty-Five Minutes From Broadway 1906

The Mascot of the Troop
Music by Victor Herbert
Lyrics by Henry Blossom
Mlle. Modiste 1905

Masculinity
Music and lyrics by Jack Lawrence
and Don Walker
Courtin' Time 1951

Masculinity
Music and lyrics by Jerry Herman
La Cage aux Folles 1983

Mash Notes
Music by Frank Grey
Lyrics by McElbert Moore
The Matinee Girl 1926

Masochism Tango
Music and lyrics by Tom Lehrer
Tomfoolery (OB) 1981

The Mason
Music and lyrics by Craig Carnelia
Working 1978

Mason Cares
Music by Bob James
Lyrics by Jack O'Brien
The Selling of the President 1972

The Masque
Music by Richard Rodgers
Lyrics by Sheldon Harnick
Rex 1976

Masquerade
Music and lyrics by Charles Herbert
Two for Tonight (OB) 1939

Masquerade
Music by John Clifton
Lyrics by John Clifton and Ben Tarver
Man With a Load of Mischief (OB) 1966

Massacre
Music and lyrics by Gene Curty, Nitra Scharfman
and Chuck Strand
The Lieutenant 1975

The Master of the Greatest Art of All
Music by Sammy Fain
Lyrics by Marilyn and Alan Bergman
Something More 1964

The Master Plan
Music and lyrics by Irving Burgie
Ballad for Bimshire (OB) 1963

Mata Hari
Music and lyrics by Rick Besoyan
Little Mary Sunshine (OB) 1959

Matchmaker, Matchmaker
Music by Jerry Bock
Lyrics by Sheldon Harnick
Fiddler on the Roof 1964

Mathilde
Music by Jacques Brel
English lyrics by Eric Blau and Mort Shuman
*Jacques Brel Is Alive and Well
and Living in Paris* (OB) 1968

Matilda
Music and lyrics by James Shelton
Dance Me a Song 1950

The Matinee
Music and lyrics by Billy Barnes
The Billy Barnes People 1961

The Matrimonial Handicap
Music by George Gershwin
Lyrics by B.G. DeSylva
Sweet Little Devil 1924

The Matrimonial Stomp
Music by Gene de Paul
Lyrics by Johnny Mercer
Li'l Abner 1956

Matrimony
Music by Franz Lehár
Lyrics by Harry B. and Robert B. Smith
Gypsy Love 1911

A Matter of Time
Music by Mary Rodgers
Lyrics by Martin Charnin
Hot Spot 1963

Matters Culinary
Music by Lehman Engel
Lyrics by Agnes Morgan
A Hero Is Born 1937

Maud, the Bawd
Music and lyrics by Deed Meyer
She Shall Have Music (OB) 1959

Max the Millionaire
Music by Tommy Wolf
Lyrics by Fran Landesman
The Nervous Set 1959

Maxie
Music and lyrics by Harry Chapin
The Night That Made America Famous 1975

The Maxim Girl
Music by Ivan Caryll
Lyrics by C.M.S. McLellan
Oh! Oh! Delphine 1912

Maxim's
Music by Franz Lehár
Lyrics by Adrian Ross
The Merry Widow 1907

Maxine!
Music by Kenn Long and Jim Crozier
Lyrics by Kenn Long
Touch (OB) 1970

Maxixe-Habanera
Music by Don Gohman
Lyrics by Hal Hackady
Ambassador 1972

May I Dance With You?
Music and lyrics by John Raniello
Movie Buff (OB) 1977

May I Have My Gloves?
Music by Ray Henderson
Lyrics by Jack Yellen
George White's Scandals (1936)

May I Say I Love You?
Music by J. Fred Coots
Lyrics by Arthur Swanstrom and Benny Davis
Sons o' Guns 1929

May I Suggest Romance?
Music by Frederick Loewe
Lyrics by Earle Crooker
Great Lady 1938

May in Manhattan
Music by Ruth Cleary Patterson
Lyrics by Tom Romano
Russell Patterson's Sketch Book (OB) 1960

May Moon
Music by Armand Vecsey
Lyrics by P.G. Wodehouse
The Nightingale 1927

May the Best Man Win
Music by Jimmy Van Heusen
Lyrics by Johnny Burke
Nellie Bly 1946

Maybe
Music by George Gershwin
Lyrics by Ira Gershwin
Oh, Kay! 1926

Maybe
Music by Charles Strouse
Lyrics by Martin Charnin
Annie 1977

Maybe for Instance
Music by Joe Ercole
Lyrics by Bruce Kluger
Ka-Boom (OB) 1980

Maybe I Should Change My Ways
Music by Duke Ellington
Lyrics by John Latouche
Beggar's Holiday 1946

Maybe I Will
Music by Harold Orlob
Lyrics by Irving Caesar
Talk About Girls 1927

Maybe I'll Baby You
Music by Dave Stamper
Lyrics by Gene Buck
Take the Air 1927

Maybe I'm Doing It Wrong
Music and lyrics by Randy Newman
Maybe I'm Doing It Wrong (1st edition) (OB) 1981

Maybe It's Me
Music by Richard Rodgers
Lyrics by Lorenz Hart
Peggy-Ann 1926

Maybe It's Time for Me
Music by Laurence Rosenthal
Lyrics by James Lipton
Sherry! 1967

Maybe, Maybe, Maybe
Music by Richard Rodgers
Lyrics by Martin Charnin
I Remember Mama 1979

Dropped from production

Maybe Means Yes
Music by Jimmy McHugh
Lyrics by Dorothy Fields
Hello Daddy 1928

Maybe So
Music by Alberta Nichols
Lyrics by Mann Holiner
Angela 1928

Maybe Some Other Time
Music and lyrics by Ervin Drake
What Makes Sammy Run? 1964

Maybe This Is Love
Music by Ray Henderson
Lyrics by B.G. DeSylva
Three Cheers 1928

Maybe This Time
Music by John Kander
Lyrics by Fred Ebb
Cabaret (film version, 1972)

Mayfair
Music by Raymond Hubbell
Lyrics by Anne Caldwell
Yours Truly 1927

Mayfair
Music by William Waliter
Lyrics by Rowland Leigh
Walk a Little Faster 1932

Mayfair Affair
Music and lyrics by Robert Wright
and George Forrest
Kean 1961

Mayflower
Music by J. Fred Coots, Maury Rubens
and Pat Thayer
Lyrics by Clifford Grey
Mayflowers 1925

The Mayor's Chair
Music by Mitch Leigh
Lyrics by William Alfred and Phyllis Robinson
Cry for Us All 1970

The Maze
Music by Charles Strouse
Lyrics by David Rogers
Charlie and Algernon 1980

Mazeltov
Music and lyrics by Jerry Herman
The Grand Tour 1979

Mazuma
Music by Leo Fall
Lyrics by Harold Atteridge
The Rose of Stamboul 1922

McInerney's Farm
Music by Sammy Fain
Lyrics by George Marion, Jr.
Toplitzky of Notre Dame 1946

Me
Music by Jerome Kern
Lyrics by Edgar Allan Woolf
Head Over Heels 1918

Me
Music and lyrics by Johnny Brandon
Who's Who, Baby? (OB) 1968

Me
Music and lyrics by Billy Solly
Boy Meets Boy (OB) 1975

Me, a Big Heap Indian
Music and lyrics by Rick Besoyan
Little Mary Sunshine (OB) 1959

Me Alone
Music by Coleridge-Taylor Perkinson
Lyrics by Errol Hill
Man Better Man (OB) 1969

Me an' My Bundle
Music and lyrics by Irving Berlin
Miss Liberty 1949

Me and Dorothea
Music by David Baker
Lyrics by Sheldon Harnick
Smiling, the Boy Fell Dead (OB) 1961

Me and Lee
Music by Giuseppe Verdi (adapted by Hans
Spialek)
Lyrics by Charles Friedman
My Darlin' Aïda 1952

Me and Love
Music by David Baker
Lyrics by David Craig
Copper and Brass 1957

Me and Marie
Music and lyrics by Cole Porter
Jubilee 1935

Me and My Baby
Music by John Kander
Lyrics by Fred Ebb
Chicago 1975

Me and My Horse
Music and lyrics by Norman Dean
Autumn's Here (OB) 1966

Me and My Old World Charm
Music by Thomas (Fats) Waller
Lyrics by George Marion, Jr.
Early to Bed 1943

Me and My Town
Music and lyrics by Stephen Sondheim
Anyone Can Whistle 1964

Me and the Elements
Music by Moose Charlap
Lyrics by Eddie Lawrence
Kelly 1965

Me and the Role and You
Music by Jerome Kern
Lyrics by Oscar Hammerstein II
Very Warm for May 1939

Dropped from production

Me Atahualpa
Music by Ray Haney
Lyrics by Alfred Aiken
We're Civilized? (OB) 1962

Me for You
Music by Richard Rodgers
Lyrics by Lorenz Hart
Heads Up! 1929

Me for You Forever
Music by Richard Myer
Lyrics by Edward Heyman
Murder at the Vanities 1933

Me, the Moonlight and Me
Music by Maury Rubens
Lyrics by Clifford Grey
The Madcap 1928

Meadowlark
Music by Bronislaw Kaper (based on Chopin)
Lyrics by John Latouche
Polonaise 1945

Mean
Music by Gordon Duffy
Lyrics by Harry M. Haldane
Happy Town 1959

Mean
Music and lyrics by Walter Marks
Bajour 1964

Mean Ole Lion
Music and lyrics by Charlie Smalls
The Wiz 1975

The Meanest Man in Town
Music and lyrics by Robert Dahdah
Curley McDimple (OB) 1967

Meanwhile Back in Yonkers
Music by Rob Fremont
Lyrics by Doris Willens
Piano Bar (OB) 1978

Measure the Valleys
Music by Judd Woldin
Lyrics by Robert Brittan
Raisin 1973

Meat and Potatoes
Music and lyrics by Irving Berlin
Mr. President 1962

Mechanical Man
Music by Alma Sanders
Lyrics by Monte Carlo
Mystery Moon 1930

Medea in Disneyland
Music by Lloyd Norlin
Lyrics by Sheldon Harnick
Shoestring Revue (1955) (OB)

Medea Tango
Music by Manos Hadjidakis
Lyrics by Joe Darion
Illya Darling 1967

Meditation
Music by Gary Geld
Lyrics by Peter Udell
Shenandoah 1975

Mediteranee
Music by Dov Seltzer
Lyrics by David Paulsen
To Live Another Summer 1971

The Meek Shall Inherit
Music by Alan Menken
Lyrics by Howard Ashman
Little Shop of Horrors (OB) 1982

Meerahlah
Music and lyrics by Cole Porter
Around the World 1946

Meeskite
Music by John Kander
Lyrics by Fred Ebb
Cabaret 1966

Meet Me at the Fair
Music by Arthur Schwartz
Lyrics by Albert Stillman
Virginia 1937

Meet Me Tonight
Music by Don Pippin
Lyrics by Steve Brown
Fashion (OB) 1974

Meet Miss Blendo
Music and lyrics by Johnny Mercer
Top Banana 1951

Meet My Seester
Music by Jule Styne
Lyrics by Sammy Cahn
Look to the Lilies 1970

Meet the Boyfriend
Music by Vincent Youmans
Lyrics by Billy Rose and Edward Eliscu
Great Day! 1929

Dropped from production

Meet the People
Music by Jay Gorney
Lyrics by Henry Myers
Meet the People 1940

The Meeting
Music by Robert Kessler
Lyrics by Lola Pergament
O Marry Me! (OB) 1961

Meg
Music by Monty Norman
Lyrics by Julian More
The Moony Shapiro Songbook 1981

Meilinki Meilchick
Music and lyrics by Leslie Bricusse
and Anthony Newley
Stop the World—I Want to Get Off 1962

Mein Herr
Music by John Kander
Lyrics by Fred Ebb
Cabaret (film version, 1972)

Mein Kleine Akrobat
Music by Arthur Schwartz
Lyrics by Howard Dietz
Flying Colors 1932

Melican Papa
Music by Jerome Kern
Lyrics by Anne Caldwell
Good Morning, Dearie 1921

Melinda
Music by Burton Lane
Lyrics by Alan Jay Lerner
On a Clear Day You Can See Forever 1965

Melinda Schecker
Music by Diane Leslie
Lyrics by William Gleason
The Coolest Cat in Town (OB) 1978

Melisande
Music by Harvey Schmidt
Lyrics by Tom Jones
110 in the Shade 1963

Melodies of May
Music by Jerome Kern
Lyrics by Oscar Hammerstein II
Music in the Air 1932

Choral setting of Beethoven's Piano Sonata Opus 2, No. 3 (second movement)

Melodies Within My Heart
Music by Karl Hajos (based on Chopin)
Lyrics by Harry B. Smith
White Lilacs 1928

Melody
Music by Sigmund Romberg
Lyrics by Irving Caesar
Melody 1933

Melody
Music and lyrics by Matt Dubey and Dean Fuller
Smith (OB) 1973

Melody in Four F
Music and lyrics by Sylvia Fine
and Max Liebman
Let's Face It! 1941

The Melody of Love
Music by Franz Lehár
Lyrics by Harry B. and Robert B. Smith
Gypsy Love 1911

Melody of Manhattan
Music and lyrics by Ronnie Britton
Greenwich Village Follies (OB) 1976

Melody Triste
Music by Sigmund Romberg
Lyrics by Dorothy Donnelly
Blossom Time 1921

Melt Us!
Music by Charles Strouse
Lyrics by Lee Adams
All American 1962

Memories
Music by Joseph Meyer and Philip Charig
Lyrics by Leo Robin
Just Fancy 1927

Memories
Music by Ray Henderson
Lyrics by B.G. DeSylva and Lew Brown
Manhattan Mary 1927

Memories of Madison Square Garden
Music by Richard Rodgers
Lyrics by Lorenz Hart
Jumbo 1935

Memories of You
Music by Eubie Blake
Lyrics by Andy Razaf
Blackbirds of 1930

Memory
Music and lyrics by Jerry Herman
Dear World 1969

Memory
Music by Andrew Lloyd Webber
Lyrics by Trevor Nunn, based on poems by T. S. Eliot
Cats 1982

Men
Music by John Green
Lyrics by George Marion, Jr.
Beat the Band 1942

Men
Music by Frank Black
Lyrics by Gladys Shelley
The Duchess Misbehaves 1946

Men
Music by Moose Charlap
Lyrics by Norman Gimbel
Whoop-Up 1958

Men
Music by Jule Styne
Lyrics by Betty Comden and Adolph Green
Lorelei 1974

Men
Music and lyrics by Stan Daniels
So Long, 174th Street 1976

Men About Town
Music and lyrics by Noël Coward
Tonight at 8:30 ("Red Peppers") 1936

Men About Town
Music by Alma Sanders
Lyrics by Monte Carlo
Louisiana Lady 1947

Men Are a Pain in the Neck
Music by Frederico Valerio
Lyrics by Elizabeth Miele
Hit the Trail 1954

Men Are Men
Music and lyrics by Al Carmines
The Evangelist (OB) 1982

Men Awake
Music and lyrics by Harold Rome
Pins and Needles (OB) 1937

Men Grow Older
Music by Jean Gilbert
Lyrics by Harry Graham and Cyrus Wood
The Lady in Ermine 1922

The Men in My Life
Music by David Martin
Lyrics by Langston Hughes
Simply Heavenly 1957

Men of China
Music by Franz Lehár
Lyrics by Harry Graham
Yours Is My Heart 1946

Men of Hades
Music by Alma Sanders
Lyrics by Monte Carlo
The Houseboat on the Styx 1928

Men of the Water-Mark
Music by Jay Gorney
Lyrics by Jean and Walter Kerr
Touch and Go 1949

The Men Who Run the Country
Music and lyrics by Johnny Mercer
Saratoga 1959

Mene, Mene, Tekel
Music and lyrics by Harold Rome
Pins and Needles (OB) 1937

Added during run

Menu Song
Music and lyrics by Cass Morgan
and Debra Monk
Pump Boys and Dinettes 1982

Meow! Meow! Meow!
Music by Victor Herbert
Lyrics by James O'Dea
The Lady of the Slipper 1912

Mercenary Mary
Music by Con Conrad
Lyrics by William B. Friedlander
Mercenary Mary 1925

Merci, Bon Dieu
Music by Larry Grossman
Lyrics by Hal Hackady
Goodtime Charley 1975

Merely Marvelous
Music by Albert Hague
Lyrics by Dorothy Fields
Redhead 1959

Merrily We Roll Along
Music and lyrics by Stephen Sondheim
Merrily We Roll Along 1981

Merrily We Waltz Along
Music by Henry Sullivan
Lyrics by Earle Crooker
Thumbs Up! 1934

Merry Andrew (instrumental)
Music by George Gershwin
Rosalie 1928

Merry Christmas
Music by C. Luckey Roberts
Lyrics by Alex C. Rogers
My Magnolia 1926

The Merry Go Round
Music by Seymour Furth and Lee Edwards
Lyrics by R.F. Carroll
Bringing Up Father 1925

Merry-Go-Round
Music by H. Maurice Jacquet
Lyrics by William Brady
The Silver Swan 1929

Merry-Go-Round
Music and lyrics by Ronnie Britton
Greenwich Village Follies (OB) 1976

Merry Little Minuet
Music and lyrics by Sheldon Harnick
John Murray Anderson's Almanac (1953)

Merry May
Music and lyrics by Rick Besoyan
The Student Gypsy (OB) 1963

Merry Old Land of Oz
Music by Harold Arlen
Lyrics by E.Y. Harburg
The Wizard of Oz (1939) F

Merry Wedding Bells
Music by Jean Schwartz
Lyrics by Edward Madden
The Fascinating Widow 1911

Mesdames and Messieurs
Music and lyrics by Cole Porter
Du Barry Was a Lady 1939

The Message of the Violet
Music by Gustav Luders
Lyrics by Frank Pixley
The Prince of Pilsen 1903

Messages
Music by Monty Norman
Lyrics by Julian More
The Moony Shapiro Songbook 1981

Messin' Around
Music by Jimmy Johnson
Lyrics by Perry Bradford
Messin' Around 1929

Messin' Round
Music by Werner Janssen
Lyrics by Mann Holiner and J. Keirn Brennan
Boom-Boom 1929

Metamorphosis
Music by John Addison
Lyrics by John Cranko
Cranks 1956

Metaphor
Music by Harvey Schmidt
Lyrics by Tom Jones
The Fantasticks (OB) 1960

Metaphorically Speaking
Music by Lee Pockriss
Lyrics by Anne Croswell
Ernest in Love (OB) 1960

Metropolitan Nights
Music and lyrics by Irving Berlin
Watch Your Step 1914

Mexican Bad Men
Music by Maria Grever
Lyrics by Raymond Leveen
Viva O'Brien 1941

Mexican Blues
Music by Joe Jordan
Lyrics by Homer Tutt and Henry Creamer
Deep Harlem 1929

Mexico
Music by Martin Broones
Lyrics by Ballard MacDonald
Rufus Lemaire's Affairs 1927

Mexico
Music by Sigmund Romberg
Lyrics by Dorothy Donnelly
My Maryland 1927

The Mexiconga
Music by Sammy Fain
Lyrics by Jack Yellen and Herb Magidson
George White's Scandals (1939)

Mi Chiquita
Music by Joseph Meyer and Philip Charig
Lyrics by Leo Robin
Just Fancy 1927

Mi! Mi!
Music by Frank D'Armond
Lyrics by Will Morrissey
Saluta 1934

Mia Luna
Music by G. Puccini [not Giacomo]
Lyrics by E. Ray Goetz
Naughty Cinderella 1925

Miani
Music and lyrics by Ed Tyler
Sweet Miani (OB) 1962

Mickey
Music by Sam Morrison
Lyrics by Dolph Singer
Summer Wives 1936

The Micromaniac
Music and lyrics by Harold Rome
Ziegfeld Follies (1943)

The Midas Touch
Music by Jule Styne
Lyrics by Betty Comden and Adolph Green
Bells Are Ringing 1956

Middle Age Blues
Music by Charles Strouse
Lyrics by Lee Adams
Bring Back Birdie 1981

The Middle Class
Music by Jacques Brel
English lyrics by Eric Blau and Mort Shuman
*Jacques Brel Is Alive and Well
and Living in Paris* (OB) 1968

Middle-Class-Liberal-Blues
Music and lyrics by Johnny Brandon
Love! Love! Love! (OB) 1977

Middle Class Revolution
Music by Wally Harper
Lyrics by Paul Zakrzewski
Sensations (OB) 1970

Middle of the Sea
Music and lyrics by Ed Tyler
Sweet Miani (OB) 1962

The Middle Years
Music and lyrics by Hal Hester and Danny Apolinar
Your Own Thing (OB) 1968

Midnight Bells
Music by George Gershwin
Lyrics by Otto Harbach and Oscar Hammerstein II
Song of the Flame 1925

Midnight Cabaret
Music and lyrics by Porter Grainger
and Freddie Johnson
Lucky Sambo 1925

Midnight Daddy
Music by Will Morrisey
Lyrics by Edmund Joseph
Polly of Hollywood 1927

Midnight Deadline Blastoff
Music and lyrics by John Phillips
Man on the Moon 1975

Midnight-Hot Blood
Music and lyrics by Cliff Jones
Rockabye Hamlet 1976

Midnight Lullabye
Music by Jim Steinman
Lyrics by Michael Weller and Jim Steinman
More Than You Deserve (OB) 1973

Midnight Mass
Music and lyrics by Cliff Jones
Rockabye Hamlet 1976

Midnight Matinee
Music and lyrics by Noël Coward
Set to Music 1939

Midnight Riding
Music by Charles Strouse
Lyrics by David Rogers
Charlie and Algernon 1980

The Midnight Supper
Music by Richard Rodgers
Lyrics by Lorenz Hart
Poor Little Ritz Girl 1920

In Boston production but dropped before Broadway
opening

Midnight Waltz
Music by Robert Stolz (adapted from Johann
Strauss)
Lyrics by Robert Sour
Mr. Strauss Goes to Boston 1945

Midsummer Night
Music and lyrics by Rick Besoyan
Babes in the Wood (OB) 1964

Midsummer Night
Music by Richard Rodgers
Lyrics by Martin Charnin
I Remember Mama 1979

Dropped from production

Midsummer's Eve
Music and lyrics by Robert Wright and George
Forrest
Song of Norway 1944

Based on Grieg's *'Twas on a Lovely Evening in
June* and Scherzo in E minor

Midtown
Music by Max Rich
Lyrics by Jack Scholl
Keep Moving 1934

A Mighty Fortress
Music by Coleridge-Taylor Perkinson
Lyrics by Ray McIver
God Is a (Guess What?) (OB) 1968

Mighty Girl
Music by Karl Hoschna
Lyrics by Otto Harbach
The Fascinating Widow 1911

Mighty Whitey
Music and lyrics by Oscar Brown, Jr.
Buck White 1969

Mignonette
Music by Victor Herbert
Lyrics by Henry Blossom
The Red Mill 1906

The Military Ball (orchestral)
Music by Victor Herbert
Lyrics by Glen MacDonough
Babes in Toyland 1903

Military Dancing Drill
Music by George Gershwin
Lyrics by Ira Gershwin
Strike Up the Band 1930

Military Life
Music and lyrics by Harold Rome
Call Me Mister 1946

Military Men I Love
Music by Edward Künneke
Lyrics by Harry B. Smith
The Love Song 1925

Milk and Honey
Music and lyrics by Jerry Herman
Milk and Honey 1961

Milk, Milk, Milk
Music and lyrics by Cole Porter
Let's Face It! 1941

Milkmaid
Music by Galt MacDermot
Lyrics by John Guare
Two Gentlemen of Verona 1971

Milkmaids of Broadway
Music by Alma Sanders
Lyrics by Monte Carlo
Mystery Moon 1930

Milkmaid's Song
Music by Reginald De Koven
Lyrics by Harry B. Smith
Robin Hood 1891

The Milky Way
Music and lyrics by Gene Lockhart
Bunk of 1926

Millefleurs
Music by Sigmund Romberg
Lyrics by Rowland Leigh
My Romance 1948

The Miller's Son
Music and lyrics by Stephen Sondheim
A Little Night Music 1973

Million Dollar Smile
Music by Morton Gould
Lyrics by Betty Comden and Adolph Green
Billion Dollar Baby 1945

A Million Dollars
Music by Dave Stamper
Lyrics by Fred Herendeen
Orchids Preferred 1937

A Million Eyes
Music by Jean Schwartz
Lyrics by Alfred Bryan
A Night in Spain 1927

A Million Good Reasons
Music by Joseph Meyer
Lyrics by William Moll
Jonica 1930

A Million Miles Away Behind the Door
Music by André Previn
Lyrics by Alan Jay Lerner
Paint Your Wagon (film version, 1969)

Million Songs
Music and lyrics by Stephen H. Lemberg
Jazzbo Brown 1980

A Million Windows and I
Music by Alec Wilder
Lyrics by Norman Gimbel
Shoestring Revue (1955) (OB)

The Millionaire
Music by Leslie Stuart
Lyrics by Ernest Boyd-Jones
Florodora 1900

Mimi
Music by Richard Rodgers
Lyrics by Lorenz Hart
Love Me Tonight (1932) F

Mind If I Make Love to You
Music and lyrics by Cole Porter
High Society (1956) F

Mind Over Matter
Music by David Shire
Lyrics by Richard Maltby, Jr.
The Sap of Life (OB) 1961

The Mind Reader
Music by Raymond Hubbell
Lyrics by Glen MacDonough
The Jolly Bachelors 1910

Mine
Music by George Gershwin
Lyrics by Ira Gershwin
Let 'Em Eat Cake 1933

Mine
Music by Cy Coleman
Lyrics by Betty Comden and Adolph Green
On the Twentieth Century 1978

Mine Song
Music by John Kander
Lyrics by Fred Ebb
Zorba (1983 revival)

Mine 'til Monday
Music by Arthur Schwartz
Lyrics by Dorothy Fields
A Tree Grows in Brooklyn 1951

Mineola
Music by Sammy Fain
Lyrics by Marilyn and Alan Bergman
Something More 1964

Minnie
Music by Sigmund Romberg
Lyrics by Oscar Hammerstein II
East Wind 1931

Minnie's Boys
Music by Larry Grossman
Lyrics by Hal Hackady
Minnie's Boys 1970

Minsky
Music by Dave Stamper
Lyrics by Fred Herendeen
Orchids Preferred 1937

Minsky's Metropolitan Grand Opera
Music by Michael H. Cleary
Lyrics by Max and Nathaniel Lief
Hey Nonny Nonny! 1932

The Minstrel
Music by Mary Rodgers
Lyrics by Marshall Barer
Once Upon a Mattress 1959

Minstrel Days
Music and lyrics by Irving Berlin
The Cocoanuts 1925

The Minstrel Parade
Music and lyrics by Irving Berlin
Watch Your Step 1914

Minstrel Parade
Music by Kurt Weill
Lyrics by Alan Jay Lerner
Love Life 1948

Minstrel Song
Music by Mel Marvin
Lyrics by Christopher Durang
A History of the American Film 1978

The Minuet of the Minute
Music by Herbert Stothart
Lyrics by Oscar Hammerstein II and Otto Harbach
Rose Marie 1924

Mio Fratello
Music by Frank Fields
Lyrics by Armand Aulicino
The Shoemaker and the Peddler (OB) 1960

Mira
Music and lyrics by Bob Merrill
Carnival 1961

Miracle of Miracles
Music by Jerry Bock
Lyrics by Sheldon Harnick
Fiddler on the Roof 1964

Miracle Song
Music and lyrics by Stephen Sondheim
Anyone Can Whistle 1964

Miracle Town
Music by Steve Jankowski
Lyrics by Kenny Morris
Francis (OB) 1982

Miranda
Music by Milton Schafer
Lyrics by Ronny Graham
Bravo Giovanni 1962

Mirror
Music and lyrics by Earl Wilson, Jr.
Let My People Come (OB) 1974

Mirror, Mirror
Music by Cole Porter
Lyrics by T. Lawrason Riggs and Cole Porter
See America First 1916

Mirror, Mirror on the Wall
Music and lyrics by Melvin Van Peebles
Ain't Supposed to Die a Natural Death 1971

Misalliance
Music by Donald Swann
Lyrics by Michael Flanders
At the Drop of a Hat 1959

Mischa, Jascha, Toscha, Sascha
Music by George Gershwin
Lyrics by Ira Gershwin

The Gershwins wrote this circa 1921 about their distinguished friends, the violinists, Mischa Elman, Jascha Heifetz, Toscha Seidel and Sascha Jacobsen. (The song was never in a show):
    Names like Sammy, Max and Moe
    Never bring the heavy dough
    Like Mischa, Jascha, Toscha, Sascha,
    Fiddle-lee
    Diddle-lee
    Dee.

Miserable With You
Music by Arthur Schwartz
Lyrics by Howard Dietz
The Band Wagon 1931

Miserere
Music by Leonard Bernstein
Lyrics by Stephen Sondheim
Candide 1956

Miserere
Music by Meyer Kupferman
Lyrics by Paul Goodman
Jonah (OB) 1966

Misery Is
Music by Mary Rodgers
Lyrics by Marshall Barer
The Mad Show (OB) 1966

Mis'ry's Comin' Around'
Music by Jerome Kern
Lyrics by Oscar Hammerstein II
Show Boat 1927

Dropped from production

Miss America
Music by Nancy Ford
Lyrics by Gretchen Cryer
I'm Getting My Act Together and Taking It on the Road 1978

Miss America
Music and lyrics by Ann Harris
Sky High (OB) 1979

Miss Blush
Music by Paul A. Rubens
Lyrics by Paul A. Rubens and Arthur Wimperis
The Sunshine Girl 1913

Miss Bubbles
Music and lyrics by Jeanne Napoli, Doug Frank and Gary Portnoy
Marilyn 1983

Miss Euclid Avenue
Music and lyrics by Jerry Herman
Madame Aphrodite (OB) 1961

Miss Follies
Music by Colin Romoff
Lyrics by David Rogers
Ziegfeld Follies (1957)

Miss Follies of 192-
Music and lyrics by Herman Hupfeld
Ziegfeld Follies (1957)

Miss Langley's School for Girls
Music by Frederick Loewe
Lyrics by Alan Jay Lerner
What's Up? 1943

Miss Liberty
Music and lyrics by Irving Berlin
Miss Liberty 1949

Miss Lorelei Lee
Music by Jule Styne
Lyrics by Betty Comden and Adolph Green
Lorelei 1974

Miss Marmelstein
Music and lyrics by Harold Rome
I Can Get It for You Wholesale 1962

Miss Mere
Music by James Bredt
Lyrics by Edward Eager
The Happy Hypocrite (OB) 1968

Miss Mimsey
Music and lyrics by Irvin Graham
New Faces of 1936

Miss Otis Regrets
Music and lyrics by Cole Porter

Monty Woolley suggested this title to Porter,
betting him that he couldn't write a song to it.
Porter did and dedicated it to Elsa Maxwell. Later in
the year (1934) the song went into a London revue,
Hi Diddle Diddle. Among those who adopted the
song as their own was the late "Bricktop" (Ada
Beatrice Queen Victoria Louise Virginia Smith), a
much beloved American entertainer whose café in
Paris was a favorite spot of Porter's.

Miss Platt Selects Mate
Music by Jay Gorney
Lyrics by Jean and Walter Kerr
Touch and Go 1949

Miss Truth
Music and lyrics by Glory Van Scott
Miss Truth (OB) 1979

A "Miss You" Kiss
Music by Victor Young
Lyrics by Stella Unger
Seventh Heaven 1955

Missed America
Music and lyrics by Kenny Solms and Gail Parent
New Faces of 1968

Mission Control
Music and lyrics by John Phillips
Man on the Moon 1975

M-i-s-s-i-s-s-i-p-p-i
Music by Harry Tierney
Lyrics by Ben Ryan and Bert Hanlon
Hitchy-koo 1917

Mississippi
Music by Jimmy Johnson
Lyrics by Perry Bradford
Messin' Around 1929

Mississippi Joys
Music and lyrics by Al Wilson, Charles Weinberg
and Ken Macomber
Yeah Man 1932

Missouri
Music and lyrics by Nat Reed
Brown Buddies 1930

Missouri Mule
Music by Paul Klein
Lyrics by Fred Ebb
Morning Sun (OB) 1963

A Mist is Over the Moon
Music by Ben Oakland
Lyrics by Oscar Hammerstein II
The Lady Objects (1938) F

Mister Boy
Music and lyrics by C. Jackson and James Hatch
Fly Blackbird (OB) 1962

Mister Cellophane
Music by John Kander
Lyrics by Fred Ebb
Chicago 1975

Mister Destiny
Music by Monty Norman
Lyrics by Julian More
The Moony Shapiro Songbook 1981

Mister Drummer Man
Music by Louis A. Hirsch
Lyrics by Rennold Wolf
The Rainbow Girl 1918

Mister Washington! Uncle George
Music by Morton Gould
Lyrics by Dorothy Fields
Arms and the Girl 1950

Misunderstood
Music by Jerome Kern
Lyrics by Otto Harbach
The Cat and the Fiddle 1931

Dropped from production

Mitzi's Lullaby
Music by Jerome Kern
Lyrics by Edgar Allan Woolf
Head Over Heels 1918

The Mix
Music and lyrics by Elizabeth Swados
Dispatches (OB) 1979

Mix and Mingle
Music and lyrics by Harold Rome
Wish You Were Here 1952

The Mix-Up Rag
Music by Jerome Kern
Lyrics by Paul Dickey and Charles W. Goddard
Miss Information 1915

Moanin' in the Mornin'
Music by Harold Arlen
Lyrics by E.Y. Harburg
Hooray for What! 1937

Moanin' Low
Music by Ralph Rainger
Lyrics by Howard Dietz
The Little Show (1st edition) 1929

Mock Turtle Lament
Music and lyrics by Elizabeth Swados
Alice in Concert (OB) 1980

The Mocking Bird
Music by Sigmund Romberg
Lyrics by Dorothy Donnelly
My Maryland 1927

Mocking Bird
Music by Richard Rodgers
Lyrics by Lorenz Hart
Simple Simon 1930

The Model Hasn't Changed
Music and lyrics by Harold Rome
Michael Todd's Peep Show 1950

Model Married Pair
Music by Jean Gilbert
Lyrics by Harry B. and Robert B. Smith
Modest Suzanne 1912

Models
Music by Ray Henderson
Lyrics by Jack Yellen
George White's Scandals (1936)

Modern Madrigal
Music by Warburton Guilbert
Lyrics by Viola Brothers Shore and June Sillman
New Faces of 1934

Modern Maiden's Prayer
Music by James Hanley
Lyrics by Ballard MacDonald
Ziegfeld Follies of 1917

The Modern Pirate
Music by Gustav Luders
Lyrics by Frank Pixley
The Prince of Pilsen 1903

Modernistic Moe
Music by Vernon Duke
Lyrics by Ira Gershwin
Ziegfeld Follies (1936)

A Modest Little Thing
Music and lyrics by Gene Lockhart
Bunk of 1926

The Modiste
Music by Richard Rodgers
Lyrics by Lorenz Hart
I Married an Angel 1938

Moi
Music and lyrics by Deed Meyer
She Shall Have Music (OB) 1959

Molasses to Rum
Music and lyrics by Sherman Edwards
1776 1969

Mollie O'Donahue
Music by Jerome Kern
Lyrics by Oscar Hammerstein II
Sweet Adeline 1929

Molly
Music and lyrics by Ron Dante and Gene Allan
Billy 1969

Molly Malone
Music and lyrics by George M. Cohan
The Merry Malones 1927

Molly O'Reilly
Music and lyrics by Charles Gaynor
Lend an Ear 1948

A Moment Ago
Music by Moose Charlap
Lyrics by Eddie Lawrence
Kelly 1965

The Moment Has Passed
Music by Al Carmines
Lyrics by Maria Irene Fornes
Promenade (OB) 1969

The Moment I Looked in Your Eyes
Music and lyrics by Joan Edwards
and Lyn Duddy
Tickets Please 1950

The Moment I Saw You
Music by Arthur Schwartz
Lyrics by Howard Dietz
Three's a Crowd 1930

The Moment I Saw You
Music by Manning Sherwin
Lyrics by Harold Purcell
Under the Counter 1947

The Moment Is Now
Music and lyrics by Bob Goodman
Wild and Wonderful 1971

A Moment of Truth
Music and lyrics by Jack Holmes
New Faces of 1962

A Moment of Your Love
Music by Jimmy Van Heusen
Lyrics by Johnny Burke
Carnival in Flanders 1953

A Moment With You
Music and lyrics by Stephen Sondheim
Marry Me a Little (OB) 1981

Moments
Music by Vincent Youmans
Lyrics by Anne Caldwell
Oh, Please! 1926

Dropped from production

The Moments of Happiness
Music by Andrew Lloyd Webber
Cats 1982

Lyrics based on T.S. Eliot's *Old Possum's Book of Practical Cats*

The Moments of the Dance
Music by Jerome Kern
Lyrics by Edgar Allan Woolf
Head Over Heels 1918

Momma, Look Sharp
Music and lyrics by Sherman Edwards
1776 1969

Momma, Momma
Music and lyrics by Harold Rome
I Can Get It for You Wholesale 1962

Momma's Turn
Music and lyrics by Douglas Bernstein
and Denis Markell
Upstairs at O'Neal's (OB) 1982

Mommy Dear Has Dropped Dead in Her Sleep
Music and lyrics by William Finn
In Trousers (OB) 1981

Moms and Dads
Music by Rob Fremont
Lyrics by Doris Willens
Piano Bar (OB) 1978

Mon Ami, My Friend
Music by Kurt Weill
Lyrics by Paul Green
Johnny Johnson 1936

Mona
Music and lyrics by Jim Swann
Pump Boys and Dinettes 1982

Mona From Arizona
Music by Arthur Schwartz
Lyrics by Dorothy Fields
By the Beautiful Sea 1954

Money
Music by Louis A. Hirsch
Lyrics by Otto Harbach
Mary 1920

Money Doesn't Mean a Thing
Music by Lewis E. Gensler and Milton Schwarzwald
Lyrics by George S. Kaufman, Marc Connelly
and Ira Gershwin
Be Yourself 1924

Money in the Bank
Music by Stanley Silverman
Lyrics by Tom Hendry
Doctor Selavy's Magic Theatre (OB) 1972

Money Isn't Everything
Music by Robert Emmett Dolan
Lyrics by Johnny Mercer
Foxy 1964

Money Isn't Ev'rything
Music by Richard Rodgers
Lyrics by Oscar Hammerstein II
Allegro 1947

Money, Money, Money!
Music by George Gershwin
Lyrics by Arthur J. Jackson and B.G. DeSylva
La, La, Lucille 1919

Money, Money, Money
Music by Jule Styne
Lyrics by E.Y. Harburg
Darling of the Day 1968

Money, Money, Money
Music and lyrics by Oscar Brown, Jr.
Buck White 1969

Money, Money, Money
Music by John Kander
Lyrics by Fred Ebb
Cabaret (film version, 1972)

This song replaced "The Money Song" from the stage production.

The Money Rings Out Like Freedom
Music by André Previn
Lyrics by Alan Jay Lerner
Coco 1969

The Money Song
Music by John Kander
Lyrics by Fred Ebb
Cabaret 1966

Money to Burn
Music and lyrics by David Heneker
Half a Sixpence 1965

The Money Tree
Music by John Kander
Lyrics by Fred Ebb
The Act 1977

Monica
Music by Cy Coleman
Lyrics by Michael Stewart
I Love My Wife 1977

Monica, Monica
Music and lyrics by Gian-Carlo Menotti
The Medium 1947

The Monkey Doodle-Doo
Music and lyrics by Irving Berlin
The Cocoanuts 1925

Monkey in the Mango Tree
Music by Harold Arlen
Lyrics by E.Y. Harburg
Jamaica 1957

Monkey Land
Music by Ford Dabney
Lyrics by Jo Trent
Rang-Tang 1927

The Monkey Sat in the Coconut Tree
Music by Harold Arlen
Lyrics by Leo Robin
Casbah (1948) F

A Monkey When He Loves
Music by Baldwin Bergersen
Lyrics by William Archibald
The Crystal Heart (OB) 1960

Monotonous
Music by Arthur Siegel
Lyrics by June Carroll
New Faces of 1952

Monsoon
Music and lyrics by Ervin Drake
What Makes Sammy Run? 1964

Montana
Music by Moose Charlap
Lyrics by Norman Gimbel
Whoop-Up 1958

Montana Moon
Music and lyrics by Ring Lardner
June Moon 1929

Monte Carlo Moon
Music by Jerome Kern
Lyrics by Edward Madden
La Belle Paree 1911

Monte Martre
Music and lyrics by Irving Berlin
Music Box Revue (2nd edition) 1922

Monte, the Model
Music and lyrics by Gene Lockhart
Bunk of 1926

A Month of Sundays
Music by Robert Emmett Dolan
Lyrics by Johnny Mercer
Texas, Li'l Darlin' 1949

Montmart'
Music and lyrics by Cole Porter
Can-Can 1953

Moo Cow
Music by Jerome Kern
Lyrics by Harry B. Smith
Love o' Mike 1917

Mood of the Moment
Music by Maria Grever
Lyrics by Raymond Leveen
Viva O'Brien 1941

Moon About Town
Music by Dana Suesse
Lyrics by E.Y. Harburg
Ziegfeld Follies (1934)

Moon-Faced, Starry-Eyed
Music by Kurt Weill
Lyrics by Langston Hughes
Street Scene 1947

Moon Flower
Music by Sigmund Romberg
Lyrics by Arthur Wimperis
Louie the 14th 1925

Moon in My Window
Music by Richard Rodgers
Lyrics by Stephen Sondheim
Do I Hear a Waltz? 1965

The Moon is on the Sea
Music by George Gershwin
Lyrics by Ira Gershwin
Oh, Kay! 1926

Dropped from production

Moon Madness
Music and lyrics by Rick Besoyan
Babes in the Wood (OB) 1964

Moon, Moon, Moon
Music by Raymond Hubbell
Lyrics by Glen MacDonough
The Jolly Bachelors 1910

Moon of Love
Music by Jerome Kern
Lyrics by Anne Caldwell
Hitchy-Koo 1920

Moon of My Delight
Music by Richard Rodgers
Lyrics by Lorenz Hart
Chee-Chee 1928

Originally written as "Thank You in Advance."
  Thank You in Advance,
    For Keeping Me Around to Cheer You
  Thank You in Advance,
    For Letting No One Else Come Near You.

Moon Song
Music by Jerome Kern
Lyrics by P.G. Wodehouse
Oh, Lady! Lady!! 1918

The Moon Song
Music by Clay Warnick
Lyrics by Edward Eager
Dream With Music 1944

The Moon, the Wind and the Sea
Music by Lewis E. Gensler
Lyrics by Owen Murphy and Robert A.Simon
The Gang's All Here l931

Moonbeams
Music by Victor Herbert
Lyrics by Henry Blossom
The Red Mill 1906

Moonglade
Music by David Baker
Lyrics by Will Holt
Come Summer 1969

Mooning
Music and lyrics by Jim Jacobs and Warren Casey
Grease 1972

Moonland
Music by Jimmy Van Heusen
Lyrics by Eddie De Lange
Swingin' the Dream 1939

Moonlight
Music by Seymour Furth and Lee Edwards
Lyrics by R.F. Carroll
Bringing Up Father 1925

Moonlight
Music and lyrics by Ron Eliran
Don't Step on My Olive Branch (OB) 1976

Moonlight and Violins
Music by Sigmund Romberg
Lyrics by Otto Harbach
Forbidden Melody 1936

Moonlight Memories
Music and lyrics by Irving Berlin
Follow The Fleet (1936) F

Dropped from film

Moonlight Soliloquy
Music by Bronislaw Kaper (based on Chopin)
Lyrics by John Latouche
Polonaise 1945

Moonshine Lullaby
Music and lyrics by Irving Berlin
Annie Get Your Gun 1946

Moonstruck
Music and lyrics by Lionel Monckton
Our Miss Gibbs 1910

Moosh, Moosh
Music and lyrics by James Rado
Rainbow (OB) 1972

Moral Rearmament
Music and lyrics by Jack Holmes
New Faces of 1962

Morality
Music by Robert Kessler
Lyrics by Lola Pergament
O Marry Me! (OB) 1961

More and More
Music by William Heagney
Lyrics by William Heagney and Tom Connell
There You Are 1932

More and More
Music by Jerome Kern
Lyrics by E. Y. Harburg
Can't Help Singing (1944) F

More and More
Music by Fred Stamer
Lyrics by Gen Genovese
Buttrio Square 1952

More and More, Less and Less
Music and lyrics by Jerry Herman
The Grand Tour 1979

More Better Go Easy
Music and lyrics by Eaton Magoon, Jr.
Heathen 1972

More I Cannot Wish You
Music and lyrics by Frank Loesser
Guys and Dolls 1950

The More I See of Others, Dear, the Better I Love You
Music by Victor Herbert
Lyrics by Henry Blossom
The Only Girl 1914

The More I See People
Music by Bert Keyes and Bob Larimer
Lyrics by Bob Larimer
But Never Jam Today 1979

More Incredible Happenings
Music and lyrics by Ronald Jeans
Wake Up and Dream 1929

More Love Than Your Love
Music by Arthur Schwartz
Lyrics by Dorothy Fields
By the Beautiful Sea 1954

More of Me to Love
Music and lyrics by Barbara Schottenfeld
I Can't Keep Running in Place (OB) 1981

More of the Same
Music and lyrics by Oscar Brand
How to Steal an Election (OB) 1968

More of the Same
Music by Billy Goldenberg
Lyrics by Alan and Marilyn Bergman
Ballroom 1978

More Precious Far
Music by Larry Grossman
Lyrics by Hal Hackady
Minnie's Boys 1970

More Than Ever
Music by Vincent Youmans
Lyrics by Harold Adamson and Clifford Grey
Smiles 1930

Dropped from production

More Than Ever Now
Music by David Baker
Lyrics by Sheldon Harnick
Smiling, the Boy Fell Dead (OB) 1961

More Than Friends
Music by William Dyer
Lyrics by Don Parks and William Dyer
Jo (OB) 1964

More Than Just a Friend
Music and lyrics by Richard Rodgers
State Fair (re-make, 1962) F

More Than One More Day
Music by Sol Kaplan
Lyrics by Edward Eliscu
The Banker's Daughter (OB) 1962

More Than One Way
Music by Jimmy Van Heusen
Lyrics by Sammy Cahn
Skyscraper 1965

A More Than Ordinary Glorious Vocabulary
Music by Jacques Urbont
Lyrics by Bruce Geller
All in Love (OB) 1961

More Than These
Music by John Mundy
Lyrics by Edward Eager
Sing Out, Sweet Land 1944

More Than You Deserve
Music by Jim Steinman
Lyrics by Michael Weller and Jim Steinman
More Than You Deserve (OB) 1973

More Than You Know
Music by Vincent Youmans
Lyrics by Billy Rose and Edward Eliscu
Great Day! 1929

The More You Get
Music by Stanley Silverman
Lyrics by Tom Hendry
Doctor Selavy's Magic Theatre (OB) 1972

Morgan Le Fay
Music by Richard Rodgers
Lyrics by Lorenz Hart
A Connecticut Yankee 1927

Dropped from production

A Mormon Life
Music by Jerome Kern
Lyrics by Howard Dietz
Dear Sir 1924

Morning
Music by Johann Strauss
Lyrics by Desmond Carter
The Great Waltz 1934

Morning
Music and lyrics by Clark Gesner
The Utter Glory of Morrissey Hall 1979

Morning
Music by Michael Dansicker
Lyrics by Sarah Schlesinger
On The Swing Shift (OB) 1983

The Morning After
Music by Susan Hulsman Bingham
Lyrics by Myrna Lamb
Mod Donna (OB) 1970

Morning Anthem
Music by Kurt Weill
Lyrics by Marc Blitzstein
The Threepenny Opera (OB) 1954

Morning Glory
Music by Jerome Kern
Lyrics by Anne Caldwell
The Bunch and Judy 1922

Morning Glory Mountain
Music by Harris Wheeler
Lyrics by Mary L. Fisher
Blue Plate Special (OB) 1983

Morning Glow
Music and lyrics by Stephen Schwartz
Pippin 1972

Morning in Madrid
Music by Frank Black
Lyrics by Gladys Shelley
The Duchess Misbehaves 1946

Morning Is Midnight
Music by Richard Rodgers
Lyrics by Lorenz Hart

Dropped from *Lido Lady* (London, 1926) and *She's My Baby* (1928)

The Morning Music of Montmartre
Music and lyrics by Jay Livingston and Ray Evans
Oh Captain! 1958

Morning Prayer
Music by Louis Bellson and Will Irwin
Lyrics by Richard Ney
Portofino 1958

Morning Sun
Music by Paul Klein
Lyrics by Fred Ebb
Morning Sun (OB) 1963

Morning Sun
Music by Wally Harper
Lyrics by Paul Zakrzewski
Sensations (OB) 1970

Mornings at Seven
Music by Richard Rodgers
Lyrics by Lorenz Hart
Higher And Higher 1940

Mornings at Seven
Music by James Bredt
Lyrics by Edward Eager
The Happy Hypocrite (OB) 1968

The Most Beautiful Girl in the World
Music by Richard Rodgers
Lyrics by Lorenz Hart
Jumbo 1935

A Most Disagreeable Man
Music by Richard Rodgers
Lyrics by Martin Charnin
I Remember Mama 1979

Dropped from production

The Most Expensive Statue in the World
Music and lyrics by Irving Berlin
Miss Liberty 1949

Most Gentlemen Don't Like Love
Music and lyrics by Cole Porter
Leave It to Me 1938

The Most Happy Fella
Music and lyrics by Frank Loesser
The Most Happy Fella 1956

Most Omniscient Maid
Music by John Philip Sousa
Lyrics by Leonard Liebling
The American Maid 1913

Most Popular and Most Likely to Succeed
Music and lyrics by Kelly Hamilton
Trixie True Teen Detective (OB) 1980

Most Unusual Pair
Music and lyrics by Ronnie Britton
Greenwich Village Follies (OB) 1976

The Moth and the Flame
Music and lyrics by Elizabeth Swados
Lullabye and Goodnight 1982

The Moth and the Moon
Music by Victor Herbert
Lyrics by Harry B. Smith
Miss Dolly Dollars 1905

The Moth Song
Music by George Kleinsinger
Lyrics by Joe Darion
Shinbone Alley 1957

Mother
Music by Sigmund Romberg
Lyrics by Dorothy Donnelly
My Maryland 1927

Mother
Music and lyrics by Rick Besoyan
Babes in the Wood (OB) 1964

Mother
Music by Elizabeth Swados
Lyrics by Garry Trudeau
Doonesbury 1983

Mother Africa's Day
Music and lyrics by Oscar Brown, Jr. and Sivuca
Joy (OB) 1970

Mother, Angel, Darling
Music and lyrics by Charles Gaynor
Irene (1973 revival)

Mother Earth
Music and lyrics by Johnny Brandon
Billy Noname (OB) 1970

Mother Eve
Music by George Gershwin
Lyrics by Arthur Jackson
George White's Scandals (1921)

Mother Goose
Music by Victor Herbert
Lyrics by Robert B. Smith
Sweethearts 1913

Mother Grows Younger
Music by Richard Rodgers
Lyrics by Lorenz Hart
Heads Up! 1929

Mother Isn't Getting Any Younger
Music by Richard Lewine
Lyrics by Ted Fetter
The Fireman's Flame (OB) 1937

Mother, Mother, Are You There?
Music and lyrics by Gian-Carlo Menotti
The Medium 1947

Mother Nature
Music by Ray Haney
Lyrics by Alfred Aiken
We're Civilized? (OB) 1962

Mother Told Me So
Music by Arthur Schwartz
Lyrics by Howard Dietz
Flying Colors 1932

Motherhood
Music and lyrics by Jerry Herman
Hello, Dolly 1964

Motherly Love
Music by Robert Kessler
Lyrics by Lola Pergament
O Marry Me! (OB) 1961

Mother's Complaint
Music and lyrics by Noël Coward
This Year of Grace 1928

Mother's Day
Music and lyrics by Johnny Brandon
Love! Love! Love! (OB) 1977

Mother's Day
Music by Larry Grossman
Lyrics by Hal Hackady
Snoopy (OB) 1982

Mother's Getting Nervous
Music by Kurt Weill
Lyrics by Alan Jay Lerner
Love Life 1948

A Mother's Heart
Music by Albert Hague
Lyrics by Marty Brill
Café Crown 1964

Mothers-in-Law
Music and lyrics by Al Carmines
The Faggot (OB) 1973

A Mother's Love
Music by Al Carmines
Lyrics by Maria Irene Fornes
Promenade (OB) 1969

Mothers of the World
Music by Alfred Goodman, Maury Rubens
and J. Fred Coots
Lyrics by Clifford Grey
Artists and Models (1925)

Mother's Prayer
Music and lyrics by Melvin Van Peebles
Waltz of the Stork (OB) 1982

Motor Perpetuo
Music by Donald Swann
Lyrics by Michael Flanders
At the Drop of Another Hat 1966

Motoring Along the Old Post Road
Music by Jerome Kern
Lyrics by Herbert Reynolds
Rock-a-Bye Baby 1918

Mountain Greenery
Music by Richard Rodgers
Lyrics by Lorenz Hart
The Garrick Gaieties (2nd edition) 1926

Also in the London production of *The Girl Friend* (1927) and, instrumentally, as the music at the college dance in Rodgers' and Hammerstein's *Allegro* (1947).

Mountain High, Valley Low
Music by Raymond Scott
Lyrics by Bernard Hanighen
Lute Song 1946

The Mountains
Music by Galt MacDermot
Lyrics by Gerome Ragni
Dude 1972

The Mounted Messenger
Music by Kurt Weill
Lyrics by Marc Blitzstein
The Threepenny Opera (OB) 1954

The Mounties
Music by Rudolf Friml and Herbert Stothart
Lyrics by Oscar Hammerstein II and Otto Harbach
Rose Marie 1924

Mouse Meets Girl
Music by Clay Warnick
Lyrics by Edward Eager
Dream With Music 1944

Move On
Music and lyrics by Stephen Sondheim
Sunday in the Park With George (OB) 1983

Move Over, New York
Music and lyrics by Walter Marks
Bajour 1964

Move (You're Steppin' on My Heart)
Music by Henry Krieger
Lyrics by Tom Eyen
Dreamgirls 1981

A Mover's Life
Music by Cy Coleman
Lyrics by Michael Stewart
I Love My Wife 1977

The Movie Ball
Music by Harry Ruby
Lyrics by Bert Kalmar
The Ramblers 1926

The Movie Cowboy
Music and lyrics by John Raniello
Movie Buff (OB) 1977

Movie House
Music and lyrics by Al Carmines
The Faggot (OB) 1973

Movie House in Manhattan
Music by Richard Lewine
Lyrics by Arnold B. Horwitt
Make Mine Manhattan 1948

Movie Star Mansion
Music by Gary William Friedman
Lyrics by Will Holt
Platinum 1978

Movie Stars
Music and lyrics by John Raniello
Movie Buff (OB) 1977

Movies Were Movies
Music and lyrics by Jerry Herman
Mack and Mabel 1974

Movietown USA
Music and lyrics by John Raniello
Movie Buff (OB) 1977

Movin'
Music by Frederick Loewe
Lyrics by Alan Jay Lerner
Paint Your Wagon 1951

Movin'
Music and lyrics by Johnny Brandon
Billy Noname (OB) 1970

Movin' Out
Music by Charles Strouse
Lyrics by Lee Adams
Bring Back Birdie 1981

Moving Day
Music by James P. Johnson
Lyrics by Flournoy Miller
Sugar Hill 1931

The Moving Men
Music by Jean Schwartz
Lyrics by Joseph W. Herbert and Harold Atteridge
The Honeymoon Express 1913

Moving On
Music and lyrics by Gary Portnoy
and Judy Hart Angelo
Preppies (OB) 1983

Mozambamba
Music by Maria Grever
Lyrics by Raymond Leveen
Viva O'Brien 1941

Mozambique
Music by Eubie Blake
Lyrics by Andy Razaf
Blackbirds of 1930

Mr. and Missus Fitch
Music and lyrics by Cole Porter
Gay Divorce 1932

Mr. and Mrs. Dick Dickerson
Music and lyrics by Kelly Hamilton
Trixie True Teen Detective (OB) 1980

Mr. and Mrs. Rorer
Music by Jerome Kern
Lyrics by P. G. Wodehouse
Sitting Pretty 1924

Mr. and Mrs. Sipkin
Music by George Gershwin
Lyrics by B.G. DeSylva and Ira Gershwin
Tell Me More 1925

Mr. and Mrs. Smith
Music and lyrics by Cole Porter
Jubilee 1935

Mr. and Mrs. Wrong
Music by Clay Warnick
Lyrics by Edward Eager
Dream With Music 1944

Mr. Baiello
Music by Sol Berkowitz
Lyrics by James Lipton
Nowhere to Go But Up 1962

Mr. Banjo Man
Music and lyrics by Arthur Malvin
Sugar Babies 1979

Mr. Brown, Miss Dupree
Music by Jay Gorney
Lyrics by Jean and Walter Kerr
Touch and Go 1949

Mr. Bunbury
Music by Lee Pockriss
Lyrics by Anne Croswell
Ernest in Love (OB) 1960

Mr. Chigger
Music by Paul Klein
Lyrics by Fred Ebb
Morning Sun (OB) 1963

Mr. Clown
Music and lyrics by Hugo Peretti, Luigi Creatore
and George David Weiss
Maggie Flynn 1968

Mr. Cupid
Music by Sigmund Romberg
Lyrics by Dorothy Donnelly
My Maryland 1927

Mr. Dolan Is Passing Through
Music by Richard Rodgers
Lyrics by Lorenz Hart
America's Sweetheart 1931

Mr. Flynn
Music and lyrics by Johnny Burke
Donnybrook! 1961

Mr. Gallagher and Mr. Shean
Music and lyrics by Edward Gallagher
and Al Shean
Ziegfeld Follies of 1922

Mr. Goldstone
Music by Jule Styne
Lyrics by Stephen Sondheim
Gypsy 1959

Mr. Henry Jones
Music and lyrics by Steve Allen
Sophie 1963

Mr. James Dillingham Young
Music and lyrics by Ronnie Britton
Gift of the Magi (OB) 1975

Mr. Jessel
Music and lyrics by Charlotte Kent
Sweet and Low 1930

Mr. Know It All
Music by Diane Leslie
Lyrics by William Gleason
The Coolest Cat in Town (OB) 1978

Mr. Livingstone
Music by Harold Karr
Lyrics by Matt Dubey
Happy Hunting 1956

Mr. Mammy Man
Music and lyrics by J.C. Johnson
Change Your Luck 1930

Mr. Might've Been
Music and lyrics by Oscar Brand
How to Steal an Election (OB) 1968

Mr. Mistoffolees
Music by Andrew Lloyd Webber
Cats 1982

Lyrics based on T.S. Eliot's *Old Possum's
Book of Practical Cats*

Mr. Moon
Music and lyrics by Lloyd Waner, Lupin Feine
and Moe Jaffe
A Little Racketeer 1932

Mr. Phelps
Music by Al Carmines
Lyrics by Maria Irene Fornes
Promenade (OB) 1969

Mr. President
Music and lyrics by Randy Newman
Maybe I'm Doing It Wrong (2nd edition)
(OB) 1982

Mr. Right
Music by Kurt Weill
Lyrics by Alan Jay Lerner
Love Life 1948

Mr. Right
Music by Frederico Valerio
Lyrics by Elizabeth Miele
Hit the Trail 1954

Mr. Strauss Goes to Boston
Music by Robert Stolz
Lyrics by Robert Sour
Mr. Strauss Goes to Boston 1945

Mr. Tanner
Music and lyrics by Harry Chapin
The Night That Made America Famous 1975

Mr. Wonderful
Music and lyrics by Jerry Bock, George Weiss
and Larry Holofcener
Mr. Wonderful 1956

Mrs. Bodie
Music and lyrics by William Roy
The Penny Friend (OB) 1966

Mrs. Grudden's Goodbye
Music and lyrics by Stephen Oliver
The Life and Times of Nicholas Nickleby 1981

Mrs. Grundy
Music by Victor Herbert
Lyrics by George V. Hobart
Old Dutch 1909

Mrs. Krause's Blue-Eyed Baby Boy
Music by Ray Henderson
Lyrics by B.G. DeSylva and Lew Brown
Flying High 1930

Mrs. Larry, Tell Me This
Music by Mischa and Wesley Portnoff
Lyrics by Donagh MacDonagh
Happy as Larry 1950

Mrs. Patterson
Music and lyrics by James Shelton
Mrs. Patterson 1954

Mrs. S. L. Jacobowsky
Music and lyrics by Jerry Herman
The Grand Tour 1979

Mrs. Sally Adams
Music and lyrics by Irving Berlin
Call Me Madam 1950

Much as I Love You
Music and lyrics by Oscar Brown, Jr.
and Luis Henrique
Joy (OB) 1970

Much More
Music by Harvey Schmidt
Lyrics by Tom Jones
The Fantasticks (OB) 1960

Much Too Soon
Music and lyrics by Robert Dennis, Peter Schickele,
Stanley Walden and Jacques Levy
Oh! Calcutta! 1969

Muchacha
Music by Vernon Duke and Jay Gorney
Lyrics by E.Y. Harburg
Shoot the Works 1931

Mu-Cha-Cha
Music by Jule Styne
Lyrics by Betty Comden and Adolph Green
Bells Are Ringing 1956

The Muffin Song
Music by Lee Pockriss
Lyrics by Anne Croswell
Ernest in Love (OB) 1960

Muffy and the Topsiders
Music by Elizabeth Swados
Lyrics by Garry Trudeau
Doonesbury 1983

Muito Bom
Music by Mitch Leigh
Lyrics by N. Richard Nash
Saravá 1979

Mulhaney's Song
Music by Jeanne Bargy
Lyrics by Jeanne Bargy, Frank Gehrecke

and Herb Corey
Greenwich Village U.S.A. (OB) 1960

Mulunghu Tabu
Music by Emmerich Kálmán and Herbert Stothart
Lyrics by Otto Harbach and Oscar Hammerstein II
Golden Dawn 1927

Mumbo Jumbo
Music and lyrics by Leslie Bricusse
and Anthony Newley
Stop the World—I Want to Get Off 1962

**Mummy, Mummy, Dear, You Must
Not Cry For Me**
Music and lyrics by Gian-Carlo Menotti
The Medium 1947

Munchkinland
Music by Harold Arlen
Lyrics by E.Y. Harburg
The Wizard of Oz (1939) F

Mungojerrie and Rumpleteazer
Music by Andrew Lloyd Webber
Cats 1982

Lyrics based on T.S. Eliot's *Old Possum's
Book of Practical Cats*

Murder
Music by Louis A. Hirsch
Lyrics by Otto Harbach
The O'Brien Girl 1921

Murder in Parkwold
Music by Kurt Weill
Lyrics by Maxwell Anderson
Lost in the Stars 1949

Museum Song
Music by Cy Coleman
Lyrics by Michael Stewart
Barnum 1980

Mushari's Waltz
Music by Alan Menken
Lyrics by Howard Ashman
God Bless You, Mr. Rosewater (OB) 1979

Mushnik and Son
Music by Alan Menken
Lyrics by Howard Ashman
Little Shop of Horrors (OB) 1982

The Music and the Mirror
Music by Marvin Hamlisch
Lyrics by Edward Kleban
A Chorus Line 1975

The Music Call
Music by Karl Hajos (based on Chopin)
Lyrics by Harry B. Smith
White Lilacs 1928

Music for Madame
Music and lyrics by Jack Lawrence
and Richard Myers
Ziegfeld Follies (1957)

Music Hath'nt
Music by Robert Kessler
Lyrics by Martin Charnin
Fallout (OB) 1959

Music in My Fingers
Music by Richard Myers
Lyrics by Edward Heyman
Here Goes the Bride 1931

Music in My Heart
Music by Warburton Guilbert
Lyrics by June Sillman
New Faces of 1934

Music in the Air
Music by Lehman Engel
Lyrics by Agnes Morgan
A Hero Is Born 1937

Music in the House
Music and lyrics by Marc Blitzstein
Juno 1959

Music in the Night
Music by Erich Korngold
Lyrics by Oscar Hammerstein II
Give Us This Night (1936) F

Music Is
Music by Richard Adler
Lyrics by Will Holt
Music Is 1976

Music Makes Me
Music by Vincent Youmans
Lyrics by Edward Eliscu and Gus Kahn
Flying Down to Rio (1933) F

The Music of a Rippling Stream
Music by Cliff Friend
Lyrics by Lew Brown
Piggy 1927

The Music of Home
Music and lyrics by Frank Loesser
Greenwillow 1960

The Music of Love
Music by Paul Rubens
Lyrics by Percy Greenbank
The Girl From Utah 1914

The Music That Makes Me Dance
Music by Jule Styne
Lyrics by Bob Merrill
Funny Girl 1964

The Music Thrills Me
Music by Emmerich Kálmán
Lyrics by Harry B. Smith
Countess Maritza 1926

Musical Chairs
Music and lyrics by Tom Savage
Musical Chairs 1980

A Musical Lesson
Music by George Lessner
Lyrics by Miriam Battista and Russell Maloney
Sleepy Hollow 1948

The Musical Moon
Music and lyrics by George M. Cohan
The Little Millionaire 1911

The Musical Snore
Music by Rudolf Friml
Lyrics by Otto Harbach and Edward Clark
You're In Love 1917

Musical Tour of the City
Music by Jay Gorney
Lyrics by Barry Trivers
Heaven on Earth 1948

Musketeers
Music by Harry Ruby
Lyrics by Bert Kalmar
Animal Crackers 1928

Must Be Given to You
Music by Moose Charlap
Lyrics by Norman Gimbel
The Conquering Hero 1961

Must It Be Love?
Music and lyrics by Walter Marks
Bajour 1964

Mustapha
Music and lyrics by Sandy Wilson
Valmouth (OB) 1960

Mustapha Abdullah Abu ben al Raajid
Music by Dean Fuller
Lyrics by Marshall Barer
New Faces of 1956

Muted
Music by Ray Haney
Lyrics by Alfred Aiken
We're Civilized? (OB) 1962

Mutual Admiration Society
Music by Harold Karr
Lyrics by Matt Dubey
Happy Hunting 1956

My Arab Complex
Music by Henry Sullivan
Lyrics by Ballard MacDonald
Thumbs Up! 1934

My Arms Are Open
Music by Michael Cleary
Lyrics by Ned Washington
Earl Carroll's Vanities (1928)

My Baby and Me
Music by Gerald Jay Markoe
Lyrics by Michael Colby
Charlotte Sweet (OB) 1982

My Baby Talk Lady
Music by William B. Kernell
Lyrics by Dorothy Donnelly
Hello, Lola 1926

My Baby's Arms
Music by Harry Tierney
Lyrics by Joe McCarthy
Ziegfeld Follies of 1919

My Baby's Bored
Music by Allan Roberts
Lyrics by Lester Lee
All for Love 1949

My Bajadere
Music by Emmerich Kálmán
Lyrics by B.G. DeSylva
The Yankee Princess 1922

My Beautiful Lady
Music by Ivan Caryll
Lyrics by C.M.S. McLellan
The Pink Lady 1911

My Beautiful Rhinestone Girl
Music and lyrics by Irving Berlin
Face the Music 1932

My Ben Ali Haggin Girl
Music and lyrics by Irving Berlin
Music Box Revue (1st edition) 1921

My Best Girl
Music and lyrics by Jerry Herman
Mame 1966

My Best Love
Music by Richard Rodgers
Lyrics by Oscar Hammerstein II
Flower Drum Song 1958

Dropped from production

My Best Pal
Music by Maury Rubens
Lyrics by Clifford Grey
The Madcap 1928

My Bicycle Girl
Music by Arthur Schwartz
Lyrics by Oscar Hammerstein II
American Jubilee 1940

My Bird of Paradise
Music by Rudolf Friml
Lyrics by J. Keirn Brennan
Luana 1930

My Blanket and Me
Music and lyrics by Clark Gesner
You're a Good Man, Charlie Brown (OB) 1967

My Blue Bird's Home Again
Music by Ray Henderson
Lyrics by B.G. DeSylva and Lew Brown
Manhattan Mary 1927

My Boy and I
Music by Vincent Youmans and Herbert Stothart
Lyrics by Oscar Hammerstein II
and William Cary Duncan
Mary Jane McKane 1923

Originally a waltz ballad, Youmans changed it to
2/4 time and it became the title song of *No, No,
Nanette* (1925).

My Bridal Gown
Music by Arthur Schwartz
Lyrics by Albert Stillman and Laurence Stallings
Virginia 1937

My Brother Willie
Music by William B. Kernell
Lyrics by Dorothy Donnelly
Hello, Lola 1926

My Brother's Keeper
Music by Walt Smith
Lyrics by Leon Uris
Ari 1971

My Brudder and Me
Music by Richard Lewine
Lyrics by Arnold B. Horwitt
Make Mine Manhattan 1948

My Bus and I
Music by Heitor Villa-Lobos
Lyrics by Robert Wright and George Forrest
Magdalena 1948

My Business Man
Music by David Raksin
Lyrics by June Carroll
If the Shoe Fits 1946

My Bwanna
Music by Emmerich Kálmán and Herbert Stothart
Lyrics by Otto Harbach and Oscar Hammerstein II
Golden Dawn 1927

My Captain
Music and lyrics by Ron Dante and Gene Allan
Billy 1969

My Castle in Spain
Music and lyrics by Isham Jones
By the Way 1925

My Castle in the Air
Music by Jerome Kern
Lyrics by P.G. Wodehouse
Little Miss Springtime 1916

My City
Music by Cy Coleman
Lyrics by Dorothy Fields
Seesaw 1973

My City
Music by Howard Marren
Lyrics by Enid Futterman
Portrait of Jennie (OB) 1982

My Conviction
Music by Galt MacDermot
Lyrics by Gerome Ragni and James Rado
Hair 1968

My Cousin in Milwaukee
Music by George Gershwin
Lyrics by Ira Gershwin
Pardon My English 1933

My Cup Runneth Over
Music by Harvey Schmidt
Lyrics by Tom Jones
I Do! I Do! 1966

My Daddy Is a Dandy
Music and lyrics by James Shelton
Mrs. Patterson 1954

My Dancing Lady
Music by Jimmy McHugh
Lyrics by Dorothy Fields
Dancing Lady (1933) F

My Darlin' Aida
Music by Giuseppe Verdi (adapted by Hans
Spialek)
Lyrics by Charles Friedman
My Darlin' Aida 1952

My Darlin' Eileen
Music by Leonard Bernstein
Lyrics by Betty Comden and Adolph Green
Wonderful Town 1953

Based on an Irish folk tune.

My Darling
Music by Richard Myers
Lyrics by Edward Heyman
Earl Carroll's Vanities (1932)

My Darling I Love You March
Music by Galt MacDermot
Lyrics by Gerome Ragni
Dude 1972

My Darling, My Darling
Music and lyrics by Frank Loesser
Where's Charley? 1948

My Darling Never Is Late
Music and lyrics by Cole Porter
Les Girls (1957) F

Dropped from film

My Daughter Is Wed to a Friend of Mine
Music and lyrics by George M. Cohan
The Man Who Owns Broadway 1909

My Daughter the Countess
Music by Don Pippin
Lyrics by Steve Brown
Fashion (OB) 1974

My Day
Music by Joseph Meyer
Lyrics by Floyd Huddleston
Shuffle Along of 1952

My Dear Benvenuto
Music by Kurt Weill
Lyrics by Ira Gershwin
The Firebrand of Florence 1945

My Dearest Love
Music by Oscar Straus
Lyrics by Joseph W. Herbert
A Waltz Dream 1908

My Death
Music by Jacques Brel
English lyrics by Eric Blau and Mort Shuman
*Jacques Brel Is Alive and Well
and Living in Paris* (OB) 1968

My Defenses Are Down
Music and lyrics by Irving Berlin
Annie Get Your Gun 1946

My Doctor
Music by Vincent Youmans
Lyrics by Otto Harbach
No, No, Nanette 1925

My Dream Book of Memories
Music and lyrics by David Rose
Winged Victory 1943

My Dream for Tomorrow
Music and lyrics by Richard M. Sherman
and Robert B. Sherman
Over Here! 1974

My Dream Girl
Music by Victor Herbert
Lyrics by Rida Johnson Young
The Dream Girl 1924

My Dream of Love
Music by Leo Fall
Lyrics by George Grossmith
The Dollar Princess 1909

My Dynamo
Music by Arthur Schwartz
Lyrics by Agnes Morgan
The Grand Street Follies (1929)

My Eternal Devotion
Music by Lee Pockriss
Lyrics by Anne Croswell
Ernest in Love (OB) 1960

My Fair Lady
Music by George Gershwin
Lyrics by B.G. DeSylva and Ira Gershwin
Tell Me More 1925

My Fair Unknown
Music by Victor Herbert
Lyrics by Harry B. Smith
Miss Dolly Dollars 1905

My Faithful Stradivari
Music by Emmerich Kálmán
Lyrics by C.C.S. Cushing and E.P. Heath
Sari 1914

My Family Tree
Music and lyrics by Noël Coward
The Girl Who Came to Supper 1963

My Fatal Charm
Music by Frederico Valerio
Lyrics by Elizabeth Miele
Hit the Trail 1954

My Father Said
Music by Arthur Schwartz
Lyrics by Howard Dietz
Revenge With Music 1934

My Favorite Things
Music by Richard Rodgers
Lyrics by Oscar Hammerstein II
The Sound of Music 1959

My Feet Are Firmly Planted on the Ground
Music by Jerome Moross
Lyrics by Emanuel Eisenberg
Parade (1935)

My Feet Took t' Walkin'
Music by Jonathan Holtzman
Lyrics by Susan Cooper and Jonathan Holtzman
Foxfire 1982

My First
Music and lyrics by Paul Shyre
Ah, Men (OB) 1981

My First Love
Music by Ruth Cleary Patterson
Lyrics by Fred Heider
Russell Patterson's Sketch Book (OB) 1960

My First Love, My Last Love
Music by Sigmund Romberg
Lyrics by Irving Caesar and Otto Harbach
Nina Rosa 1930

My First Love Song
Music and lyrics by Leslie Bricusse
and Anthony Newley
*The Roar of the Greasepaint—The Smell
of the Crowd* 1965

My First Moment
Music and lyrics by Bob Goodman
Wild and Wonderful 1971

My First Promise
Music and lyrics by Hugh Martin and Ralph Blane
Best Foot Forward 1941

My Fortune Is My Face
Music by Jule Styne
Lyrics by Betty Comden and Adolph Green
Fade Out—Fade In 1964

My Friend the Night
Music by Richard Rodgers
Lyrics by Lorenz Hart
Hollywood Party (1934) F

Dropped from film

My Friends
Music and lyrics by Stephen Sondheim
Sweeney Todd 1979

My Funny Valentine
Music by Richard Rodgers
Lyrics by Lorenz Hart
Babes in Arms 1937

My Gal Is Mine Once More
Music by Arthur Schwartz
Lyrics by Howard Dietz
Inside U.S.A. 1948

My Galilee
Music by Walt Smith
Lyrics by Leon Uris
Ari 1971

My Gang
Music and lyrics by George M. Cohan
The Rise of Rosie O'Reilly 1923

My Garden
Music by Harvey Schmidt
Lyrics by Tom Jones
Celebration 1969

My Gentle Young Johnny
Music by Jerry Bock
Lyrics by Sheldon Harnick
Tenderloin 1960

My G.I. Joey
Music by Jack Holmes
Lyrics by Bill Conklin and Bob Miller
O Say Can You See! (OB) 1962

My Girl
Music by Jerome Kern
Lyrics by Oscar Hammerstein II
Show Boat 1927

Dropped from production

My Girl and I
Music by Sigmund Romberg
Lyrics by Oscar Hammerstein II
Sunny River 1941

My Girl Back Home
Music by Richard Rodgers
Lyrics by Oscar Hammerstein II
South Pacific 1949

Dropped from production, but included in film
version (1958)

My Girl Is Just Enough Woman For Me
Music by Albert Hague
Lyrics by Dorothy Fields
Redhead 1959

My God, Why Hast Thou Forsaken Me?
Music by Meyer Kupferman
Lyrics by Paul Goodman
Jonah (OB) 1966

My Gypsy Sweetheart
Music by Victor Herbert
Lyrics by George V. Hobart
Old Dutch 1909

My Handy Man Ain't Handy No More
Music by Eubie Blake
Lyrics by Andy Razaf
Blackbirds of 1930

My Hawaii
Music and lyrics by Eaton Magoon, Jr.
13 Daughters 1961

My Heart Begins to Thump! Thump!
Music by Morgan Lewis
Lyrics by Ted Fetter
The Second Little Show 1930

My Heart Belongs to Daddy
Music and lyrics by Cole Porter
Leave It to Me 1938

This song launched Mary Martin's Broadway
career. It was also in the London revue *Black
Velvet* (1939).

My Heart Controls My Head
Music by Johann Strauss I, adapted by
Oscar Straus
Lyrics by Clare Kummer
Three Waltzes 1937

My Heart Flies Homing
Music by Howard Talbot
Lyrics by Arthur Wimperis
The Arcadians 1910

My Heart Is Calling
Music by Sigmund Romberg
Lyrics by Harold Atteridge
The Rose of Stamboul 1922

My Heart Is Calling
Music by Philip Charig
Lyrics by James Dyrenforth
Nikki 1931

My Heart Is Dancing
Music by Arthur Schwartz
Lyrics by Albert Stillman
Virginia 1937

My Heart Is on a Binge
Music by Philip Charig
Lyrics by Dan Shapiro and Milton Pascal
Artists and Models (1943)

My Heart Is Part of You
Music by Arthur Schwartz
Lyrics by Howard Dietz
Flying Colors 1932

My Heart Is So Full of You
Music and lyrics by Frank Loesser
The Most Happy Fella 1956

My Heart Is Unemployed
Music and lyrics by Harold Rome
Sing Out the News 1938

My Heart Is Waking
Music by Oscar Straus
Lyrics by Edward Delaney Dunn
The Last Waltz 1921

My Heart Leaps Up
Music and lyrics by Jerry Herman
Mack and Mabel 1974

My Heart Stood Still
Music by Richard Rodgers
Lyrics by Lorenz Hart
A Connecticut Yankee 1927

Also performed in *One Dam Thing After Another*
(London, 1927). One of Rodgers' and Hart's first
hits, "My Heart Stood Still" is, along with "The Blue
Room," an example of the simplicity of their early
writing. The melody is made up entirely of half and
quarter notes, with a whole note at the end of each
eight-bar phrase. Its range is an octave and one
note, and the lyrics are, with few exceptions, one-
syllable words.

My Heart Won't Learn
Music by Baldwin Bergersen
Lyrics by William Archibald
The Crystal Heart (OB) 1960

My Heart Won't Say Goodbye
Music by Sigmund Romberg (developed by Don Walker)
Lyrics by Leo Robin
The Girl in Pink Tights 1954

My Heart's a Banjo
Music by Jay Gorney
Lyrics by E.Y. Harburg
Shoot the Works 1931

My Heart's an Open Book
Music by Harden Church
Lyrics by Edward Heyman
Caviar 1934

My Heart's an Open Door
Music and lyrics by Beth Lawrence
and Norman Thalheimer
Marilyn 1983

My Heart's Darlin'
Music and lyrics by Ralph Blane
Three Wishes for Jamie 1952

My Heart's in the Middle of July
Music by Allan Roberts
Lyrics by Lester Lee
All for Love 1949

My Heaven
Music by Alma Sanders
Lyrics by Monte Carlo
The Houseboat on the Styx 1928

My Heaven With You
Music by Rudolf Friml
Lyrics by Brian Hooker
The White Eagle 1927

My Hero
Music by Oscar Straus
Lyrics by Stanislaus Stange
The Chocolate Soldier 1909

My Hero
Music by Victor Herbert
Lyrics by Rida Johnson Young
The Dream Girl 1924

My High School Sweetheart
Music and lyrics by William Finn
In Trousers (OB) 1981

My Holiday
Music by Nancy Ford
Lyrics by Gretchen Cryer
Now Is the Time for All Good Men (OB) 1967

My Home Is in My Shoes
Music and lyrics by Johnny Mercer
Top Banana 1951

My Home Town
Music and lyrics by Tom Lehrer
Tomfoolery (OB) 1981

My Home Town in Kansas
Music by Harry Archer
Lyrics by Harlan Thompson
Little Jessie James 1923

My Home's a Highway
Music and lyrics by Ralph Blane
Three Wishes for Jamie 1952

My Hometown
Music and lyrics by Ervin Drake
What Makes Sammy Run? 1964

My House
Music and lyrics by Leonard Bernstein
Peter Pan 1950

My Houseboat on the Harlem
Music by Jerome Kern
Lyrics by Howard Dietz
Dear Sir 1924

My Husband Makes Movies
Music and lyrics by Maury Yeston
Nine 1982

My Husband's First Wife
Music by Jerome Kern
Lyrics by Oscar Hammerstein II
Sweet Adeline 1929

My Icy Floe
Music by Randall Thompson
Lyrics by Agnes Morgan
The Grand Street Follies (1926) (OB)

My Indian Family
Music by Sammy Fain
Lyrics by Paul Francis Webster
Christine 1960

My Intuition
Music by Arthur Schwartz
Lyrics by Howard Dietz
The Second Little Show 1930

My Jewels
Music by Ray Henderson
Lyrics by B.G. DeSylva and Lew Brown
George White's Scandals (1926)

My Joe
Music by Georges Bizet
Lyrics by Oscar Hammerstein II
Carmen Jones 1943

My Kind of Love
Music and lyrics by Charles Gaynor
Show Girl 1961

My Kind of Night
Music by Kurt Weill
Lyrics by Alan Jay Lerner
Love Life 1948

My Knees Are Weak
Music by Galt MacDermot
Lyrics by Rochelle Owens
The Karl Marx Play 1973

My Lady
Music by George Gershwin
Lyrics by Arthur Jackson
George White's Scandals (1920)

My Lady
Music and lyrics by Frank Crumit
and Ben Jerome
Yes, Yes, Yvette 1927

My Lady Love
Music by Alma Sanders
Lyrics by Monte Carlo
Oh! Oh! Nurse 1925

My Lady of the Nile
Music by Jerome Kern
Lyrics by Gene Buck
Ziegfeld Follies of 1916

My Lady's Dress
Music by Jerome Kern
Lyrics by Harry B. Smith
Ninety in the Shade 1915

My Lady's Dress
Music by Jerome Kern
Lyrics by Anne Caldwell
Good Morning, Dearie 1921

A different song from the one in *Ninety In The Shade* (above). Dropped from production.

My Lady's Fan
Music by Seymour Furth and Lee Edwards
Lyrics by R.F. Carroll
Bringing Up Father 1925

My Lady's Hand
Music by Dave Stamper
Lyrics by Fred Herendeen
Orchids Preferred 1937

My Land
Music and lyrics by Ron Eliran
Don't Step on My Olive Branch (OB) 1976

My Last Affair
Music and lyrics by Haven Johnson
New Faces of 1934

My Last Love
Music by Frederick Loewe
Lyrics by Alan Jay Lerner
What's Up? 1943

My Late, Late Lady
Music by Dean Fuller
Lyrics by Marshall Barer
Ziegfeld Follies (1957)

My Life in Color
Music and lyrics by Ron Eliran
Don't Step on My Olive Branch (OB) 1976

My Life Is Yours
Music and lyrics by Rick Besoyan
The Student Gypsy (OB) 1963

My Lips, My Love, My Soul
Music by Percy Wenrich
Lyrics by Raymond Peck
Castles in the Air 1926

My Little Baby
Music by Gustave Kerker
Lyrics by Hugh Morton
The Belle of New York 1897

My Little Canoe
Music by Louis A. Hirsch
Lyrics by Otto Harbach
The O'Brien Girl 1921

My Little Dog Has Ego
Music and lyrics by Herman Hupfeld
Dance Me a Song 1950

My Little Ducky
Music by George Gershwin
Lyrics by B.G. DeSylva
Sweet Little Devil 1924

Dropped from production

My Little Girl
Music and lyrics by Walter Cool
Mackey of Appalachia (OB) 1965

My Little Irish Rose
Music by Victor Herbert
Lyrics by Henry Blossom
Eileen 1917

My Little Lost Girl
Music by Sammy Fain
Lyrics by Paul Francis Webster
Christine 1960

My Little Piece o' Pie
Music and lyrics by Cole Porter
Les Girls (1957) F

Dropped from film

My Little Room
Music by Bert Keyes and Bob Larimer
Lyrics by Bob Larimer
But Never Jam Today 1979

My Lord and Master
Music by Richard Rodgers
Lyrics by Oscar Hammerstein II
The King and I 1951

My Lords and Ladies
Music by Kurt Weill
Lyrics by Ira Gershwin
The Firebrand of Florence 1945

My Loulou
Music and lyrics by Cole Porter
Jubilee 1935

My Love
Music by Leonard Bernstein
Lyrics by John Latouche and Richard Wilbur
Candide 1956

My Love and I
Music by Erich Korngold
Lyrics by Oscar Hammerstein II
Give Us This Night (1936) F

My Love and My Mule
Music by Harold Arlen
Lyrics by Dorothy Fields
Mr. Imperium (1951) F

My Love Belongs to You
Music and lyrics by Melvin Van Peebles
Waltz of the Stork (OB) 1982

My Love Carries On
Music by Sam Morrison
Lyrics by Dolph Singer
Summer Wives 1936

My Love Is a Blower
Music by John Philip Sousa
Lyrics by Leonard Liebling
The American Maid 1913

My Love Is a Married Man
Music by Frederick Loewe
Lyrics by Alan Jay Lerner
The Day Before Spring 1945

My Love Is a Wanderer
Music and lyrics by Bart Howard
John Murray Anderson's Almanac (1953)

My Love Is on the Way
Music by Jerome Moross
Lyrics by John Latouche
The Golden Apple 1954

My Love Is Young
Music by Irvin Graham
Lyrics by Bickley Reichner
New Faces of 1936

My Love, My Love
Music and lyrics by Walter Cool
Mackey of Appalachia (OB) 1965

My Love Will Come By
Music and lyrics by Irving Burgie
Ballad for Bimshire (OB) 1963

My Loved One
Music by Robert Stolz
Lyrics by Rowland Leigh
Night of Love 1941

My Lover
Music by Vincent Youmans
Lyrics by B.G. DeSylva
Take a Chance 1932

Dropped from production

My Love's So Good
Music and lyrics by Micki Grant
Don't Bother Me, I Can't Cope (OB) 1972

My Luck Is Changing
Music by Henry Krieger
Lyrics by Robert Lorick
The Tap Dance Kid 1983

My Lucky Lover
Music by George Lessner
Lyrics by Miriam Battista and Russell Maloney
Sleepy Hollow 1948

My Lucky Star
Music by Richard Rodgers
Lyrics by Lorenz Hart
She's My Baby 1928

My Lucky Star
Music by Ray Henderson
Lyrics by B.G. DeSylva and Lew Brown
Follow Thru 1929

My Lungs
Music and lyrics by James Rado
Rainbow (OB) 1972

My Magnolia
Music by C. Luckey Roberts
Lyrics by Alex C. Rogers
My Magnolia 1926

My Mammy
Music by Walter Donaldson
Lyrics by Irving Caesar
Sinbad (1918)

My Man
Music by Maurice Yvain
Lyrics by Channing Pollock
Ziegfeld Follies of 1921

My Man Is on the Make
Music by Richard Rodgers
Lyrics by Lorenz Hart
Heads Up! 1929

My Man's Gone Now
Music by George Gershwin
Lyrics by DuBose Heyward
Porgy and Bess 1935

My Melody Man
Music by Peter de Rose
Lyrics by Charles Tobias and Henry Clare
Pleasure Bound 1929

My Memories Started With You
Music by Baldwin Bergersen
Lyrics by June Sillman
All in Fun 1940

My Mimosa
Music by Sigmund Romberg
Lyrics by Dorothy Donnelly
My Princess 1927

My Mindanao Chocolate Soldier
Music by Jerome Kern
Lyrics by Clare Kummer
Ninety in the Shade 1915

My Miss Mary
Music by Jerry Bock
Lyrics by Sheldon Harnick
Tenderloin 1960

My Missus
Music by Richard Rodgers
Lyrics by Lorenz Hart
Betsy 1926

My Model Girl
Music by Sigmund Romberg
Lyrics by Harold Atteridge
The Blue Paradise 1915

My Most Important Moments Go By
Music by Nancy Ford
Lyrics by Gretchen Cryer
The Last Sweet Days of Isaac (OB) 1970

My Most Intimate Friend
Music and lyrics by Cole Porter
Jubilee 1935

My Mother Said
Music by Helen Miller
Lyrics by Eve Merriam
Inner City 1971

My Mother Told Me Not to Trust a Soldier
Music by Vincent Youmans
Lyrics by Oscar Hammerstein II
Rainbow 1928

My Mother Would Love You
Music and lyrics by Cole Porter
Panama Hattie 1940

My Mother's Wedding Day
Music by Frederick Loewe
Lyrics by Alan Jay Lerner
Brigadoon 1947

My Motter
Music by Howard Talbot
Lyrics by Arthur Wimperis
The Arcadians 1910

My Name
Music and lyrics by Lionel Bart
Oliver! 1963

My Name Is Can
Music and lyrics by John Phillips
Man on the Moon 1975

My Name Is Leda Pearl
Music by C.C. Courtney
Lyrics by C.C. Courtney and Ragan Courtney
Earl of Ruston 1971

My Name Is Man
Music and lyrics by Micki Grant
Don't Bother Me, I Can't Cope (OB) 1972

My Name Is Samuel Cooper
Music by Kurt Weill
Lyrics by Alan Jay Lerner
Love Life 1948

My Number Is Eleven
Music by Al Carmines
Lyrics by Rosalyn Drexler
Home Movies (OB) 1964

My Old Friends
Music and lyrics by Mel Mandel and Norman Sachs
My Old Friends (OB) 1979

My Old Hoss
Music by Harry Akst
Lyrics by Lew Brown
Calling All Stars 1934

My Old Kentucky Home
Music and lyrics by Randy Newman
Maybe I'm Doing It Wrong (1st edition) (OB) 1981

My Old Virginia Home (On the River Nile)
Music by Vernon Duke
Lyrics by John Latouche
Cabin in the Sky 1940

My One and Only
Music by George Gershwin
Lyrics by Ira Gershwin
Funny Face 1927

Also the title of a 1983 Broadway musical, with a new book and seventeen songs from stage and film scores by George and Ira Gershwin.

My One and Only Highland Fling
Music by Harry Warren
Lyrics by Ira Gershwin
The Barkleys of Broadway (1949) F

My One Girl
Music and lyrics by Frank E. Harling
Say When 1928

My Only Romance
Music by Frank Black
Lyrics by Gladys Shelley
The Duchess Misbehaves 1946

My Own
Music by Harry Archer
Lyrics by Harlan Thompson
Merry-Merry 1925

My Own Best Friend
Music by John Kander
Lyrics by Fred Ebb
Chicago 1975

My Own Brass Bed
Music and lyrics by Meredith Willson
The Unsinkable Molly Brown 1960

My Own Light Infantry
Music by Jerome Kern
Lyrics by Herbert Reynolds
Rock-a-Bye Baby 1918

My Own Morning
Music by Jule Styne
Lyrics by Betty Comden and Adolph Green
Hallelujah, Baby! 1967

My Own Space
Music by John Kander
Lyrics by Fred Ebb
The Act 1977

My Palace of Dreams
Music by Rudolf Friml
Lyrics by Rowland Leigh and John Shubert
Music Hath Charms 1934

My Paradise
Music by Rudolf Friml
Lyrics by Otto Harbach
Katinka 1915

My Paramount-Publix-Roxy Rose
Music by Harold Arlen
Lyrics by Ira Gershwin and E.Y. Harburg
Life Begins at 8:40 1934

My Passion Flower
Music by Sigmund Romberg
Lyrics by Dorothy Donnelly
My Princess 1927

My Personal Property
Music by Cy Coleman
Lyrics by Dorothy Fields
Sweet Charity (film version, 1970)

My Picture in the Papers
Music by Jerome Moross
Lyrics by John Latouche
The Golden Apple 1954

My Pleasure
Music and lyrics by Eaton Magoon, Jr.
13 Daughters 1961

My Prince
Music by Richard Rodgers
Lyrics by Lorenz Hart
Too Many Girls 1939

My Prince
Music by Sam Pottle
Lyrics by Tom Whedon
All Kinds of Giants (OB) 1961

My Prince Came Riding
Music by Emmerich Kálmán
Lyrics by George Marion, Jr.
Marinka 1945

My Raggyadore
Music by Jean Schwartz
Lyrics by Joseph W. Herbert and Harold Atteridge
The Honeymoon Express 1913

My Rainbow
Music by Jeanne Hackett
Lyrics by Lester Lee
Harry Delmar's Revels 1927

My Rainbow Girl
Music by Louis A. Hirsch
Lyrics by Rennold Wolf
The Rainbow Girl 1918

My Real Ideal
Music by Burton Lane
Lyrics by Samuel Lerner
Artists and Models (1930)

My Red-Letter Day
Music by Vernon Duke
Lyrics by Ira Gershwin
Ziegfeld Follies (1936)

My Red Riding Hood
Music by Jule Styne
Lyrics by Bob Merrill
*The Dangerous Christmas of
Red Riding Hood* (1965) TV

My Regular Man
Music and lyrics by J.C. Johnson
Change Your Luck 1930

My Religion
Music and lyrics by Glory Van Scott
Miss Truth (OB) 1979

My Road
Music by Lewis E. Gensler and Milton Schwarzwald
Lyrics by George S. Kaufman, Marc Connelly
and Ira Gershwin
Be Yourself 1924

My Romance
Music by Richard Rodgers
Lyrics by Lorenz Hart
Jumbo 1935

My Rose of Spain
Music by Jean Schwartz
Lyrics by Alfred Bryan
A Night in Spain 1927

My Secret Dream
Music by Harvey Schmidt
Lyrics by Tom Jones
Philemon (OB) 1975

My Sergeant and I Are Buddies
Music and lyrics by Irving Berlin
This Is the Army 1942

My Shining Hour
Music by Harold Arlen
Lyrics by Johnny Mercer
The Sky's the Limit (1943) F

My Ship
Music by Kurt Weill
Lyrics by Ira Gershwin
Lady in the Dark 1941

My Silhouette
Music by Jean Gilbert
Lyrics by Harry Graham and Cyrus Wood
The Lady in Ermine 1922

My Silver Tree
Music by Raymond Hubbell
Lyrics by Anne Caldwell
Three Cheers 1928

My Sister Bess
Music by Galt MacDermot
Lyrics by William Dumaresq
The Human Comedy (OB) 1983

My Sister-in-Law
Music by Paul Klein
Lyrics by Fred Ebb
Morning Sun (OB) 1963

My Son-in-Law
Music by Arthur Schwartz
Lyrics by Ira Gershwin
Park Avenue 1946

My Son the Druggist
Music and lyrics by Stan Daniels
So Long, 174th Street 1976

My Son, the Lawyer
Music by John Kander
Lyrics by James Goldman, John Kander and
William Goldman
A Family Affair 1962

My Son, Uphold the Law
Music by Milton Schafer
Lyrics by Ira Levin
Drat! The Cat! 1965

My Song
Music by Ray Henderson
Lyrics by B.G. DeSylva and Lew Brown
George White's Scandals (1931)

My Spies Tell Me (You Love Nobody But Me)
Music by Gerald Marks
Lyrics by Irving Caesar and Sam Lerner
My Dear Public 1943

My Springtime Thou Art
Music by Sigmund Romberg
Lyrics by Dorothy Donnelly
Blossom Time 1921

Based on Schubert's Waltz op. 9 no. 2

My Star
Music by Sam Pottle
Lyrics by Tom Whedon
All Kinds of Giants (OB) 1961

My State
Music and lyrics by Meredith Willson
Here's Love 1963

My Sugar Plum
Music by Joseph Meyer and J. Fred Coots
Lyrics by B.G. DeSylva
Gay Paree 1925

My Sumurun Girl
Music by Louis A. Hirsch
Lyrics by Harold Atteridge
The Whirl of Society 1912

My Sunday Fella
Music by George Gershwin
Lyrics by Gus Kahn and Ira Gershwin
Show Girl 1929

My Sunny South
Music and lyrics by Abner Silver
Earl Carroll's Sketch Book (1929)

My Sweet
Music by Richard Rodgers
Lyrics by Lorenz Hart
America's Sweetheart 1931

My Sweet Tomorrow
Music and lyrics by Eaton Magoon, Jr.
Heathen 1972

My Sweetheart Mamie
Music by Harry Ruby
Lyrics by Bert Kalmar
High Kickers 1941

My Sweetheart 'Tis of Thee
Music by John Green
Lyrics by Edward Heyman
Here Goes the Bride 1931

My Sword
Music by Rudolf Friml
Lyrics by P.G. Wodehouse and Clifford Grey
The Three Musketeers 1928

My Talking Day
Music and lyrics by Sandy Wilson
Valmouth (OB) 1960

My Tambourine Girl
Music and lyrics by Irving Berlin
Ziegfeld Follies of 1919

My Time
Music and lyrics by Tom Savage
Musical Chairs 1980

My Time of Day
Music and lyrics by Frank Loesser
Guys and Dolls 1950

My Title Song
Music by Don Pippin
Lyrics by Steve Brown
Fashion (OB) 1974

My Top Sergeant
Music by Vernon Duke
Lyrics by Howard Dietz
Jackpot 1944

My True Heart
Music and lyrics by Marc Blitzstein
Juno 1959

My Very First Impression
Music by Lee Pockriss
Lyrics by Anne Croswell
Ernest in Love (OB) 1960

My Violin
Music by Sigmund Romberg
Lyrics by Alex Gerber
Poor Little Ritz Girl 1920

My Walking Stick
Music and lyrics by Irving Berlin
Alexander's Ragtime Band (1938) F

My Way
Music and lyrics by Leslie Bricusse
and Anthony Newley
*The Roar of the Greasepaint—The Smell
of the Crowd* 1965

My Wedding
Music by Joseph Meyer
Lyrics by Edward Eliscu
Lady Fingers 1929

My Weight in Gold
Music by Robert Emmett Dolan
Lyrics by Johnny Mercer
Foxy 1964

My White Knight
Music and lyrics by Meredith Willson
The Music Man 1957

My Wish
Music and lyrics by Meredith Willson
Here's Love 1963

My Woman's Heart
Music by Rudolf Friml
Lyrics by Otto Harbach
High Jinks 1913

My Yellow Flower
Music by Jerome Moross
Lyrics by John Latouche
Ballet Ballads 1948

Mysterious Lady
Music by Jule Styne
Lyrics by Betty Comden and Adolph Green
Peter Pan 1954

Mystery Moon
Music by Alma Sanders
Lyrics by Monte Carlo
Mystery Moon 1930

The Mystery of the Moon
Music and lyrics by Kelly Hamilton
Trixie True Teen Detective (OB) 1980

The Mystery Play
Music and lyrics by George M. Cohan
Little Nellie Kelly 1922

N

Nag! Nag! Nag!
Music and lyrics by Leslie Bricusse and Anthony
Newley
Stop the World—I Want to Get Off 1962

Najla's Song
Music by Sammy Fain
Lyrics by E.Y. Harburg
Flahooley 1951

Name: Cockian
Music by Harvey Schmidt
Lyrics by Tom Jones
Philemon (OB) 1975

Name: Emily Adam
Music by Sol Berkowitz
Lyrics by James Lipton
Miss Emily Adam (OB) 1960

The Name of Kelly
Music and lyrics by George M. Cohan
Little Nellie Kelly 1922

Namely You
Music by Gene de Paul
Lyrics by Johnny Mercer
Li'l Abner 1956

Names I Love to Hear
Music by George Gershwin
Lyrics by Brian Hooker
Our Nell 1922

The Name's La Guardia
Music by Jerry Bock
Lyrics by Sheldon Harnick
Fiorello! 1959

The Naming of Cats
Music by Andrew Lloyd Webber
Cats 1982

Lyrics based on T.S. Eliot's *Old Possum's
Book of Practical Cats*

Nancy's Farewell
Music by Fritz Kreisler
Lyrics by William LeBaron
Apple Blossoms 1919

Nanty Puts Her Hair Up
Music by Arthur Siegel
Lyrics by Herbert Farjeon
New Faces of 1952

Napoleon
Music by Jerome Kern
Lyrics by P.G. Wodehouse
Have a Heart 1917

Napoleon
Music by Will Irwin
Lyrics by Norman Zeno
Fools Rush In 1934

Napoleon
Music by Harold Arlen
Lyrics by E.Y. Harburg
Jamaica 1957

Napoleon's a Pastry
Music by Harold Arlen
Lyrics by E.Y. Harburg
Hooray for What! 1937

Nashville Nightingale
Music by George Gershwin
Lyrics by Irving Caesar
Nifties of 1923

Natacha
Music and lyrics by Berton Braley, M. de Jari
and Alex James
Earl Carroll's Vanities (1926)

Natchitoches, Louisiana
Music and lyrics by C. Jackson and James Hatch
Fly Blackbird (OB) 1962

National Brotherhood Week
Music and lyrics by Tom Lehrer
Tomfoolery (OB) 1981

The National Pastime
Music by Bob Brush
Lyrics by Martin Charnin
The First 1981

Natural High
Music by Nancy Ford
Lyrics by Gretchen Cryer
I'm Getting My Act Together and Taking It on the Road 1978

Nature Played a Dirty Trick on You
Music by Manning Sherwin
Lyrics by Arthur Lippmann and Milton Pascal
Everybody's Welcome 1931

Natuscha
Music by Franz Steininger (adapted from Tchaikovsky)
Lyrics by Forman Brown
Music in My Heart 1947

Naughty Bird Tarantella
Music by Frank Fields
Lyrics by Armand Aulicino
The Shoemaker and the Peddler (OB) 1960

Naughty Boy
Music by Joseph Meyer and Philip Charig
Lyrics by Leo Robin
Just Fancy 1927

Naughty Boy
Music by Jerome Kern
Lyrics by Oscar Hammerstein II
Sweet Adeline 1929

Naughty Eyes
Music by Tom Johnstone
Lyrics by Phil Cook
When You Smile 1925

Naughty Little Step
Music by J. Fred Coots
Lyrics by Clifford Grey
June Days 1925

Naughty Marietta
Music by Victor Herbert
Lyrics by Rida Johnson Young
Naughty Marietta 1910

Naughty-Naught
Music by Richard Lewine
Lyrics by Ted Fetter
Naughty-Naught (OB) 1937

Naughty, Naughty Nancy
Music and lyrics by Rick Besoyan
Little Mary Sunshine (OB) 1959

The Naughty Nineties
Music by Max Ewing
Lyrics by Agnes Morgan
The Grand Street Follies (1927) (OB)

The Naughty Nobleman
Music by Jerome Kern
Lyrics by Anne Caldwell
The Bunch and Judy 1922

Naughty Riquette
Music by Maury Rubens and Kendall Burgess
Lyrics by Harry B. Smith
Naughty Riquette 1926

Nausea Before the Game
Music and lyrics by William Finn
In Trousers (OB) 1981

Navajo Woman
Music and lyrics by Al Carmines
The Evangelist (OB) 1982

The Navy Foxtrot Man
Music by Jerome Kern
Lyrics by Anne Caldwell
She's a Good Fellow 1919

Nazi Party Pooper
Music by Monty Norman
Lyrics by Julian More
The Moony Shapiro Songbook 1981

Neapolitan Love Song
Music by Victor Herbert
Lyrics by Henry Blossom
The Princess Pat 1915

The Near Future
Music and lyrics by Irving Berlin
Ziegfeld Follies of 1919

Near to You
Music and lyrics by Richard Adler and Jerry Ross
Damn Yankees 1955

Nearing the Day
Music by Harry Tierney
Lyrics by Joseph McCarthy
Up She Goes 1922

Neat to Be a Newsboy
Music and lyrics by Stephen Schwartz
Working 1978

'Neath the Southern Moon
Music by Victor Herbert
Lyrics by Rida Johnson Young
Naughty Marietta 1910

'Neath Thy Window
Music by Victor Herbert
Lyrics by Harry B. Smith
Cyrano de Bergerac 1899

Necessity
Music by Burton Lane
Lyrics by E.Y. Harburg
Finian's Rainbow 1947

Needles
Music by Con Conrad
Lyrics by Gus Kahn
Kitty's Kisses 1926

The Neighborhood Song
Music and lyrics by Jack Lawrence
and Stan Freeman
I Had a Ball 1964

Nellie Bly
Music by Jimmy Van Heusen
Lyrics by Johnny Burke
Nellie Bly 1946

Nellie Kelly, I Love You
Music and lyrics by George M. Cohan
Little Nellie Kelly 1922

Nelson
Music and lyrics by Jerry Herman
A Day in Hollywood, a Night in the Ukraine 1979

Nero, Caesar, Napoleon
Music by Sol Kaplan
Lyrics by Edward Eliscu
The Banker's Daughter (OB) 1962

Nervous
Music by Lawrence Hurwit
Lyrics by Lee Goldsmith
Sextet 1974

Nesting in a New York Tree
Music and lyrics by George M. Cohan
Little Johnny Jones 1904

Nesting Time in Flatbush
Music by Jerome Kern
Lyrics by P.G. Wodehouse and Jerome Kern
Oh, Boy! 1917

Network
Music by Ted Simons
Lyrics by Elinor Guggenheimer
Potholes (OB) 1979

Neurotic You and Psychopathic Me
Music and lyrics by Charles Gaynor
Lend an Ear 1948

Nevada
Music by Arthur Schwartz
Lyrics by Ira Gershwin
Park Avenue 1946

Nevada Hoe Down
Music by Frederico Valerio
Lyrics by Elizabeth Miele
Hit the Trail 1954

Nevada Moonlight
Music by Richard A. Whiting
Lyrics by Oscar Hammerstein II
Free for All 1931

Never
Music by Cy Coleman
Lyrics by Betty Comden and Adolph Green
On the Twentieth Century 1978

Never a Dull Moment
Music by Arthur Schwartz
Lyrics by Dorothy Fields
Stars in Your Eyes 1939

Never Again
Music and lyrics by Norman Gregg
A La Carte 1927

Never Again
Music and lyrics by Noël Coward
Set to Music 1939

Never Be-Devil the Devil
Music by Jacques Offenbach (adapted by Robert
De Cormier)
Lyrics by E.Y. Harburg
The Happiest Girl in the World 1961

Never Before
Music by Moose Charlap
Lyrics by Norman Gimbel
Whoop-Up 1958

Never Do a Bad Thing
Music by Alfred Brooks
Lyrics by Ira J. Bilowit
Of Mice and Men (OB) 1958

Never Give Anything Away
Music and lyrics by Cole Porter
Can-Can 1953

Never Go There Anymore
Music by Moose Charlap
Lyrics by Eddie Lawrence
Kelly 1965

Never Go to Argentina
Music by Richard Rodgers
Lyrics by Lorenz Hart
Never Go to Argentina (1941) F

Never Gonna Dance
Music by Jerome Kern
Lyrics by Dorothy Fields
Swing Time (1936) F

Never Gonna Make Me Fight
Music and lyrics by Hugo Peretti, Luigi Creatore
and George David Weiss
Maggie Flynn 1968

Never Had an Education
Music by Sigmund Romberg
Lyrics by Irving Caesar
Melody 1933

Never Let Her Go
Music by George Lessner
Lyrics by Miriam Battista and Russell Maloney
Sleepy Hollow 1948

Never Marry a Dancer
Music by Arthur Schwartz
Lyrics by Howard Dietz
Revenge With Music 1934

Never Mention Love When We're Alone
Music by Victor Herbert
Lyrics by Robert B. Smith
The Debutante 1914

Never Met a Girl Like You
Music and lyrics by George M. Cohan
The Rise of Rosie O'Reilly 1923

Never Mind, Bo-Peep
Music by Victor Herbert
Lyrics by Glen MacDonough
Babes in Toyland 1903

Never, Never
Music and lyrics by Bob Ost
Everybody's Gettin' Into the Act (OB) 1981

Never, Never Be an Artist
Music and lyrics by Cole Porter
Can-Can 1953

Never Never Land
Music and lyrics by Leonard Bernstein
Peter Pan 1950

Never Never Land
Music by Jule Styne
Lyrics by Betty Comden and Adolph Green
Peter Pan 1954

Never on Sunday
Music by Manos Hadjidakis
Lyrics by Joe Darion
Illya Darling 1967

Never Play Croquet
Music and lyrics by Elizabeth Swados
Alice in Concert (OB) 1980

Never Say Never
Music by Harris Wheeler
Lyrics by Mary L. Fisher
Blue Plate Special (OB) 1983

Never Say No
Music by Harvey Schmidt
Lyrics by Tom Jones
The Fantasticks (OB) 1960

Never Say No To A Man
Music and lyrics by Richard Rodgers
State Fair (remake 1962) F

Never Say the World Was Made to Cry
Music by Maury Rubens
Lyrics by Clifford Grey
The Great Temptations 1926

Never Too Late Cha-Cha
Music by Jerry Bock
Lyrics by Sheldon Harnick
Never Too Late 1962

Never Too Late For Love
Music and lyrics by Harold Rome
Fanny 1954

Never Trouble Trouble
Music by Robert Hood Bowers
Lyrics by Francis DeWitt
Oh, Ernest! 1927

Never Trust a Virgin
Music by Jacques Offenbach (adapted by Robert De Cormier)
Lyrics by E.Y. Harburg
The Happiest Girl in the World 1961

Never Try Too Hard
Music by Alec Wilder
Lyrics by Arnold Sundgaard
Kittiwake Island (OB) 1960

Never Wait for Love
Music by David Baker
Lyrics by David Craig
Phoenix '55 (OB)

Never Was There a Girl So Fair
Music by George Gershwin
Lyrics by Ira Gershwin
Of Thee I Sing 1931

Never Was There Such a Lover
Music by Oscar Straus
Lyrics by Stanislaus Stange
The Chocolate Soldier 1909

Never Will I Marry
Music and lyrics by Frank Loesser
Greenwillow 1960

Nevermore
Music by John Philip Sousa
Lyrics by Leonard Liebling
The American Maid 1913

Nevermore
Music and lyrics by Noël Coward
Conversation Piece 1934

Nevermore
Music by Gerald Marks
Lyrics by Sam Lerner
Hold It! 1948

Neville
Music and lyrics by Tony Geiss
Wet Paint (OB) 1965

A New Argentina
Music by Andrew Lloyd Webber
Lyrics by Tim Rice
Evita 1979

New Art Is True Art
Music by Kurt Weill
Lyrics by Ogden Nash
One Touch of Venus 1943

**The New Ashmolean Marching Society
and Students' Conservatory Band**
Music and lyrics by Frank Loesser
Where's Charley? 1948

New Blue
Music by John Addison
Lyrics by John Cranko
Cranks 1956

New Boy in Town
Music by Paul Klein
Lyrics by Fred Ebb
Morning Sun (OB) 1963

New Day
Music and lyrics by James MacDonald, David Vos
and Robert Gerlach
Something's Afoot 1976

A New Deal for Christmas
Music by Charles Strouse
Lyrics by Martin Charnin
Annie 1977

New Dreams for Old
Music by Louis Bellson and Will Irwin
Lyrics by Richard Ney
Portofino 1958

New Evaline
Music and lyrics by Tom Sankey
The Golden Screw (OB) 1967

New Faces
Music by Martha Caples
Lyrics by Nancy Hamilton
New Faces of 1934

New Faces
Music by Alex Fogarty
Lyrics by Edwin Gilbert
New Faces of 1936

New Fangled Preacher Man
Music by Gary Geld
Lyrics by Peter Udell
Purlie 1970

A New-Fangled Tango
Music by Harold Karr
Lyrics by Matt Dubey
Happy Hunting 1956

A New Generation
Music and lyrics by Oscar Brown, Jr.
and Luis Henrique
Joy (OB) 1970

New Hollywood Plots
Music by Sammy Fain
Lyrics by Paul Webster
Catch a Star! 1955

New Jerusalem
Music by Galt MacDermot
Lyrics by Christopher Gore
Via Galactica 1972

New Kind of Rhythm
Music by Will Morrisey
Lyrics by Edmund Joseph
Polly of Hollywood 1927

A New Life Coming
Music by David Shire
Lyrics by Richard Maltby, Jr.
Starting Here, Starting Now (OB) 1977

The New Look
Music and lyrics by Hugh Martin
Look Ma, I'm Dancin'! 1948

New Look Feeling
Music by Frederico Valerio
Lyrics by Elizabeth Miele
Hit the Trail 1954

New Love
Music by Lewis E. Gensler
Lyrics by B.G. DeSylva
Captain Jinks 1925

A New Love Is Old
Music by Jerome Kern
Lyrics by Otto Harbach
The Cat and the Fiddle 1931

New Loves for Old
Music by Albert T. Viola
Lyrics by William S. Kilborne, Jr.
Head Over Heels 1981

New Madness
Music by Steve Jankowski
Lyrics by Kenny Morris
Francis (OB) 1982

New Math
Music and lyrics by Tom Lehrer
Tomfoolery (OB) 1981

The New Me
Music and lyrics by William Roy
Maggie 1953

New New York
Music by Arthur Schwartz
Lyrics by Howard Dietz
The Second Little Show 1930

New Orleans Jeunesse Dorée
Music by Victor Herbert
Lyrics by Rida Johnson Young
Naughty Marietta 1910

A New Pair of Shoes
Music and lyrics by Ervin Drake
What Makes Sammy Run? 1964

New Prisoner's Song
Music and lyrics by Bland Simpson and Jim Wann
(Based on traditional folk music)
Diamond Studs (OB) 1975

New Sensation
Music by Will Irwin
Lyrics by Norman Zeno
Fools Rush In 1934

New Sun in the Sky
Music by Arthur Schwartz
Lyrics by Howard Dietz
The Band Wagon 1931

New to Me
Music by Ken Welch
Lyrics by Bud McCreery
Shoestring Revue (1955) (OB)

A New Town Is a Blue Town
Music and lyrics by Richard Adler and Jerry Ross
The Pajama Game 1954

A New Waltz
Music by Fred Hellerman
Lyrics by Fran Minkoff
New Faces of 1968

New Words for an Old Love Song
Music by Dave Stamper
Lyrics by Frederick Herendeen
Provincetown Follies (OB) 1935

New World
Music by Ann Sternberg
Lyrics by Gertrude Stein
Gertrude Stein's First Reader (OB) 1969

New Year's Eve
Music by Larry Grossman
Lyrics by Betty Comden and Adolph Green
A Doll's Life 1982

New York
Music and lyrics by George M. Cohan
Billie 1928

New York
Music by Tommy Wolf
Lyrics by Fran Landesman
The Nervous Set 1959

New York Cliché
Music by Rob Fremont
Lyrics by Doris Willens
Piano Bar (OB) 1978

New York From the Air
Music by Hank Beebe
Lyrics by Bill Heyer
*Tuscaloosa's Calling Me
But I'm Not Going!* (OB) 1975

New York Is the Same Old Place
Music by Victor Herbert
Lyrics by B.G. DeSylva
Orange Blossoms 1922

New York, New York
Music by Leonard Bernstein
Lyrics by Betty Comden and Adolph Green
On the Town 1944

New York, New York
Music by John Kander
Lyrics by Fred Ebb
New York, New York (1977) F

New York Serenade
Music by George Gershwin
Lyrics by Ira Gershwin and P.G. Wodehouse
Rosalie 1928

New York '69
Music by Hank Beebe
Lyrics by Bill Heyer
*Tuscaloosa's Calling Me
But I'm Not Going!* (OB) 1975

New York Town
Music by Henry Souvaine and Jay Gorney
Lyrics by Morrie Ryskind and Howard Dietz
Merry-Go-Round 1927

The New Yorker
Music by Milton Ager
Lyrics by Jack Yellen
John Murray Anderson's Almanac (1929)

New Yorkers
Music and lyrics by George M. Cohan
The Little Millionaire 1911

Newlywed Express
Music by Alma Sanders
Lyrics by Monte Carlo
Oh! Oh! Nurse 1925

Newlyweds
Music by Albert Von Tilzer
Lyrics by Neville Fleeson
The Gingham Girl 1922

News
Music by Harry Ruby
Lyrics by Bert Kalmar
Animal Crackers 1928

Next
Music by A. Baldwin Sloane
Lyrics by E. Ray Goetz
The Hen Pecks 1911

Next
Music by Jacques Brel
English lyrics by Eric Blau and Mort Shuman
*Jacques Brel Is Alive and Well
and Living in Paris* (OB) 1968

Next
Music and lyrics by Stephen Sondheim
Pacific Overtures 1976

The Next Dance With You
Music by Oscar Straus
Lyrics by Edward Delaney Dunn
The Last Waltz 1921

The Next May Be the Right
Music by Heinrich Reinhardt
Lyrics by Robert B. Smith
The Spring Maid 1910

The Next Time I Care
Music by Bronislaw Kaper
Lyrics by John Latouche
Polonaise 1945

The Next Time I Love
Music and lyrics by Jerry Herman
Parade (OB) 1960

The Next Time It Happens
Music by Richard Rodgers
Lyrics by Oscar Hammerstein II
Pipe Dream 1955

The Next-to-Last Supper
Music by Scott Killian and Kim D. Sherman
Lyrics by Kenneth Robins, Scott Killian
and Kim D. Sherman
Lenny and the Heartbreakers (OB) 1983

Next to Lovin' (I Like Fightin')
Music by Gary Geld
Lyrics by Peter Udell
Shenandoah 1975

Next to Texas, I Love You
Music by Jule Styne
Lyrics by Sammy Cahn
High Button Shoes 1947

Niagara Falls
Music by Jerome Kern
Lyrics by Anne Caldwell
Good Morning, Dearie 1921

Nice as Any Man Can Be
Music by William Dyer
Lyrics by Don Parks and William Dyer
Jo (OB) 1964

Nice Baby! (Come to Papa!)
Music by George Gershwin
Lyrics by Ira Gershwin
Tip-Toes 1925

Nice Fella
Music by Alfred Brooks
Lyrics by Ira J. Bilowit
Of Mice and Men (OB) 1958

Nice Girl
Music by Charles M. Schwab
Lyrics by Henry Myers
Bare Facts of 1926

Nice House We Got Here
Music by Alfred Brooks
Lyrics by Ira J. Bilowit
Of Mice and Men (OB) 1958

A Nice Little Plot for a Play
Music and lyrics by George M. Cohan
The Man Who Owns Broadway 1909

Nice Work If You Can Get It
Music by George Gershwin
Lyrics by Ira Gershwin
A Damsel in Distress (1937) F

It was Ira Gershwin's theory that song titles could
be found everywhere. This one, he remembered,
was the punch line of an old music hall joke about
two Cockney street walkers.

The Nicest Thing
Music and lyrics by Jay Livingston and Ray Evans
Let It Ride 1961

Nicholas
Music by Herman Darewski
Lyrics by Arthur Wimperis
Charlot's Revue 1924

A Nickel to My Name
Music by Vernon Duke
Lyrics by John Latouche
Banjo Eyes 1941

Nickel Under the Foot
Music and lyrics by Marc Blitzstein
The Cradle Will Rock 1938

Nicodemus
Music by Vincent Youmans
Lyrics by Anne Caldwell
Oh, Please! 1926

Nigger Heaven Blues
Music by Alfred Nathan
Lyrics by George Oppenheimer
The Manhatters 1927

Night
Music by Frank D'Armond
Lyrics by Will Morrissey
Saluta 1934

Night
Music by Johann Strauss
Lyrics by Desmond Carter
The Great Waltz 1934

Night After Night
Music by Arthur Schwartz
Lyrics by Howard Dietz
Three's a Crowd 1930

Night After Night
Music by David Raksin
Lyrics by June Carroll
If the Shoe Fits 1946

Night and Day
Music and lyrics by Cole Porter
Gay Divorce 1932

Ring Lardner was a life-long observer and
occasional practitioner of the craft of lyric writing.
He was struck by what he called the sheer
magnificence of the lines:
    Night and day, under the hide of me,
    There's an Oh, such a hungry yearning,
    Burning inside of me.
and wrote several versions of his own:
    Night and day, under the bark of me,
    There's an Oh, such a mob of microbes
    Making a park of me.
and:
    Night and day, under my dermis, dear
    There's a spot just as hot as coffee
    Kept in a thermos, dear.

The Night and the Sea
Music and lyrics by Ron Dante and Gene Allan
Billy 1969

The Night Before the Morning After
Music by Arthur Schwartz
Lyrics by Howard Dietz
Between the Devil 1937

Night Birds
Music by Jean Gilbert
Lyrics by Harry Graham
Katja 1926

Night Club Nights
Music by Henry Sullivan
Lyrics by Edward Eliscu
A Little Racketeer 1932

Night Flies By
Music by Jerome Kern
Lyrics by Oscar Hammerstein II
Music in the Air 1932

Has the same melody as "One More Dance" in the
same show.

The Night Gondolfi Got Married
Music and lyrics by Robert Larimer
King of the Whole Damn World (OB) 1962

A Night in the Orient
Music by Sigmund Romberg
Lyrics by Harold Atteridge
Sinbad (1918)

The Night Is Filled With Music
Music and lyrics by Irving Berlin
Carefree (1938) F

The Night Is Young
Music by Sigmund Romberg
Lyrics by Oscar Hammerstein II
The Night Is Young (1935) F

The Night It Happened
Music by Joseph Meyer
Lyrics by William Moll
Jonica 1930

Night Letter
Music by Galt MacDermot
Lyrics by John Guare
Two Gentlemen of Verona 1971

The Night May Be Dark
Music by Arthur Schwartz
Lyrics by Howard Dietz
Jennie 1963

Night May Have Its Sadness
Music by Ivor Novello
Lyrics by Collie Knox
Charlot's Revue 1924

A Night of Masquerade
Music and lyrics by George M. Cohan
The Merry Malones 1927

Night of My Nights
Music and lyrics by Robert Wright
and George Forrest
Kismet 1953

Based on Borodin's *Serenade*

The Night of the Embassy Ball
Music by Harold Arlen
Lyrics by E.Y. Harburg
Hooray for What! 1937

Night on the Town
Music by Michael Dansicker
Lyrics by Sarah Schlesinger
On The Swing Shift (OB) 1983

Night People
Music by Tommy Wolf
Lyrics by Fran Landesman
The Nervous Set 1959

Night Song
Music by Charles Strouse
Lyrics by Lee Adams
Golden Boy 1964

The Night That Made America Famous
Music and lyrics by Harry Chapin
The Night That Made America Famous 1975

The Night They Invented Champagne
Music by Frederick Loewe
Lyrics by Alan Jay Lerner
Gigi (1958) F

Also in stage version (1973)

The Night Time
Music by Jerome Kern
Lyrics by Clifford Grey
Sally 1920

Night Time in Araby
Music by George Gershwin
Lyrics by B.G. DeSylva
George White's Scandals (1924)

Night Waltz (instrumental)
Music and lyrics by Stephen Sondheim
A Little Night Music 1973

Sung as "The Sun Won't Set"

The Night Was All to Blame
Music by Alma Sanders
Lyrics by Monte Carlo
Louisiana Lady 1947

The Night Was Made for Love
Music by Jerome Kern
Lyrics by Otto Harbach
French lyrics by Robert Russell Bennett
The Cat and the Fiddle 1931

Nightie-Night
Music by George Gershwin
Lyrics by Ira Gershwin
Tip-Toes 1925

Nightingale
Music by Edward Earle
Lyrics by Yvonne Tarr
The Decameron (OB) 1961

The Nightingale and the Star
Music by Victor Herbert
Lyrics by Henry Blossom
Mlle. Modiste 1905

Nightingale, Bring Me a Rose
Music by Henry Sullivan
Lyrics by John Murray Anderson
John Murray Anderson's Almanac (1953)

The Nightingale Song
Music by Milton Ager
Lyrics by Jack Yellen
John Murray Anderson's Almanac (1929)

Nightlife
Music by Charles Strouse
Lyrics by Lee Adams
All American 1962

The Nightmare
Music by Frank Black
Lyrics by Gladys Shelley
The Duchess Misbehaves 1946

The Nightmare
Music by Frank Fields
Lyrics by Armand Aulicino
The Shoemaker and the Peddler (OB) 1960

The Nightmare
Music by Harvey Schmidt
Lyrics by Tom Jones
Philemon (OB) 1975

The Nightmare Was Me
Music and lyrics by Elizabeth Swados
Lullabye and Goodnight 1982

The Nighttime Is No Time for Thinking
Music by Kurt Weill
Lyrics by Ira Gershwin
The Firebrand of Florence 1945

Nightwind
Music by Harden Church
Lyrics by Edward Heyman
Caviar 1934

Nijigo Novgo Glide
Music by Harry Ruby
Lyrics by Bert Kalmar
Helen of Troy, New York 1923

The Nile
Music and lyrics by Xaver Leroux
A Night in Paris 1926

Nina
Music and lyrics by Herbert Stothart, Bert Kalmar
and Harry Ruby
Good Boy 1928

Nina
Music by Werner Janssen
Lyrics by Mann Holiner and J. Keirn Brennan
Boom-Boom 1929

Nina
Music and lyrics by Cole Porter
The Pirate (1948) F

Nina Rosa
Music by Sigmund Romberg
Lyrics by Irving Caesar
Nina Rosa 1930

The Nina, the Pinta, the Santa Maria
Music by Kurt Weill
Lyrics by Ira Gershwin
Where Do We Go from Here? (1945) F

Nine
Music and lyrics by Maury Yeston
Nine 1982

Nine o'Clock
Music and lyrics by Bob Merrill
Take Me Along 1959

The 1908 Life
Music by Ray Henderson
Lyrics by B.G. DeSylva and Lew Brown
Follow Thru 1929

1945
Music by Gary William Friedman
Lyrics by Will Holt
Platinum 1978

1934 Hot Chocolate Jazz Babies Revue
Music by Charles Strouse
Lyrics by Lee Adams
A Broadway Musical 1978

Nineteen Twenty-Seven
Music by Harold Orlob
Lyrics by Irving Caesar
Talk About Girls 1927

Ninety Again!
Music by Richard Rodgers
Lyrics by Martin Charnin
Two by Two 1970

Ninety Minutes Is a Long, Long Time
Music and lyrics by Noël Coward
Together With Music (1955) TV

99 Per Cent Pure
Music by Arthur Schwartz
Lyrics by Henry Myers
The New Yorkers 1927

Nippy
Music by Vivian Ellis
Lyrics by Graham John
By the Way 1925

Niri-Esther
Music and lyrics by Sandy Wilson
Valmouth (OB) 1960

Nitchevo
Music by Lee Pockriss
Lyrics by Anne Croswell
Tovarich 1963

Nize Baby
Music by James F. Hanley
Lyrics by Ballard MacDonald
No Foolin' 1926

No
Music by David Baker
Lyrics by Will Holt
Come Summer 1969

No
Music by John Kander
Lyrics by Fred Ebb
Chicago 1975

No Bad News
Music and lyrics by Charlie Smalls
The Wiz 1975

No Better Way to Start a Case
Music by George Gershwin
Lyrics by Ira Gershwin
Let 'Em Eat Cake 1933

No Boom Boom
Music by John Kander
Lyrics by Fred Ebb
Zorba 1968

No Champagne
Music by Joseph Raposo
Lyrics by Erich Segal
Sing Muse! (OB) 1961

No Comprenez, No Capish, No Versteh!
Music by George Gershwin
Lyrics by Ira Gershwin
Let 'Em Eat Cake 1933

No Foolin'
Music by James F. Hanley
Lyrics by Gene Buck
No Foolin' 1926

No Goodbyes
Music and lyrics by Richard M. Sherman
and Robert B. Sherman
Over Here! 1974

No Hearts for Sale
Music by Alma Sanders
Lyrics by Monte Carlo
Oh! Oh! Nurse 1925

No Holds Barred
Music and lyrics by Jim Wann and Cass Morgan
Pump Boys and Dinettes 1982

No, I Won't
Music by Alma Sanders
Lyrics by Monte Carlo
Oh! Oh! Nurse 1925

No Ketchup
Music by Alfred Brooks
Lyrics by Ira J. Bilowit
Of Mice and Men (OB) 1958

No Lies
Music and lyrics by Carol Hall
The Best Little Whorehouse in Texas 1978

No Life
Music and lyrics by Stephen Sondheim
Sunday in the Park With George (OB) 1983

No Lookin' Back
Music by Jay Gorney
Lyrics by Henry Myers and Edward Eliscu
Meet the People 1940

No Lover
Music and lyrics by Cole Porter
Out of This World 1950

No Man Is Worth It
Music by Charles Strouse
Lyrics by Alan Jay Lerner
Dance a Little Closer 1983

No Matter Where
Music by Richard Adler
Lyrics by Will Holt
Music Is 1976

No More
Music by Charles Strouse
Lyrics by Lee Adams
Golden Boy 1964

No More Candy
Music by Jerry Bock
Lyrics by Sheldon Harnick
She Loves Me 1963

No More Mornings
Music by Larry Grossman
Lyrics by Betty Comden and Adolph Green
A Doll's Life 1982

No More Waiting
Music and lyrics by Richard Rodgers
Androcles and the Lion (1967) TV

No More You
Music by Ray Henderson
Lyrics by B.G. DeSylva and Lew Brown
Follow Thru 1929

No, Mother, No
Music by Richard Rodgers
Lyrics by Lorenz Hart
By Jupiter 1942

No News Today
Music by Jimmy Van Heusen
Lyrics by Johnny Burke
Nellie Bly 1946

No, No, Mamselle
Music by Alma Sanders
Lyrics by Monte Carlo
Louisiana Lady 1947

No, No, Nanette
Music by Vincent Youmans
Lyrics by Otto Harbach
No, No, Nanette 1925

No! No! No!
Music by Franz Steininger (adapted from
Tchaikovsky)
Lyrics by Forman Brown
Music in My Heart 1947

No! No! No!
Music by Frederico Valerio
Lyrics by Elizabeth Miele
Hit the Trail 1954

No! No! No!
Music by Lee Pockriss
Lyrics by Anne Croswell
Tovarich 1963

No One
Music by Galt MacDermot
Lyrics by Gerome Ragni
Dude 1972

No One Cares for Dreams
Music by Alma Sanders
Lyrics by Monte Carlo
Louisiana Lady 1947

No One Ever Told Me Love Would Be So Hard
Music by Ronald Melrose
Lyrics by Bill Russell
Fourtune (OB) 1980

No One Knows
Music by Jerome Kern
Lyrics by Anne Caldwell
The City Chap 1925

No One Knows Me
Music by Leon Pober
Lyrics by Bud Freeman
Beg, Borrow or Steal 1960

No One Loves Me
Music by Mischa and Wesley Portnoff
Lyrics by Donagh MacDonagh
Happy as Larry 1950

No One'll Ever Love You
Music by Leroy Anderson
Lyrics by Joan Ford and Walter and Jean Kerr
Goldilocks 1958

No One's Ever Kissed Me
Music by Vivian Ellis
Lyrics by Graham John
By the Way 1925

No One's Perfect, Dear
Music and lyrics by Hal Hester and Danny Apolinar
Your Own Thing (OB) 1968

No One's Tried to Kiss Me
Music by Manning Sherwin
Lyrics by Harold Purcell
Under the Counter 1947

No Other Love
Music by Emile Berté and Maury Rubens
Lyrics by J. Keirn Brennan
Music in May 1929

No Other Love
Music by Richard Rodgers
Lyrics by Oscar Hammerstein II
Me and Juliet 1953

The melody was written as one of the themes in
Rodgers' score for the television series *Victory at
Sea* in 1952. The music, a tango, was written for
the episode "Beneath the Southern Cross."

No Place for Me
Music by Wally Harper
Lyrics by Paul Zakrzewski
Sensations (OB) 1970

No Place Like Home
Music by Roger Wolfe Kahn
Lyrics by Irving Caesar
Americana (1928)

No Place Like London
Music and lyrics by Stephen Sondheim
Sweeney Todd 1979

No Place to Go
Music by Ray Haney
Lyrics by Alfred Aiken
We're Civilized? (OB) 1962

No Questions
Music by Sammy Fain
Lyrics by Marilyn and Alan Bergman
Something More 1964

No Room in My Heart
Music by Ray Perkins
Lyrics by Max and Nathaniel Lief
Say When 1928

No Room No Room
Music and lyrics by Elizabeth Swados
Alice in Concert (OB) 1980

No Song More Pleasing
Music by Richard Rodgers
Lyrics by Sheldon Harnick
Rex 1976

No Strings
Music and lyrics by Irving Berlin
Top Hat (1935) F

No Strings
Music and lyrics by Richard Rodgers
No Strings 1962

No Surprises
Music by Charles Strouse
Lyrics by David Rogers
Charlie and Algernon 1980

No Talent
Music and lyrics by Oscar Brand and Paul Nassau
A Joyful Noise 1966

No, Thank You
Music by Michael J. Lewis
Lyrics by Anthony Burgess
Cyrano 1933

No Tickee, No Washee
Music by George Gershwin
Lyrics by Ira Gershwin
Pardon My English 1933

Dropped from production

No Time
Music by Baldwin Bergersen
Lyrics by Phyllis McGinley
Small Wonder 1948

No Time
Music by Robert Waldman
Lyrics by Alfred Uhry
Here's Where I Belong 1968

No Time at All
Music and lyrics by Stephen Schwartz
Pippin 1972

No Time for Nothin' But Love
Music by Allan Roberts
Lyrics by Lester Lee
All for Love 1949

No True Love
Music and lyrics by Deed Meyer
She Shall Have Music (OB) 1959

No Two People
Music and lyrics by Frank Loesser
Hans Christian Andersen (1952) F

No Understand
Music by Richard Rodgers
Lyrics by Stephen Sondheim
Do I Hear a Waltz? 1965

No Use Pretending
Music by Sigmund Romberg
Lyrics by Otto Harbach
Forbidden Melody 1936

No Way in Hell
Music and lyrics by Eaton Magoon, Jr.
Heathen 1972

No Way to Stop It
Music by Richard Rodgers
Lyrics by Oscar Hammerstein II
The Sound of Music 1959

No Wedding Bells for Me
Music by Louis Bellson and Will Irwin
Lyrics by Richard Ney
Portofino 1958

No Wonder I'm Blue
Music by Louis Alter
Lyrics by Oscar Hammerstein II
Ballyhoo 1930

No Wonder Taxes Are High
Music and lyrics by Cole Porter
Aladdin (1958) TV

No (You Can't Have My Heart)
Music and lyrics by Dana Suesse
You Never Know 1938

Noah's Ark
Music by Naomi Shemer
Lyrics by David Paulsen
To Live Another Summer 1971

Nobility
Music by Jerry Bock
Lyrics by Sheldon Harnick
The Body Beautiful 1958

Nobles of Castilian Birth
Music by John Philip Sousa
Lyrics by Tom Frost and John Philip Sousa
El Capitan 1896

Nobody Breaks My Heart
Music by Kay Swift
Lyrics by Paul James
Fine and Dandy 1930

Nobody But You
Music by George Gershwin
Lyrics by Arthur J. Jackson and B.G. DeSylva
La, La, Lucille 1919

Nobody Does It Like Me
Music by Cy Coleman
Lyrics by Dorothy Fields
Seesaw 1973

Nobody Does My Thing
Music and lyrics by Oscar Brown, Jr.
Buck White 1969

Nobody Else But Me
Music by Jerome Kern
Lyrics by Oscar Hammerstein II
Show Boat (1946 revival)

Written expressly for this revival, it was to be
Kern's very last song. He died on November 11,
1945.

Nobody Else But You
Music by Albert Hague
Lyrics by Arnold B. Horwitt
The Girls Against the Boys 1959

Nobody Ever Died for Dear Old Rutgers
Music by Jule Styne
Lyrics by Sammy Cahn
High Button Shoes 1947

Nobody Ever Pins Me Up
Music by Vernon Duke
Lyrics by Howard Dietz
Jackpot 1944

Nobody Loves a Riveter
Music by Richard Rodgers
Lyrics by Lorenz Hart
The Hot Heiress (1931) F

Nobody Makes a Pass at Me
Music and lyrics by Harold Rome
Pins and Needles (OB) 1937

Nobody Really Do
Music by Garry Sherman
Lyrics by Peter Udell
Comin' Uptown 1979

Nobody Steps on Kafritz
Music and lyrics by Bob Merrill
Henry, Sweet Henry 1967

Nobody Tells Me How
Music by Mary Rodgers
Lyrics by Susan Birkenhead
Working 1978

Nobody Throw Those Bull
Music by Moose Charlap
Lyrics by Norman Gimbel
Whoop-Up 1958

Nobody to Cry To
Music and lyrics by Johnny Brandon
Who's Who, Baby? (OB) 1968

Nobody Told Me
Music by Baldwin Bergersen
Lyrics by Phyllis McGinley
Small Wonder 1948

Nobody Told Me
Music and lyrics by Richard Rodgers
No Strings 1962

Nobody Wants Me
Music by Philip Charig
Lyrics by Irving Caesar
Polly 1929

Nobody Will Remember Him
Music by Elmer Bernstein
Lyrics by Don Black
Merlin 1983

Nobody's Chasing Me
Music and lyrics by Cole Porter
Out of This World 1950

Nobody's Heart
Music by Richard Rodgers
Lyrics by Lorenz Hart
By Jupiter 1942

Nobody's Heart But Mine
Music by Jimmy McHugh
Lyrics by Harold Adamson
As the Girls Go 1948

Nobody's Listening
Music and lyrics by Oscar Brand
How to Steal an Election (OB) 1968

Nobody's Perfect
Music by Harvey Schmidt
Lyrics by Tom Jones
I Do! I Do! 1966

Nobody's Perfect
Music by Rob Fremont
Lyrics by Doris Willens
Piano Bar (OB) 1978

Nocturne
Music by Rudolf Friml
Lyrics by Brian Hooker
The Vagabond King 1925

Nodding Roses
Music by Jerome Kern
Lyrics by Schuyler Greene and Herbert Reynolds
Very Good Eddie 1915

Kern slyly interpolated a phrase from Richard
Strauss' opera *Der Rosenkavalier* into the
orchestration of this song.

Noises in the Street
Music by Richard Lewine
Lyrics by Peter Barry and
David Greggory
'Tis of Thee 1940

Later rewritten (with additional lyrics by Arnold B.
Horwitt) for *Make Mine Manhattan* (1948).

Noisy Neighbors
Music by James P. Johnson
Lyrics by Flournoy Miller
Sugar Hill 1931

Nookie Time
Music and lyrics by Al Carmines
The Faggot (OB) 1973

Nora Malone
Music by Silvio Hein
Lyrics by George V. Hobart
The Yankee Girl 1910

Nordraak's Farewell
Music and lyrics by Robert Wright and George
Forrest
Song of Norway 1944

Based on Grieg's song *Springtide*

Normal American Boy
Music by Charles Strouse
Lyrics by Lee Adams
Bye Bye Birdie 1960

Normandy
Music by Mary Rodgers
Lyrics by Marshall Barer
Once Upon a Mattress 1959

North American Shmear
Music and lyrics by Robert Swerdlow
Love Me, Love My Children (OB) 1971

Northern Blues
Music by Walter [Gustave] Haenschen
Lyrics by Robert A. Simon
The Grand Street Follies (1926) (OB)

Northfield Minnesota
Music and lyrics by Bland Simpson and Jim Wann
Diamond Studs (OB) 1975

Noses
Music by Galt MacDermot
Lyrics by William Dumaresq
The Human Comedy (OB) 1983

Nostalgia
Music by Monty Norman
Lyrics by Julian More
The Moony Shapiro Songbook 1981

Not a Care in the World
Music by Vernon Duke
Lyrics by John Latouche
Banjo Eyes 1941

Also in the OB revival of *Cabin in the Sky* (1964).

Not a Day Goes By
Music and lyrics by Stephen Sondheim
Merrily We Roll Along 1981

Not Another Day Like This
Music by Charles Strouse
Lyrics by David Rogers
Charlie and Algernon 1980

Not Anymore
Music by Judd Woldin
Lyrics by Robert Brittan
Raisin 1973

Not Every Day of the Week
Music by John Kander
Lyrics by Fred Ebb
Flora, the Red Menace 1965

Not for All the Rice in China
Music and lyrics by Irving Berlin
As Thousands Cheer 1933

Not for Him
Music by Sigmund Romberg
Lyrics by Otto Harbach and Oscar Hammerstein II
The Desert Song 1926

Dropped from production

Not Guilty
Music and lyrics by Harold Rome
Destry Rides Again 1959

Not Here! Not Here!
Music by Jerome Kern
Lyrics by M.E. Rourke
The Dollar Princess 1909

A lively number in this show, it was rewritten as a romantic ballad "The Land of Let's Pretend," with lyrics by Harry B. Smith, for *The Girl From Utah* (1914).

Not in Business Hours
Music by Vincent Youmans and Herbert Stothart
Lyrics by Oscar Hammerstein II
and William Cary Duncan
Mary Jane McKane 1923

Not Me
Music and lyrics by Oscar Brand and Paul Nassau
A Joyful Noise 1966

Not Mine
Music by Jule Styne
Lyrics by Betty Comden and Adolph Green
Hallelujah, Baby! 1967

Not My Problem
Music by Harvey Schmidt
Lyrics by Tom Jones
Celebration 1969

Not Now, But Later
Music by Rudolf Friml
Lyrics by Otto Harbach
High Jinks 1913

Not Now, Not Here
Music by Edward Thomas
Lyrics by Martin Charnin
Ballad for a Firing Squad (OB) 1968

Not on Your Nellie
Music by Jule Styne
Lyrics by E.Y. Harburg
Darling of the Day 1968

Not on Your Tintype
Music by Richard Lewine
Lyrics by John Latouche
Murder in the Old Red Barn (OB) 1936

Not Since Chaplin
Music and lyrics by Maury Yeston
Nine 1982

Not Since Nineveh
Music and lyrics by Robert Wright and George Forrest
Kismet 1953

Based on Borodin's *Polovetsian Dances*

Not So Bad to Be Good
Music by Vernon Duke
Lyrics by John Latouche
Cabin in the Sky (1964 OB revival)

Not So Long Ago
Music and lyrics by Porter Grainger
and Freddie Johnson
Lucky Sambo 1925

Not Tabu
Music and lyrics by Ed Tyler
Sweet Miani (OB) 1962

Not That I Care
Music by Richard A. Whiting
Lyrics by Oscar Hammerstein II
Free for All 1931

Not That Sort of Person
Music by Lionel Monckton
Lyrics by George Grossmith, Jr.
Our Miss Gibbs 1910

Not Tomorrow
Music by Don Gohman
Lyrics by Hal Hackady
Ambassador 1972

Not While I'm Around
Music and lyrics by Stephen Sondheim
Sweeney Todd 1979

Not Yet
Music by Jerome Kern
Lyrics by P.G. Wodehouse
Oh, Lady! Lady!! 1918

Nothin' for Nothin'
Music by Morton Gould
Lyrics by Dorothy Fields
Arms and the Girl 1950

Nothin' Up
Music by Robert Waldman
Lyrics by Alfred Uhry
The Robber Bridegroom 1975

Nothing
Music by Marvin Hamlisch
Lyrics by Edward Kleban
A Chorus Line 1975

Nothing at All
Music by Sammy Fain
Lyrics by Dan Shapiro
Ankles Aweigh 1955

Nothing at All, at All
Music and lyrics by Paul Rubens
The Girl From Utah 1914

Nothing But a Fool
Music and lyrics by Oscar Brown, Jr.
and Luis Henrique
Joy (OB) 1970

Nothing But Love
Music by Ray Henderson
Lyrics by B.G. DeSylva and Lew Brown
Manhattan Mary 1927

Nothing But "Yes" in My Eyes
Music and lyrics by E. Ray Goetz
Naughty Cinderella 1925

Nothing But You
Music by Richard Rodgers
Lyrics by Lorenz Hart
Higher And Higher 1940

Nothing Can Ever Happen in New York
Music by James F. Hanley
Lyrics by Eddie Dowling
Sidewalks of New York 1927 •

Nothing Can Replace a Man
Music by Sammy Fain
Lyrics by Dan Shapiro
Ankles Aweigh 1955

Nothing Can Stop Me Now!
Music and lyrics by Leslie Bricusse
and Anthony Newley
*The Roar of the Greasepaint—The Smell
of the Crowd* 1965

Nothing Could Be Sweeter
Music by Vincent Youmans
Lyrics by Leo Robin and Clifford Grey
Hit the Deck (1927)

Later published as "Why, Oh Why?"

Nothing Ever Happens in Angel's Roost
Music by Jerome Moross
Lyrics by John Latouche
The Golden Apple 1954

Nothing in Common
Music by Gordon Duffy
Lyrics by Harry M. Haldane
Happy Town 1959

Nothing in Common
Music and lyrics by Meredith Willson
Here's Love 1963

Nothing Is Impossible
Music by Burton Lane
Lyrics by Ira Gershwin
Give a Girl a Break (1953) F

Nothing Is Working Quite Right
Music by Alec Wilder
Lyrics by Arnold Sundgaard
Kittiwake Island (OB) 1960

Nothing Left But Dreams
Music by Edgar Fairchild
Lyrics by Henry Myers
The New Yorkers 1927

Nothing Like a Darned Good Cry
Music and lyrics by George M. Cohan
The Rise of Rosie O'Reilly 1923

Nothing Man Cannot Do
Music and lyrics by Eaton Magoon, Jr.
13 Daughters 1961

Nothing Matters
Music by Jacques Belasco
Lyrics by Kay Twomey
The Girl From Nantucket 1945

Nothing More
Music by Michael Leonard
Lyrics by Herbert Martin
The Yearling 1965

Nothing More to Look Forward To
Music and lyrics by Richard Adler
Kwamina 1961

Nothing, Only Love
Music by Peter Link
Lyrics by Jacob Brackman
King of Hearts 1978

Nothing Really Happened
Music and lyrics by Craig Carnelia
Is There Life After High School? 1982

Nothing to Do
Music by Armando Trovaioli
Lyrics by Pietro Garinei and Sandro Giovannini
(Lyric translation by Edward Eager)
Rugantino 1964

Nothing to Do But Relax
Music by Richard Rodgers
Lyrics by Lorenz Hart
By Jupiter 1942

Dropped from production

Nothing's Left of God
Music by Stanley Silverman
Lyrics by Arthur Miller
Up From Paradise (OB) 1983

Nothing's Missing
Music by Mitch Leigh
Lyrics by N. Richard Nash
Saravá 1979

Nothing's Wrong
Music by Richard Rodgers
Lyrics by Lorenz Hart
A Connecticut Yankee 1927

Nothin's Gonna Change
Music and lyrics by Johnny Brandon
Who's Who, Baby? (OB) 1968

The Notorious Colonel Blake
Music by Richard Rodgers
Lyrics by Lorenz Hart
Mississippi (1935) F

Dropped from film

November Song
Music by Jule Styne
Lyrics by Bob Merrill
Sugar 1972

Now
Music by Vernon Duke
Lyrics by Ted Fetter
The Show Is On 1936

Now
Music and lyrics by Robert Wright and George
Forrest
Song of Norway 1944

Based on Grieg's Waltz op. 12 and Violin Sonata
No. 2

Now
Music and lyrics by C. Jackson and James Hatch
Fly Blackbird (OB) 1962

Now!
Music by Susan Hulsman Bingham
Lyrics by Myrna Lamb
Mod Donna (OB) 1970

Now
Music and lyrics by Stephen Sondheim
A Little Night Music 1973

Now
Music by Charles Strouse
Lyrics by David Rogers
Charlie and Algernon 1980

Now and Then
Music by Mischa and Wesley Portnoff
Lyrics by Donagh MacDonagh
Happy as Larry 1950

Now Fades My Golden Love Dream
Music by Oscar Straus
Lyrics by Edward Delaney Dunn
The Last Waltz 1921

The Now Generation
Music and lyrics by Hal Hester and Danny Apolinar
Your Own Thing (OB) 1968

Now I Have Everything
Music by Jerry Bock
Lyrics by Sheldon Harnick
Fiddler on the Roof 1964

Now I Know
Music by Philip Charig
Lyrics by James Dyrenforth
Nikki 1931

Now I Know
Music by Harold Arlen
Lyrics by Ted Koehler
Up in Arms (1944) F

Now I Know Your Face By Heart
Music by Bronislaw Kaper (based on Chopin)
Lyrics by John Latouche
Polonaise 1945

Now I Lay Me
Music by Helen Miller
Lyrics by Eve Merriam
Inner City 1971

Now I Lay Me Down to Sleep
Music by Garry Sherman
Lyrics by Peter Udell
Comin' Uptown 1979

Now I'm Ready for a Frau
Music by Arthur Schwartz
Lyrics by Howard Dietz
The Gay Life 1961

Now Is the South Wind Blowing
Music by Victor Herbert
Lyrics by David Stevens
and Justin Huntly McCarthy
The Madcap Duchess 1913

Now Is the Time
Music by Max Rich
Lyrics by Jack Scholl
Keep Moving 1934

Now It Can Be Told
Music and lyrics by Irving Berlin
Alexander's Ragtime Band (1938) F

Now It's Fall
Music and lyrics by Skip Redwine and Larry Frank
Frank Merriwell, or Honor Challenged 1971

Now, Morris
Music by John Kander
Lyrics by James Goldman, John Kander
and William Goldman
A Family Affair 1962

Now, O Lips, Say Goodbye
Music and lyrics by Gian-Carlo Menotti
The Consul 1950

Now That I Am Forty
Music by Leon Carr
Lyrics by Earl Shuman
The Secret Life of Walter Mitty (OB) 1964

Now That I Know You
Music by Richard Rodgers
Lyrics by Lorenz Hart

See note on "I'd Rather be Right"

Now That I'm Free
Music by Irving Caesar
Lyrics by Irma Hollander
My Dear Public 1943

Now That I've Got My Strength
Music by Richard Rodgers
Lyrics by Lorenz Hart
By Jupiter 1942

Now We Pray
Music by Joe Ercole
Lyrics by Bruce Kluger
Ka-Boom (OB) 1980

Now You Are One of the Family
Music and lyrics by Elizabeth Swados
Lullabye and Goodnight 1982

Now You Has Jazz
Music by lyrics by Cole Porter
High Society (1956) F

Now You Know
Music and lyrics by Stephen Sondheim
Merrily We Roll Along 1981

Now You Leave
Music by Richard Rodgers
Lyrics by Oscar Hammerstein II
The King and I 1951

Dropped from production

Nowadays
Music by John Kander
Lyrics by Fred Ebb
Chicago 1975

Nowhere
Music by Albert T. Viola
Lyrics by William S. Kilborne, Jr.
Head Over Heels 1981

Nowhere to Go But Up
Music by Sol Berkowitz
Lyrics by James Lipton
Nowhere to Go But Up 1962

Now's the Time
Music by Jule Styne
Lyrics by Betty Comden and Adolph Green
Hallelujah, Baby! 1967

The Nub of the Nation
Music by Helen Miller
Lyrics by Eve Merriam
Inner City 1971

Nude With Violin
Music and lyrics by Ronnie Britton
Greenwich Village Follies (OB) 1976

Nuevo Laredo
Music and lyrics by Will Holt
That 5 A.M. Jazz (OB) 1964

#X9RL220
Music by Jerry Powell
Lyrics by Michael McWhinney
New Faces of 1968

Numbers
Music by Gary William Friedman
Lyrics by Will Holt
The Me Nobody Knows (OB) 1970

Numbers
Music by Helen Miller
Lyrics by Eve Merriam
Inner City 1971

Nursery
Music and lyrics by Charles Herbert
Two for Tonight (OB) 1939

Nuthin' for Nuthin'
Music and lyrics by John Dooley
Hobo (OB) 1961

Nutmeg Insurance
Music by Harry Revel
Lyrics by Arnold B. Horwitt
Are You With It? 1945

Nuts
Music by Paul A. Rubens
Lyrics by Paul A. Rubens and Arthur Wimperis
The Sunshine Girl 1913

N.Y.C.
Music by Charles Strouse
Lyrics by Martin Charnin
Annie 1977

O

O, Heart of Love
Music by Kurt Weill
Lyrics by Paul Green
Johnny Johnson 1936

O Heart of My Country
Music by Bronislaw Kaper (based on Chopin)
Lyrics by John Latouche
Polonaise 1945

O Leo
Music by Arthur Schwartz
Lyrics by Howard Dietz
At Home Abroad 1935

O Marry Me!
Music by Robert Kessler
Lyrics by Lola Pergament
O Marry Me! (OB) 1961

O Miserere
Music by Leonard Bernstein
Lyrics by Stephen Sondheim
Candide (added to 1973 revival)
Same music as "It Must Be So."

O, Mistress Mine
Music by Galt MacDermot
Lyrics by Rochelle Owens
The Karl Marx Play (OB) 1973

O Pallas Athene
Music by Joseph Raposo
Lyrics by Erich Segal
Sing Muse! (OB) 1961

O Rock Eternal
Music by Michael Valenti
Lyrics by John Lewin
Blood Red Roses 1970

O Say Can You See!
Music by Jack Holmes
Lyrics by Bill Conklin and Bob Miller
O Say Can You See! (OB) 1962

O Tixo, Tixo, Help Me
Music by Kurt Weill
Lyrics by Maxwell Anderson
Lost in the Stars 1949

O, What a War
Music by Jim Steinman
Lyrics by Michael Weller and Jim Steinman
More Than You Deserve (OB) 1973

Oak Leaf Memorial Park
Music by Jerry Livingston
Lyrics by Mack David
Molly 1973

The Oasis
Music and lyrics by Walter Marks
Broadway Follies 1981

Obedian March
Music by Sol Berkowitz
Lyrics by James Lipton
Miss Emily Adam (OB) 1960

Obedience
Music and lyrics by James Rado
Rainbow (OB) 1972

Oblivia
Music by Ernest G. Schweikert
Lyrics by Frank Reardon
Rumple 1957

The O'Brien Girl
Music by Louis A. Hirsch
Lyrics by Otto Harbach
The O'Brien Girl 1921

The Ocarina
Music and lyrics by Irving Berlin
Call Me Madam 1950

Occasional Flight of Fancy
Music by Jimmy Van Heusen
Lyrics by Sammy Cahn
Skyscraper 1965

An Occasional Man
Music and Lyrics by Hugh Martin
and Ralph Blane
Girl Rush (1955) F

Oceanography and Old Astronomy
Music by Alec Wilder
Lyrics by Arnold Sundgaard
Kittiwake Island (OB) 1960

October
Music by Mischa and Wesley Portnoff
Lyrics by Donagh MacDonagh
Happy as Larry 1950

Octopus Song
Music and lyrics by Harold Rome
Fanny 1954

Odds
Music by Jacques Urbont
Lyrics by Bruce Geller
All in Love (OB) 1961

The Odds and Ends of Love
Music by Sol Berkowitz
Lyrics by James Lipton
Nowhere to Go But Up 1962

Ode to a Key
Music by Sammy Fain
Lyrics by Marilyn and Alan Bergman
Something More 1964

Ode to Lola
Music by Walter Kent
Lyrics by Kim Gannon
Seventeen 1951

Ode to the Bridge
Music by Moose Charlap
Lyrics by Eddie Lawrence
Kelly 1965

Ode to the Styx
Music by Alma Sanders
Lyrics by Monte Carlo
The Houseboat on the Styx 1928

Odle-De-O
Music by Maury Rubens
Lyrics by Clifford Grey
The Madcap 1928

Oedipus Rex
Music and lyrics by Tom Lehrer
Tomfoolery (OB) 1981

Of Thee I Sing
Music by George Gershwin
Lyrics by Ira Gershwin
Of Thee I Sing 1931

Of V We Sing
Music by Lou Cooper
Lyrics by Arthur Zipser
Of V We Sing 1942

Off Again, On Again
Music by Vernon Duke
Lyrics by E.Y. Harburg
Walk a Little Faster 1932

Off on a Weekend Cruise
Music by Michael Cleary
Lyrics by Arthur Swanstrom
Sea Legs 1937

Off the Record
Music by Richard Rodgers
Lyrics by Lorenz Hart
I'd Rather Be Right 1937

Lorenz Hart, having already written four long
choruses of lyric, wrote a fifth for James Cagney to
sing in the film *Yankee Doodle Dandy* (1942).

Off Time
Music by Thomas (Fats) Waller and Harry Brooks
Lyrics by Andy Razaf
Hot Chocolates 1929

Off to Gluckstein
Music by Lehman Engel
Lyrics by Agnes Morgan
A Hero Is Born 1937

Off to See New York
Music by Alfred Nathan
Lyrics by George Oppenheimer
The Manhatters 1927

Off to the Derby
Music and lyrics by George M. Cohan
Little Johnny Jones 1904

Office Hours
Music and lyrics by Irving Berlin
Watch Your Step 1914

Oh! Argentina
Music by Rudolf Friml
Lyrics by Rida Johnson Young
Sometime 1918

Oh, Baby
Music by Cliff Friend
Lyrics by Lew Brown
Piggy 1927

Oh, Baby!
Music and lyrics by Owen Murphy
Rain or Shine 1928

Oh, Beautiful Land of Spain
Music by John Philip Sousa
Lyrics by Tom Frost and John Philip Sousa
El Capitan 1896

Oh, Bess, Oh Where's My Bess
Music by George Gershwin
Lyrics by Ira Gershwin
Porgy and Bess 1935

Oh, Black Swan
Music and lyrics by Gian-Carlo Menotti
The Medium 1947

Oh, Boy
Music by Albert Hague
Lyrics by Allen Sherman
The Fig Leaves Are Falling 1969

Oh Boy, Can We Deduct
Music by Lee Wainer
Lyrics by Robert Sour
Sing for Your Supper 1939

Oh, Brother
Music by Michael Valenti
Lyrics by Donald Driver
Oh, Brother 1981

Oh Brother
Music by Steve Jankowski
Lyrics by Kenny Morris
Francis (OB) 1982

Oh But I Do
Music by Arthur Schwartz
Lyrics by Leo Robin
The Time, the Place and the Girl (1946) F

Oh, Captain, My Captain
Music by Stan Harte, Jr.
Leaves of Grass (OB) 1971

Oh, Come Away, Away!
Music by Franz Lehár
Lyrics by Adrian Ross
The Merry Widow 1907

Oh, Daddy, Please
Music by Jerome Kern
Lyrics by P.G. Wodehouse
Oh, Boy! 1917

Oh, de Lawd Shake de Heaven
Music by George Gershwin
Lyrics by DuBose Heyward
Porgy and Bess 1935

Oh, Diogenes
Music by Richard Rodgers
Lyrics by Lorenz Hart
The Boys From Syracuse 1938

Oh, Doctor Jesus
Music by George Gershwin
Lyrics by DuBose Heyward and Ira Gershwin
Porgy and Bess 1935

Oh, Donna Clara
Music by J. Petersburski
Lyrics by Irving Caesar
The Wonder Bar 1931

Oh, Fabulous One
Music by Kurt Weill
Lyrics by Ira Gershwin
Lady in the Dark 1941

Oh, for the Life of a Cowboy
Music by James F. Hanley
Lyrics by Eddie Dowling
Sidewalks of New York 1927

Oh, Gee!
Music and lyrics by Bill and Patti Jacob
Jimmy 1969

Oh Gee, Oh Gosh
Music by William Daly
Lyrics by Arthur Jackson
For Goodness Sake 1922

Oh Gee! Oh Joy!
Music by George Gershwin
Lyrics by Ira Gershwin and P.G. Wodehouse
Rosalie 1928

Oh, Give Me the Good Old Days
Music and lyrics by Harold Rome
Pins and Needles (OB) 1937

Added during run

Oh God I'm Thirty
Music by Patrick Rose
Lyrics by Merv Campone and Richard Ouzounian
A Bistro Car on the CNR (OB) 1978

Oh, Gosh
Music by Ray Henderson
Lyrics by B.G. DeSylva and Lew Brown
Hold Everything! 1928

Oh, Happy Day
Music by Gene de Paul
Lyrics by Johnny Mercer
Li'l Abner 1956

Oh, Happy We
Music by Leonard Bernstein
Lyrics by Richard Wilbur
Candide 1956

Oh, How Happy We'll Be
Music by Lewis E. Gensler
Lyrics by Robert A. Simon and Clifford Grey
Ups-a-Daisy 1928

Oh, How I Adore Your Name
Music by John Morris
Lyrics by Gerald Freedman
A Time for Singing 1966

Oh, How I Hate to Get Up in the Morning
Music and lyrics by Irving Berlin
Yip, Yip, Yaphank 1918

Sung by Sergeant Irving Berlin. Later used in *This Is the Army* (1942), again sung by the composer.

Oh, How I Long to Belong to You
Music by Vincent Youmans
Lyrics by B.G. DeSylva
Take a Chance 1932

Oh, How I Miss You Blues
Music by Lewis E. Gensler
Lyrics by Robert A. Simon and Clifford Grey
Ups-a-Daisy 1928

Oh, How That Man Can Love
Music and lyrics by Lillian Roth and Herb Magidson
Earl Carroll's Vanities (1928)

Oh, How Unfortunate You Mortals Be
Music by Allan Roberts
Lyrics by Lester Lee
All for Love 1949

Oh! How We Love Our Alma Mater
Music by Harry Ruby
Lyrics by Bert Kalmar
The Ramblers 1926

Oh, How We Love You, Mrs. Cornwall
Music by Baldwin Bergersen
Lyrics by William Archibald
Rosa (OB) 1978

Oh, I Am a Fork
Music and lyrics by James Rado
Rainbow (OB) 1972

Oh, I Can't Sit Down
Music by George Gershwin
Lyrics by Ira Gershwin
Porgy and Bess 1935

Oh, Kay!
Music by George Gershwin
Lyrics by Ira Gershwin and Howard Dietz
Oh, Kay! 1926

Oh, Lady
Music by Sam Stept
Lyrics by Herb Magidson
George White's Music Hall Varieties 1932

Oh, Lady, Be Good!
Music by George Gershwin
Lyrics by Ira Gershwin
Lady, Be Good! 1924

Oh, Lady! Lady!!
Music by Jerome Kern
Lyrics by P.G. Wodehouse
Oh, Lady! Lady!! 1918

Oh, Lonely One
Music by Baldwin Bergersen
Lyrics by William Archibald
Carib Song 1945

Oh, Look at Me!
Music by Julian Slade
Lyrics by Dorothy Reynolds and Julian Slade
Salad Days (OB) 1958

Oh Lord
Music by Joe Ercole
Lyrics by Bruce Kluger
Ka-Boom (OB) 1980

Oh Me, Oh My, Oh You
Music by Vincent Youmans
Lyrics by Arthur Francis (Ira Gershwin)
Two Little Girls in Blue 1921

Oh, Mein Liebchen
Music by Arthur Schwartz
Lyrics by Howard Dietz
The Gay Life 1961

Oh, Mrs. Larry
Music by Mischa and Wesley Portnoff
Lyrics by Donagh MacDonagh
Happy as Larry 1950

Oh, Mrs. Lynde
Music by Norman Campbell
Lyrics by Donald Harron and Norman Campbell
Anne of Green Gables (OB) 1971

Oh, My Age
Music by Wally Harper
Lyrics by Paul Zakrzewski
Sensations (OB) 1970

Oh, My Rose
Music and lyrics by Mel Mandel and Norman Sachs
My Old Friends (OB) 1979

Oh! Oh! Delphine
Music by Ivan Caryll
Lyrics by C.M.S. McLellan
Oh! Oh! Delphine 1912

Oh, Oh, Oh
Music and lyrics by James Rado
Rainbow (OB) 1972

Oh, Oh, Oh, O'Sullivan
Music by Earl Robinson
Lyrics by Waldo Salt
Sandhog (OB) 1954

Oh, Papa!
Music by Ivan Caryll
Lyrics by Anne Caldwell
Jack O' Lantern 1917

Oh, Peggy
Music by Harry Akst
Lyrics by Benny Davis
Artists and Models (1927)

Oh, Pity the Man
Music by George Fischoff
Lyrics by Verna Tomasson
The Prince and the Pauper (OB) 1963

Oh, Please
Music and lyrics by Bob Merrill
Take Me Along 1959

Oh P-P-Poor Bouchotte
Music by Ivan Caryll
Lyrics by C.M.S. McLellan
Oh! Oh! Delphine 1912

Oh, Promise Me
Music by Reginald De Koven
Lyrics by Clement Scott
Robin Hood 1891

Written two years before the show's premiere, but
added to the score at the insistence of the leading
contralto. The song has since become by far the
best-known number from the score and, like
"Through the Years," is occasionally sung at
weddings.

Oh! Sam
Music by J. Fred Coots and Maury Rubens
Lyrics by Clifford Grey
Mayflowers 1925

Oh Say, Can You See?
Music by Robert Kessler
Lyrics by Martin Charnin
Fallout (OB) 1959

Oh, See the Lambkins Play
Music by Reginald De Koven
Lyrics by Harry B. Smith
Robin Hood 1891

Oh, Sky, Goodbye
Music by Giuseppe Verdi (adapted by Hans
Spialek)
Lyrics by Charles Friedman
My Darlin' Aïda 1952

Oh, So Gently
Music by Ivan Caryll
Lyrics by C.M.S. McLellan
The Pink Lady 1911

Oh, So Lovely
Music by Richard Rodgers
Lyrics by Lorenz Hart
Simple Simon 1930

Dropped from production

Oh, So Nice
Music by George Gershwin
Lyrics by Ira Gershwin
Treasure Girl 1928

Oh! Sonny
Music by Gustave Kerker
Lyrics by Hugh Morton
The Belle of New York 1897

Oh, Spare a Daughter
Music by John Philip Sousa
Lyrics by Tom Frost and John Philip Sousa
El Capitan 1896

Oh Sun
Music and lyrics by Clark Gesner
The Utter Glory of Morrissey Hall 1979

Oh, Teach Me How to Kiss
Music by Gustave Kerker
Lyrics by Hugh Morton
The Belle of New York 1897

Oh, the Shame
Music by Sol Berkowitz
Lyrics by James Lipton
Miss Emily Adam (OB) 1960

Oh, Theobold, Oh, Elmer
Music by Niclas Kempner
Lyrics by Graham John
The Street Singer 1929

Oh, to Be a Movie Star
Music by Jerry Bock
Lyrics by Sheldon Harnick
The Apple Tree 1966

Oh, Up! It's Up!
Music by Victor Herbert
Lyrics by David Stevens
and Justin Huntly McCarthy
The Madcap Duchess 1913

Oh, Warrior Grim
Music by John Philip Sousa
Lyrics by Tom Frost and John Philip Sousa
El Capitan 1896

Oh, Wasn't It Lovely?
Music by Harry Archer
Lyrics by Harlan Thompson
Merry-Merry 1925

Oh, What a Beautiful Mornin'
Music by Richard Rodgers
Lyrics by Oscar Hammerstein II
Oklahoma! 1943

Oscar Hammerstein believed in going to the
underlying work, when there was one, for song
ideas. Here he took Lynn Riggs' description at the
start of the play *Green Grow the Lilacs*, on which

the show was based: "It is a radiant summer morning."

Oh What a Circus!
Music by Andrew Lloyd Webber
Lyrics by Tim Rice
Evita 1979

Oh, What a Girl
Music by Tom Johnstone
Lyrics by Phil Cook
When You Smile 1925

Oh! What a Little Whopper
Music by Rudolf Friml
Lyrics by Bide Dudley and Otto Harbach
The Little Whopper 1919

Oh, What a Lovely Dance
Music and lyrics by Gian-Carlo Menotti
The Consul 1950

Oh, What a Man
Music and lyrics by Herbert Stothart, Bert Kalmar and Harry Ruby
Good Boy 1928

Oh, What a Playmate You Could Make
Music and lyrics by Leon DeCosta
The Blonde Sinner 1926

Oh, What She Hangs Out (She Hangs Out in Our Alley)
Music by George Gershwin
Lyrics by B.G. DeSylva
George White's Scandals (1922)

Oh, Woe Is Me
Music by Jean Gilbert
Lyrics by Harry Graham
Katja 1926

Oh, You!
Music by Milton Susskind
Lyrics by Paul Porter and Benjamin Hapgood Burt
Florida Girl 1925

Oh, You Beautiful Person!
Music by Jerome Kern
Lyrics by Anne Caldwell
She's a Good Fellow 1919

Oh, You Beautiful Spring
Music by Jerome Kern
Lyrics by M. E. Rourke
The Red Petticoat 1912

Oh, You Lady!
Music by George Gershwin
Lyrics by Brian Hooker
Our Nell 1922

Oh, You Major Scales
Music by Rudolf Friml
Lyrics by Bide Dudley and Otto Harbach
The Little Whopper 1919

Oh, You Wonderful Girl
Music and lyrics by George M. Cohan
The Little Millionaire 1911

Oh, You're a Wonderful Person
Music by Morgan Lewis
Lyrics by Nancy Hamilton
Three to Make Ready 1946

Ohhh! Ahhh!
Music by John Green
Lyrics by Edward Heyman
Here Goes the Bride 1931

Ohio
Music by Leonard Bernstein
Lyrics by Betty Comden and Adolph Green
Wonderful Town 1953

Ohrbach's, Bloomingdale's, Best and Saks
Music by André Previn
Lyrics by Alan Jay Lerner
Coco 1969

Oisgetzaychnet
Music and lyrics by Harold Rome
The Zulu and the Zayda 1965

O.K. for T.V.
Music and lyrics by Johnny Mercer
Top Banana 1951

O.K. Goodbye
Music and lyrics by James Rado
Rainbow (OB) 1972

O.K., Mr. Major
Music by Arthur Schwartz
Lyrics by Howard Dietz
A Bell for Adano (1956) TV

Okay for Sound
Music by Arthur Schwartz
Lyrics by Dorothy Fields
Stars in Your Eyes 1939

Oklahoma
Music by Richard Rodgers
Lyrics by Oscar Hammerstein II
Oklahoma! 1943

Ol' Man River
Music by Jerome Kern
Lyrics by Oscar Hammerstein II
Show Boat 1927

Ol' Pease Puddin'
Music by George Fischoff
Lyrics by Carole Bayer
Georgy 1970

Old Boy Neutral
Music by Jerome Kern
Lyrics by Schuyler Greene
Very Good Eddie 1915

An Old City Boy at Heart
Music by Richard Rodgers
Lyrics by Martin Charnin
I Remember Mama 1979

Dropped from production

The Old Clarinet
Music by Jerome Kern
Lyrics by Harry B. Smith
Oh, I Say! 1913

Old Deuteronomy
Music by Andrew Lloyd Webber
Cats 1982

Lyrics based on T.S. Eliot's *Old Possum's Book of Practical Cats*

Old Devil Moon
Music by Burton Lane
Lyrics by E.Y. Harburg
Finian's Rainbow 1947

The Old Dope Peddler
Music and lyrics by Tom Lehrer
Tomfoolery (OB) 1981

Old Enough to Love
Music by Richard Rodgers
Lyrics by Lorenz Hart
Dearest Enemy 1925

Old Enough to Love
Music by Arthur Schwartz
Lyrics by Dorothy Fields
By the Beautiful Sea 1954

Old Enough to Marry
Music by Maury Rubens
Lyrics by Clifford Grey
The Madcap 1928

Old Fashioned Cakewalk
Music and lyrics by George M. Cohan
Hello, Broadway 1914

The Old-Fashioned Cakewalk
Music and lyrics by Donald Heywood
Africana 1927

Old Fashioned Dances
Music by Jerome Kern
Lyrics by Anne Caldwell
Hitchy-Koo 1920

Old-Fashioned Garden
Music and lyrics by Cole Porter
Hitchy-Koo 1920

Old Fashioned Garden
Music by Victor Herbert
Lyrics by Gene Buck
Ziegfeld Follies of 1923

An Old-Fashioned Girl
Music by Richard Rodgers
Lyrics by Edith Meiser
The Garrick Gaieties (1st edition) 1925

An Old-Fashioned Girl
Music by Ray Henderson
Lyrics by B.G. DeSylva and Lew Brown
George White's Scandals (1928)

Old-Fashioned Girl
Music by Richard Lewine
Lyrics by Arnold B. Horwitt
The Girls Against the Boys 1959

Old Fashioned Girl
Music and lyrics by Rick Besoyan
Babes in the Wood (OB) 1964

An Old-Fashioned Glimmer in Your Eye
Music and lyrics by Jack Lawrence and Don Walker
Courtin' Time 1951

Old Fashioned Husband
Music and lyrics by Paul Nassau and Oscar Brand
The Education of H*y*m*a*n K*a*p*l*a*n 1968

Old Fashioned Love
Music and lyrics by James Johnson
and Cecil Mack
Runnin' Wild 1923

Old-Fashioned Mothers
Music by Sammy Fain
Lyrics by Dan Shapiro
Ankles Aweigh 1955

Old Fashioned Song
Music by Albert Hague
Lyrics by Allen Sherman
The Fig Leaves Are Falling 1969

Old-Fashioned Wedding
Music by Lewis E. Gensler
Lyrics by E.Y. Harburg
Ballyhoo 1932

An Old-Fashioned Wedding
Music and lyrics by Irving Berlin
Annie Get Your Gun (1966 revival)

For the revival Berlin added this show-stopping contrapuntal duet for Ethel Merman and Bruce Yarnell.

An Old-Fashioned Wife
Music by Jerome Kern
Lyrics by P.G. Wodehouse
Oh, Boy! 1917

An Old Flame Never Dies
Music by Arthur Schwartz
Lyrics by Albert Stillman and Laurence Stallings
Virginia 1937

Old Folks
Music by Jacques Brel
English lyrics by Eric Blau and Mort Shuman
Jacques Brel Is Alive and Well and Living in Paris (OB) 1968

Old Folks
Music by John Kander
Lyrics by Fred Ebb
70, Girls, 70 1971

Old Friend
Music by Nancy Ford
Lyrics by Gretchen Cryer
I'm Getting My Act Together and Taking It on the Road 1978

Old Friends
Music and lyrics by Stephen Sondheim
Merrily We Roll Along 1981

The Old Gumbie Cat
Music by Andrew Lloyd Webber
Cats 1982

Lyrics based on T.S. Eliot's *Old Possum's Book of Practical Cats*

Old Jitterbug
Music by Jimmy McHugh
Lyrics by Al Dubin
Keep Off the Grass 1940

Old John Barleycorn
Music by Sigmund Romberg
Lyrics by Dorothy Donnelly
My Maryland 1927

The Old Lake Trail
Music by Harry Tierney
Lyrics by Joseph McCarthy
Kid Boots 1923

Old Long John
Music by John Morris
Lyrics by Gerald Freedman
A Time for Singing 1966

Old Love and Brand New Love
Music by Don Walker
Lyrics by Clay Warnick
Memphis Bound 1945

Old Maid
Music by Harvey Schmidt
Lyrics by Tom Jones
110 in the Shade 1963

An Old Man
Music by Richard Rodgers
Lyrics by Martin Charnin
Two by Two 1970

Old Man
Music by Hank Beebe
Lyrics by Bill Heyer
Tuscaloosa's Calling Me But I'm Not Going! (OB) 1975

The Old Man
Music and lyrics by Randy Newman
Maybe I'm Doing It Wrong (1st edition) (OB) 1981

Old Man Danube
Music by Emmerich Kálmán
Lyrics by George Marion, Jr.
Marinka 1945

The Old Man in the Moon
Music by Jerome Kern
Lyrics by P.G. Wodehouse
Miss 1917

An Old Man Shouldn't Be Born
Music by Murray Rumshinsky
Lyrics by Jacob Jacobs
The President's Daughter 1970

Old Man Subway
Music by Robert Russell Bennett
Lyrics by Owen Murphy and Robert A. Simon
Hold Your Horses 1933

Old Man's Darling—Young Man's Slave
Music and lyrics by Irving Berlin
Louisiana Purchase 1940

Old Melodies
Music by Monte Carlo and Alma Sanders
Lyrics by Howard Johnson
Tangerine 1921

The Old Military Canal
Music and lyrics by David Heneker
Half a Sixpence 1965

Old New York
Music by Jerome Kern
Lyrics by Anne Caldwell
Hitchy-Koo 1920

The Old Park Bench
Music by Jimmy McHugh
Lyrics by Howard Dietz
Keep Off the Grass 1940

Old Sayin's
Music and lyrics by Marc Blitzstein
Juno 1959

The Old Soft Shoe
Music by Morgan Lewis
Lyrics by Nancy Hamilton
Three to Make Ready 1946

Old Songs
Music by Victor Herbert
Lyrics by Rida Johnson Young
The Dream Girl 1924

Old Spanish Custom
Music by Harry Revel
Lyrics by Mack Gordon
Smiling Faces 1932

Old Time Swing
Music by Eubie Blake
Lyrics by J. Milton Reddie and Cecil Mack
Swing It 1937

Old Timer
Music by Burton Lane
Lyrics by E.Y. Harburg
Hold On to Your Hats 1940

Old Times, Good Times
Music by Gary William Friedman
Lyrics by Will Holt
Platinum 1978

Old White Tom
Music and lyrics by C. Jackson and James Hatch
Fly Blackbird (OB) 1962

Old World Charm
Music by Duke Ellington
Lyrics by Marshall Barer and Fred Tobias
Pousse-Café 1966

The Oldest Established
Music and lyrics by Frank Loesser
Guys and Dolls 1950

The Oldest Trick in the World
Music and lyrics by Jay Thompson
Double Entry (OB) 1961

Ole Ole
Music by Frank Black
Lyrics by Gladys Shelley
The Duchess Misbehaves 1946

Ole Soft Core
Music and lyrics by Ronnie Britton
Greenwich Village Follies (OB) 1976

Olive Oil
Music by Frederic Norton
Lyrics by Oscar Asche
Chu Chin Chow 1917

The Olive Tree
Music and lyrics by Robert Wright
and George Forrest
Kismet 1953

Based on a theme from Borodin's *Prince Igor*

Oliver!
Music and lyrics by Lionel Bart
Oliver! 1963

The Olympics
Music by Jacques Offenbach (adapted by Robert
De Cormier)
Lyrics by E.Y. Harburg
The Happiest Girl in the World 1961

Olympics '36
Music by Monty Norman
Lyrics by Julian More
The Moony Shapiro Songbook 1981

Om Mani Padme Hum
Music by Harry Warren
Lyrics by Jerome Lawrence and Robert E. Lee
Shangri-La 1956

Omaha I'm Here
Music and lyrics by Al Carmines
The Evangelist (OB) 1982

The Omen Bird
Music by Heitor Villa-Lobos
Lyrics by Robert Wright and George Forrest
Magdalena 1948

On a Clear Day You Can See Forever
Music by Burton Lane
Lyrics by Alan Jay Lerner
On a Clear Day You Can See Forever 1965

On a Day Like This
Music and lyrics by Marc Blitzstein
Juno 1959

On a Desert Island With Thee
Music by Richard Rodgers
Lyrics by Lorenz Hart
A Connecticut Yankee 1927

On a Desert Island With You
Music by Jerome Kern
Lyrics by P. G. Wodehouse
Sitting Pretty 1924

On a Holiday
Music and lyrics by George M. Cohan
The Rise of Rosie O'Reilly 1923

On a Hundred Different Ships
Music and lyrics by George M. Cohan
The Man Who Owns Broadway 1909

On a Pony for Two
Music by James F. Hanley
Lyrics by Gene Buck
Take the Air 1927

On a Roof in Manhattan
Music and lyrics by Irving Berlin
Face the Music 1932

On a Sunday by the Sea
Music by Jule Styne
Lyrics by Sammy Cahn
High Button Shoes 1947

On Account of I Love You
Music by Philip Charig
Lyrics by James Dyrenforth
Nikki 1931

On and On and On
Music by George Gershwin
Lyrics by Ira Gershwin
Let 'Em Eat Cake 1933

On Any Street
Music by Ray Henderson
Lyrics by Lew Brown
Strike Me Pink 1933

On, Comrades
Music by Sigmund Romberg
Lyrics by Harry B. Smith
Princess Flavia 1925

On Cupid's Green
Music by Sigmund Romberg
Lyrics by Harold Atteridge
Sinbad (1918)

On Double Fifth Avenue
Music by Abel Baer
Lyrics by Sam Lewis and Joe Young
Lady Do 1927

On Fifth Avenue
Music and lyrics by Irving Berlin
Ziegfeld Follies of 1920

On It Goes
Music by Gerald Jay Markoe
Lyrics by Michael Colby
Charlotte Sweet (OB) 1982

On Leave for Love
Music and lyrics by Ann Ronell
Count Me In 1942

On Living
Music and lyrics by Elizabeth Swados
Nightclub Cantata (OB) 1977

On Love Alone
Music by Johann Strauss
Lyrics by Desmond Carter
The Great Waltz 1934

On My Mind a New Love
Music by Joseph Meyer and Roger Wolfe Kahn
Lyrics by Irving Caesar
Here's Howe 1928

On My Mind the Whole Night Long
Music by George Gershwin
Lyrics by Arthur Jackson
George White's Scandals (1920)

On My Nude Ranch With You
Music by Michael H. Cleary
Lyrics by Max and Nathaniel Lief
Hey Nonny Nonny! 1932

On My Own
Music by Jule Styne
Lyrics by Betty Comden and Adolph Green
Bells Are Ringing 1956

On My Own
Music by Nancy Ford
Lyrics by Gretchen Cryer
Now Is the Time for All Good Men (OB) 1967

On My Own
Music by Robert Kole
Lyrics by Sandi Merle
I Take These Women (OB) 1982

On, On, On
Music by Peter Link
Lyrics by Michael Cacoyannis
Lysistrata 1972

On Parade
Music by Victor Herbert
Lyrics by Robert B. Smith
Sweethearts 1913

On Parade
Music by Jerome Moross
Lyrics by Paul Peters and George Sklar
Parade 1935

On Revient de Chantilly
Music by Lionel Monckton
Lyrics by Adrian Ross
The Quaker Girl 1911

On Ten Square Miles by the Potomac River
Music by Leonard Bernstein
Lyrics by Alan Jay Lerner
1600 Pennsylvania Avenue 1976

On That Day
Music and lyrics by Robert Wright and George Forrest (based on Rachmaninoff)
Anya 1965

On the Atchison, Topeka and the Santa Fe
Music by Harry Warren
Lyrics by Johnny Mercer
The Harvey Girls (1946) F

Academy Award winner

On the Avenue
Music and lyrics by Irving Berlin
On the Avenue (1937) F

Dropped from film

On the Balcony of the Casa Rosada
Music by Andrew Lloyd Webber
Lyrics by Tim Rice
Evita 1979

On the Banks of the Bronx
Music by Victor Jacobi
Lyrics by William LeBaron
Apple Blossoms 1919

On the Beach
Music by Robert Hood Bowers
Lyrics by Francis DeWitt
Oh, Ernest! 1927

(On the Beach at) How've-You-Been
Music by George Gershwin
Lyrics by B.G. DeSylva
George White's Scandals (1923)

On the Beach at Narragansett
Music by Gustave Kerker
Lyrics by Hugh Morton
The Belle of New York 1897

On the Beam
Music by Jerome Kern
Lyrics by Johnny Mercer
You Were Never Lovelier (1942) F

On the Border Line
Music by Harry Ruby
Lyrics by Bert Kalmar
Top Speed 1929

On the Brim of Her Old-Fashioned Bonnet
Music by George Gershwin
Lyrics by E. Ray Goetz
Snapshots of 1921

On the Campus
Music by Ray Henderson
Lyrics by B.G. DeSylva and Lew Brown
Good News 1927

On the Corner of the Rue Cambon
Music by André Previn
Lyrics by Alan Jay Lerner
Coco 1969

On the Day When the World Goes Boom
Music and lyrics by John Dooley
Hobo (OB) 1961

On the Farm
Music and lyrics by Bob Merrill
New Girl in Town 1957

On the Golden Trail
Music by Vincent Youmans
Lyrics by Oscar Hammerstein II
Rainbow 1928

On the Ground at Last
Music by Mel Marvin
Lyrics by Robert Montgomery
Green Pond (OB) 1977

On the Levee
Music by Johnson
Lyrics by Henry Creamer
Keep Shufflin' 1928

On the Other Hand
Music by Martha Caples
Lyrics by Nancy Hamilton
New Faces of 1934

On the Relative Merits of Education and Experience
Music by Paul Hoffert
Lyrics by David Secter
Get Thee to Canterbury (OB) 1969

On the Right Track
Music and lyrics by Stephen Schwartz
Pippin 1972

On the Riviera
Music by Victor Herbert
Lyrics by B.G. DeSylva
Orange Blossoms 1922

On the Road
Music by Ronald Melrose
Lyrics by Bill Russell
Fourtune (OB) 1980

On the Shore at Le Lei Wi
Music by Henry Kailimai and Jerome Kern
Lyrics by Herbert Reynolds
Very Good Eddie 1915

On the Side of the Angels
Music by Jerry Bock
Lyrics by Sheldon Harnick
Fiorello! 1959

On the S.S. Bernard Cohn
Music by Burton Lane
Lyrics by Alan Jay Lerner
On a Clear Day You Can See Forever 1965

On the Stage
Music by Carl Millöcker (revised by Theo Mackeben)
Lyrics by Rowland Leigh
The Dubarry 1932

On the Street Where You Live
Music by Frederick Loewe
Lyrics by Alan Jay Lerner
My Fair Lady 1956

On the Sunny Side of the Street
Music by Jimmy McHugh
Lyrics by Dorothy Fields
Lew Leslie's International Revue 1930

On the Track
Music by Heinrich Reinhardt
Lyrics by Robert B. Smith
The Spring Maid 1910

On the Twentieth Century
Music by Cy Coleman
Lyrics by Betty Comden and Adolph Green
On the Twentieth Century 1978

On the Willows
Music and lyrics by Stephen Schwartz
Godspell (OB) 1971

On the Winning Side
Music by Bob James
Lyrics by Jack O'Brien
The Selling of the President 1972

On the Wrong Side of the Railroad Tracks
Music by Duke Ellington
Lyrics by John Latouche
Beggar's Holiday 1946

On This Night of a Thousand Stars
Music by Andrew Lloyd Webber
Lyrics by Tim Rice
Evita 1979

On This Rock
Music by Helen Miller
Lyrics by Eve Merriam
Inner City 1971

On This Wedding Day
Music by Albert Hague
Lyrics by Marty Brill
Café Crown 1964

On to Africa!
Music by Sigmund Romberg
Lyrics by Irving Caesar
Melody 1933

On to Hollywood
Music by James F. Hanley
Lyrics by Eddie Dowling
Honeymoon Lane 1926

On Top
Music by Werner Janssen
Lyrics by Mann Holiner and J. Keirn Brennan
Boom-Boom 1929

On Top of the World
Music by Charles Strouse
Lyrics by Alan Jay Lerner
Dance a Little Closer 1983

On Trial for My Life
Music and lyrics by Gene Curty, Nitra Scharfman
and Chuck Strand
The Lieutenant 1975

On With the Dance
Music by Jerome Kern
Lyrics by Clifford Grey
Sally 1920

On With the Dance
Music by Richard Rodgers
Lyrics by Lorenz Hart
The Garrick Gaieties (1st edition) 1925

On With the Dance
Music by Philip Charig
Lyrics by Irving Caesar
Polly 1929

On With the Dance
Music by Richard Rodgers
Lyrics by Lorenz Hart
Simple Simon 1930

On With the Game
Music by Harry Tierney
Lyrics by Joseph McCarthy
Kid Boots 1923

On With the Show
Music by Frederico Valerio
Lyrics by Elizabeth Miele
Hit the Trail 1954

On Your Toes
Music by Richard Rodgers
Lyrics by Lorenz Hart
On Your Toes 1936

Once
Music by George Gershwin
Lyrics by B.G. DeSylva and Ira Gershwin
Tell Me More 1925

Dropped from production. Later used in *Funny Face* (1927).

Once a Year Day
Music and lyrics by Richard Adler and Jerry Ross
The Pajama Game 1954

Once in a Blue Moon
Music by Jerome Kern
Lyrics by Anne Caldwell
Stepping Stones 1923

Once in a Blue Moon
Music and lyrics by Rick Besoyan
Little Mary Sunshine (OB) 1959

Once in a Lifetime
Music by Jesse Greer
Lyrics by Raymond Klages
Earl Carroll's Vanities (1928)

Once in a Lifetime
Music and lyrics by Leslie Bricusse
and Anthony Newley
Stop the World—I Want to Get Off 1962

Once in a Million Moons
Music by Jerome Kern
Lyrics by E. Y. Harburg
Can't Help Singing (1944) F

Dropped from film

Once-in-a-While
Music by Arthur Schwartz
Lyrics by Howard Dietz
Revenge With Music 1934

Once in a While
Music and lyrics by Richard O'Brien
The Rocky Horror Show 1975

Once in Love With Amy
Music and lyrics by Frank Loesser
Where's Charley? 1948

Once in September
Music by Armand Vecsey
Lyrics by Clifford Grey
The Nightingale 1927

Once in the Highlands
Music by Frederick Loewe
Lyrics by Alan Jay Lerner
Brigadoon 1947

Once in 2.7 Years
Music by Ernest Gold
Lyrics by Anne Croswell
I'm Solomon 1968

Once Knew a Fella
Music and lyrics by Harold Rome
Destry Rides Again 1959

Once, Only Once
Music by James Bredt
Lyrics by Edward Eager
The Happy Hypocrite (OB) 1968

Once the Man You Laughed At
Music by Michael Leonard
Lyrics by Herbert Martin
How to Be a Jewish Mother 1967

Once Upon a Long Ago
Music by Arthur Schwartz
Lyrics by Maxwell Anderson
High Tor 1956 TV

Once Upon a Time
Music by Harold Levey
Lyrics by Zelda Sears
The Clinging Vine 1922

Once Upon a Time
Music by Morgan Lewis
Lyrics by Nancy Hamilton
One for the Money 1939

Once Upon a Time
Music by Franz Steininger (adapted from
Tchaikovsky)
Lyrics by Forman Brown
Music in My Heart 1947

Once Upon a Time
Music by Sol Berkowitz
Lyrics by James Lipton
Miss Emily Adam (OB) 1960

Once Upon a Time
Music by Charles Strouse
Lyrics by Lee Adams
All American 1962

Once Upon a Time
Music and lyrics by Johnny Brandon
Cindy (OB) 1964

Once Upon a Time
Music and lyrics by Elizabeth Swados
Runaways 1978

Once Upon a Time Today
Music and lyrics by Irving Berlin
Call Me Madam 1950

Once Upon the Natchez Trace
Music by Robert Waldman
Lyrics by Alfred Uhry
The Robber Bridegroom 1975

Once You've Had a Little Taste
Music by John Clifton
Lyrics by John Clifton and Ben Tarver
Man With a Load of Mischief (OB) 1966

Once You've Seen Everything
Music by Al Carmines
Lyrics by Rosalyn Drexler
Home Movies (OB) 1964

One
Music by Franz Lehár
Lyrics by Edward Eliscu
Frederika 1937

One
Music by Marvin Hamlisch
Lyrics by Edward Kleban
A Chorus Line 1975

One Alone
Music by Sigmund Romberg
Lyrics by Otto Harbach and Oscar Hammerstein II
The Desert Song 1926

One Baby
Music by Charles Rosoff
Lyrics by Leo Robin
Judy 1927

One Beating a Day
Music by Paul Horner
Lyrics by Peggy Lee
Peg 1983

One Big Happy Family
Music by Kenneth Jacobson
Lyrics by Rhoda Roberts
Show Me Where the Good Times Are (OB) 1970

One Big Happy Family
Music and lyrics by Jill Williams
Rainbow Jones 1974

One Big Union for Two
Music and lyrics by Harold Rome
Pins and Needles (OB) 1937

One Boy
Music by Charles Strouse
Lyrics by Lee Adams
Bye Bye Birdie 1960

One Boy's Enough for Me
Music by Harold Orlob
Lyrics by Irving Caesar
Talk About Girls 1927

One Brick at a Time
Music by Cy Coleman
Lyrics by Michael Stewart
Barnum 1980

One Brief Moment
Music by Arthur Schwartz
Lyrics by Dorothy Fields
Stars in Your Eyes 1939

One by One
Music by Billy Goldenberg
Lyrics by Alan and Marilyn Bergman
Ballroom 1978

One Cell
Music and lyrics by Ann Harris
Sky High (OB) 1979

One Day, One Day, Congotay
Music by Coleridge-Taylor Perkinson
Lyrics by Errol Hill
Man Better Man (OB) 1969

One Day We Dance
Music by Cy Coleman
Lyrics by Carolyn Leigh
Wildcat 1960

One Extraordinary Thing
Music and lyrics by Jerry Herman
The Grand Tour 1979

One Flag
Music by Walt Smith
Lyrics by Leon Uris
Ari 1971

One Flower Grows Alone in Your Garden
Music by Sigmund Romberg
Lyrics by Otto Harbach and Oscar Hammerstein II
The Desert Song 1926

One Foot, Other Foot
Music by Richard Rodgers
Lyrics by Oscar Hammerstein II
Allegro 1947

One for All
Music by Albert Sirmay and Arthur Schwartz
Lyrics by Arthur Swanstrom
Princess Charming 1930

One for My Baby (And One More for the Road)
Music by Harold Arlen
Lyrics by Johnny Mercer
The Sky's the Limit (1943) F

One Girl
Music and lyrics by Irving Berlin
Music Box Revue (3rd edition) 1923

The One Girl
Music by Vincent Youmans
Lyrics by Oscar Hammerstein II
Rainbow 1928

One Golden Hour
Music by Rudolf Friml
Lyrics by Otto Harbach and Oscar Hammerstein II
The Wild Rose 1926

One Good Friend
Music by Frank Grey
Lyrics by Earle Crooker and McElbert Moore
Happy 1927

One Good Man Gone Wrong
Music by Sigmund Romberg
Lyrics by Otto Harbach and Oscar Hammerstein II
The Desert Song 1926

One Hallowe'en
Music by Charles Strouse
Lyrics by Lee Adams
Applause 1970

One Hand, One Heart
Music by Leonard Bernstein
Lyrics by Stephen Sondheim
West Side Story 1957

One Heart
Music by Sam H. Stept
Lyrics by Bud Green
Shady Lady 1933

One Hour Ahead of the Posse
Music by Philip Charig
Lyrics by Ray Golden and Dave Ormont
Catch a Star! 1955

One Hundred and Fifteen
Music and lyrics by Melvin Van Peebles
Waltz of the Stork (OB) 1982

One Hundred Easy Ways
Music by Leonard Bernstein
Lyrics by Betty Comden and Adolph Green
Wonderful Town 1953

The One I'm Looking For
Music by Emmerich Kálmán
Lyrics by Harry B. Smith
Countess Maritza 1926

One in a Million
Music by Harry Revel
Lyrics by Mack Gordon
Everybody's Welcome 1931

One in a Million
Music by Harden Church
Lyrics by Edward Heyman
Caviar 1934

One in a Million
Music by Arthur Schwartz
Lyrics by Oscar Hammerstein II
American Jubilee 1940

One in a Million
Music and lyrics by Bill and Patti Jacob
Jimmy 1969

The One Indispensable Man
Music by Kurt Weill
Lyrics by Maxwell Anderson
Knickerbocker Holiday 1938

One Is a Lonely Number
Music by Albert Hague
Lyrics by Maurice Valency
Dance Me a Song 1950

One Is a Lonely Number
Music by Fred Stamer
Lyrics by Gen Genovese
Buttrio Square 1952

One Kind Word
Music and lyrics by Marc Blitzstein
Juno 1959

One Kiss
Music by Sigmund Romberg
Lyrics by Oscar Hammerstein II
The New Moon 1928

One Kiss
Music by Diane Leslie
Lyrics by William Gleason
The Coolest Cat in Town (OB) 1978

One Last Kiss
Music by Charles Strouse
Lyrics by Lee Adams
Bye Bye Birdie 1960

One Last Love Song
Music by Emmerich Kálmán
Lyrics by George Marion, Jr.
Marinka 1945

One Life to Live
Music by Kurt Weill
Lyrics by Ira Gershwin
Lady in the Dark 1941

One Little Brick at a Time
Music by Jule Styne
Lyrics by Sammy Cahn
Look to the Lilies 1970

One Little Girl
Music by Tom Johnstone
Lyrics by Phil Cook
When You Smile 1925

One Little World Apart
Music by Milton Schafer
Lyrics by Ronny Graham
Bravo Giovanni 1962

One Little Year
Music by Larry Grossman
Lyrics by Hal Hackady
Goodtime Charley 1975

One Long Last Look
Music by Sammy Fain
Lyrics by Marilyn and Alan Bergman
Something More 1964

One Love
Music by Vincent Youmans
Lyrics by Billy Rose and Edward Eliscu
Great Day! 1929

Dropped from production

One Love
Music by Harold Arlen
Lyrics by Ted Koehler
Earl Carroll's Vanities (1930)

One Man
Music by George Gershwin
Lyrics by Gus Kahn and Ira Gershwin
Show Girl 1929

One Man
Music by Lance Mulcahy
Lyrics by Paul Cherry
Park 1970

One Man
Music by Helen Miller
Lyrics by Eve Merriam
Inner City 1971

One Man
Music and lyrics by Al Kasha and Joel Hirschorn
Seven Brides for Seven Brothers 1982

One Man Ain't Quite Enough
Music by Harold Arlen
Lyrics by Harold Arlen and Truman Capote
House of Flowers 1954

The One Man I Need
Music by Robert Stolz
Lyrics by Rowland Leigh
Night of Love 1941

One Man's Death Is Another Man's Living
Music by Kurt Weill
Lyrics by Ira Gershwin
The Firebrand of Florence 1945

One Misty, Moisty Morning
Music by Helen Miller
Lyrics by Eve Merriam
Inner City 1971

One Moment Alone
Music by Jerome Kern
Lyrics by Otto Harbach
The Cat and the Fiddle 1931

One More Angel in Heaven
Music by Andrew Lloyd Webber
Lyrics by Tim Rice
*Joseph and the Amazing
Technicolor Dreamcoat* 1982

One More Dance
Music by Jerome Kern
Lyrics by Oscar Hammerstein II
Music in the Air 1932

Has the same melody as "Night Flies By" from the
same show.

One More Day
Music by Sol Kaplan
Lyrics by Edward Eliscu
The Banker's Daughter (OB) 1962

One More for the Last One
Music and lyrics by Stan Freeman
and Franklin Underwood
Lovely Ladies, Kind Gentlemen 1970

One More Kiss
Music and lyrics by Stephen Sondheim
Follies 1971

One More Time
Music and lyrics by Michael Brown
Different Times 1972

One More Tomorrow
Music and lyrics by Harry Chapin
Cotton Patch Gospel (OB) 1981

One More Walk Around the Garden
Music by Burton Lane
Lyrics by Alan Jay Lerner
Carmelina 1979

One Mother Each
Music by Moose Charlap
Lyrics by Norman Gimbel
The Conquering Hero 1961

One Night
Music by H. Maurice Jacquet
Lyrics by Preston Sturges
The Well of Romance 1930

One Night in the Rain
Music by Alma Sanders
Lyrics by Monte Carlo
Mystery Moon 1930

One Night of Love
Music by Maury Rubens
Lyrics by J. Keirn Brennan
A Night in Venice 1929

One Night Only
Music by Henry Krieger
Lyrics by Tom Eyen
Dreamgirls 1981

One of a Kind
Music by Charles Strouse
Lyrics by Lee Adams
Applause 1970

One of the Boys
Music by John Kander
Lyrics by Fred Ebb
Woman of the Year 1981

One of These Fine Days
Music and lyrics by Harold Rome
Sing Out the News 1938

One of Those Days
Music and lyrics by Billy Barnes
The Billy Barnes Revue 1959

One of Those Moments
Music by Elmer Bernstein
Lyrics by Carolyn Leigh
How Now, Dow Jones 1967

One of Us
Music and lyrics by Peter Copani
New York City Street Show (OB) 1977

One of Us Should Be Two
Music by Richard Rodgers
Lyrics by Lorenz Hart
Betsy 1926

One Perfect Moment
Music and lyrics by Marshall Barer, Dean Fuller
and Leslie Julian-Jones
New Faces of 1956

One Person
Music and lyrics by Jerry Herman
Dear World 1969

One Promise
Music by Michael Leonard
Lyrics by Herbert Martin
The Yearling 1965

One Room
Music by Jerry Bock
Lyrics by Sheldon Harnick
The Rothschilds 1970

One Second of Sex
Music by John Green
Lyrics by Edward Heyman
Here Goes the Bride 1931

One Side of World
Music and lyrics by Stan Freeman
and Franklin Underwood
Lovely Ladies, Kind Gentlemen 1970

One Step
Music by David Shire
Lyrics by Richard Maltby, Jr.
Starting Here, Starting Now (OB) 1977

One Step Away
Music and lyrics by Gary Portnoy
and Judy Hart Angelo
Preppies (OB) 1983

One Step Into Love
Music by Sigmund Romberg
Lyrics by Herbert Reynolds
The Blue Paradise 1915

One Step Nearer the Moon
Music by Joseph Meyer
Lyrics by William Moll
Jonica 1930

One Step to Heaven
Music by Jesse Greer
Lyrics by Raymond Klages
Say When 1928

One Step–Two Step
Music by Harold Arlen
Lyrics by Johnny Mercer
Saratoga 1959

One Sunny Day
Music by Jean Schwartz
Lyrics by Clifford Grey and William Cary Duncan
Sunny Days 1928

One Sweet Moment
Music and lyrics by Deed Meyer
She Shall Have Music (OB) 1959

1001
Music and lyrics by Peter Link and C.C. Courtney
Salvation (OB) 1969

One Touch of Alchemy
Music by Kurt Weill
Lyrics by Maxwell Anderson
Knickerbocker Holiday 1938

One Touch of Venus
Music by Kurt Weill
Lyrics by Ogden Nash
One Touch of Venus 1943

One Touch of Vienna
Music by Emmerich Kálmán
Lyrics by George Marion, Jr.
Marinka 1945

One Track Mind
Music by Morton Gould
Lyrics by Betty Comden and Adolph Green
Billion Dollar Baby 1945

One, Two
Music by Helen Miller
Lyrics by Eve Merriam
Inner City 1971

One, Two, Three
Music by Jerome Kern
Lyrics by Herbert Reynolds
Rock-a-Bye Baby 1918

One, Two, Three
Music by George Gershwin
Lyrics by Ira Gershwin
The Shocking Miss Pilgrim (1947) F

Adapted by Kay Swift and Ira Gershwin from the
manuscripts of George Gershwin.

One! Two! Three!
Music by Sonny Burke
Lyrics by Paul Francis Webster and Ray Golden
Alive and Kicking 1950

One, Two, Three
Music by Coleridge-Taylor Perkinson
Lyrics by Errol Hill
Man Better Man (OB) 1969

One Two Three
Music by Rob Fremont
Lyrics by Doris Willens
Piano Bar (OB) 1978

One Way Street
Music by Walter Donaldson
Lyrics by Ballard MacDonald
Sweetheart Time 1926

One Way Ticket to Hell
Music by Garry Sherman
Lyrics by Peter Udell
Comin' Uptown 1979

One Who Will Understand
Music by Rudolf Friml
Lyrics by Otto Harbach
Katinka 1915

One Wife
Music and lyrics by Richard Adler
Kwamina 1961

One Word From You
Music by Victor Herbert
Lyrics by Harry B. Smith
The Enchantress 1911

One Word Led to Another
Music by Hal Borne
Lyrics by Ray Golden
Alive and Kicking 1950

The One You Love
Music by Frank Grey
Lyrics by McElbert Moore and Frank Grey
The Matinee Girl 1926

Ongsay and Anceday
Music by Richard Rodgers
Lyrics by Lorenz Hart
Heads Up! 1929

Onh-Honh-Honh!
Music and lyrics by Matt Dubey and Dean Fuller
Smith (OB) 1973

Only a Day Dream
Music and lyrics by Walter Cool
Mackey of Appalachia (OB) 1965

Only a Dream
Music by Edward Künneke
Lyrics by Harry B. Smith
The Love Song 1925

Only a Kiss
Music by Herbert Stothart
Lyrics by Oscar Hammerstein II and Otto Harbach
Rose Marie 1924

Only a Man
Music and lyrics by Howard Blankman
By Hex (OB) 1956

Only a Passing Phase
Music and lyrics by Sandy Wilson
Valmouth (OB) 1960

Only a Rose
Music by Rudolf Friml
Lyrics by Brian Hooker
The Vagabond King 1925

Only a Smile
Music by Jean Gilbert
Lyrics by Harry B. Smith
The Red Robe 1928

Only Another Boy and Girl
Music and lyrics by Cole Porter
Seven Lively Arts 1944

The Only Boy
Music by Harold Orlob
Lyrics by Irving Caesar
Talk About Girls 1927

The Only Dance I Know
Music and lyrics by Irving Berlin
Mr. President 1962

Only for Americans
Music and lyrics by Irving Berlin
Miss Liberty 1949

The Only Game That I Would Play
Music by H. Maurice Jacquet
Lyrics by William Brady
The Silver Swan 1929

The Only Home I Know
Music by Gary Geld
Lyrics by Peter Udell
Shenandoah 1975

Only if You're in Love
Music and lyrics by Johnny Mercer
Top Banana 1951

Only in the Play
Music by Victor Herbert
Lyrics by Harry B. Smith
The Fortune Teller 1898

Only Love
Music and lyrics by Jerry Herman
Madame Aphrodite (OB) 1961

Only Love
Music by John Kander
Lyrics by Fred Ebb
Zorba 1968

Only Love
Music and lyrics by Ron Eliran
Don't Step on My Olive Branch (OB) 1976

The Only Man for the Job
Music and lyrics by Jill Williams
Rainbow Jones 1974

Only More!
Music and lyrics by Lionel Bart
La Strada 1969

Only One
Music by Sigmund Romberg
Lyrics by Harry B. Smith
Princess Flavia 1925

Only One
Music by Frank Grey
Lyrics by McElbert Moore and Frank Grey
The Matinee Girl 1926

The Only One
Music by Johann Strauss II, adapted by Oscar
Straus
Lyrics by Clare Kummer
Three Waltzes 1937

The Only One
Music by Lee Pockriss
Lyrics by Anne Croswell
Tovarich 1963

The Only One for Me
Music by Lewis E. Gensler
Lyrics by B.G. DeSylva
Captain Jinks 1925

The Only One for Me
Music by Harry Akst
Lyrics by Benny Davis
Artists and Models 1927

Only One Love Ever Fills My Heart
Music by Sigmund Romberg
Lyrics by Dorothy Donnelly
Blossom Time 1921

Only One of Anything
Music by Victor Herbert
Lyrics by Glen MacDonough
Algeria 1908

The Only Place for Me
Music and lyrics by Mel Mandel and Norman Sachs
My Old Friends (OB) 1979

Only Rainbows
Music by Moose Charlap
Lyrics by Norman Gimbel
The Conquering Hero 1961

Only Right Here in New York City
Music by Hank Beebe
Lyrics by Bill Heyer
*Tuscaloosa's Calling Me
But I'm Not Going!* (OB) 1975

Only Time Will Tell
Music and lyrics by Harold Rome
Destry Rides Again 1959

Only to You
Music and lyrics by Paul Rubens
The Girl From Utah 1914

Only With You
Music and lyrics by Maury Yeston
Nine 1982

Only You
Music by Tom Johnstone
Lyrics by Will B. Johnstone
I'll Say She Is 1924

Oo, How I Love to Be Loved by You
Music by George Gershwin
Lyrics by Lou Paley
La, La, Lucille 1919

Also in *Ed Wynn's Carnival* (1920)

Oo, How I Love You
Music by Harold Orlob
Lyrics by Irving Caesar
Talk About Girls 1927

Oo-la-la
Music by Oscar Straus
Lyrics by Edward Delaney Dunn
The Last Waltz 1921

Oo-Ooo-Oo
Music by Jerome Kern
Lyrics by Paul West
The Red Petticoat 1912

The Oof Dah Man
Music by C. Luckey Roberts
Lyrics by Alex C. Rogers
My Magnolia 1926

Ooh, Do You Love You!
Music by Charles Strouse
Lyrics by Lee Adams
It's a Bird, It's a Plane, It's Superman 1966

Ooh, I'm Thinking
Music by Ray Henderson
Lyrics by Lew Brown
Strike Me Pink 1933

Ooh, Maybe It's You
Music and lyrics by Irving Berlin
Ziegfeld Follies (1927)

Ooh, My Feet
Music and lyrics by Frank Loesser
The Most Happy Fella 1956

Ooh, Ooh, Ooh, What You Do to Me
Music by Walter Kent
Lyrics by Kim Gannon
Seventeen 1951

Ooh! That Kiss
Music by Harry Warren
Lyrics by Mort Dixon and Joe Young
The Laugh Parade 1931

Ooh! What You Said
Music by Hoagy Carmichael
Lyrics by Johnny Mercer
Walk With Music 1940

Oom-Pah-Pah
Music and lyrics by Lionel Bart
Oliver! 1963

OOOO-EEEE
Music and lyrics by Paul Nassau and Oscar Brand
The Education of H*y*m*a*n K*a*p*l*a*n 1968

'Op in the 'Ansom
Music and lyrics by George M. Cohan
Little Johnny Jones 1904

Opec Maiden
Music by Michael Valenti
Lyrics by Donald Driver
Oh, Brother 1981

Open a New Window
Music and lyrics by Jerry Herman
Mame 1966

Open and Shut Idea
Music by Emile Berté and Maury Rubens
Lyrics by J. Keirn Brennan
Music in May 1929

Open Book
Music by Joseph Meyer
Lyrics by Edward Eliscu
Lady Fingers 1929

Open That Door
Music and lyrics by J.C. Johnson
Change Your Luck 1930

Open the Gates of Madrid
Music by Morris Hamilton
Lyrics by Grace Henry
Earl Carroll's Vanities 1926

Open the Window
Music by Norman Campbell
Lyrics by Donald Harron and Norman Campbell
Anne of Green Gables (OB) 1971

Open Up Your Heart
Music by Vincent Youmans
Lyrics by Billy Rose and Edward Eliscu
Great Day! 1929

Open Your Eyes
Music by Burton Lane
Lyrics by Alan Jay Lerner
Royal Wedding (1951) F

Open Your Heart
Music and lyrics by James Johnson and Cecil Mack
Runnin' Wild 1923

Open Your Window
Music by Emile Berté and Maury Rubens
Lyrics by J. Keirn Brennan
Music in May 1929

Opening Doors
Music and lyrics by Stephen Sondheim
Merrily We Roll Along 1981

An Opening for a Princess
Music by Mary Rodgers
Lyrics by Marshall Barer
Once Upon a Mattress 1959

An Opening for Everybody
Music by Jay Gorney
Lyrics by Jean and Walter Kerr
Touch and Go 1949

Opening Night
Music by Lee Wainer
Lyrics by Robert Sour
Sing for Your Supper 1939

The Opera Ain't Over
Music by Bob Brush
Lyrics by Martin Charnin
The First 1981

Opium Song
Music and lyrics by Ann Harris
Sky High (OB) 1979

Opportunity!
Music by Gordon Duffy
Lyrics by Harry M. Haldane
Happy Town 1959

Opportunity Knocks But Once
Music and lyrics by Cole Porter
Aladdin (1958) TV

The Opposite Sex
Music by Michael Cleary
Lyrics by Arthur Swanstrom
Sea Legs 1937

Opposites
Music by Jimmy Van Heusen
Lyrics by Sammy Cahn
Skyscraper 1965

Or Thereabouts
Music by Hugo Felix
Lyrics by Adrian Ross
The Quaker Girl 1911

Or What Have You?
Music by Morris Hamilton
Lyrics by Grace Henry
The Little Show (1st edition) 1929

Orange Blossom Home
Music by Raymond Hubbell
Lyrics by Anne Caldwell
Three Cheers 1928

Orange Blossoms
Music by Jean Schwartz
Lyrics by Clifford Grey and William Cary Duncan
Sunny Days 1928

An Orange Grove in California
Music and lyrics by Irving Berlin
Music Box Revue (3rd edition) 1923

Oranges
Music by Milton Susskind
Lyrics by Paul Porter and Benjamin Hapgood Burt
Florida Girl 1925

Orchids
Music and lyrics by Donald Heywood
Black Rhythm 1936

Orchids In the Moonlight
Music by Vincent Youmans
Lyrics by Edward Eliscu and Gus Kahn
Flying Down to Rio (1933) F

An Ordinary Couple
Music by Richard Rodgers
Lyrics by Oscar Hammerstein II
The Sound of Music 1959

Ordinary Guy
Music and lyrics by Harold Rome
Sing Out the News 1938

Ordinary People
Music and lyrics by Richard Adler
Kwamina 1961

Ordinary Things
Music and lyrics by Al Carmines
The Faggot (OB) 1973

Ore From a Gold Mine
Music by Duke Ellington
Lyrics by John Latouche
Beggar's Holiday 1946

Orienta
Music by Vincent Youmans and Paul Lannin
Lyrics by Arthur Francis
Two Little Girls in Blue 1921

Oriental Blues
Music and lyrics by Noble Sissle and Eubie Blake
Shuffle Along 1921

Oriental Memories
Music by Alfred Goodman, Maury Rubens
and J. Fred Coots
Lyrics by Clifford Grey
Artists and Models 1925

Oriental Moon
Music by Jerome Kern
Lyrics by Oscar Hammerstein II
Sweet Adeline 1929

Oriental Nights
Music by Mann Holiner
Lyrics by Alberta Nichols
Gay Paree 1926

Original Sin
Music by Don McAfee
Lyrics by Nancy Leeds
Great Scot! (OB) 1965

An Orphan, I Am
Music by Galt MacDermot
Lyrics by William Dumaresq
The Human Comedy (OB) 1983

Orphan in the Storm
Music by Harvey Schmidt
Lyrics by Tom Jones
Celebration 1969

An Orphan Is the Girl for Me
Music by Vincent Youmans
Lyrics by Zelda Sears
Lollipop 1924

An Orthodox Fool
Music and lyrics by Richard Rodgers
No Strings 1962

Ostende Nobis Tosca
Music by Mel Marvin
Lyrics by Christopher Durang
A History of the American Film 1978

The Other Fellow
Music by Karl Hoschna
Lyrics by Otto Harbach
Madame Sherry 1910

The Other Fellow's Girl
Music by Percy Wenrich
Lyrics by Raymond Peck
Castles in the Air 1926

The Other Generation
Music by Richard Rodgers
Lyrics by Oscar Hammerstein II
Flower Drum Song 1958

The Other Half of Me
Music and lyrics by Jack Lawrence
and Stan Freeman
I Had a Ball 1964

Other Hands, Other Hearts
Music and lyrics by Harold Rome
Fanny 1954

The Other One
Music by Arthur Siegel
Lyrics by June Carroll
New Faces of 1962

The Other Part of Me
Music by Paul Horner
Lyrics by Peggy Lee
Peg 1983

Other People
Music and lyrics by Tom Savage
Musical Chairs 1980

Other People's Houses
Music by Patrick Rose
Lyrics by Merv Campone and Richard Ouzounian
A Bistro Car on the CNR (OB) 1978

The Other Side of the Sky
Music by Galt MacDermot
Lyrics by Christopher Gore
Via Galactica 1972

The Other Side of the Tracks
Music by Cy Coleman
Lyrics by Carolyn Leigh
Little Me 1962

The Other Side of the Wall
Music and lyrics by Bruce Montgomery
The Amorous Flea (OB) 1964

Oui, Oui
Music by Alberta Nichols
Lyrics by Mann Holiner
Angela 1928

Our Ancestors
Music by Sigmund Romberg
Lyrics by Harold Atteridge
Sinbad (1918)

Our Ancient Liberties
Music by Kurt Weill
Lyrics by Maxwell Anderson
Knickerbocker Holiday 1938

Our Bridal Night
Music by Sigmund Romberg
Lyrics by Dorothy Donnelly
My Princess 1927

Our Castle in Spain
Music by Victor Herbert
Lyrics by Glen MacDonough
Babes in Toyland 1903

Our Child
Music by C. Luckey Roberts
Lyrics by Alex C. Rogers
My Magnolia 1926

Our Children
Music by Charles Strouse
Lyrics by Lee Adams
All American 1962

Our City of Dreams
Music by Louis A. Hirsch
Lyrics by P.G. Wodehouse
Oh, My Dear! 1918

Our Crown
Music and lyrics by Cole Porter
Jubilee 1935

Our Farm
Music by Ivan Caryll
Lyrics by Lionel Monckton
Our Miss Gibbs 1910

Our First Kiss
Music by Sammy Fain
Lyrics by Jack Yellen
George White's Scandals 1939

Our Floral Queen
Music by Gustav Luders
Lyrics by Frank Pixley
The Prince of Pilsen 1903

Our Heroes Come
Music by Oscar Straus
Lyrics by Stanislaus Stange
The Chocolate Soldier 1909

Our Home
Music by Richard Lewine
Lyrics by Ted Fetter
The Girl From Wyoming (OB) 1938

Our Home Town
Music and lyrics by Ballard MacDonald
and Harry Carroll
Ziegfeld Follies of 1921

Our Jimmy
Music and lyrics by Bill and Patti Jacob
Jimmy 1969

Our Language of Love
Music by Marguerite Monnot
Lyrics by Julian More, David Heneker
and Monte Norman
Irma la Douce 1960

Our Last Waltz Together
Music by Oscar Straus
Lyrics by Clare Kummer
Three Waltzes 1937

Our Little Captain
Music by George Gershwin
Lyrics by Ira Gershwin
Tip-Toes 1925

Our Little Kingdom
Music by Rudolf Friml
Lyrics by Otto Harbach and Oscar Hammerstein II
The Wild Rose 1926

Our Little Lady Upstairs
Music by Sigmund Romberg
Lyrics by Irving Caesar
Melody 1933

Our Little Nest
Music by Jerome Kern
Lyrics by P.G. Wodehouse
Oh, Lady! Lady!! 1918

Our Little Secret
Music by Burt Bacharach
Lyrics by Hal David
Promises, Promises 1968

Our Love Has Flown Away
Music and lyrics by Rick Besoyan
The Student Gypsy (OB) 1963

Our Love Is Here to Stay
Music by George Gershwin
Lyrics by Ira Gershwin
Goldwyn Follies (1938) F

This was the last song George Gershwin wrote
before his death on July 11, 1937. Vernon Duke
finished the score of the film—with Ira Gershwin's
lyrics of course. He wrote several verses to already
completed choruses of songs and a song of his
own, "Spring Again."

Our Lovely Rose
Music by Jerome Kern
Lyrics by Anne Caldwell
Stepping Stones 1923

As in his song "Nodding Roses" Kern made
musical reference in this song to Richard Strauss'
opera *Der Rosenkavalier*.

Our Night
Music and lyrics by Gary Portnoy
and Judy Hart Angelo
Preppies (OB) 1983

Our Own Way of Going Along
Music and lyrics by George M. Cohan
The Merry Malones 1927

Our Private World
Music by Cy Coleman
Lyrics by Betty Comden and Adolph Green
On the Twentieth Century 1978

Our Song
Music by Jerome Kern
Lyrics by Dorothy Fields
When You're in Love (1937) F

Our Song
Music by Maria Grever
Lyrics by Raymond Leveen
Viva O'Brien 1941

Our State Fair
Music by Richard Rodgers
Lyrics by Oscar Hammerstein II
State Fair (1945) F

Our Time
Music and lyrics by Stephen Sondheim
Merrily We Roll Along 1981

Our Time Together
Music and lyrics by Mel Mandel and Norman Sachs
My Old Friends (OB) 1979

Our Town
Music and lyrics by James Shelton
The Straw Hat Revue 1939

Our Wedding Day
Music and lyrics by Irving Berlin
As Thousands Cheer 1933

Ours
Music and lyrics by Cole Porter
Red, Hot and Blue! 1936

The Ousing Cha-Cha
Music and lyrics by C. Jackson and James Hatch
Fly Blackbird (OB) 1962

Out for No Good
Music by Philip Charig
Lyrics by Dan Shapiro and Milton Pascal
Follow the Girls 1944

Out in the Open Air
Music by Burton Lane
Lyrics by Howard Dietz
Three's a Crowd 1930

Out in the Sun
Music by Franz Lehár
Lyrics by Edward Eliscu
Frederika 1937

Out of a Clear Blue Sky
Music by Harold Arlen
Lyrics by Ted Koehler
Earl Carroll's Vanities 1930

Out of Breath
Music by Everett Miller
Lyrics by Johnny Mercer
The Garrick Gaieties (3rd edition) 1930

Out of Breath
Music by Julian Slade
Lyrics by Dorothy Reynolds and Julian Slade
Salad Days (OB) 1958

Out of My Dreams
Music by Richard Rodgers
Lyrics by Oscar Hammerstein II
Oklahoma! 1943

Out of Sight, Out of Mind
Music by John Mundy
Lyrics by Edward Eager
The Liar 1950

Out of Sight, Out of Mind
Music by Sol Berkowitz
Lyrics by James Lipton
Nowhere to Go But Up 1962

Out of the Blue
Music by Jerome Kern
Lyrics by Oscar Hammerstein II
Sweet Adeline 1929

Out of the Clear Blue Sky
Music by Vernon Duke
Lyrics by Ogden Nash
Two's Company 1952

Out of the Way
Music by Sigmund Romberg (developed by Don Walker)
Lyrics by Leo Robin
The Girl in Pink Tights 1954

Out of This World
Music by Harold Arlen
Lyrics by Johnny Mercer
Out of This World (1945) F

Out of Town Buyers
Music by Albert Von Tilzer
Lyrics by Neville Fleeson
Bye Bye, Bonnie 1927

Out of Towner
Music by Hank Beebe
Lyrics by Bill Heyer
*Tuscaloosa's Calling Me
But I'm Not Going!* (OB) 1975

Out on the Loose
Music by Harry Tierney
Lyrics by Joseph McCarthy
Rio Rita 1927

Out on the Street
Music and lyrics by Micki Grant
It's So Nice to Be Civilized 1980

Out on the Streets
Music by Robert Mitchell
Lyrics by Elizabeth Perry
Bags (OB) 1982

Out There
Music by Cy Coleman
Lyrics by Michael Stewart
Barnum 1980

Out to Launch
Music by Joseph Raposo
Lyrics by Erich Segal
Sing Muse! (OB) 1961

Out Where the Blues Begin
Music by Jimmy McHugh
Lyrics by Dorothy Fields
Hello Daddy 1928

An Outdoor Man for My Indoor Sports
Music by Ray Henderson
Lyrics by B.G. DeSylva and Lew Brown
Hold Everything! 1928

Outlaw Man
Music and lyrics by Al Carmines
Wanted (OB) 1972

Outracing Light
Music by Wally Harper
Lyrics by Paul Zakrzewski
Sensations (OB) 1970

Outside Looking In
Music by Harry Archer
Lyrics by Edward Eliscu
Sweet and Low 1930

Outside of That I Love You
Music and lyrics by Irving Berlin
Louisiana Purchase 1940

Over a Garden Wall
Music by Con Conrad
Lyrics by William B. Friedlander
Mercenary Mary 1925

Over and Over
Music and lyrics by Hugh Martin
Make a Wish 1951

Over and Over
Music and lyrics by Jerry Herman
I Feel Wonderful (OB) 1954

Over and Over Again
Music by Richard Rodgers
Lyrics by Lorenz Hart
Jumbo 1935

Over at the Frankenstein Place
Music and lyrics by Richard O'Brien
The Rocky Horror Show 1975

Over Here
Music by J. Fred Coots
Lyrics by Arthur Swanstrom and Benny Davis
Sons o' Guns 1929

Over Here
Music by Arthur Schwartz
Lyrics by Howard Dietz
Jennie 1963

Over Here
Music and lyrics by Richard M. Sherman
and Robert B. Sherman
Over Here! 1974

Over in Europe
Music by Kurt Weill
Lyrics by Paul Green
Johnny Johnson 1936

Over on the Jersey Side
Music and lyrics by Nora Bayes and Jack Norworth
Ziegfeld Follies of 1908

Over the Garden Wall
Music by Robert Hood Bowers
Lyrics by Francis DeWitt
Oh, Ernest! 1927

Over the Hill
Music by Gary Geld
Lyrics by Peter Udell
Shenandoah 1975

Over the Hills
Music by Jerome Kern
Lyrics by Anne Caldwell
She's a Good Fellow 1919

Dropped from production

Over the Mountains
Music by Victor Herbert
Lyrics by Harry B. Smith
Cyrano de Bergerac 1899

Over the Phone
Music and lyrics by George M. Cohan
Little Nellie Kelly 1922

Over the Rainbow
Music by Harold Arlen
Lyrics by E.Y. Harburg
The Wizard of Oz (1939) F

Academy Award winner

Over the River and Into the Woods
Music and lyrics by Jack Holmes
New Faces of 1962

Overflow
Music by George Gershwin
Lyrics by DuBose Heyward
Porgy and Bess 1935

Overnight
Music by Louis Alter
Lyrics by Billy Rose and Charlotte Kent
Sweet and Low 1930

Overspend
Music by Richard Lewine
Lyrics by Arnold B. Horwitt
The Girls Against the Boys 1959

Oxford Bags
Music by Philip Braham
Lyrics by Arthur Wimperis
Charlot's Revue of 1926

Oxford Days
Music by Alfred Goodman
Sky High 1925

Oyez, Oyez, Oyez
Music by George Gershwin
Lyrics by Ira Gershwin
Let 'Em Eat Cake 1933

Oysters
Music by Galt MacDermot
Lyrics by Christopher Gore
Via Galactica 1972

Oysters, Cockles and Mussels
Music and lyrics by Harold Rome
Fanny 1954

The Ozarks Are Calling Me Home
Music and lyrics by Cole Porter
Red, Hot and Blue! 1936

Pablo
Music by Sigmund Romberg
Lyrics by Irving Caesar
Nina Rosa 1930

Pablo, You Are My Heart
Music by Richard Rodgers
Lyrics by Lorenz Hart
Mississippi (1935) F

Dropped from film

Pack Up Your Blues and Smile
Music by Peter de Rose and Albert Von Tilzer
Lyrics by Jo Trent
Yes, Yes, Yvette 1927

Pack Up Your Sins and Go to the Devil
Music and lyrics by Irving Berlin
Music Box Revue (2nd edition) 1922

A Package of Seeds
Music by Jerome Kern
Lyrics by P.G. Wodehouse
Oh, Boy! 1917

Paddy MacNeil and His Automobile
Music and lyrics by Noël Coward
The Girl Who Came to Supper 1963

Padlock Your Blues
Music by Ray Perkins
Lyrics by Max and Nathaniel Lief
The Greenwich Village Follies (1928)

Paducah
Music by Shelley Mowell
Lyrics by Mike Stewart
Shoestring Revue (1955) (OB)

Pageant Song
Music by Norman Campbell
Lyrics by Donald Harron and Norman Campbell
Anne of Green Gables (OB) 1971

Paint a Rainbow
Music and lyrics by Ervin Drake
What Makes Sammy Run? 1964

Paint Me a Rainbow
Music by Sam Pottle
Lyrics by Tom Whedon
All Kinds of Giants (OB) 1961

Painting a Vanities Girl
Music and lyrics by Ernie Golden
Earl Carroll's Vanities (1928)

A Pair of Ordinary Coons
Music and lyrics by Irving Berlin
Stop! Look! Listen! 1915

The Pajama Game
Music and lyrics by Richard Adler and Jerry Ross
The Pajama Game 1954

Pal Joey
Music by Richard Rodgers
Lyrics by Lorenz Hart
Pal Joey 1940

A Pal Like You
Music by Jerome Kern
Lyrics by P.G. Wodehouse
Oh, Boy! 1917

Palace of Dreams
Music by Albert Sirmay and Arthur Schwartz
Lyrics by Arthur Swanstrom
Princess Charming 1930

The Pale Venetian Moon
Music by Jerome Kern
Lyrics by Anne Caldwell
The Bunch and Judy 1922

Palm Beach Baby
Music and lyrics by Herman Hupfeld
A La Carte 1927

The Palm Beach Girl
Music by Jerome Kern
Lyrics by P.G. Wodehouse
Miss 1917

Palm Beach Walk
Music by Walter G. Samuels
Lyrics by Morrie Ryskind
Ned Wayburn's Gambols 1929

Palomino Pal
Music by John Kander
Lyrics by Fred Ebb
Flora, the Red Menace 1965

Pals of the Pentagon
Music and lyrics by Harold Rome
Alive and Kicking 1950

The Pampas
Music and lyrics by Walter Marks
Broadway Follies 1981

Panache
Music by Jule Styne
Lyrics by E.Y. Harburg
Darling of the Day 1968

Panassociative
Music by Susan Hulsman Bingham
Lyrics by Myrna Lamb
Mod Donna (OB) 1970

Pancho Villa
Music and lyrics by Bland Simpson and Jim Wann
Diamond Studs (OD) 1975

Pandora
Music and lyrics by Ronnie Britton
Greenwich Village Follies (OB) 1976

Panic
Music by Elmer Bernstein
Lyrics by Carolyn Leigh
How Now, Dow Jones 1967

Panic in Panama
Music by Harry Ruby
Lyrics by Bert Kalmar
High Kickers 1941

The Panic's On
Music by Albert Sirmay and Arthur Schwartz
Lyrics by Arthur Swanstrom
Princess Charming 1930

Panisse and Son
Music and lyrics by Harold Rome
Fanny 1954

Pansies on Parade
Music and lyrics by Porter Grainger
Fast and Furious 1931

Pansy
Music and lyrics by Maceo Pinkard
Pansy 1929

Pantalettes
Music by Carl Millöcker (revised by Theo Mackeben)
Lyrics by Rowland Leigh
The Dubarry 1932

Pants
Music and lyrics by Randy Newman
Maybe I'm Doing It Wrong (2nd edition)
(OB) 1982

Papa-De-Da-Da
Music and lyrics by Spencer Williams, Clarence Todd and Clarence Williams
Blackbirds of 1930

Papa, Let's Do It Again
Music and lyrics by Johnny Brandon
Cindy (OB) 1964

Papa Lewis, Mama Green
Music and lyrics by Harold Rome
Pins and Needles (OB) 1937

Added during run

Papa Likes a Hot Papoose
Music by Jay Gorney
Lyrics by E.Y. Harburg
Earl Carroll's Sketch Book (1929)

Papa, Won't You Dance With Me?
Music by Jule Styne
Lyrics by Sammy Cahn
High Button Shoes 1947

Papa Would Persist in Picking Peaches
Music by Jerome Kern
Lyrics by P.G. Wodehouse
Miss 1917

Papa's Gonna Make It Alright
Music by Gary Geld
Lyrics by Peter Udell
Shenandoah 1975

Papa's Got a Job
Music by Ned Lehak
Lyrics by Robert Sour
Sing for Your Supper 1939

Papa's Return
Music and lyrics by Ann Ronell
Count Me In 1942

Paper Bag Rag
Music and lyrics by Walter Marks
Broadway Follies 1981

Paper of Gold
Music and lyrics by Eaton Magoon, Jr.
13 Daughters 1961

The Papers
Music by Harry Ruby
Lyrics by Bert Kalmar
Top Speed 1929

A Parade in Town
Music and lyrics by Stephen Sondheim
Anyone Can Whistle 1964

Parade Night
Music by Will Irwin
Lyrics by Norman Zeno
The Show Is On 1936

Parade of the Christmas Dinner
Music by C. Luckey Roberts
Lyrics by Alex C. Rogers
My Magnolia 1926

Parade of the Wooden Soldiers (orchestral)
Music by Leon Jessel
Chauve-Souris 1922

Paradise
Music and lyrics by Eaton Magoon, Jr.
Heathen 1972

Paradise Stolen
Music by Sigmund Romberg
Lyrics by Rowland Leigh
My Romance 1948

Paragraphs (Hansel and Gretel)
Music by Leo Fall
Lyrics by George Grossmith
The Dollar Princess 1909

Parasol Lady
Music and lyrics by Al Carmines
Wanted (OB) 1972

Pardon Me, Madame
Music by Herbert Stothart
Lyrics by Gus Kahn
Rose Marie (film version, 1936)

Pardon Me, Sir
Music and lyrics by Irving Burgie
Ballad for Bimshire (OB) 1963

Pardon Me While I Dance
Music and lyrics by John Jennings
Riverwind (OB) 1962

Pardon My English
Music by George Gershwin
Lyrics by Ira Gershwin
Pardon My English 1933

Pardon Our French
Music by Victor Young
Lyrics by Edward Heyman
Pardon Our French 1950

Paree
Music by Arthur Schwartz
Lyrics by Howard Dietz
At Home Abroad 1935

Paree
Music by Johann Strauss II, adapted by Oscar Straus
Lyrics by Clare Kummer
Three Waltzes 1937

Paree Has the Fever Now
Music and lyrics by Vincent Valentini
Parisiana 1928

Paree, What Did You Do to Me?
Music and lyrics by Cole Porter
Fifty Million Frenchmen 1929

The Parents' Farewell
Music and lyrics by Gary Portnoy
and Judy Hart Angelo
Preppies (OB) 1983

Paris
Music by Jean Gilbert
Lyrics by Harry B. and Robert B. Smith
Modest Suzanne 1912

Paris
Music by Emmerich Kálmán
Lyrics by C.C.S. Cushing and E.P. Heath
Sari 1914

Paris
Music and lyrics by E. Ray Goetz and Louis Alter
Paris 1928

Paris
Music by Howard Marren
Lyrics by Enid Futterman
Portrait of Jennie (OB) 1982

Paris Cuisine
Music by Michael J. Lewis
Lyrics by Anthony Burgess
Cyrano 1973

Paris, France
Music and lyrics by Hugh Martin
Make a Wish 1951

Paris Gown
Music by Jule Styne
Lyrics by Bob Hilliard
Hazel Flagg 1953

Paris Green
Music and lyrics by Vincent Valentini
Parisiana 1928

Paris Is a Lonely Town
Music by Harold Arlen
Lyrics by E. Y. Harburg
Gay Purr-ee (1962) F

Paris Is a Paradise for Coons
Music by Jerome Kern
Lyrics by Edward Madden
La Belle Paree 1911

The melody reappeared in *Love o'Mike* (1917) as "Look in the Book" (lyrics by Harry B. Smith).

Paris Is Paris Again
Music by Frederick Loewe
Lyrics by Alan Jay Lerner
Gigi (stage version, 1973)

Paris Is Really Divine
Music by Richard Rodgers
Lyrics by Lorenz Hart
Peggy-Ann 1926

Dropped from production

Paris Loves Lovers
Music and lyrics by Cole Porter
Silk Stockings 1955

Paris Original
Music and lyrics by Frank Loesser
How to Succeed in Business Without Really Trying 1961

Paris Sings Again
Music by Paul Durand
Lyrics by Harry Graham
Yours Is My Heart 1946

Paris Taught Me 'Zis
Music by Abel Baer
Lyrics by Sam Lewis and Joe Young
Lady Do 1927

Paris Wakes Up and Smiles
Music and lyrics by Irving Berlin
Miss Liberty 1949

Parisian Pierrot
Music and lyrics by Noël Coward
Charlot's Revue 1924

Parisiana Roses
Music and lyrics by Vincent Valentini
Parisiana 1928

The Parisians
Music by Frederick Loewe
Lyrics by Alan Jay Lerner
Gigi (1958) F

Dropped from stage version

Park
Music by Lance Mulcahy
Lyrics by Paul Cherry
Park 1970

Park Avenue Strut
Music by Phil Baker and Maury Rubens
Lyrics by Moe Jaffe and Harold Atteridge
Pleasure Bound 1929

Park Avenue's Going to Town
Music by Edgar Fairchild
Lyrics by Milton Pascal
The Illustrators' Show 1936

A Parking Meter Like Me
Music by Menachem Zur
Lyrics by Herbert Appleman
Unfair to Goliath (OB) 1970

Parting
Music by Galt MacDermot
Lyrics by William Dumaresq
The Human Comedy (OB) 1983

Partners
Music by Louis A. Hirsch
Lyrics by Otto Harbach
The O'Brien Girl 1921

The Party Gets Going
Music by Richard Rodgers
Lyrics by Oscar Hammerstein II
Pipe Dream 1955

A Party in Southampton
Music and lyrics by Bob Ost
Everybody's Gettin' Into the Act (OB) 1981

The Party Is Where I Am
Music by Arthur Siegel
Lyrics by Mae Richard
Tallulah (OB) 1983

Party Song
Music by Tommy Wolf
Lyrics by Fran Landesman
The Nervous Set 1959

Party Talk
Music by Sammy Fain
Lyrics by Marilyn and Alan Bergman
Something More 1964

The Party That We're Gonna Have Tomorrow Night
Music by Richard Rodgers
Lyrics by Oscar Hammerstein II
Pipe Dream 1955

Party's Gonna End
Music by Stanley Silverman
Lyrics by Tom Hendry
Doctor Selavy's Magic Theatre (OB) 1972

The Party's on the House
Music and lyrics by David Heneker
Half a Sixpence 1965

The Party's Over
Music by Jule Styne
Lyrics by Betty Comden and Adolph Green
Bells Are Ringing 1956

The Party's Over Now
Music and lyrics by Noël Coward
Set to Music 1939

Pas de Deux
Music by Charles Strouse
Lyrics by Alan Jay Lerner
Dance a Little Closer 1983

Pass a Little Love Around
Music and lyrics by Micki Grant
It's So Nice to Be Civilized 1980

Pass That Peace Pipe
Music and lyrics by Roger Edens, Hugh Martin
and Ralph Blane
Good News (film version, 1947)

Pass the Cross to Me
Music by Gary Geld
Lyrics by Peter Udell
Shenandoah 1975

Pass the Football
Music by Leonard Bernstein
Lyrics by Betty Comden and Adolph Green
Wonderful Town 1953

A Passacaglia
Music by Bob James
Lyrics by Jack O'Brien
The Selling of the President 1972

Passatella (The Drinking Game)
Music by Armando Trovaioli
Lyrics by Pietro Garinei and Sandro Giovannini
(Lyric translation by Edward Eager)
Rugantino 1964

The Passenger's Always Right
Music and lyrics by Noël Coward
Sail Away 1961

Passing By
Music by Patrick Rose
Lyrics by Merv Campone and Richard Ouzounian
A Bistro Car on the CNR (OB) 1978

The Passing of Time
Music by Al Carmines
Lyrics by Maria Irene Fornes
Promenade (OB) 1969

Passion
Music by Stanley Silverman
Lyrics by Arthur Miller
Up From Paradise (OB) 1983

Past My Prime
Music by Gene de Paul
Lyrics by Johnny Mercer
Li'l Abner 1956

Pastrami Brothers
Music and lyrics by Elizabeth Swados
Nightclub Cantata (OB) 1977

Patience
Music and lyrics by Norman Dean
Autumn's Here (OB) 1966

Patiently Smiling
Music by Franz Lehár
Lyrics by Harry Graham
Yours Is My Heart 1946

Patriotic Song
Music and lyrics by Stephen Oliver
The Life and Times of Nicholas Nickleby 1981

Patron Saints
Music and lyrics by James Quinn and Alaric Jans
Do Patent Leather Shoes Really Reflect Up? 1982

Patsy
Music and lyrics by Steve Allen
Sophie 1963

Pay Day
Music by C. Luckey Roberts
Lyrics by Alex C. Rogers
My Magnolia 1926

Pay Day
Music by Sigmund Romberg
Lyrics by Irving Caesar
Nina Rosa 1930

Pay Day on the Levee
Music and lyrics by James Johnson
and Cecil Mack
Runnin' Wild 1923

Pay Day Pauline
Music by Vincent Youmans
Lyrics by Otto Harbach
No, No, Nanette 1925

Pay Heed
Music by Vernon Duke
Lyrics by John Latouche
Cabin in the Sky 1940

Pay Some Attention to Me
Music by George Gershwin
Lyrics by Ira Gershwin
A Damsel in Distress (1937) F

Dropped from film

Payador
Music by Sigmund Romberg
Lyrics by Irving Caesar
Nina Rosa 1930

Payday
Music by Arthur Schwartz
Lyrics by Dorothy Fields
A Tree Grows in Brooklyn 1951

Paying Off
Music by Dave Stamper
Lyrics by Fred Herendeen
Orchids Preferred 1937

Peace, Brother
Music by Jimmy Van Heusen
Lyrics by Eddie De Lange
Swingin' the Dream 1939

Peace Celebration
Music by Baldwin Bergersen
Lyrics by William Archibald
Rosa (OB) 1978

Peace Come to Every Heart
Music by John Morris
Lyrics by Gerald Freedman
A Time for Singing 1966

Peace Love and Good Damn
Music by Ron Steward and Neal Tate
Lyrics by Ron Steward
Sambo (OB) 1969

Peace Peace
Music by Galt MacDermot
Lyrics by Gerome Ragni
Dude 1972

Peace Teachers
Music and lyrics by Harry Chapin
The Night That Made America Famous 1975

Peace to My Lonely Heart
Music by Sigmund Romberg
Lyrics by Dorothy Donnelly
Blossom Time 1921

Based on Schubert's *Ave Maria*

Peace Will Come
Music and lyrics by David Langston Smyrl
On the Lock-In (OB) 1977

Peach Girl
Music by Jerome Kern
Lyrics by Anne Caldwell
The Bunch and Judy 1922

A Peach of a Life
Music by Jerome Kern
Lyrics by P. G. Wodehouse
Leave It to Jane 1917

Peach on the Beach
Music by Vincent Youmans
Lyrics by Otto Harbach
No, No, Nanette 1925

Peaches
Music by Jean Gilbert
Lyrics by Harry B. and Robert B. Smith
Modest Suzanne 1912

Peaches and Cream
Music by Jerome Kern
Lyrics by Paul West
The Red Petticoat 1912

Peanut Song
Music by Al Carmines
Lyrics by Rosalyn Drexler
Home Movies (OB) 1964

Peanuts and Kisses
Music by Robert Russell Bennett
Lyrics by Owen Murphy and Robert A. Simon
Hold Your Horses 1933

Pear Tree Quintet
Music by Richard Hill and John Hawkins
Lyrics by Nevill Coghill
Canterbury Tales 1969

Pearl of Broadway
Music by Jerome Kern
Lyrics by Bert Kalmar and Harry Ruby
Lucky 1927

Pearls
Music and lyrics by Jerry Herman
Dear World 1969

Pearls
Music by Galt MacDermot
Lyrics by John Guare
Two Gentlemen of Verona 1971

Pears and Peaches
Music by Galt MacDermot
Lyrics by Gerome Ragni
Dude 1972

The Pears of Anjou
Music by Richard Rodgers
Lyrics by Sheldon Harnick
Rex 1976

Dropped from production

Pebble Waltz
Music by Paul Klein
Lyrics by Fred Ebb
Morning Sun (OB) 1963

Peculiar State of Affairs
Music by Ernest G. Schweikert
Lyrics by Frank Reardon
Rumple 1957

Pedro, Ichabod
Music by George Lessner
Lyrics by Miriam Battista and Russell Maloney
Sleepy Hollow 1948

Peepin' Tommy
Music and lyrics by Vincent Valentini
Parisiana 1928

Peggy, Peggy
Music by Richard Rodgers
Lyrics by Lorenz Hart
Peggy-Ann 1926

Dropped from production

Peggy's a Creature of Moods
Music by Victor Herbert
Lyrics by Robert B. Smith
The Debutante 1914

The Penalty of Love
Music by Porter Grainger
Lyrics by Donald Heywood
Hot Rhythm 1930

Penelope's Hand
Music by Mitch Leigh
Lyrics by Charles Burr and Forman Brown
Home Sweet Homer 1976

Penis Envy
Music and lyrics by Barbara Schottenfeld
I Can't Keep Running in Place (OB) 1981

Penniless Blues
Music by Jule Styne
Lyrics by Bob Merrill
Sugar 1972

Penny Candy
Music by Arthur Siegel
Lyrics by June Carroll
New Faces of 1952

A Penny for Your Thoughts
Music by Vernon Duke
Lyrics by E.Y. Harburg
Walk a Little Faster 1932

The Penny Friend
Music and lyrics by William Roy
The Penny Friend (OB) 1966

Penny Plain, Twopence Colored
Music and lyrics by Robert Wright
and George Forrest
Kean 1961

A Penny Saved
Music and lyrics by Ronnie Britton
Gift of the Magi (OB) 1975

Penthouse of Your Mind
Music and lyrics by John Phillips
Man on the Moon 1975

Pents-un-Wreckum
Music by Al Carmines
Lyrics by Rosalyn Drexler
Home Movies (OB) 1964

People
Music by Jule Styne
Lyrics by Bob Merrill
Funny Girl 1964

People Collecting Things
Music and lyrics by Alan Menken
Real Life Funnies (OB) 1981

People Don't Do That
Music and lyrics by Matt Dubey and Dean Fuller
Smith (OB) 1973

People in Love
Music and lyrics by William Roy
Maggie 1953

People Like Us
Music and lyrics by Gary Portnoy
and Judy Hart Angelo
Preppies (OB) 1983

People of Taste
Music by Martha Caples
Lyrics by Nancy Hamilton
New Faces of 1934

People Stink
Music and lyrics by James Rado
Rainbow (OB) 1972

People Watchers
Music and lyrics by Bob Merrill
Henry, Sweet Henry 1967

People Who Are Nice
Music by Jimmy Van Heusen
Lyrics by Sammy Cahn
Walking Happy 1966

People Will Say We're in Love
Music by Richard Rodgers
Lyrics by Oscar Hammerstein II
Oklahoma! 1943

The People's Choice
Music by Norman Martin
Lyrics by Fred Ebb
Put It in Writing (OB) 1963

Pep
Music by Sigmund Romberg
Lyrics by Arthur Wimperis
Louie the 14th 1925

Pepita
Music by George Gershwin
Lyrics by B.G. DeSylva
Sweet Little Devil 1924

Dropped from production

Pepper and Salt
Music by Alma Sanders
Lyrics by Monte Carlo
Mystery Moon 1930

Per Favore
Music and lyrics by Cole Porter
Les Girls (1957) F

Dropped from film

Percolatin'
Music and lyrics by J.C. Johnson
Change Your Luck 1930

Percussion
Music by Don Elliott
Lyrics by James Costigan
The Beast in Me 1963

Percy With Perseverance
Music by Edward Ward
Lyrics by George Waggner
Tattle Tales 1933

Perennial Debutantes
Music and lyrics by Cole Porter
Red, Hot and Blue! 1936

A Perfect Evening
Music by Glenn Paxton
Lyrics by Robert Goldman and George Weiss
First Impressions 1959

Perfect Young Ladies
Music and lyrics by Sandy Wilson
The Boy Friend 1954

Perfection
Music by Lee Pockriss
Lyrics by Anne Croswell
Ernest in Love (OB) 1960

Perfection
Music by Baldwin Bergersen
Lyrics by William Archibald
Rosa (OB) 1978

Perfection
Music by Albert T. Viola
Lyrics by William S. Kilborne, Jr.
Head Over Heels 1981

Perfection
Music and lyrics by Bob Ost
Everybody's Gettin' Into the Act (OB) 1981

Perfectly Lovely Couple
Music by Richard Rodgers
Lyrics by Stephen Sondheim
Do I Hear a Waltz? 1965

Perfectly Marvelous
Music by John Kander
Lyrics by Fred Ebb
Cabaret 1966

The Perfume of Love
Music and lyrics by Cole Porter
Silk Stockings 1955

Dropped from production

Perhaps
Music by Richard Rodgers
Lyrics by Stephen Sondheim
Do I Hear a Waltz? 1965

Dropped from production

Perish the Baubles
Music by Robert Kessler
Lyrics by Lola Pergament
O Marry Me! (OB) 1961

Pernambuco
Music and lyrics by Frank Loesser
Where's Charley? 1948

Peron's Latest Flame
Music by Andrew Lloyd Webber
Lyrics by Tim Rice
Evita 1979

Perpetual Anticipation
Music and lyrics by Stephen Sondheim
A Little Night Music 1973

The Persian Way of Life
Music by Don Walker
Lyrics by George Marion, Jr.
Allah Be Praised! 1944

Personal Heaven
Music and lyrics by Eugene and Ralph Berton
Two for Tonight (OB) 1939

Personality
Music by Victor Herbert
Lyrics by Henry Blossom
The Only Girl 1914

Personality
Music and lyrics by George M. Cohan
Billie 1928

Personally Yours
Music by Michael H. Cleary
Lyrics by Max and Nathaniel Lief
Hey Nonny Nonny! 1932

Personals
Music by Rob Fremont
Lyrics by Doris Willens
Piano Bar (OB) 1978

Perspiration
Music by Lee Wainer
Lyrics by John Latouche
Sing for Your Supper 1939

The Persuasion
Music by Frederick Loewe
Lyrics by Alan Jay Lerner
Camelot 1960

Pet Me, Poppa
Music and lyrics by Frank Loesser
Guys and Dolls (film version, 1955)

Peteca!
Music by Heitor Villa-Lobos
Lyrics by Robert Wright and George Forrest
Magdalena 1948

Peter Pan
Music by Carroll Gibbons
Lyrics by Billy Rose and James Dyrenforth
Crazy Quilt 1931

Peter, Peter
Music and lyrics by Leonard Bernstein
Peter Pan 1950

Peter's Denial
Music by Andrew Lloyd Webber
Lyrics by Tim Rice
Jesus Christ Superstar 1971

Petite Belle Lily
Music by Coleridge-Taylor Perkinson
Lyrics by Errol Hill
Man Better Man (OB) 1969

Pets
Music and lyrics by Cole Porter
Let's Face It!

Dropped from production 1941

Petticoat High
Music by Harold Arlen
Lyrics by Johnny Mercer
Saratoga 1959

Petty Crime
Music and lyrics by Bob Goodman
Wild and Wonderful 1971

Pffft!
Music by Jerry Bock
Lyrics by Sheldon Harnick
The Body Beautiful 1958

Phantom of the Opera
Music and lyrics by Frederick Silver
Gay Company (OB) 1974

Pharaoh's Dream Explained
Music by Andrew Lloyd Webber
Lyrics by Tim Rice
*Joseph and the Amazing
Technicolor Dreamcoat* 1982

Pharaoh's Story
Music by Andrew Lloyd Webber
Lyrics by Tim Rice
*Joseph and the Amazing
Technicolor Dreamcoat* 1982

Phil the Fiddler
Music by Richard Lewine
Lyrics by Arnold B. Horwitt
Make Mine Manhattan 1948

Philadelphia
Music by Richard Rodgers
Lyrics by Stephen Sondheim
Do I Hear a Waltz? 1965

Dropped from production

Philological Waltz
Music by Donald Swann
Lyrics by Michael Flanders
At the Drop of a Hat 1959

Philosophy
Music by Carl Friberg
Lyrics by Hal Hackady
New Faces of 1968

Phoebe Snow
Music by Louis A. Hirsch
Lyrics by P.G. Wodehouse
Oh, My Dear! 1918

The Phoney Game
Music and lyrics by Melvin Van Peebles
Don't Play Us Cheap 1972

Phooey
Music and lyrics by Don Tucker
Red, White and Maddox 1969

Phrenology
Music by Leslie Stuart
Lyrics by Ernest Boyd-Jones
Florodora 1900

Physical Fitness
Music by Charles Strouse
Lyrics by Lee Adams
All American 1962

Piano Lesson
Music and lyrics by Meredith Willson
The Music Man 1957

Piccadilly
Music and lyrics by Walter Marks
Broadway Follies 1981

Piccaninny Pie
Music and lyrics by Harold Orlob
Hairpin Harmony 1943

The Piccolino
Music and lyrics by Irving Berlin
Top Hat (1935) F

Piccolo
Music by Oscar Straus
Lyrics by Joseph W. Herbert
A Waltz Dream 1908

Pick a Husband
Music by Emmerich Kálmán
Lyrics by C.C.S. Cushing and E.P. Heath
Sari 1914

Pick 'Em Up and Lay 'Em Down
Music by Werner Janssen
Lyrics by Mann Holiner and J. Keirn Brennan
Boom-Boom 1929

Pick-Me-Up!
Music by Gordon Duffy
Lyrics by Harry M. Haldane
Happy Town 1959

Pick More Daisies
Music by Gary William Friedman
Lyrics by Will Holt
Taking My Turn (OB) 1983

Pick Yourself a Flower
Music by Claibe Richardson
Lyrics by Kenward Elmslie
The Grass Harp 1971

Pick Yourself Up
Music by Jerome Kern
Lyrics by Dorothy Fields
Swing Time (1936) F

Kern's melody is based on a Bohemian folk tune
whose theme had been used both by Bedrich
Smetana and by Jaromir Weinberger in "Schwanda
Der Dudelsackpfeifer [The Bagpipe Player]."

Pickalittle
Music and lyrics by Meredith Willson
The Music Man 1957

The Pickers Are Comin'
Music by Gary Geld
Lyrics by Peter Udell
Shenandoah 1975

Pickin' Cotton
Music by Ray Henderson
Lyrics by B.G. DeSylva and Lew Brown
George White's Scandals (1928)

Picking Peaches
Music by Rudolf Friml
Lyrics by Rida Johnson Young
Sometime 1918

The Pickpocket
Music by Helen Miller
Lyrics by Eve Merriam
Inner City 1971

Pick-Pocket Tango
Music by Albert Hague
Lyrics by Dorothy Fields
Redhead 1959

The Pickwickians
Music by Cyril Ornadel
Lyrics by Leslie Bricusse
Pickwick 1965

The Picnic
Music by Norman Campbell
Lyrics by Donald Harron and Norman Campbell
Anne of Green Gables (OB) 1971

Picnic Party With You
Music by John Egan
Lyrics by Dorothy Donnelly
Poppy 1923

A Picture I Want to See
Music by Jerome Kern
Lyrics by P G. Wodehouse
Miss 1917 1917

Dropped during run. Also titled "That's The Picture
I Want To See"

The Picture of Happiness
Music by Jerry Bock
Lyrics by Sheldon Harnick
Tenderloin 1960

A Picture of Me Without You
Music and lyrics by Cole Porter
Jubilee 1935

Pictures in the Smoke
Music by Gustav Luders
Lyrics by Frank Pixley
The Prince of Pilsen 1903

Piddle, Twiddle and Resolve
Music and lyrics by Sherman Edwards
1776 1969

Pie
Music by Jerome Kern
Lyrics by Anne Caldwell
Stepping Stones 1923

Pie-Eyed Piper
Music by Sammy Fain
Lyrics by Irving Kahal
Everybody's Welcome 1931

Pie in the Sky
Music by Michael H. Cleary
Lyrics by Max and Nathaniel Lief
Shoot the Works 1931

Pièce de Résistance
Music by Heitor Villa-Lobos
Lyrics by Robert Wright and George Forrest
Magdalena 1948

A Piece of a Girl
Music by Vernon Duke
Lyrics by Howard Dietz
Jackpot 1944

A Piece of the Rainbow
Music by Jerry Livingston
Lyrics by Leonard Adelson
Molly 1973

Pierre
Music by Alma Sanders
Lyrics by Monte Carlo
Oh! Oh! Nurse 1925

Pierrette and Pierrot
Music by Franz Lehár
Lyrics by Basil Hood
The Count of Luxembourg 1912

Pigeon-Hole Time
Music by Rob Fremont
Lyrics by Doris Willens
Piano Bar (OB) 1978

Pigeon Run
Music and lyrics by Harry Chapin
The Night That Made America Famous 1975

Pigtails and Freckles
Music and lyrics by Irving Berlin
Mr. President 1962

Pilate and Christ
Music by Andrew Lloyd Webber
Lyrics by Tim Rice
Jesus Christ Superstar 1971

Pilate's Dream
Music by Andrew Lloyd Webber
Lyrics by Tim Rice
Jesus Christ Superstar 1971

The Pilgrim Fathers
Music by Serge Walter
Lyrics by Agnes Morgan
The Grand Street Follies (1929)

Pilgrims of Love
Music by Victor Herbert
Lyrics by Robert B. Smith
Sweethearts 1913

A Pilgrim's Primer
Music and lyrics by Frederick Silver
Gay Company (OB) 1974

Pilgrims' Procession
Music by Leonard Bernstein
Lyrics by Richard Wilbur
Candide 1956

A Pill a Day
Music by Jerome Kern
Lyrics by Anne Caldwell
The City Chap 1925

Pill Parade
Music and lyrics by Jay Thompson
From A to Z 1960

Pillar to Post
Music and lyrics by Bob Merrill
Henry, Sweet Henry 1967

A Pillow for His Royal Head
Music by Fred Spielman and Arthur Gershwin
Lyrics by Stanley Adams
A Lady Says Yes 1945

A Pin Cushion
Music by Maury Rubens
Lyrics by Clifford Grey
The Great Temptations 1926

Pinching Myself
Music and lyrics by Alexander Hill
Hummin' Sam 1933

Pine Cones and Holly Berries
Music and lyrics by Meredith Willson
Here's Love 1963

Pinpipi's Sob of Love
Music and lyrics by Sandy Wilson
Valmouth (OB) 1960

Pioneers
Music by Stan Harte, Jr.
Leaves of Grass (OB) 1971

Pipe Dreaming
Music and lyrics by Cole Porter
Around the World 1946

Pipes of Pan Americana
Music by Gerald Marks
Lyrics by Irving Caesar
My Dear Public 1943

The Pipes of Pan Are Calling
Music by Lionel Monckton
Lyrics by Arthur Wimperis
The Arcadians 1910

Pipes of Pansy
Music by Richard Rodgers
Lyrics by Lorenz Hart
She's My Baby 1928

Dropped from production. Originally written for
Dearest Enemy (1925), but dropped. It was also
dropped from *The Girl Friend* (1926) and
Peggy-Ann (1926).

Piraeus, My Love
Music by Manos Hadjidakis
Lyrics by Joe Darion
Illya Darling 1967

Pirate Jenny
Music by Kurt Weill
Lyrics by Marc Blitzstein
The Threepenny Opera (OB) 1954

The Pirate Song
Music and lyrics by Leonard Bernstein
Peter Pan 1950

Pirate Song
Music by Mark Charlap
Lyrics by Carolyn Leigh
Peter Pan 1954

The Pirates' Life
Music and lyrics by Bland Simpson and Jim Wann
Hot Grog (OB) 1977

The Pirate's Song
Music by Edward Earle
Lyrics by Yvonne Tarr
The Decameron (OB) 1961

Pirelli's Magical Elixir
Music and lyrics by Stephen Sondheim
Sweeney Todd 1979

The Piscean
Music by Ron Steward and Neal Tate
Lyrics by Ron Steward
Sambo (OB) 1969

Pistachio
Music and lyrics by Mark Lawrence
Small Wonder 1948

Pitter Patter
Music and lyrics by Hugo Peretti, Luigi Creatore
and George David Weiss
Maggie Flynn 1968

Pity the Poor
Music by Leonard Bernstein
Lyrics by Alan Jay Lerner
1600 Pennsylvania Avenue 1976

Pity the Sunset
Music by Harold Arlen
Lyrics by E.Y. Harburg
Jamaica 1957

Pizarro Was a Very Narrow Man
Music by Sigmund Romberg
Lyrics by Irving Caesar
Nina Rosa 1930

Place in Space
Music and lyrics by John Phillips
Man on the Moon 1975

Place in the Country
Music by George Gershwin
Lyrics by Ira Gershwin
Treasure Girl 1928

A Place of My Own
Music by Baldwin Bergersen
Lyrics by William Archibald
Rosa (OB) 1978

Places, Everybody
Music by Arthur Schwartz
Lyrics by Dorothy Fields
Stars in Your Eyes 1939

Plain, Clean, Average Americans
Music by Alan Menken
Lyrics by Howard Ashman
God Bless You, Mr. Rosewater (OB) 1979

Plain We Live
Music by Albert Hague
Lyrics by Arnold B. Horwitt
Plain and Fancy 1955

Plan It by the Planets
Music by Heitor Villa-Lobos
Lyrics by Robert Wright and George Forrest
Magdalena 1948

Planet of No Thigh Bulge
Music by Cheryl Hardwick
Lyrics by Marilyn Suzanne Miller
Girls, Girls, Girls (OB) 1980

Planet Shmanet Janet
Music and lyrics by Richard O'Brien
The Rocky Horror Show 1975

The Plank
Music and lyrics by Leonard Bernstein
Peter Pan 1950

Plant a Radish
Music by Harvey Schmidt
Lyrics by Tom Jones
The Fantasticks (OB) 1960

Plant You Now, Dig You Later
Music by Richard Rodgers
Lyrics by Lorenz Hart
Pal Joey 1940

Plantation in Philadelphia
Music by Morton Gould
Lyrics by Dorothy Fields
Arms and the Girl 1950

The Plastic Alligator
Music and lyrics by Meredith Willson
Here's Love 1963

Plastic Surgery
Music by Frank Grey
Lyrics by Earle Crooker and McElbert Moore
Happy 1927

Platinum Dreams
Music by Gary William Friedman
Lyrics by Will Holt
Platinum 1978

Play a Simple Melody
Music and lyrics by Irving Berlin
Watch Your Step 1914

Play Ball With the Lord
Music by Stanley Lebowsky
Lyrics by Fred Tobias
Gantry 1970

Play Boy
Music by Richard Rodgers
Lyrics by Lorenz Hart
Heads Up! 1929

A Play-Fair Man
Music by Harry Tierney
Lyrics by Joseph McCarthy
Kid Boots 1923

Play Gypsies, Dance Gypsies
Music by Emmerich Kálmán
Lyrics by Harry B. Smith
Countess Maritza 1926

The Play Is the Bunk
Music by Max Rich
Lyrics by Jack Scholl
Keep Moving 1934

Play It as It Lays
Music and lyrics by Melvin Van Peebles
Waltz of the Stork (OB) 1982

Play Me a Bagpipe Tune
Music by Seymour Furth and Lee Edwards
Lyrics by R.F. Carroll
Bringing Up Father 1925

Play Me a New Tune
Music by J. Fred Coots and Maury Rubens
Lyrics by Clifford Grey
Mayflowers 1925

Play Me an Old Time Two-Step
Music by Sam Morrison
Lyrics by Dolph Singer
Summer Wives 1936

Play, Orchestra, Play!
Music and lyrics by Noël Coward
Tonight at 8:30 ("Shadow Play") 1936

Play the Game
Music by Vincent Youmans
Lyrics by Billy Rose and Edward Eliscu
Great Day! 1929

Play the Queen
Music by Mitch Leigh
Lyrics by N. Richard Nash
Saravá 1979

Play Us a Polka, Dot
Music by Jerome Kern
Lyrics by Oscar Hammerstein II
Sweet Adeline 1929

A Play Without a Bedroom
Music and lyrics by Irving Berlin
Music Box Revue (1st edition) 1921

Playground in the Sky
Music by James F. Hanley
Lyrics by Eddie Dowling
Sidewalks of New York 1927

Playing Croquet
Music and lyrics by Rick Besoyan
Little Mary Sunshine (OB) 1959

Playthings of Love
Music by Emil Gerstenberger
Lyrics by Howard Johnson
The Lace Petticoat 1927

Plaza 6-9423
Music and lyrics by Harold Rome
Sing Out the News 1938

The Plaza Song
Music by David Shire
Lyrics by Richard Maltby, Jr.
Baby 1983

Pleasant Beach House
Music and lyrics by Bob Merrill
Take Me Along 1959

Pleasant Company
Music by Mel Marvin
Lyrics by Robert Montgomery
Green Pond (OB) 1977

Pleasantly Plump
Music and lyrics by Alan Menken
Real Life Funnies (OB) 1981

Please Be Human
Music by Richard Adler
Lyrics by Will Holt
Music Is 1976

Please Come to My House
Music and lyrics by William Finn
March of the Falsettos (OB) 1981

Please Don't Make Me Be Good
Music and lyrics by Cole Porter
Fifty Million Frenchmen 1929

Dropped from production

Please Don't Monkey With Broadway
Music and lyrics by Cole Porter
Broadway Melody of 1940 (1940) F

Please Hello
Music and lyrics by Stephen Sondheim
Pacific Overtures 1976

Please Let Me Read
Music by Joseph Raposo
Lyrics by Erich Segal
Sing Muse! (OB) 1961

Please Let Me Tell You
Music and lyrics by Frank Loesser
The Most Happy Fella 1956

Please Let Us Have Our Seance, Madame Flora
Music and lyrics by Gian-Carlo Menotti
The Medium 1947

Please Stay
Music by John Kander
Lyrics by Fred Ebb
The Happy Time 1968

Please, Teacher
Music by J. Fred Coots
Lyrics by Clifford Grey
June Days 1925

Please Turn Your Backs
Music by Ivan Caryll
Lyrics by C.M.S. McLellan
Oh! Oh! Delphine 1912

Pleased With Myself
Music by David Shire
Lyrics by Richard Maltby, Jr.
Starting Here, Starting Now (OB) 1977

Pleasure and Privilege
Music by Jerry Bock
Lyrics by Sheldon Harnick
The Rothschilds 1970

Pleasures
Music and lyrics by John Driver
Ride the Winds 1974

The Pleasure's About to Be Mine
Music by Elmer Bernstein
Lyrics by Carolyn Leigh
How Now, Dow Jones 1967

Plenty Bambini
Music and lyrics by Frank Loesser
The Most Happy Fella 1956

Plenty of Pennsylvania
Music by Albert Hague
Lyrics by Arnold B. Horwitt
Plain and Fancy 1955

Plot and Counterplot
Music and lyrics by Robert Swerdlow
Love Me, Love My Children (OB) 1971

A Plot to Catch a Man In
Music by John Mundy
Lyrics by Edward Eager
The Liar 1950

The Plumed Knight
Music and lyrics by Oscar Brand
How to Steal an Election (OB) 1968

The Plundering of the Town
Music by Jimmy Van Heusen
Lyrics by Johnny Burke
Carnival in Flanders 1953

Plymouth Rock
Music by Dave Stamper
Lyrics by Channing Pollock
Ziegfeld Follies of 1921

Po' Lil' Black Chile
Music by Frank Harling
Lyrics by Laurence Stallings
Deep River 1926

Po, Po, Po
Music by Manos Hadjidakis
Lyrics by Joe Darion
Illya Darling 1967

Pocketful of Dreams
Music and lyrics by Harold Rome
Michael Todd's Peep Show 1950

Poems
Music and lyrics by Stephen Sondheim
Pacific Overtures 1976

Poetry and All That Jazz
Music by Leon Pober
Lyrics by Bud Freeman
Beg, Borrow or Steal 1960

The Poetry of Motion
Music by George Gershwin
Lyrics by B.G. DeSylva and Ira Gershwin
Tell Me More 1925

Poisoning Pigeons
Music and lyrics by Tom Lehrer
Tomfoolery (OB) 1981

The Pokenhatchit Public Protest Committee
Music by Monty Norman
Lyrics by Julian More
The Moony Shapiro Songbook 1981

The Poker Game
Music by John Kander
Lyrics by Fred Ebb
Woman of the Year 1981

The Poker-Polka
Music by Victor Young
Lyrics by Edward Heyman
Pardon Our French 1950

Poker Polka
Music by Harvey Schmidt
Lyrics by Tom Jones
110 in the Shade 1963

The Polar Bear Strut
Music by Arthur Schwartz
Lyrics by Theodore Goodwin
The Grand Street Follies (1926) (OB)

Police Song
Music and lyrics by Matt Dubey and Dean Fuller
Smith (OB) 1973

The Policeman's Ball
Music and lyrics by Irving Berlin
Miss Liberty 1949

Political Science
Music and lyrics by Randy Newman
Maybe I'm Doing It Wrong (1st edition)
(OB) 1982

Politicians' Song
Music by Ted Simons
Lyrics by Elinor Guggenheimer
Potholes (OB) 1979

Politics
Music by Robert Emmett Dolan
Lyrics by Johnny Mercer
Texas, Li'l Darlin' 1949

Politics and Poker
Music by Jerry Bock
Lyrics by Sheldon Harnick
Fiorello! 1959

The Polka
Music by Harold Arlen
Lyrics by Johnny Mercer
Saratoga 1959

The Polka Dot
Music by Jerome Kern
Lyrics by P.G. Wodehouse
Sitting Pretty 1924

The Polka Dot
Music by Henry Sullivan
Lyrics by Clifford Orr
John Murray Anderson's Almanac (1929)

Pollution
Music and lyrics by Tom Lehrer
Tomfoolery (OB) 1981

Polly
Music by Philip Charig
Lyrics by Irving Caesar
Polly 1929

Polly From Hollywood
Music and lyrics by Irving Berlin
Music Box Revue (4th edition) 1924

Polly of Hollywood
Music by Will Morrisey
Lyrics by Edmund Joseph
Polly of Hollywood 1927

Polly, Put the Kettle On
Music by Harry Tierney
Lyrics by Joseph McCarthy
Kid Boots 1923

Pollyanna
Music by Robert Hood Bowers
Lyrics by Francis DeWitt
Oh, Ernest! 1927

Polly's Song
Music by Kurt Weill
Lyrics by Marc Blitzstein
The Threepenny Opera (OB) 1954

Pompadour
Music by Sigmund Romberg
Lyrics by Irving Caesar
Melody 1933

Pompanola
Music by Ray Henderson
Lyrics by B.G. DeSylva
Three Cheers 1928

Poncho de Panther From Brazil
Music by Georges Bizet
Lyrics by Oscar Hammerstein II
Carmen Jones 1943

Ponies on Parade
Music and lyrics by Clarence Gaskill
Earl Carroll's Vanities (1925)

Pool of Love
Music by Winthrop Cortelyou
Lyrics by Derick Wulff
Kiss Me 1927

Poontang
Music and lyrics by Earl Wilson, Jr.
Let My People Come (OB) 1974

Poor
Music by Jacques Urbont
Lyrics by Bruce Geller
All in Love (OB) 1961

Poor
Music by Hank Beebe
Lyrics by Bill Heyer
*Tuscaloosa's Calling Me
But I'm Not Going!* (OB) 1975

The Poor Apache
Music by Richard Rodgers
Lyrics by Lorenz Hart
Love Me Tonight (1932) F

Poor as a Church Mouse
Music by Vernon Duke
Lyrics by Howard Dietz
Sadie Thompson 1944

Poor Baby
Music and lyrics by Stephen Sondheim
Company 1970

Poor Boy
Music by Stanley Silverman
Lyrics by Tom Hendry
Doctor Selavy's Magic Theatre (OB) 1972

Poor Butterfly
Music by Raymond Hubbell
Lyrics by John Golden
The Big Show 1916

The Lyrics tell the story of Puccini's Opera
Madama Butterfly, which was adapted from David
Belasco's play, which was in turn based on a story
by John Luther Long.

Poor Everybody Else
Music by Cy Coleman
Lyrics by Dorothy Fields
Seesaw 1973

Poor Jerusalem
Music by Andrew Lloyd Webber
Lyrics by Tim Rice
Jesus Christ Superstar 1971

Poor Joe
Music by Richard Rodgers
Lyrics by Oscar Hammerstein II
Allegro 1947

Poor John
Music by Jerome Kern
Lyrics by Ira Gershwin
Cover Girl (1944) F

Poor Little Boy
Music and lyrics by Robert Larimer
King of the Whole Damn World (OB) 1962

Poor Little Doorstep Baby
Music by Michael H. Cleary
Lyrics by Max and Nathaniel Lief
Shoot the Works 1931

Poor Little Hollywood Star
Music by Cy Coleman
Lyrics by Carolyn Leigh
Little Me 1962

Poor Little Marie
Music by James F. Hanley
Lyrics by Gene Buck
No Foolin' 1926

Poor Little Me
Music by Harry Revel
Lyrics by Arnold B. Horwitt
Are You With It? 1945

Poor Little Person
Music and lyrics by Bob Merrill
Henry, Sweet Henry 1967

Poor Little Pierrette
Music and lyrics by Sandy Wilson
The Boy Friend 1954

Poor Little Rich Girl
Music and lyrics by Noël Coward
Charlot's Revue of 1926

Poor Little Ritz Girl
Music by Sigmund Romberg
Lyrics by Alex Gerber
Poor Little Ritz Girl 1920

Poor Little, Shy Little, Demure Little Me
Music by Harry Revel
Lyrics by Mack Gordon
Smiling Faces 1932

Poor Man
Music by George Lessner
Lyrics by Miriam Battista and Russell Maloney
Sleepy Hollow 1948

A Poor Man
Music by Al Carmines
Lyrics by Maria Irene Fornes
Promenade (OB) 1969

Poor Michael! Poor Golo!
Music by George Gershwin
Lyrics by Ira Gershwin
Pardon My English 1933

Dropped from production

Poor Old World
Music and lyrics by George M. Cohan
The Rise of Rosie O'Reilly 1923

Poor Pierrot
Music by Harry Archer
Lyrics by Harlan Thompson
Merry-Merry 1925

Poor Pierrot
Music by Jerome Kern
Lyrics by Otto Harbach
The Cat and the Fiddle 1931

Poor, Poor Joseph
Music by Andrew Lloyd Webber
Lyrics by Tim Rice
*Joseph and the Amazing Technicolor
Dreamcoat* 1982

Poor, Poor Pharaoh
Music by Andrew Lloyd Webber
Lyrics by Tim Rice
*Joseph and the Amazing Technicolor
Dreamcoat* 1982

Poor Porgy
Music by Sylvan Green
Lyrics by Frederick Herendeen
Provincetown Follies (OB) 1935

The Poor Rich
Music and lyrics by Cole Porter
The New Yorkers 1930

Poor Sweet Baby
Music by Larry Grossman
Lyrics by Hal Hackady
Snoopy (OB) 1982

Poor Thing
Music and lyrics by Stephen Sondheim
Sweeney Todd 1979

Poor Tied Up Darlin'
Music by Robert Waldman
Lyrics by Alfred Uhry
The Robber Bridegroom 1975

Popcapdedious
Music by Michael J. Lewis
Lyrics by Anthony Burgess
Cyrano 1973

Poppa Knows Best
Music by Richard Rodgers
Lyrics by Martin Charnin
Two by Two 1970

Poppy Dear
Music by Stephen Jones and Arthur Samuels
Lyrics by Dorothy Donnelly
Poppy 1923

Poppy the Dream Girl
Music by Seymour Furth and Lee Edwards
Lyrics by R.F. Carroll
Bringing Up Father 1925

Poppyland
Music by George Gershwin
Lyrics by B.G. Desylva and John Henry Mears
Morris Gest Midnight Whirl 1919

The Popular Pests
Music and lyrics by Gene Buck and Dave Stamper
Ziegfeld Follies of 1919

Porcelain Maid
Music and lyrics by Irving Berlin
Music Box Revue (2nd edition) 1922

Pore Jud Is Daid
Music by Richard Rodgers
Lyrics by Oscar Hammerstein II
Oklahoma! 1943

Porgy
Music by Jimmy McHugh
Lyrics by Dorothy Fields
Blackbirds of 1928

Port Authority
Music and lyrics by Elizabeth Swados
Lullabye and Goodnight 1982

Porterology
Music and lyrics by Porter Grainger
and Freddie Johnson
Lucky Sambo 1925

Portofino
Music by Louis Bellson and Will Irwin
Lyrics by Richard Ney
Portofino 1958

Portrait of Jennie
Music by Howard Marren
Lyrics by Enid Futterman
Portrait of Jennie (OB) 1982

Posing for Venus
Music by Ivan Caryll
Lyrics by C.M.S. McLellan
Oh! Oh! Delphine 1912

Postage Stamp Principality
Music by Harold Karr
Lyrics by Matt Dubey
Happy Hunting 1956

Posterity Is Just Around the Corner
Music by George Gershwin
Lyrics by Ira Gershwin
Of Thee I Sing 1931

Potiphar
Music by Andrew Lloyd Webber
Lyrics by Tim Rice
Joseph and the Amazing Technicolor Dreamcoat 1982

The Pots
Music by Richard Rodgers
Lyrics by Lorenz Hart
Hollywood Party (1934) F

Dropped from film

Pottawatomie
Music by Richard Rodgers
Lyrics by Lorenz Hart
Too Many Girls 1939

Pour le Sport
Music and lyrics by Stephen Sondheim
Marry Me a Little (OB) 1981

Poverty Program
Music by Helen Miller
Lyrics by Eve Merriam
Inner City 1971

Poverty Row or Luxury Lane
Music by Gus Edwards
Lyrics by Howard Johnson
Broadway Sho-window 1936

Pow! Bam! Zonk!
Music by Charles Strouse
Lyrics by Lee Adams
It's a Bird, It's a Plane, It's Superman 1966

Pow-Wow Polka
Music by Jule Styne
Lyrics by Betty Comden and Adolph Green
Peter Pan 1954

Powder Puff
Music by J. Fred Coots and Maury Rubens
Lyrics by Clifford Grey and McElbert Moore
A Night in Paris 1926

Power
Music by Wally Harper
Lyrics by Paul Zakrzewski
Sensations (OB) 1970

Power
Music by Larry Grossman
Lyrics by Betty Comden and Adolph Green
A Doll's Life 1982

The Power of Negative Thinking
Music and lyrics by Bud McCreery
The Littlest Revue (OB) 1956

The Power of the Human Eye
Music by Victor Herbert
Lyrics by Harry B. Smith
The Fortune Teller 1898

A Power Stronger Than Will
Music by Al Carmines
Lyrics by Rosalyn Drexler
Home Movies (OB) 1964

A Pox Upon the Traitor's Brow
Music by Milton Schafer
Lyrics by Ira Levin
Drat! The Cat! 1965

P** P* B**** B** D******
Music by Donald Swann
Lyrics by Michael Flanders
At the Drop of Another Hat 1966

Practical
Music and lyrics by William Roy
Maggie 1953

Practising Up on You
Music by Philip Charig
Lyrics by Howard Dietz
Three's a Crowd 1930

Prairie Blues
Music by Russell Tarbox
Lyrics by Charles O. Locke
Hello, Paris 1930

Praise the Lord
Music and lyrics by Al Carmines
Joan (OB) 1972

Praises to the Sun
Music by Steve Jankowski
Lyrics by Kenny Morris
Francis (OB) 1982

Prayer
Music by Jerome Kern
Lyrics by Oscar Hammerstein II
Music in the Air 1932

Prayer
Music by Richard Rodgers
Lyrics by Lorenz Hart
Hollywood Party (1934) F

Dropped from film, in which it was to have been
sung by Jean Harlow. Rewritten as "The Bad in
Every Man," "Manhattan Melodrama," and finally as
"Blue Moon."

Prayer
Music by Sigmund Romberg
Lyrics by Rowland Leigh
My Romance 1948

Prayer
Music by Buster Davis
Lyrics by Steven Vinaver
Diversions (OB) 1958

Prayer
Music by Burton Lane
Lyrics by Alan Jay Lerner
Carmelina 1979

Prayers in the Delta
Music and lyrics by Elizabeth Swados
Dispatches (OB) 1979

Preacher Man
Music and lyrics by Johnny Brandon
Love! Love! Love! (OB) 1977

Precious Little Darkness
Music by Tom Mandel
Lyrics by Louisa Rose
The Bar That Never Closes (OB) 1972

Precious Patterns
Music and lyrics by Stephen H. Lemberg
Jazzbo Brown 1980

Prehistoric Complaint
Music by Donald Swann
Lyrics by Michael Flanders
At the Drop of Another Hat 1966

Prelude
Music by Michael Valenti
Lyrics by John Lewin
Blood Red Roses 1970

Preludium
Music by Richard Rodgers
Lyrics by Oscar Hammerstein II
The Sound of Music 1959

Prepare Ye the Way of the Lord
Music and lyrics by Stephen Schwartz
Godspell (OB) 1971

Preposterous
Music by Ernest Gold
Lyrics by Anne Croswell
I'm Solomon 1968

Presenting Clara Spencer
Music by Leon Pober
Lyrics by Bud Freeman
Beg, Borrow or Steal 1960

The President Jefferson Sunday Luncheon Party March
Music by Leonard Bernstein
Lyrics by Alan Jay Lerner
1600 Pennsylvania Avenue 1976

The President's Daughter
Music by Murray Rumshinsky
Lyrics by Jacob Jacobs
The President's Daughter 1970

Press Conference
Music by Henry Krieger
Lyrics by Tom Eyen
Dreamgirls 1981

Pretending
Music by Victor Herbert
Lyrics by George V. Hobart
Old Dutch 1909

Pretty as a Picture
Music by Victor Herbert
Lyrics by Robert B. Smith
Sweethearts 1913

Pretty as a Picture
Music by Harold Arlen
Lyrics by E.Y. Harburg
Bloomer Girl 1944

Pretty Butterfly
Music by Franz Lehár
Lyrics by Basil Hood
The Count of Luxembourg 1912

Pretty Face
Music by Monty Norman
Lyrics by Julian More
The Moony Shapiro Songbook 1981

Pretty Flower
Music by Ron Steward and Neal Tate
Lyrics by Ron Steward
Sambo (OB) 1969

Pretty Girl
Music by Tom Johnstone
Lyrics by Will B. Johnstone
I'll Say She Is 1924

Pretty Girl
Music by Morris Hamilton
Lyrics by Grace Henry
Earl Carroll's Vanities (1928)

A Pretty Girl Is Like a Melody
Music and lyrics by Irving Berlin
Ziegfeld Follies of 1919

A Pretty Girl (Is Like a Pretty Girl)
Music by Richard Lewine
Lyrics by Arnold B. Horwitt
Ziegfeld Follies (1957)

Dropped from production

Pretty Kitty
Music by George Kleinsinger
Lyrics by Joe Darion
Shinbone Alley 1957

Pretty Lady
Music and lyrics by Ronnie Britton
Gift of the Magi (OB) 1975

Pretty Lady
Music and lyrics by Stephen Sondheim
Pacific Overtures 1976

Pretty Little China Girl
Music by Gustave Kerker
Lyrics by Hugh Morton
The Belle of New York 1897

Pretty Little Missus Bell
Music and lyrics by Cole Porter
Seven Lively Arts 1944

Dropped from production

Pretty Little Picture
Music and lyrics by Stephen Sondheim
A Funny Thing Happened on the Way to the Forum 1962

Pretty Little So-and-So
Music by Edgar Fairchild
Lyrics by Henry Myers
The New Yorkers 1927

Pretty Little Stranger
Music by Charles Rosoff
Lyrics by Leo Robin
Judy 1927

The Pretty Milliners
Music by Jerome Kern
Lyrics by Edward Madden
La Belle Paree 1911

Pretty Ming Toy
Music by Sigmund Romberg
Lyrics by Alex Gerber
Poor Little Ritz Girl 1920

Pretty, Petite and Sweet
Music by Harry Archer
Lyrics by Walter O'Keefe
Just a Minute 1928

Pretty Piggy
Music and lyrics by Elizabeth Swados
Alice in Concert (OB) 1980

Pretty Pin-Up
Music by Mel Marvin
Lyrics by Christopher Durang
A History of the American Film 1978

Pretty Polly with a Past
Music by Irving Berlin
Lyrics by George M. Cohan
The Cohan Revue of 1918

Pretty Things
Music by Rudolf Friml
Lyrics by Oscar Hammerstein II and Otto Harbach
Rose Marie 1924

Pretty to Walk With
Music by Harold Arlen
Lyrics by E.Y. Harburg
Jamaica 1957

Pretty Women
Music by Galt MacDermot
Lyrics by Rochelle Owens
The Karl Marx Play (OB) 1973

Pretty Women
Music and lyrics by Stephen Sondheim
Sweeney Todd 1979

Priam's Little Congai
Music by Will Irwin
Lyrics by Agnes Morgan
The Grand Street Follies (1929)

Priceless Relics
Music by Mel Marvin
Lyrics by Robert Montgomery
Green Pond (OB) 1977

Pricklepear Bloom
Music by Robert Waldman
Lyrics by Alfred Uhry
The Robber Bridegroom 1975

Pride and Freedom
Music and lyrics by Stephen H. Lemberg
Jazzbo Brown 1980

Prigio Don't Know
Music by Lehman Engel
Lyrics by Agnes Morgan
A Hero Is Born 1937

Prim and Proper
Music and lyrics by Skip Redwine and Larry Frank
Frank Merriwell, or Honor Challenged 1971

Prince Charming
Music by Sigmund Romberg
Lyrics by Dorothy Donnelly
My Princess 1927

Prince Charming
Music by Walter Kollo
Lyrics by Harry B. Smith
Three Little Girls 1930

Prince Charming
Music by Harden Church
Lyrics by Edward Heyman
Caviar 1934

The Prince Is Giving a Ball
Music by Richard Rodgers
Lyrics by Oscar Hammerstein II
Cinderella (1957) TV

The Prince Is Mad
Music by George Fischoff
Lyrics by Verna Tomasson
The Prince and the Pauper (OB) 1963

The Prince Of Humbug
Music by Cy Coleman
Lyrics by Michael Stewart
Barnum 1980

A Princely Scheme
Music by Mark Charlap
Lyrics by Carolyn Leigh
Peter Pan 1954

Princes and Princesses
Music and lyrics by Noël Coward
Tonight at 8:30 ("Family Album") 1936

The Prince's Farewell
Music by Cy Coleman
Lyrics by Carolyn Leigh
Little Me 1962

Princes' Street
Music by Don McAfee
Lyrics by Nancy Leeds
Great Scot! (OB) 1965

Princess of Dollar Princesses
Music by Leo Fall
Lyrics by George Grossmith, Jr.
The Dollar Princess 1909

Princess of Far Away
Music by Victor Herbert
Lyrics by James O'Dea
The Lady of the Slipper 1912

The Princess of Pure Delight
Music by Kurt Weill
Lyrics by Ira Gershwin
Lady in the Dark 1941

Priorities
Music by Lou Cooper
Lyrics by Roslyn Harvey
Of V We Sing 1942

Prisms
Music by Carl Friberg
Lyrics by Hal Hackady
New Faces of 1968

A Prisoner of Love
Music by Jerome Kern
Lyrics by Paul West
The Red Petticoat 1912

Prisoners in Niggertown
Music by Galt MacDermot
Lyrics by Gerome Ragni and James Rado
Hair 1968

Private Hunting Ground
Music and lyrics by Norman Dean
Autumn's Here (OB) 1966

Probably
Music and lyrics by C.C. and Ragan Courtney
Earl of Ruston 1971

Probably in Love
Music by Jack Urbont
Lyrics by Bruce Geller
Livin' the Life (OB) 1957

Problem
Music by Alan Friedman
Lyrics by Dennis Marks
Fallout (OB) 1959

Procession
Music by Coleridge-Taylor Perkinson
Lyrics by Errol Hill
Man Better Man (OB) 1969

Professor Cupid
Music by Victor Herbert
Lyrics by Robert B. Smith
The Debutante 1914

Progress
Music by Kurt Weill
Lyrics by Alan Jay Lerner
Love Life 1948

Progress
Music by Robert Waldman
Lyrics by Alfred Uhry
Here's Where I Belong 1968

Progress Is the Root of All Evil
Music by Gene de Paul
Lyrics by Johnny Mercer
Li'l Abner 1956

Prologue
Music by Arthur Schwartz
Lyrics by Howard Dietz
The Show Is On 1936

Prologue
Music by Leonard Bernstein
Lyrics by Stephen Sondheim
West Side Story 1957

A Promenade
Music by Frederick Loewe
Lyrics by Earle Crooker
Great Lady 1938

Promenade
Music by Peter Link
Lyrics by Jacob Brackman
King of Hearts 1978

Promenade
Music and lyrics by Clark Gesner
The Utter Glory of Morrissey Hall 1979

The Promenade
Music and lyrics by Jerry Herman
La Cage aux Folles 1983

Promenade the Esplanade
Music by Jean Schwartz
Lyrics by Alfred Bryan
A Night in Spain 1927

The Promenade Walk at the Beach
Music by Alfred Goodman, Maury Rubens
and J. Fred Coots
Lyrics by Clifford Grey
Artists and Models (1925)

Promise Me a Rose
Music and lyrics by Bob Merrill
Take Me Along 1959

Promise Not to Stand Me Up Again
Music by Albert Von Tilzer
Lyrics by Neville Fleeson
Bye Bye, Bonnie 1927

The Promise of What I Could Be
Music by Stanley Lebowsky
Lyrics by Fred Tobias
Gantry 1970

Promise Your Kisses
Music by Con Conrad
Lyrics by Gus Kahn
Kitty's Kisses 1926

Promises, Promises
Music by Burt Bacharach
Lyrics by Hal David
Promises, Promises 1968

Proper Due
Music by Robert Kessler
Lyrics by Lola Pergament
O Marry Me! (OB) 1961

A Proper Gentleman
Music and lyrics by David Heneker
Half a Sixpence 1965

Propinquity
Music by Sonny Burke
Lyrics by Paul Francis Webster and Ray Golden
Alive and Kicking 1950

Proposal Duet
Music by Laurence Rosenthal
Lyrics by James Lipton
Sherry! 1967

The Protest
Music by Harvey Schmidt
Lyrics by Tom Jones
Philemon (OB) 1975

Proud, Erstwhile, Upright, Fair
Music and lyrics by Clark Gesner
The Utter Glory of Morrissey Hall 1979

Proud of You
Music by John Green
Lyrics by George Marion, Jr.
Beat the Band 1942

The Psalm
Music by Mitch Leigh
Lyrics by Joe Darion
Man of La Mancha 1965

The Psychiatry Song
Music by Kurt Weill
Lyrics by Paul Green
Johnny Johnson 1936

Ptolemy
Music and lyrics by Ervin Drake
Her First Roman 1968

Public Enemy Number One
Music and lyrics by Cole Porter
Anything Goes 1934

Public Enemy No.1
Music and lyrics by Harold Rome
Pins and Needles (OB) 1937

Puddin' 'n Tame
Music and lyrics by Al Carmines
The Faggot (OB) 1973

Puka Puka Pants
Music and lyrics by Eaton Magoon, Jr.
13 Daughters 1961

The Pulitzer Prize
Music and lyrics by Irving Berlin
Miss Liberty 1949

Dropped from production

Pull the Boat for Eli
Music by Richard Lewine
Lyrics by Ted Fetter
Naughty-Naught (OB) 1937

Pull Yourself Together
Music by Philip Charig and Richard Myers
Lyrics by Leo Robin
Allez-Oop 1927

Pulverize the Kaiser
Music by Robert Waldman
Lyrics by Alfred Uhry
Here's Where I Belong 1968

Pump Boys
Music and lyrics by Jim Swann
Pump Boys and Dinettes 1982

Punch and Judy Man
Music by Harry Warren
Lyrics by Mort Dixon and Joe Young
The Laugh Parade 1931

Punk
Music by Cheryl Hardwick
Lyrics by Marilyn Suzanne Miller
Girls, Girls, Girls (OB) 1980

Puns
Music by Gerald Alters
Lyrics by Herbert Hartig
Wet Paint (OB) 1965

Puppet Dream
Music by Meyer Kupferman
Lyrics by Paul Goodman
Jonah (OB) 1966

The Pure in Heart
Music and lyrics by Skip Redwine and Larry Frank
Frank Merriwell, or Honor Challenged 1971

Purefoy's Lament
Music by Milton Schafer
Lyrics by Ira Levin
Drat! The Cat! 1965

The Purity Brigade
Music by Gustave Kerker
Lyrics by Hugh Morton
The Belle of New York 1897

Purlie
Music by Gary Geld
Lyrics by Peter Udell
Purlie 1970

Purple Rose
Music by Vernon Duke
Lyrics by Ogden Nash
Two's Company 1952

Purse Snatch
Music by Hank Beebe
Lyrics by Bill Heyer
*Tuscaloosa's Calling Me
But I'm Not Going!* (OB) 1975

Pursuit
Music and lyrics by Marian Grudeff
and Raymond Jessel
Baker Street 1965

A Purty Little Thing
Music by Philip Broughton
Lyrics by Will B. Johnstone
Nine-Fifteen Revue 1930

Push a Button in a Hutton
Music by Jay Gorney
Lyrics by Barry Trivers
Heaven on Earth 1948

Push Around
Music by Richard Rodgers
Lyrics by Lorenz Hart
Betsy 1926

Push de Button
Music by Harold Arlen
Lyrics by E.Y. Harburg
Jamaica 1957

Pussy Cat Song
Music by Al Carmines
Lyrics by Rosalyn Drexler
Home Movies (OB) 1964

The Pussy Foot
Music by Leroy Anderson
Lyrics by Joan Ford and Walter and Jean Kerr
Goldilocks 1958

Put a Curse on You
Music and lyrics by Melvin Van Peebles
Ain't Supposed to Die a Natural Death 1971

Put a Little Magic in Your Life
Music by Elmer Bernstein
Lyrics by Don Black
Merlin 1983

Put 'Em Back
Music by Gene de Paul
Lyrics by Johnny Mercer
Li'l Abner 1956

Put Him Away
Music by Richard Rodgers
Lyrics by Martin Charnin
Two by Two 1970

Put in a Package and Sold
Music by Nancy Ford
Lyrics by Gretchen Cryer
I'm Getting My Act Together and Taking It on the Road 1978

Put It Away Till Spring
Music by Peter Nolan
Lyrics by Joshua Titzell
The Garrick Gaieties (3rd edition) 1930

Put It in the Book
Music and lyrics by Leslie Bricusse and Anthony Newley
The Roar of the Greasepaint—The Smell of the Crowd 1965

Put It in Writing
Music and lyrics by Alan Kohan
Put It in Writing (OB) 1963

Put It Where the Moon Don't Shine
Music and lyrics by Bland Simpson and Jim Wann
Diamond Studs (OB) 1975

Put Me to the Test
Music by George Gershwin
Lyrics by Ira Gershwin
A Damsel in Distress (1937) F

Dropped from film

Put Me to the Test
Music by Jerome Kern
Lyrics by Ira Gershwin
Cover Girl (1944) F

Ira Gershwin thought his lyric, dropped from his brother's score for *A Damsel in Distress*, might be suitable as a Gene Kelly number for *Cover Girl*, which he was writing with Kern. The composer managed to turn out a completely new tune for the complicated lyric without necessitating a single change in words or rhythm.

Put on a Happy Face
Music by Charles Strouse
Lyrics by Lee Adams
Bye Bye Birdie 1960

Put on Your Sunday Clothes
Music and lyrics by Jerry Herman
Hello, Dolly 1964

Put Your Arms Around Me
Music by Kerry Lewis
Lyrics by S.M. Lewis
The Fascinating Widow 1911

Put Your Best Foot Forward
Music by Victor Herbert
Lyrics by James O'Dea
The Lady of the Slipper 1912

Put Your Heart in a Song
Music by Ray Henderson
Lyrics by Ted Koehler
Say When 1934

Put Your Mind Right on It
Music by Jimmy Johnson
Lyrics by Perry Bradford
Messin' Around 1929

Put Your Troubles in a Candy Box
Music by J. Fred Coots
Lyrics by Clifford Grey
Mayflowers 1925

Putting It Together
Music and lyrics by Stephen Sondheim
Sunday in the Park With George (OB) 1983

Puttin' on the Ritz
Music and lyrics by Irving Berlin
Puttin' on the Ritz (1929) F

Putting on the Ritz
Music by Ray Henderson
Lyrics by B.G. DeSylva
Three Cheers 1928

Putty in Your Hands
Music by Laurence Rosenthal
Lyrics by James Lipton
Sherry! 1967

A Puzzlement
Music by Richard Rodgers
Lyrics by Oscar Hammerstein II
The King and I 1951

Q

Quaint Toys
Music by Ivan Caryll
Lyrics by Anne Caldwell and James O'Dea
Chin-Chin 1914

A Quaker Girl
Music by Lionel Monckton
Lyrics by Adrian Ross
The Quaker Girl 1911

Quakers' Meeting
Music by Lionel Monckton
Lyrics by Adrian Ross
The Quaker Girl 1911

Quakin' and Shakin'
Music and lyrics by Elizabeth Swados
Dispatches (OB) 1979

Qualifications
Music and lyrics by Porter Grainger
Yeah Man 1932

The Quarrel
Music by Ivan Caryll
Lyrics by C.M.S. McLellan
Oh! Oh! Delphine 1912

Quarrel for Three
Music by Duke Ellington
Lyrics by John Latouche
Beggar's Holiday 1946

Quarrel-tet
Music by Moose Charlap
Lyrics by Norman Gimbel
Whoop-Up 1958

Quartet Agonistes
Music by Gerald Jay Markoe
Lyrics by Michael Colby
Charlotte Sweet (OB) 1982

Quartet Erotica
Music by Harold Arlen
Lyrics by Ira Gershwin and E.Y. Harburg
Life Begins at 8:40 1934

Quartet Finale
Music by Leonard Bernstein
Lyrics by Richard Wilbur
Candide 1956

Quartet for Losers
Music and lyrics by Ronnie Britton
Greenwich Village Follies (OB) 1976

Que Pasa
Music and lyrics by John Clifton
El Bravo! (OB) 1981

Queen Alice
Music and lyrics by Elizabeth Swados
Alice in Concert (OB) 1980

Queen Cobra
Music and lyrics by Ann Harris
Sky High (OB) 1979

Queen Elizabeth
Music by Richard Rodgers
Lyrics by Lorenz Hart
The Garrick Gaieties (2nd edition) 1926

Queen Esther
Music by George Kleinsinger
Lyrics by Beatrice Goldsmith
Of V We Sing 1942

Queen for a Day
Music and lyrics by Richard Adler and Jerry Ross
John Murray Anderson's Almanac (1953)

Queen of My Heart
Music by Rudolf Friml
Lyrics by P.G. Wodehouse and Clifford Grey
The Three Musketeers 1928

Queen of Spain
Music by Harvey Schmidt
Lyrics by Tom Jones
Shoestring '57 (OB)

The Queen of Terre Haute
Music and lyrics by Cole Porter
Fifty Million Frenchmen 1929

Dropped from production

Queen of the Burlesque Wheel
Music and lyrics by Steve Allen
Sophie 1963

The Queen of the Philippine Islands
Music by Leslie Stuart
Florodora 1900

Queen of the Ring
Music by Victor Herbert
Lyrics by Harry B. Smith
Miss Dolly Dollars 1905

Queenie's Ballyhoo (C'mon, Folks)
Music by Jerome Kern
Lyrics by Oscar Hammerstein II
Show Boat 1927

Queenly Comments
Music by Gerald Jay Markoe
Lyrics by Michael Colby
Charlotte Sweet (OB) 1982

Queer Little Insect
Music by George Kleinsinger
Lyrics by Joe Darion
Shinbone Alley 1957

Quelque Chose
Music and lyrics by Cole Porter
Paris 1928

Dropped from production

Querida
Music by Maury Rubens
Lyrics by Clifford Grey
The Great Temptations 1926

A Question of Gait
Music by Lehman Engel
Lyrics by Thomas Burke
A Hero Is Born 1937

Questions
Music and lyrics by Micki Grant
Don't Bother Me, I Can't Cope (OB) 1972

Questions Questions
Music and lyrics by James Rado
Rainbow (OB) 1972

Queue at Drury Lane
Music and lyrics by Robert Wright
and George Forrest
Kean 1961

Quick Henry, the Flit
Music by Harry Revel
Lyrics by Mack Gordon
Smiling Faces 1932

Quickly
Music by Jacques Urbont
Lyrics by Bruce Geller
All in Love (OB) 1961

Quiet
Music by Leonard Bernstein
Lyrics by Richard Wilbur
Candide 1956

Quiet
Music by Mary Rodgers
Lyrics by Marshall Barer
Once Upon a Mattress 1959

Quiet Afternoon
Music by Harry Archer
Lyrics by Harlan Thompson
Little Jessie James 1923

Quiet Country
Music by Kenn Long and Jim Crozier
Lyrics by Kenn Long
Touch (OB) 1970

A Quiet Girl
Music by Leonard Bernstein
Lyrics by Betty Comden and Adolph Green
Wonderful Town 1953

A Quiet Land
Music and lyrics by Robert Wright and George
Forrest (based on Rachmaninoff)
Anya 1965

A Quiet Life
Music and lyrics by Johnny Burke
Donnybrook! 1961

Quiet Morning
Music and lyrics by Ronnie Britton
Gift of the Magi (OB) 1975

Quiet Night
Music by Richard Rodgers
Lyrics by Lorenz Hart
On Your Toes 1936

Quiet Street
Music by George Kleinsinger
Lyrics by Joe Darion
Shinbone Alley 1957

A Quiet Thing
Music by John Kander
Lyrics by Fred Ebb
Flora, the Red Menace 1965

Quit Kiddin'
Music by Raymond Hubbell
Lyrics by Anne Caldwell
Yours Truly 1927

Quite a Party
Music by George Gershwin
Lyrics by B.G. DeSylva
Sweet Little Devil 1924

Quite Parisian
Music by Franz Lehár
Lyrics by Adrian Ross
The Merry Widow 1907

Quittin' Time
Music and lyrics by John Rox
All in Fun 1940

Quittin' Time
Music by Nancy Ford
Lyrics by Gretchen Cryer
Now Is the Time for All Good Men (OB) 1967

Quitting Time
Music and lyrics by Melvin Van Peebles
Don't Play Us Cheap 1972

R

Rabbit Song
Music by Armand Vecsey
Lyrics by P.G. Wodehouse
The Nightingale 1927

Rabbit's Excuse
Music and lyrics by Elizabeth Swados
Alice in Concert (OB) 1980

The Rabbit's House
Music and lyrics by Elizabeth Swados
Alice in Concert (OB) 1980

The Race Is Over
Music by Joseph Meyer and James F. Hanley
Lyrics by B.G. DeSylva
Big Boy 1925

Racin' Form
Music by Harold Arlen
Lyrics by Johnny Mercer
St. Louis Woman 1946

Racing With the Clock
Music and lyrics by Richard Adler and Jerry Ross
The Pajama Game 1954

Rackety Coo!
Music by Rudolf Friml
Lyrics by Otto Harbach
Katinka 1915

Radio
Music and lyrics by Gene Buck and Dave Stamper
Ziegfeld Follies of 1922

Radio City, I Love You
Music by Lee Wainer
Lyrics by June Carroll
New Faces of 1943

Radziwill
Music and lyrics by Ralph Benatzky
Meet My Sister 1930

Rafesville, U.S.A.
Music by Leon Pober
Lyrics by Bud Freeman
Beg, Borrow or Steal 1960

Raffles
Music by Vernon Duke
Lyrics by Al Dubin
Keep Off the Grass 1940

Rag Offen the Bush
Music by Gene de Paul
Lyrics by Johnny Mercer
Li'l Abner 1956

Raga
Music and lyrics by Elizabeth Swados
Nightclub Cantata (OB) 1977

Raggedy Ann
Music by Jerome Kern
Lyrics by Anne Caldwell
Stepping Stones 1923

Raggedy Rag
Music and lyrics by Gene Buck and Dave Stamper
Ziegfeld Follies of 1921

Rags
Music and lyrics by Deed Meyer
'Toinette (OB) 1961

Rags and Tatters
Music by Richard Rodgers
Lyrics by Lorenz Hart
Simple Simon 1930

The Ragtime College Girl
Music by Kerry Mills
Lyrics by S.M. Lewis
The Fascinating Widow 1911

Ragtime College Turkey Trot
Music by Percy Wenrich
Lyrics by Julian Eltinge and Jack Mahoney
The Fascinating Widow 1911

The Ragtime Express
Music by Jean Schwartz
Lyrics by Joseph W. Herbert and Harold Atteridge
The Honeymoon Express 1913

Ragtime Melodrama
Music and lyrics by Irving Berlin
Stop! Look! Listen! 1915

The Ragtime Restaurant
Music by Jerome Kern
Lyrics by Paul West
The Red Petticoat 1912

Ragtime Romeo
Music by James Mundy
Lyrics by John Latouche
The Vamp 1955

Ragtime Temple Bells
Music by Ivan Caryll
Lyrics by Anne Caldwell and James O'Dea
Chin-Chin 1914

Rah, Rah, Rah
Music by Sam Stept
Lyrics by Irving Caesar and Herb Magidson
George White's Music Hall Varieties 1932

Rahadlakum
Music and lyrics by Robert Wright and George
Forrest (based on Alexander Borodin)
Kismet 1953

Railbird
Music by Gary Geld
Lyrics by Peter Udell
Angel 1978

Rain
Music by Lewis E. Gensler and Milton Schwarzwald
Lyrics by George S. Kaufman, Marc Connelly
and Ira Gershwin
Be Yourself 1924

The Rain in Spain
Music by Frederick Loewe
Lyrics by Alan Jay Lerner
My Fair Lady 1956

Rain on the Roof
Music and lyrics by Stephen Sondheim
Follies 1971

Rain on the Sea
Music by Irving Caesar and Sam Lerner
Lyrics by Gerald Marks
My Dear Public 1943

Rain or Shine
Music by Milton Ager
Lyrics by Jack Yellen
Rain or Shine 1928

The Rain Song
Music by Harvey Schmidt
Lyrics by Tom Jones
110 in the Shade 1963

Rain Your Love on Me
Music by Nancy Ford
Lyrics by Gretchen Cryer
Now Is the Time for All Good Men (OB) 1967

Rainbow
Music by Harold Levey
Lyrics by Zelda Sears
Rainbow Rose 1926

Rainbow
Music and lyrics by Ann Harris
Sky High (OB) 1979

Rainbow Girl
Music by Louis A. Hirsch
Lyrics by Rennold Wolf
The Rainbow Girl 1918

Rainbow High
Music by Andrew Lloyd Webber
Lyrics by Tim Rice
Evita 1979

Rainbow of Girls
Music and lyrics by Irving Berlin
Ziegfeld Follies (1927)

The Rainbow of Your Smile
Music by Percy Wenrich
Lyrics by Raymond Peck
Castles in the Air 1926

Rainbow Tour
Music by Andrew Lloyd Webber
Lyrics by Tim Rice
Evita 1979

Raining in My Heart
Music by Jim Wise
Lyrics by George Haimsohn and Robin Miller
Dames at Sea (OB) 1968

Rainy Afternoon Girls
Music by George Gershwin
Lyrics by Ira Gershwin
Lady, Be Good! 1924

Rainy Day
Music by Tom Johnstone
Lyrics by Will B. Johnstone
I'll Say She Is 1924

A Rainy Day
Music by Arthur Schwartz
Lyrics by Howard Dietz
Flying Colors 1932

Rainy Night in Rio
Music by Arthur Schwartz
Lyrics by Leo Robin
The Time, the Place and the Girl (1946) F

Raise the Dust
Music by Joseph Meyer
Lyrics by Edward Eliscu
Lady Fingers 1929

Raise the Flag of Dixie
Music by Gary Geld
Lyrics by Peter Udell
Shenandoah 1975

Raising Cain
Music by Robert Waldman
Lyrics by Alfred Uhry
Here's Where I Belong 1968

Rakish Young Man With the Whiskers
Music by Harold Arlen
Lyrics by E.Y. Harburg
Bloomer Girl 1944

Rally Round Me
Music by Vincent Youmans
Lyrics by Ring Lardner
Smiles 1930

Rambler Rose
Music by Louis A. Hirsch
Lyrics by Gene Buck and Dave Stamper
Ziegfeld Follies of 1922

Ramona's Lament
Music by Harris Wheeler
Lyrics by Mary L. Fisher
Blue Plate Special (OB) 1983

Rancho Mexicano
Music and Lyrics by Tatanacho
The Garrick Gaieties (1st edition) 1925

Rang-Tang
Music by Ford Dabney
Lyrics by Jo Trent
Rang-Tang 1927

The Rangers' Song
Music by Harry Tierney
Lyrics by Joseph McCarthy
Rio Rita 1927

The Ranger's Song
Music by Sigmund Romberg
Lyrics by Harry B. Smith
The Love Call 1927

The Rap
Music by Henry Krieger
Lyrics by Tom Eyen
Dreamgirls 1981

Rap Tap on Wood
Music and lyrics by Cole Porter
Born to Dance (1936) F

The Rape of Miss Goldberg
Music and lyrics by William Finn
In Trousers (OB) 1981

Raquel
Music and lyrics by George Whiting and Joe Burke
Earl Carroll's Vanities (1928)

Rare Wines
Music by Larry Grossman
Lyrics by Betty Comden and Adolph Green
A Doll's Life 1982

Rat-Tat-Tat-Tat
Music by Jule Styne
Lyrics by Bob Merrill
Funny Girl 1964

Raunchy
Music by Harvey Schmidt
Lyrics by Tom Jones
110 in the Shade 1963

Raven the Magnet
Music and lyrics by Al Carmines
The Evangelist (OB) 1982

Raving Beauty
Music and lyrics by Hugh Martin and Ralph Blane
Best Foot Forward (1963 OB revival)

Razzle Dazzle
Music by John Kander
Lyrics by Fred Ebb
Chicago 1975

Reach Out
Music by Claibe Richardson
Lyrics by Kenward Elmslie
The Grass Harp 1971

Reach Out
Music and lyrics by Johnny Brandon
Love! Love! Love! (OB) 1977

Reaching for the Moon
Music by Harry Ruby
Lyrics by Bert Kalmar
Top Speed 1929

Reaching for the Moon
Music and lyrics by Irving Berlin
Reaching for the Moon (1930) F

Reaching, Touching
Music by Kenn Long and Jim Crozier
Lyrics by Kenn Long
Touch (OB) 1970

Read It in the Weekly
Music by Keith Hermann
Lyrics by Charlotte Anker and Irene Rosenberg
Onward Victoria 1980

Read What the Papers Say
Music by Ray Henderson
Lyrics by B.G. DeSylva and Lew Brown
George White's Scandals (1925)

Readin', Writin' and Rythmatic
Music by Leo Edwards
Lyrics by Herman Timberg
You'll See Stars 1942

Reading
Music by Charles Strouse
Lyrics by David Rogers
Charlie and Algernon 1980

Reading, Writing and a Little Bit of Rhythm
Music by Jimmy McHugh
Lyrics by Al Dubin
The Streets of Paris 1939

Ready Cash
Music by Sammy Fain
Lyrics by Dan Shapiro
Ankles Aweigh 1955

Ready or Not
Music by Patrick Rose
Lyrics by Merv Campone and Richard Ouzounian
A Bistro Car on the CNR (OB) 1978

The Real American Folk Song (Is a Rag)
Music by George Gershwin
Lyrics by Ira Gershwin
Ladies First 1918

These were Ira Gershwin's first lyrics in any
production.

A Real American Tune
Music by Ray Henderson
Lyrics by B.G. DeSylva and Lew Brown
George White's Scandals (1928)

Real Estate
Music by Elizabeth Swados
Lyrics by Garry Trudeau
Doonesbury 1983

Real Life Funnies
Music and lyrics by Alan Menken
Real Life Funnies (OB) 1981

A Real Life Lullabye
Music by Bert Keyes and Bob Larimer
Lyrics by Bob Larimer
But Never Jam Today 1979

Real Live Girl
Music by Cy Coleman
Lyrics by Carolyn Leigh
Little Me 1962

The Real Me
Music by Charles Strouse
Lyrics by Lee Adams
All American 1962

Real Rich Ladies
Music and lyrics by Jay Thompson
Double Entry (OB) 1961

A Real Slow Drag
Music and lyrics by Scott Joplin
Treemonisha 1975

Written in 1909

The Real Spring Drive
Music by Jerome Kern
Lyrics by Herbert Reynolds
Rock-a-Bye Baby 1918

The Real Thing
Music by Mary Rodgers
Lyrics by Marshall Barer
The Mad Show (OB) 1966

Really and Truly
Music by Jean Schwartz
Lyrics by Clifford Grey and William Cary Duncan
Sunny Days 1928

Recipe for Love
Music by Tom Mandel
Lyrics by John Braswell
The Bar That Never Closes (OB) 1972

Reciprocity
Music by Walter Kent
Lyrics by Kim Gannon
Seventeen 1951

Reckless
Music by Jerome Kern
Lyrics by Oscar Hammerstein II
Reckless (1935) F

The Reckoning
Music by Gerald Jay Markoe
Lyrics by Michael Colby
Charlotte Sweet (OB) 1982

The Red Ball Express
Music and lyrics by Harold Rome
Call Me Mister 1946

The Red Baron
Music and lyrics by Clark Gesner
You're a Good Man, Charlie Brown (OB) 1967

Red-Blooded American Boy
Music and lyrics by Jack Lawrence
and Stan Freeman
I Had a Ball 1964

Red Blues
Music and lyrics by Cole Porter
Silk Stockings 1955

Red Caps Cappers
Music and lyrics by James Johnson and Cecil Mack
Runnin' Wild 1923

Red-Collar Job
Music by Louis Bellson and Will Irwin
Lyrics by Richard Ney
Portofino 1958

The Red Cross Girl
Music by Raymond Hubbell
Lyrics by Glen MacDonough
The Jolly Bachelors 1910

A Red-Headed Woman
Music by George Gershwin
Lyrics by Ira Gershwin
Porgy and Bess 1935

Red, Hot and Blue
Music and lyrics by Cole Porter
Red, Hot and Blue! 1936

Red Hot and Blue Rhythm
Music by J. Fred Coots
Lyrics by Arthur Swanstrom and Benny Davis
Sons o' Guns 1929

Red Hot Chicago
Music by Ray Henderson
Lyrics by B.G. DeSylva and Lew Brown
Flying High 1930

Red Hot Mama
Music and lyrics by Steve Allen
Sophie 1963

Red Hot Trumpet
Music by Richard Rodgers
Lyrics by Lorenz Hart
Spring Is Here 1929

Red Letter Day
Music by Ernest G. Schweikert
Lyrics by Frank Reardon
Rumple 1957

Red Lover Wrist Watch
Music by Galt MacDermot
Lyrics by Rochelle Owens
The Karl Marx Play (OB) 1973

Red Queen
Music and lyrics by Elizabeth Swados
Alice in Concert (OB) 1980

Red River
Music by Alma Sanders
Lyrics by Monte Carlo
The Houseboat on the Styx 1928

Red, White and Blue
Music by Jerome Kern
Lyrics by Adrian Ross
The Dollar Princess 1909

The Red, White and Blue
Music by Mel Marvin
Lyrics by Christopher Durang
A History of the American Film 1978

The Red White and Blues
Music by Leonard Bernstein
Lyrics by Alan Jay Lerner
1600 Pennsylvania Avenue 1976

Red, White and Maddox Kazoo March
Music and lyrics by Don Tucker
Red, White and Maddox 1969

Red Wine
Music by Rudolf Friml
Lyrics by P.G. Wodehouse and Clifford Grey
The Three Musketeers 1928

Redecorate
Music by Abraham Ellstein
Lyrics by Walter Bullock
Great to Be Alive 1950

Reflection
Music and lyrics by Clark Gesner
The Utter Glory of Morrissey Hall 1979

Reflections
Music and lyrics by Robert Swerdlow
Love Me, Love My Children (OB) 1971

Reflections in a Mirror
Music and lyrics by John Raniello
Movie Buff (OB) 1977

Reform
Music by Jerry Bock
Lyrics by Sheldon Harnick
Tenderloin 1960

The Regal Romp
Music by Alberta Nichols
Lyrics by Mann Holiner
Angela 1928

Regardez-Moi
Music by Sigmund Romberg
Lyrics by Oscar Hammerstein II
East Wind 1931

Regency Rakes
Music and lyrics by Noël Coward
Conversation Piece 1934

The Regiment Loves the Girls
Music by Edward Künneke
Lyrics by Clifford Grey
Mayflowers 1925

Regimental Band
Music by Sigmund Romberg
Lyrics by Arthur Wimperis
Louie the 14th 1925

Regimental Song
Music by Rudolf Friml
Lyrics by Brian Hooker
The White Eagle 1927

A Regular Guy
Music by Jerome Kern
Lyrics by Harry B. Smith
Ninety in the Shade 1915

Rehearsal Tap
Music and lyrics by Buster Davis
Doctor Jazz 1975

Rehearse!
Music by Leonard Bernstein
Lyrics by Alan Jay Lerner
1600 Pennsylvania Avenue 1976

Reincarnation
Music by Richard Rodgers
Lyrics by Lorenz Hart and Jimmy Durante
Hollywood Party (1934) F

Rejoice
Music by Gary William Friedman
Lyrics by Will Holt
The Me Nobody Knows (OB) 1970

A Relatively Simple Affair
Music by Jerry Bock
Lyrics by Sheldon Harnick
The Body Beautiful 1958

Relax
Music and lyrics by Harold Rome
Wish You Were Here 1952

Relax and Enjoy It
Music by Clay Warnick
Lyrics by Edward Eager
Dream With Music 1944

Religion in My Feet
Music and lyrics by J.C. Johnson
Change Your Luck 1930

The Religious Establishment
Music and lyrics by Al Carmines
Joan (OB) 1972

The Reluctant Cannibal
Music by Donald Swann
Lyrics by Michael Flanders
At the Drop of a Hat 1959

Remarkable Fellow
Music by Victor Young
Lyrics by Stella Unger
Seventh Heaven 1955

Remarkable People We
Music by John Green
Lyrics by Edward Heyman
Here Goes the Bride 1931

Remember?
Music and lyrics by Stephen Sondheim
A Little Night Music 1973

Remember
Music by Mitch Leigh
Lyrics by N. Richard Nash
Saravá 1979

Remember Always to Give
Music by Galt MacDermot
Lyrics by William Dumaresq
The Human Comedy (OB) 1983

Remember Joplin
Music and lyrics by Al Carmines
The Evangelist (OB) 1982

Remember Me (Love Song)
Music by Edward Künneke
Lyrics by Harry B. Smith
The Love Song 1925

Remember, Remember
Music by Frank Fields
Lyrics by Armand Aulicino
The Shoemaker and the Peddler (OB) 1960

Remember That Day
Music and lyrics by John Driver
Ride the Winds 1974

Remember That I Care
Music by Kurt Weill
Lyrics by Langston Hughes
Street Scene 1947

Remember the Dancing
Music by David Baker
Lyrics by David Craig
Copper and Brass 1957

Remember the Night
Music by Frederico Valerio
Lyrics by Elizabeth Miele
Hit the Trail 1954

Remember Today
Music by Howard Marren
Lyrics by Enid Futterman
Portrait of Jennie (OB) 1982

Remember When I Hated You?
Music by Al Carmines
Lyrics by Rosalyn Drexler
Home Movies (OB) 1964

Remembering You
Music by J. Fred Coots
Lyrics by Clifford Grey
June Days 1925

Remembrances of Things Past
Music and lyrics by Frederick Silver
Gay Company (OB) 1974

Remembering
Music and lyrics by Vivian Duncan
and Rosetta Duncan
Topsy and Eva   1924

Remind Me
Music by Jerome Kern
Lyrics by Dorothy Fields
One Night in the Tropics (1940) F

Written four years earlier for an unproduced film
entitled *Riviera*.

Rendezvous
Music by Sigmund Romberg
Lyrics by Irving Caesar
Melody 1933

Rendezvous Time in Paris
Music by Jimmy McHugh
Lyrics by Al Dubin
The Streets of Paris 1939

Renita Renata
Music by Emil Gerstenberger and Carle Carlton
Lyrics by Howard Johnson
The Lace Petticoat 1927

Repent
Music by Cy Coleman
Lyrics by Betty Comden and Adolph Green
On the Twentieth Century 1978

Requiem
Music and lyrics by Ron Dante and Gene Allan
Billy 1969

Requiem
Music by Stanley Silverman
Lyrics by Tom Hendry
Doctor Selavy's Magic Theatre (OB) 1972

Requiem for Evita
Music by Andrew Lloyd Webber
Lyrics by Tim Rice
Evita 1979

The Rescue
Music by John Clifton
Lyrics by John Clifton and Ben Tarver
Man With a Load of Mischief (OB) 1966

The Rescue
Music and lyrics by Scott Joplin
Treemonisha 1975

Written in 1909

Respectability
Music and lyrics by Harold Rome
Destry Rides Again 1959

Respectable
Music by Keith Hermann
Lyrics by Charlotte Anker and Irene Rosenberg
Onward Victoria 1980

The Rest of Michael Davis
Music and lyrics by Walter Marks
Broadway Follies 1981

Rest Room Rose
Music by Richard Rodgers
Lyrics by Lorenz Hart
Crazy Quilt 1931

A Rested Body Is a Rested Mind
Music and lyrics by Charlie Smalls
The Wiz 1975

Restless
Music by Ray Henderson
Lyrics by Lew Brown
Strike Me Pink 1933

Restless
Music and lyrics by Joan Edwards and Lyn Duddy
Tickets Please 1950

Restless Heart
Music and lyrics by Harold Rome
Fanny 1954

The Return
Music by Jean Gilbert
Lyrics by Harry B. and Robert B. Smith
Modest Suzanne 1912

Reuben
Music by Harry Archer
Lyrics by Harlan Thompson
Twinkle Twinkle 1926

Reunion
Music and lyrics by Craig Carnelia
Is There Life After High School? 1982

Revenge
Music and lyrics by Cole Porter
Let's Face It! 1941

Dropped from production

Revenge
Music by John Kander
Lyrics by James Goldman, John Kander
and William Goldman
A Family Affair 1962

Revenge
Music by Charles Strouse
Lyrics by Lee Adams
It's a Bird, It's a Plane, It's Superman 1966

Revenge Song
Music and lyrics by Elizabeth Swados
Runaways 1978

Reveries
Music by Victor Herbert
Lyrics by Henry Blossom
Eileen 1917

Dropped from production

Reviewing the Situation
Music and lyrics by Lionel Bart
Oliver! 1963

The Revival
Music by Peter Link
Lyrics by C.C. Courtney and Ragan Courtney
Earl of Ruston 1971

Revival Day
Music by Will Irwin
Lyrics by Malcolm McComb
Sweet and Low 1930

Rex
Music by Richard Rodgers
Lyrics by Sheldon Harnick
Rex 1976

Dropped from production

Rhapsody
Music by Morgan Lewis
Lyrics by Nancy Hamilton
One for the Money 1939

Rhapsody of Love
Music by H. Maurice Jacquet
Lyrics by Preston Sturges
The Well of Romance 1930

Rhode Island Is Famous for You
Music by Arthur Schwartz
Lyrics by Howard Dietz
Inside U.S.A. 1948

Rhode Island Tango
Music by Alan Menken
Lyrics by Dennis Green
God Bless You, Mr. Rosewater (OB) 1979

The Rhumba Jumps
Music by Hoagy Carmichael
Lyrics by Johnny Mercer
Walk With Music 1940

A Rhyme for Angela
Music by Kurt Weill
Lyrics by Ira Gershwin
The Firebrand of Florence 1945

Rhymes Have I
Music and lyrics by Robert Wright and George
Forrest
Kismet 1953

Based on a theme from Borodin's Symphony No. 2
in B minor

Rhythm
Music by Richard Rodgers
Lyrics by Lorenz Hart
The Show Is On 1936

Rhythm Feet
Music and lyrics by J.C. Johnson
Change Your Luck 1930

Rhythm in My Hair
Music by Will Irwin
Lyrics by Norman Zeno
Fools Rush In 1934

Rhythm Is a Racket
Music by Eubie Blake
Lyrics by J. Milton Reddie and Cecil Mack
Swing It 1937

The Rhythm Is Red an' White an' Blue
Music by Al Moss
Lyrics by David Greggory
Tis of Thee 1940

Rhythm of America
Music by Eubie Blake
Lyrics by Noble Sissle
Shuffle Along of 1952

Rhythm of Life
Music by Cy Coleman
Lyrics by Dorothy Fields
Sweet Charity 1966

Rhythm of the Day
Music by Owen Murphy
Lyrics by Donald Lindley
Earl Carroll's Vanities (1925)

Rhythm of the Day
Music by Richard Rodgers
Lyrics by Lorenz Hart
Dancing Lady (1933) F

Rhythm of the Waves
Music by Vincent Rose
Lyrics by Charles and Harry Tobias
Earl Carroll's Sketch Book (1929)

Ribbons and Bows
Music and lyrics by Irving Berlin
Ziegfeld Follies (1927)

Ribbons Down My Back
Music and lyrics by Jerry Herman
Hello, Dolly 1964

Rice and Shoes
Music by Vincent Youmans
Lyrics by Arthur Francis and Schuyler Greene
Two Little Girls in Blue 1921

The Rich
Music and lyrics by Marc Blitzstein
The Cradle Will Rock 1938

The Rich
Music and lyrics by Bob Merrill
Carnival 1961

Rich and Famous
Music by Ronald Melrose
Lyrics by Bill Russell
Fourtune (OB) 1980

Rich and Happy
Music and lyrics by Stephen Sondheim
Merrily We Roll Along 1981

Rich Butterfly
Music by Richard Lewine
Lyrics by Arnold B. Horwitt
The Girls Against the Boys 1959

Rich Is
Music by Larry Grossman
Lyrics by Hal Hackady
Minnie's Boys 1970

Rich Man, Poor Man
Music by Jerome Kern
Lyrics by Clare Kummer
Ninety in the Shade 1915

Rich Man! Poor Man!
Music by Richard Rodgers
Lyrics by Lorenz Hart
Spring Is Here 1929

Rich Man, Poor Man, Beggar-Man, Thief
Music by Victor Herbert
Lyrics by George V. Hobart
Old Dutch 1909

Rich Man's Frug
Music by Cy Coleman
Lyrics by Dorothy Fields
Sweet Charity 1966

Rich or Poor
Music by Kay Swift
Lyrics by Paul James
Fine and Dandy 1930

Rich, Rich, Rich
Music by Mary Rodgers
Lyrics by Martin Charnin
Hot Spot 1963

Riches
Music by Robert Waldman
Lyrics by Alfred Uhry
The Robber Bridegroom 1975

Riddle-Diddle Me This
Music and lyrics by Cole Porter
Something for the Boys 1943

Dropped before Broadway opening

Riddle Me This
Music by Lewis E. Gensler
Lyrics by E.Y. Harburg
Ballyhoo 1932

The Riddle of You
Music and lyrics by Robert Larimer
King of the Whole Damn World (OB) 1962

Riddle Song
Music by Helen Miller
Lyrics by Eve Merriam
Inner City 1971

Ride, Baby, Ride
Music by Gary William Friedman
Lyrics by Will Holt
Platinum 1978

Ride, Cowboy, Ride
Music by Richard Lewine
Lyrics by Ted Fetter
The Girl From Wyoming (OB) 1938

Ride 'Em, Cowboy
Music by Robert Emmett Dolan
Lyrics by Johnny Mercer
Texas, Li'l Darlin' 1949

Ride Out the Storm
Music by Cy Coleman
Lyrics by Dorothy Fields
Seesaw 1973

Ride the Winds
Music and lyrics by John Driver
Ride the Winds 1974

Rider In the Rain
Music and lyrics by Randy Newman
Maybe I'm Doing It Wrong (1st edition) (OB) 1981

Ridin' High
Music and lyrics by Cole Porter
Red, Hot and Blue! 1936

Ridin' on the Breeze
Music by Jerome Moross
Lyrics by John Latouche
Ballet Ballads 1948

Ridin' on the Moon
Music by Harold Arlen
Lyrics by Johnny Mercer
St. Louis Woman 1946

Riding for a Fall
Music by Bert Keyes and Bob Larimer
Lyrics by Bob Larimer
But Never Jam Today 1979

Riding Habit
Music by Arthur Schwartz
Lyrics by Howard Dietz
Flying Colors 1932

The Riding Lesson
Music by Leo Fall
Lyrics by George Grossmith, Jr.
The Dollar Princess 1909

The Riff Song
Music by Sigmund Romberg
Lyrics by Otto Harbach and Oscar Hammerstein II
The Desert Song 1926

Right
Music by Marvin Hamlisch
Lyrics by Carole Bayer Sager
They're Playing Our Song 1979

Right About Here
Music and lyrics by Arthur Siegel
New Faces of 1968

Right as the Rain
Music by Harold Arlen
Lyrics by E.Y. Harburg
Bloomer Girl 1944

Right at the Start of It
Music by Arthur Schwartz
Lyrics by Howard Dietz
Three's a Crowd 1930

The Right Finger of My Left Hand
Music by Albert Hague
Lyrics by Dorothy Fields
Redhead 1959

The Right Girl
Music and lyrics by Stephen Sondheim
Follies 1971

Right Girls
Music by John Kander
Lyrics by James Goldman, John Kander
and William Goldman
A Family Affair 1962

Right Hand Man
Music and lyrics by Stan Freeman
and Franklin Underwood
Lovely Ladies, Kind Gentlemen 1970

The Right Man
Music by Maury Rubens and Sam Timberg
Lyrics by Moe Jaffe
Broadway Nights 1929

The Right Man
Music and lyrics by Oscar Brand
How to Steal an Election (OB) 1968

Right Out of Heaven
Music by Harry Tierney
Lyrics by Joseph McCarthy
Cross My Heart 1928

The Right Place for a Girl
Music by Rudolf Friml
Lyrics by Paul Francis Webster
Rose Marie (film version, 1954)

The Right Romance
Music by Jerome Kern
Lyrics by Leo Robin
Centennial Summer (1946) F

Right This Way
Music by Bradford Greene
Lyrics by Marianne Brown Waters
Right This Way 1938

The Right Time, the Right Place
Music by Don Gohman
Lyrics by Hal Hackady
Ambassador 1972

Right Way
Music and lyrics by C. Jackson
and James Hatch
Fly Blackbird (OB) 1962

Rigo's Last Lullaby
Music and lyrics by Evelyn Adler
Tales of Rigo 1927

Ring a Ding a Ding Dong Dell
Music by George Gershwin
Lyrics by Ira Gershwin
Strike Up the Band 1930

Ring Iron
Music by Earl Robinson
Lyrics by Waldo Salt
Sandhog (OB) 1954

Ring On
Music by Vincent Youmans
Lyrics by Billy Rose and Edward Eliscu
Great Day! 1929

Dropped from production

Ring on the Finger
Music and lyrics by Harold Rome
Destry Rides Again 1959

Ring Out the Bells
Music by Burton Lane
Lyrics by Alan Jay Lerner
On a Clear Day You Can See Forever 1965

Ring the Bell
Music by Jimmy Van Heusen
Lyrics by Johnny Burke
Carnival in Flanders 1953

A Ring to the Name of Rosie
Music and lyrics by George M. Cohan
The Rise of Rosie O'Reilly 1923

Ringalevio
Music by Richard Lewine
Lyrics by Arnold B. Horwitt
Make Mine Manhattan 1948

Ringmaster Song
Music and lyrics by Ann Harris
Sky High (OB) 1979

Rinka Tinka Man
Music by Lew Kesler
Lyrics by June Sillman
Who's Who 1938

Rin-tin-tin
Music by Sigmund Romberg
Lyrics by Arthur Wimperis
Louie the 14th 1925

Rio Rita
Music by Harry Tierney
Lyrics by Joseph McCarthy
Rio Rita 1927

Rip Van Winkle
Music by Sigmund Romberg
Lyrics by Dorothy Fields
Up in Central Park 1945

Rip Van Winkle and His Little Men
Music by Jerome Kern
Lyrics by Anne Caldwell
The Night Boat 1920

Dropped from production

Rise 'n' Shine
Music by Vincent Youmans
Lyrics by B.G. DeSylva
Take a Chance 1932

Rise Up and Stand Again
Music by Garry Sherman
Lyrics by Peter Udell
Amen Corner 1983

Rising Star
Music by Franz Lehár
Lyrics by Edward Eliscu
Frederika 1937

Rit, Tit, Tat
Music and lyrics by William Finn
In Trousers (OB) 1981

Rita From Argentina
Music and lyrics by Kelly Hamilton
Trixie True Teen Detective (OB) 1980

Ritz Roll and Rock
Music and lyrics by Cole Porter
Silk Stockings (film version, 1957)

The River Bank
Music by Moose Charlap
Lyrics by Norman Gimbel
The Conquering Hero 1961

River Song
Music by Harry Tierney
Lyrics by Joseph McCarthy
Rio Rita 1927

River Song
Music by Vincent Youmans
Lyrics by Billy Rose and Edward Eliscu
Great Day! 1929

Dropped from production

The River Song
Music by Richard Addinsell
Lyrics by Clemence Dane
Come of Age 1934

River Song
Music by Heitor Villa-Lobos
Lyrics by Robert Wright and George Forrest
Magdalena 1948

Rivers of Roses
Music and lyrics by Al Carmines
Joan (OB) 1972

Rivers of Tears
Music and lyrics by Harold Rome
The Zulu and the Zayda 1965

Rivers to the South
Music and lyrics by C. Jackson
and James Hatch
Fly Blackbird (OB) 1962

Riverside Bus
Music by Con Conrad
Lyrics by J.P. McEvoy
Americana (1926)

Riverside Drive
Music and lyrics by Bill and Patti Jacob
Jimmy 1969

Riverwind
Music and lyrics by John Jennings
Riverwind (OB) 1962

Riviera
Music by Rudolf Friml
Lyrics by Otto Harbach and Oscar Hammerstein II
The Wild Rose 1926

The Riviera
Music and lyrics by Sandy Wilson
The Boy Friend 1954

The Riviera Rage
Music by Wally Harper
Lyrics by Joseph McCarthy
Irene (1973 revival)

Road of Dreams
Music by Pat Thayer
Lyrics by Donovan Parsons and Clifford Grey
Mayflowers 1925

The Road That Lies Before
Music by Jerome Kern
Lyrics by P.G. Wodehouse
Have a Heart 1917

Road to Hampton
Music by David Baker
Lyrics by Will Holt
Come Summer 1969

The Road to Happiness
Music by Carl Millöcker (revised by Theo Mackeben)
Lyrics by Rowland Leigh
The Dubarry 1932

The Road to Home
Music by Vincent Youmans
Lyrics by Edward Heyman
Through the Years 1932

See note on "If I Told You"

The Road to Paradise
Music by Sigmund Romberg
Lyrics by Rida Johnson Young
Maytime 1917

The Road to Paradise
Music by Steve Jankowski
Lyrics by Kenny Morris
Francis (OB) 1982

The Road Tour
Music by Charles Strouse
Lyrics by Lee Adams
Golden Boy 1964

The Road You Didn't Take
Music and lyrics by Stephen Sondheim
Follies 1971

The Roaring Twenties Strike Back
Music and lyrics by Harold Rome
Bless You All 1950

The Robber-Baron Minstrel Parade
Music by Leonard Bernstein
Lyrics by Alan Jay Lerner
1600 Pennsylvania Avenue 1976

The Robbers' March
Music by Frederic Norton
Lyrics by Oscar Asche
Chu Chin Chow 1917

The Robbery
Music by Frank Fields
Lyrics by Armand Aulicino
The Shoemaker and the Peddler (OB) 1960

Robert, Alvin, Wendell and Jo Jo
Music by Gary William Friedman
Lyrics by Will Holt
The Me Nobody Knows (OB) 1970

Robert the Roué
Music by Jimmy McHugh
Lyrics by Al Dubin
The Streets of Paris 1939

Robinson Crusoe
Music by Alec Wilder
Lyrics by Arnold Sundgaard
Kittiwake Island (OB) 1960

The Rochelle Hudson Tango
Music by Claibe Richardson
Lyrics by Paul Rosner
Shoestring '57 (OB)

Rock Back the Clock
Music by Diane Leslie
Lyrics by William Gleason
The Coolest Cat in Town (OB) 1978

Rock Island
Music and lyrics by Meredith Willson
The Music Man 1957

Rock 'n' Roll Party Queen
Music and lyrics by Jim Jacobs and Warren Casey
Grease 1972

Rock n' Roll Star
Music and lyrics by Ronnie Britton
Greenwich Village Follies (OB) 1976

Rock, Rock, Rock
Music by Jimmy McHugh
Lyrics by Harold Adamson
As the Girls Go 1948

Rock-a-Bye Baby
Music and lyrics by Irving Berlin
Music Box Revue (4th edition) 1924

Rock-a-Bye, Baby Dear
Music by Jerome Kern
Lyrics by Herbert Reynolds
Rock-a-Bye Baby 1918

Rockabye Hamlet
Music and lyrics by Cliff Jones
Rockabye Hamlet 1976

Rock-A-Bye Your Baby to a Dixie Melody
Music by Jean Schwartz
Lyrics by Joe Young and Sam Lewis
Sinbad (1918)

Rockin'
Music by David Baker
Lyrics by Will Holt
Come Summer 1969

Rockin' in Rhythm
Music by Harold Arlen
Lyrics by Ted Koehler
Earl Carroll's Vanities (1932)

Rocking the Boat
Music by Jimmy Horowitz
Lyrics by Leo Rost and Jimmy Horowitz
Marlowe 1981

Rococo Rag
Music by Don Pippin
Lyrics by Steve Brown
Fashion (OB) 1974

The Roebling Plan
Music by Scott MacLarty
Lyrics by Dorothy Chansky
The Brooklyn Bridge (OB) 1983

The Rogue Song
Music by Herbert Stothart
Lyrics by Clifford Grey
The Rogue Song (1930) F

Role-Playing
Music by Steve Sterner
Lyrics by Peter del Valle
Lovers (OB) 1975

Roll Along, Sadie
Music by Vernon Duke
Lyrics by Ogden Nash
Two's Company 1952

The Roll Call in the Morning
Music by Alma Sanders
Lyrics by Monte Carlo
The Houseboat on the Styx 1928

Roll 'Em
Music by Gerald Marks
Lyrics by Sam Lerner
Hold It! 1948

Roll Jordan
Music by Eubie Blake
Lyrics by Andy Razaf
Blackbirds of 1930

Roll Mississippi
Music by Richard Rodgers
Lyrics by Lorenz Hart
Mississippi (1935) F

Roll of the Drum
Music by Jean Gilbert
Lyrics by Harry B. Smith
The Red Robe 1928

Roll Out the Hose, Boys
Music by Sigmund Romberg (developed by Don Walker)
Lyrics by Leo Robin
The Girl in Pink Tights 1954

Roll Up the Ribbons
Music by Harvey Schmidt
Lyrics by Tom Jones
I Do! I Do! 1966

Roll Yer Socks Up
Music and lyrics by Bob Merrill
New Girl in Town 1957

Rolled Into One
Music by Jerome Kern
Lyrics by P.G. Wodehouse
Oh, Boy! 1917

The Roller Skate Rag
Music by Jule Styne
Lyrics by Bob Merrill
Funny Girl (film version, 1968)

Rollin'
Music and lyrics by Randy Newman
Maybe I'm Doing It Wrong (1st edition) (OB) 1981

Rollin' in Gold
Music by Robert Emmett Dolan
Lyrics by Johnny Mercer
Foxy 1964

Rolling Home
Music and lyrics by Cole Porter
Born to Dance (1936) F

Roma
Music by Armando Trovaioli
Lyrics by Pietro Garinei and Sandro Giovannini
(Lyric translation by Edward Eager)
Rugantino 1964

Romance
Music by Sigmund Romberg
Lyrics by Otto Harbach and Oscar Hammerstein II
The Desert Song 1926

Romance
Music by Sigmund Romberg
Lyrics by Harry B. Smith
Cherry Blossoms 1927

Romance
Music by Rudolf Friml
Lyrics by Rowland Leigh and John Shubert
Music Hath Charms 1934

Romance
Music and lyrics by Rick Besoyan
The Student Gypsy (OB) 1963

Romance!
Music by John Clifton
Lyrics by John Clifton and Ben Tarver
Man With a Load of Mischief (OB) 1966

Romance
Music by David Shire
Lyrics by Richard Maltby, Jr.
Baby 1983

Romance and Musketeer
Music by Kurt Weill
Lyrics by Maxwell Anderson
Knickerbocker Holiday 1938

Romance Is Calling
Music by Edward A. Horan
Lyrics by Frederick Herendeen
All the King's Horses 1934

A Romantic Atmosphere
Music by Jerry Bock
Lyrics by Sheldon Harnick
She Loves Me 1963

Romany
Music by Arthur Schwartz
Lyrics by Henry Myers
The New Yorkers 1927

Romany Life
Music by Victor Herbert
Lyrics by Harry B. Smith
The Fortune Teller 1898

Rome
Music by Milton Schafer
Lyrics by Ronny Graham
Bravo Giovanni 1962

Romeo
Music by Rudolf Friml
Lyrics by Otto Harbach
High Jinks 1913

Roof Space
Music and lyrics by Marian Grudeff
and Raymond Jessel
Baker Street 1965

Roof Tree
Music by Harry Tierney
Lyrics by Joseph McCarthy
Up She Goes 1922

Room Enough for Me
Music by Ray Henderson
Lyrics by B.G. DeSylva and Lew Brown
George White's Scandals (1925)

A Room in Bloomsbury
Music and lyrics by Sandy Wilson
The Boy Friend 1954

Room in My Heart
Music by Sammy Fain
Lyrics by Paul Francis Webster
Christine 1960

A Room With a Bath
Music by Max Ewing
Lyrics by Agnes Morgan
The Grand Street Follies (1929)

A Room With a View
Music and lyrics by Noël Coward
This Year of Grace 1928

The title was, in Coward's words, "unblushingly pinched" from E.M. Forster's novel.

A Room Without Windows
Music and lyrics by Ervin Drake
What Makes Sammy Run? 1964

The Rooster and the Hen
Music by Menachem Zur
Lyrics by Herbert Appleman
Unfair to Goliath (OB) 1970

Rootless
Music by Leon Pober
Lyrics by Bud Freeman
Beg, Borrow or Steal 1960

Rootsie-Pootsie
Music by Franz Lehár
Lyrics by Basil Hood
The Count of Luxembourg 1912

Ropin' Dogies
Music by Ted Simons
Lyrics by Elinor Guggenheimer
Potholes (OB) 1979

Rosa
Music by Baldwin Bergersen
Lyrics by William Archibald
Rosa (OB) 1978

Rosabella
Music and lyrics by Frank Loesser
The Most Happy Fella 1956

Rosalie
Music by George Gershwin
Lyrics by Ira Gershwin
Rosalie 1928

Dropped from production

Rosalie
Music and lyrics by Cole Porter
Rosalie (1937) F

Porter wrote six title songs for this MGM film before coming up with one that he thought would satisfy Louis B. Mayer. But the Big Boss wasn't satisfied and told Porter to go home and write something good and corny. Enraged, Porter did just that in less than three hours, and always hated the song even though it sold half a million copies.

Rosamund's Dream
Music by Robert Waldman
Lyrics by Alfred Uhry
The Robber Bridegroom 1975

The Rose
Music by Mitch Leigh
Lyrics by Charles Burr and Forman Brown
Home Sweet Homer 1976

The Rose Aria
Music by Emil Gerstenberger and Carle Carlton
Lyrics by Howard Johnson
The Lace Petticoat 1927

Rose in the Heather
Music by Franz Lehár
Lyrics by Edward Eliscu
Frederika 1937

A Rose Is a Rose
Music and lyrics by Harold Rome
Bless You All 1950

Rose Lovejoy of Paradise Alley
Music and lyrics by Harold Rome
Destry Rides Again 1959

Rose, Lucky Rose
Music by Victor Herbert
Lyrics by Harry B. Smith
The Enchantress 1911

Rose-Marie
Music by Jerome Kern
Lyrics by Anne Caldwell
Good Morning, Dearie 1921

Rose Marie
Music by Rudolf Friml
Lyrics by Oscar Hammerstein II and Otto Harbach
Rose Marie 1924

Rose of Arizona (musical scene)
Music by Richard Rodgers
Lyrics by Lorenz Hart
The Garrick Gaieties (2nd edition) 1926

Rose of Delight
Music by Jerome Kern
Lyrics by Anne Caldwell and Otto Harbach
Criss-Cross 1926

Rose of Iran
Music by Winthrop Cortelyou
Lyrics by Derick Wulff
Kiss Me 1927

Rose of Madrid
Music by George Gershwin
Lyrics by B.G. DeSylva
George White's Scandals (1924)

Rose of Stamboul
Music by Leo Fall
Lyrics by Harold Atteridge
The Rose of Stamboul 1922

Rose of the World
Music by Victor Herbert
Lyrics by Glen MacDonough
Algeria 1908

Rose of the World
Music by Morris Hamilton
Lyrics by Grace Henry
Earl Carroll's Vanities (1928)

Rose of Washington Square
Music by James F. Hanley
Lyrics by Ballard MacDonald
Ziegfeld Midnight Frolic 1920

Rose Ruby
Music by Jerome Kern
Lyrics by Anne Caldwell
Good Morning, Dearie 1921

Dropped from production

Rose-Time
Music by Ray Henderson
Lyrics by B.G. DeSylva and Lew Brown
George White's Scandals (1925)

Roseland
Music by Lawrence Hurwit
Lyrics by Lee Goldsmith
Sextet 1974

Rosemary
Music and lyrics by Frank Loesser
*How to Succeed in Business
Without Really Trying* 1961

Rosencrantz and Guildenstern Boogie
Music and lyrics by Cliff Jones
Rockabye Hamlet 1976

Roses
Music by Harry Tierney
Lyrics by Joseph McCarthy
Rio Rita 1927

Roses Are Nodding
Music by Jerome Kern
Lyrics by P.G. Wodehouse
Sitting Pretty 1924

Dropped from production

Roses, Lovely Roses
Music by Emmerich Kálmán
Lyrics by B.G. DeSylva
The Yankee Princess 1922

Roses of Red
Music and lyrics by G. Romilli
Fioretta 1929

Roses Out of Breath
Music by Oscar Straus
Lyrics by Edward Delaney Dunn
The Last Waltz 1921

Rose's Turn
Music by Jule Styne
Lyrics by Stephen Sondheim
Gypsy 1959

Roses Understand
Music and lyrics by George M. Cohan
The Merry Malones 1927

The Rosewater Foundation
Music by Alan Menken
Lyrics by Howard Ashman
God Bless You, Mr. Rosewater (OB) 1979

Rosie
Music by Charles Strouse
Lyrics by Lee Adams
Bye Bye Birdie 1960

Rosita Rodriguez; Serenade
Music by Al Carmines
Lyrics by Maria Irene Fornes
Promenade (OB) 1969

Rothschild and Sons
Music by Jerry Bock
Lyrics by Sheldon Harnick
The Rothschilds 1970

The Rotisserie
Music by Alfred Goodman, Maury Rubens
and J. Fred Coots
Lyrics by Clifford Grey
Artists and Models (1925)

Rough Stuff
Music by Ivor Novello
Lyrics by Ronald Jeans
Charlot's Revue 1924

Rough Times
Music by Moose Charlap
Lyrics by Norman Gimbel
The Conquering Hero 1961

Roulette
Music and lyrics by Ida Hoyt Chamberlain
Enchanted Isle 1927

Roumania
Music by Harold Levey
Lyrics by Zelda Sears
The Clinging Vine 1922

Round and Round
Music by Harvey Schmidt
Lyrics by Tom Jones
The Fantasticks (OB) 1960

'Round the Corner
Music by Rudolf Friml
Lyrics by Bide Dudley and Otto Harbach
The Little Whopper 1919

Roundabout
Music by Vernon Duke
Lyrics by Ogden Nash
Two's Company 1952

Roust-about
Music by Jimmy Johnson
Lyrics by Perry Bradford
Messin' Around 1929

Roustabouts
Music and lyrics by James Johnson
and Cecil Mack
Runnin' Wild 1923

Roustabout's Song
Music by Milton Ager and Owen Murphy
Rain or Shine 1928

Row, Row, Row
Music by Jimmy Monaco
Lyrics by William Jerome
Ziegfeld Follies of 1912

Row 10, Aisle 6, Bench 114
Music by Michael Dansicker
Lyrics by Sarah Schlesinger
On The Swing Shift (OB) 1983

Roxana
Music by Michael J. Lewis
Lyrics by Anthony Burgess
Cyrano 1973

Roxie
Music by John Kander
Lyrics by Fred Ebb
Chicago 1975

The Royal Bangkok Academy
Music by Richard Rodgers
Lyrics by Oscar Hammerstein II
The King and I 1951

Rub a Dub Dub
Music by Helen Miller
Lyrics by Eve Merriam
Inner City 1971

Rub-a-Dub Your Rabbit's Foot
Music and lyrics by Frank Marcus
and Bernard Maltin
Bamboola 1929

Rub Your Lamp
Music and lyrics by Cole Porter
Let's Face It! 1941

Rue de la Paix
Music by Walter Donaldson
Lyrics by Ballard MacDonald
Sweetheart Time 1926

Rugantino in the Stocks
Music by Armando Trovaioli
Lyrics by Pietro Garinei and Sandro Giovannini
(Lyric translation by Edward Eager)
Rugantino 1964

Rules and Regulations
Music by Duke Ellington
Lyrics by Marshall Barer and Fred Tobias
Pousse-Café 1966

The Rum Tum Tugger
Music by Andrew Lloyd Webber
Cats 1982

Lyrics based on T.S. Eliot's *Old Possum's Book of Practical Cats*

Rumba Rhythm
Music by Jimmy Johnson
Lyrics by Stella Unger
Earl Carroll's Vanities (1930)

The Rumble of the Subway
Music by Vincent Youmans and Herbert Stothart
Lyrics by Oscar Hammerstein II
and William Cary Duncan
Mary Jane McKane 1923

Rumble, Rumble, Rumble
Music by Rudolf Friml
Lyrics by Otto Harbach and Oscar Hammerstein II
The Wild Rose 1926

Dropped from production.

Rumbola
Music by James P. Johnson
Lyrics by Flournoy Miller
Sugar Hill 1931

Rumson
Music by Frederick Loewe
Lyrics by Alan Jay Lerner
Paint Your Wagon 1951

Run Between the Raindrops
Music and lyrics by Jeanne Napoli
and Gary Portnoy
Marilyn 1983

Run for Your Life
Music by Jimmy Van Heusen
Lyrics by Sammy Cahn
Skyscraper 1965

Run, Indian, Run
Music by Victor Ziskin
Lyrics by Joan Javits
Young Abe Lincoln 1961

Run, Musashi, Run
Music and lyrics by John Driver
Ride the Winds 1974

Run on the Bank
Music and lyrics by Noble Sissle and Eubie Blake
The Chocolate Dandies 1924

Run, Run, Run
Music and lyrics by Jay Livingston and Ray Evans
Let It Ride 1961

Run, Run, Run Cinderella
Music by Robert Emmett Dolan
Lyrics by Johnny Mercer
Foxy 1964

Run to Me, My Love
Music by Allan Roberts
Lyrics by Lester Lee
All for Love 1949

Runaway Colts
Music by Jerome Kern
Lyrics by Berton Braley
Toot-Toot! 1918

A Runaway Match
Music by Lionel Monckton
Lyrics by Adrian Ross
The Quaker Girl 1911

Runnin'
Music and lyrics by Porter Grainger
and Freddie Johnson
Lucky Sambo 1925

Runnin' to Meet the Man
Music by Judd Woldin
Lyrics by Robert Brittan
Raisin 1973

Running Down the Sun
Music and lyrics by Robert Swerdlow
Love Me, Love My Children (OB) 1971

Russian Blues
Music and lyrics by Noël Coward
Charlot's Revue of 1926

The Rustle of Your Bustle
Music by Will Irwin
Lyrics by Norman Zeno
Earl Carroll's Sketch Book (1935)

S

'S Wonderful
Music by George Gershwin
Lyrics by Ira Gershwin
Funny Face 1927

Sabbath Prayer
Music by Jerry Bock
Lyrics by Sheldon Harnick
Fiddler on the Roof 1964

The Sabra
Music by Menachem Zur
Lyrics by Herbert Appleman
Unfair to Goliath (OB) 1970

The Sabre Song
Music by Sigmund Romberg
Lyrics by Otto Harbach and Oscar Hammerstein II
The Desert Song 1926

The Sacred Tree
Music and lyrics by Scott Joplin
Treemonisha 1975

Written in 1909

Sacrifice
Music by Susan Hulsman Bingham
Lyrics by Myrna Lamb
Mod Donna (OB) 1970

The Sacrifice
Music by Dov Seltzer
Lyrics by David Paulsen
To Live Another Summer 1971

Sad Is The Life
Music by Arthur Schwartz
Lyrics by Maxwell Anderson
High Tor (1956) TV

Sad Was the Day
Music and lyrics by Johnny Burke
Donnybrook! 1961

The Sadder-But-Wiser Girl
Music and lyrics by Meredith Willson
The Music Man 1957

Sadie, Sadie
Music by Jule Styne
Lyrics by Bob Merrill
Funny Girl 1964

Safe in Your Arms
Music by William Heagney
Lyrics by William Heagney and Tom Connell
There You Are 1932

Safety in Numbers
Music by J. Fred Coots
Lyrics by Clifford Grey
June Days 1925

Safety in Numbers
Music and lyrics by Sandy Wilson
The Boy Friend 1954

The Saga of Carmen
Music by Ray Henderson
Lyrics by Jack Yellen
Ziegfeld Follies (1943)

The Saga of the Haganah
Music by Walt Smith
Lyrics by Leon Uris
Ari 1971

Sahara Moon
Music and lyrics by Harry Denny
and Dave Ringle
Footlights 1927

Sail Away
Music and lyrics by Noël Coward
Sail Away 1961

Sail Away
Music and lyrics by Randy Newman
Maybe I'm Doing It Wrong (1st edition) (OB) 1981

Sailing
Music and lyrics by Ed Tyler
Sweet Miani (OB) 1962

Sailing at Midnight
Music by Vernon Duke
Lyrics by Howard Dietz
Sadie Thompson 1944

The Sailor of My Dreams
Music by Jim Wise
Lyrics by George Haimsohn
Dames at Sea (OB) 1968

Sailor Song
Music and lyrics by Irving Berlin
Stop! Look! Listen! 1915

Sailors of St. Hurrah
Music and lyrics by George M. Cohan
Little Johnny Jones 1904

Sailors of the Sea
Music and lyrics by Steve Allen
Sophie 1963

Sailor's Round
Music by Meyer Kupferman
Lyrics by Paul Goodman
Jonah (OB) 1966

The Sailor's Tango
Music by Kurt Weill
Lyrics by Bertolt Brecht (adapted by Michael
Feingold)
Happy End 1977

Saint Lazare
Music by Aristide Bruant
Lyrics by Kay Swift
Paris '90 1952

The Saints Come Flying (Sci-Fi)
Music by Scott Killian
and Kim D. Sherman
Lyrics by Kenneth Robins, Scott Killian
and Kim D. Sherman
Lenny and the Heartbreakers (OB) 1983

Salaaming the Raja
Music by Harry Tierney
Lyrics by Joseph McCarthy
Cross My Heart 1928

Salamaggis Birthday
Music and lyrics by Melvin Van Peebles
Ain't Supposed to Die a Natural Death 1971

Sales Reproach
Music and lyrics by Jerry Herman
Madame Aphrodite (OB) 1961

Salesmanship
Music by Philip Springer
Lyrics by Carolyn Leigh
Ziegfeld Follies (1957)

Salley Gardens
Music by John Duffy
Lyrics by Rocco Bufano and John Duffy
Horseman, Pass By (OB) 1969

Sally
Music by Jerome Kern
Lyrics by Clifford Grey
Sally 1920

Sally
Music by Jimmy McHugh
Lyrics by Arthur Malvin
Sugar Babies 1979

Sally
Music and lyrics by Tom Savage
Musical Chairs 1980

Sally, Won't You Come Back
Music and lyrics by Gene Buck and Dave Stamper
Ziegfeld Follies of 1921

Salomee
Music by Jule Styne
Lyrics by Bob Hilliard
Hazel Flagg 1953

The Saloon
Music and lyrics by Walter Marks
Broadway Follies 1981

Saloon Piano
Music and lyrics by Bland Simpson and Jim Wann
Diamond Studs (OB) 1975

Salt Air
Music and lyrics by Cole Porter
Gay Divorce 1932

The Saltarello
Music by Armando Trovaioli
Lyrics by Pietro Garinei and Sandro Giovannini
(Lyric translation by Edward Eager)
Rugantino 1964

Salvation
Music and lyrics by Peter Link and C.C. Courtney
Salvation (OB) 1969

Salzburg
Music by Jule Styne
Lyrics by Betty Comden and Adolph Green
Bells Are Ringing 1956

Sam and Delilah
Music by George Gershwin
Lyrics by Ira Gershwin
Girl Crazy 1930

Samarkand
Music by Jerome Kern
Lyrics by P.G. Wodehouse
Have a Heart 1917

Sambo Was a Bad Boy
Music by Ron Steward and Neal Tate
Lyrics by Ron Steward
Sambo (OB) 1969

Sambo's Banjo
Music by Ford Dabney
Lyrics by Jo Trent
Rang-Tang 1927

The Same Old Game
Music and lyrics by Mellor, Gifford and Godfrey
Very Good Eddie 1915

Same Old Love Songs
Music by Emmerich Kálmán
Lyrics by Harry B. Smith
The Circus Princess 1927

The Same Old Me
Music by Victor Ziskin
Lyrics by Joan Javits
Young Abe Lincoln 1961

The Same Old Moon
Music by Harry Ruby
Lyrics by Bert Kalmar and Otto Harbach
Lucky 1927

Same Old Moon
Music by Henry Sullivan
Lyrics by John Murray Anderson and Clifford Orr
John Murray Anderson's Almanac (1929)

The Same Old South
Music by Jay Gorney
Lyrics by Henry Myers
Meet the People 1940

The Same Old Story
Music by George Gershwin
Lyrics by B.G. DeSylva
Sweet Little Devil 1924

The Same Old Tune
Music and lyrics by Stephen H. Lemberg
Jazzbo Brown 1980

The Same Old Two
Music by Victor Herbert
Lyrics by Glen MacDonough
Algeria 1908

The Same Old Way
Music by Harry Tierney
Lyrics by Joseph McCarthy
Kid Boots 1923

Same Sort of Girl
Music by Jerome Kern
Lyrics by Harry B. Smith
The Girl From Utah 1914

Sammy and Topsy
Music by Ford Dabney
Lyrics by Jo Trent
Rang-Tang 1927

Samson and Delilah
Music by James Mundy
Lyrics by John Latouche
The Vamp 1955

San Pasquale
Music by Armando Trovaioli
Lyrics by Pietro Garinei and Sandro Giovannini
(Lyric translation by Edward Eager)
Rugantino 1964

San Toy
Music by Tom Johnstone
Lyrics by Will B. Johnstone
I'll Say She Is 1924

Sand in My Eyes
Music by Julian Slade
Lyrics by Dorothy Reynolds and Julian Slade
Salad Days (OB) 1958

Sandhog Song
Music by Earl Robinson
Lyrics by Waldo Salt
Sandhog (OB) 1954

Sands of Time
Music and lyrics by Robert Wright
and George Forrest
Kismet 1953

Based on Borodin's *In the Steppes of Central Asia*

Sandwich for Two
Music by Gerard Calvi
Lyrics by Harold Rome
La Grosse Valise 1965

The Sandwich Man
Music and lyrics by Hugh Martin and Timothy Gray
High Spirits 1964

The Sandwich Men
Music by Richard Rodgers
Lyrics by Lorenz Hart
A Connecticut Yankee 1927

Sans Souci
Music and lyrics by Johnny Mercer
Top Banana 1951

Santa Claus
Music by Vincent Youmans
No, No, Nanette 1925

Dropped from production

Santa Evita
Music by Andrew Lloyd Webber
Lyrics by Tim Rice
Evita 1979

Santo Dinero
Music by Richard Stutz
Lyrics by Milton Pascal
Along Fifth Avenue 1949

Santo Domingo
Music and lyrics by Charles Gaynor
Lend an Ear 1948

Sapphire Seas
Music by Rudolf Friml
Lyrics by Otto Harbach
The Firefly 1912

Saratoga
Music by Harold Arlen
Lyrics by Johnny Mercer
Saratoga 1959

Saravá
Music by Mitch Leigh
Lyrics by N. Richard Nash
Saravá 1979

Sascha's Got a Girl
Music and lyrics by Irvin Graham
Crazy With the Heat 1941

Saskatchewan
Music by Clinton Ballard
Lyrics by Carolyn Richter
The Ballad of Johnny Pot (OB) 1971

Satan Rules
Music by Elmer Bernstein
Lyrics by Don Black
Merlin 1983

Satanic Strut
Music and lyrics by Edward Pola
and Eddie Brandt
Woof, Woof 1929

Satan's Li'l Lamb
Music by Harold Arlen
Lyrics by E.Y. Harburg and Johnny Mercer
Americana (1932)

Satellite Moon
Music by Donald Swann
Lyrics by Michael Flanders
At the Drop of a Hat 1959

Satin and Silk
Music and lyrics by Cole Porter
Silk Stockings 1955

Satisfaction Guaranteed
Music by Harris Wheeler
Lyrics by Mary L. Fisher
Blue Plate Special (OB) 1983

Saturday Afternoon
Music by Eubie Blake
Lyrics by Noble Sissle
Shuffle Along of 1933

Saturday Morning
Music by David Shire
Lyrics by Richard Maltby, Jr.
The Sap of Life (OB) 1961

Saturday Night
Music and lyrics by Melvin Van Peebles
Don't Play Us Cheap 1972

Saturday Night
Music and lyrics by Stephen Sondheim
Marry Me a Little (OB) 1981

Saturday Night at the Rose and Crown
Music and lyrics by Noël Coward
The Girl Who Came to Supper 1963

Saturday Night in Central Park
Music by Richard Lewine
Lyrics by Arnold B. Horwitt
Make Mine Manhattan 1948

Saturday's Child
Music by Baldwin Bergersen
Lyrics by Phyllis McGinley
Small Wonder 1948

The Saucer Song
Music by Julian Slade
Lyrics by Dorothy Reynolds and Julian Slade
Salad Days (OB) 1958

Savage Serenade
Music and lyrics by Herman Hupfeld
Murder at the Vanities 1933

Savannah
Music by Raymond Hubbell
Lyrics by Glen MacDonough
The Jolly Bachelors 1910

Savannah
Music by Vernon Duke
Lyrics by John Latouche
Cabin in the Sky 1940

Savannah
Music by Harold Arlen
Lyrics by E.Y. Harburg
Jamaica 1957

Savannah Stomp
Music by Walter G. Samuels
Lyrics by Morrie Ryskind
Ned Wayburn's Gambols 1929

Savannah's Wedding
Music by Harold Arlen
Lyrics by E.Y. Harburg
Jamaica 1957

Save a Kiss
Music by Leroy Anderson
Lyrics by Joan Ford and Walter and Jean Kerr
Goldilocks 1958

Save Me From Caesar
Music and lyrics by Ervin Drake
Her First Roman 1968

Save the People
Music and lyrics by Stephen Schwartz
Godspell (OB) 1971

Save the Village
Music and lyrics by Jerry Herman
Parade (OB) 1960

Saxophone Man
Music by Victor Herbert
Lyrics by Rida Johnson Young
The Dream Girl 1924

Say a Prayer for Me Tonight
Music by Frederick Loewe
Lyrics by Alan Jay Lerner
Gigi (1958) F

Originally written for Eliza to sing just before the
ball scene in *My Fair Lady*, but dropped before
Broadway opening.

Say, Darling
Music by Jule Styne
Lyrics by Betty Comden and Adolph Green
Say, Darling 1958

Say It With a Sable
Music by Ray Henderson
Lyrics by B.G. DeSylva and Lew Brown
George White's Scandals (1925)

Say It With a Solitaire
Music by Jimmy Monaco
Lyrics by Billy Rose and Ballard MacDonald
Harry Delmar's Revels 1927

Say It With Gin
Music and lyrics by Cole Porter
The New Yorkers 1930

Say It With Girls
Music by Morris Hamilton
Lyrics by Grace Henry
Earl Carroll's Vanities (1928)

Say It With Music
Music and lyrics by Irving Berlin
Music Box Revue (1st edition) 1921

Say It With Your Feet
Music by Thomas (Fats) Waller and Harry Brooks
Lyrics by Andy Razaf
Hot Chocolates 1929

Say No More
Music by Sol Kaplan
Lyrics by Edward Eliscu
The Banker's Daughter (OB) 1962

Say Not Love Is a Dream
Music by Franz Lehár
Lyrics by Basil Hood
The Count of Luxembourg 1912

Say "Oui" Chérie
Music by Vincent Youmans
Lyrics by George Waggner
and J. Russel Robinson
What a Widow! (1930) F

Say So
Music by George Gershwin
Lyrics by P.G. Wodehouse and Ira Gershwin
Rosalie 1928

Say That You Love Me
Music by Richard Myers
Lyrics by Leo Robin
Hello, Yourself! 1928

Say the Word
Music by Burton Lane
Lyrics by Harold Adamson
The Third Little Show 1931

Say the Word That Will Make You Mine
Music by Porter Grainger
Lyrics by Donald Heywood
Hot Rhythm 1930

Say the Words
Music and lyrics by Stan Daniels
So Long, 174th Street 1976

Say "Uncle"
Music and lyrics by Rick Besoyan
Little Mary Sunshine (OB) 1959

Say (What I Wanna Hear You Say)
Music by Ray Henderson
Lyrics by Lew Brown
Hot-Cha! 1932

Say When
Music by Jesse Greer
Lyrics by Raymond Klages
Say When 1928

Say When
Music by Ray Henderson
Lyrics by Ted Koehler
Say When 1934

Say Yes, Look No
Music by Robert Kessler
Lyrics by Lola Pergament
O Marry Me! (OB) 1961

Say Yes, Sweetheart
Music by Emmerich Kálmán
Lyrics by Harry B. Smith
Countess Maritza 1926

Say You'll Stay
Music by Lee Pockriss
Lyrics by Anne Croswell
Tovarich 1963

Say, Young Man of Manhattan
Music by Vincent Youmans
Lyrics by Harold Adamson and Clifford Grey
Smiles 1930

Scandal
Music by Johann Strauss II, adapted by Oscar
Straus
Lyrics by Clare Kummer
Three Waltzes 1937

Scandal Walk
Music by George Gershwin
Lyrics by Arthur Jackson
George White's Scandals (1920)

Scarecrows
Music by Vincent Youmans
Lyrics by Billy Rose and Edward Eliscu
Great Day! 1929

Scared
Music by Clinton Ballard
Lyrics by Carolyn Richter
The Ballad of Johnny Pot (OB) 1971

Scarlet Trimmings
Music and lyrics by Deed Meyer
She Shall Have Music (OB) 1959

The Scars
Music by Kurt Weill
Lyrics by Maxwell Anderson
Knickerbocker Holiday 1938

The Scene Is in a Garden
Music by Jerome Kern
Lyrics by Oscar Hammerstein II
Sweet Adeline 1929

Scenes From Some Marriages
Music by Rob Fremont
Lyrics by Doris Willens
Piano Bar (OB) 1978

Scheherezade
Music and lyrics by Harold Goldman
The Garrick Gaieties (3rd edition) 1930

The Schnitza-Komisski
Music by Jerome Kern
Lyrics by Clifford Grey
Sally 1920

School Don't Mean a Damn Thing
Music and lyrics by Voices, Inc.
The Believers (OB) 1968

The Schoolhouse Blues
Music and lyrics by Irving Berlin
Music Box Revue (1st edition) 1921

Schrafft's
Music by Richard Lewine
Lyrics by Arnold B. Horwitt
Make Mine Manhattan 1948

Schrafft's University
Music by Henry Sullivan
Lyrics by Edward Eliscu
John Murray Anderson's Almanac (1929)

Schroeder
Music and lyrics by Clark Gesner
You're a Good Man, Charlie Brown (OB) 1967

Schwartz
Music and lyrics by Peter Link and C.C. Courtney
Salvation (OB) 1969

Schwesters
Music by Robert Mitchell
Lyrics by Elizabeth Perry
Bags (OB) 1982

Science Fiction
Music and lyrics by Richard O'Brien
The Rocky Horror Show 1975

Scotch Archer's Song
Music by Rudolf Friml
Lyrics by Brian Hooker
The Vagabond King 1925

Scotch Lassie
Music by Leo Edwards
Lyrics by Blanche Merrill
Ziegfeld Follies of 1921

Scratch My Back
Music by Dean Fuller
Lyrics by Marshall Barer
New Faces of 1956

Scream
Music by Cy Coleman
Lyrics by Michael Stewart
I Love My Wife 1977

Screwy Little Tune
Music by Philip Charig
Lyrics by James Dyrenforth
Nikki 1931

The Scrimmage of Life
Music by Duke Ellington
Lyrics by John Latouche
Beggar's Holiday 1946

Sea Breeze
Music and lyrics by Bland Simpson and Jim Wann
Hot Grog (OB) 1977

Sea Chantey
Music and lyrics by Cole Porter
Around the World 1946

Sea Fever
Music by Donald Swann
Lyrics by Michael Flanders
At the Drop of a Hat 1959

The Sea Is All Around Us
Music by David Baker
Lyrics by Sheldon Harnick
Shoestring Revue (1955) (OB)

Sea Legs
Music by Lewis E. Gensler
Lyrics by B.G. DeSylva
Captain Jinks 1925

Sea Song
Music by John Addison
Lyrics by John Cranko
Cranks 1956

The Sea Song (By the Beautiful Sea)
Music by Arthur Schwartz
Lyrics by Dorothy Fields
By the Beautiful Sea 1954

Seagull, Starfish, Pebble
Music and lyrics by Lionel Bart
La Strada 1969

Seal It With a Kiss
Music by Arthur Schwartz
Lyrics by Edward Heyman
That Girl from Paris (1937) F

The Search
Music by Kurt Weill
Lyrics by Maxwell Anderson
Lost in the Stars 1949

Search for Wisdom
Music by Mel Marvin
Lyrics by Christopher Durang
A History of the American Film 1978

The Search Is Through
Music by Harold Arlen
Lyrics by Ira Gershwin
The Country Girl (1954) F

Searching for Love
Music and lyrics by Johnny Brandon
Love! Love! Love! (OB) 1977

Searching for Yesterdays
Music and lyrics by Johnny Brandon
Love! Love! Love! (OB) 1977

A Season at the Shore
Music by Gustav Luders
Lyrics by Frank Pixley
The Prince of Pilsen 1903

The Season Ended
Music by Michael H. Cleary
Lyrics by Max and Nathaniel Lief
Hey Nonny Nonny! 1932

Second Avenue and 12th Street Rag
Music by Vernon Duke
Lyrics by Ogden Nash
The Littlest Revue (OB) 1956

Second Best
Music and lyrics by Billy Barnes
The Billy Barnes People 1961

Second Campaign Song
Music and lyrics by Don Tucker
Red, White and Maddox 1969

Second Hand Rose
Music by James Hanley
Lyrics by Grant Clarke
Ziegfeld Follies of 1921

The Second Honeymoon
Music by Susan Hulsman Bingham
Lyrics by Myrna Lamb
Mod Donna (OB) 1970

The Second Last Supper
Music by Scott Killian and Kim D. Sherman
Lyrics by Kenneth Robins, Scott Killian
and Kim D. Sherman
Lenny and the Heartbreakers (OB) 1983

Second Thoughts
Music and lyrics by Craig Carnelia
Is There Life After High School? 1982

Second Time in Love
Music by Harry Warren
Lyrics by Jerome Lawrence and Robert E. Lee
Shangri-La 1956

The Second Violin
Music by Fritz Kreisler
Lyrics by William LeBaron
Apple Blossoms 1919

Based on Kreisler's violin piece "Marche Miniature Viennoise"

he Secret Life
Music by Leon Carr
Lyrics by Earl Shuman
The Secret Life of Walter Mitty (OB) 1964

The Secret of My Life
Music by Sigmund Romberg
Lyrics by Irving Caesar
Nina Rosa 1930

The Secret of Success
Music by Lehman Engel
Lyrics by Agnes Morgan
A Hero Is Born 1937

The Secret of the Tapping Shoes
Music and lyrics by Kelly Hamilton
Trixie True Teen Detective (OB) 1980

The Secret Service
Music and lyrics by Irving Berlin
Mr. President 1962

Secret Song
Music by Baldwin Bergersen
Lyrics by George Marion, Jr.
Allah Be Praised! 1944

A Secretary Is Not a Toy
Music and lyrics by Frank Loesser
*How to Succeed in Business
Without Really Trying* 1961

Secrets
Music by Howard Marren
Lyrics by Enid Futterman
Portrait of Jennie (OB) 1982

Secrets of the Household
Music and lyrics by George M. Cohan
The Man Who Owns Broadway 1909

Security
Music by Jule Styne
Lyrics by Sammy Cahn
High Button Shoes 1947

Seduction
Music and lyrics by Johnny Brandon
Billy Noname (OB) 1970

Seduction Second Degree
Music by Susan Hulsman Bingham
Lyrics by Myrna Lamb
Mod Donna (OB) 1970

See
Music and lyrics by Robert Swerdlow
Love Me, Love My Children (OB) 1971

See America First
Music by Cole Porter
Lyrics by T. Lawrason Riggs and Cole Porter
See America First 1916

See Everything New
Music by Nancy Ford
Lyrics by Gretchen Cryer
Now Is the Time for All Good Men (OB) 1967

See Her First
Music by Harold Orlob
Lyrics by Harry L. Cort and George E. Stoddard
Listen, Lester 1918

See No Evil
Music by Mitch Leigh
Lyrics by William Alfred and Phyllis Robinson
Cry for Us All 1970

See Seattle
Music by Arthur Schwartz
Lyrics by Howard Dietz
Jennie 1963

See That You're Born in Texas
Music and lyrics by Cole Porter
Something for the Boys 1943

See the Blue
Music and lyrics by Clark Gesner
The Utter Glory of Morrissey Hall 1979

See the Light
Music by John Kander
Lyrics by Fred Ebb
70, Girls, 70 1971

See the Monkey
Music by Raymond Scott
Lyrics by Bernard Hanighen
Lute Song 1946

See What It Gets You
Music and lyrics by Stephen Sondheim
Anyone Can Whistle 1964

See You in the Funny Papers
Music by John Kander
Lyrics by Fred Ebb
Woman of the Year 1981

See Yourselves in the Mirror
Music by Harold Levey
Lyrics by Owen Murphy
The Greenwich Village Follies (1925)

The Seed of God
Music by Heitor Villa-Lobos
Lyrics by Robert Wright and George Forrest
Magdalena 1948

Seeing Dickie Home
Music by George Gershwin
Lyrics by Ira Gershwin
Lady, Be Good! 1924

Dropped from production

Seeing the Sights
Music and lyrics by Michael Brown
Different Times 1972

Seeing Things
Music by John Kander
Lyrics by Fred Ebb
The Happy Time 1968

Seek the Spy
Music by Oscar Straus
Lyrics by Stanislaus Stange
The Chocolate Soldier 1909

Seena
Music by Leonard Bernstein
Lyrics by Alan Jay Lerner
1600 Pennsylvania Avenue 1976

Seizure to Roam
Music and lyrics by Bland Simpson and Jim Wann
Hot Grog (OB) 1977

Self-Expression
Music by Arthur Schwartz
Lyrics by Henry Myers
The New Yorkers 1927

The Self-Made Family
Music by Victor Herbert
Lyrics by Harry B. Smith
Miss Dolly Dollars 1905

Self-Made Maiden
Music by Leo Fall
Lyrics by George Grossmith, Jr.
The Dollar Princess 1909

Self Made Man
Music by Arthur Schwartz
Lyrics by Dorothy Fields
Stars in Your Eyes 1939

Self-Made Woman
Music and lyrics by Glory Van Scott
Miss Truth (OB) 1979

Selling a Song
Music by Dave Stamper
Lyrics by Fred Herendeen
Orchids Preferred 1937

Selling Gowns
Music by Sigmund Romberg
Lyrics by Rida Johnson Young
Maytime 1917

Selling Sex
Music by Jerome Moross
Lyrics by Kyle Crichton
Parade (1935) 1935

Seminary Song
Music by Al Carmines
Lyrics by Rosalyn Drexler
Home Movies (OB) 1964

Semiramis
Music by Jerome Kern
Lyrics by Anne Caldwell
She's a Good Fellow 1919

Dropped from production

Senate in Session
Music by Jay Gorney
Lyrics by Henry Myers
Meet the People 1940

The Senatorial Roll Call
Music by George Gershwin
Lyrics by Ira Gershwin
Of Thee I Sing 1931

The Senators' Song
Music and lyrics by Harold Rome
Call Me Mister 1946

Send a Boy
Music by Morgan Lewis
Lyrics by Nancy Hamilton
One for the Money 1939

Send for Me
Music by Richard Rodgers
Lyrics by Lorenz Hart
Simple Simon 1930

Same music as "I Must Love You" from *Chee-Chee* (1928)

Send for the Militia
Music and lyrics by Marc Blitzstein
Parade (1935)

Send in the Clowns
Music and lyrics by Stephen Sondheim
A Little Night Music 1973

Send One Angel Down
Music by Arthur Schwartz
Lyrics by Albert Stillman
Virginia 1937

Send the Marines
Music and lyrics by Tom Lehrer
Tomfoolery (OB) 1981

Send Us Back to the Kitchen
Music by Harry Revel
Lyrics by Arnold B. Horwitt
Are You With It? 1945

Senoras de la Noche
Music and lyrics by Elizabeth Swados
Runaways 1978

Sensations
Music by Wally Harper
Lyrics by Paul Zakrzewski
Sensations (OB) 1970

The Sensible Thing to Do
Music and lyrics by Jack Lawrence and Don Walker
Courtin' Time 1951

Sensitivity
Music by Mary Rodgers
Lyrics by Marshall Barer
Once Upon a Mattress 1959

Sentimental Me
Music by Richard Rodgers
Lyrics by Lorenz Hart
The Garrick Gaieties (1st edition) 1925

Sentimental Melody
Music by J. Fred Coots
Lyrics by Arthur Swanstrom and Benny Davis
Sons o' Guns 1929

Sentimental Silly
Music by Henry Souvaine and Jay Gorney
Lyrics by Morrie Ryskind and Howard Dietz
Merry-Go-Round 1927

Sentimental Weather
Music by Vernon Duke
Lyrics by Ira Gershwin
Ziegfeld Follies (1936)

September Song
Music by Kurt Weill
Lyrics by Maxwell Anderson
Knickerbocker Holiday 1938

Written especially for the distinguished dramatic
actor Walter Huston, Kurt Weill kept the song's
range within Huston's limited vocal capacity.
Despite a huge personal success with the song
Huston, who had never been in a musical before,
never appeared in one again.

Sera Sera Jim
Music and lyrics by Melvin Van Peebles
Ain't Supposed to Die a Natural Death 1971

Serenade
Music by Reginald De Koven
Lyrics by Harry B. Smith
Robin Hood 1891

Serenade
Music by Sigmund Romberg
Lyrics by Dorothy Donnelly
Blossom Time 1921

Based on Schubert's *Serenade*

Serenade
Music by Harold Levey
Lyrics by Zelda Sears
The Clinging Vine 1922

Serenade
Music by Sigmund Romberg
Lyrics by Dorothy Donnelly
The Student Prince 1924

Serenade
Music by Rudolf Friml
Lyrics by Brian Hooker
The Vagabond King 1925

Serenade
Music by H. Maurice Jacquet
Lyrics by Preston Sturges
The Well of Romance 1930

Serenade
Music and lyrics by Al Carmines
The Evangelist (OB) 1982

Serenade
Music by Steve Jankowski
Lyrics by Kenny Morris
Francis (OB) 1982

Serenade Creole
Music by Frank Harling
Lyrics by Laurence Stallings
Deep River 1926

Serenade for You
Music by Robert Stolz
Lyrics by Rowland Leigh
Night of Love 1941

Serenade of Love
Music by Sigmund Romberg
Lyrics by Irving Caesar
Nina Rosa 1930

Serenade to the Emperor
Music by Ralph Benatzky
Lyrics by Irving Caesar
White Horse Inn 1936

Serenade With Asides
Music and lyrics by Frank Loesser
Where's Charley? 1948

The Sermon
Music and lyrics by Frank Loesser
Greenwillow 1960

Service for Service
Music and lyrics by Robert Wright
and George Forrest
Kean 1961

Set 'em Sadie
Music and lyrics by James Johnson and Cecil Mack
Runnin' Wild 1923

Set It Right
Music and lyrics by Cliff Jones
Rockabye Hamlet 1976

Set Me Free
Music by Frederico Valerio
Lyrics by Elizabeth Miele
Hit the Trail 1954

Set Those Sails
Music and lyrics by William Finn
In Trousers (OB) 1981

Settle Down in a One-Horse Town
Music and lyrics by Irving Berlin
Watch Your Step 1914

Settle Down, Travel Around
Music by Harry Tierney
Lyrics by Joseph McCarthy
Up She Goes 1922

7 1/2 Cents
Music and lyrics by Richard Adler and Jerry Ross
The Pajama Game 1954

Seven Days
Music by Jerome Kern
Lyrics by Howard Dietz
Dear Sir 1924

Seven Days
Music by Edward Kunneke
Lyrics by Clifford Grey
Mayflowers 1925

The Seven Deadly Virtues
Music by Frederick Loewe
Lyrics by Alan Jay Lerner
Camelot 1960

Seven Million Crumbs
Music and lyrics by Frank Loesser
The Most Happy Fella 1956

**Seven Sheep, Four Red Shirts
and a Bottle of Gin**
Music and lyrics by Richard Adler
Kwamina 1961

A Seventeen-Gun Salute
Music by Jimmy Van Heusen
Lyrics by Johnny Burke
Carnival in Flanders 1953

Seventeen Summers
Music by Paul Klein
Lyrics by Fred Ebb
Morning Sun (OB) 1963

Seventh Heaven Waltz
Music and lyrics by Rick Besoyan
The Student Gypsy (OB) 1963

70, Girls, 70
Music by John Kander
Lyrics by Fred Ebb
70, Girls, 70 1971

Seventy-Six Trombones
Music and lyrics by Meredith Willson
The Music Man 1957

See note on "Goodnight, My Someone"

Sevilla
Music by Ray Henderson
Lyrics by B.G. DeSylva and Lew Brown
George White's Scandals (1926)

Sevilla
Music by Ned Lehak
Lyrics by Edward Eliscu
The Third Little Show 1931

Sew the Buttons On
Music and lyrics by John Jennings
Riverwind (OB) 1962

The Sew-Up
Music and lyrics by Walter Marks
Bajour 1964

Sex Appeal
Music by Harold Orlob
Lyrics by Irving Caesar
Talk About Girls 1927

Sex Marches On
Music and lyrics by Irving Berlin
Louisiana Purchase 1940

Sextet
Music by John Clifton
Lyrics by John Clifton and Ben Tarver
Man With a Load of Mischief (OB) 1966

Sextet
Music by Cy Coleman
Lyrics by Betty Comden and Adolph Green
On the Twentieth Century 1978

Sexually Free
Music by Cy Coleman
Lyrics by Michael Stewart
I Love My Wife 1977

Sez I
Music and lyrics by Johnny Burke
Donnybrook! 1961

Sez You? Sez I!
Music by Lewis E. Gensler
Lyrics by B. G. DeSylva
Queen High 1926

The Shade of the Palm
Music by Leslie Stuart
Lyrics by Ernest Boyd-Jones and Paul Rubens
Florodora 1900

Shadow of the Moon
Music by Jerome Kern
Lyrics by P. G. Wodehouse
Sitting Pretty 1924

Shadow of the Sun
Music by Helen Miller
Lyrics by Eve Merriam
Inner City 1971

Shadows
Music by Sigmund Romberg
Lyrics by Otto Harbach
Forbidden Melody 1936

Shadows
Music by Paul Hoffert
Lyrics by David Secter
Get Thee to Canterbury (OB) 1969

Shadows on the Wall
Music by Harry Revel
Lyrics by Mack Gordon
Fast and Furious 1931

Shady Dan
Music and lyrics by Al Wilson, Charles Weinberg
and Ken Macomber
Yeah Man 1932

Shady Lady Bird
Music and lyrics by Hugh Martin and Ralph Blane
Best Foot Forward 1941

Shaganola
Music by Sammy Fain
Lyrics by Charles Tobias
Hellzapoppin 1938

Shake a Leg
Music and lyrics by Maceo Pinkard
Pansy 1929

Shake, Brother!
Music by Joseph Meyer and Philip Charig
Lyrics by Leo Robin
Just Fancy 1927

Shake High, Shake Low
Music by Werner Janssen
Lyrics by Mann Holiner and J. Keirn Brennan
Boom-Boom 1929

Shake Well Before Using
Music by John Green
Lyrics by Edward Heyman
Here Goes the Bride 1931

Shake Your Duster
Music by C. Luckey Roberts
Lyrics by Alex C. Rogers
My Magnolia 1926

Shake Your Feet
Music and lyrics by Gene Buck and Dave Stamper
Ziegfeld Follies of 1923

Shake Your Music
Music and lyrics by Al Wilson, Charles Weinberg
and Ken Macomber
Yeah Man 1932

Shake Yourself Out of Here
Music and lyrics by Clarence Gaskill
Earl Carroll's Vanities (1925)

Shakespeare Lied
Music by Elmer Bernstein
Lyrics by Carolyn Leigh
How Now, Dow Jones 1967

Shakin' at the High School Hop
Music and lyrics by Jim Jacobs and Warren Casey
Grease 1972

Shakin' the Shakespeare
Music by Harry Revel
Lyrics by Mack Gordon
Smiling Faces 1932

Shaking Hands With the Wind
Music and lyrics by Ron Dante and Gene Allan
Billy 1969

Shaking the Blues Away
Music by Mann Holiner
Lyrics by Alberta Nichols
Gay Paree 1926

Shaking the Blues Away
Music and lyrics by Irving Berlin
Ziegfeld Follies (1927)

Shall I Take My Heart and Go?
Music by Leroy Anderson
Lyrics by Joan Ford and Walter and Jean Kerr
Goldilocks 1958

Shall I Tell Him?
Music by Karl Hajos (based on Tchaikovsky)
Lyrics by Harry B. Smith
Natja 1925

Shall I Tell You What I Think of You?
Music by Richard Rodgers
Lyrics by Oscar Hammerstein II
The King and I 1951

Shall We Dance
Music by George Gershwin
Lyrics by Ira Gershwin
Shall We Dance (1937) F

Shall We Dance?
Music by Richard Rodgers
Lyrics by Oscar Hammerstein II
The King and I 1951

Shall We Dance?
Music and lyrics by Cliff Jones
Rockabye Hamlet 1976

Shall We Friend?
Music by Galt MacDermot
Lyrics by Christopher Gore
Via Galactica 1972

Shall We Join the Ladies?
Music by Vivian Ellis
Lyrics by Graham John
By the Way 1925

Shall We Say Farewell?
Music by Jacques Offenbach (adapted by Robert
De Cormier)
Lyrics by E.Y. Harburg
The Happiest Girl in the World 1961

Shalom
Music and lyrics by Jerry Herman
Milk and Honey 1961

Shame
Music and lyrics by Glory Van Scott
Miss Truth (OB) 1979

Shangri-La
Music by Harry Warren
Lyrics by Jerome Lawrence and Robert E. Lee
Shangri-La 1956

Shanty Town Romance
Music by Mel Marvin
Lyrics by Christopher Durang
A History of the American Film 1978

The Shape of Things
Music and lyrics by Sheldon Harnick
The Littlest Revue (OB) 1956

Shauny O'Shay
Music and lyrics by Hugh Martin
Look Ma, I'm Dancin'! 1948

She Came, She Saw, She Can Canned
Music by Burton Lane
Lyrics by E.Y. Harburg
Hold On to Your Hats 1940

She Can't Really Be
Music by Don Pippin
Lyrics by Steve Brown
The Contrast (OB) 1972

She Could Shake the Maracas
Music by Richard Rodgers
Lyrics by Lorenz Hart
Too Many Girls 1939

She Didn't Say "Yes"
Music by Jerome Kern
Lyrics by Otto Harbach
The Cat and the Fiddle 1931

She Goes Right, He Goes Left
Music by Franz Lehár
Lyrics by Basil Hood
The Count of Luxembourg 1912

She Got Him
Music by Sigmund Romberg
Lyrics by Oscar Hammerstein II
Sunny River 1941

She Hadda Go Back
Music and lyrics by Meredith Willson
Here's Love 1963

She Is a Diamond
Music by Andrew Lloyd Webber
Lyrics by Tim Rice
Evita 1979

She Is My Ideal
Music and lyrics by Ralph Benatzky
Meet My Sister 1930

She Is Not Thinking of Me

See Waltz at Maxim's

She Is the Belle of New York
Music by Gustave Kerker
Lyrics by Hugh Morton
The Belle of New York 1897

She Likes Basketball
Music by Burt Bacharach
Lyrics by Hal David
Promises, Promises 1968

She Loves Me
Music by Tom Johnstone
Lyrics by Phil Cook
When You Smile 1925

She Loves Me
Music by Jerry Bock
Lyrics by Sheldon Harnick
She Loves Me 1963

She Loves Me Not
Music by Arthur Schwartz
Lyrics by Edward Heyman
She Loves Me Not 1933

She Loves Me Not
Music by David Shire
Lyrics by Richard Maltby, Jr.
The Sap of Life (OB) 1961

She Makes You Think of Home
Music and lyrics by William Roy
The Penny Friend (OB) 1966

She Never Told Her Love
Music and lyrics by Hal Hester and Danny Apolinar
Your Own Thing (OB) 1968

She or Her
Music by Moose Charlap
Lyrics by Norman Gimbel
Whoop-Up 1958

She Passed My Way
Music by Don Gohman
Lyrics by Hal Hackady
Ambassador 1972

She Says It With Her Eyes
Music by Rudolf Friml
Lyrics by Otto Harbach
High Jinks 1913

She Shall Have Music
Music and lyrics by Deed Meyer
She Shall Have Music (OB) 1959

She Shook Him in Chicago
Music by Karl Hoschna
Lyrics by Otto Harbach
Madame Sherry 1910

She Thinks That's the Answer
Music by Larry Grossman
Lyrics by Betty Comden and Adolph Green
A Doll's Life 1982

She Touched Me
Music by Milton Schafer
Lyrics by Ira Levin
Drat! The Cat! 1965

She Was a Wonderful Queen
Music by Vincent Youmans
Lyrics by Anne Caldwell
Oh, Please! 1926

Dropped from production

She Was Very Dear to Me
Music and Lyrics by Ben Burt
Tangerine 1921

She Wasn't You
Music by Burton Lane
Lyrics by Alan Jay Lerner
On a Clear Day You Can See Forever 1965

The Sheep's Song
Music by Leonard Bernstein
Lyrics by Stephen Sondheim
Candide (Added to 1973 revival)

Sheik Song
Music and lyrics by Ann Harris
Sky High (OB) 1979

A "Shell" Game
Music and lyrics by Rick Besoyan
Little Mary Sunshine (OB) 1959

She'll Get the Business in the End
Music and lyrics by Ann Harris
Sky High (OB) 1979

The Shepherd Song
Music by Erich Wolfgang Korngold (based on
Jacques Offenbach)
Lyrics by Herbert Baker
Helen Goes to Troy 1944

Shepherd's Song
Music and lyrics by Jerry Herman
Milk and Honey 1961

Sherry
Music by Laurence Rosenthal
Lyrics by James Lipton
Sherry! 1967

She's a Nut
Music by Cy Coleman
Lyrics by Betty Comden and Adolph Green
On the Twentieth Century 1978

She's Exciting
Music by Morton Gould
Lyrics by Dorothy Fields
Arms and the Girl 1950

She's Gonna Come Home With Me
Music and lyrics by Frank Loesser
The Most Happy Fella 1956

She's Got Everything
Music by Dean Fuller
Lyrics by Marshall Barer
New Faces of 1956

She's Got the Lot
Music by Marguerite Monnot
Lyrics by Julian More, David Heneker
and Monte Norman
Irma la Douce 1960

She's Innocent
Music by Vincent Youmans and Paul Lannin
Lyrics by Arthur Francis
Two Little Girls in Blue 1921

She's Just a Baby
Music by George Gershwin
Lyrics by Arthur Jackson
George White's Scandals (1921)

She's Just Another Girl
Music by Harold Karr
Lyrics by Matt Dubey
Happy Hunting 1956

She's My Girl
Music by Nancy Ford
Lyrics by Gretchen Cryer
Shelter 1973

She's My Girl
Music and lyrics by Tom Lehrer
Tomfoolery (OB) 1981

She's My Love
Music and lyrics by Bob Merrill
Carnival 1961

She's No Longer a Gypsy
Music by Charles Strouse
Lyrics by Lee Adams
Applause 1970

She's Nuts About Me
Music by Nacio Herb Brown and Richard Whiting
Lyrics by B.G. DeSylva
Take a Chance 1932

She's on Her Way
Music by Jerome Kern
Lyrics by Anne Caldwell and Otto Harbach
Criss-Cross 1926

She's Roses
Music by Milton Schafer
Lyrics by Ira Levin
Drat! The Cat! 1965

She's Spanish
Music by Jerome Kern
Lyrics by Anne Caldwell
The Night Boat 1920

Dropped from production

She's Such a Comfort to Me
Music by Arthur Schwartz
Lyrics by Douglas Furber, Max and Nathaniel Lief
and Donovan Parsons
Wake Up and Dream 1929

She's Talking Out
Music by Leon Carr
Lyrics by Earl Shuman
The Secret Life of Walter Mitty (OB) 1964

She's Too Far Above Me
Music and lyrics by David Heneker
Half a Sixpence 1965

Shh!
Music and lyrics by Edward Pola and Eddie Brandt
Woof, Woof 1929

Shika Shika
Music and lyrics by Harold Rome
Fanny 1954

Shimmy Town
Music and lyrics by Gene Buck and Dave Stamper
Ziegfeld Follies of 1919

Shinbone Alley
Music by George Kleinsinger
Lyrics by Joe Darion
Shinbone Alley 1957

Shine
Music by Eubie Blake
Lyrics by J. Milton Reddie and Cecil Mack
Swing It 1937

Shine It On
Music by John Kander
Lyrics by Fred Ebb
The Act 1977

Shine On, Harvest Moon
Music by Nora Bayes and Jack Norworth
Lyrics by Jack Norworth
Ziegfeld Follies of 1908

A Shine on Your Shoes
Music by Arthur Schwartz
Lyrics by Howard Dietz
Flying Colors 1932

The Ship Has Sailed
Music by Sam Stept
Lyrics by Lew Brown and Charles Tobias
Yokel Boy 1939

Ship of Love
Music by Walter G. Samuels
Lyrics by Morrie Ryskind
Ned Wayburn's Gambols 1929

A Ship Without a Sail
Music by Richard Rodgers
Lyrics by Lorenz Hart
Heads Up! 1929

Shipoopi
Music and lyrics by Meredith Willson
The Music Man 1957

Shirts by the Millions
Music by George Gershwin
Lyrics by Ira Gershwin
Let 'Em Eat Cake 1933

Shoein' the Mare
Music by Harold Arlen
Lyrics by Ira Gershwin and E.Y. Harburg
Life Begins at 8:40 1934

Shoeless Joe From Hannibal, Mo.
Music and lyrics by Richard Adler and Jerry Ross
Damn Yankees 1955

Shoes
Music by Will Irwin
Lyrics by Norman Zeno
Fools Rush In 1934

Shoes
Music by Will Irwin
Lyrics by June Carroll
New Faces of 1943

Shoes
Music and lyrics by John Clifton
El Bravo! (OB) 1981

The Shoes of Husband Number One
Music by Victor Herbert
Lyrics by Henry Blossom
The Princess Pat 1915

Shoes With Wings On
Music by Harry Warren
Lyrics by Ira Gershwin
The Barkleys of Broadway (1940) F

Sholom Aleichem
Music by Joseph Rumshinsky
Lyrics by L. Wolfe Gilbert
The Singing Rabbi 1931

Sho'Nuff
Music and lyrics by Harry Chapin
Cotton Patch Gospel (OB) 1981

Shootin' the Pistol
Music by Clarence Williams
Lyrics by Chris Smith
Bottomland 1927

Shootin' the Works for Uncle Sam
Music and lyrics by Cole Porter
You'll Never Get Rich (1941) F

Shooting Stars
Music by Alma Sanders
Lyrics by Monte Carlo
Oh! Oh! Nurse 1925

Shop
Music by Jerome Kern
Lyrics by P.G. Wodehouse
Have a Heart 1917

Shop Girls and Mannikins
Music by George Gershwin
Lyrics by B.G. DeSylva and Ira Gershwin
Tell Me More 1925

Dropped from production

Shopping Around
Music and lyrics by Harold Rome
Wish You Were Here 1952

Shopping in the Orient
Music by Ivan Caryll
Lyrics by Anne Caldwell and James O'Dea
Chin-Chin 1914

Shore Leave
Music by Vincent Youmans
Lyrics by Leo Robin and Clifford Grey
Hit the Deck 1927

Shore Leave
Music by Rudolf Friml
Lyrics by J. Keirn Brennan
Luana 1930

Short People
Music and lyrics by Randy Newman
Maybe I'm Doing It Wrong (1st edition) (OB) 1981

The Shortest Day of the Year
Music by Richard Rodgers
Lyrics by Lorenz Hart
The Boys From Syracuse 1938

The Shorty George
Music by Jerome Kern
Lyrics by Johnny Mercer
You Were Never Lovelier (1942) F

Should I Be Sweet?
Music by Vincent Youmans
Lyrics by B.G. DeSylva
Take a Chance 1932

Should I Speak of Loving You?
Music by Richard Adler
Lyrics by Will Holt
Music Is 1976

Should I Tell You I Love You?
Music and lyrics by Cole Porter
Around the World 1946

Shoulders to Lean On
Music and lyrics by Melvin Van Peebles
Waltz of the Stork (OB) 1982

Shout On!
Music by Jimmy Johnson
Lyrics by Perry Bradford
Messin' Around 1929

Shoutin' Sinners
Music and lyrics by Frank Marcus
and Bernard Maltin
Bamboola 1929

Show a Little Pep
Music by Alma Sanders
Lyrics by Monte Carlo
Oh! Oh! Nurse 1925

Show a Little Something New
Music by Harold Orlob
Lyrics by Harry L. Cort and George E. Stoddard
Listen, Lester 1918

Show Business
See There's No Business Like Show Business

The Show Business Nobody Knows
Music and lyrics by Earl Wilson, Jr.
Let My People Come (OB) 1974

Show Girls (I Love 'Em All)
Music by Charles Strouse
Lyrics by Lee Adams
Bring Back Birdie 1981

Show Him the Way
Music by Stanley Lebowsky
Lyrics by Fred Tobias
Gantry 1970

The Show Is On
Music by Hoagy Carmichael
Lyrics by Ted Fetter
The Show Is On 1936

Show Me
Music by Frederick Loewe
Lyrics by Alan Jay Lerner
My Fair Lady 1956

Show Me
Music by Al Carmines
Lyrics by Rosalyn Drexler
Home Movies (OB) 1964

Show Me How to Make Love
Music by Richard Rodgers
Lyrics by Lorenz Hart
Betsy 1926

Dropped from production

Show Me That Special Gene
Music and lyrics by Micki Grant
Don't Bother Me, I Can't Cope (OB) 1972

Show Me the Town
Music by George Gershwin
Lyrics by Ira Gershwin
Rosalie 1928

Written for *Oh, Kay!* (1926) but dropped from production

Show Me Where the Good Times Are
Music by Kenneth Jacobson
Lyrics by Rhoda Roberts
Show Me Where the Good Times Are (OB) 1970

The Show Must Go On
Music by Jerome Kern
Lyrics by Ira Gershwin
Cover Girl (1944) F

Show Off
Music and lyrics by Albert Selden
Small Wonder 1948

Show Train
Music by Jule Styne
Lyrics by Betty Comden and Adolph Green
Two on the Aisle 1951

Show Tune in 2/4 Time
Music and lyrics by Jerry Herman
Parade (OB) 1960

Rewritten as "It's Today" for *Mame* (1966)

Show Us How to Do the Fox-trot
Music and lyrics by Irving Berlin
Watch Your Step 1914

Shower Chorus
Music by Howard Talbot
Lyrics by Arthur Wimperis
The Arcadians 1910

Shower of Rice
Music by Jerome Kern
Lyrics by Berton Braley
Toot-Toot! 1918

Showstopper
Music and lyrics by Johnny Myers
Wet Paint (OB) 1965

Shuffle
Music by Richard Rodgers
Lyrics by Lorenz Hart
Betsy 1926

Shuffle Along
Music and lyrics by Noble Sissle and Eubie Blake
Shuffle Along 1921

Shuffle Off to Buffalo
Music by Harry Warren
Lyrics by Al Dubin
Forty-Second Street (1933) F

Shuffle Your Feet and Roll Along
Music by Jimmy McHugh
Lyrics by Dorothy Fields
Blackbirds of 1928

Shufflin' Sam
Music by Jerome Kern
Lyrics by P. G. Wodehouse
Sitting Pretty 1924

Shuffling Bill
Music by Raymond Hubbell
Lyrics by Anne Caldwell
Yours Truly 1927

Shunned
Music and lyrics by Howard Blankman
By Hex (OB) 1956

Shut Up Gerald
Music by John Kander
Lyrics by Fred Ebb
Woman of the Year 1981

Shy
Music by Mary Rodgers
Lyrics by Marshall Barer
Once Upon a Mattress 1959

Si, Si, Señor
Music by Vincent Youmans
Lyrics by Billy Rose and Edward Eliscu
Great Day! 1929

Siberia
Music and lyrics by Cole Porter
Silk Stockings 1955

Sid, Ol' Kid
Music and lyrics by Bob Merrill
Take Me Along 1959

Side by Side by Side
Music and lyrics by Stephen Sondheim
Company 1970

Side of Fries
Music by Harris Wheeler
Lyrics by Mary L. Fisher
Blue Plate Special (OB) 1983

A Side Street off Broadway
Music by Edgar Fairchild
Lyrics by Henry Myers
The New Yorkers 1927

The Sidestep
Music and lyrics by Carol Hall
The Best Little Whorehouse in Texas 1978

Sidewalk Tree
Music by Judd Woldin
Lyrics by Robert Brittan
Raisin 1973

Siegal Marching Song
Music by John Kander
Lyrics by James Goldman, John Kander
and William Goldman
A Family Affair 1962

Sigh by Night
Music by Emmerich Kálmán
Lyrics by George Marion, Jr.
Marinka 1945

**Sigmund Freud's Impersonation of
Albert Einstein in America**
Music and lyrics by Randy Newman
Maybe I'm Doing It Wrong (2nd edition)
(OB) 1982

Sign Here
Music by John Kander
Lyrics by Fred Ebb
Flora, the Red Menace 1965

The Signal
Music by George Gershwin
Lyrics by Otto Harbach and Oscar Hammerstein II
Song of the Flame 1925

Signed, Peeled and Delivered
Music and lyrics by Ronald Melrose
Upstairs at O'Neal's (OB) 1982

Signor Mons. Muldoni
Music by Victor Herbert
Lyrics by Harry B. Smith
The Fortune Teller 1898

Signora Campbell
Music by Burton Lane
Lyrics by Alan Jay Lerner
Carmelina 1979

Signora Pandolfi
Music by Milton Schafer
Lyrics by Ronny Graham
Bravo Giovanni 1962

Silent Cal
Music and lyrics by Oscar Brand
How to Steal an Election (OB) 1968

Silent E
Music and lyrics by Tom Lehrer
Tomfoolery (OB) 1981

The Silent Years
Music by Mel Marvin
Lyrics by Christopher Durang
A History of the American Film 1978

Silenzio
Music by Jerome Kern
Lyrics by Anne Caldwell
The Bunch and Judy 1922

Silhouette
Music by Emmerich Kálmán
Lyrics by Harry B. Smith
The Circus Princess 1927

Silhouettes Under the Stars
Music and lyrics by Charles Tobias, Charles
Newman and Murray Mencher
Earl Carroll's Sketch Book (1935)

Silk Stockings
Music and lyrics by Cole Porter
Silk Stockings 1955

Silly People
Music and lyrics by Stephen Sondheim
A Little Night Music 1973

Dropped from production and used in *Marry Me a
Little* (1981)

The Silly Season
Music by Vincent Youmans and Paul Lannin
Lyrics by Arthur Francis
Two Little Girls in Blue 1921

Silly, Silly Cavalier
Music by Franz Lehár
Lyrics by Adrian Ross
The Merry Widow 1907

Silver Earring
Music and lyrics by Irving Burgie
Ballad for Bimshire (OB) 1963

Silver Moon
Music by Sigmund Romberg
Lyrics by Dorothy Donnelly
My Maryland 1927

Silver Sails
Music by Harden Church
Lyrics by Edward Heyman
Caviar 1934

Silver Screen
Music and lyrics by John Raniello
Movie Buff (OB) 1977

The Silver Star of Love
Music by Leslie Stuart
Lyrics by Ernest Boyd-Jones and Paul Rubens
Florodora 1900

Silver Threads
Music and lyrics by Irving Berlin
Yip, Yip, Yaphank 1918

Silver Wings
Music by Dave Stamper
Lyrics by Gene Buck
Take the Air 1927

Silvers Theme
Music by Peter Link
Lyrics by C.C. Courtney and Ragan Courtney
Earl of Ruston 1971

Silvery Days
Music and lyrics by Ed Tyler
Sweet Miani (OB) 1962

Simon Legree
Music by Harold Arlen
Lyrics by E.Y. Harburg
Bloomer Girl 1944

Simon Smith and the Amazing Dancing Bear
Music and lyrics by Randy Newman
Maybe I'm Doing It Wrong (1st edition) (OB) 1981

Simon Zealots
Music by Andrew Lloyd Webber
Lyrics by Tim Rice
Jesus Christ Superstar 1971

Simpatica
Music by Richard Rodgers
Lyrics by Lorenz Hart
They Met in Argentina (1941) F

Simple
Music and lyrics by Stephen Sondheim
Anyone Can Whistle 1964

Simple
Music and lyrics by Maury Yeston
Nine 1982

Simple Ain't Easy
Music by Moose Charlap
Lyrics by Eddie Lawrence
Kelly 1965

Simple Joys
Music and lyrics by Stephen Schwartz
Pippin 1972

The Simple Joys of Maidenhood
Music by Frederick Loewe
Lyrics by Alan Jay Lerner
Camelot 1960

The Simple Life
Music by Richard Rodgers
Lyrics by Lorenz Hart
The Girl Friend 1926

A Simple Life
Music by Nancy Ford
Lyrics by Gretchen Cryer
Now Is the Time for All Good Men (OB) 1967

Simple Little Things
Music by Harvey Schmidt
Lyrics by Tom Jones
110 in the Shade 1963

Simple Little Tune
Music by Jerome Kern
Lyrics by Harry B. Smith
Love o' Mike 1917

Simple Little Village Maid
Music by Emmerich Kálmán
Lyrics by C.C.S. Cushing and E.P. Heath
Sari 1914

A Simple Man
Music by Mitch Leigh
Lyrics by N. Richard Nash
Saravá 1979

Simple Simon
Music by Helen Miller
Lyrics by Eve Merriam
Inner City 1971

Simple Spanish Maid
Music by Jean Schwartz
Lyrics by Alfred Bryan
A Night in Spain 1927

A Simple Wife
Music by Paul Hoffert
Lyrics by David Secter
Get Thee to Canterbury (OB) 1969

Simple Word
Music and lyrics by Stan Freeman
and Franklin Underwood
Lovely Ladies, Kind Gentlemen 1970

Simply Heavenly
Music by David Martin
Lyrics by Langston Hughes
Simply Heavenly 1957

Simply Paranoia
Music by Kurt Weill
Lyrics by Ogden Nash
One Touch of Venus 1943

Dropped from production

The Simpson Sisters
Music by Albert Hague
Lyrics by Dorothy Fields
Redhead 1959

Since Eve
Music and lyrics by Jerry Herman
I Feel Wonderful (OB) 1954

Since I Am Not for Thee
Music by Victor Herbert
Lyrics by Harry B. Smith
Cyrano de Bergerac 1899

Since I Kissed My Baby Goodbye
Music and lyrics by Cole Porter
You'll Never Get Rich (1941) F

Since Nora Brought Her Angora Around
Music and lyrics by Vincent Valentini
Parisiana 1928

Since the Days of Grandmama
Music by Jerome Kern
Lyrics by Paul West
The Red Petticoat 1912

Since the Time We Met
Music by Michael Leonard
Lyrics by Herbert Martin
How to Be a Jewish Mother 1967

Since You Came to This Town
Music by Alan Menken
Lyrics by Dennis Green
God Bless You, Mr. Rosewater (OB) 1979

Since You're Alone
Music by H. Maurice Jacquet
Lyrics by Preston Sturges
The Well of Romance 1930

Since You're Not Around
Music and lyrics by Richard M. Sherman
and Robert B. Sherman
Over Here! 1974

Sincere
Music and lyrics by Meredith Willson
The Music Man 1957

Sincere Replies
Music and lyrics by Robert Dennis, Peter Schickele
and Stanley Walden
Oh! Calcutta! 1969

Sing
Music by Richard Rodgers
Lyrics by Lorenz Hart
Betsy 1926

Added to *Lady Fingers* (1929)

Sing!
Music by Marvin Hamlisch
Lyrics by Edward Kleban
A Chorus Line 1975

Sing a Christmas Song
Music by Garry Sherman
Lyrics by Peter Udell
Comin' Uptown 1979

Sing a Little Jingle
Music by Harry Warren
Lyrics by Mort Dixon
Crazy Quilt 1931

Sing a Little Song
Music by Lucien Denni
Lyrics by Helena Evans
Happy Go Lucky 1926

Sing a Little Song
Music by George Gershwin
Lyrics by Ira Gershwin
Funny Face 1927

Sing a Song in the Rain
Music by Harry Rosenthal
Lyrics by Douglas Furber and Irving Caesar
Polly 1929

Sing a Song of Sambo
Music by Ron Steward and Neal Tate
Lyrics by Ron Steward
Sambo (OB) 1969

Sing Alone
Music and lyrics by Cliff Jones
Rockabye Hamlet 1976

Sing American Tunes
Music by Edward Ward
Lyrics by Frank Fay and William Walsh
Tattle Tales 1933

Sing and Dance Your Troubles Away
Music by Eubie Blake
Lyrics by Noble Sissle
Shuffle Along of 1933

Sing, Brothers!
Music by Jack Waller and Joseph Tunbridge
Lyrics by R.P. Weston and Bert Lee
Tell Her the Truth 1932

Sing, Dance and Smile
Music by Philip Charig
Lyrics by Ben Jerome
Yes, Yes, Yvette 1927

Sing for Your Supper
Music by Richard Rodgers
Lyrics by Lorenz Hart
The Boys From Syracuse 1938

Sing Happy
Music by John Kander
Lyrics by Fred Ebb
Flora, the Red Menace 1965

Sing Hi
Music by Richard Adler
Lyrics by Will Holt
Music Is 1976

Sing Jubilee
Music and lyrics by Cole Porter
Jubilee 1935

Dropped from production

Sing Me a Song With Social Significance
Music and lyrics by Harold Rome
Pins and Needles (OB) 1937

Sing Me Not a Ballad
Music by Kurt Weill
Lyrics by Ira Gershwin
The Firebrand of Florence 1945

Sing Muse
Music by Joseph Raposo
Lyrics by Erich Segal
Sing Muse! (OB) 1961

Sing My Heart
Music by Harold Arlen
Lyrics by Ted Koehler
Love Affair (1939) F

Sing of Spring
Music by George Gershwin
Lyrics by Ira Gershwin
A Damsel in Distress (1937) F

Sing Out, Sweet Land (As I Was Going Along)
Music by Elie Siegmeister
Lyrics by Edward Eager
Sing Out, Sweet Land 1944

Sing Sing for Sing Sing
Music and lyrics by Cole Porter
The New Yorkers 1930

Sing, Sing, You Tetrazzini
Music by Jerome Kern
Lyrics by Paul West
The Red Petticoat 1912

Sing Something Simple
Music and lyrics by Herman Hupfeld
The Second Little Show 1930

Sing-Song Girl
Music by Jerome Kern
Lyrics by Anne Caldwell
Good Morning, Dearie 1921

Sing Sorrow
Music by Earl Robinson
Lyrics by Waldo Salt
Sandhog (OB) 1954

Sing! South! Sing!
Music by Giuseppe Verdi (adapted by Hans Spialek)
Lyrics by Charles Friedman
My Darlin' Aïda 1952

Sing the Merry
Music by Sammy Fain
Lyrics by E.Y. Harburg
Flahooley 1951

Sing to Me, Guitar
Music and lyrics by Cole Porter
Mexican Hayride 1944

Sing Trovatore
Music by Jerome Kern
Lyrics by Edward Madden
La Belle Paree 1911

Singapore Sue
Music by Jim Wise
Lyrics by George Haimsohn
Dames at Sea (OB) 1968

The Singer's Career, Ha! Ha!
Music by Percy Wenrich
Lyrics by Raymond Peck
Castles in the Air 1926

Singin' Pete
Music by George Gershwin
Lyrics by Ira Gershwin
Lady, Be Good! 1924

Dropped from production

Singin' the Blues
Music by Jimmy McHugh
Lyrics by Dorothy Fields
Singin' the Blues 1931

Singing a Love Song
Music by Richard Rodgers
Lyrics by Lorenz Hart
Chee-Chee 1928

A new lyric "I Still Believe in You" was written for the score of *Simple Simon* (1930).

Singin' in the Rain
Music by Nacio Herb Brown
Lyrics by Arthur Freed
Hollywood Revue of 1929 (1929) F

Later used in the film *Singin' in the Rain* (1952)

Singing Mermaids
Music and lyrics by Ann Harris
Sky High (OB) 1979

Singing Nurses
Music and lyrics by Porter Grainger
and Freddie Johnson
Lucky Sambo 1925

Singing to You
Music and lyrics by Ben Oakland, Margot Millham
and Robert A. Simon
Hold Your Horses 1933

The Singing Tree
Music by Heitor Villa-Lobos
Lyrics by Robert Wright and George Forrest
Magdalena 1948

Singing Wheels
Music by Ruth Cleary Patterson
Lyrics by Fred Heider
Russell Patterson's Sketch Book (OB) 1960

The Single Bird
Music by Raymond Hubbell
Lyrics by Glen MacDonough
The Jolly Bachelors 1910

A Single Dream
Music and lyrics by Jeanne Napoli and Doug Frank
Marilyn 1983

A Single Life
Music by Mitch Leigh
Lyrics by N. Richard Nash
Saravá 1979

Singles Bar
Music by Hank Beebe
Lyrics by Bill Heyer
*Tuscaloosa's Calling Me
But I'm Not Going!* (OB) 1975

Singspielia
Music and lyrics by Rick Besoyan
The Student Gypsy (OB) 1963

'Sippi
Music by Jimmy Johnson
Lyrics by Henry Creamer
Keep Shufflin' 1928

Sir Galahad
Music by Jerome Kern
Lyrics by P. G. Wodehouse
Leave It to Jane 1917

Sir or Ma'am
Music and lyrics by Noël Coward
The Girl Who Came to Supper 1963

Siren of the Tropics
Music by Vernon Duke
Lyrics by Howard Dietz
Sadie Thompson 1944

The Sirens' Song
Music by Jerome Kern
Lyrics by P. G. Wodehouse
Leave It to Jane 1917

Sister Mine
Music by Emmerich Kálmán
Lyrics by Harry B. Smith
Countess Maritza 1926

Sister Paradise
Music and lyrics by David Langston Smyrl
On the Lock-In (OB) 1977

Sisters
Music and lyrics by Cass Morgan
Pump Boys and Dinettes 1982

Sisters Under the Skin
Music by Frederick Loewe
Lyrics by Earle Crooker
Great Lady 1938

Sisters Under the Skin
Music by Baldwin Bergersen
Lyrics by Sylvia Marks
Of V We Sing 1942

Sit Down, John
Music and lyrics by Sherman Edwards
1776 1969

The Sit Down Song
Music by Coleridge-Taylor Perkinson
Lyrics by Ray McIver
God Is a (Guess What?) (OB) 1968

Sit Down, You're Rockin' the Boat
Music and lyrics by Frank Loesser
Guys and Dolls 1950

Sit In—Wade In
Music and lyrics by Johnny Brandon
Billy Noname (OB) 1970

Sitting in the Park
Music by Kenn Long and Jim Crozier
Lyrics by Kenn Long
Touch (OB) 1970

Sitting in the Sun
Music by J. Fred Coots
Lyrics by Al Dubin
White Lights 1927

Sitting in the Sun (Just Wearing a Smile)
Music and lyrics by Cliff Friend and George White
George White's Scandals (1929)

Sitting on the Back Porch
Music by Richard Rodgers
Lyrics by Oscar Hammerstein II
Pipe Dream 1955

Dropped from production

Sitting on Your Status Quo
Music and lyrics by Harold Rome
Pins and Needles (OB) 1937

Added during run

Sitting Over There
Music by Will Irwin
Lyrics by Norman Zeno
Fools Rush In 1934

Sitting Pretty
Music by Jerome Kern
Lyrics by P. G. Wodehouse
Sitting Pretty 1924

Dropped from production

Six
Music and lyrics by Charles Strouse
Six (OB) 1971

Six Blocks From the Bridge
Music by Moose Charlap
Lyrics by Eddie Lawrence
Kelly 1965

Six Fucking Shades of Green
Music and lyrics by Elizabeth Swados
Dispatches (OB) 1979

Six Lillies of the Valley
Music and lyrics by Noël Coward
The Girl Who Came to Supper 1963

Six Little Kitzels
Music by Richard Rodgers
Lyrics by Lorenz Hart
Betsy 1926

Dropped from production

Six Months Out of Every Year
Music and lyrics by Richard Adler and Jerry Ross
Damn Yankees 1955

Six o'Clock
Music by Philip Charig
Lyrics by Irving Caesar
Yes, Yes, Yvette 1927

Six Palaces
Music and lyrics by Robert Wright and George
Forrest (based on Rachmaninoff)
Anya 1965

Six-String Orchestra
Music and lyrics by Harry Chapin
The Night That Made America Famous 1975

Sixteen Going On Seventeen
Music by Richard Rodgers
Lyrics by Oscar Hammerstein II
The Sound of Music 1959

1617 Broadway
Music and lyrics by Jerry Bock, George Weiss
and Larry Holofcener
Mr. Wonderful 1956

Sixteen Sweet Sixteen
Music and lyrics by Irving Berlin
Music Box Revue (4th edition) 1924

Sixteenth Summer
Music by Robert Kessler
Lyrics by Martin Charnin
Fallout (OB) 1959

Sixty-Second Romance
Music by Bud Harris
Lyrics by Lawrence Harris
Fools Rush In 1934

Skid Row
Music by Alan Menken
Lyrics by Howard Ashman
Little Shop of Horrors (OB) 1982

Skiddle-de-Scow
Music by Jimmy Johnson
Lyrics by Perry Bradford
Messin' Around 1929

Skidikiscatch
Music by Rudolf Friml
Lyrics by Otto Harbach
Katinka 1915

Skiing at Saks
Music and lyrics by Irvin Graham
Who's Who 1938

Skimbleshanks
Music by Andrew Lloyd Webber
Cats 1982

Lyrics based on T.S. Eliot's *Old Possum's
Book of Practical Cats*

Skin and Bones
Music by David Baker
Lyrics by Will Holt
Come Summer 1969

Skinnin' a Cat
Music by Gary Geld
Lyrics by Peter Udell
Purlie 1970

Skip the Build-Up
Music by Sammy Fain
Lyrics by Dan Shapiro
Ankles Aweigh 1955

Skull and Bones
Music by George Gershwin
Lyrics by Ira Gershwin
Treasure Girl 1928

Sky and Sea
Music and lyrics by Oscar Brown, Jr.
and Johnny Alf
Joy (OB) 1970

Sky City
Music by Richard Rodgers
Lyrics by Lorenz Hart
Heads Up! 1929

Dropped from production

The Sky Girl
Music by Jean Schwartz
Lyrics by Alfred Bryan
A Night in Spain 1927

Sky High
Music by Jimmy Van Heusen
Lyrics by Johnny Burke
Nellie Bly 1946

Skye Boat Song
Music and lyrics by Bland Simpson and Jim Wann
Hot Grog (OB) 1977

Skyrocket
Music by Harry Tierney
Lyrics by Joseph McCarthy
Irene 1919

Skyscraper Blues
Music by Gordon Jenkins
Lyrics by Tom Adair
Along Fifth Avenue 1949

Slap My Face
Music by Alex Fogarty
Lyrics by Edwin Gilbert
New Faces of 1936

Slap on the Greasepaint
Music by Berenice Kazounoff
Lyrics by John Latouche
Two for Tonight (OB) 1939

Slap That Bass
Music by George Gershwin
Lyrics by Ira Gershwin
Shall We Dance (1937) F

Slatey Fork
Music and lyrics by Walter Cool
Mackey of Appalachia (OB) 1965

Slaughter on Tenth Avenue (ballet)
Music by Richard Rodgers
On Your Toes 1936

Slave Madonna
Music and lyrics by Al Carmines
Joan (OB) 1972

The Slave of Love
Music and lyrics by Noble Sissle and Eubie Blake
The Chocolate Dandies 1924

Slaves of Broadway
Music by Ray Perkins
Lyrics by Max and Nathaniel Lief
The Greenwich Village Follies (1928)

Sleep, Baby, Don't Cry
Music by Baldwin Bergersen
Lyrics by William Archibald
Carib Song 1945

Sleep Little Mouse
Music by Meyer Kupferman
Lyrics by Paul Goodman
Jonah (OB) 1966

Sleep, My Baby, Sleep
Music by Nancy Ford
Lyrics by Gretchen Cryer
Shelter 1973

Sleep, O Sleep
Music by Sol Kaplan
Lyrics by Edward Eliscu
The Banker's Daughter (OB) 1962

Sleep Peaceful, Mr. Used-to-Be
Music by Harold Arlen
Lyrics by Johnny Mercer
St. Louis Woman 1946

Sleep-Tite
Music and lyrics by Richard Adler and Jerry Ross
The Pajama Game 1954

A Sleepin' Bee
Music by Harold Arlen
Lyrics by Harold Arlen and Truman Capote
House of Flowers 1954

Sleeping Beauty
Music by Richard Rodgers
Lyrics by Lorenz Hart
Hallelujah, I'm a Bum (1933) F

Dropped from film

Sleepyhead
Music by Richard Rodgers
Lyrics by Lorenz Hart
The Garrick Gaieties (2nd edition) 1926

Written for *The Girl Friend* (1926), but dropped from the production.

Sleepy Hollow
Music and lyrics by Norman Dean
Autumn's Here (OB) 1966

Sleepy Man
Music by Robert Waldman
Lyrics by Alfred Uhry
The Robber Bridegroom 1975

Sleepy Time Down South
Music and lyrics by Bland Simpson and Jim Wann
Diamond Studs (OB) 1975

The Slice
Music by Jule Styne
Lyrics by Betty Comden and Adolph Green
Hallelujah, Baby! 1967

Slide Boy, Slide
Music by Harold Arlen
Lyrics by Harold Arlen and Truman Capote
House of Flowers 1954

Slide Some Oil to Me
Music and lyrics by Charlie Smalls
The Wiz 1975

Sliding Down a Silver Cloud
Music by Lee David
Lyrics by J. Keirn Brennan
A Night in Venice 1929

A Slight Case of Ecstasy
Music by Sammy Fain
Lyrics by George Marion, Jr.
Toplitzky of Notre Dame 1946

Slightly Less Than Wonderful
Music by Thomas (Fats) Waller
Lyrics by George Marion, Jr.
Early to Bed 1943

Slightly Perfect
Music by Harry Revel
Lyrics by Arnold B. Horwitt
Are You With It? 1945

Slippy Sloppy Shoes
Music by Gerard Calvi
Lyrics by Harold Rome
La Grosse Valise 1965

Slogan Song
Music and lyrics by Johnny Mercer
Top Banana 1951

Sloth
Music by Donald Swann
Lyrics by Michael Flanders
At the Drop of Another Hat 1966

Slow River
Music by Charles M. Schwab
Lyrics by Henry Myers
The New Yorkers 1927

Slow Train
Music by Donald Swann
Lyrics by Michael Flanders
At the Drop of Another Hat 1966

Slumber Song (Good Night)
Music by Richard A. Whiting
Lyrics by Oscar Hammerstein II
Free for All 1931

Slumming on Park Avenue
Music and lyrics by Irving Berlin
On the Avenue (1937) F

Small Apartment
Music and lyrics by Deed Meyer
'Toinette (OB) 1961

A Small Cartel
Music by Lee Pockriss
Lyrics by Anne Croswell
Tovarich 1963

Small Hotel
See There's a Small Hotel

Small Talk
Music and lyrics by Richard Adler and Jerry Ross
The Pajama Game 1954

Small Town
Music by David Baker
Lyrics by Sheldon Harnick
Smiling, the Boy Fell Dead (OB) 1961

A Small Town Gal
Music and lyrics by George M. Cohan
Fifty Miles From Boston 1908

Small World
Music by Jule Styne
Lyrics by Stephen Sondheim
Gypsy 1959

Smart Little Girls
Music by Sammy Fain
Lyrics by Jack Yellen
George White's Scandals (1939)

Smart People
Music by Richard Rodgers
Lyrics by Lorenz Hart
She's My Baby 1928

Added during the run

Smart Set
Music by Harry Revel
Lyrics by Mack Gordon
Smiling Faces 1932

Smart Set
Music by Will Irwin
Lyrics by Paul Peters and George Sklar
Parade (1935)

Smart to Be Smart
Music by Vernon Duke
Lyrics by E.Y. Harburg
Ziegfeld Follies (1934)

Smash Him
Music and lyrics by Melvin Van Peebles
Don't Play Us Cheap 1972

The Smell of Christmas
Music by Larry Grossman
Lyrics by Hal Hackady
Minnie's Boys 1970

Smellin' of Vanilla (Bamboo Cage)
Music by Harold Arlen
Lyrics by Harold Arlen and Truman Capote
House of Flowers 1954

The Smew Song
Music by Alec Wilder
Lyrics by Arnold Sundgaard
Kittiwake Island (OB) 1960

Smile
Music and lyrics by Donald Heywood
Africana 1927

Smile
Music by Vincent Youmans
Lyrics by Harold Adamson and Clifford Grey
Smiles 1930

Dropped from production

Smile
Music by Nancy Ford
Lyrics by Gretchen Cryer
*I'm Getting My Act Together and Taking It
on the Road* 1978

Smile
Music by Joe Ercole
Lyrics by Bruce Kluger
Ka-Boom (OB) 1980

A Smile, a Kiss
Music by Rudolf Friml
Lyrics by Rowland Leigh and John Shubert
Music Hath Charms 1934

Smile at Me
Music and lyrics by Edward J. Lambert
Smile at Me 1935

Smile, Darn You, Smile
Music by Rudolf Friml
Lyrics by Brian Hooker
The White Eagle 1927

Smile for Me
Music and lyrics by William Roy
Maggie 1953

Smile for the Press
Music by Hoagy Carmichael
Lyrics by Johnny Mercer
Walk With Music 1940

Smile, Girls
Music by Jule Styne
Lyrics by Stephen Sondheim
Gypsy 1959

Dropped from production

A Smile Is Up
Music and lyrics by Jack Bussins
and Ellsworth Olin
Be Kind to People Week (OB) 1975

Smile On
Music by Milton Susskind
Lyrics by Paul Porter and Benjamin Hapgood Burt
Florida Girl 1925

The Smile She Means for You
Music by Karl Hoschna
Lyrics by Otto Harbach
Madame Sherry 1910

Smile, Smile
Music by Jule Styne
Lyrics by Betty Comden and Adolph Green
Hallelujah, Baby! 1967

Smiles
Music by Mary Rodgers
Lyrics by Martin Charnin
Hot Spot 1963

Smoke
Music by Jerome Kern
Lyrics by Berton Braley
Toot-Toot! 1918

Smoke and Fire
Music by Charles Strouse
Lyrics by Lee Adams
A Broadway Musical 1978

Smoke Gets in Your Eyes
Music by Jerome Kern
Lyrics by Otto Harbach
Roberta 1933

Originally written (but not used) for a tap dance
sequence in *Show Boat* (1927), this melody then
turned up as a march theme for a 1932 NBC series
that never materialized.

Smoke Rings
Music by Rudolf Friml
Lyrics by Otto Harbach
The Blue Kitten 1922

Smokin' Reefers
Music by Arthur Schwartz
Lyrics by Howard Dietz
Flying Colors 1932

Smoky Rhythm
Music and lyrics by George Hickman
New Faces of 1934

A Snake in the Grass
Music by Frederick Loewe
Lyrics by Alan Jay Lerner
The Little Prince (1975) F

Snap Into It
Music by Abel Baer
Lyrics by Sam Lewis and Joe Young
Lady Do 1927

Snap Out of It
Music by Harry Akst
Lyrics by Benny Davis
Artists and Models (1927)

Snap Your Finger
Music by Rudolf Friml
Lyrics by Bide Dudley and Otto Harbach
The Little Whopper 1919

Snappy Show in Town
Music by Vincent Youmans
Lyrics by Anne Caldwell
Oh, Please! 1926

Snatched From the Cradle
Music by Rudolf Friml
Lyrics by Otto Harbach and Edward Clark
You're In Love 1917

Snip, Snip, Snip
Music by Jerome Kern
Lyrics by Anne Caldwell
She's a Good Fellow 1919

Sniper
Music and lyrics by Harry Chapin
The Night That Made America Famous 1975

Snoopy
Music and lyrics by Clark Gesner
You're a Good Man, Charlie Brown (OB) 1967

Snoopy's Song
Music by Larry Grossman
Lyrics by Hal Hackady
Snoopy (OB) 1982

Snow Flakes
Music by George Gershwin
Lyrics by Arthur Jackson
Broadway Brevities (1920)

Snowflakes and Sweethearts
Music and lyrics by Robert Wright and George
Forrest (based on Rachmaninoff)
Anya 1965

Snowtime
Music and lyrics by James Johnson
and Cecil Mack
Runnin' Wild 1923

So Am I
Music by George Gershwin
Lyrics by Ira Gershwin
Lady, Be Good! 1924

So Are You!
Music by George Gershwin
Lyrics by Gus Kahn and Ira Gershwin
Show Girl 1929

So Beautiful
Music by Don Elliott
Lyrics by James Costigan
The Beast in Me 1963

So Close
Music and lyrics by Bob Ost
Everybody's Gettin' Into the Act (OB) 1981

So Do I
Music by Jean Schwartz
Lyrics by Clifford Grey and William Cary Duncan
Sunny Days 1928

So Do I
Music by Vincent Youmans
Lyrics by B. G. DeSylva
Take a Chance 1932

So Far
Music by Richard Rodgers
Lyrics by Oscar Hammerstein II
Allegro 1947

So Far
Music by Don Pippin
Lyrics by Steve Brown
The Contrast (OB) 1972

So Hard to Keep When They're Beautiful
Music by Harry Tierney
Lyrics by Joseph McCarthy
Ziegfeld Follies of 1920

So I Give You
Music by Galt MacDermot
Lyrics by Rochelle Owens
The Karl Marx Play (OB) 1973

So I Married the Guy
Music by Sam Stept
Lyrics by Herb Magidson
George White's Music Hall Varieties 1932

So I (Ode to Virginity)
Music by Jimmy Horowitz
Lyrics by Leo Rost and Jimmy Horowitz
Marlowe 1981

So I'll Tell Her
Music by Jerry Livingston
Lyrics by Leonard Adelson
Molly 1973

So in Love
Music and lyrics by Cole Porter
Kiss Me, Kate 1948

So Little Time
Music and lyrics by Micki Grant
Don't Bother Me, I Can't Cope (OB) 1972

So Lonesome
Music by Joe Jordan
Lyrics by Rosamond Johnson
Fast and Furious 1931

So Long As It Isn't Shakespeare
Music by Albert Hague
Lyrics by Marty Brill
Café Crown 1964

So Long, Baby
Music by Leonard Bernstein
Lyrics by Betty Comden and Adolph Green
On the Town 1944

So Long, Big Guy
Music by Charles Strouse
Lyrics by Lee Adams
It's a Bird, It's a Plane, It's Superman 1966

So Long, Dearie
Music and lyrics by Jerry Herman
Hello, Dolly 1964

So Long Dude
Music by Galt MacDermot
Lyrics by Gerome Ragni
Dude 1972

So Long, Farewell
Music by Richard Rodgers
Lyrics by Oscar Hammerstein II
The Sound of Music 1959

So Long For Ever So Long
Music by Ray Henderson
Lyrics by Ted Koehler
Say When 1934

So Long, Mary
Music and lyrics by George M. Cohan
Forty-Five Minutes From Broadway 1906

So Long Mom
Music and lyrics by Tom Lehrer
Tomfoolery (OB) 1981

So Long 174th Street
Music and lyrics by Stan Daniels
So Long, 174th Street 1976

So Long, Sammy
Music and lyrics by Micki Grant
Don't Bother Me, I Can't Cope (OB) 1972

So Long, San Antonio
Music and lyrics by Cole Porter
Something for the Boys 1943

Dropped before Broadway opening

So Long Sing Song
Music and lyrics by George M. Cohan
Little Johnny Jones 1904

So Low
Music by Donald Honrath
Lyrics by Nancy Hamilton and June Sillman
New Faces of 1934

So Many People
Music and lyrics by Stephen Sondheim
Marry Me a Little (OB) 1981

Dropped from *Follies* (1971)

So Much for Marriage
Music by Robert Mitchell
Lyrics by Elizabeth Perry
Bags (OB) 1982

So Much World
Music by David Baker
Lyrics by Will Holt
Come Summer 1969

So Much You Loved Me
Music by Richard Rodgers
Lyrics by Sheldon Harnick
Rex 1976

Same music as "From Afar," which was dropped from production.

So Near and Yet So Far
Music and lyrics by Cole Porter
You'll Never Get Rich (1941) F

So Nonchalant
Music by Vernon Duke
Lyrics by E.Y. Harburg
Walk a Little Faster 1932

So Proud
Music and lyrics by Robert Wright and George
Forrest (based on Rachmaninoff)
Anya 1965

So Raise the Banner High
Music by Alec Wilder
Lyrics by Arnold Sundgaard
Kittiwake Island (OB) 1960

So They Call It New York
Music by Don Pippin
Lyrics by Steve Brown
The Contrast (OB) 1972

So This Is Mexico
Music by Ray Henderson
Lyrics by Lew Brown
Hot-Cha! 1932

So What?
Music by George Gershwin
Lyrics by Ira Gershwin
Pardon My English 1933

So What?
Music and lyrics by Cole Porter
High Society (1955) F

Original title "Why Not?" Dropped from film

So What?
Music by John Kander
Lyrics by Fred Ebb
Cabaret 1966

So What?
Music by George Fischoff
Lyrics by Carole Bayer
Georgy 1970

So What?
Music by Diane Leslie
Lyrics by William Gleason
The Coolest Cat in Town (OB) 1978

So What Else Is New?
Music by John Kander
Lyrics by Fred Ebb
Woman of the Year 1981

So Would I
Music by Milton Ager
Lyrics by Jack Yellen
Rain or Shine 1928

So You Wanted to Meet the Wizard
Music and lyrics by Charlie Smalls
The Wiz 1975

Soap Operetta
Music by Seth Friedman
Lyrics by David L. Crane, Seth Friedman
and Marta Kauffman
Upstairs at O'Neal's (OB) 1982

Soapbox Sillies
Music by Bradford Greene
Lyrics by Marianne Brown Waters
Right This Way 1938

Sobbin' Women
Music by Gene dePaul
Lyrics by Johnny Mercer
Seven Brides for Seven Brothers 1982

The Social
Music and lyrics by Harold Rome
Destry Rides Again 1959

Social Director
Music and lyrics by Harold Rome
Wish You Were Here 1952

The Social Whirl
Music and lyrics by Robert Wright
and George Forrest
Kean 1961

The Society Farmerettes
Music by Victor Herbert
Lyrics by P.G. Wodehouse
Miss 1917 1917

Society Ladder
Music by Harry Ruby
Lyrics by Bert Kalmar
The Five o'Clock Girl 1927

Sock Life in the Eye
Music and lyrics by Michael Brown
Different Times 1972

Sodomy
Music by Galt MacDermot
Lyrics by Gerome Ragni and James Rado
Hair 1968

Soft in de Moonlight
Music by Frank Harling
Lyrics by Laurence Stallings
Deep River 1926

Soft Is the Sparrow
Music by Robert Waldman
Lyrics by Alfred Uhry
Here's Where I Belong 1968

Soft Lights and Sweet Music
Music and lyrics by Irving Berlin
Face the Music 1932

Soft Music
Music and lyrics by Richard M. Sherman
and Robert B. Sherman
Over Here! 1974

The Soft Spot
Music by Joe Ercole
Lyrics by Bruce Kluger
Ka-Boom (OB) 1980

Softly, as in a Morning Sunrise
Music by Sigmund Romberg
Lyrics by Oscar Hammerstein II
The New Moon 1928

Softly thro' the Summer Night
Music by Emmerich Kálmán
Lyrics by C.C.S. Cushing and E.P. Heath
Sari 1914

Sold
Music by Harry Tierney
Lyrics by Joseph McCarthy
Cross My Heart 1928

The Soldier and the Washerworker
Music and lyrics by Ronald Melrose
Upstairs at O'Neal's (OB) 1982

Soldier Boy
Music by Shep Camp
Lyrics by Frank DuPree and Harry B. Smith
Half a Widow 1927

A Soldier of Fortune
Music by Jean Gilbert
Lyrics by Harry B. Smith
The Red Robe 1928

Soldier of Love
Music by Gerald Marks
Lyrics by Irving Caesar
Thumbs Up! 1934

A Soldier Stole Her Love
Music by Oscar Straus
Lyrics by Joseph W. Herbert
A Waltz Dream 1908

A Soldier Takes Pride in Saluting His Captain
Music by John Duffy
Lyrics by Rocco Bufano and John Duffy
Horseman, Pass By (OB) 1969

Soldiers Anthem
Music by Michael Valenti
Lyrics by John Lewin
Blood Red Roses 1970

Soldiers' March (instrumental)
Music by George Gershwin
Strike Up the Band 1930

Soldiers True
Music by A. Baldwin Sloane
Lyrics by Harry Cort and George E. Stoddard
China Rose 1925

Soliciting Subscriptions
Music by Richard Rodgers
Lyrics by Lorenz Hart
The Garrick Gaieties (1st edition) 1925

Solid Silver Platform Shoes
Music and lyrics by Stephen Schwartz
The Magic Show 1974

Soliloquies
Music and lyrics by Noël Coward
The Girl Who Came to Supper 1963

Soliloquy
Music by Vincent Youmans
Lyrics by Oscar Hammerstein II
Rainbow 1928

Soliloquy
Music by Richard Rodgers
Lyrics by Oscar Hammerstein II
Carousel 1945

Soliloquy
Music by Robert Kole
Lyrics by Sandi Merle
I Take These Women (OB) 1982

Solomon Song
Music by Kurt Weill
Lyrics by Marc Blitzstein
The Threepenny Opera (OB) 1954

Some Bright Morning
Music by Charles Strouse
Lyrics by David Rogers
Charlie and Algernon 1980

Some Day
Music by Rudolf Friml
Lyrics by Brian Hooker
The Vagabond King 1925

Some Day
Music by Ford Dabney
Lyrics by Jo Trent
Rang-Tang 1927

Some Day
Music by Rudi Revil
Lyrics by Kurt Kasznar and Carl Kent
Crazy With the Heat 1941

Some Day I'll Find You
Music and lyrics by Noël Coward
Private Lives 1931

Some Day I'm Gonna Fly
Music by Michael Leonard
Lyrics by Herbert Martin
The Yearling 1965

Some Days Everything Goes Wrong
Music and lyrics by Ervin Drake
What Makes Sammy Run? 1964

Some Days It Seems That It Don't Even Pay to Get Out of Bed
Music and lyrics by Melvin Van Peebles
Don't Play Us Cheap 1972

Some Enchanted Evening
Music by Richard Rodgers
Lyrics by Oscar Hammerstein II
South Pacific 1949

Some Fine Day
Music by Jerome Kern
Lyrics by Anne Caldwell
The Night Boat 1920

Some Girl Is on Your Mind
Music by Jerome Kern
Lyrics by Oscar Hammerstein II
Sweet Adeline 1929

Some Girls Can Bake a Pie
Music by George Gershwin
Lyrics by Ira Gershwin
Of Thee I Sing 1931

Some Kind of Man
Music by Jule Styne
Lyrics by Sammy Cahn
Look to the Lilies 1970

Some Like to Hunt
Music by Herbert Stothart
Lyrics by Otto Harbach and Oscar Hammerstein II
Wildflower 1923

Some Little People
Music by Leon Pober
Lyrics by Bud Freeman
Beg, Borrow or Steal 1960

Some Other Day
Music by J. Fred Coots
Lyrics by Al Dubin
White Lights 1927

Some Other Time
Music by Leonard Bernstein
Lyrics by Betty Comden and Adolph Green
On the Town 1944

Some Party
Music by Jerome Kern
Lyrics by Anne Caldwell
She's a Good Fellow 1919

Some People
Music by Jule Styne
Lyrics by Stephen Sondheim
Gypsy 1959

Some Said They Were Crazy
Music by Earl Robinson
Lyrics by Waldo Salt
Sandhog (OB) 1954

Some Sort of Somebody
Music by Jerome Kern
Lyrics by Elsie Janis
Miss Information 1915

Elsie Janis herself sang this song in *Miss Information,* which closed in six weeks. Kern immediately put it into *Very Good Eddie* (1915).

Some Sunday
Music and lyrics by Will Holt
That 5 A.M. Jazz (OB) 1964

Some Sweet Someone
Music and lyrics by Herbert Stothart, Bert Kalmar and Harry Ruby
Good Boy 1928

Some Things
Music and lyrics by Harold Rome
The Zulu and the Zayda 1965

Some Wonderful Sort of Someone
Music by George Gershwin
Lyrics by Schuyler Greene
Ladies First 1918

Somebody
Music by Leslie Stuart
Lyrics by Ernest Boyd-Jones and Paul Rubens
Florodora 1900

Somebody
Music by Harvey Schmidt
Lyrics by Tom Jones
Celebration 1969

Somebody Did Alright for Herself
Music by Billy Goldenberg
Lyrics by Alan and Marilyn Bergman
Ballroom 1978

Somebody Else
Music by Raymond Hubbell
Lyrics by Anne Caldwell
Yours Truly 1927

Somebody Else
Music by Gary William Friedman
Lyrics by Will Holt
Taking My Turn (OB) 1983

Somebody From Somewhere
Music by George Gershwin
Lyrics by Ira Gershwin
Delicious (1931) F

Somebody Like Me
Music and lyrics by Frank Marcus and Bernard Maltin
Bamboola 1929

Somebody Loves Me
Music by George Gershwin
Lyrics by B.G. DeSylva and Ballard MacDonald
George White's Scandals (1924)

Somebody New
Music by Charles Strouse
Lyrics by David Rogers
Charlie and Algernon 1980

Somebody Ought to Be Told
Music by Sigmund Romberg
Lyrics by Oscar Hammerstein II
May Wine 1935

Somebody Ought to Wave a Flag
Music by Richard Rodgers
Lyrics by Lorenz Hart
The Phantom President (1932) F

Somebody, Somebody Hold Me
Music by Steve Sterner
Lyrics by Peter del Valle
Lovers (OB) 1975

Somebody, Somewhere
Music and lyrics by Frank Loesser
The Most Happy Fella 1956

Somebody Write Me a Love Song
Music by Patrick Rose
Lyrics by Merv Campone and Richard Ouzounian
A Bistro Car on the CNR (OB) 1978

Somebody's Going to Throw a Big Party
Music and lyrics by Cole Porter
Fifty Million Frenchmen 1929

Somebody's Stepping on My Olive Branch
Music and lyrics by Ron Eliran
Don't Step on My Olive Branch (OB) 1976

Someday
Music and lyrics by Alan Menken
Real Life Funnies (OB) 1981

Someday
Music by Henry Krieger
Lyrics by Robert Lorick
The Tap Dance Kid 1983

Someday, if We Grow Up
Music by Norman Curtis
Lyrics by Patricia Taylor Curtis
Walk Down Mah Street! (OB) 1968

Someday I'll Walk
Music and lyrics by John Driver
Ride the Winds 1974

Someday, Maybe
Music and lyrics by Deed Meyer
She Shall Have Music (OB) 1959

Somehow I Never Could Believe
Music by Kurt Weill
Lyrics by Langston Hughes
Street Scene 1947

Somehow I'm Taller
Music by Steve Sterner
Lyrics by Peter del Valle
Lovers (OB) 1975

Somehow It Seldom Comes True
Music by George Gershwin
Lyrics by Arthur J. Jackson and B.G. DeSylva
La, La, Lucille 1919

Somehow I've Always Known
Music by Frederico Valerio
Lyrics by Elizabeth Miele
Hit the Trail 1954

Someone
Music by George Gershwin
Lyrics by Arthur Francis (Ira Gershwin)
For Goodness Sake 1922

Someone
Music by Alfred Goodman and Maury Rubens
Lyrics by Harry B. Smith
Naughty Riquette 1926

Someone
Music by Jack Urbont
Lyrics by Bruce Geller
Livin' the Life (OB) 1957

Someone a Lot Like You
Music by Jack Holmes
Lyrics by Bill Conklin and Bob Miller
O Say Can You See! (OB) 1962

Someone at Last
Music by Harold Arlen
Lyrics by Ira Gershwin
A Star Is Born (1954) F

Someone in a Tree
Music and lyrics by Stephen Sondheim
Pacific Overtures 1976

Someone in April
Music by Burton Lane
Lyrics by Alan Jay Lerner
Carmelina 1979

Someone in the Know
Music and lyrics by Ann Ronell
Count Me In 1942

Someone Is Sending Me Flowers
Music by David Baker
Lyrics by Sheldon Harnick
Shoestring Revue (1955) (OB)

Someone Is Waiting
Music and lyrics by Stephen Sondheim
Company 1970

Someone I've Already Found
Music by Stanley Lebowsky
Lyrics by Fred Tobias
Gantry 1970

Someone Like Me
Music by Ernest Gold
Lyrics by Anne Croswell
I'm Solomon 1968

Someone Like You
Music by Alma Sanders
Lyrics by Monte Carlo
The Houseboat on the Styx 1928

Someone Like You
Music by Richard Rodgers
Lyrics by Stephen Sondheim
Do I Hear a Waltz? 1965

Someone Loves You After All
Music by Harry Tierney
Lyrics by Joseph McCarthy
Kid Boots 1923

Someone Must Try
Music by John Morris
Lyrics by Gerald Freedman
A Time for Singing 1966

Someone Needs Me
Music by Harvey Schmidt
Lyrics by Tom Jones
I Do! I Do! 1966

Someone Nice Like You
Music and lyrics by Leslie Bricusse
and Anthony Newley
Stop the World—I Want to Get Off 1962

Someone Should Tell Them
Music by Richard Rodgers
Lyrics by Lorenz Hart
A Connecticut Yankee 1927

Dropped from production and re-titled "There's
So Much More" for *America's Sweetheart* (1931)

Someone to Admire, Someone to Adore
Music by Serge Walter
Lyrics by Agnes Morgan
The Grand Street Follies (1928)

Someone to Care For
Music by Duke Ellington
Lyrics by Marshall Barer and Fred Tobias
Pousse-Café 1966

Someone to Come Home With Me Tonight
Music and lyrics by Alan Menken
Real Life Funnies (OB) 1981

Someone to Count On
Music and lyrics by Deed Meyer
'Toinette (OB) 1961

Someone to Love
Music by Lawrence Hurwit
Lyrics by Lee Goldsmith
Sextet 1974

Someone to Watch Over Me
Music by George Gershwin
Lyrics by Ira Gershwin
Oh, Kay! 1926

Originally written in an exciting, jazzy tempo. When George casually slowed it down one day both he and Ira realized that it was better as a warm and charming ballad. The title was suggested by Howard Dietz.

Someone Waiting
Music by Robert Kessler
Lyrics by Martin Charnin
Fallout (OB) 1959

Someone Who Believes in You
Music by George Gershwin
Lyrics by B.G. DeSylva
Sweet Little Devil 1924

Someone Will Make You Smile
Music by Rudolf Sieczynski
Lyrics by Irving Caesar
Poppy 1923

Dropped from production. The music is the same as that of "Wien, du Stadt Meiner Träume," better known as "Wien, Wein, Nur du Allein."

Someone Woke Up
Music by Richard Rodgers
Lyrics by Stephen Sondheim
Do I Hear a Waltz? 1965

Someone Wonderful I Missed
Music by Cy Coleman
Lyrics by Michael Stewart
I Love My Wife 1977

Someone You Know
Music by Victor Ziskin
Lyrics by Joan Javits
Young Abe Lincoln 1961

Something
Music by Rudolf Friml
Lyrics by Otto Harbach
The Firefly 1912

Something
Music and lyrics by Douglas Bernstein and Denis Markell
Upstairs at O'Neal's (OB) 1982

Something About a Uniform
Music and lyrics by George M. Cohan
The Man Who Owns Broadway 1909

Something About Love
Music by George Gershwin
Lyrics by Lou Paley
The Lady in Red (1919)

Added to London production of *Lady, Be Good!* (1926)

Something Beautiful
Music by Gary William Friedman
Lyrics by Will Holt
The Me Nobody Knows (OB) 1970

Something Big
Music and lyrics by Richard Adler
Kwamina 1961

Something Big
Music by Sam Pottle
Lyrics by David Axelrod
New Faces of 1968

Something Doesn't Happen
Music by Richard Rodgers
Lyrics by Martin Charnin
Two by Two 1970

Something for Nothing
Music by Joseph Meyer and James F. Hanley
Lyrics by B.G. DeSylva
Big Boy 1925

Something for Nothing
Music by Claibe Richardson
Lyrics by Kenward Elmslie
The Grass Harp 1971

Something for the Boys
Music and lyrics by Cole Porter
Something for the Boys 1943

Something Good
Music and lyrics by Richard Rodgers
The Sound of Music (film version, 1965)

Something Greater
Music by Charles Strouse
Lyrics by Lee Adams
Applause 1970

Something Had to Happen
Music by Jerome Kern
Lyrics by Otto Harbach
Roberta 1933

Something Has Happened
Music by Harvey Schmidt
Lyrics by Tom Jones
I Do! I Do! 1966

Something Holy
Music by Bob James
Lyrics by Jack O'Brien
The Selling of the President 1972

Something I Dreamed Last Night
Music by Sammy Fain
Lyrics by Jack Yellen and Herb Magidson
George White's Scandals (1939)

Something in His Eyes
Music by Ernest Gold
Lyrics by Anne Croswell
I'm Solomon 1968

Something in the Air of May
Music by Sigmund Romberg
Lyrics by Oscar Hammerstein II
May Wine 1935

Something Is Coming to Tea
Music and lyrics by Hugh Martin and Timothy Gray
High Spirits 1964

Something More
Music by Sammy Fain
Lyrics by Marilyn and Alan Bergman
Something More 1964

Something More
Music by Don Gohman
Lyrics by Hal Hackady
Ambassador 1972

Something More
Music by Elmer Bernstein
Lyrics by Don Black
Merlin 1983

Something New
Music and lyrics by Howard Blankman
By Hex (OB) 1956

Something New Is in My Heart
Music by Sigmund Romberg
Lyrics by Oscar Hammerstein II
May Wine 1935

Something Nice Is Going to Happen
Music and lyrics by Robert Dahdah
Curley McDimple (OB) 1967

Something Peculiar
Music by George Gershwin
Lyrics by Ira Gershwin
Girl Crazy 1930

Dropped from production

Something Seems Tingle-ingle-ing
See "High Jinks"

Something Seems to Tell Me
Music by Robert Katscher
Lyrics by Irving Caesar
The Wonder Bar 1931

Something, Somewhere
Music by Richard Rodgers
Lyrics by Martin Charnin
Two by Two 1970

Something Sort of Grandish
Music by Burton Lane
Lyrics by E.Y. Harburg
Finian's Rainbow 1947

Something Spanish in Your Eyes
Music by Philip Charig
Lyrics by Irving Caesar
Polly 1929

Something Special
Music by Gordon Duffy
Lyrics by Harry M. Haldane
Happy Town 1959

Something Special
Music by George Fischoff
Lyrics by Carole Bayer
Georgy 1970

Something Tells Me
Music by Henry Souvaine and Jay Gorney
Lyrics by Morrie Ryskind and Howard Dietz
Merry-Go-Round 1927

Something Tells Me
Music and lyrics by Hugh Martin and Timothy Gray
High Spirits 1964

Something Tells Me I'm in Love
Music by Harold Levey
Lyrics by Owen Murphy
Rainbow Rose 1926

Something That I Can't Explain
Music by Jean Schwartz
Lyrics by William Jerome
The Fascinating Widow 1911

Something to Believe In
Music and lyrics by John Raniello
Movie Buff (OB) 1977

Something to Dance About
Music and lyrics by Irving Berlin
Call Me Madam 1950

Something to Do Tonight
Music by Michael Dansicker
Lyrics by Sarah Schlesinger
On The Swing Shift (OB) 1983

Something to Live For
Music by Joseph Meyer
Lyrics by Edward Eliscu
Lady Fingers 1929

Something to Live For
Music and lyrics by Ervin Drake
What Makes Sammy Run? 1964

Something to Point To
Music and lyrics by Craig Carnelia
Working 1978

Something to Remember You By
Music by Arthur Schwartz
Lyrics by Howard Dietz
Three's a Crowd 1930

First written in a bright tempo as "I Have No

Words" (lyrics by Desmond Carter) for the London revue *Little Tommy Tucker* (1929).

Something to Shout About
Music and lyrics by Cole Porter
Something to Shout About (1943) F

Something to Sing About
Music by Vincent Youmans
Lyrics by Harold Adamson and Clifford Grey
Smiles 1930

Something to Tell
Music by Maury Rubens and J. Fred Coots
Lyrics by Clifford Grey
The Madcap 1928

Something Very Strange
Music and lyrics by Noël Coward
Sail Away 1961

Something Was Missing
Music by Charles Strouse
Lyrics by Martin Charnin
Annie 1977

Something Will Turn Up
Music and lyrics by Al Kasha and Joel Hirschhorn
Copperfield 1981

Something Wonderful
Music by Richard Rodgers
Lyrics by Oscar Hammerstein II
The King and I 1951

Something Wonderful Can Happen
Music and lyrics by Bob Goodman
Wild and Wonderful 1971

Something Wrong With Me
Music by J. Fred Coots
Lyrics by Clifford Grey
June Days 1925

Something You Lack
Music by Warburton Guilbert
Lyrics by Nancy Hamilton and June Sillman
New Faces of 1934

Something You Never Had Before
Music by Arthur Schwartz
Lyrics by Howard Dietz
The Gay Life 1961

Something's Afoot
Music and lyrics by James MacDonald, David Vos and Robert Gerlach
Something's Afoot 1976

Something's Always Happening on the River
Music by Jule Styne
Lyrics by Betty Comden and Adolph Green
Say, Darling 1958

Something's Brewing in Gainesville
Music and lyrics by Harry Chapin
Cotton Patch Gospel (OB) 1981

Something's Coming
Music by Leonard Bernstein
Lyrics by Stephen Sondheim
West Side Story 1957

Something's Going to Happen to You
Music by James P. Johnson
Lyrics by Flournoy Miller
Sugar Hill 1931

Something's Gone Wrong
Music and lyrics by Gene Curty, Nitra Scharfman and Chuck Strand
The Lieutenant 1975

Something's Got to Be Done
Music and lyrics by George M. Cohan
Little Nellie Kelly 1922

Something's Got to Be Done
Music by Cole Porter
Lyrics by T. Lawrason Riggs and Cole Porter
See America First 1916

Something's Got to Give
Music and lyrics by Johnny Mercer
Daddy Long Legs (1955) F

Something's Happened to Rosie
Music and lyrics by George M. Cohan
The Rise of Rosie O'Reilly 1923

Something's Rotten in Denmark
Music and lyrics by Cliff Jones
Rockabye Hamlet 1976

Sometime
Music by Rudolf Friml
Lyrics by Rida Johnson Young
Sometime 1918

Sometimes
Music by Harvey Schmidt
Lyrics by Tom Jones
Philemon (OB) 1975

Sometimes
Music and lyrics by Elizabeth Swados
Runaways 1978

Sometimes a Day Goes By
Music by John Kander
Lyrics by Fred Ebb
Woman of the Year 1981

Sometimes I Feel Just Like Grandpa
Music by Emmerich Kálmán
Lyrics by P.G. Wodehouse
The Riviera Girl 1917

Sometimes I Wonder
Music by Frank Fields
Lyrics by Armand Aulicino
The Shoemaker and the Peddler (OB) 1960

Sometimes I'm Happy
Music by Vincent Youmans
Lyrics by Irving Caesar
Hit the Deck 1927

The original lyric, titled "Come On and Pet Me," written by Oscar Hammerstein II and William Cary Duncan, was intended for the score of *Mary Jane McKane* (1923). The song was dropped from the show before the New York opening and new lyrics were written by Irving Caesar for a show called *A Night Out*, which opened and closed in Philadelphia in 1925. The song survived, however. As "Sometimes I'm Happy" it was the hit of *Hit the Deck*.

Sometimes You're Up
Music by Paul Horner
Lyrics by Peggy Lee
Peg 1983

Somewhere
Music by Lionel Monckton
Lyrics by Arthur Wimperis
The Arcadians 1910

Somewhere
Music by Harry Warren
Lyrics by Jerome Lawrence and Robert E. Lee
Shangri-La 1956

Somewhere
Music by Leonard Bernstein
Lyrics by Stephen Sondheim
West Side Story 1957

Somewhere
Music and lyrics by Rick Besoyan
The Student Gypsy (OB) 1963

Somewhere Along the Road
Music and lyrics by Johnny Brandon
Love! Love! Love! (OB) 1977

Somewhere Close By
Music by Garry Sherman
Lyrics by Peter Udell
Amen Corner 1983

Somewhere in Lovers' Land
Music by Carlton Kelsey and Maury Rubens
Lyrics by Clifford Grey
Sky High 1925

Somewhere in the Past
Music by Bill Weeden
Lyrics by David Finkle
Hurry, Harry 1972

Somewhere in Your Eyes
Music and lyrics by John Dooley
Hobo (OB) 1961

Somewhere Is Here
Music by Peter Link
Lyrics by Jacob Brackman
King of Hearts 1978

Somewhere, Someone
Music by Galt MacDermot
Lyrics by William Dumaresq
The Human Comedy (OB) 1983

Somewhere That's Green
Music by Alan Menken
Lyrics by Howard Ashman
Little Shop of Horrors (OB) 1982

Somewhere There's a Little Bluebird
Music and lyrics by Charles Gaynor
Show Girl 1961

Somewhere Under the Rainbow
Music and lyrics by James Rado
Rainbow (OB) 1972

Son of a Billionaire
Music and lyrics by George M. Cohan
The Merry Malones 1927

The Son of a Gun Is Nothing But a Tailor
Music by Richard Rodgers
Lyrics by Lorenz Hart
Love Me Tonight (1932) F

Son of Africa
Music by Ron Steward and Neal Tate
Lyrics by Ron Steward
Sambo (OB) 1969

Son of Man
Music by Dov Seltzer
Lyrics by David Axelrod
To Live Another Summer 1971

Son of the Ma
Music and lyrics by Marc Blitzstein
Juno 1959

Son of the Sun
Music by Rudolf Friml
Lyrics by J. Keirn Brennan
Luana 1930

A Song About Love
Music by Arthur Schwartz
Lyrics by Henry Myers
The New Yorkers 1927

A Song for Dancin'
Music by Billy Goldenberg
Lyrics by Alan and Marilyn Bergman
Ballroom 1978

A Song From Somewhere
Music and lyrics by Robert Wright and George
Forrest (based on Rachmaninoff)
Anya 1965

The Song Is You
Music by Jerome Kern
Lyrics by Oscar Hammerstein II
Music in the Air 1932

Song of a Child Prostitute
Music and lyrics by Elizabeth Swados
Runaways 1978

Song of a Summer Night
Music and lyrics by Frank Loesser
The Most Happy Fella 1956

Song of Greater Britain
Music by Michael Valenti
Lyrics by John Lewin
Blood Red Roses 1970

Song of Harlem
Music and lyrics by Frank Marcus
and Bernard Maltin
Bamboola 1929

Song of Love
Music by Sigmund Romberg
Lyrics by Dorothy Donnelly
Blossom Time 1921

Based on Schubert's Unfinished Symphony

Song of Love
Music by Mary Rodgers
Lyrics by Marshall Barer
Once Upon a Mattress 1959

Song of Me
Music by David Shire
Lyrics by Richard Maltby, Jr.
Starting Here, Starting Now (OB) 1977

Song of My Heart
Music by Franklin Hauser
Lyrics by Brian Hooker
The O'Flynn 1934

Song of Myself
Music by Stan Harte, Jr.
Leaves of Grass (OB) 1971

The Song of Norway
Music and lyrics by Robert Wright
and George Forrest
Song of Norway 1944

Based on Grieg's Piano Concerto in A minor

A Song of Patriotic Prejudice
Music by Donald Swann
Lyrics by Michael Flanders
At the Drop of Another Hat 1966

The Song of Prigio
Music by Lehman Engel
Lyrics by Agnes Morgan
A Hero Is Born 1937

Song of Reproduction
Music by Donald Swann
Lyrics by Michael Flanders
At the Drop of a Hat 1959

The Song of Sallah Shabeti
Music by Menachem Zur
Lyrics by Herbert Appleman
Unfair to Goliath (OB) 1970

Song of the Bends
Music by Earl Robinson
Lyrics by Waldo Salt
Sandhog (OB) 1954

Song of the Big Shot
Music by Kurt Weill
Lyrics by Bertolt Brecht
(adapted by Michael Feingold)
Happy End 1977

Song of the Brass Key
Music by Sigmund Romberg
Lyrics by Otto Harbach and Oscar Hammerstein II
The Desert Song 1926

Song of the City of Hope
Music by Jim Steinman
Lyrics by Michael Weller and Jim Steinman
More Than You Deserve (OB) 1973

Song of the Claque
Music by Franz Steininger (adapted from
Tchaikovsky)
Lyrics by Forman Brown
Music in My Heart 1947

Song of the Cotton Fields
Music by Thomas (Fats) Waller and Harry Brooks
Lyrics by Andy Razaf
Hot Chocolates 1929

Song of the Fair Dissenter Lass
Music by Michael Valenti
Lyrics by John Lewin
Blood Red Roses 1970

Song of the Flame
Music by George Gershwin and Herbert Stothart
Lyrics by Otto Harbach and Oscar Hammerstein II
Song of the Flame 1925

Song of the Foreign Legion
Music by Ray Henderson
Lyrics by B.G. DeSylva and Lew Brown
George White's Scandals (1931)

Song of the Frog
Music and lyrics by Matt Dubey and Dean Fuller
Smith (OB) 1973

Song of the Goddess
Music by Kurt Weill
Lyrics by Paul Green
Johnny Johnson 1936

Song of the Golden Egg
Music by Jim Steinman
Lyrics by Michael Weller and Jim Steinman
More Than You Deserve (OB) 1973

Song of the Guns
Music by Kurt Weill
Lyrics by Paul Green
Johnny Johnson 1936

Song of the King
Music by Andrew Lloyd Webber
Lyrics by Tim Rice
Joseph and the Amazing Technicolor Dreamcoat 1982

Song of the LURP
Music and lyrics by Elizabeth Swados
Dispatches (OB) 1979

Song of the Malcontents
Music and lyrics by Don Tucker
Red, White and Maddox 1969

The Song of the Mask
Music by James Bredt
Lyrics by Edward Eager
The Happy Hypocrite (OB) 1968

Song of the Matadors
Music by Ray Henderson
Lyrics by Lew Brown
Hot-Cha! 1932

Song of the Moonbeams
Music by Vincent Rose
Lyrics by Charles and Harry Tobias
Earl Carroll's Sketch Book (1929)

Song of the Navy
Music by Maurice Levi
Lyrics by Harry B. Smith
Ziegfeld Follies of 1908

Song of the Nose
Music by Victor Herbert
Lyrics by Harry B. Smith
Cyrano de Bergerac 1899

Song of the Open Road
Music by Stan Harte, Jr.
Leaves of Grass (OB) 1971

Song of the Poet
Music by Victor Herbert
Lyrics by Glen MacDonough
Babes in Toyland 1903

Song of the Riveter
Music by Arthur Schwartz
Lyrics by Lew Levenson
The Little Show (1st edition) 1929

The Song of the Roustabouts
Music by Richard Rodgers
Lyrics by Lorenz Hart
Jumbo 1935

Song of the Sarong
Music and lyrics by Dorcas Cochran
and Charles Rosoff
Earl Carroll's Vanities (1940)

The Song of the Scimitar
Music by Frederic Norton
Lyrics by Oscar Asche
Chu Chin Chow 1917

Song of the Setting Sun
Music by Walter Donaldson
Lyrics by Gus Kahn
Whoopee 1928

Song of the Thirteen Colonies
Music and lyrics by Norman Dean
Autumn's Here (OB) 1966

Song of the Troika
Music by Franz Steininger (adapted from Tchaikovsky)
Lyrics by Forman Brown
Music in My Heart 1947

Song of the Vagabonds
Music by Rudolf Friml
Lyrics by Brian Hooker
The Vagabond King 1925

A Song of the Weather
Music by Donald Swann
Lyrics by Michael Flanders
At the Drop of a Hat 1959

Song of the Woodman
Music by Harold Arlen
Lyrics by E.Y. Harburg
The Show Is On 1936

Song of the Wounded Frenchman
Music by Kurt Weill
Lyrics by Paul Green
Johnny Johnson 1936

Song of Two Islands
Music by John Green
Lyrics by George Marion, Jr.
Beat the Band 1942

Song of Victory
Music by Sigmund Romberg
Lyrics by Dorothy Donnelly
My Maryland 1927

Song of Welcome
Music by Richard Hill and John Hawkins
Lyrics by Nevill Coghill
Canterbury Tales 1969

Song of Yesterday
Music and lyrics by John Raniello
Movie Buff (OB) 1977

Song on the Sand
Music and lyrics by Jerry Herman
La Cage aux Folles 1983

Song to Endangered Species
Music by Robert Mitchell
Lyrics by Elizabeth Perry
Bags (OB) 1982

Song to Sing
Music and lyrics by James Rado
Rainbow (OB) 1972

A Song to Sing
Music by Galt MacDermot
Lyrics by Gerome Ragni
Dude 1972

Song Without Words
Music by Harold Levey
Lyrics by Zelda Sears
The Clinging Vine 1922

Songbook
Music by Monty Norman
Lyrics by Julian More
The Moony Shapiro Songbook 1981

The Song's for Free
Music by Sammy Fain
Lyrics by Jack Yellen
George White's Scandals (1939)

The Songs of Long Ago
Music by George Gershwin
Lyrics by Arthur Jackson
George White's Scandals (1920)

The Sonny-Boy Slave Song
Music by Coleridge-Taylor Perkinson
Lyrics by Ray McIver
God Is a (Guess What?) (OB) 1968

Sons
Music by Jerry Bock
Lyrics by Sheldon Harnick
The Rothschilds 1970

Sons and Daughters of the Sea
Music by Eubie Blake
Lyrics by J. Milton Reddie and Cecil Mack
Swing It 1937

Sons Of
Music by Jacques Brel
English lyrics by Eric Blau and Mort Shuman

*Jacques Brel Is Alive and Well
and Living in Paris* (OB) 1968

Sons of France
Music by Marguerite Monnot
Lyrics by Julian More, David Heneker
and Monte Norman
Irma la Douce 1960

Sons of Greentree
Music by David Baker
Lyrics by Sheldon Harnick
Smiling, the Boy Fell Dead (OB) 1961

The Sons of Old Black Joe
Music and lyrics by Noble Sissle and Eubie Blake
The Chocolate Dandies 1924

Sons of the Sea
Music by Jacques Belasco
Lyrics by Kay Twomey
The Girl From Nantucket 1945

Soon
Music by George Gershwin
Lyrics by Ira Gershwin
Strike Up the Band 1930

Soon
Music by Richard Rodgers
Lyrics by Lorenz Hart
Mississippi (1935) F

Soon
Music and lyrics by Walter Marks
Bajour 1964

Soon
Music and lyrics by Stephen Sondheim
A Little Night Music 1973

Soon as I Get Home
Music and lyrics by Charlie Smalls
The Wiz 1975

Soon It's Gonna Rain
Music by Harvey Schmidt
Lyrics by Tom Jones
The Fantasticks (OB) 1960

Soon We'll Be Seen Upon the Screen
Music by Louis A. Hirsch
Lyrics by Rennold Wolf
The Rainbow Girl 1918

Soon You Gonna Leave Me, Joe
Music and lyrics by Frank Loesser
The Most Happy Fella 1956

Sooner or Later
Music and lyrics by Lionel Bart
La Strada 1969

Sophia
Music by George Gershwin
Lyrics by Ira Gershwin
Kiss Me Stupid (1964) F

Same music as "Wake Up Brother and Dance"
from the film *Shall We Dance* (1937).

Sophie
Music by William B. Kernell
Lyrics by Dorothy Donnelly
Hello, Lola 1926

Sophie in New York
Music and lyrics by Steve Allen
Sophie 1963

Sorry for Myself
Music by Moose Charlap
Lyrics by Norman Gimbel
Whoop-Up 1958

Sorry-Grateful
Music and lyrics by Stephen Sondheim
Company 1970

Sorry That I Strayed Away From You
Music by Jimmy Johnson
Lyrics by Perry Bradford
Messin' Around 1929

Sorry We Won
Music by David Krivoshei
Lyrics by David Paulsen
To Live Another Summer 1971

Sort o' Lonesome
Music and lyrics by Herman Hupfeld
A La Carte 1927

A Sort of Courting Song
Music by Don Pippin
Lyrics by Steve Brown
The Contrast (OB) 1972

So's Your Old Man
Music by Jerome Kern
Lyrics by Otto Harbach and Oscar Hammerstein II
Sunny 1925

Soul
Music by Paul Horner
Lyrics by Peggy Lee
Peg 1983

Soul Mates
Music by Alma Sanders
Lyrics by Monte Carlo
The Houseboat on the Styx 1928

Soul Saving Sadie
Music by Joseph Meyer
Lyrics by Billy Rose and Ballard MacDonald
Ziegfeld Follies (1934)

Soulless a Faery Dies
Music by John Duffy
Lyrics by Rocco Bufano and John Duffy
Horseman, Pass By (OB) 1969

Sound and Light
Music by Ted Simons
Lyrics by Elinor Guggenheimer
Potholes (OB) 1979

The Sound of Money
Music and lyrics by Harold Rome
I Can Get It for You Wholesale 1962

The Sound of Music
Music by Richard Rodgers
Lyrics by Oscar Hammerstein II
The Sound of Music 1959

The Sound of the Drum
Music by William Heagney
Lyrics by William Heagney and Tom Connell
There You Are 1932

Sounds
Music by Gary William Friedman
Lyrics by Will Holt
The Me Nobody Knows (OB) 1970

Sounds
Music by Wally Harper
Lyrics by Paul Zakrzewski
Sensations (OB) 1970

South America, Take It Away
Music and lyrics by Harold Rome
Call Me Mister 1946

South American Way
Music by Jimmy McHugh
Lyrics by Al Dubin
The Streets of Paris 1939

South American Way
Music by Norman Martin
Lyrics by Norman Martin and Fred Ebb
From A to Z 1960

South American Way
Music and lyrics by Ann Harris
Sky High (OB) 1979

South Sea Island Blues
Music by Monte Carlo and Alma Sanders
Lyrics by Howard Johnson
Tangerine 1921

South Sea Isles (Sunny South Sea Islands)
Music by George Gershwin
Lyrics by Arthur Jackson
George White's Scandals (1921)

South Sea Moon
Music and lyrics by Gene Buck and Dave Stamper
Ziegfeld Follies of 1922

South Wind Is Calling
Music by Emil Gerstenberger and Carle Carlton
Lyrics by Howard Johnson
The Lace Petticoat 1927

Southern Hospitality
Music by Bob Brush
Lyrics by Martin Charnin
The First 1981

Souvenir
Music by Richard Rodgers
Lyrics by Lorenz Hart
Poor Little Ritz Girl 1920

Included in Boston production, but dropped before
Broadway opening

Souvenir
Music by Sigmund Romberg
Lyrics by Rowland Leigh
My Romance 1948

Spanglish
Music by Cy Coleman
Lyrics by Dorothy Fields
Seesaw 1973

Spanish Love
Music by George Gershwin
Lyrics by Irving Caesar
Broadway Brevities of 1920

Spanish Love
Music by Sigmund Romberg
Lyrics by Harry B. Smith
The Love Call 1927

Spanish Maid
Music by Rudolf Friml
Lyrics by Rida Johnson Young
Sometime 1918

The Spanish Mick
Music by Harry Archer
Lyrics by Harlan Thompson
Merry-Merry 1925

Spanish Moon
Music by Tom Johnstone
Lyrics by Phil Cook
When You Smile 1925

Spanish Panic
Music by Mary Rodgers
Lyrics by Marshall Barer
Once Upon a Mattress 1959

Spanish Rose
Music by Charles Strouse
Lyrics by Lee Adams
Bye Bye Birdie 1960

Spanish Shawl
Music by Harry Tierney
Lyrics by Joseph McCarthy
Rio Rita 1927

A Spanish Shawl
Music by Jean Schwartz
Lyrics by Alfred Bryan
A Night in Spain 1927

Spare a Little Love
Music by Melville Gideon
Lyrics by Clifford Grey
The Optimists 1928

Spare That Building
Music by Jimmy Van Heusen
Lyrics by Sammy Cahn
Skyscraper 1965

Speak Easy
Music by Lewis E. Gensler
Lyrics by Owen Murphy and Robert A.Simon
The Gang's All Here l931

Speak Low
Music by Kurt Weill
Lyrics by Ogden Nash
One Touch of Venus 1943

The first line of the lyric, "Speak low, when you
speak love," was borrowed from Shakespeare's
Much Ado About Nothing.

Speaking of Love
Music by Vernon Duke
Lyrics by E.Y. Harburg
Walk a Little Faster 1932

Speaking of Pals
Music by Morton Gould
Lyrics by Betty Comden and Adolph Green
Billion Dollar Baby 1945

Speaking of You
Music by Lewis E. Gensler
Lyrics by Owen Murphy and Robert A.Simon
The Gang's All Here l931

A Special Announcement
Music and lyrics by Leslie Bricusse
and Anthony Newley
Stop the World—I Want to Get Off 1962

A Special Boy
Music and lyrics by Frederick Silver
Gay Company (OB) 1974

Special Bulletin
Music by Susan Hulsman Bingham
Lyrics by Myrna Lamb
Mod Donna (OB) 1970

Special Delivery!
Music and lyrics by Frank Loesser
The Most Happy Fella 1956

A Special Man
Music and lyrics by Peter Copani
New York City Street Show (OB) 1977

Specially Made for You
Music by Joseph Meyer
Lyrics by William Moll
Jonica 1930

Speed
Music by Vincent Youmans and Herbert Stothart
Lyrics by Oscar Hammerstein II
and William Cary Duncan
Mary Jane McKane 1923

Speed of Light
Music and lyrics by John Phillips
Man on the Moon 1975

The Spell of Those Harlem Nights
Music and lyrics by Al Wilson, Charles Weinberg
and Ken Macomber
Yeah Man 1932

Spend It
Music by C. Luckey Roberts
Lyrics by Alex C. Rogers
My Magnolia 1926

Spic and Spanish
Music by Richard Rodgers
Lyrics by Lorenz Hart
Too Many Girls 1939

The Spider and the Fly
Music by Duke Ellington
Lyrics by Marshall Barer and Fred Tobias
Pousse-Café 1966

The Spider's Web
Music by Milton Schwarzwald
Lyrics by Clifford Grey
The Great Temptations 1926

The Spiel
Music by James Mundy
Lyrics by John Latouche
The Vamp 1955

The Spirit Is Moving
Music and lyrics by Michael Brown
Different Times 1972

Spirit of Capsulanti
Music by Sammy Fain
Lyrics by E.Y. Harburg
Flahooley 1951

The Spirit of Education
Music by Helen Miller
Lyrics by Eve Merriam
Inner City 1971

Spitball
Music and lyrics by Harry Chapin
Cotton Patch Gospel (OB) 1981

Splendor in the Grass
Music by Jacques Urbont
Lyrics by David Newburger
Stag Movie (OB) 1971

Spoken Aria
Music and lyrics by Al Carmines
Joan (OB) 1972

Sport Is Sport
Music by Harry Revel
Lyrics by Mack Gordon
Smiling Faces 1932

Sposalizio
Music and lyrics by Frank Loesser
The Most Happy Fella 1956

Spread a Little Sunshine
Music and lyrics by Stephen Schwartz
Pippin 1972

Spring
Music by John Mundy
Lyrics by Edward Eager
The Liar 1950

Spring Again
Music by Vernon Duke
Lyrics by Ira Gershwin
Goldwyn Follies (1938) F

Spring Beauties
Music by Al Carmines
Lyrics by Maria Irene Fornes
Promenade (OB) 1969

Spring Doth Let Her Colours Fly
Music by Charles Strouse
Lyrics by Lee Adams
The Littlest Revue (OB) 1956

Spring Fever
Music by Harold Levey
Lyrics by Zelda Sears
The Clinging Vine 1922

Spring Fever
Music by Harold Arlen
Lyrics by Ira Gershwin and E.Y. Harburg
Life Begins at 8:40 1934

Spring Has Sprung
Music by Arthur Schwartz
Lyrics by Dorothy Fields
Excuse My Dust (1951) F

Spring in Autumn
Music by Will Ortman
Lyrics by Gus Kahn and Raymond B. Egan
Holka-Polka 1925

Spring in the City
Music and lyrics by Paul Nassau and Oscar Brand
*The Education of H*y*m*a*n K*a*p*l*a*n* 1968

Spring in Vienna
Music by Richard Rodgers
Lyrics by Lorenz Hart
I'd Rather Be Right 1937

The title was changed to "Spring in Milwaukee" during the run.

Spring Is Here
Music by Jerome Kern
Lyrics by Oscar Hammerstein II
Sweet Adeline 1929

Spring Is Here
Music by Richard Rodgers
Lyrics by Lorenz Hart
Spring Is Here 1929

The first of two Rogers and Hart songs with this title, the first lively, the second reflective.

Spring Is Here
Music by Richard Rodgers
Lyrics by Lorenz Hart
I Married an Angel 1938

Spring Is in the Air
Music by Henry Souvaine and Jay Gorney
Lyrics by Morrie Ryskind and Howard Dietz
Merry-Go-Round 1927

Spring Is in the Air
Music by Gus Edwards
Lyrics by Eugene Conrad
Broadway Sho-window 1936

Spring Love Is in the Air
Music and lyrics by Cole Porter
Rosalie (1937) F

The Spring of Next Year
Music and lyrics by Jerry Herman
Dear World 1969

Spring Song
Music by Warburton Guilbert
Lyrics by Viola Brothers Shore and June Sillman
New Faces of 1934

Spring Time of the Year
Music and lyrics by Oscar Brand and Paul Nassau
A Joyful Noise 1966

Spring Tra La
Music and lyrics by Lloyd Waner, Lupin Feine and Moe Jaffe
A Little Racketeer 1932

Spring Will Be a Little Late This Year
Music and lyrics by Frank Loesser
Christmas Holiday (1944) F

Springtime
Music by Lewis E. Gensler
Lyrics by B.G. DeSylva
Queen High 1926

The Springtime Cometh
Music by Sammy Fain
Lyrics by E.Y. Harburg
Flahooley 1951

Springtime Is in the Air
Music by Johann Strauss I, adapted by Oscar Straus
Lyrics by Clare Kummer
Three Waltzes 1937

The Springtime of Life Is Fairest
Music by Victor Herbert
Lyrics by Robert B. Smith
The Debutante 1914

Spunk
Music by Lawrence Hurwit
Lyrics by Lee Goldsmith
Sextet 1974

The Squabble Song
Music and lyrics by Bill and Patti Jacob
Jimmy 1969

St. Bridget
Music and lyrics by Jerry Herman
Mame 1966

St. Patrick's Day Parade
Music by Ted Simons
Lyrics by Elinor Guggenheimer
Potholes (OB) 1979

St. Pierre
Music by John Kander
Lyrics by Fred Ebb
The Happy Time 1968

Stability
Music by Jerry Bock
Lyrics by Sheldon Harnick
The Rothschilds 1970

Stag Movie
Music by Jacques Urbont
Lyrics by David Newburger
Stag Movie (OB) 1971

Stage Managers' Chorus
Music by Richard Rodgers
Lyrics by Dudley Digges and Lorenz Hart
The Garrick Gaieties (1st edition) 1925

Stage Society
Music and lyrics by George M. Cohan
The Rise of Rosie O'Reilly 1923

Stan' Up and Fight
Music by Georges Bizet
Lyrics by Oscar Hammerstein II
Carmen Jones 1943

Stand Around the Band
Music by Don Walker
Lyrics by Clay Warnick
Memphis Bound 1945

Stand Back
Music by Earl Robinson
Lyrics by Waldo Salt
Sandhog (OB) 1954

Stand Up and Fight
Music by George Gershwin
Lyrics by Ira Gershwin
The Shocking Miss Pilgrim (1947) F

Adapted by Kay Swift and Ira Gershwin from
manuscripts of George Gershwin

Stand Up on Your Feet and Dance
Music by Charles M. Schwab
Lyrics by Henry Myers
Bare Facts of 1926

Standing
Music by Peter Link
Lyrics by C.C. Courtney and Ragan Courtney
Earl of Ruston 1971

Standing on the Corner
Music and lyrics by Frank Loesser
The Most Happy Fella 1956

Star and Garter Girls
Music by Lester Lee
Lyrics by Jerry Seelen
Star and Garter 1942

Star in the Twilight
Music by Karl Hajos (based on Chopin)
Lyrics by Harry B. Smith
White Lilacs 1928

Star Light, Star Bright
Music by Victor Herbert
Lyrics by Harry B. Smith
The Wizard of the Nile 1895

The Star of Hitchy-Koo
Music by Jerome Kern
Lyrics by Anne Caldwell
Hitchy-Koo 1920

Star of Love
Music by Fritz Kreisler
Lyrics by William LeBaron
Apple Blossoms 1919

Based on Kreisler's violin piece "La Gitana"

Star of Stars
Music by Philip Charig and Richard Myers
Lyrics by Leo Robin
Allez-Oop 1927

Star of the North State
Music by Sidney Lippman
Lyrics by Sylvia Dee
Barefoot Boy With Cheek 1947

The Star of This War
Music and lyrics by Gene Curty, Nitra Scharfman
and Chuck Strand
The Lieutenant 1975

A Star on the Monument
Music by Nancy Ford
Lyrics by Gretchen Cryer
Now Is the Time for All Good Men (OB) 1967

Star Song
Music and lyrics by James Rado
Rainbow (OB) 1972

Star Stepping Stranger
Music and lyrics by John Phillips
Man on the Moon 1975

Star Tar
Music by Jim Wise
Lyrics by George Haimsohn and Robin Miller
Dames at Sea (OB) 1968

Starbust
Music and lyrics by John Phillips
Man on the Moon 1975

Stardust Waltz
Music by Billy Goldenberg
Lyrics by Alan and Marilyn Bergman
Ballroom 1978

Starlight
Music by Albert Von Tilzer
Lyrics by Neville Fleeson
Bye Bye, Bonnie 1927

Starlight, Starbright
Music by Helen Miller
Lyrics by Eve Merriam
Inner City 1971

The Starlit Hour
Music by Peter de Rose
Lyrics by Mitchell Parrish
Earl Carroll's Vanities (1940)

Starry Old Night
Music and lyrics by James Rado
Rainbow (OB) 1972

Starry Sky
Music by Dimitri Tiomkin
Lyrics by Edward Eliscu
A Little Racketeer 1932

Stars and Bars
Music and lyrics by James Rado
Rainbow (OB) 1972

Stars and Lovers
Music and lyrics by Robert Dahdah
Curley McDimple (OB) 1967

Stars and Rosebuds
Music by Victor Herbert
Lyrics by Henry Blossom
Eileen 1917

Dropped from production

Stars Have Blown My Way
Music by Tommy Wolf
Lyrics by Fran Landesman
The Nervous Set 1959

Stars of Glory
Music by Bob James
Lyrics by Jack O'Brien
The Selling of the President 1972

Stars of the Stage
Music by Emmerich Kálmán
Lyrics by B.G. DeSylva
The Yankee Princess 1922

The Stars Remain
Music by Jay Gorney
Lyrics by Henry Myers
Meet the People 1940

Stars With Stripes
Music by Max Ewing
Lyrics by Dorothy Sands and Marc Loebell
The Grand Street Follies (1927) (OB)

Start Dancing
Music by Jimmy Van Heusen
Lyrics by Johnny Burke
Nellie Bly 1946

Start Stompin'
Music by Charles Rosoff
Lyrics by Leo Robin
Judy 1927

Start the Ball Rollin'
Music by David Raksin
Lyrics by June Carroll
If the Shoe Fits 1946

Starting at the Bottom
Music by Kay Swift
Lyrics by Paul James
Fine and Dandy 1930

Starting Here, Starting Now
Music by David Shire
Lyrics by Richard Maltby, Jr.
Starting Here, Starting Now (OB) 1977

Starting Out Again
Music and lyrics by Elizabeth Swados
Alice in Concert (OB) 1980

Starved
Music by Ted Simons
Lyrics by Elinor Guggenheimer
Potholes (OB) 1979

State of the Kingdom
Music by Sam Pottle
Lyrics by Tom Whedon
All Kinds of Giants (OB) 1961

The Stately Homes of England
Music and lyrics by Noël Coward
Set to Music 1939

Station L–O–V–E
Music by Manning Sherwin
Lyrics by Arthur Herzog, Jr.
Bad Habits of 1926 (OB)

Statistics
Music by Helen Miller
Lyrics by Eve Merriam
Inner City 1971

The Statue
Music by Jacques Brel
English lyrics by Eric Blau and Mort Shuman
*Jacques Brel Is Alive and Well
and Living in Paris* (OB) 1968

Stay
Music by Richard Rodgers
Lyrics by Stephen Sondheim
Do I Hear a Waltz? 1965

Stay as We Are
Music by Arthur Schwartz
Lyrics by Ira Gershwin
Park Avenue 1946

Stay Awhile
Music by Arthur Siegel
Lyrics by Mae Richard
Tallulah (OB) 1983

Stay East, Young Man
Music by Richard Lewine
Lyrics by Ted Fetter
The Girl From Wyoming (OB) 1938

Stay Out, Sammy
Music and lyrics by Harold Rome
Pins and Needles (OB) 1937

Added during run

Stay Well
Music by Kurt Weill
Lyrics by Maxwell Anderson
Lost in the Stars 1949

Stay With Me, Nora
Music by Larry Grossman
Lyrics by Betty Comden and Adolph Green
A Doll's Life 1982

Stay With the Happy People
Music by Jule Styne
Lyrics by Bob Hilliard
Michael Todd's Peep Show 1950

Staying Alive
Music by Kenneth Jacobson
Lyrics by Rhoda Roberts
Show Me Where the Good Times Are (OB) 1970

Staying Young
Music and lyrics by Bob Merrill
Take Me Along 1959

Steady, Steady
Music by Milton Schafer
Lyrics by Ronny Graham
Bravo Giovanni 1962

Steal With Style
Music by Robert Waldman
Lyrics by Alfred Uhry
The Robber Bridegroom 1975

Steam Heat
Music and lyrics by Richard Adler and Jerry Ross
The Pajama Game 1954

The Steam Is on the Beam
Music by John Green
Lyrics by George Marion, Jr.
Beat the Band 1942

Steamboat
Music by Jack Urbont
Lyrics by Bruce Geller
Livin' the Life (OB) 1957

Steamboat Days
Music and lyrics by Clarence Williams
Bottomland 1927

The Steamboat Whistle
Music by Arthur Schwartz
Lyrics by Howard Dietz
At Home Abroad 1935

The Steely Glint in My Eye
Music by Richard Rodgers
Lyrics by Lorenz Hart
Mississippi (1935) F

Dropped from film

Step Across That Line
Music and lyrics by Oscar Brown, Jr.
Buck White 1969

Step Into My World
Music and lyrics by Micki Grant
It's So Nice to Be Civilized 1980

Step on It
Music by Joseph Meyer
Lyrics by Irving Caesar
Sweetheart Time 1926

Step on the Blues
Music by Con Conrad and Will Donaldson
Lyrics by Otto Harbach
Kitty's Kisses 1926

Step on the Gasoline
Music by William B. Kernell
Lyrics by Dorothy Donnelly
Hello, Lola 1926

Step, Step Sisters
Music by Harry Archer
Lyrics by Harlan Thompson
Merry-Merry 1925

Step, Step, Step
Music and lyrics by Jack Murray and Joe Brandfon
Half a Widow 1927

Step to Paris Blues
Music by Maury Rubens
Lyrics by Clifford Grey
The Madcap 1928

Step to the Rear
Music by Elmer Bernstein
Lyrics by Carolyn Leigh
How Now, Dow Jones 1967

Step Up and Pep Up the Party
Music by Harry Tierney
Lyrics by Joseph McCarthy
Cross My Heart 1928

Steppin' Along
Music and lyrics by Alexander Hill
Hummin' Sam 1933

Steppin' Baby
Music by Harold Levey
Lyrics by Owen Murphy
Rainbow Rose 1926

Steppin' Back
Music and lyrics by Bob Ost
Everybody's Gettin' Into the Act (OB) 1981

Steppin' Out with My Baby
Music and lyrics by Irving Berlin
Easter Parade (1948) F

Steppin' to the Bad Side
Music by Henry Krieger
Lyrics by Tom Eyen
Dreamgirls 1981

Stepping Around
Music by Stephen Jones and Arthur Samuels
Lyrics by Dorothy Donnelly
Poppy 1923

Stepping Stones
Music by Jerome Kern
Lyrics by Anne Caldwell
Stepping Stones 1923

Stepping to the Stars
Music and lyrics by John Phillips
Man on the Moon 1975

The Steps of the Capitol
Music and lyrics by Burton Lane
Laffing Room Only 1944

Stepsisters' Lament
Music by Richard Rodgers
Lyrics by Oscar Hammerstein II
Cinderella (1957) TV

Stereophonic Sound
Music and lyrics by Cole Porter
Silk Stockings 1955

Stetson
Music by Walter Donaldson
Lyrics by Gus Kahn
Whoopee 1928

Stick Around
Music by Charles Strouse
Lyrics by Lee Adams
Golden Boy 1964

Stick to Your Dancing, Mabel
Music and lyrics by Charlotte Kent
The Little Show (1st edition) 1929

Stick to Your Knitting
Music by Vincent Youmans and Herbert Stothart
Lyrics by Oscar Hammerstein II
and William Cary Duncan
Mary Jane McKane 1923

Stiff Upper Lip
Music by George Gershwin
Lyrics by Ira Gershwin
A Damsel in Distress (1937) F

Still I'd Love You
Music by Ray Henderson
Lyrics by B.G. DeSylva and Lew Brown
Follow Thru 1929

Stiochket
Music by Murray Rumshinsky
Lyrics by Jacob Jacobs
The President's Daughter 1970

Stitching, Stitching
Music by Jerome Kern
Lyrics by Herbert Reynolds
Rock-a-Bye Baby 1918

Stock Report
Music by Norman Martin
Lyrics by Fred Ebb
Put It in Writing (OB) 1963

Stolen Dreams
Music by Jerome Kern
Lyrics by Otto Harbach
Men of the Sky (1931) F

Stolen Kisses
Music by Franz Steininger (adapted from
Tchaikovsky)
Lyrics by Forman Brown
Music in My Heart 1947

Stomach and Stomachs
Music by John Mundy
Lyrics by Edward Eager
The Liar 1950

Stompin' 'Em Down
Music and lyrics by Alexander Hill
Hummin' Sam 1933

The Stone Bridge at Eight
Music by James F. Hanley
Lyrics by Eddie Dowling
Honeymoon Lane 1926

Stone the Crows
Music by Andrew Lloyd Webber
Lyrics by Tim Rice
*Joseph and the Amazing
Technicolor Dreamcoat* 1982

Stoned in Saigon
Music and lyrics by Elizabeth Swados
Dispatches (OB) 1979

Stonewall Moskowitz March
Music by Richard Rodgers
Lyrics by Irving Caesar
Betsy 1926

Stools
Music and lyrics by Martin Charnin
Upstairs at O'Neal's (OB) 1982

Stoopid
Music and lyrics by Harry Chapin
The Night That Made America Famous 1975

Stop
Music and lyrics by Porter Grainger
and Freddie Johnson
Lucky Sambo 1925

Stop, Go!
Music by Maury Rubens and J. Fred Coots
Lyrics by Clifford Grey
The Madcap 1928

Stop Holding Me Back
Music by John Mundy
Lyrics by Edward Eager
The Liar 1950

Stop It, Stop It!
Music by Emmerich Kálmán
Lyrics by C.C.S. Cushing and E.P. Heath
Sari 1914

Stop, Look and Listen
Music by Victor Herbert
Lyrics by Rida Johnson Young
The Dream Girl 1924

Stop! Look! Listen
Music and lyrics by Irving Berlin
Stop! Look! Listen! 1915

Stop That Dancing
Music and lyrics by Burton Lane
Laffing Room Only 1944

Stop That "Rag"
Music by Raymond Hubbell
Lyrics by Glen MacDonough
The Jolly Bachelors 1910

Store-Bought Suit
Music by Jerome Moross
Lyrics by John Latouche
The Golden Apple 1954

Storefront Church
Music and lyrics by Micki Grant
Don't Bother Me, I Can't Cope (OB) 1972

The Stork Don't Come Around Any More
Music and lyrics by B. Laidlaw
A Night in Venice 1929

A Storm in My Heart
Music by Monty Norman
Lyrics by Julian More
The Moony Shapiro Songbook 1981

Stormy Love
Music by Franz Lehár
Lyrics by Edward Eliscu
Frederika 1937

The Story Goes On
Music by David Shire
Lyrics by Richard Maltby, Jr.
Baby 1983

The Story of a Carrot
Music by Sidney Lippman
Lyrics by Sylvia Dee
Barefoot Boy With Cheek 1947

The Story of a Horn
Music by Lee Wainer
Lyrics by Robert Sour
Sing for Your Supper 1939

The Story of Alice
Music by Jerry Bock
Lyrics by Larry Holofcener
Catch a Star! 1955

The Story of Lucy and Jessie
Music and lyrics by Stephen Sondheim
Follies 1971

The Story of Marie
Music and lyrics by Charles Gaynor
Show Girl 1961

Stouthearted Men
Music by Sigmund Romberg
Lyrics by Oscar Hammerstein II
The New Moon 1928

A Strain on the Name
Music by Peter Link
Lyrics by Jacob Brackman
King of Hearts 1978

Stranded Again
Music by Cy Coleman
Lyrics by Betty Comden and Adolph Green
On the Twentieth Century 1978

Strange Duet
Music by Jule Styne
Lyrics by Betty Comden and Adolph Green
Subways Are for Sleeping 1961

Strange Music
Music and lyrics by Robert Wright and George
Forrest
Song of Norway 1944

Based on Grieg's Nocturne from the *Lyric Suite*
and *Wedding Day at Troldhaugen*

Strange New Look
Music and lyrics by James Shelton
Dance Me a Song 1950

Dropped from production

Strange New World
Music and lyrics by Paul Nassau and Oscar Brand
*The Education of H*y*m*a*n K*a*p*l*a*n* 1968

Strange Thing Mystifying
Music by Andrew Lloyd Webber
Lyrics by Tim Rice
Jesus Christ Superstar 1971

Strangely
Music by Alfred Brooks
Lyrics by Ira J. Bilowit
Of Mice and Men (OB) 1958

Stranger
Music by Bronislaw Kaper (based on Chopin)
Lyrics by John Latouche
Polonaise 1945

Stranger in Paradise
Music and lyrics by Robert Wright
and George Forrest
Kismet 1953

Based on a theme from Borodin's *Polovetsian
Dances*

A Stranger Interlude
Music and lyrics by Maceo Pinkard
Pansy 1929

Strangers
Music and lyrics by Richard Rodgers
Androcles and the Lion (1967) TV

Straw Hat in the Rain
Music by Harry Akst
Lyrics by Lew Brown
Calling All Stars 1934

The Straw That Broke the Camel's Back
Music by Sammy Fain
Lyrics by Marilyn and Alan Bergman
Something More 1964

Strawberries, Pickles and Ice Cream
Music and lyrics by Peter Copani
New York City Street Show (OB) 1977

Strawberry-Blueberry
Music by Stanley Silverman
Lyrics by Tom Hendry
Doctor Selavy's Magic Theatre (OB) 1972

Strawberry Jam
Music by Sigmund Romberg
Lyrics by Dorothy Donnelly
My Maryland 1927

Streamlined Pompadour
Music by Robert Stolz
Lyrics by Rowland Leigh
Night of Love 1941

Street Corner Song
Music by Robert Mitchell
Lyrics by Elizabeth Perry
Bags (OB) 1982

Street Cries
Music and lyrics by Irving Burgie
Ballad for Bimshire (OB) 1963

Street Cries (Strawberry Woman, Crab Man)
Music by George Gershwin
Lyrics by DuBose Heyward
Porgy and Bess 1935

Street Lady
Music by Cheryl Hardwick
Lyrics by Marilyn Suzanne Miller
Girls, Girls, Girls (OB) 1980

Street Music
Music by Patrick Rose
Lyrics by Merv Campone and Richard Ouzounian
A Bistro Car on the CNR (OB) 1978

Street People's Anthem
Music by Robert Mitchell
Lyrics by Elizabeth Perry
Bags (OB) 1982

Street Sermon
Music by Helen Miller
Lyrics by Eve Merriam
Inner City 1971

Street Song
Music by James Bredt
Lyrics by Edward Eager
The Happy Hypocrite (OB) 1968

The Streets of Antioch
Music by Harvey Schmidt
Lyrics by Tom Jones
Philemon (OB) 1975

The Streets of Bed-Stuy
Music and lyrics by Johnny Brandon
Love! Love! Love! (OB) 1977

The Streets of New York (In Old New York)
Music by Victor Herbert
Lyrics by Henry Blossom
The Red Mill 1906

The Streets of Paris
Music by Jimmy McHugh
Lyrics by Al Dubin
The Streets of Paris 1939

Strength Is My Weakness
Music and lyrics by Richard Rodgers
Androcles and the Lion (1967) TV

Strictly Confidential
Music by Dave Stamper
Lyrics by Fred Herendeen
Orchids Preferred 1937

The Strike
Music by Harry Tierney
Lyrics by Joseph McCarthy
Up She Goes 1922

Strike
Music by J. Fred Coots
Lyrics by Clifford Grey
June Days 1925

Strike!
Music by Frederick Loewe
Lyrics by Alan Jay Lerner
Paint Your Wagon 1951

Strike Me Pink
Music by Ray Henderson
Lyrics by Lew Brown
Strike Me Pink 1933

Strike, Strike, Strike
Music by George Gershwin
Lyrics by B.G. DeSylva
Sweet Little Devil 1924

Strike Up the Band
Music by George Gershwin
Lyrics by Ira Gershwin
Strike Up the Band 1930

String Quartet
Music and lyrics by Paul Nassau
Fallout (OB) 1959

A Stroll on the Plaza 'ana
Music and lyrics by Cole Porter
Panama Hattie 1940

Strollers
Music by Ivan Caryll
Lyrics by Anne Caldwell and James O'Dea
Chin-Chin 1914

Strolling
Music and lyrics by Porter Grainger
and Freddie Johnson
Lucky Sambo 1925

Strolling on the Lido
Music by Lee David and Maury Rubens
Lyrics by J. Keirn Brennan and Moe Jaffe
A Night in Venice 1929

Strolling, or What Have You?
Music by Jerome Kern
Lyrics by Otto Harbach and Oscar Hammerstein II
Sunny 1925

Strolling Thru the Park
Music by Sammy Fain
Lyrics by Charles Tobias
Hellzapoppin 1938

Strolling With the One I Love the Best
Music by Sigmund Romberg
Lyrics by Dorothy Donnelly
My Maryland 1927

Strong Woman Number
Music by Nancy Ford
Lyrics by Gretchen Cryer
*I'm Getting My Act Together and Taking It
on the Road* 1978

The Stronger Sex
Music by Jimmy Van Heusen
Lyrics by Johnny Burke
Carnival in Flanders 1953

The Strongest Man in the World
Music by Charles Strouse
Lyrics by Lee Adams
It's a Bird, It's a Plane, It's Superman 1966

Struttin' Time
Music by C. Luckey Roberts
Lyrics by Alex C. Rogers
My Magnolia 1926

Stuck-Up
Music by Nancy Ford
Lyrics by Gretchen Cryer
Now Is the Time for All Good Men (OB) 1967

Stuck With Each Other
Music by Lee Pockriss
Lyrics by Anne Croswell
Tovarich 1963

Student Life
Music by Sigmund Romberg
Lyrics by Dorothy Donnelly
The Student Prince 1924

The Student Robin Hood of Pilsen
Music by Randall Thompson
Lyrics by Perry Ivins
Bad Habits of 1926 (OB)

Study of the Human Figure
Music by Scott Killian and Kim D. Sherman
Lyrics by Kenneth Robins, Scott Killian
and Kim D. Sherman
Lenny and the Heartbreakers (OB) 1983

Stuttering Song
Music by Al Carmines
Lyrics by Rosalyn Drexler
Home Movies (OB) 1964

Style
Music and lyrics by Stephen Schwartz
The Magic Show 1974

Sub-Babylon
Music and lyrics by Elizabeth Swados
Lullabye and Goodnight 1982

Sub-Debs' First Fling
Music by Dave Stamper
Lyrics by Fred Herendeen
Orchids Preferred 1937

Suburban Fugue
Music by Hank Beebe
Lyrics by Bill Heyer
*Tuscaloosa's Calling Me
But I'm Not Going!* (OB) 1975

Suburban Retreat
Music by David Baker
Lyrics by David Craig
Phoenix '55 (OB)

Subway Directions; Ride Through the Night
Music by Jule Styne
Lyrics by Betty Comden and Adolph Green
Subways Are for Sleeping 1961

Subway Dream
Music by Helen Miller
Lyrics by Eve Merriam
Inner City 1971

Subway Rag
Music by Buster Davis
Lyrics by Steven Vinaver
Diversions (OB) 1958

Subway Rider
Music and lyrics by Micki Grant
It's So Nice to Be Civilized 1980

Subway Song
Music by Richard Lewine
Lyrics by Arnold B. Horwitt
Make Mine Manhattan 1948

The Subway Sun
Music by Ray Perkins
Lyrics by Max and Nathaniel Lief
The Greenwich Village Follies (1928)

Subways Are for Sleeping
Music by Jule Styne
Lyrics by Betty Comden and Adolph Green
Subways Are for Sleeping 1961

Success
Music by Jule Styne
Lyrics by Betty Comden and Adolph Green
Do Re Mi 1960

Such a Beautiful World
Music by Sol Kaplan
Lyrics by Edward Eliscu
The Banker's Daughter (OB) 1962

Such a Merry Party
Music and lyrics by Rick Besoyan
Little Mary Sunshine (OB) 1959

Such a Sociable Sort
Music by Jimmy Van Heusen
Lyrics by Sammy Cahn
Walking Happy 1966

Such Good Fun
Music by Richard Rodgers
Lyrics by Martin Charnin
I Remember Mama 1979

Dropped from production

Such Is Life in a Love Song
Music by Harry Archer
Lyrics by Harlan Thompson
Little Jessie James 1923

Such Stuff As Dreams Are Made Of
Music by Sammy Fain
Lyrics by Irving Kahal
Boys and Girls Together 1940

Sudden Death Overtime
Music by Patrick Rose
Lyrics by Merv Campone and Richard Ouzounian
A Bistro Car on the CNR (OB) 1978

Sudden Lilac
Music by Richard Adler
Lyrics by Will Holt
Music Is 1976

The Sudden Thrill
Music by Jimmy Van Heusen
Lyrics by Johnny Burke
Carnival in Flanders 1953

Suddenly
Music by Vernon Duke
Lyrics by E.Y. Harburg and Billy Rose
Ziegfeld Follies (1934)

Suddenly, It's Spring
Music by Jimmy Van Heusen
Lyrics by Johnny Burke
Lady in the Dark (film version, 1944)

Suddenly Love
Music and lyrics by Tom Savage
Musical Chairs 1980

Suddenly, Seymour
Music by Alan Menken
Lyrics by Howard Ashman
Little Shop of Horrors (OB) 1982

Suddenly She Was There
Music by Ted Simons
Lyrics by Elinor Guggenheimer
Potholes (OB) 1979

Suddenly Stop and Think
Music by Sam Pottle
Lyrics by Tom Whedon
All Kinds of Giants (OB) 1961

Sue Me
Music and lyrics by Frank Loesser
Guys and Dolls 1950

Sugar
Music by Jule Styne
Lyrics by Bob Merrill
Sugar 1972

Sugar Babe
Music by Eubie Blake
Lyrics by Noble Sissle
Shuffle Along of 1933

The Sugar Baby Bounce
Music and lyrics by Jay Livingston and Ray Evans
Sugar Babies 1979

Sugarfoot
Music by Vernon Duke
Lyrics by Howard Dietz
Jackpot 1944

Suicide Song
Music by George Kleinsinger
Lyrics by Joe Darion
Shinbone Alley 1957

Suite for Five Letters
Music and lyrics by Robert Dennis, Peter Schickele
and Stanley Walden
Oh! Calcutta! 1969

Suits Me Fine
Music and lyrics by Hugh Martin
Make a Wish 1951

Sullivan Street Flat
Music and lyrics by Ronnie Britton
Gift of the Magi (OB) 1975

Sullivan's Got a Job
Music by Jerry Livingston
Lyrics by Mack David
Molly 1973

Summer Afternoon
Music and lyrics by Harold Rome
Wish You Were Here 1952

Summer Day
Music and lyrics by Marc Blitzstein
Regina 1949

Summer Dresses
Music and lyrics by Harold Rome
Bless You All 1950

Summer Is
Music by Jerry Bock
Lyrics by Sheldon Harnick
The Body Beautiful 1958

Summer Is A-Comin' In
Music by Vernon Duke
Lyrics by John Latouche
The Lady Comes Across 1942

Later in *The Littlest Revue* (1956)

Summer Is Over
Music by John Kander
Lyrics by James Goldman, John Kander
and William Goldman
A Family Affair 1962

Summer Nights
Music by Ford Dabney
Lyrics by Jo Trent
Rang-Tang 1927

Summer Nights
Music by Helen Miller
Lyrics by Eve Merriam
Inner City 1971

Summer Nights
Music and lyrics by Jim Jacobs
and Warren Casey
Grease 1972

Summer Pastimes
Music by Karl Hoschna
Lyrics by Otto Harbach
Three Twins 1908

Summer, Summer
Music by Galt MacDermot
Lyrics by John Guare
Two Gentlemen of Verona 1971

The Summer Time
Music by William B. Kernell
Lyrics by Dorothy Donnelly
Hello, Lola 1926

Summer Time
Music by Rudolf Friml
Lyrics by P.G. Wodehouse and Clifford Grey
The Three Musketeers 1928

Summertime
Music by George Gershwin
Lyrics by DuBose Heyward
Porgy and Bess 1935

Summertime
Music and lyrics by Gary Portnoy
and Judy Hart Angelo
Preppies (OB) 1983

Summertime Is Summertime
Music by Walter Kent
Lyrics by Kim Gannon
Seventeen 1951

Summertime Love
Music and lyrics by Frank Loesser
Greenwillow 1960

The Sun About to Rise
Music by Jerome Kern
Lyrics by Oscar Hammerstein II
Sweet Adeline 1929

Sun at My Window, Love at My Door
Music by Victor Young
Lyrics by Stella Unger
Seventh Heaven 1955

The Sun Has Fallen
Music and lyrics by Gian-Carlo Menotti
The Medium 1947

The Sun Is Beginning to Crow
Music and lyrics by Richard Adler
Kwamina 1961

Sun on My Face
Music by Jule Styne
Lyrics by Bob Merrill
Sugar 1972

The Sun Rises
Music by Sol Kaplan
Lyrics by Edward Eliscu
The Banker's Daughter (OB) 1962

The Sun Shines Brighter
Music by Jerome Kern
Lyrics by P. G. Wodehouse
Leave It to Jane 1917

The Sun Starts to Shine Again
Music by Jerome Kern
Lyrics by P.G. Wodehouse
Oh, Lady! Lady!! 1918

The Sun Will Shine
Music by Arthur Schwartz
Lyrics by Morrie Ryskind
Ned Wayburn's Gambols 1929

The Sun Won't Set
Music and lyrics by Stephen Sondheim
A Little Night Music 1973

Same music as "Night Waltz"

Sun Worship
Music by A. Baldwin Sloane
Lyrics by Harry Cort and George E. Stoddard
China Rose 1925

Sunday
Music by J. Fred Coots
Lyrics by Clifford Grey
The Merry World 1926

Sunday
Music by Richard Rodgers
Lyrics by Oscar Hammerstein II
Flower Drum Song 1958

Sunday
Music and lyrics by Stephen Sondheim
Sunday in the Park With George (OB) 1983

Sunday Afternoon
Music by Harry Archer
Lyrics by Harlan Thompson
Twinkle Twinkle 1926

Sunday in Cicero Falls
Music by Harold Arlen
Lyrics by E.Y. Harburg
Bloomer Girl 1944

Sunday in the Park
Music and lyrics by Harold Rome
Pins and Needles (OB) 1937

Sunday in the Park With George
Music and lyrics by Stephen Sondheim
Sunday in the Park With George (OB) 1983

Sunday Morning
Music by Ray Henderson
Lyrics by Ted Koehler
Say When 1934

Sunday Morning
Music and lyrics by Johnny Burke
Donnybrook! 1961

Sunday Morning Breakfast Time
Music and lyrics by Cole Porter
Jubilee 1935

Sunday Morning Churchman
Music by Richard Lewine
Lyrics by Norman Zeno
Entre-Nous (OB) 1935

Sunday Morning in June
Music by Paul McGrane
Lyrics by Neville Fleeson
Who's Who 1938

Sunday Morning Sunshine
Music and lyrics by Harry Chapin
The Night That Made America Famous 1975

Sunday Night in New York
Music and lyrics by Charles Tobias, Charles
Newman and Murray Mencher
Earl Carroll's Sketch Book (1935)

Sundown Serenade
Music by C. Luckey Roberts
Lyrics by Alex C. Rogers
My Magnolia 1926

The Sun'll Be Up in the Morning
Music by Sammy Fain
Lyrics by Jack Yellen
Boys and Girls Together 1940

Sunny
Music by Jerome Kern
Lyrics by Otto Harbach and Oscar Hammerstein II
Sunny 1925

Sunny California
Music and lyrics by Burton Lane
Laffing Room Only 1944

Sunny Disposish
Music by Philip Charig
Lyrics by Ira Gershwin
Americana (1926)

Sunny Moon
Music and lyrics by John Phillips
Man on the Moon 1975

Sunny River
Music by Sigmund Romberg
Lyrics by Oscar Hammerstein II
Sunny River 1941

Sunny Side of You
Music by Frank Grey
Lyrics by Earle Crooker and McElbert Moore
Happy 1927

Sunny Side Up
Music by Ray Henderson
Lyrics by B.G. DeSylva and Lew Brown
Sunny Side Up (1929) F

Sunny Southern Smile
Music by Harry Revel
Lyrics by Mack Gordon
Ziegfeld Follies (1931)

Sunrise
Music by Vincent Youmans
Lyrics by Oscar Hammerstein II
Rainbow 1928

Dropped from production

Sunrise
Music by Nancy Ford
Lyrics by Gretchen Cryer
Shelter 1973

Sunrise on Sunset
Music by Baldwin Bergersen
Lyrics by George Marion, Jr.
Allah Be Praised! 1944

Sunrise, Sunset
Music by Jerry Bock
Lyrics by Sheldon Harnick
Fiddler on the Roof 1964

The Suns That Daily Rise
Music by Meyer Kupferman
Lyrics by Paul Goodman
Jonah (OB) 1966

Sunset
Music by Bob James
Lyrics by Jack O'Brien
The Selling of the President 1972

Sunset
Music by Gary William Friedman
Lyrics by Will Holt
Platinum 1978

Sunset Tree
Music by Jule Styne
Lyrics by E.Y. Harburg
Darling of the Day 1968

Sunshine
Music by Jerome Kern
Lyrics by Otto Harbach and Oscar Hammerstein II
Sunny 1925

See note for "I Can't Forget Your Eyes"

Sunshine
Music by Jule Styne
Lyrics by Leo Robin
Gentlemen Prefer Blondes 1949

Sunshine
Music by Ann Sternberg
Lyrics by Gertrude Stein
Gertrude Stein's First Reader (OB) 1969

Sunshine Face
Music and lyrics by Steve Allen
Sophie 1963

Sunshine Girl
Music and lyrics by Bob Merrill
New Girl in Town 1957

Sunup
Music by Percy Wenrich
Lyrics by Harry Clarke
Who Cares? 1930

Super Heroes
Music and lyrics by Richard O'Brien
The Rocky Horror Show 1975

Supersational Day
Music by Jack Urbont
Lyrics by Bruce Geller
Livin' the Life (OB) 1957

Superstar
Music by Andrew Lloyd Webber
Lyrics by Tim Rice
Jesus Christ Superstar 1971

Superstar
Music by Diane Leslie
Lyrics by William Gleason
The Coolest Cat in Town (OB) 1978

Superstition
Music by Max Rich
Lyrics by Jack Scholl
Keep Moving 1934

Superstition
Music and lyrics by Scott Joplin
Treemonisha 1975

Written in 1909

Supper Time
Music and lyrics by Irving Berlin
As Thousands Cheer 1933

Suppertime
Music and lyrics by Clark Gesner
You're a Good Man, Charlie Brown (OB) 1967

Suppertime
Music by Alan Menken
Lyrics by Howard Ashman
Little Shop of Horrors (OB) 1982

Supple Couple
Music by Thomas (Fats) Waller
Lyrics by George Marion, Jr.
Early to Bed 1943

Suppose I Had Never Met You
Music by Harry Archer
Lyrics by Harlan Thompson
Little Jessie James 1923

Sur La Plage
Music and lyrics by Sandy Wilson
The Boy Friend 1954

Surabaya Johnny
Music by Kurt Weill
Lyrics by Bertolt Brecht (adapted by Michael
Feingold)
Happy End 1977

Sure Sign You Really Love Me
Music and lyrics by Harry Denny
Footlights 1927

Sure Thing
Music by Jerome Kern
Lyrics by Ira Gershwin
Cover Girl (1944) F

Surplus Blues
Music and lyrics by Harold Rome
Call Me Mister 1946

Surprise
Music and lyrics by Jay Livingston
and Ray Evans
Oh Captain! 1958

Surprise
Music by Don Gohman
Lyrics by Hal Hackady
Ambassador 1972

Surprise
Music and lyrics by Scott Joplin
Treemonisha 1975

Written in 1909

Surprise! Surprise!
Music by Gerald Jay Markoe
Lyrics by Michael Colby
Charlotte Sweet (OB) 1982

The Surrey With the Fringe on Top
Music by Richard Rodgers
Lyrics by Oscar Hammerstein II
Oklahoma! 1943

Survive
Music by Harvey Schmidt
Lyrics by Tom Jones
Celebration 1969

The Susan Belle
Music by Eubie Blake
Lyrics by J. Milton Reddie and Cecil Mack
Swing It 1937

Susan Brown From a Country Town
Music by Jerome Kern
Lyrics by Edward Madden
La Belle Paree 1911

Susannah's Squeaking Shoes
Music by Muriel Lillie
Lyrics by Arthur Weigall
Charlot's Revue of 1926

Susan's Song
Music by Kenn Long and Jim Crozier
Lyrics by Kenn Long
Touch (OB) 1970

Suspended Animation
Music by Diane Leslie
Lyrics by William Gleason
The Coolest Cat in Town (OB) 1978

Suspicious
Music and lyrics by James MacDonald, David Vos
and Robert Gerlach
Something's Afoot 1976

Suzanne, Suzanne
Music by Jean Gilbert
Lyrics by Harry B. and Robert B. Smith
Modest Suzanne 1912

Suzie
Music by Jerome Kern
Lyrics by Anne Caldwell
Criss-Cross 1926

Suzie Moon
Music by Galt MacDermot
Lyrics by Gerome Ragni
Dude 1972

Suzy Is a Good Thing
Music by Richard Rodgers
Lyrics by Oscar Hammerstein II
Pipe Dream 1955

The Swallows
Music by Richard Rodgers
Lyrics by Lorenz Hart
She's My Baby 1928

The Swamps of Home
Music by Mary Rodgers
Lyrics by Marshall Barer
Once Upon a Mattress 1959

The Swan
Music by Jule Styne
Lyrics by Bob Merrill
Funny Girl (film version, 1968)

Swanee
Music by George Gershwin
Lyrics by Irving Caesar
Sinbad 1919 (road tour only)

Swanee Moon
Music by Eubie Blake
Lyrics by Noble Sissle
Shuffle Along of 1952

Swanee River Blues
Music and lyrics by Gene Buck and Dave Stamper
Ziegfeld Follies of 1923

Swanee River Melody
Music by Charles Weinberg
Lyrics by Al Wilson
Americana (1926)

Swanee Strut
Music and lyrics by Buster Davis
Doctor Jazz 1975

Swapping Sweet Nothings With You
Music by Robert Russell Bennett
Lyrics by Owen Murphy and Robert A. Simon
Hold Your Horses 1933

Sweat Song
Music by Earl Robinson
Lyrics by Waldo Salt
Sandhog (OB) 1954

Sweep
Music and lyrics by Jay Thompson
Double Entry (OB) 1961

Sweet and Hot
Music by Harold Arlen
Lyrics by Jack Yellen
You Said It 1931

Sweet and Low-Down
Music by George Gershwin
Lyrics by Ira Gershwin
Tip-Toes 1925

Ira Gershwin's slangy lyrics were his trademark and
unmistakable style. He was pleased with his
invention of the phrase "Sweet and Low-Down,"
which became part of the language of the twenties.
He had borrowed "Sweet and Low" from a
sentimental Victorian song with words by Tennyson
and combined the phrase with the current jazz term
"low-down."

Sweet as Sugar Cane
Music by Vincent Youmans
Lyrics by Billy Rose and Edward Eliscu
Great Day! 1929

See note on "If I Told You"

Sweet as You Can Be
Music by Rudolf Friml
Lyrics by Otto Harbach
The Blue Kitten 1922

Sweet Beginning
Music and lyrics by Leslie Bricusse
and Anthony Newley
*The Roar of the Greasepaint—The Smell
of the Crowd* 1965

The Sweet By and By
Music by Victor Herbert
Lyrics by Rida Johnson Young
Naughty Marietta 1910

Sweet Charity
Music by Ruth Cleary Patterson
Lyrics by Les Kramer
Russell Patterson's Sketch Book (OB) 1960

Sweet Charity
Music by Cy Coleman
Lyrics by Dorothy Fields
Sweet Charity 1966

Sweet Cookie
Music by Albert Von Tilzer
Lyrics by Neville Fleeson
The Gingham Girl 1922

Sweet Danger
Music and lyrics by Robert Wright
and George Forrest
Kean 1961

Sweet Dreams
Music by Rudolf Friml
Lyrics by Bide Dudley and Otto Harbach
The Little Whopper 1919

Sweet Dreams
Music by Galt MacDermot
Lyrics by Gerome Ragni
Dude 1972

Sweet Evening Breeze
Music by Ford Dabney
Lyrics by Jo Trent
Rang-Tang 1927

Sweet Fool
Music by Rudolf Friml
Lyrics by Rowland Leigh and John Shubert
Music Hath Charms 1934

Sweet Geraldine
Music by Richard Rodgers
Lyrics by Lorenz Hart
America's Sweetheart 1931

Sweet Helen
Music by Erich Wolfgang Korngold (based on
Jacques Offenbach)
Lyrics by Herbert Baker
Helen Goes to Troy 1944

Sweet Lady
Music by Frank Crumit and Dave Zoob
Lyrics by Howard Johnson
Tangerine 1921

Sweet Liar
Music by Herbert Stothart
Lyrics by Irving Caesar
Polly 1929

Sweet Liar
Music and lyrics by Irving Caesar
George White's Music Hall Varieties 1932

Sweet Little Baby o'Mine
Music and lyrics by J.C. Johnson
Change Your Luck 1930

Sweet Little Devil
Music by George Gershwin
Lyrics by B.G. DeSylva
Sweet Little Devil 1924

Dropped from production

Sweet Little Stranger
Music by Harry Revel
Lyrics by Mack Gordon
Smiling Faces 1932

Sweet Longings
Music by Gary William Friedman
Lyrics by Will Holt
Taking My Turn (OB) 1983

Sweet Madness
Music by Victor Young
Lyrics by Ned Washington
Murder at the Vanities 1933

Sweet Melody of Night
Music by Erich Korngold
Lyrics by Oscar Hammerstein II
Give Us This Night (1936) F

Sweet Memory
Music by George Fischoff
Lyrics by Carole Bayer
Georgy 1970

Sweet Music
Music by Arthur Schwartz
Lyrics by Howard Dietz
The Band Wagon 1931

Sweet Old-Fashioned Waltz
Music by Walter G. Samuels
Lyrics by Morrie Ryskind
Ned Wayburn's Gambols 1929

Sweet One
Music by Lewis E. Gensler
Lyrics by Robert A. Simon
Ups-a-Daisy 1928

Sweet Packard
Music by George Gershwin
Lyrics by Ira Gershwin
The Shocking Miss Pilgrim (1947) F

Adapted by Kay Swift and Ira Gershwin from
manuscripts of George Gershwin.

Sweet Peter
Music by Richard Rogers
Lyrics by Lorenz Hart
Dearest Enemy 1925

Sweet Popopper
Music by C. Luckey Roberts
Lyrics by Alex C. Rogers
My Magnolia 1926

Sweet Savannah Sue
Music by Thomas (Fats) Waller and Harry Brooks
Lyrics by Andy Razaf
Hot Chocolates 1929

Sweet Simplicitas
Music by Howard Talbot
Lyrics by Arthur Wimperis
The Arcadians 1910

Sweet Sixteen
Music and lyrics by Gene Buck and Dave Stamper
Ziegfeld Follies of 1919

Sweet Sixty-Five
Music by Richard Rodgers
Lyrics by Lorenz Hart
I'd Rather Be Right 1937

Sweet So and So
Music by Philip Charig and Joseph Meyer
Lyrics by Ira Gershwin
Sweet and Low 1930

Sweet Stuff
Music by Harold Orlob
Lyrics by Harry L. Cort and George E. Stoddard
Listen, Lester 1918

Sweet Sue's
Music by Rob Fremont
Lyrics by Doris Willens
Piano Bar (OB) 1978

Sweet, Sweet, Sweet
Music and lyrics by Stephen Schwartz
The Magic Show 1974

Sweet Talker
Music by Jonathan Holtzman
Lyrics by Susan Cooper and Jonathan Holtzman
Foxfire 1982

Sweet Thursday
Music by Richard Rodgers
Lyrics by Oscar Hammerstein II
Pipe Dream 1955

Sweet Time
Music and lyrics by Will Holt
That 5 A.M. Jazz (OB) 1964

Sweet Time
Music by Judd Woldin
Lyrics by Robert Brittan
Raisin 1973

Sweet Transvestite
Music and lyrics by Richard O'Brien
The Rocky Horror Show 1975

Sweet William
Music by Frederick Loewe
Lyrics by Earle Crooker
Great Lady 1938

Sweet William
Music by David Baker
Lyrics by David Craig
Copper and Brass 1957

Sweet Words
Music and lyrics by Elizabeth Swados
Lullabye and Goodnight 1982

Sweetenheart
Music by Richard Rodgers
Lyrics by Lorenz Hart
Simple Simon 1930

Sweeter Than You
Music by Harry Ruby
Lyrics by Bert Kalmar
Twinkle Twinkle 1926

Also in *Top Speed* (1929)

Sweetest Maid of All
Music by Oscar Straus
Lyrics by Joseph W. Herbert
A Waltz Dream 1908

Sweetest of the Roses
Music by Lewis E. Gensler
Lyrics by Robert A. Simon
Ups-a-Daisy 1928

The Sweetest Sounds
Music and lyrics by Richard Rodgers
No Strings 1962

The Sweetest Thing in Life
Music by Jerome Kern
Lyrics by B.G. DeSylva
Peter Pan 1924

Sweetheart
Music by John Philip Sousa
Lyrics by Leonard Liebling
The American Maid 1913

Sweetheart, I'm Waiting
Music by John Philip Sousa
Lyrics by Tom Frost and John Philip Sousa
El Capitan 1896

Sweetheart, My Own Sweetheart
Music by Reginald De Koven
Lyrics by Harry B. Smith
Robin Hood 1891

A Sweetheart of My Own
Music by Ivan Caryll
Lyrics by Anne Caldwell
Jack O' Lantern 1917

Sweetheart of Our Student Corps
Music by Emile Berté and Maury Rubens
Lyrics by J. Keirn Brennan
Music in May 1929

The Sweetheart of Your Dream
Music by Percy Wenrich
Lyrics by Raymond Peck
Castles in the Air 1926

Sweetheart Time
Music by Joseph Meyer
Lyrics by Irving Caesar
Sweetheart Time 1926

Sweethearts
Music by Victor Herbert
Lyrics by Robert B. Smith
Sweethearts 1913

Sweethearts
Music by Harry Tierney
Lyrics by Joseph McCarthy
Rio Rita 1927

The Sweethearts of the Team
Music by Richard Rodgers
Lyrics by Lorenz Hart
Too Many Girls 1939

Sweeties
Music by Jerome Kern
Lyrics by Anne Caldwell
Hitchy-Koo 1920

Sweetness
Music and lyrics by John Dooley
Hobo (OB) 1961

Swept Away
Music and lyrics by Robert Wright
and George Forrest
Kean 1961

Swing!
Music by Leonard Bernstein
Lyrics by Betty Comden and Adolph Green
Wonderful Town 1953

Swing-a-Ding-a-Ling
Music and lyrics by Robert Dahdah
Curley McDimple (OB) 1967

Swing Low, Sweet Harriet
Music by Philip Charig
Lyrics by Dan Shapiro and Milton Pascal
Artists and Models (1943)

Swing Me High, Swing Me Low
Music by Victor Hollander
Lyrics by Ballard MacDonald
Ziegfeld Follies of 1910

Swing Shift
Music and lyrics by Beth Lawrence
and Norman Thalheimer
Marilyn 1983

Swing Song
Music and lyrics by Noël Coward
The Girl Who Came to Supper 1963

Swing That Swing
Music and lyrics by Cole Porter
Jubilee 1935

Swing Your Bag
Music by Mitch Leigh
Lyrics by William Alfred and Phyllis Robinson
Cry for Us All 1970

Swing Your Lady, Mr. Hemingway
Music by Ray Henderson
Lyrics by Jack Yellen
Ziegfeld Follies (1943)

Swing Your Projects
Music by Jule Styne
Lyrics by Betty Comden and Adolph Green
Subways Are for Sleeping 1961

Swing Your Sweetheart Round the Fire
Music by Jerome Kern
Lyrics by E. Y. Harburg
Can't Help Singing (1944) F

Swing Your Tails
Music by Arthur Schwartz
Lyrics by Howard Dietz
The Second Little Show 1930

Swingin' a Dream
Music by Jimmy Van Heusen
Lyrics by Eddie De Lange
Swingin' the Dream 1939

Swingin' the Jinx Away
Music and lyrics by Cole Porter
Born to Dance (1936) F

Swinging a Dance
Music and lyrics by Oscar Brand and Paul Nassau
A Joyful Noise 1966

Swinging on the Gate
Music by William B. Kernell
Lyrics by Dorothy Donnelly
Hello, Lola 1926

Swingy Little Thingy
Music by Sam H. Stept
Lyrics by Stanley Adams
Shady Lady 1933

Swiss Miss
Music by George Gershwin
Lyrics by Ira Gershwin and Arthur Jackson
Lady, Be Good! 1924

Switchblade Bess
Music and lyrics by Charles Gaynor
Show Girl 1961

Swoop of the Moopem
Music by Al Carmines
Lyrics by Rosalyn Drexler
Home Movies (OB) 1964

A Sword for the King
Music by Albert Sirmay and Arthur Schwartz
Lyrics by Arthur Swanstrom
Princess Charming 1930

The Sword of Damocles
Music and lyrics by Richard O'Brien
The Rocky Horror Show 1975

Sword, Rose and Cape
Music and lyrics by Bob Merrill
Carnival 1961

Sympathetic Someone
Music by Jerome Kern
Lyrics by Anne Caldwell
The City Chap 1925

Sympathy
Music by Oscar Straus
Lyrics by Stanislaus Stange
The Chocolate Soldier 1909

Sympathy
Music by Rudolf Friml
Lyrics by Otto Harbach
The Firefly 1912

Sympathy
Music and lyrics by John Dooley
Hobo (OB) 1961

Symphony
Music by Galt MacDermot
Lyrics by John Guare
Two Gentlemen of Verona 1971

A Syncopated Cocktail
Music and lyrics by Irving Berlin
Ziegfeld Follies of 1919

The Syncopated Vamp
Music and lyrics by Irving Berlin
Ziegfeld Follies of 1920

The Syncopated Walk
Music and lyrics by Irving Berlin
Watch Your Step 1914

Syncopatia Land
Music by Jean Schwartz
Lyrics by Joseph W. Herbert and Harold Atteridge
The Honeymoon Express 1913

Syncopatin'
Music and lyrics by Johnny Brandon
Who's Who, Baby? (OB) 1968

Synergy
Music and lyrics by Peter Stampfel and Antonia
Operation Sidewinder 1970

System
Music by George Gershwin
Lyrics by B.G. DeSylva
Sweet Little Devil 1924

T

Ta Ra Ra Boom De Ay
Music and lyrics by Noël Coward
Bitter Sweet 1929

Ta Ta, Ol' Bean
Music by Manning Sherwin
Lyrics by Edward Eliscu
Nine-Fifteen Revue 1930

Also in *Everybody's Welcome* (1931)

Table Talk
Music by John Kander
Lyrics by Fred Ebb
Woman of the Year 1981

Tabloid Papers
Music by Con Conrad
Lyrics by J.P. McEvoy
Americana (1926)

Tact
Music by Leslie Stuart
Lyrics by Paul Rubens
Florodora 1900

Tact
Music by Rudolf Friml
Lyrics by Otto Harbach
The Blue Kitten 1922

Taffy
Music by Helen Miller
Lyrics by Eve Merriam
Inner City 1971

Tailor-Made Babies
Music and lyrics by Frank Marcus
and Bernard Maltin
Bamboola 1929

The Tailor, Motel Kamzoil
Music by Jerry Bock
Lyrics by Sheldon Harnick
Fiddler on the Roof 1964

Taisez-Vous
Music by Victor Herbert
Lyrics by Rida Johnson Young
Naughty Marietta 1910

The Tait School Song
Music by Ray Henderson
Lyrics by B.G. DeSylva and Lew Brown
Good News 1927

Take a Bow
Music and lyrics by Stephen H. Lemberg
Jazzbo Brown 1980

Take a Crank Letter
Music by Robert Emmett Dolan
Lyrics by Johnny Mercer
Texas, Li'l Darlin' 1949

Take a Good Look Around
Music and lyrics by Jerry Herman
Madame Aphrodite (OB) 1961

Take a Job
Music by Jule Styne
Lyrics by Betty Comden and Adolph Green
Do Re Mi 1960

Take a Knife
Music by Susan Hulsman Bingham
Lyrics by Myrna Lamb
Mod Donna (OB) 1970

Take a Little Baby Home With You
Music by Alfred Goodman, Maury Rubens
and J. Fred Coots
Lyrics by Clifford Grey
Artists and Models (1925)

Take a Little Dip
Music by Milton Susskind
Lyrics by Paul Porter and Benjamin Hapgood Burt
Florida Girl 1925

Take a Little One-Step
Music by Vincent Youmans
Lyrics by Zelda Sears
Lollipop 1924

Also added to 1971 revival of *No, No Nanette.*

Take a Little Sip
Music by Claibe Richardson
Lyrics by Kenward Elmslie
The Grass Harp 1971

Take a Little Stroll With Me
Music by J. Fred Coots and Maury Rubens
Lyrics by Clifford Grey
Mayflowers 1925

Take a Little Wife
Music and lyrics by Irving Berlin
Music Box Revue (2nd edition) 1922

Take a Pick
Music by Paul Hoffert
Lyrics by David Secter
Get Thee to Canterbury (OB) 1969

Take a Poem
Music by George Kleinsinger
Lyrics by Norman Corwin
Of V We Sing 1942

Take-a-Tour, Congressman
Music by Helen Miller
Lyrics by Eve Merriam
Inner City 1971

Take a Trip to Candyland
Music by Ivan Caryll
Lyrics by Anne Caldwell
Jack O' Lantern 1917

Take a Trip to Harlem
Music by Eubie Blake
Lyrics by Andy Razaf
Blackbirds of 1930

Take a Vacation
Music and lyrics by Nick Branch
An Evening With Joan Crawford (OB) 1981

Take a Walk With Me
Music by Edward Künneke
Lyrics by Harry B. Smith
The Love Song 1925

Take and Take and Take
Music by Richard Rodgers
Lyrics by Lorenz Hart
I'd Rather Be Right 1937

Take Back Your Mink
Music and lyrics by Frank Loesser
Guys and Dolls 1950

Take Care of This House
Music by Leonard Bernstein
Lyrics by Alan Jay Lerner
1600 Pennsylvania Avenue 1976

Take Courage, Daughter
Music and lyrics by Al Carmines
Joan (OB) 1972

Take 'Em to the Door Blues
Music by J. Fred Coots
Lyrics by Clifford Grey
June Days 1925

Take Him
Music by Richard Rodgers
Lyrics by Lorenz Hart
Pal Joey 1940

Take Him to Jail
Music and lyrics by Porter Grainger
and Freddie Johnson
Lucky Sambo 1925

Take Hold the Crutch
Music by Gary William Friedman
Lyrics by Will Holt
The Me Nobody Knows (OB) 1970

Take It Away
Music by Fred Stamer
Lyrics by Gen Genovese
Buttrio Square 1952

Take It Easy
Music and lyrics by Cole Porter
Something to Shout About (1943) F

Dropped from film

Take It in Your Stride
Music and lyrics by Irving Berlin
Annie Get Your Gun 1946

Dropped from production

Take It Slow, Joe
Music by Harold Arlen
Lyrics by E.Y. Harburg
Jamaica 1957

Take Kids
Music by Jack Urbont
Lyrics by Bruce Geller
Livin' the Life (OB) 1957

Take Love Easy
Music by Duke Ellington
Lyrics by John Latouche
Beggar's Holiday 1946

Take Me
Music by Don Pippin
Lyrics by Steve Brown
Fashion (OB) 1974

Take Me Along
Music and lyrics by Bob Merrill
Take Me Along 1959

Take Me Away
Music by Peter Tinturin
Lyrics by Sidney Clare and Charles Tobias
Earl Carroll's Vanities (1932)

Take Me Back
Music by Sol Berkowitz
Lyrics by James Lipton
Nowhere to Go But Up 1962

Take Me Back to Manhattan
Music and lyrics by Cole Porter
The New Yorkers 1930

Take Me Back to Texas
Music by Jack Holmes
Lyrics by Bill Conklin and Bob Miller
O Say Can You See! (OB) 1962

Take Me Back to Texas With You
Music and lyrics by Hugh Martin
Make a Wish 1951

Take Me, Dear
Music by Heinrich Reinhardt
Lyrics by Robert B. Smith
The Spring Maid 1910

Take Me Down to Coney Island
Music by Gustave Kerker
Lyrics by Hugh Morton
The Belle of New York 1897

Take Me for a Honeymoon Ride
Music by Jerome Kern
Lyrics by Oscar Hammerstein II
Sweet Adeline 1929

Take Me Home With You
Music and lyrics by Earl Wilson, Jr.
Let My People Come (OB) 1974

Take Me to the World
Music and lyrics by Stephen Sondheim
Evening Primrose (1966) TV

Take My Advice
Music by Erich Wolfgang Korngold (based on Jacques Offenbach)
Lyrics by Herbert Baker
Helen Goes to Troy 1944

Take My Hand
Music by Bob James
Lyrics by Jack O'Brien
The Selling of the President 1972

Take My Heart With You
Music by Fred Spielman and Arthur Gershwin
Lyrics by Stanley Adams
A Lady Says Yes 1945

Take Off a Little Bit
Music and lyrics by Irving Berlin
Stop! Look! Listen! 1915

Take Off the Coat
Music and lyrics by Harold Rome
Bless You All 1950

Take the Air
Music by Dave Stamper
Lyrics by Gene Buck
Take the Air 1927

Take the Glamor Out of War
Music and lyrics by Elizabeth Swados
Dispatches (OB) 1979

Take the Moment
Music by Richard Rodgers
Lyrics by Stephen Sondheim
Do I Hear a Waltz? 1965

Take the Night Boat to Albany
Music by Sigmund Romberg
Lyrics by Harold Atteridge
Sinbad (1918)

Take the Steamer to Nantucket
Music by Jacques Belasco
Lyrics by Kay Twomey
The Girl From Nantucket 1945

Take the Word of a Gentleman
Music by Jimmy Van Heusen
Lyrics by Johnny Burke
Carnival in Flanders 1953

Take Them All Away
Music and lyrics by Jack Strachey
Charlot's Revue of 1926

Take Your Hat Off
Music by Galt MacDermot
Lyrics by Christopher Gore
Via Galactica 1972

Take Your Time
Music by Frederico Valerio
Lyrics by Elizabeth Miele
Hit the Trail 1954

Take Your Time and Take Your Pick
Music by Albert Hague
Lyrics by Arnold B. Horwitt
Plain and Fancy 1955

Take Yourself a Trip
Music by Alex Fogarty
Lyrics by Edwin Gilbert
You Never Know 1938

Taken by Surprise
Music by Robert Hood Bowers
Lyrics by Francis DeWitt
Oh, Ernest! 1927

Taken for a Ride
Music by Michael H. Cleary
Lyrics by Max and Nathaniel Lief
Shoot the Works 1931

Takes a Heap o' Love
Music by Harry Tierney
Lyrics by Joseph McCarthy
Up She Goes 1922

Takin' My Time
Music and lyrics by Spider John Koerner
and John Foley
Pump Boys and Dinettes 1982

Taking a Chance on Love
Music by Vernon Duke
Lyrics by John Latouche and Ted Fetter
Cabin in the Sky 1940

Ethel Waters, who sang this song, was responsible
for its presence in the show. Playing the put-upon
wife of a ne'er-do-well husband, she wanted a song
to express her belief in his promise to reform. A
few days before the Broadway opening, Vernon
Duke played her a song he had written a few years
earlier entitled "Fooling Around With Love" which
had lyrics by Ted Fetter. Ethel Waters wanted the
song, but with a different title. John Latouche, the
show's lyricist, gave the song its new title and
wrote some additional lyrics for it. The song went
in at the last minute and became a major standard.

Taking a Wife
Music by Sigmund Romberg
Lyrics by Arthur Wimperis
Louie the 14th 1925

Taking Care of You
Music and lyrics by Walter Marks
Golden Rainbow 1968

Taking No Chances
Music by Kurt Weill
Lyrics by Alan Jay Lerner
Love Life 1948

Taking Off
Music by Philip Charig
Lyrics by James Dyrenforth
Nikki 1931

Taking Our Turn
Music by Gary William Friedman
Lyrics by Will Holt
Taking My Turn (OB) 1983

Taking the Cure
Music by William Dyer
Lyrics by Don Parks and William Dyer
Jo (OB) 1964

The Tale of a Coat
Music by Oscar Straus
Lyrics by Stanislaus Stange
The Chocolate Soldier 1909

The Tale of a Shirt
Music and lyrics by Irving Berlin
The Cocoanuts 1925

The Tale of an Oyster
Music and lyrics by Cole Porter
Fifty Million Frenchmen 1929

The Tale of the Seashell
Music by Gustav Luders
Lyrics by Frank Pixley
The Prince of Pilsen 1903

Talent Is What the Public Wants
Music by Ray Henderson
Lyrics by B.G. DeSylva and Lew Brown
George White's Scandals (1926)

The Tales
Music by Mitch Leigh
Lyrics by Charles Burr and Forman Brown
Home Sweet Homer 1976

The Tales of Hoffman
Music and lyrics by Irving Caesar and A. Segal
Betsy 1926

Talk
Music by Edward Earle
Lyrics by Yvonne Tarr
The Decameron (OB) 1961

Talk
Music by Cyril Ornadel
Lyrics by Leslie Bricusse
Pickwick 1965

Talk About a Busy Little Household
Music and lyrics by George M. Cohan
The Merry Malones 1927

Talk About Girls
Music by Stephen Jones
Lyrics by Irving Caesar
Talk About Girls 1927

Talk About This—Talk About That
Music by Victor Herbert
Lyrics by Robert B. Smith
Sweethearts 1913

Dropped from production

The Talk of the Town
Music by Harry Tierney
Lyrics by Joseph McCarthy
Irene 1919

Talk to Him
Music and lyrics by Jerry Bock, George Weiss
and Larry Holofcener
Mr. Wonderful 1956

Talk to Me
Music by Richard Lewine
Lyrics by Arnold B. Horwitt
Make Mine Manhattan 1948

Talk to Me
Music by Sol Berkowitz
Lyrics by James Lipton
Miss Emily Adam (OB) 1960

Talk to Me About Love
Music by Galt MacDermot
Lyrics by Gerome Ragni
Dude 1972

Talk to Me, Baby
Music by Robert Emmett Dolan
Lyrics by Johnny Mercer
Foxy 1964

Talk With Your Heel and Your Toe
Music by Oscar Levant
Lyrics by Irving Caesar
Ripples 1930

Talkative Toes
Music by Vernon Duke
Lyrics by Howard Dietz
Three's a Crowd 1930

Talkin' Blues
Music and lyrics by David Langston Smyrl
On the Lock-In (OB) 1977

Talkin' 'Bout You
Music by Gordon Duffy
Lyrics by Harry M. Haldane
Happy Town 1959

Talkin' in Tongues
Music by Claibe Richardson
Lyrics by Kenward Elmslie
The Grass Harp 1971

Talkin' With Your Feet
Music by Harry Warren
Lyrics by Jerome Lawrence and Robert E. Lee
Shangri-La 1956

Talking Picture Show
Music by Monty Norman
Lyrics by Julian More
The Moony Shapiro Songbook 1981

Talking to You
Music and lyrics by Hugh Martin and Timothy Gray
High Spirits 1964

Talking to Yourself
Music by Jule Styne
Lyrics by Betty Comden and Adolph Green
Hallelujah, Baby! 1967

Tall Hope
Music by Cy Coleman
Lyrics by Carolyn Leigh
Wildcat 1960

Tallulah
Music by Arthur Siegel
Lyrics by Mae Richard
Tallulah (OB) 1983

Tallulahbaloo
Music by Arthur Siegel
Lyrics by Mae Richard
Tallulah (OB) 1983

Tally-Ho
Music by Alberta Nichols
Lyrics by Mann Holiner
Angela 1928

Tamboree
Music by Edward A. Horan
Lyrics by Frederick Herendeen
All the King's Horses 1934

Tambourine
Music by Carl Sigman
Lyrics by Bob Hilliard
Angel in the Wings 1947

Tampa
Music by Henry Souvaine and Jay Gorney
Lyrics by Morrie Ryskind and Howard Dietz
Merry-Go-Round 1927

Tampico Tap
Music by Albert Von Tilzer
Lyrics by Neville Fleeson
Bye Bye, Bonnie 1927

Tampico Tune
Music and lyrics by Frank Marcus
and Bernard Maltin
Bamboola 1929

Tangled Tangents
Music and lyrics by James Rado
Rainbow (OB) 1972

Tangles
Music by Robert Hood Bowers
Lyrics by Francis DeWitt
Oh, Ernest! 1927

Tango
Music by Sam Pottle
Lyrics by David Axelrod
New Faces of 1968

Tango Ballad
Music by Kurt Weill
Lyrics by Marc Blitzstein
The Threepenny Opera (OB) 1954

Tango Melody
Music and lyrics by Irving Berlin
The Cocoanuts 1925

Tango Tragique
Music by Jerry Bock
Lyrics by Sheldon Harnick
She Loves Me 1963

Tanz mit Mir
Music and lyrics by Bob Merrill
Carnival 1961

Tap My Way to the Stars
Music and lyrics by Walter Marks
Broadway Follies 1981

The Tap, Tap
Music by Jesse Greer
Lyrics by Billy Rose and Ballard MacDonald
Padlocks of 1927

Tap Tap
Music by Henry Krieger
Lyrics by Robert Lorick
The Tap Dance Kid 1983

Tap the Plate
Music and lyrics by Oscar Brown, Jr.
Buck White 1969

Tap the Toe
Music by Joseph Meyer and James F. Hanley
Lyrics by B.G. DeSylva
Big Boy 1925

Tap Your Troubles Away
Music and lyrics by Jerry Herman
Mack and Mabel 1974

Tappin' the Barrel
Music by Victor Young
Lyrics by Joseph Young and Ned Washington
Blackbirds of 1934

Tappin' the Toe
Music by J. Fred Coots
Lyrics by Al Dubin
White Lights 1927

Taps
Music by Walter Donaldson
Lyrics by Gus Kahn
Whoopee 1928

Tarantella
Music by Mark Charlap
Lyrics by Carolyn Leigh
Peter Pan 1954

Tarantella Rhythm
Music by Frank D'Armond
Lyrics by Will Morrissey
Saluta 1934

Tartar
Music by George Gershwin and Herbert Stothart
Lyrics by Otto Harbach and Oscar Hammerstein II
Song of the Flame 1925

The Tartar Song
Music by Richard Rodgers
Lyrics by Lorenz Hart
Chee-Chee 1928

Tarts and Flowers
Music by Harden Church
Lyrics by Edward Heyman
Caviar 1934

Taste
Music and lyrics by Walter Marks
Golden Rainbow 1968

A Taste of Forever
Music by Keith Hermann
Lyrics by Charlotte Anker and Irene Rosenberg
Onward Victoria 1980

A Taste of the Sea
Music by Henry Sullivan
Lyrics by Earle Crooker
Thumbs Up! 1934

Tavern Song
Music by Sigmund Romberg
Lyrics by Oscar Hammerstein II
The New Moon 1928

Tax the Bachelors
Music by Raymond Hubbell
Lyrics by Glen MacDonough
The Jolly Bachelors 1910

Taxi
Music and lyrics by Harry Chapin
The Night That Made America Famous 1975

Taxi Drivers' Lament
Music by Randall Thompson
Lyrics by Agnes Morgan
The Grand Street Follies (1926) (OB)

Te Deum
Music by Richard Rodgers
Lyrics by Sheldon Harnick
Rex 1976

Tea for Two
Music by Vincent Youmans
Lyrics by Irving Caesar
No, No, Nanette 1925

Youmans played his catchy tune for Caesar late
one night and then took a short nap. Caesar wrote
what he meant to be a "dummy" lyric ("Picture you
upon my knee,"), intending to write the actual lyric
next morning. On waking, Youmans was delighted
with the dummy lyric and, to Caesar's amazement,
insisted that it be used.

Tea in Chicago
Music and lyrics by James Shelton
Mrs. Patterson 1954

Tea in the Rain
Music by Nancy Ford
Lyrics by Gretchen Cryer
Now Is the Time for All Good Men (OB) 1967

Tea Party
Music by Baldwin Bergersen
Lyrics by William Archibald
The Crystal Heart (OB) 1960

Tea Time
Music by Charles M. Schwab
Lyrics by Henry Myers
Bare Facts of 1926

Tea Time Tap
Music by Harry Ruby
Lyrics by Bert Kalmar
The Five o'Clock Girl 1927

Teach Me How to Love
Music and lyrics by Irving Berlin
Stop! Look! Listen! 1915

Teach Me to Dance Like Grandma
Music and lyrics by Noël Coward
This Year of Grace 1928

Teacher, Teacher
Music by Jerome Kern
Lyrics by Anne Caldwell
She's a Good Fellow 1919

T.E.A.M. (The Baseball Game)
Music and lyrics by Clark Gesner
You're a Good Man, Charlie Brown (OB) 1967

Tear the Town Apart
Music by Jule Styne
Lyrics by Bob Merrill
Sugar 1972

Tears
Music by Stan Harte, Jr.
Leaves of Grass (OB) 1971

Tears of Ice
Music by Tom Mandel
Lyrics by Louisa Rose,
The Bar That Never Closes (OB) 1972

Teasing
Music by Jerome Kern
Lyrics by Edward Madden
La Belle Paree 1911

Teasing Mama
Music by Jimmy Johnson
Lyrics by Henry Creamer
Keep Shufflin' 1928

The Teddy Toddle
Music by Jerome Kern
Lyrics by Anne Caldwell
Good Morning, Dearie 1921

Tee-Oodle-Um-Bum-Bo
Music by George Gershwin
Lyrics by Arthur J. Jackson and B.G. DeSylva
La, La, Lucille 1919

Tee Teedle Tum Di Dum
Music and lyrics by George M. Cohan
The Merry Malones 1927

Teeny Bopper
Music by Norman Curtis
Lyrics by Patricia Taylor Curtis
Walk Down Mah Street! (OB) 1968

Teeter Totter Tessie
Music by Morgan Lewis
Lyrics by Nancy Hamilton
One for the Money 1939

Telephone Girlie
Music by Vincent Youmans
Lyrics by Otto Harbach
No, No, Nanette 1925

The Telephone Hour
Music by Charles Strouse
Lyrics by Lee Adams
Bye Bye Birdie 1960

Telephone Song
Music by John Kander
Lyrics by Fred Ebb
Cabaret 1966

Telephone Tango
Music by John Addison
Lyrics by John Cranko
Cranks 1956

Tell a Handsome Stranger
Music and lyrics by Rick Besoyan
Little Mary Sunshine (OB) 1959

Tell a Little Lie or Two
Music and lyrics by John Raniello
Movie Buff (OB) 1977

Tell Her
Music by Arthur Siegel
Lyrics by June Carroll
New Faces of 1956

Tell Her
Music by John Morris
Lyrics by Gerald Freedman
A Time for Singing 1966

Tell Her
Music by Michael J. Lewis
Lyrics by Anthony Burgess
Cyrano 1973

Tell Her in the Springtime
Music and lyrics by Irving Berlin
Music Box Revue (4th edition) 1924

Tell Her the Truth
Music by Jack Waller and Joseph Tunbridge
Lyrics by R.P. Weston and Bert Lee
Tell Her the Truth 1932

Tell Her While the Waltz Is Playing
Music by Albert Von Tilzer
Lyrics by Neville Fleeson
The Gingham Girl 1922

Tell It All Over Again
Music by Victor Herbert
Lyrics by Henry Blossom
The Only Girl 1914

Tell It to the Marines
Music by Richard Rodgers
Lyrics by Lorenz Hart
Present Arms 1928

Tell Me
Music by Richard Rodgers
Lyrics by Sheldon Harnick
Rex 1976

Dropped from production

Tell Me a Bedtime Story
Music and lyrics by Irving Berlin
Music Box Revue (3rd edition) 1923

Tell Me Again
Music by Shep Camp
Lyrics by Frank DuPree
Half a Widow 1927

Tell Me All Your Troubles, Cutie
Music by Jerome Kern
Lyrics by P.G. Wodehouse
Miss 1917

Tell Me, Daisy
Music by Sigmund Romberg
Lyrics by Dorothy Donnelly
Blossom Time 1921

Based on the second movement of Schubert's
Unfinished Symphony

Tell Me Goodbye
Music by Paul Klein
Lyrics by Fred Ebb
Morning Sun (OB) 1963

Tell Me How
Music by Frederico Valerio
Lyrics by Elizabeth Miele
Hit the Trail 1954

Tell Me, Little Gypsy
Music and lyrics by Irving Berlin
Ziegfeld Follies of 1920

Tell Me More!
Music by George Gershwin
Lyrics by B.G. DeSylva and Ira Gershwin
Tell Me More 1925

Tell Me Not That You Are Forgetting
Music by Edward Künneke
Lyrics by Harry B. Smith
The Love Song 1925

Tell Me, Pretty Maiden
Music by Leslie Stuart
Lyrics by Ernest Boyd-Jones and Paul Rubens
Florodora 1900

Also known as *The Florodora Sextet*

Tell Me, Pretty Maiden
Music and lyrics by Harold Rome
Sing Out the News 1938

Tell Me Something About Yourself
Music by Michael H. Cleary
Lyrics by Max and Nathaniel Lief
Hey Nonny Nonny! 1932

Tell Me the Story
Music by Morgan Lewis
Lyrics by Nancy Hamilton
Three to Make Ready 1946

Tell Me, What Can This Be?
Music and lyrics by Ralph Benatzky
Meet My Sister 1930

Tell Me, What Is Love?
Music and lyrics by Noël Coward
Bitter Sweet 1929

Tell Me Who You Are
Music by Lewis E. Gensler
Lyrics by Robert A. Simon
Ups-a-Daisy 1928

Tell Sweet Saroyana
Music by Michael Valenti
Lyrics by Donald Driver
Oh, Brother 1981

Tell the Doc
Music by George Gershwin
Lyrics by Ira Gershwin
Funny Face 1927

Tell the Town "Hello" Tonight
Music by Sigmund Romberg
Lyrics by Harold Atteridge
The Blue Paradise 1915

Tell the World I'm Through
Music by Harry Ruby
Lyrics by Bert Kalmar
The Five o'Clock Girl 1927

Temperance Polka
Music by David Baker
Lyrics by Sheldon Harnick
Smiling, the Boy Fell Dead (OB) 1961

The Temple
Music by Andrew Lloyd Webber
Lyrics by Tim Rice
Jesus Christ Superstar 1971

Tempt Me Not
Music by Richard Rodgers
Lyrics by Lorenz Hart
Too Many Girls 1939

The Temptation Strut
Music by Earl Lindsay and Maury Rubens
Lyrics by Clifford Grey
The Great Temptations 1926

Tempting Salome
Music by Galt MacDermot
Lyrics by Rochelle Owens
The Karl Marx Play (OB) 1973

Ten Cents a Dance
Music by Richard Rodgers
Lyrics by Lorenz Hart
Simple Simon 1930

The Ten Commandments of Love
Music by George Gershwin
Lyrics by Arthur J. Jackson and B.G. DeSylva
La, La, Lucille 1919

Ten Days Ago
Music and lyrics by James Rado
Rainbow (OB) 1972

Ten Minutes Ago
Music by Richard Rodgers
Lyrics by Oscar Hammerstein II
Cinderella (1957) TV

Ten Minutes in Bed
Music by Ned Lehak
Lyrics by Allen Boretz
Sweet and Low 1930

Ten o'Clock Town
Music by Michael Cleary
Lyrics by Arthur Swanstrom
Sea Legs 1937

Ten Percent
Music by John Kander
Lyrics by Fred Ebb
Chicago 1975

Tender Shepherd
Music by Mark Charlap
Lyrics by Carolyn Leigh
Peter Pan 1954

A Tender Spot
Music and lyrics by Ervin Drake
What Makes Sammy Run? 1964

Tender Understanding
Music and lyrics by Ted Hayes
Waltz of the Stork (OB) 1982

Tengu
Music and lyrics by John Driver
Ride the Winds 1974

Tennessee Dan
Music by Richard Rodgers
Lyrics by Lorenz Hart
America's Sweetheart 1931

Tennessee Fish Fry
Music by Arthur Schwartz
Lyrics by Oscar Hammerstein II
American Jubilee 1940

Tennis
Music by Leo Fall
Lyrics by George Grossmith
The Dollar Princess 1909

Tennis
Music by Percy Wenrich
Lyrics by Harry Clarke
Who Cares? 1930

Tennis Champs
Music by Richard Rodgers
Lyrics by Lorenz Hart
The Garrick Gaieties (2nd edition) 1926

Tennis Song
Music by Richard Adler
Lyrics by Will Holt
Music Is 1976

The Tennis Tournament
Music by Jean Schwartz
Lyrics by Joseph W. Herbert and Harold Atteridge
The Honeymoon Express 1913

Tenth and Greenwich
Music and lyrics by Melvin Van Peebles
Ain't Supposed to Die a Natural Death 1971

Tequila
Music and lyrics by Cole Porter
Mexican Hayride 1944

Dropped from production

Terminix
Music by Bob James
Lyrics by Jack O'Brien
The Selling of the President 1972

Terre Haute High
Music by Galt MacDermot
Lyrics by Christopher Gore
Via Galactica 1972

Terribly Attractive
Music by Arthur Schwartz
Lyrics by Dorothy Fields
Stars in Your Eyes 1939

A Terrific Band and a Real Nice Crowd
Music by Billy Goldenberg
Lyrics by Alan and Marilyn Bergman
Ballroom 1978

Tess's Torch Song
Music by Harold Arlen
Lyrics by Ted Koehler
Up in Arms (1944) F

The Test
Music by Kenneth Jacobson
Lyrics by Rhoda Roberts
Show Me Where the Good Times Are (OB) 1970

Texas Has a Whorehouse in It
Music and lyrics by Carol Hall
The Best Little Whorehouse in Texas 1978

Texas, Li'l Darlin'
Music by Robert Emmett Dolan
Lyrics by Johnny Mercer
Texas, Li'l Darlin' 1949

Texas Stomp
Music by Will Morrisey
Lyrics by Edmund Joseph
Polly of Hollywood 1927

The Textile Troops
Music by Max Ewing
Lyrics by Agnes Morgan
The Grand Street Follies (1929)

Thank God
Music and lyrics by James Quinn and Alaric Jans
Do Patent Leather Shoes Really Reflect Up? 1982

Thank God for the Volunteer Fire Brigade
Music by Alan Menken
Lyrics by Dennis Green
God Bless You, Mr. Rosewater (OB) 1979

Thank God I'm Old
Music by Cy Coleman
Lyrics by Michael Stewart
Barnum 1980

Thank Heaven for Little Girls
Music by Frederick Loewe
Lyrics by Alan Jay Lerner
Gigi (1958) F

Also in stage version (1973)

Thank Heaven for You
Music and lyrics by Micki Grant
Don't Bother Me, I Can't Cope (OB) 1972

Thank You
Music by Al Carmines
Lyrics by Maria Irene Fornes
Promenade (OB) 1969

Thank You, Don't Mention It
Music by Harry Revel
Lyrics by Mack Gordon
Smiling Faces 1932

Thank You for a Lovely Evening
Music by Jimmy McHugh
Lyrics by Dorothy Fields
Have a Heart (1934) F

Thank You, Ma'am
Music by Duke Ellington
Lyrics by Marshall Barer and Fred Tobias
Pousse-Café 1966

Thank You, Madam
Music by Jerry Bock
Lyrics by Sheldon Harnick
She Loves Me 1963

Thank You, Mrs. Butterfield
Music by Abraham Ellstein
Lyrics by Walter Bullock
Great to Be Alive 1950

Thank You, No
Music by Don Gohman
Lyrics by Hal Hackady
Ambassador 1972

Thank You So Much
Music by Richard Rodgers
Lyrics by Stephen Sondheim
Do I Hear a Waltz? 1965

Thank You So Much, Mrs. Lowsborough–Goodby
Music and lyrics by Cole Porter

This song, written independently of a stage or film production, is a bread-and-butter letter after a disastrous weekend.

The Thank You Song
Music and lyrics by Hugo Peretti, Luigi Creatore and George David Weiss
Maggie Flynn 1968

Thank You, South America
Music by Sammy Fain
Lyrics by Jack Yellen
Sons o' Fun 1941

Thank Your Father
Music by Ray Henderson
Lyrics by B.G. DeSylva and Lew Brown
Flying High 1930

Thank Your Lucky Stars
Music by Arthur Schwartz
Lyrics by Frank Loesser
Thank Your Lucky Stars (1943) F

Thanks
Music by Stan Harte, Jr.
Leaves of Grass (OB) 1971

Thanks a Lot
Music and lyrics by Michael Brown
Different Times 1972

Thanks for a Darn Nice Time
Music by Harry Tierney
Lyrics by Joseph McCarthy
Cross My Heart 1928

Thanks for a Lousy Evening
Music by Philip Charig
Lyrics by Dan Shapiro and Milton Pascal
Follow the Girls 1944

Thanks for the Francs
Music by Jimmy McHugh
Lyrics by Al Dubin
The Streets of Paris 1939

Thanks, Sweet Jesus!
Music by Stanley Lebowsky
Lyrics by Fred Tobias
Gantry 1970

Thanks to You
Music by Henry Sullivan
Lyrics by Edward Eliscu
A Little Racketeer 1932

That American Boy of Mine
Music by George Gershwin
Lyrics by Irving Caesar
The Dancing Girl (1923)

That Big-Bellied Bottle
Music by Don McAfee
Lyrics by Nancy Leeds
Great Scot! (OB) 1965

That Certain Feeling
Music by George Gershwin
Lyrics by Ira Gershwin
Tip-Toes 1925

That Certain Party
Music by William B. Kernell
Lyrics by Dorothy Donnelly
Hello, Lola 1926

That Certain Thing
Music and lyrics by Edward Pola
and Eddie Brandt
Woof, Woof 1929

That Charleston Dance
Music and lyrics by Noble Sissle
and Eubie Blake
The Chocolate Dandies 1924

That Deviling Tune
Music by Jerome Kern
Lyrics by Edward Madden
La Belle Paree 1911

That Dirty Old Man
Music and lyrics by Stephen Sondheim
*A Funny Thing Happened on the Way
to the Forum* 1962

That Face!
Music and lyrics by Hugh Martin
Make a Wish 1951

That Face
Music by Lee Pockriss
Lyrics by Anne Croswell
Tovarich 1963

That Farm Out in Kansas
Music by Louis A. Hirsch
Lyrics by Otto Harbach
Mary 1920

That Fellow Manuelo
Music by Arthur Schwartz
Lyrics by Howard Dietz
Revenge With Music 1934

That First Hello
Music and lyrics by Bob Ost
Everybody's Gettin' Into the Act (OB) 1981

That Gal of Mine
Music by Jean Schwartz
Lyrics by Joseph W. Herbert and Harold Atteridge
The Honeymoon Express 1913

That Girl With the Curls
Music and lyrics by Ronnie Britton
Greenwich Village Follies (OB) 1976

That Great Come and Get It Day
Music by Burton Lane
Lyrics by E.Y. Harburg
Finian's Rainbow 1947

That Guilty Feeling
Music by Bill Weeden
Lyrics by David Finkle
I'm Solomon 1968

That Hula Hula
Music and lyrics by Irving Berlin
Stop! Look! Listen! 1915

That Is Art
Music by Victor Herbert
Lyrics by David Stevens
and Justin Huntly McCarthy
The Madcap Duchess 1913

That Is Love
Music by Victor Herbert
Lyrics by George V. Hobart
Old Dutch 1909

That It Should Come to This
Music and lyrics by Cliff Jones
Rockabye Hamlet 1976

That Latin Lure
Music and lyrics by John Clifton
El Bravo! (OB) 1981

That Lindy Hop
Music by Eubie Blake
Lyrics by Andy Razaf
Blackbirds of 1930

That Little Monosyllable
Music by Don Pippin
Lyrics by Steve Brown
The Contrast (OB) 1972

That Little Something
Music by Jerome Kern
Lyrics by Bert Kalmar and Harry Ruby
Lucky 1927

That Lost Barbershop Chord
Music by George Gershwin
Lyrics by Ira Gershwin
Americana (1926)

That Lucky Fellow
Music by Jerome Kern
Lyrics by Oscar Hammerstein II
Very Warm for May 1939

That Man and Woman Thing
Music by Baldwin Bergersen
Lyrics by John Rox
All in Fun 1940

That Man Over There
Music and lyrics by Meredith Willson
Here's Love 1963

That Means Nothing to Me
Music and lyrics by A. L. Keith and Lee Sterling
Naughty Cinderella 1925

That Might Have Satisfied Grandma
Music by Louis A. Hirsch
Lyrics by Otto Harbach
Mary 1920

That Mister Man of Mine
Music by Jim Wise
Lyrics by George Haimsohn and Robin Miller
Dames at Sea (OB) 1968

That Moment of Moments
Music by Vernon Duke
Lyrics by Ira Gershwin
Ziegfeld Follies (1936)

That Naughty Little Song
Music by Victor Herbert
Lyrics by Harry B. Smith
The Enchantress 1911

That Naughty Show From Gay Paree
Music by Sigmund Romberg
(developed by Don Walker)

Lyrics by Leo Robin
The Girl in Pink Tights 1954

That Old Black Magic
Music by Harold Arlen
Lyrics by Johnny Mercer
Star Spangled Rhythm (1942) F

That Old Familiar Ring
Music and lyrics by Bill and Patti Jacob
Jimmy 1969

That Old Piano
Music by Paul Horner
Lyrics by Peggy Lee
Peg 1983

That Old Time Crowd
Music by Moose Charlap
Lyrics by Eddie Lawrence
Kelly 1965

That Prelude!
Music and lyrics by Robert Wright and George
Forrest (based on Rachmaninoff)
Anya 1965

That Rhythm Man
Music by Thomas (Fats) Waller and Harry Brooks
Lyrics by Andy Razaf
Hot Chocolates 1929

That Russian Winter
Music and lyrics by Irving Berlin
This Is the Army 1942

That Slavery Is Love
Music by Mitch Leigh
Lyrics by William Alfred and Phyllis Robinson
Cry for Us All 1970

That Something Extra Special
Music by Jule Styne
Lyrics by E.Y. Harburg
Darling of the Day 1968

That Special Day
Music by Don McAfee
Lyrics by Nancy Leeds
Great Scot! (OB) 1965

That Terrible Tune
Music by Morgan Lewis
Lyrics by Nancy Hamilton
Two for the Show 1940

That Terrific Rainbow
Music by Richard Rodgers
Lyrics by Lorenz Hart
Pal Joey 1940

That Tired Feeling
Music by Louis Alter
Lyrics by Harry Ruskin and Leighton K. Brill
Ballyhoo 1930

That Touch
Music and lyrics by John Driver
Ride the Winds 1974

That Was Yesterday
Music and lyrics by Jerry Herman
Milk and Honey 1961

That Week in Paris
Music by Ben Oakland
Lyrics by Oscar Hammerstein II
The Lady Objects (1938) F

That Woman Can't Play No Piano
Music by Garry Sherman
Lyrics by Peter Udell
Amen Corner 1983

That Wonderful Melody
Music and lyrics by Noël Coward
Bitter Sweet 1929

That Would Be Lovely
Music by Oscar Straus
Lyrics by Stanislaus Stange
The Chocolate Soldier 1909

That'll Be the Day
Music by Jacques Offenbach
(adapted by Robert De Cormier)
Lyrics by E.Y. Harburg
The Happiest Girl in the World 1961

That'll Be the Day
Music and lyrics by Johnny Brandon
Who's Who, Baby? (OB) 1968

That'll Show Him
Music and lyrics by Stephen Sondheim
*A Funny Thing Happened on the Way
to the Forum* 1962

That's a Beginning
Music by John Kander
Lyrics by Fred Ebb
Zorba (1983 revival)

That's a Crime
Music by Marguerite Monnot
Lyrics by Julian More, David Heneker
and Monte Norman
Irma la Douce 1960

That's a Very Interesting Question
Music by Galt MacDermot
Lyrics by John Guare
Two Gentlemen of Verona 1971

That's All Right for McGilligan
Music by Jerome Kern
Lyrics by M.E. Rourke
La Belle Paree 1911

That's All There Is
Music by Harry Tierney
Lyrics by Joseph McCarthy
Kid Boots 1923

That's Broadway
Music and lyrics by Gene Herbert and Teddy Hall
Bright Lights of 1944

That's Class
Music by Jimmy Van Heusen
Lyrics by Johnny Burke
Nellie Bly 1946

That's Entertainment
Music by Arthur Schwartz
Lyrics by Howard Dietz
The Band Wagon (film version, 1953)

That's Fine
Music by Jack Waller and Joseph Tunbridge
Lyrics by R.P. Weston and Bert Lee
Tell Her the Truth 1932

That's for Me
Music by Richard Rodgers
Lyrics by Oscar Hammerstein II
State Fair (1945) F

That's for Sure
Music and lyrics by Johnny Mercer
Top Banana 1951

That's Good Enough for Me
Music by Elmer Bernstein
Lyrics by Carolyn Leigh
How Now, Dow Jones 1967

That's Good—That's Bad
Music by Mary Rodgers
Lyrics by Martin Charnin
Hot Spot 1963

That's Him
Music by Kurt Weill
Lyrics by Ogden Nash
One Touch of Venus 1943

That's Him
Music by Michael Valenti
Lyrics by Donald Driver
Oh, Brother 1981

That's How I Learned to Sing the Blues
Music by Paul Horner
Lyrics by Peggy Lee
Peg 1983

That's How I Love the Blues
Music and lyrics by Hugh Martin and Ralph Blane
Best Foot Forward 1941

That's How It Goes
Music by Arthur Schwartz
Lyrics by Dorothy Fields
A Tree Grows in Brooklyn 1951

That's How It Is
Music by George Fischoff
Lyrics by Carole Bayer
Georgy 1970

That's How It Starts
Music and lyrics by Bob Merrill
Take Me Along 1959

That's How Young I Feel
Music and lyrics by Jerry Herman
Mame 1966

That's Life
Music by Vernon Duke
Lyrics by E.Y. Harburg
Walk a Little Faster 1932

That's Love
Music by Richard Rodgers
Lyrics by Lorenz Hart
Nana (1934) F

Commissioned by Sam Goldwyn for his film based
on the Emile Zola novel, which was to star Anna
Sten. When Rodgers played the song for Goldwyn
and members of his staff, screen writer Frances
Marion pronounced it "the essence of Paris."
Goldwyn, delighted, turned to Alfred Newman the
conductor and commanded: "Newman, in the
orchestra eight French horns!"

That's Love
Music by Louis Bellson and Will Irwin
Lyrics by Richard Ney
Portofino 1958

That's My Approach to Love
Music and lyrics by Harold Orlob
Hairpin Harmony 1943

That's My Fella
Music by Morton Gould
Lyrics by Dorothy Fields
Arms and the Girl 1950

That's My Man
Music by Harold Orlob
Lyrics by Irving Caesar
Talk About Girls 1927

That's Not Cricket
Music by Arthur Schwartz
Lyrics by Howard Dietz
At Home Abroad 1935

That's Religion
Music and lyrics by Porter Grainger
Yeah Man 1932

That's Right!
Music by Paul Klein
Lyrics by Fred Ebb
Morning Sun (OB) 1963

That's Right, Mr. Syph
Music by Mildred Kayden
Lyrics by Frank Gagliano
Paradise Gardens East (OB) 1969

That's the Best of All
Music by Jerome Kern
Lyrics by Ira Gershwin
Cover Girl (1944) F

Dropped from film

That's the Irish in Her
Music by Seymour Furth and Lee Edwards
Lyrics by R.F. Carroll
Bringing Up Father 1925

That's the Kind of Baby for Me
Music by Jack Egan
Lyrics by Alfred Harrison
Ziegfeld Follies of 1917

That's the Law
Music by Cyril Ornadel
Lyrics by Leslie Bricusse
Pickwick 1965

That's the Life for Me
Music by Jean Schwartz
Lyrics by Joseph W. Herbert and Harold Atteridge
The Honeymoon Express 1913

That's the Life for Me
Music by Albert Hague
Lyrics by Marty Brill
Café Crown 1964

That's the Picture I Want to See
Music by Jerome Kern
Lyrics by P.G. Wodehouse
Miss 1917

That's the Song of Paree
Music by Richard Rodgers
Lyrics by Lorenz Hart
Love Me Tonight (1932) F

That's the Time When I Miss You
Music by Alexander Fogarty
Lyrics by Seymour Morris
Cape Cod Follies 1929

That's the Way It Happens
Music by Richard Rodgers
Lyrics by Oscar Hammerstein II
Me and Juliet 1953

That's What He Did
Music by George Gershwin
Lyrics by Ira Gershwin
Let 'Em Eat Cake 1933

That's What I Got for Not Listening to My Mother
Music by Ruth Cleary Patterson
Lyrics by Floria Vestoff
Russell Patterson's Sketch Book (OB) 1960

That's What I Need
Music by Don Gohman
Lyrics by Hal Hackady
Ambassador 1972

That's What I Told Him Last Night
Music by Morton Gould
Lyrics by Dorothy Fields
Arms and the Girl 1950

That's What I Want for Janie
Music by Cy Coleman
Lyrics by Carolyn Leigh
Wildcat 1960

That's What I'd Like for Christmas
Music by Cyril Ornadel
Lyrics by Leslie Bricusse
Pickwick 1965

That's What It Is to Be Young
Music and lyrics by Leslie Bricusse
and Anthony Newley
*The Roar of the Greasepaint—The Smell
of the Crowd* 1965

**That's What the Well Dressed Man
in Harlem Will Wear**
Music and lyrics by Irving Berlin
This Is the Army 1942

That's What Young Ladies Do
Music by John Morris
Lyrics by Gerald Freedman
A Time for Singing 1966

That's What's Happening, Baby
Music and lyrics by Johnny Brandon
Who's Who, Baby? (OB) 1968

That's Where a Man Fits In
Music by James Mundy
Lyrics by John Latouche
The Vamp 1955

That's Where We Come In
Music by Samuel Pokrass
Lyrics by E.Y. Harburg
Ziegfeld Follies (1934)

That's Why Darkies Were Born
Music by Ray Henderson
Lyrics by B.G. DeSylva and Lew Brown
George White's Scandals (1931)

That's Why I Love You
Music and lyrics by Cole Porter
Fifty Million Frenchmen 1929

Dropped from production

That's Why I Love You
Music by Rudolf Friml
Lyrics by Otto Harbach and Oscar Hammerstein II
The Wild Rose 1926

Dropped from production

That's Why I Want to Go Home
Music by Alma Sanders
Lyrics by Monte Carlo
Louisiana Lady 1947

That's Why I'm Here Tonight
Music by Ruth Cleary Patterson
Lyrics by Les Kramer
Russell Patterson's Sketch Book (OB) 1960

That's Why We Misbehave
Music by Alexander Fogarty
Lyrics by Edith Lois and Urana Clarke
Cape Cod Follies 1929

That's Why We're Dancing
Music by Jimmy McHugh
Lyrics by Dorothy Fields
Lew Leslie's International Revue 1930

That's Your Funeral
Music and lyrics by Lionel Bart
Oliver! 1963

That's Your Thing, Baby
Music and lyrics by Tom Sankey
The Golden Screw (OB) 1967

The Theatre Is a Lady
Music by Vernon Duke
Lyrics by Ogden Nash
Two's Company 1952

Theatre Quadrille
Music and lyrics by Deed Meyer
She Shall Have Music (OB) 1959

Theatre/Theatre
Music by Galt MacDermot
Lyrics by Gerome Ragni
Dude 1972

Them and They
Music by Jule Styne
Lyrics by Sammy Cahn
Look to the Lilies 1970

Them Was the Childhood Days
Music by Victor Herbert
Lyrics by James O'Dea
The Lady of the Slipper 1912

Then
Music and lyrics by Noël Coward
Tonight at 8:30 ("Shadow Play") 1936

Then All Come Along
Music by Ivan Caryll
Lyrics by C.M.S. McLellan
Oh! Oh! Delphine 1912

Then Came the War
Music and lyrics by Ben Black
The Vanderbilt Revue 1930

Then Comes the Dawning
Music by Victor Herbert
Lyrics by B.G. DeSylva
Orange Blossoms 1922

Then I'll Have Time for You
Music by Ray Henderson
Lyrics by B.G. DeSylva and Lew Brown
Follow Thru 1929

Then You Go?
Music by Leo Fall
Lyrics by George Grossmith, Jr.
The Dollar Princess 1909

Then You May Take Me to the Fair
Music by Frederick Loewe
Lyrics by Alan Jay Lerner
Camelot 1960

Then You Were Never in Love
Music by Burton Lane
Lyrics by E.Y. Harburg
Hold On to Your Hats 1940

Then You Will Know
Music by Sigmund Romberg
Lyrics by Otto Harbach and Oscar Hammerstein II
The Desert Song 1926

Theophilus
Music by Karl Hoschna
Lyrics by Otto Harbach
Madame Sherry 1910

There
Music and lyrics by Jerry Bock, George Weiss
and Larry Holofcener
Mr. Wonderful 1956

There
Music and lyrics by Melvin Van Peebles
Waltz of the Stork (OB) 1982

There Ain't No Busy Signals
Music and lyrics by Harry Chapin
Cotton Patch Gospel (OB) 1981

There Ain't No Color Line Around the Rainbow
Music by Irving Caesar
Lyrics by Gerald Marks and Sam Lerner
My Dear Public 1943

There Ain't No Flies on Jesus
Music and lyrics by Peter Link and C.C. Courtney
Salvation (OB) 1969

There Ain't No Flies on Me
Music and lyrics by Bob Merrill
New Girl in Town 1957

There Are Days and There Are Days
Music by Bob Brush
Lyrics by Martin Charnin
The First 1981

There Are Times
Music by Ivor Novello
Lyrics by Ronald Jeans
Charlot's Revue 1924

There Are Worse Things I Could Do
Music and lyrics by Jim Jacobs and Warren Casey
Grease 1972

There Are Yanks (From the Banks of the Wabash)
Music by Vernon Duke
Lyrics by Howard Dietz
Jackpot 1944

There Aren't Many Ladies in the Mile End Road
Music and lyrics by Johnny Brandon
Who's Who, Baby? (OB) 1968

There But for You Go I
Music by Frederick Loewe
Lyrics by Alan Jay Lerner
Brigadoon 1947

There Comes a Time
Music and lyrics by Jerry Herman
Madame Aphrodite (OB) 1961

There Comes a Time
Music by Jule Styne
Lyrics by Sammy Cahn
Look to the Lilies 1970

There Goes a Mad Old Man
Music and lyrics by Bruce Montgomery
The Amorous Flea (OB) 1964

There Goes My Gal
Music and lyrics by Walter Cool
Mackey of Appalachia (OB) 1965

There Had to Be the Waltz
Music by Frederick Loewe
Lyrics by Earle Crooker
Great Lady 1938

There He Goes, Mr. Phileas Fogg
Music and lyrics by Cole Porter
Around the World 1946

There I Go Dreaming Again
Music by Ray Henderson
Lyrics by Lew Brown
Hot-Cha! 1932

There I'd Be
Music by Morton Gould
Lyrics by Betty Comden and Adolph Green
Billion Dollar Baby 1945

There Is a Curious Paradox
Music by Harvey Schmidt
Lyrics by Tom Jones
The Fantasticks (OB) 1960

There Is a Garden in Loveland
Music by Karl Hajos (based on Tchaikovsky)
Lyrics by Harry B. Smith
Natja 1925

There Is a Land of Fancy
Music by Franz Lehár
Lyrics by Harry B. and Robert B. Smith
Gypsy Love 1911

There Is a Sucker Born Ev'ry Minute
Music by Cy Coleman
Lyrics by Michael Stewart
Barnum 1980

There Is Always You
Music by Steve Sterner
Lyrics by Peter del Valle
Lovers (OB) 1975

There Is Beautiful You Are
Music by John Morris
Lyrics by Gerald Freedman
A Time for Singing 1966

There Is Magic in a Smile
Music by Victor Herbert
Lyrics by Robert B. Smith
Sweethearts 1913

There Is No Other Way
Music and lyrics by Stephen Sondheim
Pacific Overtures 1976

There Is Nothin' Like a Dame
Music by Richard Rodgers
Lyrics by Oscar Hammerstein II
South Pacific 1949

There Is Nothing Too Good for You
Music by George Gershwin
Lyrics by B.G. DeSylva and E. Ray Goetz
George White's Scandals (1923)

There Is Only One Paris for That
Music by Marguerite Monnot
Lyrics by Julian More, David Heneker
and Monte Norman
Irma la Douce 1960

There Is Only One Thing to Be Sure Of
Music by Edward Thomas
Lyrics by Martin Charnin
Ballad For a Firing Squad (OB) 1968

There Is That in Me
Music by Stan Harte, Jr.
Leaves of Grass (OB) 1971

There Isn't One Girl
Music by Jerome Kern
Lyrics by P. G. Wodehouse
Sitting Pretty 1924

There It Is Again
Music by Jerome Kern
Lyrics by P. G. Wodehouse
Leave It to Jane 1917

Same music as "When the Orchestra is Playing
Your Favorite Dance": dropped from *Oh, Boy*
(1917)

There Must Be Someone for Me
Music and lyrics by Cole Porter
Mexican Hayride 1944

There Must Be Somethin' Better Than Love
Music by Morton Gould
Lyrics by Dorothy Fields
Arms and the Girl 1950

There Never Was a Town Like Paris
Music by Mann Holiner
Lyrics by Alberta Nichols
Gay Paree 1926

There Never Was a Woman
Music by Leroy Anderson
Lyrics by Joan Ford and Walter and Jean Kerr
Goldilocks 1958

There Once Was a Man
Music and lyrics by Richard Adler and Jerry Ross
The Pajama Game 1954

There She Is
Music by Larry Grossman
Lyrics by Betty Comden and Adolph Green
A Doll's Life 1982

There Was a Hen
Music by Galt MacDermot
Lyrics by Rochelle Owens
The Karl Marx Play (OB) 1973

There Was a Little Man
Music by Helen Miller
Lyrics by Eve Merriam
Inner City 1971

There Was Once a Little Village by the Sea
Music and lyrics by Noël Coward
Conversation Piece 1934

There When I Need Him
Music by John Kander
Lyrics by Fred Ebb
The Act 1977

There Will Be a Girl
Music by Harry Revel
Lyrics by Mack Gordon
Smiling Faces 1932

There Won't Be Trumpets
Music and lyrics by Stephen Sondheim
Marry Me a Little (OB) 1981

Dropped from *Anyone Can Whistle* (1964)

There You Are
Music by William Heagney
Lyrics by William Heagney and Tom Connell
There You Are 1932

There You Are
Music and lyrics by Tom Savage
Musical Chairs 1980

There You Go Again
Music and lyrics by Ronnie Britton
Gift of the Magi (OB) 1975

There'll Always Be a Lady Fair
Music and lyrics by Cole Porter
Anything Goes 1934

There'll Be Life, Love, and Laughter
Music by Kurt Weill
Lyrics by Ira Gershwin
The Firebrand of Florence 1945

There'll Be Trouble
Music by Kurt Weill
Lyrics by Langston Hughes
Street Scene 1947

There'll Have to Be Changes Made
Music by Giuseppe Verdi (adapted by Hans
Spialek)
Lyrics by Charles Friedman
My Darlin' Aïda 1952

There'll Never Be Another Girl Like Daisy
Music by Emmerich Kálmán
Lyrics by P.G. Wodehouse
The Riviera Girl 1917

There's a Big Job Waiting for You
Music and lyrics by Matt Dubey and Dean Fuller
Smith (OB) 1973

There's a Boat Dat's Leavin' Soon for New York
Music by George Gershwin
Lyrics by Ira Gershwin
Porgy and Bess 1935

The title and idea came from lines in the play *Porgy*
by Dorothy and Dubose Heyward on which *Porgy
and Bess* is based. In the play Sportin' Life says to
Bess, "Dere'a a boat to New York tomorra . . .
and I'm goin' . . . "

There's a Boy in Harlem
Music by Richard Rodgers
Lyrics by Lorenz Hart
Fools for Scandal (1938) F

There's a Brand New Beat in Heaven
Music by Charles Strouse
Lyrics by Lee Adams
Bring Back Birdie 1981

There's a Brand New Hero
Music by Louis A. Hirsch
Lyrics by Otto Harbach
Going Up 1917

There's a Broadway up in Heaven
Music by Gerald Dolin
Lyrics by Edward J. Lambert
Smile at Me 1935

There's a Building Going Up
Music by Sammy Fain
Lyrics by Paul Francis Webster and Ray Golden
Alive and Kicking 1950

There's a Chill in the Air
Music by Frank D'Armond
Lyrics by Will Morrissey
Saluta 1934

There's a Circus in Town
Music and lyrics by Lionel Bart
La Strada 1969

There's a Coach Comin' In
Music by Frederick Loewe
Lyrics by Alan Jay Lerner
Paint Your Wagon 1951

There's a Comin' Together
Music by George Fischoff
Lyrics by Carole Bayer
Georgy 1970

There's a Girl
Music and lyrics by Rick Besoyan
Babes in the Wood (OB) 1964

There's a Great Day Coming, Manana
Music by Burton Lane
Lyrics by E.Y. Harburg
Hold On to Your Hats 1940

There's a Happy Land in the Sky
Music and lyrics by Cole Porter
Something for the Boys 1943

There's a Hill Beyond a Hill
Music by Jerome Kern
Lyrics by Oscar Hammerstein II
Music in the Air 1932

There's a Hollywood That's Good
Music and lyrics by Cole Porter
Silk Stockings 1955

Dropped from production

**There's a Lot of Things You Can Do With Two
(But Not With Three)**
Music by Sidney Lippman
Lyrics by Sylvia Dee
Barefoot Boy With Cheek 1947

There's a Man in My Life
Music by Thomas (Fats) Waller
Lyrics by George Marion, Jr.
Early to Bed 1943

There's a Muddle
Music by Robert Hood Bowers
Lyrics by Francis DeWitt
Oh, Ernest! 1927

There's a New Deal on the Way
Music by Jerry Livingston
Lyrics by Leonard Adelson
Molly 1973

There's a Rainbow on the Way
Music by J. Fred Coots
Lyrics by Arthur Swanstrom and Benny Davis
Sons o' Guns 1929

There's a Riot in Havana
Music by Sigmund Romberg
Lyrics by Oscar Hammerstein II
The Night Is Young (1935) F

There's a Small Hotel
Music by Richard Rodgers
Lyrics by Lorenz Hart
On Your Toes 1936

First written as "I Love You Today" for *Jumbo.* ("I
Love you today/More than yesterday")

There's a Sunbeam for Every Drop of Rain
Music by Monte Carlo and Alma Sanders
Lyrics by Howard Johnson
Tangerine 1921

There's a War Going On
Music by Michael Dansicker
Lyrics by Sarah Schlesinger
On The Swing Shift (OB) 1983

There's Always a Woman
Music and lyrics by Stephen Sondheim
Anyone Can Whistle 1964

Dropped from production

There's Always One You Can't Forget
Music by Charles Strouse
Lyrics by Alan Jay Lerner
Dance a Little Closer 1983

**There's Always Something Fishy
About the French**
Music and lyrics by Noël Coward
Conversation Piece 1934

There's Art in My Revenge
Music by Scott Killian and Kim D. Sherman
Lyrics by Kenneth Robins, Scott Killian
and Kim D. Sherman
Lenny and the Heartbreakers (OB) 1983

There's Going to Be a Wedding
Music by Nancy Ford
Lyrics by Gretchen Cryer
Now Is the Time for All Good Men (OB) 1967

There's Gold on the Trees
Music by Jerry Livingston
Lyrics by Leonard Adelson
Molly 1973

There's Got to Be Love
Music and lyrics by Walter Cool
Mackey of Appalachia (OB) 1965

There's Gotta Be a Villain
Music and lyrics by Robert Larimer
King of the Whole Damn World (OB) 1962

There's Gotta Be a Wedding
Music by Jimmy Van Heusen
Lyrics by Eddie De Lange
Swingin' the Dream 1939

There's Gotta Be Something Better Than This
Music by Cy Coleman
Lyrics by Dorothy Fields
Sweet Charity 1966

There's History to Be Made
Music by George Lessner
Lyrics by Miriam Battista and Russell Maloney
Sleepy Hollow 1948

There's Life in the Old Folks Yet
Music and lyrics by Rick Besoyan
The Student Gypsy (OB) 1963

There's Life in the Old Girl Yet
Music and lyrics by Noël Coward
Charlot's Revue 1924

There's Love in the Heart I Hold
Music by Emile Berté and Maury Rubens
Lyrics by J. Keirn Brennan
Music in May 1929

There's More to the Kiss than the X-X-X
Music by George Gershwin
Lyrics by Irving Caesar
La, La, Lucille 1919

Also in *Good Morning, Judge* (1919)

There's Music in a Kiss
Music and lyrics by Al Sherman, Al Lewis
and Abner Silver
Earl Carroll's Sketch Book (1935)

There's Music in You
Music by Richard Rodgers
Lyrics by Oscar Hammerstein II
Main Street to Broadway (1953) F

There's Never Been Anything Like Us
Music by Charles Strouse
Lyrics by Alan Jay Lerner
Dance a Little Closer 1983

There's No Better Use for Time Than Kissing
Music by Jerome Kern
Lyrics by Herbert Reynolds
Rock-a-Bye Baby 1918

There's No Business Like Show Business
Music and lyrics by Irving Berlin
Annie Get Your Gun 1946

This was the song (now the unofficial anthem of
show business) that persuaded Ethel Merman, as
Annie Oakley, to join Buffalo Bill's Wild West Show.
Getting Sitting Bull to invest in the show hadn't
been as easy, although he finally agreed. His earlier
reaction had been: "Sitting Bull live by three rules—
no eat red meat, no get feet wet, no put money in
show business."

There's No Getting Away From You
Music by Jimmy McHugh
Lyrics by Harold Adamson
As the Girls Go 1948

There's No Holding Me
Music by Arthur Schwartz
Lyrics by Ira Gershwin
Park Avenue 1946

There's No Man Like a Snowman
Music by Victor Young
Lyrics by Edward Heyman
Pardon Our French 1950

There's No Other Solution
Music and lyrics by Gene Curty, Nitra Scharfman
and Chuck Strand
The Lieutenant 1975

There's No Place as Grand as Bandana Land
Music and lyrics by Noble Sissle and Eubie Blake
The Chocolate Dandies 1924

There's No Place Like the Country
Music by Arthur Jones
Lyrics by Gen Genovese
Buttrio Square 1952

There's No Reason in the World
Music and lyrics by Jerry Herman
Milk and Honey 1961

There's No School Like Our School
Music and lyrics by Skip Redwine and Larry Frank
Frank Merriwell, or Honor Challenged 1971

There's Nothin' So Bad for a Woman
Music by Richard Rodgers
Lyrics by Oscar Hammerstein II
Carousel 1945

There's Nothing Like a Model T
Music by Jule Styne
Lyrics by Sammy Cahn
High Button Shoes 1947

There's Nothing Like It
Music by Abraham Ellstein
Lyrics by Walter Bullock
Great to Be Alive 1950

There's Nothing Like Marriage for People
Music by Arthur Schwartz
Lyrics by Ira Gershwin
Park Avenue 1946

There's Nothing Like Swimming
Music and lyrics by Cole Porter
Jubilee 1935

Dropped from production

There's Nothing Like Travel
Music by Jimmy Van Heusen
Lyrics by Johnny Burke
Nellie Bly 1946

There's Nothing New in Old New York
Music by Harry Akst
Lyrics by Benny Davis
Artists and Models (1927)

There's Nothing New Under the Sun
Music by Vivian Ellis
Lyrics by Graham John
By the Way 1925

There's Nothing New Under the Sun
Music by Meyer Kupferman
Lyrics by Paul Goodman
Jonah (OB) 1966

There's Nothing Nicer Than People
Music and lyrics by Harold Rome
Wish You Were Here 1952

There's Nothing the Matter With Me
Music by Ray Henderson
Lyrics by Lew Brown
Hot-Cha! 1932

There's Nothing Wrong With a Kiss
Music by Oscar Levant
Lyrics by Irving Caesar and Graham John
Ripples 1930

There's Nothing Wrong With Our Values
Music and lyrics by Billy Barnes
The Billy Barnes People 1961

There's Nowhere to Go but Up
Music by Kurt Weill
Lyrics by Maxwell Anderson
Knickerbocker Holiday 1938

There's Only One Thing to Do
Music by Rudolf Friml
Lyrics by Bide Dudley and Otto Harbach
The Little Whopper 1919

There's Room Enough for Us
Music by Gene de Paul
Lyrics by Johnny Mercer
Li'l Abner 1956

There's Room in My House
Music by John Kander
Lyrics by James Goldman, John Kander
and William Goldman
A Family Affair 1962

There's So Much More
Music by Richard Rodgers
Lyrics by Lorenz Hart
America's Sweetheart 1931

There's Something About a Horse
Music and lyrics by Jay Livingston and Ray Evans
Let It Ride 1961

There's Something About Me They Like
Music by Vincent Youmans
Lyrics by Arthur Francis and Fred Jackson
Two Little Girls in Blue 1921

There's Something About You
Music by Emmerich Kálmán
Lyrics by Harry B. Smith
The Circus Princess 1927

There's Something About You
Music by Cyril Ornadel
Lyrics by Leslie Bricusse
Pickwick 1965

There's Something About You
Music by Jim Wise
Lyrics by George Haimsohn and Robin Miller
Dames at Sea (OB) 1968

There's Something Spanish in Your Eyes
Music and lyrics by Cliff Friend and George White
George White's Scandals (1929)

There's the Moon
Music by Richard Hill and John Hawkins
Lyrics by Nevill Coghill
Canterbury Tales 1969

There's "Yes" in the Air
Music by Thomas (Fats) Waller
Lyrics by George Marion, Jr.
Early to Bed 1943

Thermodynamic Duo
Music by Donald Swann
Lyrics by Michael Flanders
At the Drop of Another Hat 1966

These Are Worth Fighting For
Music by Jack Holmes
Lyrics by Bill Conklin and Bob Miller
O Say Can You See! (OB) 1962

These Charming People
Music by George Gershwin
Lyrics by Ira Gershwin
Tip-Toes 1925

The title and lyric are a spoof of a highly
sophisticated Michael Arlen comedy that was
playing on Broadway at the time.

These Four Walls
Music by Stanley Lebowsky
Lyrics by Fred Tobias
Gantry 1970

These Southern States That I Love
Music and lyrics by Bland Simpson and Jim Wann
Diamond Studs (OB) 1975

These Things I Know Are True
Music and lyrics by Jennifer Konecky
Wet Paint (OB) 1965

These Tropics
Music by Sigmund Romberg
Lyrics by Oscar Hammerstein II
East Wind 1931

These Were the Faces
Music and lyrics by Elizabeth Swados
Dispatches (OB) 1979

They
Music by Bert Keyes and Bob Larimer
Lyrics by Bob Larimer
But Never Jam Today 1979

They Ain't Done Right by Our Nell
Music and lyrics by Cole Porter
Panama Hattie 1940

They All Fall in Love
Music and lyrics by Cole Porter
The Battle of Paris (1929) F

They All Follow Me
Music by Gustave Kerker
Lyrics by Hugh Morton
The Belle of New York 1897

They All Laughed
Music by George Gershwin
Lyrics by Ira Gershwin
Shall We Dance (1937) F

They All Look Good When They're Far Away
Music by Victor Herbert
Lyrics by Harry B. Smith
The Enchantress 1911

They All Love Me
Music by William Heagney
Lyrics by William Heagney and Tom Connell
There You Are 1932

They Always Follow Me Around
Music and lyrics by Irving Berlin
Watch Your Step 1914

They Call It Dancing
Music and lyrics by Irving Berlin
Music Box Revue (1st edition) 1921

They Call Me the Virgin Mary
Music and lyrics by Al Carmines
Joan (OB) 1972

They Call the Wind Maria
Music by Frederick Loewe
Lyrics by Alan Jay Lerner
Paint Your Wagon 1951

They Can't Prohibit Love
Music by Mel Marvin
Lyrics by Christopher Durang
A History of the American Film 1978

They Can't Take That Away From Me
Music by George Gershwin
Lyrics by Ira Gershwin
Shall We Dance (1937) F

They Couldn't Compare to You
Music and lyrics by Cole Porter
Out of This World 1950

They Didn't Believe Me
Music by Jerome Kern
Lyrics by Herbert Reynolds
The Girl From Utah 1914

They Don't Make 'Em Like That Anymore
Music by Elmer Bernstein
Lyrics by Carolyn Leigh
How Now, Dow Jones 1967

They Don't Make 'Em That Way Any More
Music by Lewis E. Gensler and Milton Schwarzwald
Lyrics by Ira Gershwin
Be Yourself 1924

They Fall in Love
Music and lyrics by George M. Cohan
Billie 1928

They Just Got Married
Music and lyrics by Randy Newman
Maybe I'm Doing It Wrong (2nd edition)
(OB) 1982

They Keep Comin'
Music and lyrics by Micki Grant
Don't Bother Me, I Can't Cope (OB) 1972

They Learn About Women From Me
Music by Harold Arlen
Lyrics by Jack Yellen
You Said It 1931

They Like Ike
Music and lyrics by Irving Berlin
Call Me Madam 1950

Irving Berlin, who had already cornered the market for holiday songs ("Easter Parade" and "White Christmas"), and had begun to invade George M. Cohan territory with a patriotic song ("God Bless America"), now had a political campaign song. With a small change it was widely sung as "I Like Ike" during the Eisenhower campaign of 1952.

They Love Me
Music and lyrics by Irving Berlin
Mr. President 1962

They Never Hear What I Say
Music by Henry Krieger
Lyrics by Robert Lorick
The Tap Dance Kid 1983

They Never Proved a Thing
Music and lyrics by Bill and Patti Jacob
Jimmy 1969

They Pass By Singing
Music by George Gershwin
Lyrics by DuBose Heyward
Porgy and Bess 1935

They Say
Music by Lehman Engel
Lyrics by Agnes Morgan
A Hero Is Born 1937

They Say
Music by Jerry Bock
Lyrics by Sheldon Harnick
The Rothschilds 1970

They Say It's Wonderful
Music and lyrics by Irving Berlin
Annie Get Your Gun 1946

They Still Look Good
Music by Con Conrad
Lyrics by William B. Friedlander
Mercenary Mary 1925

They Talk a Different Language
Music by Robert Emmett Dolan
Lyrics by Johnny Mercer
Texas, Li'l Darlin' 1949

They Were You
Music by Harvey Schmidt
Lyrics by Tom Jones
The Fantasticks (OB) 1960

They Won't Know Me
Music and lyrics by Harold Rome
Wish You Were Here 1952

They're All My Boys
Music and lyrics by George M. Cohan
Little Nellie Kelly 1922

They're All My Friends
Music and lyrics by George M. Cohan
Little Johnny Jones 1904

They're Blaming the Charleston
Music and lyrics by Irving Berlin
The Cocoanuts 1925

They're Either Too Young or Too Old
Music by Arthur Schwartz
Lyrics by Frank Loesser
Thank Your Lucky Stars (1943) F

They're Hot Now up in Iceland
Music and lyrics by Vincent Valentini
Parisiana 1928

They're Off
Music and lyrics by Alexander Hill
Hummin' Sam 1933

They're Playing Our Song
Music by Marvin Hamlisch
Lyrics by Carole Bayer Sager
They're Playing Our Song 1979

They've Got a Lot to Learn
Music and lyrics by Steve Allen
Sophie 1963

Thief in the Night
Music by Arthur Schwartz
Lyrics by Howard Dietz
At Home Abroad 1935

Thimbleful
Music and lyrics by William Roy
Maggie 1953

Thine Alone
Music by Victor Herbert
Lyrics by Henry Blossom
Eileen 1917

Things
Music by Harold Arlen
Lyrics by Ira Gershwin and E.Y. Harburg
Life Begins at 8:40 1934

Things Ain't as Nice
Music and lyrics by Walter Cool
Mackey of Appalachia (OB) 1965

Things Are Going Well Today
Music by Arthur Siegel
Lyrics by June Carroll
Shoestring Revue (1955) (OB)

Things Are Gonna Hum This Summer
Music by Walter Kent
Lyrics by Kim Gannon
Seventeen 1951

Things Are Looking Up
Music by George Gershwin
Lyrics by Ira Gershwin
A Damsel in Distress (1937) F

Things I Didn't Know I Loved
Music and lyrics by Elizabeth Swados
Nightclub Cantata (OB) 1977

Things I Learned in High School
Music and lyrics by Craig Carnelia
Is There Life After High School? 1982

The Things I Want
Music by Jerome Kern
Lyrics by Oscar Hammerstein II
High, Wide and Handsome (1937) F

The Things That Lovers Say
Music by George Lessner
Lyrics by Miriam Battista and Russell Maloney
Sleepy Hollow 1948

Things That They Must Not Do
Music by Rudolf Friml
Lyrics by Otto Harbach and Edward Clark
You're In Love 1917

The Things That Were Made for Love
Music by Peter de Rose
Lyrics by Charles Tobias and Irving Kahal
Pleasure Bound 1929

Things to Remember
Music and lyrics by Leslie Bricusse
and Anthony Newley
*The Roar of the Greasepaint—The Smell
of the Crowd* 1965

The Things We Think We Are
Music and lyrics by Ervin Drake
Her First Roman 1968

Things Were Out
Music by Hank Beebe
Lyrics by Bill Heyer
*Tuscaloosa's Calling Me
But I'm Not Going!* (OB) 1975

Think
Music by Leon Pober
Lyrics by Bud Freeman
Beg, Borrow or Steal 1960

Think Beautiful
Music and lyrics by Jack Lawrence
and Stan Freeman
I Had a Ball 1964

Think Big Rich
Music by Claibe Richardson
Lyrics by Kenward Elmslie
The Grass Harp 1971

Think How It's Gonna Be
Music by Charles Strouse
Lyrics by Lee Adams
Applause 1970

Think It Over
Music by Arthur Schwartz
Lyrics by Howard Dietz
Revenge With Music 1934

Think Mink
Music and lyrics by Johnny Brandon
Cindy (OB) 1964

Think of My Reputation
Music by Harry Revel
Lyrics by Mack Gordon
Smiling Faces 1932

Think of Something Else
Music by Jimmy Van Heusen
Lyrics by Sammy Cahn
Walking Happy 1966

Think of the Time I Save
Music and lyrics by Richard Adler and Jerry Ross
The Pajama Game 1954

Think Spring
Music by David Baker
Lyrics by Will Holt
Come Summer 1969

Thinkin'
Music by Richard Rodgers
Lyrics by Oscar Hammerstein II
Pipe Dream 1955

Thinking
Music by Richard Rodgers
Lyrics by Stephen Sondheim
Do I Hear a Waltz? 1965

Thinking of Me
Music and lyrics by Noble Sissle and Eubie Blake
The Chocolate Dandies 1924

Thinking of You
Music by Con Conrad
Lyrics by Gus Kahn
Kitty's Kisses 1926

Thinking of You
Music by Harry Ruby
Lyrics by Bert Kalmar
The Five o'Clock Girl 1927

Thinking Out Loud
Music by Harry Akst
Lyrics by Lew Brown
Calling All Stars 1934

Third Avenue L
Music and lyrics by Michael Brown
The Littlest Revue (OB) 1956

The Third From the End
Music by Charles M. Schwab
Lyrics by Henry Myers
Bare Facts of 1926

Thirteen Collar
Music by Jerome Kern
Lyrics by Schuyler Greene
Very Good Eddie 1915

13 Daughters
Music and lyrics by Eaton Magoon, Jr.
13 Daughters 1961

1348
Music by Edward Earle
Lyrics by Yvonne Tarr
The Decameron (OB) 1961

13 Old Maids
Music and lyrics by Eaton Magoon, Jr.
13 Daughters 1961

The Thirties
Music by Jule Styne
Lyrics by Betty Comden and Adolph Green
Fade Out—Fade In 1964

Thirty-Five Summers Ago
Music by Ray Henderson
Lyrics by Jack Yellen
Ziegfeld Follies (1943)

Thirty Miles From the Banks of the Ohio
Music by Alan Menken
Lyrics by Howard Ashman
God Bless You, Mr. Rosewater (OB) 1979

This Amazing London Town
Music by Jerry Bock
Lyrics by Sheldon Harnick
The Rothschilds 1970

This Can't Be Love
Music by Richard Rodgers
Lyrics by Lorenz Hart
The Boys From Syracuse 1938

This Cornucopian Land
Music by Mitch Leigh
Lyrics by William Alfred and Phyllis Robinson
Cry for Us All 1970

This Could Go On for Years
Music by George Gershwin
Lyrics by Ira Gershwin
Strike Up the Band 1930

This Dream
Music and lyrics by Leslie Bricusse
and Anthony Newley

The Roar of the Greasepaint—The Smell of the Crowd 1965

This Funny World
Music by Richard Rodgers
Lyrics by Lorenz Hart
Betsy 1926

This Goes Up
Music by Richard Rodgers
Lyrics by Lorenz Hart
She's My Baby 1928

This Great Purple Butterfly
Music by John Duffy
Lyrics by Rocco Bufano and John Duffy
Horseman, Pass By (OB) 1969

This Had Better Be Love
Music by Jay Gorney
Lyrics by Jean and Walter Kerr
Touch and Go 1949

This Had Better Come to a Stop
Music and lyrics by William Finn
March of the Falsettos (OB) 1981

This Has Never Been Done Before
Music and lyrics by Jerry Herman
I Feel Wonderful (OB) 1954

This Heat
Music by Paul Klein
Lyrics by Fred Ebb
Morning Sun (OB) 1963

This House
Music by Harvey Schmidt
Lyrics by Tom Jones
I Do! I Do! 1966

This Is a Darned Fine Funeral
Music and lyrics by Charles Gaynor
Show Girl 1961

This Is a Great Country
Music and lyrics by Irving Berlin
Mr. President 1962

This Is a Night Club
Music and lyrics by Clarence Gaskill
Earl Carroll's Vanities (1925)

This Is a Tough Neighborhood
Music by Moose Charlap
Lyrics by Eddie Lawrence
Kelly 1965

This Is a Very Special Day
Music and lyrics by Glory Van Scott
Miss Truth (OB) 1979

This Is All Very New to Me
Music by Albert Hague
Lyrics by Arnold B. Horwitt
Plain and Fancy 1955

This Is as Far as I Go
Music and lyrics by Burton Lane
Laffing Room Only 1944

This Is Different, Dear
Music by Michael H. Cleary
Lyrics by Max and Nathaniel Lief
Hey Nonny Nonny! 1932

This Is How It Feels
Music by Richard Rodgers
Lyrics by Oscar Hammerstein II
South Pacific 1949

This Is Indeed My Lucky Day
Music and lyrics by Kelly Hamilton
Trixie True Teen Detective (OB) 1980

This Is It
Music by Arthur Schwartz
Lyrics by Dorothy Fields
Stars in Your Eyes 1939

This Is It
Music by Ray Henderson
Lyrics by Jack Yellen
Ziegfeld Follies (1943)

This Is My Beloved
Music by Harry Revel
Lyrics by Arnold B. Horwitt
Are You With It? 1945

This Is My Busy Day
Music by John Philip Sousa
Lyrics by Leonard Liebling
The American Maid 1913

This Is My Holiday
Music by Frederick Loewe
Lyrics by Alan Jay Lerner
The Day Before Spring 1945

This Is My House
Music by Robert Kole
Lyrics by Sandi Merle
I Take These Women (OB) 1982

This Is My Kind of Love
Music and lyrics by Robert Wright and George Forrest (based on Rachmaninoff)
Anya 1965

This Is My Night to Howl
Music by Richard Rodgers
Lyrics by Lorenz Hart
A Connecticut Yankee (1943 revival)

This Is My Night to Howl
Music by Robert Emmett Dolan
Lyrics by Johnny Mercer
Foxy 1964

This Is My Song
Music by Gary William Friedman
Lyrics by Will Holt
Taking My Turn (OB) 1983

This Is My Wedding Day
Music by Abel Baer
Lyrics by Sam Lewis and Joe Young
Lady Do 1927

This Is New
Music by Kurt Weill
Lyrics by Ira Gershwin
Lady in the Dark 1941

This Is Not a Song
Music by Vernon Duke
Lyrics by E.Y. Harburg and E. Hartman
Ziegfeld Follies (1934)

This Is Only the Beginning
Music by Harold Arlen
Lyrics by Ted Koehler
Let's Fall in Love (1934) F

This Is Our Private Love Song
Music by Irving Caesar
Lyrics by Sam Lerner
My Dear Public 1943

This Is Quite a Perfect Night
Music by Dean Fuller
Lyrics by Marshall Barer
New Faces of 1956

This Is So Nice
Music by Thomas (Fats) Waller
Lyrics by George Marion, Jr.
Early to Bed 1943

This Is Someone I Could Love
Music and lyrics by Eaton Magoon, Jr.
Heathen 1972

This Is Spring
Music by Jimmy McHugh
Lyrics by Al Dubin
Keep Off the Grass 1940

This Is the Army, Mr. Jones
Music and lyrics by Irving Berlin
This Is the Army 1942

This Is the End of the Story
Music by David Raksin
Lyrics by June Carroll
If the Shoe Fits 1946

This Is the Girl for Me
Music and lyrics by Norman Dean
Autumn's Here (OB) 1966

This Is the Life
Music by Kurt Weill
Lyrics by Alan Jay Lerner
Love Life 1948

This Is the Life
Music by Charles Strouse
Lyrics by Lee Adams
Golden Boy 1964

This Is the Missus
Music by Ray Henderson
Lyrics by B.G. DeSylva and Lew Brown
George White's Scandals (1931)

This Is the Way We Go to School
Music by Helen Miller
Lyrics by Eve Merriam
Inner City 1971

This Is What I Call Love
Music by Harold Karr
Lyrics by Matt Dubey
Happy Hunting 1956

This Is Where I Came In
Music by Vernon Duke
Lyrics by John Latouche
The Lady Comes Across 1942

This Is Where We Met
Music by Robert Mitchell
Lyrics by Elizabeth Perry
Bags (OB) 1982

This Is Winter
Music by Jimmy McHugh
Lyrics by Al Dubin
Keep Off the Grass 1940

This Isn't Heaven
Music and lyrics by Richard Rodgers
State Fair (remake, 1962) F

This Jesus Must Die
Music by Andrew Lloyd Webber
Lyrics by Tim Rice
Jesus Christ Superstar 1971

This Kind of a Girl
Music by Arthur Schwartz
Lyrics by Howard Dietz
The Gay Life 1961

This Little Yankee
Music by Mary Rodgers
Lyrics by Martin Charnin
Hot Spot 1963

This Merry Christmas
Music by Morgan Lewis
Lyrics by Nancy Hamilton
Two for the Show 1940

This Much I Know
Music by Harold Karr
Lyrics by Matt Dubey
Happy Hunting 1956

This Nearly Was Mine
Music by Richard Rodgers
Lyrics by Oscar Hammerstein II
South Pacific 1949

This Old Ship
Music and lyrics by Voices, Inc.
The Believers (OB) 1968

This One Day
Music by Claibe Richardson
Lyrics by Kenward Elmslie
The Grass Harp 1971

This Particular Party
Music by George Gershwin
Lyrics by Ira Gershwin
Treasure Girl 1928

Dropped from production

This Plum Is Too Ripe
Music by Harvey Schmidt
Lyrics by Tom Jones
The Fantasticks (OB) 1960

This Really Isn't Me
Music by Glenn Paxton
Lyrics by Robert Goldman and George Weiss
First Impressions 1959

This Same Heart
Music by Rudolf Friml
Lyrics by Johnny Burke
The Vagabond King (film version, 1956)

This State of Affairs
Music and lyrics by Rick Besoyan
Babes in the Wood (OB) 1964

This Time
Music and lyrics by Irving Berlin
This Is the Army 1942

This Time
Music and lyrics by Stan Freeman
and Franklin Underwood
Lovely Ladies, Kind Gentlemen 1970

This Time It's Love
Music by Victor Herbert
Lyrics by B.G. DeSylva
Orange Blossoms 1922

This Time It's True Love
Music and lyrics by Noël Coward
The Girl Who Came to Supper 1963

This Time of the Year
Music by Burton Lane
Lyrics by E.Y. Harburg
Finian's Rainbow 1947

This Time the Dream's on Me
Music by Harold Arlen
Lyrics by Johnny Mercer
Blues in the Night (1941) F

This Tuxedo Is Mine!
Music by David Baker
Lyrics by David Craig
Phoenix '55 (OB)

This War Gets Old
Music and lyrics by Elizabeth Swados
Dispatches (OB) 1979

This Was a Real Nice Clambake
Music by Richard Rodgers
Lyrics by Oscar Hammerstein II
Carousel 1945

This Was Just Another Day
Music by Walter Kent
Lyrics by Kim Gannon
Seventeen 1951

This Week Americans
Music by Richard Rodgers
Lyrics by Stephen Sondheim
Do I Hear a Waltz? 1965

This Woman
Music by Baldwin Bergersen
Lyrics by William Archibald
Carib Song 1945

This World
Music by Gary William Friedman
Lyrics by Will Holt
The Me Nobody Knows (OB) 1970

This World
Music by Leonard Bernstein
Lyrics by Stephen Sondheim
Candide (Added to 1973 revival)

This Year's Kisses
Music and lyrics by Irving Berlin
On the Avenue (1937) F

Thistledown
Music by Vincent Youmans and Herbert Stothart
Lyrics by Oscar Hammerstein II
and William Cary Duncan
Mary Jane McKane 1923

Thither, Thother
Music by Michael J. Lewis
Lyrics by Anthony Burgess
Cyrano 1973

Those ABC's
Music by Joe Ercole
Lyrics by Bruce Kluger
Ka-Boom (OB) 1980

Those Canaan Days
Music by Andrew Lloyd Webber
Lyrics by Tim Rice
Joseph and the Amazing Technicolor Dreamcoat 1982

Those Eyes
Music by George Gershwin
Lyrics by Ira Gershwin
Funny Face 1927

Dropped from production

Those Eyes So Tender
Music by Jean Gilbert
Lyrics by Harry Graham
Katja 1926

Those Magic Changes
Music and lyrics by Jim Jacobs and Warren Casey
Grease 1972

Those Mammy Singers
Music and lyrics by Gene Lockhart
Bunk of 1926

Those Sheik-of-Araby Blues
Music and lyrics by Buster Davis
Doctor Jazz 1975

Those Were the Days
Music and lyrics by Will Holt
That 5 A.M. Jazz (OB) 1964

Those Were the Good Old Days
Music and lyrics by Richard Adler and Jerry Ross
Damn Yankees 1955

Those Who Speak
Music and lyrics by John Driver
Ride the Winds 1974

Thou, Julia, Thou Has Metamorphosed Me
Music by Galt MacDermot
Lyrics by John Guare
Two Gentlemen of Verona 1971

Also performed in show as "Thou, Proteus, Thou Has Metamorphosed Me."

Thou Shalt Not Be Afraid
Music and lyrics by Elizabeth Swados
Dispatches (OB) 1979

Thou Swell
Music by Richard Rodgers
Lyrics by Lorenz Hart
A Connecticut Yankee 1927

Though I'm a Little Angel
Music and lyrics by John Phillips
Man on the Moon 1975

Though Tongues May Wag
Music by Frederick Loewe
Lyrics by Earle Crooker
Great Lady 1938

The Thought of You
Music and lyrics by Harold Rome
Fanny 1954

Thoughtless
Music by Jerry Livingston
Lyrics by Mack David
Bright Lights of 1944

Thoughts Will Come to Me
Music by Sigmund Romberg
Lyrics by Dorothy Donnelly
The Student Prince 1924

A Thousand and One Arabian Nights
Music by Sigmund Romberg
Lyrics by Harold Atteridge
Sinbad (1918)

Thousand Islands Song
Music by Carl Sigman
Lyrics by Bob Hilliard
Angel in the Wings 1947

Thousand, Thousand
Music by Coleridge-Taylor Perkinson
Lyrics by Errol Hill
Man Better Man (OB) 1969

A Thousand Times
Music by Shep Camp
Lyrics by Frank DuPree and Harry B. Smith
Half a Widow 1927

Thousands of Miles
Music by Kurt Weill
Lyrics by Maxwell Anderson
Lost in the Stars 1949

Thousands of Trumpets
Music and lyrics by Craig Carnelia
Is There Life After High School? 1982

The Three B's
Music by Richard Rodgers
Lyrics by Lorenz Hart
On Your Toes 1936

The Three B's
Music and lyrics by Hugh Martin and Ralph Blane
Best Foot Forward 1941

The Three Bears
Music and lyrics by Herbert Stothart, Bert Kalmar and Harry Ruby
Good Boy 1928

Three Boxes of Longs, Please
Music and lyrics by Melvin Van Peebles
Ain't Supposed to Die a Natural Death 1971

Three Cheers for the Red, White and Blue
Music and lyrics by Irving Berlin
Music Box Revue (2nd edition) 1922

Three Cheers for the Union!
Music by George Gershwin
Lyrics by Ira Gershwin
Strike Up the Band 1930

Three Coins in the Fountain
Music by Jule Styne
Lyrics by Sammy Cahn
Three Coins in the Fountain (1954) F

Academy Award winner

Three Girls in a Boat
Music by Frederick Loewe
Lyrics by Alan Jay Lerner
What's Up? 1943

Three Is a Bore
Music by Victor Jacobi
Lyrics by William LeBaron
Apple Blossoms 1919

Three Letters
Music by Jerry Bock
Lyrics by Sheldon Harnick
She Loves Me 1963

Three Little Columnists
Music by Michael H. Cleary
Lyrics by Max and Nathaniel Lief
Hey Nonny Nonny! 1932

Three Little Debutantes
Music and lyrics by Noël Coward
Set to Music 1939

Three Little Maids
Music by Sigmund Romberg
Lyrics by Dorothy Donnelly
Blossom Time 1921

Based on Schubert's *Rosamunde* ballet

Three Little Maids
Music by Max Ewing
Lyrics by Agnes Morgan
The Grand Street Follies (1927) (OB)

Three Little Maids
Music by Jimmy McHugh
Lyrics by Al Dubin
The Streets of Paris 1939

Three Little Maids From School
Music by Jimmy McHugh
Lyrics by Dorothy Fields
Hello Daddy 1928

Three Little Queens of the Silver Screen
Music and lyrics by Charles Gaynor
Lend an Ear 1948

Three Little Words
Music by Bert Kalmar
Lyrics by Harry Ruby
Check and Double Check (1930) F

Three Loves
Music and lyrics by Robert Wright and George Forrest
Song of Norway 1944

Based on Grieg's *Albumblatt* op. 12, no. 7 and *Poème Erotique*

Three Loves
Music by Charles Strouse
Lyrics by Mike Stewart
Shoestring Revue (1955) (OB)

Three Men on a Date
Music and lyrics by Hugh Martin and Ralph Blane
Best Foot Forward 1941

Three Menu Songs
Music by Stanley Silverman
Lyrics by Tom Hendry
Doctor Selavy's Magic Theatre (OB) 1972

The Three Musketeers
Music by Richard Rodgers
Lyrics by Lorenz Hart
The Garrick Gaieties (1st edition) 1925

Three o'Clock in the Morning
Music and lyrics by Dorothy Terris
and Julian Robeldo
Greenwich Village Follies (1921)

Three Old Ladies From Hades
Music by Mischa and Wesley Portnoff
Lyrics by Donagh MacDonagh
Happy as Larry 1950

Three Paradises
Music and lyrics by Jay Livingston and Ray Evans
Oh Captain! 1958

Three Quarter Time
Music by George Gershwin
Lyrics by Ira Gershwin
Pardon My English 1933

Three Questions
Music by David Raksin
Lyrics by June Carroll
If the Shoe Fits 1946

The Three R's
Music and lyrics by Henry Russell and Morry Olsen
Orchids Preferred 1937

The Three Riddles
Music by Ernest Gold
Lyrics by Erich Segal
I'm Solomon 1968

Three Rousing Cheers
Music by Vernon Duke
Lyrics by John Latouche
The Lady Comes Across 1942

Three Ships
Music by John Morris
Lyrics by Gerald Freedman
A Time for Singing 1966

The Three Sisters Who Are Not Sisters
Music by Ann Sternberg
Lyrics by Gertrude Stein
Gertrude Stein's First Reader (OB) 1969

Three Stones to Stand On
Music by Giuseppe Verdi
(adapted by Hans Spialek)
Lyrics by Charles Friedman
My Darlin' Aïda 1952

Three Times a Day
Music by George Gershwin
Lyrics by B.G. DeSylva and Ira Gershwin
Tell Me More 1925

Three Trees (recitation with accompaniment)
Music by Heinrich Reinhardt
Lyrics by Robert B. Smith
The Spring Maid 1910

Three White Feathers
Music and lyrics by Noël Coward
Set to Music 1939

Three Wishes for Christmas
Music by Jule Styne
Lyrics by Stephen Sondheim
Gypsy 1959

Dropped from production

Three's a Crowd
Music by Franz Steininger (adapted from
Tchaikovsky)
Lyrics by Forman Brown
Music in My Heart 1947

The Thrill Is Gone
Music by Ray Henderson
Lyrics by B.G. DeSylva and Lew Brown
George White's Scandals (1931)

Thrill Me
Music by Lewis E. Gensler
Lyrics by E.Y. Harburg
Ballyhoo 1932

The Thrill of a Kiss
Music by Jean Gilbert
Lyrics by Harry B. Smith
The Red Robe 1928

The Thrill of First Love
Music and lyrics by William Finn
March of the Falsettos (OB) 1981

Throttle Throttlebottom
Music by George Gershwin
Lyrics by Ira Gershwin
Let 'Em Eat Cake 1933

Through a Thousand Dreams
Music by Arthur Schwartz
Lyrics by Leo Robin
The Time, the Place and the Girl (1946) F

Through the Bamboo
Music by A. Baldwin Sloane
Lyrics by Harry Cort and George E. Stoddard
China Rose 1925

Through the Night
Music by Frank Grey
Lyrics by Earle Crooker and McElbert Moore
Happy 1927

Through the Years
Music by Vincent Youmans
Lyrics by Edward Heyman
Through the Years 1932

The composer's own favorite of all his songs.

Through Thick and Thin
Music and lyrics by Cole Porter
Something to Shout About (1943) F

Throw a Petal
Music and lyrics by Eaton Magoon, Jr.
13 Daughters 1961

Throw Her in High!
Music by George Gershwin
Lyrics by B.G. DeSylva and E. Ray Goetz
George White's Scandals (1923)

Throw It Out the Window
Music by Louis Alter
Lyrics by Harry Ruskin and Leighton K. Brill
Ballyhoo 1930

Throw Me a Kiss
Music by Louis A. Hirsch
Lyrics by Gene Buck and Dave Stamper
Ziegfeld Follies of 1922

Throw Me a Rose
Music by Emmerich Kálmán
Lyrics by P.G. Wodehouse and M.E. Rourke
Miss Springtime 1916

Throw the Anchor Away
Music by Arthur Schwartz
Lyrics by Dorothy Fields
By the Beautiful Sea 1954

Throwing a Party
Music by Henry Sullivan
Lyrics by Edward Eliscu
A Little Racketeer 1932

Thumbelina
Music and lyrics by Frank Loesser
Hans Christian Andersen (1952) F

Tickets Please
Music by Clay Warnick
Lyrics by Mel Tolkin and Lucille Kallen
Tickets Please 1950

Tickets' Song
Music by Ted Simons
Lyrics by Elinor Guggenheimer
Potholes (OB) 1979

Ticketyboo
Music and lyrics by Ann Ronell
Count Me In 1942

Tickle Me
Music and lyrics by Randy Newman
Maybe I'm Doing It Wrong (1st edition) (OB) 1981

The Tickle Toe
Music by Louis A. Hirsch
Lyrics by Otto Harbach
Going Up 1917

Tickled Pink
Music by Nacio Herb Brown and Richard Whiting
Lyrics by B.G. DeSylva
Take a Chance 1932

Tickling the Ivories
Music and lyrics by Irving Berlin
Ziegfeld Follies 1927

The Tide Pool
Music by Richard Rodgers
Lyrics by Oscar Hammerstein II
Pipe Dream 1955

Tie a String Around Your Finger
Music by Vincent Youmans
Lyrics by Zelda Sears
Lollipop 1924

Tie-Up
Music by Harry Tierney
Lyrics by Joseph McCarthy
Up She Goes 1922

Tie Your Cares to a Melody
Music by Joseph Meyer
Lyrics by William Moll
Jonica 1930

Tiger Lady
Music and lyrics by Elizabeth Swados
Dispatches (OB) 1979

Tiger, Tiger
Music by Jerry Bock
Lyrics by Sheldon Harnick
The Apple Tree 1966

A Tight-Knit Family
Music and lyrics by William Finn
March of the Falsettos (OB) 1981

Til the Big Fat Moon Falls Down
Music by Moose Charlap
Lyrics by Norman Gimbel
Whoop-Up 1958

Till Good Luck Comes My Way
Music by Jerome Kern
Lyrics by Oscar Hammerstein II
Show Boat 1927

Till I Met You
Music by H. Maurice Jacquet
Lyrics by William Brady and Alonso Price
The Silver Swan 1929

Till My Luck Comes Rolling Along
Music and lyrics by George M. Cohan
Little Nellie Kelly 1922

Till the Clouds Roll By
Music by Jerome Kern
Lyrics by P.G. Wodehouse, Jerome Kern
and Guy Bolton
Oh, Boy! 1917

Till the Real Thing Comes Along
Music by Alberta Nichols
Lyrics by Mann Holiner and Sammy Cahn
Rhapsody in Black 1931

Till Then
Music and lyrics by Sherman Edwards
1776 1969

Till There Was You
Music and lyrics by Meredith Willson
The Music Man 1957

Till Tomorrow
Music by Jerry Bock
Lyrics by Sheldon Harnick
Fiorello! 1959

Till Tomorrow
Music and lyrics by Ronnie Britton
Gift of the Magi (OB) 1975

**Tiller, Foster, Hoffman, Hale
and Albertina Rasch**
Music by Henry Sullivan
Lyrics by Henry Myers
John Murray Anderson's Almanac (1929)

Tillie of Longacre Square
Music by James F. Hanley
Lyrics by Harold Atteridge and Ballard MacDonald
Gay Paree 1925

Time
Music and lyrics by Oscar Brown, Jr.
Joy (OB) 1970

Time
Music by Richard Rodgers
Lyrics by Martin Charnin
I Remember Mama 1979

Time Ain't Very Long
Music and lyrics by Donald Heywood
Africana 1927

Time and a Half for Overtime
Music by Vincent Youmans
Lyrics by Zelda Sears
Lollipop 1924

The Time, and the Place, and the Girl
Music by Victor Herbert
Lyrics by Henry Blossom
Mlle. Modiste 1905

Time and Tide
Music by Vernon Duke
Lyrics by E.Y. Harburg
Walk a Little Faster 1932

Time and Tide
Music by Robert Kessler
Lyrics by Lola Pergament
O Marry Me! (OB) 1961

Time and Time Again
Music by George Gershwin
Lyrics by DuBose Heyward
Porgy and Bess 1935

Time and Time Again
Music by Leo Edwards
Lyrics by Herman Timberg
You'll See Stars 1942

Time and Time Again
Music by David Shire
Lyrics by Richard Maltby, Jr.
The Sap of Life (OB) 1961

Time Brings About a Change
Music and lyrics by Micki Grant
Don't Bother Me, I Can't Cope (OB) 1972

Time-Clock Slaves
Music by Vincent Youmans and Herbert Stothart
Lyrics by Oscar Hammerstein II
and William Cary Duncan
Mary Jane McKane 1923

Time for Jukin'
Music by Walter Kent
Lyrics by Lew Brown and Charles Tobias
Yokel Boy 1939

A Time for Singing
Music by John Morris
Lyrics by Gerald Freedman
A Time for Singing 1966

Time for Tea
Music by Arthur Siegel
Lyrics by June Carroll
New Faces of 1952

Time Goes Faster
Music by Baldwin Bergersen
Lyrics by William Archibald
Rosa (OB) 1978

Time Heals Everything
Music and lyrics by Jerry Herman
Mack and Mabel 1974

The Time Is Now
Music by Mark Bucci
Lyrics by David Rogers
Vintage '60 (OB) 1960

The Time Is Ripe for Loving
Music by Richard Adler
Lyrics by Will Holt
Music Is 1976

Time Is Standing Still
Music by Sigmund Romberg
Lyrics by Oscar Hammerstein II
Sunny River 1941

Time Marches On!
Music by Vernon Duke
Lyrics by Ira Gershwin
Ziegfeld Follies (1936)

The Time of My Life
Music by Julian Slade
Lyrics by Dorothy Reynolds and Julian Slade
Salad Days (OB) 1958

The Time of Your Life
Music by William Provost
Lyrics by Peter K. Smith
Crazy With the Heat 1941

Time, Oh Time
Music by Emmerich Kálmán
Lyrics by C.C.S. Cushing and E.P. Heath
Sari 1914

Time on My Hands
Music by Vincent Youmans
Lyrics by Harold Adamson and Mack Gordon
Smiles 1930

Marilyn Miller hated this song, for whatever reason, and refused to sing it as written. The solution: Ring Lardner wrote an alternate lyric for her with the same tune:
   What can I say
   Is there a way
   I can get gay with you?

Time Remembered
Music and lyrics by Vernon Duke
Time Remembered 1957

Time Stands Still
Music by George Lessner
Lyrics by Miriam Battista and Russell Maloney
Sleepy Hollow 1948

Time Stands Still in Truro
Music by Howard Marren
Lyrics by Enid Futterman
Portrait of Jennie (OB) 1982

Time Step
Music by Paul Klein
Lyrics by Fred Ebb
From A to Z 1960

Time: the Present
Music by Jerome Kern
Lyrics by Ira Gershwin
Cover Girl (1944) F

Dropped from film

Time to Call It Quits
Music by Jeanne Bargy
Lyrics by Jeanne Bargy, Frank Gehrecke
and Herb Corey
Greenwich Village U.S.A. (OB) 1960

Time to Let Go
Music by Ernest Gold
Lyrics by Anne Croswell
I'm Solomon 1968

The Time to Sing
Music by Harry Ruby
Lyrics by Bert Kalmar
High Kickers 1941

Time Warp
Music and lyrics by Richard O'Brien
The Rocky Horror Show 1975

Time Will Be
Music by William Dyer
Lyrics by Don Parks and William Dyer
Jo (OB) 1964

Time Will Tell
Music and lyrics by Noël Coward
The Girl Who Came to Supper 1963

Dropped from production

Times Square
Music by Jerome Kern
Lyrics by Anne Caldwell
The Bunch and Judy 1922

Times Square Dance
Music by Sammy Fain
Lyrics by Jack Yellen
Boys and Girls Together 1940

Timid Frieda
Music by Jacques Brel
English lyrics by Eric Blau and Mort Shuman
*Jacques Brel Is Alive and Well
and Living in Paris* (OB) 1968

Tin Pan Alley
Music by Cy Coleman
Lyrics by Joseph McCarthy, Jr.
John Murray Anderson's Almanac (1953)

Ting-a-Ling-Dearie
Music and lyrics by Rick Besoyan
The Student Gypsy (OB) 1963

Ting-a-Ling, the Bells'll Ring
Music and lyrics by Irving Berlin
The Cocoanuts 1925

Tinkers' Song
Music by Reginald De Koven
Lyrics by Harry B. Smith
Robin Hood 1891

Tinkle! Tinkle!
Music by Milton Ager
Lyrics by Jack Yellen
John Murray Anderson's Almanac (1929)

Tinkle Tune
Music by Adorjan Otvos and Louis Breau
Lyrics by Ballard MacDonald
Battling Buttler 1923

Tiny Room
Music and lyrics by Hugh Martin
Look Ma, I'm Dancin'! 1948

Tiny, the Champion
Music by Coleridge-Taylor Perkinson
Lyrics by Errol Hill
Man Better Man (OB) 1969

Tiny Touch
Music by Paul A. Rubens
Lyrics by Paul A. Rubens and Arthur Wimperis
The Sunshine Girl 1913

Tip Your Hat
Music by Bradford Greene
Lyrics by Marianne Brown Waters
Right This Way 1938

Tippecanoe and Tyler Too
Music and lyrics by Oscar Brand
How to Steal an Election (OB) 1968

Tippy Tippy Toes
Music by Cy Coleman
Lyrics by Carolyn Leigh
Wildcat 1960

Tips
Music and lyrics by Debra Monk
and Cass Morgan
Pump Boys and Dinettes 1982

Tiptoe
Music by Lionel Monckton
Lyrics by Adrian Ross
The Quaker Girl 1911

Tip-Toe Tap-Tap
Music by Irving Actman
Lyrics by Jean Herbert
Earl Carroll's Sketch Book (1929)

Tip-Toes
Music by George Gershwin
Lyrics by Ira Gershwin
Tip-Toes 1925

Tired of the South
Music by Gerald Dolin
Lyrics by Edward J. Lambert
Smile at Me 1935

Tirrallallera
Music by Armando Trovaioli
Lyrics by Pietro Garinei and Sandro Giovannini
(Lyric translation by Edward Eager)
Rugantino 1964

'Tis Love
Music by Sigmund Romberg
Lyrics by Harry B. Smith
The Love Call 1927

Tis of Thee
Music by Alex North
Lyrics by Alfred Hayes
Tis of Thee 1940

Tis Pity, Tis True
Music and lyrics by Cliff Jones
Rockabye Hamlet 1976

'Tis the End, so Farewell!
Music by Rudolf Friml
Lyrics by Otto Harbach
Katinka 1915

Titania's Philosophy
Music and lyrics by Rick Besoyan
Babes in the Wood (OB) 1964

Titina
Music by Leo Daniderff
Lyrics by Bertal-Maubon and E. Ronn
Puzzles of 1925

Tkambuza
Music and lyrics by Harold Rome
The Zulu and the Zayda 1965

T'morra, T'morra
Music by Harold Arlen
Lyrics by E.Y. Harburg
Bloomer Girl 1944

T.N.D.P.W.A.M.
Music and lyrics by Jim Swann
Pump Boys and Dinettes 1982

TNT
Music by Duke Ellington
Lyrics by John Latouche
Beggar's Holiday 1946

To Adjust Is a Must
Music by Ernest G. Schweikert
Lyrics by Frank Reardon
Rumple 1957

To an Isle in the Water
Music by John Duffy
Lyrics by Rocco Bufano and John Duffy
Horseman, Pass By (OB) 1969

To Bath Derry-O
Music by Jacques Urbont
Lyrics by Bruce Geller
All in Love (OB) 1961

To Be a King
Music by Sam Pottle
Lyrics by Tom Whedon
All Kinds of Giants (OB) 1961

To Be Alone With You
Music and lyrics by Jerry Herman
Ben Franklin in Paris 1964

To Be Artistic
Music and lyrics by Bob Merrill
Henry, Sweet Henry 1967

To Be or Not to Be
Music and lyrics by Irving Berlin
As Thousands Cheer 1933

To Be or Not to Be in Love
Music by Philip Charig
Lyrics by Ray Golden, Danny Shapiro
and Milton Pascal
Catch a Star! 1955

To Do a Little Good
Music by Jule Styne
Lyrics by Sammy Cahn
Look to the Lilies 1970

To Each His Dulcinea
Music by Mitch Leigh
Lyrics by Joe Darion
Man of La Mancha 1965

To Feel So Needed
Music by Jim Steinman
Lyrics by Michael Weller and Jim Steinman
More Than You Deserve (OB) 1973

To Follow Every Fancy
Music by Cole Porter
Lyrics by T. Lawrason Riggs and Cole Porter
See America First 1916

To Get Away
Music and lyrics by Cole Porter
Jubilee 1935

To Get Out of This World Alive
Music by Jule Styne
Lyrics by E.Y. Harburg
Darling of the Day 1968

To Have and to Hold
Music by Richard Rodgers
Lyrics by Oscar Hammerstein II
Allegro 1947

To Heaven on the Bronx Express
Music and lyrics by George M. Cohan
The Merry Malones 1927

To Keep My Love Alive
Music by Richard Rodgers
Lyrics by Lorenz Hart
A Connecticut Yankee (1943 revival)

One of six new songs written by Rodgers and Hart
for the revival and the last lyric Hart wrote. He died
five days after the Broadway opening.

To Keep You in Your Seats
Music by Louis A. Hirsch
Lyrics by Otto Harbach
The O'Brien Girl 1921

To Know You Is to Love You
Music by Ray Henderson
Lyrics by B.G. DeSylva and Lew Brown
Hold Everything! 1928

To Life
Music by Jerry Bock
Lyrics by Sheldon Harnick
Fiddler on the Roof 1964

To Live Another Summer, to Pass Another Winter
Music by Dov Seltzer
Lyrics by David Paulsen
To Live Another Summer 1971

To Look Upon My Love
Music and lyrics by Robert Wright
and George Forrest
Kean 1961

To Love Is to Live
Music by Johann Strauss II, adapted by Oscar
Straus
Lyrics by Clare Kummer
Three Waltzes 1937

To Love Is to Live
Music and lyrics by Jack Bussins
and Ellsworth Olin
Be Kind to People Week (OB) 1975

To Love or Not to Love
Music and lyrics by Cole Porter
Rosalie (1937) F

Dropped from film

To Make a Boy a Man
Music by Larry Grossman
Lyrics by Hal Hackady
Goodtime Charley 1975

To My Wife
Music and lyrics by Harold Rome
Fanny 1954

To Paradise We'll Gaily Trip
Music by Edmund Eysler
Lyrics by Herbert Reynolds
The Blue Paradise 1915

To Prove My Love
Music by Maria Grever
Lyrics by Raymond Leveen
Viva O'Brien 1941

To Take a Dip in the Ocean
Music by Kerry Mills
Lyrics by S.M. Lewis
The Fascinating Widow 1911

To the Beat of My Heart
Music by Samuel Pokrass
Lyrics by E.Y. Harburg
Ziegfeld Follies (1934)

To the Dance
Music by Richard Myers
Lyrics by Leo Robin
Hello, Yourself! 1928

To the Ends of the Earth
Music and lyrics by Matt Dubey and Dean Fuller
Smith (OB) 1973

To the Fair
Music by Jerome Kern
Lyrics by Howard Dietz
Dear Sir 1924

To the Garden
Music by Harvey Schmidt
Lyrics by Tom Jones
Celebration 1969

To the Harbormaster
Music and lyrics by Elizabeth Swados
Nightclub Cantata (OB) 1977

To the Inn We're Marching
Music by Sigmund Romberg
Lyrics by Dorothy Donnelly
The Student Prince 1924

To the Land of My Own Romance
Music by Victor Herbert
Lyrics by Harry B. Smith
The Enchantress 1911

To the Top
Music and lyrics by Oscar Brand and Paul Nassau
A Joyful Noise 1966

To Think He Remembered Me
Music by Jerome Kern
Lyrics by Otto Harbach and Oscar Hammerstein II
Sunny 1925

Dropped from production

To This We've Come
Music and lyrics by Gian-Carlo Menotti
The Consul 1950

To Touch the Sky
Music by Peter Link
Lyrics by Michael Cacoyannis
Lysistrata 1972

To War!
Music by Kurt Weill
Lyrics by Maxwell Anderson
Knickerbocker Holiday 1938

To Whom It May Concern
Music by Frederick Loewe
Lyrics by Earle Crooker
Great Lady 1938

To Whom It May Concern Me
Music by Galt MacDermot
Lyrics by John Guare
Two Gentlemen of Verona 1971

To Wit
Music and lyrics by Bob Ost
Everybody's Gettin' Into the Act (OB) 1981

The Toast
Music and lyrics by Hugh Martin
Look Ma, I'm Dancin'! 1948

The Toast of the Boys at the Post
Music by Vernon Duke
Lyrics by John Latouche
Banjo Eyes 1941

Toast of the Town
Music and lyrics by Ann Harris
Sky High (OB) 1979

A Toast to Alpha Cholera
Music by Sidney Lippman
Lyrics by Sylvia Dee
Barefoot Boy With Cheek 1947

A Toast to the Bride
Music and lyrics by Johnny Burke
Donnybrook! 1961

A Toast to Volstead
Music and lyrics by Cole Porter
Fifty Million Frenchmen 1929

A Toast to Woman's Eyes
Music by Sigmund Romberg
Lyrics by Herbert Reynolds
The Blue Paradise 1915

The Tobacco Blues
Music by Mischa and Wesley Portnoff
Lyrics by Donagh MacDonagh
Happy as Larry 1950

Toby
Music and lyrics by Gian-Carlo Menotti
The Medium 1947

Today
Music by Carl Millöcker (revised by Theo Mackeben)
Lyrics by Rowland Leigh
The Dubarry 1932

Today
Music by Rob Fremont
Lyrics by Doris Willens
Piano Bar (OB) 1978

Today at Your House, Tomorrow at Mine
Music and lyrics by Jack Lawrence and Don Walker
Courtin' Time 1951

Today I Am a Glamour Girl
Music by Hoagy Carmichael
Lyrics by Johnny Mercer
Walk With Music 1940

Today I Is So Happy
Music by Baldwin Bergersen
Lyrics by William Archibald
Carib Song 1945

Today I Love Ev'rybody
Music by Harold Arlen
Lyrics by Dorothy Fields
The Farmer Takes a Wife (1953) F

Today I Saw a Rose
Music by Albert Hague
Lyrics by Allen Sherman
The Fig Leaves Are Falling 1969

Today Is a Day for a Band to Play
Music by Milton Schafer
Lyrics by Ira Levin
Drat! The Cat! 1965

Today Is Spring
Music by Jerome Kern
Lyrics by Edgar Allan Woolf
Head Over Heels 1918

Today Is the First Day of the Rest of My Life
Music by David Shire
Lyrics by Richard Maltby, Jr.
Starting Here, Starting Now (OB) 1977

Today Will Be Yesterday Tomorrow
Music by Philip Charig
Lyrics by Dan Shapiro and Milton Pascal
Follow the Girls 1944

Toddlin' Along
Music by George Gershwin
Lyrics by Ira Gershwin
Nine-Fifteen Revue 1930

Toddling the Todalo
Music by A. Baldwin Sloane
Lyrics by E. Ray Goetz
The Hen Pecks 1911

Together
Music by Charles Strouse
Lyrics by Lee Adams
A Broadway Musical 1978

Together
Music by Cy Coleman
Lyrics by Betty Comden and Adolph Green
On the Twentieth Century 1978

Together At Last
Music by George Gershwin
Lyrics by Ira Gershwin
Pardon My English 1933

Dropped from production

Together Forever
Music by Harvey Schmidt
Lyrics by Tom Jones
I Do! I Do! 1966

Together Wherever We Go
Music by Jule Styne
Lyrics by Stephen Sondheim
Gypsy 1959

Together With Music
Music and lyrics by Noël Coward
Together With Music (1955) TV

Togetherness
Music and lyrics by Dickson Hughes
and Everett Sloane
From A to Z 1960

Togetherness
Music and lyrics by Mavor Moore
New Faces of 1962

'Toinette
Music and lyrics by Deed Meyer
'Toinette (OB) 1961

Tokay
Music and lyrics by Noël Coward
Bitter Sweet 1929

Tokyo Blues
Music and lyrics by Irving Berlin
Music Box Revue (4th edition) 1924

Tom, Dick or Harry
Music and lyrics by Cole Porter
Kiss Me, Kate 1948

Tom, Tom
Music by Helen Miller
Lyrics by Eve Merriam
Inner City 1971

Tom Tom Toddle
Music by Louis A. Hirsch
Lyrics by Otto Harbach
Mary 1920

Tommy Atkins
Music by Rudolf Friml
Lyrics by Otto Harbach
The Firefly 1912

Tommy, Tommy
Music by Jerry Bock
Lyrics by Sheldon Harnick
Tenderloin 1960

Tommy, Won't You Teach Me the Tango
Music by Jean Schwartz
Lyrics by Joseph W. Herbert and Harold Atteridge
The Honeymoon Express 1913

Tomorrow
Music by A. Baldwin Sloane
Lyrics by Harry Cort and George E. Stoddard
China Rose 1925

Tomorrow
Music by Con Conrad
Lyrics by William B. Friedlander
Mercenary Mary 1925

Adapted from Chopin's Nocturne No. 12

Tomorrow
Music by Rudolf Friml
Lyrics by Brian Hooker
The Vagabond King 1925

Tomorrow
Music and lyrics by Cole Porter
Leave It to Me 1938

Tomorrow
Music by Alex North
Lyrics by Alfred Hayes
Tis of Thee 1940

Tomorrow
Music by Mitch Leigh
Lyrics by Charles Burr and Forman Brown
Home Sweet Homer 1976

Tomorrow
Music and lyrics by John Raniello
Movie Buff (OB) 1977

Tomorrow
Music by Charles Strouse
Lyrics by Martin Charnin
Annie 1977

Tomorrow Belongs to Me
Music by John Kander
Lyrics by Fred Ebb
Cabaret 1966

Tomorrow I'm Gonna Be Old
Music by Gary Geld
Lyrics by Peter Udell
Angel 1978

Tomorrow Is Here
Music by David Baker
Lyrics by David Craig
Phoenix '55 (OB)

**Tomorrow Is the First Day
of the Rest of My Life**
Music and lyrics by Peter Link
and C.C. Courtney
Salvation (OB) 1969

Tomorrow Is the Time
Music by Arthur Schwartz
Lyrics by Ira Gershwin
Park Avenue 1946

Tomorrow Morning
Music and lyrics by Harold Rome
Destry Rides Again 1959

Tomorrow Morning
Music by John Kander
Lyrics by Fred Ebb
The Happy Time 1968

Tomorrow Mountain
Music by Duke Ellington
Lyrics by John Latouche
Beggar's Holiday 1946

Tomorrow Night
Music by Rob Fremont
Lyrics by Doris Willens
Piano Bar (OB) 1978

Tomorrow Will Be the Same
Music by Lance Mulcahy
Lyrics by Paul Cherry
Park 1970

Tongalango Tap
Music by Jean Gilbert
Lyrics by Harry B. and Robert B. Smith
Modest Suzanne 1912

Tonight
Music by Richard A. Whiting
Lyrics by Oscar Hammerstein II
Free for All 1931

Tonight
Music by George Gershwin
Lyrics by Ira Gershwin
Pardon My English 1933

Later published as one of the *Two Waltzes in C* for two pianos.

Tonight
Music by Leonard Bernstein
Lyrics by Stephen Sondheim
West Side Story 1957

Tonight at Eight
Music by Jerry Bock
Lyrics by Sheldon Harnick
She Loves Me 1963

Tonight at the Mardi Gras
Music and lyrics by Irving Berlin
Louisiana Purchase 1940

Tonight I Love You More
Music and lyrics by Cole Porter
Out of This World 1950

Dropped from production

Tonight Is Opening Night
Music by Nacio Herb Brown and Richard Whiting
Lyrics by B.G. DeSylva
Take a Chance 1932

Tonight May Never Come Again
Music by Sigmund Romberg
Lyrics by Irving Caesar
Melody 1933

Tonight or Never
Music by Joseph Meyer
Lyrics by William Moll
Jonica 1930

Tonight or Never
Music and lyrics by Jack Meskill, Raymond Klages
and Vincent Rose
Earl Carroll's Vanities (1931)

Tonight or Never
Music by Robert Stolz
Lyrics by Rowland Leigh
Night of Love 1941

Tonight You Are in Paree
Music and lyrics by Hugh Martin
Make a Wish 1951

Tonight's the Fight
Music by Joseph Raposo
Lyrics by Erich Segal
Sing Muse! (OB) 1961

Tonight's the Night
Music by Alex Fogarty
Lyrics by June Sillman
New Faces of 1936

Tonight's the Night
Music and lyrics by Johnny Brandon
Cindy (OB) 1964

Tonight's the Night
Music and lyrics by Tom Savage
Musical Chairs 1980

Tonsils
Music by Jerome Kern
Lyrics by Otto Harbach and Oscar Hammerstein II
Sunny 1925

Dropped from production

Tony From America
Music and lyrics by Lionel Monckton
The Quaker Girl 1911

Tony, Tony, Tony
Music by Sigmund Romberg
Lyrics by Harry B. Smith
The Love Call 1927

Tony's Thoughts
Music and lyrics by Frank Loesser
The Most Happy Fella 1956

Too Bad
Music by Alfred Nathan
Lyrics by George Oppenheimer
The Manhatters 1927

Too Bad
Music and lyrics by Cole Porter
Silk Stockings 1955

Too Charming
Music by Mark Sandrich, Jr.
Lyrics by Sidney Michaels
Ben Franklin in Paris 1964

Too Close for Comfort
Music and lyrics by Jerry Bock, George Weiss
and Larry Holofcener
Mr. Wonderful 1956

Too Darn Hot
Music and lyrics by Cole Porter
Kiss Me, Kate 1948

Too Good
Music and lyrics by Bob Ost
Everybody's Gettin' Into the Act (OB) 1981

Too Good for the Average Man
Music by Richard Rodgers
Lyrics by Lorenz Hart
On Your Toes 1936

Too Good to Be True
Music by Ray Henderson
Lyrics by B.G. DeSylva and Lew Brown
Hold Everything! 1928

Too Late Now
Music by Burton Lane
Lyrics by Alan Jay Lerner
Royal Wedding (1951) F

Too Little Time for Love
Music by Louis Bellson and Will Irwin
Lyrics by Richard Ney
Portofino 1958

Too Long at the Fair
Music and lyrics by Billy Barnes
The Billy Barnes Revue 1959

Too Many Girls
Music by Richard Rodgers
Lyrics by Lorenz Hart
Too Many Girls 1939

Too Many Mirrors
Music by Gary William Friedman
Lyrics by Will Holt
Platinum 1978

Too Many Mornings
Music and lyrics by Stephen Sondheim
Follies 1971

Too Many People Alone
Music by Harvey Schmidt
Lyrics by Tom Jones
110 in the Shade 1963

Dropped from production

Too Many Questions
Music and lyrics by Paul Nassau
Fallout (OB) 1959

Too Many Rings Around Rosie
Music by Vincent Youmans
Lyrics by Irving Caesar
No, No, Nanette 1925

Too Many Tomorrows
Music by Cy Coleman
Lyrics by Dorothy Fields
Sweet Charity 1966

Too Much Money Blues
Music and lyrics by Julian Neil and Lee Sparks
An Evening With Joan Crawford (OB) 1981

Too Much to Forgive
Music by Don Gohman
Lyrics by Hal Hackady
Ambassador 1972

Too Much Work
Music by Richard Addinsell
Lyrics by Clemence Dane
Come of Age 1934

Too Much World
Music and lyrics by Harry Chapin
The Night That Made America Famous 1975

Too Nice a Day to Go to School
Music by Sidney Lippman
Lyrics by Sylvia Dee
Barefoot Boy With Cheek 1947

Too Old
Music by Ray Haney
Lyrics by Alfred Aiken
We're Civilized? (OB) 1962

Too Soon
Music and lyrics by Harold Rome
I Can Get It for You Wholesale 1962

Too, Too Divine
Music by Vernon Duke
Lyrics by E.Y. Harburg
The Garrick Gaieties (3rd edition) 1930

Too Young to Live
Music by Richard Lewine
Lyrics by Arnold B. Horwitt
The Girls Against the Boys 1959

Toodle-oo
Music by Vincent Youmans and Herbert Stothart
Lyrics by Oscar Hammerstein II
and William Cary Duncan
Mary Jane McKane 1923

Toodle-oo
Music by Albert Von Tilzer
Lyrics by Neville Fleeson
Bye Bye, Bonnie 1927

Toot-Toot!
Music by Jerome Kern
Lyrics by Berton Braley
Toot-Toot! 1918

Tooth and Claw
Music by Duke Ellington
Lyrics by John Latouche
Beggar's Holiday 1946

Top Banana
Music and lyrics by Johnny Mercer
Top Banana 1951

Top Hat, White Tie and Tails
Music and lyrics by Irving Berlin
Top Hat (1935) F

The Top of the Hill
Music by John Kander
Lyrics by Fred Ebb
Zorba 1968

Top of the Morning
Music by Silvio Hein
Lyrics by George V. Hobart
The Yankee Girl 1910

Top of the Train
Music by Robert Waldman
Lyrics by Alfred Uhry
Here's Where I Belong 1968

Topple Down
Music and lyrics by Edward Pola and Eddie Brandt
Woof, Woof 1929

Torch Parade
Music by Ray Henderson
Lyrics by Ted Koehler
Say When 1934

The Torch Singer (What Do You Think My Heart Is Made Of?)
Music by Henry Sullivan
Lyrics by Earle Crooker
Thumbs Up! 1934

The Torch Song
Music by Harry Warren
Lyrics by Mort Dixon and Joe Young
The Laugh Parade 1931

Torch Song
Music and lyrics by Irving Berlin
Face the Music 1932

Torture
Music and lyrics by John Clifton
El Bravo! (OB) 1981

Tosy and Cosh
Music by Burton Lane
Lyrics by Alan Jay Lerner
On a Clear Day You Can See Forever 1965

Totem Tom-Tom
Music by Rudolf Friml and Herbert Stothart;
Lyrics by Oscar Hammerstein II and Otto Harbach
Rose Marie 1924

Touch and Go
Music by Buster Davis
Lyrics by Steven Vinaver
Diversions (OB) 1958

Touch and Go
Music by Elmer Bernstein
Lyrics by Carolyn Leigh
How Now, Dow Jones 1967

The Touch of a Woman's Hand
Music by Louis A. Hirsch
Lyrics by Otto Harbach
Going Up 1917

The Touch of Your Hand
Music by Jerome Kern
Lyrics by Otto Harbach
Roberta 1933

Touched in the Head
Music by Michael Cleary
Lyrics by Arthur Swanstrom
Sea Legs 1937

Touching Your Hand Is Like Touching Your Mind
Music by Nancy Ford
Lyrics by Gretchen Cryer
The Last Sweet Days of Isaac (OB) 1970

Toujours Gai
Music by George Kleinsinger
Lyrics by Joe Darion
Shinbone Alley 1957

The Tour Must Go On
Music and lyrics by Hugh Martin
Make a Wish 1951

Tour of the Town
Music by George Gershwin (posthumous—from manuscript)
Lyrics by Ira Gershwin
The Shocking Miss Pilgrim (1946) F

Dropped from film

Tourist Madrigal
Music by Richard B. Chodosh
Lyrics by Barry Alan Grael
The Streets of New York (OB) 1963

Tower of Babble
Music and lyrics by Stephen Schwartz
Godspell (OB) 1971

Town Hall Tonight
Music by Richard Rodgers
Lyrics by Lorenz Hart
The Girl Friend 1926

The Townsfolks' Lament
Music and lyrics by Al Kasha and Joel Hirschorn
Seven Brides for Seven Brothers 1982

Toyland
Music by Victor Herbert
Lyrics by Glen MacDonough
Babes in Toyland 1903

Toyland
Music and lyrics by Gene P. Bissell
New Faces of 1968

The Toyshop
Music and lyrics by Walter Marks
Broadway Follies 1981

Tra Gog in Dein Whole (I Will Not Tell a Soul)
Music and lyrics by Elizabeth Swados
Runaways 1978

Tra-La-La
Music by George Gershwin
Lyrics by Arthur Francis
For Goodness Sake 1922

Tra La La
Music by Lehman Engel
Lyrics by Agnes Morgan
A Hero Is Born 1937

Tra-la-la-la
Music and lyrics by Elsie Janis and Vincent Scotto
Puzzles of 1925

Tradition
Music by Jerry Bock
Lyrics by Sheldon Harnick
Fiddler on the Roof 1964

Trailing a Shooting Star
Music by Albert Sirmay and Arthur Schwartz
Lyrics by Arthur Swanstrom
Princess Charming 1930

The Train
Music and lyrics by Irving Berlin
Miss Liberty 1949

Train Time
Music by Baldwin Bergersen
Lyrics by June Sillman
Who's Who 1938

Train to Johannesburg
Music by Kurt Weill
Lyrics by Maxwell Anderson
Lost in the Stars 1949

The Train With the Cushioned Seats
Music and lyrics by William Roy
Maggie 1953

Tramp, Tramp, Tramp
Music by Victor Herbert
Lyrics by Rida Johnson Young
Naughty Marietta 1910

Tramping Along
Music by Richard Rodgers
Lyrics by Lorenz Hart
Peggy-Ann 1926

Dropped from production

Trample Your Troubles
Music by Jean Schwartz
Lyrics by Clifford Grey and William Cary Duncan
Sunny Days 1928

Tramps of the Desert
Music by Ford Dabney
Lyrics by Jo Trent
Rang-Tang 1927

A Transparent Crystal Moment
Music by Nancy Ford
Lyrics by Gretchen Cryer
The Last Sweet Days of Isaac (OB) 1970

A Transport of Delight
Music by Donald Swann
Lyrics by Michael Flanders
At the Drop of a Hat 1959

Trapped
Music by Susan Hulsman Bingham
Lyrics by Myrna Lamb
Mod Donna (OB) 1970

Travel
Music by David Shire
Lyrics by Richard Maltby, Jr.
Starting Here, Starting Now (OB) 1977

Travel the Road of Love
Music by Tommy Wolf
Lyrics by Fran Landesman
The Nervous Set 1959

Travel, Travel, Travel
Music by Milton Susskind
Lyrics by Paul Porter and Benjamin Hapgood Burt
Florida Girl 1925

Travel, Travel, Travel
Music by Heitor Villa-Lobos
Lyrics by Robert Wright and George Forrest
Magdalena 1948

Travellin'
Music and lyrics by J.C. Johnson
Change Your Luck 1930

Treasure Island
Music by Jerome Kern
Lyrics by Anne Caldwell
Hitchy-Koo 1920

Treasure Island
Music by George Gershwin
Lyrics by Ira Gershwin
Treasure Girl 1928

Dropped from production

Treasure to Bury/One of Us
Music and lyrics by Bland Simpson and Jim Wann
Hot Grog (OB) 1977

Treat a Woman Like a Drum
Music by Emmerich Kálmán
Lyrics by George Marion, Jr.
Marinka 1945

Treat 'Em Rough
Music by Charles M. Schwab
Lyrics by Henry Myers
Bare Facts of 1926

Treat Me Rough
Music by George Gershwin
Lyrics by Ira Gershwin
Girl Crazy 1930

The Tree
Music by Gary William Friedman
Lyrics by Will Holt
The Me Nobody Knows (OB) 1970

The Tree and the Sun
Music by George Fischoff
Lyrics by Verna Tomasson
The Prince and the Pauper (OB) 1963

A Tree in the Park
Music by Richard Rodgers
Lyrics by Lorenz Hart
Peggy-Ann 1926

Treemonisha in Peril
Music and lyrics by Scott Joplin
Treemonisha 1975

Written in 1909

Treemonisha's Bringing Up
Music and lyrics by Scott Joplin
Treemonisha 1975

Written in 1909

Treemonisha's Return
Music and lyrics by Scott Joplin
Treemonisha 1975

Written in 1909

The Tremont Avenue Cruisewear Fashion Show
Music by Jerry Livingston
Lyrics by Mack David
Molly 1973

Trial Before Pilate
Music by Andrew Lloyd Webber
Lyrics by Tim Rice
Jesus Christ Superstar 1971

The Trial Song
Music by H. Maurice Jacquet
Lyrics by William Brady
The Silver Swan 1929

Trials and Tribulations/I Like You
Music by Gary William Friedman
Lyrics by Will Holt
Platinum 1978

The Triangle
Music by Jerome Kern
Lyrics by Guy Bolton
Very Good Eddie 1915

Triangle
Music by Charles M. Schwab
Lyrics by Henry Myers
The New Yorkers 1927

Tried by the Centre Court
Music by Donald Swann
Lyrics by Michael Flanders
At the Drop of a Hat 1959

Trilogy
Music and lyrics by Bud McCreery
Put It in Writing (OB) 1963

Trina's Song
Music and lyrics by William Finn
March of the Falsettos (OB) 1981

Trinity
Music by Susan Hulsman Bingham
Lyrics by Myrna Lamb
Mod Donna (OB) 1970

Trio
Music by Frederick Loewe
Lyrics by Alan Jay Lerner
Paint Your Wagon 1951

Trip
Music and lyrics by Charles Strouse
Six (OB) 1971

A Trip Doesn't Care at All
Music by Philip Kadison
Lyrics by Thomas Howell
Along Fifth Avenue 1949

A Trip Through My Mind
Music by Bill Weeden
Lyrics by David Finkle
Hurry, Harry 1972

A Trip to Bermuda
Music by Rudolf Friml
Lyrics by Otto Harbach
The Firefly 1912

A Trip to the Library
Music by Jerry Bock
Lyrics by Sheldon Harnick
She Loves Me 1963

Triplets
Music by Arthur Schwartz
Lyrics by Howard Dietz
Between the Devil 1937

Also sung in the London revue *Better Late* (1946)
and later in the film *The Band Wagon* (1953),
performed by Fred Astaire, Jack Buchanan and
Nanette Fabray. The film used the title of the
successful Schwartz and Dietz revue (1931), seven
songs from the revue, and eleven other Schwartz-
Dietz songs including "That's Entertainment," which
they wrote for the film.

Tripping
Music by Kenn Long and Jim Crozier
Lyrics by Kenn Long
Touch (OB) 1970

Tripping the Light Fantastic
Music and lyrics by Harold Rome
Wish You Were Here 1952

Trixie True Teen Detective
Music and lyrics by Kelly Hamilton
Trixie True Teen Detective (OB) 1980

Trixie's on the Case!
Music and lyrics by Kelly Hamilton
Trixie True Teen Detective (OB) 1980

The Trojan Horse
Music by Richard Rodgers
Lyrics by Lorenz Hart
Simple Simon 1930

The Trolley Song
Music and lyrics by Hugh Martin and Ralph Blane
Meet Me in St. Louis (1944) F

Tropic Vamps
Music by Monte Carlo and Alma Sanders
Lyrics by Howard Johnson
Tangerine 1921

Tropical Night
Music by Jerome Kern
Lyrics by Ira Gershwin
Cover Girl (1944) F

Dropped from film

Trottin' to the Fair
Music and lyrics by Ralph Blane
Three Wishes for Jamie 1952

Trouble
Music by Milton Susskind
Lyrics by Paul Porter and Benjamin Hapgood Burt
Florida Girl 1925

Trouble
Music and lyrics by Meredith Willson
The Music Man 1957

Trouble Man
Music by Kurt Weill
Lyrics by Maxwell Anderson
Lost in the Stars 1949

The Trouble With Me
Music and lyrics by Howard Blankman
By Hex (OB) 1956

The Trouble With Women
Music by Kurt Weill
Lyrics by Ogden Nash
One Touch of Venus 1943

Truck Stop
Music and lyrics by Paul Shyre
Ah, Men (OB) 1981

Truckers Ball
Music and lyrics by Donald Heywood
Black Rhythm 1936

Truckin' in My Tails
Music by Ray Henderson
Lyrics by Jack Yellen
George White's Scandals (1936)

The Trucks
Music by Steve Sterner
Lyrics by Peter del Valle
Lovers (OB) 1975

True Blue
Music by Richard Myers
Lyrics by Leo Robin
Hello, Yourself! 1928

True Confession
Music and lyrics by Frederick Silver
Gay Company (OB) 1974

True Hearts
Music by Sigmund Romberg
Lyrics by Arthur Wimperis
Louie the 14th 1925

True Love
Music by Joseph Meyer and James F. Hanley
Lyrics by B.G. DeSylva
Big Boy 1925

True Love
Music and lyrics by Cole Porter
High Society (1956) F

True Love
See I Had Myself a True Love

True Love Will Never Grow Cold
Music by Vincent Youmans and Herbert Stothart
Lyrics by Otto Harbach and Oscar Hammerstein II
Wildflower 1923

Dropped from production

True Romance
Music by George Kleinsinger
Lyrics by Joe Darion
Shinbone Alley 1957

True to Them All
Music by George Gershwin
Lyrics by Ira Gershwin
Rosalie 1928

Dropped from production

The Trumpeter and the Lover
Music by Vincent Youmans
Lyrics by Edward Heyman
Through the Years 1932

Trumpeter, Blow Your Golden Horn
Music by George Gershwin
Lyrics by Ira Gershwin
Of Thee I Sing 1931

Trust Your Destiny to a Star
Music and lyrics by Cole Porter
Aladdin (1958) TV

Truth
Music by John Mundy
Lyrics by Edward Eager
The Liar 1950

Truth
Music by Moose Charlap
Lyrics by Norman Gimbel
The Conquering Hero 1961

The Truth
Music by Cy Coleman
Lyrics by Carolyn Leigh
Little Me 1962

Truth Cannot Be Treason
Music and lyrics by John Phillips
Man on the Moon 1975

Truth Is So Beautiful
Music by Lionel Monckton
Lyrics by Arthur Wimperis
The Arcadians 1910

Try a Trio
Music by Jacques Urbont
Lyrics by David Newburger
Stag Movie (OB) 1971

Try Again
Music by Louis A. Hirsch
Lyrics by P.G. Wodehouse
Oh, My Dear! 1918

Try Again Tomorrow
Music by Richard Rodgers
Lyrics by Lorenz Hart
She's My Baby 1928

Try Dancing
Music by Harry Ruby
Lyrics by Bert Kalmar
Top Speed 1929

Try Her Out at Dances
Music by Sigmund Romberg
Lyrics by Oscar Hammerstein II
The New Moon 1928

Try Me
Music by Jerry Bock
Lyrics by Sheldon Harnick
She Loves Me 1963

Try This on Your Pianna, Anna
Music by A. Baldwin Sloane
Lyrics by E. Ray Goetz
The Hen Pecks 1911

Try to Forget
Music by Jerome Kern
Lyrics by Otto Harbach
The Cat and the Fiddle 1931

Try to Love Me Just As I Am
Music by Jule Styne
Lyrics by Betty Comden and Adolph Green
Say, Darling 1958

Try to Remember
Music by Harvey Schmidt
Lyrics by Tom Jones
The Fantasticks (OB) 1960

Tschaikowsky
Music by Kurt Weill
Lyrics by Ira Gershwin
Lady in the Dark 1941

Tsing-la-la
Music by Erich Wolfgang Korngold (based on
Jacques Offenbach)
Lyrics by Herbert Baker
Helen Goes to Troy 1944

Tu Reviendras
Music and lyrics by Gian-Carlo Menotti
The Consul 1950

Tu Sais
Music by Max Ewing and Serge Walter
Lyrics by Agnes Morgan
The Grand Street Follies (1928)

Tulip Time
Music and lyrics by Gene Buck and Dave Stamper
Ziegfeld Follies of 1919

Tulip Time in Sing Sing
Music by Jerome Kern
Lyrics by P.G. Wodehouse
Sitting Pretty 1924

Tum On and Tiss Me
Music by George Gershwin
Lyrics by Arthur Jackson
George White's Scandals (1920)

Tune In to Station J.O.Y.
Music by George Gershwin
Lyrics by B.G. DeSylva
George White's Scandals (1924)

The Tune They Croon in the U.S.A.
Music and lyrics by Cecil Lean
The Blue Paradise 1915

The Tune You Can't Forget
Music by Rudolf Friml
Lyrics by Rida Johnson Young
Sometime 1918

Turkey Lurkey Time
Music by Burt Bacharach
Lyrics by Hal David
Promises, Promises 1968

Turn Around
Music by Peter Link
Lyrics by Jacob Brackman
King of Hearts 1978

Turn Back, O Man
Music and lyrics by Stephen Schwartz
Godspell (OB) 1971

Turn Her Out
Music and lyrics by Elizabeth Swados
Lullabye and Goodnight 1982

Turn It Around
Music and lyrics by Harry Chapin
Cotton Patch Gospel (OB) 1981

Turn It On
Music by John Kander
Lyrics by Fred Ebb
The Act 1977

Turn Me Loose on Broadway
Music by Vernon Duke
Lyrics by Ogden Nash
Two's Company 1952

Turn My Little Millwheel
Music by Paul Delmet
Lyrics by Kay Swift
Paris '90 1952

Turn On the Charm
Music by Emmerich Kálmán
Lyrics by George Marion, Jr.
Marinka 1945

Turn on the Heat
Music and lyrics by B.G. DeSylva, Lew Brown
and Ray Henderson
Sunny Side Up (1929) F

Turn Out the Light
Music by Nacio Herb Brown and Richard Whiting
Lyrics by B.G. DeSylva
Take a Chance 1932

Turn to Me
Music by Joseph Meyer
Lyrics by Edward Eliscu
Lady Fingers 1929

Turoola
Music and lyrics by Ed Tyler
Sweet Miani (OB) 1962

Turtle Song
Music by Harold Arlen
Lyrics by Harold Arlen and Truman Capote
House of Flowers 1954

Tuscaloosa's Calling Me, But I'm Not Going
Music by Hank Beebe
Lyrics by Bill Heyer
*Tuscaloosa's Calling Me
But I'm Not Going!* (OB) 1975

'Twas Not So Long Ago
Music by Jerome Kern
Lyrics by Oscar Hammerstein II
Sweet Adeline 1929

Tweedledee for President
Music by George Gershwin
Lyrics by Ira Gershwin
Let 'Em Eat Cake 1933

The campaign song for John P. Tweedledee, who

is running for President against the incumbent, John P. Wintergreen. The music is a counterpoint melody to "Wintergreen for President," from the Gershwins' earlier political satire *Of Thee I Sing*, to which this show is a sequel. Both are sung together at the show's opening.

Tweedledum and Tweedledee
Music and lyrics by Elizabeth Swados
Alice in Concert (OB) 1980

Tweet Tweet
Music by Ray Henderson
Lyrics by B.G. DeSylva and Lew Brown
George White's Scandals (1926)

Twelve Days to Christmas
Music by Jerry Bock
Lyrics by Sheldon Harnick
She Loves Me 1963

Twelve o'Clock and All Is Well
Music by Philip Charig
Lyrics by Dan Shapiro and Milton Pascal
Follow the Girls 1944

Twelve o'Clock Song
Music and lyrics by Deed Meyer
She Shall Have Music (OB) 1959

Twelve Rooftops Leaping
Music by Helen Miller
Lyrics by Eve Merriam
Inner City 1971

Twentieth Century Blues
Music and lyrics by Noël Coward
Cavalcade (1932) F

Twenty-Eight
Music and lyrics by Gene Curty, Nitra Scharfman and Chuck Strand
The Lieutenant 1975

28 Men
Music by Earl Robinson
Lyrics by Waldo Salt
Sandhog (OB) 1954

Twenty-Eight Men
Music by Stan Harte, Jr.
Leaves of Grass (OB) 1971

Twenty Fans
Music and lyrics by Carol Hall
The Best Little Whorehouse in Texas 1978

Twenty-Five Miles
Music by Patrick Rose
Lyrics by Merv Campone and Richard Ouzounian
A Bistro Car on the CNR (OB) 1978

Twenty-Four Hours of Lovin'
Music and lyrics by Carol Hall
The Best Little Whorehouse in Texas 1978

Twenty Happy Years
Music by Charles Strouse
Lyrics by Lee Adams
Bring Back Birdie 1981

Twenty-One Chateaux
Music by Richard Adler
Lyrics by Will Holt
Music Is 1976

Twenty Thousand Pounds
Music by Franz Lehár
Lyrics by Basil Hood
The Count of Luxembourg 1912

Twenty Tons of T.N.T
Music by Donald Swann
Lyrics by Michael Flanders
At the Drop of Another Hat 1966

Twenty Years
Music by Stan Harte, Jr.
Leaves of Grass (OB) 1971

Twenty Years
Music by Steve Sterner
Lyrics by Peter del Valle
Lovers (OB) 1975

Twenty Years Ago
Music by Ray Henderson
Lyrics by B.G. DeSylva and Lew Brown
George White's Scandals (1926)

Twice as Nice
Music by Harris Wheeler
Lyrics by Mary L. Fisher
Blue Plate Special (OB) 1983

Twice Shy
Music by Donald Swann
Lyrics by Michael Flanders
At the Drop of Another Hat 1966

Twilight
Music by William Daly and Paul Lannin
Lyrics by Arthur Jackson
For Goodness Sake 1922

Twilight
Music by Morris Hamilton
Lyrics by Grace Henry
Earl Carroll's Vanities (1926)

Twilight in Barakeesh
Music by Victor Herbert
Lyrics by Glen MacDonough
Algeria 1908

Twilight Song
Music and lyrics by C. Jackson and James Hatch
Fly Blackbird (OB) 1962

Twilight Voices
Music by Sigmund Romberg
Lyrics by Harry B. Smith
Princess Flavia 1925

'Twill Never Be the Same
Music by John Mundy
Lyrics by Edward Eager
The Liar 1950

Twin Soliloquies
Music by Richard Rodgers
Lyrics by Oscar Hammerstein II
South Pacific 1949

The Twinkle in Your Eye
Music by Albert Von Tilzer
Lyrics by Neville Fleeson
The Gingham Girl 1922

A Twinkle in Your Eye
Music by Richard Rodgers
Lyrics by Lorenz Hart
I Married an Angel 1938

Twinkle, Little Star
Music by Rudolf Friml
Lyrics by Bide Dudley and Otto Harbach
The Little Whopper 1919

Twinkle Twinkle
Music by Harry Archer
Lyrics by Harlan Thompson
Twinkle Twinkle 1926

Twinkle, Twinkle Little Star
Music by Bert Keyes and Bob Larimer
Lyrics by Bob Larimer
But Never Jam Today 1979

Twins
Music by Earl Robinson
Lyrics by Waldo Salt
Sandhog (OB) 1954

Twist Her Mind
Music and lyrics by Cliff Jones
Rockabye Hamlet 1976

Twist My Arm
Music by Sammy Fain
Lyrics by Paul Webster
Catch a Star! 1955

Two a Day
Music and lyrics by Jerry Herman
Parade (OB) 1960

Two-a-Day for Keith
Music by Richard Rodgers
Lyrics by Lorenz Hart
On Your Toes 1936

Two a Day on the Milky Way
Music by Dean Fuller
Lyrics by Marshall Barer
Ziegfeld Follies (1957)

Two Big Eyes
Music and lyrics by Cole Porter
Miss Information 1915

Two Blind Loves
Music by Harold Arlen
Lyrics by E. Y. Harburg
At the Circus (1939) F

Two Boys
Music by Ray Henderson
Lyrics by B.G. DeSylva
Three Cheers 1928

Two by Two
Music by David Baker
Lyrics by Sheldon Harnick
Smiling, the Boy Fell Dead (OB) 1961

Two by Two
Music by Richard Rodgers
Lyrics by Stephen Sondheim
Do I Hear a Waltz? 1965

Dropped from production

Two by Two
Music by Richard Rodgers
Lyrics by Martin Charnin
Two by Two 1970

Two Cigarettes and a Dog
Music by Lew Pollack
Lyrics by Paul Francis Webster
Kill That Story! 1934

Two-Faced Woman
Music by Arthur Schwartz
Lyrics by Howard Dietz
Flying Colors 1932

Two Faces in the Dark
Music by Albert Hague
Lyrics by Dorothy Fields
Redhead 1959

Two Fairy Tales
Music and lyrics by Stephen Sondheim
Marry Me a Little (OB) 1981

Dropped from *A Little Night Music* (1973)

Two Falls to a Finish
Music by Al Carmines
Lyrics by Rosalyn Drexler
Home Movies (OB) 1964

Two Feet in Two-Four Time
Music by Harold Arlen
Lyrics by Irving Caesar
George White's Music Hall Varieties 1932

Two Fellows and a Girl
Music by Con Conrad
Lyrics by Gus Kahn
Kitty's Kisses 1926

Two Gentlemen of Verona
Music by Galt MacDermot
Lyrics by John Guare
Two Gentlemen of Verona 1971

Two Get Together
Music by Will Irwin
Lyrics by Norman Zeno
Fools Rush In 1934

Two Girls From the Chorus
Music and lyrics by George M. Cohan
The Rise of Rosie O'Reilly 1923

Two Heads
Music by Robert Waldman
Lyrics by Alfred Uhry
The Robber Bridegroom 1976

Two Hearts Are Better Than One
Music by Jerome Kern
Lyrics by Leo Robin
Centennial Summer (1946) F

Two in a Taxi
Music by Jimmy McHugh
Lyrics by Howard Dietz
Keep Off the Grass 1940

Two Is Company
Music by Harold Orlob
Lyrics by Harry L. Cort and George E. Stoddard
Listen, Lester 1918

Two Is Company
Music by Winthrop Cortelyou
Lyrics by Derick Wulff
Kiss Me 1927

Two Is Plenty
Music by Oscar Straus
Lyrics by Joseph W. Herbert
A Waltz Dream 1908

Two Keys
Music by Steve Jankowski
Lyrics by Kenny Morris
Francis (OB) 1982

Two Ladies
Music by John Kander
Lyrics by Fred Ebb
Cabaret 1966

Two Ladies and a Man
Music by Sigmund Romberg
Lyrics by Otto Harbach
Forbidden Melody 1936

Two Ladies in de Shade of de Banana Tree
Music by Harold Arlen
Lyrics by Harold Arlen and Truman Capote
House of Flowers 1954

Two Laughing Irish Eyes
Music by Victor Herbert
Lyrics by Henry Blossom
The Princess Pat 1915

Two Little Angels
Music by Al Carmines
Lyrics by Maria Irene Fornes
Promenade (OB) 1969

Two Little Babes in the Wood
Music and lyrics by Cole Porter
Paris 1928

Two Little Bluebirds
Music by Jerome Kern
Lyrics by Otto Harbach and Oscar Hammerstein II
Sunny 1925

Two Little Girls
Music by Vincent Youmans
Lyrics by Arthur Francis
Two Little Girls in Blue 1921

Two Little Love Bees
Music by Heinrich Reinhardt
Lyrics by Robert B. Smith
The Spring Maid 1910

Two Little Pals
Music by Walter L. Rosemont
Lyrics by Ballard MacDonald
Battling Buttler 1923

Two Little Pussycats
Music by Leon Carr
Lyrics by Earl Shuman
The Secret Life of Walter Mitty (OB) 1964

Two Little Ships
Music by Armand Vecsey
Lyrics by P.G. Wodehouse
The Nightingale 1927

Two Little Stars
Music by Frank Harling
Lyrics by Laurence Stallings
Deep River 1926

Two Lost Souls
Music and lyrics by Richard Adler and Jerry Ross
Damn Yankees 1955

Two Lovers
Music by Jimmy Horowitz
Lyrics by Leo Rost and Jimmy Horowitz
Marlowe 1981

Two Loving Arms
Music by Joseph Meyer and Philip Charig
Lyrics by Leo Robin
Just Fancy 1927

Two Make a Home
Music by Stephen Jones and Arthur Samuels
Lyrics by Dorothy Donnelly
Poppy 1923

Two of Me
Music by Gary William Friedman
Lyrics by Will Holt
Taking My Turn (OB) 1983

The Two of Us
Music and lyrics by George M. Cohan
Billie 1928

Two People in Love
Music by David Shire
Lyrics by Richard Maltby, Jr.
Baby 1983

Two Perfect Lovers
Music by Burton Lane
Lyrics by Samuel Lerner
Artists and Models (1930)

Two Strangers
Music and lyrics by Frederick Silver
Gay Company (OB) 1974

2000 Miles
Music and lyrics by Tom Sankey
The Golden Screw (OB) 1967

Two Unfortunate Orphans
Music by Richard Rodgers
Lyrics by Lorenz Hart
America's Sweetheart 1931

Two Years in the Making
Music by Leroy Anderson
Lyrics by Joan Ford, Walter Kerr and Jean Kerr
Goldilocks 1958

Two's Company
Music and lyrics by Stephen Schwartz
The Magic Show 1974

Typewriter
Music by Leo Fall
Lyrics by George Grossmith
The Dollar Princess 1909

Typical New Yorkers
Music by Ted Simons
Lyrics by Elinor Guggenheimer
Potholes (OB) 1979

A Typical Self-Made American
Music by George Gershwin
Lyrics by Ira Gershwin
Strike Up the Band 1930

The Typical Tune of Zanzibar
Music by John Philip Sousa
Lyrics by Tom Frost and John Philip Sousa
El Capitan 1896

Typically English
Music and lyrics by Leslie Bricusse
and Anthony Newley
Stop the World—I Want to Get Off 1962

Typische Deutsche
Music and lyrics by Leslie Bricusse
and Anthony Newley
Stop the World—I Want to Get Off 1962

U

"U," Dearie
Music by Victor Herbert
Lyrics by George V. Hobart
Old Dutch 1909

Ugg-a-Wugg
Music by Jule Styne
Lyrics by Betty Comden and Adolph Green
Peter Pan 1954

The Ugly Duckling
Music and lyrics by Frank Loesser
Hans Christian Andersen (1952) F

Uh-Huh, Oh, Yeah!
Music by Jerry Bock
Lyrics by Sheldon Harnick
The Body Beautiful 1958

Uh-Oh!
Music by Lee Pockriss
Lyrics by Anne Croswell
Tovarich 1963

Uh-Uh!
Music by Milton Schwarzwald
Lyrics by George S. Kaufman, Marc Connelly
and Ira Gershwin
Be Yourself 1924

Ukulele Lorelei
Music by George Gershwin
Lyrics by B.G. DeSylva and Ira Gershwin
Tell Me More 1925

Ultivac
Music by Sol Berkowitz
Lyrics by James Lipton
Miss Emily Adam (OB) 1960

Umble
Music and lyrics by Al Kasha and Joel Hirschhorn
Copperfield 1981

Un, Deux, Trois
Music and lyrics by Deed Meyer
'Toinette (OB) 1961

Un Mejor Dia Vendra
Music by James Taylor
Lyrics by Grace Daniele and Matt Landers
Working 1978

Unaccustomed As I Am
Music by Max Ewing
Lyrics by Agnes Morgan
The Grand Street Follies (1927) (OB)

Unaccustomed As I Am
Music by Vernon Duke
Lyrics by E.Y. Harburg
Walk a Little Faster 1932

Unafraid
Music by John Kander
Lyrics by Fred Ebb
Flora, the Red Menace 1965

Uncle Chris
Music by Richard Rodgers
Lyrics by Raymond Jessel
I Remember Mama 1979

The Uncle Sam Rag
Music by Albert Hague
Lyrics by Dorothy Fields
Redhead 1959

Uncle Sam's Lullaby
Music by Sam Stept
Lyrics by Lew Brown and Charles Tobias
Yokel Boy 1939

Uncle Says I Mustn't, So I Won't
Music by Karl Hoschna
Lyrics by Otto Harbach
Madame Sherry 1910

Uncle Tom and Old Black Joe
Music and lyrics by Noble Sissle and Eubie Blake
Shuffle Along 1921

The Undecided Blues
Music and lyrics by Elsie Janis
Puzzles of 1925

Under a One-Man Top
Music by George Gershwin
Lyrics by B.G. DeSylva
Sweet Little Devil 1924

Under a Spell
Music by Louis Bellson and Will Irwin
Lyrics by Richard Ney
Portofino 1958

Under a Tree
Music by Alec Wilder
Lyrics by Arnold Sundgaard
Kittiwake Island (OB) 1960

Under My Skin
Music by Harry Archer
Lyrics by Will B. Johnstone
Entre-Nous (OB) 1935

Under My Umbrella
Music by Alma Sanders
Lyrics by Monte Carlo
Oh! Oh! Nurse 1925

Under the Bamboo Tree
Music and lyrics by Robert Cole
Sally in our Alley 1902

Under the Clock at the Astor
Music by Manning Sherwin
Lyrics by Ned Wever
Crazy Quilt 1931

Under the Midsummer Moon
Music by Shep Camp
Lyrics by Harry B. Smith
Half a Widow 1927

Under the Sky
Music by Jerome Kern
Lyrics by Otto Harbach and Oscar Hammerstein II
Sunny 1925

Dropped from production

Under the Sleeping Volcano
Music by Jay Gorney
Lyrics by Jean and Walter Kerr
Touch and Go 1949

Under the Sun
Music and lyrics by Oscar Brown, Jr.
Joy (OB) 1970

Under the Tree
Music by Harvey Schmidt
Lyrics by Tom Jones
Celebration 1969

Under Your Spell
Music by Arthur Schwartz
Lyrics by Howard Dietz
Under Your Spell (1936) F

Underneath It All
Music by Larry Grossman
Lyrics by Hal Hackady
Minnie's Boys 1970

The Undiscovered Son
Music and lyrics by Elizabeth Swados
Runaways 1978

Undo
Music by Galt MacDermot
Lyrics by Gerome Ragni
Dude 1972

Undressing Girls With My Eyes
Music and lyrics by Stan Daniels
So Long, 174th Street 1976

Unescorted Women
Music by Keith Hermann
Lyrics by Charlotte Anker and Irene Rosenberg
Onward Victoria 1980

Unexpectedly
Music by Sol Kaplan
Lyrics by Edward Eliscu
The Banker's Daughter (OB) 1962

Unfair
Music by Jerry Bock
Lyrics by Sheldon Harnick
Fiorello 1959

Unfortunate Rose
Music and lyrics by Vincent Valentini
Parisiana 1928

UNICEF Song
Music by Sammy Fain
Lyrics by Paul Francis Webster
Christine 1960

Union Label
Music by Jay Gorney
Lyrics by Henry Myers
Meet the People 1940

Union Square
Music by George Gershwin
Lyrics by Ira Gershwin
Let 'Em Eat Cake 1933

Unlucky in Love
Music and lyrics by Irving Berlin
Music Box Revue (4th edition) 1924

Unmistakable Sign
Music by David Baker
Lyrics by David Craig
Copper and Brass 1957

Unnecessary Town
Music by Gene de Paul
Lyrics by Johnny Mercer
Li'l Abner 1956

The Unofficial Spokesman
Music by George Gershwin
Lyrics by Ira Gershwin
Strike Up the Band 1930

Unreconstructed Rebel
Music and lyrics by Jan Davidson
Diamond Studs (OB) 1975

Unrequited Love
Music by Al Carmines
Lyrics by Maria Irene Fornes
Promenade (OB) 1969

Unrequited Love March
Music and lyrics by Ronny Graham
Wet Paint (OB) 1965

Unseen Buds
Music by Stan Harte, Jr.
Leaves of Grass (OB) 1971

The Untalented Relative
Music by Arthur Siegel
Lyrics by Joey Carter and Richard Maury
New Faces of 1962

Until Today
Music and lyrics by Oscar Brand
and Paul Nassau
A Joyful Noise 1966

Until You Get Somebody Else
Music by Walter Donaldson
Lyrics by Gus Kahn
Whoopee 1928

Unto Your Heart
Music by Emile Berté and Maury Rubens
Lyrics by J. Keirn Brennan
Music in May 1929

Untogether Cinderella
Music by Ron Steward and Neal Tate
Lyrics by Ron Steward
Sambo (OB) 1969

The Untrue Pigeon
Music and lyrics by Elizabeth Swados
Runaways 1978

Unusual Way
Music and lyrics by Maury Yeston
Nine 1982

Up Among the Chimney Pots
Music by Kay Swift
Lyrics by Paul James
Nine-Fifteen Revue 1930

Up and at 'Em! On to Vict'ry
Music by George Gershwin
Lyrics by Ira Gershwin
Let 'Em Eat Cake 1933

Up and Down
Music by Wally Harper
Lyrics by Paul Zakrzewski
Sensations (OB) 1970

Up Chickamauga Hill
Music by Kurt Weill
Lyrics by Paul Green
Johnny Johnson 1936

Up From the Gutter
Music by Sigmund Romberg
Lyrics by Dorothy Fields
Up in Central Park 1945

Up in the Clouds
Music by Harry Ruby
Lyrics by Bert Kalmar
The Five o'Clock Girl 1927

Up in the Elevated Railway
Music by Sigmund Romberg (developed by Don
Walker)
Lyrics by Leo Robin
The Girl in Pink Tights 1954

Up in the Sky
Music and lyrics by Gian-Carlo Menotti
The Medium 1947

Up on High
Music by Alfred Nathan
Lyrics by George Oppenheimer
The Manhatters 1927

Up on the Hudson Shore
Music by Jean Schwartz
Lyrics by Joseph W. Herbert and Harold Atteridge
The Honeymoon Express 1913

Up on Your Toes
Music by Harry Ruby
Lyrics by Bert Kalmar
Helen of Troy, New York 1923

Up She Goes
Music by Harry Tierney
Lyrics by Joseph McCarthy
Up She Goes 1922

Up the Ladder
Music and lyrics by Al Kasha and Joel Hirschhorn
Copperfield 1981

Up to His Old Tricks
Music and lyrics by Stephen Schwartz
The Magic Show 1974

Up Where the People Are
Music and lyrics by Meredith Willson
The Unsinkable Molly Brown 1960

Up With the Lark
Music by Jerome Kern
Lyrics by Leo Robin
Centennial Summer (1946) F

Up With the Stars
Music by Harry Tierney
Lyrics by Joseph McCarthy
Up She Goes 1922

Upon a Moonlight Night in May
Music by Franz Lehár
Lyrics by Harry Graham
Yours Is My Heart 1946

Ups-a-Daisy
Music by Lewis E. Gensler
Lyrics by Robert A. Simon
Ups-a-Daisy 1928

Upstairs
Music by Burt Bacharach
Lyrics by Hal David
Promises, Promises 1968

Upstairs at O'Neal's
Music and lyrics by Martin Charnin
Upstairs at O'Neal's (OB) 1982

Uptown Downtown
Music and lyrics by Stephen Sondheim
Marry Me a Little 1981

Dropped from *Follies* (1971)

Urban Renewal
Music by Helen Miller
Lyrics by Eve Merriam
Inner City 1971

Uriti
Music by Milton Schafer
Lyrics by Ronny Graham
Bravo Giovanni 1962

Us on a Bus
Music by Vee Lawnhurst
Lyrics by Tot Seymour
Summer Wives 1936

Us Two
Music by Jack Holmes
Lyrics by Bill Conklin and Bob Miller
O Say Can You See! (OB) 1962

Use Your Imagination
Music and lyrics by Cole Porter
Out of This World 1950

Use Your Noggin
Music by Jimmy Van Heusen
Lyrics by Sammy Cahn
Walking Happy 1966

Useful Phrases
Music and lyrics by Noël Coward
Sail Away 1961

Useless Song
Music by Kurt Weill
Lyrics by Marc Blitzstein
The Threepenny Opera (OB) 1954

The Usher From the Mezzanine
Music by Jule Styne
Lyrics by Betty Comden and Adolph Green
Fade Out—Fade In 1964

V

Vacation
Music and lyrics by Jim Swann
Pump Boys and Dinettes 1982

Vacation in the Store
Music by Gordon Jenkins
Lyrics by Tom Adair
Along Fifth Avenue 1949

Vadinho Is Gone
Music by Mitch Leigh
Lyrics by N. Richard Nash
Saravá 1979

The Vagabond Song
Music by Alex Fry
Lyrics by Lyon Phelps
Do You Know the Milky Way? 1961

Valencia
Music by José Padilla
Lyrics by Clifford Grey
The Great Temptations 1926

Valmouth
Music and lyrics by Sandy Wilson
Valmouth (OB) 1960

Val's Ballad
Music by Cheryl Hardwick
Lyrics by Marilyn Suzanne Miller
Girls, Girls, Girls (OB) 1980

Valse Anglaise
Music by John Addison
Lyrics by John Cranko
Cranks 1956

Valse Julian
Music by Kerry Mills
The Fascinating Widow 1911

Valse Milieu
Music by Marguerite Monnot

Lyrics by Julian More, David Heneker
and Monte Norman
Irma la Douce 1960

Valse Triste
Music and lyrics by Bob Ost
Everybody's Gettin' Into the Act (OB) 1981

Vamp Your Men
Music by Sigmund Romberg
Lyrics by Arthur Wimperis
Louie the 14th 1925

The Vamps
Music by James Mundy
Lyrics by John Latouche
The Vamp 1955

Van Buren
Music and lyrics by Oscar Brand
How to Steal an Election (OB) 1968

Vaniteaser
Music and lyrics by Michael Cleary
and Paul Jones
Earl Carroll's Vanities (1928)

The Varsity Drag
Music by Ray Henderson
Lyrics by B.G. DeSylva and Lew Brown
Good News 1927

The Vatican Rag
Music and lyrics by Tom Lehrer
Tomfoolery (OB) 1981

Vaudeville
Music and lyrics by Walter Marks
Broadway Follies 1981

Ve Vouldn't Gonto Do It
Music by Kurt Weill
Lyrics by Maxwell Anderson
Knickerbocker Holiday 1938

591

Vedi la Vita
Music by Frank Fields
Lyrics by Armand Aulicino
The Shoemaker and the Peddler (OB) 1960

Vegetable Reggie
Music by Gerald Jay Markoe
Lyrics by Michael Colby
Charlotte Sweet (OB) 1982

Velasquez
Music and lyrics by Noël Coward
This Year of Grace 1928

Velvet Paws
Music and lyrics by Richard Rodgers
Androcles and the Lion (1967) TV

Ven I Valse
Music and lyrics by Bob Merrill
New Girl in Town 1957

Vendors' Calls
Music by Frederick Loewe
Lyrics by Alan Jay Lerner
Brigadoon 1947

Vendor's Song
Music and lyrics by Irving Burgie
Ballad for Bimshire (OB) 1963

Venetian Wedding Moon
Music by Al Goodman, J. Fred Coots
and Maury Rubens
Lyrics by Clifford Grey
Gay Paree 1925

Venezia and Her Three Lovers
Music by Victor Young
Lyrics by Edward Heyman
Pardon Our French 1950

Venice
Music by Victor Herbert
Lyrics by Gene Buck
Ziegfeld Follies of 1920

Venice
Music and lyrics by Cole Porter
The New Yorkers 1930

Ventriloquist and Dummy
Music and lyrics by Elizabeth Swados
Nightclub Cantata (OB) 1977

The Venus Waltz
Music by Ivan Caryll
Lyrics by C.M.S. McLellan
Oh! Oh! Delphine 1912

The Verandah Waltz
Music by Mitch Leigh
Lyrics by William Alfred and Phyllis Robinson
Cry for Us All 1970

The Verdict
Music and lyrics by Gene Curty, Nitra Scharfman
and Chuck Strand
The Lieutenant 1975

Veronica Takes Over
Music by Jack Holmes
Lyrics by Bill Conklin and Bob Miller
O Say Can You See! (OB) 1962

Veronique
Music by Cy Coleman
Lyrics by Betty Comden and Adolph Green
On the Twentieth Century 1978

Very
Music by Cyril Ornadel
Lyrics by Leslie Bricusse
Pickwick 1965

A Very Full and Productive Day
Music and lyrics by William Roy
The Penny Friend (OB) 1966

A Very Good Baby in the Daytime
Music by Harold Orlob
Lyrics by Harry L. Cort and George E. Stoddard
Listen, Lester 1918

Very Much in Love
Music and lyrics by Rick Besoyan
The Student Gypsy (OB) 1963

The Very Necessary You
Music by Jimmy Van Heusen
Lyrics by Johnny Burke
Carnival in Flanders 1953

The Very Next Man
Music by Jerry Bock
Lyrics by Sheldon Harnick
Fiorello! 1959

A Very Nice Man
Music and lyrics by Bob Merrill
Carnival 1961

A Very Proper Town
Music and lyrics by Jay Livingston and Ray Evans
Oh Captain! 1958

Very Soft Shoes
Music by Mary Rodgers
Lyrics by Marshall Barer
Once Upon a Mattress 1959

A Very Special Day
Music by Richard Rodgers
Lyrics by Oscar Hammerstein II
Me and Juliet 1953

Very, Very, Very
Music by Kurt Weill
Lyrics by Ogden Nash
One Touch of Venus 1943

Vesper Bell
Music by Rudolf Friml
Lyrics by P.G. Wodehouse and Clifford Grey
The Three Musketeers 1928

Via Galactica
Music by Galt MacDermot
Lyrics by Christopher Gore
Via Galactica 1972

Vicki Lawrence
Music by Cheryl Hardwick
Lyrics by Marilyn Suzanne Miller
Girls, Girls, Girls (OB) 1980

Victim of the Voodoo Drums
Music by Victor Young
Lyrics by Joseph Young and Ned Washington
Blackbirds of 1934

The Victoria Trio
Music and lyrics by Paul Nassau
Fallout (OB) 1959

Victoria's Banner
Music by Keith Hermann
Lyrics by Charlotte Anker and Irene Rosenberg
Onward Victoria 1980

Victory
Music by Monty Norman
Lyrics by Julian More
The Moony Shapiro Songbook 1981

Video Bleeptones
Music by Scott Killian and Kim D. Sherman
Lyrics by Kenneth Robins, Scott Killian
and Kim D. Sherman
Lenny and the Heartbreakers (OB) 1983

Video Dreamboy
Music by Scott Killian and Kim D. Sherman
Lyrics by Kenneth Robins, Scott Killian
and Kim D. Sherman
Lenny and the Heartbreakers (OB) 1983

Video Enigma
Music by Scott Killian and Kim D. Sherman
Lyrics by Kenneth Robins, Scott Killian
and Kim D. Sherman
Lenny and the Heartbreakers (OB) 1983

Vienna
Music by Jerome Kern
Lyrics by Adrian Ross
A Waltz Dream 1908

Vienna Girls
Music by Rudolf Friml
Lyrics by Otto Harbach
Katinka 1915

Vienna Gossip
Music by Johann Strauss I, adapted by Oscar
Strauss

Lyrics by Clare Kummer
Three Waltzes 1937

Vienna, How D'Ye Do
Music by Edmund Eysler
Lyrics by Herbert Reynolds
The Blue Paradise 1915

Vienna, Vienna
Music by Edmund Eysler
Lyrics by Herbert Reynolds
The Blue Paradise 1915

Viennese
Music by Ladislas Kun
Lyrics by Lorenz Hart
The Garrick Gaieties (2nd edition) 1926

Vigil
Music by Larry Grossman
Lyrics by Hal Hackady
Snoopy (OB) 1982

The Vigilantes
Music by Jerome Kern
Lyrics by Paul West
The Red Petticoat 1912

Dropped from production

Vilia
Music by Franz Lehár
Lyrics by Adrian Ross
The Merry Widow 1907

The Villain Always Gets It
Music by Sammy Fain
Lyrics by Dan Shapiro
Ankles Aweigh 1955

Villainy Is the Matter
Music and lyrics by Al Kasha and Joel Hirschhorn
Copperfield 1981

The Vineyards of Manhattan
Music by Arthur Schwartz
Lyrics by Agnes Morgan
The Grand Street Follies (1929)

Violet
Music by Ivan Caryll
Lyrics by Anne Caldwell and James O'Dea
Chin-Chin 1914

Violets
Music by Edward Künneke
Lyrics by Harry B. Smith
The Love Song 1925

Violets and Silverbells
Music by Gary Geld
Lyrics by Peter Udell
Shenandoah 1975

Violins From Nowhere
Music by Sammy Fain
Lyrics by Herb Magidson
Michael Todd's Peep Show 1950

V.I.P.
Music by Jule Styne
Lyrics by Betty Comden and Adolph Green
Do Re Mi 1960

The Virgin Polka
Music and lyrics by John Dooley
Hobo (OB) 1961

Virginia
Music by Vincent Youmans
Lyrics by Oscar Hammerstein II
Rainbow 1928

See note on "If I Told You"

Virginia
Music by Arthur Schwartz
Lyrics by Albert Stillman
Virginia 1937

Virginia (Don't Go Too Far)
Music by George Gershwin
Lyrics by B.G. DeSylva
Sweet Little Devil 1924

Virgins Wrapped in Cellophane
Music by John Jacob Loeb
Lyrics by Paul Francis Webster
Murder at the Vanities 1933

Virtue Arrivederci
Music by Milton Schafer
Lyrics by Ronny Graham
Bravo Giovanni 1962

Virtue Is Its Own Reward
Music by Jean Gilbert
Lyrics by Harry B. and Robert B. Smith
Modest Suzanne 1912

A Vision of the Future
Music by Joseph Rumshinsky
Lyrics by L. Wolfe Gilbert
The Singing Rabbi 1931

Vision Song
Music by Raymond Scott
Lyrics by Bernard Hanighen
Lute Song 1946

Visions and Voices
Music by Larry Grossman
Lyrics by Hal Hackady
Goodtime Charley 1975

Visit Panama
Music and lyrics by Cole Porter
Panama Hattie 1940

Visiting Rights
Music by Lawrence Hurwit
Lyrics by Lee Goldsmith
Sextet 1974

The Visitors
Music by Harry Tierney
Lyrics by Joseph McCarthy
Up She Goes 1922

Visitors Ashore
Music by Warburton Guilbert
Lyrics by Everett Marcy and Nancy Hamilton
New Faces of 1934

Vite, Vite, Vite
Music and lyrics by Cole Porter
Leave It to Me 1938

Viva a Vida
Music by Mitch Leigh
Lyrics by N. Richard Nash
Saravá 1979

Viva for Geneva
Music by Harold Arlen
Lyrics by E.Y. Harburg
Hooray for What! 1937

Viva Vitamins
Music by Fred Spielman and Arthur Gershwin
Lyrics by Stanley Adams
A Lady Says Yes 1945

Vivaldi
Music by Gary William Friedman
Lyrics by Will Holt
Taking My Turn (OB) 1983

Vive la Différence
Music by John Kander
Lyrics by Fred Ebb
Zorba 1968

Vive la Virtue
Music by Jacques Offenbach (adapted by Robert De Cormier)
Lyrics by E.Y. Harburg
The Happiest Girl in the World 1961

Vive la You
Music by Rudolf Friml
Lyrics by Johnny Burke
The Vagabond King (film version, 1956)

Vivienne
Music and lyrics by Cole Porter
Paris 1928

Vodka
Music by George Gershwin and Herbert Stothart
Lyrics by Otto Harbach and Oscar Hammerstein II
Song of the Flame 1925

Vodka, Vodka!
Music and lyrics by Robert Wright and George
Forrest (based on Rachmaninoff)
Anya 1965

The Voice in My Heart
Music and lyrics by George M. Cohan
Little Nellie Kelly 1922

The Voice of the City
Music and lyrics by Herbert Stothart, Bert Kalmar
and Harry Ruby
Good Boy 1928

Voice of the High Sierras
Music and lyrics by Ida Hoyt Chamberlain
Enchanted Isle 1927

Voices
Music and lyrics by Jerry Herman
Dear World 1969

Volley of Indecision
Music by Gerald Jay Markoe
Lyrics by Michael Colby
Charlotte Sweet (OB) 1982

Voodoo
Music and lyrics by Cole Porter
The Pirate (1948) F

Dropped from film

Voodoo
Music and lyrics by Johnny Brandon
Who's Who, Baby? (OB) 1968

Voodoo of the Zulu Isle
Music by J. Fred Coots and Maury Rubens
Lyrics by Clifford Grey and McElbert Moore
A Night in Paris 1926

Vorderveele
Music by Jerome Kern
Lyrics by Edgar Allan Woolf
Head Over Heels 1918

Vote for Lincoln
Music by Victor Ziskin
Lyrics by Joan Javits
Young Abe Lincoln 1961

W

Wabash 4-7473
Music by G. Wood
Lyrics by Bruce Kirby
Shoestring Revue (1955) (OB)

Waddya Say—We Steal Away
Music by James F. Hanley
Lyrics by Eddie Dowling
Honeymoon Lane 1926

Wade in the Water
Music by Vernon Duke
Lyrics by John Latouche
Cabin in the Sky (1964 OB revival)

Wah-Wah
Music by Martin Broones
Lyrics by Ballard MacDonald
Rufus Lemaire's Affairs 1927

Wah Wah
Music by Galt MacDermot
Lyrics by Gerome Ragni
Dude 1972

Wahoo!
Music and lyrics by Al Carmines
Wanted (OB) 1972

Wait
Music and lyrics by Stephen Sondheim
Sweeney Todd 1979

Wait a Little While
Music and lyrics by Jill Williams
Rainbow Jones 1974

Wait and See
Music by Peter Copani and Ed Vogel
Lyrics by Peter Copani
New York City Street Show (OB) 1977

Wait for Me
Music and lyrics by Bob Goodman
Wild and Wonderful 1971

Wait for Me Marlena
Music and lyrics by Richard M. Sherman
and Robert B. Sherman
Over Here! 1974

Wait for the Happy Ending
Music by Milton Ager
Lyrics by Jack Yellen
John Murray Anderson's Almanac (1929)

Wait for Tomorrow
Music by Bronislaw Kaper (based on Chopin)
Lyrics by John Latouche
Polonaise 1945

Wait 'Till We're Sixty-Five
Music by Burton Lane
Lyrics by Alan Jay Lerner
On a Clear Day You Can See Forever 1965

Wait Till the Cows Come Home
Music by Ivan Caryll
Lyrics by Anne Caldwell
Jack O' Lantern 1917

Wait Till Tomorrow
Music by Jerome Kern
Lyrics by P.G. Wodehouse
Leave It to Jane 1917

Wait Till You See Her
Music by Richard Rodgers
Lyrics by Lorenz Hart
By Jupiter 1942

Dropped during Broadway run

Wait Till You See Me in the Morning
Music by Hoagy Carmichael
Lyrics by Johnny Mercer
Walk With Music 1940

Waiters
Music by Emmerich Kálmán
Lyrics by Harry B. Smith
The Circus Princess 1927

Waitin'
Music by Harold Arlen
Lyrics by Harold Arlen and Truman Capote
House of Flowers 1954

Waitin' for My Dearie
Music by Frederick Loewe
Lyrics by Alan Jay Lerner
Brigadoon 1947

Waitin' for the Evening Train
Music by Arthur Schwartz
Lyrics by Howard Dietz
Jennie 1963

Waiting
Music by Harold Orlob
Lyrics by Harry L. Cort and George E. Stoddard
Listen, Lester 1918

Waiting
Music by Louis A. Hirsch
Lyrics by Otto Harbach
Mary 1920

Waiting
Music by Richard Rodgers
Lyrics by Oscar Hammerstein II
The King and I 1951

Dropped from production

Waiting
Music and lyrics by Elizabeth Swados
Nightclub Cantata (OB) 1977

Waiting All the Time for You
Music by Frank Grey
Lyrics by McElbert Moore and Frank Grey
The Matinee Girl 1926

Waiting Around the Corner
Music by Jerome Kern
Lyrics by P.G. Wodehouse
Oh, Lady! Lady!! 1918

Also published as "Some Little Girl."

Waiting at the End of the Road
Music and lyrics by Irving Berlin
Hallelujah (1929) F

Waiting for the Bride
Music by Victor Herbert
Lyrics by Robert B. Smith
Sweethearts 1913

Waiting for the Girls Upstairs
Music and lyrics by Stephen Sondheim
Follies 1971

Waiting for the Men
Music by Earl Robinson
Lyrics by Waldo Salt
Sandhog (OB) 1954

Waiting for the Sun to Come Out
Music by George Gershwin
Lyrics by Arthur Francis (Ira Gershwin)
The Sweetheart Shop 1920

Waiting for the Train
Music by George Gershwin
Lyrics by Ira Gershwin
Tip-Toes 1925

Waiting for the Whistle to Blow
Music by Eubie Blake
Lyrics by Noble Sissle
Shuffle Along of 1933

Waiting for You
Music by Vincent Youmans
Lyrics by Otto Harbach
No, No, Nanette 1925

Same melody as "You Started Something" (lyrics
by Arthur Francis) in *Two Little Girls in Blue.*

Waiting in a Queue
Music and lyrics by Noël Coward
This Year of Grace 1928

Waiting, Waiting
Music by Jule Styne
Lyrics by Betty Comden and Adolph Green
Do Re Mi 1960

Wake Me Up a Star
Music by Michael Cleary
Lyrics by Arthur Swanstrom
Sea Legs 1937

Wake Up
Music and lyrics by C. Jackson and James Hatch
Fly Blackbird (OB) 1962

Wake Up and Dream
Music and lyrics by Cole Porter
Wake Up and Dream 1929

Wake Up, Brother And Dance
Music by George Gershwin
Lyrics by Ira Gershwin
Shall We Dance (1937) F

Dropped from film. (Same music as "Sophia")

Wake Up, Sleepy Moon
Music by Max Rich
Lyrics by Jack Scholl
Keep Moving 1934

Wake-Up Sun
Music and lyrics by Micki Grant
It's So Nice to Be Civilized 1980

Waking This Morning
Music and lyrics by Elizabeth Swados
Nightclub Cantata (OB) 1977

Waking Up Sun
Music by Robert Waldman
Lyrics by Alfred Uhry
Here's Where I Belong 1968

Walk Away
Music by Elmer Bernstein
Lyrics by Carolyn Leigh
How Now, Dow Jones 1967

Walk Down My Street
Music by Norman Curtis
Lyrics by Patricia Taylor Curtis
Walk Down Mah Street! (OB) 1968

Walk Him Up the Stairs
Music by Gary Geld
Lyrics by Peter Udell
Purlie 1970

Walk Into Heaven
Music by Claibe Richardson
Lyrics by Kenward Elmslie
The Grass Harp 1971

Walk Like a Sailor
Music by Sammy Fain
Lyrics by Dan Shapiro
Ankles Aweigh 1955

Walk, Lordy, Walk
Music by Norman Curtis
Lyrics by Patricia Taylor Curtis
Walk Down Mah Street! (OB) 1968

Walk Sweet
Music by Harry Warren
Lyrics by Jerome Lawrence and Robert E. Lee
Shangri-La 1956

Walk This Way
Music by Raymond Hubbell
Lyrics by Glen MacDonough
The Jolly Bachelors 1910

Walk Through That Golden Gate
Music and lyrics by Ann Harris
Sky High (OB) 1979

Walk Together, Children
Music and lyrics by J.C. Johnson
Change Your Luck 1930

Walk, Walk, Walk
Music by Jerome Kern
Lyrics by Paul West
The Red Petticoat 1912

The Walker Walk
Music and lyrics by Bill and Patti Jacob
Jimmy 1969

Walkin' Along Mindin' My Business
Music by Burton Lane
Lyrics by E.Y. Harburg
Hold On to Your Hats 1940

Walkin' on Air
Music by Harry Revel
Lyrics by Mack Gordon
Fast and Furious 1931

Walkin' the Track
Music by Con Conrad
Lyrics by Gus Kahn
Kitty's Kisses

Walking All the Way to Rome
Music by Steve Jankowski
Lyrics by Kenny Morris
Francis (OB) 1982

Walking Away Whistling
Music and lyrics by Frank Loesser
Greenwillow 1960

Walking Dogs Around
Music by Ray Henderson
Lyrics by B.G. DeSylva and Lew Brown
George White's Scandals (1926)

Walking Down the Road
Music and lyrics by Alan Kohan
and William Angelos
Put It in Writing (OB) 1963

Walking Happy
Music by Jimmy Van Heusen
Lyrics by Sammy Cahn
Walking Happy 1966

Walking Home With Angeline
Music by George Gershwin
Lyrics by Brian Hooker
Our Nell 1922

Walking Home With Josie
Music by Jerome Kern
Lyrics by Anne Caldwell
The City Chap 1925

Walking in Space
Music by Galt MacDermot
Lyrics by Gerome Ragni and James Rado
Hair 1968

Walking the Deck
Music by Frank D'Armond
Lyrics by Will Morrissey
Saluta 1934

Walking the Dog (instrumental)
Music by George Gershwin
Shall We Dance (1937) F

Later published as "Promenade"

Walking With Peninnah
Music by Leon Carr
Lyrics by Earl Shuman
The Secret Life of Walter Mitty (OB) 1964

Walking With You, Two by Two
Music by Tom Mandel
Lyrics by Louisa Rose
The Bar That Never Closes (OB) 1972

Walks
Music by Victor Herbert
Lyrics by Harry B. Smith
Miss Dolly Dollars 1905

Wall Street
Music by Jim Wise
Lyrics by George Haimsohn and Robin Miller
Dames at Sea (OB) 1968

Wall Street Blues
Music by Tom Johnstone
Lyrics by Will B. Johnstone
I'll Say She Is 1924

Wall Street Reel
Music by Arthur Siegel
Lyrics by Jim Fuerst
New Faces of 1962

Wall Street Zoo
Music by Lucien Denni
Lyrics by Helena Evans
Happy Go Lucky 1926

The Walla Walla Boola
Music and lyrics by Noël Coward
The Girl Who Came to Supper 1963

The Walrus and the Carpenter
Music and lyrics by Elizabeth Swados
Alice in Concert (OB) 1980

The Walter Mitty March
Music by Leon Carr
Lyrics by Earl Shuman
The Secret Life of Walter Mitty (OB) 1964

Walt's Truth
Music by Rob Fremont
Lyrics by Doris Willens
Piano Bar (OB) 1978

Waltz at Maxim's (She Is Not Thinking of Me)
Music by Frederick Loewe
Lyrics by Alan Jay Lerner
Gigi (1958) F

Also in stage version (1973)

Waltz Down the Aisle
Music and lyrics by Cole Porter

Dropped from *Anything Goes* (1934) and *Jubilee* (1935)

Waltz Eternal
Music and lyrics by Robert Wright and George Forrest
Song of Norway 1944

Based on Grieg's *Waltz Caprice*

Waltz for a Ball
Music by Richard Rodgers
Cinderella (1957) TV

Waltz for Eva and Che
Music by Andrew Lloyd Webber
Lyrics by Tim Rice
Evita 1979

The Waltz I Heard in a Dream
Music and lyrics by Kay Swift
Paris '90 1952

Waltz in Swingtime
Music by Jerome Kern
Lyrics by Dorothy Fields
Swing Time (1936) F

The Waltz Is Made for Love
Music by Emmerich Kálmán
Lyrics by B.G. DeSylva
The Yankee Princess 1922

The Waltz of Long Ago
Music and lyrics by Irving Berlin
Music Box Revue (3rd edition) 1923

The Waltz of Love
Music by Richard Fall
Lyrics by Irving Caesar
White Horse Inn 1936

Waltz of the Season
Music by Edmund Eysler
Lyrics by Herbert Reynolds
The Blue Paradise 1915

The Waltz That Brought You Back to Me
Music by Carmen Lombardo
Lyrics by Irving Caesar
George White's Music Hall Varieties 1932

The Waltz Time Girl
Music by Jerome Kern
Lyrics by Paul West
The Red Petticoat 1912

A Waltz Was Born in Vienna
Music by Frederick Loewe
Lyrics by Earle Crooker
The Illustrators' Show 1936

Waltz With Me
Music and lyrics by George M. Cohan
Fifty Miles From Boston 1908

Waltz With Me
Music by Walter Kollo
Lyrics by Harry B. Smith
Three Little Girls 1930

Waltzing in the Moonlight
Music by Harry Ruby
Lyrics by Bert Kalmar
High Kickers 1941

Waltzing Is Better Sitting Down
Music by George Gershwin
Lyrics by Ira Gershwin
The Shocking Miss Pilgrim (1947) F

Adapted by Kay Swift and Ira Gershwin from
manuscripts of George Gershwin.

Wanapoo Bay
Music by Rudolf Friml
Lyrics by J. Keirn Brennan
Luana 1930

Wander Away
Music by Herbert Stothart
Lyrics by Otto Harbach and Oscar Hammerstein II
Song of the Flame 1925

Wandering in Dreamland
Music by Martin Broones
Lyrics by Ballard MacDonald
Rufus Lemaire's Affairs 1927

Wand'rin' Star
Music by Frederick Loewe
Lyrics by Alan Jay Lerner
Paint Your Wagon 1951

Wandr'ing Heart
Music by Arthur Schwartz
Lyrics by Howard Dietz
Revenge With Music 1934

Want to Get Retarded?
Music by Norman Curtis
Lyrics by Patricia Taylor Curtis
Walk Down Mah Street! (OB) 1968

Wanta, Hope to Feel at Home
Music by Alfred Brooks
Lyrics by Ira J. Bilowit
Of Mice and Men (OB) 1958

Wanting Things
Music by Burt Bacharach
Lyrics by Hal David
Promises, Promises 1968

Wanting You
Music by Will Morrisey
Lyrics by Edmund Joseph
Polly of Hollywood 1927

Wanting You
Music by Sigmund Romberg
Lyrics by Oscar Hammerstein II
The New Moon 1928

War and Rebellion
Music by Coleridge-Taylor Perkinson
Lyrics by Errol Hill
Man Better Man (OB) 1969

War Babies
Music by Gary William Friedman
Lyrics by Will Holt
The Me Nobody Knows (OB) 1970

War Is a Science
Music and lyrics by Stephen Schwartz
Pippin 1972

War Is Good Business
Music by Wally Harper
Lyrics by Paul Zakrzewski
Sensations (OB) 1970

War Is War
Music by Richard Rodgers
Lyrics by Lorenz Hart
Dearest Enemy 1925

Warm All Over
Music and lyrics by Frank Loesser
The Most Happy Fella 1956

Warm and Willing
Music by Jimmy Mchugh
Lyrics by Jay Livingston and Ray Evans
Sugar Babies 1979

Warm Breezes at Twilight
Music and lyrics by Ed Tyler
Sweet Miani (OB) 1962

The Wart Song
Music and lyrics by Cliff Jones
Rockabye Hamlet 1976

Wartime Wedding
Music and lyrics by Richard M. Sherman
and Robert B. Sherman
Over Here! 1974

Was I?
Music by Chick Endor
Lyrics by Charles Farrell
Ziegfeld Follies (1931)

Was I Wazir?
Music and lyrics by Robert Wright and George
Forrest (based on Alexander Borodin)
Kismet 1953

Was She Prettier than I?
Music and lyrics by Hugh Martin and Timothy Gray
High Spirits 1964

Washed Away
Music by Nancy Ford
Lyrics by Gretchen Cryer
Now Is the Time for All Good Men (OB) 1967

Washington Square
Music by Clay Warnick
Lyrics by Mel Tolkin and Lucille Kallen
Tickets Please 1950

Washington Square
Music and lyrics by Ronnie Britton
Gift of the Magi (OB) 1975

Washington Square Dance
Music and lyrics by Irving Berlin
Call Me Madam 1950

The Washington Twist
Music and lyrics by Irving Berlin
Mr. President 1962

Wasn't It a Simply Lovely Wedding?
Music by Glenn Paxton
Lyrics by Robert Goldman and George Weiss
First Impressions 1959

Wasn't It Beautiful While It Lasted?
Music by Ray Henderson
Lyrics by B.G. DeSylva and Lew Brown
Flying High 1930

Wasn't It Great?
Music by Richard Rodgers
Lyrics by Lorenz Hart
She's My Baby 1928

Dropped from production

Wasn't It Nice?
Music by Rudolf Friml
Lyrics by Irving Caesar
No Foolin' 1926

The Wasp Nest
Music and lyrics by Scott Joplin
Treemonisha 1975

Written in 1909

Wasting Away
Music and lyrics by J.C. Johnson
Change Your Luck 1930

Watch Dog Theme
Music and lyrics by Carol Hall
The Best Little Whorehouse in Texas 1978

Watch My Baby Walk
Music by Peter de Rose
Lyrics by Jo Trent
Earl Carroll's Vanities 1928

Watch My Dust
Music by Jule Styne
Lyrics by Betty Comden and Adolph Green
Hallelujah, Baby! 1967

Watch Out for Claggart/Work
Music and lyrics by Ron Dante and Gene Allan
Billy 1969

Watch the Birdies
Music by Emil Gerstenberger and Carle Carlton
Lyrics by Howard Johnson
The Lace Petticoat 1927

Watching
Music by Kenn Long and Jim Crozier
Lyrics by Kenn Long
Touch (OB) 1970

Watching the Big Parade Go By
Music by David Shire
Lyrics by Richard Maltby, Jr.
The Sap of Life (OB) 1961

Also used in *Starting Here, Starting Now* (OB) 1977.

Watching the Clouds Roll By
Music by Harry Ruby
Lyrics by Bert Kalmar
Animal Crackers 1928

Watching the World Go By
Music and lyrics by Cole Porter
Fifty Million Frenchmen 1929

Dropped from production

Water Movin' Slow
Music by Baldwin Bergersen
Lyrics by William Archibald
Carib Song 1945

Water Under the Bridge
Music by Vernon Duke
Lyrics by E.Y. Harburg
Ziegfeld Follies (1934)

The Water Wears Down the Stone
Music and lyrics by Harold Rome
The Zulu and the Zayda 1965

Wave a Hand
Music by Stanley Lebowsky
Lyrics by Fred Tobias
Gantry 1970

Way Back in 1939 A.D.
Music by Hoagy Carmichael
Lyrics by Johnny Mercer
Walk With Music 1940

Way Back When
Music and lyrics by Clark Gesner
The Utter Glory of Morrissey Hall 1979

Way Down Blues
Music by George Kleinsinger
Lyrics by Joe Darion
Shinbone Alley 1957

Way Down Town
Music by Jerome Kern
Lyrics by Anne Caldwell
Good Morning, Dearie 1921

Way Down Town
Music by James F. Hanley
Lyrics by Eddie Dowling
Sidewalks of New York 1927

The Way It Might Have Been
Music and lyrics by Hugh Martin
Look Ma, I'm Dancin'! 1948

The Way My Ancestors Went
Music and lyrics by Ann Ronell
Count Me In 1942

The Way of My Father
Music and lyrics by Alan Menken
Real Life Funnies (OB) 1981

Way Out in Rainbow Land
Music by Alma Sanders
Lyrics by Monte Carlo
Oh! Oh! Nurse 1925

Way Out West
Music by Richard Rodgers
Lyrics by Lorenz Hart
Babes in Arms 1937

Way Out West in Jersey
Music by Victor Herbert
Lyrics by B.G. DeSylva
Orange Blossoms 1922

Way Out West in Jersey
Music by Kurt Weill
Lyrics by Ogden Nash
One Touch of Venus 1943

Way Out West Where the East Begins
Music by Burton Lane
Lyrics by E.Y. Harburg
Hold On to Your Hats 1940

The Way Things Are
Music and lyrics by Harold Rome
I Can Get It for You Wholesale 1962

Way Up North in Dixie
Music by Philip Charig
Lyrics by Dan Shapiro and Milton Pascal
Artists and Models (1943)

The Way You Look Tonight
Music by Jerome Kern
Lyrics by Dorothy Fields
Swing Time (1936) F

Academy Award winner

Wayside Flower
Music by Sigmund Romberg
Lyrics by Arthur Wimperis
Louie the 14th 1925

Wayside Inn
Music by John Clifton
Lyrics by John Clifton and Ben Tarver
Man With a Load of Mischief (OB) 1966

We
Music by George Gershwin
Lyrics by Ira Gershwin
Tip-Toes 1925

Dropped from production

We
Music by Albert Hague
Lyrics by Allen Sherman
The Fig Leaves Are Falling 1969

We All Need Love
Music and lyrics by Jill Williams
Rainbow Jones 1974

We Are Cut in Twain
Music by Kurt Weill
Lyrics by Maxwell Anderson
Knickerbocker Holiday 1938

We Are Friends
Music and lyrics by Walter Cool
Mackey of Appalachia (OB) 1965

We Are Marching Through the Night
Music by Oscar Straus
Lyrics by Stanislaus Stange
The Chocolate Soldier 1909

We Are Not Strangers
Music and lyrics by Elizabeth Swados
Runaways 1978

We Are One
Music by Galt MacDermot
Lyrics by Christopher Gore
Via Galactica 1972

We Are Only Poor Weak Mortals
Music by Karl Hoschna
Lyrics by Otto Harbach
Madame Sherry 1910

We Are the Clouds
Music and lyrics by James Rado
Rainbow (OB) 1972

We Are the Ones
Music and lyrics by Beth Lawrence
and Norman Thalheimer
Marilyn 1983

We Are the Show Girls
Music by Morris Hamilton
Lyrics by Grace Henry
Earl Carroll's Vanities (1926)

We Are the Waiters
Music and lyrics by Clarence Gaskill
Earl Carroll's Vanities (1925)

We Are the Whores
Music by Susan Hulsman Bingham
Lyrics by Myrna Lamb
Mod Donna (OB) 1970

We Are What We Are
Music by Robert Waldman
Lyrics by Alfred Uhry
Here's Where I Belong 1968

We Are What We Are
Music and lyrics by Jerry Herman
La Cage aux Folles 1983

We Beg Your Kind Consideration
Music by John Philip Sousa
Lyrics by Tom Frost and John Philip Sousa
El Capitan 1896

We Believe
Music by Lehman Engel
Lyrics by Agnes Morgan
A Hero Is Born 1937

We Belong to Old Broadway
Music by Karl Hoschna
Lyrics by Otto Harbach
Three Twins 1908

We Belong Together
Music by Jerome Kern
Lyrics by Oscar Hammerstein II
Music in the Air 1932

We Beseech Thee
Music and lyrics by Stephen Schwartz
Godspell (OB) 1971

We Both Reached for the Gun
Music by John Kander
Lyrics by Fred Ebb
Chicago 1975

We Bring Ye Fruits
Music by Frederic Norton
Lyrics by Oscar Asche
Chu Chin Chow 1917

We Came in Chains
Music and lyrics by Oscar Brown, Jr.
Buck White 1969

We Came Together
Music by Jacques Urbont
Lyrics by David Newburger
Stag Movie (OB) 1971

We Can All Give Love
Music by Stanley Lebowsky
Lyrics by Fred Tobias
Gantry 1970

We Can Be Proud
Music and lyrics by Marc Blitzstein
Juno 1959

We Can Talk to Each Other
Music by David Shire
Lyrics by Richard Maltby, Jr.
Starting Here, Starting Now (OB) 1977

We Chant a Song of Labor
Music by John Philip Sousa
Lyrics by Leonard Liebling
The American Maid 1913

We Clearly Requested
Music by Norman Campbell
Lyrics by Donald Harron and Norman Campbell
Anne of Green Gables (OB) 1971

We Come This Way
Music by Gustave Kerker
Lyrics by Hugh Morton
The Belle of New York 1897

We Could Be Close
Music by Jule Styne
Lyrics by Bob Merrill
Sugar 1972

We Deserve Each Other
Music by Richard Rodgers
Lyrics by Oscar Hammerstein II
Me and Juliet 1953

We Detest a Fiesta
Music and lyrics by Cole Porter
Panama Hattie 1940

We Did It Before
Music and lyrics by Charlie Tobias and Cliff Friend
Banjo Eyes 1941

We Do Not Belong Together
Music and lyrics by Stephen Sondheim
Sunday in the Park With George (OB) 1983

We Do the Dirty Work
Music and lyrics by George M. Cohan
The Little Millionaire 1911

We Don't Matter at All
Music by Charles Strouse
Lyrics by Lee Adams
It's a Bird, It's a Plane, It's Superman 1966

We Don't Understand Our Children
Music by Julian Slade
Lyrics by Dorothy Reynolds and Julian Slade
Salad Days (OB) 1958

We Doubt You, Papa
Music by Galt MacDermot
Lyrics by Rochelle Owens
The Karl Marx Play (OB) 1973

We Drink to You, J. H. Brody
Music and lyrics by Cole Porter
Leave It to Me 1938

We Fear You Will Not Do, Lady Wetherell
Music by Louis A. Hirsch
Lyrics by Rennold Wolf
The Rainbow Girl 1918

We Feel Our Man Is Definitely You
Music by Sidney Lippman
Lyrics by Sylvia Dee
Barefoot Boy With Cheek 1947

We Get Up at 8 A.M.
Music by Leslie Stuart
Lyrics by Ernest Boyd-Jones and Paul Rubens
Florodora 1900

We Go To Church on Sunday
Music by George Gershwin
Lyrics by Brian Hooker
Our Nell 1922

We Go Together
Music and lyrics by Jim Jacobs
and Warren Casey
Grease 1972

We Gon' Jump Up
Music and lyrics by Irving Burgie
Ballad for Bimshire (OB) 1963

We Got a Future
Music by Alfred Brooks
Lyrics by Ira J. Bilowit
Of Mice and Men (OB) 1958

We Got a Good Thing Goin'
Music by Garry Sherman
Lyrics by Peter Udell
Amen Corner 1983

We Got a Job to Do
Music by Michael Dansicker
Lyrics by Sarah Schlesinger
On The Swing Shift (OB) 1983

We Got It
Music and lyrics by Richard M. Sherman
and Robert B. Sherman
Over Here! 1974

We Got Love
Music by Jeanne Bargy
Lyrics by Jeanne Bargy, Frank Gehrecke
and Herb Corey
Greenwich Village U.S.A. (OB) 1960

We Got to Get Organized
Music and lyrics by Harry Chapin
Cotton Patch Gospel (OB) 1981

We Got Troubles
Music and lyrics by Walter Cool
Mackey of Appalachia (OB) 1965

We Got Us
Music and lyrics by Walter Marks
Golden Rainbow 1968

We Gotta Make It Through the Winter
Music by Gene dePaul
Lyrics by Johnny Mercer
Seven Brides for Seven Brothers 1982

We Had a House in France
Music and lyrics by Gian-Carlo Menotti
The Medium 1947

We Had to Rehearse
Music by Arthur Schwartz
Lyrics by Albert Stillman
Virginia 1937

We Have a Date
Music by Lou Cooper
Lyrics by Roslyn Harvey
Of V We Sing 1942

We Haven't Fought a Battle in Years
Music by Elmer Bernstein
Lyrics by Don Black
Merlin 1983

We Haven't Got a Pot to Cook In
Music by Jimmy McHugh
Lyrics by Al Dubin
The Streets of Paris 1939

We Hope to Make a Hit
Music by Seymour Furth and Lee Edwards
Lyrics by R.F. Carroll
Bringing Up Father 1925

We Incorporated
Music by Frank D'Armond
Lyrics by Will Morrissey
Saluta 1934

We Kiss in a Shadow
Music by Richard Rodgers
Lyrics by Oscar Hammerstein II
The King and I 1951

We Know It's Wrong to Flirt
Music by Gustav Luders
Lyrics by Frank Pixley
The Prince of Pilsen 1903

We Know Love
Music by Jim Steinman
Lyrics by Michael Weller and Jim Steinman
More Than You Deserve (OB) 1973

We Know Reno
Music by John Green
Lyrics by Edward Heyman
Here Goes the Bride 1931

We Know What You Want and We Got It
Music by Ruth Cleary Patterson
Lyrics by Floria Vestoff
Russell Patterson's Sketch Book (OB) 1960

We Lend It, Spend It, End It
Music by Franz Lehár
Lyrics by Basil Hood
The Count of Luxembourg 1912

We Like It Over Here
Music by Arthur Schwartz
Lyrics by Oscar Hammerstein II
American Jubilee 1940

We Love a Conference
Music and lyrics by Ron Eliran
Don't Step on My Olive Branch (OB) 1976

We Love an Old Story
Music by Michael Valenti
Lyrics by Donald Driver
Oh, Brother 1981

We Love to Go to Work
Music by Muriel Pollock
Lyrics by Max and Nathaniel Lief
and Harold Atteridge
Pleasure Bound 1929

We Love You, Conrad!
Music by Charles Strouse
Lyrics by Lee Adams
Bye Bye Birdie 1960

We Loves Ya, Jimey
Music by Albert Hague
Lyrics by Dorothy Fields
Redhead 1959

We Make a Beautiful Pair
Music by Gary Geld
Lyrics by Peter Udell
Shenandoah 1975

We Make a Promise
Music and lyrics by Johnny Brandon
Billy Noname (OB) 1970

We Make the Show
Music by Carlton Kelsey and Maury Rubens
Lyrics by Clifford Grey
Sky High 1925

The We Makin' Dough You So and So Rag
Music by Sol Berkowitz
Lyrics by James Lipton
Nowhere to Go But Up 1962

We May Meet Again
Music by Rudolf Friml
Lyrics by Bide Dudley and Otto Harbach
The Little Whopper 1919

We Might Play Tiddle de Winks
Music by Richard Myers
Lyrics by Leo Robin
Hello, Yourself! 1928

We Must Have a Ball
Music by Leonard Bernstein
Lyrics by Alan Jay Lerner
1600 Pennsylvania Avenue 1976

We Need a Little Christmas
Music and lyrics by Jerry Herman
Mame 1966

We Need Him
Music by Charles Strouse
Lyrics by Lee Adams
It's a Bird, It's a Plane, It's Superman 1966

We Never Sleep
Music by Oscar Levant
Lyrics by Irving Caesar and Graham John
Ripples 1930

We Open in Venice
Music and lyrics by Cole Porter
Kiss Me, Kate 1948

We Pirates From Weehawken
Music by Richard Rodgers
Lyrics by Lorenz Hart
Peggy-Ann 1926

We Prize Most the Things We Miss
Music by Ralph Benatzky
Lyrics by Irving Caesar
White Horse Inn 1936

We Said We Wouldn't Look Back
Music by Julian Slade
Lyrics by Dorothy Reynolds and Julian Slade
Salad Days (OB) 1958

We Sail the Seas
Music by Mark Sandrich, Jr.
Lyrics by Sidney Michaels
Ben Franklin in Paris 1964

We Saw the Sea
Music and lyrics by Irving Berlin
Follow the Fleet (1936) F

We Shall Meet in the Great Hereafter
Music by Nancy Ford
Lyrics by Gretchen Cryer
Now Is the Time for All Good Men (OB) 1967

We Shall Meet to Part, No Never
Music by Harold Arlen
Lyrics by Johnny Mercer
St. Louis Woman 1946

We Shall Never Be Younger
Music and lyrics by Cole Porter
Kiss Me, Kate 1948

Dropped from production

We Should Care
Music and lyrics by Irving Berlin
The Cocoanuts 1925

We Sing America
Music and lyrics by Harold Rome
Pins and Needles (OB) 1937

Added during run

We Speak the Same Language
Music by Charles Strouse
Lyrics by Lee Adams
All American 1962

We Start Today
Music by David Shire
Lyrics by Richard Maltby, Jr.
Baby 1983

We Strut Our Band
Music by Gerald Jay Markoe
Lyrics by Michael Colby
Charlotte Sweet (OB) 1982

We Two
Music by Emmerich Kálmán and Herbert Stothart
Lyrics by Otto Harbach and Oscar Hammerstein II
Golden Dawn 1927

We Two
Music by Murray Rumshinsky
Lyrics by Jacob Jacobs
The President's Daughter 1970

We 'Uns From Dixie
Music by Raymond Hubbell
Lyrics by Glen MacDonough
The Jolly Bachelors 1910

We Wanna Star
Music and lyrics by Ronnie Britton
Greenwich Village Follies (OB) 1976

We Want Our Breakfast
Music by Harold Levey
Lyrics by Owen Murphy
Rainbow Rose 1926

We Want to Laugh
Music by Jerome Kern
Lyrics by P.G. Wodehouse
Miss 1917

We Want You
Music by Harry Ruby
Lyrics by Bert Kalmar
The Five o'Clock Girl 1927

Also in *Top Speed* (1929)

We Were a Wow
Music by Harry Archer
Lyrics by Harlan Thompson
Merry-Merry 1925

We Were Dancing
Music and lyrics by Noël Coward
Tonight at 8:30 ("We Were Dancing") 1936

We Were So Young
Music by Jerome Kern
Lyrics by Oscar Hammerstein II
Sweet Adeline (film version, 1935)

We Will All Go Together
Music and lyrics by Tom Lehrer
Tomfoolery (OB) 1981

We Will Be Together
Music by Richard Rodgers
Lyrics by Oscar Hammerstein II
State Fair (1945) F

Dropped from film

We Will Rest Awhile
Music and lyrics by Scott Joplin
Treemonisha 1975

Written in 1909

We Will Trust You as Our Leader
Music and lyrics by Scott Joplin
Treemonisha 1975

Written in 1909

We Wish You a Pleasant Journey
Music by Sigmund Romberg
Lyrics by Herbert Reynolds
The Blue Paradise 1915

We Won't Charleston
Music by Harry Ruby
Lyrics by Bert Kalmar
The Ramblers 1926

We Won't Discuss It
Music by Milton Schafer
Lyrics by Ronny Graham
Bravo Giovanni 1962

We Won't Forget to Write
Music and lyrics by Oscar Brand and Paul Nassau
A Joyful Noise 1966

We Won't Let It Happen Here
Music by Sammy Fain
Lyrics by Charles Tobias
Hellzapoppin 1938

We Won't Take It Back
Music by Arthur Schwartz
Lyrics by Howard Dietz
Inside U.S.A. 1948

The Weaker Sex
Music by Lewis E. Gensler
Lyrics by B. G. DeSylva
Queen High 1926

The Weaker Sex
Music by Alberta Nichols
Lyrics by Mann Holiner
Angela 1928

Wealth
Music by Jerry Bock
Lyrics by Sheldon Harnick
The Apple Tree 1966

Wear Your Sunday Smile
Music by Charles Rosoff
Lyrics by Leo Robin
Judy 1927

Wearing of the Blue
Music by David Baker
Lyrics by David Craig
Copper and Brass 1957

Weary Feet
Music and lyrics by Donald Heywood
Africana 1927

Weary Near to Dyin'
Music and lyrics by Bob Merrill
Henry, Sweet Henry 1967

Weather Man
Music by George Gershwin
Lyrics by Ira Gershwin
Lady, Be Good! 1924

Weatherbee's Drug Store
Music by Walter Kent
Lyrics by Kim Gannon
Seventeen 1951

Weaving
Music by Victor Herbert
Lyrics by Gene Buck
Ziegfeld Follies of 1922

We'd Like to Thank You
Music by Charles Strouse
Lyrics by Martin Charnin
Annie 1977

We'd Rather Be Right
Music by Harold Rome
Lyrics by Arthur Kramer
Pins and Needles (OB) 1937

We'd Rather Dance Than Eat
Music by Dave Stamper
Lyrics by Gene Buck
Take the Air 1927

The Wedding
Music and lyrics by Jerry Herman
Milk and Honey 1961

The Wedding
Music by John Kander
Lyrics by James Goldman, John Kander
and William Goldman
A Family Affair 1962

The Wedding
Music by Duke Ellington
Lyrics by Marshall Barer and Fred Tobias
Pousse-Café 1966

The Wedding
Music and lyrics by Cliff Jones
Rockabye Hamlet 1976

A Wedding! A Wedding!
Music by William Dyer
Lyrics by Don Parks and William Dyer
Jo (OB) 1964

Wedding Anthem
Music and lyrics by Stephen Oliver
The Life and Times of Nicholas Nickleby 1981

Wedding Bells
Music by Vincent Youmans
Lyrics by Billy Rose and Edward Eliscu
Great Day! 1929

Dropped from production

Wedding Bells
Music by Kay Swift
Lyrics by Paul James
Fine and Dandy 1930

Wedding Bells Are Calling Me
Music by Jerome Kern
Lyrics by Harry B. Smith
Very Good Eddie 1915

The Wedding Bells Ring On
Music by Vincent Youmans
Lyrics by Billy Rose and Edward Eliscu
Great Day! 1929

Wedding Cake-Walk
Music and lyrics by Cole Porter
You'll Never Get Rich (1941) F

The Wedding Ceremony
Music by Louis A. Hirsch
Lyrics by Rennold Wolf
The Rainbow Girl 1918

Wedding Chimes
Music by Seymour Furth and Lee Edwards
Lyrics by R.F. Carroll
Bringing Up Father 1925

Wedding Conversation
Music and lyrics by Jerry Herman
The Grand Tour 1979

Wedding Dance
Music by Jerry Bock
Lyrics by Sheldon Harnick
Fiddler on the Roof 1964

Wedding Gifts of Silver
Music by Ivan Caryll
Lyrics by Anne Caldwell and James O'Dea
Chin-Chin 1914

A Wedding in Cherokee County
Music and lyrics by Randy Newman
Maybe I'm Doing It Wrong (2nd edition)
(OB) 1982

Wedding in the Park
Music by Jay Gorney
Lyrics by Barry Trivers
Heaven on Earth 1948

Wedding in the Spring
Music by Jerome Kern
Lyrics by Johnny Mercer
You Were Never Lovelier (1942) F

The Wedding Knell
Music by Jerome Kern
Lyrics by Otto Harbach and Oscar Hammerstein II
Sunny 1925

Wedding of the Year
Music and lyrics by Ervin Drake
What Makes Sammy Run? 1964

Wedding-of-the-Year Blues
Music by Harold Karr
Lyrics by Matt Dubey
Happy Hunting 1956

The Wedding Parade
Music by Joseph Meyer
Lyrics by William Moll
Jonica 1930

Wedding Song
Music by Kurt Weill
Lyrics by Marc Blitzstein
The Threepenny Opera (OB) 1954

The Wedding Song
Music by Michael Leonard
Lyrics by Herbert Martin
How to Be a Jewish Mother 1967

Wedding Song
Music and lyrics by Richard O'Brien
The Rocky Horror Show 1975

Weddings and Funerals
Music and lyrics by Mark Barkan
Waltz of the Stork (OB) 1982

Wedgewood Maid
Music by Al Goodman, Maury Rubens
and J. Fred Coots

Lyrics by Clifford Grey
Gay Paree 1925

The Wee Golden Warrior
Music by Richard Rodgers
Lyrics by Sheldon Harnick
Rex 1976

A Weekend Affair
Music and lyrics by Cole Porter
Gay Divorce 1932

Dropped from production

A Weekend in July
Music by Vincent Youmans
Lyrics by Anne Caldwell
Oh, Please! 1926

Dropped from production

A Weekend in the Country
Music and lyrics by Stephen Sondheim
A Little Night Music 1973

The Weekly Wedding
Music by Rudolf Friml
Lyrics by Otto Harbach
Katinka 1915

Weep No More
Music by Gordon Jenkins
Lyrics by Tom Adair
Along Fifth Avenue 1949

Weep No More, My Baby
Music by John Green
Lyrics by Edward Heyman
Murder at the Vanities 1933

Weeping Willow Tree
Music by Jerome Kern
Lyrics by Howard Dietz
Dear Sir 1924

Welcome
Music by Arthur Schwartz
Lyrics by Howard Dietz
Jennie 1963

Welcome
Music by Mary Rodgers
Lyrics by Martin Charnin
Hot Spot 1963

Welcome
Music by Ted Simons
Lyrics by Elinor Guggenheimer
Potholes (OB) 1979

Welcome Banana
Music and lyrics by James Rado
Rainbow (OB) 1972

Welcome Hinges
Music by Harold Arlen
Lyrics by E.Y. Harburg
Bloomer Girl 1944

Welcome Home
Music by Joseph Meyer and James F. Hanley
Lyrics by B.G. DeSylva
Big Boy 1925

Welcome Home
Music by Winthrop Cortelyou
Lyrics by Derick Wulff
Kiss Me 1927

Welcome Home
Music and lyrics by Harold Rome
Fanny 1954

Welcome Home
Music and lyrics by Richard Adler
Kwamina 1961

Welcome Home
Music and lyrics by Rick Besoyan
The Student Gypsy (OB) 1963

Welcome Home
Music and lyrics by Stephen Schwartz
Pippin 1972

Welcome Home Again
Music by Victor Ziskin
Lyrics by Joan Javits
Young Abe Lincoln 1961

Welcome Home Miz Adams
Music by Leonard Bernstein
Lyrics by Alan Jay Lerner
1600 Pennsylvania Avenue 1976

Welcome, Little One
Music by Lor Crane
Lyrics by John B. Kuntz
Whispers on the Wind (OB) 1970

Welcome Mr. Anderson
Music and lyrics by Micki Grant
It's So Nice to Be Civilized 1980

Welcome, Mr. Golden!
Music by Murray Rumshinsky
Lyrics by Jacob Jacobs
The President's Daughter 1970

Welcome on the Landing Stage
Music by Ralph Benatzky
Lyrics by Irving Caesar
White Horse Inn 1936

Welcome Song
Music by Sammy Fain
Lyrics by Paul Francis Webster
Christine 1960

Welcome Song
Music and lyrics by Irving Burgie
Ballad for Bimshire (OB) 1963

Welcome to a New World
Music by Nancy Ford
Lyrics by Gretchen Cryer
Shelter 1973

Welcome to Holiday Inn!
Music by Cy Coleman
Lyrics by Dorothy Fields
Seesaw 1973

Welcome to Jerry
Music and lyrics by Cole Porter
Panama Hattie 1940

Welcome to Kanagawa
Music and lyrics by Stephen Sondheim
Pacific Overtures 1976

Welcome to Pootzie Van Doyle
Music and lyrics by Noël Coward
The Girl Who Came to Supper 1963

Welcome to Sludgepool
Music and lyrics by Leslie Bricusse
and Anthony Newley
Stop the World—I Want to Get Off 1962

Welcome to Sunvale
Music and lyrics by Leslie Bricusse
and Anthony Newley
Stop the World—I Want to Get Off 1962

Welcome to the Moon
Music and lyrics by John Phillips
Man on the Moon 1975

Welcome to the Queen
Music by Rudolf Friml
Lyrics by P.G. Wodehouse and Clifford Grey
The Three Musketeers 1928

Welcome to the Theater
Music by Charles Strouse
Lyrics by Lee Adams
Applause 1970

Welcome, Welcome
Music and lyrics by Frederick Silver
Gay Company (OB) 1974

Welcoming the Bride
Music by Victor Herbert
Lyrics by Robert B. Smith
Sweethearts 1913

Welfare Rag
Music and lyrics by Harry Chapin
The Night That Made America Famous 1975

We'll Be the Same
Music by Richard Rodgers
Lyrics by Lorenz Hart
America's Sweetheart 1931

We'll Be There
Music by J. Fred Coots
Lyrics by Arthur Swanstrom and Benny Davis
Sons o' Guns 1929

We'll Build a Brand New Bamboo Bungalow
Music by A. Baldwin Sloane
Lyrics by Harry Cort and George E. Stoddard
China Rose 1925

Well, Did You Evah!
Music and lyrics by Cole Porter
Du Barry Was a Lady 1939

Also used in the film *High Society* (1958)

We'll Do the Riviera
Music by Harry Tierney
Lyrics by Joseph McCarthy
Up She Goes 1922

We'll Drift Along
Music by Rudolf Friml
Lyrics by Otto Harbach and Edward Clark
You're In Love 1917

We'll Find a Way
Music by Joseph Raposo
Lyrics by Erich Segal
Sing Muse! (OB) 1961

We'll Get Along
Music by Muriel Pollock
Lyrics by Max and Nathaniel Lief
and Harold Atteridge
Pleasure Bound 1929

We'll Go Away Together
Music by Kurt Weill
Lyrics by Langston Hughes
Street Scene 1947

We'll Have a Model Factory
Music by Harry Ruby
Lyrics by Bert Kalmar
Helen of Troy, New York 1923

We'll Have a New Home in the Morning
Music by Willard Robison
Lyrics by J. Russel Robinson and Gene Buck
Take the Air 1927

We'll Have a Wonderful Party
Music by Louis A. Hirsch
Lyrics by Otto Harbach
Mary 1920

We'll Have Our Good Days
Music by Harry Tierney
Lyrics by Joseph McCarthy
Cross My Heart 1928

We'll Help You Through the Night
Music and lyrics by Jeanne Napoli, Dawsen
and Turner
Marilyn 1983

Well, I'm Not!
Music by Charles Strouse
Lyrics by Lee Adams
Bring Back Birdie 1981

Well It Ain't
Music by Mary Rodgers
Lyrics by Larry Siegel and Stan Hart
The Mad Show (OB) 1966

We'll Just Be Two Commuters
Music by Harry Archer
Lyrics by Walter O'Keefe
Just a Minute 1928

A Well-Known Fact
Music by Harvey Schmidt
Lyrics by Tom Jones
I Do! I Do! 1966

We'll Live All Over Again
Music by Vernon Duke
Lyrics by John Latouche
Cabin in the Sky (1964 OB revival)

We'll Make a Bet
Music by Jerome Kern
Lyrics by Anne Caldwell
Hitchy-Koo 1920

We'll Never Grow Old
Music by Monte Carlo and Alma Sanders
Lyrics by Howard Johnson
Tangerine 1921

The Well of Romance
Music by H. Maurice Jacquet
Lyrics by Preston Sturges
The Well of Romance 1930

We'll See
Music by Jerome Kern
Lyrics by Harry B. Smith
Love o' Mike 1917

We'll Swing It Through
Music by Lee Wainer
Lyrics by John Lund
New Faces of 1943

Well, This Is Jolly
Music by Jerome Kern
Lyrics by Harry B. Smith
Oh, I Say! 1913

Well, Well!
Music by Lee Wainer
Lyrics by June Carroll
New Faces of 1943

Well, You See
Music by John Green
Lyrics by Edward Heyman
Here Goes the Bride 1931

Wells Fargo Wagon
Music and lyrics by Meredith Willson
The Music Man 1957

Wendy
Music by Jule Styne
Lyrics by Betty Comden and Adolph Green
Peter Pan 1954

We're a Couple of Salesmen
Music by Eubie Blake
Lyrics by Noble Sissle
Shuffle Along of 1933

We're a Home
Music by Robert Waldman
Lyrics by Alfred Uhry
Here's Where I Belong 1968

We're a Little Family
Music by Galt MacDermot
Lyrics by William Dumaresq
The Human Comedy (OB) 1983

We're About to Start Big Rehearsin'
Music and lyrics by Cole Porter
Red, Hot and Blue! 1936

We're Alive
Music and lyrics by Marc Blitzstein
Juno 1959

We're All in the Same Boat
Music by Sigmund Romberg (developed by Don Walker)
Lyrics by Leo Robin
The Girl in Pink Tights 1954

We're Almost There
Music and lyrics by Jerry Herman
The Grand Tour 1979

We're Betting on You
Music by Robert Kessler
Lyrics by Martin Charnin
Fallout (OB) 1959

We're Calling On Mr. Brooks
Music by Ray Henderson
Lyrics by B.G. DeSylva and Lew Brown
Hold Everything! 1928

We're Civilized
Music by Ray Haney
Lyrics by Alfred Aiken
We're Civilized? (OB) 1962

We're Crooks
Music by Jerome Kern
Lyrics by P.G. Wodehouse
Miss 1917

We're for Love
Music and lyrics by Ralph Blane
Three Wishes for Jamie 1952

We're Getting Away With It
Music by Harry Tierney
Lyrics by Joseph McCarthy
Irene 1919

We're Goin' Around
Music and lyrics by Scott Joplin
Treemonisha 1975

Written in 1909

We're Going Away
Music and lyrics by Gene Lockhart
Bunk of 1926 1926

We're Going to Atlanta
Music and lyrics by Harry Chapin
Cotton Patch Gospel (OB) 1981

We're Going to Balance the Budget
Music by Richard Rodgers
Lyrics by Lorenz Hart
I'd Rather Be Right 1937

We're Going to Des Moines
Music and lyrics by Al Carmines
The Evangelist (OB) 1982

We're Going to Make a Man of You
Music by Rudolf Friml
Lyrics by Otto Harbach
The Firefly 1912

We're Going to Make Boom-Boom
Music by Werner Janssen
Lyrics by Mann Holiner and J. Keirn Brennan
Boom-Boom 1929

We're Gonna Be All Right
Music by Richard Rodgers
Lyrics by Stephen Sondheim
Do I Hear a Waltz? 1965

We're Gonna Have a Wedding
Music by Don McAfee
Lyrics by Nancy Leeds
Great Scot! (OB) 1965

We're Gonna Live It Together
Music by Bob James
Lyrics by Jack O'Brien
The Selling of the President 1972

We're Gonna Love It
Music and lyrics by Harry Chapin
Cotton Patch Gospel (OB) 1981

We're Gonna Turn on Freedom
Music and lyrics by Johnny Brandon
Billy Noname (OB) 1970

We're Gonna Win
Music and lyrics by Oscar Brand
How to Steal an Election (OB) 1968

We're Gonna Work It Out
Music by John Kander
Lyrics by Fred Ebb
Woman of the Year 1981

We're Having a Baby
Music by Vernon Duke
Lyrics by Harold Adamson
Banjo Eyes 1941

We're Having a Party
Music and lyrics by Walter Cool
Mackey of Appalachia (OB) 1965

We're Having Our Fling
Music by Jerry Livingston
Lyrics by Mack David
Bright Lights of 1944

We're Here
Music and lyrics by J.C. Johnson
Change Your Luck 1930

We're Here Because
Music by George Gershwin
Lyrics by Ira Gershwin
Lady, Be Good! 1924

We're Home
Music and lyrics by Bob Merrill
Take Me Along 1959

We're in a Salad
Music by Mel Marvin
Lyrics by Christopher Durang
A History of the American Film 1978

We're Jumping Into Something
Music and lyrics by Blanche Merrill
Puzzles of 1925

We're Looking for a Piano
Music by Julian Slade
Lyrics by Dorothy Reynolds and Julian Slade
Salad Days (OB) 1958

We're Not Children
Music and lyrics by Jay Livingston and Ray Evans
Oh Captain! 1958

We're Off
Music by Richard Lewine
Lyrics by Ted Fetter
The Fireman's Flame (OB) 1937

We're Off on a Wonderful Trip
Music by Youmans and Paul Lannin
Lyrics by Arthur Francis
Two Little Girls in Blue 1921

We're Off to Feathermore
Music and lyrics by Cole Porter
Jubilee 1935

We're Off to India
Music by Youmans and Paul Lannin
Lyrics by Arthur Francis
Two Little Girls in Blue 1921

We're Off to See the Wizard
Music by Harold Arlen
Lyrics by E.Y. Harburg
The Wizard of Oz (1939) F

We're on Our Way
Music by Jerome Kern
Lyrics by Schuyler Greene
Very Good Eddie 1915

We're on Our Way to France
Music and lyrics by Irving Berlin
Yip, Yip, Yaphank 1918

We're on the Map
Music by Harry Ruby
Lyrics by Bert Kalmar
Twinkle Twinkle 1926

We're Sharin' Sharon
Music by Stanley Lebowsky
Lyrics by Fred Tobias
Gantry 1970

We're Still Friends
Music by Cy Coleman
Lyrics by Michael Stewart
I Love My Wife 1977

We're Still on the Map
Music and lyrics by Ann Ronell
Count Me In 1942

We're the Berries
Music by Eubie Blake
Lyrics by Andy Razaf
Blackbirds of 1930

We're the Girls You Can't Forget
Music by James F. Hanley
Lyrics by Eddie Dowling
Sidewalks of New York 1927

Were Thine That Special Face
Music and lyrics by Cole Porter
Kiss Me, Kate 1948

Were This to Prove a Feather in My Hat
Music by Alec Wilder
Lyrics by Arnold Sundgaard
Kittiwake Island (OB) 1960

We're Today
Music by Norman Curtis
Lyrics by Patricia Taylor Curtis
Walk Down Mah Street! (OB) 1968

Wernher von Braun
Music and lyrics by Tom Lehrer
Tomfoolery (OB) 1981

West End Avenue
Music and lyrics by Stephen Schwartz
The Magic Show 1974

West Point Song
Music by Sigmund Romberg
Lyrics by P.G. Wodehouse
Rosalie 1928

West Wind
Music by Vincent Youmans
Lyrics by J. Russel Robinson

Added to *Song of the West* (1930), the film version
of *Rainbow* (1928)

West Wind
Music by Kurt Weill
Lyrics by Ogden Nash
One Touch of Venus 1943

Western People Funny
Music by Richard Rodgers
Lyrics by Oscar Hammerstein II
The King and I 1951

Westward Ho!
Music and lyrics by Dorcas Cochran
and Charles Rosoff
Earl Carroll's Vanities (1940)

We've Chosen You, Lieutenant
Music and lyrics by Gene Curty, Nitra Scharfman
and Chuck Strand
The Lieutenant 1975

We've Decided to Stay
Music by Harry Warren
Lyrics by Jerome Lawrence and Robert E. Lee
Shangri-La 1956

We've Got Connections
Music and lyrics by Buster Davis
Doctor Jazz 1975

We've Got Each Other
Music and lyrics by Gary Portnoy
and Judy Hart Angelo
Preppies (OB) 1983

We've Got Him
Music and lyrics by George M. Cohan
The Merry Malones 1927

We've Got It
Music by Cy Coleman
Lyrics by Dorothy Fields
Seesaw 1973

We've Got the Song
Music and lyrics by Harold Rome
Sing Out the News 1938

We've Had a Grand Old Time
Music and lyrics by George M. Cohan
The Merry Malones 1927

We've Just Begun
Music by Harold Rome
Lyrics by Harold Rome and Charles Friedman
Pins and Needles (OB) 1937

Wha'd You Come to College For?
Music by Harold Arlen
Lyrics by Jack Yellen
You Said It 1931

Whaddaya Say, Kid?
Music by Clinton Ballard
Lyrics by Carolyn Richter
The Ballad of Johnny Pot (OB) 1971

What a Blessing
Music and lyrics by Frank Loesser
Greenwillow 1960

What a Case I've Got on You
Music by Arthur Schwartz
Lyrics by Howard Dietz
The Second Little Show 1930

What a Charming Couple
Music by Arthur Schwartz
Lyrics by Howard Dietz
The Gay Life 1961

What a Country!
Music by Charles Strouse
Lyrics by Lee Adams
All American 1962

What a Crazy Way to Spend Sunday
Music and lyrics by Cole Porter
Mexican Hayride 1944

What a Day!
Music by Abraham Ellstein
Lyrics by Walter Bullock
Great to Be Alive 1950

What a Delightful
Music by Sammy Fain
Lyrics by Paul Francis Webster and Ray Golden
Alive and Kicking 1950

What a Difference a Uniform Will Make
Music and lyrics by Irving Berlin
Yip, Yip, Yaphank 1918

What a Girl
Music by Richard Rodgers
Lyrics by Lorenz Hart
Spring Is Here 1929

What a Girl
Music by Werner Janssen
Lyrics by Mann Holiner and J. Keirn Brennan
Boom-Boom 1929

What a Good Day Is Saturday
Music by John Morris
Lyrics by Gerald Freedman
A Time for Singing 1966

What a Great Pair We'll Be
Music and lyrics by Cole Porter
Red, Hot and Blue! 1936

What a Happy Day
Music by Michael Leonard
Lyrics by Herbert Martin
The Yearling 1965

What a Jamboree
Music and lyrics by Ida Hoyt Chamberlain
Enchanted Isle 1927

What a Life!
Music by Harry Archer
Lyrics by Harlan Thompson
Merry-Merry 1925

What a Long Cold Winter!
Music by William Dyer
Lyrics by Don Parks and William Dyer
Jo (OB) 1964

What a Lovely Day for a Wedding
Music by Richard Rodgers
Lyrics by Oscar Hammerstein II
Allegro 1947

What a Lovely Day for a Wedding
Music by Burton Lane
Lyrics by Alan Jay Lerner
Royal Wedding (1951) F

What a Lovely Night
Music by Frank Grey
Lyrics by Earle Crooker and McElbert Moore
Happy 1927

What a Man!
Music and lyrics by Leslie Bricusse
and Anthony Newley
*The Roar of the Greasepaint—The Smell
of the Crowd* 1965

What a Man
Music and lyrics by Lionel Bart
La Strada 1969

What a Nice Idea
Music by Galt MacDermot
Lyrics by John Guare
Two Gentlemen of Verona 1971

What a Nice Municipal Park
Music and lyrics by Cole Porter
Jubilee 1935

What a Night This Is Going to Be
Music and lyrics by Marian Grudeff
and Raymond Jessel
Baker Street 1965

What a Party
Music by John Morris
Lyrics by Gerald Freedman
A Time for Singing 1966

What a Piece of Work Is Man
Music by Galt MacDermot
Lyrics by Gerome Ragni and James Rado
Hair 1968

What a Pretty Baby You Are
Music by Leo Edwards
Lyrics by Herman Timberg
You'll See Stars 1942

What a Priceless Pleasure [The Waiters]
Music and lyrics by Cole Porter
You Never Know 1938

Dropped from production

What a Shame
Music by Don McAfee
Lyrics by Nancy Leeds
Great Scot! (OB) 1965

What a Song Can Do
Music and lyrics by Bernie Wayne and Lee Morris
Catch a Star! 1955

What a Waste
Music by Leonard Bernstein
Lyrics by Betty Comden and Adolph Green
Wonderful Town 1953

What a Wedding
Music and lyrics by Johnny Brandon
Cindy (OB) 1964

**What a Whale of a Difference
a Woman Can Make**
Music by Charles Rosoff
Lyrics by Leo Robin
Judy 1927

What a Wonderful World
Music by Arthur Schwartz
Lyrics by Howard Dietz
At Home Abroad 1935

What a World This Would Be
Music by Ray Henderson
Lyrics by B.G. DeSylva and Lew Brown
George White's Scandals (1925)

What-a-Ya Say?
Music and lyrics by Harold Orlob
Hairpin Harmony 1943

What About Me?
Music by Clinton Ballard
Lyrics by Carolyn Richter
The Ballad of Johnny Pot (OB) 1971

What About Today?
Music by David Shire
Lyrics by David Shire
Starting Here, Starting Now (OB) 1977

What Abraham Lincoln Once Said
Music by Menachem Zur
Lyrics by Herbert Appleman
Unfair to Goliath (OB) 1970

What Am I Going to Do to Make You Love Me?
Music by Raymond Hubbell
Lyrics by Glen MacDonough
The Jolly Bachelors 1910

What Am I Supposed to Do?
Music by Galt MacDermot
Lyrics by William Dumaresq
The Human Comedy (OB) 1983

What Am I to Do?
Music and lyrics by Cole Porter
The Man Who Came to Dinner 1939

What America Means to Me
Music and lyrics by Don Tucker
Red, White and Maddox 1969

What Are Little Husbands Made Of?
Music and lyrics by Cole Porter
Let's Face It! 1941

Dropped from production

What Are the Basic Things?
Music by Dov Seltzer
Lyrics by Lillian Durstein
To Live Another Summer 1971

What Are They Doing to Us Now?
Music and lyrics by Harold Rome
I Can Get It for You Wholesale 1962

What Are We Doing in Egypt?
Music and lyrics by Ervin Drake
Her First Roman 1968

What Are We Gonna Do Tonight?
Music by Leon Pober
Lyrics by Bud Freeman
Beg, Borrow or Steal 1960

What Are We Here For?
Music by George Gershwin
Lyrics by Ira Gershwin
Treasure Girl 1928

What Are You Doing the Rest of Your Life
Music by Burton Lane
Lyrics by Ted Koehler
Hollywood Canteen (1944) F

What Are You Going to Do About It?
Music by Charles Strouse
Lyrics by Alan Jay Lerner
Dance a Little Closer 1983

What Are You Going to Do About Love?
Music by Dave Stamper
Lyrics by Fred Herendeen
Orchids Preferred 1937

What Are You Proposing?
Music by Stanley Silverman
Lyrics by Tom Hendry
Doctor Selavy's Magic Theatre (OB) 1972

What Became of the People We Were?
Music by Jim Steinman
Lyrics by Michael Weller and Jim Steinman
More Than You Deserve (OB) 1973

What Better Time for Love?
Music by Garry Sherman
Lyrics by Peter Udell
Comin' Uptown 1979

What Can I Do for You?
Music and lyrics by James Rado
Rainbow (OB) 1972

What Can I Give You?
Music by Phillip Broughton
Lyrics by Will B. Johnstone
Entre-Nous (OB) 1935

What Can It Be?
Music by Jacques Urbont
Lyrics by Bruce Geller
All in Love (OB) 1961

What Can They See in Dancing?
Music by Vivian Ellis
Lyrics by Graham John
By the Way 1925

What Can You Do With a Man?
Music by Richard Rodgers
Lyrics by Lorenz Hart
The Boys From Syracuse 1938

What Can You Say in a Love Song?
Music by Harold Arlen
Lyrics by Ira Gershwin and E.Y. Harburg
Life Begins at 8:40 1934

What Care I?
Music by Sigmund Romberg
Lyrics by Harry B. Smith
Princess Flavia 1925

What Care We?
Music and lyrics by Ben Schwartz
Tales of Rigo 1927

What Causes That?
Music by George Gershwin
Lyrics by Ira Gershwin
Treasure Girl 1928

What Chance Have I?
Music and lyrics by Irving Berlin
Louisiana Purchase 1940

What Could Be Better?
Music by David Shire
Lyrics by Richard Maltby, Jr.
Baby 1983

What Could I Do?
Music by Werner Janssen
Lyrics by Mann Holiner and J. Keirn Brennan
Boom-Boom 1929

What Could I Do, But Fall in Love With You?
Music by Alma Sanders
Lyrics by Monte Carlo
Mystery Moon 1930

What Did Della Wear?
Music by Arthur Schwartz
Lyrics by Agnes Morgan and Albert Carroll
The Grand Street Follies (1929)

What Did Dey Do to my Goil?
Music by Paul Horner
Lyrics by Peggy Lee
Peg 1983

What Did I Ever See in Him?
Music by Charles Strouse
Lyrics by Lee Adams
Bye Bye Birdie 1960

What Did I Have That I Don't Have?
Music by Burton Lane
Lyrics by Alan Jay Lerner
On a Clear Day You Can See Forever 1965

What Did We Do Wrong?
Music and lyrics by Johnny Brandon
Love! Love! Love! (OB) 1977

What Did William Tell?
Music by Philip Charig and Richard Myers
Lyrics by Leo Robin
Allez-Oop 1927

What Difference Does It Make?
Music by Constance Shepard
Lyrics by McElbert Moore and Frank Grey
The Matinee Girl 1926

What Do I Care?
Music and lyrics by Billy Solly
Boy Meets Boy (OB) 1975

What Do I Do Now?
Music by Claibe Richardson
Lyrics by Kenward Elmslie
The Grass Harp 1971

What Do I Do Now?
Music by Ronald Melrose
Lyrics by Bill Russell
Fourtune (OB) 1980

What Do I Know?
Music and lyrics by Ralph Blane
Three Wishes for Jamie 1952

What Do I Know?
Music and lyrics by Hal Hester and Danny Apolinar
Your Own Thing (OB) 1968

What Do I Tell People This Time?
Music by Michael Valenti
Lyrics by Donald Driver
Oh, Brother 1981

What Do I Want With Love?
Music by Eubie Blake
Lyrics by J. Milton Reddie and Cecil Mack
Swing It 1937

What Do I Want With Love?
Music and lyrics by Sandy Wilson
Valmouth (OB) 1960

What Do the Neighbors Say?
Music and lyrics by Harold Orlob
Hairpin Harmony 1943

What Do the Simple Folk Do?
Music by Frederick Loewe
Lyrics by Alan Jay Lerner
Camelot 1960

What Do We Care?
Music by Harold Arlen
Lyrics by Jack Yellen
You Said It 1931

What Do We Care?
Music by George Kleinsinger
Lyrics by Joe Darion
Shinbone Alley 1957

What Do We Do? We Fly!
Music by Richard Rodgers
Lyrics by Stephen Sondheim
Do I Hear a Waltz? 1965

What Do We Have to Hold On To?
Music and lyrics by Billy Barnes
The Billy Barnes People 1961

What Do Women Want?
Music by Richard Hill and John Hawkins
Lyrics by Nevill Coghill
Canterbury Tales 1969

What Do You Do Sunday, Mary?
Music by Stephen Jones
Lyrics by Irving Caesar
Poppy 1923

**What Do You Give to a Man
Who's Had Everything?**
Music by Jule Styne
Lyrics by Bob Merrill
Sugar 1972

What Do You Have to Do?
Music by Rudolf Friml
Lyrics by Rida Johnson Young
Sometime 1918

What Do You Say?
Music by Don Elliott
Lyrics by James Costigan
The Beast in Me 1963

What Do You Think About Men?
Music and lyrics by Cole Porter
Out of This World 1950

Dropped from production

What Do You Think I Am?
Music and lyrics by Hugh Martin and Ralph Blane
Best Foot Forward 1941

What Do You Want with Money?
Music by Richard Rodgers
Lyrics by Lorenz Hart
Hallelujah, I'm a Bum (1933) F

What Does a Lover Pack?
Music by Galt MacDermot
Lyrics by John Guare
Two Gentlemen of Verona 1971

What Does Atlanta Mean to Me?
Music and lyrics by Harry Chapin
Cotton Patch Gospel (OB) 1981

What Does He Look Like?
Music and lyrics by Irving Berlin
This Is the Army 1942

What Does He Want of Me?
Music by Mitch Leigh
Lyrics by Joe Darion
Man of La Mancha 1965

What Does It Mean?
Music by Philip Charig and Richard Myers
Lyrics by Leo Robin
Allez-Oop 1927

What Does That Dream Mean?
Music by Harold Karr
Lyrics by Matt Dubey
New Faces of 1956

What Does Your Servant Dream About?
Music and lyrics by Cole Porter
Kiss Me, Kate 1948

Dropped from production

What D'Ya Say?
Music by Henry Souvaine and Jay Gorney
Lyrics by Morrie Ryskind and Howard Dietz
Merry-Go-Round 1927

What D'Ya Say?
Music by Jesse Greer
Lyrics by Raymond Klages
The Circus Princess 1927

What D'Ya Say?
Music by Ray Henderson
Lyrics by B.G. DeSylva and Lew Brown
George White's Scandals (1928)

What Ever Happened to Saturday Night?
Music and lyrics by Richard O'Brien
The Rocky Horror Show 1975

What Every Little Girl Should Know
Music by Arthur Schwartz
Lyrics by Henry Myers
The Little Show (1st edition) 1929

What Every Old Girl Should Know
Music by Harry Warren
Lyrics by Jerome Lawrence and Robert E. Lee
Shangri-La 1956

What Every Woman Knows
Music and lyrics by William Roy
Maggie 1953

What Fun
Music and lyrics by Cole Porter
Les Girls (1957) F

Dropped from film

What Good Does It Do
Music by Harold Arlen
Lyrics by E.Y. Harburg
Jamaica 1957

What Good Is Love?
Music and lyrics by Harold Rome
Pins and Needles (OB) 1937

What Good Would the Moon Be?
Music by Kurt Weill
Lyrics by Langston Hughes
Street Scene 1947

What Great Big Eyes You Have
Music by Henry Sullivan
Lyrics by Edward Eliscu
A Little Racketeer 1932

What Great Men Cannot Do
Music by R.P. Weston
Lyrics by Bert Lee
Naughty Riquette 1926

What Happened?
Music by Vernon Duke
Lyrics by Howard Dietz
Jackpot 1944

What Happened Nobody Knows
Music by Richard Rodgers
Lyrics by Lorenz Hart
Poor Little Ritz Girl 1920

What Happened to Me Tonight?
Music and lyrics by Richard Adler
Kwamina 1961

What Happened to Paris?
Music by Don Gohman
Lyrics by Hal Hackady
Ambassador 1972

What Happens to Life
Music by Gary William Friedman
Lyrics by Will Holt
The Me Nobody Knows (OB) 1970

What Has Happened?
Music and lyrics by Rick Besoyan
Little Mary Sunshine (OB) 1959

What Has He Got?
Music by Vernon Duke
Lyrics by Ted Fetter
The Show Is On 1936

What Has Made the Movies?
Music by Maury Rubens
Lyrics by Clifford Grey
The Madcap 1928

What Have I Done?
Music and lyrics by J.C. Johnson
Change Your Luck 1930

What Have I Done?
Music by James P. Johnson
Lyrics by Flournoy Miller
Sugar Hill 1931

What Have You Done to Me?
Music by Lewis E. Gensler
Lyrics by Owen Murphy and Robert A.Simon
The Gang's All Here l931

What Have You Got to Have?
Music by Lewis E. Gensler
Lyrics by E.Y. Harburg
Ballyhoo 1932

What Ho, Mrs. Brisket
Music and lyrics by Noël Coward
The Girl Who Came to Supper 1963

What I Could Have Done Tonight
Music and lyrics by Tom Savage
Musical Chairs 1980

What I Did for Love
Music by Marvin Hamlisch
Lyrics by Edward Kleban
A Chorus Line 1975

What I Love to Hear
Music by Jerome Kern
Lyrics by Ira Gershwin
Cover Girl (1944) F

What I Mean to Say
Music by Moose Charlap
Lyrics by Norman Gimbel
Whoop-Up 1958

What I Say Goes
Music by John Kander
Lyrics by James Goldman, John Kander
and William Goldman
A Family Affair 1962

What I Was Warned About
Music and lyrics by Hugh Martin
Make a Wish 1951

What I Wonder
Music and lyrics by Al Carmines
Joan (OB) 1972

What if We
Music and lyrics by Barbara Schottenfeld
I Can't Keep Running in Place (OB) 1981

What I'm Longing to Say
Music by Jerome Kern
Lyrics by P. G. Wodehouse
Leave It to Jane 1917

What in the World Did You Want?
Music and lyrics by Hugh Martin and Timothy Gray
High Spirits 1964

What Is a Friend?
Music and lyrics by Oscar Brown, Jr.
and Luis Henrique
Joy (OB) 1970

What Is a Friend For?
Music by Harold Arlen
Lyrics by Harold Arlen and Truman Capote
House of Flowers 1954

What Is a Letter?
Music and lyrics by Elizabeth Swados
Alice in Concert (OB) 1980

What Is a Man
Music by Richard Rodgers
Lyrics by Lorenz Hart

Originally written as "Love Is My Friend"

What Is a Queen?
Music and lyrics by Al Carmines
The Faggot (OB) 1973

What Is a Woman?
Music by Harvey Schmidt
Lyrics by Tom Jones
I Do! I Do! 1966

What Is It?
Music by Richard Rodgers
Lyrics by Lorenz Hart
The Girl Friend 1926

What Is Life Without Love
Music by Rudolf Friml
Lyrics by Otto Harbach
High Jinks 1913

What Is Love?
Music and lyrics by Howard Blankman
By Hex (OB) 1956

What Is That Tune?
Music and lyrics by Cole Porter
You Never Know 1938

What Is the Good
Music by Lew Kesler
Lyrics by Clifford Grey
Ned Wayburn's Gambols 1929

What Is the Stars?
Music and lyrics by Marc Blitzstein
Juno 1959

What Is There to Say?
Music by Vernon Duke
Lyrics by E.Y. Harburg
Ziegfeld Follies (1934)

What Is There to Say?
Music and lyrics by Johnny Brandon
Love! Love! Love! (OB) 1977

What Is There to Sing About?
Music and lyrics by Charles Strouse
Six (OB) 1971

What Is This Feeling in the Air?
Music by Jule Styne
Lyrics by Betty Comden and Adolph Green
Subways Are for Sleeping 1961

What Is This Thing Called Love?
Music and lyrics by Cole Porter
Wake Up and Dream 1929

What It's All About
Music by Richard Rodgers
Lyrics by Lorenz Hart
I'd Rather Be Right 1937

Added to production after Broadway opening

What It's Like to Be a Legend
Music and lyrics by Nick Branch
An Evening With Joan Crawford (OB) 1981

What I've Always Wanted
Music by Charles Strouse
Lyrics by Lee Adams
It's a Bird, It's a Plane, It's Superman 1966

What Kind of a Place Is This?
Music by Jerome Kern
Lyrics by Edward Madden
La Belle Paree 1911

What Kind of Baby
Music by Menachem Zur
Lyrics by Herbert Appleman
Unfair to Goliath (OB) 1970

What Kind of Fool Am I?
Music and lyrics by Leslie Bricusse
and Anthony Newley
Stop the World—I Want to Get Off 1962

What Kind of Life Is That?
Music by Norman Martin
Lyrics by Fred Ebb
Put It in Writing (OB) 1963

What Kind of Man Is He?
Music by Don Pippin
Lyrics by Steve Brown
Fashion (OB) 1974

What Kind of Parents
Music by Wally Harper
Lyrics by Paul Zakrzewski
Sensations (OB) 1970

What Makes a Business Man Wear
Music by Harry Ruby
Lyrics by Bert Kalmar
Helen of Troy, New York 1923

What Makes a Marriage Merry
Music by Jule Styne
Lyrics by E.Y. Harburg
Darling of the Day 1968

What Makes It Happen?
Music by Jimmy Van Heusen
Lyrics by Sammy Cahn
Walking Happy 1966

What Makes Me Love Him?
Music by Jerry Bock
Lyrics by Sheldon Harnick
The Apple Tree 1966

What Makes You So Wonderful
Music and lyrics by Herbert Stothart, Bert Kalmar
and Harry Ruby
Good Boy 1928

What Might Have Been
Music by Edward Thomas
Lyrics by Martin Charnin
Ballad for a Firing Squad (OB) 1968

What More Can a General Do?
Music by George Gershwin
Lyrics by Ira Gershwin
Let 'Em Eat Cake 1933

What More Do I Need?
Music by Murray Rumshinsky
Lyrics by Jacob Jacobs
The President's Daughter 1970

What Next?
Music by Charles Zwar
Lyrics by Alan Melville
From A to Z 1960

What—No Dixie?
Music by Victor Young
Lyrics by Joseph Young and Ned Washington
Blackbirds of 1934

What Shadows We Are
Music by Norman Curtis
Lyrics by Patricia Taylor Curtis
Walk Down Mah Street! (OB) 1968

What Shall I Believe in Now?
Music and lyrics by Voices, Inc.
The Believers (OB) 1968

What Shall I Do?
Music by Cole Porter
Lyrics by Rowland Leigh
You Never Know 1938

What She Wanted and What She Got
Music by Victor Herbert
Lyrics by Robert B. Smith
Sweethearts 1913

Dropped from production

What Sort of Wedding Is This?
Music by George Gershwin
Lyrics by Ira Gershwin
Pardon My English 1933

What Style!
Music by John Clifton
Lyrics by John Clifton and Ben Tarver
Man With a Load of Mischief (OB) 1966

What Takes My Fancy
Music by Cy Coleman
Lyrics by Carolyn Leigh
Wildcat 1960

What the Girls Will Wear
Music by Harry Ruby
Lyrics by Bert Kalmar
Helen of Troy, New York 1923

What the Hell
Music by George Kleinsinger
Lyrics by Joe Darion
Shinbone Alley 1957

What the Hell Am I Doing Here?
Music by Lawrence Hurwit
Lyrics by Lee Goldsmith
Sextet 1974

What Then?
Music by Edward Thomas
Lyrics by Martin Charnin
Ballad for a Firing Squad (OB) 1968

What Then?
Music by John Duffy
Lyrics by Rocco Bufano and John Duffy
Horseman, Pass By (OB) 1969

What There Is
Music and lyrics by Elizabeth Swados
Alice in Concert (OB) 1980

What This Party Needs
Music by Harold Rome
Lyrics by Harold Rome and Arthur Kramer
Pins and Needles (OB) 1937

Added to run

What Thrills Can There Be?
Music by Stamper
Lyrics by Harry Ruskin
Ziegfeld Follies of 1923

What to Do?
Music and lyrics by Robert Larimer
King of the Whole Damn World (OB) 1962

What We Need Around Here
Music and lyrics by Mel Mandel and Norman Sachs
My Old Friends (OB) 1979

What We Pick Up
Music by Alfred Nathan
Lyrics by George Oppenheimer
The Manhatters 1927

What Will Become of Our England?
Music and lyrics by Cole Porter
Gay Divorce 1932

What Will It Be?
Music and lyrics by Marc Blitzstein
Regina 1949

What Will the Future Say?
Music by Erich Wolfgang Korngold (based on
Jacques Offenbach)
Lyrics by Herbert Baker
Helen Goes to Troy 1944

What Would I Care
Music by Harry Ruby
Lyrics by Bert Kalmar
Top Speed 1929

What Would I Do if I Could Feel?
Music and lyrics by Charlie Smalls
The Wiz 1975

What Would We Do Without You
Music and lyrics by Stephen Sondheim
Company 1970

What Would You Do?
Music by John Kander
Lyrics by Fred Ebb
Cabaret 1966

What Would You Do?
Music by Murray Rumshinsky
Lyrics by Jacob Jacobs
The President's Daughter 1970

What You Go Through
Music by Charles Strouse
Lyrics by Lee Adams
A Broadway Musical 1978

What You Want With Bess?
Music by George Gershwin
Lyrics by DuBose Heyward
Porgy and Bess 1935

What You Will
Music by Richard Adler
Lyrics by Will Holt
Music Is 1976

Whatever Became of Old Temple?
Music by Mark Sandrich, Jr.
Lyrics by Sidney Michaels
Ben Franklin in Paris 1964

Whatever Happened to the Good Old Days?
Music and lyrics by Jack Bussins
and Ellsworth Olin
Be Kind to People Week (OB) 1975

Whatever It Happens to Be
Music and lyrics by David Langston Smyrl
On the Lock-In (OB) 1977

Whatever Lola Wants
Music and lyrics by Richard Adler and Jerry Ross
Damn Yankees 1955

Whatever That May Be
Music by Jacques Offenbach (adapted by Robert
De Cormier)
Lyrics by E.Y. Harburg
The Happiest Girl in the World 1961

Whatever Time There Is
Music by Charles Strouse
Lyrics by David Rogers
Charlie and Algernon 1980

Whatever Turns You On
Music and lyrics by Earl Wilson, Jr.
Let My People Come (OB) 1974

What'll I Do?
Music and lyrics by Irving Berlin
Music Box Revue (3rd edition) 1923

Added to the score during the run and sung by
Grace Moore and John Steel.

What'll They Think of Next?
Music by Hoagy Carmichael
Lyrics by Johnny Mercer
Walk With Music 1940

What's a Girl Supposed to Do?
Music by Robert Stolz
Lyrics by Robert Sour
Mr. Strauss Goes to Boston 1945

What's a Guy Like You Doin' in a Place Like This?
Music by Nancy Ford
Lyrics by Gretchen Cryer
Now Is the Time for All Good Men (OB) 1967

What's a Kiss Among Friends?
Music by Vincent Youmans
Lyrics by Leo Robin and Clifford Grey
Hit the Deck 1927

What's a Mama For?
Music and lyrics by Robert Larimer
King of the Whole Damn World (OB) 1962

What's a Nice Girl Like Her
Music by Galt MacDermot
Lyrics by John Guare
Two Gentlemen of Verona 1971

What's a Sailor Got?
Music by Jacques Belasco
Lyrics by Kay Twomey
The Girl From Nantucket 1945

What's a Show?
Music by Shelley Mowell
Lyrics by Mike Stewart
Shoestring '57 (OB)

What's Become of the Bowery?
Music and lyrics by Vincent Valentini
Parisiana 1928

What's Cooking?
Music by Norman Martin
Lyrics by Fred Ebb
Put It in Writing (OB) 1963

What's Goin' On Here?
Music by Frederick Loewe
Lyrics by Alan Jay Lerner
Paint Your Wagon 1951

What's Going On Inside?
Music and lyrics by Lionel Bart
La Strada 1969

What's Gonna Be Tomorrow
Music by Albert Hague
Lyrics by Marty Brill
Café Crown 1964

What's Good About Goodbye?
Music by Harold Arlen
Lyrics by Leo Robin
Casbah (1948) F

What's Good About Good Night?
Music by Jerome Kern
Lyrics by Dorothy Fields
The Joy of Living (1938) F

What's Good for General Bullmoose
Music by Gene de Paul
Lyrics by Johnny Mercer
Li'l Abner 1956

What's He Like?
Music by Jacques Belasco
Lyrics by Kay Twomey
The Girl From Nantucket 1945

What's in a Name?
Music by John Mundy
Lyrics by Edward Eager
The Liar 1950

What's in It for Me?
Music and lyrics by Harold Rome
I Can Get It for You Wholesale 1962

What's in It for You?
Music by Jerry Bock
Lyrics by Sheldon Harnick
Tenderloin 1960

What's in Store for You
Music and lyrics by Leon DeCosta
Kosher Kitty Kelly 1925

What's in the Air
Music by Nancy Ford
Lyrics by Gretchen Cryer
Now Is the Time for All Good Men (OB) 1967

What's Keeping My Prince Charming?
Music by Alberta Nichols
Lyrics by Mann Holiner
Rhapsody in Black 1931

What's Mine Is Thine
Music by Al Moss
Lyrics by Alfred Hayes
Tis of Thee 1940

What's Mine Is Yours
Music by Vernon Duke
Lyrics by Howard Dietz
Jackpot 1944

What's My Man Gonna Be Like?
Music and lyrics by Cole Porter
The Vanderbilt Revue 1930

What's New at the Zoo?
Music by Jule Styne
Lyrics by Betty Comden and Adolph Green
Do Re Mi 1960

What's New in New York
Music by Baldwin Bergersen
Lyrics by George Marion, Jr.
Allah Be Praised! 1944

What's the Buzz?
Music by Andrew Lloyd Webber
Lyrics by Tim Rice
Jesus Christ Superstar 1971

What's the Difference?
Music by John Green
Lyrics by Edward Heyman
Here Goes the Bride 1931

What's the Matter With a Nice Beef Stew?
Music and lyrics by Noël Coward
The Girl Who Came to Supper 1963

Dropped from production

What's the Matter With Buffalo?
Music by Albert Hague
Lyrics by Marty Brill
Café Crown 1964

What's the Matter With Our City?
Music by Jay Gorney
Lyrics by Barry Trivers
Heaven on Earth 1948

What's the Reason?
Music by Maury Rubens
Lyrics by Harold Atteridge
The Greenwich Village Follies (1928)

What's the Use?
Music by Jerome Kern
Lyrics by Howard Dietz
Dear Sir 1924

What's the Use?
Music by Leonard Bernstein
Lyrics by Richard Wilbur
Candide 1956

What's the Use of Talking?
Music by Richard Rodgers
Lyrics by Lorenz Hart
The Garrick Gaieties (2nd edition) 1926

What's the Use of Wond'rin'
Music by Richard Rodgers
Lyrics by Oscar Hammerstein II
Carousel 1945

What's the Younger Generation Coming To?
Music by David Raksin
Lyrics by June Carroll
If the Shoe Fits 1946

What's to Lose?
Music by Tommy Wolf
Lyrics by Fran Landesman
The Nervous Set 1959

What's Wrong With Me?
Music and lyrics by Richard Adler
Kwamina 1961

What's Wrong With Me?
Music by Edward Earle
Lyrics by Yvonne Tarr
The Decameron (OB) 1961

Wheatless Day
Music by Jerome Kern
Lyrics by P.G. Wodehouse
Oh, Lady! Lady!! 1918

Wheels
Music by Morris Hamilton
Lyrics by Grace Henry
Earl Carroll's Vanities (1928)

Wheels of Steel
Music by Kay Swift
Lyrics by Paul James
Fine and Dandy 1930

When
Music by Manning Sherwin
Lyrics by Arthur Herzog, Jr.
Bad Habits of 1926 (OB)

When
Music by Cliff Friend
Lyrics by Lew Brown
Piggy 1927

When
Music and lyrics by Harold Rome
Bless You All 1950

When
Music and lyrics by Stephen Sondheim
Evening Primrose (1966) TV

When
Music by Richard Rodgers
Lyrics by Martin Charnin
I Remember Mama 1979

Dropped from production

When a Black Man's Blue
Music and lyrics by George A. Little, Art Sizemore
and Ed G. Nelson
Brown Buddies 1930

When a Brother Is a Mother to His Sister
Music by Monty Norman
Lyrics by Julian More
The Moony Shapiro Songbook 1981

When a Fella Needs a Friend
Music by Sol Berkowitz
Lyrics by James Lipton
Nowhere to Go But Up 1962

When a Fellow Meets a Flapper on Broadway
Music by Philip Charig
Lyrics by Irving Caesar
Polly 1929

When a Girl Forgets to Scream
Music by Sigmund Romberg
Lyrics by Otto Harbach
Forbidden Melody 1936

When a Good Man Takes to Drink
Music by Harry Revel
Lyrics by Arnold B. Horwitt
Are You With It? 1945

When a Hick Chick Meets a City Slicker
Music by Jacques Belasco
Lyrics by Burt Milton
The Girl From Nantucket 1945

When a Maid Comes Knocking at Your Heart
Music by Rudolf Friml
Lyrics by Otto Harbach
The Firefly 1912

When a Maiden Weds
Music by Reginald De Koven
Lyrics by Harry B. Smith
Robin Hood 1891

When a Man Cries
Music by Bill Weeden
Lyrics by David Finkle
Hurry, Harry 1972

When a Man Is Twenty-one
Music by Gustave Kerker
Lyrics by Hugh Morton
The Belle of New York 1897

When a Pansy Was a Flower
Music by Will Irwin
Lyrics by Billy Rose and Malcolm McComb
Sweet and Low 1930

When a Pimp Meets a Whore
Music and lyrics by Elizabeth Swados
Lullabye and Goodnight 1982

When a Pullet Is Plump
Music by Frederic Norton
Lyrics by Oscar Asche
Chu Chin Chow 1917

When a Robin Leaves Chicago
Music by Alec Wilder
Lyrics by Arnold Sundgaard
Kittiwake Island (OB) 1960

When a Woman Has a Baby
Music by Kurt Weill
Lyrics by Langston Hughes
Street Scene 1947

When After You Pass My Door
Music and lyrics by Paul Shyre
Ah, Men (OB) 1981

When Am I Going to Meet Your Mother?
Music and lyrics by Richard Adler and Jerry Ross
John Murray Anderson's Almanac (1953)

When an Interfering Person
Music by Leslie Stuart
Lyrics by Paul Rubens
Florodora 1900

**When Any Woman Makes a Running Issue
Out of Her Flesh**
Music and lyrics by Elizabeth Swados
Lullabye and Goodnight 1982

When Cadets Parade
Music by George Gershwin
Lyrics by Ira Gershwin
Rosalie 1928

Dropped from production

When Daddy Goes A-Hunting
Music by Vincent Youmans
Lyrics by Anne Caldwell
Oh, Please! 1926

Dropped from production

When Did I Fall in Love?
Music by Jerry Bock
Lyrics by Sheldon Harnick
Fiorello! 1959

When Do We Dance?
Music by George Gershwin
Lyrics by Ira Gershwin
Tip-Toes 1925

When Does This Feeling Go Away?
Music and lyrics by Hugh Martin
Make a Wish 1951

When East Meets West
Music by George Gershwin
Lyrics by Arthur Jackson
George White's Scandals (1921)

When Everything Is Hunky-Dory
Music by Niclas Kempner
Lyrics by Graham John
The Street Singer 1929

When First I Saw My Lady's Face
Music by Richard Adler
Lyrics by Will Holt
Music Is 1976

When Foreign Princes Come to Visit Us
Music and lyrics by Noël Coward
The Girl Who Came to Supper 1963

When Gaby Did the Gaby Glide
Music by Jean Schwartz
Lyrics by Joseph W. Herbert and Harold Atteridge
The Honeymoon Express 1913

When Gemini Meets Capricorn
Music and lyrics by Harold Rome
I Can Get It for You Wholesale 1962

**When Gentlemen Grew Whiskers
and Ladies Grew Old**
Music by Charles Rosoff
Lyrics by Leo Robin
Judy 1927

When He Calls Half-Hour
Music and lyrics by Ann Harris
Sky High (OB) 1979

When He Looks at Me
Music by John Morris
Lyrics by Gerald Freedman
A Time for Singing 1966

When Hearts Are Young
Music by Sigmund Romberg
Lyrics by Harry Graham and Cyrus Wood
The Lady in Ermine 1922

When I Am Free to Love
Music by Sigmund Romberg (developed by Don Walker)
Lyrics by Leo Robin
The Girl in Pink Tights 1954

When I Am Lost
Music by Galt MacDermot
Lyrics by William Dumaresq
The Human Comedy (OB) 1983

When I Dance With the Person I Love
Music by Mark Sandrich, Jr.
Lyrics by Sidney Michaels
Ben Franklin in Paris 1964

When I Die
Music and lyrics by Stephen H. Lemberg
Jazzbo Brown 1980

When I Discover My Man
Music by Jerome Kern
Lyrics by Alice Duer Miller
The Charm School 1920

When I Discovered You
Music and lyrics by Irving Berlin
Watch Your Step 1914

When I Do a Dance for You
Music by Arthur Siegel
Lyrics by Mae Richard
Tallulah (OB) 1983

When I Drink With My Love
Music by Baldwin Bergersen
Lyrics by William Archibald
The Crystal Heart (OB) 1960

When I Fall in Love
Music and lyrics by Albert Selden
Small Wonder 1948

When I Feel Like Moving
Music and lyrics by Micki Grant
Don't Bother Me, I Can't Cope (OB) 1972

When I Fell in Love
Music by Jerome Kern
Lyrics by Anne Caldwell
The City Chap 1925

When I First Saw You
Music by Henry Krieger
Lyrics by Tom Eyen
Dreamgirls 1981

When I Found You
Music by Sigmund Romberg
Lyrics by Alex Gerber
Poor Little Ritz Girl 1920

When I Get Back to the U.S.A.
Music and lyrics by Irving Berlin
Stop! Look! Listen! 1915

When I Get the Call
Music and lyrics by Bland Simpson and Jim Wann
Diamond Studs (OB) 1975

When I Go on the Stage
Music by Richard Rodgers
Lyrics by Lorenz Hart
She's My Baby 1928

When I Grow Too Old to Dream
Music by Sigmund Romberg
Lyrics by Oscar Hammerstein II
The Night Is Young (1935) F

When I Grow Up (The G-Man Song)
Music and lyrics by Harold Rome
Pins and Needles (OB) 1937

Added during run

When I Hear a Syncopated Tune
Music by Louis Hirsch
Lyrics by Gene Buck
Ziegfeld Follies of 1918

When I Leave Town
Music by Leslie Stuart
Lyrics by Paul Rubens
Florodora 1900

When I Look Up
Music and lyrics by Harry Chapin
The Night That Made America Famous 1975

When I Look Up
Music and lyrics by Harry Chapin
Cotton Patch Gospel (OB) 1981

When I Love Again
Music and lyrics by Jerry Herman
I Feel Wonderful (OB) 1954

When I Love, I Love
Music by Ray Henderson
Lyrics by B.G. DeSylva and Lew Brown
Hold Everything! 1928

When I Make a Million for You
Music by Lucien Denni
Lyrics by Helena Evans
Happy Go Lucky 1926

When I March With April in May
Music by Clarence Williams
Lyrics by Spencer Williams
Bottomland 1927

When I Marry Mr. Snow
Music by Richard Rodgers
Lyrics by Oscar Hammerstein II
Carousel 1945

When I Played Carmen
Music by Victor Herbert
Lyrics by Robert B. Smith
The Debutante 1914

When I Rise
Music and lyrics by Micki Grant
It's So Nice to Be Civilized 1980

When I Take You All to London
Music by Sigmund Romberg
Lyrics by Harry B. Smith
The Love Call 1927

When I Used to Lead the Ballet
Music by Cole Porter
Lyrics by T. Lawrason Riggs and Cole Porter
See America First 1916

When I Walk With You
Music by Duke Ellington
Lyrics by John Latouche
Beggar's Holiday 1946

When I Waltz With You
Music by Rudolf Friml
Lyrics by Otto Harbach
The Blue Kitten 1922

When I Was a Cowboy
Music and lyrics by Bland Simpson and Jim Wann
(Based on traditional folk music)
Diamond Studs (OB) 1975

When I Was a Girl Like You
Music by Sigmund Romberg
Lyrics by Dorothy Donnelly
My Princess 1927

When I Was a Little Cuckoo
Music and lyrics by Cole Porter
Seven Lively Arts 1944

When I Was Born the Stars Stood Still
Music by Gustave Kerker
Lyrics by Hugh Morton
The Belle of New York 1897

When I Was Young
Music by Jule Styne
Lyrics by Sammy Cahn
Look to the Lilies 1970

When I Went to School
Music by Jerome Kern
Lyrics by Anne Caldwell
Stepping Stones 1923

Dropped from production

When I'm Alone
Music by Don Elliott
Lyrics by James Costigan
The Beast in Me 1963

When I'm Being Born Again
Music by Burton Lane
Lyrics by Alan Jay Lerner
On a Clear Day You Can See Forever 1965

When I'm in a Quiet Mood
Music by David Martin
Lyrics by Langston Hughes
Simply Heavenly 1957

When I'm in Love
Music and lyrics by Steve Allen
Sophie 1963

When I'm in Paree
Music by Maurice Yvain
Lyrics by Max and Nathaniel Lief
Luckee Girl 1928

When I'm Looking at You
Music by Herbert Stothart
Lyrics by Clifford Grey
The Rogue Song (1930) F

When I'm Not Near the Girl I Love
Music by Burton Lane
Lyrics by E.Y. Harburg
Finian's Rainbow 1947

When I'm Out With You
Music and lyrics by Irving Berlin
Stop! Look! Listen! 1915

When I'm Waltzing With You
Music by Franz Lehár
Lyrics by Harry B. and Robert B. Smith
Gypsy Love 1911

When I'm With the Girls
Music by Vincent Youmans
Lyrics by Arthur Francis
Two Little Girls in Blue 1921

**When Ireland Stands Among
the Nations of the World**
Music by Victor Herbert
Lyrics by Henry Blossom
Eileen 1917

When It Dries
Music by Richard Rodgers
Lyrics by Martin Charnin
Two by Two 1970

When It Gets Dark
Music by Seymour Furth and Lee Edwards
Lyrics by R.F. Carroll
Bringing Up Father 1925

When It's All Said and Done
Music and lyrics by Cole Porter
Leave It to Me 1938

When It's Cactus Time in Arizona
Music by George Gershwin
Lyrics by Ira Gershwin
Girl Crazy 1930

When June Comes Along With a Song
Music and lyrics by George M. Cohan
The Rise of Rosie O'Reilly 1923

When Love Awakes
Music by Victor Herbert
Lyrics by Henry Blossom
Eileen 1917

When Love Beckoned (in Fifty-Second Street)
Music and lyrics by Cole Porter
Du Barry Was a Lady 1939

When Love Comes Swingin' Along
Music by Ray Henderson
Lyrics by Ted Koehler
Say When 1934

When Love Comes Your Way
Music and lyrics by Cole Porter
Jubilee 1935

When Love Is Near
Music by Will Ortman
Lyrics by Gus Kahn and Raymond B. Egan
Holka-Polka 1925

When Love's in the Air
Music by Jean Gilbert
Lyrics by Harry Graham
Katja 1926

When Mabel Comes in the Room
Music and lyrics by Jerry Herman
Mack and Mabel 1974

When Maudey Wants a Man
Music and lyrics by Harry Chapin
The Night That Made America Famous 1975

When McGregor Sings Off Key
Music by Sammy Fain
Lyrics by Charles Tobias
Hellzapoppin 1938

When Me, Mowgli, Love
Music and lyrics by Cole Porter
Jubilee 1935

When Men Are Alone
Music by Stephen Jones and Arthur Samuels
Lyrics by Dorothy Donnelly
Poppy 1923

When Moses Spake to Goldstein
Music by Menachem Zur
Lyrics by Herbert Appleman
Unfair to Goliath (OB) 1970

When My Baby Goes to Town
Music and lyrics by Cole Porter
Something for the Boys 1943

When My Dreams Come True
Music and lyrics by Irving Berlin
The Cocoanuts (film version, 1929)

When My Eyes Meet Yours
Music and lyrics by Arthur Brander
The Seventh Heart 1927

When My Little Ship Comes In
Music by Frank Grey
Lyrics by McElbert Moore and Frank Grey
The Matinee Girl 1926

When My Man Returns
Music by George Moustaki
Lyrics by David Paulsen
To Live Another Summer 1971

When My Violin Is Calling
Music by Edward Künneke
Lyrics by Harry B. Smith
The Love Song 1925

When Night Starts to Fall
Music by Stanley Silverman
Lyrics by Arthur Miller
Up From Paradise (OB) 1983

When One Deems a Lady Sweet
Music by Alec Wilder
Lyrics by Arnold Sundgaard
Kittiwake Island (OB) 1960

When Opportunity Knocks
Music by Richard Lewine
Lyrics by Ted Fetter
Entre-Nous (OB) 1935

When Sammy Sang the Marseillaise
Music by Rudolf Friml
Lyrics by Otto Harbach
High Jinks 1913

When She Walks in the Room
Music by Sigmund Romberg
Lyrics by Dorothy Fields
Up in Central Park 1945

When Some Serious Affliction
Music by John Philip Sousa
Lyrics by Tom Frost and John Philip Sousa
El Capitan 1896

When Somebody Cares
Music by William Daly and Paul Lannin
Lyrics by Arthur Jackson
For Goodness Sake 1922

When Someone You Love Loves You
Music and lyrics by Charles Gaynor
Lend an Ear 1948

When the Baby Comes
Music by John Morris
Lyrics by Gerald Freedman
A Time for Singing 1966

When the Bluebirds Fly All Over the World
Music by Jack Holmes
Lyrics by Bill Conklin and Bob Miller
O Say Can You See! (OB) 1962

When the Bo-Tree Blossoms Again
Music by Jerome Kern
Lyrics by Bert Kalmar and Harry Ruby
Lucky 1927

When the Boys Come Home
Music by Harold Arlen
Lyrics by E.Y. Harburg
Bloomer Girl 1944

When the Cat's Away the Mice Will Play
Music by Victor Herbert
Lyrics by Henry Blossom
Mlle. Modiste 1905

When the Children Are Asleep
Music by Richard Rodgers
Lyrics by Oscar Hammerstein II
Carousel 1945

When the Cocoanuts Call
Music by Harry Tierney
Lyrics by Joseph McCarthy
Kid Boots 1923

When the Debbies Go By
Music by George Gershwin
Lyrics by B.G. DeSylva and Ira Gershwin
Tell Me More 1925

When the Duchess Is Away
Music by Kurt Weill
Lyrics by Ira Gershwin
The Firebrand of Florence 1945

When the Hen Stops Laying
Music and lyrics by Cole Porter
Leave It to Me 1938

Dropped from production

When the Honeymoon Stops Shining
Music by Jean Schwartz
Lyrics by Joseph W. Herbert and Harold Atteridge
The Honeymoon Express 1913

When the Hurdy Gurdy Plays
Music by Harold Levey
Lyrics by Owen Murphy
Rainbow Rose 1926

When the Idle Poor Become the Idle Rich
Music by Burton Lane
Lyrics by E.Y. Harburg
Finian's Rainbow 1947

When the Kids Get Married
Music by Harvey Schmidt
Lyrics by Tom Jones
I Do! I Do! 1966

When the Lights Are Low
Music by Jerome Kern
Lyrics by Gene Buck
Ziegfeld Follies of 1916

When the Nylons Bloom Again
Music by Thomas (Fats) Waller
Lyrics by George Marion, Jr.
Early to Bed 1943

**When the Orchestra is Playing
Your Favorite Dance**
Music by Jerome Kern
Lyrics by P.G. Wodehouse
Oh, Boy! 1917

Dropped from production.
See "There It Is Again."

When the Party Gives a Party
Music by Sigmund Romberg
Lyrics by Dorothy Fields
Up in Central Park 1945

When the Right Man Sings Tra-La
Music by Victor Herbert
Lyrics by Harry B. Smith
The Enchantress 1911

When the Right One Comes Along
Music by George Gershwin
Lyrics by Ira Gershwin
Rosalie 1928

Dropped from production

When the Shadows Fall
Music by Harold Orlob
Lyrics by Harry L. Cort and George E. Stoddard
Listen, Lester 1918

When the Shaker Plays a Cocktail Tune
Music by James F. Hanley
Lyrics by Gene Buck
No Foolin' 1926

When the Sheets Come Back From the Laundry
Music by Abraham Ellstein
Lyrics by Walter Bullock
Great to Be Alive 1950

When the Ships Come Home
Music by Jerome Kern
Lyrics by P.G. Wodehouse
Oh, Lady! Lady!! 1918

When the Song of Love Is Heard
Music by Oscar Straus
Lyrics by Joseph W. Herbert
A Waltz Dream 1908

When the Spring Is in the Air
Music by Jerome Kern
Lyrics by Oscar Hammerstein II
Music in the Air 1932

When the Sun Kissed the Rose Goodbye
Music by Gitz Rice
Lyrics by Paul Porter
Nic-Nax of 1926

When the Sun Meets the Moon in Finale-Land
Music by Charles M. Schwab
Lyrics by Henry Myers
The Garrick Gaieties (3rd edition) 1930

When the Tall Man Talks
Music by Moose Charlap
Lyrics by Norman Gimbel
Whoop-Up 1958

When the Time Is Right
Music by Gordon Duffy
Lyrics by Harry M. Haldane
Happy Town 1959

When the Vampire Exits Laughing
Music by Louis A. Hirsch
Lyrics by Otto Harbach
Mary 1920

When the Wedding Bells Are Ringing
Music by Victor Jacobi
Lyrics by William LeBaron
Apple Blossoms 1919

When the Wings of the Wind Take Me Home
Music by Ruth Cleary Patterson
Lyrics by Les Kramer
Russell Patterson's Sketch Book (OB) 1960

When They Start Again
Music and lyrics by Michael Brown
Different Times 1972

When Things Are Bright and Rosy
Music by Harry Ruby
Lyrics by Bert Kalmar
Animal Crackers 1928

When Things Come Your Way
Music by Harold Orlob
Lyrics by Harry L. Cort and George E. Stoddard
Listen, Lester 1918

When Time Takes Your Hand
Music and lyrics by Bruce Montgomery
The Amorous Flea (OB) 1964

When Tomorrow Comes
Music by Kenneth Jacobson
Lyrics by Rhoda Roberts
Show Me Where the Good Times Are (OB) 1970

When Tomorrow Comes
Music by Michael Dansicker
Lyrics by Sarah Schlesinger
On The Swing Shift (OB) 1983

When Velma Takes the Stand
Music by John Kander
Lyrics by Fred Ebb
Chicago 1975

When Villains Ramble Far and Near
Music and lyrics by Scott Joplin
Treemonisha 1975

Written in 1909

When We Are Married
Music by Gustave Kerker
Lyrics by Hugh Morton
The Belle of New York 1897

When We Are Married
Music by Vincent Youmans
Lyrics by Zelda Sears
Lollipop 1924

When We Are on the Stage
Music and lyrics by Paul Rubens
Florodora 1900

When We Get Our Divorce
Music by Jerome Kern
Lyrics by Otto Harbach and Oscar Hammerstein II
Sunny 1925

When We Hear the Call for Battle
Music by John Philip Sousa
Lyrics by Tom Frost and John Philip Sousa
El Capitan 1896

When We Meet Again
Music and lyrics by Harold Rome
Call Me Mister 1946

When We See a Pretty Girl We Whistle
Music and lyrics by Jack Bussins
and Ellsworth Olin
Be Kind to People Week (OB) 1975

When We're Bride and Groom
Music by Harry Archer
Lyrics by Harlan Thompson
Twinkle Twinkle 1926

When We're Home on the Range
Music and lyrics by Cole Porter
Something for the Boys 1943

When We're in Love
Music by Richard Lewine
Lyrics by Ted Fetter
Naughty-Naught (OB) (1946 revival)

When Will Grown-Ups Grow Up?
Music by Charles Strouse
Lyrics by Lee Adams
Bring Back Birdie 1981

When Will I Learn?
Music and lyrics by Paul Nassau and Oscar Brand
*The Education of H*y*m*a*n K*a*p*l*a*n* 1968

When You and I Were Young, Maggie Blues
Music by Jimmy McHugh
Lyrics by Jack Frost
Sugar Babies 1979

When You Are Close to Me
Music by Alma Sanders
Lyrics by Monte Carlo
Louisiana Lady 1947

When You Are Old and Grey
Music and lyrics by Tom Lehrer
Tomfoolery (OB) 1981

When You Are Together
Music by David McHugh
Lyrics by Peter Copani
New York City Street Show (OB) 1977

When You Are Young
Music by Sigmund Romberg
Lyrics by Oscar Hammerstein II
East Wind 1931

When You Carry Your Own Suitcase
Music and lyrics by Steve Allen
Sophie 1963

When You Change Your Name to Mine
Music by John Philip Sousa
Lyrics by Leonard Liebling
The American Maid 1913

When You Do the Hinky Dee
Music and lyrics by George M. Cohan
Little Nellie Kelly 1922

When You Get to Congress
Music by Albert Von Tilzer
Lyrics by Neville Fleeson
Bye Bye, Bonnie 1927

When You Go Down by Miss Jenny's
Music by Duke Ellington
Lyrics by John Latouche
Beggar's Holiday 1946

When You Grow Up
Music by Giuseppe Verdi
(adapted by Hans Spialek)
Lyrics by Charles Friedman
My Darlin' Aïda 1952

When You Hear the Wind
Music and lyrics by Eaton Magoon, Jr.
13 Daughters 1961

When You Live in a Furnished Flat
Music by George Gershwin
Lyrics by Arthur J. Jackson and B.G. DeSylva
La, La, Lucille 1919

When You Live on an Island
Music by Vernon Duke
Lyrics by Howard Dietz
Sadie Thompson 1944

When You Look in Your Looking Glass
Music by Paul Mann and Stephen Weiss
Lyrics by Sam Lewis
Hellzapoppin 1938

When You Love Only One
Music by Arthur Schwartz
Lyrics by Howard Dietz
Revenge With Music 1934

When You Meet a Man in Chicago
Music by Jule Styne
Lyrics by Bob Merrill
Sugar 1972

When You Run the Show
Music and lyrics by Beth Lawrence
and Norman Thalheimer
Marilyn 1983

When You Say No to Love
Music and lyrics by Vincent Valentini
Parisiana 1928

When You Smile
Music by Tom Johnstone
Lyrics by Phil Cook
When You Smile 1925

When You Smile
Music by George Gershwin
Lyrics by Ira Gershwin
Funny Face 1927

Dropped from production

When You Wake Up Dancing
Music by Jerome Kern
Lyrics by Berton Braley
Toot-Toot! 1918

When You Want Me
Music and lyrics by Noël Coward
Sail Away 1961

When Your Boy Becomes a Man
Music by Richard A. Whiting
Lyrics by Oscar Hammerstein II
Free for All 1931

When Your Lover Says Goodbye
Music by André Previn
Lyrics by Alan Jay Lerner
Coco 1969

When Your Troubles Have Started
Music and lyrics by Cole Porter
Red, Hot and Blue! 1936

Dropped from production

When You're Away
Music by Victor Herbert
Lyrics by Henry Blossom
The Only Girl 1914

When You're Dancing the Waltz
Music by Richard Rodgers
Lyrics by Lorenz Hart
Dancing Pirate (1936) F

When You're Driving Through the Moonlight
Music by Richard Rodgers
Lyrics by Oscar Hammerstein
Cinderella (1957) TV

When You're Far Away From New York Town
Music by Arthur Schwartz
Lyrics by Howard Dietz
Jennie 1963

When You're In Love
Music by Arthur Schwartz
Lyrics by Maxwell Anderson
High Tor (1956) TV

When You're in My Arms
Music by Marvin Hamlisch
Lyrics by Carole Bayer Sager
They're Playing Our Song 1979

When You're in Rome
Music by William Daly and Paul Lannin
Lyrics by Arthur Jackson
For Goodness Sake 1922

When You're in the Room
Music by Ben Oakland
Lyrics by Oscar Hammerstein II
The Lady Objects (1938) F

When You're Pretty and the World Is Fair
Music by Victor Herbert
Lyrics by Henry Blossom
The Red Mill 1906

When You're Right, You're Right
Music by John Kander
Lyrics by Fred Ebb
Woman of the Year 1981

When You're Single
Music by George Gershwin
Lyrics by Ira Gershwin
Funny Face 1927

Dropped from production

When You're the Only One
Music by Scott MacLarty
Lyrics by Dorothy Chansky
The Brooklyn Bridge (OB) 1983

When You're Wearing the Ball and Chain
Music by Victor Herbert
Lyrics by Henry Blossom
The Only Girl 1914

When You're Young and in Love
Music and lyrics by Hal Hester and Danny Apolinar
Your Own Thing (OB) 1968

When You've Loved Your Man
Music and lyrics by Stephen H. Lemberg
Jazzbo Brown 1980

When Yuba Plays the Rumba on His Tuba
Music and lyrics by Herman Hupfeld
The Third Little Show 1931

Whenever I Dream
Music by Con Conrad
Lyrics by Gus Kahn
Kitty's Kisses 1926

Where?
Music by John Mundy
Lyrics by Edward Eager
Sing Out, Sweet Land 1944

Where?
Music and lyrics by Marc Blitzstein
Juno 1959

Where Am I Going?
Music by Cy Coleman
Lyrics by Dorothy Fields
Sweet Charity 1966

Where Are the Blossoms
Music by Paul Hoffert
Lyrics by David Secter
Get Thee to Canterbury (OB) 1969

Where Are the Girls of Yesterday?
Music by Richard Hill and John Hawkins
Lyrics by Nevill Coghill
Canterbury Tales 1969

Where Are the Men?
Music and lyrics by Cole Porter
Anything Goes 1934

Where Are the Snows?
Music by Harvey Schmidt
Lyrics by Tom Jones
I Do! I Do! 1966

Where Are They?
Music by Jerry Bock
Lyrics by Sheldon Harnick
The Body Beautiful 1958

Where Are Those People Who Did "Hair"?
Music and lyrics by Elizabeth Swados
Runaways 1978

Where Are Your Children?
Music and lyrics by Billy Barnes
The Billy Barnes Revue 1959

Where Can He Be?
Music by Arthur Schwartz
Lyrics by Howard Dietz
The Band Wagon 1931

Where Can I Go From You?
Music by Baldwin Bergersen
Lyrics by Virginia Faulkner
All in Fun 1940

Where Can the Baby Be?
Music by Richard Rodgers
Lyrics by Lorenz Hart
She's My Baby 1928

Where Can the Rich and Poor Be Friends?
Music by Richard B. Chodosh
Lyrics by Barry Alan Grael
The Streets of New York (OB) 1963

Where Can You Take a Girl?
Music by Burt Bacharach
Lyrics by Hal David
Promises, Promises 1968

Where Did It Go?
Music by Harvey Schmidt
Lyrics by Tom Jones
Celebration 1969

Where Did It Go?
Music by Jim Steinman
Lyrics by Michael Weller and Jim Steinman
More Than You Deserve (OB) 1973

Where Did That Little Dog Go?
Music by Larry Grossman
Lyrics by Hal Hackady
Snoopy (OB) 1982

Where Did the Bird Hear That?
Music by Jerome Kern
Lyrics by Paul West
The Red Petticoat 1912

Where Did the Dream Go?
Music and lyrics by Johnny Brandon
Love! Love! Love! (OB) 1977

Where Did the Good Times Go?
Music and lyrics by Richard M. Sherman
and Robert B. Sherman
Over Here! 1974

Where Did the Night Go?
Music and lyrics by Harold Rome
Wish You Were Here 1952

Where Did the Summer Go To?
Music by Norman Campbell
Lyrics by Donald Harron and Norman Campbell
Anne of Green Gables (OB) 1971

Where Did We Go? Out
Music by Richard Lewine
Lyrics by Arnold B. Horwitt
The Girls Against the Boys 1959

Where Do I Go?
Music by Galt MacDermot
Lyrics by Gerome Ragni and James Rado
Hair 1968

Where Do I Go From Here?
Music by Jerry Bock
Lyrics by Sheldon Harnick
Fiorello! 1959

Dropped from production

Where Do I Go From Here?
Music and lyrics by Voices, Inc.
The Believers (OB) 1968

Where Do I Go From Here?
Music by Steve Sterner
Lyrics by Peter del Valle
Lovers (OB) 1975

Where Do Mosquitos Go?
Music by Harry Tierney
Lyrics by Joseph McCarthy
Ziegfeld Follies of 1920

Where Do People Go?
Music and lyrics by Elizabeth Swados
Runaways 1978

Where Do They Get Those Guys?
Music by Sigmund Romberg
Lyrics by Harold Atteridge
Sinbad (1918)

Where Do You Get Your Greens?
Music by Morgan Lewis
Lyrics by Nancy Hamilton
Two for the Show 1940

Where Do You Travel?
Music and lyrics by Hugh Martin and Ralph Blane
Best Foot Forward 1941

Where Does a Man Begin?
Music by Don McAfee
Lyrics by Nancy Leeds
Great Scot! (OB) 1965

Where Has My Hubby Gone Blues
Music by Vincent Youmans
Lyrics by Irving Caesar
No, No, Nanette 1925

Where Has Tom Gone?
Music by John Addison
Lyrics by John Cranko
Cranks 1956

Where Have I Been?
Music by Robert Waldman
Lyrics by Alfred Uhry
Here's Where I Belong 1968

Where Have We Met Before?
Music by Vernon Duke
Lyrics by E.Y. Harburg
Walk a Little Faster 1932

Where Have You Been?
Music and lyrics by Cole Porter
The New Yorkers 1930

Where Have You Been All My Life?
Music by Philip Charig and Richard Myers
Lyrics by Leo Robin
Allez-Oop 1927

Where Have You Been All Night?
Music and lyrics by Gian-Carlo Menotti
The Medium 1947

Where Have You Been Up to Now?
Music and lyrics by Al Carmines
Wanted (OB) 1972

Where I Come From
Music by Howard Marren
Lyrics by Enid Futterman
Portrait of Jennie (OB) 1982

Where Is He?
Music by Arthur Siegel
Lyrics by June Carroll
New Faces of 1968

Where Is Love?
Music by Erich Wolfgang Korngold (based on Jacques Offenbach)
Lyrics by Herbert Baker
Helen Goes to Troy 1944

Where Is Love?
Music and lyrics by Lionel Bart
Oliver! 1963

Where Is Matthew Going?
Music by Norman Campbell
Lyrics by Donald Harron and Norman Campbell
Anne of Green Gables (OB) 1971

Where Is My Little Old New York?
Music and lyrics by Irving Berlin
Music Box Revue (4th edition) 1924

Where Is My Son?
Music by Richard Rodgers
Lyrics by Sheldon Harnick
Rex 1976

Where Is She?
Music by George Gershwin
Lyrics by B.G. DeSylva
George White's Scandals (1923)

Where Is That Rainbow?
Music by Don McAfee
Lyrics by Nancy Leeds
Great Scot! (OB) 1965

Where Is That Someone for Me?
Music by Victor Young
Lyrics by Stella Unger
Seventh Heaven 1955

Where Is the Clown?
Music and lyrics by Billy Barnes
The Billy Barnes People 1961

Where Is the Life That Late I Led?
Music and lyrics by Cole Porter
Kiss Me, Kate 1948

The title is taken from a speech by Petruchio in *The Taming of the Shrew.*

Where Is the Man?
Music and lyrics by John Raniello
Movie Buff (OB) 1977

Where Is the Man I Married?
Music and lyrics by Hugh Martin and Timothy Gray
High Spirits 1964

Where Is the Man of My Dreams?
Music by George Gershwin
Lyrics by B.G. DeSylva and E. Ray Goetz
George White's Scandals (1922)

Where Is the Reason?
Music and lyrics by Cliff Jones
Rockabye Hamlet 1976

Where Is the She for Me?
Music and lyrics by Charles Gaynor
Lend an Ear 1948

Where Is the Tribe for Me?
Music and lyrics by Walter Marks
Bajour 1964

Where Is the Waltz?
Music by Alonzo Levister
Lyrics by Paul Nassau
New Faces of 1968

Where Love Grows
Music by Jean Gilbert
Lyrics by Harry B. Smith
The Red Robe 1928

Where, Oh, Where
Music and lyrics by Gian-Carlo Menotti
The Medium 1947

Where, Oh Where
Music and lyrics by Cole Porter
Out of This World 1950

Where Oh Where
Music by Robert Waldman
Lyrics by Alfred Uhry
The Robber Bridegroom 1975

Where, Oh Where Can I Find Love?
Music by Jesse Greer
Lyrics by Stanley Adams
Shady Lady 1933

Where or When
Music by Richard Rodgers
Lyrics by Lorenz Hart
Babes in Arms 1937

Where Shall I Find Him?
Music and lyrics by Noël Coward
Sail Away 1961

Where Shall I Go?
Music and lyrics by Voices, Inc.
The Believers (OB) 1968

Where the Honeymoon Alone Can See
Music by Rudolf Friml
Lyrics by Otto Harbach
The Blue Kitten 1922

Where the Hudson River Flows
Music by Richard Rodgers
Lyrics by Lorenz Hart
Dearest Enemy 1925

Where the Morning Glories Twine
Music by Martin Broones
Lyrics by Ballard MacDonald
Rufus Lemaire's Affairs 1927

Where the Red, Red Roses Grow
Music by Jean Schwartz
Lyrics by Joseph W. Herbert and Harold Atteridge
The Honeymoon Express 1913

Where the Trees Are Green With Parrots
Music and lyrics by Sandy Wilson
Valmouth (OB) 1960

Where There's Smoke
Music and lyrics by Frederick Silver
Gay Company (OB) 1974

Where Was I?
Music by Jimmy Van Heusen
Lyrics by Sammy Cahn
Walking Happy 1966

Where Was I When They Passed Out Luck?
Music by Larry Grossman
Lyrics by Hal Hackady
Minnie's Boys 1970

Where We Came From
Music by Richard Rodgers
Lyrics by Raymond Jessel
I Remember Mama 1979

Dropped from production

Where We Can Be in Love
Music and lyrics by Leon DeCosta
Kosher Kitty Kelly 1925

Where Were You—Where Was I?
Music and lyrics by George M. Cohan
Billie 1928

Where Will I Be Next Wednesday Night?
Music and lyrics by Barbara Schottenfeld
I Can't Keep Running in Place (OB) 1981

Where Would You Be Without Me?
Music and lyrics by Leslie Bricusse
and Anthony Newley
The Roar of the Greasepaint—The Smell of the Crowd 1965

Where Would You Get Your Coat?
Music and lyrics by Cole Porter
Fifty Million Frenchmen 1929

Where You Are
Music by Philip Charig
Lyrics by Dan Shapiro and Milton Pascal
Follow the Girls 1944

Where You Are
Music by Raymond Scott
Lyrics by Bernard Hanighen
Lute Song 1946

Where You Are
Music by Arthur Schwartz
Lyrics by Howard Dietz
Jennie 1963

Where You Been Hiding Till Now?
Music by Stanley Silverman
Lyrics by Tom Hendry
Doctor Selavy's Magic Theatre (OB) 1972

Where You Go I Go
Music by George Gershwin
Lyrics by Ira Gershwin
Pardon My English 1933

Where You Lead
Music by Rudolf Friml
Lyrics by J. Keirn Brennan
Luana 1930

Where Your Name Is Carved With Mine
Music by Ray Henderson
Lyrics by B.G. DeSylva and Lew Brown
George White's Scandals (1928)

Whereas
Music and lyrics by Bob Merrill
Henry, Sweet Henry 1967

Where'd Marilla Come From?
Music by Norman Campbell
Lyrics by Donald Harron and Norman Campbell
Anne of Green Gables (OB) 1971

Wherefore Art Thou, Juliet?
Music and lyrics by Charlotte Kent
The Illustrators' Show 1936

Where's Charley?
Music and lyrics by Frank Loesser
Where's Charley? 1948

Where's Mama?
Music by Silvio Hein
Lyrics by George V. Hobart
The Yankee Girl 1910

Where's My Happy Ending?
Music by Harry Revel
Lyrics by Mack Gordon and Harold Adamson
Fast and Furious 1931

Where's My Love A'Wandering?
Music by Baldwin Bergersen
Lyrics by William Archibald
Rosa (OB) 1978

Where's My Shoe?
Music by Jerry Bock
Lyrics by Sheldon Harnick
She Loves Me 1963

Where's My Wife?
Music by Frederick Loewe
Lyrics by Alan Jay Lerner
The Day Before Spring 1945

Where's North?
Music by Galt MacDermot
Lyrics by John Guare
Two Gentlemen of Verona 1971

Where's That Rainbow?
Music by Richard Rodgers
Lyrics by Lorenz Hart
Peggy-Ann 1926

Where's the Boy? Here's the Girl!
Music by George Gershwin
Lyrics by Ira Gershwin
Treasure Girl 1928

Where's the Boy I Saved for a Rainy Day?
Music by Baldwin Bergersen
Lyrics by John Rox
All in Fun 1940

Where's the Girl for Me?
Music by Jerome Kern
Lyrics by Harry B. Smith
Ninety in the Shade 1915

Wherever He Ain't
Music and lyrics by Jerry Herman
Mack and Mabel 1974

Wherever I May Go
Music by Frederico Valerio
Lyrics by Elizabeth Miele
Hit the Trail 1954

Wherever They Fly the Flag of Old England
Music and lyrics by Cole Porter
Around the World 1946

Wherever You Are
Music by James F. Hanley
Lyrics by Eddie Dowling
Sidewalks of New York 1927

Which?
Music and lyrics by Cole Porter
Paris (film version, 1930)

Which Door?
Music by Jerry Bock
Lyrics by Sheldon Harnick
The Apple Tree 1966

Which Shall It Be?
Music by Frank Grey
Lyrics by Ethelberta Hasbrook
Happy 1927

Which Way?
Music by Charles Strouse
Lyrics by Lee Adams
All American 1962

Which Way Do I Go?
Music by Mitch Leigh
Lyrics by N. Richard Nash
Saravá 1979

Which Witch?
Music by Charles Zwar
Lyrics by Allen Melville
John Murray Anderson's Almanac (1953)

Whichaway'd They Go?
Music by Robert Emmett Dolan
Lyrics by Johnny Mercer
Texas, Li'l Darlin' 1949

The Whichness of the Whatness
Music by William Daly and Paul Lannin
Lyrics by Arthur Jackson
For Goodness Sake 1922

While the City Sleeps
Music by Charles Strouse
Lyrics by Lee Adams
Golden Boy 1964

While There's a Song to Sing
Music by Franz Steininger
(adapted from Tchaikovsky)
Lyrics by Forman Brown
Music in My Heart 1947

While You Are Young
Music by Harold Arlen
Lyrics by Jack Yellen
You Said It 1931

While You Love Me
Music by Johann Strauss
Lyrics by Desmond Carter
The Great Waltz 1934

Whiling My Time Away
Music by Henry Sullivan
Lyrics by Edward Eliscu
A Little Racketeer 1932

The Whip
Music by Emmerich Kálmán and Herbert Stothart
Lyrics by Otto Harbach and Oscar Hammerstein II
Golden Dawn 1927

The Whip Hand
Music by Oscar Straus
Lyrics by Edward Delaney Dunn
The Last Waltz 1921

Whip-Poor-Will
Music by Jerome Kern
Lyrics by B.G. DeSylva
Sally 1920

Whirled Into Happiness
Music by Carlton Kelsey and Maury Rubens
Lyrics by Clifford Grey
Sky High 1925

Whiskey Bug
Music by Jack Urbont
Lyrics by Bruce Geller
Livin' the Life (OB) 1957

The Whispering Song
Music and lyrics by Leon DeCosta
The Blonde Sinner 1926

Whispering to You
Music and lyrics by Al Carmines
Wanted (OB) 1972

Whispering Trees
Music by Maury Rubens and J. Fred Coots
Lyrics by Herbert Reynolds
The Merry World 1926

Whistle
Music by Harry Ruby
Lyrics by Bert Kalmar
Twinkle Twinkle 1926

Whistle Away Your Blues
Music by Richard Myers
Lyrics by Leo Robin
The Greenwich Village Follies (1925)

Whistle It
Music by Victor Herbert
Lyrics by Henry Blossom
The Red Mill 1906

Whistle While You Work, Boys
Music by Walter Kollo
Lyrics by Harry B. Smith
Three Little Girls 1930

A Whistle Works
Music and lyrics by Rick Besoyan
The Student Gypsy (OB) 1963

Whistling Boy
Music by Jerome Kern
Lyrics by Dorothy Fields
When You're in Love (1937) F

Whistling for a Kiss
Music by Richard Myers
Lyrics by E.Y. Harburg and Johnny Mercer
Americana (1932)

White Boys
Music by Galt MacDermot
Lyrics by Gerome Ragni and James Rado
Hair 1968

White Christmas
Music and lyrics by Irving Berlin
Holiday Inn (1942) F

Academy Award winner

The White Dove
Music by Franz Lehar and Herbert Stothart
Lyrics by Clifford Grey
The Rogue Song (1930) F

White Heat
Music by Arthur Schwartz
Lyrics by Howard Dietz
The Band Wagon 1931

White Horse Inn
Music by Ralph Benatzky
Lyrics by Irving Caesar
White Horse Inn 1936

White Is the Dove
Music by Buster Davis
Lyrics by Steven Vinaver
Diversions (OB) 1958

White Knight
Music and lyrics by Elizabeth Swados
Alice in Concert (OB) 1980

White Light Alley
Music by A. Baldwin Sloane
Lyrics by E. Ray Goetz
The Hen Pecks 1911

White Lights
Music by J. Fred Coots
Lyrics by Al Dubin
White Lights 1927

White Lights Were Coming
Music by Maury Rubens and Sam Timberg
Lyrics by Moe Jaffe
Broadway Nights 1929

White Lilacs
Music by Karl Hajos (based on Chopin)
Lyrics by Harry B. Smith
White Lilacs 1928

White Queen
Music and lyrics by Elizabeth Swados
Alice in Concert (OB) 1980

White Roses, Red
Music and lyrics by Elizabeth Swados
Alice in Concert (OB) 1980

White Sheeting
Music by Galt MacDermot
Lyrics by Rochelle Owens
The Karl Marx Play (OB) 1973

The White Slavery Fandango
Music and lyrics by Jay Thompson
Double Entry (OB) 1961

The White Witch of Jamaica
Music by Arthur Siegel
Lyrics by June Carroll
New Faces of 1956

Whither Thou Goest
Music and lyrics by Oscar Brand and Paul Nassau
A Joyful Noise 1966

Whizzer Brown
Music and lyrics by William Finn
In Trousers (OB) 1981

Whizzin' Away Along de Track
Music by Georges Bizet
Lyrics by Oscar Hammerstein II
Carmen Jones 1943

Who
Music and lyrics by Irving Berlin
Music Box Revue (4th edition) 1924

Who?
Music by Jerome Kern
Lyrics by Otto Harbach and Oscar Hammerstein II
Sunny 1925

Jerome Kern felt that the success of the song was due in large part to its title, the first word of the chorus. A highly singable word, it is sustained for two and a quarter bars and then repeated insistently five more times in the lyric.

Who Am I?
Music by Emmerich Kálmán
Lyrics by Harry B. Smith
Countess Maritza 1926

Who Am I?
Music by Kurt Weill
Lyrics by Ogden Nash
One Touch of Venus 1943

Dropped from production

Who Am I?
Music and lyrics by Leonard Bernstein
Peter Pan 1950

Who Am I?
Music and lyrics by Johnny Brandon
Cindy (OB) 1964

Who Am I? (That You Should Care for Me)
Music by Vincent Youmans
Lyrics by Gus Kahn
Rainbow 1928

Dropped from production

Who Am I Thinking Of?
Music by A. Baldwin Sloane
Lyrics by Harry Cort and George E. Stoddard
China Rose 1925

Who Am I, Who Are You, Who Are We?
Music and lyrics by William Roy
The Penny Friend (OB) 1966

Who Are We?
Music and lyrics by James Rado
Rainbow (OB) 1972

Who Are We Kidding?
Music and lyrics by Steve Allen
Sophie 1963

Who Are You?
Music by Richard Rodgers
Lyrics by Lorenz Hart
The Boys From Syracuse (film version, 1940)

Who Are You?
Music and lyrics by Deed Meyer
She Shall Have Music (OB) 1959

Who Are You Now?
Music by Jule Styne
Lyrics by Bob Merrill
Funny Girl 1964

Who Bites the Hole in Schweitzer Cheese?
Music by Alma Sanders
Lyrics by Monte Carlo
Oh! Oh! Nurse 1925

Who But You?
Music and lyrics by Cole Porter
Red, Hot and Blue! 1936

Dropped from production, and later dropped from
the film *Born to Dance* (1936). The lyric idea is
similar to Porter's "After You" in the score of *Gay
Divorce* (1932).

Who Can I Turn To? (When Nobody Needs Me)
Music and lyrics by Leslie Bricusse
and Anthony Newley
*The Roar of the Greasepaint—The Smell
of the Crowd* 1965

Who Can Say?
Music and lyrics by Peter Copani
New York City Street Show (OB) 1977

Who Can Tell?
Music by Fritz Kreisler
Lyrics by William LeBaron
Apple Blossoms 1919

The same melody as "Stars in My Eyes" (lyrics by
Dorothy Fields), which was sung by Grace Moore in
the 1936 film *The King Steps Out*.

Who Can? You Can!
Music by Arthur Schwartz
Lyrics by Howard Dietz
The Gay Life 1961

Who Cares?
Music by Percy Wenrich
Lyrics by Harry Clarke
Who Cares? 1930

Who Cares?
Music by Haydn Wood, Joseph Tunbridge
and Jack Waller
Lyrics by Dion Titheradge
Artists and Models (1930)

Who Cares?
Music by George Gershwin
Lyrics by Ira Gershwin
Of Thee I Sing 1931

Who Committed the Murder?
Music by Richard Myer
Lyrics by Edward Heyman
Murder at the Vanities 1933

Who Could Be Blue?
Music and lyrics by Stephen Sondheim
Marry Me a Little (OB) 1981

Dropped from *Follies* (1971)

Who Did? You Did
Music by Harry Ruby
Lyrics by Bert Kalmar
The Five o'Clock Girl 1927

Who Do You Love, I Hope
Music and lyrics by Irving Berlin
Annie Get Your Gun 1946

Who Do You Think You Are?
Music by Sidney Lippman
Lyrics by Sylvia Dee
Barefoot Boy With Cheek 1947

Who Do You Think You Are?
Music and lyrics by Charlie Smalls
The Wiz 1975

Who Done It?
Music by Abraham Ellstein
Lyrics by Walter Bullock
Great to Be Alive 1950

Who Ever You Are
Music and lyrics by Stan Daniels
So Long, 174th Street 1976

Who Fills the Bill?
Music by Sammy Fain
Lyrics by Marilyn and Alan Bergman
Something More 1964

Who Gives a Sou?
Music and lyrics by Hugh Martin
Make a Wish 1951

Who Hit Me?
Music and lyrics by Charles Gaynor
Lend an Ear 1948

Who Is General Staff?
Music and lyrics by Ann Ronell
Count Me In 1942

Who Is It Always There?
Music by John Addison
Lyrics by John Cranko
Cranks 1956

Who Is Samuel Cooper?
Music by Kurt Weill
Lyrics by Alan Jay Lerner
Love Life 1948

Who Is She?
Music and lyrics by Al Carmines
The Evangelist (OB) 1982

Who Is Sylvia?
Music by Galt MacDermot
Lyrics by John Guare
Two Gentlemen of Verona 1971

Who Is the Bravest?
Music by Jule Styne
Lyrics by Bob Hilliard
Hazel Flagg 1953

Who Is the Lucky Girl to Be?
Music by George Gershwin
Lyrics by Ira Gershwin
Of Thee I Sing 1931

Who Killed Nobody?
Music by Helen Miller
Lyrics by Eve Merriam
Inner City 1971

Who Knows?
Music and lyrics by Cole Porter
Rosalie (1937) F

Who Knows?
Music by Robert Stolz
Lyrics by Robert Sour
Mr. Strauss Goes to Boston 1945

Who Knows?
Music and lyrics by Harold Rome
I Can Get It for You Wholesale 1962

Who Knows What Might Have Been?
Music by Jule Styne
Lyrics by Betty Comden and Adolph Green
Subways Are for Sleeping 1961

Who Makes Much of a Miracle
Music by Stan Harte, Jr.
Leaves of Grass (OB) 1971

Who Needs It?
Music and lyrics by Deed Meyer
She Shall Have Music (OB) 1959

Who Needs the Love of a Woman?
Music and lyrics by Jill Williams
Rainbow Jones 1974

Who Put Out the Light That Lit the Candle . . .
Music and lyrics by John Dooley
Hobo (OB) 1961

Who Said There Is No Santa Claus?
Music by Sammy Fain
Lyrics by E.Y. Harburg
Flahooley 1951

Who Started the Rhumba?
Music by Vernon Duke
Lyrics by John Latouche
Banjo Eyes 1941

Who Taught Her Everything?
Music by Jule Styne
Lyrics by Bob Merrill
Funny Girl 1964

Who to Love If Not a Stranger
Music by Mitch Leigh
Lyrics by William Alfred and Phyllis Robinson
Cry for Us All 1970

Who Walks Like a Scarecrow
Music and lyrics by Norman Dean
Autumn's Here (OB) 1966

Who Wants to Be a Millionaire?
Music and lyrics by Cole Porter
High Society (1956) F

Who Wants to Love Spanish Ladies?
Music by Vincent Youmans
Lyrics by Oscar Hammerstein II
Rainbow 1928

Who Was Chasing Paul Revere?
Music by Joseph Meyer and James F. Hanley
Lyrics by B.G. DeSylva
Big Boy 1925

Who Was the Last Girl?
Music by Harold Orlob
Lyrics by Harry L. Cort and George E. Stoddard
Listen, Lester 1918

(Who, Who, Who, Who) Who Is She?
Music by Jerry Bock
Lyrics by Sheldon Harnick
The Apple Tree 1966

Who Will Be the Children?
Music by Galt MacDermot
Lyrics by Gerome Ragni
Dude 1972

Who Will Buy?
Music and lyrics by Lionel Bart
Oliver! 1963

Who Will the Next Fool Be?
Music and lyrics by Charlie Rich
Pump Boys and Dinettes 1982

Who Would Have Dreamed
Music and lyrics by Cole Porter
Panama Hattie 1940

Who Would Refuse?
Music by Richard Rodgers
Lyrics by Oscar Hammerstein II
The King and I 1951

Dropped from production

Who Wouldn't?
Music and lyrics by Vincent Valentini
Parisiana 1928

Who? You!
Music by Lewis E. Gensler
Lyrics by B.G. DeSylva
Queen High 1926

Whoa, Emma!
Music by Edward Künneke
Lyrics by Clifford Grey
Mayflowers 1925

Whoa, Gal
Music and lyrics by Ida Hoyt Chamberlain
Enchanted Isle 1927

Who'd Believe?
Music by Kenneth Jacobson
Lyrics by Rhoda Roberts
Show Me Where the Good Times Are (OB) 1970

Whoever You Are
Music by Burt Bacharach
Lyrics by Hal David
Promises, Promises 1968

A Whole Lotta Sunlight
Music by Judd Woldin
Lyrics by Robert Brittan
Raisin 1973

The Whole World Loves
Music by Sigmund Romberg
Lyrics by Irving Caesar
Melody 1933

Who'll Buy?
Music by Kurt Weill
Lyrics by Maxwell Anderson
Lost in the Stars 1949

Who'll Mend a Broken Heart?
Music by Lewis E. Gensler
Lyrics by B.G. DeSylva
Queen High 1926

Whoop Daddy Ooden Dooden Day
Music by Silvio Hein
Lyrics by George V. Hobart
The Yankee Girl 1910

Whoopin' and A-Hollerin'
Music by Robert Emmett Dolan
Lyrics by Johnny Mercer
Texas, Li'l Darlin' 1949

Whoopsie
Music by Richard Rodgers
Lyrics by Lorenz Hart
She's My Baby 1928

Dropped from production

Whoop-Ti-Ay
Music by Frederick Loewe
Lyrics by Alan Jay Lerner
Paint Your Wagon 1951

Whooshin' Through My Flesh
Music by Claibe Richardson
Lyrics by Kenward Elmslie
The Grass Harp 1971

Who's Been Listening to My Heart?
Music by Harry Ruby
Lyrics by Bert Kalmar
Animal Crackers 1928

Who's Been Sitting in My Chair?
Music by Leroy Anderson
Lyrics by Joan Ford and Walter and Jean Kerr
Goldilocks 1958

Who's Complaining?
Music by Jerome Kern
Lyrics by Ira Gershwin
Cover Girl (1944) F

Who's Doing What to Erwin?
Music and lyrics by Jay Livingston and Ray Evans
Let It Ride 1961

Who's Goin' to Get You?
Music by Milton Ager
Lyrics by Jack Yellen
Rain or Shine 1928

Who's Going to Teach the Children?
Music and lyrics by Micki Grant
It's So Nice to Be Civilized 1980

Who's Gonna Be the Winner?
Music by Morton Gould
Lyrics by Betty Comden and Adolph Green
Billion Dollar Baby 1945

Who's Got the Pain?
Music and lyrics by Richard Adler and Jerry Ross
Damn Yankees 1955

Who's It?
Music by Galt MacDermot
Lyrics by Gerome Ragni
Dude 1972

Who's My Little Baby Lamb?
Music by Franz Lehár
Lyrics by Harry B. and Robert B. Smith
Gypsy Love 1911

Who's Next?
Music and lyrics by Tom Lehrer
Tomfoolery (OB) 1981

Who's on Our Side?
Music and lyrics by Al Carmines and David Epstein
Wanted (OB) 1972

Who's Perfect?
Music and lyrics by Robert Larimer
King of the Whole Damn World (OB) 1962

Who's Perfect for You?
Music and lyrics by Robert Larimer
King of the Whole Damn World (OB) 1962

Who's That Girl?
Music by Charles Strouse
Lyrics by Lee Adams
Applause 1970

Who's That Woman?
Music and lyrics by Stephen Sondheim
Follies 1971

Who's the Boss?
Music by Paul A. Rubens
Lyrics by Paul A. Rubens and Arthur Wimperis
The Sunshine Girl 1913

Who's the Boy?
Music by Ray Perkins
Lyrics by Max and Nathaniel Lief
The Greenwich Village Follies (1928)

Who's the Fool?
Music and lyrics by C. Jackson and James Hatch
Fly Blackbird (OB) 1962

Who's the Greatest—?
Music by George Gershwin
Lyrics by Ira Gershwin
Let 'Em Eat Cake 1933

Who's the Thief?
Music by Andrew Lloyd Webber
Lyrics by Tim Rice
Joseph and the Amazing Technicolor Dreamcoat 1982

Who's Who?
Music by Walter Donaldson
Lyrics by Ballard MacDonald
Sweetheart Time 1926

Who's Who
Music by Baldwin Bergersen
Lyrics by June Sillman
Who's Who 1938

Who's Who
Music by John Addison
Lyrics by John Cranko
Cranks 1956

Who's Who
Music and lyrics by Tom Savage
Musical Chairs 1980

Who's Who With You?
Music by Vincent Youmans
Lyrics by Arthur Francis
Two Little Girls in Blue 1921

Who's Zoo in Girl Land
Music by Jerome Kern
Lyrics by P.G. Wodehouse
Miss 1917

Whose Baby Are You?
Music by Jerome Kern
Lyrics by Anne Caldwell
The Night Boat 1920

Whose Little Angry Man
Music by Judd Woldin
Lyrics by Robert Brittan
Raisin 1973

The Whosis-Whatsis
Music by Ray Henderson
Lyrics by B.G. DeSylva and Lew Brown
George White's Scandals (1925)

Why?
Music by J. Fred Coots
Lyrics by Arthur Swanstrom and Benny Davis
Sons o' Guns 1929

Why?
Music by Don Elliott
Lyrics by James Costigan
The Beast in Me 1963

Why?
Music by Paul Klein
Lyrics by Fred Ebb
Morning Sun (OB) 1963

Why?
Music by Richard Rodgers
Lyrics by Sheldon Harnick
Rex 1976

Why?
Music by Robert Kole
Lyrics by Sandi Merle
I Take These Women (OB) 1982

Why Ain't I Home?
Music by Vincent Youmans
Lyrics by Ring Lardner
Smiles 1930

Why Ain't We Free?
Music by Giuseppe Verdi
adapted by Hans Spialek)
Lyrics by Charles Friedman
My Darlin' Aida 1952

Why Am I a Hit With the Ladies?
Music and lyrics by Irving Berlin
The Cocoanuts 1925

Why Am I Me?
Music by Gary Geld
Lyrics by Peter Udell
Shenandoah 1975

Why Am I So Gone about That Girl?
Music and lyrics by Cole Porter
Les Girls (1957) F

Why Are They Following Me?
Music by Carlton Kelsey and Maury Rubens
Lyrics by Clifford Grey
Sky High 1925

Why Are We Invited Here?
Music by Sigmund Romberg
Lyrics by Herbert Reynolds
The Blue Paradise 1915

Why Be Afraid to Dance?
Music and lyrics by Harold Rome
Fanny 1954

Why Can't He See?
Music by Jule Styne
Lyrics by Sammy Cahn
Look to the Lilies 1970

Why Can't I?
Music by Richard Rodgers
Lyrics by Lorenz Hart
Spring Is Here 1929

Why Can't I Speak?
Music by John Kander
Lyrics by Fred Ebb
Zorba 1968

Why Can't I Walk Away?
Music and lyrics by Hugo Peretti, Luigi Creatore
and George David Weiss
Maggie Flynn 1968

Why Can't It Happen Again?
Music by Michel Emer
Lyrics by Sammy Gallup
All for Love 1949

Why Can't It Happen to Me?
Music by Maury Rubens
Lyrics by Clifford Grey
The Madcap 1928

Why Can't Me and You?
Music and lyrics by Micki Grant
It's So Nice to Be Civilized 1980

Why Can't the English?
Music by Frederick Loewe
Lyrics by Alan Jay Lerner
My Fair Lady 1956

Why Can't the World Go and Leave Us Alone
Music by Charles Strouse
Lyrics by Alan Jay Lerner
Dance a Little Closer 1983

Why Can't They Hand It to Me?
Music by Jerome Kern
Lyrics by P.G. Wodehouse
Oh, Boy! 1917

Dropped from production

Why Can't This Night Last Forever?
Music by Frederick Loewe
Lyrics by Earle Crooker
Great Lady 1938

Why Can't We All Be Nice?
Music by Larry Grossman
Lyrics by Hal Hackady
Goodtime Charley 1975

Why Can't We Be Unhappy?
Music by Jeanne Bargy
Lyrics by Jeanne Bargy, Frank Gehrecke
and Herb Corey
Greenwich Village U.S.A. (OB) 1960

Why Can't You Behave?
Music and lyrics by Cole Porter
Kiss Me, Kate 1948

Why Couldn't We Incorporate?
Music by Alma Sanders
Lyrics by Monte Carlo
Mystery Moon 1930

Why Did He Have to Die?
Music and lyrics by Cliff Jones
Rockabye Hamlet 1976

Why Did I Choose You?
Music by Michael Leonard
Lyrics by Herbert Martin
The Yearling 1965

Why Did We Marry Soldiers?
Music by Sigmund Romberg
Lyrics by Otto Harbach and Oscar Hammerstein II
The Desert Song 1926

Why Did You Do It?
Music by Arthur Schwartz
Lyrics by Howard Dietz
Between the Devil 1937

Why Did You Kiss My Heart Awake?
Music by Franz Lehár
Lyrics by Edward Eliscu
Frederika 1937

Why Didn't You Tell Me?
Music and lyrics by Edward Pola and Eddie Brandt
Woof, Woof 1929

Why Do I?
Music by Richard Rodgers
Lyrics by Lorenz Hart
The Girl Friend 1926

Why Do I Love You?
Music by George Gershwin
Lyrics by B.G. DeSylva and Ira Gershwin
Tell Me More 1925

Why Do I Love You?
Music by Jerome Kern
Lyrics by Oscar Hammerstein II
Show Boat 1927

Oscar Hammerstein, knowing that Jerome Kern couldn't stand the world "Cupid" in a lyric, decided to have a bit of fun with his collaborator before submitting the real lyric for "Why Do I Love You?" On the first sheet of paper he wrote:

Cupid knows the way
He's the naked boy
Who can make you prey
To love's own joy.
When he shoots his little arrow
He can thrill you to the marrow . . .

Angry at first, Kern saw the joke and laughed raucously. Later he framed the verse and hung it in his study.

Why Do the Wrong People Travel?
Music and lyrics by Noël Coward
Sail Away 1961

**Why Do They Die at the End
of a Classical Dance?**
Music by Leo Fall
Lyrics by Harold Atteridge
The Rose of Stamboul 1922

Why Do They Make 'Em So Beautiful?
Music by A. Baldwin Sloane
Lyrics by Harry Cort and George E. Stoddard
China Rose 1925

Why Do They Say They're the Fair Sex?
Music and lyrics by Ann Ronell
Count Me In 1942

Why Do Women Have to Call It Love?
Music by Don Gohman
Lyrics by Hal Hackady
Ambassador 1972

Why Do Ya Roll Those Eyes?
Music by Philip Charig
Lyrics by Morrie Ryskind
Americana (1926)

Why Do You Suppose?
Music by Richard Rodgers
Lyrics by Lorenz Hart
Heads Up! 1929

Originally written as "How Was I to Know?" for *She's My Baby* (1928) but dropped from production.

Why Do You Tease Me?
Music by Muriel Pollock
Lyrics by Max and Nathaniel Lief
and Harold Atteridge
Pleasure Bound 1929

Why Does It Have to Be You?
Music by James Mundy
Lyrics by John Latouche
The Vamp 1955

Why Does the Whole Damn World Adore Me?
Music by Laurence Rosenthal
Lyrics by James Lipton
Sherry! 1967

Why Don't They Dance the Polka Anymore?
Music by Jerome Kern
Lyrics by Harry B. Smith
The Girl From Utah 1914

Why Don't They Hand It to Me?
Music by Emmerich Kálmán
Lyrics by P.G. Wodehouse
The Riviera Girl 1917

Why Don't We?
Music by Maury Rubens and Sam Timberg
Lyrics by Moe Jaffe
Broadway Nights 1929

Why Don't We Switch?
Music by George Fischoff
Lyrics by Verna Tomasson
The Prince and the Pauper (OB) 1963

Why Don't We Try Staying Home?
Music and lyrics by Cole Porter
Fifty Million Frenchmen 1929

Dropped from production

Why Fight This?
Music and lyrics by Johnny Mercer
Saratoga 1959

Why Go Anywhere at All?
Music by Arthur Schwartz
Lyrics by Howard Dietz
The Gay Life 1961

Why Her?
Music by David Baker
Lyrics by David Craig
Copper and Brass 1957

Why Him?
Music by Burton Lane
Lyrics by Alan Jay Lerner
Carmelina 1979

Why Is Love?
Music by J. Fred Coots
Lyrics by Clifford Grey
June Days 1925

Why Is the Desert (Lovely to See)?
Music by Frederick Loewe
Lyrics by Alan Jay Lerner
The Little Prince (1975) F

Why Is the World So Changed Today?
Music by Emmerich Kálmán
Lyrics by Harry B. Smith
Countess Maritza 1926

Why Marry Them?
Music and lyrics by Cole Porter
Gay Divorce 1932

Why Me?
Music by Richard Rodgers
Lyrics by Martin Charnin
Two by Two 1970

Why Must We Always Be Dreaming?
Music by Sigmund Romberg
Lyrics by P.G. Wodehouse
Rosalie 1928

Why Not?
Music by Al Carmines
Lyrics by Maria Irene Fornes
Promenade (OB) 1969

Why Not for Marriage?
Music by Louis Bellson and Will Irwin
Lyrics by Richard Ney
Portofino 1958

Why Not Katie?
Music by Albert Hague
Lyrics by Arnold B. Horwitt
Plain and Fancy 1955

Why Not Surrender?
Music by Arthur Schwartz
Lyrics by Howard Dietz
A Bell For Adano (1956) TV

Why Should I Care?
Music and lyrics by Cole Porter
Rosalie (1937) F

Why, Oh Why?
Music by Vincent Youmans
Lyrics by Leo Robin and Clifford Grey
Hit the Deck 1927

Later re-written as "Nothing Could Be Sweeter"

Why Should I Wake Up?
Music by John Kander
Lyrics by Fred Ebb
Cabaret 1966

Why Should They Know About Paris?
Music by Don Pippin
Lyrics by Steve Brown
Fashion (OB) 1974

Why Shouldn't I?
Music and lyrics by Cole Porter
Jubilee 1935

Why Shouldn't I?
Music and lyrics by Deed Meyer
'Toinette (OB) 1961

Why Shouldn't I Have You?
Music and lyrics by Cole Porter
Fifty Million Frenchmen 1929

Why Shouldn't We?
Music by Herbert Stothart;
Lyrics by Oscar Hammerstein II and Otto Harbach
Rose Marie 1924

Why Shouldn't You Tell Me That?
Music by Ivan Caryll
Lyrics by C.M.S. McLellan
Oh! Oh! Delphine 1912

Why Speak of Money?
Music by George Gershwin
Lyrics by Ira Gershwin
Let 'Em Eat Cake 1933

Why They Made Him King
Music and lyrics by George M. Cohan
The Man Who Owns Broadway 1909

Why Try Hard to Be Good?
Music by Alfred Brooks
Lyrics by Ira J. Bilowit
Of Mice and Men (OB) 1958

Why Was I Born?
Music by Jerome Kern
Lyrics by Oscar Hammerstein II
Sweet Adeline 1929

Why Was I Born on a Farm?
Music by George Lessner
Lyrics by Miriam Battista and Russell Maloney
Sleepy Hollow 1948

Why We Do It?
Music and lyrics by Elizabeth Swados
Lullabye and Goodnight 1982

Why Wives
Music by Jacques Urbont
Lyrics by Bruce Geller
All in Love (OB) 1961

Why Would Anyone Want to Get Married?
Music by John Morris
Lyrics by Gerald Freedman
A Time for Singing 1966

Why Wouldn't I Do?
Music by Ivor Novello
Lyrics by Ivor Novello and Desmond Carter
Wake Up and Dream 1929

A Wicked Man
Music by Lee Pockriss
Lyrics by Anne Croswell
Ernest in Love (OB) 1960

Wicked, Unwholesome, Expensive
Music and lyrics by John Rox
Fools Rush In 1934

Wide-Awake Morning
Music by Frank Fields
Lyrics by Armand Aulicino
The Shoemaker and the Peddler (OB) 1960

The Wide Open Spaces
Music by Frederico Valerio
Lyrics by Elizabeth Miele
Hit the Trail 1954

Wide Pants Willie
Music by James F. Hanley
Lyrics by Harold Atteridge and Henry Creamer
Gay Paree 1925

The Widow
Music by Gustav Luders
Lyrics by Frank Pixley
The Prince of Pilsen 1903

The Widow
Music by Fritz Kreisler
Lyrics by William LeBaron
Apple Blossoms 1919

The Widow Fascinating
Music by Percy Wenrich
Lyrics by Julian Eltinge and Jack Mahoney
The Fascinating Widow 1911

A Widow Has Ways
Music by Victor Herbert
Lyrics by Henry Blossom
The Red Mill 1906

Widows
Music by Jerome Kern
Lyrics by Edward Madden
La Belle Paree 1911

Wife Beating Song
Music and lyrics by Elizabeth Swados
Lullabye and Goodnight 1982

A Wifie of Your Own
Music by Jerome Kern
Lyrics by Harry B. Smith
Oh, I Say! 1913

Wild About Music
Music by Maurice Yvain
Lyrics by Max and Nathaniel Lief
Luckee Girl 1928

Wild and Reckless
Music by Milton Schafer
Lyrics by Ira Levin
Drat! The Cat! 1965

Wild and Wonderful
Music and lyrics by Bob Goodman
Wild and Wonderful 1971

The Wild and Woolly West
Music by Dave Stamper
Lyrics by Gene Buck
Take the Air 1927

Wild Birds Calling
Music by David Baker
Lyrics by Will Holt
Come Summer 1969

Wild Cats
Music and lyrics by Irving Berlin
Music Box Revue (4th edition) 1924

The Wild Justice
Music by Kurt Weill
Lyrics by Maxwell Anderson
Lost in the Stars 1949

Wild Rose
Music by Jerome Kern
Lyrics by Clifford Grey
Sally 1920

The Wild Rose
Music by Rudolf Friml
Lyrics by Otto Harbach and Oscar Hammerstein II
The Wild Rose 1926

Wildcat
Music by Cy Coleman
Lyrics by Carolyn Leigh
Wildcat 1960

Wildcats
Music by Richard Rodgers
Lyrics by Oscar Hammerstein II
Allegro 1947

Wildflower
Music by Vincent Youmans
Lyrics by Otto Harbach and Oscar Hammerstein II
Wildflower 1923

Wildflowers
Music by Ann Sternberg
Lyrics by Gertrude Stein
Gertrude Stein's First Reader (OB) 1969

Wilkes-Barre, Pa.
Music by Lee Pockriss
Lyrics by Anne Croswell
Tovarich 1963

Will He Like Me?
Music by Jerry Bock
Lyrics by Sheldon Harnick
She Loves Me 1963

Will I Ever Tell You
Music and lyrics by Meredith Willson
The Music Man 1957

Will She Come From the East?
Music and lyrics by Irving Berlin
Music Box Revue (2nd edition) 1922

Will We Ever Know Each Other?
Music by Bob Brush
Lyrics by Martin Charnin
The First 1981

Will You Forget?
Music by Emmerich Kálmán
Lyrics by P.G. Wodehouse
The Riviera Girl 1917

Will You Forgive Me?
Music by Richard Rodgers
Lyrics by Lorenz Hart
Poor Little Ritz Girl 1920

Included in Boston production, but dropped before
Broadway opening.

Will You Marry Me?
Music by Walter L. Rosemont
Lyrics by Ballard MacDonald
Battling Buttler 1923

Will You Marry Me?
Music by Richard Rodgers
Lyrics by Oscar Hammerstein II
Pipe Dream 1955

Will You Marry Me Tomorrow, Maria?
Music by Jerome Kern
Lyrics by Oscar Hammerstein II
High, Wide and Handsome (1937) F

Will You Remember?
Music by Sigmund Romberg
Lyrics by Rida Johnson Young
Maytime 1917

Will You Remember Me?
Music by George Gershwin
Lyrics by Ira Gershwin
Lady, Be Good! 1924

Dropped from production

Will You Remember Me?
Music by Kurt Weill
Lyrics by Maxwell Anderson
Knickerbocker Holiday 1938

Will You Remember? Will You Forget?
Music by Lewis E. Gensler
Lyrics by Robert A. Simon and Clifford Grey
Ups-a-Daisy 1928

Will You Think of Me Tomorrow?
Music and lyrics by Bill and Patti Jacob
Jimmy 1969

The Will-o'-the-Wisp
Music by Victor Herbert
Lyrics by Robert B. Smith
The Debutante 1914

Willa
Music by Leon Carr
Lyrics by Earl Shuman
The Secret Life of Walter Mitty (OB) 1964

William McKinley High
Music by Albert Selden
Lyrics by Burt Shevelove
Small Wonder 1948

William's Song
Music by Henry Krieger
Lyrics by Robert Lorick
The Tap Dance Kid 1983

Willie Was a Gay Boy
Music by Leslie Stuart
Lyrics by Alfred Murray
Florodora 1900

Willie's Little Whistle
Music by Will Irwin
Lyrics by Norman Zeno
Fools Rush In 1934

Willing and Eager
Music and lyrics by Richard Rodgers
State Fair (remake, 1962) F

Willkommen
Music by John Kander
Lyrics by Fred Ebb
Cabaret 1966

Willow Tree
Music by Raymond Scott
Lyrics by Bernard Hanighen
Lute Song 1946

Willow, Willow, Willow
Music and lyrics by Robert Wright
and George Forrest
Kean 1961

Wimmen's Ways
Music and lyrics by Oscar Brown, Jr.
Joy (OB) 1970

Win for Me
Music by Harry Tierney
Lyrics by Joseph McCarthy
Kid Boots 1923

Windchild
Music and lyrics by Gary Graham
Touch (OB) 1970

Windflowers
Music by Jerome Moross
Lyrics by John Latouche
The Golden Apple 1954

The Window Cleaners
Music by Harry Ruby
Lyrics by Bert Kalmar
The Greenwich Village Follies (1925)

Windows
Music and lyrics by Eugene and Ralph Berton
Two for Tonight (OB) 1939

Windy City Marmalade
Music by Jule Styne
Lyrics by Bob Merrill
Sugar 1972

Wine Maid Divine
Music by A. Baldwin Sloane
Lyrics by E. Ray Goetz
The Hen Pecks 1911

Wine, Woman and Song
Music by Gustave Kerker
Lyrics by Hugh Morton
The Belle of New York 1897

Wine, Women and Song
Music by Jerome Kern
Lyrics by Anne Caldwell
She's a Good Fellow 1919

Dropped from production

Winged Love
Music by Victor Herbert
Lyrics by David Stevens
and Justin Huntly McCarthy
The Madcap Duchess 1913

Winged Victory
Music and lyrics by David Rose
Winged Victory 1943

Wings of the Morning
Music by William Heagney
Lyrics by William Heagney and Tom Connell
There You Are 1932

Wino Will
Music by Helen Miller
Lyrics by Eve Merriam
Inner City 1971

Winona
Music by Rudolf Friml
Lyrics by Brian Hooker
The White Eagle 1927

Winter and Spring
Music by Rudolf Friml
Lyrics by Edward Eliscu
Nine-Fifteen Revue 1930

Winter and Summer
Music by Harvey Schmidt
Lyrics by Tom Jones
Celebration 1969

Winter in Central Park
Music by Jerome Kern
Lyrics by Oscar Hammerstein II
Sweet Adeline 1929

Winter Nights
Music by Helen Miller
Lyrics by Eve Merriam
Inner City 1971

Winter of the Mind
Music by Howard Marren
Lyrics by Enid Futterman
Portrait of Jennie (OB) 1982

Wintergreen for President
Music by George Gershwin
Lyrics by Ira Gershwin
Of Thee I Sing 1931

This 2/4 time march is the campaign song at the opening of the show. The title itself is repeated nine more times in the chorus, and the lines, "He's the Man the People choose/Loves the Irish and the Jews," are used twice; that, along with some vocal "ta, ta, tas" to the music of old-time campaign songs, comprises the entire lyric. In *Let 'Em Eat Cake,* the sequel to *Of Thee I Sing,* candidate John P. Tweedledee is running against the incumbent Wintergreen; his supporters have their own campaign song, "Tweedledee for President," which they sing in counterpoint to "Wintergreen."

Winter's Here
Music and lyrics by Skip Redwine and Larry Frank
Frank Merriwell, or Honor Challenged 1971

Wisdom
Music by Helen Miller
Lyrics by Eve Merriam
Inner City 1971

Wish
Music by Ernest G. Schweikert
Lyrics by Frank Reardon
Rumple 1957

Wish
Music by Howard Marren
Lyrics by Enid Futterman
Portrait of Jennie (OB) 1982

Wish I May
Music and lyrics by Hugh Martin and Ralph Blane
Best Foot Forward (1963 OB revival)

Wish Me Luck
Music by Jay Gorney
Lyrics by Jean and Walter Kerr
Touch and Go 1949

Wish Them Well
Music by Richard Rodgers
Lyrics by Oscar Hammerstein II
Allegro 1947

Wish You Were Here
Music and lyrics by Harold Rome
Wish You Were Here 1952

Wisha Wurra
Music and lyrics by Johnny Burke
Donnybrook! 1961

Wishing Song
Music and lyrics by John Jennings
Riverwind (OB) 1962

Witch Song
Music by Ray Haney
Lyrics by Alfred Aiken
We're Civilized? (OB) 1962

Witches' Brew
Music by Jule Styne
Lyrics by Betty Comden and Adolph Green
Hallelujah, Baby! 1967

With a Little Bit of Luck
Music by Frederick Loewe
Lyrics by Alan Jay Lerner
My Fair Lady 1956

With a Smile On My Face
Music and lyrics by Irving Berlin
Follow The Fleet (1936) F

Dropped from film

With a Snap of My Finger
Music and lyrics by Stan Freeman
and Franklin Underwood
Lovely Ladies, Kind Gentlemen 1970

With a Song in My Heart
Music by Richard Rodgers
Lyrics by Lorenz Hart
Spring Is Here 1929

With a Sword in My Buckle
Music by George Fischoff
Lyrics by Verna Tomasson
The Prince and the Pauper (OB) 1963

With a Twist of the Wrist
Music and lyrics by Irvin Graham
Crazy With the Heat 1941

With a Wave of My Wand
Music by David Raksin
Lyrics by June Carroll
If the Shoe Fits 1946

With a World to Conquer
Music by Joe Ercole
Lyrics by Bruce Kluger
Ka-Boom (OB) 1980

With All My Heart
Music by Johann Strauss
Lyrics by Desmond Carter
The Great Waltz 1934

With Anne on My Arm
Music and lyrics by Jerry Herman
La Cage aux Folles 1983

Also sung as "With You on My Arm"

With Downcast Eyes
Music by Karl Hoschna
Lyrics by Otto Harbach
The Fascinating Widow 1911

With Lowered Heads
Music by Emmerich Kálmán
Lyrics by C.C.S. Cushing and E.P. Heath
Sari 1914

With My Head in the Clouds
Music and lyrics by Irving Berlin
This Is the Army 1942

With Papers Duly Signed
Music by Leo Fall
Lyrics by Harold Atteridge
The Rose of Stamboul 1922

With So Little to Be Sure Of
Music and lyrics by Stephen Sondheim
Anyone Can Whistle 1964

With the Dawn
Music by Sigmund Romberg
Lyrics by Irving Caesar
Nina Rosa 1930

With the One I Love
Music and lyrics by Al Kasha
and Joel Hirschhorn
Copperfield 1981

With This Ring
Music by Laurence Rosenthal
Lyrics by James Lipton
Sherry! 1967

With Type a-Ticking
Music by Jerome Kern
Lyrics by Edgar Allan Woolf
Head Over Heels 1918

With You
Music and lyrics by Irving Berlin
Puttin' on the Ritz (1929) F

With You
Music and lyrics by Steve Allen
Sophie 1963

With You
Music and lyrics by Stephen Schwartz
Pippin 1972

With You
Music by David Shire
Lyrics by Richard Maltby, Jr.
Baby 1983

With You, With Me
Music and lyrics by Richard Lewine
Entre-Nous (OB) 1935

With Your Hand in My Hand
Music by Ernest Gold
Lyrics by Anne Croswell
I'm Solomon 1968

Within This Empty Space
Music by Harvey Schmidt
Lyrics by Tom Jones
Philemon (OB) 1975

Without a Caress
Music by Fred Spielman and Arthur Gershwin
Lyrics by Stanley Adams
A Lady Says Yes 1945

Without a Mother
Music by Murray Rumshinsky
Lyrics by Jacob Jacobs
The President's Daughter 1970

Without a Shadow of a Doubt
Music and lyrics by Ord Hamilton
Artists and Models (1930)

Without a Song
Music by Vincent Youmans
Lyrics by Billy Rose and Edward Eliscu
Great Day! 1929

Without a Sponsor
Music and lyrics by Harold Orlob
Hairpin Harmony 1943

Without a Stitch
Music by Mischa and Wesley Portnoff
Lyrics by Donagh MacDonagh
Happy as Larry 1950

Without Love
Music by Ray Henderson
Lyrics by B.G. DeSylva and Lew Brown
Flying High 1930

Without Love
Music and lyrics by Cole Porter
Silk Stockings 1955

Without Me
Music by John Kander
Lyrics by Fred Ebb
The Happy Time 1968

Without My Money
Music by Richard Rodgers
Lyrics by Martin Charnin
Two by Two 1970

Dropped from production

Without You
Music by Dave Stamper
Lyrics by Gene Buck
Ziegfeld Follies of 1914

Without You
Music by Robert Stolz
Lyrics by Rowland Leigh
Night of Love 1941

Without You
Music by Frederick Loewe
Lyrics by Alan Jay Lerner
My Fair Lady 1956

Without You I'm Nothing
Music and lyrics by Jerry Bock, George Weiss
and Larry Holofcener
Mr. Wonderful 1956

Without Your Love
Music by Carl Millöcker (revised by Theo
Mackeben)
Lyrics by Rowland Leigh
The Dubarry 1932

Woe Is Me
Music by Lehman Engel
Lyrics by Agnes Morgan
A Hero Is Born 1937

Woke Up Today
Music by Nancy Ford
Lyrics by Gretchen Cryer
Shelter 1973

Wolf Time
Music by Sammy Fain
Lyrics by George Marion, Jr.
Toplitzky of Notre Dame 1946

Woman
Music by Edward Künneke
Lyrics by Clifford Grey
Mayflowers 1925

Woman
Music by John Kander
Lyrics by Fred Ebb
Zorba (1983 revival)

Woman Against the World
Music by Clay Warnick
Lyrics by Edward Eager
Dream With Music 1944

A Woman Alone
Music by Larry Grossman
Lyrics by Betty Comden and Adolph Green
A Doll's Life 1982

The Woman for the Man
Music by Charles Strouse
Lyrics by Lee Adams
It's a Bird, It's a Plane, It's Superman 1966

The Woman I Love
Music and lyrics by Al Carmines
Joan (OB) 1972

The Woman I Was Before
Music by Sammy Fain
Lyrics by Paul Francis Webster
Christine 1960

The Woman in His Room
Music and lyrics by Frank Loesser
Where's Charley? 1948

A Woman in Love
Music and lyrics by Frank Loesser
Guys and Dolls (film version, 1955)

Woman in Love
Music and lyrics by Bob Merrill
Henry, Sweet Henry 1967

Woman Is a Rascal
Music by Baldwin Bergersen
Lyrics by William Archibald
Carib Song 1945

A Woman Is a Sometime Thing
Music by George Gershwin
Lyrics by DuBose Heyward
Porgy and Bess 1935

A Woman Is a Woman Is a Woman
Music and lyrics by Rick Besoyan
The Student Gypsy (OB) 1963

A Woman Is How She Loves
Music by André Previn
Lyrics by Alan Jay Lerner
Coco 1969

A Woman Is Only a Woman, But a Good Cigar Is a Smoke
Music by Victor Herbert
Lyrics by Harry B. Smith
Miss Dolly Dollars 1905

Title taken from Rudyard Kipling's *The Betrothed*

A Woman Must Never Grow Old
Music and lyrics by John Jennings
Riverwind (OB) 1962

A Woman Must Think of These Things
Music and lyrics by John Jennings
Riverwind (OB) 1962

A Woman Needs Something Like That
Music by Richard Rodgers
Lyrics by Lorenz Hart
Love Me Tonight (1932) F

The Woman of the Year
Music and lyrics by Ann Ronell
Count Me In 1942

Woman of the Year
Music by John Kander
Lyrics by Fred Ebb
Woman of the Year 1981

Woman on the Run
Music by Nancy Ford
Lyrics by Gretchen Cryer
Shelter 1973

A Woman Ought to Know Her Place
Music and lyrics by Al Kasha and Joel Hirschorn
Seven Brides for Seven Brothers 1982

A Woman Rarely Ever
Music by Don Pippin
Lyrics by Steve Brown
The Contrast (OB) 1972

Woman to Lady
Music by George Gershwin
Lyrics by DuBose Heyward
Porgy and Bess 1935

Woman to Woman
Music by Mel Marvin
Lyrics by Robert Montgomery
Green Pond (OB) 1977

A Woman Waits for Me
Music by Stan Harte, Jr.
Leaves of Grass (OB) 1971

The Woman Who Lived up There
Music by Kurt Weill
Lyrics by Langston Hughes
Street Scene 1947

A Woman Who Thinks I'm Wonderful
Music by Charles Strouse
Lyrics by Alan Jay Lerner
Dance a Little Closer 1983

A Woman Wouldn't Be a Woman
Music by George Kleinsinger
Lyrics by Joe Darion
Shinbone Alley 1957

A Woman's Career
Music and lyrics by Cole Porter
Kiss Me, Kate 1948

Dropped from production

A Woman's Hands
Music by Peter Link
Lyrics by Michael Cacoyannis
Lysistrata 1972

A Woman's Heart
Music by Jerome Kern
Lyrics by Harry B. Smith
Oh, I Say! 1913

A Woman's Kiss
Music by Rudolf Friml
Lyrics by Robert Wright and George Forrest
The Firefly (film version, 1937)

A Woman's Prerogative
Music by Harold Arlen
Lyrics by Johnny Mercer
St. Louis Woman 1946

A Woman's Smile
Music by Rudolf Friml
Lyrics by Otto Harbach
The Firefly 1912

The Woman's Touch
Music by George Gershwin
Lyrics by Ira Gershwin
Oh, Kay! 1926

Women
Music by Franz Lehár
Lyrics by Adrian Ross
The Merry Widow 1907

Women
Music by Richard Rodgers
Lyrics by Lorenz Hart
Jumbo 1935

Women!
Music by Edward Earle
Lyrics by Yvonne Tarr
The Decameron (OB) 1961

Women
Music by David Baker
Lyrics by Will Holt
Come Summer 1969

Women and Men
Music by Lawrence Hurwit
Lyrics by Lee Goldsmith
Sextet 1974

Women in Love
Music by Ronald Melrose
Lyrics by Bill Russell
Fourtune (OB) 1980

Women Simple
Music by Jacques Urbont
Lyrics by Bruce Geller
All in Love (OB) 1961

Women Weaving
Music by Heitor Villa-Lobos
Lyrics by Robert Wright and George Forrest
Magdalena 1948

Women With Women—Men With Men
Music and lyrics by Al Carmines
The Faggot (OB) 1973

Women, Women, Women
Music by Duke Ellington
Lyrics by John Latouche
Beggar's Holiday 1946

Women's Club Blues
Music by Kurt Weill
Lyrics by Alan Jay Lerner
Love Life 1948

Women's Liberation
Music by Murray Rumshinsky
Lyrics by Jacob Jacobs
The President's Daughter 1970

Women's Work
Music by Lehman Engel
Lyrics by Edward Eager
The Liar 1950

Women's Work Is Never Done
Music by George Gershwin and Herbert Stothart
Lyrics by Otto Harbach and Oscar Hammerstein II
Song of the Flame 1925

The Wompom
Music by Donald Swann
Lyrics by Michael Flanders
At the Drop of a Hat 1959

A Wonder
Music by John Clifton
Lyrics by John Clifton and Ben Tarver
Man With a Load of Mischief (OB) 1966

Wonder Where My Heart Is
Music and lyrics by Deed Meyer
She Shall Have Music (OB) 1959

Wonder Why
Music by Philip Charig
Lyrics by James Dyrenforth
Nikki 1931

Wonderful
Music by Lionel Monckton
Lyrics by Adrian Ross
The Quaker Girl 1911

Wonderful Copenhagen
Music and lyrics by Frank Loesser
Hans Christian Andersen (1952) F

Wonderful Dad
Music by Jerome Kern
Lyrics by Anne Caldwell
Stepping Stones 1923

A Wonderful Day Like Today
Music and lyrics by Leslie Bricusse
and Anthony Newley
*The Roar of the Greasepaint—The Smell
of the Crowd* 1965

Wonderful Days
Music by Jerome Kern
Lyrics by Harry B. Smith
Ninety in the Shade 1915

Wonderful Girls
Music by Al Goodman and J. Fred Coots
Lyrics by Clifford Grey
Gay Paree 1925

Wonderful Good
Music and lyrics by Howard Blankman
By Hex (OB) 1956

The Wonderful Machine
Music by David Baker
Lyrics by Sheldon Harnick
Smiling, the Boy Fell Dead (OB) 1961

Wonderful, Marvelous You
Music by Moose Charlap
Lyrics by Norman Gimbel
The Conquering Hero 1961

Wonderful Music
Music by Harvey Schmidt
Lyrics by Tom Jones
110 in the Shade 1963

A Wonderful Party
Music by George Gershwin
Lyrics by Ira Gershwin
Lady, Be Good! 1924

Wonderful Party
Music by John Kander

Lyrics by James Goldman, John Kander
and William Goldman
A Family Affair 1962

Wonderful Rhythm
Music by Tom Johnstone
Lyrics by Phil Cook
When You Smile 1925

The Wonderful Thing We Call Love
Music by Albert Von Tilzer
Lyrics by Neville Fleeson
The Gingham Girl 1922

Wonderful U
Music and lyrics by Walter Marks
Broadway Follies 1981

A Wonderful Way of Life
Music by Ruth Cleary Patterson
Lyrics by Les Kramer and Floria Vestoff
Russell Patterson's Sketch Book (OB) 1960

Wonderful, Wonderful Day
Music by Gene dePaul
Lyrics by Johnny Mercer
Seven Brides for Seven Brothers 1982

Wonderful Yesterday
Music by Tom Johnstone
Lyrics by Phil Cook
When You Smile 1925

Wondering Who
Music by Alexander Fogarty
Lyrics by George Fitch
Cape Cod Follies 1929

Wondrin'
Music by Norman Campbell
Lyrics by Donald Harron and Norman Campbell
Anne of Green Gables (OB) 1971

Won't I Do?
Music and lyrics by Edward Pola and Eddie Brandt
Woof, Woof 1929

Won't Some Nice Boy Marry Me?
Music by Louis A. Hirsch
Lyrics by Rennold Wolf
The Rainbow Girl 1918

Won't Some One Take Me Home?
Music by Karl Hoschna
Lyrics by Otto Harbach
Madame Sherry 1910

Won't You Charleston With Me?
Music and lyrics by Sandy Wilson
The Boy Friend 1954

Won't You Come Across?
Music by Rudolf Friml
Lyrics by Otto Harbach and Oscar Hammerstein II
The Wild Rose 1926

Won't You Come to the Party?
Music and lyrics by William Roy
The Penny Friend (OB) 1966

Won't You Have a Little Feather
Music by Jerome Kern
Lyrics by Paul West
Peter Pan 1924

Won't You Marry Me?
Music by Sigmund Romberg
Lyrics by Dorothy Donnelly
My Maryland 1927

Won't You Marry Me?
Music by Moose Charlap
Lyrics by Norman Gimbel
The Conquering Hero 1961

Won't You Tell Me
Music by Charles M. Schwab
Lyrics by Henry Myers
Bare Facts of 1926

Won't You Tell Me Why?
Music by Jack Waller and Joseph Tunbridge
Lyrics by R.P. Weston and Bert Lee
Tell Her the Truth 1932

Wooden Wedding
Music by Kurt Weill
Lyrics by Ogden Nash
One Touch of Venus 1943

Woodman, Woodman, Spare That Tree
Music and lyrics by Irving Berlin
Ziegfeld Follies of 1911

Woof
Music by Will Irwin
Lyrics by Norman Zeno
The Show Is On 1936

A Word a Day
Music and lyrics by Johnny Mercer
Top Banana 1951

A Word in Edgewise
Music by Richard Rodgers
Lyrics by Lorenz Hart
Spring Is Here 1929

Dropped from production

The Word Is Love
Music by David Shire
Lyrics by Richard Maltby, Jr.
Starting Here, Starting Now (OB) 1977

The Word of the Lord
Music and lyrics by Eaton Magoon, Jr.
Heathen 1972

The Words
Music by Norman Campbell
Lyrics by Donald Harron and Norman Campbell
Anne of Green Gables (OB) 1971

Words Are Not Needed
Music by Jerome Kern
Lyrics by P.G. Wodehouse
Oh, Boy! 1917

The Words I Never Said
Music and lyrics by Michael Brown
Different Times 1972

Words, Music, Cash
Music by Karl Hajos (based on Chopin)
Lyrics by Harry B. Smith
White Lilacs 1928

Words Without Music
Music by Vernon Duke
Lyrics by Ira Gershwin
Ziegfeld Follies (1936)

Words, Words, Words
Music and lyrics by Walter Marks
Bajour 1964

Work Alike
Music by Frank Grey
Lyrics by Earle Crooker
The Little Whopper 1919

Work Song
Music by Earl Robinson
Lyrics by Waldo Salt
Sandhog (OB) 1954

The Worker and the Shirker
Music by Susan Hulsman Bingham
Lyrics by Myrna Lamb
Mod Donna (OB) 1970

Workin' It Out
Music by Marvin Hamlisch
Lyrics by Carole Bayer Sager
They're Playing Our Song 1979

Workout
Music by Charles Strouse
Lyrics by Lee Adams
Golden Boy 1964

The World According to Snoopy
Music by Larry Grossman
Lyrics by Hal Hackady
Snoopy (OB) 1982

The World Belongs to the Young
Music by André Previn
Lyrics by Alan Jay Lerner
Coco 1969

World Creation
Music by Galt MacDermot
Lyrics by Rochelle Owens
The Karl Marx Play (OB) 1973

The World Is Beautiful Today
Music by Jule Styne
Lyrics by Bob Hilliard
Hazel Flagg 1953

The World Is Comin' to a Start
Music by Gary Geld
Lyrics by Peter Udell
Purlie 1970

The World Is Full of Loneliness
Music by Galt MacDermot
Lyrics by William Dumaresq
The Human Comedy (OB) 1983

The World Is Full of Villains
Music by Kurt Weill
Lyrics by Ira Gershwin
The Firebrand of Florence 1945

The World Is in My Arms
Music by Burton Lane
Lyrics by E.Y. Harburg
Hold On to Your Hats 1940

The World Is Mean
Music by Kurt Weill
Lyrics by Marc Blitzstein
The Threepenny Opera (OB) 1954

The World Is Mine
Music by George Gershwin
Lyrics by Ira Gershwin
Funny Face 1927

Dropped from production and later in score of
Nine-Fifteen Revue (1930) under the title "Toddlin'
Along."

The World Is My Oyster
Music by Richard Rodgers
Lyrics by Lorenz Hart
I'd Rather Be Right 1937

Dropped from production

The World Is Round
Music and lyrics by James Rado
Rainbow (OB) 1972

The World Is Your Balloon
Music by Sammy Fain
Lyrics by E.Y. Harburg
Flahooley 1951

The World Keeps Going Round
Music and lyrics by Micki Grant
It's So Nice to Be Civilized 1980

The World Must Be Bigger Than an Avenue
Music by Wally Harper
Lyrics by Jack Lloyd
Irene (1973 revival)

World of Dreams
Music by Victor Herbert
Lyrics by Edward Eliscu
Nine-Fifteen Revue 1930

The World Outside
Music by Harry Warren
Lyrics by Jerome Lawrence and Robert E. Lee
Shangri-La 1956

World, Take Me Back
Music and lyrics by Jerry Herman
Hello, Dolly 1964

See note on "Love, Look In My Window"

A World to Win
Music by David Baker
Lyrics by Sheldon Harnick
Smiling, the Boy Fell Dead (OB) 1961

The World Today
Music and lyrics by William Roy
The Penny Friend (OB) 1966

World Weary
Music and lyrics by Noël Coward
This Year of Grace 1928

Worlds Apart
Music by Jerry Bock
Lyrics by Sheldon Harnick
Man in the Moon 1963

The World's Greatest Musical Act
Music and lyrics by Ron Eliran
Don't Step on My Olive Branch (OB) 1976

The World's Worst Women
Music by Herbert Stothart
Lyrics by Otto Harbach and Oscar Hammerstein II
Wildflower 1923

The Worm Germ
Music by Galt MacDermot
Lyrics by Christopher Gore
Via Galactica 1972

Worries
Music by Jerome Kern
Lyrics by P. G. Wodehouse
Sitting Pretty 1924

The Worst Pies in London
Music and lyrics by Stephen Sondheim
Sweeney Todd 1979

Worthy of You
Music by Harry Tierney
Lyrics by Joseph McCarthy
Irene 1919

Would You Be So Kindly
Music by Burton Lane
Lyrics by E.Y. Harburg
Hold On to Your Hats 1940

Would You Let Me Know?
Music by John Addison
Lyrics by John Cranko
Cranks 1956

Would You Like to Take a Walk?
Music by Harry Warren
Lyrics by Mort Dixon and Billy Rose
Sweet and Low 1930

Also in *Crazy Quilt* (1931)

Would-ja?
Music by Manning Sherwin
Lyrics by Arthur Herzog, Jr.
Bad Habits of 1926 (OB)

Would'ja for a Big Red Apple
Music by Henry Souvaine
Lyrics by Everett Miller and Johnny Mercer
Americana (1932)

Wouldn't I?
Music by Don Pippin
Lyrics by Steve Brown
The Contrast (OB) 1972

Wouldn't It Be Fun
Music and lyrics by Cole Porter
Aladdin (1957) TV

Dropped from the production before the broadcast, although it was sung by Basil Rathbone on the cast album, which had been made in advance. It was the last song written for the production and, as it turned out, the last song Porter wrote. He was never active again and died on October 15, 1964.

Wouldn't It Be Loverly?
Music by Frederick Loewe
Lyrics by Alan Jay Lerner
My Fair Lady 1956

Wouldn't That Be Wonderful
Music and lyrics by Herman Hupfeld
Hey Nonny Nonny! 1932

Wouldn't You Like to Be on Broadway?
Music by Kurt Weill
Lyrics by Langston Hughes
Street Scene 1947

Wow Wow Wow
Music and lyrics by Elizabeth Swados
Alice in Concert (OB) 1980

Wow-Ooh-Wolf
Music and lyrics by Cole Porter
Seven Lively Arts 1944

Wrap Me in Your Serape
Music by Maria Grever
Lyrics by Raymond Leveen
Viva O'Brien 1941

Wrapped in a Ribbon and Tied in a Bow
Music by Kurt Weill
Lyrics by Langston Hughes
Street Scene 1947

Wrapped Up in You
Music by Ben Oakland
Lyrics by Jack Murray and Barry Trivers
Ziegfeld Follies (1931)

The Wrath of Achilles
Music by Joseph Raposo
Lyrics by Erich Segal
Sing Muse! (OB) 1961

The Wreath
Music and lyrics by Scott Joplin
Treemonisha 1975

Written in 1909

The Wreck of a Mec
Music by Marguerite Monnot
Lyrics by Julian More, David Heneker
and Monte Norman
Irma la Douce 1960

A Writer Writes at Night
Music by Richard Rodgers
Lyrics by Martin Charnin
I Remember Mama 1979

Written in Your Hand
Music by Sigmund Romberg
Lyrics by Rowland Leigh
My Romance 1948

Wrong!
Music by Jimmy Van Heusen
Lyrics by Sammy Cahn
Skyscraper 1965

Wrong Is Never Right
Music and lyrics by Scott Joplin
Treemonisha 1975

Written in 1909

Wrong Note Rag
Music by Leonard Bernstein
Lyrics by Betty Comden and Adolph Green
Wonderful Town 1953

The Wrong Thing at the Right Time
Music by Milton Schwarzwald
Lyrics by George S. Kaufman, Marc Connelly
and Ira Gershwin
Be Yourself 1924

Wunderbar
Music and lyrics by Cole Porter
Kiss Me, Kate 1948

X

Xanadu
Music by Gerard Calvi
Lyrics by Harold Rome
La Grosse Valise 1965

#X9RL220

See (Number) X9RL220

Y

Y' Can't Win
Music by Gordon Duffy
Lyrics by Harry M. Haldane
Happy Town 1959

Ya Chara
Music by Manos Hadjidakis
Lyrics by Joe Darion
Illya Darling 1967

Ya Got Me
Music by Leonard Bernstein
Lyrics by Betty Comden and Adolph Green
On the Town 1944

The Yahoo Step
Music and lyrics by Charles Gaynor
Lend An Ear 1948

Also in *Show Girl* (1961)

Y'all Got It!
Music and lyrics by Charlie Smalls
The Wiz 1975

Yaller
Music by Charles M. Schwab
Lyrics by Henry Myers
Three's a Crowd 1930

The Yam
Music and lyrics by Irving Berlin
Carefree (1938) F

The Yama-Yama Man
Music by Karl Hoschna
Lyrics by Collin Davis
Three Twins 1908

Hoschna had written this song much earlier for a vaudeville sketch. The show's star, Bessie McCoy (Davis) made a huge hit with it, and was from then on known as "The Yama-Yama Girl."

Yankee Dollar
Music by Harold Arlen
Lyrics by E.Y. Harburg
Jamaica 1957

Yankee Doodle Dandy
Music and lyrics by George M. Cohan
Little Johnny Jones 1904

Yankee Doodle Rhythm
Music by George Gershwin
Lyrics by Ira Gershwin
Rosalie 1928

Dropped from production

Yankee Doodles Are Coming to Town
Music by Burton Lane
Lyrics by Alan Jay Lerner
Carmelina 1979

The Yankee Father in the Yankee Home
Music and lyrics by George M. Cohan
The Merry Malones 1927

The Yankee Girl
Music by Silvio Hein
Lyrics by George V. Hobart
The Yankee Girl 1910

Yankee, Go Home
Music and lyrics by Richard Rodgers
No Strings 1962

Dropped from production

Yankee Stay
Music by Ray Haney
Lyrics by Alfred Aiken
We're Civilized? (OB) 1962

Yankyula
Music by Rudolf Friml
Lyrics by J. Keirn Brennan
Luana 1930

Yasni Kozkolai
Music and lyrics by Noël Coward
The Girl Who Came to Supper 1963

Y'assou
Music by John Kander
Lyrics by Fred Ebb
Zorba 1968

Ya-ta-ta
Music by Galt MacDermot
Lyrics by Rochelle Owens
The Karl Marx Play (OB) 1973

Yatata, Yatata, Yatata
Music by Richard Rodgers
Lyrics by Oscar Hammerstein II
Allegro 1947

Ye Birds in Azure Winging
Music by Reginald De Koven
Lyrics by Harry B. Smith
Robin Hood 1891

Ye Lunchtime Follies
Music by Richard Rodgers
Lyrics by Lorenz Hart
A Connecticut Yankee (1943 revival)

Year After Year
Music by George Gershwin
Lyrics by B.G. DeSylva
George White's Scandals (1924)

A Year From Today
Music by Jerome Kern
Lyrics by P. G. Wodehouse
Sitting Pretty 1924

A Year Is a Day
Music by Baldwin Bergersen
Lyrics by William Archibald
The Crystal Heart (OB) 1960

A Year Is a Long, Long Time
Music by Rudolf Friml
Lyrics by Otto Harbach and Edward Clark
You're In Love 1917

Year of Jubilo
Music and lyrics by Bland Simpson and Jim Wann
(Based on traditional folk music)
Diamond Studs (OB) 1975

The Years Before Us
Music and lyrics by Frank Loesser
Where's Charley? 1948

Yeemy Yeemy
Music by James Mundy
Lyrics by John Latouche
The Vamp 1955

Yellow Drum
Music by Claibe Richardson
Lyrics by Kenward Elmslie
The Grass Harp 1971

Yellow Man
Music and lyrics by Randy Newman
Maybe I'm Doing It Wrong (1st edition)
(OB) 1982

Yenta Power
Music by Charles Strouse
Lyrics by Lee Adams
A Broadway Musical 1978

Yer My Friend, Aintcha?
Music and lyrics by Bob Merrill
New Girl in Town 1957

Yerushaliam
Music by Walt Smith
Lyrics by Leon Uris
Ari 1971

Yes
Music by John Kander
Lyrics by Fred Ebb
70, Girls, 70 1971

Yes, Aunt
Music by Baldwin Bergersen
Lyrics by William Archibald
The Crystal Heart (OB) 1960

Yes, I Know That I'm Alive
Music by Nancy Ford
Lyrics by Gretchen Cryer
The Last Sweet Days of Isaac (OB) 1970

Yes, I Love You Honey
Music by Jerry Livingston
Lyrics by Mack David
Bright Lights of 1944

Yes I See the Woman
Music and lyrics by Bob Ost
Everybody's Gettin' Into the Act (OB) 1981

Yes Me
Music by Richard Rodgers
Lyrics by Lorenz Hart and Jimmy Durante
Hollywood Party (1934) F

Dropped from film

Yes, My Heart
Music and lyrics by Bob Merrill
Carnival 1961

Yes or No
Music by Edward Künneke
Lyrics by Harry B. Smith
The Love Song 1925

Yes or No
Music by Sigmund Romberg
Lyrics by Harry B. Smith
Princess Flavia 1925

Yes, Sir, I've Made a Date
Music by Lee Wainer
Lyrics by J.B. Rosenberg
New Faces of 1943

Yes, Yes, Yes
Music and lyrics by Cole Porter
You Never Know 1938

Yes, Yes, Yvette
Music by Philip Charig
Lyrics by Irving Caesar
Yes, Yes, Yvette 1927

Yesterday I Left the Earth
Music and lyrics by John Phillips
Man on the Moon 1975

Yesterday I Loved You
Music by Mary Rodgers
Lyrics by Marshall Barer
Once Upon a Mattress 1959

Yesterday Was Such a Lovely Day
Music and lyrics by Irving Burgie
Ballad for Bimshire (OB) 1963

Yesterdays
Music by Jerome Kern
Lyrics by Otto Harbach
Roberta 1933

Yesterday's Champagne
Music by Robert Kole
Lyrics by Sandi Merle
I Take These Women (OB) 1982

Yesterday's Lover
Music by Patrick Rose
Lyrics by Merv Campone and Richard Ouzounian
A Bistro Car on the CNR (OB) 1978

Yip Ahoy
Music and lyrics by Harold Rome
Sing Out the News 1938

Yoga and Yoghurt
Music by Ted Simons
Lyrics by Elinor Guggenheimer
Potholes (OB) 1979

The Yoo-Hoo Blues
Music by Morgan Lewis
Lyrics by Nancy Hamilton
One for the Money 1939

You
Music by Albert Sirmay and Arthur Schwartz
Lyrics by Arthur Swanstrom
Princess Charming 1930

You
Music by Richard Rodgers
Lyrics by Martin Charnin
Two by Two 1970

Y–O–U
Music by Galt MacDermot
Lyrics by Gerome Ragni
Dude 1972

You Ain't Gonna Pick Up Where You Left Off
Music by Garry Sherman
Lyrics by Peter Udell
Amen Corner 1983

You Ain't Got No Savoir Faire
Music by Richard Rodgers
Lyrics by Lorenz Hart
America's Sweetheart 1931

You Ain't No Astronaut
Music and lyrics by Melvin Van Peebles
Ain't Supposed to Die a Natural Death 1971

You Ain't So Hot
Music by Jerome Moross
Lyrics by Paul Peters and George Sklar
Parade (1935)

You Alone Would Do
Music by Jerome Kern
Lyrics by P. G. Wodehouse
Sitting Pretty 1924

Dropped from production

You Always Love the Same Girl
Music by Richard Rodgers
Lyrics by Lorenz Hart
A Connecticut Yankee (1943 revival)

You Always Talk of Friendship
Music by Alma Sanders
Lyrics by Monte Carlo
Mystery Moon 1930

You and I
Music by Paul A. Rubens
Lyrics by Paul A. Rubens and Arthur Wimperis
The Sunshine Girl 1913

You and I
Music by George Gershwin
Lyrics by B.G. DeSylva, E. Ray Goetz
and Ballard MacDonald
George White's Scandals (1923)

You and I Are Passersby
Music by Jean Gilbert
Lyrics by Harry B. Smith
The Red Robe 1928

You and I Could Be Just Like That
Music by Henry Sullivan
Lyrics by Edward Eliscu
A Little Racketeer 1932

You and I Know
Music by Arthur Schwartz
Lyrics by Albert Stillman and Laurence Stallings
Virginia 1937

You and I, Love
Music by John Kander
Lyrics by Fred Ebb
70, Girls, 70 1971

You and I Love You and Me
Music by Albert Von Tilzer
Lyrics by Neville Fleeson
Bye Bye, Bonnie 1927

You and the Night and the Music
Music by Arthur Schwartz
Lyrics by Howard Dietz
Revenge With Music 1934

Originally written in 3/4 time and called "Tonight," with lyrics by Desmond Carter, it was sung by Anna Neagle in the film *The Queen's Affair* (1934).

You and Your Kiss
Music by Jerome Kern
Lyrics by Dorothy Fields
One Night in the Tropics (1940) F

You Appeal to Me
Music by Sigmund Romberg
Lyrics by Harry B. Smith
The Love Call 1927

You Are
Music by Richard Rodgers
Lyrics by Lorenz Hart
Hollywood Party (1934) F

Dropped from film

You Are
Music and lyrics by Clark Gesner
New Faces of 1968

You Are All I've Wanted
Music by Sigmund Romberg
Lyrics by Otto Harbach
Forbidden Melody 1927

You Are Beautiful
Music by Richard Rodgers
Lyrics by Oscar Hammerstein II
Flower Drum Song 1958

The original title, *She Is Beautiful,* was changed during the tryout.

You Are for Loving
Music and lyrics by Hugh Martin and Ralph Blane
Best Foot Forward (1963 OB revival)

You Are Free
Music by Victor Jacobi
Lyrics by William LeBaron
Apple Blossoms 1919

You Are Love
Music by Jerome Kern
Lyrics by Oscar Hammerstein II
Show Boat 1927

You Are My Darlin' Bride
Music by Giuseppe Verdi (adapted by Hans Spialek)
Lyrics by Charles Friedman
My Darlin' Aïda 1952

You Are My Day Dream
Music and lyrics by Cliff Friend and George White
George White's Scandals (1929)

You Are My Downfall
Music by Sammy Fain
Lyrics by George Marion, Jr.
Toplitzky of Notre Dame 1946

You Are My Songs
Music by Johann Strauss
Lyrics by Desmond Carter
The Great Waltz 1934

You Are My Woman
Music by Sigmund Romberg
Lyrics by Oscar Hammerstein II
East Wind 1931

You Are Never Away
Music by Richard Rodgers
Lyrics by Oscar Hammerstein II
Allegro 1947

You Are Not Real
Music by Jerry Bock
Lyrics by Sheldon Harnick
The Apple Tree 1966

You Are One of a Kind
Music and lyrics by Joseph Church
An Evening With Joan Crawford (OB) 1981

You Are Romance
Music by Philip Charig
Lyrics by Dan Shapiro and Milton Pascal
Artists and Models (1943)

You Are So Beyond
Music and lyrics by Jeanne Napoli and Doug Frank
Marilyn 1983

You Are So Fair
Music by Richard Rodgers
Lyrics by Lorenz Hart
Babes in Arms 1937

You Are So Lovely and I'm So Lonely
Music by Richard Rodgers
Lyrics by Lorenz Hart
Something Gay 1935

You Are Something Very Special
Music and lyrics by John Raniello
Movie Buff (OB) 1977

You Are Still My Boy
Music and lyrics by Harry Chapin
Cotton Patch Gospel (OB) 1981

You Are the Song
Music by Sigmund Romberg
Lyrics by Irving Caesar
Melody 1933

You Are Too Beautiful
Music by Richard Rodgers
Lyrics by Lorenz Hart
Hallelujah, I'm a Bum (1933) F

You Are What You Feel
Music by Andrew Lloyd Webber
Lyrics by Tim Rice
Joseph and the Amazing Technicolor Dreamcoat 1982

You Are Woman
Music by Jule Styne
Lyrics by Bob Merrill
Funny Girl 1964

You Are You
Music by George Gershwin and Herbert Stothart
Lyrics by Otto Harbach and Oscar Hammerstein II
Song of the Flame 1925

Dropped from production

You Are You
Music by John Kander
Lyrics by Fred Ebb
Flora, the Red Menace 1965

You Are You
Music by Joe Ercole
Lyrics by Bruce Kluger
Ka-Boom (OB) 1980

You Beautiful So and So
Music by Ted Snyder
Lyrics by Billy Rose
Earl Carroll's Sketch Book (1929)

You Become Me
Music and lyrics by William Roy
Maggie 1953

You Build a Fire Down in My Heart
Music and lyrics by Irving Berlin
The Fascinating Widow 1911

You Burn Me Up
Music by Jean Gilbert
Lyrics by Harry B. Smith
Marching By 1932

You Came Along
Music by Joseph Meyer and Philip Charig
Lyrics by Leo Robin
Just Fancy 1927

You Came to Me as a Young Man
Music by Steve Sterner
Lyrics by Peter del Valle
Lovers (OB) 1975

You Can Always Find Another Partner
Music by Vincent Youmans
Lyrics by Otto Harbach and Oscar Hammerstein II
Wildflower 1923

You Can Dance
Music by Victor Ziskin
Lyrics by Joan Javits
Young Abe Lincoln 1961

You Can Dance With Any Girl at All
Music by Vincent Youmans
Lyrics by Irving Caesar
No, No, Nanette 1925

You Can Do No Wrong
Music and lyrics by Cole Porter
The Pirate (1948) F

You Can Do Nothing About It
Music by Galt MacDermot
Lyrics by Gerome Ragni
Dude 1972

You Can Hang Your Hat Here
Music by Ray Haney
Lyrics by Alfred Aiken
We're Civilized? (OB) 1962

You Can Have Him
Music and lyrics by Irving Berlin
Miss Liberty 1949

You Can Leave Your Hat On
Music and lyrics by Randy Newman
Maybe I'm Doing It Wrong (1st edition) (OB) 1981

You Can Make My Life a Bed of Roses
Music by Ray Henderson
Lyrics by Lew Brown
Hot-Cha! 1932

You Can Never Blame a Girl for Dreaming
Music by Herbert Stothart
Lyrics by Otto Harbach and Oscar Hammerstein II
Wildflower 1923

You Can Never Go Back
Music by Charles Strouse
Lyrics by Lee Adams
Bring Back Birdie 1981

You Can Never Tell
Music by Niclas Kempner
Lyrics by Graham John
The Street Singer 1929

You Can Reach the Sun
Music and lyrics by Bob Goodman
Wild and Wonderful 1971

You Can Trust Me
Music and lyrics by Ervin Drake
What Makes Sammy Run? 1964

You Cannot Drown the Dreamer
Music by Keith Hermann
Lyrics by Charlotte Anker and Irene Rosenberg
Onward Victoria 1980

You Cannot Make Your Shimmy Shake on Tea
Music and lyrics by Irving Berlin and Rennold Wolf
Ziegfeld Follies of 1919

You Cannot Send Him Away
Music and lyrics by Gian-Carlo Menotti
The Medium 1947

You Can't Blame Your Uncle Sammy
Music by Jimmy McHugh
Lyrics by Al Dubin and Irwin Dash
Sugar Babies 1979

You Can't Brush Me Off
Music and lyrics by Irving Berlin
Louisiana Purchase 1940

You Can't Eye a Shy Baby
Music by Abel Baer
Lyrics by Sam Lewis and Joe Young
Lady Do 1927

You Can't Fool the People
Music by George Kleinsinger
Lyrics by Alfred Hayes
Of V We Sing 1942

You Can't Fool Your Dreams
Music by Richard Rodgers
Lyrics by Lorenz Hart
Poor Little Ritz Girl 1920

Same music as "Don't Love Me Like Othello," In the Columbia Varsity show *Fly With Me*.

You Can't Get a Man With a Gun
Music and lyrics by Irving Berlin
Annie Get Your Gun 1946

**You Can't Get Up Before Noon
Without Being a Square**
Music and lyrics by Melvin Van Peebles
Ain't Supposed to Die a Natural Death 1971

You Can't Keep a Good Girl Down
Music by Jerome Kern
Lyrics by Clifford Grey and P. G. Wodehouse
Sally 1920

You Can't Make Love
Music by Lee Pockriss
Lyrics by Anne Croswell
Ernest in Love (OB) 1960

You Can't Miss It
Music by Albert Hague
Lyrics by Arnold B. Horwitt
Plain and Fancy 1955

You Can't Overdo a Good Thing
Music by Joseph Meyer
Lyrics by Floyd Huddleston
Shuffle Along of 1952

You Can't Play Every Instrument in the Band
Music by John Golden
Lyrics by Joseph Cawthorn
The Sunshine Girl 1913

You Can't Put Catsup on the Moon
Music by Sammy Fain
Lyrics by Irving Kahal
Boys and Girls Together 1940

You Can't Stop Me From Loving You
Music by Alberta Nichols
Lyrics by Mann Holiner
Rhapsody in Black 1931

You Can't Take It With You
Music and lyrics by Joan Edwards and Lyn Duddy
Tickets Please 1950

You Can't Unscramble Scrambled Eggs
Music by George Gershwin
Lyrics by Ira Gershwin
Girl Crazy 1930

Dropped from production

You Can't Walk Back From an Aeroplane
Music and lyrics by Irving Bibo
and William B. Friedlander
Footlights 1927

You Click With Me
Music by Bradford Greene
Lyrics by Marianne Brown Waters
Right This Way 1938

You Could Drive a Person Crazy
Music and lyrics by Stephen Sondheim
Company 1970

You Could Not Please Me More
Music by Richard Rodgers
Lyrics by Martin Charnin
I Remember Mama 1979

You Couldn't Be Cuter
Music by Jerome Kern
Lyrics by Dorothy Fields
The Joy of Living (1938) F

You Couldn't Blame Me for That
Music by Harry Ruby
Lyrics by Bert Kalmar
Top Speed 1929

You Cut Up the Clothes in the Closet of My Dreams
Music and lyrics by Melvin Van Peebles
Don't Play Us Cheap 1972

You Deserve Me
Music and lyrics by Jack Lawrence
and Stan Freeman
I Had a Ball 1964

You Did It
Music by Frederick Loewe
Lyrics by Alan Jay Lerner
My Fair Lady 1956

You Do
Music by Mitch Leigh
Lyrics by N. Richard Nash
Saravá 1979

You Do Something to Me
Music and lyrics by Cole Porter
Fifty Million Frenchmen 1929

You Do This
Music and lyrics by Al Carmines
Wanted (OB) 1972

You Do-Do-Do It Good
Music by Bob Brush
Lyrics by Martin Charnin
The First 1981

You Done Right
Music by Judd Woldin
Lyrics by Robert Brittan
Raisin 1973

You Don't Dance
Music by Philip Charig
Lyrics by Dan Shapiro and Milton Pascal
Follow the Girls 1944

You Don't Have to Do It for Me
Music by Larry Grossman
Lyrics by Hal Hackady
Minnie's Boys 1970

You Don't Know
Music and lyrics by Meredith Willson
Here's Love 1963

You Don't Know Him
Music and lyrics by Jay Livingston and Ray Evans
Oh Captain! 1958

You Don't Know Paree
Music and lyrics by Cole Porter
Fifty Million Frenchmen 1929

You Don't Look for Love
Music by Eubie Blake
Lyrics by Noble Sissle
Shuffle Along of 1933

You Don't Remind Me
Music and lyrics by Cole Porter
Out of This World 1950

Dropped from production

You Don't Take a Sandwich to a Banquet
Music and lyrics by Worton David and J.P. Long
Nobody Home 1915

You Don't Tell Me
Music and lyrics by Richard Rodgers
No Strings 1962

The You-Don't-Want-to-Play-With-Me Blues
Music and lyrics by Sandy Wilson
The Boy Friend 1954

You Fell Out of the Sky
Music and lyrics by James MacDonald, David Vos and Robert Gerlach
Something's Afoot 1976

You Forgot Your Gloves
Music by Ned Lehak
Lyrics by Edward Eliscu
The Third Little Show 1931

You Found Me and I Found You
Music by Jerome Kern
Lyrics by P.G. Wodehouse
Oh, Lady! Lady!! 1918

You Gave Me Love
Music and lyrics by Elizabeth Swados
Lullabye and Goodnight 1982

You Got to Be Clever
Music and lyrics by James Rado
Rainbow (OB) 1972

You Gotta Be Holdin' Out Five Dollars on Me
Music and lyrics by Melvin Van Peebles
Ain't Supposed to Die a Natural Death 1971

You Gotta Have a Gimmick
Music by Jule Styne
Lyrics by Stephen Sondheim
Gypsy 1959

You Gotta Have Dancing
Music by Charles Strouse
Lyrics by Lee Adams
A Broadway Musical 1978

You Gotta Keep Saying "No"
Music by Harry Revel
Lyrics by Arnold B. Horwitt
Are You With It? 1945

You Have Cast Your Shadow on the Sea
Music by Richard Rodgers
Lyrics by Lorenz Hart
The Boys From Syracuse 1938

You Have Everything
Music by Arthur Schwartz
Lyrics by Howard Dietz
Between the Devil 1937

You Have Got to Have a Rudder on the Ark
Music by Richard Rodgers
Lyrics by Martin Charnin
Two by Two 1970

You Have Made Me Love
Music by Michael J. Lewis
Lyrics by Anthony Burgess
Cyrano 1973

You Have Me—I Have You
Music by Harold Levey
Lyrics by Owen Murphy
The Greenwich Village Follies (1925)

You Have My Heart
Music by Frank D'Armond
Lyrics by Will Morrissey
Saluta 1934

You Have to Do What You Do Do
Music by Kurt Weill
Lyrics by Ira Gershwin
The Firebrand of Florence 1945

You Have to Have a Part to Make a Hit
Music by Victor Herbert
Lyrics by Henry Blossom
The Only Girl 1914

You Haven't Changed at All
Music by Frederick Loewe
Lyrics by Alan Jay Lerner
The Day Before Spring 1945

You Haven't Got Time for Love
Music and lyrics by Kelly Hamilton
Trixie True Teen Detective (OB) 1980

You Haven't Lived Until You've Played the Palace
Music and lyrics by Charles Gaynor
Show Girl 1961

You Help Me
Music and lyrics by Ervin Drake
What Makes Sammy Run? 1964

You I Like
Music and lyrics by Jerry Herman
Madame Aphrodite (OB) 1961

Also in *The Grand Tour* (1979)

You in Your Room; I in Mine
Music by Winthrop Cortelyou
Lyrics by Derick Wulff
Kiss Me 1927

You Interest Me
Music by Larry Grossman
Lyrics by Betty Comden and Adolph Green
A Doll's Life 1982

You Irritate Me So
Music and lyrics by Cole Porter
Let's Face It! 1941

You Keep Coming Back Like a Song
Music and lyrics by Irving Berlin
Blue Skies (1946) F

You Kissed Me
Music by Morton Gould
Lyrics by Dorothy Fields
Arms and the Girl 1950

You Know and I Know
Music by Jerome Kern
Lyrics by Harry B. Smith
Nobody Home 1915

You Know How It Is
Music by George Gershwin
Lyrics by Ira Gershwin and P.G. Wodehouse
Rosalie 1928

Dropped from production

You Know, I Know
Music by Harry Archer
Lyrics by Harlan Thompson
Twinkle Twinkle 1926

You Know, Oh Lord
Music by Baldwin Bergersen
Lyrics by William Archibald
Carib Song 1945

You Like Monkey, You
Music and lyrics by Robert Dahdah
Curley McDimple (OB) 1967

You Live in Flowers
Music and lyrics by James Rado
Rainbow (OB) 1972

You Look Like Me
Music by Al Carmines
Lyrics by Rosalyn Drexler
Home Movies (OB) 1964

You Lost Your Opportunity
Music by Charles M. Schwab
Lyrics by Henry Myers
The Garrick Gaieties (3rd edition) 1930

You Love Me
Music and lyrics by Herman Hupfeld
Murder at the Vanities 1933

You Love Me
Music by Lee Pockriss
Lyrics by Anne Croswell
Tovarich 1963

You Made Me Love You
Music by James Monaco
Lyrics by Joseph McCarthy
Irene (1973 revival)

You Make Me Laugh
Music by Richard Rodgers
Lyrics by Lorenz Hart
Heads Up! 1929

Dropped from production

You Marry a Marionette
Music by Victor Herbert
Lyrics by Rida Johnson Young
Naughty Marietta 1910

You May Be the Someone
Music and lyrics by Norman Dean
Autumn's Here (OB) 1966

You May Have Planted Many a Lily
Music by Alma Sanders
Lyrics by Monte Carlo
Oh! Oh! Nurse 1925

You Might as Well Pretend
Music by Morgan Lewis
Lyrics by Edward Eliscu and Ted Fetter
The Third Little Show 1931

You Must Be Born With It
Music and lyrics by Irving Berlin
Face the Music 1932

You Must Come Over
Music by Jerome Kern
Lyrics by B.G. DeSylva
Ziegfeld Follies of 1921

You Must Come Over Blues
Music by Lewis E. Gensler
Lyrics by B.G. DeSylva and Ira Gershwin
Captain Jinks 1925

You Must Learn the Latest Dances
Music by Albert Von Tilzer
Lyrics by Neville Fleeson
The Gingham Girl 1922

You Must Meet My Wife
Music and lyrics by Stephen Sondheim
A Little Night Music 1973

You Mustn't Be Discouraged
Music by Jule Styne
Lyrics by Betty Comden and Adolph Green
Fade Out—Fade In 1964

You Mustn't Kick It Around
Music by Richard Rodgers
Lyrics by Lorenz Hart
Pal Joey 1940

You Need a Hobby
Music and lyrics by Irving Berlin
Mr. President 1962

You Need a Lift!
Music by Arthur Siegel
Lyrics by Mae Richard
Tallulah (OB) 1983

You Need a Song
Music and lyrics by Matt Dubey and Dean Fuller
Smith (OB) 1973

You Never Can Tell
Music by Jerome Kern
Lyrics by Harry B. Smith
The Girl From Utah 1914

You Never Can Tell
Music by Mary Rodgers
Lyrics by Steven Vinaver
The Mad Show (OB) 1966

You Never Can Tell About a Woman
Music by Victor Herbert
Lyrics by Henry Blossom
The Red Mill 1906

You Never Knew About Me
Music by Jerome Kern
Lyrics by P.G. Wodehouse
Oh, Boy! 1917

You Never Know
Music by Louis A. Hirsch
Lyrics by P.G. Wodehouse
Oh, My Dear! 1918

You Never Know
Music and lyrics by Cole Porter
You Never Know 1938

You Never Know What Comes Next
Music by Robert Stolz
Lyrics by Robert Sour
Mr. Strauss Goes to Boston 1945

You Never Know What Hit You
Music and lyrics by Harold Rome
Bless You All 1950

You Never Met a Feller Like Me
Music by Cyril Ornadel
Lyrics by Leslie Bricusse
Pickwick 1965

You Never Miss the Water
Music and lyrics by Norman Dean
Autumn's Here (OB) 1966

You Never Really Know
Music and lyrics by Voices, Inc.
The Believers (OB) 1968

You Never Saw That Before
Music by Jimmy Van Heusen
Lyrics by Johnny Burke
Nellie Bly 1946

You Never Say Yes
Music by Richard Rodgers
Lyrics by Lorenz Hart
Spring Is Here 1929

You Never Take Me Anywhere
Music and lyrics by Bob Ost
Everybody's Gettin' Into the Act (OB) 1981

You-oo Just You
Music by George Gershwin
Lyrics by Irving Caesar
Hitchy-koo 1918

You or No One
Music by Harold Arlen
Lyrics by Johnny Mercer
Saratoga 1959

You, or Nobody!
Music and lyrics by Irving Caesar
Yes, Yes, Yvette 1927

You Ought to Know
Music and lyrics by Noble Sissle and Eubie Blake
The Chocolate Dandies 1924

You Ought to See Sweet Marguerite
Music by Jerome Kern
Lyrics by Otto Harbach
Men of the Sky (1931) F

You Poor Thing
Music and lyrics by Marc Blitzstein
Juno 1959

You Remind Me of My Mother
Music and lyrics by George M. Cohan
Little Nellie Kelly 1922

You Remind Me of You
Music by Larry Grossman
Lyrics by Hal Hackady
Minnie's Boys 1970

You Said It
Music by Harold Arlen
Lyrics by Jack Yellen
You Said It 1931

You Said It
Music and lyrics by Cole Porter
Panama Hattie 1940

You Said Something
Music by Jerome Kern
Lyrics by P.G. Wodehouse
Have a Heart 1917

You Say the Nicest Things, Baby
Music by Jimmy McHugh
Lyrics by Harold Adamson
As the Girls Go 1948

You Say—They Say
Music and lyrics by Stan Freeman
and Franklin Underwood
Lovely Ladies, Kind Gentlemen 1970

You Say You Care
Music by Jule Styne
Lyrics by Leo Robin
Gentlemen Prefer Blondes 1949

You See Before You What Fashion Can Do
Music by Don Pippin
Lyrics by Steve Brown
Fashion (OB) 1974

You See in Me
Music by John Philip Sousa
Lyrics by Tom Frost and John Philip Sousa
El Capitan 1896

You See in Me a Bobby
Music by Gerald Jay Markoe
Lyrics by Michael Colby
Charlotte Sweet (OB) 1982

You Set My Heart to Music
Music and lyrics by Eaton Magoon, Jr.
13 Daughters 1961

You Should Be Set to Music
Music and lyrics by Irvin Graham
Crazy With the Heat 1941

You Should Know
Music and lyrics by J.C. Johnson
Change Your Luck 1930

You Should See Yourself
Music by Cy Coleman
Lyrics by Dorothy Fields
Sweet Charity 1966

You Show Me Yours
Music and lyrics by Ronnie Britton
Greenwich Village Follies (OB) 1976

You Smiled at Me
Music by Harry Ruby
Lyrics by Bert Kalmar
The Ramblers 1926

You Started It
Music by George Gershwin
Lyrics by Ira Gershwin
Delicious (1931) F

Dropped from film

You Started Something
Music by Vincent Youmans
Lyrics by Arthur Francis
Two Little Girls in Blue 1921

Same music as "Waiting for You" in *No, No, Nanette* (1925)

You Still Have a Long Way to Go
Music by Larry Grossman
Lyrics by Hal Hackady
Goodtime Charley 1975

You Still Love Me
Music by C.C. Courtney
Lyrics by C.C. and Ragan Courtney
Earl of Ruston 1971

You Talk Just Like My Maw
Music by Georges Bizet
Lyrics by Oscar Hammerstein II
Carmen Jones 1943

You Think I Got Rhythm?
Music and lyrics by Micki Grant
Don't Bother Me, I Can't Cope (OB) 1972

You Told Me That You Loved Me, But You Never Told Me Why
Music and lyrics by Gene Lockhart
Bunk of 1926

You Too Can Be a Puppet
Music by Sammy Fain
Lyrics by E.Y. Harburg
Flahooley 1951

You Took Advantage of Me
Music by Richard Rodgers
Lyrics by Lorenz Hart
Present Arms 1928

Sung by Busby Berkeley, who was also the choreographer of the show.

You Took Me by Surprise
Music by Vernon Duke
Lyrics by John Latouche
The Lady Comes Across 1942

You Took Possession of Me
Music by Gerald Marks
Lyrics by Sam Lerner
Hold It! 1948

You Touched Her
Music and lyrics by Stan Daniels
So Long, 174th Street 1976

You Treacherous Men
Music by Jerry Bock
Lyrics by Sheldon Harnick
Man in the Moon 1963

You Turn Me On
Music by Robert Kole
Lyrics by Sandi Merle
I Take These Women (OB) 1982

You Wait and Wait and Wait
Music by Sigmund Romberg
Lyrics by Oscar Hammerstein II
May Wine 1935

You Walked Out
Music by David Baker
Lyrics by David Craig
Copper and Brass 1957

You Want to Mourn
Music by Earl Robinson
Lyrics by Waldo Salt
Sandhog (OB) 1954

You Wanted Me, I Wanted You
Music by Harold Arlen
Lyrics by Ted Koehler
Nine-Fifteen Revue 1930

You Wash and I'll Dry
Music by Frederick Loewe
Lyrics by Alan Jay Lerner
What's Up? 1943

You Were Dead, You Know
Music by Leonard Bernstein
Lyrics by John Latouche and Richard Wilbur
Candide 1956

You Were Meant For Me
Music and lyrics by Noble Sissle and Eubie Blake
Charlot's Revue 1924

You Were Never Lovelier
Music by Jerome Kern
Lyrics by Johnny Mercer
You Were Never Lovelier (1942) F

You Were There
Music and lyrics by Noël Coward
Tonight at 8:30 ("Shadow Play") 1936

You Will Know When the Time Has Arrived
Music and lyrics by Clark Gesner
The Utter Glory of Morrissey Hall 1979

You Will Never Be Lonely
Music by Arthur Schwartz
Lyrics by Howard Dietz
The Gay Life 1961

You Will Never Know
Music by Vincent Youmans
Lyrics by Paul James
Nine-Fifteen Revue 1930

You Will Remember Vienna
Music by Sigmund Romberg
Lyrics by Oscar Hammerstein II
Viennese Nights (1930) F

You Will, Won't You?
Music by Jerome Kern
Lyrics by Anne Caldwell and Otto Harbach
Criss-Cross 1926

You Wonder How These Things Begin
Music by Harvey Schmidt
Lyrics by Tom Jones
The Fantasticks (OB) 1960

You Won't Be an Orphan for Long
Music by Charles Strouse
Lyrics by Martin Charnin
Annie 1977

You Won't Be Happy
Music by Bill Weeden
Lyrics by David Finkle
Hurry, Harry 1972

You Won't Say No
Music and lyrics by Tom Sankey
The Golden Screw (OB) 1967

You Would Say
Music and lyrics by Clark Gesner
The Utter Glory of Morrissey Hall 1979

You Wouldn't Fool Me, Would You?
Music by Ray Henderson
Lyrics by B.G. DeSylva and Lew Brown
Follow Thru 1929

You'd Be Amazed
Music by John Clifton
Lyrics by John Clifton and Ben Tarver
Man With a Load of Mischief (OB) 1966

You'd Be Hard to Replace
Music by Harry Warren
Lyrics by Ira Gershwin
The Barkleys of Broadway (1949) F

You'd Be So Nice to Come Home To
Music and lyrics by Cole Porter
Something to Shout About (1943) F

You'd Be Surprised
Music and lyrics by Irving Berlin
Ziegfeld Follies (1919)

You'd Better Dance
Music by Jerry Livingston
Lyrics by Mack David
Bright Lights of 1944

You'd Better Go Now
Music by Irvin Graham
Lyrics by Bickley Reichner
New Faces of 1936

You'd Better Love Me
Music and lyrics by Hugh Martin and Timothy Gray
High Spirits 1964

You'd Better Tell Her
Music and lyrics by Ronnie Britton
Gift of the Magi (OB) 1975

You'd Like Nebraska
Music by Mary Rodgers
Lyrics by Martin Charnin
Hot Spot 1963

You'd Think You Were in Paris
Music and lyrics by George M. Cohan
The Man Who Owns Broadway 1909

You'll Call the Next Love the First
Music by Jean Schwartz
Lyrics by Joseph W. Herbert and Harold Atteridge
The Honeymoon Express 1913

You'll Do
Music by Harold Arlen
Lyrics by Jack Yellen
You Said It 1931

You'll Feel Better Then
Music by Victor Herbert
Lyrics by Glen MacDonough
Algeria 1908

You'll Find Mice
Music by Helen Miller
Lyrics by Eve Merriam
Inner City 1971

You'll Have to Guess
Music by Karl Hajos (based on Tchaikovsky)
Lyrics by Harry B. Smith
Natja 1925

You'll Kill 'Em
Music by Harry Archer
Lyrics by Walter O'Keefe
Just a Minute 1928

You'll Know That It's Me
Music by Philip Charig
Lyrics by Dan Shapiro and Milton Pascal
Artists and Models (1943)

You'll Make an Elegant Butler
Music and lyrics by Joan Javits and Philip Springer
Tovarich 1963

You'll Never Get Away From Me
Music by Jule Styne
Lyrics by Stephen Sondheim
Gypsy 1959

Jule Styne's melody had two other titles and sets of words before ending up in *Gypsy*. Sammy Cahn wrote a lyric called "Why Did I Have to Wait So Long?" for a film that was never produced; later, with Leo Robin's words, it became "I'm in Pursuit of Happiness" for a 1957 television musical *Ruggles of Red Gap*.

You'll Never Know
Music by Lewis E. Gensler
Lyrics by B. G. DeSylva
Queen High 1926

You'll Never Walk Alone
Music by Richard Rodgers
Lyrics by Oscar Hammerstein II
Carousel 1945

You'll Think of Someone
Music by Burt Bacharach
Lyrics by Hal David
Promises, Promises 1968

Young
Music by Charles Strouse
Lyrics by Lee Adams
Bring Back Birdie 1981

Young and Foolish
Music by Albert Hague
Lyrics by Arnold B. Horwitt
Plain and Fancy 1955

Young and Healthy
Music by Harry Warren
Lyrics by Al Dubin
Forty-Second Street (1933) F

Young Black Joe
Music by Roger Wolfe Kahn
Lyrics by Irving Caesar
Americana (1928)

Young Days
Music and lyrics by Ron Eliran
Don't Step on My Olive Branch (OB) 1976

Young Enough to Dream
Music by Ron Steward and Neal Tate
Lyrics by Ron Steward
Sambo (OB) 1969

Young Ideas
Music and lyrics by Charles Tobias, Charles
Newman and Murray Mencher
Earl Carroll's Sketch Book (1935)

Young Man in Love
Music by Sigmund Romberg
Lyrics by Oscar Hammerstein II
East Wind 1931

Dropped from production

A Young Man's Fancy
Music by Milton Ager
Lyrics by John Murray Anderson and Jack Yellen

What's in a Name? 1956

Young People
Music and lyrics by Frank Loesser
The Most Happy Fella 1956

Young People Think About Love
Music by Kurt Weill
Lyrics by Maxwell Anderson
Knickerbocker Holiday 1938

A Young Pretty Girl Like You
Music by Burt Bacharach
Lyrics by Hal David
Promises, Promises 1968

Young With Him
Music by Don Gohman
Lyrics by Hal Hackady
Ambassador 1972

Younger Generation
Music by Aaron Copland
Lyrics by Ira Gershwin
The North Star (1943) F

The Younger Set
Music by James F. Hanley
Lyrics by Eddie Dowling
Sidewalks of New York 1927

The Younger Set
Music by J. Fred Coots
Lyrics by Arthur Swanstrom and Benny Davis
Sons o' Guns 1929

Younger Than Springtime
Music by Richard Rodgers
Lyrics by Oscar Hammerstein II
South Pacific 1949

The Youngest President
Music by Robert Kessler
Lyrics by Martin Charnin
Put It in Writing (OB) 1963

Your Broadway and Mine
Music by Maury Rubens
Lyrics by Moe Jaffe
Broadway Nights 1929

Your Country Needs You
Music by Edward Künneke
Lyrics by Harry B. Smith
The Love Song 1925

Your Daddy's Gone Away
Music and lyrics by Cliff Jones
Rockabye Hamlet 1976

Your Disposition Is Mine
Music by Jimmy McHugh
Lyrics by Dorothy Fields
Hello Daddy 1928

Your Dream (Is the Same as My Dream)
Music by Jerome Kern
Lyrics by Oscar Hammerstein II and Otto Harbach
One Night in the Tropics (1940) F

Your Eyes
Music by Rudolf Friml
Lyrics by P.G. Wodehouse and Clifford Grey
The Three Musketeers 1928

Your Eyes Are Blue
Music and lyrics by Stephen Sondheim
Marry Me a Little (OB) 1981

Dropped from *A Funny Thing Happened on the
Way to the Forum* (1962)

Your Face Is So Familiar
Music by Alex Fogarty
Lyrics by Edwin Gilbert
New Faces of 1936

Your Face Is Your Fortune
Music by Jerry Livingston
Lyrics by Mack David
Bright Lights of 1944

Your Fatal Fascination
Music by Jacques Belasco
Lyrics by Kay Twomey
The Girl From Nantucket 1945

Your Good Morning
Music and lyrics by Jerry Herman
Parade (OB) 1960

Your Hand in Mine
Music and lyrics by Jerry Herman
Parade (OB) 1960

Your Hat and My Hat
Music and lyrics by Irving Berlin
Music Box Revue (3rd edition) 1923

Your High Note!
Music by Gerald Jay Markoe
Lyrics by Michael Colby
Charlotte Sweet (OB) 1982

Your Home Away From Home
Music and lyrics by Frederick Silver
Gay Company (OB) 1974

Your Land and My Land
Music by Sigmund Romberg
Lyrics by Dorothy Donnelly
My Maryland 1927

Your Life, My Little Girl
Music by Gustave Kerker
Lyrics by Hugh Morton
The Belle of New York 1897

Your Love I Crave
Music by Jimmy Johnson
Lyrics by Perry Bradford
Messin' Around 1929

Your Loving Eyes
Music and lyrics by Jonathan Hogan
Fifth of July 1980

Your Majesties
Music by Richard Rodgers
Lyrics by Oscar Hammerstein II
Cinderella (1957) TV

Your Mother's Son-in-Law
Music by Albert Nichols
Lyrics by Mann Holiner
Blackbirds of 1934

Your Name May Be Paris
Music by Joseph Raposo
Lyrics by Erich Segal
Sing Muse! (OB) 1961

Your Photo
Music by Rudolf Friml
Lyrics by Otto Harbach
Katinka 1915

Your Prince Was Not So Charming
Music by Harden Church
Lyrics by Edward Heyman
Caviar 1934

Your Smiles, Your Tears
Music by Sigmund Romberg
Lyrics by Irving Caesar
Nina Rosa 1930

Your Time Is Different to Mine
Music by Monty Norman
Lyrics by Julian More
The Moony Shapiro Songbook 1981

Your Type Is Coming Back
Music by Sam H. Stept
Lyrics by Bud Green
Shady Lady 1933

Your Way of Loving
Music and lyrics by Al Carmines
The Faggot (OB) 1973

Your Wonderful U.S.A.
Music by Paul Lannin
Lyrics by Arthur Francis
Two Little Girls in Blue 1921

You're a Bad Influence on Me
Music and lyrics by Cole Porter
Red, Hot and Blue! 1936

You're a Builder Upper
Music by Harold Arlen
Lyrics by Ira Gershwin and E.Y. Harburg
Life Begins at 8:40 1934

You're a Child
Music by Frederick Loewe
Lyrics by Alan Jay Lerner
The Little Prince (1975) F

You're a Good Man, Charlie Brown
Music and lyrics by Clark Gesner
You're a Good Man, Charlie Brown (OB) 1967

You're a Grand Old Flag
Music and lyrics by George M. Cohen
George Washington, Jr. 1906

You're a Liar
Music by Cy Coleman
Lyrics by Carolyn Leigh
Wildcat 1960

You're a Little Young for the Job
Music by Galt MacDermot
Lyrics by William Dumaresq
The Human Comedy 1983

You're a Long, Long Way From America
Music and lyrics by Noël Coward
Sail Away 1961

You're a Lovable Lunatic
Music by Cy Coleman
Lyrics by Dorothy Fields
Seesaw 1973

You're a Magician
Music by Gerald Dolin
Lyrics by Edward J. Lambert
Smile at Me 1935

You're a Man
Music and lyrics by Rick Besoyan
The Student Gypsy (OB) 1963

You're a Queer One, Julie Jordan
Music by Richard Rodgers
Lyrics by Oscar Hammerstein II
Carousel 1945

You're a Stranger in This Neighborhood
Music by Albert Hague
Lyrics by Marty Brill
Café Crown 1964

You're a Wonderful Girl
Music by Shep Camp
Lyrics by Frank DuPree and Harry B. Smith
Half a Widow 1927

You're All the World to Me
Music by Harold Levey
Lyrics by Owen Murphy
Rainbow Rose 1926

You're All the World to Me
Music and lyrics by Edward Pola and Eddie Brandt
Woof, Woof 1929

You're All the World to Me
Music by Burton Lane
Lyrics by Alan Jay Lerner
Royal Wedding (1951) F

You're Always in My Arms
Music by Harry Tierney
Lyrics by Joseph McCarthy
Rio Rita (film version, 1929)

You're an Old Smoothie
Music by Nacio Herb Brown and Richard Whiting
Lyrics by B.G. DeSylva
Take a Chance 1932

You're as English As
Music and lyrics by Richard Adler
Kwamina 1961

You're Asking Me
Music by Edward A. Horan
Lyrics by Frederick Herendeen
All the King's Horses 1934

You're Beautiful
Music and lyrics by Billy Solly
Boy Meets Boy (OB) 1975

You're Colossal
Music by James Mundy
Lyrics by John Latouche
The Vamp 1955

You're Dead!
Music by Jimmy Van Heusen
Lyrics by Johnny Burke
Carnival in Flanders 1953

You're Delicious
Music by Don Elliott
Lyrics by James Costigan
The Beast in Me 1963

You're Devastating
Music by Jerome Kern
Lyrics by Otto Harbach
Roberta 1933

The melody had been used by Kern for the song "Do I Do Wrong," with lyrics by Graham John, in his 1928 London musical *Blue Eyes*, sung by Evelyn Laye and Geoffrey Gwyther.

You're Divine
Music and lyrics by Jack Bussins
and Ellsworth Olin
Be Kind to People Week (OB) 1975

You're Dreaming
Music and lyrics by Robert Swerdlow
Love Me, Love My Children (OB) 1971

You're Easy to Dance With
Music and lyrics by Irving Berlin
Holiday Inn (1942) F

You're Everywhere
Music by Vincent Youmans
Lyrics by Edward Heyman
Through the Years 1932

You're False
Music by Giuseppe Verdi (adapted by Hans Spialek)
Lyrics by Charles Friedman
My Darlin' Aïda 1952

You're Far From Wonderful
Music by Vernon Duke
Lyrics by Ogden Nash
The Littlest Revue (OB) 1956

You're Far too Near Me
Music by Kurt Weill
Lyrics by Ira Gershwin
The Firebrand of Florence 1945

You're Getting to Be a Habit With Me
Music by Harry Warren
Lyrics by Al Dubin
Forty-Second Street (1933) F

You're Gonna Dance With Me, Willie
Music by Jule Styne
Lyrics by Bob Hilliard
Hazel Flagg 1953

You're Gonna Love Tomorrow
Music and lyrics by Stephen Sondheim
Follies 1971

You're Here and I'm Here
Music by Jerome Kern
Lyrics by Harry B. Smith
The Marriage Market 1914

You're in Love
Music by Franz Lehár
Lyrics by Adrian Ross
Gypsy Love 1911

You're in Love
Music by Rudolf Friml
Lyrics by Otto Harbach and Edward Clark
You're In Love 1917

You're in Love
Music and lyrics by Cole Porter
Gay Divorce 1932

You're in Love
Music by Joseph Raposo
Lyrics by Erich Segal
Sing Muse! (OB) 1961

You're in New York Now
Music and lyrics by Matt Dubey and Dean Fuller
Smith (OB) 1973

You're in Paris
Music by Mark Sandrich, Jr.
Lyrics by Sidney Michaels
Ben Franklin in Paris 1964

You're Just in Love
Music and lyrics by Irving Berlin
Call Me Madam 1950

You're Just Too, Too
Music and lyrics by Cole Porter
Les Girls (1957) F

You're Laughing At Me
Music and lyrics by Irving Berlin
On the Avenue (1937) F

You're Like
Music by Ray Haney
Lyrics by Alfred Aiken
We're Civilized? (OB) 1962

You're Lonely and I'm Lonely
Music and lyrics by Irving Berlin
Louisiana Purchase 1940

You're Loving Me
Music and lyrics by John Driver
Ride the Winds 1974

You're Lucky
Music and lyrics by Hugh Martin and Ralph Blane
Best Foot Forward (1963 OB revival)

You're Lucky to Me
Music by Eubie Blake
Lyrics by Andy Razaf
Blackbirds of 1930

You're Mine, All Mine
Music by Fred Stamer
Lyrics by Gen Genovese
Buttrio Square 1952

You're Momma's
Music by Robert Waldman
Lyrics by Alfred Uhry
Here's Where I Belong 1968

You're More than a Name and Address
Music by Fred Spielman and Arthur Gershwin
Lyrics by Stanley Adams
A Lady Says Yes 1945

You're Musical
Music and lyrics by Lionel Bart
La Strada 1969

You're My Everything
Music by Harry Warren
Lyrics by Mort Dixon and Joe Young
The Laugh Parade 1931

You're My Favorite Lullabye
Music and lyrics by Elizabeth Swados
Lullabye and Goodnight 1982

You're My Girl
Music by Jule Styne
Lyrics by Sammy Cahn
High Button Shoes 1947

You're My Happiness
Music by Kenneth Jacobson
Lyrics by Rhoda Roberts
Show Me Where the Good Times Are (OB) 1970

You're My Last Chance
Music by Diane Leslie
Lyrics by William Gleason
The Coolest Cat in Town (OB) 1978

You're My Man
Music by Robert Kessler
Lyrics by Martin Charnin
Fallout (OB) 1959

You're My Relaxation
Music by Charles Schwab
Lyrics by Robert Sour
New Faces of 1934

You're Nearer
Music by Richard Rodgers
Lyrics by Lorenz Hart
Too Many Girls (1940) F

Added to film version

You're Never Fully Dressed Without a Smile
Music by Charles Strouse
Lyrics by Martin Charnin
Annie 1977

You're No Good
Music and lyrics by Ervin Drake
What Makes Sammy Run? 1964

You're Not
Music by Leon Carr
Lyrics by Earl Shuman
The Secret Life of Walter Mitty (OB) 1964

You're Not Alone
Music by Jacques Brel
English lyrics by Eric Blau and Mort Shuman
Jacques Brel Is Alive and Well and Living in Paris (OB) 1968

You're Not Foolin' Me
Music by Harvey Schmidt
Lyrics by Tom Jones
110 in the Shade 1963

You're Not Pretty But You're Mine
Music by Burton Lane
Lyrics by E.Y. Harburg
Americana (1932)

You're Not the One
Music by Jesse Greer
Lyrics by Stanley Adams
Shady Lady 1933

You're Not the Type
Music by Arthur Schwartz
Lyrics by Howard Dietz
The Gay Life 1961

You're Nothing
Music by Buster Davis
Lyrics by Steven Vinaver
Diversions (OB) 1958

You're on My Mind
Music by Harry Ruby
Lyrics by Bert Kalmar
High Kickers 1941

You're Perf
Music by Philip Charig
Lyrics by Dan Shapiro and Milton Pascal
Follow the Girls 1944

You're Perfect
Music by Joseph Meyer
Lyrics by Edward Eliscu
Lady Fingers 1929

You're Perfect
Music and lyrics by Michael Brown
Different Times 1972

You're Right, You're Right
Music by Jimmy Van Heusen
Lyrics by Sammy Cahn
Walking Happy 1966

You're Sensational
Music and lyrics by Cole Porter
High Society (1956) F

You're So Beautiful That—
Music and lyrics by Johnny Mercer
Top Banana 1951

You're So Much a Part of Me
Music and lyrics by Richard Adler and Jerry Ross
John Murray Anderson's Almanac (1953)

You're So Near (So Near and Yet So Far)
Music by Jay Gorney
Lyrics by Barry Trivers
Heaven on Earth 1948

You're So Nice to Remember
Music and lyrics by David Rose
Winged Victory 1943

Dropped from production

You're So Right for Me
Music and lyrics by Jay Livingston and Ray Evans
Oh Captain! 1958

You're the Better Half of Me
Music by Jimmy McHugh
Lyrics by Dorothy Fields
The Vanderbilt Revue 1930

You're the Cats
Music by Richard Rodgers
Lyrics by Lorenz Hart
The Hot Heiress (1931) F

You're the Cream in My Coffee
Music by Ray Henderson
Lyrics by B.G. DeSylva and Lew Brown
Hold Everything! 1928

You're the Cure for What Ails Me
Music by Harold Arlen
Lyrics by E.Y. Harburg
The Singing Kid (1935) F

You're the Fairest Flower
Music and lyrics by Rick Besoyan
Little Mary Sunshine (OB) 1959

**You're the Fellow the Fortune Teller
Told Me All About**
Music by Lucien Denni
Lyrics by Helena Evans
Happy Go Lucky 1926

You're the First Cup of Coffee
Music by Jay Gorney
Lyrics by Barry Trivers
Heaven on Earth 1948

You're the Lord of Any Manor
Music by Fred Spielman and Arthur Gershwin
Lyrics by Stanley Adams
A Lady Says Yes 1945

You're the Most Impossible Person
Music and lyrics by Deed Meyer
'Toinette (OB) 1961

You're the Mother Type
Music by Richard Rodgers
Lyrics by Lorenz Hart
Betsy 1926

Dropped from production

You're the One
Music by Harry Archer
Lyrics by Harlan Thompson
Merry-Merry 1925

You're the One I'm For
Music and lyrics by Clark Gesner
New Faces of 1968

You're the Only One
Music by Clarence Williams
Lyrics by Len Gray
Bottomland 1927

You're the Only One
Music by Don McAfee
Lyrics by Nancy Leeds
Great Scot! (OB) 1965

You're the Only One for Me
Music by Victor Herbert
Lyrics by Henry Blossom
The Only Girl 1914

You're the Prize Guy of Guys
Music and lyrics by Cole Porter
Les Girls (1957) F

Dropped from film

You're the Reason
Music and lyrics by Harold Orlob
Hairpin Harmony 1943

You're the Sunrise
Music by Arthur Schwartz
Lyrics by Howard Dietz
The Second Little Show 1930

You're the Top
Music and lyrics by Cole Porter
Anything Goes 1934

In spite of the complexity of the song's rhyme scheme, Porter wrote seven choruses of lyric. There is also, and perhaps inevitably, a salacious parody not written by Porter. Though witty and well-known, its authorship is unclaimed.

You're Too Smart
Music and lyrics by Walter Cool
Mackey of Appalachia (OB) 1965

You're What I Need
Music by Richard Rodgers
Lyrics by Lorenz Hart
She's My Baby 1928

Written for *A Connecticut Yankee* (1927) but dropped from production

You're Wonderful
Music by Frederick Loewe
Lyrics by Alan Jay Lerner
The Day Before Spring 1945

You're Wonderful
Music by Buster Davis
Lyrics by Steven Vinaver
Diversions (OB) 1958

You're You
Music by Arthur Siegel
Lyrics by Mae Richard
Tallulah (OB) 1983

Yours
Music and lyrics by Cole Porter
Jubilee 1935

Dropped from production

Yours, All Yours
Music by Moose Charlap
Lyrics by Norman Gimbel
The Conquering Hero 1961

Yours Is My Heart Alone
Music by Franz Lehár
Lyrics by Harry B. Smith
Yours Is My Heart 1946

Yours Sincerely
Music by Richard Rodgers
Lyrics by Lorenz Hart
Spring Is Here 1929

Yours, Yours, Yours
Music and lyrics by Sherman Edwards
1776 1969

The Youth of the Heart
Music by Donald Swann
Lyrics by Sydney Carter
At the Drop of a Hat 1959

You've Broken a Fine Woman's Heart
Music and lyrics by Stan Freeman
and Franklin Underwood
Lovely Ladies, Kind Gentlemen 1970

You've Built a Fire Down in My Heart
Music and lyrics by Irving Berlin
Ziegfeld Follies of 1911

You've Come Home
Music by Cy Coleman
Lyrics by Carolyn Leigh
Wildcat 1960

You've Got a Hold on Me
Music by Frederick Loewe
Lyrics by Alan Jay Lerner
What's Up? 1943

You've Got a Lease on My Heart
Music by Sammy Fain
Lyrics by Irving Kahal
Everybody's Welcome 1931

You've Got a Way With You
Music by Richard Myers
Lyrics by Leo Robin
Hello, Yourself! 1928

You've Got It All
Music and lyrics by Ann Ronell
Count Me In 1942

You've Got Me Up a Tree
Music by Alberta Nichols
Lyrics by Mann Holiner
Angela 1928

You've Got Possibilities
Music by Charles Strouse
Lyrics by Lee Adams
It's a Bird, It's a Plane, It's Superman 1966

You've Got Something
Music and lyrics by Cole Porter
Red, Hot and Blue! 1936

You've Got Something to Say
Music by Leon Pober
Lyrics by Bud Freeman
Beg, Borrow or Steal 1960

You've Got Something to Sing About
Music by Al Moss
Lyrics by Alfred Hayes
Tis of Thee 1940

You've Got That
Music by Richard Rodgers
Lyrics by Lorenz Hart
Hollywood Party (1934) F

Dropped from film

You've Got That Kind of a Face
Music by George Lessner
Lyrics by Miriam Battista and Russell Maloney
Sleepy Hollow 1948

You've Got That Thing
Music and lyrics by Cole Porter
Fifty Million Frenchmen 1929

You've Got to Appease With a Strip Tease
Music by Toby Sacher
Lyrics by Lewis Allen
Of V We Sing 1942

You've Got to Be a Lady
Music and lyrics by Steve Allen
Sophie 1963

You've Got to Be a Little Crazy
Music by Sigmund Romberg (developed by Don Walker)
Lyrics by Leo Robin
The Girl in Pink Tights 1954

You've Got to Dance
Music and lyrics by Elsie Janis
Puzzles of 1925

You've Got to Have Heart
Music and lyrics by Richard Adler and Jerry Ross
Damn Yankees 1955

You've Got to Have Koo Wah
Music by Eubie Blake
Lyrics by Noble Sissle
Shuffle Along of 1933

You've Got to Keep Building
Music and lyrics by Mel Mandel and Norman Sachs
My Old Friends (OB) 1979

You've Got to Know Just How to Make Love
Music by Alma Sanders
Lyrics by Monte Carlo
The Houseboat on the Styx 1928

You've Got to Pick a Pocket or Two
Music and lyrics by Lionel Bart
Oliver! 1963

You've Got to Sell Yourself
Music by Henry Sullivan
Lyrics by Edward Eliscu
A Little Racketeer 1932

You've Got to Surrender
Music by Richard Rodgers
Lyrics by Lorenz Hart
Heads Up! 1929

You've Got What Gets Me
Music by George Gershwin
Lyrics by Ira Gershwin
Girl Crazy (film version, 1932)

You've Got What I Need
Music by Charles Strouse
Lyrics by Lee Adams
It's a Bird, It's a Plane, It's Superman 1966

You've Made Me Happy Today!
Music by Niclas Kempner
Lyrics by Graham John
The Street Singer 1929

You've Never Been Loved
Music by Sammy Stept
Lyrics by Dan Shapiro
Michael Todd's Peep Show 1950

You've Stolen My Heart
Music by John Mundy
Lyrics by Edward Eager
The Liar 1950

Yucatana
Music by Maria Grever
Lyrics by Raymond Leveen
Viva O'Brien 1941

Yuletide, Park Avenue
Music and lyrics by Harold Rome
Call Me Mister 1946

Yum Ticky-Ticky
Music and lyrics by Bob Merrill
Carnival 1961

Yvonne
Music and lyrics by Clarence Gaskill
Earl Carroll's Vanities (1925)

Z

Ze English Language
Music by Victor Herbert
Lyrics by Henry Blossom
Mlle. Modiste 1905

Zebekiko
Music by Manos Hadjidakis
Lyrics by Joe Darion
Illya Darling 1967

Zen Is When
Music by Leon Pober
Lyrics by Bud Freeman
Beg, Borrow or Steal 1960

Zigeuner
Music and lyrics by Noël Coward
Bitter Sweet 1929

Zim Zam Zee
Music by Richard Lewine
Lyrics by Ted Fetter
Naughty-Naught (OB) 1937

Zing, Went the Strings of My Heart
Music and Lyrics by James F. Hanley
Thumbs Up! 1934

Zip
Music by Lucien Denni
Lyrics by Helena Evans
Happy Go Lucky 1926

Zip
Music by Richard Rodgers
Lyrics by Lorenz Hart
Pal Joey 1940

Zita
Music and lyrics by Ben Schwartz
Tales of Rigo 1927

Zulu Love Song
Music and lyrics by Harold Rome
The Zulu and the Zayda 1965

Shows

A LA CARTE
August 17, 1927 (46)
Music and lyrics by Herman Hupfeld

Hors d'Oeuvres • Give Trouble the Air (Music by
Louis Alter; lyrics by Leo Robin) • Palm Beach Baby
• Baby's Blue • Never Again (Music and lyrics by
Norman Gregg) • Kangaroo (Music by James P.
Johnson; lyrics by Henry Creamer) • Sort o'
Lonesome • The Calinda

THE ACT
October 29, 1977 (233)
Music by John Kander
Lyrics by Fred Ebb

Shine It On • It's the Strangest Thing • Bobo's •
Turn It On • Little Do They Know • Arthur in the
Afternoon • Hollywood, California • The Money Tree
• City Lights • There When I Need Him • Hot
Enough for You? • My Own Space

RA

AFRICANA
July 11, 1927 (72)
Music and lyrics by Donald Heywood

Weary Feet • The Old-Fashioned Cakewalk • Time
Ain't Very Long • Smile • Clorinda • The Africana
Stomp • I'm Comin', Virginia (Lyrics by Will Marion
Cook and Heywood)

AH, MEN (OB)
May 11, 1981 (28)
Music and lyrics by Paul Shyre

Ah, Men • Man Is for the Woman Made • When
After You Pass My Door • My First • The Last
Minute Waltz • Truck Stop • Illusions • Daddy Blues

AIN'T SUPPOSED TO DIE A NATURAL DEATH
October 20, 1971 (325)
Music and lyrics by Melvin Van Peebles

Just Don't Make No Sense • Coolest Place in Town

• You Can't Get Up Before Noon Without Being a
Square • Mirror, Mirror on the Wall • Come Raising
Your Leg on Me • You Gotta Be Holdin' Out Five
Dollars on Me • Sera Sera Jim • Catch That on the
Corner • The Dozens • Funky Girl on Motherless
Broadway • Tenth and Greenwich • Heh Heh Good
Mornin' Sunshine • You Ain't No Astronaut • Three
Boxes of Longs, Please • Lily Has Done the
Zampoughi Every Time I Pulled Her Coattail • I Got
the Blood • Salamaggis Birthday • Come On Feet,
Do Your Thing • Put a Curse on You

RA

ALGERIA[1]
August 31, 1908 (48)
Music by Victor Herbert
Lyrics by Glen MacDonough

The Same Old Two • The Boule' Miche' • I've Been
Decorated • You'll Feel Better Then • The Great
White Easiest Way • Rose of the World • Love Is
Like a Cigarette • Ask Her While the Band Is
Playing • Only One of Anything • Twilight in
Barakeesh • The Foolish Gardener • Little Bird of
Paradise • Goodbye, Bohemia

VS

[1] With a revised book and a new cast, Algeria
re-opened on September 20, 1909 as The Rose
of Algeria, by which title it is now generally
known. In spite of these revisions, the second
production ran for only 40 additional
performances.

ALICE IN CONCERT (OB)
December 9, 1980 (32)
Music and lyrics by Elizabeth Swados

Based on Lewis Carroll's Alice in Wonderland and
Through the Looking Glass

What There Is • Rabbit's Excuse • Down Down
Down • Drink Me • Goodbye Feet • The Rabbit's
House • Bill's Lament • Caterpillar's Advice •
Beautiful Soup • Wow Wow Wow • Pretty Piggy •

Cheshire Puss • If You Knew Time • No Room No Room • Starting Out Again • White Roses, Red • Alphabet • Red Queen • Never Play Croquet • Mock Turtle Lament • Lobster Quadrille • Eating Mushrooms • Child of Pure Unclouded Brow • Jabberwocky • Bird Song • Humpty Dumpty • Tweedledum and Tweedledee • The Walrus and the Carpenter • White Queen • White Knight • An Aged Aged Man • The Examination • The Lion and the Unicorn • Queen Alice • What Is a Letter?

ALIVE AND KICKING
January 17, 1950 (46)

Alive and Kicking (Music by Hal Borne; lyrics by Ray Golden and Sid Kuller) • Pals of the Pentagon (Music and lyrics by Harold Rome) • What a Delightful (Music by Sammy Fain; lyrics by Paul Francis Webster and Ray Golden) • Abou Ben Adhem (Music and lyrics by Ray Golden) • Cry, Baby, Cry (Music and lyrics by Harold Rome) • One Word Led to Another (Music by Hal Borne; lyrics by Ray Golden) • Love, It Hurts So Good (Music and lyrics by Harold Rome) • There's a Building Going Up (Music by Sammy Fain; lyrics by Paul Francis Webster and Ray Golden) • Propinquity (Music by Sonny Burke; lyrics by Paul Francis Webster and Ray Golden) • I'm All Yours (Music by Leo Schumer; lyrics by Mike Stuart) • One! Two! Three! (Music by Sonny Burke; lyrics by Paul Francis Webster and Ray Golden) • French With Tears (Music and lyrics by Harold Rome)

ALL AMERICAN
March 19, 1962 (80)
Music by Charles Strouse
Lyrics by Lee Adams

Melt Us! • What a Country! • Our Children • Animal Attraction • We Speak the Same Language • I Can Teach Them • It's Fun to Think • Once Upon a Time • Nightlife • I've Just Seen Her • Physical Fitness • The Fight Song • I Couldn't Have Done It Alone • If I Were You • Have a Dream • I'm Fascinating • The Real Me • Which Way? • It's Up to Me

RA, SEL

ALL FOR LOVE
January 22, 1949 (121)
Music by Allan Roberts
Lyrics by Lester Lee

All for Love • My Baby's Bored • The Big Four (Music and lyrics by Peter Howard Weiss) • Why Can't It Happen Again? (Music by Michel Emer; lyrics by Sammy Gallup) • My Heart's in the Middle of July • It's a Living • Run to Me, My Love • No Time for Nothin' but Love • Dreamer With a Penny • The Farrell Girl • Oh, How Unfortunate You Mortals Be

ALL IN FUN
December 27, 1940 (3)
Music by Baldwin Bergersen

It's All in Fun (Lyrics by S.K. Russel) • Where Can I Go From You? (Lyrics by Virginia Faulkner) • Love

and I (Lyrics by Irvin Graham and June Sillman) • April in Harrisburg (Lyrics by Virginia Faulkner) • That Man and Woman Thing (Lyrics by John Rox) • It's a Big, Wide, Wonderful World (Music and lyrics by John Rox) • How Did It Get So Late So Early? (Music by Will Irwin; lyrics by June Sillman) • Where's the Boy I Saved for a Rainy Day? (Lyrics by John Rox) • My Memories Started With You (Lyrics by June Sillman) • Macumba (Lyrics by June Sillman) • Quittin' Time (Music and lyrics by John Rox)

ALL IN LOVE (OB)
November 10, 1961 (141)
Music by Jacques Urbont
Lyrics by Bruce Geller

Based on the play The Rivals by Richard Brinsley Sheridan

To Bath Derry-O • Poor • What Can It Be? • Odds • I Love a Fool • A More Than Ordinary Glorious Vocabulary • Women Simple • The Lady Was Made to Be Loved • The Good Old Ways • Honour • I Found Him • Day Dreams • Don't Ask Me • Why Wives • Quickly • All in Love

RA

ALL KINDS OF GIANTS (OB)
December 18, 1961 (16)
Music by Sam Pottle
Lyrics by Tom Whedon

State of the Kingdom • My Prince • Paint Me a Rainbow • Logic! • If I Were Only Someone • To Be a King • Suddenly Stop and Think • My Star • All Kinds of Giants • Friends • Here We Are • Be Yourself

ALL THE KING'S HORSES
January 30, 1934 (120)
Music by Edward A. Horan
Lyrics by Frederick Herendeen

Fame Is a Phoney • Tamboree • The Hair of the Heir • You're Asking Me • Evening Star • I Found a Song • Langenstein in Spring • Charming • I've Gone Nuts Over You • Mamazelle Papazelle • Romance Is Calling

ALLAH BE PRAISED!
April 20, 1944 (20)
Music by Don Walker and Baldwin Bergersen
Lyrics by George Marion, Jr.

The Persian Way of Life (Music by Walker) • Allah Be Praised (Music by Walker) • What's New in New York (Music by Bergersen) • Leaf in the Wind (Music by Bergersen) • Katinka to Eva to Frances (Music by Walker) • Let's Go Too Far (Music by Walker) • Getting Oriental Over You (Music by Walker) • Secret Song (Music by Bergersen) • Sunrise on Sunset (Music by Bergersen)

ALLEGRO
October 10, 1947 (315)
Music by Richard Rodgers
Lyrics by Oscar Hammerstein II

Joseph Taylor, Jr. • I Know It Can Happen Again • One Foot, Other Foot • Poor Joe • A Fellow Needs a Girl • A Darn Nice Campus • Wildcats • So Far • You Are Never Away • What a Lovely Day for a Wedding • It May Be a Good Idea • To Have and to Hold • Wish Them Well • Money Isn't Ev'rything • Yatata, Yatata, Yatata • The Gentleman Is a Dope • Allegro • Come Home

RA,VS

ALLEZ-OOP
August 2, 1927 (120)
Music by Philip Charig and Richard Myers
Lyrics by Leo Robin

What Does It Mean? • Hoof, Hoof • Where Have You Been All My Life? • A Kiss With a Kick • Pull Yourself Together • Doin' the Gorilla • Star of Stars • Blow Hot and Heavy • In the Heart of Spain • What Did William Tell?

ALONG FIFTH AVENUE
January 13, 1949 (180)

Fifth Avenue (Music by Gordon Jenkins; lyrics by Tom Adair) • The Best Time of Day (Music by Gordon Jenkins; lyrics by Tom Adair) • If This Is Glamour! (Music by Richard Stutz; lyrics by Rick French) • Skyscraper Blues (Music by Gordon Jenkins; lyrics by Tom Adair) • I Love Love in New York (Music by Gordon Jenkins; lyrics by Tom Adair) • The Fugitive From Fifth Avenue (Music by Richard Stutz; lyrics by Nat Hiken) • Santo Dinero (Music by Richard Stutz; lyrics by Milton Pascal) • In the Lobby (Music by Gordon Jenkins; lyrics by Tom Adair) • Weep No More (Music by Gordon Jenkins; lyrics by Tom Adair) • Chant d'Amour (Music by Gordon Jenkins; lyrics by Nat Hiken) • Vacation in the Store (Music by Gordon Jenkins; lyrics by Tom Adair) • Call It Applefritters (Music by Richard Stutz; lyrics by Milton Pascal) • A Trip Doesn't Care at All (Music by Philip Kadison; lyrics by Thomas Howell)

AMBASSADOR
November 9, 1972 (9)
Music by Don Gohman
Lyrics by Hal Hackady

Based on the novel *The Ambassadors* by Henry James

Lilas • Lambert's Quandary • I Know the Man • The Right Time, the Right Place • She Passed My Way • Something More • Love Finds the Lonely • Kyrie Eleison • Surprise • Happy Man • What Happened to Paris? • Young With Him • Too Much to Forgive • Why Do Women Have to Call It Love? • Mama • That's What I Need • Maxixe-Habanera • Gossip • Not Tomorrow • All of My Life • Thank You, No

RA

AMEN CORNER
November 10, 1983 (28)

Music by Garry Sherman
Lyrics by Peter Udell

Based on the play by James Baldwin

Amen Corner • That Woman Can't Play No Piano • In the Real World • You Ain't Gonna Pick Up Where You Left Off • We Got a Good Thing Goin' • In His Own Good Time • Heat Sensation • Everytime We Call It Quits • Somewhere Close By • Leanin' on the Lord • I'm Already Gone • Rise Up and Stand Again

AMERICAN JUBILEE[1]
May 12, 1940
Music by Arthur Schwartz
Lyrics by Oscar Hammerstein II

Another New Day • We Like It Over Here • Jenny Lind • How Can I Ever Be Alone? • My Bicycle Girl • Tennessee Fish Fry • One in a Million

[1] Produced at the New York World's Fair (1940) where it was performed several times daily for the Fair's duration.

THE AMERICAN MAID
March 3, 1913 (16)
Music by John Philip Sousa
Lyrics by Leonard Liebling

This Is My Busy Day • Nevermore • Most Omniscient Maid • We Chant a Song of Labor • My Love Is a Blower • Cheer Up • The Dinner Pail • The Crystal Lute • The American Girl • From Maine to Oregon • I Can't Get 'Em Up • When You Change Your Name to Mine • Sweetheart

AMERICANA (1926)
July 26, 1926 (224)

American Revue Girls (Music by Con Conrad; lyrics by J.P. McEvoy) • Sunny Disposish (Music by Philip Charig; lyrics by Ira Gershwin) • Kosher Kleagle (Music by Philp Charig; lyrics by J.P. McEvoy) • That Lost Barbershop Chord (Music by George Gershwin; lyrics by Ira Gershwin) • Blowin' the Blues Away (Music by Philip Charig; lyrics by Ira Gershwin) • Dreaming (Music by Con Conrad and Henry Souvaine; lyrics by J.P. McEvoy) • Riverside Bus (Music by Con Conrad; lyrics by J.P. McEvoy) • Tabloid Papers (Music by Con Conrad; lyrics by J.P. McEvoy) • Why Do Ya Roll Those Eyes? (Music by Philip Charig; lyrics by Morrie Ryskind) • Swanee River Melody (Music by Charles Weinberg; lyrics by Al Wilson)

AMERICANA (1928)
October 30, 1928 (12)
Music by Roger Wolfe Kahn
Lyrics by Irving Caesar

Life as a Twosome* (Music by Joseph Meyer and Roger Wolfe Kahn) • Jazz City (Music by Henry Souvaine; lyrics by J.P. McEvoy) • The Ameri-can-can • No Place Like Home • Young Black Joe • Hot Pants

AMERICANA (1932)
October 5, 1932 (76)

Would'ja for a Big Red Apple (Music by Henry Souvaine; lyrics by Everett Miller and Johnny Mercer) • Whistling for a Kiss (Music by Richard Myers; lyrics by E.Y. Harburg and Johnny Mercer) • Satan's Li'l Lamb (Music by Harold Arlen; lyrics by E.Y. Harburg and Johnny Mercer) • You're Not Pretty but You're Mine (Music by Burton Lane; lyrics by E.Y. Harburg) • Brother, Can You Spare a Dime? (Music by Jay Gorney; lyrics by E.Y. Harburg) • Let Me Match My Private Life With Yours (Music by Vernon Duke; lyrics by E.Y. Harburg) • Five Minutes of Spring (Music by Jay Gorney; lyrics by E.Y. Harburg) • Get That Sun Into You (Music by Richard Myers; lyrics by E.Y. Harburg)

AMERICA'S SWEETHEART
February 10, 1931 (135)
Music by Richard Rodgers
Lyrics by Lorenz Hart

Mr. Dolan Is Passing Through • In Californ-i-a • My Sweet • I've Got Five Dollars • Sweet Geraldine • There's So Much More • We'll Be the Same • How About It? • Innocent Chorus Girls of Yesterday • A Lady Must Live • You Ain't Got No Savoir Faire • Two Unfortunate Orphans • I Want a Man • Tennessee Dan

Dropped from production
God Gave Me Eyes

THE AMOROUS FLEA (OB)
February 17, 1964 (93)
Music and lyrics by Bruce Montgomery

Based on the play *The School for Wives* by Molière

All About Me • Learning Love • There Goes a Mad Old Man • Dialogue on Dalliance • March of the Vigilant Vassals • Lessons on Life • Man Is a Man's Best Friend • The Other Side of the Wall • Closeness Begets Closeness • It's a Stretchy Day • When Time Takes Your Hand • The Amorous Flea

ANGEL
May 10, 1978 (5)
Music by Gary Geld
Lyrics by Peter Udell

Based on the play by Ketti Frings and the novel *Look Homeward, Angel* by Thomas Wolfe

Angel Theme • All the Comforts of Home • Like the Eagles Fly • Make a Little Sunshine • Fingers and Toes • Fatty • Astoria Gloria • Railbird • If I Ever Loved Him • A Dime Ain't Worth a Nickel • I Got a Dream to Sleep On • Drifting • I Can't Believe It's You • Feelin' Loved • Tomorrow I'm Gonna Be Old • How Do You Say Goodbye? • Gant's Waltz

RA,SEL

ANGEL IN THE WINGS
December 11, 1947 (308)
Music by Carl Sigman
Lyrics by Bob Hilliard

Long Green Blues • Holler Blue Murder • Breezy • Civilization • Tambourine • If It Were Easy to Do • Thousand Islands Song • The Big Brass Band From Brazil

ANGELA
December 3, 1928 (40)
Music by Alberta Nichols
Lyrics by Mann Holiner

The Weaker Sex • Love Is Like That • Don't Forget Your Etiquette • The Baron, the Duchess, and the Count • The Regal Romp • Tally-Ho • I Can't Believe It's True • Bundle of Love • Maybe So • You've Got Me Up a Tree • Bearing Silver Platters • Oui, Oui

ANIMAL CRACKERS
October 23, 1928 (191)
Music by Harry Ruby
Lyrics by Bert Kalmar

News • Hooray for Captain Spalding! • Who's Been Listening to My Heart? • The Long Island Low Down • Go Places and Do Things • Watching the Clouds Roll By • When Things Are Bright and Rosy • Cool Off • Musketeers

ANKLES AWEIGH
April 18, 1955 (176)
Music by Sammy Fain
Lyrics by Dan Shapiro

Italy • Old-Fashioned Mothers • Skip the Build-Up • Nothing at All • Walk Like a Sailor • Headin' for the Bottom • Nothing Can Replace a Man • Here's to Dear Old Us • His and Hers • La Fiesta • Ready Cash • Kiss Me and Kill Me With Love • Honeymoon • The Villain Always Gets It • The Code • Eleven o'Clock Song

RA

ANNE OF GREEN GABLES (OB)
December 21, 1971 (16)
Music by Norman Campbell
Lyrics by Donald Harron and Norman Campbell

Based on the novel by L.M. Montgomery

Great Workers for the Cause • Where Is Matthew Going? • Gee, I'm Glad I'm No One Else But Me • We Clearly Requested • The Facts • Where'd Marilla Come From? • Humble Pie • Oh, Mrs. Lynde • Avonlea, We Love Thee • Wondrin' • Did You Hear? • Ice Cream • The Picnic • Where Did the Summer Go To? • Kindred Spirits • Open the Window • The Words • I'll Show Him • General Store • Pageant Song • If It Hadn't Been for Me • Anne of Green Gables

RA

ANNIE[1]
April 21, 1977 (2377)
Music by Charles Strouse
Lyrics by Martin Charnin

Based on the comic strip *Little Orphan Annie* by Harold Gray

Maybe • It's the Hard-knock Life • Tomorrow • We'd Like to Thank You • Little Girls • I Think I'm Gonna Like It Here • N.Y.C. • Easy Street • You Won't Be an Orphan for Long • You're Never Fully Dressed Without a Smile • Something Was Missing • I Don't Need Anything but You • Annie • A New Deal for Christmas

RA,VS,SEL

[1] Tony Award for Best Musical and Best Score

ANNIE GET YOUR GUN[1]
May 16, 1946 (1147)
Music and lyrics by Irving Berlin

Buffalo Bill • I'm a Bad, Bad Man • Doin' What Comes Natur'lly • The Girl That I Marry • You Can't Get a Man With a Gun • There's No Business Like Show Business • They Say It's Wonderful • Moonshine Lullaby • I'll Share It All With You • My Defenses Are Down • I'm an Indian Too • I Got Lost in His Arms • Who Do You Love, I Hope • I Got the Sun in the Morning • Anything You Can Do

Dropped from production
Take It in Your Stride

Added to 1966 revival
An Old-Fashioned Wedding*

RA,VS,SEL

[1] The show was planned as a starring vehicle for Ethel Merman, and was to have music by Jerome Kern and lyrics by Dorothy Fields. Miss Fields, with her brother Herbert, would also write the book. Jerome Kern died on November 11, 1945, without having begun work on the project, and the producers, Rodgers and Hammerstein, persuaded Irving Berlin to write the score.

ANYA
November 29, 1965 (16)
Music and lyrics by Robert Wright and George Forrest (based on Rachmaninoff)

Based on the play *Anastasia* by Marcelle Maurette and Guy Bolton

Anya • A Song From Somewhere • Vodka, Vodka! • So Proud • Homeward • Snowflakes and Sweethearts • On That Day • Six Palaces • Hand in Hand • This Is My Kind of Love • That Prelude! • A Quiet Land • Here Tonight, Tomorrow Where? • Leben Sie Wohl • If This Is Goodbye • Little Hands • All Hail the Empress

RA

ANYONE CAN WHISTLE
April 4, 1964 (9)
Music and lyrics by Stephen Sondheim

I'm Like the Bluebird • Me and My Town • Miracle Song • Simple • A-1 March • Come Play Wiz Me • Anyone Can Whistle • A Parade in Town • Everybody Says Don't • I've Got You to Lean On • See What It Gets You • With So Little to Be Sure Of

Dropped from production
There Won't Be Trumpets •

• There's Always a Woman

RA,VS,SEL

ANYTHING GOES[1]
November 21, 1934 (420)
Music and lyrics by Cole Porter

I Get a Kick Out of You* • Bon Voyage • All Through the Night • There'll Always Be a Lady Fair • Where Are the Men? • You're the Top* • Anything Goes • Public Enemy Number One • Blow, Gabriel, Blow • Be Like the Bluebird • Buddy, Beware • The Gypsy in Me

Dropped from production
Waltz Down the Aisle

RA,VS,SEL

[1] The original story was described in a press release as a "humorous shipwreck" but the sinking of the S.S. *Morro Castle* as the show went into rehearsal dictated a complete change of plan. The original writers were no longer available and Howard Lindsay, who was to write the new book, suggested Russel Crouse as his collaborator. So began that very durable partnership, and the show, with Cole Porter's score, was one of the most successful of the 1930s.

APPLAUSE[1]
March 30, 1970 (896)
Music by Charles Strouse
Lyrics by Lee Adams

Based on the film *All About Eve* (1950) by Joseph Mankiewicz, which had been adapted from the short story "The Wisdom of Eve" by Mary Orr

Backstage Babble • Think How It's Gonna Be • But Alive • The Best Night of My Life • Who's That Girl? • Applause • Hurry Back • Fasten Your Seat Belts • Welcome to the Theater • Inner Thoughts • Good Friends • She's No Longer a Gypsy • One of a Kind • One Hallowe'en • Something Greater

RA,VS,SEL

[1] Tony Award for Best Musical

APPLE BLOSSOMS
October 7, 1919 (256)
Music by Fritz Kreisler and Victor Jacobi
Lyrics by William LeBaron

Brothers (Music by Jacobi) • Who Can Tell?* (Music by Kreisler) • Three Is a Bore (Music by Jacobi) • The Letter Song (Music by Kreisler) • On the Banks of the Bronx (Music by Jacobi) • I'll Be True to You (Music by Jacobi) • Nancy's Farewell (Music by Kreisler) • The Marriage Knot (Music by Kreisler) • When the Wedding Bells Are Ringing (Music by Jacobi) • Little Girls, Goodbye (Music by Jacobi) • You Are Free (Music by Jacobi) • The Widow (Music by Kreisler) • The Happy Wedding Day (Music by Jacobi) • Star of Love* (Music by Kreisler) • A Girl, a Man, a Night, a Dance* (Music by Kreisler) • I Am

in Love (Music by Kreisler) • The Second Violin[*]
(Music by Kreisler)

VS,SEL

THE APPLE TREE
October 18, 1966 (463)
Music by Jerry Bock
Lyrics by Sheldon Harnick

Part I—The Diary of Adam and Eve

Based on *The Diary of Adam and Eve* by Mark
Twain

Here in Eden • Feelings • Eve • Friends • The Apple
Tree (Forbidden Fruit) • Beautiful, Beautiful World •
It's a Fish • Go to Sleep Whatever You Are • What
Makes Me Love Him?

Part II—The Lady or the Tiger

Based on *The Lady or the Tiger* by Frank Stockton

I'll Tell You a Truth • Make Way • Forbidden Love (in
Gaul) • I've Got What You Want • Tiger, Tiger •
Which Door?

Part III—Passionella

Based on the play *Passionella* by Jules Feiffer

Oh, to Be a Movie Star • Gorgeous • (Who, Who,
Who, Who) Who Is She? • Wealth • You Are Not
Real • George L.

RA,VS,SEL

THE ARCADIANS
January 17, 1910 (136)
Music by Howard Talbot and Lionel Monckton
Lyrics by Arthur Wimperis

I Quite Forgot Arcadia (Music by Monckton) • The
Joy of Life (Music by Talbot) • Look, What Hovers
There (Music by Talbot) • The Pipes of Pan Are
Calling (Music by Monckton) • All a Lie! (Music by
Talbot) • Sweet Simplicitas (Music by Talbot) • Back
Your Fancy! (Music by Monckton) • The Girl With a
Brogue (Music by Monckton) • Shower Chorus
(Music by Talbot) • Arcady Is Ever Young (Music by
Monckton; lyrics by Monckton and Wimperis) •
Somewhere (Music by Monckton) • Charming
Weather (Music by Monckton) • I Like London
(Music by Talbot) • Half-Past Two (Music by Talbot;
lyrics by Percy Greenbank and Wimperis) • Cheer
for Simplicitas! (Music by Monckton) • All Down
Piccadilly (Music by Monckton; lyrics by Wimperis
and Monckton) • Truth Is So Beautiful (Music by
Monckton) • My Motter (Music by Talbot) • My Heart
Flies Homing (Music by Talbot) • Bring Me a Rose
(Music by Monckton; lyrics by Monckton and
Wimperis)

VS

ARE YOU WITH IT?
November 10, 1945 (264)
Music by Harry Revel
Lyrics by Arnold B. Horwitt

Five More Minutes in Bed • Nutmeg Insurance •
Slightly Perfect • When a Good Man Takes to Drink
• Poor Little Me • Are You With It? • This Is My
Beloved • Send Us Back to the Kitchen • Here I Go
Again • You Gotta Keep Saying "No" • Just Beyond
the Rainbow • In Our Cozy Little Cottage of
Tomorrow

ARI
January 15, 1971 (19)
Music by Walt Smith
Lyrics by Leon Uris

Based on the novel *Exodus* by Leon Uris

Children's Lament • Yerushaliam • The Saga of the
Haganah • Give Me One Good Reason • Dov's
Nightmare • Karen's Lullaby • Aphrodite • My Galilee
• The Lord Helps Those Who Help Themselves •
The Alphabet Song • My Brother's Keeper • The
Exodus • He'll Never Be Mine • One Flag • I See
What I Choose to See • Ari's Promise

ARMS AND THE GIRL
February 2, 1950 (134)
Music by Morton Gould
Lyrics by Dorothy Fields

Based on the play *The Pursuit of Happiness* by
Lawrence Langner and Armina Marshall

A Girl With a Flame • That's What I Told Him Last
Night • I Like It Here • That's My Fella • A Cow and
a Plough and a Frau • Nothin' for Nothin' • He Will
Tonight • Plantation in Philadelphia • You Kissed Me
• Don't Talk • I'll Never Learn • There Must Be
Somethin' Better than Love • She's Exciting • Mister
Washington! Uncle George

RA

AROUND THE WORLD
May 31, 1946 (74)
Music and lyrics by Cole Porter

Based on the novel *Around the World in Eighty
Days* by Jules Verne

Look What I Found • There He Goes, Mr. Phileas
Fogg • Meerahlah • Sea Chantey • Should I Tell You
I Love You? • Pipe Dreaming • If You Smile at Me •
Wherever They Fly the Flag of Old England • The
Marine's Hymn

RA

ARTISTS AND MODELS (1925)
June 24, 1925 (411)
Music by Alfred Goodman, Maury Rubens and J.
Fred Coots
Lyrics by Clifford Grey

The Maid of the Milky Way • Let Me Dance •
Cellini's Dream • Take a Little Baby Home With You
• Mothers of the World • Follow Your Star • The
Magic Garden of Love • The Rotisserie • The
Promenade Walk at the Beach • Oriental Memories •
Lucita • Flexatone

ARTISTS AND MODELS (1927)
November 15, 1927 (151)

Here Am I—Broken Hearted (Music by Ray Henderson; lyrics by B.G. DeSylva and Lew Brown) • Oh, Peggy (Music by Harry Akst; lyrics by Benny Davis) • The Only One for Me (Music by Harry Akst; lyrics by Benny Davis) • Is Everybody Happy Now? (Music by Maury Rubens; lyrics by Jack Osterman and Ted Lewis) • The Call of Broadway (Music by Maury Rubens; lyrics by Jack Osterman and Ted Lewis) • The Lobster Crawl (Music by Harry Akst; lyrics by Benny Davis) • There's Nothing New in Old New York (Music by Harry Akst; lyrics by Benny Davis) • Snap Out of It (Music by Harry Akst; lyrics by Benny Davis)

ARTISTS AND MODELS (1930)[1]
June 10, 1930 (55)

My Real Ideal (Music by Burton Lane; lyrics by Samuel Lerner) • Without a Shadow of a Doubt (Music and lyrics by Ord Hamilton) • Who Cares? (Music by Haydn Wood, Joseph Tunbridge, and Jack Waller; lyrics by Dion Titheradge) • Two Perfect Lovers (Music by Burton Lane; lyrics by Samuel Lerner)

[1] Pre-Broadway title: *Dear Love*

ARTISTS AND MODELS (1943)
November 5, 1942 (27)
Music by Philip Charig
Lyrics by Dan Shapiro and Milton Pascal

Way Up North in Dixie • Swing Low, Sweet Harriet • You'll Know That It's Me • How'ja Like to Take Me Home • My Heart Is on a Binge • You Are Romance • Blowing the Top

AS THE GIRLS GO
November 13, 1948 (420)
Music by Jimmy McHugh
Lyrics by Harold Adamson

As the Girls Go • Nobody's Heart but Mine • Brighten Up and Be a Little Sunbeam • Rock, Rock, Rock • It's More Fun Than a Picnic • American Cannes • You Say the Nicest Things, Baby • I've Got the President's Ear • Holiday in the Country • There's No Getting Away From You • I Got Lucky in the Rain • Father's Day • It Takes a Woman to Take a Man

AS THOUSANDS CHEER[1]
September 30, 1933 (400)
Music and lyrics by Irving Berlin

How's Chances? • Heat Wave • Majestic Sails at Midnight • Lonely Heart • The Funnies • To Be or Not to Be • Easter Parade* • Supper Time • Our Wedding Day • Harlem on My Mind • Not for All the Rice in China

[1] For its London run in 1935, the show was

retitled *Stop Press* and several songs by Arthur Schwartz and Howard Dietz were added.

AT HOME ABROAD
September 19, 1935 (198)
Music by Arthur Schwartz
Lyrics by Howard Dietz

Get Away From It All • That's Not Cricket • Hottentot Potentate • Farewell, My Lovely • The Lady With the Tap • Thief in the Night • O Leo • Love Is a Dancing Thing • What a Wonderful World • The Steamboat Whistle • Loadin' Time • Get Yourself a Geisha • Got a Bran' New Suit

RA

AT THE DROP OF A HAT
October 8, 1959 (215)
Music by Donald Swann
Lyrics by Michael Flanders

A Transport of Delight • Song of Reproduction • The Hog Beneath the Skin • The Youth of the Heart (Lyrics by Sydney Carter) • The Wompom • Sea Fever • A Gnu • Judgement of Paris • Philological Waltz • Satellite Moon • A Happy Song • A Song of the Weather • The Reluctant Cannibal • In the Bath • Design for Living • Tried by the Centre Court • Misalliance • Kokoraki • Madeira, M'Dear? • The Hippopotamus

RA

AT THE DROP OF ANOTHER HAT
December 27, 1966 (105)
Music by Donald Swann
Lyrics by Michael Flanders

The Gas Man Cometh • From Our Bestiary • P** P* B**** B** D****** • Bilbo's Song • Slow Train • Thermodynamic Duo • Sloth • In the Desert • Los Olivados • Motor Perpetuo • A Song of Patriotic Prejudice • All Gall • Horoscope • Armadillo Idyll • Twenty Tons of T.N.T • Ill Wind • Food for Thought • Prehistoric Complaint • Twice Shy

RA

AUTUMN'S HERE (OB)
October 25, 1966 (80)
Music and lyrics by Norman Dean

Based on *The Legend of Sleepy Hollow* by Washington Irving

Sleepy Hollow • Boy, Do I Hate Horse Races • Me and My Horse • Autumn's Here • Song of the Thirteen Colonies • Patience • For the Harvest Safely Gathered • Who Walks Like a Scarecrow • This Is the Girl for Me • Do You Think I'm Pretty? • Fine Words and Fancy Phrases • Private Hunting Ground • It's a Long Road Home • Brom and Katrina • Dark New England Night • Dutch Country Table • You Never Miss the Water • Any Day Now • You May Be the Someone • Beware As You Ride Through the Hollow

BABES IN ARMS
April 14, 1937 (289)
Music by Richard Rodgers
Lyrics by Lorenz Hart

Where or When • Babes in Arms • I Wish I Were in
Love Again • All Dark People • Way Out West • My
Funny Valentine • Johnny One Note • Imagine • All at
Once • The Lady Is a Tramp • You Are So Fair

RA,VS,SEL

BABES IN THE WOOD (OB)
December 28, 1964 (45)
Music and lyrics by Rick Besoyan

Adapted from Shakespeare's *A Midsummer Night's
Dream*

This State of Affairs • Titania's Philosophy • A Lover
Waits • The Gossip Song • I'm Not for You • Mother
• Old Fashioned Girl • Love Is Lovely • Babes in the
Wood • Anyone Can Make a Mistake • Cavorting •
There's a Girl • Little Tear • Helena's Solution •
Helena • Midsummer Night • Moon Madness • The
Alphabet Song

BABES IN TOYLAND
October 13, 1903 (192)
Music by Victor Herbert
Lyrics by Glen MacDonough

Never Mind, Bo-Peep • Floretta • Barney O'Flynn •
Jane • I Can't Do That Sum • Go to Sleep, Slumber
Deep • Hail to Christmas • Song of the Poet •
Beatrice Barefacts • March of the Toys • The
Military Ball (orchestral) • Toyland • Our Castle in
Spain • Before and After • He Won't Be Happy Till
He Gets It

RA,VS,SEL

BABY
December 4, 1983[1]
Music by David Shire
Lyrics by Richard Maltby, Jr.

We Start Today • What Could Be Better? • The
Plaza Song • Baby, Baby, Baby • I Want It All • At
Night She Comes Home to Me • Fatherhood Blues •
Romance • I Chose Right • The Story Goes On • The
Ladies Singin' Their Song • Easier to Love • Two
People in Love • With You • And What If We Had
Loved Like That

RA,SEL

[1] Still running December 31, 1983

BAD HABITS OF 1926 (OB)
April 30, 1926 (19)
Music by Manning Sherwin
Lyrics by Arthur Herzog, Jr.

Are We Downhearted? • When • Gone Away Blues •
Station L–O–V–E • Would-ja? • Cinderella of Our
Block • Funeral of Charleston • Manhattan Transfer
• Chorus Girl Blues • Geisha Girl • Let Me Be
Myself • The Student Robin Hood of Pilsen (Music
by Randall Thompson; lyrics by Perry Ivins) • Keep
Your Shirt On • The Lifeguards

BAGS (OB)
April 6, 1982 (18)
Music by Robert Mitchell
Lyrics by Elizabeth Perry

It's Mine • I Was Beautiful • Bobby's Songs • The
Clean Ones • Lady Wake Up • This Is Where We
Met • So Much for Marriage • Honky Jewish Boy •
Out on the Streets • Street People's Anthem • Lucky
Me • Song to Endangered Species • Street Corner
Song • Schwesters • The Freedom Song

BAJOUR
November 23, 1964 (218)
Music and lyrics by Walter Marks

Based on stories by Joseph Mitchell

Move Over, New York • Where Is the Tribe for Me?
• Love-Line • Words, Words, Words • Mean • Must It
Be Love? • Bajour • Soon • I Can • Living Simply •

Honest Man • Guarantee • Love Is a Chance • The Sew-Up

RA,SEL

BAKER STREET
February 16, 1965 (313)
Music and lyrics by Marian Grudeff and Raymond Jessel

Adapted from stories by Sir Arthur Conan Doyle

It's So Simple • I'm in London Again • Leave It to Us, Gov • Letters • Cold Clear World • Finding Words for Spring • What a Night This Is Going to Be • London Underworld • I Shall Miss You • Roof Space • A Married Man • I'd Do It Again • Pursuit • Jewelry

RA

BALLAD FOR A FIRING SQUAD (OB)
December 11, 1968 (7)
Music by Edward Thomas
Lyrics by Martin Charnin

Ballad for a Firing Squad • Is This a Fact? • There Is Only One Thing to Be Sure Of • How Young You Were Tonight • I'm Saving Myself for a Soldier • Everyone Has Something to Hide • Fritzie • The Choice Is Yours • Maman • Not Now, Not Here • I Did Not Sleep Last Night • Hello Yank • I Don't See Him Very Much Anymore • What Then? • What Might Have Been

BALLAD FOR BIMSHIRE (OB)
October 15, 1963 (74)
Music and lyrics by Irving Burgie

Ballad for Bimshire • Street Cries • Fore Day Noon in the Mornin' • Lately I've Been Feeling So Strange • Deep in My Heart • Have You Got Charm? • Hail Britannia • Welcome Song • Belle Plain • I'm a Dandy • Silver Earring • My Love Will Come By • Chicken's a Popular Bird • Pardon Me, Sir • Yesterday Was Such a Lovely Day • The Master Plan • Chant • Vendor's Song • We Gon' Jump Up

RA

THE BALLAD OF JOHNNY POT (OB)
April 26, 1971 (16)
Music by Clinton Ballard
Lyrics by Carolyn Richter

The Ballad of Johnny Pot • Johnny's Creed • Hard Hat Stetsons • The Letter • Discarded Blues • Whaddaya Say, Kid? • Crazy • Head Down the Road • A Carol • Lonely Is the Life • What About Me? • Have Some Pot • Scared • How Wonderful It Is • Like It • Dance of Distraction • Saskatchewan • Little Sparrows • Find My Way Alone

BALLET BALLADS
May 18, 1948 (69)
Music by Jerome Moross
Lyrics by John Latouche

Ridin' on the Breeze • I've Got Me • My Yellow Flower

BALLROOM
December 14, 1978 (116)
Music by Billy Goldenberg
Lyrics by Alan and Marilyn Bergman

Based on the television play *Queen of the Stardust Ballroom* by Jerome Kass

A Terrific Band and a Real Nice Crowd • A Song for Dancin' • One by One • Dreams • Somebody Did Alright for Herself • Goodnight Is Not Goodbye • I've Been Waiting All My Life • I Love to Dance* • More of the Same • Stardust Waltz • Fifty Percent • I Wish You a Waltz

RA,SEL

BALLYHOO (1930)
December 22, 1930 (68)
Music by Louis Alter
Lyrics by Harry Ruskin and Leighton K. Brill

How I Could Go for You • That Tired Feeling • No Wonder I'm Blue (Lyrics by Oscar Hammerstein II) • Throw It Out the Window • Blow Hot—Blow Cold • If I Were You • I'm One of God's Children (Lyrics by Oscar Hammerstein II and Harry Ruskin) • Good Girls Love Bad Men

BALLYHOO (1932)
September 6, 1932 (94)
Music by Lewis E. Gensler
Lyrics by E.Y. Harburg

Falling off the Wagon • Thrill Me • Old Fashioned Wedding • How Do You Do It? • Man About Yonkers • Ballyhujah • Love, Nuts and Noodles • Riddle Me This • What Have You Got to Have?

BAMBOOLA
June 26, 1929 (27)
Music and lyrics by Frank Marcus and Bernard Maltin

Evenin' • Ace of Spades • Dixie Vagabond • Rub-a-Dub Your Rabbit's Foot • Bamboola • Somebody Like Me • Tailor-Made Babies • African Whoopee • Tampico Tune • Song of Harlem • Shoutin' Sinners • Anna • Hot Patootie Wedding Night

THE BAND WAGON
June 3, 1931 (260)
Music by Arthur Schwartz
Lyrics by Howard Dietz

It Better Be Good • Sweet Music • High and Low • Hoops • Confession • New Sun in the Sky • Miserable With You • I Love Louisa • Dancing in the Dark • Where Can He Be? • White Heat • The Beggar Waltz (instrumental)*

Added to film version (1953)
That's Entertainment

RA

BANJO EYES
December 25, 1941 (126)
Music by Vernon Duke
Lyrics by John Latouche

Based on the play *Three Men on a Horse* by John Cecil Holm and George Abbott

The Greeting Cards • I'll Take the City • The Toast of the Boys at the Post • I've Got to Hand It to You • A Nickel to My Name • Who Started the Rhumba? • It Could Only Happen in the Movies (Lyrics by Harold Adamson) • Make With the Feet (Lyrics by Harold Adamson) • We're Having a Baby (Lyrics by Harold Adamson) • Banjo Eyes • We Did It Before (Music and lyrics by Charlie Tobias and Cliff Friend) • Not a Care in the World*

THE BANKER'S DAUGHTER (OB)
January 22, 1962 (68)
Music by Sol Kaplan
Lyrics by Edward Eliscu

Based on the play *The Streets of New York* by Dion Boucicault

One More Day • Gentlemen's Understanding • Such a Beautiful World • Genteel • In a Brownstone Mansion • Both Ends Against the Middle • The Sun Rises • Father's Daughter • Say No More • More Than One More Day • Nero, Caesar, Napoleon • Head in the Stars • Sleep, O Sleep • Unexpectedly • A Carriage for Alida • It's So Heart-Warming

THE BAR THAT NEVER CLOSES (OB)
December 3, 1972 (33)
Music by Tom Mandel
Lyrics by Louisa Rose, John Braswell and Tom Mandel

Walking With You, Two by Two (Lyrics by Rose) • Do It (Lyrics by Braswell) • Recipe for Love (Lyrics by Braswell) • Kaleidoscope (Lyrics by Rose) • I Don't Think I'll Ever Love You (Lyrics by Braswell) • Dear Dear (Lyrics by Mandel) • Tears of Ice (Lyrics by Rose) • Circus of Jade (Lyrics by Braswell) • Precious Little Darkness (Lyrics by Rose)

BARE FACTS OF 1926
July 16, 1926 (107)
Music by Charles M. Schwab
Lyrics by Henry Myers

Won't You Tell Me? • Stand Up on Your Feet and Dance • Treat 'Em Rough • The Third From the End • Cradle Song • Nice Girl • Tea Time

BAREFOOT BOY WITH CHEEK
April 3, 1947 (108)
Music by Sidney Lippman
Lyrics by Sylvia Dee

Based on the novel by Max Shulman

A Toast to Alpha Cholera • We Feel Our Man Is Definitely You • The Legendary Eino Fflliikkiinnenn • Too Nice a Day to Go to School • I Knew I'd Know •

I'll Turn a Little Cog • Who Do You Think You Are? • Everything Leads Right Back to Love • Little Yetta's Gonna Get a Man • Alice in Boogieland • After Graduation Day • There's a Lot of Things You Can Do With Two (but Not With Three) • The Story of a Carrot • Star of the North State • It Couldn't Be Done (but We Did It)

BARNUM
April 30, 1980 (854)
Music by Cy Coleman
Lyrics by Michael Stewart

There Is a Sucker Born Ev'ry Minute • Thank God I'm Old • The Colors of My Life • One Brick at a Time • Museum Song • I Like Your Style • Bigger Isn't Better • Love Makes Such Fools of Us All • Out There • Come Follow the Band • Black and White • The Prince Of Humbug • Join the Circus

RA,SEL

BATTLING BUTTLER
October 8, 1923 (313)
Music by Walter L. Rosemont
Lyrics by Ballard MacDonald

If Every Day Was Sunday (Music by Adorjan Otvos) • Apples, Bananas and You • Two Little Pals • Will You Marry Me? • Tinkle Tune (Music by Adorjan Otvos and Louis Breau) • Dancing Honeymoon (Music and lyrics by Philip Braham) • As We Leave the Years Behind (Music by Joseph Meyer) • In the Spring (Music by Adorjan Otvos)

BE KIND TO PEOPLE WEEK (OB)
March 23, 1975 (100)
Music and lyrics by Jack Bussins and Ellsworth Olin

Whatever Happened to the Good Old Days? • I Will Give Him Love • Mad About You Manhattan • I Have a Friend at the Chase Manhattan Bank • All I Got Is You • I'm in Like With You • When We See a Pretty Girl We Whistle • Ecology • I Need You • To Love Is to Live • Freud Is a Fraud • Black Is Beautiful • A Smile Is Up • You're Divine • Be Kind to People Week

BE YOURSELF
September 3, 1924 (93)
Music by Lewis E. Gensler and Milton Schwarzwald
Lyrics by George S. Kaufman, Marc Connelly, and Ira Gershwin

Rain • High in the Hills • My Road • Little Bit of This • A Good Hand Organ and a Sidewalk • The Decent Thing to Do • A Flapper Too • I Came Here (Music by Gensler) • The Wrong Thing at the Right Time (Music by Schwarzwald) • Uh-Uh! (Music by Schwarzwald) • Money Doesn't Mean a Thing • Do It Now • Bonga Boo (Music by Owen Murphy) • Can't You See I'm in Love? (Music by Owen Murphy) • All of Them Was Friends of Mine (Lyrics by Connelly and Gershwin) • They Don't Make 'Em That Way Any More (Lyrics by Gershwin) • Life in Town

THE BEAST IN ME
May 16, 1963 (4)
Music by Don Elliott
Lyrics by James Costigan

Based on *Fables for Our Time* by James Thurber

Percussion • So Beautiful • You're Delicious • I Owe Ohio • Go, Go, Go • Eat Your Breakfast • Eat Your Nice Lily, Unicorn • Bacchanale • Calypso Kitty • Glorious Cheese • Why? • J'ai • What Do You Say? • When I'm Alone • Hallelujah

BEAT THE BAND
October 14, 1942 (68)
Music by John Green
Lyrics by George Marion, Jr.

Down Through the Agents • Free, Cute and Size Fourteen • Song of Two Islands • Keep It Casual • Proud of You • Break It Up • Let's Comb Beaches • The Hula Girl • America Loves a Band • The Afternoon of a Phoney • Men • The Steam Is on the Beam • I'm Physical, You're Cultured • Ev'ry Other Heartbeat • The Four Freedoms—Calypso

BEG, BORROW OR STEAL
February 10, 1960 (5)
Music by Leon Pober
Lyrics by Bud Freeman

Some Little People • Rootless • What Are We Gonna Do Tonight? • Poetry and All That Jazz • Don't Stand Too Close to the Picture • Beg, Borrow or Steal • No One Knows Me • Zen Is When • Clara • You've Got Something to Say • Presenting Clara Spencer • I Can't Stop Talking • It's All in Your Mind • In Time • Think • Little People • Rafesville, U.S.A. • Let's Be Strangers Again

RA

BEGGAR'S HOLIDAY
December 26, 1946 (111)
Music by Duke Ellington
Lyrics by John Latouche

Based on *The Beggar's Opera* by John Gay

When You Go Down by Miss Jenny's • I've Got Me • TNT • Take Love Easy • I Wanna Be Bad • When I Walk With You • The Scrimmage of Life • Ore From a Gold Mine • Tooth and Claw • Maybe I Should Change My Ways • On the Wrong Side of the Railroad Tracks • Tomorrow Mountain • Girls Want a Hero • Lullaby for Junior • Quarrel for Three • Brown Penny* • Women, Women, Women • The Hunted

THE BELIEVERS (OB)
May 9, 1968 (295)
Music and lyrics by Voices, Inc.

African Sequence • Believers' Chants • Believers' Laments • This Old Ship • Where Shall I Go? • What Shall I Believe in Now? • I Just Got in the City • City Blues • You Never Really Know • Early One Morning

Blues • Daily Buzz • Children's Games • School Don't Mean a Damn Thing • I'm Gonna Do My Things • Where Do I Go From Here? • Burn This Town • Learn to Love

RA

THE BELLE OF NEW YORK[1]
September 28, 1897 (56)
Music by Gustave Kerker
Lyrics by Hugh Morton

When a Man Is Twenty-one • When I Was Born the Stars Stood Still • Little Sister Kissie • Oh, Teach Me How to Kiss • We Come This Way • The Anti-Cigarette Society • Wine, Woman and Song • La Belle Parisienne • My Little Baby • Pretty Little China Girl • They All Follow Me • She Is the Belle of New York • Your Life, My Little Girl • Oh! Sonny • When We Are Married • The Purity Brigade • I Do, So There! • Take Me Down to Coney Island • On the Beach at Narragansett • For the Twentieth Time We'll Drink • At Ze Naughty Folies Bergères • For in the Field • Father of the Queen of Comic Opera

VS

[1] This was the first American musical to enjoy an extended run in London, where it ran for for 697 performances.

BELLE PAREE *See* LA BELLE PAREE

BELLS ARE RINGING
November 29, 1956 (924)
Music by Jule Styne
Lyrics by Betty Comden and Adolph Green

Bells Are Ringing • It's a Perfect Relationship • On My Own • It's a Simple Little System • Is It a Crime? • Hello, Hello There • I Met a Girl • Long Before I Knew You • Mu-Cha-Cha • Just in Time • Drop That Name • The Party's Over • Salzburg • The Midas Touch • I'm Going Back • Independent

RA,VS

BEN FRANKLIN IN PARIS
October 27, 1964 (215)
Music by Mark Sandrich, Jr.
Lyrics by Sidney Michaels

We Sail the Seas • I Invented Myself • Too Charming • Whatever Became of Old Temple? • Half the Battle • A Balloon Is Ascending • To Be Alone With You (Music and lyrics by Jerry Herman) • You're in Paris • How Laughable It Is • Hic Haec Hoc • God Bless the Human Elbow • When I Dance With the Person I Love • Diane Is • Look for Small Pleasures • I Love the Ladies

RA,SEL

BEST FOOT FORWARD
October 1, 1941 (326)
Music and lyrics by Hugh Martin and Ralph Blane

Don't Sell the Night Short • Three Men on a Date •

That's How I Love the Blues • The Three B's • Ev'ry Time • The Guy Who Brought Me • I Know You by Heart • Shady Lady Bird • Buckle Down, Winsocki • My First Promise • What Do You Think I Am? • Just a Little Joint With a Juke Box • Where Do You Travel? • I'd Gladly Trade

Added to 1963 Off-Broadway production (224)
Wish I May • Hollywood Story • Alive and Kicking • You're Lucky • Raving Beauty • You Are for Loving

RA

THE BEST LITTLE WHOREHOUSE IN TEXAS
April 17, 1978[1] (1,584)
Music and lyrics by Carol Hall

Twenty Fans • Lil' Ole Bitty Pissant Country Place • Girl, You're a Woman • Watch Dog Theme • Texas Has a Whorehouse in It • Twenty-four Hours of Lovin' • Doatsey Mae • Angelette March • The Aggie Song • Bus From Amarillo • The Sidestep • No Lies • Good Old Girls • Hard Candy Christmas

RA,SEL

[1] Opened this date Off Broadway, moved to Broadway June 19, 1979. Reopened on Broadway May 31, 1982.

BETSY
December 28, 1926 (39)
Music by Richard Rodgers
Lyrics by Lorenz Hart

The Kitzel Engagement • My Missus • Stonewall Moskowitz March (Lyrics by Irving Caesar) • One of Us Should Be Two • Sing • In Our Parlor on the Third Floor Back • This Funny World • The Tales of Hoffman (Music and lyrics by Irving Caesar and Al Segal) • Follow On • Push Around • Bugle Blow • Cradle of the Deep • If I Were You • Blue Skies (Music and lyrics by Irving Berlin) • Leave It to Levy (Music and lyrics by Irving Caesar) • Birds on High • Shuffle

Dropped from production
Come and Tell Me* • Show Me How to Make Love • At the Saskatchewan • Ladies' Home Companion • You're the Mother Type • Six Little Kitzels • In Variety • Is My Girl Refined?

BETWEEN THE DEVIL
December 22, 1937 (93)
Music by Arthur Schwartz
Lyrics by Howard Dietz

I See Your Face Before Me • The Night Before the Morning After • I've Made Up My Mind • Don't Go Away, Monsieur • Experience • Five O'Clock • Triplets* • Fly by Night • You Have Everything • Bye-Bye Butterfly Lover • Celina Couldn't Say "No" • Front Page News • Why Did You Do It? • By Myself • The Gendarme • I'm Against Rhythm

BIG BOY
January 7, 1925 (48)
Music by Joseph Meyer and James F. Hanley
Lyrics by B.G. DeSylva

As Long As I've Got My Mammy • Born and Bred in Old Kentucky • Hello, Tucky • Lackawanna • Who Was Chasing Paul Revere? • The Dance From Down Yonder • Welcome Home • Lead 'Em On • The Day I Rode Half Fare • True Love • Tap the Toe • Cookies and Bookies • The Race Is Over • Come On and Play • Something for Nothing • It all Depends On You* (Music by Ray Henderson; lyrics by Lew Brown and DeSylva)

BILLIE
October 1, 1928 (112)
Music and lyrics by George M. Cohan

Based on Cohan's play *Broadway Jones*

New York • Come to St. Thomas' • Happy • Billie • Go Home Ev'ry Once in a While • Friends • The Cause of the Situation • Ev'ry Boy in Town's My Sweetheart • They Fall in Love • Where Were You— Where Was I? • The Jones' Family Friends • I'm a One-Girl Man • Personality • Bluff • The Two of Us

BILLION DOLLAR BABY
December 21, 1945 (219)
Music by Morton Gould
Lyrics by Betty Comden and Adolph Green

Million Dollar Smile • Who's Gonna Be the Winner? • Dreams Come True • Charleston • Broadway Blossom • Speaking of Pals • There I'd Be • One Track Mind • Bad Timing • A Lovely Girl • Havin' a Time • Faithless • I'm Sure of Your Love • A Life With Rocky

BILLY
March 22, 1969 (1)
Music and lyrics by Ron Dante and Gene Allan

Suggested by the story *Billy Budd* by Herman Melville

Molly • Chanty • Watch Out for Claggart/Work • Shaking Hands With the Wind • Billy • It Ain't Us Who Make the Wars • The Bridge to Nowhere • The Night and the Sea • In the Arms of a Stranger • The Fiddlers' Green • My Captain • Requiem

THE BILLY BARNES PEOPLE
June 13, 1961 (7)
Music and lyrics by Billy Barnes

If It Wasn't for People • There's Nothing Wrong With Our Values • Don't Bother • Damn-Alot • What Do We Have to Hold On To? • I Like You • Before and After • Let's Get Drunk • It's Not Easy • The Matinee • The End? • Second Best • Dolls • Where Is the Clown? • Marital Infidelity

THE BILLY BARNES REVUE
June 9, 1959 (199 including Off-Broadway run)
Music and lyrics by Billy Barnes

Do a Revue • Where Are Your Children? • Foolin' Ourselves • Las Vegas • Too Long at the Fair • Listen to the Beat! • City of the Angels • Blocks • One of Those Days

RA

BILLY NONAME (OB)
March 2, 1970 (48)
Music and lyrics by Johnny Brandon

King Joe • Seduction • Billy Noname • Boychild • A Different Drummer • Look Through the Window • It's Our Time Now • Hello World • At the End of the Day • I Want to Live • Manchild • Color Me White • We're Gonna Turn on Freedom • Mother Earth • Sit In—Wade In • Movin' • The Dream • Black Boy • Burn, Baby, Burn • We Make a Promise • Get Your Slice of Cake

RA

A BISTRO CAR ON THE CNR (OB)
March 23, 1978 (82)
Music by Patrick Rose
Lyrics by Merv Campone and Richard Ouzounian

C.N.R. • Twenty-five Miles • Passing By • Madame La Chanson • Oh God I'm Thirty • Ready or Not • Sudden Death Overtime • Bring Back Swing • Yesterday's Lover • Four-Part Invention • La Belle Province • Dewey and Sal • Here I Am Again • Street Music • Other People's Houses • Genuine Grade A Canadian Superstar • I Don't Live Anywhere Anymore • The Lady Who Loved to Sing • Somebody Write Me a Love Song

BITTER SWEET
November 5, 1929 (159)
Music and lyrics by Noël Coward

That Wonderful Melody • The Call of Life • If You Could Only Come With Me • I'll See You Again* • Tell Me, What Is Love? • The Last Dance • Life in the Morning • Ladies of the Town • If Love Were All • Evermore and a Day • Dear Little Cafe • Tokay • Bonne Nuit, Merci • Kiss Me • Ta Ra Ra Boom De Ay • Alas, the Time Is Past • Green Carnations • Zigeuner

RA,VS,SEL

BLACK RHYTHM
December 19, 1936 (6)
Music and lyrics by Donald Heywood

Truckers Ball • Bow Down, Sinners • Orchids • Here 'Tis • Black Rhythm • Doin' the Toledo • Emaline

BLACKBERRIES OF 1932
April 4, 1932 (24)
Music and lyrics by Donald Heywood

The Answer Is No • Blackberries • Brown Sugar • First Thing in the Morning • Harlem Mania • Love Me More—Love Me Less (Music by Tom Peluso; lyrics by Ben Bernard)

BLACKBIRDS OF 1928
May 9, 1928 (518)
Music by Jimmy McHugh
Lyrics by Dorothy Fields

Digga Digga Do • I Can't Give You Anything But Love* • Bandanna Babies • Porgy • Magnolia's

Wedding Day • Doin' the New Low-Down • Here Comes My Blackbird • Dixie • Shuffle Your Feet and Roll Along

Dropped from production
Baby!

RA

BLACKBIRDS OF 1930
October 22, 1930 (57)
Music by Eubie Blake
Lyrics by Andy Razaf

Roll Jordan • Cabin Door • Memories of You • Mozambique • Green Pastures (Lyrics by Will Morrissey and Razaf) • You're Lucky to Me • Papa-De-Da-Da (Music and lyrics by Spencer Williams, Clarence Todd and Clarence Williams) • My Handy Man Ain't Handy No More • Take a Trip to Harlem • We're the Berries • That Lindy Hop • Dianna Lee

BLACKBIRDS OF 1934
December 2, 1933 (25)

I'm Walkin' the Chalk Line (Music by Alberta Nichols; lyrics by Mann Holiner) • I Just Couldn't Take It, Baby (Music by Alberta Nichols; lyrics by Mann Holiner) • A Hundred Years From Today (Music by Victor Young; lyrics by Joseph Young and Ned Washington) • Your Mother's Son-in-Law (Music by Albert Nichols; lyrics by Mann Holiner) • Tappin' the Barrel (Music by Victor Young; lyrics by Joseph Young and Ned Washington) • Victim of the Voodoo Drums (Music by Victor Young; lyrics by Joseph Young and Ned Washington) • Doin' the Shim Sham (Music by Alberta Nichols; lyrics by Mann Holiner) • Let Me Be Born Again (Music by Victor Young; lyrics by Joseph Young and Ned Washington) • What—No Dixie? (Music by Victor Young; lyrics by Joseph Young and Ned Washington)

BLESS YOU ALL
December 14, 1950 (84)
Music and lyrics by Harold Rome

Bless You All • Do You Know a Better Way to Make a Living? • Don't Wanna Write About the South • I Can Hear It Now • When • Little Things Meant So Much to Me • A Rose Is a Rose • Love Letter to Manhattan • Summer Dresses • Take Off the Coat • The Desert Flame • You Never Know What Hit You • The Roaring Twenties Strike Back

THE BLONDE SINNER
July 14, 1926 (173)
Music and lyrics by Leon DeCosta

Don't You Cheat • Oh, What a Playmate You Could Make • If You Said What You Thought • Man Is a Mistake • The Whispering Song • Lips • Bye-Bye Babe

BLOOD RED ROSES
March 22, 1970 (1)
Music by Michael Valenti
Lyrics by John Lewin

The Cream of English Youth • A Garden in the Sun • In the Country Where I Come From • Black Dog Rum • How Fucked Up Things Are • The English Rose • O Rock Eternal • Soldiers Anthem • Prelude • Blood Red Roses • The Fourth Light Dragoons • Song of Greater Britain • Song of the Fair Dissenter Lass

BLOOMER GIRL
October 5, 1944 (654)
Music by Harold Arlen
Lyrics by E.Y. Harburg

When the Boys Come Home • Evelina • Welcome Hinges • Farmer's Daughter • It Was Good Enough for Grandma • The Eagle and Me • Right as the Rain • T'morra, T'morra • The Rakish Young Man With the Whiskers • Pretty as a Picture • Sunday in Cicero Falls • I Got a Song • Lullaby (Satin Gown and Silver Shoe) • Simon Legree • Liza Crossing the Ice • I Never Was Born • Man for Sale • Civil War Ballet

RA,SEL

BLOSSOM TIME[1]
September 29, 1921 (592)
Music by Sigmund Romberg
Lyrics by Dorothy Donnelly

Melody Triste • Three Little Maids[*] • Serenade[*] • My Springtime Thou Art[*] • Song of Love[*] • Love Is a Riddle • Let Me Awake • Tell Me, Daisy[*] • Only One Love Ever Fills My Heart • Keep It Dark • Peace to My Lonely Heart[*]

RA,VS

[1] A very free adaptation of a still-popular Viennese operetta, *Das Dreimäderlhaus*, based on the life and music of Franz Schubert. The British version (1922) of this operetta, *Lilac Time*, was adapted by G. H. Clutsam, who used different Schubert melodies, and was truer to the original than the Romberg adaptations. See individual song titles for notes on the specific musical sources.

THE BLUE KITTEN
January 13, 1922 (140)
Music by Rudolf Friml
Lyrics by Otto Harbach

Adapted from the farce *Le Chasseur de Chez Maxim* by Yves Mirand and Gustave Quinson

I Could Do a Lot for You • Tact • Cutie • I Found a Bud Among the Roses • Her Love Is Always the Same • Where the Honeymoon Alone Can See • The Best I Ever Get Is the Worst of It • Smoke Rings • The Blue Kitten Blues (Me-Ow!) • Sweet as You Can Be • When I Waltz With You

RA

THE BLUE PARADISE[1]
August 5, 1915 (356)

Music by Edmund Eysler and Sigmund Romberg[2]
Lyrics by Herbert Reynolds

A Toast to Woman's Eyes (Music by Romberg) • Here's to You, My Sparkling Wine (Music by Leo Edwards; lyrics by Blanche Merrill) • To Paradise We'll Gaily Trip (Music by Eysler) • Tell the Town "Hello" Tonight (Music by Romberg; lyrics by Harold Atteridge) • Auf Wiedersehn! (Music by Romberg) • We Wish You a Pleasant Journey (Music by Romberg) • Vienna, Vienna (Music by Eysler) • I'm From Chicago (Music by Romberg) • Just a Pretty Widow (Music by Eysler) • One Step Into Love (Music by Romberg) • Vienna, How D'Ye Do (Music by Eysler) • Why Are We Invited Here? (Music by Romberg) • I Had a Dog (Music by Leo Edwards) • My Model Girl (Music by Romberg; lyrics by Harold Atteridge) • Waltz of the Season (Music by Eysler) • The Tune They Croon in the U.S.A. (Music and lyrics by Cecil Lean) • I'm Dreaming of a Wonderful Night (Music by Eysler)

[1] The show gave a marvelous opportunity to Vivienne Segal, then an eighteen-year-old vocal student at Philadelphia's Curtis Institute of Music, to play the role of the heroine on opening night with only four days' rehearsal, when the original leading lady proved unsatisfactory.

[2] After writing songs for a succession of Shubert revues, *The Blue Paradise* gave Romberg his first opportunity to compose operetta, the field of music in which he was to become renowned.

BLUE PLATE SPECIAL (OB)
November 15, 1983 (16)
Music by Harris Wheeler
Lyrics by Mary L. Fisher

Morning Glory Mountain • At the Bottom Lookin' Up • Ramona's Lament • Never Say Never • Halfway to Heaven • Satisfaction Guaranteed • Blue Plate Special • Twice as Nice • All American Male • Side of Fries • Honky Tonk Queens • I Ain't Looking Back • I'm Gonna Miss Those Tennessee Nights

THE BODY BEAUTIFUL
January 23, 1958 (60)
Music by Jerry Bock
Lyrics by Sheldon Harnick

Where Are They? • The Body Beautiful • Pffft! • Fair Warning • Leave Well Enough Alone • Blonde Blues • Uh-huh, Oh, Yeah! • All of These and More • Nobility • Summer Is • The Honeymoon Is Over • Just My Luck • The Art of Conversation • Gloria • A Relatively Simple Affair

SEL

BOOM-BOOM
January 28, 1929 (72)
Music by Werner Janssen
Lyrics by Mann Holiner and J. Keirn Brennan

Based on the play *Mlle. Ma Mère* by Louis Verneuil

What Could I Do? • On Top • Be That Way • Shake High, Shake Low • Nina • What a Girl • Just a Big-

Hearted Man • He's Just My Ideal • Pick 'Em Up and Lay 'Em Down • Messin' Round • We're Going to Make Boom-Boom • Blow the Blues Away

BOTTOMLAND
June 27, 1927 (21)
Music by Clarence Williams

Steamboat Days (Lyrics by Clarence Williams) • Shootin' the Pistol (Lyrics by Chris Smith) • Bottomland (Lyrics by Jo Trent) • You're the Only One (Lyrics by Len Gray) • Come On Home (Music and lyrics by Donald Heywood) • Dancing Girl (Lyrics by Spencer Williams) • Any Time (Lyrics by Joe Jordan) • When I March With April in May (Lyrics by Spencer Williams)

THE BOY FRIEND
September 30, 1954 (485)
Music and lyrics by Sandy Wilson

Perfect Young Ladies • The Boy Friend • Won't You Charleston With Me? • Fancy Forgetting • I Could Be Happy With You • Sur La Plage • A Room in Bloomsbury • The You-Don't-Want-to-Play-With-Me Blues • Safety in Numbers • The Riviera • It's Never Too Late to Fall in Love • Poor Little Pierrette

RA,VS,SEL

BOY MEETS BOY (OB)
September 17, 1975 (463)
Music and lyrics by Billy Solly

Boy Meets Boy • Giving It Up for Love • Me • English Rose • Marry an American • It's a Boy's Life • Does Anybody Love You? • You're Beautiful • Let's Dance • Just My Luck • It's a Dolly • What Do I Care? • Clarence's Turn

RA

BOYS AND GIRLS TOGETHER
October 1, 1940 (191)
Music by Sammy Fain
Lyrics by Irving Kahal and Jack Yellen

Liable to Catch On • Such Stuff As Dreams Are Made Of (Lyrics by Kahal) • I Want to Live (Lyrics by Yellen) • Times Square Dance (Lyrics by Yellen) • You Can't Put Catsup on the Moon (Lyrics by Kahal) • The Sun'll Be Up in the Morning (Lyrics by Yellen) • The Latin in Me

THE BOYS FROM SYRACUSE
November 23, 1938 (235)
Music by Richard Rodgers
Lyrics by Lorenz Hart

Based on Shakespeare's *The Comedy of Errors*

I Had Twins • Dear Old Syracuse • What Can You Do With a Man? • Falling in Love With Love* • The Shortest Day of the Year • This Can't Be Love • Let Antipholus In • Ladies of the Evening • He and She • You Have Cast Your Shadow on the Sea • Come With Me • Big Brother • Sing for Your Supper • Oh, Diogenes

Added to film version (1940)
Who Are You? • The Greeks Have No Word for It

RA,VS,SEL

BRAVO *See* **EL BRAVO**

BRAVO GIOVANNI
May 19, 1962 (76)
Music by Milton Schafer
Lyrics by Ronny Graham

Based on the novel by Howard Shaw

Rome • Uriti • Breachy's Law • I'm All I've Got • The Argument • Signora Pandolfi • The Kangaroo • If I Were the Man • Steady, Steady • We Won't Discuss It • Ah! Camminare • Virtue Arrivederci • Bravo, Giovanni • One Little World Apart • Jump In • Miranda

RA,SEL

BRIGADOON
March 13, 1947 (581)
Music by Frederick Loewe
Lyrics by Alan Jay Lerner

Once in the Highlands • Brigadoon • Vendors' Calls • Down on MacConnachy Square • Waitin' for My Dearie • I'll Go Home With Bonnie Jean • The Heather on the Hill • The Love of My Life • Jeannie's Packin' Up • Come to Me, Bend to Me • Almost Like Being in Love • The Chase • There but for You Go I • My Mother's Wedding Day • From This Day On

RA,VS,SEL

BRIGHT LIGHTS OF 1944
September 16, 1943 (4)
Music by Jerry Livingston
Lyrics by Mack David

Haven't We Met Before? • You'd Better Dance • Thoughtless • Don't Forget the Girl From Punxsutawney • That's Broadway (Music and lyrics by Gene Herbert and Teddy Hall) • We're Having Our Fling • Back Bay Beat • Your Face Is Your Fortune • Yes, I Love You Honey • A Lick, and a Riff, and a Slow Bounce

BRING BACK BIRDIE
March 5, 1981 (4)
Music by Charles Strouse
Lyrics by Lee Adams

Twenty Happy Years • Movin' Out • Half of a Couple • I Like What I Do • Bring Back Birdie • Baby, You Can Count on Me • A Man Worth Fightin' For • You Can Never Go Back • Filth • Back in Show Biz Again • Middle Age Blues • Inner Peace • There's a Brand New Beat in Heaven • Well, I'm Not! • When Will Grown-Ups Grow Up? • Young • Show Girls (I Love 'Em All)

BRINGING UP FATHER
March 30, 1925 (24)
Music by Seymour Furth and Lee Edwards

Lyrics by R.F. Carroll

Based on the cartoon strip by George McManus

An Angel Without Wings • That's the Irish in Her • When It Gets Dark • We Hope to Make a Hit • Play Me a Bagpipe Tune • The Girls of New York • The Gainsboro Glide • The Merry Go Round • Moonlight • A Lady Bred in the Purple • Poppy the Dream Girl • My Lady's Fan • Wedding Chimes

BROADWAY FOLLIES
March 15, 1981 (1)
Music and lyrics by Walter Marks

Broadway Follies • Vaudeville • Wonderful U • Piccadilly • The Oasis • The Pampas • The Toyshop • Paper Bag Rag • At Home With the Clinkers • The Barnyard • The Saloon • Tap My Way to the Stars • The Rest of Michael Davis • Grand Parade

A BROADWAY MUSICAL
December 21, 1978 (1)
Music by Charles Strouse
Lyrics by Lee Adams

Broadway, Broadway • A Broadway Musical • I Hurry Home to You • Smoke and Fire • Lawyers • Yenta Power • Let Me Sing My Song • 1934 Hot Chocolate Jazz Babies Revue • It's Time for a Cheer-Up Song • You Gotta Have Dancing • What You Go Through • Don't Tell Me • Together

BROADWAY NIGHTS
July 15, 1929 (40)
Music by Maury Rubens and Sam Timberg
Lyrics by Moe Jaffe

Why Don't We? • Hotsy Totsy Hats • The Right Man • White Lights Were Coming • Arabian Nights • Come Hit Your Baby • Your Broadway and Mine (Music by Rubens) • Heart of a Rose • Baby-Doll Dance (Music by Rubens and Phil Svigals; lyrics by J. Keirn Brennan and Jaffe)

BROADWAY SHO-WINDOW
April 12, 1936 (24)

Hitch Your Wagon to a Star (Music by Richard Lewine; lyrics by Ted Fetter) • Poverty Row or Luxury Lane (Music by Gus Edwards; lyrics by Howard Johnson) • Spring Is in the Air (Music by Gus Edwards; lyrics by Eugene Conrad)

THE BROOKLYN BRIDGE (OB)
August 27, 1983 (35)
Music by Scott MacLarty
Lyrics by Dorothy Chansky

Brooklyn • Love Means • Can I Do It All? • Bridge to the Future • Cash Politics • The Roebling Plan • Keep Me Out of the Caisson • When You're the Only One • Ain't No Women There • Every Day for Four Years • A Man in the Window • All That I Know

BROWN BUDDIES
October 7, 1930 (111)

Give Me a Man Like That (Music and lyrics by George A. Little and Art Sizemore) • When a Black Man's Blue (Music and lyrics by George A. Little, Art Sizemore and Ed G. Nelson) • Missouri (Music and lyrics by Nat Reed) • I Hate Myself (for Falling in Love With You) (Music and lyrics by Abner Silver and Dave Oppenheim) • Happy (Music by Nat Reed; lyrics by Bob Joffe) • Don't Leave Your Little Blackbird Blue (Music and lyrics by Joe Jordan, Porter Grainger and Sheldon Brooks) • Darky Rhythm (Music by Peter Tinturin; lyrics by Joe Young) • Dancin' 'Way Your Sin (Music and lyrics by J.C. Johnson) • Betty Lou (Music by Joe Jordan; lyrics by Rosamond Johnson)

BUCK WHITE
December 2, 1969 (7)
Music and lyrics by Oscar Brown, Jr.

Based on the play *Big Time Buck White* by Joseph Dolan Tuotti

Honey Man Song • Money, Money, Money • Nobody Does My Thing • Step Across That Line • H.N.I.C. • Beautiful Allelujah Days • Tap the Plate • Big Time Buck White Chant • Better Far • We Came in Chains • Black Balloons • Look at Them • Mighty Whitey • Get Down

THE BUNCH AND JUDY
November 28, 1922 (63)
Music by Jerome Kern
Lyrics by Anne Caldwell

Silenzio • The Naughty Nobleman • The Pale Venetian Moon • Peach Girl • Morning Glory • Lovely Lassie • Every Day in Every Way • Times Square • "Have You Forgotten Me" Blues • How Do You Do, Katinka?

Dropped from production
Hot Dog

BUNK OF 1926
February 16, 1926 (104)
Music and lyrics by Gene Lockhart

Bunk • You Told Me That You Loved Me, but You Never Told Me Why • Monte, the Model • Those Mammy Singers • A Modest Little Thing • Cuddle Up • We're Going Away • The Milky Way • Chatter • How Very Long Ago • Do You Do the Charleston?

BUT NEVER JAM TODAY
July 31, 1979 (8)
Music by Bert Keyes and Bob Larimer
Lyrics by Bob Larimer

Adapted from the works of Lewis Carroll

Curiouser and Curiouser • Twinkle, Twinkle Little Star • Long Live the Queen • A Real Life Lullabye • The More I See People • My Little Room • But Never Jam Today • Riding for a Fall • All the Same to Me • I've Got My Orders • God Could Give Me Anything • I Like to Win • And They Call the Hatter Mad • Jumping From Rock to Rock • They

BUTTRIO SQUARE
October 14, 1952 (7)
Music by Fred Stamer
Lyrics by Gen Genovese • Every Day Is a Holiday • Let's Make It Forever • I'll Tell the World • There's No Place Like the Country (Music by Arthur Jones) • Take It Away • Get Me Out • I'm Gonna Be a Pop • One Is a Lonely Number • Love Swept Like a Storm • I Keep Telling Myself (Music by Arthur Jones) • More and More • You're Mine, All Mine

BY HEX (OB)
June 18, 1956 (40)
Music and lyrics by Howard Blankman

Market Day • Shunned • Ferhuddled and Ferhexed • Wonderful Good • What Is Love? • I Can Learn • Only a Man • An Amishman • I Have Lived • I Know My Love • The Trouble With Me • Something New • It Takes Time

BY JUPITER[1]
June 2, 1942 (427)
Music by Richard Rodgers
Lyrics by Lorenz Hart

Based on the play *The Warrior's Husband* by Julian F. Thompson

For Jupiter and Greece • Jupiter Forbid • Life With Father • Nobody's Heart • The Gateway of the Temple of Minerva • Here's a Hand • No, Mother, No • The Boy I Left Behind Me • Ev'rything I've Got • Bottoms Up • Careless Rhapsody • Wait Till You See Her • Now That I've Got My Strength

Dropped from production
Fool Meets Fool • Nothing to Do but Relax • Life Was Monotonous

Dropped during Broadway run
Wait Till You See Her

RA

[1] Pre-Broadway title: *All's Fair*. This was the last full score of the Rodgers and Hart collaboration. (In the 1943 revival of *A Connecticut Yankee* six new songs were added to the original score.) *By Jupiter* had the longest run of any of their musicals and could have run longer had not the star, Ray Bolger, left the cast to join an overseas USO troupe.

BY THE BEAUTIFUL SEA
April 8, 1954 (270)
Music by Arthur Schwartz
Lyrics by Dorothy Fields

Mona From Arizona • The Sea Song (By the Beautiful Sea) • Old Enough to Love • Coney Island Boat • Alone Too Long • Happy Habit • Good Time Charlie • I'd Rather Wake Up by Myself • Hooray for George the Third • Hang Up! • More Love Than Your Love • Throw the Anchor Away

RA

BY THE WAY
December 28, 1925 (176)
Music by Vivian Ellis
Lyrics by Graham John

By the Way • Shall We Join the Ladies? • What Can They See in Dancing? • My Castle in Spain (Music and lyrics by Isham Jones) • The Beauty of Bath • Gather Roses While You May • In the Same Way I Love You (Music by H M. Tennent; lyrics by Eric Little) • I Know Someone Loves Me • High Street, Africa • Hum a Little Tune • No One's Ever Kissed Me • Nippy • There's Nothing New Under the Sun

BYE BYE BIRDIE
April 14, 1960 (607)
Music by Charles Strouse
Lyrics by Lee Adams

An English Teacher • The Telephone Hour • How Lovely to Be a Woman • We Love You, Conrad! • Put on a Happy Face • Normal American Boy • One Boy • Honestly Sincere • Hymn for a Sunday Evening • One Last Kiss • What Did I Ever See in Him? • A Lot of Livin' to Do • Kids • Baby, Talk to Me • Spanish Rose • Rosie

RA,VS,SEL

BYE BYE, BONNIE
January 13, 1927 (125)
Music by Albert Von Tilzer
Lyrics by Neville Fleeson

Have You Used Soft Soap? • Promise Not to Stand Me Up Again • Love Is Like a Blushing Rose • Out of Town Buyers • You and I Love You and Me • Just Cross the River From Queens • Bye Bye, Bonnie • I Like to Make It Cozy • Toodle-Oo • When You Get to Congress • In My Arms Again • Lovin' off My Mind • Look in Your Engagement Book • Starlight • Tampico Tap

C

CABARET[1]
November 20, 1966 (1,166)
Music by John Kander
Lyrics by Fred Ebb

Based on the play *I Am a Camera,* John Van Druten's adaptation of stories by Christopher Isherwood

Willkommen • So What? • Don't Tell Mama • Telephone Song • Perfectly Marvelous • Two Ladies • It Couldn't Please Me More • Tomorrow Belongs to Me • Why Should I Wake Up? • The Money Song • Married • Meeskite • If You Could See Her • What Would You Do? • Cabaret

RA,VS,SEL

Added to film version (1972)
Mein Herr • Maybe This Time • Money

[1] Tony Award for Best Score

CABIN IN THE SKY
October 25, 1940 (156)
Music by Vernon Duke
Lyrics by John Latouche

The General's Song • Pay Heed • Taking a Chance on Love (Lyrics by Latouche and Ted Fetter)* • Cabin in the Sky • Do What You Wanna Do • My Old Virginia Home (On the River Nile) • Love Me Tomorrow • Love Turned the Light Out • Honey in the Honeycomb • Savannah

Added to film version (1943)
Happiness Is a Thing Called Joe (Music by Harold Arlen; lyrics by E.Y. Harburg)

Added to 1964 Off-Broadway production (47)
Wade in the Water • Make Way • The Man Upstairs • We'll Live All Over Again • Not So Bad to Be Good • Living It Up (Lyrics by Vernon Duke) • Not a Care in the World* • Gospel: Great Day

RA

CAFÉ CROWN
April 17, 1964 (3)

Music by Albert Hague
Lyrics by Marty Brill

Based on the play by Hy Kraft

You're a Stranger in This Neighborhood • What's the Matter With Buffalo? • All Those Years • Au Revoir Poland—Hello New York • Make the Most of Spring • So Long As It Isn't Shakespeare • A Lifetime Love • I'm Gonna Move • A Mother's Heart • On This Wedding Day • What's Gonna Be Tomorrow • A Man Must Have Something to Live For • That's the Life for Me • Magical Things in Life

CAGE AUX FOLLES *See* **LA CAGE AUX FOLLES**

CALL ME MADAM
October 12, 1950 (644)
Music and lyrics by Irving Berlin

Mrs. Sally Adams • Hostess With the Mostes' on the Ball • Washington Square Dance • Lichtenburg • Can You Use Any Money Today? • Marrying for Love • The Ocarina • It's a Lovely Day Today • The Best Thing for You • Something to Dance About • Once Upon a Time Today • They Like Ike* • You're Just in Love

RA,VS

CALL ME MISTER
April 18, 1946 (734)
Music and lyrics by Harold Rome

Goin' Home Train • Along With Me • Surplus Blues • The Drug Store Song • The Red Ball Express • Military Life • Call Me Mister • Yuletide, Park Avenue • When We Meet Again • The Face on the Dime • A Home of Our Own • His Old Man • South America, Take It Away • The Senators' Song

RA,SEL

CALLING ALL STARS
December 13, 1934 (36)
Music by Harry Akst
Lyrics by Lew Brown

Calling All Stars • Thinking Out Loud • I've Nothing to Offer • If It's Love • I Don't Want to Be President • I'd Like to Dunk You in My Coffee • I'm Stepping Out of the Picture • He Just Beats a Tom-Tom • My Old Hoss • Just Mention Joe • Straw Hat in the Rain

CAMELOT
December 3, 1960 (873)
Music by Frederick Loewe
Lyrics by Alan Jay Lerner

Based on *The Once and Future King* by T.H. White

I Wonder What the King Is Doing Tonight • The Simple Joys of Maidenhood • Camelot • Follow Me • C'est Moi • The Lusty Month of May • Then You May Take Me to the Fair • How to Handle a Woman • The Jousts • Before I Gaze at You Again • If Ever I Would Leave You • The Seven Deadly Virtues • What Do the Simple Folk Do? • The Persuasion • Fie on Goodness • I Loved You Once in Silence • Guenevere

RA,VS,SEL

CAN-CAN
May 7, 1953 (892)
Music and lyrics by Cole Porter

Maidens Typical of France • Never Give Anything Away • C'est Magnifique • Come Along With Me • Live and Let Live • I Am in Love • If You Loved Me Truly • Montmart' • Allez-Vous En • Never, Never Be an Artist • It's All Right With Me • Every Man Is a Stupid Man • I Love Paris • Can-Can

RA,VS,SEL

CANDIDE
December 1, 1956 (73)
Music by Leonard Bernstein

Based on Voltaire's satire

The Best of All Possible Worlds (Lyrics by Richard Wilbur) • Oh, Happy We (Lyrics by Richard Wilbur) • It Must Be So (Lyrics by Richard Wilbur) • Lisbon Sequence (Lyrics by Leonard Bernstein) • It Must Be Me (Lyrics by Richard Wilbur) • Glitter and Be Gay (Lyrics by Richard Wilbur) • You Were Dead, You Know (Lyrics by John Latouche and Richard Wilbur) • Pilgrims' Procession (Lyrics by Richard Wilbur) • My Love (Lyrics by John Latouche and Richard Wilbur) • I Am Easily Assimilated (Lyrics by Leonard Bernstein) • Quartet Finale (Lyrics by Richard Wilbur) • Quiet (Lyrics by Richard Wilbur) • Eldorado (Lyrics by Lillian Hellman) • Bon Voyage (Lyrics by Richard Wilbur) • What's the Use? (Lyrics by Richard Wilbur) • Gavotte (Lyrics by Dorothy Parker) • Make Our Garden Grow (Lyrics by Richard Wilbur)

Added to 1973 revival (740)
Life Is Happiness Indeed (Lyrics by Stephen Sondheim) • Auto Da Fé—What a Day (Lyrics by Stephen Sondheim and John Latouche) • This World (Lyrics by Stephen Sondheim) • The Sheep's Song (Lyrics by Stephen Sondheim) • O Miserere (Lyrics by Stephen Sondheim)

RA,VS,SEL

CANTERBURY TALES
February 3, 1969 (121)
Music by Richard Hill and John Hawkins
Lyrics by Nevill Coghill

Based on a translation from Geoffrey Chaucer

Song of Welcome • Good Night Hymn • Canterbury Day • I Have a Noble Cock • Darling, Let Me Teach You How to Kiss • There's the Moon • It Depends on What You're At • Love Will Conquer All • Beer Is Best • Come On and Marry Me Honey • Where Are the Girls of Yesterday? • Hymen, Hymen • If She Has Never Loved Before • I'll Give My Love a Ring • Pear Tree Quintet • I Am All A-Blaze • What Do Women Want? • April Song

RA,SEL

CAPE COD FOLLIES
September 18, 1929 (29)
Music by Alexander Fogarty

Clutching at Shadows (Lyrics by Seymour Morris) • That's Why We Misbehave (Lyrics by Edith Lois and Urana Clarke) • That's the Time When I Miss You (Lyrics by Seymour Morris) • Wondering Who (Lyrics by George Fitch) • Looking at Life Through a Rainbow (Music by Kenneth Burton; lyrics by Walter Craig)

CAPITAN *See* EL CAPITAN

CAPTAIN JINKS
September 8, 1925 (167)
Music by Lewis E. Gensler
Lyrics by B.G. DeSylva

Based on the play *Captain Jinks of the Horse Marines* by Clyde Fitch

Ain't Love Wonderful? • Fond of You • I Do • Kiki • New Love • The Only One for Me • Sea Legs • You Must Come Over Blues (Lyrics by DeSylva and Ira Gershwin)

CARIB SONG
September 27, 1945 (36)
Music by Baldwin Bergersen
Lyrics by William Archibald

Go Sit by the Body • This Woman • Water Movin' Slow • Basket, Make a Basket • Woman Is a Rascal • A Girl She Can't Remain • Market Song • Sleep, Baby, Don't Cry • Today I Is So Happy • Can't Stop the Sea • You Know, Oh Lord • Go Down to the River (Washer Woman) • Oh, Lonely One

RA

CARMELINA
April 8, 1979 (17)
Music by Burton Lane
Lyrics by Alan Jay Lerner

Based on the film *Buona Sera, Mrs. Campbell*

Prayer • It's Time for a Love Song • Why Him? • I

Must Have Her • Someone in April • Signora Campbell • Love Before Breakfast • Yankee Doodles Are Coming to Town • One More Walk Around the Garden • All That He Wants Me to Be • Carmelina • The Image of Me • I'm a Woman

RA

CARMEN JONES[1]
December 2, 1943 (502)
Music by Georges Bizet
Lyrics by Oscar Hammerstein II

Based on Meilhac and Halévy's adaptation of Prosper Mérimée's *Carmen*

Lif' 'Em Up and Put 'Em Down • Honey Gal o' Mine • Good Luck • Dat's Love • You Talk Just Like My Maw • Carmen Jones Is Goin' to Jail • Dere's a Café on de Corner • Beat Out Dat Rhythm on a Drum • Stan' Up and Fight • Whizzin' Away Along de Track • Dis Flower • If You Would Only Come Away • De Cards Don't Lie • Dat Ol' Boy • Poncho de Panther From Brazil • My Joe • Get Yer Program for de Big Fight • Dat's Our Man

RA,SEL

[1] In this modernized version Oscar Hammerstein retained most of Bizet's score, adapting much of it into Americanized songs. The show had an all-black cast and the locale was transferred to the deep south in wartime America. The cigarette factory became a parachute factory, Don José an Army corporal and Escamillo a prize-fighter. Hammerstein's enthusiasm for the project was due in large part to the opportunity to present an all-black cast in a serious Broadway musical at a time when such an event was a rarity.

CARNIVAL
April 13, 1961 (719)
Music and lyrics by Bob Merrill

Based on the film *Lili*, based in turn on the story *The Seven Souls of Clement O'Reilly* by Paul Gallico

Direct From Vienna • A Very Nice Man • I've Got to Find a Reason • Mira • Sword, Rose and Cape • Humming • Yes, My Heart • Everybody Likes You • Magic, Magic • Tanz mit Mir • Yum Ticky-Ticky • The Rich • Beautiful Candy • Her Face • Grand Imperial Cirque de Paris • I Hate Him • Love Makes the World Go Round • Always Always You • She's My Love

RA,SEL

CARNIVAL IN FLANDERS
September 8, 1953 (6)
Music by Jimmy Van Heusen
Lyrics by Johnny Burke

Based on the film *La Kermesse Héroïque*

Ring the Bell • The Very Necessary You • It's a Fine Old Institution • I'm One of Your Admirers • The Plundering of the Town • The Stronger Sex • The Sudden Thrill • It's an Old Spanish Custom • A

Seventeen-Gun Salute • You're Dead! • Here's That Rainy Day • Take the Word of a Gentleman • A Moment of Your Love • How Far Can a Lady Go?

CAROUSEL
April 19, 1945 (890)
Music by Richard Rodgers[1]
Lyrics by Oscar Hammerstein II

Based on the play *Liliom* by Ferenc Molnár, as adapted by Benjamin F. Glazer

Carousel Waltz (Instrumental) • You're a Queer One, Julie Jordan • When I Marry Mr. Snow • If I Loved You* • June Is Bustin' Out All Over • When the Children Are Asleep • Blow High, Blow Low • Soliloquy • This Was a Real Nice Clambake • Geraniums in the Winder • There's Nothin' So Bad for a Woman • What's the Use of Wond'rin' • You'll Never Walk Alone • The Highest Judge of All

RA,VS,SEL

[1] In his autobiography (1975) Richard Rodgers called the score of *Carousel* "the most satisfying" he had ever written.

CASTLES IN THE AIR
September 6, 1926 (160)
Music by Percy Wenrich
Lyrics by Raymond Peck

I Don't Blame 'Em • Love's Refrain • Lantern of Love • The Singer's Career, Ha! Ha! • The Other Fellow's Girl • If You Are in Love With a Girl • The Sweetheart of Your Dream • I Would Like to Fondle You • The Rainbow of Your Smile • Baby • Latavia • Land of Romance • My Lips, My Love, My Soul • The Latavian Chant • Girls and the Gimmies • Love Rules the World

THE CAT AND THE FIDDLE
October 15, 1931 (395)
Music by Jerome Kern
Lyrics by Otto Harbach

She Didn't Say "Yes" • The Night Was Made for Love* • I Watch the Love Parade • The Breeze Kissed Your Hair • One Moment Alone • Try to Forget • Poor Pierrot • A New Love Is Old • Ha! Cha! Cha!

Dropped from production
Don't Ask Me Not to Sing • Misunderstood

RA,VS

CATCH A STAR!
September 6, 1955 (23)

Catch a Star! (Music by Sammy Fain; lyrics by Paul Webster) • Everybody Wants to Be in Show Business (Music and lyrics by Ray Golden, Bud Burtson and Philip Charig) • A Little Traveling Music (Music by Hal Borne; lyrics by Paul Webster and Ray Golden) • One Hour Ahead of the Posse (Music by Philip Charig; lyrics by Ray Golden and Dave Ormont) • Las Vegas (Music and lyrics by Ray Golden, Sy Kleinman and Lee Adams) • To Be or

Not to Be in Love (Music by Philip Charig; lyrics by Ray Golden, Danny Shapiro, and Milton Pascal) • The Story of Alice (Music by Jerry Bock; lyrics by Larry Holofcener) • What a Song Can Do (Music and lyrics by Bernie Wayne and Lee Morris) • Carnival in Court (Music by Jay Navarre; lyrics by Ray Golden and I.A.L. Diamond) • Twist My Arm (Music by Sammy Fain; lyrics by Paul Webster) • Foreign Cars (Music and lyrics by Norman Martin) • New Hollywood Plots (Music by Sammy Fain; lyrics by Paul Webster) • Gruntled (Music and lyrics by Ray Golden, Sy Kleinman and Philip Charig) • Fly, Little Heart (Music by Jerry Bock; lyrics by Larry Holofcener) • Bachelor Hoedown (Music by Jerry Bock; lyrics by Larry Holofcener) • Boffola (Music by Philip Charig; lyrics by Danny Shapiro, Milton Pascal and Ray Golden)

CATS[1]

October 2, 1982[2]
Music by Andrew Lloyd Webber

Based on *Old Possum's Book of Practical Cats* by T.S. Eliot

Jellicle Songs for Jellicle Cats (Lyrics by Trevor Nunn and Richard Stilgoe, based on poems by T.S. Eliot) • The Naming of Cats • The Invitation to the Jellicle Ball • The Old Gumbie Cat • The Rum Tum Tugger • Grizabella, the Glamour Cat • Bustopher Jones • Mungojerrie and Rumpleteazer • Old Deuteronomy • Awefull Battle of the Pekes and Pollicles • The Marching Song of the Pollicle Dogs • The Jellicle Ball • Memory (Lyrics by Trevor Nunn, based on poems by T.S. Eliot) • The Moments of Happiness • Gus: The Theatre Cat • Growltiger's Last Stand • Skimbleshanks • Macavity • Mr. Mistoffolees • The Journey to the Heaviside Layer • The Ad-dressing of Cats

RA,SEL

[1] Tony Award for Best Score

[2] Still running December 31, 1983

CAVIAR

June 7, 1934 (20)
Music by Harden Church
Lyrics by Edward Heyman

One in a Million • Dream Kingdom • Here's to You • My Heart's an Open Book • Silver Sails • Nightwind • Tarts and Flowers • Prince Charming • Gypsy • I Feel Sorta— • Your Prince Was Not So Charming • Haywire (Music by Edward Heyman)

CELEBRATION

January 22, 1969 (109)
Music by Harvey Schmidt
Lyrics by Tom Jones

Celebration • Orphan in the Storm • Survive • Somebody • Bored • My Garden • Where Did It Go? • Love Song • To the Garden • I'm Glad to See You've Got What You Want • It's You Who Makes Me Young • Not My Problem • Fifty Million Years Ago • Under the Tree • Winter and Summer

RA,VS,SEL

CHANGE YOUR LUCK

June 6, 1930 (17)
Music and lyrics by J.C. Johnson

Sweet Little Baby o'Mine • Can't Be Bothered Now • Ain't Puttin' Out Nothin' • Religion in My Feet • You Should Know • Wasting Away • Walk Together, Children • Honesty • Mr. Mammy Man • My Regular Man • I'm Honest • We're Here • Open That Door • Change Your Luck • Percolatin' • Travellin' • What Have I Done? • Rhythm Feet

CHARLIE AND ALGERNON

September 14, 1980 (17)
Music by Charles Strouse
Lyrics by David Rogers

Based on the novel *Flowers for Algernon* by Daniel Keyes

Have I the Right? • I Got a Friend • Some Bright Morning • Jelly Donuts and Chocolate Cake • Hey, Look at Me • Reading • No Surprises • Midnight Riding • Dream Safe With Me • Not Another Day Like This • Somebody New • I Can't Tell You • Now • Charlie and Algernon • The Maze • Whatever Time There Is • Everything Was Perfect • Charlie, I Really Loved You

RA

CHARLOT'S REVUE

January 9, 1924 (298)

Parisian Pierrot (Music and lyrics by Noël Coward) • Nicholas (Music by Herman Darewski; lyrics by Arthur Wimperis) • You Were Meant for Me (Music and lyrics by Noble Sissle and Eubie Blake) • I Don't Know (Music by Philip Braham; lyrics by Ronald Jeans) • There's Life in the Old Girl Yet (Music and lyrics by Noël Coward) • I Might (Music by Philip Braham; lyrics by Ronald Jeans) • Rough Stuff (Music by Ivor Novello; lyrics by Ronald Jeans) • March With Me (Music by Ivor Novello; lyrics by Douglas Furber) • Limehouse Blues* (Music by Philip Braham; lyrics by Douglas Furber) • Night May Have Its Sadness (Music by Ivor Novello; lyrics by Collie Knox) • There Are Times (Music by Ivor Novello; lyrics by Ronald Jeans)

CHARLOT'S REVUE OF 1926

November 10, 1925 (138)

How D'You Do? (Music by Philip Braham; lyrics by Eric Blore and Dion Titheradge) • Let's All Go Raving Mad (Music by Philip Braham; lyrics by Hugh E. Wright) • Gigolette (Music by Franz Lehár; lyrics by Irving Caesar) • Russian Blues (Music and lyrics by Noël Coward) • Take Them All Away (Music and lyrics by Jack Strachey) • Poor Little Rich Girl (Music and lyrics by Noël Coward) • Susannah's Squeaking Shoes (Music by Muriel Lillie; lyrics by Arthur Weigall) • Oxford Bags (Music by Philip Braham; lyrics by Arthur Wimperis) • March With Me! (Music by Ivor Novello; lyrics by

Douglas Furber) • A Cup of Coffee, a Sandwich and You (Music by Joseph Meyer; lyrics by Billy Rose and Al Dubin) • The Fox Has Left His Lair (Music by Peggy Connor; lyrics by Douglas Furber) • Carrie (Music and lyrics by Noël Coward)

CHARLOTTE SWEET (OB)
August 12, 1982 (102)
Music by Gerald Jay Markoe
Lyrics by Michael Colby

At the Music Hall • Charlotte Sweet • A Daughter of Valentine's Day • Forever • Liverpool Sunset • Layers of Underwear • Quartet Agonistes • We Strut Our Band • The Circus of Voices • Keep It Low • Bubbles in Me Bonnet • Vegetable Reggie • My Baby and Me • A-Weaving • Your High Note! • Katinka/The Darkness • On It Goes • You See in Me a Bobby • A Christmas Buche • The Letter (Me Charlotte Dear) • Dover • Volley of Indecision • Good Things Come • It Could Only Happen in the Theatre • Lonely Canary • Queenly Comments • Surprise! Surprise! • The Reckoning • Farewell to Auld Lang Syne

RA,SEL

CHEE-CHEE
September 25, 1928 (31)
Music by Richard Rodgers
Lyrics by Lorenz Hart

Adapted from the novel *The Son of the Grand Eunuch* by Charles Petit

I Must Love You* • Dear, Oh Dear • Moon of My Delight* • Better Be Good to Me • The Tartar Song • Singing a Love Song*

RA

CHERRY BLOSSOMS
March 28, 1927 (56)
Music by Sigmund Romberg
Lyrics by Harry B. Smith

Based on the play *The Willow Tree* by Benrimo and Harrison Rhodes

I'll Peek-a-Boo You • Legend Song • If You Know What I Think • Feast of the Lanterns • Cigarette Song • Happy Rickshaw Man • Japanese Serenade • I Want to Be There • Romance

CHICAGO
June 1, 1975 (898)
Music by John Kander
Lyrics by Fred Ebb

Based on the play *Roxie Hart* by Maurine Dallas Watkins

All That Jazz • Funny Honey • Cell Block Tango • Ten Percent • No • All I Care About • A Little Bit of Good • We Both Reached for the Gun • Roxie • I Can't Do It Alone • Chicago After Midnight • My Own Best Friend • I Know a Girl • Me and My Baby • Mister Cellophane • When Velma Takes the Stand • Razzle Dazzle • Class • Nowadays • Keep It Hot

RA,SEL

CHINA ROSE
January 19, 1925 (96)
Music by A. Baldwin Sloane
Lyrics by Harry Cort and George E. Stoddard

Sun Worship • Soldiers True • Maiden Fair • Chinese Potentate • We'll Build a Brand New Bamboo Bungalow • I'm High, I'm Low • China Rose • I'm All Alone • Who Am I Thinking Of? • I Like the Girls • Through the Bamboo • Chinese Lantern Man • Home • China Bogie Man • Just a Kiss • Hail the Bridegroom • Tomorrow • Great White Way in China • I'm No Butterfly • Calling You My Own • Why Do They Make 'Em So Beautiful? • Happy Bride

CHIN-CHIN
October 20, 1914 (295)
Music by Ivan Caryll
Lyrics by Anne Caldwell and James O'Dea

Quaint Toys • Shopping in the Orient • The Chinese Honeymoon • Chipper • China Chaps • Good-Bye Girls, I'm Through (Lyrics by John Golden) • Go Gar Sig Gong-Jue • In an Oriental Way • Violet • Ragtime Temple Bells • Wedding Gifts of Silver • The Grey Dove • Love Moon • Strollers • Chin-Chin

VS

THE CHOCOLATE DANDIES
September 1, 1924 (96)
Music and lyrics by Noble Sissle and Eubie Blake

Mammy's Little Choc'late Cullud Chile • Have a Good Time Everybody • That Charleston Dance • The Slave of Love • I'll Find My Love in D–I–X–I–E • There's No Place as Grand as Bandana Land • The Sons of Old Black Joe • Jassamine Lane • Dumb Luck • Jump Steady • Breakin' 'Em Down • Jockey's Life for Mine • Dixie Moon • Down in the Land of Dancing Pickaninnies • Thinking of Me • All the Wrongs You've Done to Me • Manda • Run on the Bank • Chocolate Dandies • You Ought to Know • Jazztime Baby

THE CHOCOLATE SOLDIER
September 13, 1909 (296)
Music by Oscar Straus
Lyrics by Stanislaus Stange

Based on the play *Arms and the Man* by George Bernard Shaw[1]

We Are Marching Through the Night • My Hero • Sympathy • Seek the Spy • Our Heroes Come • Alexius the Heroic • Never Was There Such a Lover • The Tale of a Coat • That Would Be Lovely • Falling in Love • The Letter Song

RA,VS

[1] Although he had reluctantly given permission for a musical version of his play, Shaw insisted that the program carry this disclaimer: "With apologies to Mr. George Bernard Shaw for an unauthorized parody of one of his comedies."

A Chorus Line[1]
July 25, 1975[2]
Music by Marvin Hamlisch
Lyrics by Edward Kleban

I Hope I Get It • I Can Do That • And • At the Ballet • Sing! • Hello Twelve, Hello Thirteen, Hello Love • Nothing • The Music and the Mirror • One • What I Did for Love

RA,VS,SEL

[1] Tony Award for Best Score; Pulitzer Prize winner

[2] First opened Off Broadway April 15, 1975 (101). On September 29, 1983, this became the longest running show in Broadway history (3,389 performances); still running December 31, 1983.

Christine
May 7, 1960 (12)
Music by Sammy Fain
Lyrics by Paul Francis Webster

Adapted from *My Indian Family* by Hilda Wernher

Welcome Song • My Indian Family • A Doctor's Soliloquy • UNICEF Song • My Little Lost Girl • I'm Just a Little Sparrow • How to Pick a Man a Wife • The Lovely Girls of Akbarabad • Room in My Heart • I Never Meant to Fall in Love • Freedom Can Be a Most Uncomfortable Thing • Ireland Was Never Like This • He Loves Her • Christine • I Love Him • Kathakali • Bharatha Natyan • The Woman I Was Before

RA

Chu Chin Chow
October 22, 1917 (208)
Music by Frederic Norton
Lyrics by Oscar Asche

Here Be Oysters Stewed in Honey • I Am Chu Chin Chow of China • Cleopatra's Nile • Corraline • When a Pullet Is Plump • The Robbers' March • I Shiver and Shake With Fear • Beans, Beans, Beans • All My Days Till End of Time • At Siesta Time • Any Time's Kissing Time • If I Liken Thy Shape • The Song of the Scimitar • The Cobbler's Song • We Bring Ye Fruits • From Cairo, Bagdad • How Dear Is Our Day • Olive Oil

RA,VS

Cindy (OB)
March 19, 1964 (428)
Music and lyrics by Johnny Brandon

Once Upon a Time • Let's Pretend • Is There Something to What He Said? • Papa, Let's Do It Again • A Genuine Feminine Girl • Cindy • Think Mink • Tonight's the Night • Who Am I? • If You've Got It, You've Got It • The Life That I Planned for Him • If It's Love • Got the World in the Palm of My Hand • Call Me Lucky • Laugh It Up • What a Wedding

RA

The Circus Princess
April 25, 1927 (192)
Music by Emmerich Kálmán
Lyrics by Harry B. Smith

But Who Cares? • Silhouette • Bravo, Bravo • There's Something About You • Dear Eyes That Haunt Me • Same Old Love Songs • I Dare to Speak of Love to You • Girls, I Am True to All of You • Joy Bells • The Hussars' Song • Like You • I Like the Boys • What D'Ya Say? (Music by Jesse Greer; lyrics by Raymond Klages) • Guarded • Waiters • I'll Be Waiting

VS

The City Chap
October 26, 1925 (72)
Music by Jerome Kern
Lyrics by Anne Caldwell

Based on the play *The Fortune Hunter* by Winchell Smith

Like the Nymphs of Spring • The Go-Getter • Journey's End (Lyrics by P.G. Wodehouse) • Sympathetic Someone • The City Chap • He Is the Type • If You Are as Good as You Look • The Fountain of Youth • A Pill a Day • Walking Home With Josie • Bubbles of Bliss • No One Knows • When I Fell in Love

The Clinging Vine
December 25, 1922 (184)
Music by Harold Levey
Lyrics by Zelda Sears

A Little Bit of Paint • Grandma • Roumania • Once Upon a Time • Lady Luck • Spring Fever • Age of Innocence • The Clinging Vine • Cupid • Homemade Happiness • Serenade • Song Without Words

Coco
December 18, 1969 (332)
Music by André Previn
Lyrics by Alan Jay Lerner

But That's the Way You Are • The World Belongs to the Young • Let's Go Home • Mademoiselle Cliché de Paris • On the Corner of the Rue Cambon • The Money Rings Out Like Freedom • A Brand New Dress • A Woman Is How She Loves • Gabrielle • Coco • Fiasco • When Your Lover Says Goodbye • Ohrbach's, Bloomingdale's, Best and Saks • Always Mademoiselle

RA,VS

The Cocoanuts
December 8, 1925 (375)
Music and lyrics by Irving Berlin

The Guests • The Bellhops • Family Reputation • Lucky Boy • Why Am I a Hit With the Ladies? • A Little Bungalow • Florida by the Sea • The Monkey Doodle-Doo • Five O'Clock Tea • They're Blaming the Charleston • We Should Care • Minstrel Days • Tango Melody • The Tale of a Shirt • Ting-a-Ling, the Bells'll Ring

Added to film version (1929)
When My Dreams Come True

COLETTE (OB)
May 6, 1970 (101)
Music by Harvey Schmidt
Lyrics by Tom Jones

Based on *Earthly Paradise,* Robert Phelps'
collection of Colette's autobiographical writings

The Bouilloux Girls • Femme du Monde • Earthly
Paradise

RA

COME OF AGE
January 12, 1934 (35)
Music by Richard Addinsell
Lyrics by Clemence Dane

I Came to Your Room • I Come Out of a Dream •
I'm Afraid of the Dark • The River Song • Too Much
Work

COME ON STRONG (Play with one song)
October 4, 1962 (36)
Music by Jimmy Van Heusen
Lyrics by Sammy Cahn

Come On Strong

COME SUMMER
March 18, 1969 (7)
Music by David Baker
Lyrics by Will Holt

Good Time Charlie • Think Spring • Wild Birds
Calling • Goodbye, My Bachelor • Fine, Thank You,
Fine • Road to Hampton • Come Summer • Let Me
Be • Feather in My Shoe • The Loggers' Song •
Jude's Holler • Faucett Falls Fancy • Rockin' • Skin
and Bones • Moonglade • Women • No • So Much
World

COMIN' UPTOWN
December 20, 1979 (45)
Music by Garry Sherman
Lyrics by Peter Udell

Christmas Is Comin' Uptown • Now I Lay Me Down
to Sleep • Get Your Act Together • Lifeline • What
Better Time for Love? • It Won't Be Long • Get
Down, Brother, Get Down • Sing a Christmas Song
• Have I Finally Found My Heart? • Nobody Really
Do • Goin' Gone • One Way Ticket to Hell • Born
Again

COMPANY[1]
April 26, 1970 (690)
Music and lyrics by Stephen Sondheim

Company • The Little Things You Do Together •
Sorry-Grateful • You Could Drive a Person Crazy •
Have I Got a Girl for You • Someone Is Waiting •
Another Hundred People • Getting Married Today •
Side by Side by Side • What Would We Do Without

You • Poor Baby • Barcelona • The Ladies Who
Lunch • Being Alive

Dropped from production
Happily Ever After • Marry Me a Little

RA,VS,SEL

[1] Tony Award for Best Score

A CONNECTICUT YANKEE
November 3, 1927 (418)
Music by Richard Rodgers
Lyrics by Lorenz Hart

Based on the novel *A Connecticut Yankee in King
Arthur's Court* by Mark Twain

A Ladies' Home Companion • My Heart Stood Still*
• Thou Swell • At the Round Table • On a Desert
Island With Thee • Nothing's Wrong • I Feel at Home
With You • The Sandwich Men • Evelyn, What Do
You Say?

Dropped from production
I Blush • Britain's Own Ambassadors • You're What
I Need* • Someone Should Tell Them* • Morgan Le
Fay

Added to 1943 production (135)
This Is My Night to Howl • To Keep My Love Alive*
• Ye Lunchtime Follies • Can't You Do a Friend a
Favor? • You Always Love the Same Girl • The
Camelot Samba

RA,SEL

THE CONQUERING HERO
January 16, 1961 (8)
Music by Moose Charlap
Lyrics by Norman Gimbel

Based on the film *Hail, the Conquering Hero* (1944)
directed by Preston Sturges

Girls! Girls! • Five Shots of Whiskey • Hail, the
Conquering Hero! • Must Be Given to You •
Wonderful, Marvelous You • Truth • Won't You
Marry Me? • The River Bank • Only Rainbows • The
Campaign • One Mother Each • I'm Beautiful •
Rough Times • Yours, All Yours

THE CONSUL
March 15, 1950 (269)
Music and lyrics by Gian-Carlo Menotti

Tu Reviendras • Now, O Lips, Say Goodbye • In
Endless Waiting Rooms • Lullaby (Sleep, My Love) •
Oh, What a Lovely Dance • To This We've Come •
All the Documents Must Be Signed • Death's
Frontiers Are Open

RA,VS

THE CONTRAST (OB)
November 28, 1972 (24)
Music by Don Pippin
Lyrics by Steve Brown

Based on the play by Royall Tyler

A Woman Rarely Ever • A House Full of People • Keep Your Little Eye Upon the Main Chance, Mary • So They Call It New York • Dear Lord Chesterfield • A Sort of Courting Song • So Far • She Can't Really Be • Wouldn't I? • A Hundred Thousand Ways • That Little Monosyllable • It's Too Much • I Was in the Closet

CONVERSATION PIECE
October 23, 1934 (55)
Music and lyrics by Noël Coward

I'll Follow My Secret Heart* • Regency Rakes • Charming, Charming • Dear Little Soldiers • There's Always Something Fishy About the French • English Lesson • There Was Once a Little Village by the Sea • Nevermore

RA,VS

THE COOLEST CAT IN TOWN (OB)
June 22, 1978 (21)
Music by Diane Leslie
Lyrics by William Gleason

Disco Rag • Born to Rock and Roll • Don't Say Shoo-Be-DoBop • Melinda Schecker • Superstar • One Kiss • Suspended Animation • Lost My Cool • Rock Back the Clock • The Bop Will Never Die • Let's Live It Over Again • You're My Last Chance • Hula Hoop • The Coolest Cat in Town • Mr. Know It All • So What?

COPPER AND BRASS
October 17, 1957 (36)
Music by David Baker
Lyrics by David Craig

Career Guidance • Wearing of the Blue • I Need All the Help I Can Get • Cool Combo Mambo • You Walked Out • Cool Credo • Bringing Up Daughter • Don't Look Now • Baby's Baby • Call the Police • Unmistakable Sign • Why Her? • Me and Love • Remember the Dancing • Sweet William • Little Woman

COPPERFIELD
April 16, 1981 (13)
Music and lyrics by Al Kasha and Joel Hirschhorn

Based on the novel *David Copperfield* by Charles Dickens

I Don't Want a Boy • Mama Don't Get Married • Copperfield • Bottle Song • Something Will Turn Up • Anyone • Here's a Book • Umble • The Circle Waltz • Up the Ladder • I Wish He Knew • The Lights of London • Villainy Is the Matter • With the One I Love

COTTON PATCH GOSPEL (OB)
October 21, 1981 (193)
Music and lyrics by Harry Chapin

Based on *The Cotton Patch Version of Matthew and John* by Clarence Jordan

Something's Brewing in Gainesville • I Did It • Mama Is Here • It Isn't Easy • Sho' Nuff • Turn It Around • When I Look Up • There Ain't No Busy Signals • Spitball • We're Going to Atlanta • What Does Atlanta Mean to Me? • Are We Ready? • You Are Still My Boy • We Got to Get Organized • We're Gonna Love It • Jubilation • One More Tomorrow • I Wonder

COUNT ME IN
October 8, 1942 (61)
Music and lyrics by Ann Ronell

All-Out Bugle Call • The Way My Ancestors Went • Someone in the Know • On Leave for Love • You've Got It All • Why Do They Say They're the Fair Sex? • We're Still on the Map • Ticketyboo • Who Is General Staff? • The Woman of the Year • Papa's Return

THE COUNT OF LUXEMBOURG
September 16, 1912 (120)
Music by Franz Lehár
Lyrics by Basil Hood

Bohemia • Pierrette and Pierrot • We Lend It, Spend It, End It • A Carnival for Life • I Am in Love • Love, Good-Bye! • Cousins of the Czar • Twenty Thousand Pounds • She Goes Right, He Goes Left • Pretty Butterfly • Her Glove • In Society • Love Breaks Every Bond • Say Not Love Is a Dream • Rootsie-Pootsie • Are You Going to Dance? • Boys

RA,VS

COUNTESS MARITZA
September 18, 1926 (321)
Music by Emmerich Kálmán
Lyrics by Harry B. Smith

Dear Home of Mine, Goodbye • Hola, Follow, Follow Me • In the Days Gone By • Make Up Your Mind • The Music Thrills Me • Sister Mine • The One I'm Looking For • Play Gypsies, Dance Gypsies • Say Yes, Sweetheart • Don't Tempt Me • Love Has Found My Heart (Melody revised by Alfred Goodman) • I'll Keep On Dreaming • Who Am I? • Why Is the World So Changed Today? • Brown-Eyed Girl

RA,VS

COURTIN' TIME
June 14, 1951 (37)
Music and lyrics by Jack Lawrence and Don Walker

Based on the play *The Farmer's Wife* by Eden Phillpotts

Today at Your House, Tomorrow at Mine • Fixin' for a Long Cold Winter • Araminto to Herself • An Old-Fashioned Glimmer in Your Eye • Goodbye, Dear Friend • I Do! He Doesn't! • Golden Moment • Johnny Ride the Sky • The Sensible Thing to Do • Masculinity • Maine Will Remember the Maine • Heart in Hand

THE CRADLE WILL ROCK
January 3, 1938 (108)
Music and lyrics by Marc Blitzstein

Croon-Spoon • Honolulu • Gus and Sadie Love
Song • Nickel Under the Foot • The Cradle Will Rock
• Joe Worker • Art for Art's Sake • Doctor and Ella •
Drugstore Scene • The Freedom of the Press •
Leaflets • The Rich

RA

CRANKS
November 26, 1956 (40)
Music by John Addison
Lyrics by John Cranko

Who's Who • Adrift • Where Has Tom Gone? • Cold
Comfort • Who Is It Always There? • Chiromancy •
New Blue • Valse Anglaise • Don't Let Him Know
You • Sea Song • Telephone Tango • I'm the Boy
You Should Say "Yes" To • Metamorphosis • Would
You Let Me Know? • Dirge • Arthur, Son of Martha •
Goodnight

RA

CRAZY QUILT
May 19, 1931 (67)

Sing a Little Jingle (Music by Harry Warren; lyrics
by Mort Dixon) • I Found a Million Dollar Baby
(Music by Harry Warren; lyrics by Billy Rose and
Mort Dixon) • I Want to Do a Number With the Boys
(Music by Roland Wilson; lyrics by Ned Wever) •
Under the Clock at the Astor (Music by Manning
Sherwin; lyrics by Ned Wever) • In the Merry Month
of Maybe (Music by Harry Warren; lyrics by Ira
Gershwin and Billy Rose) • Kept in Suspense
(Music by Carroll Gibbons; lyrics by Billy Rose and
James Dyrenforth) • Crazy Quilt (Music by Harry
Warren; lyrics by Bud Green) • Would You Like to
Take a Walk? (Music by Harry Warren; lyrics by
Billy Rose and Mort Dixon) • Peter Pan (Music by
Carroll Gibbons; lyrics by Billy Rose and James
Dyrenforth) • Rest Room Rose (Music by Richard
Rodgers; lyrics by Lorenz Hart)

CRAZY WITH THE HEAT
January 14, 1941 (99)

With a Twist of the Wrist (Music and lyrics by Irvin
Graham) • Sascha's Got a Girl (Music and lyrics by
Irvin Graham) • Some Day (Music by Rudi Revil;
lyrics by Kurt Kasznar and Carl Kent) • The Time of
Your Life (Music by William Provost; lyrics by Peter
K. Smith) • Crazy With the Heat (Music by Rudi
Revil; lyrics by Irvin Graham) • You Should Be Set
to Music (Music and lyrics by Irvin Graham)

CRISS-CROSS
October 12, 1926 (210)
Music by Jerome Kern
Lyrics by Anne Caldwell and Otto Harbach

Cinderella Girl • Cinderella's Ride • She's on Her
Way • Flap-a-Doodle • In Araby With You • Rose of
Delight • You Will, Won't You? • Suzie (Lyrics by
Anne Caldwell) • The Ali Baba Babies

Dropped from production
Criss Cross • Bread and Butter • Kiss a Four Leaf
Clover

CROSS MY HEART
September 17, 1928 (64)
Music by Harry Tierney
Lyrics by Joseph McCarthy

Step Up and Pep Up the Party • Sold • Dream
Sweetheart • Salaaming the Raja • Right Out of
Heaven • Hot Sands • In the Gardens of Noor-Ed-
Deen • Lady Whippoorwill • Come Along, Sunshine •
We'll Have Our Good Days • Thanks for a Darn
Nice Time

CRY FOR US ALL
April 8, 1970 (9)
Music by Mitch Leigh
Lyrics by William Alfred and Phyllis Robinson

Based on the play *Hogan's Goat* by William Alfred

See No Evil • The End of My Race • How Are You
Since? • The Mayor's Chair • The Cruelty Man • The
Verandah Waltz • Home Free All • The Broken
Heart, or the Wages of Sin • The Confessional •
Who to Love If Not a Stranger • Cry for Us All •
Swing Your Bag • Call In to Her • That Slavery Is
Love • I Lost It • Aggie, Oh Aggie • The Leg of the
Duck • This Cornucopian Land

RA

THE CRYSTAL HEART (OB)
February 15, 1960 (8)
Music by Baldwin Bergersen
Lyrics by William Archibald

A Year Is a Day • A Monkey When He Loves •
Handsome Husbands • Yes, Aunt • A Girl With a
Ribbon • I Must Paint • I Wanted to See the World •
Fireflies • How Strange the Silence • When I Drink
With My Love • Desperate • Lovely Island • Bluebird
• Agnes and Me • Madam, I Beg You! • My Heart
Won't Learn • Tea Party • Lovely Bridesmaids • It
Took Them • D–o–g

RA

CURLEY McDIMPLE (OB)
November 22, 1967 (931)
Music and lyrics by Robert Dahdah

A Cup of Coffee • I Try • Curley McDimple • Love Is
the Loveliest Love Song • Are There Any More
Rosie O'Gradys? • Dancing in the Rain • Be Grateful
for What You've Got • At the Playland Jamboree •
I've Got a Little Secret • You Like Monkey, You •
Stars and Lovers • The Meanest Man in Town •
Something Nice Is Going to Happen • Swing-a-Ding-
a-Ling • Hi de hi de hi, hi de hi de ho • Dwarf's Song

SEL

CYRANO
May 13, 1973 (49)
Music by Michael J. Lewis
Lyrics by Anthony Burgess

Based on the play *Cyrano de Bergerac* by Edmond Rostand

Cyrano's Nose • La France, la France • Tell Her • From Now Till Forever • Bergerac • Popcapdedious • No, Thank You • Roxana • It's She and It's Me • You Have Made Me Love • Thither, Thother • Paris Cuisine • Love Is Not Love • Autumn Carol • I Never Loved You

RA

CYRANO DE BERGERAC
September 18, 1899 (28)

Music by Victor Herbert
Lyrics by Harry B. Smith

Based on the play by Edmond Rostand

Come the Gallants of the Court • I Am a Court Coquette • I Come From Gascony • I Must Marry a Handsome Man • The King's Musketeers • Since I Am Not for Thee • Song of the Nose • Cadets of Gascony • I Wonder • Diplomacy • Over the Mountains • 'Neath Thy Window • Let the Sun of Thine Eyes

VS

D

DAMES AT SEA (OB)
December 20, 1968 (575)
Music by Jim Wise
Lyrics by George Haimsohn and Robin Miller

Wall Street • It's You • Broadway Baby • That Mister Man of Mine • Choo-Choo Honeymoon • The Sailor of My Dreams (Lyrics by Haimsohn) • Singapore Sue (Lyrics by Haimsohn) • Good Times Are Here to Stay (Lyrics by Haimsohn) • Dames at Sea • The Beguine • Raining in My Heart • There's Something About You • The Echo Waltz (Lyrics by Haimsohn) • Star Tar • Let's Have a Simple Wedding

RA,SEL

DAMN YANKEES[1]
May 5, 1955 (1,019)
Music and lyrics by Richard Adler and Jerry Ross

Based on the novel *The Year the Yankees Lost the Pennant* by Douglass Wallop

Six Months out of Every Year • Goodbye, Old Girl • Heart • Shoeless Joe From Hannibal, Mo. • A Little Brains—a Little Talent • A Man Doesn't Know • Who's Got the Pain? • The Game • Near to You • Those Were the Good Old Days • Two Lost Souls

RA,VS,SEL

[1] Tony Award for Best Score

DANCE A LITTLE CLOSER
May 11, 1983 (1)
Music by Charles Strouse
Lyrics by Alan Jay Lerner

Based on the play *Idiot's Delight* by Robert E. Sherwood

It Never Would've Worked • Happy, Happy New Year • No Man Is Worth It • What Are You Going to Do About It? • A Woman Who Thinks I'm Wonderful • Pas de Deux • There's Never Been Anything Like Us • Another Life • Why Can't the World Go and Leave Us Alone • He Always Comes Home to Me • I Got a New Girl • Dance a Little Closer • There's Always One You Can't Forget • Homesick • Mad • I Don't Know • Auf Wiedersehen • I Never Want to See You Again • On Top of the World

RA

DANCE ME A SONG
January 20, 1950 (35)
Music and lyrics by James Shelton

It's the Weather • I'm the Girl • Love • One Is a Lonely Number (Music by Albert Hague; lyrics by Maurice Valency) • My Little Dog Has Ego (Music and lyrics by Herman Hupfeld) • Lilac Wine • Matilda • Dance Me a Song

Dropped from production
Strange New Look

DARLING OF THE DAY
January 27, 1968 (32)
Music by Jule Styne
Lyrics by E.Y. Harburg

Based on the novel *Buried Alive* by Arnold Bennett

Mad for Art • He's a Genius • To Get Out of This World Alive • It's Enough to Make a Lady Fall in Love • A Gentleman's Gentleman • Double Soliloquy • Let's See What Happens • Panache • I've Got a Rainbow Working for Me • Money, Money, Money • That Something Extra Special • What Makes a Marriage Merry • Not on Your Nellie • Sunset Tree • Butler in the Abbey

RA

THE DAY BEFORE SPRING
November 22, 1945 (167)
Music by Frederick Loewe
Lyrics by Alan Jay Lerner

The Day Before Spring • God's Green World • You Haven't Changed at All • My Love Is a Married Man • Friends to the End • You're Wonderful • He

Follows Me Around • A Jug of Wine • I Love You This Morning • Where's My Wife? • This Is My Holiday

A DAY IN HOLLYWOOD, A NIGHT IN THE UKRAINE[1]
March 28, 1979 (588)
Music by Frank Lazarus
Lyrics by Dick Vosburgh

Just Go to the Movies (Music and lyrics by Jerry Herman) • Nelson (Music and lyrics by Jerry Herman) • The Best in the World (Music and lyrics by Jerry Herman) • I Love a Film Cliché (Music by Trevor Lyttleton) • It All Comes Out of the Piano (Lyrics by Vosburgh and Lazarus)

RA,SEL

[1] The show also included a number of well-known songs from films.

DEAR SIR[1]
September 23, 1924 (15)
Music by Jerome Kern
Lyrics by Howard Dietz

Grab a Girl • What's the Use? • I Want to Be There • A Mormon Life • Dancing Time • To the Fair • My Houseboat on the Harlem • All Lanes Must Reach a Turning • Seven Days • If You Think It's Love You're Right • Weeping Willow Tree

[1] Except for one interpolation in a 1923 show, this was Howard Dietz's first work for the musical theater.

DEAR WORLD
February 6, 1969 (132)
Music and lyrics by Jerry Herman

Based on the play *The Madwoman of Chaillot* by Jean Giraudoux, as adapted by Maurice Valency

The Spring of Next Year • Each Tomorrow Morning • I Don't Want to Know • I've Never Said I Love You • Garbage • Dear World • Kiss Her Now • Memory • Pearls • Dickie • Voices • And I Was Beautiful • One Person

RA,SEL

DEAREST ENEMY
September 18, 1925 (286)
Music by Richard Rodgers
Lyrics by Lorenz Hart

Heigh-Ho, Lackaday! • War Is War • I Beg Your Pardon • Cheerio • Full Blown Roses • The Hermits • Here in My Arms* • Gavotte • I'd Like to Hide It • Where the Hudson River Flows • Bye and Bye • Old Enough to Love • Sweet Peter • Here's a Kiss

Dropped from production
Ale, Ale • The Pipes of Pansy* • Dear Me

RA

THE DEBUTANTE
December 7, 1914 (48)

Music by Victor Herbert
Lyrics by Robert B. Smith

Love Is a Battle • Married Life • Professor Cupid • All for the Sake of a Girl • The Golden Age • The Love of the Lorelei • Peggy's a Creature of Moods • Never Mention Love When We're Alone • When I Played Carmen • The Baker's Boy and the Chimney Sweep • The Cubist Opera • Call Around Again • The Will-o'-the-Wisp • The Dancing Lesson • The Face Behind the Mask • Burlesque Modern Opera • Fate • The Springtime of Life Is Fairest

VS

THE DECAMERON (OB)
April 12, 1961 (39)
Music by Edward Earle
Lyrics by Yvonne Tarr

Based on the tales of Boccaccio

1348 • Talk • Deceive Me • Ballad of Tancred • Golden Goblet • What's Wrong With Me? • Women! • Love Is Paradise • I Know, I Know • Cuckold's Delight • Barnabo • The Pirate's Song • Nightingale • Come, Sweet Love

DEEP HARLEM
January 7, 1929 (8)
Music by Joe Jordan
Lyrics by Homer Tutt and Henry Creamer

Deep Harlem • Mexican Blues • I Shall Love You • Deliver • Kentucky

DEEP RIVER
October 4, 1926 (32)
Music by Frank Harling
Lyrics by Laurence Stallings

Ashes and Fire • Cherokee Rose • De Old Clay Road • Dis Is de Day • Love Lasts a Day • Po' Lil' Black Chile • Serenade Creole • Soft in de Moonlight • Two Little Stars

THE DESERT SONG[1]
November 30, 1926 (471)
Music by Sigmund Romberg
Lyrics by Otto Harbach and Oscar Hammerstein II

The Riff Song • Margot • I'll Be a Buoyant Girl • Why Did We Marry Soldiers? • French Military Marching Song • Romance • Then You Will Know • I Want a Kiss • "It" • The Desert Song • Song of the Brass Key • One Good Man Gone Wrong • Let Love Go • One Flower Grows Alone in Your Garden • One Alone • The Sabre Song • Farewell • Let's Have a Love Affair

Dropped from production
Love's Dear Yearning • Not for Him • Ali-Up • Love Is a Two-Edged Sword

RA,VS,SEL

[1] Pre-Broadway title: *Lady Fair*

DESTRY RIDES AGAIN
April 23, 1959 (473)
Music and lyrics by Harold Rome

Based on the film (1939)

Bottleneck • Ladies • Hoop-de-Dingle • Tomorrow Morning • Ballad of the Gun • The Social • I Know Your Kind • I Hate Him • Rose Lovejoy of Paradise Alley • Anyone Would Love You • Once Knew a Fella • Every Once in a While • Fair Warning • Are You Ready, Gyp Watson? • Not Guilty • Only Time Will Tell • Respectability • Ring on the Finger • I Say Hello

RA,VS

DIAMOND STUDS (OB)
January 14, 1975 (232)
Music and lyrics by Bland Simpson and Jim Wann

Jesse James Robbed This Train • These Southern States That I Love • Year of Jubilo (Based on traditional folk music) • Unreconstructed Rebel (Music and lyrics by Jan Davidson) • Mama Fantastic • Saloon Piano • I Don't Need a Man to Know I'm Good • Northfield Minnesota • King Cole (Based on traditonal folk music) • New Prisoner's Song (Based on traditional folk music) • K.C. Line (Based on traditional folk music) • Cakewalk Into Kansas City • When I Was a Cowboy (Based on traditional folk music) • Pancho Villa • Put It Where the Moon Don't Shine • Sleepy Time Down South • Bright Morning Star (Based on traditional folk music) • When I Get the Call

DIFFERENT TIMES
May 1, 1972 (24)
Music and lyrics by Michael Brown

Different Times • Seeing the Sights • The Spirit Is Moving • Here's Momma • Everything in the World Has a Place • I Wish I Didn't Love Him • Forward Into Tomorrow • You're Perfect • Marianne • Daddy, Daddy • I Feel Grand • Sock Life in the Eye • I'm Not Through • I Miss Him • One More Time • I Dreamed About Roses • The Words I Never Said • The Life of a Woman • He Smiles • Genuine Plastic • Thanks a Lot • When They Start Again

DISPATCHES (OB)
April 19, 1979 (77)
Music and lyrics by Elizabeth Swados

Crazy • Thou Shalt Not Be Afraid • Breathing In • These Were the Faces • The Ground Was Always in Play • Song of the LURP • Helicopter, Helicopter • Stoned in Saigon • Beautiful for Once • Tiger Lady • Prayers in the Delta • Flip Religion • Quakin' and Shakin' • Six Fucking Shades of Green • Bougainvillea • The Mix • I See a Road • Take the Glamor Out of War • This War Gets Old • Back in the World Now • Freezing and Burning

DIVERSIONS (OB)[1]
November 7, 1958 (85)
Music by Buster Davis
Lyrics by Steven Vinaver

You're Nothing • Touch and Go • Subway Rag • Here Comes the Ballad • White Is the Dove • Prayer • He Follows Me Around • You're Wonderful

[1] Obie Award for Best Musical

DO I HEAR A WALTZ?
March 18, 1965 (220)
Music by Richard Rodgers
Lyrics by Stephen Sondheim

Based on the play *The Time of the Cuckoo* by Arthur Laurents

Someone Woke Up • This Week Americans • What Do We Do? We Fly! • Someone Like You • Bargaining • Here We Are Again • Thinking • No Understand • Take the Moment • Moon in My Window • We're Gonna Be All Right • Do I Hear a Waltz? • Stay • Perfectly Lovely Couple • Thank You So Much

Dropped from production
Philadelphia • Two by Two • Perhaps • Everybody Loves Leona

RA,VS,SEL

DO PATENT LEATHER SHOES REALLY REFLECT UP?
May 27, 1982 (5)
Music and lyrics by James Quinn and Alaric Jans

Get Ready Eddie • The Greatest Gift • It's the Nuns • Little Fat Girls • Cookie Cutters • Patron Saints • How Far Is Too Far? • Doo-Waa Doo-Wee • I Must Be in Love • Friends the Best Of • Mad Bombers and Prom Queens • Late Bloomer • Thank God

DO RE MI
December 26, 1960 (400)
Music by Jule Styne
Lyrics by Betty Comden and Adolph Green

Waiting, Waiting • All You Need Is a Quarter • Take a Job • The Juke Box Hop • It's Legitimate • I Know About Love • Cry Like the Wind • Ambition • Success • Fireworks • What's New at the Zoo? • Asking for You • The Late, Late Show • Adventure • Make Someone Happy • V.I.P. • All of My Life

RA,VS,SEL

DO YOU KNOW THE MILKY WAY?
October 16, 1961 (16)
Music by Alex Fry
Lyrics by Lyon Phelps

Do You Know the Milky Way? • The Child's Song • The Vagabond Song

DOCTOR JAZZ
March 19, 1975 (5)
Music and lyrics by Buster Davis

Dr. Jazz • We've Got Connections • Georgia Shows 'Em How • Cleopatra Had a Jazz Band • Juba Dance • Charleston Rag • I've Got Elgin Watch Movements in My Hips • Blues My Naughty Sweetie Gave to Me • Good-Time Flat Blues • Evolution Papa •

Rehearsal Tap • I Love It • Anywhere the Wind Blows • Those Sheik-of-Araby Blues • Look Out for Lil • Swanee Strut • All I Want Is My Black Baby Back • Everybody Leaves You • Free and Easy

RA

DOCTOR SELAVY'S MAGIC THEATRE (OB)
November 23, 1972 (144)
Music by Stanley Silverman
Lyrics by Tom Hendry

I Live by My Wits • Three Menu Songs • Bankrupt Blues • Future for Sale • Life on the Inside • Strawberry-Blueberry • The More You Get • Money in the Bank • Long Live Free Enterprise • Doesn't It Bug You? • Dusky Shadows • Poor Boy • Dearest Man • Where You Been Hiding Till Now? • Fireman's Song • What Are You Proposing? • Party's Gonna End • Requiem • Let's Hear It for Daddy Moola

RA

THE DOLLAR PRINCESS
September 6, 1909 (288)
Music by Leo Fall
Lyrics by George Grossmith, Jr.

Self-Made Maiden • The Marquis de Jolifontaine • The Riding Lesson • My Dream of Love • Inspection • Hip, Hip, Hurrah! • I Danced With You One Night • Tennis • Typewriter • Chewska • Paragraphs (Hansel and Gretel) • Love! Love! Love! (Music by Frank E. Tours; lyrics by Adrian Ross) • The Dollar Princesses • Not Here! Not Here!* (Music by Jerome Kern; lyrics by M.E. Rourke) • Love's a Race • Red, White and Blue (Music by Jerome Kern; lyrics by Adrian Ross) • A Boat Sails on Wednesday (Music by Jerome Kern; lyrics by Adrian Ross and Grossmith) • The Lion's Queen (Music by Richard Fall) • Then You Go? • Princess of Dollar Princesses

VS

A DOLL'S LIFE
September 23, 1982 (4)
Music by Larry Grossman
Lyrics by Betty Comden and Adolph Green

An imaginary sequel to Ibsen's *A Doll's House*

A Woman Alone • Letter to the Children • New Year's Eve • Stay With Me, Nora • She Thinks That's the Answer • The Arrival • Loki and Baldur • You Interest Me • The Departure • Letter From Klemnacht • Learn to Be Lonely • Hats and Mice and Fish • Jailer, Jailer • Rare Wines • No More Mornings • There She Is • Power • At Last • The Grand Cafe • Can You Hear Me Now?

RA,SEL

DONNYBROOK!
May 18, 1961 (68)
Music and lyrics by Johnny Burke

Based on the film *The Quiet Man* (1952) by Maurice Walsh

Sez I • The Day the Snow Is Meltin' • Sad Was the Day • Donnybrook • Ellen Roe • Sunday Morning • The Lovable Irish • I Wouldn't Bet One Penny • He Makes Me Feel I'm Lovely • I Have My Own Way • A Toast to the Bride • Wisha Wurra • A Quiet Life • Mr. Flynn • Dee-lightful Is the Word • For My Own

RA

DON'T BOTHER ME, I CAN'T COPE (OB)
April 19, 1972 (1065)
Music and lyrics by Micki Grant

I Gotta Keep Movin' • Harlem Streets • Lock Up the Doors • Lookin' Over From Your Side • Don't Bother Me, I Can't Cope • Children's Rhymes • When I Feel Like Moving • Ghetto Life • So Long, Sammy • You Think I Got Rhythm? • Time Brings About a Change • So Little Time • Thank Heaven for You • Show Me That Special Gene • My Love's So Good • They Keep Comin' • My Name Is Man • All I Need • Questions • It Takes a Whole Lot of Human Feeling • Love Mississippi • Good Vibrations • Storefront Church • Fighting for Pharaoh

RA

DON'T PLAY US CHEAP
May 16, 1972 (18)
Music and lyrics by Melvin Van Peebles

Some Days It Seems That It Don't Even Pay to Get Out of Bed • Break That Party • Eight Day Week • Saturday Night • I'm a Bad Character • You Cut Up the Clothes in the Closet of My Dreams • It Makes No Difference • Quitting Time • Ain't Love Grand • The Book of Life • Know Your Business • Big Future • Feast on Me • The Phoney Game • Smash Him

DON'T STEP ON MY OLIVE BRANCH (OB)
November 1, 1976 (16)
Music and lyrics by Ron Eliran

Moonlight • The World's Greatest Musical Act • I Believe • Only Love • My Land • We Love a Conference • I Hear a Song • My Life in Color • Young Days • Somebody's Stepping on My Olive Branch • It Was Worth It • Jerusalem

DOONESBURY
November 21, 1983[1]
Music by Elizabeth Swados
Lyrics by Garry Trudeau

Based on the comic strip by Garry Trudeau

Graduation • Just One Night • I Came to Tan • Guilty • I Can Have It All • Get Together • Baby Boom Boogie Boy • Another Memorable Meal • Just a House • Complicated Man • Real Estate • Mother • It's the Right Time to Be Rich • Muffy and the Topsiders • Just One Night

RA

[1] Still running December 31, 1983

DOUBLE ENTRY (OB)
February 20, 1961 (56)

Music and lyrics by Jay Thompson

Sweep • Kinda Sorta Doin' Nothing • Real Rich Ladies • The Oldest Trick in the World • Dear Madame Scarlatina • The Fortune • The White Slavery Fandango • All the Young Men

DRAT! THE CAT!
October 10, 1965 (8)
Music by Milton Schafer
Lyrics by Ira Levin

Drat! The Cat! • My Son, Uphold the Law • Holmes and Watson • She Touched Me • Wild and Reckless • She's Roses • Dancing With Alice • Purefoy's Lament • A Pox Upon the Traitor's Brow • Deep in Your Heart • Let's Go • It's Your Fault • Today Is a Day for a Band to Play • I Like Him • Justice Triumphant

SEL

THE DREAM GIRL
August 20, 1924 (117)
Music by Victor Herbert[1]
Lyrics by Rida Johnson Young

Making a Venus • All Year Round • Dancing Round • My Dream Girl • Old Songs • Maiden, Let Me In • Gypsy Life • Stop, Look and Listen • The Broad Highway (Music by Sigmund Romberg) • My Hero • I Want to Go Home • Bubbles • Saxophone Man

[1] Victor Herbert died on May 26, 1924 before completing the score. Sigmund Romberg agreed to finish it but asked that he not be credited as composer. It is known, however, that "The Broad Highway" is the work of Romberg.

DREAM WITH MUSIC
May 18, 1944 (28)
Music by Clay Warnick
Lyrics by Edward Eager

Be Glad You're Alive • I'm Afraid I'm in Love • Baby, Don't Count on Me • Give, Sinbad, Give • I'll Take the Solo • Love at Second Sight • Relax and Enjoy It • Come With Me • Battle of the Genie • Mr. and Mrs. Wrong • The Lion and the Lamb • Mouse Meets Girl • The Moon Song • Woman Against the World

DREAMGIRLS
December 20, 1981[1]
Music by Henry Krieger
Lyrics by Tom Eyen

Move (You're Steppin' on My Heart) • Fake Your Way to the Top • Cadillac Car • Steppin' to the Bad Side • Family • Dreamgirls • Press Conference • And I'm Telling You I'm Not Going • Ain't No Party • When I First Saw You • I Am Changing • I Meant

You No Harm • The Rap • Firing of Jimmy • I Miss You Old Friend • One Night Only • Hard to Say Goodbye, My Love

RA,SEL

[1] Still running December 31, 1983

DU BARRY WAS A LADY[1]
December 6, 1939 (408)
Music and lyrics by Cole Porter

Ev'ry Day a Holiday • It Ain't Etiquette • When Love Beckoned (in Fifty-Second Street) • Come On In • Mesdames and Messieurs • But in the Morning, No! • Do I Love You? • Du Barry Was a Lady • Give Him the Oo-La-La • Well, Did You Evah!* • It Was Written in the Stars • L'Apres-Midi d'un Boeuf • Katie Went to Haiti • Friendship

[1] The story was originally written for the movies, with Mae West in mind for the leading role. Hollywood turned it down, however, and in its transition to the Broadway stage Cole Porter was signed to write the score and Ethel Merman to take over the lead.

THE DUBARRY
November 22, 1932 (87)
Music by Carl Millöcker (revised by Theo Mackeben)
Lyrics by Rowland Leigh

Today • On the Stage • Without Your Love • If I Am Dreaming • Happy Little Jeanne • Pantalettes • Dance for the Gentlemen • I Give My Heart • Beauty • The Road to Happiness • Ga-Ga • The Dubarry

THE DUCHESS MISBEHAVES
February 13, 1946 (5)
Music by Frank Black
Lyrics by Gladys Shelley

Art • My Only Romance • Broadminded • I Hate Myself in the Morning • Men • Couldn't Be More in Love • Ole Ole • Katie Did in Madrid • Morning in Madrid • Lost • The Honeymoon Is Over • Fair Weather Friends • The Nightmare

DUDE
October 9, 1972 (16)
Music by Galt MacDermot
Lyrics by Gerome Ragni

Theatre/Theatre • A-Stage • The Mountains • Pears and Peaches • Eat It • Wah Wah • Suzie Moon • Y–O–U • I Love My Boo Boo • Humdrum Life • Who's It? • Talk to Me About Love • Goodbyes • I'm Small • You Can Do Nothing About It • The Handsomest Man • Electric Prophet • No One • Who Will Be the Children? • Go, Holy Ghost • A Song to Sing • A Dawn • The Days of This Life • I Never Knew • Air Male • Undo • The Earth • My Darling I Love You March • So Long Dude • Peace Peace • Jesus Hi • Baby Breath • Sweet Dreams

RA

E

EARL CARROLL'S SKETCH BOOK (1929)
July 1, 1929 (400)

Legs, Legs, Legs (Music by Jay Gorney; lyrics by E.Y. Harburg) • For Someone I Love (Music by Ted Snyder; lyrics by Benny Davis) • Song of the Moonbeams (Music by Vincent Rose; lyrics by Charles and Harry Tobias) • Kinda Cute (Music by Jay Gorney; lyrics by E.Y. Harburg) • Fascinating You (Music and lyrics by Benee Russell, Vincent Rose, and Charles and Harry Tobias) • Like Me Less, Love Me More (Music by Jay Gorney; lyrics by E.Y. Harburg) • Crashing the Golden Gate (Music by Jay Gorney and Phil Cohan; lyrics by E.Y. Harburg) • Rhythm of the Waves (Music by Vincent Rose; lyrics by Charles and Harry Tobias) • You Beautiful So and So (Music by Ted Snyder; lyrics by Billy Rose) • Don't Hang Your Dreams on a Rainbow (Music by Arnold Johnson; lyrics by Irving Kahal) • Tip-Toe Tap-Tap (Music by Irving Actman; lyrics by Jean Herbert) • Papa Likes a Hot Papoose (Music by Jay Gorney; lyrics by E.Y. Harburg) • My Sunny South (Music and lyrics by Abner Silver)

EARL CARROLL'S SKETCH BOOK (1935)
June 4, 1935 (207)

Let's Swing It (Music and lyrics by Charles Tobias, Charles Newman and Murray Mencher) • Anna Louise of Louisiana (Music by Will Irwin; lyrics by Norman Zeno) • At Last (Music by Henry Tobias; lyrics by Charles Tobias and Sam Lewis) • Gringola (Music and lyrics by Charles Tobias, Charles Newman and Murray Mencher) • There's Music in a Kiss (Music and lyrics by Al Sherman, Al Lewis and Abner Silver) • Young Ideas (Music and lyrics by Charles Tobias, Charles Newman and Murray Mencher) • Let the Man Who Makes the Gun (Music by Gerald Marks; lyrics by Raymond B. Egan) • The Rustle of Your Bustle (Music by Will Irwin; lyrics by Norman Zeno) • Silhouettes Under the Stars (Music and lyrics by Charles Tobias, Charles Newman and Murray Mencher) • Mardi Gras Day in New Orleans (Music by Will Irwin; lyrics by Norman Zeno) •

Sunday Night in New York (Music and lyrics by Charles Tobias, Charles Newman and Murray Mencher)

EARL CARROLL'S VANITIES (1925)
July 6, 1925 (390)
Music and lyrics by Clarence Gaskill

We Are the Waiters • Beautiful Ladies of the Night • This Is a Night Club • The Chow Mein Girls • A Kiss in the Moonlight • I Thank You • Ponies on Parade • Dorothy • At the Gate of Roses • Rhythm of the Day (Music by Owen Murphy; lyrics by Donald Lindley) • Yvonne • Shake Yourself Out of Here

EARL CARROLL'S VANITIES (1926)
August 24, 1926 (303)
Music by Morris Hamilton
Lyrics by Grace Henry

Open the Gates of Madrid • Cool 'Em Off • We Are the Show Girls • Natacha (Music and lyrics by Berton Braley, M. de Jari and Alex James) • Adorable (Music and lyrics by Tom Ford and Ray Wynburn) • Climbing Up the Ladder of Love (Music by Jesse Greer; lyrics by Raymond Klages) • The Lament of Shakespeare • All Is Vanity • Twilight • Hugs and Kisses (Music by Louis Alter; lyrics by Raymond Klages) • The Chinese Idol (Music and lyrics by Berton Braley, M. de Jari and Alex James) • Alabama Stomp (Music by James P. Johnson; lyrics by Henry Creamer) • Broadway to Madrid

EARL CARROLL'S VANITIES (1928)
August 6, 1928 (203)
Music by Morris Hamilton
Lyrics by Grace Henry

Say It With Girls • Pretty Girl • Rose of the World • Flutterby Baby • Wheels • Vaniteaser (Music and lyrics by Michael Cleary and Paul Jones) • Getting the Beautiful Girls (Music by Michael Cleary; lyrics by Ned Washington) • Raquel (Music and lyrics by George Whiting and Joe Burke) • My Arms Are

711

Open (Music by Michael Cleary; lyrics by Ned Washington) • Blue Shadows (Music by Louis Alter; lyrics by Raymond Klages) • Oh, How That Man Can Love (Music and lyrics by Lillian Roth and Herb Magidson) • Watch My Baby Walk (Music by Peter de Rose; lyrics by Jo Trent) • Once in a Lifetime (Music by Jesse Greer; lyrics by Raymond Klages) • Painting a Vanities Girl (Music and lyrics by Ernie Golden) • I'm Flyin' High (Music and lyrics by Abner Silver, Jack Le Soir and Roy Doll)

EARL CARROLL'S VANITIES (1930)
July 1, 1930 (215)

Knee Deep in June (Music by Jay Gorney; lyrics by E.Y. Harburg) • One Love (Music by Harold Arlen; lyrics by Ted Koehler) • Hittin' the Bottle (Music by Harold Arlen; lyrics by Ted Koehler) • The March of Time (Music by Harold Arlen; lyrics by Ted Koehler) • Love Boats (Music by Jay Gorney; lyrics by E.Y. Harburg) • I Came to Life (Music by Jay Gorney; lyrics by E.Y. Harburg) • Rumba Rhythm (Music by Jimmy Johnson; lyrics by Stella Unger) • Out of a Clear Blue Sky (Music by Harold Arlen; lyrics by Ted Koehler) • Going Up (Music by Jay Gorney; lyrics by E.Y. Harburg) • Contagious Rhythm (Music by Harold Arlen; lyrics by Ted Koehler)

EARL CARROLL'S VANITIES (1931)
August 27, 1931 (278)
Music by Burton Lane
Lyrics by Harold Adamson

It's Great to Be in Love (Music and lyrics by Cliff Friend) • Have a Heart • Going to Town With Me • Tonight or Never (Music and lyrics by Jack Meskill, Raymond Klages and Vincent Rose) • The Mahoneyphone • Love Came Into My Heart • I'm Back in Circulation Again (Music by Michael H. Cleary; lyrics by Max and Nathaniel Lief) • Heigh Ho, the Gang's All Here

EARL CARROLL'S VANITIES (1932)
September 27, 1932 (87)

My Darling (Music by Richard Myers; lyrics by Edward Heyman) • Along Came Love (Music by Henry Tobias; lyrics by Charles Tobias and Haven Gillespie) • Love Is My Inspiration (Music by André Renaud; lyrics by Ted Koehler) • I've Got a Right to Sing the Blues (Music by Harold Arlen; lyrics by Ted Koehler) • Take Me Away (Music by Peter Tinturin; lyrics by Sidney Clare and Charles Tobias) • Forsaken (Music by Richard Myers; lyrics by Edward Heyman) • Rockin' in Rhythm (Music by Harold Arlen; lyrics by Ted Koehler)

EARL CARROLL'S VANITIES (1940)
January 13, 1940 (25)
Music and lyrics by Dorcas Cochran and Charles Rosoff

The Lady Has Oomph • Angel (Music by Peter de Rose; lyrics by Mitchell Parrish) • Charming • The Starlit Hour (Music by Peter de Rose; lyrics by

Mitchell Parrish) • Westward Ho! • Can the Can-Can • I Want My Mama (Music by Jararaca and Vincent Paiva; lyrics by Al Stillman) • Song of the Sarong

EARL OF RUSTON
May 5, 1971 (5)
Music by Peter Link
Lyrics by C.C. Courtney and Ragan Courtney

Just Your Old Friend • Earl Is Crazy • Guitar Song • Easy to Be Lonely • Standing • Probably (Music by C.C. and Ragan Courtney) • Mama, Earl Done Ate the Tooth Paste Again (Music by C.C. and Ragan Courtney) • Silvers Theme • Mama, Mama, Mama • I've Been Sent Back to the First Grade (Music by C.C. Courtney) • The Revival • My Name Is Leda Pearl (Music by C.C. Courtney) • Insane Poontang (Music by C.C. and Ragan Courtney) • You Still Love Me (Music by C.C. Courtney) • Earl Was Ahead

EARLY TO BED
June 17, 1943 (380)
Music by Thomas (Fats) Waller
Lyrics by George Marion, Jr.

A Girl Who Doesn't Ripple When She Bends • There's a Man in My Life • Me and My Old World Charm • Supple Couple • Slightly Less Than Wonderful • This Is So Nice • The Ladies Who Sing With a Band • There's "Yes" in the Air • Get Away, Young Man • Long Time No Song • Early to Bed • When the Nylons Bloom Again

EAST WIND
October 27, 1931 (23)
Music by Sigmund Romberg
Lyrics by Oscar Hammerstein II

It's a Wonderful World • East Wind • I Saw Your Eyes • These Tropics • Are You Love? • You Are My Woman • Minnie • Embrace Me • The Americans Are Coming • I'd Be a Fool • Regardez-Moi • When You Are Young

Dropped from production
Young Man in Love

THE EDUCATION OF H*Y*M*A*N K*A*P*L*A*N
April 4, 1968 (28)
Music and lyrics by Paul Nassau and Oscar Brand

Based on the stories by Leo Rosten

Strange New World • OOOO-EEEE • A Dedicated Teacher • Lieben Dich • Loving You • The Day I Met Your Father • Anything Is Possible • Spring in the City • Old Fashioned Husband • Julius Caesar • I Never Felt Better in My Life • When Will I Learn? • All American

EILEEN
March 19, 1917 (64)
Music by Victor Herbert
Lyrics by Henry Blossom

Free Trade and a Misty Moon • My Little Irish Rose

• Eileen, Alanna Asthore • When Love Awakes • If Eve Had Left the Apple on the Bough • Life's a Game at Best • In Erin's Isle • Thine Alone • The Irish Have a Great Day Tonight • When Ireland Stands Among the Nations of the World

Dropped from production
Cupid, the Cunnin' Paudeen • Stars and Rosebuds • Reveries

VS,SEL

EL BRAVO! (OB)
June 16, 1981 (48)
Music and lyrics by John Clifton

El Bravo • Cuchifrito Restaurant • Que Pasa • Honest John's Game • Chiquita Bonita • Shoes • Hey Chico! • Criminal • He Says • Gotta Get Out • Adios Barrio • Fairy Tales • Torture • That Latin Lure • Congratulations! • Bailar! • And Furthermore

EL CAPITAN
April 20, 1896 (112)
Music by John Philip Sousa[1]
Lyrics by Tom Frost and John Philip Sousa

Nobles of Castilian Birth • Oh, Beautiful Land of Spain • From Peru's Majestic Mountains • Don Medigua, All for Thy Coming Wait • If You Examine Human Kind • When We Hear the Call for Battle • Oh, Spare a Daughter • Lo, the Awful Man Approaches • You See in Me • Bah! Bah! • Ditty of the Drill • Behold El Capitan • I've a Most Decided Notion • Bowed With Tribulation • Oh, Warrior Grim • Don Medigua, Here's Your Wife • He Can Not, Must Not, Shall Not • Sweetheart, I'm Waiting • When Some Serious Affliction • The Typical Tune of Zanzibar • We Beg Your Kind Consideration

VS

[1] Although today Sousa is remembered primarily for his marches, he composed in many musical forms, including ten operettas, and even wrote three novels and an autobiography. The familiar "El Capitan March" is actually a medley of several tunes from this score.

ENCHANTED ISLE
September 19, 1927 (32)
Music and lyrics by Ida Hoyt Chamberlain

Hacienda Garden • Enchanted Castle • Jazz • Business Is Business • Whoa, Gal • Julianne • Close in Your Arms • California • Dream Girl • Enchanted Isle • Abandon • Cowboy Potentate • Love Thought Garden • What a Jamboree • Voice of the High Sierras • Dream Boat • Roulette • Down to the Sea • Could I Forget?

THE ENCHANTRESS
October 19, 1911 (72)
Music by Victor Herbert
Lyrics by Harry B. Smith

When the Right Man Sings Tra-La • They All Look Good When They're Far Away • If You Can't Be as

Happy as You'd Like to Be • And That Little Girl Is You • To the Land of My Own Romance • I've Been Looking for a Perfect Man • Rose, Lucky Rose • Art Is Calling Me (I Want to Be a Prima Donna) • Come, Little Fishes • Come to Sunny Spain • One Word From You • Dreaming Princess • That Naughty Little Song • All Your Own Am I

VS

ENTRE-NOUS (OB)
December 30, 1935 (47)
Music by Richard Lewine
Lyrics by Will B. Johnstone

Entre-Nous • Let's Go High Hat • I'll See You Home (Music by Harry Archer) • Let's Get Married or Something (Lyrics by Ted Fetter) • With You, With Me (Music and lyrics by Lewine) • Kick in the Pants (Music by Harry Archer) • Sunday Morning Churchman (Lyrics by Norman Zeno) • Under My Skin (Music by Harry Archer) • What Can I Give You? (Music by Phillip Broughton) • A.J. (Music by Harry Archer) • Am I? (Music by Harry Archer) • When Opportunity Knocks (Lyrics by Ted Fetter)

ERNEST IN LOVE (OB)
May 4, 1960 (111)
Music by Lee Pockriss
Lyrics by Anne Croswell

Based on the play *The Importance of Being Earnest* by Oscar Wilde

Come Raise Your Cup • How Do You Find the Words? • The Hat • Mr. Bunbury • Perfection • A Handbag Is Not a Proper Mother • A Wicked Man • Metaphorically Speaking • You Can't Make Love • Lost • My Very First Impression • The Muffin Song • My Eternal Devotion

RA

THE EVANGELIST (OB)
March 31, 1982 (16)
Music and lyrics by Al Carmines

Hymns From the Darkness • Everything God Does Is Perfect • Holy Ghost Ride • I Was a Black Sheep • Home • I Am a Preacher of the Lord • Remember Joplin • Omaha I'm Here • Cardboard Madonna • Blame It on the Moon • Little Children on the Grass • Clinging to the Rock • Goodbye • Brother Blues • Serenade • I Love You • Do I Do It Through God? • Buds of May • Men Are Men • We're Going to Des Moines • Who Is She? • Garland Is My Man • I Am an Evangelist • The Light • Navajo Woman • Raven the Magnet

AN EVENING WITH JOAN CRAWFORD (OB)
January 28, 1981 (15)
Music and lyrics by Joseph Church and Nick Branch

The Devil's Song (Music and lyrics by Branch) • Hollywood Lullabye (Music and lyrics by Church) • Give 'Em Hell (Music by Church; lyrics by Kristine

Zbornik) • Too Much Money Blues (Music and lyrics by Julian Neil and Lee Sparks) • You Are One of a Kind (Music and lyrics by Church) • Ain't No Place Like Home (Music and lyrics by Branch) • Take a Vacation (Music and lyrics by Branch) • What It's Like to Be a Legend (Music and lyrics by Branch) • Blame It All on Me (Music by Church; lyrics by Church and Richard Schill)

EVERYBODY'S GETTIN' INTO THE ACT (OB)
September 27, 1981 (23)
Music and lyrics by Bob Ost

Everybody's Gettin' Into the Act • That First Hello • Perfection • Too Good • So Close • Steppin' Back • I'm Available • Love Me Just a Little Bit • Looks Like Love • You Never Take Me Anywhere • Yes I See the Woman • To Wit • A Party in Southampton • It Always Seems to Rain • Never, Never • Keepin' It Together • Ballad of the Victim • Alive and Well • Valse Triste • And I'm There! • Don't I Know You?

EVERYBODY'S WELCOME
October 13, 1931 (139)

Based on the play *Up Pops the Devil* by Albert Hackett and Frances Goodrich

One in a Million (Music by Harry Revel; lyrics by Mack Gordon) • All Wrapped Up in You (Music by Harry Revel; lyrics by Mack Gordon and Harold Adamson) • Pie-Eyed Piper (Music by Sammy Fain; lyrics by Irving Kahal) • Ta Ta, Old Bean (Music by Manning Sherwin; lyrics by Edward Eliscu) • As Time Goes By (Music and lyrics by Herman Hupfeld)* • Even As You and I (Music by Sammy Fain; lyrics by Irving Kahal) • Feather in a Breeze (Music by Sammy Fain; lyrics by Irving Kahal) • You've Got a Lease on My Heart (Music by Sammy Fain; lyrics by Irving Kahal) • Nature Played a Dirty Trick on You (Music by Manning Sherwin; lyrics by Arthur Lippmann and Milton Pascal) • I Shot the Works (Music by Manning Sherwin; lyrics by Arthur Lippmann and Milton Pascal) • Is Rhythm Necessary? (Music by Sammy Fain; lyrics by Irving Kahal)

EVITA[1]
September 25, 1979 (1,759)
Music by Andrew Lloyd Webber
Lyrics by Tim Rice

Requiem for Evita • Oh What a Circus! • On This Night of a Thousand Stars • Eva, Beware of the City • Buenos Aires • Goodnight and Thank You • The Art of the Possible • I'd Be Surprisingly Good for You • Another Suitcase in Another Hall • Peron's Latest Flame • A New Argentina • On the Balcony of the Casa Rosada • Don't Cry for Me Argentina • High Flying Adored • Rainbow High • Rainbow Tour • The Actress Hasn't Learned • And the Money Kept Rolling In • Santa Evita • Waltz for Eva and Che • She Is a Diamond • Dice Are Rolling • Lament

RA,SEL

[1] Tony Award for Best Score

F

FACE THE MUSIC
February 17, 1932 (165)
Music and lyrics by Irving Berlin

Lunching at the Automat • Let's Have Another Cup of Coffee • Torch Song • You Must Be Born With It • On a Roof in Manhattan • My Beautiful Rhinestone Girl • Soft Lights and Sweet Music • I Say It's Spinach • Drinking Song • Dear Old Crinoline Days • I Don't Want to Be Married • Manhattan Madness

FADE OUT—FADE IN
May 26, 1964 (271)
Music by Jule Styne
Lyrics by Betty Comden and Adolph Green

The Thirties • It's Good to Be Back Home • Fear • Call Me Savage • The Usher From the Mezzanine • I'm With You • My Fortune Is My Face • Lila Tremaine • Go Home Train • Close Harmony • You Mustn't Be Discouraged • The Dangerous Age • The Fiddler and the Fighter • Fade Out—Fade In

RA,SEL

THE FAGGOT (OB)
June 18, 1973 (203)
Music and lyrics by Al Carmines

Movie House • Women With Women—Men With Men • The Hustler • I'll Take My Fantasy • Mothers-in-Law • Hari Krishna • Desperation • A Gay Bar Cantata • Nookie Time • Your Way of Loving • Fag Hag • Puddin' 'n Tame • Ordinary Things • Art Song • What Is a Queen?

FALLOUT (OB)
May 20, 1959 (31)
Music by Robert Kessler
Lyrics by Martin Charnin

We're Betting on You • String Quartet (Music and lyrics by Paul Nassau) • Sixteenth Summer • Someone Waiting • The Victoria Trio (Music and lyrics by Paul Nassau) • I Think I'd Like to Fall in Love (Music and lyrics by Charnin) • Clandestine • Music Hath'nt • Look • Too Many Questions (Music and lyrics by Paul Nassau) • Problem (Music by Alan Friedman; lyrics by Dennis Marks) • You're My Man • Individuals (Music by Jerry Alters; lyrics by Herb Hartig) • Oh Say, Can You See? • Love Is (Music and lyrics by Martin Charnin)

A FAMILY AFFAIR
January 27, 1962 (65)
Music by John Kander
Lyrics by James Goldman, John Kander and William Goldman

Anything for You • Beautiful • My Son, the Lawyer • Every Girl Wants to Get Married • Right Girls • Kalua Bay • There's Room in My House • Siegal Marching Song • Harmony • Now, Morris • Wonderful Party • Revenge • Summer Is Over • I'm Worse Than Anybody • What I Say Goes • The Wedding

RA,SEL

FANNY
November 4, 1954 (888)
Music and lyrics by Harold Rome

Based on the trilogy of plays by Marcel Pagnol

Never Too Late for Love • Cold Cream Jar Song • Octopus Song • Restless Heart • Why Be Afraid to Dance? • Shika Shika • Welcome Home • I Like You • I Have to Tell You • Fanny • Oysters, Cockles and Mussels • Panisse and Son • Birthday Song • To My Wife • The Thought of You • Love Is a Very Light Thing • Other Hands, Other Hearts • Be Kind to Your Parents • Cesario's Party

RA,VS,SEL

THE FANTASTICKS (OB)
May 3, 1960[1]
Music by Harvey Schmidt
Lyrics by Tom Jones

Suggested by the play *Les Romanesques* by Edmond Rostand

Try to Remember • Much More • Metaphor • Never Say No • It Depends on What You Pay • You Wonder How These Things Begin • Soon It's Gonna Rain • Happy Ending • This Plum Is Too Ripe • I Can See It • Plant a Radish • Round and Round • There Is a Curious Paradox • They Were You

RA,VS,SEL

[1] On December 31, 1983 the show played its 8,846th performance, making it by far the longest-running theatrical production in the United States.

THE FASCINATING WIDOW[1]
September 11, 1911 (56)

Always Keep a Fellow Guessing If You Want His Love (Music by Kerry Mills; lyrics by S.M. Lewis) • Clinging Vine (Music by Percy Wenrich; lyrics by Otto Harbach[2]) • Don't Take Your Beau to the Seashore (Music by Irving Berlin; lyrics by E. Ray Goetz) • You Build a Fire Down in My Heart (Music and lyrics by Irving Berlin) • Don't You Make a Noise (Music by Kerry Mills; lyrics by S.M. Lewis) • The Eltinge Moorish Dance (Music by Kerry Mills) • Everybody Likes a College Girl (Music by Kerry Mills; lyrics by S.M. Lewis) • The Fascinating Widow Waltz (Music by Kerry Mills) • Girlies You've Kissed in Dreams (Music by Karl Hoschna; lyrics by Otto Harbach) • Hindu (Music by Percy Wenrich; lyrics by Jack Mahoney) • If Only Someone Would Teach Me (Music by Karl Hoschna; lyrics by Otto Harbach) • Cute In My Bathing Suit (Music by Percy Wenrich; lyrics by Julian Eltinge and Jack Mahoney) • I'm Only a Fair Sun Bather (Music by Kerry Mills; lyrics by S.M. Lewis) • I'm to Be a Blushing Bride (Music by Kerry Mills; lyrics by S.M. Lewis) • Jack O'Lantern Moon (Music by Percy Wenrich; lyrics by Julian Eltinge) • Love Is the Theme of Your Dreams (Music and lyrics by Kerry Mills) • Merry Wedding Bells (Music by Jean Schwartz; lyrics by Edward Madden) • Mighty Girl (Music by Karl Hoschna; lyrics by Otto Harbach) • Put Your Arms Around Me (Music by Kerry Lewis; lyrics by S.M. Lewis) • The Ragtime College Girl (Music by Kerry Mills; lyrics by S.M. Lewis) • Ragtime College Turkey Trot (Music by Percy Wenrich; lyrics by Julian Eltinge and Jack Mahoney) • Something That I Can't Explain (Music by Jean Schwartz; lyrics by William Jerome) • To Take a Dip in the Ocean (Music by Kerry Mills; lyrics by S.M. Lewis) • Valse Julian (Music by Kerry Mills) • The Widow Fascinating (Music by Percy Wenrich; lyrics by Julian Eltinge and Jack Mahoney) • With Downcast Eyes (Music by Karl Hoschna; lyrics by Otto Harbach)

[1] The show starred Julian Eltinge, a famous female impersonator.

[2] Then known as Otto Hauerbach.

FASHION (OB)
February 17, 1974 (94)[1]
Music by Don Pippin
Lyrics by Steve Brown

Based on the play by Anna Cora Mowatt

Rococo Rag • You See Before You What Fashion Can Do • It Was for Fashion's Sake • The Good Old American Way • What Kind of Man Is He? • My Daughter the Countess • Take Me • Why Should They Know About Paris? • I Must Devise a Plan • Meet Me Tonight • My Title Song • A Life Without Her

[1] Reopened off Broadway April 17, 1974 (32).

FAST AND FURIOUS
September 15, 1931 (6)
Music by Harry Revel
Lyrics by Mack Gordon

Fast and Furious • Walkin' on Air • So Lonesome (Music by Joe Jordan; lyrics by Rosamond Johnson) • Frowns • Doing the Dumbbell • Shadows on the Wall • Where's My Happy Ending? (Lyrics by Gordon and Harold Adamson) • Hot, Hot Mama (Music and lyrics by Porter Grainger) • Boomerang (Music by Joe Jordan; lyrics by Rosamond Johnson) • Pansies on Parade (Music and lyrics by Porter Grainger) • Hot Feet • Let's Raise Hell (Music and lyrics by Porter Grainger)

FIDDLER ON THE ROOF[1]
September 22, 1964 (3242)
Music by Jerry Bock
Lyrics by Sheldon Harnick

Based on stories by Sholom Aleichem

Tradition • Matchmaker, Matchmaker • If I Were a Rich Man • Sabbath Prayer • To Life • Miracle of Miracles • The Tailor, Motel Kamzoil • Sunrise, Sunset • Wedding Dance • Now I Have Everything • Do You Love Me? • I Just Heard • Far From the Home I Love • Anatevka • Epilogue

RA,VS,SEL

[1] Tony Award for Best Score

FIFTH OF JULY (Play with one song)
November 5, 1980 (511)
Music and lyrics by Jonathan Hogan

Your Loving Eyes

FIFTY MILES FROM BOSTON
February 3, 1908 (32)
Music and lyrics by George M. Cohan

Jack and Jill • A Small Town Gal • Boys Who Fight the Flames • Waltz With Me • Ain't It Awful • Harrigan

FIFTY MILLION FRENCHMEN
November 27, 1929 (254)
Music and lyrics by Cole Porter

A Toast to Volstead • You Do Something to Me • The American Express • You've Got That Thing • Find Me a Primitive Man • Where Would You Get Your Coat? • Do You Want to See Paris? • At Longchamps Today • The Happy Heaven of Harlem • Why Shouldn't I Have You? • Somebody's Going

to Throw a Big Party • It Isn't Done • I'm in Love •
The Tale of an Oyster • Paree, What Did You Do to
Me? • You Don't Know Paree • I'm Unlucky at
Gambling • Let's Step Out • The Boy Friend Back
Home

Dropped from production
I Worship You • Please Don't Make Me Be Good •
The Queen of Terre Haute • Watching the World Go
By • Down With Everybody but Us • Why Don't We
Try Staying Home? • That's Why I Love You

THE FIG LEAVES ARE FALLING
January 2, 1969 (4)
Music by Albert Hague
Lyrics by Allen Sherman

All Is Well in Larchmont • Lillian • Like Yours • All of
My Laughter • Give Me a Cause • Today I Saw a
Rose • We • For Our Sake • Light One Candle • Oh,
Boy • The Fig Leaves Are Falling • For the Rest of
My Life • I Like It • Old Fashioned Song • Did I Ever
Really Live?

FINE AND DANDY
September 23, 1930 (246)
Music by Kay Swift
Lyrics by Paul James[1]

Rich or Poor • Fine and Dandy • Wheels of Steel •
Starting at the Bottom • Can This Be Love? • I'll Hit
a New High • Let's Go Eat Worms in the Garden •
The Jig Hop • Nobody Breaks My Heart • Wedding
Bells

[1] The name Paul James was a pseudonym for
James Paul Warburg, a New York banker.

FINIAN'S RAINBOW
January 10, 1947 (725)
Music by Burton Lane
Lyrics by E.Y. Harburg

This Time of the Year • How Are Things in Glocca
Morra? • If This Isn't Love • Look to the Rainbow •
Old Devil Moon • Something Sort of Grandish •
Necessity • When the Idle Poor Become the Idle
Rich • The Begat • When I'm Not Near the Girl I
Love • That Great Come and Get It Day

RA,VS,SEL

FIORELLO![1]
November 23, 1959 (795)
Music by Jerry Bock
Lyrics by Sheldon Harnick

On the Side of the Angels • Politics and Poker •
Unfair • Marie's Law • The Name's La Guardia • The
Bum Won • I Love a Cop • Till Tomorrow • Home
Again • When Did I Fall in Love? • Gentleman Jimmy
• Little Tin Box • The Very Next Man

Dropped from production
Where Do I Go From Here?

RA,SEL

[1] Pulitzer Prize winner. Tony Award for Best
Score (tied with *The Sound of Music*).

FIORETTA
February 5, 1929 (111)

Dream Boat (Music by George Bagby; lyrics by
Grace Henry and Jo Trent) • Fioretta (Music and
lyrics by G. Romilli) • Blade of Mine (Music by
George Bagby; lyrics by Grace Henry) • Alone With
You (Music by G. Romilli; lyrics by Grace Henry and
Jo Trent) • Roses of Red (Music and lyrics by G.
Romilli) • Carissima (Music by G. Romilli; lyrics by
Grace Henry)

THE FIREBRAND OF FLORENCE
March 22, 1945 (43)
Music by Kurt Weill
Lyrics by Ira Gershwin

Based on the play *The Firebrand* by Edwin Justus
Mayer

One Man's Death Is Another Man's Living • Come
to Florence* • My Lords and Ladies • There'll Be
Life, Love, and Laughter • You're Far too Near Me •
Alessandro the Wise • I Am Happy Here • Sing Me
Not a Ballad • When the Duchess Is Away • I Know
Where There's a Cozy Nook • The Nighttime Is No
Time for Thinking • Dizzily, Busily • The Little Naked
Boy • My Dear Benvenuto • Just in Case • A Rhyme
for Angela • The World Is Full of Villains • You Have
to Do What You Do Do • Love Is My Enemy • Come
to Paris

RA

THE FIREFLY[1]
December 2, 1912 (120)
Music by Rudolf Friml
Lyrics by Otto Harbach

A Trip to Bermuda • He Says "Yes," She Says "No"
• Call Me Uncle • Love Is Like a Firefly • Something
• Giannina Mia • Sapphire Seas • Tommy Atkins •
Sympathy • A Woman's Smile • De Trop • We're
Going to Make a Man of You • The Beautiful Ship
From Toyland • When a Maid Comes Knocking at
Your Heart • An American Beauty Rose • The Latest
Thing From Paris • Kiss Me, and 'Tis Day

Added to film version (1937)
The Donkey Serenade (Music by Rudolf Friml,
adapted by Herbert Stothart; lyrics by Robert
Wright and George Forrest) • He Who Loves and
Runs Away (Music by Rudolf Friml; lyrics by Gus
Kahn) • A Woman's Kiss (Music by Rudolf Friml;
lyrics by Robert Wright and George Forrest)

VS

[1] Victor Herbert was to have composed this
score for Emma Trentini, who had starred so
brilliantly in his *Naughty Marietta*. But, following
a violent quarrel with the temperamental prima
donna during the run of that operetta, he swore
he would never write another note for her. This
provided an ideal opportunity for young Rudolf
Friml to make an auspicious debut as an
operetta composer; he turned out the score in
less than a month! *The Firefly* was also the
producing debut of Arthur Hammerstein, who
had previously been general manager for his
father, the impresario Oscar Hammerstein I.

THE FIREMAN'S FLAME (OB)
October 9, 1937 (204)
Music by Richard Lewine
Lyrics by Ted Fetter

Hose Boys • The Fireman's Flame • Fire Belles' Gallop • Doin' the Waltz • We're Off • Do My Eyes Deceive Me? • Mother Isn't Getting Any Younger • It's a Lovely Night on the Hudson River • I Like the Nose on Your Face

VS

THE FIRST
November 17, 1981 (37)
Music by Bob Brush
Lyrics by Martin Charnin

Based on the career of Jackie Robinson

Bums • Jack Roosevelt Robinson • The National Pastime • Will We Ever Know Each Other? • The First • Bloat • Southern Hospitality • It Ain't Gonna Work • The Brooklyn Dodger Strike • Is This Year Next Year? • You Do-Do-Do It Good • There Are Days and There Are Days • It's a Beginning • The Opera Ain't Over

FIRST IMPRESSIONS
March 19, 1959 (84)
Music by Glenn Paxton
Lyrics by Robert Goldman and George Weiss

Based on the novel *Pride and Prejudice* by Jane Austen

Five Daughters • I'm Me • Have You Heard the News? • A Perfect Evening • As Long as There's a Mother • Love Will Find Out the Way • A Gentleman Never Falls Wildly in Love • Fragrant Flower • I Feel Sorry for the Girl • I Suddenly Find It Agreeable • This Really Isn't Me • Wasn't It a Simply Lovely Wedding? • A House in Town • The Heart Has Won the Game • Let's Fetch the Carriage

RA

THE FIVE O'CLOCK GIRL
October 10, 1927 (280)
Music by Harry Ruby
Lyrics by Bert Kalmar

I'm One Little Party • We Want You* • Thinking of You • Happy Go Lucky • Up in the Clouds • Any Little Thing • Following in Father's Footsteps • Lonesome Romeos • Tea Time Tap • Who Did? You Did • Society Ladder • Tell the World I'm Through

FLAHOOLEY
May 14, 1951 (40)
Music by Sammy Fain
Lyrics by E.Y. Harburg

You Too Can Be a Puppet • Here's to Your Illusions • B.G. Bigelow, Inc. • Najla's Song • Who Said There Is No Santa Claus? • Flahooley • The World Is Your Balloon • He's Only Wonderful • Arabian for "Get Happy" • Jump, Little Chillun • Spirit of

Capsulanti • Happy Hunting • The Springtime Cometh • Sing the Merry

RA

FLORA, THE RED MENACE
May 11, 1965 (87)
Music by John Kander
Lyrics by Fred Ebb

Based on the novel *Love Is Just Around the Corner* by Lester Atwell

Unafraid • All I Need Is One Good Break • Not Every Day of the Week • Sign Here • The Flame • Palomino Pal • A Quiet Thing • Hello, Waves • Dear Love • Express Yourself • Knock, Knock • Sing Happy • You Are You

RA

FLORIDA GIRL
November 2, 1925 (40)
Music by Milton Susskind
Lyrics by Paul Porter and Benjamin Hapgood Burt

Travel, Travel, Travel • Oranges • Lady of My Heart • Smile On • Into Society • Daphne • Take a Little Dip • Oh, You! • Trouble • Chinky China Charleston • As a Troubador

FLORODORA[1]
November 12, 1900 (553)
Music by Leslie Stuart

Flowers A-Blooming So Gay (Lyrics by Ernest Boyd-Jones) • The Credit's Due to Me (Lyrics by Ernest Boyd-Jones) • The Silver Star of Love (Lyrics by Ernest Boyd-Jones and Paul Rubens) • Somebody (Lyrics by Ernest Boyd-Jones and Paul Rubens) • Come and See Our Island (Lyrics by Ernest Boyd-Jones and Paul Rubens) • When I Leave Town (Lyrics by Paul Rubens) • Galloping (Lyrics by Ernest Boyd-Jones) • I Want to Marry a Man, I Do (Lyrics by Paul Rubens) • The Fellow Who Might (Lyrics by J. Hickory Wood) • Phrenology (Lyrics by Ernest Boyd-Jones) • When an Interfering Person (Lyrics by Paul Rubens) • The Shade of the Palm (Lyrics by Ernest Boyd-Jones and Paul Rubens) • Tact (Lyrics by Paul Rubens) • The Millionaire (Lyrics by Ernest Boyd-Jones) • Tell Me, Pretty Maiden* (Lyrics by Ernest Boyd-Jones and Paul Rubens) • I've an Inkling (Music and lyrics by Paul Rubens) • The Queen of the Philippine Islands (Music and lyrics by Paul Rubens) • We Get Up at 8 A.M. (Lyrics by Ernest Boyd-Jones and Paul Rubens) • I Want to Be a Military Man (Lyrics by Frank A. Clement) • He Loves Me, He Loves Me Not (Lyrics by Ernest Boyd-Jones) • Willie Was a Gay Boy (Lyrics by Alfred Murray) • When We Are on the Stage (Music and lyrics by Paul Rubens) • The Island of Love (Music by Ivan Caryll; lyrics by Aubrey Hopwood)

VS

[1] The title is not the name of the heroine but that of a small island in the Philippines on which the action takes place.

FLOWER DRUM SONG
December 1, 1958 (600)
Music by Richard Rodgers
Lyrics by Oscar Hammerstein II

Based on the novel by C.Y. Lee

You Are Beautiful* • A Hundred Million Miracles • I Enjoy Being a Girl • I Am Going to Like It Here • Like a God • Chop Suey • Don't Marry Me • Grant Avenue • Love, Look Away • Fan Tan Fannie • Gliding Through My Memoree • The Other Generation • Sunday

Dropped from production
My Best Love

RA,VS,SEL

FLY BLACKBIRD (OB)[1]
February 5, 1962 (127)
Music and lyrics by C. Jackson and James Hatch

Everything Comes to Those Who Wait • Now • Big Betty's Song • I'm Sick of the Whole Damn Problem • Who's the Fool? • Couldn't We? • Right Way • The Ousing Cha-Cha • Natchitoches, Louisiana • Fly Blackbird • The Gong Song • Rivers to the South • Lilac Tree • Twilight Song • The Love Elixir • Mister Boy • Old White Tom • Wake Up

RA

[1] Obie Award for Best Musical

FLYING COLORS
September 15, 1932 (188)
Music by Arthur Schwartz
Lyrics by Howard Dietz

Two-Faced Woman • A Rainy Day • Mother Told Me So • A Shine on Your Shoes • Alone Together • Louisiana Hayride • Mein Kleine Akrobat • Smokin' Reefers • Fatal Fascination • It Was Never Like This • Day After Day • All's Well • Riding Habit • My Heart Is Part of You

FLYING HIGH
March 3, 1930 (357)
Music by Ray Henderson
Lyrics by B.G. DeSylva and Lew Brown

I'll Know Him • Wasn't It Beautiful While It Lasted? • Air-Minded • The First Time for Me • Flying High • Thank Your Father • Happy Landing • Good for You—Bad for Me • Red Hot Chicago • Without Love • Mrs. Krause's Blue-Eyed Baby Boy • I'll Get My Man

FOLLIES[1]
April 4, 1971 (522)
Music and lyrics by Stephen Sondheim

Beautiful Girls • Don't Look at Me • Waiting for the Girls Upstairs • Rain on the Roof • Ah, Paris! • Broadway Baby • The Road You Didn't Take • Bolero d'Amour • In Buddy's Eyes • Who's That Woman? • I'm Still Here • Too Many Mornings • The Right Girl • One More Kiss • Could I Leave You? • Loveland • You're Gonna Love Tomorrow • Love Will See Us Through • The God-Why-Don't-You-Love-Me Blues • Losing My Mind • The Story of Lucy and Jessie • Live, Laugh, Love

Dropped from production
Can That Boy Foxtrot! • Uptown Downtown • Who Could Be Blue? • Little White House • So Many People • It Wasn't Meant to Happen

RA,VS,SEL

[1] Tony Award for Best Score

FOLLIES OF 1907 *See* ZIEGFELD FOLLIES

FOLLOW THE GIRLS
April 8, 1944 (882)
Music by Philip Charig
Lyrics by Dan Shapiro and Milton Pascal

At the Spotlight Canteen • You Don't Dance • Thanks for a Lousy Evening • You're Perf • Twelve o'Clock and All Is Well • Out for No Good • Where You Are • Follow the Girls • John Paul Jones • I Wanna Get Married • Today Will Be Yesterday Tomorrow • I'm Gonna Hang My Hat

FOLLOW THRU
January 9, 1929 (403)
Music by Ray Henderson
Lyrics by B.G. DeSylva and Lew Brown

The Daring Gibson Girl • The 1908 Life • It's a Great Sport • My Lucky Star • Button Up Your Overcoat • You Wouldn't Fool Me, Would You? • He's a Man's Man • Then I'll Have Time for You • I Want to Be Bad • Married Men and Single Men • No More You • I Could Give Up Anything but You • Follow Thru • Still I'd Love You

FOOLS RUSH IN
December 25, 1934 (14)
Music by Will Irwin
Lyrics by Norman Zeno

I Want to Dance • Napoleon • Jim Dandy • Sitting Over There • Love, Come Take Me • Shoes • New Sensation • Rhythm in My Hair • Willie's Little Whistle • Two Get Together • Ghost Town • I'm So in Love • Building Up to a Let-Down (Lyrics by Norman Zeno and Lee Brody) • Ça, c'est Sixth Avenue (Music and lyrics by Lee Brody and Richard Jones) • Sixty-Second Romance (Music by Bud Harris; lyrics by Lawrence Harris) • Let's Hold Hands (Music by Richard Lewine; lyrics by June Sillman) • Wicked, Unwholesome, Expensive (Music and lyrics by John Rox)

FOOTLIGHTS
August 19, 1927 (43)

Sure Sign You Really Love Me (Music and lyrics by Harry Denny) • Just When I Thought I Had You All to Myself (Music and lyrics by Harry Denny and Joe Fletcher) • Footlight Walk (Music and lyrics by Harry Denny) • You Can't Walk Back From an Aeroplane (Music and lyrics by Irving Bibo and William B.

Friedlander) • Gypsy Sweetheart (Music and lyrics by Irving Kahal, Francis Wheeler and Ted Snyder) • I Adore You (Music and lyrics by Ballard MacDonald, Sam Coslow and René Mercier) • Sahara Moon (Music and lyrics by Harry Denny and Dave Ringle)

FOR GOODNESS SAKE[1]
February 20, 1922 (103)
Music by William Daly and Paul Lannin
Lyrics by Arthur Jackson

All to Myself • Someone (Music by George Gershwin; lyrics by Arthur Francis) • Tra-La-La (Music by George Gershwin; lyrics by Arthur Francis) • When You're in Rome • Every Day (Music by Daly) • Twilight • The Greatest Team of All • Oh Gee, Oh Gosh (Music by Daly) • In the Days of Wild Romance • When Somebody Cares • The French Pastry Walk (Lyrics by Jackson and Arthur Francis) • The Whichness of the Whatness

[1] This was the first appearance of the name "Arthur Francis," the pseudonym of Ira Gershwin.

FORBIDDEN MELODY
November 2, 1936 (32)
Music by Sigmund Romberg
Lyrics by Otto Harbach

Bucharest • Lady in the Window • Just Hello • Moonlight and Violins • Two Ladies and a Man • You Are All I've Wanted • How Could a Fellow Want More? • No Use Pretending • Hear the Gypsies Playing • Shadows • When a Girl Forgets to Scream • Blame It All on the Night

THE FORTUNE TELLER
September 26, 1898 (40)
Music by Victor Herbert
Lyrics by Harry B. Smith[1]

Always Do as People Say You Should • Hungaria's Hussars • Ho! Ye Townsmen • Romany Life • Signor Mons. Muldoni • Gypsy Love Song • Only in the Play • Gypsy Jan • The Power of the Human Eye • The Lily and the Nightingale

VS,SEL

[1] See note on Marching By (1932).

FORTY-FIVE MINUTES FROM BROADWAY
January 1, 1906 (90)
Music and lyrics by George M. Cohan

Gentlemen of the Press • I Want to Be a Popular Millionaire • Mary's a Grand Old Name • So Long, Mary • Forty-Five Minutes From Broadway

FOURTUNE (OB)
April 27, 1980 (242)
Music by Ronald Melrose
Lyrics by Bill Russell

Four-Part Harmony • Rich and Famous • Women in Love • Fantasy • Funky Love • No One Ever Told Me

Love Would Be So Hard • I'd Rather Be a Fairy Than a Troll • Complications • On the Road • What Do I Do Now? • Making It • I'll Try It Your Way • Fortune

FOXFIRE   (Play with songs)
November 11, 1982 (213)
Music by Jonathan Holtzman
Lyrics by Susan Cooper and Jonathan Holtzman

Sweet Talker • Dear Lord • My Feet Took t'Walkin'

SEL

FOXY
February 16, 1964 (72)
Music by Robert Emmett Dolan
Lyrics by Johnny Mercer

Suggested by Ben Jonson's Volpone

Many Ways to Skin a Cat • Rollin' in Gold • My Weight in Gold • Money Isn't Everything • Larceny and Love • Ebenezer McAfee III • Talk to Me, Baby • This Is My Night to Howl • Bon Vivant • It's Easy When You Know How • Run, Run, Run Cinderella • I'm Way Ahead of the Game • A Case of Rape • In Loving Memory

FRANCIS (OB)
January 24, 1982 (30)
Music by Steve Jankowski
Lyrics by Kenny Morris

Miracle Town • The Legend of Old Rufino • The Legend of King Arthur • Serenade • Canticle of Pleasure • I'm Ready Now! • The Fire in My Heart • For the Good of Brotherhood • New Madness • Bidding the World Farewell • Oh Brother • All the Time in the World • Walking All the Way to Rome • Two Keys • The Road to Paradise • Francis • Praises to the Sun

FRANK MERRIWELL, OR HONOR CHALLENGED
April 24, 1971 (1)
Music and lyrics by Skip Redwine and Larry Frank

Based on the novel Frank Merriwell's School Days by Burt L. Standish (Gilbert Patten)

There's No School Like Our School • Howdy, Mr. Sunshine • Prim and Proper • Inza • Look for the Happiness Ahead • I'd Be Crazy to Be Crazy Over You • Now It's Fall • The Fallin'-Out-of-Love Rag • Frank, Frank, Frank • In Real Life • The Broadway of My Heart • Winter's Here • The Pure in Heart • Don't Turn His Picture to the Wall • Manuel Your Friend

FREDERIKA
February 4, 1937 (95)
Music by Franz Lehár
Lyrics by Edward Eliscu

Out in the Sun • I Asked My Heart • Rising Star • One • Rose in the Heather • Stormy Love • A Kiss to Remind You • Jealousy Begins at Home • Why Did You Kiss My Heart Awake? • The Bane of Man

VS

FREE FOR ALL
September 8, 1931 (15)
Music by Richard A. Whiting
Lyrics by Oscar Hammerstein II

I Love Him, the Rat • Free for All • The Girl Next Door • Living in Sin • Just Eighteen • Not That I Care • Slumber Song (Good Night) • When Your Boy Becomes a Man • Tonight • Nevada Moonlight

FROM A TO Z
April 20, 1960 (21)

Best Gold (Music and lyrics by Jerry Herman) • Pill Parade (Music and lyrics by Jay Thompson) • Togetherness (Music and lyrics by Dickson Hughes and Everett Sloane) • Balloons (Music and lyrics by Jack Holmes) • Hire a Guy (Music by Mary Rodgers; lyrics by Marshall Barer) • I Said to Love (Music by Paul Klein; lyrics by Fred Ebb) • Charlie (Music and lyrics by Fred Ebb and Norman Martin) • Grand Jury Jump (Music by Paul Klein; lyrics by Fred Ebb) • South American Way (Music by Norman Martin; lyrics by Norman Martin and Fred Ebb) • Time Step (Music by Paul Klein; lyrics by Fred Ebb) • Countermelody (Music by Mary Rodgers and Jay Thompson; lyrics by Marshall Barer) • Four for the Road (Music by Paul Klein; lyrics by Lee Goldsmith and Fred Ebb) • What Next? (Music by Charles Zwar; lyrics by Alan Melville)

FUNNY FACE[1]
November 22, 1927 (244)
Music by George Gershwin
Lyrics by Ira Gershwin

Birthday Party • Once • Funny Face • High Hat • 'S Wonderful • Let's Kiss and Make Up • In the Swim • He Loves and She Loves • Tell the Doc • My One and Only* • Sing a Little Song • The Babbitt and the Bromide*

Dropped from production

Dance Alone With You* • The World Is Mine* •

Aviator • When You Smile • When You're Single • Those Eyes • Dancing Hour • How Long Has This Been Going On?*

RA,SEL

[1] Pre-Broadway title: *Smarty*

FUNNY GIRL
March 26, 1964 (1348)
Music by Jule Styne
Lyrics by Bob Merrill

If a Girl Isn't Pretty • I'm the Greatest Star • Cornet Man • Who Taught Her Everything? • His Love Makes Me Beautiful • I Want to Be Seen With You Tonight • Henry Street • People • You Are Woman • Don't Rain on My Parade • Sadie, Sadie • Find Yourself a Man • Rat-Tat-Tat-Tat • Who Are You Now? • The Music That Makes Me Dance

Added to film version (1968):
The Swan • Roller Skate Rag • Funny Girl

RA,VS,SEL

A FUNNY THING HAPPENED ON THE WAY TO THE FORUM
May 8, 1962 (964)
Music and lyrics by Stephen Sondheim

Comedy Tonight • Love, I Hear • Free • The House of Marcus Lycus • Lovely • Pretty Little Picture • Everybody Ought to Have a Maid • I'm Calm • Impossible • Bring Me My Bride • That Dirty Old Man • That'll Show Him • Funeral Sequence

Dropped from production
Love Is in the Air • Love Story (Your Eyes Are Blue) • The Echo Song

Added to 1972 revival
Farewell

RA,VS,SEL

THE GANG'S ALL HERE
February 18, 1931 (23)
Music by Lewis E. Gensler
Lyrics by Owen Murphy and Robert A.Simon

What Have You Done to Me? • The Gang's All Here • Dumb Girl • Gypsy Rose • Baby Wanna Go Bye-Bye • Adorable Julie • Husband, Lover, and Wife • Speaking of You • By Special Permission of the Copyright Owners, I Love You • The Moon, the Wind and the Sea • It Always Takes Two • How Can I Get Rid of Those Blues? • Speak Easy

GANTRY
February 14, 1970 (1)
Music by Stanley Lebowsky
Lyrics by Fred Tobias

Based on the novel *Elmer Gantry* by Sinclair Lewis

Wave a Hand • He Was There • Play Ball With the Lord • Katie Jonas • Thanks, Sweet Jesus! • Someone I've Already Found • He's Never Too Busy • We're Sharin' Sharon • We Can All Give Love • Foresight • These Four Walls • Show Him the Way • The Promise of What I Could Be

THE GARRICK GAIETIES (1ST EDITION)[1]
May 17, 1925 (211)
Music by Richard Rodgers
Lyrics by Lorenz Hart

Soliciting Subscriptions • Gilding the Guild • Butcher, Baker, Candlestick-Maker (Music by Mana-Zucca; lyrics by Benjamin M. Kaye) • An Old-Fashioned Girl (Lyrics by Edith Meiser) • April Fool • Stage Managers' Chorus (Lyrics by Dudley Digges and Lorenz Hart) • The Joy Spreader • Rancho Mexicano (Music and Lyrics by Tatanacho) • Ladies of the Box Office • Manhattan* • The Three Musketeers • Do You Love Me? • On With the Dance • Black and White • Sentimental Me

[1] Planned for only two performances at the Garrick Theatre, the show featured the Theatre Guild Junior Players. It was a surprise hit and continued to run, at the same time establishing the new young team of Rodgers and Hart. For Rodgers it was an especially significant turning point: it encouraged him to turn down a job in the childrens' underwear field, one which in deep despair he had decided to accept.

THE GARRICK GAIETIES (2ND EDITION)
May 10, 1926 (174)
Music by Richard Rodgers
Lyrics by Lorenz Hart

Mountain Greenery* • Keys to Heaven • Sleepyhead* • Rose of Arizona (musical scene) • Viennese (Music by Ladislas Kun) • What's the Use of Talking? • Idles of the King • Queen Elizabeth • Gigolo • Four Little Song Pluggers • Tennis Champs • Allez-Oop

Dropped from production
Little Souvenir

THE GARRICK GAIETIES (3RD EDITION)
June 4, 1930 (155)

Ankle Up the Altar With Me (Music by Richard Myers; lyrics by Edward Eliscu) • You Lost Your Opportunity (Music by Charles M. Schwab; lyrics by Henry Myers) • Do Tell (Music by Charles M. Schwab; lyrics by Henry Myers) • Lazy Levee Loungers (Music and lyrics by Willard Robison) • Out of Breath (Music by Everett Miller; lyrics by Johnny Mercer) • I Am Only Human After All (Music by Vernon Duke; lyrics by Ira Gershwin and E.Y. Harburg) • Just a Sister (Music and lyrics by Thomas McKnight) • I'm Grover (Music by Vernon Duke; lyrics by Newman Levy) • Johnny Wanamaker (Music by Kay Swift; lyrics by Paul James) • Beauty (Music by Ned Lehak; lyrics by Allen Boretz) • Put It Away Till Spring (Music by Peter Nolan; lyrics by Joshua Titzell) • I've Got It Again (Music by Ned Lehak; lyrics by Allen Boretz) • Scheherezade (Music and lyrics by Harold Goldman) • Too, Too Divine (Music by Vernon Duke; lyrics by E.Y. Harburg) • When the Sun Meets the Moon in Finale-Land (Music by Charles M. Schwab; lyrics by Henry Myers) • Love Is Like That (Music by Ned Lehak; lyrics by Allen Boretz)

GAY COMPANY (OB)
October 29, 1974 (244)
Music and lyrics by Frederick Silver

Welcome, Welcome • A Pilgrim's Primer • A Special Boy • Handsome Stranger • True Confession • Where There's Smoke • I Met My Love • Lament • Phantom of the Opera • Your Home Away From Home • Two Strangers • Remembrances of Things Past • The Days of Dancing • I've Just Been to a Wedding • If He'd Only Be Gentle • Freddy Liked to Fugue

SEL

GAY DIVORCE
November 29, 1932 (248)
Music and lyrics by Cole Porter

After You • Why Marry Them? • Salt Air • I Still Love the Red, White and Blue • Night and Day* • How's Your Romance? • What Will Become of Our England? • I've Got You on My Mind • Mr. and Missus Fitch • You're in Love

Dropped from production
A Weekend Affair • Fate*

Added to film version (The Gay Divorcee, 1934)
The Continental[1] (Music by Con Conrad; lyrics by Herb Magidson)

SEL

[1] Academy Award winner

THE GAY LIFE
November 18, 1961 (113)
Music by Arthur Schwartz
Lyrics by Howard Dietz

Suggested by the play *Anatol* by Arthur Schnitzler

What a Charming Couple • Why Go Anywhere at All? • Bring Your Darling Daughter • Now I'm Ready for a Frau • Magic Moment • Who Can? You Can! • Oh, Mein Liebchen • The Label on the Bottle • This Kind of a Girl • The Bloom Is Off the Rose • I'm Glad I'm Single • Something You Never Had Before • You Will Never Be Lonely • You're Not the Type • Come A-Wandering With Me • I Never Had a Chance • I Wouldn't Marry You • For the First Time

RA

GAY PAREE
August 18, 1925 (190)

Wide Pants Willie (Music by James F. Hanley; lyrics by Harold Atteridge and Henry Creamer) • Tillie of Longacre Square (Music by James F. Hanley; lyrics by Harold Atteridge and Ballard MacDonald) • My Sugar Plum (Music by Joseph Meyer and J. Fred Coots; lyrics by B.G. DeSylva) • Give Me the Rain (Music by Maury Rubens; lyrics by Lester Allen and Henry Creamer) • Bamboo Babies (Music by Joseph Meyer and James F. Hanley; lyrics by Ballard MacDonald) • Venetian Wedding Moon (Music by Al Goodman, J. Fred Coots and Maury Rubens; lyrics by Clifford Grey) • I Was Meant for Someone (Music by James F. Hanley; lyrics by Ballard MacDonald) • Wedgewood Maid (Music by Al Goodman, Maury Rubens and J. Fred Coots; lyrics by Clifford Grey) • Wonderful Girls (Music by Al Goodman and J. Fred Coots; lyrics by Clifford Grey) • Every Girl Must Have a Little Bull (Music by Al Goodman and J. Fred Coots; lyrics by Clifford Grey) • Baby's Baby Grand (Music by Al Goodman and J. Fred Coots; lyrics by Clifford Grey)

GAY PAREE
November 9, 1926 (175)
Music by Mann Holiner
Lyrics by Alberta Nichols

College Days • Fine Feathers • Bad Little Boy With Dancing Legs • Broken Rhythm • Kandahar Isle • Oriental Nights • Shaking the Blues Away • There Never Was a Town Like Paris • Do That Doo-Da (Music by Maury Rubens; lyrics by J. Keirn Brennan) • "Je t'Aime" Means I Love You (Music and lyrics by Powers Gouraud)

GENTLEMEN PREFER BLONDES
December 8, 1949 (740)
Music by Jule Styne
Lyrics by Leo Robin

Based on the novel by Anita Loos

It's High Time • Bye Bye Baby • A Little Girl From Little Rock • Just a Kiss Apart • I Love What I'm Doing • It's Delightful Down in Chile • You Say You Care • I'm a'Tingle, I'm a'Glow • Sunshine • Diamonds Are a Girl's Best Friend • Mamie Is Mimi • Homesick Blues • Gentlemen Prefer Blondes • Keeping Cool With Coolidge

RA,VS

GEORGE WHITE'S MUSIC HALL VARIETIES
November 22, 1932 (71)

Birds of a Feather (Music by Carmen Lombardo; lyrics by Irving Caesar) • So I Married the Guy (Music by Sam Stept; lyrics by Herb Magidson) • The Waltz That Brought You Back to Me (Music by Carmen Lombardo; lyrics by Irving Caesar) • Sweet Liar (Music and lyrics by Irving Caesar) • Cabin in the Cotton (Music by Harold Arlen; lyrics by Irving Caesar and George White) • Two Feet in Two-Four Time (Music by Harold Arlen; lyrics by Irving Caesar) • Rah, Rah, Rah (Music by Sam Stept; lyrics by Irving Caesar and Herb Magidson) • Oh, Lady (Music by Sam Stept; lyrics by Herb Magidson) • Hold Me Closer (Music and lyrics by Max Rich, Frank Littau and Jack Scholl) • A Bottle and a Bird (Music and lyrics by Irving Caesar) • Let's Put Out the Lights and Go to Sleep * (Music and lyrics by Herman Hupfeld)

GEORGE WHITE'S SCANDALS (1920)
June 7, 1920 (134)
Music by George Gershwin
Lyrics by Arthur Jackson

My Lady • Everybody Swat the Profiteer • On My

Mind the Whole Night Long • Turn On and Tiss Me • Scandal Walk • The Songs of Long Ago • Idle Dreams

GEORGE WHITE'S SCANDALS (1921)
July 11, 1921 (97)
Music by George Gershwin
Lyrics by Arthur Jackson

Mother Eve • I Love You • South Sea Isles (Sunny South Sea Islands) • Drifting Along With the Tide • She's Just a Baby • When East Meets West

GEORGE WHITE'S SCANDALS (1922)
August 28, 1922 (88)
Music by George Gershwin
Lyrics by B.G. DeSylva and E. Ray Goetz

Oh, What She Hangs Out (She Hangs Out in Our Alley) (Lyrics by DeSylva) • Cinderelatives (Lyrics by DeSylva) • I Found a Four-Leaf Clover (Lyrics by DeSylva) • I Can't Tell Where They're From When They Dance • I'll Build a Stairway to Paradise* (Lyrics by DeSylva and Arthur Francis) • Across the Sea • Argentina • Where Is the Man of My Dreams?

Dropped from production[1]
Blue Monday Blues • Has Anyone Seen My Joe? • I'm Gonna See My Mother

RA

[1] These songs are from the one-act opera *Blue Monday* (RA), which opened the second act of the show but was withdrawn after opening night. "Has Anybody Seen My Joe?" is based on a theme from Gershwin's 1919 string quartet, known and recorded separately as "Lullaby" (RA).

GEORGE WHITE'S SCANDALS (1923)
June 18, 1923 (168)
Music by George Gershwin
Lyrics by B.G. DeSylva, E. Ray Goetz and Ballard MacDonald

Little Scandal Dolls • You and I • Katinka • Lo-La-Lo (Lyrics by DeSylva) • There Is Nothing Too Good for You (Lyrics by DeSylva and Goetz) • Throw Her in High! (Lyrics by DeSylva and Goetz) • Let's Be Lonesome Together (Lyrics by DeSylva and Goetz) • Look in the Looking Glass • Where Is She? (Lyrics by DeSylva) • Laugh Your Cares Away • (On the Beach at) How've-You-Been (Lyrics by DeSylva) • Garden of Love

GEORGE WHITE'S SCANDALS (1924)
June 23, 1924 (192)
Music by George Gershwin
Lyrics by B.G. DeSylva

Just Missed the Opening Chorus • I Need a Garden • Night Time in Araby • I'm Going Back • Year After Year • Somebody Loves Me (Lyrics by DeSylva and Ballard MacDonald) • Tune In to Station J.O.Y. • Mah-Jongg • Lovers of Art • Rose of Madrid • I Love You, My Darling • Kongo Kate

GEORGE WHITE'S SCANDALS (1925)
June 22, 1925 (169)
Music by Ray Henderson
Lyrics by B.G. DeSylva and Lew Brown

Read What the Papers Say • Rose-Time • Fly, Butterfly • I Want a Lovable Baby • Say It With a Sable • Even As You and I • Room Enough for Me • The Girl of Tomorrow • The Whosis-Whatsis • What a World This Would Be • Give Us the Charleston • Beware of the Girl With the Fan

GEORGE WHITE'S SCANDALS (1926)[1]
June 14, 1926 (424)
Music by Ray Henderson
Lyrics by B.G. DeSylva and Lew Brown

Talent Is What the Public Wants • Lucky Day • Tweet Tweet • Lady Fair • Walking Dogs Around • Black Bottom • The Birth of the Blues • Sevilla • David and Lenore • The Girl Is You and the Boy Is Me • My Jewels • Twenty Years Ago

[1] It was with this score, and the score for the 1925 *Scandals,* that DeSylva, Brown and Henderson emerged as one of the top writing teams of the day. For the next decade they were to write a series of highly successful Broadway and film scores.

GEORGE WHITE'S SCANDALS (1928)
July 2, 1928 (230)
Music by Ray Henderson
Lyrics by B.G. DeSylva and Lew Brown

I'm on the Crest of a Wave • An Old-Fashioned Girl • Pickin' Cotton • A Real American Tune • Where Your Name Is Carved With Mine • What D'Ya Say?

GEORGE WHITE'S SCANDALS (1929)
September 23, 1929 (161)
Music and lyrics by Cliff Friend and George White

Bigger and Better Than Ever • Sitting in the Sun (Just Wearing a Smile) • Bottoms Up • You Are My Day Dream • Drop Your Kerchief • Love Birds • 18 Days Ago (Music and lyrics by B.G. DeSylva, Friend and White) • Is Izzy Azzy Woz? • There's Something Spanish in Your Eyes

GEORGE WHITE'S SCANDALS (1931)
September 14, 1931 (202)
Music by Ray Henderson
Lyrics by B.G. DeSylva and Lew Brown

Life Is Just a Bowl of Cherries • Beginning of Love • The Thrill Is Gone • This Is the Missus • Ladies and Gentlemen, That's Love • That's Why Darkies Were Born • Song of the Foreign Legion • Here It Is • My Song • Back From Hollywood • The Good Old Days

GEORGE WHITE'S SCANDALS (1936)
December 25, 1935 (110)
Music by Ray Henderson
Lyrics by Jack Yellen

Life Begins at Sweet Sixteen • Boondoggling •

Cigarette • I Like It With Music • Truckin' in My Tails • May I Have My Gloves? • I'm the Fellow Who Loves You • Models • I've Got to Get Hot • Anything Can Happen (Lyrics by Yellen and Ballard MacDonald)

GEORGE WHITE'S SCANDALS (1939)
August 28, 1939 (120)
Music by Sammy Fain
Lyrics by Jack Yellen

Are You Havin' Any Fun? • Smart Little Girls • Our First Kiss • The Mexiconga (Lyrics by Yellen and Herb Magidson) • Good Night, My Beautiful • Something I Dreamed Last Night (Lyrics by Yellen and Herb Magidson) • In Waikiki • The Song's for Free

GEORGY
February 26, 1970 (4)
Music by George Fischoff
Lyrics by Carole Bayer

Based on the novel by Margaret Forster and the screenplay by Margaret Forster and Peter Nichols

Howdjadoo • Make It Happen Now • Ol' Pease Puddin' • Just for the Ride • So What? • Georgy • A Baby • That's How It Is • There's a Comin' Together • Something Special • Half of Me • Gettin' Back to Me • Sweet Memory • Life's a Holiday

GERTRUDE STEIN'S FIRST READER (OB)
December 15, 1969 (40)
Music by Ann Sternberg
Lyrics by Gertrude Stein

Sunshine • Wildflowers • A Dog • The Blackberry Vine • Big Bird • The Three Sisters Who Are Not Sisters • Be Very Careful • New World • Jenny • How They Do, Do • In a Garden

RA

GET THEE TO CANTERBURY (OB)
January 25, 1969 (20)
Music by Paul Hoffert
Lyrics by David Secter

Based on The Canterbury Tales by Geoffrey Chaucer

Get Thee to Canterbury • The Journey • Take a Pick • Death Beware • Buy My Pardons • Dreams • Canter Banter • Day of Judgement • Ballad of Sir Topaz • Bottom's Up • A Simple Wife • Shadows • Alison Dear • Where Are the Blossoms? • On the Relative Merits of Education and Experience • Everybody Gets It in the End

GIFT OF THE MAGI (OB)
December 1, 1975 (48)
Music and lyrics by Ronnie Britton

Based on the short story by O. Henry

Magi Waltz • There You Go Again • The Gift • Della's Desire • Mr. James Dillingham Young • Day After

Day • Kids Are Out • Sullivan Street Flat • Beautiful Children • You'd Better Tell Her • Washington Square • Till Tomorrow • Quiet Morning • Brave You • A Penny Saved • I've Got Something Better • Pretty Lady • He Did It, She Did It • Make Him Think I'm Still Pretty

GIGI (Stage version)
November 13, 1973 (103)
Music by Frederick Loewe
Lyrics by Alan Jay Lerner

Adapted by Alan Jay Lerner from his screenplay, which was based, in turn, on Colette's novel

Songs retained from film version
Thank Heaven for Little Girls • It's a Bore • (Waltz at Maxim's) She Is Not Thinking of Me • The Night They Invented Champagne • I Remember It Well • Gigi[*] • I'm Glad I'm Not Young Any More

Added to stage version
The Earth and Other Minor Things • Paris Is Paris Again • I Never Want to Go Home Again • The Contract • In This Wide Wide World

Dropped from production
The Parisians

[1] Tony Award for Best Score

THE GINGHAM GIRL
August 28, 1922 (422)
Music by Albert Von Tilzer
Lyrics by Neville Fleeson

The Down East Flapper • The Twinkle in Your Eye • You Must Learn the Latest Dances • As Long as I Have You • The 42nd Street and Broadway Strut • Down Greenwich Village Way • Tell Her While the Waltz Is Playing • The Wonderful Thing We Call Love • Libby • Sweet Cookie • Newlyweds • Love and Kisses

GIRL CRAZY[1]
October 14, 1930 (272)
Music by George Gershwin
Lyrics by Ira Gershwin

The Lonesome Cowboy • Bidin' My Time[*] • Could You Use Me? • Broncho Busters • Barbary Coast • Embraceable You[*] • Sam and Delilah • I Got Rhythm[*] • Land of the Gay Caballero • But Not for Me[*] • Treat Me Rough • Boy! What Love Has Done to Me! • When It's Cactus Time in Arizona

Dropped from production
The Gambler of the West • And I Have You • Something Peculiar • You Can't Unscramble Scrambled Eggs

Added to film version (1932)
You've Got What Gets Me

RA,VS,SEL

[1] In addition to its many other attractions the show had among its pit musicians Red Nichols, Benny Goodman, Glenn Miller, Jimmy Dorsey, Gene Krupa, and Jack Teagarden — probably

the greatest jazz instrumentalists ever assembled to play in a Broadway pit band.

THE GIRL FRIEND
March 17, 1926 (301)
Music by Richard Rodgers
Lyrics by Lorenz Hart

Hey! Hey! • The Simple Life • The Girl Friend • Good-bye, Lenny! • The Blue Room • Cabarets • Why Do I? • The Damsel Who Done All the Dirt • He's a Winner • Town Hall Tonight • Good Fellow, Mine • Creole Crooning Song • I'd Like to Take You Home • What Is It?

Dropped from production
Sleepyhead • The Pipes of Pansy*

THE GIRL FROM NANTUCKET
November 8, 1945 (12)
Music by Jacques Belasco
Lyrics by Kay Twomey

I Want to See More of You • Take the Steamer to Nantucket • What's He Like? • What's a Sailor Got? • Magnificent Failure (Music and lyrics by Hughie Prince and Dick Rogers) • When a Hick Chick Meets a City Slicker (Lyrics by Burt Milton) • Your Fatal Fascination • Let's Do and Say We Didn't (Music and lyrics by Hughie Prince and Dick Rogers) • Nothing Matters • Sons of the Sea • Isn't It a Lovely View? • From Morning Till Night • I Love That Boy • Hammock in the Blue • Boukra Fill Mish Mish

THE GIRL FROM UTAH
August 24, 1914 (120)

The Land of Let's Pretend (Music by Jerome Kern; lyrics by Harry B. Smith) • Only to You (Music and lyrics by Paul Rubens) • Gilbert the Filbert (Music by Herman Finck; lyrics by Arthur Wimperis) • Same Sort of Girl (Music by Jerome Kern; lyrics by Harry B. Smith) • Florrie Was a Flapper (Music by Herman Finck; lyrics by Arthur Wimperis) • Nothing at All, at All (Music and lyrics by Paul Rubens) • The Music of Love (Music by Paul Rubens; lyrics by Percy Greenbank) • You Never Can Tell (Music by Jerome Kern; lyrics by Harry B. Smith) • They Didn't Believe Me (Music by Jerome Kern; lyrics by Herbert Reynolds)* • At Our Tango Tea (Music by Bert Lee; lyrics by Worton David) • Why Don't They Dance the Polka Anymore? (Music by Jerome Kern; lyrics by Harry B. Smith)

THE GIRL FROM WYOMING (OB)
October 29, 1938 (86)
Music by Richard Lewine
Lyrics by Ted Fetter

Boston in the Spring • Ride, Cowboy, Ride • Hats Off • Manuelo • The Dying Cowboy • Lullaby of the Plain • Our Home • Stay East, Young Man • Kickin' the Corn Around

THE GIRL IN PINK TIGHTS
March 5, 1954 (115)

Music by Sigmund Romberg[1] (developed by Don Walker)
Lyrics by Leo Robin

That Naughty Show From Gay Paree • Lost in Loveliness • I Promised Their Mothers • Up in the Elevated Railway • In Paris and in Love • You've Got to Be a Little Crazy • When I Am Free to Love • Out of the Way • Roll Out the Hose, Boys • My Heart Won't Say Goodbye • We're All in the Same Boat • Love Is the Funniest Thing • The Cardinal's Guard Are We

RA

[1] Romberg was working on this score at the time of his death on November 10, 1951.

THE GIRL WHO CAME TO SUPPER
December 8, 1963 (112)
Music and lyrics by Noël Coward

Based on the play *The Sleeping Prince* by Terence Rattigan

Swing Song • Yasni Kozkolai • My Family Tree • I've Been Invited to a Party • When Foreign Princes Come to Visit Us • Sir or Ma'am • Soliloquies • Lonely • London Is a Little Bit of All Right • What Ho, Mrs. Brisket • Don't Take Our Charlie for the Army • Saturday Night at the Rose and Crown • Coronation Chorale • How Do You Do, Middle Age? • Here and Now • Curt, Clear and Concise • Welcome to Pootzie Van Doyle • The Coconut Girl • Paddy MacNeil and His Automobile • Six Lillies of the Valley • The Walla Walla Boola • This Time It's True Love • I'll Remember Her

Dropped from production
Long Live the King–If He Can* • Time Will Tell • If Only Mrs. Applejohn Were Here • What's the Matter With a Nice Beef Stew?

RA

THE GIRLS AGAINST THE BOYS
November 2, 1959 (16)
Music by Richard Lewine
Lyrics by Arnold B. Horwitt

The Girls Against the Boys • Rich Butterfly • I Gotta Have You • Lolita • Where Did We Go? Out • Too Young to Live • Overspend • Girls and Boys • Old-Fashioned Girl • Nobody Else but You (Music by Albert Hague)

GIRLS, GIRLS, GIRLS (OB)
October 4, 1980 (30)
Music by Cheryl Hardwick
Lyrics by Marilyn Suzanne Miller

The Betty Song • High School • Vicki Lawrence • Punk • Frances' Ballad • Lovers • Credit Card • Divorce • Planet of No Thigh Bulge • Street Lady • Man/Woman • Val's Ballad

GIRLS OF SUMMER (Play with one song)
November 19, 1956 (56)
Music and lyrics by Stephen Sondheim

Girls of Summer

GOD BLESS YOU, MR. ROSEWATER (OB)
October 14, 1979 (49)
Music by Alan Menken
Lyrics by Howard Ashman
Additional lyrics by Dennis Green

The Rosewater Foundation • Dear Ophelia (Lyrics by Green) • Thank God for the Volunteer Fire Brigade (Lyrics by Green) • Mushari's Waltz • Thirty Miles From the Banks of the Ohio • Look Who's Here • Cheese Nips • Plain, Clean, Average Americans • Rhode Island Tango (Lyrics by Green) • Eliot . . . Sylvia • Since You Came to This Town (Lyrics by Green) • A Firestorm Consuming Indianapolis • I, Eliot Rosewater

GOD IS A (GUESS WHAT?) (OB)
December 17, 1968 (32)
Music by Coleridge-Taylor Perkinson
Lyrics by Ray McIver

A Mighty Fortress • The Lynch-Him Song • The Sonny-Boy Slave Song • The Black-Black Song • The Golden Rule Song • God Will Take Care • The Darkies Song • The Sit Down Song • The Lyncher's Prayer

GODSPELL (OB)
May 17, 1971 (2,651)[1]
Music and lyrics by Stephen Schwartz

Based on the Gospel according to St. Matthew

Tower of Babble • Prepare Ye the Way of the Lord • Save the People • Day by Day* • Learn Your Lessons Well • Bless the Lord • All for the Best • All Good Gifts • Light of the World • Turn Back, O Man • Alas for You • By My Side (Music by Peggy Gordon; lyrics by Jay Hamburger) • We Beseech Thee • On the Willows

RA,VS,SEL

[1] Moved to Broadway June 22, 1976 (527).

GOING UP
December 25, 1917 (351)
Music by Louis A. Hirsch
Lyrics by Otto Harbach

I'll Bet You • I Want a Boy • If You Look in Her Eyes • Going Up • The Touch of a Woman's Hand • Down! Up! Left! Right! • Do It for Me • The Tickle Toe • Kiss Me • There's a Brand New Hero • Here's to the Two of You

VS

THE GOLDEN APPLE[1]
April 20, 1954 (173)[2]
Music by Jerome Moross
Lyrics by John Latouche

Nothing Ever Happens in Angel's Roost • My Love Is on the Way • It Was a Glad Adventure • Come Along, Boys • It's the Going Home Together • Helen Is Always Willing • Introducin' Mr. Paris • Lazy Afternoon • My Picture in the Papers • Windflowers • Store-Bought Suit • Goona-Goona • Doomed, Doomed, Doomed • Circe, Circe

RA

[1] A re-telling of the *Iliad* and the *Odyssey* in turn-of-the-century America.

[2] First opened Off Broadway March 11, 1954 (48).

GOLDEN BOY
October 20, 1964 (569)
Music by Charles Strouse
Lyrics by Lee Adams

Based on the play by Clifford Odets

Workout • Night Song • Everything's Great • Gimme Some • Stick Around • Don't Forget 127th Street • Lorna's Here • The Road Tour • This Is the Life • Golden Boy • While the City Sleeps • Colorful • I Want to Be With You • No More • Can't You See It? • The Fight

RA,SEL

GOLDEN DAWN
November 30, 1927 (184)
Music by Emmerich Kálmán and Herbert Stothart
Lyrics by Otto Harbach and Oscar Hammerstein II

The Whip • We Two • Here in the Dark • My Bwanna • Consolation • Africa • Dawn (Music by Robert Stolz and Stothart) • Jungle Shadows • Mulunghu Tabu • It's Always the Way

GOLDEN RAINBOW
February 4, 1968 (385)
Music and lyrics by Walter Marks

Based on the play *A Hole in the Head* by Arnold Schulman

Golden Rainbow • We Got Us • He Needs Me Now • Kid • For Once in Your Life • Taking Care of You • I've Got to Be Me • Taste • Desert Moon • All in Fun • It's You Again • How Could I Be So Wrong

RA,SEL

THE GOLDEN SCREW (OB)
January 27, 1967 (40)
Music and lyrics by Tom Sankey

New Evaline • 2000 Miles • Jesus Come Down • You Won't Say No • The Beautiful People • I Heard My Mother Crying • I Can't Make It Anymore • Can I Touch You? • That's Your Thing, Baby • I Can't Remember • Bottom End of Bleecker Street • Flippin' Out • Little White Dog

GOLDILOCKS
October 11, 1958 (161)
Music by Leroy Anderson
Lyrics by Joan Ford and Walter and Jean Kerr

Lazy Moon • Give the Little Lady a Great Big Hand • Save a Kiss • No One'll Ever Love You • Who's Been Sitting in My Chair? • There Never Was a Woman • The Pussy Foot • Lady in Waiting • The Beast in You • Shall I Take My Heart and Go? • I Can't Be in Love • Bad Companions • I Never Know When • Two Years in the Making • Heart of Stone

RA

GOOD BOY
September 5, 1928 (253)
Music and lyrics by Herbert Stothart, Bert Kalmar and Harry Ruby

What Makes You So Wonderful? • Good Boy • The Voice of the City • Manhattan Walk • Some Sweet Someone • I Have My Moments • I Wanna Be Loved by You • The Three Bears • Oh, What a Man • Good Boy Wedding March • Nina

GOOD MORNING, DEARIE
November 1, 1921 (347)
Music by Jerome Kern
Lyrics by Anne Caldwell

Every Girl • Way Down Town • Rose-Marie • Didn't You Believe? • The Teddy Toddle • Sing-Song Girl • Blue Danube Blues • Easy Pickin's • Melican Papa • Niagara Falls • Ka-lu-a • Good Morning, Dearie • Le Sport American

Dropped from production
My Lady's Dress* • Green River Glide • Rose Ruby

GOOD NEWS
September 6, 1927 (551)
Music by Ray Henderson
Lyrics by B.G. DeSylva and Lew Brown

He's a Ladies' Man • The Tait School Song • Flaming Youth • Happy Days • Just Imagine • The Best Things in Life Are Free • On the Campus • The Varsity Drag • Baby! What? • Lucky in Love • A Girl of the Pi Beta Phi • In the Meantime • Good News

RA,VS

Added to film version (1947)
The French Lesson (Music by Roger Edens; lyrics by Betty Comden and Adolph Green) • Pass That Peace Pipe (Music and lyrics by Roger Edens, Hugh Martin and Ralph Blane)

RA

GOODTIME CHARLEY
March 3, 1975 (104)
Music by Larry Grossman
Lyrics by Hal Hackady

History • Goodtime Charley • Visions and Voices • Bits and Pieces • To Make a Boy a Man • Why Can't We All Be Nice? • Born Lover • I Am Going to Love (The Man You're Going to Be) • Castles of the Loire (Music by Arthur B. Rubinstein) • Coronation • You Still Have a Long Way to Go • Merci, Bon Dieu • Confessional • One Little Year • I Leave the World

RA

THE GRAND STREET FOLLIES (1926) (OB)
June 15, 1926 (55)

Fixed for Life (Music by Randall Thompson; lyrics by Agnes Morgan) • Little Igloo for Two (Music by Arthur Schwartz; lyrics by Agnes Morgan) • The Boosters' Song of the Far North (Music by Randall Thompson; lyrics by Agnes Morgan) • Aurory Bory Alice (Music by Lily Hyland; lyrics by Agnes Morgan) • Taxi Drivers' Lament (Music by Randall Thompson; lyrics by Agnes Morgan) • The Discontented Bandits (Music by Lily Hyland; lyrics by Agnes Morgan) • Beatrice Lillie Ballad (Music by Randall Thompson; lyrics by Agnes Morgan) • My Icy Floe (Music by Randall Thompson; lyrics by Agnes Morgan) • If You Know What I Mean (Music by Arthur Schwartz; lyrics by Theodore Goodwin and Albert Carroll) • The Polar Bear Strut (Music by Arthur Schwartz; lyrics by Theodore Goodwin) • Northern Blues (Music by Walter [Gustave] Haenschen; lyrics by Robert A. Simon)

THE GRAND STREET FOLLIES (1927) (OB)
May 19, 1927 (148)
Music by Max Ewing
Lyrics by Agnes Morgan

Stars With Stripes (Lyrics by Dorothy Sands and Marc Loebell) • La Prisonnière (Lyrics by Albert Carroll) • Three Little Maids • Don't Ask Her Another • If You Haven't Got "It" • A Bedtime Story • The Naughty Nineties • Unaccustomed as I Am • The Banquet

THE GRAND STREET FOLLIES (1928)
May 28, 1928 (144)
Music by Max Ewing and Serge Walter
Lyrics by Agnes Morgan

Command to Love (Music by Walter) • Tu Sais (Music by Walter) • Just a Little Love Song (Music and lyrics by Ewing) • Someone to Admire, Someone to Adore (Music by Walter) • The Briny Blues (Music by Walter) • Husky, Dusky Annabelle (Music by Ewing) • Hey, Nonny, Hey (Music by Ewing)

THE GRAND STREET FOLLIES (1929)
May 1, 1929 (85)
Lyrics by Agnes Morgan

The Amoeba's Lament (Music by Arthur Schwartz) • The Double Standard (Music by Arthur Schwartz) • The Vineyards of Manhattan (Music by Arthur Schwartz) • Priam's Little Congai (Music by Will Irwin) • I've Got You on My Mind (Music and lyrics by Max Ewing) • British Maidens (Music by Max Ewing) • A Room With a Bath (Music by Max Ewing) • The Girl I Might Have Been (Music and lyrics by Max Ewing) • I Need You So (Music by Arthur Schwartz; lyrics by David Goldberg and Howard Dietz) • Don't Do It (Music by Arthur Schwartz) • I Love You and I Like You (Music by Arthur Schwartz; lyrics by Max and Nathaniel Lief) • The Pilgrim Fathers (Music by Serge Walter) • The Textile Troops (Music by Max Ewing) • What Did

Della Wear? (Music by Arthur Schwartz; lyrics by Agnes Morgan and Albert Carroll) • My Dynamo (Music by Arthur Schwartz) • I'll Never Forget (Music by Max Ewing; lyrics by Albert Carroll)

THE GRAND TOUR
January 11, 1979 (61)
Music and lyrics by Jerry Herman

Based on the play *Jacobowsky and the Colonel* by S.N. Behrman, which was an adaptation of a German play by Franz Werfel

I'll Be Here Tomorrow • For Poland • I Belong Here • Marianne • We're Almost There • More and More, Less and Less • One Extraordinary Thing • Mrs. S. L. Jacobowsky • Wedding Conversation • Mazeltov • I Think, I Think • You I Like*

RA,SEL

THE GRASS HARP
November 2, 1971 (7)
Music by Claibe Richardson
Lyrics by Kenward Elmslie

Based on the novel and play by Truman Capote

Dropsy Cure Weather • This One Day • Think Big Rich • If There's Love Enough • Yellow Drum • Marry With Me • I'll Always Be in Love • Floozies • Call Me Babylove • Walk Into Heaven • Hang a Little Moolah on the Washline • Talkin' in Tongues • Whooshin' Through My Flesh • Something for Nothing • Indian Blues • Take a Little Sip • What Do I Do Now? • Pick Yourself a Flower • Reach Out

RA,SEL

GREASE
February 14, 1972[1] (3,388)
Music and lyrics by Jim Jacobs and Warren Casey

Alma Mater • Summer Nights • Those Magic Changes • Freddy, My Love • Greased Lightnin' • Mooning • Look at Me, I'm Sandra Dee • We Go Together • Shakin' at the High School Hop • It's Raining on Prom Night • Born to Hand-Jive • Beauty School Dropout • Alone at a Drive-In Movie • Rock 'n' Roll Party Queen • There Are Worse Things I Could Do • All Choked Up

RA,SEL

[1] Opened on this date Off Broadway; moved to Broadway June 7, 1972.

GREAT DAY![1]
October 17, 1929 (36)
Music by Vincent Youmans
Lyrics by Billy Rose and Edward Eliscu

Does It Pay to Be a Lady? • I Like What You Like • Happy Because I'm in Love • Great Day! • Si, Si, Señor • Open Up Your Heart • The Wedding Bells Ring On • More Than You Know • Play the Game • Sweet as Sugar Cane* • Without a Song • Scarecrows

Dropped from production
Help Us Tonight • The Homestead Must Be Sold •

Meet the Boyfriend • One Love • River Song • Wedding Bells • Ring On

[1] Pre-Broadway title: *Louisiana Lou.*

GREAT LADY
December 1, 1938 (20)
Music by Frederick Loewe
Lyrics by Earle Crooker

A Promenade • Sweet William • I Have Room in My Heart • Why Can't This Night Last Forever? • May I Suggest Romance? • In the Carefree Realm of Fancy • To Whom It May Concern • Though Tongues May Wag • Keep Your Hand on Your Heart • And So Will You • The Little Corporal • Sisters Under the Skin • There Had to Be the Waltz • I Never Saw a King Before • Madame Is at Home

THE GREAT MAGOO (Play with one song)
December 2, 1932 (11)
Music by Harold Arlen
Lyrics by Billy Rose and E.Y. Harburg

It's Only a Paper Moon*

GREAT SCOT! (OB)
November 10, 1965 (38)
Music by Don McAfee
Lyrics by Nancy Leeds

You're the Only One • Great Scot! • I'll Find a Dream Somewhere • He's Not for Me • That Special Day • Brandy in Your Champagne • I'm Gonna Have a Baby • Original Sin • I'll Still Love Jean • Where Is That Rainbow? • Princes' Street • Happy New Year • That Big-Bellied Bottle • He Knows Where to Find Me • Where Does a Man Begin? • What a Shame • I Left a Dream Somewhere • We're Gonna Have a Wedding

THE GREAT TEMPTATIONS
May 18, 1926 (197)
Music by Maury Rubens
Lyrics by Clifford Grey

Never Say the World Was Made to Cry • Any Step • The Spider's Web (Music by Milton Schwarzwald) • A Pin Cushion • The Temptation Strut (Music by Earl Lindsay and Rubens) • The Guards of Fantasy • Querida • Valencia (Music by José Padilla) • A Garden of Memories • The Chevalier of the Highway • Dancing Town • Beauty Is Vanity • The Atlantic City Girl

GREAT TO BE ALIVE
March 23, 1950 (52)
Music by Abraham Ellstein
Lyrics by Walter Bullock

When the Sheets Come Back From the Laundry • It's a Long Time Till Tomorrow • Headin' for a Weddin' • Redecorate • What a Day! • Call It Love • There's Nothing Like It • Dreams Ago • From This Day On • Who Done It? • Blue Day • Thank You, Mrs. Butterfield

THE GREAT WALTZ
September 22, 1934 (347)
Music by Johann Strauss
Lyrics by Desmond Carter

Morning • Look Before You Leap • You Are My Songs • Love Will Find You • On Love Alone • Like a Star in the Sky • With All My Heart • Night • Love's Never Lost • For We Love You Still • While You Love Me • Love and War • Danube So Blue

VS

GREEN POND (OB)
November 22, 1977 (32)
Music by Mel Marvin
Lyrics by Robert Montgomery

Green Pond • Pleasant Company • Daughter • I Live Alone • The Eyes of Egypt • How We Get Down • Alligator Meat • Priceless Relics • Woman to Woman • Brother to Brother • Hurricane • Hard to Love • On the Ground at Last

THE GREENWICH VILLAGE FOLLIES (1925)
December 24, 1925 (180)
Music by Harold Levey
Lyrics by Owen Murphy

You Have Me—I Have You • The Lady of the Snow • Life Is Like a Toy Balloon • See Yourselves in the Mirror • Whistle Away Your Blues (Music by Richard Myers; lyrics by Leo Robin) • The Window Cleaners (Music by Harry Ruby; lyrics by Bert Kalmar) • Go South (Music by Richard Myers; lyrics by Murphy) • The Life of the Party (Music by Richard Myers; lyrics by Harry Ruskin)

THE GREENWICH VILLAGE FOLLIES (1928)
April 9, 1928 (128)
Music by Ray Perkins
Lyrics by Max and Nathaniel Lief

Padlock Your Blues • Golden Gate • What's the Reason? (Music by Maury Rubens; lyrics by Harold Atteridge) • Slaves of Broadway • Get Your Man • The Subway Sun • Who's the Boy? • Down at the Village • High, High Up in the Clouds (Music by Maury Rubens)

GREENWICH VILLAGE FOLLIES (OB)
June 10, 1976 (444)
Music and lyrics by Ronnie Britton

Greenwich Village Follies • Let Me Sing! • Hello, New York • Le Grand Rape • You Show Me Yours • Quartet for Losers • Nude With Violin • We Wanna Star • Rock n' Roll Star • Long Ago, or Yesterday? • I've Been in Love • Most Unusual Pair • Melody of Manhattan • Merry-Go-Round • Bicentennial March • Look at Me • That Girl With the Curls • Ole Soft Core • The Expose • Garbage-Ella • Pandora

GREENWICH VILLAGE U.S.A. (OB)
September 28, 1960 (87)
Music by Jeanne Bargy

Lyrics by Jeanne Bargy, Frank Gehrecke and Herb Corey

Greenwich Village U.S.A. • How Can Anyone So Sweet • Happy Guy • Why Can't We Be Unhappy? • Love's Melody • We Got Love • Time to Call It Quits • Baby, You Bore Me • Love Me • Mulhaney's Song

RA

GREENWILLOW
March 8, 1960 (95)
Music and lyrics by Frank Loesser

Based on the novel by B.J. Chute

A Day Borrowed From Heaven • The Music of Home • Dorrie's Wish • Gideon Briggs, I Love You • Summertime Love • Walking Away Whistling • The Sermon • Greenwillow Christmas • Could've Been a Ring • Never Will I Marry • Faraway Boy • Clang Dang the Bell • What a Blessing • He Died Good

RA

GROSSE VALISE See LA GROSSE VALISE

GUYS AND DOLLS[1]
November 24, 1950 (1200)
Music and lyrics by Frank Loesser

Based on the story *The Idyll of Miss Sarah Brown* by Damon Runyon

Fugue for Tinhorns* • Follow the Fold • The Oldest Established • I'll Know • A Bushel and a Peck • Adelaide's Lament • Guys and Dolls • If I Were a Bell • My Time of Day • I've Never Been in Love Before • Take Back Your Mink • More I Cannot Wish You • Luck Be a Lady • Sue Me • Sit Down, You're Rockin' the Boat • Marry the Man Today

RA,VS,SEL

Added to film version (1955)
A Woman in Love • Pet Me, Poppa • Adelaide

[1] Tony Award for Best Score

GYPSY
May 21, 1959 (702)
Music by Jule Styne
Lyrics by Stephen Sondheim

Suggested by the memoirs of Gypsy Rose Lee

Let Me Entertain You • Some People • Small World • Mr. Goldstone • Little Lamb • You'll Never Get Away From Me* • Broadway • If Momma Was Married • All I Need Is the Girl • Everything's Coming Up Roses • Together Wherever We Go • You Gotta Have a Gimmick • Rose's Turn

Dropped from production
Three Wishes for Christmas • Mamma's Talkin' Soft • Smile, Girls

RA,VS,SEL

GYPSY LOVE
October 17, 1911 (31)
Music by Franz Lehár
Lyrics by Harry B. and Robert B. Smith

There Is a Land of Fancy • Love Is Like the Rose • Love's Sorcery • Lessons in Love • Love for a Year, Love for a Day • Gypsy Love (Lyrics by Adrian Ross) • The Melody of Love • Ha! Ha! Ha! That's Interesting • When I'm Waltzing With You • Who's My Little Baby Lamb? • Come as a Carrier Dove • I Will Give You All for Love • Matrimony

VS

H

HAIR
April 29, 1968 (1,742)
Music by Galt MacDermot
Lyrics by Gerome Ragni and James Rado

Aquarius • Donna • Hashish • Sodomy • Colored
Spade • Manchester • Ain't Got No • I Believe in
Love • Air • Initials • I Got Life • Going Down • Hair •
My Conviction • Easy to Be Hard • Hung • Don't Put
It Down • Frank Mills • Hare Krishna • Where Do I
Go? • Electric Blues • Black Boys • White Boys •
Walking in Space • Abie Baby • Prisoners in
Niggertown • What a Piece of Work Is Man • Good
Morning Starshine • The Bed • The Flesh Failures

RA,SEL

[1] First opened Off Broadway October 29, 1967
(94).

HAIRPIN HARMONY
October 1, 1943 (3)
Music and lyrics by Harold Orlob

Hairpin Harmony • What-a-Ya-Say • You're the
Reason • I'm Tickled Pink • I'm a Butter Hoarder •
Without a Sponsor • I Can Be Like Grandpa • That's
My Approach to Love • What Do the Neighbors
Say? • Piccaninny Pie

HALF A SIXPENCE
April 25, 1965 (512)
Music and lyrics by David Heneker

Based on the novel *Kipps* by H.G. Wells

All in the Cause of Economy • Half a Sixpence •
Money to Burn • A Proper Gentleman • She's Too
Far Above Me • If the Rain's Got to Fall • The Old
Military Canal • Long Ago • Flash Bang Wallop • I
Know What I Am • The Party's on the House

RA,VS,SEL

HALF A WIDOW
September 12, 1927 (16)
Music by Shep Camp
Lyrics by Frank DuPree and Harry B. Smith

Let's Laugh and Be Merry • Under the Midsummer
Moon (Lyrics by Smith) • It's Great to Be a
Doughboy (Lyrics by DuPree) • Longing for You
(Lyrics by DuPree) • I Wonder if She Will Remember
• Step, Step, Step (Music and lyrics by Jack
Murray and Joe Brandfon) • Tell Me Again (Lyrics
by DuPree) • A Thousand Times • Soldier Boy •
You're a Wonderful Girl • I'm Through With War •
France Will Not Forget (Music and lyrics by
Geoffrey O'Hara and Gordon Johnstone)

HALLELUJAH, BABY![1]
April 26, 1967 (293)
Music by Jule Styne
Lyrics by Betty Comden and Adolph Green

Back in the Kitchen • My Own Morning • The Slice •
Farewell, Farewell • Feet Do Yo' Stuff • Watch My
Dust • Smile, Smile • Witches' Brew • I Wanted to
Change Him • Being Good Isn't Good Enough •
Talking to Yourself • Hallelujah, Baby • Not Mine • I
Don't Know Where She Got It • Now's the Time

RA,SEL

[1] Tony Award for Best Score

THE HAPPIEST GIRL IN THE WORLD
April 3, 1961 (97)
Music by Jacques Offenbach (adapted by Robert
DeCormier)
Lyrics by E.Y. Harburg

Suggested by the works of Aristophanes and
Charles Bulfinch

The Olympics • Cheers for the Hero • The Glory
That Is Greece • The Happiest Girl in the World •
The Greek Marine • Shall We Say Farewell? • Never
Be-Devil the Devil • Whatever That May Be • Eureka
• Vive la Virtue • Adrift on a Star • That'll Be the Day
• How Soon, Oh Moon? • Love-Sick Serenade •
Five Minutes of Spring • Never Trust a Virgin

RA

HAPPY
December 5, 1927 (82)
Music by Frank Grey
Lyrics by Earle Crooker and McElbert Moore

Plastic Surgery • Check Your Troubles • Through the Night • Sunny Side of You • Lorelei • If You'll Put Up With Me • Happy • Here's to You, Jack • One Good Friend • Hitting on High • Blacksheep • Which Shall It Be? (Lyrics by Ethelberta Hasbrook) • What a Lovely Night • Mad About You

HAPPY AS LARRY
January 6, 1950 (3)
Music by Mischa and Wesley Portnoff
Lyrics by Donagh MacDonagh

No One Loves Me • Without a Stitch • Now and Then • October • Mrs. Larry, Tell Me This • A Cup of Tea • He's With My Johnny • And So He Died • Three Old Ladies From Hades • It's Pleasant and Delightful • The Dirty Dog • The Flatulent Ballad • The Loyalist Wife • Oh, Mrs. Larry • Give the Doctor the Best in the House • Double Murder, Double Death • He's a Bold Rogue • I Remember Her • The Tobacco Blues

HAPPY BIRTHDAY (Play with one song)
October 31, 1946 (564)
Music by Richard Rodgers
Lyrics by Oscar Hammerstein II

I Haven't Got a Worry in the World

HAPPY END
May 7, 1977[1] (75)
Music by Kurt Weill
Lyrics by Bertolt Brecht (adapted by Michael Feingold)

Based on a play by Elisabeth Hauptmann

The Bilbao Song • Lieutenants of the Lord • March Ahead • The Sailor's Tango • Brother, Give Yourself a Shove • Song of the Big Shot • Don't Be Afraid • In Our Childhood's Bright Endeavor • The Liquor Dealer's Dream • The Mandalay Song • Surabaya Johnny • Ballad of the Lily of Hell • The Happy End

VS

[1] First opened Off Broadway March 8, 1977 (56)

HAPPY GO LUCKY
September 30, 1926 (52)
Music by Lucien Denni
Lyrics by Helena Evans

Sing a Little Song • Free, Free, Free • Love Thoughts • How Are You, Lady Love? • When I Make a Million for You • Happy Melody • Choose Your Flowers • It's In, It's Out • Zip • It's Wonderful • Happy Go Lucky • In Vaudeville • Wall Street Zoo • You're the Fellow the Fortune Teller Told Me All About

HAPPY HUNTING
December 6, 1956 (412)

Music by Harold Karr
Lyrics by Matt Dubey

Postage Stamp Principality • Don't Tell Me • Gee, but It's Good to Be Here • Mutual Admiration Society • For Love or Money • It's Like a Beautiful Woman • Wedding-of-the-Year Blues • Mr. Livingstone • If'n • This Is What I Call Love • A New-Fangled Tango • She's Just Another Girl • The Game of Love • Happy Hunting • I'm a Funny Dame • This Much I Know • Just Another Guy • Everyone Who's "Who's Who"

RA

THE HAPPY HYPOCRITE (OB)
September 5, 1968 (17)
Music by James Bredt
Lyrics by Edward Eager

Based on the short story by Max Beerbohm

Street Song • Deep in Me • The Amorous Arrow • Echo Song • Miss Mere • Mornings at Seven • The Song of the Mask • Almost Too Good to Be True • Don't Take Sides • Hell Hath No Fury • I Must Smile • Once, Only Once • The Face of Love

THE HAPPY TIME
January 18, 1968 (286)
Music by John Kander
Lyrics by Fred Ebb

Based on the play by Samuel Taylor and the stories by Robert L. Fontaine

The Happy Time • He's Back • Catch My Garter • Tomorrow Morning • Please Stay • I Don't Remember You • St. Pierre • Without Me • Among My Yesterdays • The Life of the Party • Seeing Things • A Certain Girl • Being Alive

RA, SEL

HAPPY TOWN
October 7, 1959 (5)
Music by Gordon Duffy
Lyrics by Harry M. Haldane

It Isn't Easy • Celebration! • Something Special • The Legend of Black-Eyed Susan Grey • Opportunity! • As Busy as Anyone Can Be • Heaven Protect Me! • I Feel Like a Brother to You • Hoedown! • I Am What I Am! • The Beat of a Heart • Mean • When the Time Is Right • Pick-Me-Up! • I'm Stuck With Love • Nothing in Common • Talkin' 'Bout You • Y' Can't Win

HARRY DELMAR'S REVELS
November 28, 1927 (114)

I Love a Man in Uniform (Music by Jimmy Monaco; lyrics by Billy Rose and Ballard MacDonald) • My Rainbow (Music by Jeanne Hackett; lyrics by Lester Lee) • Say It With a Solitaire (Music by Jimmy Monaco; lyrics by Billy Rose and Ballard MacDonald) • If You Have Troubles Laugh Them Away (Music and lyrics by Lester Lee) • Irresistible

You (Music by Jimmy Monaco; lyrics by Billy Rose and Ballard MacDonald)

HAVE A HEART
January 11, 1917 (76)
Music by Jerome Kern
Lyrics by P.G. Wodehouse

Shop • I'm So Busy • Have a Heart • Look in His Eyes (Lyrics by Herbert Reynolds) • And I Am All Alone (Lyrics by Jerome Kern and P.G. Wodehouse) • I'm Here, Little Girls, I'm Here • Bright Lights • The Road That Lies Before • Samarkand • Honeymoon Inn • It's a Sure, Sure Sign • You Said Something • Daisy • Napoleon

VS

HAZEL FLAGG
February 11, 1953 (190)
Music by Jule Styne
Lyrics by Bob Hilliard

Based on the film *Nothing Sacred* (1937)

A Little More Heart • The World Is Beautiful Today • I'm Glad I'm Leaving • Hello, Hazel • Paris Gown • Every Street's a Boulevard in Old New York • How Do You Speak to an Angel? • I Feel Like I'm Gonna Live Forever • You're Gonna Dance With Me, Willie • Who Is the Bravest? • Salomee • Autograph Chant • Everybody Loves to Take a Bow • Laura De Maupassant

RA

HEAD OVER HEELS
September 29, 1918 (100)
Music by Jerome Kern
Lyrics by Edgar Allan Woolf

With Type a-Ticking • Today Is Spring • Any Girl • Mitzi's Lullaby • The Big Show • The Moments of the Dance • Head Over Heels • At the Thé Dansant • Vorderveele • All the World Is Swaying • Me • Houp-La • Every Bee Has a Bud of Its Own (Music by Harold Levey) • Ladies, Have a Care! • I Was Lonely • Funny Little Something

HEAD OVER HEELS
December 15, 1981 (22)
Music by Albert T. Viola
Lyrics by William S. Kilborne, Jr.

Based on the play *The Wonder Hat* by Kenneth Sawyer Goodman and Ben Hecht

New Loves for Old • Perfection • I'm in Love • Aqua Vitae • Nowhere • Castles in the Sand • As If • Could He Be You? • Lullabye to Myself • How Do You Keep Out of Love?

HEADS UP!
November 11, 1929 (144)
Music by Richard Rodgers
Lyrics by Lorenz Hart

You've Got to Surrender • Play Boy • Mother Grows

Younger • Why Do You Suppose?* • Me for You • Ongsay and Anceday • It Must Be Heaven • My Man Is on the Make • The Lass Who Loved a Sailor • A Ship Without a Sail • Knees

Dropped from production
Sky City • As Though You Were There • I Can Do Wonders With You • You Make Me Laugh • A Man's World • Bootlegger's Chanty

HEATHEN
May 21, 1972 (1)
Music and lyrics by Eaton Magoon, Jr.

Paradise • The Word of the Lord • My Sweet Tomorrow • A Man Among Men • Aloha • Kalialani • No Way in Hell • Battle Cry • This Is Someone I Could Love • House of Grass • Kava Ceremony • For You, Brother • Christianity • Heathen • More Better Go Easy • Eighth Day

HEAVEN ON EARTH
September 16, 1948 (12)
Music by Jay Gorney
Lyrics by Barry Trivers

In the Back of a Hack • Anything Can Happen • You're So Near (So Near and Yet So Far) • Don't Forget to Dream • Bench in the Park • The Letter • Push a Button in a Hutton • Home Is Where the Heart Is • Apple Jack • Wedding in the Park • Heaven on Earth • What's the Matter With Our City? • You're the First Cup of Coffee • Gift Number • Musical Tour of the City

HELEN GOES TO TROY
April 24, 1944 (96)
Music by Erich Wolfgang Korngold (based on Jacques Offenbach)
Lyrics by Herbert Baker

Come to the Sacrifice • Where Is Love? • Tsing-la-la • Take My Advice • The Shepherd Song • The Judgement of Paris • What Will the Future Say? • Extra! Extra! • Sweet Helen • Love at Last • Bring On the Concubines • If Menelaus Only Knew It • Is It a Dream? • A Little Chat • Advice to Husbands • Come With Me

HELEN OF TROY, NEW YORK
June 19, 1923 (191)
Music by Harry Ruby
Lyrics by Bert Kalmar

Up on Your Toes • Cry Baby • I Like a Big Town • Helen of Troy, New York • Look for a Happy Ending • What the Girls Will Wear • What Makes a Business Man Wear • Advertising • If I Never See You Again • Nijigo Novgo Glide • It Was Meant to Be • We'll Have a Model Factory • A Little Bit o' Jazz

HELLO, DADDY
December 26, 1928 (196)
Music by Jimmy McHugh
Lyrics by Dorothy Fields

Three Little Maids From School • I Want Plenty of You • Futuristic Rhythm • Let's Sit and Talk About You • Your Disposition Is Mine • In a Great Big Way • Maybe Means Yes • As Long as We're in Love • Out Where the Blues Begin

HELLO, DOLLY[1]
January 16, 1964 (2844)
Music and lyrics by Jerry Herman

Suggested by the play *The Matchmaker* by Thornton Wilder

I Put My Hand In • It Takes a Woman • Put on Your Sunday Clothes • Ribbons Down My Back • Motherhood • Dancing • Before the Parade Passes By • Elegance • Hello, Dolly* • It Only Takes a Moment • So Long, Dearie

RA,VS,SEL

Added during Broadway run
Love, Look in My Window • World, Take Me Back

[1] Tony Award for Best Score

HELLO, LOLA
January 12, 1926 (47)
Music by William B. Kernell
Lyrics by Dorothy Donnelly

Based on the novel and play *Seventeen* by Booth Tarkington

Bread and Butter and Sugar • The Summer Time • My Brother Willie • My Baby Talk Lady • Hello, Cousin Lola • Five-Foot-Two • Step on the Gasoline • Swinging on the Gate • That Certain Party • In the Dark • I Know Something • Little Boy Blue • Keep It Up • Sophie • Don't Stop

HELLO, PARIS
November 15, 1930 (33)

Based on the novel *They Had to See Paris* by Homer Croy

Deep Paradise (Music by Russell Tarbox; lyrics by Charles O. Locke) • Gotta Have Hips Now (Music by Russell Tarbox; lyrics by Charles O. Locke) • Every Bit of You (Music and lyrics by Kenneth Friede and Adrian Samish) • I Stumbled Over You (Music by Maury Rubens; lyrics by Henry Dagand) • Prairie Blues (Music by Russell Tarbox; lyrics by Charles O. Locke) • I'll Admit (Music by Maury Rubens; lyrics by Henry Dagand)

HELLO, YOURSELF!
October 30, 1928 (87)
Music by Richard Myers
Lyrics by Leo Robin

We Might Play Tiddle de Winks • Hello, Yourself • You've Got a Way With You • He Man • Say That You Love Me • True Blue • Daily Dozen • I Want the World to Know • Jericho • To the Dance

HELLZAPOPPIN
September 22, 1938 (1404)

Music by Sammy Fain
Lyrics by Charles Tobias

Hellzapoppin • Fuddle-Dee-Duddle • Strolling Thru the Park • Abe Lincoln (Music and lyrics by Earl Robinson and Alfred Hayes) • Shaganola • It's Time to Say "Aloha" • When You Look in Your Looking Glass (Music by Paul Mann and Stephen Weiss; lyrics by Sam Lewis) • Blow a Balloon Up to the Moon • Boomps-a-Daisy (Music and lyrics by Annette Mills) • We Won't Let It Happen Here • When McGregor Sings Off Key

THE HEN PECKS
February 4, 1911 (137)
Music by A. Baldwin Sloane
Lyrics by E. Ray Goetz

Don't Forget the Beau You Left Behind • Just Tell Me With Your Eyes • Hail to the Bride • The Dancing Fiddler • Toddling the Todalo • Next • It's the Skirt • Little Italy • White Light Alley • The Manicure Girl (Music by Jerome Kern; lyrics by Frederick Day) • Try This on Your Pianna, Anna • It's Not the Trick Itself, but It's the Tricky Way It's Done • He's the Wonder for Them All • Wine Maid Divine • Lasses Who Live in Glass Houses • June

HENRY, SWEET HENRY
October 23, 1967 (80)
Music and lyrics by Bob Merrill

Based on the novel *The World of Henry Orient* by Nora Johnson

Academic Fugue • In Some Little World • Pillar to Post • Here I Am • Whereas • I Wonder How It Io to Dance With a Boy • Nobody Steps on Kafritz • Henry, Sweet Henry • Woman in Love • People Watchers • Weary Near to Dyin' • Poor Little Person • I'm Blue Too • To Be Artistic • Forever • Do You Ever Go to Boston?

RA

HER FIRST ROMAN
October 20, 1968 (17)
Music and lyrics by Ervin Drake

Based on the play *Caesar and Cleopatra* by George Bernard Shaw

What Are We Doing in Egypt? • Hail Sphinx • Save Me From Caesar • Many Young Men From Now • Ptolemy • Kind Old Gentleman • Her First Roman • Magic Carpet • The Things We Think We Are • I Cannot Make Him Jealous • The Dangerous Age • In Vino Veritas • Caesar Is Wrong • Just for Today

HERE GOES THE BRIDE
November 3, 1931 (7)
Music by John Green
Lyrics by Edward Heyman

The Inside Story • Remarkable People We • My Sweetheart 'Tis of Thee • Shake Well Before Using • We Know Reno • Well, You See • What's the

Difference? • One Second of Sex • Hello, My Lover, Goodbye • It's My Nature • It Means So Little to You (Music by Richard Myers) • Music in My Fingers (Music by Richard Myers) • Ohhh! Ahhh!

HERE'S HOWE
May 1, 1928 (71)
Music by Joseph Meyer and Roger Wolfe Kahn
Lyrics by Irving Caesar

Beauty in the Movies • Life as a Twosome* • Crazy Rhythm • Imagination • I'd Rather Dance Here Than Hereafter • Here's Howe • Boston Post Road • On My Mind a New Love

HERE'S LOVE
October 3, 1963 (334)
Music and lyrics by Meredith Willson

Based on the film *Miracle on 34th Street* (1947)

The Big Clown Balloons • Arm in Arm • You Don't Know • The Plastic Alligator • The Bugle • Here's Love • My Wish • Pine Cones and Holly Berries • Look, Little Girl • Expect Things to Happen • She Hadda Go Back • That Man Over There • My State • Nothing in Common

RA, SEL

HERE'S WHERE I BELONG
March 3, 1968 (1)
Music by Robert Waldman
Lyrics by Alfred Uhry

Based on the novel *East of Eden* by John Steinbeck

We Are What We Are • Cal Gets By • Raising Cain • Soft Is the Sparrow • Where Have I Been? • No Time • Progress • Good Boy • Act Like a Lady • Top of the Train • Waking Up Sun • Pulverize the Kaiser • You're Momma's • Here's Where I Belong • We're a Home

A HERO IS BORN
October 1, 1937 (50)
Music by Lehman Engel
Lyrics by Agnes Morgan

Tra La La • Matters Culinary • Fiddle Dee Dee • Music in the Air • Magic Gifts • A Question of Gait (Lyrics by Thomas Burke) • Woe Is Me • Off to Gluckstein • Keeping Prigio Company • The Secret of Success • We Believe • A Love-Lorn Maid • They Say • The Best Dance of All • The Song of Prigio • Hurray for Life • Prigio Don't Know • The Last Word

HEY NONNY NONNY!
June 6, 1932 (32)
Music by Michael H. Cleary
Lyrics by Max and Nathaniel Lief

Personally Yours • Tell Me Something About Yourself • This Is Different, Dear • Manhattan Lullaby • Three Little Columnists • On My Nude Ranch With You • I Didn't Know That It Was Loaded

• Minsky's Metropolitan Grand Opera • The Season Ended • Hey Nonny Nonny (Music by Will Irwin; lyrics by Ogden Nash) • Be a Little Lackadaisical (Music and lyrics by Herman Hupfeld) • Lady in Waiting (Music by Alberta Nichols; lyrics by Mann Holiner) • I'm Really Not That Way (Music by Will Irwin; lyrics by Malcolm McComb) • Wouldn't That Be Wonderful (Music and lyrics by Herman Hupfeld) • In Those Good Old Horsecar Days (Music by Will Irwin; lyrics by Malcolm McComb) • Let's Go Lovin' (Music and lyrics by Herman Hupfeld)

HIGH BUTTON SHOES
October 9, 1947 (727)
Music by Jule Styne
Lyrics by Sammy Cahn

Based on Stephen Longstreet's novel *The Sisters Liked Them Handsome*

He Tried to Make a Dollar • Can't You Just See Yourself? • There's Nothing Like a Model T • Next to Texas, I Love You • Security • Bird Watcher's Song • Get Away for a Day in the Country • Papa, Won't You Dance With Me? • On a Sunday by the Sea • You're My Girl • I Still Get Jealous • Nobody Ever Died for Dear Old Rutgers

RA

HIGH JINKS
December 10, 1913 (213)
Music by Rudolf Friml
Lyrics by Otto Harbach

Something Seems Tingle-ingle-ing • Jim • Love's Own Kiss • Romeo • Chi-Chi • My Woman's Heart • Not Now, But Later • What Is Life Without Love? • She Says It With Her Eyes • The Bubble • When Sammy Sang the Marseillaise • Dicky Birds

VS

HIGH KICKERS
October 31, 1941 (171)
Music by Harry Ruby
Lyrics by Bert Kalmar

My Sweetheart Mamie • Didn't Your Mother Tell You Nothing? • You're on My Mind • Panic in Panama • The Girls • The Time to Sing • I've Got Something • Cigarettes • Waltzing in the Moonlight

HIGH SPIRITS
April 7, 1964 (375)
Music and lyrics by Hugh Martin and Timothy Gray

Based on the play *Blithe Spirit* by Noël Coward

Was She Prettier Than I? • The Bicycle Song • You'd Better Love Me • Where Is the Man I Married? • The Sandwich Man • Go Into Your Trance • Forever and a Day • Something Tells Me • I Know Your Heart • Faster Than Sound • If I Gave You • Talking to You • Home Sweet Heaven • Something Is Coming to Tea • The Exorcism • What in the World Did You Want?

RA, SEL

HIGHER AND HIGHER
April 4, 1940 (108)
Music by Richard Rodgers
Lyrics by Lorenz Hart

A Barking Baby Never Bites • From Another World • Mornings at Seven • Nothing but You • Disgustingly Rich • Blue Monday • Ev'ry Sunday Afternoon • Lovely Day for a Murder • How's Your Health? • It Never Entered My Mind • I'm Afraid

Dropped from production
It's Pretty in the City

A HISTORY OF THE AMERICAN FILM
March 30, 1978 (21)
Music by Mel Marvin
Lyrics by Christopher Durang

The Silent Years • Minstrel Song • Shanty Town Romance • They Can't Prohibit Love • We're in a Salad • Euphemism • Ostende Nobis Tosca • The Red, White and the Blue • Pretty Pin-Up • Apple Blossom Victory • Isn't It Fun to Be in the Movies • Search for Wisdom

HIT THE DECK
April 25, 1927 (352)
Music by Vincent Youmans
Lyrics by Leo Robin and Clifford Grey

Based on the play *Shore Leave* by Hubert Osborne

Join the Navy • What's a Kiss Among Friends? • The Harbor of My Heart • Shore Leave • Lucky Bird • Loo Loo • Why, Oh Why?* • Sometimes I'm Happy *(Lyrics by Irving Caesar) • Hallelujah!* • If He'll Come Back to Me • Nothing Could Be Sweeter

Written for film version (1929)
Keepin' Myself for You (Lyrics by Sidney Clare)

Written for film version (1954)
The Lady From the Bayou (Lyrics by Leo Robin)

RA,SEL

HIT THE TRAIL
December 2, 1954 (4)
Music by Frederico Valerio
Lyrics by Elizabeth Miele

On With the Show • Mr. Right • Dynamic • Blue Sierras • No! No! No! • The Wide Open Spaces • Gold Cannot Buy • Remember the Night • Tell Me How • It Was Destiny • Just a Wonderful Time • Nevada Hoe Down • New Look Feeling • Set Me Free • Somehow I've Always Known • My Fatal Charm • Men Are a Pain in the Neck • Wherever I May Go • Take Your Time • Happy Birthday

HITCHY-KOO
October 19, 1920 (71)
Music by Jerome Kern
Lyrics by Anne Caldwell

I Am Daguerre • Sweeties • Ding-Dong, It's Kissing Time • Moon of Love • Canajoharie • Buggy Riding • Old New York • We'll Make a Bet • I Want to Marry •

Treasure Island • Bring 'Em Back • The Star of Hitchy-Koo • Old Fashioned Dances • Old-Fashioned Garden (Music and lyrics by Cole Porter)

Dropped from production
Chick! Chick! Chick! • Girls in the Sea

HOBO (OB)
April 10, 1961 (32)
Music and lyrics by John Dooley

Nuthin' for Nuthin' • Jonah's Wail • Sympathy • The Virgin Polka • Cindy • Julie • From the Moment • Bleecker Street • Sweetness • On the Day When the World Goes Boom • Somewhere in Your Eyes • I Hate You • Good for Nothing • Little Birds • Who Put Out the Light That Lit the Candle . . .

HOLD EVERYTHING!
October 10, 1928 (413)
Music by Ray Henderson
Lyrics by B.G. DeSylva and Lew Brown

We're Calling On Mr. Brooks • An Outdoor Man for My Indoor Sports • Footwork • You're the Cream in My Coffee • When I Love, I Love • Too Good to Be True • To Know You Is to Love You • Don't Hold Everything • For Sweet Charity's Sake • Genealogy • Oh, Gosh • It's All Over but the Shoutin'

HOLD IT!
May 5, 1948 (46)
Music by Gerald Marks
Lyrics by Sam Lerner

Heaven Sent • Buck in the Bank • Always You • About Face • Fundamental Character • Hold It! • Nevermore • Roll 'Em • It Was So Nice Having You • Down the Well • You Took Possession of Me • Friendly Enemy

HOLD ON TO YOUR HATS
September 11, 1940 (158)
Music by Burton Lane
Lyrics by E.Y. Harburg

Way Out West Where the East Begins • Hold On to Your Hats • Walkin' Along Mindin' My Business • The World Is in My Arms • Would You Be So Kindly • Life Was Pie for the Pioneer • Don't Let It Get You Down • There's a Great Day Coming, Manana • Then You Were Never in Love • Down on the Dude Ranch • She Came, She Saw, She Can Canned • Old Timer

HOLD YOUR HORSES
September 25, 1933 (88)
Music by Robert Russell Bennett
Lyrics by Owen Murphy and Robert A. Simon

Good Evening, Mr. Man in the Moon • Galloping Through the Park • Hold Your Horses • Peanuts and Kisses • High Shoes • Singing to You (Music and lyrics by Ben Oakland, Margot Millham and Robert A. Simon) • If I Love Again (Music by Ben Oakland; lyrics by J.P. Murray) • I Guess I Love You • Happy Little Weekend • Old Man Subway • Do You? • I'd

Like to Take You Home to Meet My Mother • Swapping Sweet Nothings With You

HOLKA-POLKA
October 14, 1925 (21)
Music by Will Ortman
Lyrics by Gus Kahn and Raymond B. Egan

Home of My Heart • When Love Is Near • In a Little While • Holka-Polka • The Highway's Call • Spring in Autumn

HOME MOVIES (OB)
May 11, 1964 (72)
Music by Al Carmines
Lyrics by Rosalyn Drexler

A Mania • Peanut Song • Pents-un-Wreckum • Swoop of the Moopem • Birdies • A Power Stronger Than Will • Equipment Song • You Look Like Me • Remember When I Hated You? • Once You've Seen Everything • Darkness Song • Show Me • My Number Is Eleven • Boasting Song • I Know You Sell It • Here They Come Now • Lower the Boom • Chocolate Turkey • Daisies • Do Not Bruise the Fruit • Stuttering Song • Pussy Cat Song • Seminary Song • I'm Gwine Lie Down • Two Falls to a Finish

HOME SWEET HOMER
January 4, 1976 (1)
Music by Mitch Leigh
Lyrics by Charles Burr and Forman Brown

Loosely based on Homer's *Odyssey*

The Tales • The Future • The Departure • Home Sweet Homer • The Ball • How Could I Dare to Dream? • I Never Imagined Goodbye • Love Is the Prize • Penelope's Hand • He Will Come Home Again • Did He Really Think? • I Was Wrong • The Rose • Tomorrow • The Contest • He Sang Songs

THE HONEYMOON EXPRESS
February 6, 1913 (156)
Music by Jean Schwartz
Lyrics by Joseph W. Herbert and Harold Atteridge

The Tennis Tournament • That's the Life for Me • The Moving Men • When the Honeymoon Stops Shining • Syncopatia Land • That Gal of Mine • I Want the Strolling Good • You'll Call the Next Love the First • The Ragtime Express • Bring Back Your Love • Up on the Hudson Shore • I Want a Toy Soldier Man • Tommy, Won't You Teach Me the Tango • Where the Red, Red Roses Grow • My Raggyadore • When Gaby Did the Gaby Glide

HONEYMOON LANE
September 20, 1926 (353)
Music by James F. Hanley
Lyrics by Eddie Dowling

Little White House • Dreams for Sale • On to Hollywood • Waddya Say—We Steal Away • Head Over Heels in Love • A Little Smile, a Little Sigh • The Stone Bridge at Eight • Half a Moon (Lyrics by

Dowling and Herbert Reynolds) • Little Old New Hampshire • Mary Dear • Jersey Walk • Gee, but I'd Like to Be Bad

HOORAY FOR WHAT!
December 1, 1937 (200)
Music by Harold Arlen
Lyrics by E.Y. Harburg

Hooray for What! • God's Country • I've Gone Romantic on You • Moanin' in the Mornin' • Viva for Geneva • Life's a Dance • Napoleon's a Pastry • Down With Love • A Fashion Girl • The Night of the Embassy Ball • In the Shade of the New Apple Tree

Dropped from production
Buds Won't Bud

HORSEMAN, PASS BY (OB)
January 15, 1969 (37)
Music by John Duffy
Lyrics by Rocco Bufano and John Duffy (based on the writings of William Butler Yeats)

What Then? • This Great Purple Butterfly • Brown Penny • A Soldier Takes Pride in Saluting His Captain • Before the World Was Made • Last Confession • Mad as the Mist and Snow • Crazy Jane on the Day of Judgment • Her Anxiety • Salley Gardens • Soulless a Faery Dies • To an Isle in the Water • Consolation

HOT CHOCOLATES
June 29, 1929 (228)
Music by Thomas (Fats) Waller and Harry Brooks
Lyrics by Andy Razaf

Song of the Cotton Fields • Sweet Savannah Sue • Say It With Your Feet • Ain't Misbehavin' • Goddess of Rain • Dixie Cinderella • Black and Blue • That Rhythm Man • Can't We Get Together • Off Time

HOT GROG (OB)
October 6, 1977 (22)
Music and lyrics by Bland Simpson and Jim Wann

Seizure to Roam • Got a Notion • Come On Down to the Sea • Hot Grog • The Pirates' Life • The Difference Is Me • Change in Direction • Heaven Must Have Been Smiling • Hack 'Em • Treasure to Bury/One of Us • Sea Breeze • Skye Boat Song • Marooned • Drinking Fool • Bound Away • The Head Song

HOT RHYTHM
August 21, 1930 (73)
Music by Porter Grainger
Lyrics by Donald Heywood

Say the Word That Will Make You Mine • The Penalty of Love • Hot Rhythm • Loving You the Way I Do (Music by Eubie Blake; lyrics by Jack Scholl and Will Morrissey)

HOT SPOT
April 19, 1963 (43)
Music by Mary Rodgers

Lyrics by Martin Charnin

Don't Laugh • Welcome • This Little Yankee • Smiles • A Little Trouble • You'd Like Nebraska • Hey, Love • I Had Two Dregs • Rich, Rich, Rich • That's Good—That's Bad • I Think the World of You • Gabie • A Matter of Time • Big Meeting Tonight • A Far, Far Better Way

SEL

HOT-CHA!
March 8, 1932 (119)
Music by Ray Henderson
Lyrics by Lew Brown

You Can Make My Life a Bed of Roses • So This Is Mexico • Conchita • I Want Another Portion of That • Say (What I Wanna Hear You Say) • José, Can't You See! • Fiesta • I Make Up for That in Other Ways • There I Go Dreaming Again • There's Nothing the Matter With Me • Song of the Matadors

HOUSE OF FLOWERS
December 30, 1954 (165)
Music by Harold Arlen
Lyrics by Harold Arlen and Truman Capote

Waitin' • One Man Ain't Quite Enough • A Sleepin' Bee • Smellin' of Vanilla (Bamboo Cage) • House of Flowers • Two Ladies in de Shade of de Banana Tree • What Is a Friend For? • Slide Boy, Slide • I'm Gonna Leave Off Wearing My Shoes • Has I Let You Down? • I Never Has Seen Snow • Turtle Song • Don't Like Goodbyes • Mardi Gras

RA,SEL

THE HOUSEBOAT ON THE STYX
December 25, 1928 (103)
Music by Alma Sanders
Lyrics by Monte Carlo

Based on the story by John Kendrick Bangs

Ode to the Styx • The Houseboat on the Styx • The Roll Call in the Morning • Cleopatra, We're Fond of You • The Fountain of Youth • My Heaven • Club Song • Back in the Days of Long Ago • An Irate Pirate Am I • Red River • Soul Mates • Hell's Finest • Men of Hades • You've Got to Know Just How to Make Love • Someone Like You

How Now, Dow Jones
December 7, 1967 (220)
Music by Elmer Bernstein
Lyrics by Carolyn Leigh

A-B-C • They Don't Make 'Em Like That Anymore • Live a Little • The Pleasure's About to Be Mine • A Little Investigation • Walk Away • Goodbye, Failure, Goodbye • Step to the Rear • Shakespeare Lied • Big Trouble • Credo • One of Those Moments • He's Here! • Panic • Touch and Go • That's Good Enough for Me

RA

HOW TO BE A JEWISH MOTHER
December 28, 1967 (21)
Music by Michael Leonard
Lyrics by Herbert Martin

Based on the book by Dan Greenburg

Once the Man You Laughed At • Laugh a Little • Since the Time We Met • The Wedding Song • Child You Are

HOW TO STEAL AN ELECTION (OB)
October 13, 1968 (89)
Music and lyrics by Oscar Brand

The Plumed Knight • Clay and Frelinghuysen • Get on the Raft With Taft • Silent Cal • Nobody's Listening • The Right Man • How to Steal an Election • Van Buren • Tippecanoe and Tyler Too • Charisma • Lincoln and Soda • Lincoln and Liberty • Grant • Law and Order • Lucky Lindy • Down Among the Grass Roots • Get Out the Vote • Mr. Might've Been • We're Gonna Win • More of the Same

RA

HOW TO SUCCEED IN BUSINESS WITHOUT REALLY TRYING[1]
October 14, 1961 (1417)
Music and lyrics by Frank Loesser

Based on the book by Shepherd Mead

How To • Happy to Keep His Dinner Warm • Coffee Break • The Company Way • A Secretary Is Not a Toy • Been a Long Day • Grand Old Ivy • Paris Original • Rosemary • Cinderella, Darling • Love From a Heart of Gold • I Believe in You • Brotherhood of Man

RA,VS,SEL

[1] Pulitzer Prize winner; Tony Award for Best Score

THE HUMAN COMEDY (OB)
December 29, 1983[1]
Music by Galt MacDermot
Lyrics by William Dumaresq

Based on the novel by William Saroyan

In a Little Town in California • Hi Ya Kid • We're a Little Family • The Assyrians • Noses • You're a Little Young for the Job • I Can Carry a Tune • Happy Birthday • Happy Anniversary • I Think the Kid Will Do • Beautiful Music • Cocoanut Cream Pie • When I Am Lost • I Said, Oh No • Daddy Will Not Come Walking Through the Door • The Birds In the Sky • Remember Always to Give • Long Past Sunset • Don't Tell Me • Everything Is Changed • The World Is Full of Loneliness • How I Love Your Thingamajig • Everlasting • An Orphan, I Am • I'll Tell You About My Family • I Wish I Were a Man • Marcus, My Friend • My Sister Bess • I've Known a Lot of Guys • Diana • The Birds in the Trees/A Lot of Men • Parting • What Am I Supposed to Do? • I'm Home • Somewhere, Someone • I'll Always Love You • Fathers and Mothers (and You and Me)

[1] Still running December 31, 1983

HUMMIN' SAM
April 8, 1933 (1)
Music and lyrics by Alexander Hill

Steppin' Along • Harlem Dan • How the First Song Was Born • They're Off • Pinching Myself • Change Your Mind About Me • If I Didn't Have You • In the Stretch • Jubilee • A Little Bit of Quicksilver • Answer My Heart • Stompin' 'Em Down • I'll Be True, but I'll Be Blue • Jitters • Fifteen Minutes a Day • Ain'tcha Glad You Got Music? • Dancing, and I Mean Dancing

HURRY, HARRY
October 12, 1972 (2)
Music by Bill Weeden
Lyrics by David Finkle

I'm Gonna • When a Man Cries • A Trip Through My Mind • Life • Love Can • Africa Speaks • Somewhere in the Past • Hurry, Harry • Goodbye • You Won't Be Happy • He Is My Bag

I CAN GET IT FOR YOU WHOLESALE
March 22, 1962 (300)
Music and lyrics by Harold Rome

Based on the novel by Jerome Weidman

I'm Not a Well Man • The Way Things Are • When Gemini Meets Capricorn • Momma, Momma • The Sound of Money • The Family Way • Too Soon • Who Knows? • Have I Told You Lately? • Ballad of the Garment Trade • A Gift Today • Miss Marmelstein • A Funny Thing Happened • What's in It for Me? • What Are They Doing to Us Now? • Eat a Little Something

RA,VS,SEL

I CAN'T KEEP RUNNING IN PLACE (OB)
May 14, 1981 (187)
Music and lyrics by Barbara Schottenfeld

I'm Glad I'm Here • Don't Say Yes if You Want to Say No • I Can't Keep Running in Place • I'm on My Own • More of Me to Love • I Live Alone • I Can Count on You • Penis Envy • Get the Answer Now • What if We • Almost Maybes and Perhapses • Where Will I Be Next Wednesday Night?

RA

I DO! I DO!
December 5, 1966 (560)
Music by Harvey Schmidt
Lyrics by Tom Jones

Based on the play *The Fourposter* by Jan de Hartog

All the Dearly Beloved • Together Forever • I Do! I Do! • Good Night • I Love My Wife • Something Has Happened • My Cup Runneth Over • Love Isn't Everything • Nobody's Perfect • A Well-Known Fact • Flaming Agnes • The Honeymoon Is Over • Where Are the Snows? • When the Kids Get Married • The Father of the Bride • What Is a Woman? • Someone Needs Me • Roll Up the Ribbons • This House

RA,VS,SEL

I FEEL WONDERFUL (OB)
October 18, 1954 (49)
Music and lyrics by Jerry Herman

When I Love Again • It's Christmas Today • Over and Over • I Feel Wonderful • Lonesome in New York • This Has Never Been Done Before • Dior, Dior • Jailhouse Blues • Since Eve

I HAD A BALL
December 15, 1964 (184)
Music and lyrics by Jack Lawrence and Stan Freeman

Coney Island, U.S.A. • The Other Half of Me • Red-Blooded American Boy • I Got Everything I Want • Freud • Think Beautiful • Addie's at It Again • Faith • Can It Be Possible? • The Neighborhood Song • The Affluent Society • Boys, Boys, Boys • Fickle Finger of Fate • I Had a Ball • Almost • You Deserve Me

RA,SEL

I LOVE MY WIFE
April 17, 1977 (864)
Music by Cy Coleman
Lyrics by Michael Stewart

We're Still Friends • Monica • By Threes • A Mover's Life • Love Revolution • Someone Wonderful I Missed • Sexually Free • Hey There, Good Times • Lovers on Christmas Eve • Scream • Everybody Today Is Turning On • Married Couple Seeks Married Couple • I Love My Wife

RA,SEL

I MARRIED AN ANGEL[1]
May 11, 1938 (338)
Music by Richard Rodgers
Lyrics by Lorenz Hart

Did You Ever Get Stung? • I Married an Angel • The Modiste • I'll Tell the Man in the Street • How to Win Friends and Influence People • Spring Is Here • Angel Without Wings • A Twinkle in Your Eye • At the Roxy Music Hall

[1] Reversing the usual sequence, the show began

as a film with a screenplay by Moss Hart. It was cancelled before going into production, however, when Louis B. Mayer, the head of MGM, decided that "fantasies are not commercial." Rodgers and Hart (Lorenz, the lyricist, not Moss) took the idea to Broadway producer Dwight Wiman, who acquired the rights and produced it on Broadway. Interestingly, it became a film four years later. The studio was MGM.

I REMEMBER MAMA[1]
May 31, 1979 (108)
Music by Richard Rodgers
Lyrics by Martin Charnin
Additional lyrics by Raymond Jessel

Based on the play by John Van Druten (and stories by Kathryn Forbes) which had been produced by Richard Rodgers and Oscar Hammerstein II

I Remember Mama • A Little Bit More (Lyrics by Jessel) • A Writer Writes at Night • Ev'ry Day (Comes Something Beautiful) • You Could Not Please Me More • Uncle Chris (Lyrics by Jessel) • Lullaby • Easy Come, Easy Go (Lyrics by Jessel) • It's Not the End of the World • Mama Always Makes It Better* • Lars, Lars • Fair Trade • It's Going to Be Good to Be Gone • Time

Dropped from production
Maybe, Maybe, Maybe • Midsummer Night • A Most Disagreeable Man • An Old City Boy at Heart • A Fam'ly We Will Be • Such Good Fun • When • Where We Came From (Lyrics by Jessel) • I Don't Know How (Lyrics by Jessel)

SEL

[1] This was the last score that Richard Rodgers wrote before his death on December 30, 1979.

I TAKE THESE WOMEN (OB)
March 11, 1982 (20)
Music by Robert Kole
Lyrics by Sandi Merle

Adultery • Annie's Lament • I Am Yours • Soliloquy • Why? • This Is My House • Common Sense • I Took These Women • Yesterday's Champagne • Incomprehensible • I Like Her • You Turn Me On • On My Own

I'D RATHER BE RIGHT
November 2, 1937 (290)
Music by Richard Rodgers
Lyrics by Lorenz Hart

A Homogeneous Cabinet • Have You Met Miss Jones? • Take and Take and Take • Spring in Vienna* • A Little Bit of Constitutional Fun • Sweet Sixty-Five • We're Going to Balance the Budget • Labor Is the Thing • I'd Rather Be Right* • Off the Record * • A Baby Bond

Added to production after opening
What It's All About

Dropped from production
The World Is My Oyster • Ev'rybody Loves You

IF THE SHOE FITS
December 5, 1946 (20)
Music by David Raksin
Lyrics by June Carroll

Start the Ball Rollin' • I Wish • In the Morning • Come and Bring Your Instruments • Night After Night • Every Eve • With a Wave of My Wand • Am I a Man or a Mouse? • I'm Not Myself Tonight • Three Questions • If the Shoe Fits • What's the Younger Generation Coming to? • Have You Seen the Countess Cindy? • I Took Another Look • This Is the End of the Story • I Want to Go Back to the Bottom of the Garden • My Business Man

I'LL SAY SHE IS[1]
May 19, 1924 (313)
Music by Tom Johnstone
Lyrics by Will B. Johnstone

Do It • Pretty Girl • Give Me a Thrill • Only You • Break Into Your Heart • San Toy • Rainy Day • Wall Street Blues

[1] This show marked the Broadway debut of the four Marx Brothers.

THE ILLUSTRATORS' SHOW
January 22, 1936 (5)

I Want to Play With the Girls (Music by Edgar Fairchild; lyrics by Milton Pascal) • Let's Talk About the Weather (Music and lyrics by Charlotte Kent) • I've Walked in the Moonlight (Music by Edgar Fairchild; lyrics by Milton Pascal) • Park Avenue's Going to Town (Music by Edgar Fairchild; lyrics by Milton Pascal) • Bang, the Bell Rang! (Music by Irving Actman; lyrics by Frank Loesser) • A Waltz Was Born in Vienna (Music by Frederick Loewe; lyrics by Earle Crooker) • I'm You (Music by Irving Actman; lyrics by Frank Loesser) • Just for Tonight (Music and lyrics by Charlotte Kent) • Give Me the Wild Trumpets (Music by Irving Actman; lyrics by Frank Loesser) • Hello, Ma (Music by Michael H. Cleary; lyrics by Max and Nathaniel Lief) • I Love a Polka So (Music by Berenice Kazounoff; lyrics by Carl Randall) • Wherefore Art Thou, Juliet? (Music and lyrics by Charlotte Kent)

ILLYA DARLING
April 11, 1967 (320)
Music by Manos Hadjidakis
Lyrics by Joe Darion

Based on the film *Never on Sunday* (1959)

Po, Po, Po • Zebekiko • Piraeus, My Love • Golden Land • Love, Love, Love • I Think She Needs Me • I'll Never Lay Down Any More • After Love • Birthday Song • Medea Tango • Illya Darling • Dear Mr. Schubert • The Lesson • Never on Sunday • Ya Chara

RA

I'M GETTING MY ACT TOGETHER AND TAKING IT ON THE ROAD
June 14, 1978[1] (1165)
Music by Nancy Ford

Lyrics by Gretchen Cryer

Natural High • Smile • In a Simple Way I Love You • Miss America • Strong Woman Number • Dear Tom • Old Friend • Put in a Package and Sold • Feel the Love • Lonely Lady • Happy Birthday

RA,SEL

[1] Opened this date Off Broadway; moved to Broadway December 16, 1978.

I'M SOLOMON
April 23, 1968 (7)
Music by Ernest Gold
Lyrics by Anne Croswell

Based on the play *King Solomon and the Cobbler* by Sammy Gronemann

David and Bathsheba • Hail the Son of David • Preposterous • Have You Heard? • The Citation • In Love With a Fool • Someone Like Me • In Someone Else's Sandals • The Three Riddles (Lyrics by Erich Segal) • Once in 2.7 Years • Have You Ever Been Alone With a King Before? (Music by Bill Weeden; lyrics by David Finkle) • Time to Let Go • Lord I Am but a Little Child • Something in His Eyes • That Guilty Feeling (Music by Bill Weeden; lyrics by David Finkle) • With Your Hand in My Hand

IN TROUSERS (OB)
February 22, 1981 (15)
Music and lyrics by William Finn

I Can't Sleep • A Helluva Day • How Marvin Eats His Breakfast • My High School Sweetheart • Set Those Sails • I Swear I Won't Ever Again • Rit, Tit, Tat • I Am Wearing a Hat • Marvin's Giddy Seizures • A Breakfast Over Sugar • I'm Breaking Down • Whizzer Brown • The Rape of Miss Goldberg • Mommy Dear Has Dropped Dead in Her Sleep • Nausea Before the Game • Love Me for What I Am • How America Got It's Name • Marvin Takes a Victory Shower • Another Sleepless Night • Goodnight

RA

INNER CITY
December 19, 1971 (97)
Music by Helen Miller
Lyrics by Eve Merriam

Based on the book *The Inner City Mother Goose* by Eve Merriam

Fee Fi Fo Fum • Now I Lay Me • Locks • I Had a Little Teevee • Hushabye Baby • My Mother Said • Diddle Diddle Dumpling • Rub a Dub Dub • You'll Find Mice • Ding Dong Bell • The Brave Old City of New York • Urban Renewal • The Nub of the Nation • Mary, Mary • City Life • One Misty, Moisty Morning • Jack Be Nimble • If Wishes Were Horses • One Man • Deep in the Night • Statistics • Twelve Rooftops Leaping • Take-a-Tour, Congressman • Simple Simon • Poverty Program • One, Two • Tom,

Tom • Hickety, Pickety • Half Alive • This Is the Way We Go to School • The Spirit of Education • Little Jack Horner • Subway Dream • Christmas Is Coming • I'm Sorry Says the Machine • Jeremiah Obadiah • Riddle Song • Shadow of the Sun • Boys and Girls Come Out to Play • Summer Nights • Lucy Locket • Winter Nights • Wisdom • The Hooker • Wino Will • Man in the Doorway • Starlight, Starbright • The Cow Jumped Over the Moon • The Dealer • Taffy • Numbers • The Pickpocket • Law and Order • Kindness • As I Went Over • There Was a Little Man • Who Killed Nobody? • It's My Belief • Street Sermon • The Great If • On This Rock

RA

INSIDE U.S.A.
April 30, 1948 (399)
Music by Arthur Schwartz
Lyrics by Howard Dietz

Inside U.S.A • Come, Oh Come (to Pittsburgh) • Blue Grass • Haunted Heart • First Prize at the Fair • At the Mardi Gras • My Gal Is Mine Once More • We Won't Take It Back • Rhode Island Is Famous for You

Dropped from production
Atlanta

RA

IRENE
November 18, 1919 (670)
Music by Harry Tierney
Lyrics by Joseph McCarthy

The Family Tree • Hobbies • Alice Blue Gown* • Castle of Dreams • The Talk of the Town • Worthy of You • Irene • We're Getting Away With It • Skyrocket • The Last Part of Ev'ry Party

Added to 1973 revival (594)
The World Must Be Bigger Than an Avenue (Music by Wally Harper; lyrics by Jack Lloyd) • An Irish Girl (Music by Otis Clements; lyrics by Charles Gaynor) • Mother, Angel, Darling (Music and lyrics by Charles Gaynor) • The Riviera Rage (Music by Wally Harper) • The Great Lover Tango (Music by Otis Clements; lyrics by Charles Gaynor) • I'm Always Chasing Rainbows* (Music by Harry Carroll; lyrics by McCarthy) • You Made Me Love You (Music by James Monaco; lyrics by McCarthy)

RA,VS,SEL

IRMA LA DOUCE
September 29, 1960 (527)
Music by Marguerite Monnot
Lyrics by Julian More, David Heneker and Monty Norman

Valse Milieu • Sons of France • The Bridge of Caulaincourt • Our Language of Love • She's Got the Lot • Dis-donc, Dis-donc • Le Grisbi Is le Root of le Evil in Man • The Wreck of a Mec • That's a Crime • From a Prison Cell • Irma la Douce • There Is Only One Paris for That • But • Christmas Child

RA

IS THERE LIFE AFTER HIGH SCHOOL?
May 7, 1982 (12)
Music and lyrics by Craig Carnelia

The Kid Inside • Things I Learned in High School • Second Thoughts • Nothing Really Happened • Beer • For Them • Diary of a Homecoming Queen • Thousands of Trumpets • Reunion • High School All Over Again • Fran and Jane • I'm Glad You Didn't Know Me

RA

IT'S A BIRD, IT'S A PLANE, IT'S SUPERMAN
March 29, 1966 (129)
Music by Charles Strouse
Lyrics by Lee Adams

Based on the comic strip "Superman"

Doing Good • We Need Him • It's Superman • We Don't Matter at All • Revenge • The Woman for the Man • You've Got Possibilities • What I've Always Wanted • Everything's Easy When You Know How • It's Super Nice • So Long, Big Guy • The Strongest Man in the World • Ooh, Do You Love You! • You've Got What I Need • I'm Not Finished Yet • Pow! Bam! Zonk!

RA,SEL

IT'S SO NICE TO BE CIVILIZED
June 3, 1980 (8)
Music and lyrics by Micki Grant

Step Into My World • Keep Your Eye on the Red • Wake-Up Sun • Subway Rider • God Help Us • Who's Going to Teach the Children? • Out on the Street • Welcome Mr. Anderson • Why Can't Me and You? • When I Rise • The World Keeps Going Round • Antiquity • I've Still Got My Bite • Look at Us • The American Dream • Bright Lights • It's So Nice to Be Civilized • Like a Lady • Pass a Little Love Around

J

JACK O' LANTERN
October 16, 1917 (265)
Music by Ivan Caryll
Lyrics by Anne Caldwell

Hear the Bell • Come and Have a Swing With Me •
Wait Till the Cows Come Home • Follow the Girls
Around • Girls I've Met (Lyrics by Louis Harrison) •
Knit, Knit, Knit • I'll Take You Back to Italy (Music
and lyrics by Irving Berlin) • Take a Trip to
Candyland • Oh, Papa! • A Sweetheart of My Own •
Along Came Another Little Girl (Lyrics by Benjamin
Hapgood Burt)

JACKPOT
January 13, 1944 (67)
Music by Vernon Duke
Lyrics by Howard Dietz

The Last Long Mile • Blind Date • I Kissed My Girl
Goodbye • A Piece of a Girl • My Top Sergeant •
Sugarfoot • What Happened? • He's Good for
Nothing but Me • What's Mine Is Yours • It Was
Nice Knowing You • Nobody Ever Pins Me Up • I've
Got a One Track Mind • There Are Yanks (from the
Banks of the Wabash)

JACQUES BREL IS ALIVE AND WELL AND LIVING IN PARIS
(OB)
January 22, 1968 (1847)
Music by Jacques Brel
English lyrics by Eric Blau and Mort Shuman

Marathon • Alone • Madeleine • I Loved • Mathilde •
Bachelor's Dance • Timid Frieda • My Death • Girls
and Dogs • Jackie • The Statue • Desperate Ones •
Sons Of • Amsterdam • The Bulls • Old Folks •
Marieke • Brussels • Fannette • Funeral Tango • The
Middle Class • You're Not Alone • Next • Carousel •
If We Only Have Love

RA,SEL

JAMAICA
October 31, 1957 (558)

Music by Harold Arlen
Lyrics by E.Y. Harburg

Savannah • Savannah's Wedding • Pretty to Walk
With • Push de Button • Incompatibility • Little
Biscuit • Cocoanut Sweet • Pity the Sunset • Take It
Slow, Joe • Yankee Dollar • Monkey in the Mango
Tree • Ain't It the Truth • What Good Does It Do •
Leave the Atom Alone • Napoleon • For Every Fish •
I Don't Think I'll End It All Today

RA,SEL

JAZZBO BROWN
August 24, 1980 (44)
Music and lyrics by Stephen H. Lemberg

Jazzbo Brown • Broadway • I'm Bettin' on You •
Million Songs • Born to Sing • He Had the Callin' •
Bump, Bump, Bump • The Same Old Tune • When
You've Loved Your Man • The Best Man • Give Me
More • When I Die • Dancin' Shoes • Precious
Patterns • Funky Bessie • Harlem Follies • First Time
I Saw You • Pride and Freedom • Take a Bow

JENNIE
October 17, 1963 (82)
Music by Arthur Schwartz
Lyrics by Howard Dietz

Suggested by the biography of Laurette Taylor,
Laurette by Marguerite Courtney

Waitin' for the Evening Train • When You're Far
Away From New York Town • I Still Look at You
That Way • For Better or Worse • Born Again • Over
Here • Before I Kiss the World Goodbye • Where
You Are • The Jig • See Seattle • High Is Better
Than Low • The Night May Be Dark • I Believe in
Takin' a Chance • Welcome • Lonely Nights

RA

JESUS CHRIST SUPERSTAR
October 12, 1971 (711)
Music by Andrew Lloyd Webber
Lyrics by Tim Rice

Heaven on Their Minds • What's the Buzz? • Strange Thing Mystifying • Everything's Alright • This Jesus Must Die • Hosanna • Simon Zealots • Poor Jerusalem • Pilate's Dream • The Temple • I Don't Know How to Love Him • Damned for All Time • The Last Supper • Gethsemane • The Arrest • Peter's Denial • Pilate and Christ • King Herod's Song • Could We Start Again, Please? • Judas' Death • Trial Before Pilate • Superstar • The Crucifixion • John 19:41

RA, SEL

JIMMY
October 23, 1969 (84)
Music and lyrics by Bill and Patti Jacob

Based on *Beau James*, Gene Fowler's novel about James J. Walker, Mayor of New York

Will You Think of Me Tomorrow? • The Little Woman • The Darlin' of New York • Five Lovely Ladies • Oh, Gee! • That Old Familiar Ring • The Walker Walk • I Only Wanna Laugh • They Never Proved a Thing • Riverside Drive • The Squabble Song • One in a Million • It's a Nice Place to Visit • The Charmin' Son-of-a-Bitch • Jimmy • Our Jimmy • Life Is a One-Way Street

RA,SEL

JO (OB)
February 12, 1964 (63)
Music by William Dyer
Lyrics by Don Parks and William Dyer

Based on the novel *Little Women* by Louisa May Alcott

Harmony, Mass. • Deep in the Bosom of the Family • Hurry Home • Let's Be Elegant or Die! • Castles in the Air • Time Will Be • What a Long Cold Winter! • Afraid to Fall in Love • A Wedding! A Wedding! • I Like • Genius Burns • If You Can Find a True Love • Nice as Any Man Can Be • More Than Friends • Taking the Cure

JOAN (OB)
June 19, 1972 (64)
Music and lyrics by Al Carmines

Praise the Lord • Come On, Joan • It's So Nice • Go Back • They Call Me the Virgin Mary • Slave Madonna • The Woman I Love • Spoken Aria • Ira, My Dope Fiend • A Country of the Mind • I Live a Little • What I Wonder • The Religious Establishment • In My Silent Universe • Take Courage, Daughter • Rivers of Roses • I'm Madame Margaret, the Therapist • Look at Me, Joan • Despair • Faith Is Such a Simple Thing

JOHN MURRAY ANDERSON'S ALMANAC (1929)
August 14, 1929 (69)

The Almanac Covers (Music by Henry Sullivan; lyrics by Edward Eliscu) • The Polka Dot (Music by Henry Sullivan; lyrics by Clifford Orr) • Tinkle! Tinkle! (Music by Milton Ager; lyrics by Jack Yellen)

• I Can't Remember the Words (Music by Milton Ager and Henry Cabot Lodge; lyrics by Jack Yellen) • Wait for the Happy Ending (Music by Milton Ager; lyrics by Jack Yellen) • I May Be Wrong (but I Think You're Wonderful) (Music by Henry Sullivan; lyrics by Harry Ruskin) • The Nightingale Song (Music by Milton Ager; lyrics by Jack Yellen) • Schrafft's University (Music by Henry Sullivan; lyrics by Edward Eliscu) • The New Yorker (Music by Milton Ager; lyrics by Jack Yellen) • Same Old Moon (Music by Henry Sullivan; lyrics by John Murray Anderson and Clifford Orr) • Educate Your Feet (Music by Milton Ager; lyrics by Jack Yellen) • Getting Into the Talkies (Music by Milton Ager; lyrics by Jack Yellen) • Tiller, Foster, Hoffman, Hale and Albertina Rasch (Music by Henry Sullivan; lyrics by Henry Myers) • Builders of Dreams (Music by Henry Sullivan; lyrics by John Murray Anderson)

JOHN MURRAY ANDERSON'S ALMANAC (1953)
December 10, 1953 (227)
Music and lyrics by Richard Adler and Jerry Ross

Harlequinade • Queen for a Day • You're So Much a Part of Me • I Dare to Dream (Music by Michael Grace and Carl Tucker; lyrics by Sammy Gallup) • Nightingale, Bring Me a Rose (Music by Henry Sullivan; lyrics by John Murray Anderson) • My Love Is a Wanderer (Music and lyrics by Bart Howard) • Tin Pan Alley (Music by Cy Coleman; lyrics by Joseph McCarthy, Jr.) • Merry Little Minuet (Music and lyrics by Sheldon Harnick) • Hope You Come Back • If Every Month Were June (Music by Henry Sullivan; lyrics by John Murray Anderson) • Which Witch? (Music by Charles Zwar; lyrics by Allan Melville) • Fini • Acorn in the Meadow • When Am I Going to Meet Your Mother? • The Earth and the Sky (Music and lyrics by John Rox)

JOHNNY JOHNSON
November 19, 1936 (68)
Music by Kurt Weill
Lyrics by Paul Green

Over in Europe • Democracy's Call • Up Chickamauga Hill • Johnny's Melody • Aggie's Sewing Machine Song • O, Heart of Love • Captain Valentine's Tango • Song of the Goddess • Song of the Wounded Frenchman • Cowboy Song (Oh, the Rio Grande) • Song of the Guns • Mon Ami, My Friend • The Allied High Command • In Times of Tumult and War • Johnny's Arrest and Homecoming • How Sweetly Friendship Binds • The Psychiatry Song • Hymn to Peace • Johnny's Song (Listen to My Song)*

RA

THE JOLLY BACHELORS
January 6, 1910 (84)
Music by Raymond Hubbell
Lyrics by Glen MacDonough

Tax the Bachelors • A Little Bit of Blarney • The Red Cross Girl • The Luncheon Line • Has Anybody Here Seen Kelly?* • What Am I Going to Do to Make You

Love Me? • Stop That "Rag" • Walk This Way • Freshie, O Freshie • The Single Bird • The Mind Reader • I've Lost My Girl • We 'Uns From Dixie • Airship Joy Ride • Moon, Moon, Moon • Little Things • Savannah

JONAH (OB)
February 15, 1966 (24)
Music by Meyer Kupferman
Lyrics by Paul Goodman

Leviathan • Hey, What's This? • Sailor's Round • Evocation • Jonah's Melodrama • I'll Carry You an Inch • Puppet Dream • Sleep Little Mouse • I Cried for My Troubles • My God, Why Hast Thou Forsaken Me? • Forty Days • There's Nothing New Under the Sun • Miserere • Day After Day • The Suns That Daily Rise • I Am a Little Worm

JONICA
April 7, 1930 (40)
Music by Joseph Meyer
Lyrics by William Moll

The Night It Happened • Au Revoir • Tonight or Never • One Step Nearer the Moon • I Want Someone (Music and lyrics by William B. Friedlander) • Tie Your Cares to a Melody • Specially Made for You • Beautiful Girls • March of the Rice and Old Shoes • A Million Good Reasons • If You Were the Apple • Here in My Heart • The Wedding Parade

JOSEPH AND THE AMAZING TECHNICOLOR DREAMCOAT[1]
January 27, 1982 (743)
Music by Andrew Lloyd Webber
Lyrics by Tim Rice

Based on episodes from *Genesis*

You Are What You Feel • Joseph's Coat (The Coat of Many Colors) • Joseph's Dreams • Poor, Poor Joseph • One More Angel in Heaven • Potiphar • Close Every Door • Go, Go, Joseph • Pharaoh's Story • Poor, Poor Pharaoh • Song of the King • Pharaoh's Dream Explained • Stone the Crows • Those Canaan Days • The Brothers Come to Egypt • Grovel, Grovel • Who's the Thief? • Benjamin Calypso • Any Dream Will Do

RA,VS

[1] First performed Off Broadway on December 30, 1976. (22)

JOY (OB)
January 27, 1970 (205)
Music and lyrics by Oscar Brown, Jr.

Time • Under the Sun • Wimmen's Ways • Funny Feelin' (Music and lyrics by Oscar Brown, Jr. and Luis Henrique) • If I Only Had (Music and lyrics by Oscar Brown, Jr. and Charles Aznavour) • What Is a Friend? (Music and lyrics by Oscar Brown, Jr. and Luis Henrique) • Much as I Love You (Music and lyrics by Oscar Brown, Jr. and Luis Henrique) • Sky and Sea (Music and lyrics by Oscar Brown, Jr. and Johnny Alf) • Afro Blue (Music and lyrics by Oscar Brown, Jr. and Mongo Santamaria) • Mother Africa's Day (Music and lyrics by Oscar Brown, Jr. and Sivuca) • A New Generation (Music and lyrics by Oscar Brown, Jr. and Luis Henrique) • Brown Baby • Funky World • Nothing but a Fool (Music and lyrics by Oscar Brown, Jr. and Luis Henrique) • Flowing to the Sea • Brother, Where Are You?

RA

A JOYFUL NOISE
December 15, 1966 (12)
Music and lyrics by Oscar Brand and Paul Nassau

Based on the novel *The Innocent Breed* by Borden Deal

Longtime Travelin' • A Joyful Noise • I'm Ready • Spring Time of the Year • I Like to Look My Best • No Talent • Not Me • Until Today • Swinging a Dance • To the Top • I Love Nashville • Whither Thou Goest • We Won't Forget to Write • Ballad Maker • Barefoot Gal • Fool's Gold • The Big Guitar • Love Was • I Say Yes • Lord, You Sure Know How to Make a New Day

SEL

JUBILEE
October 12, 1935 (169)
Music and lyrics by Cole Porter

Why Shouldn't I? • The Kling-Kling Bird on the Divi-Divi Tree • We're Off to Feathermore • When Love Comes Your Way • What a Nice Municipal Park • When Me, Mowgli, Love • Gather Ye Autographs While Ye May • Begin the Beguine* • My Most Intimate Friend • A Picture of Me Without You • Everybod-ee Who's Anybod-ee • Sunday Morning Breakfast Time • Mr. and Mrs. Smith • Gay Little Wives • Me and Marie • Just One of Those Things* • Our Crown • Swing That Swing • My Loulou • Good Morning, Miss Standing • To Get Away

Dropped from production
Waltz Down the Aisle • There's Nothing Like Swimming • Yours • Sing Jubilee

RA,SEL

JUDY
February 8, 1927 (104)
Music by Charles Rosoff
Lyrics by Leo Robin

Hobohemia • Hard to Get Along With • Looking for a Thrill • Cinderella • Pretty Little Stranger • One Baby • Wear Your Sunday Smile • What a Whale of a Difference a Woman Can Make • Judy, Who D'Ya Love? • When Gentlemen Grew Whiskers and Ladies Grew Old • The Curfew Shall Not Ring Tonight • Start Stompin'

JUMBO
November 16, 1935 (233)
Music by Richard Rodgers
Lyrics by Lorenz Hart

Over and Over Again • The Circus Is on Parade • The Most Beautiful Girl in the World • Laugh • My Romance • Little Girl Blue • The Song of the Roustabouts • Women • Memories of Madison Square Garden • Diavolo • The Circus Wedding

RA (film version)

JUNE DAYS
August 6, 1925 (85)
Music by J. Fred Coots
Lyrics by Clifford Grey

Based on the play *The Charm School* by Alice Duer Miller

Something Wrong With Me • Remembering You • Lucky • June Days (Music by Stephen Jones; lyrics by Clifford Grey and Cyrus Wood) • A Busy Evening • All I Want Is Love (Music by Hal Dyson; lyrics by James Kendis) • Strike • Charming Women • Anytime, Anywhere, Anyhow (Music by Richard Rodgers; lyrics by Lorenz Hart) • How Do You Doodle Do? • Naughty Little Step • Girls Dream of One Thing • Safety in Numbers • Please, Teacher • Take 'Em to the Door Blues • Why Is Love?

JUNE MOON (Play with songs)[1]
October 9, 1929 (273)
Music and lyrics by Ring Lardner

Based on the short story *Some Like 'Em Cold* by Ring Lardner

Montana Moon • Life Is a Game • June Moon • Give Our Child a Name* • Hello, Hello Tokio!

> [1]The songs "June Moon" and "Montana Moon" were published with the byline "Eavesdropped by Ring Lardner and George S. Kaufman".

JUNO
March 9, 1959 (16)
Music and lyrics by Marc Blitzstein

Based on the play *Juno and the Paycock* by Sean O'Casey

We're Alive • I Wish It So • Son of the Ma • We Can Be Proud • Daarlin' Man • One Kind Word • Old Sayin's • What Is the Stars? • You Poor Thing • My True Heart • On a Day Like This • Bird Upon the Tree • Music in the House • It's Not Irish • The Liffey Waltz • Johnny • For Love • Where?

RA

JUST A MINUTE
October 8, 1928 (80)
Music by Harry Archer
Lyrics by Walter O'Keefe

You'll Kill 'Em • Doggone • We'll Just Be Two Commuters • Anything Your Heart Desires • Coming Out of the Garden • I've Got a Cookie Jar but No Cookies • The Break-Me-Down • Pretty, Petite and Sweet • I'm Ninety-eight Pounds of Sweetness • Heigh-Ho Cheerio • Just a Minute

JUST FANCY
October 11, 1927 (79)
Music by Joseph Meyer and Philip Charig
Lyrics by Leo Robin

Based on the play *Just Suppose* by A. E. Thomas

Ain't Love Grand • Shake, Brother! • Memories • Dressed Up for Your Sunday Beau • Two Loving Arms • Humpty-Dumpty • Naughty Boy • Mi Chiquita • I'm a Highway Gentleman • Coo-Coo • You Came Along

K

KA-BOOM (OB)
November 20, 1980 (70)
Music by Joe Ercole
Lyrics by Bruce Kluger

Now We Pray • Oh Lord • A Little Bit o' Glitter • Maybe for Instance • With a World to Conquer • Smile • Let Me Believe in Me • Believe Us, Receive Us • A Few Get Through • Ballad of Adam and Eve • Gimme a "G" • The Soft Spot • You Are You • The Light Around the Corner • Those ABC's • Judgement Day • Bump and Grind for God • Let the Show Go On!

RA

THE KARL MARX PLAY (OB)
April 2, 1973 (31)
Music by Galt MacDermot
Lyrics by Rochelle Owens

My Knees Are Weak • There Was a Hen • O, Mistress Mine • White Sheeting • Hello, Hello • Jenny Westphalen • So I Give You • Dying Child • Jenny Is Like an Angel • Pretty Women • Tempting Salome • It's Me They Talk About • He Eats • Red Lover Wrist Watch • Holy Mystery • Baby Johann • Comes the Revolution • Ya-ta-ta • We Doubt You, Papa • The Hand of Fate • World Creation

RA

KATINKA
December 23, 1915 (220)
Music by Rudolf Friml
Lyrics by Otto Harbach

Vienna Girls • The Bride • One Who Will Understand • Katinka • In a Hurry • 'Tis the End, so Farewell! • Charms Are Fairest When They're Hidden • Your Photo • Allah's Holiday • The Weekly Wedding • I Want All the World to Know • Rackety Coo! • My Paradise • I Want to Marry a Male Quartet • Skidikiscatch • I Can Tell by the Way that You Dance, Dear

VS

KATJA
October 18, 1926 (113)
Music by Jean Gilbert
Lyrics by Harry Graham

When Love's in the Air • Cruel Chief • Dance With You • All the World Loves a Lover • Just for Tonight (Music by Maury Rubens; lyrics by Clifford Grey) • I Fell Head Over Heels in Love • Congratulations • If You Cared • Those Eyes So Tender • Night Birds • Leander • In Jail • Oh, Woe Is Me

KEAN
November 2, 1961 (92)
Music and lyrics by Robert Wright and George Forrest

From a comedy by Jean-Paul Sartre, based in turn on a play by Alexandre Dumas

Penny Plain, Twopence Colored • Man and Shadow • Mayfair Affair • Sweet Danger • Queue at Drury Lane • King of London • To Look Upon My Love • Let's Improvise • Elena • The Social Whirl • The Fog and the Grog • Civilized People • Service for Service • Willow, Willow, Willow • Chime In! • Swept Away • Domesticity • Clown of London • Apology

RA

KEEP IT CLEAN
June 24, 1929 (16)

Just a Little Blue for You (Music and lyrics by James F. Hanley) • Broadway Mammy (Music and lyrics by Clarence Gaskill and Jimmy Duffy) • Doin' the Hot-cha-cha (Music and lyrics by Lester Lee) • I See You but What Do You See in Me? (Music and lyrics by Lester Lee) • All I Need Is Someone Like You (Music by Harry Archer; lyrics by Charles Tobias) • Let Me Hold You in My Arms (Music and lyrics by Clarence Gaskill)

KEEP MOVING
August 23, 1934 (21)
Music by Max Rich
Lyrics by Jack Scholl

749

The Play Is the Bunk • Wake Up, Sleepy Moon • Command to Love (Music by Henry Sullivan) • Midtown • Hot-Cha Chiquita • Superstition • Lovely, Lovely Day (Music by Max Rich and Billy Taylor) • Now Is the Time • Isn't It a Funny Thing?

KEEP OFF THE GRASS
May 23, 1940 (44)
Music by Jimmy McHugh
Lyrics by Al Dubin

The Cabby's Serenade • This Is Spring • Crazy as a Loon • I'll Applaud You With My Feet • A Fugitive From Esquire (Lyrics by Howard Dietz) • Two in a Taxi (Lyrics by Howard Dietz) • The Old Park Bench (Lyrics by Howard Dietz) • A Latin Tune, a Manhattan Moon and You • Clear out of This World • Look Out for My Heart • Old Jitterbug • Raffles (Music by Vernon Duke) • This Is Winter

KEEP SHUFFLIN'
February 27, 1928 (104)

Teasing Mama (Music by Jimmy Johnson; lyrics by Henry Creamer) • Chocolate Bar (Music by "Fats" Waller; lyrics by Andy Razaf) • Labor Day Parade (Music by Clarence Todd; lyrics by Andy Razaf) • Give Me the Sunshine (Music by Jimmy Johnson; lyrics by Henry Creamer and Con Conrad • Leg It (Music by Clarence Todd; lyrics by Henry Creamer and Con Conrad) • 'Sippi (Music by Jimmy Johnson; lyrics by Henry Creamer) • How Jazz Was Born (Music by "Fats" Waller; lyrics by Andy Razaf) • Keep Shufflin' (Music by "Fats" Waller; lyrics by Andy Razaf) • Everybody's Happy in Jimtown (Music by "Fats" Waller; lyrics by Andy Razaf) • Dusky Love (Music by Will Vodery; lyrics by Henry Creamer) • Charlie, My Back Door Man (Music by Clarence Todd; lyrics by Henry Creamer and Con Conrad) • On the Levee (Music by Jimmy Johnson; lyrics by Henry Creamer)

KELLY
February 6, 1965 (1)
Music by Moose Charlap
Lyrics by Eddie Lawrence

Ode to the Bridge • Six Blocks From the Bridge • That Old Time Crowd • Simple Ain't Easy • I'm Gonna Walk Right up to Her • A Moment Ago • This Is a Tough Neighborhood • Never Go There Anymore • Life Can Be Beautiful • Everyone Here Loves Kelly • Ballad to a Brute • Heavyweight Champ of the World • Me and the Elements

KID BOOTS
December 31, 1923 (479)
Music by Harry Tierney
Lyrics by Joseph McCarthy

A Day at the Club • Keep Your Eye on the Ball • The Same Old Way • Someone Loves You After All • Got to Have More • Polly, Put the Kettle On • Let's Do and Say We Didn't • In the Swim • The Old Lake Trail • On With the Game • Mah Jong • Bet on the One You Fancy • I'm in My Glory • A Play-Fair Man •

Win for Me • Down 'Round the 19th Hole • En Route • When the Cocoanuts Call • In the Rough • That's All There Is

THE KING AND I
March 29, 1951 (1,246)
Music by Richard Rodgers
Lyrics by Oscar Hammerstein II

Based on the novel *Anna and the King of Siam* by Margaret Landon

I Whistle a Happy Tune • My Lord and Master • Hello, Young Lovers • March of the Royal Siamese Children • A Puzzlement • The Royal Bangkok Academy • Getting to Know You* • We Kiss in a Shadow • Shall I Tell You What I Think of You? • Something Wonderful • Western People Funny • I Have Dreamed • The King's Song • Shall We Dance?

Dropped from production
Waiting • Who Would Refuse? • Now You Leave

RA,VS,SEL

[1] Tony Award for Best Score

KING OF HEARTS
October 22, 1978 (48)
Music by Peter Link
Lyrics by Jacob Brackman

Based on a screenplay by Philippe de Broca, Maurice Bessy, and Daniel Boulanger

A Strain on the Name • Déjà Vu • Promenade • Turn Around • Nothing, Only Love • King of Hearts • Close Upon the Hour • A Brand New Day • Le Grand Cirque de Provence • Hey, Look at Me, Mrs. Draba • Going Home Tomorrow • Somewhere Is Here • March, March, March

RA

KING OF THE WHOLE DAMN WORLD (OB)
April 12, 1962 (43)
Music and lyrics by Robert Larimer

What to Do? • Grasshop Song • Poor Little Boy • The Night Gondolfi Got Married • King of the World • Who's Perfect? • Little Dog Blue • March You Off in Style • The Riddle of You • How Do They Ever Grow Up? • What's a Mama For? • Don't Tear Up the Horse Slips • Who's Perfect for You? • Far Rockaway • There's Gotta Be a Villain

KISMET[1]
December 3, 1953 (583)
Music and lyrics by Robert Wright and George Forrest

Based on the music of Alexander Borodin[2] and the play by Edward Knoblock

Sands of Time • Rhymes Have I • Fate • Bazaar of the Caravans • Not Since Nineveh • Baubles, Bangles and Beads • Stranger in Paradise • He's in Love! • Gesticulate • Night of My Nights • Was I

Wazir? • Rahadlakum • And This Is My Beloved • The Olive Tree

RA,VS,SEL

[1] Tony Award for Best Score

[2] See individual song titles for notes on musical sources.

KISS ME
July 18, 1927 (28)
Music by Winthrop Cortelyou
Lyrics by Derick Wulff

Kiss Me • I Have Something Nice for You • Arab Maid With Midnight Eyes • You in Your Room; I in Mine • Two Is Company • Rose of Iran • Welcome Home • If You'll Always Say Yes • Pool of Love • Always Another Girl

KISS ME, KATE[1]
December 30, 1948 (1,077)
Music and lyrics by Cole Porter

Based on Shakespeare's *The Taming of the Shrew*

Another Op'nin', Another Show • Why Can't You Behave? • Wunderbar • So in Love • We Open in Venice • Tom, Dick or Harry • I've Come to Wive It Wealthily in Padua* • I Hate Men • Were Thine That Special Face • I Sing of Love • Too Darn Hot • Where Is the Life That Late I Led?* • Always True to You in My Fashion* • Bianca • Brush Up Your Shakespeare* • I Am Ashamed That Women Are So Simple* • Kiss Me, Kate

Dropped from production
We Shall Never Be Younger • It Was Great Fun the First Time • A Woman's Career • What Does Your Servant Dream About? • I'm Afraid, Sweetheart, I Love You • If Ever Married I'm

RA,VS,SEL

[1] Tony Award for Best Score

KITTIWAKE ISLAND (OB)
October 12, 1960 (7)
Music by Alec Wilder
Lyrics by Arnold Sundgaard

Were This to Prove a Feather in My Hat • It Doesn't Look Deserted • Can This Be a Toe Print? • Good Morning, Dr. Puffin • I'd Gladly Walk to Alaska • The Smew Song • Never Try Too Hard • Under a Tree • I Delight in the Sight of My Lydia • The Bard • Robinson Crusoe • Nothing Is Working Quite Right • Don't Give Up the Hunt, Dr. Puffin • If Love's Like a Lark • When One Deems a Lady Sweet • When a

Robin Leaves Chicago • So Raise the Banner High • Oceanography and Old Astronomy • It's So Easy to Say • Hail, the Mythic Smew

KITTY'S KISSES
May 6, 1926 (170)
Music by Con Conrad
Lyrics by Gus Kahn

Walkin' the Track • Choo Choo Love • Kitty's Kisses • I Love to Dance • Thinking of You • Two Fellows and a Girl • I'm in Love (Lyrics by Gus Kahn and Otto Harbach) • Promise Your Kisses • Early in the Morning • I Don't Want Him • Needles • Whenever I Dream • Bounce Me • Step on the Blues (Music by Con Conrad and Will Donaldson; lyrics by Otto Harbach)

KNICKERBOCKER HOLIDAY
October 19, 1938 (168)
Music by Kurt Weill
Lyrics by Maxwell Anderson

Clickety-Clack • It's a Law • There's Nowhere to Go but Up • It Never Was You • How Can You Tell an American? • Will You Remember Me? • One Touch of Alchemy • The One Indispensable Man • Young People Think About Love • September Song* • Ballad of the Robbers • We Are Cut in Twain • To War! • Our Ancient Liberties • Romance and Musketeer • The Scars • Dirge for a Soldier • Ve Vouldn't Gonto Do It

RA,VS

KOSHER KITTY KELLY
June 15, 1925 (105)
Music and lyrics by Leon DeCosta

Dancing Toes • Kosher Kitty Kelly • What's in Store for You • I'll Cuddle Up to You • I Want to Dance With You • Where We Can Be in Love

KWAMINA
October 23, 1961 (32)
Music and lyrics by Richard Adler

The Cocoa Bean Song • Welcome Home • The Sun Is Beginning to Crow • Did You Hear That? • You're as English As • Seven Sheep, Four Red Shirts and a Bottle of Gin • Nothing More to Look Forward To • What's Wrong With Me? • Something Big • Ordinary People • Mammy Traders • A Man Can Have No Choice • What Happened to Me Tonight? • One Wife • Another Time, Another Place • Fetish

RA

L

La Belle Paree[1]
March 20, 1911 (104)
Music by Jerome Kern
Lyrics by Edward Madden

Susan Brown From a Country Town • The Human Brush • Widows • Paris Is a Paradise for Coons* • The Pretty Milliners • Monte Carlo Moon • That Deviling Tune • Teasing • Bosphorus • The Edinburgh Wriggle (Lyrics by M.E. Rourke[2]) • Sing Trovatore • De Goblin's Glide (Lyrics by Frederick Day) • What Kind of a Place Is This? • The Duel • Look Me Over, Dearie • That's All Right for McGilligan (Lyrics by M.E. Rourke)

[1] This was the opening attraction at Broadway's Winter Garden Theatre, as well as Al Jolson's debut on the musical comedy stage. He played Erastus Sparkler, "a colored aristocrat of San Juan Hill, cutting a wide swath in Paris."

[2] Rourke changed his name to Herbert Reynolds after 1914.

La Cage aux Folles
August 21, 1983[1]
Music and lyrics by Jerry Herman

Based on the play by Jean Poiret

We Are What We Are • A Little More Mascara • With Anne on My Arm (also sung as "With You on My Arm") • The Promenade • Song on the Sand • La Cage aux Folles • I Am What I Am • Masculinity • Look Over There • Cocktail Counterpoint • The Best of Times

RA,SEL

[1] Still running December 31, 1983

La Grosse Valise
December 14, 1965 (7)
Music by Gerard Calvi
Lyrics by Harold Rome

La Grosse Valise • A Big One • C'est Defendu • Hamburg Waltz • Happy Song • For You • Sandwich for Two • La Java • Xanadu • Slippy Sloppy Shoes • Delilah Done Me Wrong • Hawaii

La, La, Lucille
May 26, 1919 (104)
Music by George Gershwin[1]
Lyrics by Arthur J. Jackson and B. G. DeSylva

When You Live in a Furnished Flat • The Best of Everything • From Now On • Money, Money, Money! • Tee-Oodle-Um-Bum-Bo • Oo, How I Love to Be Loved by You (Lyrics by Lou Paley) • It's Great to Be in Love • There's More to the Kiss than the X-X-X (Lyrics by Irving Caesar) • Somehow It Seldom Comes True • The Ten Commandments of Love • It's Hard to Tell • Nobody but You

[1] This was his first complete score.

La Strada
December 14, 1969 (1)
Music and lyrics by Lionel Bart

Based on the Federico Fellini film (1954)

Seagull, Starfish, Pebble • The Great Zampano • What's Going On Inside? • Belonging • I Don't Like You • There's a Circus in Town • You're Musical • Only More! • What a Man • Everything Needs Something (Music by Eliot Lawrence; lyrics by Martin Charnin) • Sooner or Later

The Lace Petticoat
January 4, 1927 (15)
Music by Emil Gerstenberger and Carle Carlton
Lyrics by Howard Johnson

Watch the Birdies • Renita Renata • South Wind Is Calling • The Boy in the Blue Uniform • Engagement Ring • Dear, Dear Departed • Little Lace Petticoat (Lyrics by Carlton) • Have You Forgotten? • The Rose Aria • The Heart Is Free • Playthings of Love (Music by Gerstenberger) • The Girl That I Adore (Music by Gerstenberger; lyrics by Carlton)

LADY, BE GOOD![1]
December 1, 1924 (330)
Music by George Gershwin
Lyrics by Ira Gershwin

Hang on to Me • A Wonderful Party • The End of a String • We're Here Because • Fascinating Rhythm • So Am I • Oh, Lady, Be Good! • Weather Man • Rainy Afternoon Girls • Linger in the Lobby • The Half of It, Dearie, Blues • Juanita • Leave It to Love • Little Jazz Bird • Carnival Time • Swiss Miss (Lyrics by Ira Gershwin and Arthur Jackson)

Dropped from production
The Man I Love • Seeing Dickie Home • Will You Remember Me? • Evening Star • Singin' Pete • The Bad, Bad Men

Added to London production (1926)
I'd Rather Charleston! (Lyrics by Desmond Carter) • Something About Love (Lyrics by Lou Paley) • Buy a Little Button From Us (Lyrics by Desmond Carter)

RA

[1] The show was to have been called *Black-Eyed Susan* but when librettists Guy Bolton and Harlan Thompson heard the song "Oh, Lady, Be Good!" for the first time, the name was changed on the spot. This was the first show on which the Gershwin brothers collaborated on a complete score, and the first in which Ira used his own name.

THE LADY COMES ACROSS
January 9, 1942 (3)
Music by Vernon Duke
Lyrics by John Latouche

Three Rousing Cheers • You Took Me by Surprise • Hit the Ramp • February (Music and lyrics by Danny Shapiro, Jerry Seelen, and Lester Lee) • Eenie, Meenie, Minee, Mo • This Is Where I Came In • Summer Is A-Comin' In

Dropped from production
Lady • I'd Like to Talk About the Weather

LADY DO
April 18, 1927 (56)
Music by Abel Baer
Lyrics by Sam Lewis and Joe Young

Buddy Rose • Live Today • Paris Taught Me 'Zis • On Double Fifth Avenue • You Can't Eye a Shy Baby • O Sole Mio—Whose Soul Are You? • Lady Do • Little Miss Small Town • Snap Into It • Blah! but Not Blue • In the Long Run • In My Castle in Sorrento • Dreamy Montmartre • This Is My Wedding Day • Jiggle Your Feet

LADY FINGERS
January 31, 1929 (132)
Music by Joseph Meyer
Lyrics by Edward Eliscu

Based on the play *Easy Come, Easy Go* by Owen Davis

I Want You All to Myself • Let Me Weep on Your Shoulder • Open Book • Something to Live For • Sing* (Music by Richard Rodgers; lyrics by Lorenz Hart) • Ga-Ga! • My Wedding • You're Perfect • I Love You More than Yesterday (Music by Richard Rodgers; lyrics by Lorenz Hart) • Follow Master • Turn to Me • Raise the Dust

THE LADY IN ERMINE
October 2, 1922 (232)
Music by Jean Gilbert
Lyrics by Harry Graham and Cyrus Wood

Little Boy • Lady in Ermine • My Silhouette • When Hearts Are Young (Music by Sigmund Romberg) • Childhood's Days • Dear Old Land o' Mine • How Fiercely You Dance • Men Grow Older • Marianna • Catch a Butterfly • I'll Follow You to Zanzibar

LADY IN THE DARK
January 23, 1941 (467)
Music by Kurt Weill
Lyrics by Ira Gershwin

Oh, Fabulous One • Huxley • One Life to Live • Girl of the Moment • Mapleton High Chorale • This Is New • The Princess of Pure Delight • The Greatest Show on Earth • The Best Years of His Life • Tschaikowsky • Jenny (The Saga of) • My Ship

Dropped from production
It's Never Too Late to Mendelssohn

Added to film version (1944)
Suddenly, It's Spring (Music by Jimmy Van Heusen; lyrics by Johnny Burke)

RA,VS

THE LADY OF THE SLIPPER
October 28, 1912 (232)
Music by Victor Herbert
Lyrics by James O'Dea

Fond of the Ladies • Meow! Meow! Meow! • Love Me Like a Real, Real Man • All Hallowe'en • Princess of Far Away • Them Was the Childhood Days • Bagdad • Little Girl at Home • The Lady of the Slipper • Put Your Best Foot Forward

A LADY SAYS YES
January 10, 1945 (87)
Music by Fred Spielman and Arthur Gershwin[1]
Lyrics by Stanley Adams

Viva Vitamins • You're the Lord of Any Manor • Take My Heart With You • Without a Caress • I Wonder Why You Wander • I Don't Care What They Say About Me • A Hop, a Skip, a Jump, a Look • A Pillow for His Royal Head • Don't Wake Them Up Too Soon • You're More than a Name and Address • It's the Girl Everytime, It's the Girl

[1] Younger brother of George and Ira

LAFFING ROOM ONLY
December 23, 1944 (232)
Music and lyrics by Burton Lane

Hooray for Anywhere • Go Down to Boston Harbor • Stop That Dancing • This Is as Far as I Go • Feudin' and Fightin' (Lyrics by Al Dubin and Burton Lane) • Got That Good Time Feelin' • Gotta Get Joy (Lyrics by Al Dubin and Burton Lane) • Sunny California • The Steps of the Capitol

THE LAST SWEET DAYS OF ISAAC (OB)
January 26, 1970 (485)
Music by Nancy Ford
Lyrics by Gretchen Cryer

The Last Sweet Days of Isaac • A Transparent Crystal Moment • My Most Important Moments Go By • Love You Came to Me • I Want to Walk to San Francisco • Touching Your Hand Is Like Touching Your Mind • Yes, I Know that I'm Alive

RA

THE LAST WALTZ
May 10, 1921 (223)
Music by Oscar Straus
Lyrics by Edward Delaney Dunn

Hail to Our General • The Next Dance With You • Live for Today • Charming Ladies • My Heart Is Waking • Roses out of Breath • The Last Waltz • Ladies' Choice • Bring Him My Love Thoughts • A Baby in Love (Music by Ralph Benatzky, adapted by Alfred Goodman) • Now Fades My Golden Love Dream • The Whip Hand • Oo-la-la

THE LAUGH PARADE
November 2, 1931 (231)
Music by Harry Warren
Lyrics by Mort Dixon and Joe Young

Punch and Judy Man • The Laugh Parade • Got to Go to Town • Ooh! That Kiss • The Torch Song • Excuse for Song and Dance • You're My Everything • Love Me Forever

LEAVE IT TO JANE
August 28, 1917 (167)
Music by Jerome Kern
Lyrics by P. G. Wodehouse

Based on the play The College Widow by George Ade

A Peach of a Life • Wait till Tomorrow • Just You Watch My Step • Leave It to Jane • The Crickets Are Calling • There It Is Again* • Cleopatterer • What I'm Longing to Say • Sir Galahad • The Sun Shines Brighter • The Sirens' Song • I'm Going to Find a Girl • When the Orchestra Is Playing Your Favorite Dance

RA,SEL

LEAVE IT TO ME
November 9, 1938 (307)
Music and lyrics by Cole Porter

Based on the play Clear All Wires by Samuel and Bella Spewack

How Do You Spell Ambassador? • We Drink to You, J.H. Brody • Vite, Vite, Vite • I'm Taking the Steps to Russia • Get out of Town • When It's All Said and Done • Most Gentlemen Don't Like Love • Comrade Alonzo • From Now On • I Want to Go Home • My Heart Belongs to Daddy* • Tomorrow • Far Far Away • From the U.S.A. to the U.S.S.R.

Dropped from production
When the Hen Stops Laying

LEAVES OF GRASS (OB)
September 12, 1971 (49)
Music by Stan Harte, Jr.

Based on the poems by Walt Whitman

Come, Said My Soul • There Is That in Me • Song of the Open Road • Give Me • Who Makes Much of a Miracle • Tears • Twenty-Eight Men • A Woman Waits for Me • As Adam • Do You Suppose • Enough • Dirge for Two Veterans • How Solemn • Oh, Captain, My Captain • Pioneers • Song of Myself • Excelsior • In the Prison • Twenty Years • Unseen Buds • Goodbye, My Fancy • Thanks • I Hear America Singing

LEND AN EAR
December 16, 1948 (460)
Music and lyrics by Charles Gaynor

After Hours • Give Your Heart a Chance to Sing • Neurotic You and Psychopathic Me • I'm Not in Love • Friday Dancing Class • Ballade • When Someone You Love Loves You
   The Gladiola Girl—introducing:
   (a) Join Us in a Cup of Tea*
   (b) Where Is the She for Me?
   (c) I'll Be True to You
   (d) Doin' the Old Yahoo Step*
   (e) A Little Game of Tennis
   (f) In Our Teeny Little Weeny Nest for Two*
• Santo Domingo • I'm on the Lookout • Three Little Queens of the Silver Screen • Molly O'Reilly • Who Hit Me?

LENNY AND THE HEARTBREAKERS (OB)
December 22, 1983[1]
Music by Scott Killian and Kim D. Sherman
Lyrics by Kenneth Robins, Scott Killian and Kim D. Sherman

The First Last Supper • The Saints Come Flying (Sci-Fi) • Video Dreamboy • Study of the Human Figure • Video Bleeptones • Gimme-a-Break Heartbreak • Hackney-Blue Eyes • The Second Last Supper • Video Enigma • A Light Thing • Dissection Section • I'm a Rocket Tonight • Interesting Use of Space • Di Medici Cha Cha • Angela's Flight Dream • The Next-to-Last Supper • There's Art in My Revenge • The Absolute Last Supper • Lonely in Space • Lenny and the Heartbreakers

[1] Still running December 31, 1983

LET 'EM EAT CAKE[1]
October 21, 1933 (90)
Music by George Gershwin

Lyrics by Ira Gershwin

Tweedledee for President* • Union Square • Shirts by the Millions • Comes the Revolution • Mine • Climb Up the Social Ladder • Cloistered From the Noisy City • What More Can a General Do? • On and On and On • Double Dummy Drill • Let 'Em Eat Cake • Blue, Blue, Blue • Who's the Greatest—? • No Comprenez, No Capish, No Versteh! • Why Speak of Money? • No Better Way to Start a Case • Up and at 'Em! On to Vict'ry • Oyez, Oyez, Oyez • That's What He Did • I Know a Foul Ball • Throttle Throttlebottom • A Hell of a Hole • Let'Em Eat Caviar • Hanging Throttlebottom in the Morning

Dropped from production
First Lady and First Gent

   [1] The sequel to *Of Thee I Sing* (1931)

LET IT RIDE!
October 12, 1961 (68)
Music and lyrics by Jay Livingston and Ray Evans

Based on the play *Three Men On a Horse* by John Cecil Holm and George Abbott

Run, Run, Run • The Nicest Thing • Hey, Jimmy, Joe, John, Jim, Jack • Broads Ain't People • Let It Ride! • I'll Learn Ya • Love Let Me Know • Happy Birthday • Everything Beautiful • Who's Doing What to Erwin? • I Wouldn't Have Had To • There's Something About a Horse • He Needs You • Just an Honest Mistake • His Own Little Island • If Flutterby Wins

RA

LET MY PEOPLE COME (OB)
January 8, 1974[1] (1,327)
Music and lyrics by Earl Wilson, Jr.

Mirror • Whatever Turns You On • Give It to Me • Giving Life • The Ad • Fellatio 101 • I'm Gay • Linda, Georgina, Marilyn and Me • Dirty Words • I Believe My Body • The Show Business Nobody Knows • Take Me Home With You • Choir Practice • And She Loved Me • Poontang • Doesn't Anybody Love Anymore? • Let My People Come

RA

   [1] Opened on this date Off Broadway; moved to Broadway October 2, 1976 (108).

LET'S FACE IT!
October 29, 1941 (547)
Music and lyrics by Cole Porter

Based on the play *The Cradle Snatchers* by Norma Mitchell and Russell Medcraft

Milk, Milk, Milk • A Lady Needs a Rest • Jerry, My Soldier Boy • Let's Face It • Farming • Ev'rything I Love • Ace in the Hole • You Irritate Me So • Baby Games • Rub Your Lamp • I've Got Some Unfinished Business With You • Let's Not Talk About Love • A Little Rumba Numba • I Hate You,

Darling • Melody in Four F (Music and lyrics by Sylvia Fine and Max Liebman) • Get Yourself a Girl

Dropped from production
Revenge • What Are Little Husbands Made Of? • Pets

RA

LEW LESLIE'S INTERNATIONAL REVUE
February 25, 1930 (95)
Music by Jimmy McHugh
Lyrics by Dorothy Fields

Make Up Your Mind • That's Why We're Dancing • On the Sunny Side of the Street • Big Papoose Is on the Loose • Exactly Like You • The Margineers • Gypsy Love • Keys to Your Heart • Cinderella Brown • International Rhythm

THE LIAR
May 18, 1950 (12)
Music by John Mundy
Lyrics by Edward Eager

Based on the play by Carlo Goldoni

The Ladies' Opinion • You've Stolen My Heart • The Liar's Song • Truth • Lack-a-Day • Stop Holding Me Back • What's in a Name? • Women's Work (Music by Lehman Engel) • Spring • Stomach and Stomachs • A Jewel of a Duel • Out of Sight, Out of Mind • A Plot to Catch a Man In • 'Twill Never Be the Same

THE LIEUTENANT
March 11, 1975 (9)
Music and lyrics by Gene Curty, Nitra Scharfman and Chuck Strand

The Indictment • Join the Army • Look for the Men With Potential • Kill • I Don't Want to Go Over to Vietnam • Eulogy • At 0700 Tomorrow • Massacre • Something's Gone Wrong • Twenty-Eight • Let's Believe in the Captain • Final Report • I Will Make Things Happen • He Wants to Put the Army in Jail • There's No Other Solution • I'm Going Home • We've Chosen You, Lieutenant • The Star of This War • On Trial for My Life • The Conscience of a Nation • Damned No Matter How He Turned • The Verdict

THE LIFE AND TIMES OF NICHOLAS NICKLEBY
October 4, 1981 (102)
Music and lyrics by Stephen Oliver

Journey to Portsmouth • Wedding Anthem • Patriotic Song • Mrs. Grudden's Goodbye • At the Opera

LIFE BEGINS AT 8:40
August 27, 1934 (237)
Music by Harold Arlen
Lyrics by Ira Gershwin and E.Y. Harburg

Spring Fever • You're a Builder Upper • My Paramount-Publix-Roxy Rose • Shoein' the Mare • Quartet Erotica • Fun to Be Fooled • C'est la Vie •

What Can You Say in a Love Song? • Let's Take a Walk Around the Block • Things • All the Elks and Masons • I Couldn't Hold My Man • It Was Long Ago

LI'L ABNER
November 15, 1956 (693)
Music by Gene de Paul
Lyrics by Johnny Mercer

Based on the cartoon characters created by Al Capp

It's a Typical Day • If I Had My Druthers • Jubilation T. Cornpone • Rag Offen the Bush • Namely You • What's Good for General Bullmoose • There's Room Enough for Us • Unnecessary Town • The Country's in the Very Best of Hands • Oh, Happy Day • Past My Prime • Love in a Home • Progress Is the Root of All Evil • Put 'Em Back • The Matrimonial Stomp

RA,VS,SEL

LISTEN, LESTER
December 23, 1918 (272)
Music by Harold Orlob
Lyrics by Harry L. Cort and George E. Stoddard

Show a Little Something New • When Things Come Your Way • Feather Your Nest • Waiting • Two Is Company • A Very Good Baby in the Daytime • When the Shadows Fall • I'd Love To • For a Girl Like You • Sweet Stuff • Who Was the Last Girl? • See Her First

LITTLE JESSIE JAMES
August 15, 1923 (385)
Music by Harry Archer
Lyrics by Harlan Thompson

Quiet Afternoon • Come On • Suppose I Had Never Met You • I Love You • My Home Town in Kansas • The Knocking Bookworms • Little Jack Horner • The Bluebird • Little Jessie James • From Broadway to Main Street • Such Is Life in a Love Song

LITTLE JOHNNY JONES
November 7, 1904 (52)
Music and lyrics by George M. Cohan

The Cecil in London Town • They're All My Friends • Mam'selle Fauchette • 'Op in the 'Ansom • Nesting in a New York Tree • Yankee Doodle Dandy • Off to the Derby • Girls From the U.S.A. • Sailors of St. Hurrah • Captain of the Ten-Day Boat • Goodbye, Flo • So Long Sing Song • Good Old California • A Girl I Know • Give My Regards to Broadway • March of the 'Frisco Chinks • If Mr. Boston Lawson Had His Way

LITTLE MARY SUNSHINE (OB)
November 18, 1959 (1,143)
Music and lyrics by Rick Besoyan

The Forest Rangers • Little Mary Sunshine • Look for a Sky of Blue • You're the Fairest Flower • In

Izzenschnooken on the Lovely Essenzook Zee • Playing Croquet • How Do You Do? • Tell a Handsome Stranger • Once in a Blue Moon • Colorado Love Call • Every Little Nothing • What Has Happened? • Such a Merry Party • Say "Uncle" • Me, a Big Heap Indian • Naughty, Naughty Nancy • Mata Hari • Do You Ever Dream of Vienna? • A "Shell" Game • Coo Coo

RA,VS,SEL

LITTLE ME
November 17, 1962 (257)
Music by Cy Coleman
Lyrics by Carolyn Leigh

Based on the novel by Patrick Dennis

The Truth • The Other Side of the Tracks • Birthday Party • I Love You • Deep Down Inside • Be a Performer! • Dimples • Boom—Boom • I've Got Your Number • Real Live Girl • Poor Little Hollywood Star • Little Me • The Prince's Farewell • Here's to Us

RA,SEL

THE LITTLE MILLIONAIRE
September 25, 1911 (192)
Music and lyrics by George M. Cohan

New Yorkers • Little Millionaire • We Do the Dirty Work • Drill of the Seventh • Any Place the Old Flag Flies • The Musical Moon • Oh, You Wonderful Girl • Barnum Had the Right Idea • The Dancing Wedding

LITTLE NELLIE KELLY
November 13, 1922 (276)
Music and lyrics by George M. Cohan

Over the Phone • All in the Wearing • Girls From DeVere's • Dancing My Worries Away • Nellie Kelly, I Love You • When You Do the Hinky Dee • Something's Got to Be Done • The Name of Kelly • The Busy Bees of DeVere's • The Dancing Detective • They're All My Boys • You Remind Me of My Mother • The Great New York Police • The Mystery Play • The Voice in My Heart • Till My Luck Comes Rolling Along

A LITTLE NIGHT MUSIC[1]
February 25, 1973 (601)
Music and lyrics by Stephen Sondheim

Suggested by the film *Smiles of a Summer Night* (1955) by Ingmar Bergman

Night Waltz • Later • Now • Soon • The Glamorous Life • Remember? • You Must Meet My Wife • Liaisons • In Praise of Women • Every Day a Little Death • A Weekend in the Country • The Sun Won't Set • It Would Have Been Wonderful • Perpetual Anticipation • Send in the Clowns • The Miller's Son

Dropped from production
Bang! • Silly People • Two Fairy Tales

RA,VS,SEL

[1] Tony Award for Best Score

A LITTLE RACKETEER
January 18, 1932 (32)
Music by Henry Sullivan
Lyrics by Edward Eliscu

Night Club Nights • Thanks to You • Dou, Dou • Blow, Gabriel • Mr. Moon (Music and lyrics by Lloyd Waner, Lupin Feine and Moe Jaffe) • Throwing a Party • You and I Could Be Just Like That • I'll Ballyhoo You (Music by Dimitri Tiomkin) • Danger If I Love You • I Have a Run in My Stocking • You've Got to Sell Yourself • Spring Tra La (Music and lyrics by Lloyd Waner, Lupin Feine, and Moe Jaffe) • What Great Big Eyes You Have • Starry Sky (Music by Dimitri Tiomkin) • Here's to Night • Whiling My Time Away

LITTLE SHOP OF HORRORS (OB)
May 20, 1982[1]
Music by Alan Menken
Lyrics by Howard Ashman

Little Shop of Horrors • Skid Row • Da-Doo • Grow for Me • Don't It Go to Show Ya Never Know • Somewhere That's Green • Closed for Renovations • Dentists! • Mushnik and Son • Feed Me (Git It) • Call Back in the Morning • Suddenly, Seymour • Suppertime • The Meek Shall Inherit • Don't Feed the Plants

RA,SEL

[1] Opened this date at the WPA Theatre; moved to Off Broadway July 27, 1982. Still running December 31, 1983.

THE LITTLE SHOW (1ST EDITION)
April 30, 1929 (321)

Man About Town (Music by Arthur Schwartz; lyrics by Howard Dietz) • Get Up on a New Routine (Music by Arthur Schwartz; lyrics by Howard Dietz) • Caught in the Rain (Music by Henry Sullivan; lyrics by Howard Dietz) • Or What Have You? (Music by Morris Hamilton; lyrics by Grace Henry) • I've Made a Habit of You (Music by Arthur Schwartz; lyrics by Howard Dietz) • Can't We Be Friends? (Music by Kay Swift; lyrics by Paul James) • Little Old New York (Music by Arthur Schwartz; lyrics by Howard Dietz) • Song of the Riveter (Music by Arthur Schwartz; lyrics by Lew Levenson) • What Every Little Girl Should Know (Music by Arthur Schwartz; lyrics by Henry Myers) • A Little Hut in Hoboken (Music and lyrics by Herman Hupfeld) • Stick to Your Dancing, Mabel (Music and lyrics by Charlotte Kent) • I Guess I'll Have to Change My Plan* (Music by Arthur Schwartz; lyrics by Howard Dietz) • Work Alike (Music by Frank Grey; lyrics by Earle Crooker) • Moanin' Low (Music by Ralph Rainger, lyrics by Howard Dietz)

THE LITTLE WHOPPER
October 13, 1919 (224)
Music by Rudolf Friml
Lyrics by Bide Dudley and Otto Harbach

Based on the screenplay of *Miss George Washington, Jr.*

Oh, You Major Scales • Twinkle, Little Star • Oh! What a Little Whopper • 'Round the Corner • I Have a Date • It Can't Be Wrong • It's Great to Be Married • I've Got to Leave You • I'm Lonely When I'm Alone • The Kiss • Snap Your Finger • If You Go, I'll Die • We May Meet Again • Sweet Dreams • There's Only One Thing to Do • Let It Be Soon • Good Morning, All • Work Alike (Music by Frank Grey; lyrics by Earle Crooker)

THE LITTLEST REVUE (OB)
May 22, 1956 (32)
Music by Vernon Duke
Lyrics by Ogden Nash

Good Little Girls (Lyrics by Sammy Cahn) • Second Avenue and 12th Street Rag • The Shape of Things (Music and lyrics by Sheldon Harnick) • Madly in Love • Born Too Late • Summer Is A-Comin' In (Lyrics by John Latouche)* • A Little Love, a Little Money • Third Avenue L (Music and lyrics by Michael Brown) • Fly Now, Pay Later • You're Far From Wonderful • I Lost the Rhythm (Music and lyrics by Charles Strouse) • Spring Doth Let Her Colours Fly (Music by Charles Strouse; lyrics by Lee Adams) • Love Is Still in Town • I'm Glad I'm Not a Man • The Power of Negative Thinking (Music and lyrics by Bud McCreery)

RA

LIVIN' THE LIFE (OB)
April 27, 1957 (25)
Music by Jack Urbont
Lyrics by Bruce Geller

Someone • Whiskey Bug • Livin' the Life • Steamboat • Take Kids • Probably in Love • Don't Tell Me • All of 'Em Say • Late Love • Ain't It a Shame • Supersational Day • MacDougal's Cave

LOLLIPOP[1]
January 21, 1924 (152)
Music by Vincent Youmans
Lyrics by Zelda Sears

Love in a Cottage • Honey-Bun • Time and a Half for Overtime • Take a Little One-Step* • Tie a String Around Your Finger • When We Are Married • An Orphan Is the Girl for Me • Bo Koo • Louis XIII Gavotte • Going Rowing • Deep in My Heart

Dropped from production
All She Did Was This • The Hand-Me-Down Blues • It must Be Love

[1] Pre-Broadway title: *The Left-Over.*

LOOK MA, I'M DANCIN'!
January 29, 1948 (188)
Music and lyrics by Hugh Martin

Gotta Dance • Shauny O'Shay • The Toast • I'm Tired of Texas • Tiny Room • The Little Boy Blues • The New Look • Horrible, Horrible Love • If You'll Be Mine • I'm Not So Bright • I'm the First Girl • The Way It Might Have Been

RA

LOOK TO THE LILIES
March 29, 1970 (25)
Music by Jule Styne
Lyrics by Sammy Cahn

Based on the novel *Lilies of the Field* by William E. Barrett

Gott Iss Gut • First Class Number One Bum • Himmlisher Vater • Follow the Lamb • Don't Talk About God • When I Was Young • Meet My Seester • One Little Brick at a Time • To Do a Little Good • There Comes a Time • Why Can't He See? • I'd Sure Like to Give It a Shot • Them and They • Does It Really Matter? • Look to the Lilies • I Admire You Very Much, Mr. Schmidt • Some Kind of Man • Casamagordo, New Mexico • I, Yes Me, That's Who

SEL

LORELEI[1]
January 27, 1974 (320)
Music by Jule Styne
Lyrics by Betty Comden and Adolph Green

I Won't Let You Get Away • Looking Back • Men • Miss Lorelei Lee

SEL

[1] The score also included eleven songs from *Gentlemen Prefer Blondes* (1949).

LOST IN THE STARS[1]
October 30, 1949 (273)
Music by Kurt Weill
Lyrics by Maxwell Anderson

Based on the novel *Cry, the Beloved Country* by Alan Paton

The Hills of Ixopo • Thousands of Miles • Train to Johannesburg • The Search • The Little Gray House • Who'll Buy? • Trouble Man • Murder in Parkwold • Fear • Lost in the Stars • The Wild Justice • O Tixo, Tixo, Help Me • Stay Well • Cry, the Beloved Country • Big Mole • A Bird of Passage

RA,VS

[1] This was Kurt Weill's last show. He died April 3, 1950, while it was still running.

LOUIE THE 14TH
March 3, 1925 (319)
Music by Sigmund Romberg
Lyrics by Arthur Wimperis

Market Day • Homeland • Wayside Flower • Regimental Band • Taking a Wife • The Little Blue Pig • Pep • Edelweiss (Lyrics by Clifford Grey) • Rin-tin-tin • Follow the Rajah • I'm Harold, I'm Harold • Moon Flower • Vamp Your Men • True Hearts • Little Peach

LOUISIANA LADY
June 2, 1947 (4)
Music by Alma Sanders
Lyrics by Monte Carlo

Based on the play *Creoles* by Samuel Shipman and Kenneth Perkins

Gold, Women and Laughter • That's Why I Want to Go Home • Men About Town • Just a Bit Naïve • The Cuckoo-Cheena • I Want to Live—I Want to Love • The Night Was All to Blame • Beware of Lips That Say Chérie • Louisiana's Holiday • It's Mardi Gras • No, No, Mamselle • When You Are Close to Me • No One Cares for Dreams • Mammy's Little Baby

LOUISIANA PURCHASE
May 28, 1940 (444)
Music and lyrics by Irving Berlin

Sex Marches On • Louisiana Purchase • Tomorrow Is a Lovely Day • Outside of That I Love You • You're Lonely and I'm Lonely • Tonight at the Mardi Gras • Latins Know How • What Chance Have I? • The Lord Done Fixed Up My Soul • Fools Fall in Love • Old Man's Darling—Young Man's Slave • You Can't Brush Me Off

THE LOVE CALL
October 24, 1927 (81)
Music by Sigmund Romberg
Lyrics by Harry B. Smith

Based on the play *Arizona* by Augustus Thomas

Tony, Tony, Tony • 'Tis Love • When I Take You All to London • Bonita • Eyes That Love • If That's What You Want • The Ranger's Song • The Lark • Good Pals • I Am Captured • Hear the Trumpet Call • I Live, I Die for You • You Appeal to Me • Fiesta • Spanish Love

LOVE LIFE
October 7, 1948 (252)
Music by Kurt Weill
Lyrics by Alan Jay Lerner

Who Is Samuel Cooper? • My Name Is Samuel Cooper • Here I'll Stay • Progress • I Remember It Well • Green-Up Time • Economics • Mother's Getting Nervous • My Kind of Night • Women's Club Blues • Love Song • I'm Your Man • Ho, Billy O! • Is It Him or Is It Me? • This Is the Life • Minstrel Parade • Madame Zuzu • Taking No Chances • Mr. Right

LOVE! LOVE! LOVE! (OB)
June 15, 1977 (25)
Music and lyrics by Johnny Brandon

The Great All American Power Driven Engine • Searching for Love • The Battle of Chicago • Where Did the Dream Go? • I Am You • Consenting Adults • Come On In • Preacher Man • Age Is a State of Mind • Searching for Yesterdays • Somewhere Along the Road • Reach Out • Love! Love! Love! • Empty Spaces • Look All Around You • Find Someone to Love • The Streets of Bed-Stuy • What Is There to Say? • Mother's Day • Lovin' • What Did We Do Wrong? • Law and Order • Middle-Class-Liberal-Blues

LOVE ME, LOVE MY CHILDREN (OB)
November 3, 1971 (187)
Music and lyrics by Robert Swerdlow

Don't Twist My Mind • Reflections • See • Fat City • Leave the World Behind • Don't Be a Miracle • Face to Face • Journey Home • Critics • Let Me Down Walking in the World • North American Shmear • Gingerbread Girl • Plot and Counterplot • Do the Least You Can • You're Dreaming • Running Down the Sun • Love Me, Love Me Children

RA

LOVE O' MIKE[1]
January 15, 1917 (192)
Music by Jerome Kern
Lyrics by Harry B. Smith

Drift With Me • How Was I to Know? • It Wasn't Your Fault (Lyrics by Herbert Reynolds) • Don't Tempt Me • We'll See • I Wonder Why • Moo Cow • Life's a Dance • Simple Little Tune • Hoot Mon • The Baby Vampire • Look in the Book • Lulu

[1] George Gershwin was the rehearsal pianist.

THE LOVE SONG
January 13, 1925 (167)
Music by Edward Künneke
Lyrics by Harry B. Smith

Based on the life and music of Jacques Offenbach

Tell Me Not that You Are Forgetting • All Aboard for Paris • Love Is Not for a Day • Love Will Find You Some Day • Your Country Needs You • Fair Land of Dreaming • Take a Walk With Me • Remember Me (Love Song) • A Farmer's Life • When My Violin Is Calling • Only a Dream • Military Men I Love • Yes or No • Violets

LOVELY LADIES, KIND GENTLEMEN
December 28, 1970 (16)
Music and lyrics by Stan Freeman and Franklin Underwood

Based on the novel *The Teahouse of the August Moon* by Vern J. Sneider and the play by John Patrick

With a Snap of My Finger • Right Hand Man • Find Your Own Cricket • One Side of World • Geisha • You Say—They Say • This Time • Simple Word • Garden Guaracha • If It's Good Enough for Lady Astor • Chaya • Call Me Back • Lovely Ladies, Kind Gentlemen • You've Broken a Fine Woman's Heart • One More for the Last One

SEL

LOVELY LADY
December 29, 1927 (164)
Music by Dave Stamper and Harold Levey
Lyrics by Cyrus Wood

Bad Luck, I'll Laugh at You • The Lost Step • Boy Friends • Make Believe You're Happy • Lovely Lady

(Lyrics by Harry A. Steinberg and Eddie Ward) • Breakfast in Bed • Lingerie • At the Barbecue (Lyrics by Harry A. Steinberg and Eddie Ward)

LOVERS (OB)
January 27, 1975 (118)
Music by Steve Sterner
Lyrics by Peter del Valle

Lovers • Look at Him • Make It • I Don't Want to Watch TV • Twenty Years • Somebody, Somebody Hold Me • Belt and Leather • There Is Always You • Hymn • Somehow I'm Taller • Role-Playing • Argument • Where Do I Go From Here? • The Trucks • Don't Betray His Love • You Came to Me as a Young Man

LUANA
September 17, 1930 (21)
Music by Rudolf Friml
Lyrics by J. Keirn Brennan

Based on the play *The Bird of Paradise* by Richard Walton Tully

Hoku Loa • Luana • Aloha • My Bird of Paradise • Shore Leave • Son of the Sun • By Welawela • Yankyula • Where You Lead • Magic Spell of Love • Drums of Kane • In the Clouds • Wanapoo Bay

LUCKEE GIRL
September 15, 1928 (81)
Music by Maurice Yvain
Lyrics by Max and Nathaniel Lief

Based on the play *Un Bon Garçon* by André Barde and Maurice Yvain

A Flat in Montmartre • If You'd Be Happy, Don't Fall in Love • When I'm in Paree • I Love You So • Hold Your Man • A Good Old Egg • I'll Take You to the Country • Facts of Life • Wild About Music • Chiffon • I Hate You • Come On and Make Whoopee (Music by Werner Janssen; lyrics by Mann Holiner) • Friends and Lovers • Bad Girl

LUCKY
March 22, 1927 (71)

Cingalese Girls (Music by Harry Ruby; lyrics by Bert Kalmar and Otto Harbach) • The Same Old Moon (Music by Harry Ruby; lyrics by Bert Kalmar and Otto Harbach) • When the Bo-Tree Blossoms Again (Music by Jerome Kern; lyrics by Bert Kalmar and Harry Ruby) • Lucky (Music by Jerome Kern; lyrics by Bert Kalmar and Harry Ruby) • That Little Something (Music by Jerome Kern; lyrics by Bert Kalmar and Harry Ruby) • Dancing the Devil Away (Music by Harry Ruby; lyrics by Bert Kalmar and Otto Harbach) • Pearl of Broadway (Music by Jerome Kern; lyrics by Bert Kalmar and Harry Ruby)

LUCKY SAMBO
June 6, 1925 (9)
Music and lyrics by Porter Grainger and Freddie Johnson

Happy • Stop • June • Don't Forget Bandanna Days • Anybody's Man Will Be My Man • Aunt Jemima • Coal Oil • Charley From That Charleston Dancin' School • If You Can't Bring It, You've Got to Send It • Strolling • Dreary, Dreary, Rainy Days • Take Him to Jail • Always on the Job • Singing Nurses • Dandy Dan • Porterology • Love Me While You're Gone • Keep A-Diggin' • Runnin' • Midnight Cabaret • Havin' a Wonderful Time • Not So Long Ago • Alexander's Ragtime Wedding Day

LULLABYE AND GOODNIGHT
February 9, 1982 (30)
Music and lyrics by Elizabeth Swados

Gentlemen of Leisure • Port Authority • I Am Sick of Love • When a Pimp Meets a Whore • Love Loves the Difficult Things • In the Life • The Moth and the Flame • Why We Do It? • Wife Beating Song • You're My Favorite Lullabye • When Any Woman Makes a Running Issue out of Her Flesh • Now You Are One of the Family • Turn Her Out • You Gave Me Love • Let the Day Perish When I Was Born • Keep Working • Deprogramming Song • Lies, Lies, Lies • Ladies, Look at Yourselves • Don't You Ever Give It All Away • Man That Is Born of Woman • Sub-Babylon • Getting From Day to Day • Sweet Words • The Nightmare Was Me

LUTE SONG
February 6, 1946 (142)
Music by Raymond Scott
Lyrics by Bernard Hanighen

Mountain High, Valley Low • See the Monkey • Where You Are • Willow Tree • Vision Song • Chinese Market Place • Bitter Harvest • The Lute Song

RA

LYSISTRATA
November 13, 1972 (8)
Music by Peter Link
Lyrics by Michael Cacoyannis

Based on the play by Aristophanes

A Woman's Hands • On, On, On • Many the Beasts • Are We Strong? (And Are We In?) • Lysistrata • I Miss My Man • To Touch the Sky • Eels Are a Girl's Best Friend • Let Me Tell You a Little Story • Kalimera

M

MACK AND MABEL
October 6, 1974 (66)
Music and lyrics by Jerry Herman

Movies Were Movies • Look What Happened to Mabel • Big Time • I Won't Send Roses • I Wanna Make the World Laugh • Wherever He Ain't • Hundreds of Girls • When Mabel Comes in the Room • My Heart Leaps Up • Time Heals Everything • Tap Your Troubles Away • I Promise You a Happy Ending

RA,SEL

MACKEY OF APPALACHIA (OB)
October 6, 1965 (48)
Music and lyrics by Walter Cool

Mackey of Appalachia • Judging Song • I Wonder Why • Love Me Too • You're Too Smart • There Goes My Gal • Love Will Come Your Way • It's Sad to Be Lonesome • Slatey Fork • How We Would Like Our Man • Lonely Voice • My Love, My Love • Blue and Troubled • My Little Girl • We're Having a Party • Go Up to the Mountain • There's Got to Be Love • We Got Troubles • Gotta Pay • Only a Day Dream • Things Ain't as Nice • Everybody Loves a Tree • We Are Friends

THE MAD SHOW (OB)
January 9, 1966 (871)
Music by Mary Rodgers
Lyrics by Marshall Barer, Larry Siegel and Steven Vinaver

Based on *MAD* Magazine

You Never Can Tell (Lyrics by Vinaver) • Eccch (Lyrics by Barer) • The Real Thing (Lyrics by Barer) • Well It Ain't (Lyrics by Siegel and Stan Hart) • Misery Is (Lyrics by Barer) • Hate Song (Lyrics by Vinaver) • Looking for Someone (Lyrics by Barer) • The Gift of Maggie (and Others) (Lyrics by Barer) • The Boy From (Lyrics by Stephen Sondheim)

RA

MADAME APHRODITE (OB)
December 29, 1961 (13)
Music and lyrics by Jerry Herman

I Don't Mind • Sales Reproach • Beat the World • Miss Euclid Avenue • Beautiful • You I Like* • And a Drop of Lavendar Oil • The Girls Who Sit and Wait • Afferdytie • There Comes a Time • Only Love • Take a Good Look Around

MADAME SHERRY
August 30, 1910 (231)
Music by Karl Hoschna
Lyrics by Otto Harbach

Aesthetic Dancing • Theophilus • Every Little Movement (Has a Meaning All Its Own) • Uncle Says I Mustn't, So I Won't • The Butterfly • The Smile She Means for You • Athletic Prancing • Won't Some One Take Me Home? • The Other Fellow • I'm All Right • The Birth of Passion • She Shook Him in Chicago • I'll Build for You a Little Nest • We Are Only Poor Weak Mortals

VS

THE MADCAP
January 31, 1928 (103)
Music by Maury Rubens
Lyrics by Clifford Grey

Buy Your Way • Old Enough to Marry • Birdies • What Has Made the Movies? • Honeymooning Blues • My Best Pal • Why Can't It Happen to Me? • Odle-De-O • Me, the Moonlight and Me • Honey, Be My Honey-Bee (Music by Rubens and J. Fred Coots) • Step to Paris Blues • Something to Tell (Music by Rubens and J. Fred Coots) • Stop, Go! (Music by Rubens and J. Fred Coots)

THE MADCAP DUCHESS[1]
November 11, 1913 (71)
Music by Victor Herbert
Lyrics by David Stevens and Justin Huntly McCarthy

761

Aurora Blushing Rosily • Love and I Are Playing • The Deuce, Young Man • Oh, Up! It's Up! • Love Is a Story That's Old • That Is Art • Now Is the South Wind Blowing • Babette of Beaujolais • Goddess of Mine • Winged Love • Far Up the Hill • Do You Know?

VS

[1] Originally titled *The Coquette*

MLLE. MODISTE
December 25, 1905 (202)
Music by Victor Herbert
Lyrics by Henry Blossom

When the Cat's Away the Mice Will Play • The Time, and the Place, and the Girl • If I Were on the Stage • Kiss Me Again* • Love Me, Love My Dog • Hats Make the Woman • I Want What I Want When I Want It • Ze English Language • The Mascot of the Troop • The Dear Little Girl Who Is Good • The Keokuk Culture Club • The Nightingale and the Star

RA,VS,SEL

MAGDALENA
September 20, 1948 (88)
Music by Heitor Villa-Lobos
Lyrics by Robert Wright and George Forrest

Women Weaving • Peteca! • The Omen Bird • My Bus and I • The Emerald • The Civilized People • Food for Thought • Come to Colombia • Plan It by the Planets • Bon Soir, Paris • Travel, Travel, Travel • Magdalena • The Broken Pianolita • Greeting • River Song • The Forbidden Orchid • The Singing Tree • Lost • Freedom • Pièce de Résistance • The Broken Bus • The Seed of God

RA

MAGGIE
February 18, 1953 (5)
Music and lyrics by William Roy

Based on the play *What Every Woman Knows* by Sir James M. Barrie

I Never Laughed in My Life • Long and Weary Wait • Thimbleful • He's the Man • What Every Woman Knows • Any Afternoon About Five • Smile for Me • You Become Me • It's Only Thirty Years • The New Me • The Train With the Cushioned Seats • People in Love • Practical • Charm • Fun in the Country

MAGGIE FLYNN
October 23, 1968 (81)
Music and lyrics by Hugo Peretti, Luigi Creatore and George David Weiss

Never Gonna Make Me Fight • It's a Nice Cold Morning • I Wouldn't Have You Any Other Way • Learn How to Laugh • Maggie Flynn • The Thank You Song • Look Around Your Little World • I Won't Let It Happen Again • How About a Ball? • Pitter Patter • Why Can't I Walk Away? • Mr. Clown • Don't You Think It's Very Nice?

RA,SEL

THE MAGIC SHOW
May 28, 1974 (1859)
Music and lyrics by Stephen Schwartz

Up to His Old Tricks • Solid Silver Platform Shoes • Lion Tamer • Style • Charmin's Lament • Two's Company • The Goldfarb Variations • A Bit of Villainy • West End Avenue • Sweet, Sweet, Sweet • Before Your Very Eyes

RA,SEL

MAKE A WISH
April 18, 1951 (102)
Music and lyrics by Hugh Martin

Based on the play *The Good Fairy* by Ferenc Molnár

The Tour Must Go On • I Wanna Be Good'n Bad • What I Was Warned About • Who Gives a Sou? • Tonight You Are in Paree • When Does This Feeling Go Away? • Suits Me Fine • Paris, France • That Face! • Make a Wish • I'll Never Make a Frenchman out of You • Over and Over • Take Me Back to Texas With You

RA

MAKE MINE MANHATTAN
January 15, 1948 (429)
Music by Richard Lewine
Lyrics by Arnold B. Horwitt

Anything Can Happen in New York • Phil the Fiddler • Movie House in Manhattan • Talk to Me • Schrafft's • I Don't Know Her Name • The Good Old Days (Lyrics by Horwitt and Ted Fetter) • Saturday Night in Central Park • Ringalevio • Noises in the Street* (Lyrics by Peter Barry, David Greggory and Horwitt) • I Fell in Love With You • My Brudder and Me • Gentleman Friend • Subway Song • Glad to Be Back

RA

MAMBA'S DAUGHTERS (Play with one song)
January 3, 1939 (162)

Lonesome Walls (Music by Jerome Kern; lyrics by DuBose Heyward)

MAME
May 24, 1966 (1508)
Music and lyrics by Jerry Herman

Based on the novel *Auntie Mame* by Patrick Dennis and the play by Jerome Lawrence and Robert E. Lee

St. Bridget • It's Today • Open a New Window • The Man in the Moon • My Best Girl • We Need a Little Christmas • The Fox Hunt • Mame • Bosom Buddies • Gooch's Song • That's How Young I Feel • If He Walked Into My Life

RA,VS,SEL

MAN BETTER MAN (OB)
July 2, 1969 (32)

Music by Coleridge-Taylor Perkinson

Lyrics by Errol Hill

Procession • Tiny, the Champion • I Love Petite Belle • One Day, One Day, Congotay • One, Two, Three • Man Better Man • Petite Belle Lily • Thousand, Thousand • Me Alone • Girl in the Coffee • Colie Gone • War and Rebellion • Beautiful Heaven • Briscoe, the Hero

MAN IN THE MOON
April 11, 1963 (7)
Music by Jerry Bock
Lyrics by Sheldon Harnick

Look Where I Am • Itch to Be Rich • Worlds Apart • You Treacherous Men • Ain't You Never Been Afraid?

RA

MAN OF LA MANCHA[1]
November 22, 1965 (2,329)[2]
Music by Mitch Leigh
Lyrics by Joe Darion

Suggested by the life and works of Miguel de Cervantes y Saavedra

Man of La Mancha • It's All the Same • Dulcinea • I'm Only Thinking of Him • I Really Like Him • What Does He Want of Me? • Little Bird, Little Bird • Barber's Song • Golden Helmet • To Each His Dulcinea • The Impossible Dream (The Quest) • The Combat • Knight of the Woeful Countenance • Aldonza • The Knight of the Mirrors • A Little Gossip • The Psalm

RA,VS,SEL

[1] Tony Award for Best Score

[2] Includes original OB run

MAN ON THE MOON
January 29, 1975 (5)
Music and lyrics by John Phillips

Boys From the South • Midnight Deadline Blastoff • Mission Control • Speed of Light • Though I'm a Little Angel • Girls • Canis Minor Bolero Waltz • Starbust • Penthouse of Your Mind • Champagne and Kisses • Star Stepping Stranger • Convent • My Name Is Can • American Man on the Moon • Welcome to the Moon • Sunny Moon • Love Is Coming Back • Truth Cannot Be Treason • Place in Space • Family of Man • Yesterday I Left the Earth • Stepping to the Stars

THE MAN WHO CAME TO DINNER (Play with one song)
October 16, 1939 (739)
Music and lyrics by Cole Porter

What Am I to Do?

THE MAN WHO OWNS BROADWAY
October 11, 1909 (128)
Music and lyrics by George M. Cohan

Based on Cohan's play *Popularity*

My Daughter Is Wed to a Friend of Mine • I've Always Been a Good Old Sport • I'm in Love With One of the Stars • Secrets of the Household • The Man Who Owns Broadway • You'd Think You Were in Paris • Love Will Make or Break a Man • Something About a Uniform • On a Hundred Different Ships • I'm All O.K. With K. and E. • A Nice Little Plot for a Play • In the Waldorf Halls • I'll Go the Route for You • March of the King's Amazons • Why They Made Him King

MAN WITH A LOAD OF MISCHIEF (OB)
November 6, 1966 (240)
Music by John Clifton
Lyrics by John Clifton and Ben Tarver

Based on the play by Ashley Dukes

Wayside Inn • The Rescue • Goodbye, My Sweet • Romance! • Lover Lost • Once You've Had a Little Taste • Hulla-Baloo-Balay • You'd Be Amazed • A Friend Like You • Masquerade • Man With a Load of Mischief • What Style! • A Wonder • Make Way for My Lady! • Forget • Any Other Way • Little Rag Doll • Sextet

RA

MANHATTAN MARY
September 26, 1927 (264)
Music by Ray Henderson
Lyrics by B.G. DeSylva and Lew Brown

Broadway • Hudson Duster • The Five-Step • Nothing but Love • It Won't Be Long Now • Memories • My Blue Bird's Home Again • Dawn • Manhattan Mary

THE MANHATTERS
August 3, 1927 (77)
Music by Alfred Nathan
Lyrics by George Oppenheimer

Off to See New York • Up on High • What We Pick Up • Love's Old Sweet Song • I Don't Want a Song at Twilight • Close Your Eyes • Too Bad • Every Animal Has Its Mate • Nigger Heaven Blues

MARCH OF THE FALSETTOS (OB)
March 27, 1981 (298)
Music and lyrics by William Finn

Four Jews in a Room Bitching • A Tight-Knit Family • Love Is Blind • The Thrill of First Love • Marvin at the Psychiatrist • This Had Better Come to a Stop • Please Come to My House • A Marriage Proposal • Trina's Song • March of the Falsettos • Chess Game • Making a Home • The Games I Play • Marvin Hits Trina • I Never Wanted to Love You • Father to Son

RA

MARCHING BY[1]
March 3, 1932 (12)

I Love You, My Darling (Music by Jean Gilbert; lyrics by George Hirst and Edward Eliscu) • Let Fate Decide (Music by Maury Rubens; lyrics by Harry B.

Smith) • It Might Have Been (Music and lyrics by Gus Arnheim, George Waggner and Neil Moret) • I've Gotta Keep My Eye on You (Music by Harry Revel; lyrics by Mack Gordon) • Marching By (Music by Gus Edwards; lyrics by Harry Clark and Guy Robertson) • Here We Are in Love (Music by Jean Gilbert; lyrics by Harry B. Smith) • All's Fair in Love and War (Music by Jean Gilbert; lyrics by Harry B. Smith) • You Burn Me Up (Music by Jean Gilbert; lyrics by Harry B. Smith)

[1] This was the last score with lyrics by Harry B. Smith, who was, without question, the most prolific lyricist and librettist in Broadway history. In his 45-year career he wrote the libretti for more than 300 shows and the words for more than 6000 songs. His name is little known today and yet he wrote with composers Jerome Kern, Victor Herbert, Oscar Straus, Reginald De Koven, John Philip Sousa, Sigmund Romberg and more than a dozen others. He was the first lyric writer to have his words published, as lyrics, in a hardcover volume.

MARILYN
November 20, 1983 (16)
Music and lyrics by Jeanne Napoli, Doug Frank, Gary Portnoy, Beth Lawrence and Norman Thalheimer

A Single Dream (Music and lyrics by Napoli and Frank) • Jimmy, Jimmy (Music and lyrics by Napoli and Frank) • Church Doors (Music and lyrics by Lawrence and Thalheimer) • Swing Shift (Music and lyrics by Lawrence and Thalheimer) • The Golden Dream (Music and lyrics by Lawrence and Thalheimer) • When You Run the Show (Music and lyrics by Lawrence and Thalheimer) • Cold Hard Cash (Music by Wally Harper; Lyrics by David Zippel) • I'm a Fan (Music and lyrics by Lawrence and Thalheimer) • Finally (Music and lyrics by Lawrence and Thalheimer) • It's a Premiere Night (Music and lyrics by Lawrence and Thalheimer) • We'll Help You Through the Night (Music and lyrics by Napoli, Dawsen and Turner) • Run Between the Raindrops (Music and lyrics by Napoli and Portnoy) • You Are So Beyond (Music and lyrics by Napoli and Frank) • Cultural Pursuits (Music and lyrics by Frank) • Don't Hang Up the Telephone (Music and lyrics by Napoli and Portnoy) • All Roads Lead to Hollywood (Music and lyrics by Lawrence and Thalheimer) • My Heart's an Open Door (Music and lyrics by Lawrence and Thalheimer) • Miss Bubbles (Music and lyrics by Napoli, Frank and Portnoy) • The Best of Me (Music and lyrics by Lawrence and Thalheimer) • We Are the Ones (Music and lyrics by Lawrence and Thalheimer)

MARINKA
July 18, 1945 (165)
Music by Emmerich Kálmán
Lyrics by George Marion, Jr.

One Touch of Vienna • My Prince Came Riding • Cab Song • If I Never Waltz Again • Turn On the Charm • I Admit • One Last Love Song • Old Man Danube • Sigh by Night • Treat a Woman Like a Drum

MARLOWE
October 12, 1981 (48)
Music by Jimmy Horowitz
Lyrics by Leo Rost and Jimmy Horowitz

Rocking the Boat • Because I'm a Woman • Live for the Moment • Emelia • I'm Comin' Round to Your Point of View • The Ends Justify the Means • Higher Than High • Christopher • So I (Ode to Virginity) • Two Lovers • The Funeral Dirge • Can't Leave Now • The Madrigal Blues

MARRY ME A LITTLE (OB)
March 12, 1981 (96)
Music and lyrics by Stephen Sondheim

Two Fairy Tales* • Saturday Night • Can That Boy Foxtrot!* • All Things Bright and Beautiful* • Bang!* • The Girls of Summer* • Uptown, Downtown* • Who Could Be Blue?* • Little White House* • So Many People* • Your Eyes Are Blue* • A Moment With You • Marry Me a Little* • Happily Ever After* • Pour le Sport • Silly People* • There Won't Be Trumpets* • It Wasn't Meant to Happen*

RA

MARY
October 18, 1920 (219)
Music by Louis A. Hirsch
Lyrics by Otto Harbach

That Might Have Satisfied Grandma • That Farm Out in Kansas • Anything You Want to Do Dear • Everytime I Meet a Lady • Tom Tom Toddle • The Love Nest • Mary • When the Vampire Exits Laughing • Deeper • Don't Fall Till You've Seen Them All • Waiting • Money • We'll Have a Wonderful Party

MARY JANE McKANE
December 25, 1923 (151)
Music by Vincent Youmans and Herbert Stothart
Lyrics by Oscar Hammerstein II and William Cary Duncan

The Rumble of the Subway • Speed • Not in Business Hours • Stick to Your Knitting • My Boy and I* • Toodle-oo • Down Where the Mortgages Grow • Time-Clock Slaves • Laugh It Off • Flannel Petticoat Gal • Thistledown • Mary Jane McKane

Dropped from production
Come On and Pet Me*

THE MATINEE GIRL
February 1, 1926 (25)
Music by Frank Grey
Lyrics by McElbert Moore and Frank Grey

At the Matinee • Mash Notes (Music by Grey and Moore) • Joy Ride (Music by Grey and Moore) • The One You Love • When My Little Ship Comes In • Jumping Jack • Like-a-Me, Like-a-You (Music by Grey and Moore) • Only One • His Spanish Guitar • Holding Hands • Havanola Roll • What Difference Does It Make? (Music by Constance Shepard) •

Waiting All the Time for You • A Little Bit of Spanish • The Biggest Thing in My Life • Do I Dear, I Do (Music and lyrics by Moore)

MAY WINE
December 5, 1935 (213)
Music by Sigmund Romberg
Lyrics by Oscar Hammerstein II

Based on the novel *The Happy Alienist* by Wallace Smith and Erich von Stroheim

Something in the Air of May • A Chanson in the Prater • A Doll Fantasy • You Wait and Wait and Wait • I Built a Dream One Day • Dance, My Darlings • Always Be a Gentleman • Somebody Ought to Be Told • Something New Is in My Heart • Just Once Around the Clock

MAYBE I'M DOING IT WRONG (OB) (1st edition)
March 22, 1981 (17)
Music and lyrics by Randy Newman

My Old Kentucky Home • Birmingham • Political Science • Jolly Coppers on Parade • Caroline • Maybe I'm Doing It Wrong • Simon Smith and the Amazing Dancing Bear • The Debutante's Ball • Love Story • Tickle Me • It's Money That I Love • God's Song (That's Why I Love Mankind) • Sail Away • Yellow Man • Rider In the Rain • Rollin' • You Can Leave Your Hat On • Old Man • Davy the Fat Boy • Marie • Short People • I'll Be Home • Dayton Ohio 1903

MAYBE I'M DOING IT WRONG (OB) (2nd edition)
March 14, 1982 (33)
Music and lyrics by Randy Newman

Songs added to second edition
Sigmund Freud's Impersonation of Albert Einstein in America • Burn On • Pants • They Just Got Married • A Wedding in Cherokee County • Girls in My Life • Mama Told Me Not to Come • Lonely at the Top • Mr. President • I Think It's Going to Rain Today • Let's Burn the Cornfield

MAYFLOWERS
November 24, 1925 (81)
Music by Edward Künneke
Lyrics by Clifford Grey

Based on the play *Not So Long Ago* by Arthur Richman

Whoa, Emma! • Road of Dreams (Music by Pat Thayer; lyrics by Donovan Parsons and Grey) • How Do You Do? • The Grecian Bend • Play Me a New Tune (Music by J. Fred Coots and Maury Rubens) • Foolish Wives • Take a Little Stroll With Me (Music by J. Fred Coots and Maury Rubens) • Seven Days • Oh! Sam (Music by J. Fred Coots and Maury Rubens) • Mayflower (Music by J. Fred Coots, Maury Rubens and Pat Thayer) • The Regiment Loves the Girls • Good Night Ladies • Woman • Put Your Troubles in a Candy Box (Music by J. Fred Coots)

MAYTIME
August 16, 1917 (492)
Music by Sigmund Romberg
Lyrics by Rida Johnson Young

In Our Little Home, Sweet Home • It's a Windy Day on the Battery • Gypsy Song • Will You Remember? • Jump, Jim Crow • The Road to Paradise • Selling Gowns • Dancing Will Keep You Young • Go Away, Girls

VS

ME AND JULIET
May 28, 1953 (358)
Music by Richard Rodgers
Lyrics by Oscar Hammerstein II

A Very Special Day • That's the Way It Happens • Marriage Type Love • Keep It Gay • The Big Black Giant • No Other Love* • It's Me • Intermission Talk • It Feels Good • We Deserve Each Other • I'm Your Girl

Dropped during run
The Baby You Love

RA,VS,SEL

THE ME NOBODY KNOWS (OB)
December 18, 1970[1] (378)
Music by Gary William Friedman
Lyrics by Will Holt

Dream Babies • Light Sings • This World • Numbers • What Happens to Life • Take Hold the Crutch • Flying Milk and Runaway Plates • I Love What the Girls Have • How I Feel • If I Had a Million Dollars • Fugue for Four Girls • Rejoice • Sounds • The Tree • Robert, Alvin, Wendell and Jo Jo • Jall-Life Walk • Something Beautiful • Black • The Horse • Let Me Come In • War Babies

RA,SEL

[1] First opened Off Broadway May 18, 1970 (208).

THE MEDIUM
May 1, 1947[1] (212)
Music and lyrics by Gian-Carlo Menotti

Where, Oh, Where • Behold the King of Babylon • Where Have You Been All Night? • We Had a House in France • Mother, Mother, Are You There? • Doodly, Doodly, Are You Happy? • Mummy, Mummy, Dear, You Must Not Cry for Me • But Why Be Afraid? • I Know Now! • The Sun Has Fallen • Up in the Sky • Monica, Monica • Toby • Good Evening, Madame Flora • Could That Be? • Please Let Us Have Our Seance, Madame Flora • You Cannot Send Him Away • Am I Afraid? • Oh, Black Swan

[1] Opening date on Broadway; commissioned by the Alice M. Ditson Fund of Columbia University and first presented at the University on May 8, 1946.

MEET MY SISTER
December 30, 1930 (165)
Music and lyrics by Ralph Benatzky

Love Has Faded Away • Five Thousand Francs • Tell Me, What Can This Be? • Always in My Heart • Radziwill • Look and Love Is Here • The Devil May Care • I Gotta Have My Moments • It's Money–It's Fame–It's Love • I Like You • Friendship • She Is My Ideal • Birds in the Spring

MEET THE PEOPLE
December 25, 1940 (160)
Music by Jay Gorney
Lyrics by Henry Myers

Meet the People • Senate in Session • The Stars Remain • Union Label • The Bill of Rights • American Plan • Let's Steal a Tune From Offenbach • A Fellow and a Girl (Lyrics by Edward Eliscu) • The Same Old South • No Lookin' Back (Lyrics by Myers and Edward Eliscu) • In Chichicastenango

MELODY
February 14, 1933 (80)
Music by Sigmund Romberg
Lyrics by Irving Caesar

Melody • Our Little Lady Upstairs • I'd Write a Song • Good Friends Surround Me • On to Africa! • You Are the Song • In My Garden • Rendezvous • Pompadour • Never Had an Education • The Whole World Loves • Give Me a Roll on a Drum • Tonight May Never Come Again

VS

MEMPHIS BOUND[1]
May 24, 1945 (36)
Music by Don Walker
Lyrics by Clay Warnick

Big Old River • Stand Around the Band • Old Love and Brand New Love • Growing Pains

[1] The score consisted mainly of adaptations of the Gilbert and Sullivan songs from *H.M.S. Pinafore.*

MERCENARY MARY
April 13, 1925 (136)
Music by Con Conrad
Lyrics by William B. Friedlander

Over a Garden Wall • Just You and I and the Baby • Charleston Mad • Honey, I'm in Love With You • They Still Look Good • Tomorrow* • Come On Along • Mercenary Mary • Beautiful Baby • Chaste Woman • Cherchez la Femme • Everything's Going to Be All Right

MERLIN
February 13, 1983 (199)
Music by Elmer Bernstein
Lyrics by Don Black

It's About Magic • I Can Make It Happen • Beyond My Wildest Dreams • Something More • The Elements • Fergus' Dilemma • Nobody Will Remember Him • Put a Little Magic in Your Life • He Who Knows the Way • We Haven't Fought a Battle in Years • Satan Rules

SEL

MERRILY WE ROLL ALONG
November 16, 1981 (16)
Music and lyrics by Stephen Sondheim

The Hills of Tomorrow • Merrily We Roll Along • Rich and Happy • Old Friends • Like It Was • Franklin Shepard, Inc. • Not a Day Goes By • Now You Know • Good Thing Going • Bobby and Jackie and Jack • Opening Doors • Our Time

RA,SEL

MERRY-GO-ROUND
May 31, 1927 (135)
Music by Henry Souvaine and Jay Gorney
Lyrics by Morrie Ryskind and Howard Dietz

Gabriel • Sentimental Silly • Let's Be Happy Now • If Love Should Come to Me • New York Town • Cider Ella • Tampa • Spring Is in the Air • Something Tells Me • Hogan's Alley • What D'Ya Say? • I've Got a Yes Girl

THE MERRY MALONES
September 26, 1927 (216)
Music and lyrics by George M. Cohan

Talk About a Busy Little Household • Like the Wandering Minstrel • Son of a Billionaire • Molly Malone • Honor of the Family • A Feeling in Your Heart • To Heaven on the Bronx Express • A Night of Masquerade • Behind the Mask • We've Had a Grand Old Time • Charming • We've Got Him • A Busy Little Center • Our Own Way of Going Along • The Easter Sunday Parade • Roses Understand • Gip-Gip • God Is Good to the Irish • Blue Skies, Gray Skies • Like a Little Ladylike Lady Like You • Tee Teedle Tum Di Dum • The Yankee Father in the Yankee Home

MERRY-MERRY
September 24, 1925 (197)
Music by Harry Archer
Lyrics by Harlan Thompson

It Must Be Love • What a Life! • Every Little Note • We Were a Wow • My Own • Little Girl • I Was Blue • The Spanish Mick • Oh, Wasn't It Lovely? • Step, Step Sisters • Poor Pierrot • You're the One

THE MERRY WIDOW[1]
October 21, 1907 (416)
Music by Franz Lehár
Lyrics by Adrian Ross

A Dutiful Wife • In Marsovia • Maxim's • Home • Ladies' Choice! • Oh, Come Away, Away! • Vilia • Silly, Silly Cavalier • Women • Love in My Heart • The Girls at Maxim's (Can-Can) • Quite Parisian • I Love You So

RA,VS,SEL

[1] Following an inauspicious premiere in Vienna in 1905, the producers began distributing free tickets as a last hope for the show. The tide

turned dramatically and within two years *The Merry Widow* became an international hit. It was produced successively in London, New York, Stockholm, Copenhagen, Moscow, Milan, Madrid and a half dozen other parts of the globe. On one evening in Buenos Aires in 1907 it was playing in seven theatres and in five languages. There have been several film versions (including an early Swedish one-reeler), the best known of which, in 1934, starred Maurice Chevalier and Jeanette MacDonald, with new lyrics by Lorenz Hart and Gus Kahn.

THE MERRY WORLD[1]
June 8, 1926 (85)

Deauville (Music and lyrics by Herman Hupfeld) • Don't Fall in Love With Me (Music and lyrics by Herman Hupfeld) • Golden Gates of Happiness (Music by J. Fred Coots; lyrics by Clifford Grey) • Whispering Trees (Music by Maury Rubens and J. Fred Coots; lyrics by Herbert Reynolds) • I Fell Head Over Heels in Love (Music by Pat Thayer; lyrics by Donovan Parsons) • Dancing Jim (Music by Marc Anthony; lyrics by Donovan Parsons) • Sunday (Music by J. Fred Coots; lyrics by Clifford Grey)

[1] Retitled *Passions of 1926*

MESSIN' AROUND
April 22, 1929 (33)
Music by Jimmy Johnson
Lyrics by Perry Bradford

Harlem Town • Skiddle-de-Scow • Get Away From That Window • Your Love I Crave • Shout On! • I Don't Love Nobody But You • Roust-about • Mississippi • Sorry That I Strayed Away From You • Put Your Mind Right on It • Messin' Around • I Need You

MEXICAN HAYRIDE
January 28, 1944 (481)
Music and lyrics by Cole Porter

Entrance of "Montana" • Sing to Me, Guitar • The Good-Will Movement • I Love You • There Must Be Someone for Me • Carlotta • Girls • What a Crazy Way to Spend Sunday • Abracadabra • Count Your Blessings

Dropped from production
Hereafter • It Must Be Fun to Be You • Here's a Cheer for Dear Old Ciro's • Tequila

RA

MICHAEL TODD'S PEEP SHOW
June 28, 1950 (278)

The Model Hasn't Changed (Music and lyrics by Harold Rome) • You've Never Been Loved (Music by Sammy Stept; lyrics by Dan Shapiro) • Got What It Takes (Music by Sammy Stept; lyrics by Dan Shapiro) • I Hate a Parade (Music and lyrics by Harold Rome) • Blue Night (Music and lyrics by Bhumibol-Chakraband and N. Tong Yai) • Stay With the Happy People (Music by Jule Styne; lyrics by

Bob Hilliard) • Violins From Nowhere (Music by Sammy Fain; lyrics by Herb Magidson) • Pocketful of Dreams (Music and lyrics by Harold Rome) • Gimme the Shimmy (Music and lyrics by Harold Rome)

MILK AND HONEY
October 10, 1961 (543)
Music and lyrics by Jerry Herman

Shepherd's Song • Shalom • Independence Day Hora • Milk and Honey • There's No Reason in the World • Chin Up, Ladies • That Was Yesterday • Let's Not Waste a Moment • The Wedding • Like a Young Man • I Will Follow You • Hymn to Hymie • As Simple as That

RA,VS,SEL

MINNIE'S BOYS
March 26, 1970 (76)
Music by Larry Grossman
Lyrics by Hal Hackady

Five Growing Boys • Rich Is • More Precious Far • Four Nightingales • Underneath It All • Mama, a Rainbow • You Don't Have to Do It for Me • If You Wind Me Up • Where Was I When They Passed Out Luck? • The Smell of Christmas • You Remind Me of You • Minnie's Boys • Be Happy

RA,SEL

MISS DOLLY DOLLARS
September 4, 1905 (56)
Music by Victor Herbert
Lyrics by Harry B. Smith

The Self-Made Family • An Educated Fool • Just Get Out and Walk • An American Heiress • Dolly Dollars • My Fair Unknown • It's All in the Book, You Know • Life's a Masquerade • The Moth and the Moon • Walks • A Woman Is Only a Woman, But a Good Cigar Is a Smoke* • American Music ('Tis Better Than Old "Parsifal" to Me) • Queen of the Ring

VS

MISS EMILY ADAM (OB)
March 29, 1960 (21)
Music by Sol Berkowitz
Lyrics by James Lipton

Home • Oh, the Shame • Name: Emily Adam • All Aboard • Obedian March • It's Positively You • Once Upon a Time • Talk to Me • Love Is • Ultivac • Fun • Dear Old Friend • According to Plotnik • I'm Your Valentine • At the Ball • Homeward

MISS INFORMATION
October 5, 1915 (47)
Music by Jerome Kern
Lyrics by Paul Dickey and Charles W. Goddard

Two Big Eyes (Music and lyrics by Cole Porter) • A Little Love • Some Sort of Somebody* (Lyrics by Elsie Janis) • Banks of the Wye (Music by Frank E.

Tours; lyrics by F.E. Wetherly) • The Mix-Up Rag • Constant Lover (Music by Herman Finck; lyrics by Arthur Wimperis)

MISS LIBERTY
July 15, 1949 (308)
Music and lyrics by Irving Berlin

Extra, Extra! • I'd Like My Picture Took • The Most Expensive Statue in the World • A Little Fish in a Big Pond • Let's Take an Old-Fashioned Walk • Homework • Paris Wakes Up and Smiles • Only for Americans • Just One Way to Say I Love You • Miss Liberty • The Train • You Can Have Him • The Policeman's Ball • Follow the Leader Jig • Me an' My Bundle • Falling Out of Love Can Be Fun • Give Me Your Tired, Your Poor* (Lyrics by Emma Lazarus)

Dropped from production
The Honorable Profession of the Fourth Estate • The Pulitzer Prize

RA

MISS 1917[1]
November 5, 1917 (48)
Music by Jerome Kern
Lyrics by P.G. Wodehouse

The Society Farmerettes (Music by Victor Herbert) • We're Crooks • Papa Would Persist in Picking Peaches • A Dancing M.D. • That's the Picture I Want to See • The Old Man in the Moon • The Land Where the Good Songs Go • We Want to Laugh • Falling Leaves (Ballet music by Victor Herbert) • Who's Zoo in Girl Land • The Palm Beach Girl • Go, Little Boat • Tell Me All Your Troubles, Cutie

Dropped during run
A Picture I Want to See*

[1] The show's rehearsal pianist was 19-year-old George Gershwin, who was paid $35 a week.

MISS TRUTH (OB)
June 5, 1979 (16)
Music and lyrics by Glory Van Scott

Miss Truth • Children Are for Loving • I Sing the Rainbow • Self-Made Woman • My Religion • Do Your Thing, Miss Truth • Shame • This Is a Very Special Day • Freedom Diet • Lift Every Voice and Sing

MOD DONNA (OB)
April 24, 1970 (48)
Music by Susan Hulsman Bingham
Lyrics by Myrna Lamb

Trapped • Earthworms • The Incorporation • Invitation • All the Way Down • The Deal • Liberia • The Morning After • Charlie's Plaint • Creon • The Worker and the Shirker • Food Is Love • First Act Crisis • Astrociggy • Hollow • Seduction Second Degree • Panassociative • Earth Dance • Trinity • Special Bulletin • Take a Knife • The Second Honeymoon • Jeff's Plaints • Incantation • Beautiful Man • Sacrifice • Now! • We Are the Whores

MODEST SUZANNE
January 1, 1912 (24)
Music by Jean Gilbert
Lyrics by Harry B. and Robert B. Smith

Virtue Is Its Own Reward • Model Married Pair • Paris • Peaches • Confidence • All the World Loves a Lover • Tongalango Tap • Father and Son • The Return • Suzanne, Suzanne

MOLLY
November 1, 1973 (68)
Music by Jerry Livingston
Lyrics by Leonard Adelson and Mack David

Based on the radio program "The Goldbergs"

There's a New Deal on the Way (Lyrics by Adelson) • If Everyone Got What They Wanted (Lyrics by Adelson) • A Piece of the Rainbow (Lyrics by Adelson) • Cahoots (Lyrics by Adelson) • In Your Eyes (Lyrics by Adelson) • High Class Ladies and Elegant Gentlemen (Lyrics by Adelson) • So I'll Tell Her (Lyrics by Adelson) • There's Gold on the Trees (Lyrics by Adelson) • The Mandarin Palace on the Grand Concourse (Lyrics by Adelson) • I Want to Share It With You (Lyrics by Adelson) • I See a Man (Lyrics by Adelson) • Sullivan's Got a Job (Lyrics by David) • Appointments (Lyrics by David) • Oak Leaf Memorial Park (Lyrics by David) • The Tremont Avenue Cruisewear Fashion Show (Lyrics by David) • I've Got a Molly (Lyrics by David) • Go in the Best of Health (Lyrics by David)

THE MOONY SHAPIRO SONGBOOK
May 3, 1981 (1)
Music by Monty Norman
Lyrics by Julian More

Songbook • East River Rhapsody • Talking Picture Show • Meg • Mister Destiny • Your Time Is Different to Mine • Pretty Face • Je Vous Aime • Les Halles • Olympics '36 • Nazi Party Pooper • I'm Gonna Take Her Home to Momma • Bumpity-Bump • The Girl in the Window • Victory • April in Wisconsin • It's Only a Show • Bring Back Tomorrow • Happy Hickory • When a Brother Is a Mother to His Sister • Climbin' • Don't Play That Lovesong Anymore • Lovely Sunday Mornin' • A Storm in My Heart • The Pokenhatchit Public Protest Committee • I Accuse • Messages • I Found Love • Golden Oldie • Nostalgia

MORE THAN YOU DESERVE (OB)
November 21, 1973 (63)
Music by Jim Steinman
Lyrics by Michael Weller and Jim Steinman

Give Me the Simple Life • Could She Be the One? • Where Did It Go? • Come With Me • We Know Love • Mama You Better Watch Out for Your Daughter • O, What a War • More Than You Deserve • Song of the City of Hope • To Feel So Needed • Go, Go, Go Guerillas • What Became of the People We Were? • If Only • Midnight Lullabye • Song of the Golden Egg

MORNING SUN (OB)
October 6, 1963 (9)
Music by Paul Klein
Lyrics by Fred Ebb

Based on the story by Mary Deasy

Morning Sun • This Heat • Tell Me Goodbye • New Boy in Town • Good as Anybody • Mr. Chigger • Pebble Waltz • Follow Him • Missouri Mule • Seventeen Summers • It's a Lie • My Sister-in-Law • Why? • That's Right! • For Once in My Life • All the Pretty Little Horses • I Seen It With My Very Own Eyes

MORRIS GEST MIDNIGHT WHIRL
December 27, 1919 (110)
Music by George Gershwin
Lyrics by B.G. DeSylva and John Henry Mears

I'll Show You a Wonderful World • The League of Nations • Doughnuts • Poppyland • Limehouse Nights • Let Cutie Cut Your Cuticle • Baby Dolls

THE MOST HAPPY FELLA
May 3, 1956 (676)
Music and lyrics by Frank Loesser

Based on the play *They Knew What They Wanted* by Sidney Howard

Ooh, My Feet • I Know How It Is • Seven Million Crumbs • The Letter • Somebody, Somewhere • The Most Happy Fella • Standing on the Corner • Joey, Joey, Joey • Soon You Gonna Leave Me, Joe • Rosabella • Abbondanza • Plenty Bambini • Sposalizio • Special Delivery! • Benvenuta • Aren't You Glad? • Don't Cry • Fresno Beauties (Cold and Dead) • Love and Kindness • Happy to Make Your Acquaintance • I Don't Like This Dame • Big "D" • How Beautiful the Days • Young People • Warm All Over • I Like Everybody • I Love Him • Like a Woman Loves a Man • My Heart Is So Full of You • Mama, Mama • Goodbye, Darlin' • Song of a Summer Night • Please Let Me Tell You • Tony's Thoughts • She's Gonna Come Home With Me • I Made a Fist

RA,VS,SEL

MOVIE BUFF (OB)
March 14, 1977 (21)
Music and lyrics by John Raniello

Silver Screen • Something to Believe In • Movietown USA • You Are Something Very Special • Where Is the Man? • Movie Stars • May I Dance With You? • Tell a Little Lie or Two • Song of Yesterday • The Movie Cowboy • Reflections in a Mirror • All-Talking, All-Singing, All-Dancing • Coming Attractions • Tomorrow

MR. PRESIDENT
October 20, 1962 (265)
Music and lyrics by Irving Berlin

Let's Go Back to the Waltz • In Our Hide-Away •

The First Lady • Meat and Potatoes • I've Got to Be Around • The Secret Service • It Gets Lonely in the White House • Is He the Only Man in the World? • They Love Me • Pigtails and Freckles • Don't Be Afraid of Romance • Laugh It Up • Empty Pockets Filled With Love • Glad to Be Home • You Need a Hobby • The Washington Twist • The Only Dance I Know • I'm Gonna Get Him • This Is a Great Country

RA

MR. STRAUSS GOES TO BOSTON
September 6, 1945 (12)
Music by Robert Stolz
Lyrics by Robert Sour

Can Anyone See? • For the Sake of Art • Laughing Waltz (Adaptation of Johann Strauss melody) • Mr. Strauss Goes to Boston • Down With Sin • Who Knows? • Midnight Waltz (Adaptation of Johann Strauss melody) • Into the Night • Going Back Home • You Never Know What Comes Next • What's a Girl Supposed to Do? • The Grand and Glorious Fourth

MR. WONDERFUL
March 22, 1956 (383)
Music and lyrics by Jerry Bock, George Weiss and Larry Holofcener

1617 Broadway • Without You I'm Nothing • Jacques D'Iraq • Ethel, Baby • Mr. Wonderful • Charlie Welch • Big Time • Talk to Him • Too Close for Comfort • There • I've Been Too Busy

RA,SEL

MRS. PATTERSON
December 1, 1954 (101)
Music and lyrics by James Shelton

Mrs. Patterson • If I Was a Boy • Be Good, Be Good, Be Good • My Daddy Is a Dandy • I Wish I Was a Bumble Bee • Tea in Chicago

RA

MURDER AT THE VANITIES
September 12, 1933 (298)
Music by Richard Myers
Lyrics by Edward Heyman

Sweet Madness (Music by Victor Young; lyrics by Ned Washington) • Weep No More, My Baby (Music by John Green) • Me for You Forever • Who Committed the Murder? • Savage Serenade (Music and lyrics by Herman Hupfeld) • Virgins Wrapped in Cellophane (Music by John Jacob Loeb; lyrics by Paul Francis Webster) • You Love Me (Music and lyrics by Herman Hupfeld) • Dust in Your Eyes (Music and lyrics by Irving and Lionel Newman)

MURDER IN THE OLD RED BARN (OB) (Play with two songs)
February 1, 1936 (251)
Music by Richard Lewine
Lyrics by John Latouche

Not on Your Tintype • Don't Turn Us Out of the House

MUSIC BOX REVUE (1ST EDITION)
September 22, 1921 (273)
Music and lyrics by Irving Berlin

Dancing the Seasons Away • Behind the Fan • In a Cozy Little Kitchenette Apartment • My Ben Ali Haggin Girl • A Play Without a Bedroom • Say It With Music • Everybody Step • I Am a Dumbbell • The Schoolhouse Blues • They Call It Dancing • The Legend of the Pearls

MUSIC BOX REVUE (2ND EDITION)
October 23, 1922 (330)
Music and lyrics by Irving Berlin

Take a Little Wife • Lady of the Evening • Porcelain Maid • Bring On the Pepper • Crinoline Days • Will She Come From the East? • Monte Martre • Diamond Horseshoe • The Little Red Lacquer Cage • I'm Looking for a Daddy Long Legs • Pack Up Your Sins and Go to the Devil • Dance Your Troubles Away • Three Cheers for the Red, White and Blue • Dancing Honeymoon

MUSIC BOX REVUE (3RD EDITION)
September 22, 1923 (273)
Music and lyrics by Irving Berlin

One Girl • Tell Me a Bedtime Story • Maid of Mesh • An Orange Grove in California • Learn to Do the Strut • Your Hat and My Hat • Little Butterfly • The Waltz of Long Ago • Climbing the Scale

Added during run
What'll I Do?*

MUSIC BOX REVUE (4TH EDITION)
December 1, 1924 (184)
Music and lyrics by Irving Berlin

Sixteen Sweet Sixteen • Tokyo Blues • A Couple of Senseless Censors • Don't Send Me Back • Tell Her in the Springtime • In the Shade of a Sheltering Tree • The Call of the South • Bandanna Ball • Where Is My Little Old New York? • I Want to Be a Ballet Dancer • Rock-a-Bye Baby • Wild Cats • Come Along With Alice (Alice in Wonderland) • Polly From Hollywood • Listening • Unlucky in Love • Who

MUSIC HATH CHARMS[1]
December 29, 1934 (25)
Music by Rudolf Friml
Lyrics by Rowland Leigh and John Shubert

Gondolier Song • Maria • Lovey-Dovey • It's Three o'Clock • Romance • Love Is Only What You Make It • Let Me Be Free • Sweet Fool • Cavaliers • Ladies, Beware • Exquisite Moment • My Palace of Dreams • It Happened • A Smile, a Kiss • It's You I Want to Love Tonight

[1] Pre-Broadway title: *Annina.*

MUSIC IN MAY
April 1, 1929 (80)

Music by Emile Berté and Maury Rubens
Lyrics by J. Keirn Brennan

Open Your Window • The Glory of Spring • Sweetheart of Our Student Corps • Open and Shut Idea • I Found a Friend • Unto Your Heart • High, High, High • There's Love in the Heart I Hold • I'd Like to Love Them All • I'm in Love • No Other Love • For the Papa • Lips That Laugh at Love

MUSIC IN MY HEART
October 2, 1947 (124)
Music by Franz Steininger (adapted from Tchaikovsky)
Lyrics by Forman Brown

Natuscha • Love Is a Game for Soldiers • Stolen Kisses • No! No! No! • While There's a Song to Sing • The Balalaika Serenade • Am I Enchanted? • Gossip • Once Upon a Time • Three's a Crowd • Song of the Troika • The Ballerina's Story • Song of the Claque • Love Song • Love Is the Sovereign of My Heart

MUSIC IN THE AIR
November 8, 1932 (342)
Music by Jerome Kern
Lyrics by Oscar Hammerstein II

Melodies of May* • I've Told Every Little Star* • Prayer • There's a Hill Beyond a Hill • And Love Was Born • I'm Coming Home • I'm Alone* • I Am So Eager • One More Dance* • Night Flies By* • When the Spring Is in the Air • In Egern on the Tegern See • The Song Is You • We Belong Together

RA,VS

MUSIC IS
December 20, 1976 (8)
Music by Richard Adler
Lyrics by Will Holt

Based on Shakespeare's *Twelfth Night*

Music Is • When First I Saw My Lady's Face • Lady's Choice • The Time Is Ripe for Loving • Should I Speak of Loving You? • Dance for Six • Hate to Say Goodbye to You • Big Bottom Betty • Twenty-One Chateaux • Sudden Lilac • Sing Hi • Blindman's Buff • Tennis Song • I Am It • No Matter Where • The Duel • Please Be Human • What You Will

THE MUSIC MAN[1]
December 19, 1957 (1375)
Music and lyrics by Meredith Willson

Rock Island • Iowa Stubborn • Trouble • Piano Lesson • Goodnight My Someone* • Seventy-Six Trombones • Sincere • The Sadder-but-Wiser Girl • Pickalittle • Marian the Librarian • My White Knight • Wells Fargo Wagon • It's You • Shipoopi • Lida Rose • Will I Ever Tell You • Gary, Indiana • Till There Was You

RA,VS,SEL

[1] Tony Award for Best Score

MUSICAL CHAIRS
May 14, 1980 (15)
Music and lyrics by Tom Savage

Tonight's the Night • My Time • Who's Who • If I Could Be Beautiful • What I Could Have Done Tonight • There You Are • Sally • Other People • Hit the Ladies • Musical Chairs • Suddenly Love • Better Than Broadway • Every Time the Music Starts

MY DARLIN' AIDA
October 27, 1952 (89)
Music by Giuseppe Verdi (adapted by Hans Spialek)
Lyrics by Charles Friedman

My Darlin' Aida • Love Is Trouble • Me and Lee • March On for Tennessee • Why Ain't We Free? • Knights of the White Cross • Homecoming • When You Grow Up • King Cotton • Gotta Live Free • Sing! South! Sing! • I Want to Pray • Alone • Three Stones to Stand On • You're False • There'll Have to Be Changes Made • Away • Land of Mine • I Don't Want You • You Are My Darlin' Bride • Oh, Sky, Goodbye

MY DEAR PUBLIC
September 9, 1943 (45)

Feet on the Sidewalk (Head in the Sky) (Music and lyrics by Sam Lerner and Gerald Marks) • My Spies Tell Me (You Love Nobody but Me) (Music by Gerald Marks; lyrics by Irving Caesar and Sam Lerner) • This Is Our Private Love Song (Music by Irving Caesar; lyrics by Sam Lerner) • There Ain't No Color Line Around the Rainbow (Music by Irving Caesar; lyrics by Gerald Marks and Sam Lerner) • Pipes of Pan Americana (Music by Gerald Marks; lyrics by Irving Caesar) • Love Is Such a Cheat (Music and lyrics by Irving Caesar, Gerald Marks and Irma Hollander) • I Love to Sing the Words (Music by Irving Caesar; lyrics by Gerald Marks and Sam Lerner) • Rain on the Sea (Music by Irving Caesar and Sam Lerner; lyrics by Gerald Marks) • Now That I'm Free (Music by Irving Caesar; lyrics by Irma Hollander)

MY FAIR LADY[1]
March 15, 1956 (2,717)
Music by Frederick Loewe
Lyrics by Alan Jay Lerner

Based on the play *Pygmalion* by George Bernard Shaw

Why Can't the English? • Wouldn't It Be Loverly? • With a Little Bit of Luck • I'm an Ordinary Man • Just You Wait • The Rain in Spain • I Could Have Danced All Night • Ascot Gavotte • On the Street Where You Live • Embassy Waltz • You Did It • Show Me • Get Me to the Church on Time • A Hymn to Him • Without You • I've Grown Accustomed to Her Face

Dropped from production
Come to the Ball • Say a Prayer for Me Tonight*

RA,VS,SEL

[1] Tony Award for Best Score

MY MAGNOLIA
July 8, 1926 (4)
Music by C. Luckey Roberts
Lyrics by Alex C. Rogers

At Your Service • Baby Mine • Shake Your Duster • Pay Day • My Magnolia • Hard Times • Spend It • Laugh Your Blues Away • Gallopin' Dominoes • Headin' South • Merry Christmas • Struttin' Time • Our Child • Gee Chee • Sundown Serenade • Parade of the Christmas Dinner • Baby Wants • The Oof Dah Man • Sweet Popopper

MY MARYLAND
September 12, 1927 (312)
Music by Sigmund Romberg
Lyrics by Dorothy Donnelly

Based on the play *Barbara Frietchie* by Clyde Fitch

Strolling With the One I Love the Best • Mr. Cupid • Won't You Marry Me? • Your Land and My Land • Silver Moon • The Mocking Bird • Strawberry Jam • Mexico • Old John Barleycorn • Song of Victory • Ker-choo! • Boys in Gray • Mother • Bonnie Blue Flag • Hail Stonewall Jackson

MY OLD FRIENDS (OB)
January 12, 1979[1] (100)
Music and lyrics by Mel Mandel and Norman Sachs

I'm Not Old • My Old Friends • For Two Minutes • What We Need Around Here • Oh, My Rose • I Bought a Bicycle • The Battle at Eagle Rock • Dear Jane • The Only Place for Me • I Work With Wood • Mambo '52 • A Little Starch Left • Our Time Together • You've Got to Keep Building

[1] Moved to Broadway April 12, 1979 (54).

MY PRINCESS
October 6, 1927 (20)
Music by Sigmund Romberg
Lyrics by Dorothy Donnelly

Based on the play *Princess Zin-Zin* by Edward Sheldon and Dorothy Donnelly

Gigolo • I Wonder Why • Follow the Sun to the South • When I Was a Girl Like You • Here's How • Dear Girls, Goodbye • Eviva • Our Bridal Night • My Mimosa • Prince Charming • My Passion Flower

MY ROMANCE
November 29, 1948 (95)
Music by Sigmund Romberg
Lyrics by Rowland Leigh

Based on the play *Romance* by Edward Sheldon

Souvenir • 1898 • Debutante • Written in Your Hand • Millefleurs • Love and Laughter • From Now Onward • Little Emmaline • Desire • If Only • Bella Donna • Paradise Stolen • In Love With Romance • Prayer

MYSTERY MOON
June 23, 1930 (1)
Music by Alma Sanders
Lyrics by Monte Carlo

Pepper and Salt • Mechanical Man • You Always Talk of Friendship • One Night in the Rain • What Could I Do, but Fall in Love With You? • It's All O.K. • Mystery Moon • Why Couldn't We Incorporate? • Milkmaids of Broadway • Clean Out the Corner

N

NATJA
February 16, 1925 (32)
Music by Karl Hajos (based on Tchaikovsky)
Lyrics by Harry B. Smith

Honor and Glory • Comrade, You Have a Chance Here • I Hear Love Call Me • Beside the Star of Glory • You'll Have to Guess • The Magic of Moonlight and Love • Shall I Tell Him? • March On • Eyes That Haunt Me • There Is a Garden in Loveland

NAUGHTY CINDERELLA
November 9, 1925 (121)

Nothing but "Yes" in My Eyes (Music and lyrics by E. Ray Goetz) • J'ai Deux Amants (Music by André Messager; lyrics by Sacha Guitry) • Do I Love You? (Music by Henri Christiné and E. Ray Goetz; lyrics by E. Ray Goetz) • That Means Nothing to Me (Music and lyrics by A. L. Keith and Lee Sterling) • Mia Luna (Music by G. Puccini [not Giacomo]; lyrics by E. Ray Goetz)

NAUGHTY MARIETTA
November 7, 1910 (136)
Music by Victor Herbert
Lyrics by Rida Johnson Young

Tramp, Tramp, Tramp • Taisez-Vous • Naughty Marietta • It Never, Never Can Be Love • If I Were Anybody Else but Me • 'Neath the Southern Moon • Italian Street Song • Dance of the Marionettes • You Marry a Marionette • New Orleans Jeunesse Dorée • Loves of New Orleans • The Sweet By and By • Live for Today • I'm Falling in Love With Some One • It's Pretty Soft for Simon • Ah! Sweet Mystery of Life

RA,VS,SEL

NAUGHTY-NAUGHT (OB)
January 23, 1937 (173)
Music by Richard Lewine
Lyrics by Ted Fetter

Goodbye Girls, Hello Yale • Naughty-Naught • Love Makes the World Go Round • Coney by the Sea • Zim Zam Zee • Pull the Boat for Eli

Added to 1946 revival
When We're in Love

VS,SEL

NAUGHTY RIQUETTE
September 13, 1926 (88)
Lyrics by Harry B. Smith

Naughty Riquette (Music by Maury Rubens and Kendall Burgess) • I May (Music by Maury Rubens and Kendall Burgess) • Make Believe You're Mine (Music by Oscar Straus) • In Armenia (Music by Oscar Straus) • Someone (Music by Alfred Goodman and Maury Rubens) • What Great Men Cannot Do (Music by R.P. Weston; lyrics by Bert Lee)

NED WAYBURN'S GAMBOLS
January 15, 1929 (31)
Music by Walter G. Samuels
Lyrics by Morrie Ryskind

Crescent Moon • The Church Around the Corner • I Bring My Girls Along • Little Dream That's Coming True • Palm Beach Walk • Savannah Stomp • Sweet Old-Fashioned Waltz • The Sun Will Shine (Music by Arthur Schwartz) • Ship of Love • In the Days Gone By • Gypsy Days (Music by Arthur Schwartz) • What Is the Good (Music by Lew Kesler; lyrics by Clifford Grey)

NELLIE BLY
January 21, 1946 (16)
Music by Jimmy Van Heusen
Lyrics by Johnny Burke

There's Nothing Like Travel • All Around the World • Fogarty the Great • That's Class • Nellie Bly • May the Best Man Win • How About a Date? • You Never Saw That Before • Sky High • No News Today • Just

My Luck • Aladdin's Daughter • Start Dancing • Harmony

THE NERVOUS SET
May 12, 1959 (23)
Music by Tommy Wolf
Lyrics by Fran Landesman

Man, We're Beat • New York • What's to Lose? • Stars Have Blown My Way • Fun Life • How Do You Like Your Love? • Party Song • Night People • I've Got a Lot to Learn About Life • The Ballad of the Sad Young Men • A Country Gentleman • Max the Millionaire • Travel the Road of Love • Laugh, I Thought I'd Die

RA

NEVER TOO LATE (Play with one song)
November 27, 1962 (1,007)
Music by Jerry Bock
Lyrics by Sheldon Harnick

Never Too Late Cha-Cha

NEW FACES OF 1934
March 15, 1934 (148)

New Faces (Music by Martha Caples; lyrics by Nancy Hamilton) • Something You Lack (Music by Warburton Guilbert; lyrics by Nancy Hamilton and June Sillman) • Visitors Ashore (Music by Warburton Guilbert; lyrics by Everett Marcy and Nancy Hamilton) • Lamplight (Music and lyrics by James Shelton) • Music in My Heart (Music by Warburton Guilbert; lyrics by June Sillman) • My Last Affair (Music and lyrics by Havén Johnson) • Smoky Rhythm (Music and lyrics by George Hickman) • The Gutter Song (Music and lyrics by James Shelton) • You're My Relaxation (Music by Charles Schwab; lyrics by Robert Sour) • Modern Madrigal (Music by Warburton Guilbert; lyrics by Viola Brothers Shore and June Sillman) • 'Cause You Won't Play House (Music by Morgan Lewis; lyrics by E.Y. Harburg) • People of Taste (Music by Martha Caples; lyrics by Nancy Hamilton) • So Low (Music by Donald Honrath; lyrics by Nancy Hamilton and June Sillman) • He Loves Me (Music by Cliff Allen; lyrics by Nancy Hamilton) • Spring Song (Music by Warburton Guilbert; lyrics by Viola Brothers Shore and June Sillman) • On the Other Hand (Music by Martha Caples; lyrics by Nancy Hamilton)

NEW FACES OF 1936
May 19, 1936 (193)

New Faces (Music by Alex Fogarty; lyrics by Edwin Gilbert) • Slap My Face (Music by Alex Fogarty; lyrics by Edwin Gilbert) • Tonight's the Night (Music by Alex Fogarty; lyrics by June Sillman) • Chi-Chi (Music by Irvin Graham; lyrics by June Sillman) • Miss Mimsey (Music and lyrics by Irvin Graham) • My Love Is Young (Music by Irvin Graham; lyrics by Bickley Reichner) • Lottie of the Literati (Music by Alex Fogarty; lyrics by Edwin Gilbert) • Love Is a Dancer (Music by Muriel Pollock; lyrics by Jean

Sothern) • You'd Better Go Now (Music by Irvin Graham; lyrics by Bickley Reichner) • Your Face Is So Familiar (Music by Alex Fogarty; lyrics by Edwin Gilbert)

NEW FACES OF 1943
December 22, 1942 (94)

We'll Swing It Through (Music by Lee Wainer; lyrics by John Lund) • Animals Are Nice (Music by Lee Wainer; lyrics by J.B. Rosenberg) • Love, Are You Raising Your Head? (Music by Lee Wainer; lyrics by June Carroll) • Yes, Sir, I've Made a Date (Music by Lee Wainer; lyrics by J.B. Rosenberg) • Radio City, I Love You (Music by Lee Wainer; lyrics by June Carroll) • Land of Rockefellera (Music by Lee Wainer; lyrics by John Lund) • Shoes (Music by Will Irwin; lyrics by June Carroll) • Back to Bundling (Music by Lee Wainer; lyrics by Dorothy Sachs) • Hey, Gal! (Music by Will Irwin; lyrics by June Carroll) • Well, Well! (Music by Lee Wainer; lyrics by June Carroll)

NEW FACES OF 1952
May 16, 1952 (365)

Lucky Pierre (Music and lyrics by Ronny Graham) • Guess Who I Saw Today? (Music by Murray Grand; lyrics by Elisse Boyd) • Love Is a Simple Thing (Music by Arthur Siegel; lyrics by June Carroll) • Boston Beguine (Music and lyrics by Sheldon Harnick) • Nanty Puts Her Hair Up (Music by Arthur Siegel; lyrics by Herbert Farjeon) • Time for Tea (Music by Arthur Siegel; lyrics by June Carroll) • Bal Petit Bal (Music and lyrics by Francis Lemarque) • Don't Fall Asleep (Music and lyrics by Ronny Graham) • Lizzie Borden (Music and lyrics by Michael Brown) • I'm in Love With Miss Logan (Music and lyrics by Ronny Graham) • Penny Candy (Music by Arthur Siegel; lyrics by June Carroll) • Convention Bound (Music and lyrics by Ronny Graham) • Monotonous (Music by Arthur Siegel; lyrics by June Carroll) • He Takes Me off His Income Tax (Music by Arthur Siegel; lyrics by June Carroll)

RA

NEW FACES OF 1956
June 14, 1956 (220)

And He Flipped (Music and lyrics by John Rox) • April in Fairbanks (Music and lyrics by Murray Grand) • What Does That Dream Mean? (Music by Harold Karr; lyrics by Matt Dubey) • Tell Her (Music by Arthur Siegel; lyrics by June Carroll) • Hurry (Music by Murray Grand; lyrics by Murray Grand and Elisse Boyd) • A Doll's House (Music by Arthur Siegel; lyrics by June Carroll) • Isn't She Lovely? (Music by Dean Fuller; lyrics by Marshall Barer) • Don't Wait Till It's Too Late to See Paris (Music by Arthur Siegel; lyrics by June Carroll) • Scratch My Back (Music by Dean Fuller; lyrics by Marshall Barer) • Boy Most Likely to Succeed (Music by Arthur Siegel; lyrics by June Carroll) • The Broken Kimona (Music by Robert Stringer; lyrics by Richard Maury) • This Is Quite a Perfect Night (Music by

Dean Fuller; lyrics by Marshall Barer) • The White Witch of Jamaica (Music by Arthur Siegel; lyrics by June Carroll) • The Greatest Invention (Music and lyrics by Matt Dubey, Harold Karr and Sid Silvers) • Mustapha Abdullah Abu ben al Raajid (Music by Dean Fuller; lyrics by Marshall Barer) • She's Got Everything (Music by Dean Fuller; lyrics by Marshall Barer) • One Perfect Moment (Music and lyrics by Marshall Barer, Dean Fuller and Leslie Julian-Jones • Girls 'n Girls 'n Girls (Music and lyrics by Irvin Graham)

RA

New Faces of 1962
February 1, 1962 (28)

Moral Rearmament (Music and lyrics by Jack Holmes) • In the Morning (Music and lyrics by Ronny Graham) • Happiness (Music by Marie Gordon; lyrics by David Rogers) • Togetherness (Music and lyrics by Mavor Moore) • A Moment of Truth (Music and lyrics by Jack Holmes) • I Want You to Be the First to Know (Music by Arthur Siegel; lyrics by June Carroll) • A.B.C.'s (Music by Mark Bucci; lyrics by David Rogers) • It Depends on How You Look at Things (Music by Arthur Siegel; lyrics by June Carroll) • Freedomland (Music and lyrics by Jack Holmes) • Over the River and Into the Woods (Music and lyrics by Jack Holmes) • Johnny Mishuga (Music by Mark Bucci; lyrics by David Rogers and Mark Bucci) • Collective Beauty (Music by William Roy; lyrics by Michael McWhinney) • The Other One (Music by Arthur Siegel; lyrics by June Carroll) • The Untalented Relative (Music by Arthur Siegel; lyrics by Joey Carter and Richard Maury) • Love Is Good for You (Music by Arthur Siegel; lyrics by June Carroll) • Wall Street Reel (Music by Arthur Siegel; lyrics by Jim Fuerst)

New Faces of 1968
May 2, 1968 (52)

By the Sea (Music and lyrics by Clark Gesner) • Where Is the Waltz? (Music by Alonzo Levister; lyrics by Paul Nassau) • A New Waltz (Music by Fred Hellerman; lyrics by Fran Minkoff) • The Girl in the Mirror (Music by Fred Hellerman; lyrics by Fran Minkoff) • Something Big (Music by Sam Pottle; lyrics by David Axelrod) • Love in a New Tempo (Music and lyrics by Ronny Graham) • Hungry (Music and lyrics by Murray Grand) • Luncheon Ballad (Music by Jerry Powell; lyrics by Michael McWhinney) • You're the One I'm For (Music and lyrics by Clark Gesner) • Where Is He? (Music by Arthur Siegel; lyrics by June Carroll) • Right About Here (Music and lyrics by Arthur Siegel) • Toyland (Music and lyrics by Gene P. Bissell) • Hullabaloo at Thebes (Music and lyrics by Ronny Graham) • #X9RL220 (Music by Jerry Powell; lyrics by Michael McWhinney) • You Are (Music and lyrics by Clark Gesner) • Evil (Music and lyrics by Sydney Shaw) • Prisms (Music by Carl Friberg; lyrics by Hal Hackady) • Tango (Music by Sam Pottle; lyrics by David Axelrod) • Cymbals and Tambourines (Music and lyrics by Arthur Siegel) • Philosophy (Music by

Carl Friberg; lyrics by Hal Hackady) • Das Chicago Song (Music by Michael Cohen; lyrics by Tony Geiss) • Missed America (Music and lyrics by Kenny Solms and Gail Parent) • Die Zusammenfugung (Music by Sam Pottle; lyrics by David Axelrod) • The Girl of the Minute (Music by David Shire; lyrics by Richard Maltby, Jr.)

RA

New Girl in Town
May 14, 1957 (431)
Music and lyrics by Bob Merrill

Based on the play *Anna Christie* by Eugene O'Neill

Roll Yer Socks Up • Anna Lilla • Sunshine Girl • On the Farm • Flings • It's Good to Be Alive • Look at 'Er • Yer My Friend, Aintcha? • Did You Close Your Eyes? • At the Check Apron Ball • There Ain't No Flies on Me • Ven I Valse • If That Was Love • Chess and Checkers

RA

The New Moon
September 19, 1928 (509)
Music by Sigmund Romberg
Lyrics by Oscar Hammerstein II

Marianne • The Girl on the Prow • Gorgeous Alexander • An Interrupted Love Song • Tavern Song • Softly, as in a Morning Sunrise • Stouthearted Men • One Kiss • Ladies of the Jury • Wanting You • Funny Little Sailor Man • Lover, Come Back to Me[*] • Love Is Quite a Simple Thing • Try Her Out at Dances

Dropped from production
Hot and Cold • The First Man I Kiss • A Love That Lasts • I'm Just a Sentimental Fool

RA,VS,SEL

New York City Street Show (OB)
April 28, 1977 (20)
Music and lyrics by Peter Copani

American Dream (Music by David McHugh) • Who Can Say? • God Is in the People • A Special Man • Strawberries, Pickles and Ice Cream • Hail, Hail • Kung Fu • One of Us • When You Are Together (Music by David McHugh) • If Jesus Walked • Bad but Good • Make Them Hate • Corruption • Wait and See (Music by Copani and Ed Vogel) • Hanging Out • Love Is Beautiful

The New Yorkers
March 10, 1927 (52)
Lyrics by Henry Myers

99 Per Cent Pure (Music by Arthur Schwartz) • Burn 'Em Up (Music by Edgar Fairchild) • Triangle (Music by Charles M. Schwab) • I Can't Get Into the Quota (Music by Arthur Schwartz) • Nothing Left but Dreams (Music by Edgar Fairchild) • Slow River (Music by Charles M. Schwab) • Self-Expression (Music by Arthur Schwartz) • Here Comes the

Prince of Wales (Music by Arthur Schwartz) • Pretty Little So-and-So (Music by Edgar Fairchild) • A Song About Love (Music by Arthur Schwartz) • A Side Street off Broadway (Music by Edgar Fairchild) • Floating Thru the Air (Music by Arthur Schwartz) • Romany (Music by Arthur Schwartz)

THE NEW YORKERS
December 8, 1930 (168)
Music and lyrics by Cole Porter

Go Into Your Dance • Where Have You Been? • Say It With Gin • Venice • Love for Sale* • I'm Getting Myself Ready for You • The Great Indoors • Let's Fly Away • Sing Sing for Sing Sing • Take Me Back to Manhattan • I Happen to Like New York

Dropped from production
Just One of Those Things* • The Poor Rich

NIC-NAX OF 1926
August 2, 1926 (13)
Music by Gitz Rice

Broads of Broadway (Lyrics by Paul Porter) • When the Sun Kissed the Rose Goodbye (Lyrics by Paul Porter) • I Have Forgotten You Almost (Lyrics by Anna Fitziu) • For a Girl Like You (Lyrics by Joe Goodwin) • Everything Is High Yellow Now (Lyrics by Paul Porter) • Burma Moon (Lyrics by Paul Porter)

THE NIGHT BOAT
February 2, 1920 (313)
Music by Jerome Kern
Lyrics by Anne Caldwell

Some Fine Day • Whose Baby Are You? • Left All Alone Again Blues • Good Night Boat • I'd Like a Lighthouse • Catskills, Hello • Don't You Want to Take Me? • I Love the Lassies • A Heart for Sale • Girls Are Like a Rainbow

Dropped from production
Bob White • She's Spanish • Jazz • Rip Van Winkle and His Little Men

A NIGHT IN PARIS
January 5, 1926 (335)

In Chinatown in Frisco (Music by Maurice Yvain; lyrics by Clifford Grey and McElbert Moore) • Louisiana (Music by J. Fred Coots and Maury Rubens; lyrics by McElbert Moore) • Powder Puff (Music by J. Fred Coots and Maury Rubens; lyrics by Clifford Grey and McElbert Moore) • Voodoo of the Zulu Isle (Music by J. Fred Coots and Maury Rubens; lyrics by Clifford Grey and McElbert Moore) • Bobbed-Haired Baby (Music by J. Fred Coots and Maury Rubens; lyrics by McElbert Moore) • The Black Mask (Temptation) (Music by J. J. Shubert Jr.; lyrics by Clifford Grey and McElbert Moore) • The Nile (Music and lyrics by Xaver Leroux) • Amy (Music by Roy Webb; lyrics by F. Coulon)

A NIGHT IN SPAIN
May 3, 1927 (174)

Music by Jean Schwartz
Lyrics by Alfred Bryan

Argentine • International Vamp • De-dum-dum • The Sky Girl • Promenade the Esplanade • My Rose of Spain • Hot, Hot Honey • Simple Spanish Maid • The Curfew Walk • Bambazoola • A Million Eyes • A Spanish Shawl

A NIGHT IN VENICE
May 21, 1929 (175)

Strolling on the Lido (Music by Lee David and Maury Rubens; lyrics by J. Keirn Brennan and Moe Jaffe) • I'm for You (Music by Lee David; lyrics by J. Keirn Brennan) • Loose Ankles (Music and lyrics by Moe Jaffe, Clay Boland, and Maury Rubens) • One Night of Love (Music by Maury Rubens; lyrics by J. Keirn Brennan) • Sliding Down a Silver Cloud (Music by Lee David; lyrics by J. Keirn Brennan) • The Stork Don't Come Around Any More (Music and lyrics by B. Laidlaw)

NIGHT OF LOVE
January 7, 1941 (7)
Music by Robert Stolz
Lyrics by Rowland Leigh

My Loved One • Chiquitin Trio • I'm Thinking of Love • The One Man I Need • Tonight or Never • Serenade for You • Without You • Loosen Up • Streamlined Pompadour

THE NIGHT THAT MADE AMERICA FAMOUS
February 26, 1975 (75)
Music and lyrics by Harry Chapin

Six-String Orchestra • Give Me a Road • Sunday Morning Sunshine • It's My Day • Give Me a Cause • Welfare Rag • Better Place to Be • Give Me a Wall • Peace Teachers • Pigeon Run • Changing of the Guard • When I Look Up • Sniper • Great Divide • Taxi • Cockeyed John • Mr. Tanner • Maxie • Love Can't • When Maudey Wants a Man • I'm a Wonderfully Wicked Woman • Battleground Bummer • Stoopid • Cat's in the Cradle • Too Much World • As I Grow Older • Beginning of the End • The Night That Made America Famous

NIGHTCLUB CANTATA (OB)
January 9, 1977 (145)
Music and lyrics by Elizabeth Swados

Things I Didn't Know I Loved • Bestiario • Bird Chorus • Bird Lament • Ventriloquist and Dummy • The Applicant • To the Harbormaster • Adolescents • Indecision • Dibarti • In Dreams Begin Responsibilities • Are You With Me? • Raga • Waking This Morning • Pastrami Brothers • The Ballad of the Sad Cafe • Isabella • Waiting • The Dance • On Living

THE NIGHTINGALE
January 3, 1927 (96)
Music by Armand Vecsey
Lyrics by P.G. Wodehouse

Breakfast in Bed • Josephine (Lyrics by Clifford Grey) • May Moon • Once in September (Lyrics by Clifford Grey) • Two Little Ships • Homeland • Another One Gone Wrong • Love Like Yours Is Rare Indeed • Rabbit Song

NIKKI
September 29, 1931 (40)
Music by Philip Charig
Lyrics by James Dyrenforth

Screwy Little Tune • Taking Off • Wonder Why • On Account of I Love You • Now I Know • My Heart Is Calling • The Ghost of Little Egypt

NINA ROSA
September 20, 1930 (129)
Music by Sigmund Romberg
Lyrics by Irving Caesar

Pay Day • Pablo • Nina Rosa • With the Dawn • Payador • The Secret of My Life • Your Smiles, Your Tears • Serenade of Love • Pizarro Was a Very Narrow Man • A Kiss I Must Refuse You • Latigo • A Gaucho Love Song • My First Love, My Last Love (Lyrics by Caesar and Otto Harbach)

VS

NINE[1]
May 9, 1982[2]
Music and lyrics by Maury Yeston

Not Since Chaplin • Guido's Song • The Germans at the Spa • My Husband Makes Movies • A Call From the Vatican • Only With You • Folies Bergères • Nine • De Italian • The Bells of St. Sebastian • A Man Like You • Unusual Way • The Grand Canal • Every Girl in Venice • Simple • Be on Your Own • I Can't Make This Movie • Getting Tall • Long Ago

RA,SEL

[1] Tony Award for Best Score

[2] Still running December 31, 1983

NINE-FIFTEEN REVUE
February 11, 1930 (7)

Up Among the Chimney Pots (Music by Kay Swift; lyrics by Paul James) • Toddlin' Along (Music by George Gershwin; lyrics by Ira Gershwin)* • World of Dreams (Music by Victor Herbert; lyrics by Edward Eliscu) • Ta Ta, Ol' Bean (Music by Manning Sherwin; lyrics by Edward Eliscu) • Knock on Wood (Music by Richard Myers; lyrics by Edward Eliscu) • Get Happy (Music by Harold Arlen; lyrics by Ted Koehler)* • Winter and Spring (Music by Rudolf Friml; lyrics by Edward Eliscu) • Boudoir Dolls (Music by Ned Lehak; lyrics by Edward Eliscu) • Breakfast Dance (Music by Ralph Rainger; lyrics by Edward Eliscu) • How Would a City Girl Know? (Music by Kay Swift; lyrics by Paul James) • A Purty Little Thing (Music by Philip Broughton; lyrics by Will B. Johnstone) • Gotta Find a Way to Do It (Music by Roger Wolfe Kahn; lyrics by Paul James) • You Will Never Know (Music by Vincent

Youmans; lyrics by Paul James) • Gee It's So Good, It's Too Bad (Music by Harold Arlen; lyrics by Ted Koehler) • You Wanted Me, I Wanted You (Music by Harold Arlen; lyrics by Ted Koehler)

NINETY IN THE SHADE
January 25, 1915 (40)
Music by Jerome Kern
Lyrics by Harry B. Smith

Where's the Girl for Me? • Jolly Good Fellow (Lyrics by Clare Kummer) • Lonely in Town (Music and lyrics by Clare Kummer) • I Have Been About a Bit • A Regular Guy • Rich Man, Poor Man (Lyrics by Clare Kummer) • Human Nature • My Lady's Dress • Foolishness • Wonderful Days • My Mindanao Chocolate Soldier (Lyrics by Clare Kummer)

NO FOOLIN'[1]
June 24, 1926 (108)
Music by James F. Hanley
Lyrics by Gene Buck

Honey, Be Mine • No Foolin' • Florida, the Moon and You (Music by Rudolf Friml) • Every Little Thing You Do • Wasn't It Nice? (Music by Rudolf Friml; lyrics by Irving Caesar) • Nize Baby (Lyrics by Ballard MacDonald) • Don't Do the Charleston • Poor Little Marie • When the Shaker Plays a Cocktail Tune

[1] Called *Ziegfeld Palm Beach Nights* and then *Ziegfeld's Palm Beach Girl* in its Florida premiere, the show opened on Broadway as *Ziegfeld's American Revue.* Soon after, the title became *No Foolin',* after its song hit.

NO, NO, NANETTE
September 16, 1925 (321)[1]
Music by Vincent Youmans

Based on the play *My Lady Friends* by Emil Nyitray and Frank Mandel

The Call of the Sea (Lyrics by Otto Harbach) • Too Many Rings Around Rosie (Lyrics by Irving Caesar) • Waiting for You* (Lyrics by Otto Harbach) • I Want to Be Happy (Lyrics by Irving Caesar) • No, No, Nanette* (Lyrics by Otto Harbach) • Peach on the Beach (Lyrics by Otto Harbach) • My Doctor (Lyrics by Otto Harbach) • Fight Over Me (Lyrics by Otto Harbach) • Tea for Two (Lyrics by Irving Caesar)* • You Can Dance With Any Girl at All (Lyrics by Irving Caesar) • Telephone Girlie (Lyrics by Otto Harbach) • Where Has My Hubby Gone Blues (Lyrics by Irving Caesar) • Pay Day Pauline (Lyrics by Otto Harbach)

Added to 1971 revival
I've Confessed to the Breeze (Lyrics by Otto Harbach) • Take a Little One-Step (Lyrics by Zelda Sears) • Many Rings Around Rosie (Lyrics by Irving Caesar) • Waiting for You (Lyrics by Otto Harbach) • I Want
Dropped from production
The Boy Next Door • I Don't Want a Girlie (Lyrics by B.G. DeSylva) • Lilies of the Field • Santa Claus • The Chase of the Fox

RA (1971 revival),VS,SEL

[1] The 1971 revival, December 4, 1971, ran for 861 performances, more than twice as long as the original Broadway run.

No Strings[1]
March 15, 1962 (580)
Music and lyrics by Richard Rodgers

The Sweetest Sounds • How Sad • Loads of Love • The Man Who Has Everything • Be My Host • La La La • You Don't Tell Me • Love Makes the World Go • Nobody Told Me • Look No Further • Maine • An Orthodox Fool • Eager Beaver • No Strings

Dropped from production
Yankee, Go Home

RA,VS,SEL

[1] Tony Award for Best Score

Nobody Home
April 20, 1915 (135)

You Don't Take a Sandwich to a Banquet (Music and lyrics by Worton David and J.P. Long) • You Know and I Know (Music by Jerome Kern; lyrics by Harry B. Smith) • Cupid at the Plaza (Music by Paul Rubens; lyrics by Percy Greenbank) • In Arcady (Music by Jerome Kern; lyrics by Herbert Reynolds) • The Magic Melody (Music by Jerome Kern; lyrics by Schuyler Greene) • The Chaplin Walk (Music by Jerome Kern and Otto Motzan; lyrics by Schuyler Greene) • Beautiful, Beautiful Bed (Music by Dan Lipton; lyrics by Lawrence Grossmith, C.W. Murphy and Dan Lipton) • Another Little Girl (Music by Jerome Kern; lyrics by Herbert Reynolds) • Any Old Night (Music by Jerome Kern and Otto Motzan; lyrics by Schuyler Greene and Harry B. Smith) • At That San Francisco Fair* (Music by Jerome Kern, Ford Dabney and James Europe; lyrics by Schuyler Greene)

Now Is the Time for All Good Men (OB)
September 26, 1967 (111)
Music by Nancy Ford
Lyrics by Gretchen Cryer

We Shall Meet in the Great Hereafter • Quittin' Time • What's in the Air • Keep 'Em Busy, Keep 'Em Quiet • Tea in the Rain • What's a Guy Like You Doin' in a Place Like This? • Halloween Hayride • See Everything New • All Alone • He Could Show Me • Washed Away • Stuck-Up • My Holiday • On My Own • It Was Good Enough for Grandpa • A Simple Life • A Star on the Monument • Rain Your Love on Me • There's Going to Be a Wedding

RA

Nowhere to Go But Up
November 10, 1962 (9)
Music by Sol Berkowitz
Lyrics by James Lipton

Ain't You Ashamed? • The We Makin' Dough You So and So Rag • Live a Little • Mr. Baiello • When a Fella Needs a Friend • The Odds and Ends of Love • Nowhere to Go but Up • Take Me Back • I Love You for That • Baby, Baby • Out of Sight, Out of Mind • Follow the Leader Septet • Dear Mom

O

O MARRY ME! (OB)
October 27, 1961 (21)
Music by Robert Kessler
Lyrics by Lola Pergament

Based on the play *She Stoops to Conquer* by Oliver Goldsmith

I Love Everything That's Old • Time and Tide • The Kind of Man • Ale House Song • Proper Due • Be a Lover • Perish the Baubles • The Meeting • Fashions • Say Yes, Look No • Let's All Be Exactly and Precisely What We Are • The Braggart Song • O Marry Me! • Betrayed • Motherly Love • Morality

O SAY CAN YOU SEE! (OB)
October 8, 1962 (32)
Music by Jack Holmes
Lyrics by Bill Conklin and Bob Miller

The Freedom Choo Choo Is Leaving Today • Dreamboat From Dreamland • Dogface Jive • Us Two • Take Me Back to Texas • Doughnuts for Defense • Canteen Serenade • These Are Worth Fighting For • Someone a Lot Like You • Veronica Takes Over • Buy Bonds, Buster, Buy Bonds • Chico-Chico Chico-Layo • Flim Flam Flooey • When the Bluebirds Fly All Over the World • Just the Way You Are • My G.I. Joey • O Say Can You See!

RA

THE O'BRIEN GIRL
October 3, 1921 (164)
Music by Louis A. Hirsch
Lyrics by Otto Harbach

Give, Give, Give • I'll Treat You Just Like a Sister • I Wonder How I Ever Passed You By • Learn to Smile • My Little Canoe • I'm So Excited • Murder • The Conversation Step • The O'Brien Girl • Partners • To Keep You in Your Seats

OF MICE AND MEN (OB)
December 4, 1958 (37)
Music by Alfred Brooks
Lyrics by Ira J. Bilowit

Based on the play by John Steinbeck

Nice House We Got Here • No Ketchup • We Got a Future • Buckin' Barley • Curley's Wife • Wanta, Hope to Feel at Home • Lemme Tell Ya • Just Someone to Talk To • Dudin' Up • Nice Fella • Why Try Hard to Be Good? • Never Do a Bad Thing • Is There Some Place for Me? • A Guy, A Guy, A Guy • Strangely • Candy's Lament

OF THEE I SING[1]
December 26, 1931 (441)
Music by George Gershwin
Lyrics by Ira Gershwin

Wintergreen for President* • Who Is the Lucky Girl to Be? • The Dimple on My Knee • Because, Because • Never Was There a Girl So Fair • Some Girls Can Bake a Pie • Love Is Sweeping the Country* • Of Thee I Sing • Here's a Kiss for Cinderella • I Was the Most Beautiful Blossom • Hello, Good Morning • Who Cares? • Garçon, s'Il Vous Plait • The Illegitimate Daughter • The Senatorial Roll Call • Jilted • I'm About to Be a Mother (Who Could Ask for Anything More?) • Posterity Is Just Around the Corner • Trumpeter, Blow Your Golden Horn

RA (1952 revival),VS,SEL

[1] The first musical to win the Pulitzer Prize

OF V WE SING
February 11, 1942 (76)

You Can't Fool the People (Music by George Kleinsinger; lyrics by Alfred Hayes) • Sisters Under the Skin (Music by Baldwin Bergersen; lyrics by Sylvia Marks) • Don't Sing Solo (Music by George Kleinsinger; lyrics by Roslyn Harvey) • Freedom Road (Music by Toby Sacher; lyrics by Lewis Allen) • Brooklyn Cantata (Music by George Kleinsinger; lyrics by Mike Stratton) • Take a Poem (Music by George Kleinsinger; lyrics by Norman Corwin) • Priorities (Music by Lou Cooper; lyrics by Roslyn Harvey) • Queen Esther (Music by George

779

Kleinsinger; lyrics by Beatrice Goldsmith) • Gertie the Stool Pigeon's Daughter (Music by Ned Lehak; lyrics by Joe Darion) • You've Got to Appease With a Strip Tease (Music by Toby Sacher; lyrics by Lewis Allen) • We Have a Date (Music by Lou Cooper; lyrics by Roslyn Harvey) • Juke Box (Music by Alex North; lyrics by Alfred Hayes) • Of V We Sing (Music by Lou Cooper; lyrics by Arthur Zipser)

The O'Flynn
December 27, 1934 (11)
Music by Franklin Hauser

A Lovely Lady (Lyrics by Russell Janney) • Child of Erin (Lyrics by Russell Janney) • Song of My Heart (Lyrics by Brian Hooker) • The Man I Love Is Here (Lyrics by Brian Hooker)

Oh, Boy!
February 20, 1917 (463)
Music by Jerome Kern
Lyrics by P.G. Wodehouse

Let's Make a Night of It • You Never Knew About Me • A Package of Seeds • An Old-Fashioned Wife • A Pal Like You • Till the Clouds Roll By (Lyrics by Kern, Wodehouse and Guy Bolton) • A Little Bit of Ribbon • The First Day of May • Koo-La-Loo • Rolled Into One • Oh, Daddy, Please • Nesting Time in Flatbush (Lyrics by Wodehouse and Kern) • Words Are Not Needed • Flubby Dub, the Cave Man

Dropped from production
Ain't It a Grand and a Glorious Feeling • Be a Little Sunbeam • The Bachelor • When the Orchestra Is Playing Your Favorite Dance* • Why Can't They Hand It to Me?

Oh, Brother
November 10, 1981 (3)
Music by Michael Valenti
Lyrics by Donald Driver

Based on Shakespeare's *The Comedy of Errors*

We Love an Old Story • I to the World • That's Him • How Do You Want Me? • Everybody Calls Me by My Name • Opec Maiden • A Man • Tell Sweet Saroyana • What Do I Tell People This Time? • Oh, Brother

RA

Oh! Calcutta!
June 17, 1969[1]
Music and lyrics by Robert Dennis, Peter Schickele, and Stanley Walden[2]

Sincere Replies • Don't Have a Song to Sing • I'm an Actor • I Want It • Clarence and Mildred • Much Too Soon (above writers and Jacques Levy) • Jack and Jill • Suite for Five Letters • Exchanges of Information • I Like the Look

RA

[1] Opened on this date Off Broadway; moved to Broadway September 24, 1976; still running

December 31, 1983. During the run several new songs have been added to the score and others dropped. Listed are the songs that were recorded in the cast album.

[2] Dennis, Schickele and Walden performed in the show as "The Open Window."

Oh Captain!
February 4, 1958 (192)
Music and lyrics by Jay Livingston and Ray Evans

Based on the film *The Captain's Paradise* (1953)

A Very Proper Town • Life Does a Man a Favor • Captain Henry St. James • Three Paradises • Surprise • Hey, Madame • Femininity • It's Never Quite the Same • We're Not Children • Give It All You Got • Love Is Hell • Keep It Simple • The Morning Music of Montmartre • You Don't Know Him • I've Been There and I'm Back • Double Standard • You're So Right for Me • All the Time

RA

Oh, Ernest!
May 9, 1927 (56)
Music by Robert Hood Bowers
Lyrics by Francis DeWitt

Based on the play *The Importance of Being Earnest* by Oscar Wilde

On the Beach • Taken by Surprise • Ancestry • Cupid's College • Didoes • Over the Garden Wall • Cecily • Let's Pretend • Pollyanna • Don't Scold • Give Me Someone • Little Stranger • He Knows Where the Rose Is in Bloom • Tangles • There's a Muddle • Never Trouble Trouble

Oh, I Say!
October 30, 1913 (68)
Music by Jerome Kern
Lyrics by Harry B. Smith

Each Pearl a Thought • Well, This Is Jolly • The Old Clarinet • Alone at Last • A Woman's Heart • Katy-Did • I Can't Forget Your Eyes* • A Wifie of Your Own

Oh, Kay!
November 8, 1926 (256)
Music by George Gershwin
Lyrics by Ira Gershwin

The Woman's Touch • Don't Ask! • Dear Little Girl • Maybe • Clap Yo' Hands* • Bride and Groom • Do Do Do • Someone to Watch Over Me* • Fidgety Feet • Heaven on Earth (Lyrics by Ira Gershwin and Howard Dietz) • Oh, Kay! (Lyrics by Ira Gershwin and Howard Dietz)

Dropped from production
The Moon Is on the Sea • Show Me the Town* • Ain't It Romantic • Ding Dong Dell

RA

Oh, Lady! Lady!!
February 1, 1918 (219)
Music by Jerome Kern

Lyrics by P.G. Wodehouse

Not Yet • Do It Now • Our Little Nest • When the Ships Come Home • Do Look at Him • Oh, Lady! Lady!! • You Found Me and I Found You • Moon Song • Waiting Around the Corner* • The Sun Starts to Shine Again • Before I Met You • Greenwich Village • Wheatless Day • It's a Hard World for a Man

Dropped from production
Bill*

VS

OH, MY DEAR!
November 27, 1918 (189)
Music by Louis A. Hirsch
Lyrics by P.G. Wodehouse

I Shall Be All Right Now • I Wonder Whether • Ask Dad • Our City of Dreams • Come Where Nature Calls • Phoebe Snow • Go, Little Boat (Music by Jerome Kern) • You Never Know • Try Again • It Makes a Fellow Sort of Stop and Think • Childhood Days • I'd Ask No More • If They Ever Parted Me From You

OH! OH! DELPHINE
September 30, 1912 (248)
Music by Ivan Caryll
Lyrics by C.M.S. McLellan

Based on the farce *Villa Primrose* by Georges Berr and Marcel Guillemand

Please Turn Your Backs • Posing for Venus • Oh! Oh! Delphine • Allaballa Goo-Goo • Why Shouldn't You Tell Me That? • Hush! Hush! Hush! • Oh P-P-Poor Bouchotte • Can We E'er Forget? • The Maxim Girl • Everything's at Home Except Your Wife • The Quarrel • The Venus Waltz • Then All Come Along

VS

OH! OH! NURSE
December 7, 1925 (32)
Music by Alma Sanders
Lyrics by Monte Carlo

Show a Little Pep • Love Will Keep Us Young • You May Have Planted Many a Lily • Way Out in Rainbow Land • Cleopatra • Who Bites the Hole in Schweitzer Cheese? • Keep a Kiss for Me • Pierre • My Lady Love • I'll Give the World to You • No Hearts for Sale • Is It Any Wonder? • Butter and Egg Baby • Newlywed Express • Under My Umbrella • No, I Won't • Shooting Stars

OH, PLEASE!
December 17, 1926 (75)
Music by Vincent Youmans
Lyrics by Anne Caldwell

Homely but Clean • Snappy Show in Town • Like He Loves Me • Nicodemus • I'd Steal a Star • I Know That You Know • I'm Waiting for a Wonderful Girl •

Love Me • I Can't Be Happy • The Girls of the Old Brigade

Dropped from production
When Daddy Goes A-Hunting • A Weekend in July • Lily of the Valley • Moments • Floating Along • She Was a Wonderful Queen

OKLAHOMA![1]
March 31, 1943 (2,212)
Music by Richard Rodgers
Lyrics by Oscar Hammerstein II

Based on the play *Green Grow the Lilacs* by Lynn Riggs

Oh, What a Beautiful Mornin'* • The Surrey With the Fringe on Top • Kansas City • I Cain't Say No • Many a New Day • It's a Scandal! It's a Outrage! • People Will Say We're in Love • Pore Jud Is Daid • Lonely Room • Out of My Dreams • The Farmer and the Cowman • All er Nothin' • Oklahoma

Dropped from production
Boys and Girls Like You and Me

RA,VS,SEL

[1] Tony Award for Best Score. The pre-Broadway title was *Away We Go.*

OLD DUTCH[1]
November 22, 1909 (88)
Music by Victor Herbert
Lyrics by George V. Hobart

Algy • "U," Dearie • Rich Man, Poor Man, Beggar-Man, Thief • That Is Love • I Want a Man to Love Me • I Love ze Parisienne • Pretending • My Gypsy Sweetheart • Mrs. Grundy • Honor the Brave

VS

[1] Nine-year-old Helen Hayes made her Broadway debut in this operetta. The *New York Herald* critic wrote "Miss Helen Hayes, a wee miss, won the favor of the audience by a bit of acting that was refreshing."

OLIVER![1]
January 6, 1963 (774)
Music and lyrics by Lionel Bart

Based on the novel *Oliver Twist* by Charles Dickens

Food, Glorious Food • Oliver! • I Shall Scream • Boy for Sale • That's Your Funeral • Where Is Love? • Consider Yourself • You've Got to Pick a Pocket or Two • It's a Fine Life • Be Back Soon • Oom-Pah-Pah • My Name • As Long as He Needs Me • I'd Do Anything • Who Will Buy? • Reviewing the Situation

RA,VS,SEL

[1] Tony Award for Best Score

ON A CLEAR DAY YOU CAN SEE FOREVER
October 17, 1965 (280)
Music by Burton Lane
Lyrics by Alan Jay Lerner

Hurry! It's Lovely up Here • Ring Out the Bells • Tosy and Cosh • On a Clear Day You Can See Forever • On the S.S. Bernard Cohn • Don't Tamper With My Sister • She Wasn't You • Melinda • When I'm Being Born Again • What Did I Have That I Don't Have? • Wait 'Till We're Sixty-Five • Come Back to Me

RA,VS,SEL

Added to film version (1969)
Go to Sleep • Love With All the Trimmings

RA,VS,SEL

ON THE LOCK-IN (OB)
April 14, 1977 (62)
Music and lyrics by David Langston Smyrl

Whatever It Happens to Be • Dry Mouth With No Water • Born to Lose • Sister Paradise • Peace Will Come • Circumstances • 42nd Street Blues • Talkin' Blues • Marlene • Alone

ON THE SWING SHIFT (OB)
May 17, 1983 (32)
Music by Michael Dansicker
Lyrics by Sarah Schlesinger

Morning • Row 10, Aisle 6, Bench 114 • We Got a Job to Do • There's a War Going On • Killing Time • When Tomorrow Comes • I'm Someone Now • Something to Do Tonight • Night on the Town • Evening

ON THE TOWN[1]
December 28, 1944 (463)
Music by Leonard Bernstein
Lyrics by Betty Comden and Adolph Green

I Feel Like I'm Not Out of Bed Yet • New York, New York • Come Up to My Place • I Get Carried Away • Lonely Town • Do, Re, Do • I Can Cook Too (Lyrics by Bernstein, Comden and Green) • Lucky to Be Me • So Long, Baby • I'm Blue • Ya Got Me • Some Other Time

RA,VS,SEL

[1] An elaboration of the Ballet Theatre's "Fancy Free," which, like the show, had a score by Leonard Bernstein, choreography by Jerome Robbins and settings by Oliver Smith.

ON THE TWENTIETH CENTURY[1]
February 19, 1978 (460)
Music by Cy Coleman
Lyrics by Betty Comden and Adolph Green

Based on the play *Twentieth Century* by Ben Hecht and Charles MacArthur, which was in turn based on a play by Bruce Milholland

Stranded Again • On the Twentieth Century • I Rise Again • Veronique • Together • Never • Our Private World • Repent • Mine • I've Got it All • Five Zeros • Sextet • She's a Nut • Babette • The Legacy • Lily, Oscar • Life Is Like a Train

RA,SEL
[1] Tony Award for Best Score

ON YOUR TOES
April 11, 1936 (315)
Music by Richard Rodgers
Lyrics by Lorenz Hart

Two-a-Day for Keith • The Three B's • It's Got to Be Love • Too Good for the Average Man • There's a Small Hotel* • The Heart Is Quicker Than the Eye • La Princesse Zenobia (ballet) • Quiet Night • Glad to Be Unhappy • On Your Toes • Slaughter on Tenth Avenue (ballet)

RA,VS,SEL

ONCE UPON A MATTRESS
May 11, 1959 (460)[1]
Music by Mary Rodgers
Lyrics by Marshall Barer

Based on the fairy tale *The Princess and the Pea*

Many Moons Ago • An Opening for a Princess • In a Little While • Shy • The Minstrel • The Jester and I • Sensitivity • The Swamps of Home • Normandy • Spanish Panic • Song of Love • Quiet • Happily Ever After • Man to Man Talk • Very Soft Shoes • Yesterday I Loved You • Lullaby

RA,VS,SEL

[1] Includes initial OB run

ONE FOR THE MONEY
February 4, 1939 (132)
Music by Morgan Lewis
Lyrics by Nancy Hamilton

I Only Know • Rhapsody • Teeter Totter Tessie • Send a Boy • A Little Bit Delighted With the Weather • Once Upon a Time • The Yoo-Hoo Blues • Kiss Me and We'll Both Go Home

110 IN THE SHADE
October 24, 1963 (330)
Music by Harvey Schmidt
Lyrics by Tom Jones

Based on the play *The Rainmaker* by N. Richard Nash

Another Hot Day • Lizzie's Coming Home • Love, Don't Turn Away • Poker Polka • Hungry Men • The Rain Song • You're Not Foolin' Me • Raunchy • A Man and a Woman • Old Maid • Everything Beautiful Happens at Night • Melisande • Simple Little Things • Little Red Hat • Is It Really Me? • Wonderful Music

Dropped from production
Too Many People Alone

RA,VS,SEL

ONE TOUCH OF VENUS[1]
October 7, 1943 (567)
Music by Kurt Weill
Lyrics by Ogden Nash

Based on the 19th-century novella *The Tainted Venus* by F. Anstey

New Art Is True Art • One Touch of Venus • How Much I Love You • West Wind • Way Out West in Jersey • I'm a Stranger Here Myself • Foolish Heart • The Trouble With Women • Speak Low* • Dr. Crippen • Very, Very, Very • Catch Hatch • That's Him • Wooden Wedding

Dropped from production
Simply Paranoia • Love in a Mist • Who Am I?

RA

[1] Titles considered for the show before *One Touch of Venus* included *One Man's Venus, La Belle Venus,* and, at one low point, *Who Loves Who?*

THE ONLY GIRL
November 2, 1914 (240)
Music by Victor Herbert
Lyrics by Henry Blossom

Based on the comedy *Our Wives* by Frank Mandel

The More I See of Others, Dear, the Better I Love You • When You're Away • Be Happy, Boys, Tonight • The Compact • Personality • Antoinette • Here's to the Land We Love, Boys • Tell It All Over Again • Connubial Bliss • Here's How • You Have to Have a Part to Make a Hit • When You're Wearing the Ball and Chain • Equal Rights • You're the Only One for Me

VS

ONWARD VICTORIA
December 14, 1980 (1)
Music by Keith Hermann
Lyrics by Charlotte Anker and Irene Rosenberg

The Age of Brass • Magnetic Healing • Curiosity • Beecher's Processional • I Depend on You • Victoria's Banner • Changes • A Taste of Forever • Unescorted Women • Love and Joy • Everyday I Do a Little Something for the Lord • It's Easy for Her • You Cannot Drown the Dreamer • Respectable • Another Life • Read It in the Weekly • Beecher's Defense

RA

OPERATION SIDEWINDER
March 12, 1970 (52)

Catch Me (Music and lyrics by Sam Shepard) • Alien Song (Music and lyrics by Sam Shepard) • Euphoria (Music and lyrics by Robin Remaily) • Don't Leave Me Dangling in the Dust (Music and lyrics by Robin Remaily) • Synergy (Music and lyrics by Peter Stampfel and Antonia) • Bad Karma (Music and lyrics by Peter Stampfel and Antonia) • Generalonely (Music and lyrics by Steve Weber) • Do It Girl (Music and lyrics by Peter Stampfel and Antonia) • Float Me Down Your Pipeline (Music and lyrics by Antonia) • I Disremember Quite Well (Music and lyrics by Antonia) • Hathor (Music and lyrics by Peter Stampfel) • C.I.A. Man (Music and lyrics by Tuli Kupferberg, Peter Stampfel and Antonia)

THE OPTIMISTS
January 30, 1928 (24)
Music by Melville Gideon

Amapu (Lyrics by Edward Knoblock) • I Promise I'll Be Practically True to You (Lyrics by Clifford Grey) • If I Gave You a Rose (Lyrics by Granville English) • Little Lacquer Lady (Lyrics by Clifford Seyler) • Spare a Little Love (Lyrics by Clifford Grey)

ORANGE BLOSSOMS
September 19, 1922 (95)
Music by Victor Herbert
Lyrics by B.G. DeSylva

Based on the play *The Marriage of Kitty* by Fred de Gresac and Francis de Croisset

This Time It's Love • A Kiss in the Dark • New York Is the Same Old Place • Then Comes the Dawning • I Can't Argue With You • In Hennequeville • On the Riviera • The Lonely Nest • I Missed You • Just Like That • A Dream of Orange Blossoms • Way Out West in Jersey • Let's Not Get Married

VS

ORCHIDS PREFERRED
May 11, 1937 (7)
Music by Dave Stamper
Lyrics by Fred Herendeen

I'm Leaving the Bad Girls for Good • Selling a Song • Sub-Debs' First Fling • The Dying Swan • The Three R's (Music and lyrics by Henry Russell and Morry Olsen) • A Million Dollars • Eddy-Mac • Boy, Girl, Moon • Strictly Confidential • Minsky • My Lady's Hand • Man About Town • Paying Off • The Echo of a Song • What Are You Going to Do About Love?

OUR MISS GIBBS
August 29, 1910 (64)

Hats (Music by Ivan Caryll; lyrics by Adrian Ross) • Correct (Music by Ivan Caryll; lyrics by Adrian Ross) • Mary (Music by Lionel Monckton; lyrics by Adrian Ross) • Come Tiny Goldfish to Me (Music by Harry Marlow; lyrics by Jerome Kern)* • Not That Sort of Person (Music by Lionel Monckton; lyrics by George Grossmith, Jr.) • In Yorkshire (Music by Lionel Monckton; lyrics by Lionel Monckton and Ralph Roberts) • An English Gentleman (Music by Lionel Monckton; lyrics by Percy Greenbank) • Our Farm (Music by Ivan Caryll; lyrics by Lionel Monckton) • Moonstruck (Music and lyrics by Lionel Monckton)

VS

OUR NELL
December 4, 1922 (40)
Music by George Gershwin
Lyrics by Brian Hooker

Gol-Durn! • Innocent Ingenue Baby • The Cooney County Fair • Names I Love to Hear • By and By • Madrigal • We Go To Church on Sunday • Walking Home With Angeline • Oh, You Lady! • Little Villages

Dropped from production
The Custody of the Child

OUT OF THIS WORLD
December 21, 1950 (157)
Music and lyrics by Cole Porter

Based on the Amphitryon legend

I Jupiter, I Rex • Use Your Imagination • Hail, Hail, Hail • I Got Beauty • Where, Oh Where • I Am Loved • They Couldn't Compare to You • I Sleep Easier Now • Climb Up the Mountain • No Lover • Cherry Pies Ought to Be You • Hark to the Song of the Night • Nobody's Chasing Me

Dropped from production
From This Moment On* • You Don't Remind Me • Tonight I Love You More • What Do You Think About Men?

RA

OVER HERE!
March 6, 1974 (341)
Music and lyrics by Richard M. Sherman and Robert B. Sherman

Since You're Not Around • Over Here • Buy a Victory Bond • My Dream for Tomorrow • Charlie's Place • Hey Yvette • The Grass Grows Green • The Good-Time Girl • Wait for Me Marlena • We Got It • Wartime Wedding • Don't Shoot the Hooey to Me, Louie • Where Did the Good Times Go? • Dream Drummin' • Soft Music • The Big Beat • No Goodbyes

RA

P

PACIFIC OVERTURES
January 11, 1976 (206)
Music and lyrics by Stephen Sondheim

Advantages of Floating in the Middle of the Sea • There Is No Other Way • Four Black Dragons • Chrysanthemum Tea • Poems • Welcome to Kanagawa • Someone in a Tree* • Please Hello • A Bowler Hat • Pretty Lady • Next

RA,VS,SEL

PADLOCKS OF 1927
July 5, 1927 (95)

Hot Heels (Music by Lee David; lyrics by Billy Rose and Ballard MacDonald) • If I Had a Lover (Music by Henry Tobias; lyrics by Billy Rose and Ballard MacDonald) • The Tap, Tap (Music by Jesse Greer; lyrics by Billy Rose and Ballard MacDonald)

PAINT YOUR WAGON
November 12, 1951 (289)
Music by Frederick Loewe
Lyrics by Alan Jay Lerner

I'm on My Way • Rumson • What's Goin' On Here? • I Talk to the Trees • They Call the Wind Maria • I Still See Elisa • How Can I Wait? • Trio • In Between • Whoop-Ti-Ay • Carino Mio • There's a Coach Comin' In • Hand Me Down That Can o' Beans • Another Autumn • Movin' • All for Him • Wand'rin Star • Strike!

RA,VS,SEL

Added to film version (1969)
The First Thing You Know (Music by André Previn) • A Million Miles Away Behind the Door (Music by André Previn) • The Gospel of No Name City (Music by André Previn) • The Best Things in Life Are Dirty (Music by André Previn) • Gold Fever (Music by André Previn)

RA,VS,SEL

THE PAJAMA GAME[1]
May 13, 1954 (1,063)

Music and lyrics by Richard Adler and Jerry Ross

Based on the novel *7 1/2 Cents* by Richard Bissell

The Pajama Game • Racing With the Clock • A New Town Is a Blue Town • I'm Not at All in Love • I'll Never Be Jealous Again • Hey, There • Her Is • Sleep-Tite • Once a Year Day • Small Talk • There Once Was a Man • Steam Heat • Think of the Time I Save • Hernando's Hideaway • 7 1/2 Cents

RA,VS,SEL

[1] Tony Award for Best Score

PAL JOEY
December 25, 1940 (374)
Music by Richard Rodgers
Lyrics by Lorenz Hart

Based on the stories by John O'Hara

You Mustn't Kick It Around • I Could Write a Book • Chicago • That Terrific Rainbow • Love Is My Friend* • Happy Hunting Horn • Bewitched, Bothered and Bewildered* • Pal Joey • The Flower Garden of My Heart • Zip • Plant You Now, Dig You Later • Den of Iniquity • Do It the Hard Way • Take Him

Dropped from production
I'm Talking to My Pal

RA,VS,SEL

PANAMA HATTIE
October 30, 1940 (501)
Music and lyrics by Cole Porter

Join It Right Away • Visit Panama • American Family • My Mother Would Love You • I've Still Got My Health • Fresh as a Daisy • Welcome to Jerry • Let's Be Buddies • I'm Throwing a Ball Tonight • We Detest a Fiesta • Who Would Have Dreamed • Make It Another Old-Fashioned, Please • All I've Got to Get Now Is My Man • You Said It • God Bless the Women • A Stroll on the Plaza 'ana • They Ain't Done Right by Our Nell

Dropped from production
Here's to Panama Hattie

RA

PANSY
May 14, 1929 (3)
Music and lyrics by Maceo Pinkard

It's Commencement Day • Breakin' the Rhythm •
Pansy • Campus Walk • I'd Be Happy • Gettin'
Together • Shake a Leg • If the Blues Don't Get You
• A Stranger Interlude • A Bouquet of Fond
Memories

PARADE (1935)
May 20, 1935 (40)
Music by Jerome Moross
Lyrics by Paul Peters and George Sklar

On Parade • I'm Telling You, Louie • I'm an
International Orphan • Smart Set (Music by Will
Irwin) • Life Could Be So Beautiful • Send for the
Militia (Music and lyrics by Marc Blitzstein) • You
Ain't So Hot • Boys in Blue • Fear in My Heart • My
Feet Are Firmly Planted on the Ground (Lyrics by
Emanuel Eisenberg) • Marry the Family (Lyrics by
Michael Blankfort) • Selling Sex (Lyrics by Kyle
Crichton) • Bon Voyage (Lyrics by Kyle Crichton) •
Join Our Ranks

PARADE (OB)
January 20, 1960 (95)
Music and lyrics by Jerry Herman

Show Tune in 2/4 Time* • Save the Village • Your
Hand in Mine • Confession to a Park Avenue
Mother (I'm in Love With a West Side Girl) • Two a
Day • Just Plain Folks • The Antique Man • The Next
Time I Love • Your Good Morning • Maria in Spats •
Another Candle • Jolly Theatrical Season

RA

PARADISE GARDENS EAST (OB)
March 10, 1969 (16)
Music by Mildred Kayden
Lyrics by Frank Gagliano

Harmony • The Beat of the City • I'll Bet You're a
Cat Girl • Gussy and the Beautiful People • Look at
My Sister • Black and Blue Pumps • That's Right,
Mr. Syph • The Incinerator Hour

PARDON MY ENGLISH
January 20, 1933 (46)
Music by George Gershwin
Lyrics by Ira Gershwin

Three Quarter Time • Lorelei • Pardon My English •
Dancing in the Streets • So What? • Isn't It a Pity? •
My Cousin in Milwaukee • Hail the Happy Couple •
The Dresden Northwest Mounted • Luckiest Man in
the World • What Sort of Wedding Is This? •
Tonight* • Where You Go I Go • I've Got to Be
There • He's Not Himself

Dropped from production
Bauer's House • Freud and Jung and Adler •

Together At Last • Poor Michael! Poor Golo •
Fatherland, Mother of the Band • No Tickee, No
Washee

PARDON OUR FRENCH
September 27, 1950 (100)
Music by Victor Young
Lyrics by Edward Heyman

Pardon Our French • There's No Man Like a
Snowman • I Ought to Know More About You •
Venezia and Her Three Lovers • A Face in the
Crowd • I'm Gonna Make a Fool out of April • The
Flower Song • Dolly From the Follies Bergères • The
Poker-Polka

PARIS
October 8, 1928 (195)
Music and lyrics by Cole Porter

The Land of Going to Be (Music and lyrics by E.
Ray Goetz and Walter Kollo) • Paris (Music and
lyrics by E. Ray Goetz and Louis Alter) • Two Little
Babes in the Wood • Don't Look at Me That Way •
Let's Do It, Let's Fall in Love* • Vivienne • Heaven
Hop

Dropped from production
Quelque Chose • Let's Misbehave

Added to film version (1930)
Which

PARIS '90
March 4, 1952 (87)
Music and lyrics by Kay Swift

Turn My Little Millwheel (Music by Paul Delmet) •
Lend Me a Bob Till Monday • Calliope • Saint
Lazare (Music by Aristide Bruant) • Madame Arthur
(Music by Yvette Guilbert) • The Waltz I Heard in a
Dream

RA

PARISIANA
February 9, 1928 (28)
Music and lyrics by Vincent Valentini

Keep On Dancing • When You Say No to Love •
Keep It Under Your Hat • Who Wouldn't? • Since
Nora Brought Her Angora Around • Parisiana Roses
• What's Become of the Bowery? • The Ghost of
Old Black Joe • Paris Green • In a Gondola With
You • Golliwog • Unfortunate Rose • They're Hot
Now up in Iceland • Peepin' Tommy • Paree Has the
Fever Now

PARK
April 22, 1970 (5)
Music by Lance Mulcahy
Lyrics by Paul Cherry

All the Little Things in the World Are Waiting • Hello
Is the Way Things Begin • Bein' a Kid • Elizabeth •
He Talks to Me • Tomorrow Will Be the Same • One

Man • Park • I Want It Just to Happen • I Can See • Compromise • Jamie • I'd Marry You Again

PARK AVENUE
November 4, 1946 (72)
Music by Arthur Schwartz
Lyrics by Ira Gershwin

Tomorrow Is the Time • For the Life of Me • The Dew Was on the Rose • Don't Be a Woman if You Can • Nevada • There's No Holding Me • There's Nothing Like Marriage for People • Hope for the Best • My Son-in-Law • The Land of Opportunitee • Goodbye to All That • Stay as We Are

PEG[1]
December 14, 1983 (5)
Music by Paul Horner
Lyrics by Peggy Lee

Soul • Daddy Was a Railroad Man • Mama • That Old Piano • One Beating a Day • That's How I Learned to Sing the Blues • Sometimes You're Up • He'll Make Me Believe He's Mine • The Other Part of Me • Angels on Your Pillow • What Did Dey Do to My Goil?

[1] This one-woman show, starring Peggy Lee, also included several additional songs previously written and/or made popular by her.

PEGGY-ANN
December 27, 1926 (333)
Music by Richard Rodgers
Lyrics by Lorenz Hart

Suggested by the musical comedy *Tillie's Nightmare* (1910) by Edgar Smith and A. Baldwin Sloane

Hello • A Tree in the Park • Howdy Broadway • A Little Birdie Told Me So • Charming, Charming • Where's That Rainbow? • We Pirates From Weehawken • In His Arms • Chuck It! • I'm So Humble • Havana • Maybe It's Me • Give This Little Girl a Hand

Dropped from production
Come and Tell Me • Pipes of Pansy • Peggy, Peggy • Tramping Along • Paris Is Really Divine

THE PENNY FRIEND (OB)
December 26, 1966 (32)
Music and lyrics by William Roy

Based on the play *A Kiss for Cinderella* by Sir James M. Barrie

The Penny Friend • She Makes You Think of Home • Who Am I, Who Are You, Who Are We? • Mrs. Bodie • I Am Going to Dance • Feet • The Great Unknown • How Doth the Apple Butterfly • The Diagnostician • Won't You Come to the Party? • The Grand Parade • A Very Full and Productive Day • The World Today

PETER PAN (Play with two songs)
November 26, 1924 (96)
Music by Jerome Kern

Won't You Have a Little Feather (Lyrics by Paul

West) • The Sweetest Thing in Life* (Lyrics by B.G. DeSylva)

PETER PAN
April 24, 1950 (321)
Music and lyrics by Leonard Bernstein

Based on the play by Sir James M. Barrie

Who Am I? • My House • Peter, Peter • The Pirate Song • The Plank • Never Never Land

RA,SEL

PETER PAN
October 20, 1954 (152)

Based on the play by Sir James M. Barrie

Tender Shepherd (Music by Mark Charlap; lyrics by Carolyn Leigh) • I've Gotta Crow (Music by Mark Charlap; lyrics by Carolyn Leigh) • Never Never Land (Music by Jule Styne; lyrics by Betty Comden and Adolph Green) • I'm Flying (Music by Mark Charlap; lyrics by Carolyn Leigh) • Pirate Song (Music by Mark Charlap; lyrics by Carolyn Leigh) • A Princely Scheme (Music by Mark Charlap; lyrics by Carolyn Leigh) • Indians (Music by Mark Charlap; lyrics by Carolyn Leigh) • Wendy (Music by Jule Styne; lyrics by Betty Comden and Adolph Green) • I Won't Grow Up (Music by Mark Charlap; lyrics by Carolyn Leigh) • Mysterious Lady (Music by Jule Styne; lyrics by Betty Comden and Adolph Green) • Ugg-a-Wugg (Music by Jule Styne; lyrics by Betty Comden and Adolph Green) • Pow-Wow Polka (Music by Jule Styne; lyrics by Betty Comden and Adolph Green) • Captain Hook's Waltz (Music by Jule Styne; lyrics by Betty Comden and Adolph Green) • Distant Melody (Music by Jule Styne; lyrics by Betty Comden and Adolph Green) • Captain Hook's Tango (Music by Mark Charlap; lyrics by Carolyn Leigh) • Tarantella (Music by Mark Charlap; lyrics by Carolyn Leigh)

RA,VS

PETTICOAT FEVER (Play with one song)
March 4, 1935 (137)
Music by Frederick Loewe
Lyrics by Irene Alexander

Love Tiptoed Through My Heart

PHILEMON (OB)
April 8, 1975 (48)
Music by Harvey Schmidt
Lyrics by Tom Jones

Within This Empty Space • The Streets of Antioch • Gimme a Good Digestion • Don't Kiki Me • I'd Do Almost Anything to Get Out of Here and Go Home • He's Coming • Antioch Prison • Name: Cockian • I Love Order • My Secret Dream • I Love His Face • Sometimes • The Protest • The Nightmare • Love Suffers Everything • The Confrontation

PHOENIX '55 (OB)
April 23, 1955 (97)
Music by David Baker
Lyrics by David Craig

It Says Here • Tomorrow Is Here • All Around the World • Never Wait for Love • Down to the Sea • This Tuxedo Is Mine! • Just Him • A Funny Heart • Suburban Retreat

PIANO BAR (OB)
June 8, 1978 (133)
Music by Rob Fremont
Lyrics by Doris Willens

Sweet Sue's • Today • Pigeon-Hole Time • Congratulations • Believe Me • Everywhere I Go • Dinner at the Mirklines • Scenes From Some Marriages • Personals • Nobody's Perfect • One Two Three • Greenspons • Moms and Dads • Meanwhile Back in Yonkers • Walt's Truth • New York Cliche • It's Coming Back to Me • Tomorrow Night

RA

PICKWICK
October 4, 1965 (56)
Music by Cyril Ornadel
Lyrics by Leslie Bricusse

Based on *The Pickwick Papers* by Charles Dickens

I Like the Company of Men • That's What I'd Like for Christmas • The Pickwickians • A Bit of a Character • There's Something About You • A Gentleman's Gentleman • You Never Met a Feller Like Me • I'll Never Be Lonely Again • Fizkin and Pickwick • Very • If I Ruled the World • Talk • That's the Law • Damages

RA

PIGGY
January 11, 1927 (83)
Music by Cliff Friend
Lyrics by Lew Brown

I Need a Little Bit, You Need a Little Bit • I Wanna Go Voom Voom • It Just Had to Happen • Didn't It • Oh, Baby • A Little Change of Atmosphere • It's Easy to Say Hello • The Music of a Rippling Stream • When • Let's Stroll Along and Sing a Song of Love • Ding, Dong, Dell

THE PINK LADY
March 13, 1911 (312)
Music by Ivan Caryll
Lyrics by C.M.S. McLellan

Based on the French farce *Le Satyre* by Georges Berr and Marcel Guillemand

Bring Along the Camera • Love Is Divine • By the Saskatchewan • Oh, So Gently • The Intriguers • Donny Didn't, Donny Did • The Kiss Waltz • Hide and Seek • The Duel • The Hudson Belle • I Like It • My Beautiful Lady • I'm Single for Six Weeks More

VS

PINS AND NEEDLES (OB)
November 27, 1937 (1,108)
Music and lyrics by Harold Rome

First Impression (Lyrics by Rome and Charles Friedman) • Sing Me a Song With Social Significance • Public Enemy No.1 • We'd Rather Be Right (Lyrics by Arthur Kramer) • Sunday in the Park • Nobody Makes a Pass at Me • Economics I • Men Awake • It's Not Cricket to Picket • Chain Store Daisy • What Good Is Love? • One Big Union for Two • Four Little Angels of Peace • Doin' the Reactionary • We've Just Begun (Lyrics by Rome and Charles Friedman)

Added during run
Papa Lewis, Mama Green • I've Got the Nerve to Be in Love • It's Better With a Union Man • Sitting on Your Status Quo • Mene, Mene, Tekel • Back to Work • Britannia Waives the Rules (Music by Berenice Kazounoff; lyrics by Arnold B. Horwitt and John Latouche) • Oh, Give Me the Good Old Days • When I Grow Up (The G-Man Song) • Stay Out, Sammy • We Sing America • What This Party Needs (Lyrics by Rome and Arthur Kramer) • Lorelei on the Rocks (Music by Berenice Kazounoff; lyrics by John Latouche)

RA,VS,SEL

PIPE DREAM
November 30, 1955 (246)
Music by Richard Rodgers
Lyrics by Oscar Hammerstein II

Based on the novel *Sweet Thursday* by John Steinbeck

All Kinds of People • The Tide Pool • Ev'rybody's Got a Home But Me • A Lopsided Bus • Bums' Opera • The Man I Used to Be • Sweet Thursday • Suzy Is a Good Thing • All at Once You Love Her • The Happiest House on the Block • The Party That We're Gonna Have Tomorrow Night • The Party Gets Going • I Am a Witch • Will You Marry Me? • Thinkin' • How Long? • The Next Time It Happens

Dropped from production
Sitting on the Back Porch

RA,VS

PIPPIN
October 23, 1972 (1,944)
Music and lyrics by Stephen Schwartz

Magic to Do • Corner of the Sky • Welcome Home • War Is a Science • Glory • Simple Joys • No Time at All • With You • Spread a Little Sunshine • Morning Glow • On the Right Track • Kind of Woman • Extraordinary • Love Song

RA,SEL

PLAIN AND FANCY
January 27, 1955 (461)
Music by Albert Hague
Lyrics by Arnold B. Horwitt

You Can't Miss It • It Wonders Me • Plenty of Pennsylvania • Young and Foolish • Why Not Katie? • It's a Helluva Way to Run a Love Affair • This Is All Very New to Me • Plain We Live • How Do You Raise a Barn? • Follow Your Heart • City Mouse, Country Mouse • I'll Show Him! • Take Your Time and Take Your Pick

RA,VS

PLATINUM
November 12, 1978 (33)
Music by Gary William Friedman
Lyrics by Will Holt

Back With a Beat/Nothing But • Sunset • Ride, Baby, Ride • Destiny • Disco Destiny • I Am the Light • Movie Star Mansion • Platinum Dreams • Trials and Tribulations/I Like You • 1945 • Too Many Mirrors • Old Times, Good Times

RA

PLEASURE BOUND
February 18, 1929 (136)
Music by Muriel Pollock
Lyrics by Max and Nathaniel Lief and Harold Atteridge

We Love to Go to Work • Just Suppose (Music by Phil Baker and Maury Rubens; lyrics by Sid Silvers and Moe Jaffe) • We'll Get Along • Park Avenue Strut (Music by Phil Baker and Maury Rubens; lyrics by Moe Jaffe and Harold Atteridge) • Cross Word Puzzles • My Melody Man (Music by Peter de Rose; lyrics by Charles Tobias and Henry Clare) • The Things That Were Made for Love (Music by Peter de Rose; lyrics by Charles Tobias and Irving Kahal) • Why Do You Tease Me?

POLLY
January 8, 1929 (15)
Music by Philip Charig
Lyrics by Irving Caesar

Based on the play *Polly With a Past* by David Belasco

Lots of Time for Sue • On With the Dance • Little Bo-Peep • When a Fellow Meets a Flapper on Broadway • Sing a Song in the Rain (Music by Harry Rosenthal; lyrics by Douglas Furber and Irving Caesar) • Comme Çi, Comme Ça • Nobody Wants Me • Polly • Sweet Liar (Music by Herbert Stothart) • Heel and Toe • Life Is Love • Something Spanish in Your Eyes

POLLY OF HOLLYWOOD
February 21, 1927 (24)
Music by Will Morrisey
Lyrics by Edmund Joseph

Midnight Daddy • Company Manners • Polly of Hollywood • Texas Stomp • Wanting You • New Kind of Rhythm

POLONAISE
October 6, 1945 (113)

Music by Bronislaw Kaper (based on Chopin)
Lyrics by John Latouche

Laughing Bells • O Heart of My Country • Stranger (Music by Kaper) • Au Revoir, Soldier (Music by Kaper) • Meadowlark • Hay, Hay, Hay (Music by Kaper) • Moonlight Soliloquy • Just for Tonight • Exchange for Lovers • An Imperial Conference • Now I Know Your Face by Heart • I Wonder as I Wander • The Next Time I Care (Music by Kaper) • Wait for Tomorrow

RA

POOR LITTLE RITZ GIRL[1]
July 28, 1920 (119)
Music by Richard Rodgers[2] and Sigmund Romberg
Lyrics by Lorenz Hart[2] and Alex Gerber

Poor Little Ritz Girl (Music by Romberg; lyrics by Gerber) • Mary, Queen of Scots (Music by Rodgers; lyrics by Herbert Fields. • Love Will Call (Music by Rodgers; lyrics by Hart)* • Pretty Ming Toy (Music by Romberg; lyrics by Gerber) • I Love to Say Hello to the Girls (Music by Romberg; lyrics by Gerber) • When I Found You (Music by Romberg; lyrics by Gerber) • You Can't Fool Your Dreams (Music by Rodgers; lyrics by Hart)* • What Happened Nobody Knows (Music by Rodgers; lyrics by Hart) • My Violin (Music by Romberg; lyrics by Gerber) • All You Need to Be a Star (Music by Rodgers; lyrics by Hart) • Love's Intense in Tents (Music by Rodgers; lyrics by Hart)* • The Daisy and the Lark (Music by Rodgers; lyrics by Hart) • In the Land of Yesterday (Music by Romberg; lyrics by Gerber) • The Bombay Bombashay (Music by Romberg; lyrics by Gerber)

Songs from the Boston production (opened May 28, 1920) dropped from Broadway production

The Midnight Supper (Rodgers and Hart) • Lady Raffles (Rodgers and Hart) • The Gown Is Mightier Than the Sword (Rodgers and Hart) • Let Me Drink in Your Eyes (Rodgers and Hart) • Will You Forgive Me? (Rodgers and Hart) • Souvenir (Rodgers and Hart) • Call the Doc (Rodgers and Hart) • The Lord Only Knows (Rodgers and Hart) • The Boomerang (Rodgers and Hart) • I Surrender (Rodgers and Hart)

[1] As originally presented in Boston the entire score was by Rodgers and Hart.

[2] Richard Rodgers, then eighteen years old, used his middle initial, C for Charles; Lorenz Hart used his middle initial, M for Milton.

POPPY
September 3, 1923 (346)
Music by Stephen Jones and Arthur Samuels
Lyrics by Dorothy Donnelly

Stepping Around • The Girl I've Never Met • Hang Your Sorrows in the Sun (Music by John Egan) • Two Make a Home • When Men Are Alone • Fortune Telling • Alibi Baby (Music by Samuels; lyrics by Howard Dietz) • Poppy Dear • Choose a Partner Please • What Do You Do Sunday, Mary? (Music by

Jones; lyrics by Irving Caesar) • Picnic Party With You (Music by John Egan) • The Dancing Lesson (Music by John Egan)

Dropped from production
Someone Will Make You Smile* (Music by Rudolf Sieczynski; lyrics by Irving Caesar)

PORGY AND BESS
October 10, 1935 (124)
Music by George Gershwin
Lyrics by DuBose Heyward and Ira Gershwin

Based on the play *Porgy* by DuBose and Dorothy Heyward

Jasbo Brown Blues (Piano Solo) • Summertime (Lyrics by Heyward) • A Woman Is a Sometime Thing (Lyrics by Heyward) • They Pass By Singing (Lyrics by Heyward) • Crap Game Fugue (Lyrics by Heyward) • Gone, Gone, Gone! (Lyrics by Heyward) • Overflow (Lyrics by Heyward) • My Man's Gone Now (Lyrics by Heyward) • Leavin' fo' de Promis' Lan' (Lyrics by Heyward) • It Take a Long Pull to Get There (Lyrics by Heyward) • I Got Plenty o' Nuttin' • Woman to Lady (Lyrics by Heyward) • The Buzzard Song (Lyrics by Heyward) • Bess, You Is My Woman Now • Oh, I Can't Sit Down (Lyrics by Ira Gershwin) • It Ain't Necessarily So (Lyrics by Ira Gershwin)* • What You Want With Bess? (Lyrics by Heyward) • Time and Time Again (Lyrics by Heyward) • Street Cries (Strawberry Woman, Crab Man) (Lyrics by Heyward) • I Loves You, Porgy • Oh, de Lawd Shake de Heaven (Lyrics by Heyward) • A Red-Headed Woman (Lyrics by Ira Gershwin) • Oh, Doctor Jesus • Clara, Don't You Be Downhearted (Lyrics by Heyward) • There's a Boat Dat's Leavin' Soon for New York (Lyrics by Ira Gershwin)* • Oh, Bess, Oh Where's My Bess (Lyrics by Ira Gershwin) • I'm On My Way (Lyrics by Heyward)

RA,VS,SEL

PORTOFINO
February 21, 1958 (3)
Music by Louis Bellson and Will Irwin
Lyrics by Richard Ney

Come Along • No Wedding Bells for Me • Red-Collar Job • Here I Come • New Dreams for Old • A Dream for Angela • Isn't It Wonderful? • Under a Spell • That's Love • Too Little Time for Love • It Might Be Love • Morning Prayer • The Grand Prix of Portofino • Portofino • I'm in League With the Devil • Why Not for Marriage?

PORTRAIT OF JENNIE (OB)
December 10, 1982 (16)
Music by Howard Marren
Lyrics by Enid Futterman

Based on the novel by Robert Nathan

Winter of the Mind • Where I Come From • Hammerstein's Music Hall • My City • Wish • Alhambra Nights • Secrets • Portrait of Jennie • A Green Place • Remember Today • Paris • Time Stands Still in Truro • I Love You

POTHOLES (OB)
October 9, 1979 (15)
Music by Ted Simons
Lyrics by Elinor Guggenheimer

Lost New York • Welcome • Back in the Street • Mad About • Can You Type? • Madison Avenue • Ropin' Dogies • Just Sit Back • Giant • Yoga and Yoghurt • Politicians' Song • Tickets' Song • St. Patrick's Day Parade • Starved • Fast Food • Network • Sound and Light • Looking for Someone • Suddenly She Was There • Dog Walker • Typical New Yorkers

POUSSE-CAFÉ
March 18, 1966 (3)
Music by Duke Ellington
Lyrics by Marshall Barer and Fred Tobias

The Spider and the Fly • Rules and Regulations • Follow Me up the Stairs • Goodbye Charlie • C'est Comme Ça • Thank You, Ma'am • The Eleventh Commandment • Someone to Care For • The Wedding • Let's • The Good Old Days • Easy to Take • Old World Charm

PREPPIES (OB)
August 18, 1983 (51)
Music and lyrics by Gary Portnoy and Judy Hart Angelo

People Like Us • The Chance of a Lifetime • One Step Away • Summertime • Fairy Tales • The Parents' Farewell • Bells • Moving On • Our Night • We've Got Each Other • Gonna Run • I Don't Care • Bring On the Loot

RA

PRESENT ARMS
April 26, 1928 (155)
Music by Richard Rodgers
Lyrics by Lorenz Hart

Tell It to the Marines • You Took Advantage of Me* • Do I Hear You Saying "I Love You"? • A Kiss for Cinderella • Is It the Uniform? • Crazy Elbows • Down by the Sea • I'm a Fool, Little One • Blue Ocean Blues* • Hawaii • Kohala, Welcome

THE PRESIDENT'S DAUGHTER
November 3, 1970 (72)
Music by Murray Rumshinsky
Lyrics by Jacob Jacobs

Women's Liberation • The President's Daughter • I Have What You Want! • A Lesson in Yiddish • Everything Is Possible in Life • Welcome, Mr. Golden! • Stiochket • Without a Mother • Love at Golden Years • If Only I Could Be a Kid Again • An Old Man Shouldn't Be Born • We Two • What More Do I Need? • What Would You Do?

THE PRINCE AND THE PAUPER (OB)
October 12, 1963 (158)
Music by George Fischoff
Lyrics by Verna Tomasson

Based on the story by Mark Twain

Garbage Court Round • In a Story Book • I've Been a-Begging • Why Don't We Switch? • Do This, Do That • The Prince Is Mad • Oh, Pity the Man • With a Sword in My Buckle • Ev'rybody Needs Somebody to Love • The Tree and the Sun • King Foo-Foo the First • Coronation Song

RA

THE PRINCE OF PILSEN
March 17, 1903 (143)
Music by Gustav Luders
Lyrics by Frank Pixley

The Modern Pirate • We Know It's Wrong to Flirt • Artie • A Season at the Shore • Hail to Our Noble Guest • The Message of the Violet • Heidelberg Stein Song • Biff! Bang! • The Widow • Keep It Dark • Pictures in the Smoke • The Field and Forest • He Didn't Know Exactly What to Do • The American Girl • The Tale of the Seashell • Back to the Boulevards • Our Floral Queen • Fall In!

VS

PRINCESS CHARMING
October 13, 1930 (56)
Music by Albert Sirmay and Arthur Schwartz
Lyrics by Arthur Swanstrom

Leave It All to Your Faithful Ambassador • Palace of Dreams • The Panic's On • Trailing a Shooting Star • A Sword for the King • I'll Be There • One for All • You • It's a Wonderful Thing for a King • I Love Love (Music by Robert Emmett Dolan; lyrics by Walter O'Keefe) • I'll Never Leave You • Happiness and Joy to the King

PRINCESS FLAVIA
November 2, 1925 (152)
Music by Sigmund Romberg
Lyrics by Harry B. Smith

Based on the novel The Prisoner of Zenda by Anthony Hope

Yes or No • On, Comrades • Marionettes • What Care I? • Convent Bells Are Ringing • I Dare Not Love You • By This Token • Dance With Me • Twilight Voices • Only One • I Love Them All • In Ruritania

THE PRINCESS PAT
September 29, 1915 (158)
Music by Victor Herbert
Lyrics by Henry Blossom

Allies • Make Him Guess • I'd Like to Be a Quitter • Love Is Best of All • For Better or for Worse • Neapolitan Love Song • I Wish I Was an Island in an Ocean of Girls • Flirting • All for You • In a Little World for Two • The Shoes of Husband Number One • Two Laughing Irish Eyes

VS

PRIVATE LIVES (Play with one original song)
January 27, 1931 (256)
Music and lyrics by Noël Coward

Some Day I'll Find You

RA

PROMENADE (OB)
June 4, 1969 (259)
Music by Al Carmines
Lyrics by Maria Irene Fornes

Dig, Dig, Dig • Unrequited Love • Isn't That Clear? • Don't Eat It • Four • Chicken Is He • A Flower • Rosita Rodriguez; Serenade • Après Vous I • Bliss • The Moment Has Passed • Thank You • The Clothes Make the Man • The Cigarette Song • Two Little Angels • The Passing of Time • Capricious and Fickle • Crown Me • Mr. Phelps • Madeline • Spring Beauties • A Poor Man • Why Not? • The Finger Song • Little Fool • Czardas • The Laughing Song • A Mother's Love • Listen, I Feel • I Saw a Man • All Is Well in the City

RA,SEL

PROMISES, PROMISES
December 1, 1968 (1,281)
Music by Burt Bacharach
Lyrics by Hal David

Based on the film The Apartment (1960) by Billy Wilder and I.A.L. Diamond

Half as Big as Life • Upstairs • You'll Think of Someone • Our Little Secret • She Likes Basketball • Knowing When to Leave • Where Can You Take a Girl? • Wanting Things • Turkey Lurkey Time • A Fact Can Be a Beautiful Thing • Whoever You Are • A Young Pretty Girl Like You • I'll Never Fall in Love Again • Promises, Promises

RA,VS,SEL

PROVINCETOWN FOLLIES (OB)
November 3, 1935 (63)

Poor Porgy (Music by Sylvan Green; lyrics by Frederick Herendeen) • New Words for an Old Love Song (Music by Dave Stamper; lyrics by Frederick Herendeen)

PUMP BOYS AND DINETTES
February 4, 1982 (573)[1]
Music and lyrics by Jim Swann

Highway 57 • Takin' My Time (Music and lyrics by Spider John Koerner and John Foley) • Who Will the Next Fool Be? (Music and lyrics by Charlie Rich) • Menu Song (Music and lyrics by Cass Morgan and Debra Monk) • The Best Man • Fisherman's Prayer • Catfish (Music and lyrics by Jim Wann and B. Simpson) • Mamaw • Be Good or Be Gone • Drinkin' Shoes (Music and lyrics by Mark Hardwick, Cass Morgan, and Debra Monk) • Pump Boys • Mona • T. N.D.P.W.A.M. • Tips (Music and lyrics by Debra Monk and Cass Morgan) • Sisters (Music and lyrics by Cass Morgan) • Vacation • No Holds Barred (Music and lyrics by Jim Wann and Cass Morgan) • Farmer Tan • Closing Time

RA

[1] Opened Off Broadway October 1, 1981; closed January 17, 1982 (112)

PURLIE
March 15, 1970 (688)
Music by Gary Geld
Lyrics by Peter Udell

Based on the play *Purlie Victorious* by Ossie Davis

Walk Him Up the Stairs • New Fangled Preacher Man • Skinnin' a Cat • Purlie • The Harder They Fall • Charlie's Songs • Big Fish, Little Fish • I Got Love • Great White Father • Down Home • First Thing Monday Mornin' • He Can Do It • The World Is Comin' to a Start

RA, SEL

PUT IT IN WRITING (OB)
May 13, 1963 (24)

Literary Cocktail Party (Music and lyrics by Bud McCreery) • I Hope You're Happy (Music by Norman Martin; lyrics by Fred Ebb) • Trilogy (Music and lyrics by Bud McCreery) • Give 'Em a Kiss (Music and lyrics by G. Wood) • The Ayes of Texas (Music by Norman Martin; lyrics by Fred Ebb) • Daisy (Music and lyrics by G. Wood) • The People's Choice (Music by Norman Martin; lyrics by Fred Ebb) • What's Cooking? (Music by Norman Martin; lyrics by Fred Ebb) • The Youngest President (Music by Robert Kessler; lyrics by Martin Charnin) • Emmy Lou (Music by Norman Martin; lyrics by Fred Ebb) • Stock Report (Music by Norman Martin; lyrics by Fred Ebb) • Arty (Music by James Wise; lyrics by David Bimonte) • What Kind of Life Is That? (Music by Norman Martin; lyrics by Fred Ebb) • Put It in Writing (Music and lyrics by Alan Kohan) • Walking Down the Road (Music and lyrics by Alan Kohan and William Angelos)

PUZZLES OF 1925
February 2, 1925 (104)

The Undecided Blues (Music and lyrics by Elsie Janis) • Titina (Music by Leo Daniderff; lyrics by Bertal-Maubon and E. Ronn) • Tra-la-la-la (Music and lyrics by Elsie Janis and Vincent Scotto) • You've Got to Dance (Music and lyrics by Elsie Janis) • Je Vous Aime (Music and lyrics by Arthur L. Beiner) • We're Jumping Into Something (Music and lyrics by Blanche Merrill) • Doo-Dab (Music by Harry Ruby; lyrics by Bert Kalmar)

Q

THE QUAKER GIRL
October 23, 1911 (240)
Music by Lionel Monckton
Lyrics by Adrian Ross

Quakers' Meeting • Wonderful • A Runaway Match • A Quaker Girl • A Bad Boy and a Good Girl (Lyrics by Percy Greenbank) • Tiptoe • Just as Father Used to Do (Lyrics by Percy Greenbank) • Or Thereabouts (Music by Hugo Felix) • On Revient de Chantilly • Come to the Ball • A Dancing Lesson • Barbizon • Tony From America (Lyrics by Lionel Monckton)

VS

QUEEN HIGH
September 8, 1926 (367)
Music by Lewis E. Gensler
Lyrics by B. G. DeSylva

It Pays to Advertise • Everything Will Happen for the Best • You'll Never Know • Don't Forget (Music by James F. Hanley) • Who? You! • The Weaker Sex • Cross Your Heart • Sez You? Sez I! • Beautiful Baby (Music By James F. Hanley) • Who'll Mend a Broken Heart? • Gentlemen Prefer Blondes • Springtime

R

RAIN OR SHINE
February 9, 1928 (360)
Music by Milton Ager
Lyrics by Jack Yellen

Glad Tidings • Circus Days • So Would I • Add a
Little Wiggle • Rain or Shine • Oh, Baby! (Music and
lyrics by Owen Murphy) • Roustabout's Song
(Music by Ager and Owen Murphy) • Hey, Rube •
Falling Star • Feelin' Good (Music by Owen Murphy)
• Forever and Ever • Who's Goin' to Get You? •
Breakfast With You

RAINBOW
November 21, 1928 (29)
Music by Vincent Youmans
Lyrics by Oscar Hammerstein II

On the Golden Trail • My Mother Told Me Not to
Trust a Soldier • Virginia* • I Want a Man • Soliloquy
• I Like You as You Are • The One Girl • Let Me
Give All My Love to Thee • Diamond in the Rough •
Who Wants to Love Spanish Ladies? • Hay! Straw! •
The Bride Was Dressed in White

Dropped from production
Get a Horse, Get a Mule • I Look for Love • How to
Win a Man • Who Am I? (that You Should Care for
Me) (Lyrics by Gus Kahn) • Coming Through the
Rye • Forty-Niner and His Clementine • A Faded
Rose • Sunrise

Added to film version (Song of the West) 1930
West Wind (Lyrics by J. Russel Robinson)

RAINBOW (OB)
December 18, 1972 (48)
Music and lyrics by James Rado

Who Are We? • Love Me Love My Dorothy Lamour
Sarong • Fruits and Vegetables • Welcome Banana •
Questions Questions • Song to Sing • My Lungs •
You Got to Be Clever • Tangled Tangents • What
Can I Do for You? • Oh, I Am a Fork • People Stink •
Guinea Pig • Give Your Heart to Jesus • Joke a Cola
• Mama Loves You • I Want to Make You Cry • I Am

a Cloud • A Garden for Two • Starry Old Night •
Bathroom • O.K. Goodbye • Deep in the Dark • You
Live in Flowers • I Don't Hope for Great Things •
Globligated • Be Not Afraid • Obedience • Ten Days
Ago • Oh, Oh, Oh • Moosh, Moosh • The Man • The
World Is Round • Stars and Bars • Cacophony •
Groovy Green Man Groovy • Heliopolis • I Am Not
Free • We Are the Clouds • How Dreamlike •
Somewhere Under the Rainbow • Star Song

THE RAINBOW GIRL
April 1, 1918 (160)
Music by Louis A. Hirsch
Lyrics by Rennold Wolf

Based on the comedy *The New Lady Bantock* by
Jerome K. Jerome.

Rainbow Girl • Won't Some Nice Boy Marry Me? •
Just You Alone • Alimony Blues • The Wedding
Ceremony • In a Month or Two • My Rainbow Girl •
We Fear You Will Not Do, Lady Wetherell • Let's Go
Down to the Shop • Love's Ever New • I'll Think of
You • Mister Drummer Man • I Wonder • Soon We'll
Be Seen Upon the Screen • Beautiful Lady, Tell Me

VS

RAINBOW JONES
February 13, 1974 (1)
Music and lyrics by Jill Williams

A Little Bit of Me in You • Free and Easy • Do Unto
Others • I'd Like to Know You Better • Bad Breath •
Alone, at Last, Alone • Her Name Is Leona • We All
Need Love • The Only Man for the Job • It's So Nice
• Wait a Little While • One Big Happy Family • Who
Needs the Love of a Woman?

RAINBOW ROSE
March 16, 1926 (55)
Music by Harold Levey
Lyrics by Owen Murphy

We Want Our Breakfast • Steppin' Baby • You're All

the World to Me • Jealous • First, Last, and Only • Something Tells Me I'm in Love • Going Over the Bumps • If You Were Someone Else • When the Hurdy Gurdy Plays • Dreams • Let's Run Away and Get Married • Rainbow (Lyrics by Zelda Sears)

RAISIN[1]
October 18, 1973 (847)
Music by Judd Woldin
Lyrics by Robert Brittan

Based on the play *A Raisin in the Sun* by Lorraine Hansberry

Man Say • Whose Little Angry Man • Runnin' to Meet the Man • A Whole Lotta Sunlight • Booze • Alaiyo • Sweet Time • You Done Right • He Come Down This Morning • It's a Deal • Sidewalk Tree • Not Anymore • Measure the Valleys

RA,SEL

[1] Tony Award for Best Musical

THE RAMBLERS
September 20, 1926 (291)
Music by Harry Ruby
Lyrics by Bert Kalmar

Like You Do • Oh! How We Love Our Alma Mater • Just One Kiss • All Alone Monday • Any Little Tune • California Skies • You Smiled at Me • We Won't Charleston • The Movie Ball

RANG-TANG
July 12, 1927 (119)
Music by Ford Dabney
Lyrics by Jo Trent

Everybody Shout • Sammy and Topsy • Brown • Sambo's Banjo • Some Day • Come to Africa • Jungle Rose • Monkey Land • Sweet Evening Breeze • Summer Nights • Tramps of the Desert • Harlem • Rang-Tang

REAL LIFE FUNNIES (OB)
February 11, 1981 (35)
Music and lyrics by Alan Menken

Real Life Funnies • Is It Art? • I Love Your Brains • Pleasantly Plump • Lifted • Someday • People Collecting Things • Ah Men • Every Thursday Night • Divorce Has Brought Us Together • The Way of My Father • Someone to Come Home With Me Tonight

RED, HOT AND BLUE!
October 29, 1936 (183)
Music and lyrics by Cole Porter

At Ye Olde Coffee Shoppe in Cheyenne • It's a Great Life • Perennial Debutantes • Ours • Down in the Depths, on the 90th Floor • Carry On • You've Got Something • It's De-Lovely • A Little Skipper From Heaven Above • Five Hundred Million • Ridin' High • We're About to Start Big Rehearsin' • Hymn to Hymen • What a Great Pair We'll Be • The Ozarks Are Calling Me Home • Red, Hot and Blue • You're a Bad Influence on Me

Dropped from production
Goodbye, Little Dream, Goodbye • Who But You?* • When Your Troubles Have Started • Bertie and Gertie

RA,VS,SEL

[1] Pre-Broadway titles were *But Millions;—But Millions $; Wait for Baby*

THE RED MILL
September 24, 1906 (274)[1]
Music by Victor Herbert
Lyrics by Henry Blossom

By the Side of the Mill • Mignonette • You Never Can Tell About a Woman • If You Love But Me • Whistle It • A Widow Has Ways • The Isle of Our Dreams • Go While the Goin' Is Good • When You're Pretty and the World Is Fair • Moonbeams • The Legend of the Mill • I Want You to Marry Me • Every Day Is Ladies' Day With Me • Because You're You • The Streets of New York (In Old New York) • Entrance of the Wedding Guests

[1] *The Red Mill* had the longest run of any Herbert operetta during the composer's lifetime. A 1945 Broadway revival ran 531 performances. The original production achieved further distinction by virtue of a large mill with electrically moved arms placed in front of the theater. Lights were hung on the revolving parts, thus giving Broadway its first moving electrical sign.

THE RED PETTICOAT[1]
November 13, 1912 (61)
Music by Jerome Kern
Lyrics by Paul West

Based on the play *Next* by Rida Johnson Young

Sing, Sing, You Tetrazzini • I Wonder • The Correspondence School • Dance, Dance, Dance • Little Golden Maid • Oh, You Beautiful Spring (Lyrics by M.E. Rourke[2]) • Where Did the Bird Hear That? • Peaches and Cream • The Ragtime Restaurant • A Prisoner of Love • Walk, Walk, Walk • The Joy of That Kiss • Oo-Ooo-Oo • Since the Days of Grandmama • The Waltz Time Girl

Dropped from production
The Vigilantes

[1] Titles considered before *The Red Petticoat: The Girl and the Miner* and *Look Who's Here.*

[2] Rourke adopted the professional name Herbert Reynolds beginning with the show *Nobody Home* (1915).

THE RED ROBE
December 25, 1928 (167)
Music by Jean Gilbert
Lyrics by Harry B. Smith

Based on the novel *Under the Red Robe* by Stanley Weyman

Roll of the Drum • I'll Love Them All to Death • King of the Sword (Music by Robert Stolz and Maury Rubens; lyrics by J. Keirn Brennan) • Only a Smile •

Joy or Strife • Home o' Mine • Believe in Me (Music by Arthur Schwartz) • I've Got It (Music by Alberta Nichols; lyrics by Mann Holiner) • Where Love Grows • The Thrill of a Kiss • How the Girls Adore Me • Laugh at Life (Music by Maury Rubens; lyrics by J. Delany Dunn) • A Soldier of Fortune • I Plead, Dear Heart • You and I Are Passersby

RED, WHITE AND MADDOX
January 26, 1969 (41)
Music and lyrics by Don Tucker

What America Means to Me • Givers and Getters • Jubilee Joe • Ballad of a Redneck • First Campaign Song • Hoe Down • Phooey • Second Campaign Song • God Is an American • Hip-Hooray for Washington • City Life • Song of the Malcontents • The General's Song • Little Mary Sue • Billy Joe Ju • The Impeachment Waltz • Red, White and Maddox Kazoo March

RA,SEL

REDHEAD[1]
February 5, 1959 (452)
Music by Albert Hague
Lyrics by Dorothy Fields

The Simpson Sisters • The Right Finger of My Left Hand • Just for Once • Merely Marvelous • The Uncle Sam Rag • 'Erbie Fitch's Twitch • My Girl Is Just Enough Woman for Me • Behave Yourself • Look Who's in Love • Two Faces in the Dark • I'm Back in Circulation • We Loves Ya, Jimey • Pick-Pocket Tango • I'll Try

RA,VS

[1] Tony Award for Best Score

REGINA
October 31, 1949 (56)
Music and lyrics by Marc Blitzstein

Based on the play *The Little Foxes* by Lillian Hellman

What Will It Be? • Deedle-Doodle • Summer Day • Blues • Consider the Rain • Certainly, Lord • Lionnet • Greedy Girl • Chinky Pin

RA,VS

REVENGE WITH MUSIC
November 28, 1934 (158)
Music by Arthur Schwartz
Lyrics by Howard Dietz

Based on the novel *The Three-Cornered Hat* by Pedro de Alarcón

Flamenco • When You Love Only One • Never Marry a Dancer • If There Is Someone Lovelier Than You • In the Noonday Sun • That Fellow Manuelo • Think It Over • Maria • My Father Said • You and the Night and the Music* • Once-in-a-While • In the Middle of the Night • Wandr'ing Heart

REX
April 25, 1976 (49)

Music by Richard Rodgers
Lyrics by Sheldon Harnick

Te Deum • No Song More Pleasing • Where Is My Son? • The Field of Cloth of Gold • The Chase • Away From You • As Once I Loved You • Elizabeth • Why? • Christmas at Hampton Court • The Wee Golden Warrior • The Masque • From Afar • In Time

Dropped from production
I'll Miss You • Tell Me • So Much You Loved Me* • I Brought You a Gift • Rex • Dear Jane • The Pears of Anjou

RA

RHAPSODY IN BLACK
May 4, 1931 (80)
Music by Alberta Nichols
Lyrics by Mann Holiner

What's Keeping My Prince Charming? • Eccentricity • Till the Real Thing Comes Along (Lyrics by Holiner and Sammy Cahn) • You Can't Stop Me From Loving You • Harlem Moon

RIDE THE WINDS
May 16, 1974 (3)
Music and lyrics by John Driver

Run, Musashi, Run • The Emperor Me • The Gentle Buffoon • Those Who Speak • Flower Song • You're Loving Me • Breathing the Air • Remember That Day • Tengu • Ride the Winds • Are You a Man? • Every Day • Loving You • Pleasures • Someday I'll Walk • That Touch

RIGHT THIS WAY
January 5, 1938 (14)
Music by Sammy Fain
Lyrics by Irving Kahal

I Love the Way We Fell in Love • Doughnuts and Coffee • It's Great to Be Home Again • He Can Dance • I Can Dream, Can't I? • Soapbox Sillies (Music by Bradford Greene; lyrics by Marianne Brown Waters) • Don't Listen to Your Heart (Music by Bradford Greene; lyrics by Marianne Brown Waters) • Tip Your Hat (Music by Bradford Greene; lyrics by Marianne Brown Waters) • You Click With Me (Music by Bradford Greene; lyrics by Marianne Brown Waters) • I'll Be Seeing You • Right This Way (Music by Bradford Greene; lyrics by Marianne Brown Waters)

RIO RITA[1]
February 2, 1927 (504)
Music by Harry Tierney
Lyrics by Joseph McCarthy

The Best Little Lover in Town • Sweethearts • River Song • Eight Little Gringos • Are You There? • Rio Rita • The Rangers' Song • Spanish Shawl • The Kinkajou • If You're in Love, You'll Waltz • Out on the Loose • I Can Speak Espagnol • Roses • Following the Sun Around

RA,VS

Added to film version (1929)
You're Always in My Arms

Added to film version (1942)
Long Before You Came Along (Music by Harold Arlen; lyrics by E.Y. Harburg)

[1] Jerome Kern and Oscar Hammerstein II had hoped to have their *Show Boat* ready in time to open the Ziegfeld Theatre, which had been designed by Joseph Urban and financed by William Randolph Hearst. The show was not entirely finished however and *Rio Rita* was the theatre's opening production. *Show Boat* did open at the Ziegfeld on December 27th of the same year.

RIPPLES
February 11, 1930 (55)
Music by Oscar Levant
Lyrics by Irving Caesar and Graham John

Gentlemen of the Press • Barefoot Girl • Is It Love? (Lyrics by Caesar) • We Never Sleep • I Take After Rip • Babykins • I'm Afraid (Music by Albert Sirmay) • There's Nothing Wrong With a Kiss • Girls of Long Ago • Talk With Your Heel and Your Toe (Lyrics by Caesar) • Is It Love? • I'm a Little Bit Fonder of You (Music and lyrics by Caesar)

Dropped from production
Anything May Happen Any Day (Music by Jerome Kern; lyrics by John)

THE RISE OF ROSIE O'REILLY
December 25, 1923 (87)
Music and lyrics by George M. Cohan

Never Met a Girl Like You • Born and Bred in Brooklyn • My Gang • The Arrival of Society • In the Slums of the Town • Something's Happened to Rosie • Poor Old World • Stage Society • All Night Long • Love Dreams • Just Act Natural • When June Comes Along With a Song • At Madame Regay's • On a Holiday • Let's You and I Just Say Goodbye • A Ring to the Name of Rosie • Keep a-Countin' Eight • Two Girls From the Chorus • Nothing Like a Darned Good Cry • The Italian Whirlwind

RIVERWIND (OB)
December 12, 1962 (443)
Music and lyrics by John Jennings

I Cannot Tell Her So • I Want a Surprise • Riverwind • American Family Plan • Wishing Song • Pardon Me While I Dance • Sew the Buttons On • Almost, but Not Quite • A Woman Must Think of These Things • Laughing Face • A Woman Must Never Grow Old • I'd Forgotten How Beautiful She Could Be

RA

THE RIVIERA GIRL[1]
September 24, 1917 (78)
Music by Emmerich Kálmán
Lyrics by P.G. Wodehouse

Sometimes I Feel Just Like Grandpa • The Fall of Man • There'll Never Be Another Girl Like Daisy •

Life's a Tale • Just a Voice to Call Me, Dear • Half a Married Man • Man, Man, Man • A Bungalow in Quogue (Music by Jerome Kern) • Will You Forget? • Why Don't They Hand It to Me? • Gypsy, Bring Your Fiddle

[1] The score consists mainly of songs from *Die Czárdásfürstin,* still one of the most popular works in the European operetta repertory.

THE ROAR OF THE GREASEPAINT—THE SMELL OF THE CROWD
May 16, 1965 (232)
Music and lyrics by Leslie Bricusse and Anthony Newley

The Beautiful Land • A Wonderful Day Like Today • It Isn't Enough • Things to Remember • Put It in the Book • This Dream • Where Would You Be Without Me? • Look at That Face • My First Love Song • The Joker • Who Can I Turn To? (When Nobody Needs Me) • Funny Funeral • That's What It Is to Be Young • What a Man! • Feeling Good • Nothing Can Stop Me Now! • My Way • Sweet Beginning

RA,SEL

THE ROBBER BRIDEGROOM
October 7, 1975[1] (15)
Music by Robert Waldman
Lyrics by Alfred Uhry

Based on the novella by Eudora Welty

Once Upon the Natchez Trace • Two Heads • Steal With Style • Rosamund's Dream • Pricklepear Bloom • Nothin' Up • Deeper in the Woods • Riches • Love Stolen • Poor Tied Up Darlin' • Goodbye Salome • Sleepy Man • Where Oh Where

RA,SEL

[1] Reopened October 9, 1976 for 145 performances

ROBERTA[1]
November 18, 1933 (295)
Music by Jerome Kern
Lyrics by Otto Harbach

Based on the novel *Gowns by Roberta* by Alice Duer Miller

Alpha, Beta, Pi • You're Devastating* • Let's Begin • Yesterdays • Something Had to Happen • The Touch of Your Hand • I'll Be Hard to Handle (Lyrics by Bernard Dougall) • Hot Spot • Smoke Gets in Your Eyes* • Don't Ask Me Not to Sing

RA,VS

Added to film version (1935)
I Won't Dance (Lyrics by Dorothy Fields, Oscar Hammerstein II, Harbach and Jimmy McHugh) • Lovely to Look At (Lyrics by Dorothy Fields and Jimmy McHugh)

[1] In the cast, none of them prominent at the time, were Bob Hope, who played Huckleberry Haines, Fred MacMurray, and the dancer who

would later become a senator from California, George Murphy.

ROBIN HOOD[1]
September 28, 1891 (72)[2]
Music by Reginald De Koven
Lyrics by Harry B. Smith

Auctioneer's Song • Milkmaid's Song • Entrance of Robin Hood • Come Dream So Bright • I Am the Sheriff of Nottingham • Sweetheart, My Own Sweetheart • It Takes Nine Tailors to Make a Man • Brown October Ale • Oh, Promise Me* (Lyrics by Clement Scott) • Tinkers' Song • Oh, See the Lambkins Play • Ye Birds in Azure Winging • Serenade • The Armorer's Song • When a Maiden Weds • The Legend of the Chimes • Love, Now We Never More Will Part

VS

[1] The first important American musical, and the most successful one until the Victor Herbert era.

[2] In slightly separated engagements.

ROCK-A-BYE BABY[1]
May 22, 1918 (85)
Music by Jerome Kern
Lyrics by Herbert Reynolds

Based on the farce *Baby Mine* by Margaret Mayo

Bella Mia • Hurry Now • Motoring Along the Old Post Road • One, Two, Three • I Never Thought • I Believed All She Said • A Kettle Is Singing • Stitching, Stitching • Rock-a-Bye, Baby Dear • Little Tune, Go Away • According to Dr. Holt • There's No Better Use for Time Than Kissing • The Real Spring Drive • My Own Light Infantry • I Can Trust Myself With a Lot of Girls

[1] George Gershwin was rehearsal pianist for this production.

ROCKABYE HAMLET
February 17, 1976 (7)
Music and lyrics by Cliff Jones

Based on Shakespeare's *Hamlet*

Why Did He Have to Die? • The Wedding • That It Should Come to This • Set It Right • Hello-Hello • Don't Unmask Your Beauty to the Moon • If Not to You • Have I Got a Girl for You • Tis Pity, Tis True • Shall We Dance? • All My Life • Something's Rotten in Denmark • Denmark Is Still • Twist Her Mind • Gentle Lover • Where Is the Reason? • The Wart Song • He Got It in the Ear • It Is Done • Midnight-Hot Blood • Midnight Mass • Hey! • Sing Alone • Your Daddy's Gone Away • Rockabye Hamlet • All by Yourself • Rosencrantz and Guildenstern Boogie • Laertes Coercion • The Last Blues • Didn't She Do It for Love? • If My Morning Begins

THE ROCKY HORROR SHOW
March 10, 1975 (32)
Music and lyrics by Richard O'Brien

Science Fiction • Wedding Song • Over at the Frankenstein Place • Sweet Transvestite • Time Warp • The Sword of Damocles • Charles Atlas Song • What Ever Happened to Saturday Night? • Eddie's Teddy • Once in a While • Planet Shmanet Janet • It Was Great When It All Began • Super Heroes

RA

ROSA (OB)
May 10, 1978 (12)
Music by Baldwin Bergersen
Lyrics by William Archibald

Based on the play *Dear Cavendish* by Brenda Forbes

Rosa • Be Kind to the Young • Time Goes Faster • The Herb Song • I Am Royal • A Place of My Own • Fame • Perfection • Where's My Love A'Wandering? • Let Us Charm Each Other • Fish Soup Song • Peace Celebration • From the Bottom of the Sea • Oh, How We Love You, Mrs. Cornwall • Dear Friend • Before It's Too Late

ROSALIE
January 10, 1928 (335)

Show Me the Town (Music by George Gershwin; lyrics by Ira Gershwin) • Hussars March (Music by Sigmund Romberg; lyrics by P.G. Wodehouse) • Say So (Music by George Gershwin; lyrics by P.G. Wodehouse and Ira Gershwin) • Let Me Be a Friend to You (Music by George Gershwin; lyrics by Ira Gershwin) • West Point Song (Music by Sigmund Romberg; lyrics by P.G. Wodehouse) • Oh Gee! Oh Joy! (Music by George Gershwin; lyrics by Ira Gershwin and P.G. Wodehouse) • New York Serenade (Music by George Gershwin; lyrics by Ira Gershwin and P.G. Wodehouse) • Ev'rybody Knows I Love Somebody* (Music by George Gershwin; lyrics by Ira Gershwin) • How Long Has This Been Going On? (Music by George Gershwin; lyrics by Ira Gershwin) • Merry Andrew (instrumental) (Music by George Gershwin) • Why Must We Always Be Dreaming? (Music by Sigmund Romberg; lyrics by P.G. Wodehouse)

Dropped from production
Beautiful Gypsy (Music by George Gershwin; lyrics by Ira Gershwin) • Yankee Doodle Rhythm (Music by George Gershwin; Lyrics by Ira Gershwin) • When Cadets Parade (Music by George Gershwin; lyrics by Ira Gershwin) • I Forget What I Started to Say (Music by George Gershwin; lyrics by Ira Gershwin) • You Know How It Is (Music by George Gershwin; lyrics by Ira Gershwin and P.G. Wodehouse) • The Man I Love (Music by George Gershwin; lyrics by Ira Gershwin) • True to Them All (Music by George Gershwin; lyrics by Ira Gershwin) • When the Right One Comes Along (Music by George Gershwin; lyrics by Ira Gershwin) • Rosalie (Music by George Gershwin; lyrics by Ira Gershwin)

Added during Broadway run
Follow the Drum (Music by George Gershwin; lyrics by Ira Gershwin)

ROSE BRIAR (Play with one song)
December 25, 1922 (88)
Music by Jerome Kern
Lyrics by Booth Tarkington

Love and the Moon

ROSE MARIE
September 2, 1924 (557)
Music by Rudolf Friml and Herbert Stothart
Lyrics by Oscar Hammerstein II and Otto Harbach

Hard-Boiled Herman (Music by Stothart) • Rose Marie (Music by Friml) • The Mounties (Music by Friml and Stothart) • Lak Jeem (Music by Friml) • Indian Love Call* (Music by Friml) • Pretty Things (Music by Friml) • Why Shouldn't We? (Music by Stothart) • Totem Tom-Tom • Only a Kiss (Music by Stothart) • The Minuet of the Minute (Music by Stothart) • The Door of My Dreams (Music by Friml)

Added to film version (1936)
Pardon Me, Madame (Music by Stothart; lyrics by Gus Kahn) • Just for You (Music by Stothart; lyrics by Gus Kahn)

Added to film version (1954)
I Have the Love (Music by Friml; lyrics by Paul Francis Webster) • Free to Be Free (Music by Friml; lyrics by Paul Francis Webster) • Love and Kisses (Music by Friml; lyrics by Paul Francis Webster) • The Right Place for a Girl (Music by Friml; lyrics by Paul Francis Webster)

RA,VS,SEL

ROSE OF ALGERIA *See* **ALGERIA**

THE ROSE OF STAMBOUL
March 7, 1922 (111)
Music by Leo Fall
Lyrics by Harold Atteridge

The Ladies From the Cultured West • My Heart Is Calling (Music by Sigmund Romberg) • Lovey Dove (Music by Sigmund Romberg) • A Blue Book of Girls • Rose of Stamboul • Ding-a-Ling • With Papers Duly Signed • Why Do They Die at the End of a Classical Dance? • The Love Test • Mazuma

THE ROTHSCHILDS
October 19, 1970 (505)
Music by Jerry Bock
Lyrics by Sheldon Harnick

Based on the book by Frederic Morton

Pleasure and Privilege • One Room • He Tossed a Coin • Sons • Everything • Rothschild and Sons • Allons • Give England Strength • This Amazing London Town • They Say • I'm in Love! I'm in Love! • In My Own Lifetime • Have You Ever Seen a Prettier Little Congress? • Stability • Bonds

RA,SEL

RUFUS LEMAIRE'S AFFAIRS
March 28, 1927 (56)

Music by Martin Broones
Lyrics by Ballard MacDonald

Wah-Wah • Wandering in Dreamland • I Can't Get Over a Girl Like You (Lyrics by Harry Ruskin) • Bring Back Those Minstrel Days • Mexico • Land of Broken Dreams • Where the Morning Glories Twine • Dancing by Moonlight

RUGANTINO
February 6, 1964 (28)
Music by Armando Trovaioli
Lyrics by Pietro Garinei and Sandro Giovannini
(Lyric translation by Edward Eager)

The Game of Morra • Rugantino in the Stocks • A House Is Not the Same Without a Woman • Nothing to Do • Just Look! • The Saltarello • Tirrallera • The Headsman and I • Ciumachella • Lantern Night • Roma • I'm Happy • Just Stay Alive • San Pasquale • Passatella (The Drinking Game) • It's Quick and Easy • Boy and Man

RA

RUMPLE
November 6, 1957 (45)
Music by Ernest G. Schweikert
Lyrics by Frank Reardon

It's You for Me • In Times Like These • Red Letter Day • The First Time I Spoke of You • Oblivia • Peculiar State of Affairs • How Do You Say Goodbye? • Gentlemen of the Press • To Adjust Is a Must • Coax Me • All Dressed Up • Wish

RUNAWAYS
May 13, 1978 (267)
Music and lyrics by Elizabeth Swados

Appendectomy • Where Do People Go? • Once Upon a Time • Every Now and Then • Song of a Child Prostitute • Find Me a Hero • The Undiscovered Son • The Basketball Song • Lullaby for Luis • We Are Not Strangers • Lullaby From Baby to Baby • Tra Gog in Dein Whole (I Will Not Tell a Soul) • Revenge Song • Sometimes • Where Are Those People Who Did "Hair"? • The Untrue Pigeon • Senoras de la Noche • Let Me Be a Kid • Lonesome of the Road

RUNNIN' WILD
October 29, 1923 (213)
Music and lyrics by James Johnson and Cecil Mack

Set 'em Sadie • Open Your Heart • Gingerbrown • Red Caps Cappers • Old Fashioned Love • Snowtime • Charleston • Roustabouts • Log Cabin Days • Pay Day on the Levee • Jazz Your Troubles Away

RUSSELL PATTERSON'S SKETCH BOOK (OB)
February 16, 1960 (3)
Music by Ruth Cleary Patterson

We Know What You Want and We Got It (Lyrics by Floria Vestoff) • That's Why I'm Here Tonight (Lyrics by Les Kramer) • Dancing to the Rhythm of the Raindrops (Lyrics by Gladys Shelley) • I Want to Take 'Em Off for Norman Rockwell (Lyrics by Les Kramer) • May in Manhattan (Lyrics by Tom Romano) • La Calinda (Lyrics by Gladys Shelley) • Singing Wheels (Lyrics by Fred Heider) • That's What I Got for Not Listening to My Mother (Lyrics by Floria Vestoff) • Let's Not Get Married (Lyrics by George Blake and Les Kramer) • My First Love (Lyrics by Fred Heider) • Sweet Charity (Lyrics by Les Kramer) • When the Wings of the Wind Take Me Home (Lyrics by Les Kramer) • A Wonderful Way of Life (Lyrics by Les Kramer and Floria Vestoff)

S

SADIE THOMPSON
November 16, 1944 (60)
Music by Vernon Duke
Lyrics by Howard Dietz

Based on the play *Rain* by John Colton and
Clemence Randolph (based, in turn, on the short
story "Miss Thompson" by W. Somerset Maugham)

Barrel of Beads • Fisherman's Wharf • When You
Live on an Island • Poor as a Church Mouse • The
Love I Long For • Garden in the Sky • Siren of the
Tropics • Life's a Funny Present From Someone •
Born All Over Again • Sailing at Midnight

SAIL AWAY
October 3, 1961 (167)
Music and lyrics by Noël Coward

Come to Me • Sail Away • Where Shall I Find Him? •
Beatnik Love Affair • Later Than Spring • The
Passenger's Always Right • Useful Phrases • Go
Slow, Johnny • You're a Long, Long Way From
America • Something Very Strange • The Little
Ones' ABC • Don't Turn Away From Love • When
You Want Me • Why Do the Wrong People Travel?

RA,SEL

ST. LOUIS WOMAN
March 30, 1946 (113)
Music by Harold Arlen
Lyrics by Johnny Mercer

Based on the novel *God Sends Sunday* by Arna
Bontemps

L'il Augie Is a Natural Man • Any Place I Hang My
Hat Is Home • I Feel My Luck Comin' Down • I Had
Myself a True Love • Legalize My Name • Cake
Walk Your Lady • Come Rain or Come Shine •
Chinquapin Bush • We Shall Meet to Part, No Never
• Lullaby • Sleep Peaceful, Mr. Used-to-Be • Leavin'
Time • A Woman's Prerogative • Ridin' on the Moon
• Least That's My Opinion • Racin' Form • Come
On, L'il Augie

Dropped from production
I Wonder What Became of Me

RA,SEL

SALAD DAYS (OB)
November 10, 1958 (80)
Music by Julian Slade
Lyrics by Dorothy Reynolds and Julian Slade

The Dons' Chorus • We Said We Wouldn't Look
Back • Find Yourself Something to Do • I Sit in the
Sun • Oh, Look at Me! • Hush-Hush • Out of Breath •
Cleopatra • Sand in My Eyes • It's Easy to Sing •
Let's Take a Stroll Through London • We're
Looking for a Piano • The Saucer Song • The Time
of My Life • We Don't Understand Our Children

RA,VS

SALLY
December 21, 1920 (570)
Music by Jerome Kern
Lyrics by Clifford Grey

The Night Time • On With the Dance • You Can't
Keep a Good Girl Down (Lyrics by P.G. Wodehouse
and Grey) • Look for the Silver Lining (Lyrics by
B.G. DeSylva) • Sally • Wild Rose • The Schnitza-
Komisski • Whip-Poor-Will (Lyrics by B.G. DeSylva)
• The Lorelei (Lyrics by Anne Caldwell and Grey) •
The Church 'Round the Corner (Lyrics by P.G.
Wodehouse and Grey) • The Butterfly Ballet (Music
by Victor Herbert)

Dropped from production
Bill* (Lyrics by P.G. Wodehouse)

RA,VS

SALUTA
August 28, 1934 (40)
Music by Frank D'Armond
Lyrics by Will Morrissey

Black Horse Tavern • Just Say the Word (Lyrics by
Milton Berle) • Walking the Deck • I'll Produce for
You • Night • Help the Seamen • You Have My Heart

• Tarantella Rhythm • Mi! Mi! • We Incorporated • There's a Chill in the Air • The Great Dictator and Me

SALVATION (OB)
September 24, 1969 (239)
Music and lyrics by Peter Link and C.C. Courtney

Salvation • In Between • 1001 • Honest Confession Is Good for the Soul • Ballin' • Let the Moment Slip By • Gina • If You Let Me Make Love to You Then Why Can't I Touch You? • There Ain't No Flies on Jesus • Daedalus • Deuteronomy 17, Verse 2 • For Ever • Footloose Youth and Fancy Free • Schwartz • Let's Get Lost in Now • Back to Genesis • Tomorrow Is the First Day of the Rest of My Life

RA,SEL

SAMBO (OB)
December 12, 1969 (37)
Music by Ron Steward and Neal Tate
Lyrics by Ron Steward

Sing a Song of Sambo • Hey Boy • I Am Child • Young Enough to Dream • Mama Always Said • Baddest Mammyjammy • Sambo Was a Bad Boy • Pretty Flower • I Could Dig You • Do You Care Too Much? • Be Black • Let's Go Down • Astrology • The Eternal Virgin • Boy Blue • The Piscean • Aries • Untogether Cinderella • Peace Love and Good Damn • Come On Home • Black Man • Get an Education • Ask and You Shall Receive • Son of Africa

SANDHOG (OB)
November 29, 1954 (48)
Music by Earl Robinson
Lyrics by Waldo Salt

Based on the short story St. Columbia and the River by Theodore Dreiser

Come Down • Some Said They Were Crazy • Sing Sorrow • Hey Joe • Johnny's Cursing Song • Come and Be Married • Johnny O • Good Old Days • Song of the Bends • By the Glenside • High Air • Work Song • 28 Men • Sandhog Song • Sweat Song • Fugue on a Hot Afternoon in a Small Flat • Twins • Katie O'Sullivan • Ring Iron • You Want to Mourn • Ma, Ma, Where's My Dad? • Waiting for the Men • Greathead Shield • Stand Back • Oh, Oh, Oh, O'Sullivan

RA,VS

THE SAP OF LIFE (OB)
October 2, 1961 (49)
Music by David Shire
Lyrics by Richard Maltby, Jr.

Saturday Morning • Farewell, Family • Charmed Life • Fill Up Your Life With Sunshine • Good Morning • Watching the Big Parade Go By • The Love of Your Life • A Hero's Love • Children Have It Easy • She Loves Me Not • Mind Over Matter • Time and Time Again

SARATOGA
December 7, 1959 (80)
Music by Harold Arlen
Lyrics by Johnny Mercer

Based on the novel Saratoga Trunk by Edna Ferber

I'll Be Respectable • One Step–Two Step • Gettin' a Man (Music and lyrics by Mercer) • Petticoat High • Why Fight This? (Music and lyrics by Mercer) • A Game of Poker • Love Held Lightly • The Gamblers • Saratoga • The Gossip Song • Countin' Our Chickens • You or No One • The Cure • The Men Who Run the Country (Music and lyrics by Mercer) • The Man in My Life • The Polka • Goose Never Be a Peacock • Dog Eat Dog

RA,SEL

SARAVÁ
February 23, 1979 (140)
Music by Mitch Leigh
Lyrics by N. Richard Nash

Based on the play Dona Flor and Her Two Husbands by Jorge Amado

Saravá • Makulele • Vadinho Is Gone • Hosanna • Nothing's Missing • I'm Looking for a Man • A Simple Man • Viva a Vida • Muito Bom • Play the Queen • Which Way Do I Go? • Remember • You Do • A Single Life

RA

SARI
January 13, 1914 (151)
Music by Emmerich Kálmán
Lyrics by C.C.S. Cushing and E.P. Heath

Stop It, Stop It! • Time, Oh Time • Marry Me • Pick a Husband • Paris • Love Has Wings • Ha-za-zaa • With Lowered Heads • Follow Me • Simple Little Village Maid • My Faithful Stradivari • Softly Thro' the Summer Night • Long Live the King! • Love's Own Sweet Song

VS

SAY, DARLING[1]
April 3, 1958 (332)
Music by Jule Styne
Lyrics by Betty Comden and Adolph Green

Try to Love Me Just As I Am • It's Doom • The Husking Bee • It's the Second Time You Meet That Matters • Chief of Love • Say, Darling • The Carnival Song • Dance Only With Me • Something's Always Happening on the River

RA

[1] Based on the novel of the same name by Richard Bissell, which told of his experiences in connection with the adaptation of his earlier novel 7 1/2 Cents into the musical The Pajama Game.

SAY WHEN
June 26, 1928 (15)
Music by Jesse Greer

Lyrics by Raymond Klages

My One Girl (Music and lyrics by Frank E. Harling) • How About It? • No Room in My Heart (Music by Ray Perkins; lyrics by Max and Nathaniel Lief) • Cheerio (Lyrics by James J. Walker[1]) • One Step to Heaven • In My Love Boat (Music by Ray Perkins; lyrics by Max and Nathaniel Lief) • Say When • Give Me a Night (Music and lyrics by Frank E. Harling)

[1] Then Mayor of New York City

SAY WHEN
November 8, 1934 (76)
Music by Ray Henderson
Lyrics by Ted Koehler

When Love Comes Swingin' Along • Declaration Day • It Must Have Been the Night • Say When • Don't Tell Me It's Bad • Sunday Morning • Isn't It June? • Put Your Heart in a Song • So Long for Ever So Long • Torch Parade • Let's Take Advantage of Now

SEA LEGS
May 18, 1937 (15)
Music by Michael Cleary
Lyrics by Arthur Swanstrom

Off on a Weekend Cruise • The Opposite Sex • Infatuation • A Dark Stranger • Looks Like Love Is Here to Stay • Ten o'Clock Town • Chasing Henry • Catalina • Touched in the Head • Wake Me Up a Star

THE SECOND LITTLE SHOW
September 2, 1930 (63)
Music by Arthur Schwartz
Lyrics by Howard Dietz

New New York • Swing Your Tails • Foolish Face • My Heart Begins to Thump! Thump! (Music by Morgan Lewis; lyrics by Ted Fetter) • What a Case I've Got on You • Good Clean Sport • Lucky Seven • My Intuition • I Started on a Shoestring • Sing Something Simple (Music and lyrics by Herman Hupfeld) • You're the Sunrise

THE SECRET LIFE OF WALTER MITTY (OB)
October 26, 1964 (96)
Music by Leon Carr
Lyrics by Earl Shuman

Based on the short story by James Thurber

The Secret Life • The Walter Mitty March • Now That I Am Forty • Walking With Peninnah • Drip, Drop, Tapoketa • Aggie • Don't Forget • Marriage Is for Old Folks • Hello, I Love You, Goodbye • Willa • Confidence • Two Little Pussycats • Fan the Flame • She's Talking Out • You're Not • Lonely Ones

RA

SEE AMERICA FIRST
March 28, 1916 (15)
Music by Cole Porter
Lyrics by T. Lawrason Riggs and Cole Porter[1]

Bad Men • To Follow Every Fancy • Something's Got to Be Done • I've Got an Awful Lot to Learn • See America First • The Language of Flowers • Damsel, Damsel • The Lady I've Vowed to Wed • Mirror, Mirror • Ever and Ever Yours • Lima • Buy Her a Box at the Opera • I've a Shooting-Box in Scotland • When I Used to Lead the Ballet

[1] This was Cole Porter's first score for the Broadway stage.

SEESAW
March 18, 1973 (296)
Music by Cy Coleman
Lyrics by Dorothy Fields

Based on the play Two for the Seesaw by William Gibson

Seesaw • My City • Nobody Does It Like Me • In Tune • Spanglish • Welcome to Holiday Inn! • You're a Lovable Lunatic • He's Good for Me • Ride Out the Storm • We've Got It • Poor Everybody Else • Chapter 54, Number 1909 • The Concert • It's Not Where You Start • I'm Way Ahead

RA,SEL

THE SELLING OF THE PRESIDENT
March 22, 1972 (5)
Music by Bob James
Lyrics by Jack O'Brien

Something Holy • If You Like People • Sunset • Little Moon • Come-on-a-Good Life • I've Got to Trust You • Mason Cares • On the Winning Side • Captain Terror • He's a Man • Stars of Glory • Terminix • Take My Hand • A Passacaglia • We're Gonna Live It Together • America

SENSATIONS (OB)
October 25, 1970 (16)
Music by Wally Harper
Lyrics by Paul Zakrzewski

Suggested by Shakespeare's Romeo and Juliet

Lonely Children • Sensations • Good Little Boy • The Beginning • What Kind of Parents • Power • Up and Down • Friar's Tune • Oh, My Age • Outracing Light • War Is Good Business • The Kill • Lying Here • Middle Class Revolution • I'll Stay, I'll Go • I Cannot Wait • Sounds • No Place for Me • Morning Sun • In Nomine Dei

RA

SET TO MUSIC[1]
January 18, 1939 (129)
Music and lyrics by Noël Coward

Three Little Debutantes • Mad About the Boy • The Stately Homes of England • I'm So Weary of It All • Children of the Ritz • Three White Feathers • Midnight Matinee • Never Again • I Went to a Marvelous Party* • The Party's Over Now

[1] This score consisted mainly of songs from various London shows by Coward.

SEVEN BRIDES FOR SEVEN BROTHERS
July 8, 1982 (5)
Music by Gene dePaul
Lyrics by Johnny Mercer

Based on the film (1954)

Bless Your Beautiful Hide • Wonderful, Wonderful Day • One Man (Music and lyrics by Al Kasha and Joel Hirschorn) • Goin' Courting • Love Never Goes Away (Music and lyrics by Al Kasha and Joel Hirschorn) • Sobbin' Women • The Townsfolks' Lament (Music and lyrics by Al Kasha and Joel Hirschorn) • A Woman Ought to Know Her Place (Music and lyrics by Al Kasha and Joel Hirschorn) • We Gotta Make It Through the Winter • Glad That You Were Born (Music and lyrics by Al Kasha and Joel Hirschorn)

RA (film version)

Dropped before Broadway opening
Pretty Little Missus Bell

SEVEN LIVELY ARTS
December 7, 1944 (183)
Music and lyrics by Cole Porter

Big Town • Is It the Girl? • Only Another Boy and Girl • Wow-Ooh-Wolf • Drink • When I Was a Little Cuckoo • Frahngee-Pahnee • Dancin' to a Jungle Drum • Ev'ry Time We Say Goodbye • Hence It Don't Make Sense • The Big Parade

Added during run
The Band Started Swinging a Song

SEVENTEEN
June 21, 1951 (180)
Music by Walter Kent
Lyrics by Kim Gannon

Based on the novel by Booth Tarkington

Weatherbee's Drug Store • This Was Just Another Day • Things Are Gonna Hum This Summer • How Do You Do, Miss Pratt? • Summertime Is Summertime • Reciprocity • Ode to Lola • A Headache and a Heartache • Ooh, Ooh, Ooh, What You Do to Me • Hoosier Way • I Could Get Married Today • After All, It's Spring

RA

1776[1]
March 16, 1969 (1,217)
Music and lyrics by Sherman Edwards

Sit Down, John • Piddle, Twiddle and Resolve • Till Then • The Lees of Old Virginia • But, Mrs. Adams • Yours, Yours, Yours • He Plays the Violin • Momma, Look Sharp • Cool, Cool, Considerate Men • The Egg • Molasses to Rum • Is Anybody There?

RA,SEL

[1] Tony Award for Best Musical

THE SEVENTH HEART (Play with music)
May 2, 1927 (8)
Music and lyrics by Arthur Brander

I Wonder if Love Is a Dream • Cinema Blues • For I'm in Love • When My Eyes Meet Yours

SEVENTH HEAVEN
May 26, 1955 (44)
Music by Victor Young
Lyrics by Stella Unger

Based on the play by Austin Strong

C'est la Vie • Where Is That Someone for Me? • Camille, Colette, Fifi • A Man With a Dream • Remarkable Fellow • If It's a Dream • Happy Little Crook • Sun at My Window, Love at My Door • A "Miss You" Kiss • Love, Love, Love • Love Sneaks Up on You

RA

70, GIRLS, 70
April 15, 1971 (36)
Music by John Kander
Lyrics by Fred Ebb

Based on the film *Make Mine Mink* (1960)

Old Folks • Home • Broadway, My Street • Coffee in a Cardboard Cup • You and I, Love • Do We? • Hit It, Lorraine • See the Light • Boom Ditty Boom • Believe • Go Visit • 70, Girls, 70 • The Elephant Song • Yes

RA,SEL

SEXTET
March 3, 1974 (9)
Music by Lawrence Hurwit
Lyrics by Lee Goldsmith

Nervous • What the Hell Am I Doing Here? • Keep On Dancing • Spunk • Visiting Rights • Going-Staying • I Wonder • Women and Men • I Love You All the Time • Hi • It'd Be Nice • Roseland • How Does It Start? • Someone to Love

SHADY LADY
July 5, 1933 (30)

You're Not the One (Music by Jesse Greer; lyrics by Stanley Adams) • Live, Laugh and Love (Music by Sam H. Stept; lyrics by Bud Green) • Isn't It Swell to Dream? (Music by Sam H. Stept; lyrics by Bud Green) • I'll Betcha That I'll Getcha (Music by Jesse Greer; lyrics by Stanley Adams) • Swingy Little Thingy (Music by Sam H. Stept; lyrics by Stanley Adams) • Everything but My Man (Music and lyrics by Serge Walter) • Isn't It Remarkable? (Music by Jesse Greer; lyrics by Stanley Adams) • Any Way the Wind Blows (Music by Sam H. Stept; lyrics by Bud Green) • Your Type Is Coming Back (Music by Sam H. Stept; lyrics by Bud Green) • One Heart (Music by Sam H. Stept; lyrics by Bud Green) • Hiya Sucker (Music by Jesse Greer; lyrics by Stanley Adams) • Get Hot Foot (Music by Sam H.

Stept; lyrics by Bud Green) • Where, Oh Where Can I Find Love? (Music by Jesse Greer; lyrics by Stanley Adams)

SHANGRI-LA
June 13, 1956 (21)
Music by Harry Warren
Lyrics by Jerome Lawrence and Robert E. Lee

Based on the novel *Lost Horizon* by James Hilton

Om Mani Padme Hum • Lost Horizon • The Man I Never Met • Every Time You Danced With Me • The World Outside • I'm Just a Little Bit Confused • The Beetle Race • Somewhere • What Every Old Girl Should Know • Second Time in Love • Talkin' With Your Feet • Walk Sweet • Love Is What I Never Knew • We've Decided to Stay • Shangri-La

SHE LOVES ME
April 23, 1963 (301)
Music by Jerry Bock
Lyrics by Sheldon Harnick

Based on the play *Parfumerie* by Miklos Laslo and the film *The Shop Around the Corner* (1940)

Good Morning, Good Day • Thank you, Madam • Days Gone By • No More Candy • Three Letters • Tonight at Eight • I Don't Know His Name • Goodbye, Georg • Will He Like Me? • Ilona • I Resolve • A Romantic Atmosphere • Tango Tragique • Dear Friend • Try Me • Where's My Shoe? • Ice Cream • She Loves Me • A Trip to the Library • Grand Knowing You • Twelve Days to Christmas

RA,SEL

SHE LOVES ME NOT (Play with two songs)
November 20, 1933 (360)
Music by Arthur Schwartz
Lyrics by Edward Heyman

After All, You're All I'm After • She Loves Me Not

SHE SHALL HAVE MUSIC (OB)
January 22, 1959 (54)
Music and lyrics by Deed Meyer

No True Love • Here's What a Mistress Ought to Be • Scarlet Trimmings • Someday, Maybe • Theatre Quadrille • Moi • Wonder Where My Heart Is • Twelve o'Clock Song • Who Are You? • Basic • Maud, the Bawd • She Shall Have Music • I Live to Love • One Sweet Moment • Blind Man's Buff • Who Needs It? • If I Am to Marry You

SHELTER
February 6, 1973 (31)
Music by Nancy Ford
Lyrics by Gretchen Cryer

Changing • Welcome to a New World • It's Hard to Care • Woke Up Today • Mary Margaret's House in the Country • Woman on the Run • Don't Tell Me It's Forever • Sunrise • I Bring Him Seashells • She's My Girl • He's a Fool • Going Home With My Children • Sleep, My Baby, Sleep

SHENANDOAH
January 7, 1975 (1,050)
Music by Gary Geld
Lyrics by Peter Udell

Raise the Flag of Dixie • I've Heard It All Before • Pass the Cross to Me • Why Am I Me? • Next to Lovin' (I Like Fightin') • Over the Hill • The Pickers Are Comin' • Meditation • We Make a Beautiful Pair • Violets and Silverbells • It's a Boy • Freedom • Papa's Gonna Make It Alright • The Only Home I Know

RA,VS,SEL

SHERRY!
March 27, 1967 (65)
Music by Laurence Rosenthal
Lyrics by James Lipton

Based on the play *The Man Who Came to Dinner* by George S. Kaufman and Moss Hart

In the Very Next Moment • Why Does the Whole Damn World Adore Me? • Maggie's Date • Maybe It's Time for Me • How Can You Kiss Those Times Goodbye? • With This Ring • Sherry • Au Revoir • Proposal Duet • Listen, Cosette • Christmas Eve Broadcast • Putty in Your Hands • Imagine That • Marry the Girl Myself • Harriet Sedley

SEL

SHE'S A GOOD FELLOW
May 5, 1919 (120)
Music by Jerome Kern
Lyrics by Anne Caldwell

Some Party • The Navy Foxtrot Man • The First Rose of Summer • A Happy Wedding Day • Jubilo* • Faith, Hope and Charity • Just a Little Line • Teacher, Teacher • Bullfrog Patrol • Oh, You Beautiful Person! • Snip, Snip, Snip • I Want My Little Gob • The Bumble Bee • I've Been Waiting for You All the Time

Dropped from production
A Little Pep • Wine, Women and Song • I Believe in Signs • Over the Hills • Semiramis

SHE'S MY BABY
January 3, 1928 (71)
Music by Richard Rodgers
Lyrics by Lorenz Hart

This Goes Up • My Lucky Star • You're What I Need • Here She Comes • The Swallows • When I Go on the Stage • Try Again Tomorrow • Camera Shoot • Where Can the Baby Be? • I Need Some Cooling Off • A Little House in Soho • A Baby's Best Friend • Wasn't it Great? • Whoopsie

Dropped from production
How Was I to Know?* • Pipes of Pansy* • Morning Is Midnight

Added during run
Smart People • If I Were You

SHINBONE ALLEY
April 13, 1957 (49)
Music by George Kleinsinger
Lyrics by Joe Darion

Based on the *archy and mehitabel* stories by Don Marquis

What Do We Care? • Toujours Gai • Queer Little Insect • Big Bill • True Romance • The Lightning Bug Song • I Gotta Be • Flotsam and Jetsam • Come to Mee-ow • Suicide Song • Shinbone Alley • The Moth Song • A Woman Wouldn't Be a Woman • The Lullaby • What the Hell • Pretty Kitty • Way Down Blues • The Lady Bug Song • Be a Pussycat • Quiet Street

RA,VS (published as *archie and mehitabel*)

THE SHOEMAKER AND THE PEDDLER (OB)
October 14, 1960 (43)
Music by Frank Fields
Lyrics by Armand Aulicino

Based on the Sacco and Vanzetti case

Headlines • Ah, Hum; Oh, Hum • Vedi la Vita • Wide-Awake Morning • Fish Song • Childhood Lullaby • Naughty Bird Tarantella • The Robbery • Is This the Way? • Sometimes I Wonder • Remember, Remember • Mio Fratello • The Nightmare • The Letter • Goodbye, My City • Guilty!

SHOESTRING '57 (OB)
November 5, 1956 (110)

For Critics Only (Music by Shelley Mowell; lyrics by Mike Stewart) • What's a Show? (Music by Shelley Mowell; lyrics by Mike Stewart) • Queen of Spain (Music by Harvey Schmidt; lyrics by Tom Jones) • At Twenty-Two (Music by Harvey Schmidt; lyrics by Tom Jones) • Love Is a Feeling (Music by Moose Charlap; lyrics by Norman Gimbel) • The Rochelle Hudson Tango (Music by Claibe Richardson; lyrics by Paul Rosner) • Don't Say You Like Tchaikowsky (Music by Claibe Richardson; lyrics by Paul Rosner) • Lament on Fifth Avenue (Music by Claibe Richardson; lyrics by Paul Rosner) • Best Loved Girls (Music by David Baker; lyrics by Sheldon Harnick) • Always One Day More (Music by Philip Springer; lyrics by Carolyn Leigh) • Can You See a Girl Like Me in the Role? (Music by William Howe; lyrics by Max Showalter) • Family Trouble (Music by Leopold Antelme; lyrics by Anthony Chalmers)

RA

SHOESTRING REVUE (1955) (OB)
February 28, 1955 (100)

Man's Inhumanity (Music by Charles Strouse; lyrics by Mike Stewart) • Inevitably Me (Music and lyrics by Ken Welch) • Someone Is Sending Me Flowers (Music by David Baker; lyrics by Sheldon Harnick) • Garbage (Music and lyrics by Sheldon Harnick) • Paducah (Music by Shelley Mowell; lyrics by Mike Stewart) • Kings and Queens (Music by Arthur Siegel; lyrics by June Carroll) • Wabash 4-7473

(Music by G. Wood; lyrics by Bruce Kirby) • Medea in Disneyland (Music by Lloyd Norlin; lyrics by Sheldon Harnick) • Entire History of the World in Two Minutes and Thirty-Two Seconds (Music by Charles Strouse; lyrics by Mike Stewart) • New to Me (Music by Ken Welch; lyrics by Bud McCreery) • A Million Windows and I (Music by Alec Wilder; lyrics by Norman Gimbel) • Three Loves (Music by Charles Strouse; lyrics by Mike Stewart) • Things Are Going Well Today (Music by Arthur Siegel; lyrics by June Carroll) • The Sea Is All Around Us (Music by David Baker; lyrics by Sheldon Harnick)

RA

SHOOT THE WORKS
July 21, 1931 (87)
Music by Michael H. Cleary
Lyrics by Max and Nathaniel Lief

It's in the Stars • Taken for a Ride • I Want to Chisel In on Your Heart • How Can the Night Be Good? • Pie in the Sky • Poor Little Doorstep Baby • The First Lady of the Land • Do What You Like (Music by Philip Charig; words by Leo Robin) • Hot Moonlight (Music by Jay Gorney; lyrics by E.Y. Harburg) • How's Your Uncle? (Music by Jimmy McHugh; lyrics by Dorothy Fields) • Muchacha (Music by Vernon Duke and Jay Gorney; lyrics by E.Y. Harburg) • Begging for Love (Music and lyrics by Irving Berlin) • Let's Go Out in the Open Air (Music and lyrics by Ann Ronell) • My Heart's a Banjo (Music by Jay Gorney; lyrics by E.Y. Harburg)

SHOW BOAT
December 27, 1927 (572)
Music by Jerome Kern
Lyrics by Oscar Hammerstein II

Based on the novel by Edna Ferber

Cotton Blossom • Make Believe • Ol' Man River • Can't Help Lovin' Dat Man • Life Upon the Wicked Stage* • Till Good Luck Comes My Way • I Might Fall Back on You* • Queenie's Ballyhoo (C'mon, Folks) • You Are Love • Why Do I Love You?* • In Dahomey • Bill* (Lyrics by P.G. Wodehouse and Oscar Hammerstein II) • Hey, Feller! • After the Ball (Music and lyrics by Charles K. Harris) • Goodbye, My Lady Love (Music and lyrics by Joseph E. Howard)

Dropped from production
I Would Like to Play a Lover's Part • My Girl • It's Getting Hotter in the North • Be Happy,Too • Mis'ry's Comin' Aroun' • Cheer Up*

Added to London production (1928)
Dance Away the Night

Added to 1946 revival
Nobody Else But Me*

Added to film version (1936)
I Have the Room Above • Gallivantin' Around • Ah Still Suits Me

RA,VS,SEL

SHOW GIRL[1]
July 2, 1929 (111)
Music by George Gershwin
Lyrics by Gus Kahn and Ira Gershwin

Happy Birthday • My Sunday Fella • How Could I
Forget? • Lolita • Do What You Do! • One Man • So
Are You! • I Must Be Home by Twelve o'Clock •
Black and White • Harlem Serenade • Home Blues*
• Follow the Minstrel Band • Liza (All the Clouds'll
Roll Away)*

Dropped from production
Feeling Sentimental • I Just Looked At You*

[1] George Gershwin's tone poem "An American
in Paris" was played in part as ballet music in the
show. Its slow theme was the basis of the song
"Home Blues" in the score. The full work had
had its premiere seven months earlier,
December 13, 1928, at Carnegie Hall, played by
the New York Philharmonic under Walter
Damrosch.

SHOW GIRL
January 12, 1961 (100)
Music and lyrics by Charles Gaynor

The Girl in the Show • Calypso Pete • The Girl Who
Lived in Montparnasse • Join Us in a Little Cup of
Tea* • This Is a Darned Fine Funeral • In Our Teeny
Little Weeny Nest for Two* • Love Is a Sickness •
The Yahoo Step* • Switchblade Bess • You Haven't
Lived Until You've Played the Palace • Somewhere
There's a Little Bluebird • The Story of Marie • My
Kind of Love

RA

THE SHOW IS ON
December 25, 1936 (237)

Prologue (Music by Arthur Schwartz; lyrics by
Howard Dietz) • The Show Is On (Music by Hoagy
Carmichael; lyrics by Ted Fetter) • Now (Music by
Vernon Duke; lyrics by Ted Fetter) • Rhythm (Music
by Richard Rodgers; lyrics by Lorenz Hart) • What
Has He Got? (Music by Vernon Duke; lyrics by Ted
Fetter) • Song of the Woodman (Music by Harold
Arlen; lyrics by E.Y. Harburg) • Casanova (Music by
Vernon Duke; lyrics by Ted Fetter) • Long as You've
Got Your Health (Music by Will Irwin; lyrics by E.Y.
Harburg and Norman Zeno) • Buy Yourself a
Balloon (Music and lyrics by Herman Hupfeld) •
Parade Night (Music by Will Irwin; lyrics by Norman
Zeno) • By Strauss (Music by George Gershwin;
lyrics by Ira Gershwin) • Woof (Music by Will Irwin;
lyrics by Norman Zeno) • Little Old Lady (Music by
Hoagy Carmichael; lyrics by Stanley Adams) •
Josephine Waters (Music by Harold Arlen; lyrics by
E.Y. Harburg) • Epilogue (Music by Vernon Duke;
lyrics by Ted Fetter)

SHOW ME WHERE THE GOOD TIMES ARE (OB)
March 5, 1970 (29)
Music by Kenneth Jacobson
Lyrics by Rhoda Roberts

Based on *The Imaginary Invalid* by Molière

How Do I Feel? • He's Wonderful • Look Up • Show
Me Where the Good Times Are • You're My
Happiness • Café Royale Rag Time • Staying Alive •
One Big Happy Family • Follow Your Heart • Look
Who's Throwing a Party • When Tomorrow Comes •
The Test • I'm Not Getting Any Younger • Who'd
Believe?

SHUFFLE ALONG
May 23, 1921 (504)
Music and lyrics by Noble Sissle and Eubie Blake

Election Day • I'm Just Simply Full of Jazz • Love
Will Find a Way • Bandana Days • In Honeysuckle
Time • Gypsy Blues • Shuffle Along • I'm Just Wild
About Harry* • If You've Never Been Vamped by a
Brownskin • Uncle Tom and Old Black Joe •
Everything Reminds Me of You • Oriental Blues •
I'm Craving for That Kind of Love • Daddy, Won't
You Please Come Home? • Baltimore Buzz

RA

SHUFFLE ALONG OF 1933
December 26, 1932 (17)
Music by Eubie Blake
Lyrics by Noble Sissle

Labor Day Parade • Sing and Dance Your Troubles
Away • You Don't Look for Love • Bandanna Ways •
Keep Your Chin Up • Breakin' 'Em In • In the Land
of Sunny Sunflowers • Sugar Babe • Chickens
Come Home to Roost • Waiting for the Whistle to
Blow • Saturday Afternoon • Here 'Tis • Lonesome
Man • Falling in Love • We're a Couple of Salesmen
• Dusting Around • Arabian Moon • If It's Any News
to You • You've Got to Have Koo Wah

SHUFFLE ALONG OF 1952
May 8, 1952 (4)
Music by Eubie Blake
Lyrics by Noble Sissle

Falling • City Called Heaven • Bitten by Love (Music
by Joseph Meyer; lyrics by Floyd Huddleston) •
Bongo-Boola • Swanee Moon • Rhythm of America •
It's the Gown That Makes the Gal That Makes the
Guy (Lyrics by Joan Javits) • You Can't Overdo a
Good Thing (Music by Joseph Meyer; lyrics by
Floyd Huddleston) • My Day (Music by Joseph
Meyer; lyrics by Floyd Huddleston) • Give It Love
(Music by Joseph Meyer; lyrics by Floyd
Huddleston) • Farewell With Love

SIDEWALKS OF NEW YORK
October 3, 1927 (112)
Music by James F. Hanley
Lyrics by Eddie Dowling

The Younger Set • Way Down Town • Wherever You
Are • Nothing Can Ever Happen in New York • Little
Bum • Oh, for the Life of a Cowboy • Playground in
the Sky • We're the Girls You Can't Forget • Headin'
for Harlem • Just a Little Smile From You • Goldfish
Glide

SILK STOCKINGS
February 24, 1955 (477)
Music and lyrics by Cole Porter

Based on the film *Ninotchka* (1939)

Paris Loves Lovers • Stereophonic Sound • It's a Chemical Reaction • All of You • Too Bad • Satin and Silk • Without Love • Hail, Bibinski • As On Through the Seasons We Sail • Josephine • Siberia • Silk Stockings • Red Blues

Dropped from production
The Perfume of Love • Art • There's a Hollywood That's Good

RA,SEL

Added to film version (1957)
Fated to Be Mated • Ritz Roll and Rock

RA (film version)

THE SILVER SWAN
November 27, 1929 (21)
Music by H. Maurice Jacquet
Lyrics by William Brady

The Only Game That I Would Play • A la Viennese • I Like the Military Man • The Trial Song • The Brave Deserve the Fair • Till I Met You (Lyrics by Brady and Alonzo Price) • Cigarette • Love Letters • Merry-Go-Round • The Lonely Road • I Love You, I Adore You

SIMPLE SIMON
February 18, 1930 (135)
Music by Richard Rodgers
Lyrics by Lorenz Hart

Coney Island • Don't Tell Your Folks • Magic Music • I Still Believe in You* • Send for Me* • Dull and Gay • Sweetenheart • Hunting the Fox • Mocking Bird • I Love the Woods • On With the Dance • I Can Do Wonders With You • Ten Cents a Dance • In Your Chapeau • The Trojan Horse • Rags and Tatters • Cottage in the Country

Dropped from production
Dancing on the Ceiling* • He Was Too Good to Me • Oh, So Lovely

SIMPLY HEAVENLY
May 21, 1957 (62)[1]
Music by David Martin
Lyrics by Langston Hughes

Simply Heavenly • Let Me Take You for a Ride • Broken String Blues • Did You Ever Hear the Blues? • I'm Gonna Be John Henry • When I'm in a Quiet Mood • Look for the Morning Star • Let's Ball Awhile • The Men in My Life • Good Old Girl

RA

[1] Not including original OB run

SINBAD
February 14, 1918 (164)
Music by Sigmund Romberg
Lyrics by Harold Atteridge

On Cupid's Green • A Little Bit of Every Nationality • Our Ancestors • A Thousand and One Arabian Nights • Where Do They Get Those Guys? • Beauty and the Beast • Rock-a-Bye Your Baby to a Dixie Melody (Music by Jean Schwartz; lyrics by Joe Young and Sam Lewis • Take the Night Boat to Albany • I Hail from Cairo • Swanee* (Music by George Gershwin; lyrics by Irving Caesar) • Bagdad • A Night in the Orient • Love Ahoy! • The Bedalumbo • My Mammy (Music by Walter Donaldson; lyrics by Irving Caesar) • I'll Tell the World • It's Wonderful

SING FOR YOUR SUPPER
April 24, 1939 (60)
Music by Lee Wainer
Lyrics by Robert Sour

At Long Last • Her Pop's a Cop (Music by Ned Lehak; lyrics by Irving Crane and Phil Conwit) • Opening Night • Bonnie Banks • How Can We Swing It? • Oh Boy, Can We Deduct • Imagine My Finding You Here (Music by Ned Lehak) • Papa's Got a Job (Music by Ned Lehak) • Lucky • Legitimate (Lyrics by John Latouche) • The Story of a Horn • Perspiration (Lyrics by John Latouche) • Leaning on a Shovel (Lyrics by John Latouche) • A Ballad for Americans (Music by Earl Robinson; lyrics by John Latouche)

RA

SING MUSE! (OB)
December 6, 1961 (39)
Music by Joseph Raposo
Lyrics by Erich Segal

Helen Quit Your Yellin' • Out to Launch • I Am a Traveling Poet • O Pallas Athene • Your Name May Be Paris • Sing Muse • You're in Love • The Wrath of Achilles • No Champagne • Please Let Me Read • Business Is Bad • In Our Own Little Salon • Fame! • We'll Find a Way • Tonight's the Fight • I'm to Blame

SING OUT, SWEET LAND[1]
December 27, 1944 (102)

Sing Out, Sweet Land (As I Was Going Along) (Music by Elie Siegmeister; lyrics by Edward Eager) • More Than These (Music by John Mundy; lyrics by Edward Eager) • Where? (Music by John Mundy; lyrics by Edward Eager)

RA

[1] Although consisting primarily of American folk music, the score contained three original songs.

SING OUT THE NEWS
September 24, 1938 (105)
Music and lyrics by Harold Rome

How Long Can Love Keep Laughing? • Ordinary Guy • One of These Fine Days • Tell Me, Pretty Maiden • Plaza 6-9423 • My Heart Is Unemployed • Yip Ahoy • F.D.R. Jones* • Entre-Nous • We've Got the Song

SINGIN' THE BLUES (Play with two songs)
September 16, 1931 (45)
Music by Jimmy McHugh
Lyrics by Dorothy Fields

It's the Darndest Thing • Singin' the Blues

THE SINGING RABBI
September 10, 1931 (4)
Music by Joseph Rumshinsky
Lyrics by L. Wolfe Gilbert

Sholom Aleichem • Hear O Israel • A Vision of the
Future

SITTING PRETTY
April 8, 1924 (95)
Music by Jerome Kern
Lyrics by P.G. Wodehouse

The Charity Class • Is This Not a Lovely Spot? •
Worries • Bongo on the Congo • Mr. and Mrs. Rorer
• There Isn't One Girl • A Year From Today •
Shufflin' Sam • The Polka Dot • Days Gone By • All
You Need Is a Girl • Tulip Time in Sing Sing • On a
Desert Island With You • The Enchanted Train •
Shadow of the Moon

Dropped from production
Roses Are Nodding • Coaching • You Alone Would
Do • Ladies Are Present • Sitting Pretty • Just Wait

SIX (OB)
April 12, 1971 (8)
Music and lyrics by Charles Strouse

What Is There to Sing About? • The Garden • Love
Song • Six • Coming Attractions • The Invisible Man
• The Critic • Trip • The Beginning • The Dream

1600 PENNSYLVANIA AVENUE
May 4, 1976 (7)
Music by Leonard Bernstein
Lyrics by Alan Jay Lerner

Rehearse! • If I Was a Dove • On Ten Square Miles
by the Potomac River • Welcome Home Miz Adams
• Take Care of This House • The President
Jefferson Sunday Luncheon Party March • Seena • I
Love My Wife • Auctions • The Little White Lie • We
Must Have a Ball • Forty Acres and a Mule • Bright
and Black • Duet for One (The First Lady of the
Land) • The Robber-Baron Minstrel Parade • Pity the
Poor • The Red White and Blues • I Love This Land

SEL

SKY HIGH
March 2, 1925 (217)
Music by Carlton Kelsey and Maury Rubens
Lyrics by Clifford Grey

Hello, the Little Birds Have Flown • The Best Songs
of All • Oxford Days (Music by Alfred Goodman) •
Give Your Heart in June-Time (Music by Victor
Herbert; lyrics by Grey and Harold Atteridge) • Find
a Good Time • Why Are They Following Me? •

Somewhere in Lovers' Land • We Make the Show •
The Letter Song • Man o' My Dreams (Music by
Alfred Goodman) • Let It Rain (Music and lyrics by
James Kendis and Hal Dyson) • Whirled Into
Happiness • The Barber of Seville (Music by
Rubens)

SKY HIGH (OB)
June 28, 1979 (38)
Music and lyrics by Ann Harris

Rainbow • Walk Through That Golden Gate • I'm
Mother Nature of You All • She'll Get the Business
in the End • Behold the Coming of the Sun • I'm
Betting on You • One Cell • Singing Mermaids •
South American Way • Queen Cobra • Fly Away •
When He Calls Half-Hour • Birdie Follies •
Ringmaster Song • Broadway New York • Clown
Song • Let's Go to the Dogs • Kitty Kat Song • Toast
of the Town • Gut Rocks • Au Revoir • Sheik Song •
Opium Song • I'm Lazy • Do It Yourself • Giddyup •
Miss America • Hot as Hades • Devil Man •
Champagne Song

SKYSCRAPER
November 13, 1965 (248)
Music by Jimmy Van Heusen
Lyrics by Sammy Cahn

Based on the play *Dream Girl* by Elmer Rice

Occasional Flight of Fancy • Run for Your Life •
Local 403 • Opposites • Just the Crust • Everybody
Has a Right to Be Wrong • Wrong! • More Than One
Way • Haute Couture • Don't Worry • I'll Only Miss
Her When I Think of Her • Spare That Building

RA

SLEEPY HOLLOW
June 3, 1948 (12)
Music by George Lessner
Lyrics by Miriam Battista and Russell Maloney

Based on *The Legend of Sleepy Hollow* by
Washington Irving

Time Stands Still • I Still Have to Learn • Ask Me
Again • Never Let Her Go • There's History to Be
Made • Here and Now • Why Was I Born on a
Farm? • If • My Lucky Lover • A Musical Lesson •
You've Got That Kind of a Face • I'm Lost (Lyrics
by Ruth Aarons) • Good Night • The Englishman's
Head • Pedro, Ichabod • Poor Man • The Things
That Lovers Say • Ichabod • The Gray Goose

SMALL WONDER
September 15, 1948 (134)

Count Your Blessings (Music by Baldwin
Bergersen; lyrics by Phyllis McGinley) • The
Commuters' Song (Music by Baldwin Bergersen;
lyrics by Phyllis McGinley) • Ballad for Billionaires
(Music by Albert Selden; lyrics by Burt Shevelove) •
No Time (Music by Baldwin Bergersen; lyrics by
Phyllis McGinley) • Flaming Youth (Music by Albert
Selden; lyrics by Burt Shevelove) • Show Off (Music

and lyrics by Albert Selden) • Badaroma (Music by Albert Selden; lyrics by Burt Shevelove) • Nobody Told Me (Music by Baldwin Bergersen; lyrics by Phyllis McGinley) • Pistachio (Music and lyrics by Mark Lawrence) • When I Fall in Love (Music and lyrics by Albert Selden) • Saturday's Child (Music by Baldwin Bergersen; lyrics by Phyllis McGinley) • William McKinley High (Music by Albert Selden; lyrics by Burt Shevelove) • From A to Z (Music by Albert Selden; lyrics by Burt Shevelove) • Just an Ordinary Guy (Music by Albert Selden; lyrics by Phyllis McGinley and Burt Shevelove)

SMILE AT ME
August 23, 1935 (27)
Music by Gerald Dolin
Lyrics by Edward J. Lambert

Here and There • Fiesta in Madrid • Smile at Me (Music by Lambert) • Tired of the South • Goona Goona • There's a Broadway up in Heaven • I'm Dreaming While We're Dancing • You're a Magician • Calcutta • Caribbeana • I Love to Flutter

SMILES
November 18, 1930 (63)
Music by Vincent Youmans
Lyrics by Harold Adamson and Clifford Grey

The Bowery • Say, Young Man of Manhattan • Rally Round Me (Lyrics by Ring Lardner) • Hotcha Ma Chotch • Time on My Hands* (Lyrics by Adamson and Mack Gordon) • Be Good to Me (Lyrics by Ring Lardner) • Clever, Those Chinese • Anyway, We've Had Fun (Lyrics by Ring Lardner) • Something to Sing About • Here's a Day to Be Happy • If I Were You, Love (Lyrics by Ring Lardner) • I'm Glad I Waited • La Marseilles • Why Ain't I Home? (Lyrics by Ring Lardner) • Dancing Wedding • Carry On, Keep Smiling (Lyrics by Adamson)

Dropped from production
More Than Ever • Smile • Down Where the East River Flows

SMILING FACES
August 30, 1932 (31)
Music by Harry Revel
Lyrics by Mack Gordon

Sport Is Sport • I've Fallen Out of Love • Sweet Little Stranger • Shakin' the Shakespeare • Thank You, Don't Mention It • Smart Set • Poor Little, Shy Little, Demure Little Me • There Will Be a Girl • Think of My Reputation • Quick Henry, the Flit • Can't Get Rid of Me • In a Little Stucco in the Sticks • I Stumbled Over You and Fell in Love • Old Spanish Custom

SMILING, THE BOY FELL DEAD (OB)
April 19, 1961 (22)
Music by David Baker
Lyrics by Sheldon Harnick

Sons of Greentree • Let's Evolve • The ABC's of Success • If I Felt Any Younger Today • More Than Ever Now • I've Got a Wonderful Future • Small Town • Heredity—Environment • The Gatsby Bridge March • A World to Win • The Wonderful Machine • Temperance Polka • Daydreams • Dear Old Dad • Me and Dorothea • Two by Two

SMITH (OB)
May 19, 1973 (18)
Music and lyrics by Matt Dubey and Dean Fuller

Boy Meets Girl • There's a Big Job Waiting for You • To the Ends of the Earth • Balinasia • Onh-Honh-Honh! • Police Song • You Need a Song • How Beautiful It Was • Island Ritual • People Don't Do That • You're in New York Now • It Must Be Love • Song of the Frog • G'bye • Melody

SNOOPY (OB)
December 20, 1982 (152)
Music by Larry Grossman
Lyrics by Hal Hackady

Based on the comic strip "Peanuts" by Charles M. Schulz

The World According to Snoopy • Snoopy's Song • Edgar Allan Poe • I Know Now • Vigil • Clouds • Where Did That Little Dog Go? • Dime a Dozen • Daisy Hill • Bunnies • The Great Writer • Poor Sweet Baby • Don't Be Anything Less than Everything You Can Be • The Big Bow-Wow • Just One Person • Mother's Day • Hurry Up, Face

SEL

SO LONG, 174TH STREET
April 27, 1976 (16)
Music and lyrics by Stan Daniels

Based on Joseph Stein's play *Enter Laughing*, based in turn on the novel by Carl Reiner

David Kolowitz, the Actor • It's Like • Undressing Girls With My Eyes • Bolero on Rye • Whoever You Are • Say the Words • My Son the Druggist • You Touched Her • Men • Boy Oh Boy • Butler's Song • Being With You • If You Want to Break My Father's Heart • So Long 174th Street

THE SOCIAL REGISTER (Play with one song)
November 9, 1931 (97)
Music by Lou Alter
Lyrics by Ira Gershwin

The Key to My Heart

SOMETHING FOR THE BOYS
January 7, 1943 (422)
Music and lyrics by Cole Porter

See That You're Born in Texas • When My Baby Goes to Town • Something for the Boys • When We're Home on the Range • Could It Be You? • Hey, Good-Lookin' • He's a Right Guy • The Leader of a Big-Time Band • I'm in Love With a Soldier Boy • By the Mississinewah • There's a Happy Land in the Sky

Dropped before Broadway opening

Riddle-Diddle Me This • So Long, San Antonio

SOMETHING GAY (Play with one song)
April 29, 1935 (72)
Music by Richard Rodgers
Lyrics by Lorenz Hart

You Are So Lovely and I'm So Lonely

SOMETHING MORE
November 10, 1964 (15)
Music by Sammy Fain
Lyrics by Marilyn and Alan Bergman

Based on the novel *Portofino P.T.A.* by Gerald Green

Something More • Who Fills the Bill? • The Straw That Broke the Camel's Back • Better All the Time • Don't Make a Move • No Questions • Church of My Choice • Jaded, Degraded Am I • I've Got Nothin' to Do • Party Talk • In No Time at All • The Master of the Greatest Art of All • Grazie per Niente • I Feel Like New Year's Eve • One Long Last Look • Ode to a Key • Bravo, Bravo, Novelisto • Life Is Too Short • Mineola • Comé Sta

SOMETHING'S AFOOT
May 27, 1976 (61)
Music and lyrics by James MacDonald, David Vos and Robert Gerlach

A Marvelous Weekend • Something's Afoot • Carry On • I Don't Know Why I Trust You (but I Do) • The Man With the Ginger Moustache • Suspicious • The Legal Heir • You Fell Out of the Sky • Dinghy • I Owe It All • New Day

SOMETIME
October 4, 1918 (283)
Music by Rudolf Friml
Lyrics by Rida Johnson Young

What Do You Have to Do? • Picking Peaches • Sometime • Keep On Smiling • Spanish Maid • The Tune You Can't Forget • Oh! Argentina • Beautiful Night • Little Dance • Baby Doll • Any Kind of Man

VS

SONG OF NORWAY
August 21, 1944 (860)
Music and lyrics by Robert Wright and George Forrest (based on Edvard Grieg[1])

The Legend • Hill of Dreams • Freddy and His Fiddle • Now • Strange Music • Midsummer's Eve • March of the Trollgers • Hymn of Betrothal • Bon Vivant • Three Loves • Down Your Tea • Nordraak's Farewell • Chocolate Pas de Trois • Waltz Eternal • I Love You • At Christmastime • The Song of Norway

RA,VS,SEL

[1] See individual titles for notes on derivation of songs.

SONG OF THE FLAME
December 30, 1925 (194)
Music by George Gershwin and Herbert Stothart
Lyrics by Otto Harbach and Oscar Hammerstein II

Far Away • Song of the Flame • Cossack Love Song (Don't Forget Me) • Tartar • Vodka • The Signal (Music by Gershwin) • Midnight Bells (Music by Gershwin) • Women's Work Is Never Done • Great Big Bear (Music by Stothart) • Wander Away (Music by Stothart)

Dropped from production
You Are You

SONS O' FUN
December 1, 1941 (742)
Music by Sammy Fain
Lyrics by Jack Yellen

It's a New Kind of Thing • Happy in Love • Thank You, South America • It's a Mighty Fine Country We Have Here • Manuelo • Let's Say Goodnight With a Dance

SONS O' GUNS
November 26, 1929 (295)
Music by J. Fred Coots
Lyrics by Arthur Swanstrom and Benny Davis

The Younger Set • May I Say I Love You? • I'm That Way Over You • We'll Be There • The Can-Canola • Why? • Cross Your Fingers • Red Hot and Blue Rhythm • Over Here • It's You I Love • Let's Merge • Sentimental Melody • There's a Rainbow on the Way

SOPHIE
April 15, 1963 (8)
Music and lyrics by Steve Allen

Based on the life of Sophie Tucker

Red Hot Mama • Sunshine Face • Mr. Henry Jones • Sophie in New York • Patsy • I'll Show Them All • Hold On to Your Hats • Fast Cars and Fightin' Women • Queen of the Burlesque Wheel • When You Carry Your Own Suitcase • When I'm in Love • Sailors of the Sea • I Want the Kind of a Fella • Who Are We Kidding? • Don't Look Back • I'd Know It • You've Got to Be a Lady • I Love You Today • With You • I've Got 'Em Standing in Line • They've Got a Lot to Learn

RA

THE SOUND OF MUSIC[1]
November 16, 1959 (1,443)
Music by Richard Rodgers
Lyrics by Oscar Hammerstein II

Suggested by the biography *The Trapp Family Singers* by Maria Augusta Trapp

Preludium • The Sound of Music • Maria • My Favorite Things • Do-Re-Mi • Sixteen Going on Seventeen • The Lonely Goatherd • How Can Love Survive? • So Long, Farewell • Climb Ev'ry Mountain • No Way to Stop It • An Ordinary Couple • Edelweiss*

RA,VS,SEL

Added to film version (1965)
I Have Confidence in Me (Music and lyrics by Richard Rodgers) • Something Good (Music and lyrics by Richard Rodgers)

RA (film version)

[1] Tony Award for Best Score; tied with *Fiorello*

SOUTH PACIFIC[1]
April 7, 1949 (1,925)
Music by Richard Rodgers
Lyrics by Oscar Hammerstein II

Adapted from *Tales of the South Pacific* by James A. Michener

Dites-Moi Pourquoi • A Cockeyed Optimist • Twin Soliloquies • Some Enchanted Evening • Bloody Mary • There Is Nothin' Like a Dame • Bali Ha'i • I'm Gonna Wash That Man Right Outa My Hair • I'm in Love With a Wonderful Guy[*] • Younger Than Springtime • This Is How It Feels • Happy Talk[*] • Honey Bun • Carefully Taught • This Nearly Was Mine

Dropped from production, but used in film version (1958)
My Girl Back Home

Dropped from production, but used in TV Cinderella remake (1965)
The Loneliness of Evening

RA,VS,SEL

[1] Pulitzer Prize winner; Tony Award for Best Score

SPRING IS HERE[1]
March 11, 1929 (104)
Music by Richard Rodgers
Lyrics by Lorenz Hart

Spring Is Here[*] • Yours Sincerely • You Never Say Yes • With a Song in My Heart • Baby's Awake Now • Red Hot Trumpet • What a Girl • Rich Man! Poor Man! • Why Can't I?

Dropped from production
A Cup of Tea • A Word in Edgewise • The Color of Her Eyes[*]

[1] Owen Davis adapted the libretto from his play *Shot-Gun Wedding,* which had toured but never reached New York.

THE SPRING MAID
December 26, 1910 (192)
Music by Heinrich Reinhardt
Lyrics by Robert B. Smith

The Cure • The Loving Cup (Music by Robert Hood Bowers) • The Fountain Fay Protective Institution, Limited • On the Track • The Next May Be the Right • How I Love a Pretty Face • The Fountain Fay • Two Little Love Bees • Folk Songs • Take Me, Dear • If You Want to Win a Girl • Day Dreams • Three Trees (Recitation with accompaniment) • Hungaria

VS

STAG MOVIE (OB)
January 3, 1971 (88)
Music by Jacques Urbont
Lyrics by David Newburger

Stag Movie • Looking at the Sun • I Want More Out of Life Than This • Grocery Boy • Splendor in the Grass • It's So Good • Get in Line • Try a Trio • Get Your Rocks off Rock • We Came Together

STAR AND GARTER
June 24, 1942 (605)

Star and Garter Girls (Music by Lester Lee; lyrics by Jerry Seelen) • Les Sylphides Avec la Bumpe (Music and lyrics by Irving Gordon, Alan Roberts and Jerome Brainin) • Bunny, Bunny, Bunny (Music and lyrics by Harold Rome) • For a Quarter (Music by Lester Lee; lyrics by Jerry Seelen) • The Harem (Music and lyrics by Irving Gordon, Alan Roberts and Jerome Brainin) • I Don't Get It (Music by Doris Tauber; lyrics by Sis Wilner) • Brazilian Nuts (Music by Dorival Caymmi; lyrics by Al Stillman)

STARS IN YOUR EYES
February 9, 1939 (127)
Music by Arthur Schwartz
Lyrics by Dorothy Fields

Places, Everybody • One Brief Moment • This Is It • All the Time • Self Made Man • Okay for Sound • A Lady Needs a Change • Terribly Attractive • Just a Little Bit More • As of Today • He's Goin' Home • I'll Pay the Check • Never a Dull Moment • It's All Yours

STARTING HERE, STARTING NOW (OB)
March 7, 1977 (120)
Music by David Shire
Lyrics by Richard Maltby, Jr.

The Word Is Love • Starting Here, Starting Now • A Little Bit Off • I Think I May Want to Remember Today • Beautiful • We Can Talk to Each Other • Just Across the River • Crossword Puzzle • Autumn • I Don't Remember Christmas • I Don't Believe It • I Hear Bells • Pleased With Myself • Hey There, Fans • The Girl of the Minute • A Girl You Should Know • Travel • Watching the Big Parade Go By • Flair • What About Today? (Lyrics by Shire) • One Step • Barbara • Song of Me • Today Is the First Day of the Rest of My Life • A New Life Coming

RA

STEPPING STONES
November 6, 1923 (241)
Music by Jerome Kern
Lyrics by Anne Caldwell

Little Angel Cake • Because You Love the Singer • Little Red Riding Hood • Wonderful Dad • Pie • Babbling Babette • In Love With Love • Our Lovely Rose[*] • Once in a Blue Moon • Raggedy Ann • Dear Little Peter Pan • Stepping Stones

Dropped from production
When I Went to School • Little Gypsy Lady

VS

STOP! LOOK! LISTEN!
December 25, 1915 (105)
Music and lyrics by Irving Berlin

Blow Your Horn • Give Us a Chance • I Love to Dance • And Father Wanted Me to Learn a Trade • The Girl on the Magazine Cover • I Love a Piano • That Hula Hula • A Pair of Ordinary Coons • When I'm Out With You • Take Off a Little Bit • Teach Me How to Love • The Law Must Be Obeyed • Ragtime Melodrama • When I Get Back to the U.S.A. • Stop! Look! Listen • I'll Be Coming Home With a Skate On • Everything in America Is Ragtime • Sailor Song

STOP THE WORLD—I WANT TO GET OFF
October 3, 1962 (556)
Music and lyrics by Leslie Bricusse and Anthony Newley

The A.B.C. Song • I Want to Be Rich • Typically English • A Special Announcement • Lumbered • Welcome to Sludgepool • Gonna Build a Mountain • Glorious Russian • Meilinki Meilchick • Family Fugue • Typische Deutsche • Nag! Nag! Nag! • All American • Once in a Lifetime • Mumbo Jumbo • Welcome to Sunvale • Someone Nice Like You • What Kind of Fool Am I?

RA,SEL

STRADA See LA STRADA

THE STRAW HAT REVUE
September 29, 1939 (75)
Crashing Thru (Music and lyrics by Sylvia Fine) • Four Young People (Music and lyrics by James Shelton) • Anatole of Paris (Music and lyrics by Sylvia Fine) • The Great Chandelier (Music and lyrics by Sylvia Fine) • Our Town (Music and lyrics by James Shelton)

STREET SCENE
January 9, 1947 (148)
Music by Kurt Weill
Lyrics by Langston Hughes

Based on the play by Elmer Rice

Ain't It Awful, the Heat? • I Got a Marble and a Star • Get a Load of That • When a Woman Has a Baby • Somehow I Never Could Believe • Ice Cream • Let Things Be Like They Always Was • Wrapped in a Ribbon and Tied in a Bow • Lonely House • Wouldn't You Like to Be on Broadway? • What Good Would the Moon Be? • Moon-Faced, Starry-Eyed • Remember That I Care • Catch Me if You Can • There'll Be Trouble • A Boy Like You • We'll Go Away Together • The Woman Who Lived up There • Lullaby • I Loved Her, Too • Don't Forget the Lilac Bush

RA,VS

THE STREET SINGER
September 17, 1929 (189)
Music by Niclas Kempner
Lyrics by Graham John

You Can Never Tell • I Am • When Everything Is Hunky-Dory • The Girl That I'll Adore • You've Made Me Happy Today! • Oh, Theobold, Oh, Elmer • From Now On (Music by Richard Myers; lyrics by Edward Eliscu) • Knocking on Wood

THE STREETS OF NEW YORK (OB)
October 29, 1963 (84)
Music by Richard B. Chodosh
Lyrics by Barry Alan Grael

Based on the play by Dion Boucicault

Tourist Madrigal • He'll Come to Me Crawling • If I May • Aren't You Warm? • Where Can the Rich and Poor Be Friends? • California • Christmas Carol • Laugh After Laugh • Arms for the Love of Me • Close Your Eyes • Love Wins Again

THE STREETS OF PARIS
June 19, 1939 (274)
Music by Jimmy McHugh
Lyrics by Al Dubin

The Streets of Paris • Thanks for the Francs • Danger in the Dark • Three Little Maids • Is It Possible? • Rendezvous Time in Paris • South American Way • History Is Made at Night (Music and lyrics by Harold Rome) • We Haven't Got a Pot to Cook In • Robert the Roué • Doin' the Chamberlain • Reading, Writing and a Little Bit of Rhythm • The French Have a Word for It (Music and lyrics by Harold Rome)

STRIKE ME PINK
March 4, 1933 (105)
Music by Ray Henderson
Lyrics by Lew Brown

It's Great to Be Alive • Strike Me Pink • Home to Harlem • Love and Rhythm • Let's Call It a Day • Restless • Ooh, I'm Thinking • I Hate to Think That You'll Grow Old, Baby • Hollywood, Park Avenue and Broadway • On Any Street

STRIKE UP THE BAND[1]
January 14, 1930 (191)
Music by George Gershwin
Lyrics by Ira Gershwin

Fletcher's American Chocolate Choral Society • I Mean to Say • A Typical Self-Made American • Soon • The Unofficial Spokesman • Three Cheers for the Union! • This Could Go On for Years • If I Became the President • Hangin' Around With You • Strike Up the Band! • Military Dancing Drill • Mademoiselle in New Rochelle • I've Got a Crush on You[*] • How About a Boy Like Me? • I Want to Be a War Bride • Soldiers' March (Instrumental) • Ring a Ding a Ding Dong Dell

RA,VS,SEL

[1] Like another Gershwin musical, *Girl Crazy*,

Strike Up the Band had an extraordinary group of musicians in its pit orchestra. The Red Nichols Band, as it was called, included, in addition to Nichols, Glenn Miller, Benny Goodman, Gene Krupa, Jack Teagarden and Jimmy Dorsey.

THE STUDENT GYPSY (OB)
September 30, 1963 (16)
Music and lyrics by Rick Besoyan

Welcome Home • Singspielia • Romance • Somewhere • It's a Wonderful Day to Do Nothing • The Gypsy Life • The Grenadiers' Marching Song • Greetings • Kiss Me • Ting-a-Ling-Dearie • Merry May • Seventh Heaven Waltz • You're a Man • A Whistle Works • Gypsy of Love • Our Love Has Flown Away • A Woman Is a Woman Is a Woman • Very Much in Love • My Life Is Yours • There's Life in the Old Folks Yet • The Drinking Song

THE STUDENT PRINCE
December 2, 1924 (608)
Music by Sigmund Romberg
Lyrics by Dorothy Donnelly

Based on the play *Old Heidelberg* by Rudolf Bleichman

Golden Days • To the Inn We're Marching • Drinking Song • Come, Boys • In Heidelberg Fair • Deep in My Heart, Dear • Serenade • Farmer Jacob Lay a-Snoring • Student Life • Thoughts Will Come to Me • Just We Two • The Flag That Flies Above Us • Let Us Sing a Song

RA,VS,SEL

SUBWAYS ARE FOR SLEEPING
December 27, 1961 (205)
Music by Jule Styne
Lyrics by Betty Comden and Adolph Green

Suggested by the book by Edmund G. Love

Subways Are for Sleeping • Girls Like Me • Subway Directions; Ride Through the Night • I'm Just Taking My Time • I Was a Shoo-In • Who Knows What Might Have Been? • Strange Duet • Swing Your Projects • I Said It and I'm Glad • Be a Santa • How Can You Describe a Face? • I Just Can't Wait • Comes Once in a Lifetime • What Is This Feeling in the Air?

RA

SUGAR
April 9, 1972 (505)
Music by Jule Styne
Lyrics by Bob Merrill

Based on the screenplay *Some Like It Hot* by Billy Wilder and I.A.L. Diamond

Windy City Marmalade • Penniless Blues • Tear the Town Apart • The Beauty That Drives Me Mad • We Could Be Close • Sun on My Face • November Song • Sugar • Hey, Why Not! • Beautiful Through and Through • What Do You Give to a Man Who's Had

Everything? • Magic Nights • It's Always Love • When You Meet a Man in Chicago

RA

SUGAR BABIES[1]
October 8, 1979 (1,208)
Music by Jimmy McHugh
Lyrics by Arthur Malvin

A Good Old Burlesque Show • Let Me Be Your Sugar Baby (Music and lyrics by Malvin) • In Louisiana • Goin' Back to New Orleans (Music and lyrics by Malvin) • Sally • Immigration Rose (Lyrics by Eugene West and Irwin Dash) • The Sugar Baby Bounce (Music and lyrics by Jay Livingston and Ray Evans) • Down at the Gaiety Burlesque (Music and lyrics by Malvin) • Mr. Banjo Man (Music and lyrics by Malvin) • I'm Keeping Myself Available for You • Warm and Willing (Lyrics by Jay Livingston and Ray Evans) • Every Day Another Tune (Music and lyrics by Malvin) • When You and I Were Young, Maggie Blues (Lyrics by Jack Frost) • You Can't Blame Your Uncle Sammy (Lyrics by Al Dubin and Irwin Dash)

RA,SEL

[1] The score also included well-known popular songs by Jimmy McHugh and Dorothy Fields.

SUGAR HILL
December 25, 1931 (11)
Music by James P. Johnson
Lyrics by Flournoy Miller

Noisy Neighbors • I Love You, Honey • Hanging Around Yo' Door • Hot Harlem • Boston • What Have I Done? • Hot Rhythm • Fooling Around With Love • Rumbola • Something's Going to Happen to You • Moving Day

SUMMER WIVES
April 13, 1936 (8)
Music by Sam Morrison
Lyrics by Dolph Singer

Lowen-Green Country Club, I Love You • The Chatterbox • Mickey • I Wrote a Song for You (Lyrics by Singer and William Dunham) • Play Me an Old Time Two-Step • My Love Carries On • Us on a Bus (Music by Vee Lawnhurst; lyrics by Tot Seymour)

SUNDAY IN THE PARK WITH GEORGE[1](OB)
July 6, 1983 (24)[2]
Music and lyrics by Stephen Sondheim

Sunday • No Life • Color and Light • Gossip • The Day Off • Everybody Loves Louis • Finishing the Hat • We Do Not Belong Together • Beautiful • It's Hot Up Here • Chromolume #7 • Putting It Together • Children and Art • Lesson #8 • Move On

RA

[1] Inspired by the Georges Seurat painting *Sunday Afternoon on the Island of La Grande Jatte.*

[2] A workshop production opened Off Broadway during 1983 prior to an opening on Broadway May 2, 1984, with the above songs.

SUNNY
September 22, 1925 (517)
Music by Jerome Kern
Lyrics by Otto Harbach and Oscar Hammerstein II

Sunny • Who?[*] • So's Your Old Man • Let's Say Good Night Till It's Morning • D'Ye Love Me? • The Wedding Knell • Two Little Bluebirds • When We Get Our Divorce • Sunshine • Strolling, or What Have You?

Dropped from production
To Think He Remembered Me • Under the Sky • Tonsils • It Won't Mean a Thing • Dream a Dream

RA,VS

Added to film version (1930)
I Was Alone

SUNNY DAYS
February 8, 1928 (101)
Music by Jean Schwartz
Lyrics by Clifford Grey and William Cary Duncan

A Belle, a Beau and a Boutonnière • One Sunny Day • Ginette • I'll Be Smiling • Really and Truly • I've Got to Be Good • Hang Your Hat on the Moon • So Do I • Orange Blossoms • Trample Your Troubles

SUNNY RIVER[1]
December 4, 1941 (36)
Music by Sigmund Romberg
Lyrics by Oscar Hammerstein II

My Girl and I • Call It a Dream • It Can Happen to Anyone • The Butterflies and Bees • Along the Winding Road • Bundling • Can You Sing? • Making Conversation • Let Me Live Today • Bow-Legged Sal • Sunny River • The Duello • She Got Him • Time Is Standing Still

Dropped from production
Lordy • Eleven Levee Street

[1] Pre-Broadway title: *New Orleans.*

THE SUNSHINE GIRL
February 3, 1913 (160)
Music by Paul A. Rubens
Lyrics by Paul A. Rubens and Arthur Wimperis

Get a Move on • Josephine • You and I • Kitchen Range • Ladies • Nuts • Tiny Touch • Here's to Love • Goodbye to Flirtation • You Can't Play Every Instrument in the Band (Music by John Golden; lyrics by Joseph Cawthorn) • Little Girl, Mind How You Go • Who's the Boss? • Miss Blush • Honeymoon Lane (Music by Jerome Kern; lyrics by Herbert Reynolds) • In Your Defense • A Common Little Girl • I've Been to America

SWEENEY TODD[1]
March 1, 1979 (557)
Music and lyrics by Stephen Sondheim

The Ballad of Sweeney Todd • No Place Like London • The Barber and His Wife • The Worst Pies in London • Poor Thing • My Friends • Green Finch and Linnet Bird • Ah, Miss • Johanna • Pirelli's Magical Elixir • Wait • Kiss Me • Ladies in Their Sensitivities • Pretty Women • Epiphany • A Little Priest • God, That's Good • By the Sea • Not While I'm Around • City on Fire!

RA,VS,SEL

[1] Tony Award for Best Score

SWEET ADELINE
September 2, 1929 (234)
Music by Jerome Kern
Lyrics by Oscar Hammerstein II

Play Us a Polka, Dot • 'Twas Not So Long Ago • My Husband's First Wife • Here Am I • First Mate Martin • Spring Is Here • Out of the Blue • Naughty Boy • Oriental Moon • Mollie O'Donahue • Why Was I Born? • Winter in Central Park • The Sun About to Rise • Some Girl Is on Your Mind • Don't Ever Leave Me • Take Me for a Honeymoon Ride • The Scene Is in a Garden

Dropped from production
I've Got a New Idea • I'm Dreaming

Added to film version (1935)
We Were So Young • Lonely Feet

SWEET AND LOW
November 17, 1930 (184)

Mr. Jessel (Music and lyrics by Charlotte Kent) • Dancing With Tears in Their Eyes (Music by Will Irwin; lyrics by Billy Rose and Mort Dixon) • Outside Looking In (Music by Harry Archer; lyrics by Edward Eliscu) • Cheerful Little Earful (Music by Harry Warren; lyrics by Ira Gershwin and Billy Rose) • Ten Minutes in Bed (Music by Ned Lehak; lyrics by Allen Boretz) • When a Pansy Was a Flower (Music by Will Irwin; lyrics by Billy Rose and Malcolm McComb) • Would You Like to Take a Walk?[*] (Music by Harry Warren; lyrics by Mort Dixon and Billy Rose) • Revival Day (Music by Will Irwin; lyrics by Malcolm McComb) • For I'm in Love Again (Music by Mischa Spoliansky; lyrics by Billy Rose and Mort Dixon) • I Knew Him Before He Was Spanish (Music by Dana Suesse; lyrics by Billy Rose and Ballard MacDonald) • Overnight (Music by Louis Alter; lyrics by Billy Rose and Charlotte Kent) • Sweet So and So (Music by Philip Charig and Joseph Meyer; lyrics by Ira Gershwin)

SWEET CHARITY
January 29, 1966 (608)
Music by Cy Coleman
Lyrics by Dorothy Fields

Based on the screenplay *Nights of Cabiria* by Federico Fellini, Tullio Pinelli and Ennio Flaiano

You Should See Yourself • Big Spender • Charity's Soliloquy • Rich Man's Frug • If My Friends Could See Me Now • Too Many Tomorrows • There's

Gotta Be Something Better Than This • I'm the Bravest Individual • Rhythm of Life • Baby Dream Your Dream • Sweet Charity • Where Am I Going? • I'm a Brass Band • I Love to Cry at Weddings

RA,VS,SEL

Added to film version (1970)
My Personal Property • It's a Nice Face

RA (film version)

SWEET LITTLE DEVIL[1]
January 21, 1924 (120)
Music by George Gershwin
Lyrics by B.G. DeSylva

Strike, Strike, Strike • Virginia (Don't Go Too Far) • Someone Who Believes in You • System • The Jijibo • Quite a Party • Under a One-Man Top • The Matrimonial Handicap • Just Supposing • Hey! Hey! Let 'er Go! • The Same Old Story • Hooray for the U.S.A.!

Dropped from production
Mah-Jongg • Pepita • My Little Ducky • Sweet Little Devil • Be the Life of the Crowd

[1]Pre-Broadway title: *A Perfect Lady*

SWEET MIANI (OB)
September 25, 1962 (22)
Music and lyrics by Ed Tyler

Middle of the Sea • Legend of the Islands • Black Pearls • Going Native • A Honey to Love • Sailing • Not Tabu • Maluan Moon • Canticle to the Wind • Homesick in Our Hearts • Just Sit Back and Relax • Forever and Always • Turoola • Miani • Silvery Days • Code of the Licensed Pilot • Warm Breezes at Twilight • Far Away Island

SWEETHEART TIME
January 19, 1926 (145)

Based on the play *Never Say Die* by W.H. Post and William Collier

Marian (Music by Walter Donaldson; lyrics by Ballard MacDonald) • Step on It (Music by Joseph Meyer; lyrics by Irving Caesar) • I Know That I Love You (Music by Harry Ruby; lyrics by Bert Kalmar) • Sweetheart Time (Music by Joseph Meyer; lyrics by Irving Caesar) • A Girl in Your Arms (Music by Jay

Gorney; lyrics by Irving Caesar) • One Way Street (Music by Walter Donaldson; lyrics by Ballard MacDonald) • At the Party (Music by Harry Ruby; lyrics by Bert Kalmar) • Who's Who? (Music by Walter Donaldson; lyrics by Ballard MacDonald) • Rue de la Paix (Music by Walter Donaldson; lyrics by Ballard MacDonald) • Cocktail Melody (Music by Walter Donaldson; lyrics by Ballard MacDonald)

SWEETHEARTS
September 8, 1913 (136)
Music by Victor Herbert
Lyrics by Robert B. Smith

Iron! Iron! Iron! • On Parade • There Is Magic in a Smile • Sweethearts • Every Lover Must Meet His Fate • Mother Goose • Jeannette and Her Little Wooden Shoes • The Angelus • The Game of Love • Waiting for the Bride • Pretty as a Picture • Welcoming the Bride • In the Convent They Never Taught Me That • I Don't Know How I Do It, but I Do • The Cricket on the Hearth • Pilgrims of Love

Dropped from production
What She Wanted and What She Got • Talk About This—Talk About That • The Ivy and the Oak

RA,VS

SWING IT
July 22, 1937 (60)
Music by Eubie Blake
Lyrics by J. Milton Reddie and Cecil Mack

The Susan Belle • What Do I Want With Love? • It's the Youth in Me • Ain't We Got Love? • Old Time Swing • Shine • Green and Blue • By the Sweat of Your Brow • Captain, Mate and Crew • Sons and Daughters of the Sea • Huggin' and Muggin' • Rhythm Is a Racket

SWINGIN' THE DREAM
November 29, 1939 (13)
Music by Jimmy Van Heusen
Lyrics by Eddie De Lange

Based on Shakespeare's *A Midsummer Night's Dream*

Peace, Brother • There's Gotta Be a Wedding • Swingin' a Dream • Moonland • Love's a Riddle • Darn That Dream

TAKE A CHANCE
November 26, 1932 (243)
Music by Nacio Herb Brown and Richard Whiting
Lyrics by B.G. DeSylva

The Life of the Party • Should I Be Sweet? (Music by Vincent Youmans) • So Do I (Music by Vincent Youmans) • I Got Religion (Music by Vincent Youmans) • She's Nuts About Me • Tickled Pink • Turn Out the Light • Charity • Oh, How I Long to Belong to You (Music by Vincent Youmans) • Rise 'n' Shine (Music by Vincent Youmans) • Tonight Is Opening Night • You're an Old Smoothie • Eadie Was a Lady

Dropped from production
My Lover (Music by Vincent Youmans; lyrics by B.G. DeSylva) • I Want to Be With You (Music by Vincent Youmans; lyrics by B.G. DeSylva)

TAKE ME ALONG
October 22, 1959 (448)
Music and lyrics by Bob Merrill

Based on the play *Ah, Wilderness* by Eugene O'Neill

Oh, Please • I Would Die • Sid, Ol' Kid • Staying Young • I Get Embarrassed • We're Home • Take Me Along • For Sweet Charity • Pleasant Beach House • That's How It Starts • Promise Me a Rose • Little Green Snake • Nine o'Clock • But Yours

RA

TAKE THE AIR
November 22, 1927 (296)
Music by Dave Stamper
Lyrics by Gene Buck

All Aboard for Times Square • Silver Wings • The Wild and Woolly West • Carmela • Carmen Has Nothing on Me • Maybe I'll Baby You • We'll Have a New Home in the Morning (Music by Willard Robison; lyrics by J. Russel Robinson and Buck) • Take the Air • On a Pony for Two (Music by James

F. Hanley) • Lullaby • We'd Rather Dance Than Eat • Japanese Moon • Ham and Eggs in the Morning (Music by Con Conrad and Abner Silver; lyrics by Al Dubin)

TAKING MY TURN (OB)
June 9, 1983[1]
Music by Gary William Friedman
Lyrics by Will Holt

This Is My Song • Somebody Else • Fine for the Shape I'm In • Two of Me • Janet Get Up • I Like It • I Never Made Money From Music • Vivaldi • Do You Remember? • In April • Pick More Daisies • Taking Our Turn • Sweet Longings • I Am Not Old • The Kite • Good Luck to You • In the House • It Still Isn't Over

RA

[1] Still running December 31, 1983

TALES OF RIGO (Play with songs)
May 30, 1927 (8)
Music and lyrics by Ben Schwartz

I'll Tell You All Someday • In Romany • What Care We? • Little Princess • Zita • Rigo's Last Lullaby (Music and lyrics by Evelyn Adler)

TALK ABOUT GIRLS
June 14, 1927 (15)
Music by Harold Orlob
Lyrics by Irving Caesar

In Central Park • Come to Lower Falls • The Only Boy • Oo, How I Love You • Home Town • Talk About Girls (Music by Stephen Jones) • A Lonely Girl • Maybe I Will • In Twos • Sex Appeal • That's My Man • Nineteen Twenty-Seven • One Boy's Enough for Me

TALLULAH (OB)
October 30, 1983 (40)
Music by Arthur Siegel
Lyrics by Mae Richard

Darling • Tallulah • When I Do a Dance for You • Home Sweet Home • I've Got to Try Everything Once • You're You • I Can See Him Clearly • Tallulahbaloo • The Party Is Where I Am • Stay Awhile • It's a Hit • If Only He Were a Woman • Love Is on Its Knees • Don't Ever Book a Trip on the IRT • You Need a Lift! • I'm the Woman You Wanted

TANGERINE
August 9, 1921 (337)
Music by Monte Carlo and Alma Sanders
Lyrics by Howard Johnson

It's Great to Be Married • Love Is a Business • Isle of Tangerine • Listen to Me • In Our Mountain Bower • There's a Sunbeam for Every Drop of Rain • Man Is the Lord of It All (Music by Jean Schwartz) • South Sea Island Blues • Old Melodies • Tropic Vamps • It's Your Carriage That Counts • Civilization • Sweet Lady (Music by Frank Crumit and Dave Zoob) • She Was Very Dear to Me (Music and Lyrics by Ben Burt) • We'll Never Grow Old

THE TAP DANCE KID
December 21, 1983[1]
Music by Henry Krieger
Lyrics by Robert Lorick

Based on the novel *Nobody's Family Is Going to Change* by Louise Fitzhugh

Another Day • Four Strikes Against Me • Class Act • They Never Hear What I Say • Dancing Is Everything • Crosstown • Fabulous Feet • I Could Get Used to Him • Man in the Moon • Like Him • Someday • My Luck Is Changing • I Remember How It Was • Lullabye • Tap Tap • Dance if It Makes You Happy • William's Song

RA

[1] Still running December 31, 1983

TATTLE TALES
June 1, 1933 (28)

I'll Take an Option on You (Music by Ralph Rainger; lyrics by Leo Robin) • Harlem Lullaby (Music and lyrics by Willard Robison) • Hang Up Your Hat on Broadway (Music by Bernard Grossman; lyrics by Dave Sylvester) • Percy With Perseverance (Music by Edward Ward; lyrics by George Waggner) • The First Spring Day (Music by Howard Jackson; lyrics by Edward Eliscu) • Jig Saw Jamboree (Music by Eddie Bienbryer; lyrics by William Walsh) • Sing American Tunes (Music by Edward Ward; lyrics by Frank Fay and William Walsh) • Another Case of the Blues (Music by Richard Myers; lyrics by Johnny Mercer) • Just a Sentimental Tune (Music by Louis Alter; lyrics by Max and Nathaniel Lief)

TELL HER THE TRUTH
October 28, 1932 (11)
Music by Jack Waller and Joseph Tunbridge
Lyrics by R.P. Weston and Bert Lee

Based on the play *Nothing but the Truth* by James

Montgomery, adapted from a novel by Frederick Isham

Hoch, Caroline! • Happy the Day • Won't You Tell Me Why? • Sing, Brothers! • That's Fine • Tell Her the Truth • Horrortorio

TELL ME MORE[1]
April 13, 1925 (100)
Music by George Gershwin
Lyrics by B.G. DeSylva and Ira Gershwin

Tell Me More! • Mr. and Mrs. Sipkin • When the Debbies Go By • Three Times a Day • Why Do I Love You? • How Can I Win You Now? • Kickin' the Clouds Away • Love Is in the Air • My Fair Lady • In Sardinia • Baby! • The Poetry of Motion • Ukulele Lorelei

Dropped from production
Shop Girls and Mannikins • Once* • I'm Something on Avenue A • The He-Man

[1] The pre-Broadway title, "My Fair Lady," was dropped, presumably because it was not considered commercial.

TENDERLOIN
October 17, 1960 (216)
Music by Jerry Bock
Lyrics by Sheldon Harnick

Based on the novel by Samuel Hopkins Adams

Bless This Land • Little Old New York • Dr. Brock • Artificial Flowers • What's in It for You? • Reform • Tommy, Tommy • The Picture of Happiness • Dear Friend • The Army of the Just • How the Money Changes Hands • Good Clean Fun • My Miss Mary • My Gentle Young Johnny

Dropped from production
I Wonder What It's Like • Lovely Laurie

RA,SEL

TEXAS, LI'L DARLIN'
November 25, 1949 (293)
Music by Robert Emmett Dolan
Lyrics by Johnny Mercer

Whoopin' and a-Hollerin' • Texas, Li'l Darlin' • They Talk a Different Language • A Month of Sundays • Down in the Valley • Hootin' Owl Trail • The Big Movie Show in the Sky • Horseshoes Are Lucky • Love Me, Love My Dog • Take a Crank Letter • Politics • Ride 'Em, Cowboy • Affable, Balding Me • Whichaway'd They Go? • It's Great to Be Alive

RA

THAT 5 A.M. JAZZ (OB)
October 19, 1964 (94)
Music and lyrics by Will Holt

Some Sunday • Campaign Song • Gonna Get a Woman • The Happy Daze Saloon • The All-American Two-Step • Sweet Time • Nuevo Laredo • Those Were the Days

THERE YOU ARE
May 16, 1932 (8)
Music by William Heagney
Lyrics by William Heagney and Tom Connell

Haunting Refrain • There You Are • Lover's Holiday
• They All Love Me • Aces Up • Safe in Your Arms •
Love Lives On • More and More • The Sound of the
Drum • Wings of the Morning • The Love Potion •
Just a Little Penthouse and You • Carolita • Legend
of the Mission Bells

THEY'RE PLAYING OUR SONG
February 11, 1979 (1082)
Music by Marvin Hamlisch
Lyrics by Carole Bayer Sager

Fallin' • Workin' It Out • If He Really Knew Me •
They're Playing Our Song • Right • Just for Tonight
• When You're in My Arms • I Still Believe in Love •
Fill In the Words

RA,SEL

THE THIRD LITTLE SHOW
June 1, 1931 (136)

I'll Putcha Pitcha in the Paper (Music by Michael H.
Cleary; lyrics by Max and Nathaniel Lief) • Say the
Word (Music by Burton Lane; lyrics by Harold
Adamson) • Mad Dogs and Englishmen (Music and
lyrics by Noël Coward) • Falling in Love (Music by
Henry Sullivan; lyrics by Earle Crooker) • Going,
Going, Gone! (Music by Henry Sullivan; lyrics by
Edward Eliscu) • You Forgot Your Gloves (Music by
Ned Lehak; lyrics by Edward Eliscu) • I've Lost My
Heart (Music by Morris Hamilton; lyrics by Grace
Henry) • When Yuba Plays the Rumba on His Tuba
(Music and lyrics by Herman Hupfeld) • Sevilla
(Music by Ned Lehak; lyrics by Edward Eliscu) •
African Shrieks (Music by Ned Lehak; lyrics by
Edward Eliscu) • You Might as Well Pretend (Music
by Morgan Lewis; lyrics by Edward Eliscu and Ted
Fetter) • Little Geezer (Music by Michael H. Cleary;
lyrics by Max and Nathaniel Lief and Dave
Oppenheim) • Le Five o'Clock (Music by Will Irwin;
lyrics by Carl Randall) • Cinema Lorelei (Music by
Ned Lehak; lyrics by Edward Eliscu)

Dropped from production
Any Little Fish (Music and lyrics by Noël Coward)

13 DAUGHTERS
March 2, 1961 (28)
Music and lyrics by Eaton Magoon, Jr.

Kuli Kuli • House on the Hill • 13 Daughters • Paper
of Gold • Let-a-Go Your Heart • Alphabet Song •
Throw a Petal • When You Hear the Wind • Ka
Wahine Akamai • You Set My Heart to Music • 13
Old Maids • Nothing Man Cannot Do • Hoomalimali •
My Pleasure • Puka Puka Pants • My Hawaii • Hiiaka

RA

THIS IS THE ARMY
July 4, 1942 (113)
Music and lyrics by Irving Berlin

This Is the Army, Mr. Jones • I'm Getting Tired So I
Can Sleep • My Sergeant and I Are Buddies • I Left
My Heart at the Stage Door Canteen • The Army's
Made a Man Out of Me • That Russian Winter •
That's What the Well Dressed Man in Harlem Will
Wear • American Eagles • With My Head in the
Clouds • Aryans Under the Skin • How About a
Cheer for the Navy • What Does He Look Like? •
This Time • Oh, How I Hate to Get Up in the
Morning*

RA

THIS YEAR OF GRACE[1]
November 7, 1928 (157)
Music and lyrics by Noël Coward

Waiting in a Queue • Mary Make Believe • Lorelei • A
Room With a View* • Teach Me to Dance Like
Grandma • The Lido Beach • Little Women • English
Lido • Mother's Complaint • Britannia Rules the
Waves • Dance, Little Lady • Chauve Souris • World
Weary • Velasquez • Caballero

VS

[1] A rare instance of a revue written entirely—
music, lyrics, sketches—by one man, who also
starred in it (with Beatrice Lillie) on Broadway

THREE CHEERS
October 15, 1928 (210)
Music by Ray Henderson
Lyrics by B.G. DeSylva

The Americans Are Here • Lady Luck • Maybe This
Is Love • It's an Old Spanish Custom • Pompanola •
Because You're Beautiful • Bobby and Me • My
Silver Tree (Music by Raymond Hubbell; lyrics by
Anne Caldwell) • Gee, It's Great to Be Alive • Putting
on the Ritz • Two Boys • Let's All Sing the Lard
Song (Music by Leslie Sarony; lyrics by Anne
Caldwell) • Orange Blossom Home (Music by
Raymond Hubbell; lyrics by Anne Caldwell) • Happy
Hoboes

THREE LITTLE GIRLS
April 14, 1930 (104)
Music by Walter Kollo
Lyrics by Harry B. Smith

Love's Happy Dream • Whistle While You Work,
Boys • Letter Song • Annette • I'll Tell You • Cottage
in the Country • Doll Song • Waltz With Me • Love
Comes Once in a Lifetime (Music by Harold Stern
and Harry Perella; lyrics by Stella Unger) • Prince
Charming

THE THREE MUSKETEERS
March 13, 1928 (318)
Music by Rudolf Friml
Lyrics by P.G. Wodehouse and Clifford Grey

Based on the novel by Alexandre Dumas

Summer Time • All for One and One for All • The
"He" for Me • Gascony • Heart of Mine • Vesper Bell
• Dreams • March of the Musketeers • The Colonel

and the Major • Love Is the Sun • Your Eyes •
Welcome to the Queen • Red Wine • Ma Belle • A
Kiss Before I Go • My Sword • Queen of My Heart •
Ev'ry Little While

RA,VS

THREE TO MAKE READY
March 7, 1946 (323)
Music by Morgan Lewis
Lyrics by Nancy Hamilton

It's a Nice Night for It • Tell Me the Story • The Old
Soft Shoe • Barnaby Beach • Kenosha Canoe • If It's
Love • A Lovely Lazy Kind of Day • And Why Not I?
• Oh, You're a Wonderful Person

THREE TWINS
June 15, 1908 (288)
Music by Karl Hoschna
Lyrics by Otto Harbach

Based on the farce *Incog* by R. Pancheco

Summer Pastimes • All My Girls • Good Night,
Sweetheart, Good Night • Boo-Hoo, Tee-Hee, Ta-
Ha • Cuddle Up a Little Closer, Lovey Mine • We
Belong to Old Broadway • Little Miss Up-To-Date •
The Hypnotic Kiss • The Little Girl Up There • The
Yama-Yama Man (Lyrics by Collin Davis)*

VS

THREE WALTZES
December 25, 1937 (122)
Lyrics by Clare Kummer

Springtime Is in the Air (Music by Johann Straus I,
adapted by Oscar Straus) • My Heart Controls My
Head (Music by Johann Strauss I, adapted by
Oscar Straus) • Vienna Gossip (Music by Johann
Strauss I, adapted by Oscar Straus) • Do You
Recall? (Music by Johann Strauss I, adapted by
Oscar Straus) • To Love Is to Live (Music by
Johann Strauss II, adapted by Oscar Straus) • The
Only One (Music by Johann Strauss II, adapted by
Oscar Straus) • Paree (Music by Johann Strauss II,
adapted by Oscar Straus) • I'll Can-Can All Day
(Music by Johann Strauss II, adapted by Oscar
Straus) • Scandal (Music by Johann Strauss II,
adapted by Oscar Straus) • The History of Three
Generations of Chorus Girls (Music by Oscar
Straus) • Our Last Waltz Together (Music by Oscar
Straus) • I Sometimes Wonder (Music by Oscar
Straus) • The Days of Old (Music by Oscar Straus)

THREE WISHES FOR JAMIE
March 21, 1952 (94)
Music and lyrics by Ralph Blane

Based on the novel by Charles O'Neal

The Girl That I Court in My Mind • My Home's a
Highway • We're for Love • My Heart's Darlin' •
Goin' on a Hayride • Love Has Nothing to Do With
Looks (Lyrics by Charles Lederer) • I'll Sing You a
Song • It Must Be Spring • The Army Mule Song •
What Do I Know? • It's a Wishing World • April Face
• Trottin' to the Fair

RA

THE THREEPENNY OPERA[1] (OB)
March 10, 1954 (95)

September 20, 1955 (2,611)

Music by Kurt Weill
Lyrics by Marc Blitzstein

Mack the Knife* • Morning Anthem • Instead-of
Song • The Bide-a-Wee in Soho • Wedding Song •
Army Song • Love Song • Ballad of Dependency •
The World Is Mean • Polly's Song • Pirate Jenny •
Tango Ballad • Ballad of the Easy Life • Barbara
Song • Jealousy Duet • How to Survive • Useless
Song • Solomon Song • Call From the Grave • Death
Message • The Mounted Messenger

RA,VS

[1] An earlier version, with lyrics by Gifford
Cochran and Jerrold Krimsky, opened April 13,
1933 (12).

THREE'S A CROWD
October 15, 1930 (272)

Practising Up on You (Music by Philip Charig; lyrics
by Howard Dietz) • Something to Remember You
By (Music by Arthur Schwartz; lyrics by Howard
Dietz)* • Out in the Open Air (Music by Burton
Lane; lyrics by Howard Dietz) • Je t'Aime (Music by
Arthur Schwartz; lyrics by Howard Dietz) • Talkative
Toes (music by Vernon Duke; lyrics by Howard
Dietz) • All the King's Horses (Music and lyrics by
Alec Wilder, Eddie Brandt and Howard Dietz) • Body
and Soul (Music by John Green; lyrics by Edward
Heyman, Robert Sour and Frank Eyton) • The
Moment I Saw You (Music by Arthur Schwartz;
lyrics by Howard Dietz) • Forget All Your Books
(Music by Burton Lane; lyrics by Howard Dietz) •
Yaller (Music by Charles M. Schwab; lyrics by
Henry Myers) • Night After Night (Music by Arthur
Schwartz; lyrics by Howard Dietz) • Right at the
Start of It (Music by Arthur Schwartz; lyrics by
Howard Dietz)

RA

THROUGH THE YEARS[1]
January 28, 1932 (20)
Music by Vincent Youmans
Lyrics by Edward Heyman

Based on the play *Smilin' Through* by Allan
Langdon Martin and Jane Cowl

Kathleen, Mine • An Invitation • Kinda Like You • I'll
Come Back to You • How Happy Is the Bride • It's
Every Girl's Ambition • Through the Years* • The
Trumpeter and the Lover • You're Everywhere • The
Road to Home* • Drums in My Heart

[1] Deems Taylor wrote the orchestrations for
most of the score.

THUMBS UP!
December 27, 1934 (156)

Beautiful Night (Music and lyrics by Ballard

MacDonald, Karl Stark and James F. Hanley) • Zing, Went the Strings of My Heart (Music and Lyrics by James F. Hanley) • Lily Belle May June (Music by Henry Sullivan; lyrics by Earle Crooker) • Flamenco (Music by Henry Sullivan; lyrics by Earle Crooker) • Eileen Avourneen (Music by Henry Sullivan; lyrics by John Murray Anderson) • The Torch Singer (What Do You Think My Heart Is Made Of?) (Music by Henry Sullivan; lyrics by Earle Crooker) • My Arab Complex (Music by Henry Sullivan; lyrics by Ballard MacDonald) • Soldier of Love (Music by Gerald Marks; lyrics by Irving Caesar) • Color Blind (Music by Henry Sullivan; lyrics by Earle Crooker) • Continental Honeymoon (Music by James F. Hanley; lyrics by Ballard MacDonald and James F. Hanley) • A Taste of the Sea (Music by Henry Sullivan; lyrics by Earle Crooker) • Merrily We Waltz Along (Music by Henry Sullivan; lyrics by Earle Crooker) • I've Gotta See a Man About His Daughter (Music and lyrics by Jean Herbert, Karl Stark and James F. Hanley) • Autumn in New York (Music and lyrics by Vernon Duke)

TICKETS PLEASE
April 27, 1950 (245)
Music and lyrics by Joan Edwards and Lyn Duddy

Tickets Please (Music by Clay Warnick; lyrics by Mel Tolkin and Lucille Kallen) • Washington Square (Music by Clay Warnick; lyrics by Mel Tolkin and Lucille Kallen) • Darn it, Baby, That's Love • Restless • You Can't Take It With You • Back at the Palace (Music by Clay Warnick; lyrics by Mel Tolkin and Lucille Kallen) • The Moment I Looked in Your Eyes • Maha Rogor (Music by Clay Warnick; lyrics by Mel Tolkin and Lucille Kallen)

A TIME FOR SINGING
May 21, 1966 (41)
Music by John Morris
Lyrics by Gerald Freedman

Based on the novel *How Green Was My Valley* by Richard Llewellyn

Come You Men • How Green Was My Valley • Old Long John • Here Come Your Men • What a Good Day Is Saturday • Peace Come to Every Heart • Someone Must Try • Oh, How I Adore Your Name • That's What Young Ladies Do • When He Looks at Me • Far From Home • I Wonder If • What a Party • Let Me Love You • Why Would Anyone Want to Get Married? • A Time for Singing • When the Baby Comes • I'm Always Wrong • There Is Beautiful You Are • Three Ships • Tell Her • And the Mountains Sing Back • Gone in Sorrow

RA

TIME REMEMBERED (Play with two songs)
November 12, 1957 (247)
Music and lyrics by Vernon Duke

Ages Ago • Time Remembered

TIP-TOES
December 28, 1925 (192)
Music by George Gershwin
Lyrics by Ira Gershwin

Waiting for the Train • Nice Baby! (Come to Papa!) • Looking for a Boy • Lady Luck • When Do We Dance? • These Charming People* • That Certain Feeling • Sweet and Low-Down* • Our Little Captain • Harbor of Dreams • Nightie-Night • Tip-Toes • It's a Great Little World

Dropped from production
Harbor of Dreams • Harlem River Chanty • Gather Ye Rosebuds • Dancing Hour • Life's Too Short to Be Blue • We

RA

TIS OF THEE
October 26, 1940 (1)

You've Got Something to Sing About (Music by Al Moss; lyrics by Alfred Hayes) • Lupe (Music by Alex North; lyrics by Alfred Hayes) • What's Mine Is Thine (Music by Al Moss; lyrics by Alfred Hayes) • Brooklyn Cantata* (Music by George Kleinsinger; lyrics by Mike Stratton) • After Tonight (Music by Al Moss; lyrics by Alfred Hayes) • Noises in the Street (Music by Richard Lewine; lyrics by David Greggory and Peter Barry)* • Tis of Thee (Music by Alex North; lyrics by Alfred Hayes) • The Lady (Music by Elsie Peters; lyrics by Alfred Hayes) • The Rhythm Is Red an' White an' Blue (Music by Al Moss; lyrics by David Greggory) • Tomorrow (Music by Alex North; lyrics by Alfred Hayes)

TO LIVE ANOTHER SUMMER
October 21, 1971 (173)
Music by Dov Seltzer
Lyrics by David Paulsen

Son of Man (Lyrics by David Axelrod) • The Sacrifice • What Are the Basic Things? (Lyrics by Lillian Burstein) • The Grove of Eucalyptus (Music by Naomi Shemer; lyrics by George Sherman) • The Boy With the Fiddle (Music by Alexander Argov) • Can You Hear My Voice? (Music by Samuel Kraus; lyrics by George Sherman) • Mediteranee • When My Man Returns (Music by George Moustaki) • Better Days • To Live Another Summer, to Pass Another Winter • Noah's Ark (Music by Naomi Shemer) • Don't Destroy the World • Give Shalom and Sabbath to Jerusalem • Sorry We Won (Music by David Krivoshei) • I'm Alive (Music by David Kriovshei) • Give Me a Star (Music by David Krivoshei)

RA,SEL

'TOINETTE (OB)
November 20, 1961 (31)
Music and lyrics by Deed Meyer

Based on *Le Malade Imaginaire* by Molière

Rags • Bonjour • Come On Outside and Get Some Air • Why Shouldn't I? • A Father Speaks • A Lullaby

• Honest Honore • Someone to Count On • Un, Deux, Trois • Fly Away • 'Toinette • Madly in Love With You Am I • Beat, Little Pulse • Even a Doctor Can Make a Mistake • Dr. Iatro • Small Apartment • You're the Most Impossible Person

TOMFOOLERY (OB)
December 14, 1981 (120)
Music and lyrics by Tom Lehrer

Be Prepared • Poisoning Pigeons • I Wanna Go Back to Dixie • My Home Town • Pollution • Bright College Days • Fight Fiercely, Harvard • The Elements • The Folk Song Army • In Old Mexico • She's My Girl • When You Are Old and Grey • Wernher von Braun • Who's Next? • I Got It From Agnes • National Brotherhood Week • So Long Mom • Send the Marines • Hunting Song • Irish Ballad • New Math • Silent E • Oedipus Rex • I Hold Your Hand in Mine • Masochism Tango • The Old Dope Peddler • The Vatican Rag • We Will All Go Together

TONIGHT AT 8:30
November 24, 1936 (118)
Music and lyrics by Noël Coward

Three triple bills of one-act plays. Those with songs are listed below.
We Were Dancing: We Were Dancing
Shadow Play: Then • You Were There • Play, Orchestra, Play!
Red Peppers: Has Anybody Seen Our Ship? • Men About Town
Family Album: Here's a Toast • Princes and Princesses • Let's Play a Tune on the Music Box • Hearts and Flowers

RA

TOO MANY GIRLS
October 18, 1939 (249)
Music by Richard Rodgers
Lyrics by Lorenz Hart

Heroes in the Fall • Tempt Me Not • My Prince • Pottawatomie • 'Cause We Got Cake • Love Never Went to College • Spic and Spanish • I Like to Recognize the Tune • Look Out • The Sweethearts of the Team • She Could Shake the Maracas • I Didn't Know What Time It Was • Too Many Girls • Give It Back to the Indians

Added to film version (1940)
You're Nearer

RA

TOOT-TOOT!
March 11, 1918 (40)
Music by Jerome Kern
Lyrics by Berton Braley

Adapted from the farce *Excuse Me* by Rupert Hughes

Toot-Toot! • Runaway Colts • Kan the Kaiser • Every

Girl in All America • Shower of Rice • Let's Go • It's Greek to Me • The Last Long Mile* (Music and lyrics by Emil Breitenfeld) • When You Wake Up Dancing • Girlie • Smoke • Cute Soldier Boy (Music by Anatol Friedland) • It's Immaterial to Me • If You Only Cared Enough • Indian Fox Trot

TOP BANANA
November 1, 1951 (350)
Music and lyrics by Johnny Mercer

The Man of the Year This Week • You're So Beautiful That— • Top Banana • Elevator Song • Hail to MacCracken's • Only if You're in Love • My Home Is in My Shoes • I Fought Every Step of the Way • O.K. for T.V. • Slogan Song • Meet Miss Blendo • Sans Souci • A Dog Is a Man's Best Friend • That's for Sure • A Word a Day • Be My Guest

RA

TOP SPEED
December 25, 1929 (102)
Music by Harry Ruby
Lyrics by Bert Kalmar

In the Summer • The Papers • Try Dancing • I Like to Be Liked • Keep Your Undershirt On • We Want You • Goodness Gracious • I'll Know and She'll Know • What Would I Care • Dizzy Feet • On the Border Line • Hot and Bothered • Sweeter Than You* • Reaching for the Moon • You Couldn't Blame Me for That • Fireworks

TOPLITZKY OF NOTRE DAME
December 26, 1946 (60)
Music by Sammy Fain
Lyrics by George Marion, Jr.

Let Us Gather at the Goal Line • Baby, Let's Face It • I Wanna Go to City College • Love Is a Random Thing • Common Sense • A Slight Case of Ecstasy • Wolf Time • McInerney's Farm • You Are My Downfall • All American Man

TOUCH (OB)
November 8, 1970 (422)
Music by Kenn Long and Jim Crozier
Lyrics by Kenn Long

Declaration • Windchild (Music and lyrics by Gary Graham) • City Song • Sitting in the Park • I Don't Care • Goodbyes • Come to the Road • Reaching, Touching • Guiness, Woman • Susan's Song • Maxine! • Quiet Country • Tripping • Garden Song • Watching • Hasseltown • Confrontation Song • Alphagenesis

RA

TOUCH AND GO
October 13, 1949 (176)
Music by Jay Gorney
Lyrics by Jean and Walter Kerr

An Opening for Everybody • This Had Better Be Love • American Primitive • Highbrow, Lowbrow •

Easy Does It • Be a Mess • Broadway Love Song • It'll Be All Right in a Hundred Years • Wish Me Luck • Under the Sleeping Volcano • Men of the Water-Mark • Mr. Brown, Miss Dupree • Miss Platt Selects Mate

TOVARICH
March 18, 1963 (264)
Music by Lee Pockriss
Lyrics by Anne Croswell

Based on the comedy by Jacques Deval

Nitchevo • I Go to Bed • You'll Make an Elegant Butler (Music and lyrics by Joan Javits and Philip Springer) • Stuck With Each Other • Say You'll Stay • You Love Me • That Face • Wilkes-Barre, Pa. • No! No! No! • A Small Cartel • It Used to Be • Kukla Katusha • Make a Friend • The Only One • Uh-Oh! • Managed • I Know the Feeling • All for You • Grade Polonaise

RA

TREASURE GIRL
November 8, 1928 (68)
Music by George Gershwin
Lyrics by Ira Gershwin

Skull and Bones • I've Got a Crush on You* • Oh, So Nice • According to Mr. Grimes • Place in the Country • K-ra-zy for You • I Don't Think I'll Fall in Love Today • Got a Rainbow • Feeling I'm Falling • What Are We Here For? • Where's the Boy? Here's the Girl! • What Causes That?

Dropped from production
This Particular Party • Treasure Island • Goodbye to the Old Love, Hello to the New • A-Hunting We Will Go • Dead Men Tell No Tales • I Want to Marry a Marionette

RA

A TREE GROWS IN BROOKLYN
April 19, 1951 (270)
Music by Arthur Schwartz
Lyrics by Dorothy Fields

Based on the novel by Betty Smith

Payday • Mine 'til Monday • Make the Man Love Me • I'm Like a New Broom • Look Who's Dancing • Love Is the Reason • If You Haven't Got a Sweetheart • I'll Buy You a Star • That's How It Goes • He Had Refinement • Growing Pains • Is That My Prince? • Don't Be Afraid

RA

TREEMONISHA[1]
October 21, 1975 (64)
Music and lyrics by Scott Joplin

The Bag of Luck • The Corn-Huskers • We're Goin' Around • The Wreath • The Sacred Tree • Surprise • Treemonisha's Bringing Up • Good Advice • Confusion • Superstition • Treemonisha in Peril • The Wasp Nest • The Rescue • We Will Rest Awhile

• Going Home • Aunt Dinah Has Blowed de Horn • I Want to See My Child • Treemonisha's Return • Wrong Is Never Right • Abuse • When Villains Ramble Far and Near • Conjuror's Forgiven • We Will Trust You as Our Leader • A Real Slow Drag

RA,VS,SEL

[1] Written in 1909 and published in 1911.

TRIXIE TRUE TEEN DETECTIVE (OB)
December 4, 1980 (86)
Music and lyrics by Kelly Hamilton

Trixie's on the Case! • This Is Indeed My Lucky Day • Most Popular and Most Likely to Succeed • Mr. and Mrs. Dick Dickerson • Juvenile Fiction • A Katzenjammer Kinda Song • You Haven't Got Time for Love • In Cahoots • The Mystery of the Moon • The Secret of the Tapping Shoes • Rita From Argentina • Trixie True Teen Detective

TUSCALOOSA'S CALLING ME BUT I'M NOT GOING! (OB)
December 1, 1975 (429)
Music by Hank Beebe
Lyrics by Bill Heyer

Only Right Here in New York City • I Dig Myself • Cold Cash • Things Were Out • Central Park on a Sunday Afternoon • New York From the Air • The Old Man • Backwards • Delicatessen • Out of Towner • Everything You Hate Is Right Here • Suburban Fugue • Purse Snatch • Poor • Grafitti • Singles Bar • New York '69 • Tuscaloosa's Calling Me, But I'm Not Going

RA

TWIGS (Play with one song)
November 14, 1971 (289)
Music and lyrics by Stephen Sondheim

Hollywood and Vine

TWINKLE TWINKLE
November 16, 1926 (167)
Music by Harry Archer
Lyrics by Harlan Thompson

You Know, I Know • Get a Load of This • We're on the Map (Music by Harry Ruby; lyrics by Bert Kalmar) • Reuben • Twinkle Twinkle • Hustle, Bustle • Sweeter Than You (Music by Harry Ruby; lyrics by Bert Kalmar)* • Crime • Sunday Afternoon • Whistle (Music by Harry Ruby; lyrics by Bert Kalmar) • I Hate to Talk About Myself • When We're Bride and Groom

TWO BY TWO
November 10, 1970 (343)
Music by Richard Rodgers
Lyrics by Martin Charnin

Based on the play *The Flowering Peach* by Clifford Odets

Why Me? • Put Him Away • The Gitka's Song • Something, Somewhere • You Have Got to Have a

Rudder on the Ark • Something Doesn't Happen • An Old Man • Ninety Again! • Two by Two • I Do Not Know a Day I Did Not Love You • When It Dries • You • The Golden Ram • Poppa Knows Best • As Far as I'm Concerned • Hey, Girlie • The Covenant

Dropped from production
Everything That's Gonna Be Has Been • Getting Married to a Person • Forty Nights • The Death of Me • I Can't Complain • Without My Money

RA,VS,SEL

TWO FOR THE SHOW
February 8, 1940 (124)
Music by Morgan Lewis
Lyrics by Nancy Hamilton

Calypso Joe • This Merry Christmas • That Terrible Tune • The All-Girl Band • Where Do You Get Your Greens? • At Last It's Love • Fool for Luck • How High the Moon • A House With a Little Red Barn

TWO FOR TONIGHT (OB)
December 28, 1939 (30)

Slap on the Greasepaint (Music by Berenice Kazounoff; lyrics by John Latouche) • Personal Heaven (Music and lyrics by Eugene and Ralph Berton) • Could You Use a New Friend? (Music and lyrics by Eugene and Ralph Berton) • Call of the Wild (Music by Berenice Kazounoff; lyrics by Sylvia Marks) • Masquerade (Music and lyrics by Charles Herbert) • Windows (Music and lyrics by Eugene and Ralph Berton) • Nursery (Music and lyrics by Charles Herbert) • Five O'Clock (Music by Bernie Wayne; lyrics by Ben Raleigh) • Dancing Alone (Music and lyrics by Ralph and Eugene Berton) • Blues (Music and lyrics by John Latouche) • Home Is Where You Hang Your Hat (Music by Berenice Kazounoff; lyrics by John Latouche) • Blasé (Music by Berenice Kazounoff; lyrics by John Latouche)

TWO GENTLEMEN OF VERONA
December 1, 1971 (613)
Music by Galt MacDermot
Lyrics by John Guare

Based on the play by Shakespeare

Summer, Summer • I Love My Father • That's a Very Interesting Question • I'd Like to Be a Rose • Thou, Julia, Thou Has Metamorphosed Me • Symphony • I Am Not Interested in Love • Love, Is That You? • Thou, Proteus, Thou Has Metamorphosed Me • What Does a Lover Pack? • Pearls • Two Gentlemen of Verona • Follow the Rainbow • Where's North? • Bring All the Boys Back Home • Love's Revenge • To Whom It May Concern Me • Night Letter • Calla Lily Lady • Land of Betrayal • Hot Lover • What a Nice Idea • Who Is Sylvia? • Love Me • Eglamour • Kidnapped • Mansion • What's

a Nice Girl Like Her • Don't Have the Baby • Milkmaid • Love Has Driven Me Sane

RA,VS,SEL

TWO LITTLE GIRLS IN BLUE[1]
May 3, 1921 (135)
Music by Vincent Youmans
Lyrics by Arthur Francis

We're Off on a Wonderful Trip (Music by Youmans and Paul Lannin) • Your Wonderful U.S.A. (Music by Paul Lannin) • When I'm With the Girls • Two Little Girls • The Silly Season (Music by Youmans and Paul Lannin) • Oh Me, Oh My, Oh You • You Started Something* • We're Off to India (Music by Youmans and Paul Lannin) • Here, Steward (Music by Youmans and Paul Lannin) • The Gypsy Trail (Music by Youmans and Paul Lannin) • Dolly (Lyrics by Francis and Schuyler Greene) • Who's Who With You? • Just Like You (Music by Paul Lannin) • There's Something About Me They Like (Lyrics by Francis and Fred Jackson) • Rice and Shoes (Lyrics by Francis and Schuyler Greene) • She's Innocent (Music by Youmans and Paul Lannin) • Honeymoon (Music by Paul Lannin) • I'm Tickled Silly (Music by Youmans and Paul Lannin) • Orienta (Music by Youmans and Paul Lannin)

[1] George Gershwin was originally asked to write this score. Having another commitment, he recommended the young (actually one day younger than Gershwin) Vincent Youmans. For the lyrics he suggested his brother Ira, then writing as Arthur Francis, a name derived from his brother Arthur and sister Frances. For both this was a first complete score.

TWO ON THE AISLE
July 19, 1951 (279)
Music by Jule Styne
Lyrics by Betty Comden and Adolph Green

Show Train • Here She Comes Now • If You Hadn't, but You Did • Catch Our Act at the Met • Everlasting • Give a Little, Get a Little • How Will He Know? • Hold Me—Hold Me—Hold Me

RA

TWO'S COMPANY
December 15, 1952 (91)
Music by Vernon Duke
Lyrics by Ogden Nash

The Theatre Is a Lady • Turn Me Loose on Broadway • It Just Occurred to Me (Lyrics by Sammy Cahn) • Baby Couldn't Dance • A Man's Home (Music and lyrics by Sheldon Harnick) • Roundabout • Roll Along, Sadie • Out of the Clear Blue Sky • Esther (Lyrics by Sammy Cahn) • Haunted Hot Spot • Purple Rose • Just Like a Man

RA

U

UNDER THE COUNTER
October 3, 1947 (27)
Music by Manning Sherwin
Lyrics by Harold Purcell

Everywhere • No One's Tried to Kiss Me • The Moment I Saw You • Let's Get Back to Glamour • Ai Yi Yi

UNFAIR TO GOLIATH (OB)
January 25, 1970 (73)
Music by Menachem Zur
Lyrics by Herbert Appleman

The Danger of Peace Is Over • In the Reign of Chaim • What Kind of Baby • A Parking Meter Like Me • The Sabra • The Famous Rabbi • When Moses Spake to Goldstein • The Rooster and the Hen • What Abraham Lincoln Once Said • The Song of Sallah Shabeti

THE UNSINKABLE MOLLY BROWN
November 3, 1960 (532)
Music and lyrics by Meredith Willson

I Ain't Down Yet • Belly Up to the Bar, Boys • I've A'ready Started In • I'll Never Say No • My Own Brass Bed • The Denver Police • Beautiful People of Denver • Are You Sure? • Happy Birthday, Mrs. J.J. Brown • Bon Jour • If I Knew • Chick-a-Pen • Keep-a-Hoppin' • Up Where the People Are • Dolce Far Niente

RA,VS,SEL

UP FROM PARADISE (OB)
October 25, 1983 (24)
Music by Stanley Silverman
Lyrics by Arthur Miller

Based on the play *The Creation of the World and Other Business* by Arthur Miller.

The Lord Is a Hammer of Light • How Fine It Is • When Night Starts to Fall • Bone of Thy Bones • Hallelujah • The Center of Your Mind • It's Just Like I Was You • But if Something Leads to Good • I'm Me, We're Us • Curses • Lonely Quartet • How Lovely Is Eve • I Am the River • All of That Made for Me • As Good as Paradise • It Was So Peaceful Before There Was Man • It Comes to Me • I Don't Know What Is Happening to Me • All Love • Passion • Nothing's Left of God • I Know He Wants Us to Praise His Mornings

UP IN CENTRAL PARK
January 27, 1945 (504)
Music by Sigmund Romberg
Lyrics by Dorothy Fields

Up From the Gutter • Carousel in the Park • It Doesn't Cost You Anything to Dream • Boss Tweed • When She Walks in the Room • Currier and Ives • Close as Pages in a Book • Rip Van Winkle • The Fireman's Bride • When the Party Gives a Party • The Big Back Yard • April Snow • The Birds and the Bees

RA

UP SHE GOES[1]
November 6, 1922 (256)
Music by Harry Tierney
Lyrics by Joseph McCarthy

The Visitors • Takes a Heap o' Love • Journey's End • Let's Kiss and Make Up • Nearing the Day • Bob About a Bit • Tie-Up • Roof Tree • The Strike • Lady Luck, Smile on Me • We'll Do the Riviera • Settle Down, Travel Around • Up With the Stars • Up She Goes

[1] Adapted by Frank Craven from his 1914 comedy *Too Many Cooks*, in which he played the lead.

UPS-A-DAISY
October 8, 1928 (40)
Music by Lewis E. Gensler
Lyrics by Robert A. Simon

Ups-a-Daisy • Great Little Guy • Oh, How Happy

We'll Be (Lyrics by Simon and Clifford Grey) • I've Got a Baby • Tell Me Who You Are • Will You Remember? Will You Forget? (Lyrics by Simon and Clifford Grey) • Oh, How I Miss You Blues (Lyrics by Simon and Clifford Grey) • Sweet One • Sweetest of the Roses • Hot

Dropped from production
I Can't Believe It's True

UPSTAIRS AT O'NEAL'S (OB)
October 28, 1982 (308)

Upstairs at O'Neal's (Music and lyrics by Martin Charnin) • Stools (Music and lyrics by Martin Charnin) • Cancun (Music and lyrics by John Forster and Michael Leeds) • Something (Music and lyrics by Douglas Bernstein and Denis Markell) • I Furnished My One Room Apartment (Music by Stephen Hoffman; lyrics by Michael Mooney) • Soap Operetta (Music by Seth Friedman; lyrics by David L. Crane, Seth Friedman and Marta Kauffman) • The Ballad of Cy and Beatrice (Music by Paul Trueblood; lyrics by Jim Morgan) • Signed, Peeled and Delivered (Music and lyrics by Ronald Melrose)

• The Feet (Music by Seth Friedman; lyrics by David L. Crane, Seth Friedman and Marta Kauffman) • The Soldier and the Washerworker (Music and lyrics by Ronald Melrose) • Cover Girls (Music by Seth Friedman; lyrics by David L. Crane, Seth Friedman and Marta Kauffman) • All I Can Do Is Cry (Music and lyrics by Sarah Weeks and Michael Abbott) • Momma's Turn (Music and lyrics by Douglas Bernstein and Denis Markell) • Boy, Do We Need It Now (Music and lyrics by Charles Strouse)

RA

THE UTTER GLORY OF MORRISSEY HALL
May 13, 1979 (1)
Music and lyrics by Clark Gesner

Promenade • Proud, Erstwhile, Upright, Fair • Elizabeth's Song • Way Back When • Lost • Morning • The Letter • Oh Sun • Give Me That Key • You Will Know When the Time Has Arrived • You Would Say • See the Blue • Reflection

RA

V

THE VAGABOND KING
September 21, 1925 (511)
Music by Rudolf Friml
Lyrics by Brian Hooker

Based on the play *If I Were King* by Justin Huntly McCarthy

Love for Sale • Drinking Song • Song of the Vagabonds • Some Day • Only a Rose • Hunting • Scotch Archer's Song • Tomorrow • Nocturne • Serenade • Huguette Waltz • Love Me Tonight

RA,VS,SEL

Added to film version (1930)
If I Were King (Music and lyrics by Newell Chase, Leo Robin and Sam Coslow)

Added to film version (1956)
This Same Heart (Music by Friml; lyrics by Johnny Burke) • Vive la You (Music by Friml; lyrics by Johnny Burke) • Bon Jour (Music by Friml; lyrics by Johnny Burke)

VALMOUTH (OB)
October 6, 1960 (14)
Music and lyrics by Sandy Wilson

Based on the novel by Ronald Firbank

Valmouth • Magic Fingers • Mustapha • I Loved a Man • All the Girls Were Pretty • What Do I Want With Love? • Just Once More • Lady of the Manor • Big Best Shoes • Niri-Esther • Cry of the Peacock • Little Girl Baby • The Cathedral of Clemenza • Only a Passing Phase • Where the Trees Are Green With Parrots • My Talking Day • I Will Miss You • Pinpipi's Sob of Love

RA

THE VAMP
November 10, 1955 (60)
Music by James Mundy
Lyrics by John Latouche

The Spiel • The Flickers • Keep Your Nose to the Grindstone • That's Where a Man Fits In • I've Always Loved You • You're Colossal • Fan Club Chant • Have You Met Delilah? • Yeemy Yeemy • The Vamps • Four Little Misfits • Samson and Delilah • Why Does It Have to Be You? • Ragtime Romeo • I'm Everybody's Baby • The Impossible She

THE VANDERBILT REVUE
November 5, 1930 (13)
Music by Jimmy McHugh
Lyrics by Dorothy Fields

Button Up Your Heart • Cut In • Blue Again • Ex-Gigolo (Music by Mario Braggiotti; lyrics by E.Y. Harburg) • Then Came the War (Music and lyrics by Ben Black) • I'm From Granada (Music by Mario Braggiotti; lyrics by David Sidney) • What's My Man Gonna Be Like? (Music and lyrics by Cole Porter) • Better Not Try It (Music and lyrics by Michael H. Cleary, Herb Magidson and Ned Washington) • I Give Myself Away (Music by Jacques Fray; lyrics by Edward Eliscu) • You're the Better Half of Me • Half Way to Heaven (Music by Mario Braggiotti; lyrics by David Sidney)

VERY GOOD EDDIE
December 23, 1915 (341)
Music by Jerome Kern

We're on Our Way (Lyrics by Schuyler Greene) • The Same Old Game (Music and Lyrics by Mellor, Gifford and Godfrey) • Some Sort of Somebody* (Lyrics by Elsie Janis) • Isn't It Great to be Married (Lyrics by Schuyler Greene) • Wedding Bells Are Calling Me (Lyrics by Harry B. Smith) • On the Shore at Le Lei Wi (Music by Henry Kailimai and Jerome Kern; lyrics by Herbert Reynolds) • If I Find the Girl (Lyrics by John E. Hazzard and Herbert Reynolds) • The Triangle (Lyrics by Guy Bolton) • Thirteen Collar (Lyrics by Schuyler Greene) • Old Boy Neutral (Lyrics by Schuyler Greene) • Babes in the Wood (Lyrics by Kern and Schuyler Greene) •

I'd Like to Have a Million in the Bank (Lyrics by Herbert Reynolds and John E. Hazzard) • Nodding Roses* (Lyrics by Schuyler Greene and Herbert Reynolds)

Dropped from production
I've Got to Dance* (Lyrics by Schuyler Greene)
RA,VS

VERY WARM FOR MAY
November 17, 1939 (59)
Music by Jerome Kern
Lyrics by Oscar Hammerstein II

In Other Words, Seventeen • All the Things You Are* • Heaven in My Arms (Music in My Heart) • That Lucky Fellow • In the Heart of the Dark • All in Fun

Dropped from production
Me and the Role and You • High Up in Harlem

RA

VIA GALACTICA
November 28, 1972 (7)
Music by Galt MacDermot
Lyrics by Christopher Gore

Via Galactica • We Are One • Helen of Troy • Oysters • The Other Side of the Sky • Children of the Sun • Different • Take Your Hat Off • Ilmar's Tomb • Shall We Friend? • The Lady Isn't Looking • Hush • Cross On Over • The Gospel of Gabriel Finn • Terre Haute High • Life Wins • The Great Forever Wagon • The Worm Germ • Isaac's Equation • Dance the Dark Away • Four Hundred Girls Ago • All My Good Mornings • Children of the Sun • New Jerusalem

VINTAGE '60 (OB)
September 12, 1960 (8)
The Time Is Now (Music by Mark Bucci; lyrics by David Rogers) • All American (Music by David Baker; lyrics by Sheldon Harnick) • Down in the Streets (Music and lyrics by Tommy Garlock and Alan Jeffreys) • Do It in Two (Music and lyrics by Jack Wilson and Alan Jeffreys) • Dublin Town (Music and lyrics by Fred Ebb, Paul Klein and Lee Goldsmith) • Forget Me (Music by David Baker; lyrics by Sheldon Harnick) • Afraid of Love (Music and lyrics by Alice Clark and David Morton)

VIRGINIA
September 2, 1937 (60)
Music by Arthur Schwartz
Lyrics by Albert Stillman

Virginia • We Had to Rehearse • An Old Flame Never Dies (Lyrics by Stillman and Laurence Stallings) • Send One Angel Down • My Bridal Gown (Lyrics by Stillman and Laurence Stallings) • Good and Lucky • It's Our Duty to the King • If You Were Someone Else • Goodbye, Jonah • My Heart Is Dancing • Meet Me at the Fair • You and I Know (Lyrics by Stillman and Laurence Stallings) • Fee-Fie-Fo-Fum • I'll Be Sittin' in de Lap o' de Lord

VIVA O'BRIEN
October 9, 1941 (20)
Music by Maria Grever
Lyrics by Raymond Leveen

Mozambamba • Don José O'Brien • Mood of the Moment • Mexican Bad Men • Carinito • Broken-Hearted Romeo • Wrap Me in Your Serape • Yucatana • Our Song • El Matador Terrifico • How Long? • To Prove My Love

WAKE UP AND DREAM
December 30, 1929 (136)
Music and lyrics by Cole Porter

Wake Up and Dream • She's Such a Comfort to Me
(Music by Arthur Schwartz; lyrics by Douglas
Furber, Max and Nathaniel Lief, and Donovan
Parsons) • I Loved Him but He Didn't Love Me •
More Incredible Happenings (Music and lyrics by
Ronald Jeans) • Fancy Our Meeting (Music by
Joseph Meyer and Philip Charig; lyrics by Douglas
Furber) • The Banjo That Man Joe Plays • I'm a
Gigolo • Agua Sincopada Tango • Looking at You •
What Is This Thing Called Love? • I Dream of a Girl
in a Shawl • I Want to Be Raided by You • Why
Wouldn't I Do? (Music by Ivor Novello; lyrics by Ivor
Novello and Desmond Carter)

WALK A LITTLE FASTER
December 7, 1932 (119)
Music by Vernon Duke
Lyrics by E.Y. Harburg

That's Life • Unaccustomed As I Am • Off Again, On
Again • April in Paris* • A Penny for Your Thoughts
• Where Have We Met Before? • Frisco Fanny
(Music by Henry Sullivan; lyrics by Earl Crooker) •
So Nonchalant • Time and Tide • Mayfair (Music by
William Waliter; lyrics by Rowland Leigh) • Speaking
of Love • End of a Perfect Night

WALK DOWN MAH STREET! (OB)
June 12, 1968 (135)
Music by Norman Curtis
Lyrics by Patricia Taylor Curtis

We're Today • Walk Down My Street • If You Want
to Get Ahead • Just One More Time • I'm Just a
Statistic • Someday, if We Grow Up • What
Shadows We Are • Want to Get Retarded? • Teeny
Bopper • Flower Child • For Four Hundred Years •
Don't Have to Take It Any More • Lonely Girl • Clean
Up Your Own Backyard • Walk, Lordy, Walk

WALK WITH MUSIC
June 4, 1940 (55)

Music by Hoagy Carmichael
Lyrics by Johnny Mercer

Greetings, Gates • Today I Am a Glamour Girl •
Even If I Say It Myself • I Walk With Music • Ooh!
What You Said • Everything Happens to Me • Wait
Till You See Me in the Morning • Break It Up,
Cinderella • Smile for the Press • Friend of the
Family • Way Back in 1939 A.D. • How Nice for Me •
The Rhumba Jumps • What'll They Think of Next?

WALKING HAPPY
November 26, 1966 (161)
Music by Jimmy Van Heusen
Lyrics by Sammy Cahn

Based on the play *Hobson's Choice* by Harold
Brighouse

Think of Something Else • Where Was I? • How D'ya
Talk to a Girl? • Clog and Grog • If I Be Your Best
Chance • A Joyful Thing • What Makes It Happen? •
Use Your Noggin • You're Right, You're Right • I'll
Make a Man of the Man • Walking Happy • I Don't
Think I'm in Love • Such a Sociable Sort • It Might
as Well Be Her • People Who Are Nice

RA,SEL

A WALTZ DREAM
January 27, 1908 (111)
Music by Oscar Straus
Lyrics by Joseph W. Herbert

A Soldier Stole Her Love • Love Cannot Be Bought
• A Husband's Love • The Family's Ancient Tree •
Love's Roundelay • My Dearest Love • Kissing Time
• Life Is Love and Laughter • Sweetest Maid of All •
Lesson in Love • Piccolo • When the Song of Love
Is Heard • I Love and the World Is Mine • Two Is
Plenty • Vienna (Music by Jerome Kern; lyrics by
Adrian Ross) • I'd Rather Stay at Home (Music by
Jerome Kern; lyrics by C. H. Bovill)

RA,VS

WALTZ OF THE STORK (OB)
January 15, 1982 (160)
Music and lyrics by Melvin Van Peebles

There • And I Love You • The Apple Stretching • Tender Understanding (Music and lyrics by Ted Hayes) • Mother's Prayer • My Love Belongs to You • Weddings and Funerals (Music and lyrics by Mark Barkan) • One Hundred and Fifteen • Play It as It Lays • Shoulders to Lean On

WANTED (OB)
January 19, 1972 (79)
Music and lyrics by Al Carmines

I Am the Man • Where Have You Been Up to Now? • Outlaw Man • Who's on Our Side? (Lyrics by Carmines and David Epstein) • Parasol Lady • Jailhouse Blues • I Want to Ride With You (Lyrics by Carmines and David Epstein) • You Do This • Guns Are Fun • I Do the Best I Can (Lyrics by Carmines and David Epstein) • Wahoo! • Whispering to You • I Want to Blow Up the World • The Indian Benefit Ball • The Lord Is My Light (Lyrics by Carmines and David Epstein) • It's Love • As I'm Growing Older

WATCH YOUR STEP
December 8, 1914 (175)
Music and lyrics by Irving Berlin

Office Hours • Lead Me to Love • The Dancing Teacher • The Minstrel Parade • Around the Town • They Always Follow Me Around • Show Us How to Do the Fox-trot • When I Discovered You • The Syncopated Walk • Metropolitan Nights • I Love to Have the Boys Around Me • Settle Down in a One-Horse Town • Chatter Chatter • Homeward Bound • Play a Simple Melody

THE WELL OF ROMANCE
November 7, 1930 (8)
Music by H. Maurice Jacquet
Lyrics by Preston Sturges

At Lovetime • The Well of Romance • Be Oh So Careful, Ann • Hail the King • Dream of Dreams • Since You're Alone • How Can You Tell? • I'll Never Complain • Fare Thee Well • One Night • Rhapsody of Love • For You and for Me • Serenade

WE'RE CIVILIZED? (OB)
November 8, 1962 (22)
Music by Ray Haney
Lyrics by Alfred Aiken

Brewing the Love Potion • Too Old • J.B. Pictures, Inc. • Everything Is Wonderful • Me Atahualpa • No Place to Go • Lullaby Wind • I Like • You Can Hang Your Hat Here • You're Like • Witch Song • Mother Nature • Bad If He Does, Worse If He Don't • Muted • Yankee Stay • We're Civilized

WEST SIDE STORY
September 26, 1957 (732; second run 249)
Music by Leonard Bernstein
Lyrics by Stephen Sondheim

Suggested by Shakespeare's *Romeo and Juliet*

Prologue • Jet Song • Something's Coming • Maria • Tonight • America • Cool • One Hand, One Heart • I Feel Pretty • Somewhere • Gee, Officer Krupke! • A Boy Like That • I Have a Love

RA,VS,SEL

WET PAINT (OB)
April 12, 1965 (16)

Concert Encore (Music and lyrics by Sheldon Harnick) • Neville (Music and lyrics by Tony Geiss) • Cantata (Music by Gerald Alters; lyrics by Herbert Hartig) • Cream in My Coffee (Music by Ed Scott; lyrics by Anne Croswell) • Love Affair (Music by Bob Kessler; lyrics by Martin Charnin) • Unrequited Love March (Music and lyrics by Ronny Graham) • Puns (Music by Gerald Alters; lyrics by Herbert Hartig) • I Know He'll Understand (Music and lyrics by Johnny Myers) • Canary (Music by Stan Davis; lyrics by Giles O'Connor) • Showstopper (Music and lyrics by Johnny Myers) • These Things I Know Are True (Music and lyrics by Jennifer Konecky)

WHAT MAKES SAMMY RUN?
February 27, 1964 (540)
Music and lyrics by Ervin Drake

Based on the novel by Budd Schulberg

A New Pair of Shoes • You Help Me • A Tender Spot • Lites—Camera—Platitude • My Hometown • Monsoon • I See Something • Maybe Some Other Time • You Can Trust Me • A Room Without Windows • Kiss Me No Kisses • I Feel Humble • Something to Live For • Paint a Rainbow • You're No Good • The Friendliest Thing • Wedding of the Year • Some Days Everything Goes Wrong

RA

WHAT'S UP?
November 11, 1943 (63)
Music by Frederick Loewe
Lyrics by Alan Jay Lerner

Miss Langley's School for Girls • From the Chimney to the Cellar • You've Got a Hold on Me • A Girl Is Like a Book • Joshua • Three Girls in a Boat • How Fly Times • My Last Love • You Wash and I'll Dry • The Ill-Tempered Clavichord

WHEN YOU SMILE
October 25, 1925 (49)
Music by Tom Johnstone
Lyrics by Phil Cook

Spanish Moon • Naughty Eyes • One Little Girl • Let's Have a Good Time • Gee, We Get Along • When You Smile • All Work and No Play • Keep Them Guessing • Keep Building Your Castles • Let's Dance and Make Up • Wonderful Rhythm • June • Oh, What a Girl • Wonderful Yesterday • Buy an Extra • She Loves Me

WHERE'S CHARLEY?
October 11, 1948 (792)
Music and lyrics by Frank Loesser

Based on the play *Charley's Aunt* by Brandon Thomas

The Years Before Us • Better Get Out of Here • The New Ashmolean Marching Society and Students' Conservatory Band • My Darling, My Darling • Make a Miracle • Serenade With Asides • Lovelier Than Ever • The Woman in His Room • Pernambuco • Where's Charley? • Once in Love With Amy • The Gossips • At the Red Rose Cotillion

RA,VS,SEL

THE WHIRL OF SOCIETY
March 5, 1912 (136)
Music by Louis A. Hirsch
Lyrics by Harold Atteridge

Four o'Clock Tea • Fol de Rol • I'm Saving My Kisses • My Sumurun Girl • How Do You Know? • I Want Something New to Play With • How Do You Do, Miss Ragtime? • Come Back to Me • Gaby Glide

THE WHITE EAGLE
December 26, 1927 (48)
Music by Rudolf Friml
Lyrics by Brian Hooker

Based on the play *The Squaw Man* by Edwin Milton Royle

Dance, Dance, Dance • Regimental Song • Alone (My Lover) • Gather the Rose • Bad Man Number • Give Me One Hour • Winona • Smile, Darn You, Smile • My Heaven With You • Indian Lullaby • A Home for You

RA

WHITE HORSE INN
October 1, 1936 (223)
Music by Ralph Benatzky
Lyrics by Irving Caesar

Arrival of Tourists • Leave It to Katarina (Music by Jara Benes) • I Cannot Live Without Your Love • White Horse Inn • Blue Eyes (Music by Robert Stolz) • Market Day in the Village • Goodbye, au Revoir, auf Wiedersehn* (Music by Eric Coates) • High Up on the Hills • I Would Love to Have You Love Me (Music by Irving Caesar, Sammy Lerner, and Gerald Marks) • Welcome on the Landing Stage • In a Little Swiss Chalet (Music by Will Irwin; lyrics by Norman Zeno) • Serenade to the Emperor • We Prize Most the Things We Miss • The Waltz of Love (Music by Richard Fall)

RA

WHITE LIGHTS
October 11, 1927 (31)
Music by J. Fred Coots
Lyrics by Al Dubin

Some Other Day • Tappin' the Toe • Deceiving Blue Bird • Don't Throw Me Down • White Lights • I'll

Keep On Dreaming of You • Eyeful of You • Sitting in the Sun • Better Times Are Coming (Music by Jimmie Steiger; lyrics by Dolph Singer)

WHITE LILACS
September 10, 1928 (138)
Music by Karl Hajos (based on Chopin)
Lyrics by Harry B. Smith

The Music Call • Adorable You • Words, Music, Cash • I Love Love • White Lilacs • Far Away and Long Ago • Star in the Twilight • Melodies Within My Heart • Know When to Smile • Castle of Love • I Love You and I Adore You

WHO CARES?
July 8, 1930 (32)
Music by Percy Wenrich
Lyrics by Harry Clark

Believe It or Not • Tennis • Dance of the Fan • Who Cares? • Broadway • Sunup • Dixieland • The Hunt

WHOOPEE
December 4, 1928 (379)
Music by Walter Donaldson
Lyrics by Gus Kahn

Based on the play *The Nervous Wreck* by Owen Davis

It's a Beautiful Day Today • Here's to the Girl of My Heart • I'm Bringing a Red, Red Rose • Gypsy Joe • Makin' Whoopee • Go Get 'Im • Until You Get Somebody Else • Taps • Come West, Little Girl, Come West • Love Me or Leave Me • Song of the Setting Sun • Stetson • Hallowe'en Whoopee Ball

RA,SEL

WHOOP-UP
December 22, 1958 (56)
Music by Moose Charlap
Lyrics by Norman Gimbel

Based on the novel *Stay Away, Joe* by Dan Cushman

Glenda's Place • When the Tall Man Talks • Nobody Throw Those Bull • Love Eyes • Men • Never Before • Caress Me, Possess Me, Perfume • Flattery • The Girl in His Arms • The Best of What the Country's Got • I Wash My Hands • Quarrel-tet • Sorry for Myself • Til the Big Fat Moon Falls Down • What I Mean to Say • Montana • She or Her

RA

WHO'S WHO
March 1, 1938 (23)

Who's Who (Music by Baldwin Bergersen; lyrics by June Sillman) • Skiing at Saks (Music and lyrics by Irvin Graham) • Croupier (Music by Baldwin Bergersen; lyrics by June Sillman) • Rinka Tinka Man (Music by Lew Kesler; lyrics by June Sillman) • Sunday Morning in June (Music by Paul McGrane; lyrics by Neville Fleeson) • I Dance Alone (Music and lyrics by James Shelton) • I Must Waltz (Music by Baldwin Bergersen; lyrics by Irvin Graham) • Dusky Debutante (Music by Baldwin Bergersen; lyrics by June Sillman) • The Girl With the Paint on Her Face (Music and lyrics by Irvin Graham) • Train Time (Music by Baldwin Bergersen; lyrics by June Sillman) • I Must Have a Dinner Coat (Music and lyrics by James Shelton) • It's You I Want (Music by Paul McGrane; lyrics by Al Stillman) • Let Your Hair Down With a Bang (Music by Baldwin Bergersen; lyrics by June Sillman)

WHO'S WHO, BABY? (OB)
January 29, 1968 (16)
Music and lyrics by Johnny Brandon

Island of Happiness • That'll Be the Day • Come-Along-a-Me, Babe • Nothin's Gonna Change • There Aren't Many Ladies in the Mile End Road • Syncopatin' • Voodoo • How Do You Stop Loving Someone? • Drums • Feminine-inity • That's What's Happening, Baby • Me • Nobody to Cry To

WILD AND WONDERFUL
December 7, 1971 (1)
Music and lyrics by Bob Goodman

Wild and Wonderful • My First Moment • I Spy • Desmond's Dilemma • The Moment Is Now • Something Wonderful Can Happen • Chances • Jenny • Fallen Angels • Petty Crime • Come a Little Closer • Is This My Town? • You Can Reach the Sun • A Different Kind of World • Wait for Me

THE WILD ROSE
October 20, 1926 (61)
Music by Rudolf Friml
Lyrics by Otto Harbach and Oscar Hammerstein II

Riviera • Lovely Lady • Brown Eyes • Love Me, Don't You? • It Was Fate • The Wild Rose • Lady of the Rose • One Golden Hour • Our Little Kingdom • Won't You Come Across? • The Coronation

Dropped from production
I'm the Extra Man • How Can You Keep Your Mind on Business? • Rumble, Rumble, Rumble • That's Why I Love You

WILDCAT
December 16, 1960 (172)
Music by Cy Coleman
Lyrics by Carolyn Leigh

I Hear • Hey, Look Me Over • Wildcat • You've Come Home • That's What I Want for Janie • What Takes My Fancy • You're a Liar • One Day We Dance • Give a Little Whistle • Tall Hope • Tippy Tippy Toes • El Sombrero • Corduroy Road

RA,VS,SEL

WILDFLOWER
February 7, 1923 (477)
Music by Vincent Youmans and Herbert Stothart
Lyrics by Otto Harbach and Oscar Hammerstein II

I Love You! I Love You! I Love You! (Music by Youmans) • Some Like to Hunt (Music by Stothart) • Wildflower (Music by Youmans) • Bambalina (Music by Youmans) • I'll Collaborate With You • April Blossoms (Music by Stothart) • The Best Dance I've Had Tonight • Course I Will (Music by Youmans) • Casimo (Music by Stothart) • You Can Never Blame a Girl for Dreaming (Music by Stothart) • Goodbye, Little Rosebud (Music by Stothart) • The World's Worst Women (Music by Stothart) • You Can Always Find Another Partner (Music by Youmans)

Dropped from production
True Love Will Never Grow Cold • Friends Who Understand • Everything Is All Right • If I Told You*

RA,VS

WINGED VICTORY
November 20, 1943 (212)
Music and lyrics by David Rose

My Dream Book of Memories • Winged Victory

Dropped from production
You're So Nice to Remember

WISH YOU WERE HERE
June 25, 1952 (598)
Music and lyrics by Harold Rome

Based on the play *Having Wonderful Time* by Arthur Kober

Camp Karefree • There's Nothing Nicer Than People • Social Director • Shopping Around • Bright College Days • Mix and Mingle • Could Be • Tripping the Light Fantastic • Where Did the Night Go? • Certain Individuals • They Won't Know Me • Summer Afternoon • Don José of Far Rockaway • Everybody Loves Somebody • Wish You Were Here • Relax • Flattery

Dropped from production
Glimpse of Love

RA,VS,SEL

THE WIZ[1]
January 5, 1975 (1672)
Music and lyrics by Charlie Smalls

Based on *The Wizard of Oz* by L. Frank Baum

The Feeling We Once Had • He's the Wizard • Soon as I Get Home • I Was Born on the Day Before Yesterday • Ease On Down the Road • Slide Some Oil to Me • Mean Ole Lion • Kalidah Battle • Be a Lion • So You Wanted to Meet the Wizard • What Would I Do if I Could Feel? • No Bad News • Everybody Rejoice • Funky Monkeys • Who Do You Think You Are? • If You Believe • Y'all Got It! • A Rested Body Is a Rested Mind • Home

RA,SEL

[1] Tony Awards for Best Musical and Best Score

WOMAN OF THE YEAR[1]
March 29, 1981 (770)
Music by John Kander
Lyrics by Fred Ebb

Based on a screenplay by Ring Lardner, Jr. and Michael Kanin

Woman of the Year • The Poker Game • See You in the Funny Papers • When You're Right, You're Right • Shut Up Gerald • So What Else Is New? • One of the Boys • Table Talk • It Isn't Working • I Told You So • I Wrote the Book • Happy in the Morning • Sometimes a Day Goes By • The Grass Is Always Greener • We're Gonna Work It Out

RA,SEL

[1] Tony Award for Best Musical

THE WONDER BAR
March 17, 1931 (86)
Music by Robert Katscher
Lyrics by Irving Caesar

Good Evening, Friends • I'm Falling in Love • Elizabeth • Ma Mère (Music by Harry Warren; lyrics by Al Jolson and Irving Caesar) • Oh, Donna Clara (Music by J. Petersburski) • Something Seems to Tell Me

WONDERFUL TOWN[1]
February 25, 1953 (559)
Music by Leonard Bernstein
Lyrics by Betty Comden and Adolph Green

Based on the play *My Sister Eileen* by Joseph Fields and Jerome Chodorov and the stories by Ruth McKenney

Christopher Street • Ohio • One Hundred Easy Ways • What a Waste • A Little Bit in Love • Pass the Football • Conversation Piece • A Quiet Girl • Conga! • My Darlin' Eileen* • Swing! • It's Love • Wrong Note Rag

RA

[1] Tony Award for Best Score

WOOF, WOOF
December 25, 1929 (45)
Music and lyrics by Edward Pola and Eddie Brandt

I Like It • I'll Take Care of You • That Certain Thing • I Mean What I Say • You're All the World to Me • A Girl Like You • Fair Weather • Shh! • Satanic Strut • Topple Down • Won't I Do? • Why Didn't You Tell Me? • Lay Your Bets

WORKING
May 14, 1978 (25)

Based on the poem "I Hear America Singing" by Walt Whitman

All the Livelong Day* (Music and additional lyrics by Stephen Schwartz) • The Mason (Music and lyrics by Craig Carnelia) • Neat to Be a Newsboy (Music and lyrics by Stephen Schwartz) • Nobody Tells Me How (Music by Mary Rodgers; lyrics by Susan Birkenhead) • Un Mejor Dia Vendra (Music by James Taylor; lyrics by Grace Daniele and Matt Landers) • Just a Housewife (Music and lyrics by Craig Carnelia) • Joe (Music and lyrics by Craig Carnelia) • If I Could've Been (Music and lyrics by Micki Grant) • It's an Art (Music and lyrics by Stephen Schwartz) • Brother Trucker (Music and lyrics by James Taylor) • Fathers and Sons (Music and lyrics by Stephen Schwartz) • Cleanin' Women (Music and lyrics by Micki Grant) • Something to Point To (Music and lyrics by Craig Carnelia) • Lovin' Al (Music and lyrics by Micki Grant)

RA,SEL

Y

THE YANKEE GIRL
February 10, 1910 (92)
Music by Silvio Hein
Lyrics by George V. Hobart

The Yankee Girl • Top of the Morning • Hypnotizing Rag • Where's Mama? • Louisiana Elizabeth • Maid of Sevilla • All, All Alone • I'll Make a Ring Around Rosie • Whoop Daddy Ooden Dooden Day • Nora Malone

THE YANKEE PRINCESS[1]
October 2, 1922 (80)
Music by Emmerich Kálmán
Lyrics by B.G. DeSylva

Lotus Flower • My Bajadere • The Waltz Is Made for Love • Stars of the Stage • Roses, Lovely Roses • In the Starlight • I'll Dance My Way Into Your Heart • I Still Can Dream • A Husband's Only a Husband • Friendship • Eyes So Dark and Luring • Forbidden Fruit • Can It Be That I'm in Love? • Love the Wife of Your Neighbor

[1] European title: *Die Bajadere*

YEAH MAN
May 26, 1932 (2)
Music and lyrics by Al Wilson, Charles Weinberg and Ken Macomber

Mississippi Joys • Gotta Get de Boat Loaded • Dancing Fool • That's Religion (Music and lyrics by Porter Grainger) • At the Barbecue • I'm Always Happy When I'm in Your Arms • I've Got What It Takes • Crazy Idea of Love • Qualifications (Music and lyrics by Porter Grainger) • Come to Harlem • The Spell of Those Harlem Nights • Baby, I Could Do It for You • Shady Dan • Give Me Your Love • Shake Your Music

THE YEARLING
December 10, 1965 (3)
Music by Michael Leonard
Lyrics by Herbert Martin

Based on the novel by Marjorie Kinnan Rawlings

Let Him Kick Up His Heels • Boy Talk • Bear Hunt • Some Day I'm Gonna Fly • Lonely Clearing • Everything in the World I Love • I'm All Smiles • The Kind of Man a Woman Needs • What a Happy Day • Ain't He a Joy? • Why Did I Choose You? • One Promise • Nothing More • Everything Beautiful

SEL

YES, YES, YVETTE
October 3, 1927 (40)

Based on the play *Nothing But the Truth* by James Montgomery

Pack Up Your Blues and Smile (Music by Peter de Rose and Albert Von Tilzer; lyrics by Jo Trent) • My Lady (Music and lyrics by Frank Crumit and Ben Jerome) • Yes, Yes, Yvette (Music by Philip Charig; lyrics by Irving Caesar) • How'd You Like To (Music by Stephen Jones; lyrics by Irving Caesar) • Six o'Clock (Music by Philip Charig; lyrics by Irving Caesar) • Sing, Dance and Smile (Music by Philip Charig; lyrics by Ben Jerome) • Do You Love as I Love? (Music by Joseph Meyer; lyrics by Irving Caesar) • You, or Nobody! (Music and lyrics by Irving Caesar)

YIP, YIP, YAPHANK[1]
August 19, 1918 (32)
Music and lyrics by Irving Berlin

Hello, Hello, Hello • Ding Dong • Dream On, Little Soldier Boy • Bevo • I Can Always Find a Little Sunshine in the Y.M.C.A. • Silver Threads • Oh, How I Hate to Get Up in the Morning* • What a Difference a Uniform Will Make • Kitchen Police • Mandy* • Come Along, Come Along, Come Along • We're On Our Way to France

[1] Performed by soldiers from Camp Upton, New York

YOKEL BOY
July 6, 1939 (208)
Music by Sam Stept
Lyrics by Lew Brown and Charles Tobias

A Boy Named Lem • I Know I'm Nobody • For the Sake of Lexington • Comes Love • It's Me Again • Let's Make Memories Tonight • Time for Jukin' (Music by Walter Kent) • Uncle Sam's Lullaby • Hollywood and Vine • Catherine the Great • The Ship Has Sailed • I Can't Afford to Dream

You Never Know
September 21, 1938 (78)
Music and lyrics by Cole Porter

Based on the play *Candle Light* by Siegfried Geyer

I Am Gaston • Au Revoir, Cher Baron • By Candlelight (Music by Robert Katscher; lyrics by Rowland Leigh) • Maria • You Never Know • Ladies Room (Music by Alex Fogarty; lyrics by Edwin Gilbert) • What Is That Tune? • For No Rhyme or Reason • From Alpha to Omega • Don't Let It Get You Down • What Shall I Do? (Lyrics by Rowland Leigh) • Let's Put It to Music (Music by Alex Fogarty and Edwin Gilbert; lyrics by Edwin Gilbert) • At Long Last Love* • Take Yourself a Trip (Music by Alex Fogarty; lyrics by Edwin Gilbert) • Yes, Yes, Yes • Gendarme (Music by Robert Katscher; lyrics by Rowland Leigh) • No (You Can't Have My Heart) (Music and lyrics by Dana Suesse) • Good Evening, Princess

Dropped from production
I'll Black His Eyes • I'm Yours • What a Priceless Pleasure [The Waiters] • Just One Step Ahead of Love • Ha, Ha, Ha

You Said It
January 19, 1931 (192)
Music by Harold Arlen
Lyrics by Jack Yellen

Wha'd You Come to College For? • You Said It • They Learn About Women From Me • While You Are Young • It's Different With Me • Learn to Croon • Sweet and Hot • If He Really Loves Me • What Do We Care? • You'll Do

You'll See Stars
December 29, 1942 (4)
Music by Leo Edwards
Lyrics by Herman Timberg

Future Stars • Time and Time Again • All You Have to Do Is Stand There • Dancing on a Rainbow • Betcha I Make Good • What a Pretty Baby You Are • Readin', Writin' and Rythmatic

Young Abe Lincoln
April 25, 1961 (27)
Music by Victor Ziskin
Lyrics by Joan Javits

The Same Old Me • Cheer Up! • You Can Dance • Someone You Know • I Want to Be a Little Frog in a Little Pond • Don't P-P-Point Them Guns at Me • The Captain Lincoln March • Run, Indian, Run • Welcome Home Again • Vote for Lincoln • Frontier Politics

RA

Your Own Thing (OB)
January 13, 1968 (937)
Music and lyrics by Hal Hester and Danny Apolinar

Suggested by Shakespeare's *Twelfth Night*

No One's Perfect, Dear • The Flowers • I'm Me! (I'm Not Afraid) • Baby! Baby! • Come Away, Death* • I'm on My Way to the Top • She Never Told Her Love • Be Gentle • What Do I Know? • The Now Generation • The Middle Years • When You're Young and in Love • Hunca Munca • Don't Leave Me • Do Your Own Thing

RA,SEL

You're a Good Man, Charlie Brown (OB)
March 7, 1967 (1,597)
Music and lyrics by Clark Gesner

Based on the comic strip *Peanuts* by Charles M. Schulz

You're a Good Man, Charlie Brown • Schroeder • Snoopy • My Blanket and Me • Kite • Dr. Lucy (The Doctor Is In) • Book Report • The Red Baron • T.E. A.M. (The Baseball Game) • Little Known Facts • Suppertime • Happiness

RA,VS,SEL

You're in Love[1]
February 6, 1917 (167)
Music by Rudolf Friml
Lyrics by Otto Harbach and Edward Clark

Married Life • You're in Love • Keep off the Grass • He Will Understand • Buck Up • Things That They Must Not Do • Snatched From the Cradle • We'll Drift Along • Be Sure It's Light • A Year Is a Long, Long Time • Boola Boo • Loveland • The Musical Snore • I'm Only Dreaming

[1] The show's producer, Arthur Hammerstein, gave his 21-year-old nephew, Oscar II, his first job in the theater—that of assistant stage manager at $20 a week.

Yours Is My Heart[1]
September 5, 1946 (36)
Music by Franz Lehár
Lyrics by Harry Graham

Goodbye, Paree • Free as the Air • Chinese Melody • Patiently Smiling • A Cup of China Tea • Upon a Moonlight Night in May • Love, What Has Given You This Magic Power? • Men of China • Chingo-Pingo • Yours Is My Heart Alone (Lyrics by Harry B. Smith) • Paris Sings Again (Music by Paul Durand) • Ma Petite Chèrie

VS (As *The Land of Smiles*)

[1] Also known as *The Land of Smiles*

Yours Truly
January 25, 1927 (127)
Music by Raymond Hubbell
Lyrics by Anne Caldwell

Follow the Guide • Mayfair • Shuffling Bill • Look at the World and Smile • Somebody Else • The Gunman • Lotus Flower • Quit Kiddin' • Mary Has a Little Fair • Don' Shake My Tree • I Want a Pal • Dawn of Dreams

Z

ZIEGFELD FOLLIES (1907-1918)

Outstanding Songs

FOLLIES OF 1907[1]

July 8, 1907 (70)
Budweiser's a Friend of Mine (Music by Seymour Furth; lyrics by Vincent Bryan) • Handle Me With Care (Music by Jean Schwartz; lyrics by William Jerome) • I Think I Oughtn't Auto Any More (Music by E. Ray Goetz; lyrics by Vincent Bryan) • The Gibson Bathing Girls (Music by Alfred Solomon; lyrics by Paul West) • Bye, Bye, Dear Old Broadway (Music by Gus Edwards; lyrics by Will Cobb)

[1] Although produced by Florenz Ziegfeld, this "Follies," the first in a long series, did not have the producer's name in its title. It was by far the most lavish musical produced on Broadway up to that date, costing the then enormous sum of $13,000. The title "Follies" was derived not from the French "Folies," but from a contemporary newspaper column written by Harry B. Smith, who wrote the libretto of the first show. The European star Anna Held, then Ziegfeld's wife, starred in seven editions of the Ziegfeld Follies. Later stars of the series included Fanny Brice, W.C. Fields, Marilyn Miller, Eddie Cantor, Will Rogers and Nora Bayes.

ZIEGFELD FOLLIES OF 1908

June 15, 1908 (120)

Shine On, Harvest Moon (Music by Nora Bayes and Jack Norworth; lyrics by Jack Norworth) • Song of the Navy (Music by Maurice Levi; lyrics by Harry B. Smith) • Over on the Jersey Side (Music and lyrics by Nora Bayes and Jack Norworth)

ZIEGFELD FOLLIES OF 1910

June 20, 1910 (88)

Swing Me High, Swing Me Low (Music by Victor Hollander; lyrics by Ballard MacDonald) • Goodbye, Becky Cohen (Music and lyrics by Irving Berlin) • Lovie Joe (Music and lyrics by Marion Cook and Joe Jordan)

ZIEGFELD FOLLIES OF 1911

June 26, 1911 (80)
Music and lyrics by Irving Berlin

Woodman, Woodman, Spare That Tree • Dog-Gone That Chilly Man • Ephraham Played Upon the Piano • You've Built a Fire Down in My Heart

ZIEGFELD FOLLIES OF 1912

October 21, 1912 (88)

Row, Row, Row (interpolated) (Music by Jimmy Monaco; lyrics by William Jerome) • In a Pretty Little White House of Our Own (Music by Leo Edwards; lyrics by Blanche Merrill) • Daddy Has a Sweetheart (and Mother Is Her Name) (Music by Dave Stamper; lyrics by Gene Buck)

ZIEGFELD FOLLIES OF 1913

June 16, 1913 (96)

Isle d'Amour (Music by Leo Edwards; lyrics by Earl Carroll)

ZIEGFELD FOLLIES OF 1914

June 1, 1914 (112)
Music by Dave Stamper
Lyrics by Gene Buck

Just You And I and the Moon • Everybody Must Sometime Love Somebody • Without You

ZIEGFELD FOLLIES OF 1915

June 21, 1915 (104)

Hold Me in Your Loving Arms (Music by Louis A. Hirsch; lyrics by Gene Buck) • Hello, Frisco! (Music by Louis A. Hirsch; lyrics by Gene Buck) • A Girl for Each Month of the Year (Music by Louis A. Hirsch; lyrics by Channing Pollock and Rennold Wolf)

ZIEGFELD FOLLIES OF 1916

June 12, 1916 (112)

In Florida Among the Palms (Music and lyrics by Irving Berlin) • Have a Heart* (Music by Jerome

Kern; lyrics by Gene Buck) • When the Lights Are Low (Music by Jerome Kern; lyrics by Gene Buck) • My Lady of the Nile (Music by Jerome Kern; lyrics by Gene Buck) • Ain't It Funny What a Difference a Few Drinks Make? (Music by Jerome Kern; lyrics by Gene Buck) • Bachelor Days (Music by Louis A. Hirsch; lyrics by Gene Buck)

ZIEGFELD FOLLIES OF 1917
June 12, 1917 (111)

That's the Kind of Baby for Me (Music by Jack Egan; lyrics by Alfred Harrison) • In the Beautiful Garden of Girls (Music by Raymond Hubbell; lyrics by Dave Stamper) • Can't You Hear Our Country Calling? (Music by Victor Herbert; lyrics by Gene Buck) • Modern Maiden's Prayer (Music by James Hanley; lyrics by Ballard MacDonald) • Because You're Just You* (Music by Jerome Kern; lyrics by Gene Buck)

ZIEGFELD FOLLIES OF 1918[1]
June 18, 1918 (151)

The Blue Devils of France (Music and lyrics by Irving Berlin) • I'm Gonna Pin a Medal on the Girl I Left Behind (Music and lyrics by Irving Berlin) • I Want to Jazz Dance (Music by Dave Stamper; lyrics by Gene Buck) • When I Hear a Syncopated Tune (Music by Louis A. Hirsch; lyrics by Gene Buck)

[1] The Broadway run ended at the end of World War I and the wartime songs were dropped for the subsequent road tour.

ZIEGFELD FOLLIES OF 1919
June 16, 1919 (171)
Music and lyrics by Irving Berlin

Bevo • Harem Life • I'd Rather See a Minstrel Show • I'm the Guy Who Guards the Harem • Mandy* • A Pretty Girl Is Like a Melody • My Tambourine Girl • A Syncopated Cocktail • The Near Future • The Follies Salad (Music and lyrics by Gene Buck and Dave Stamper) • Sweet Sixteen (Music and lyrics by Gene Buck and Dave Stamper) • The Popular Pests (Music and lyrics by Gene Buck and Dave Stamper) • Tulip Time (Music and lyrics by Gene Buck and Dave Stamper) • Shimmy Town (Music and lyrics by Gene Buck and Dave Stamper) • My Baby's Arms (Music by Harry Tierney; lyrics by Joseph McCarthy) • You Cannot Make Your Shimmy Shake on Tea (Lyrics by Berlin and Rennold Wolf) • You'd Be Surprised

ZIEGFELD FOLLIES OF 1920
June 22, 1920 (123)
Music and lyrics by Irving Berlin

Tell Me, Little Gypsy • The Leg of Nations • On Fifth Avenue • The Syncopated Vamp • Bells • The Girls of My Dreams • Chinese Firecrackers • Come Along Sextette • So Hard to Keep When They're Beautiful (Music by Harry Tierney; lyrics by Joseph McCarthy) • Where Do Mosquitos Go? (Music by Harry Tierney; lyrics by Joseph McCarthy) • Any Place Would Be Wonderful With You (Music and

lyrics by Gene Buck and Dave Stamper) • Mary and Doug (Music and lyrics by Gene Buck and Dave Stamper) • I'm a Vamp From East Broadway (Music and lyrics by Berlin, Bert Kalmar and Harry Ruby) • Venice (Music by Victor Herbert; lyrics by Gene Buck) • I Was a Florodora Baby (Music and lyrics by Ballard MacDonald and Harry Carroll) • I'm an Indian (Music by Leo Edwards; lyrics by Blanche Merrill) • Creation (instrumental) (Music by Victor Herbert) • The Love Boat (Music by Victor Herbert; lyrics by Gene Buck)

ZIEGFELD FOLLIES OF 1921
June 21, 1921 (119)

The Legend of the Cyclamen Tree (Music by Victor Herbert; lyrics by Gene Buck) • Second Hand Rose (Music by James Hanley; lyrics by Grant Clarke) • Plymouth Rock (Music by Dave Stamper; lyrics by Channing Pollock) • Scotch Lassie (Music by Leo Edwards; lyrics by Blanche Merrill) • Raggedy Rag (Music and lyrics by Gene Buck and Dave Stamper) • Sally, Won't You Come Back (Music and lyrics by Gene Buck and Dave Stamper) • Our Home Town (Music and lyrics by Ballard MacDonald and Harry Carroll) • The Championship of the World (Music by Victor Herbert; lyrics by Gene Buck) • Four Little Girls With a Future and Four Little Girls with a Past (Music by Rudolf Friml; lyrics by B.G. DeSylva) • Bring Back My Blushing Rose (Music by Rudolf Friml; lyrics by Gene Buck) • My Man (Music by Maurice Yvain; lyrics by Channing Pollock) • Every Time I Hear a Band Play (Music by Rudolf Friml; lyrics by Gene Buck) • You Must Come Over (Music by Jerome Kern; lyrics by B.G. DeSylva)

ZIEGFELD FOLLIES OF 1922
June 5, 1922 (541)

Blunderland (Music by Louis A. Hirsch; lyrics by Gene Buck) • 45th Street and Broadway (Music and lyrics by Gene Buck and Dave Stamper) • South Sea Moon (Music and lyrics by Gene Buck and Dave Stamper) • Rambler Rose (Music by Louis A. Hirsch; lyrics by Gene Buck and Dave Stamper) • Throw Me a Kiss (Music by Louis A. Hirsch; lyrics by Gene Buck and Dave Stamper) • It's Getting Dark on Old Broadway (Music and lyrics by Gene Buck and Dave Stamper) • Radio (Music and lyrics by Gene Buck and Dave Stamper) • Mr. Gallagher and Mr. Shean (Music and lyrics by Edward Gallagher and Al Shean) • Weaving (Music by Victor Herbert; lyrics by Gene Buck) • Bring On the Girls (Music and lyrics by Gene Buck and Dave Stamper)

ZIEGFELD FOLLIES OF 1923
October 20, 1923 (233)
Music and lyrics by Gene Buck and Dave Stamper

Glorifying the Girls • Old Fashioned Garden (Music by Victor Herbert; lyrics by Buck) • Broadway Indians • I Wonder How They Got That Way • What Thrills Can There Be? (Music by Stamper; lyrics by Harry Ruskin) • Shake Your Feet • Ben Ali Haggin (Music by Rudolf Friml; lyrics by Buck) • Chansonette* (Music by Rudolf Friml; lyrics by

Dailey Paskman, Sigmund Spaeth and Irving Caesar • Legends of the Drums (Music by Victor Herbert; lyrics by Buck) • Little Old New York (Music by Victor Herbert; lyrics by Buck) • I'm Bugs Over You • I'd Love to Waltz Through Life With You (Music by Victor Herbert; lyrics by Buck) • Swanee River Blues

ZIEGFELD FOLLIES (1927)
August 16, 1927 (168)
Music and lyrics by Irving Berlin

Ribbons and Bows • Shaking the Blues Away • Ooh, Maybe It's You • Rainbow of Girls • It All Belongs to Me • It's Up to the Band • Jimmy • Learn to Sing a Love Song • Tickling the Ivories • Jungle Jingle

ZIEGFELD FOLLIES (1931)[1]
July 1, 1931 (165)

Bring On the Follies Girls (Music by Dave Stamper; lyrics by Gene Buck) • Help Yourself to Happiness (Music by Harry Revel; lyrics by Harry Richman and Mack Gordon) • Sunny Southern Smile (Music by Harry Revel; lyrics by Mack Gordon) • Half-Caste Woman (Music and lyrics by Noël Coward) • Broadway Reverie (Music by Dave Stamper; lyrics by Gene Buck) • Was I? (Music by Chick Endor; lyrics by Charles Farrell) • Cigarettes, Cigars! (Music by Harry Revel; lyrics by Mack Gordon) • Do the New York (Music by Ben Oakland; lyrics by Jack Murray and Barry Trivers) • Mailu (Music by Jay Gorney; lyrics by E.Y. Harburg) • Changing of the Guards (Music by Ben Oakland; lyrics by Jack Murray and Barry Trivers) • Here We Are in Love (Music by Ben Oakland; lyrics by Jack Murray and Barry Trivers) • Wrapped Up in You (Music by Ben Oakland; lyrics by Jack Murray and Barry Trivers)

[1] This was the last edition of the series produced by Ziegfeld, who died July 22, 1932.

ZIEGFELD FOLLIES (1934)
January 4, 1934 (182)
Music by Vernon Duke
Lyrics by E.Y. Harburg

Smart to Be Smart • That's Where We Come In (Music by Samuel Pokrass) • Soul Saving Sadie (Music by Joseph Meyer; lyrics by Billy Rose and Ballard MacDonald) • Water Under the Bridge • Barefoot Boy (Music by James F. Hanley; lyrics by Chris Taylor) • I Like the Likes of You • What Is There to Say? • To the Beat of My Heart (Music by Samuel Pokrass) • Countess Dubinsky (Music by Joseph Meyer; lyrics by Billy Rose and Ballard MacDonald) • Suddenly (Lyrics by Harburg and Billy Rose) • Moon About Town (Music by Dana Suesse) • This Is Not a Song (Lyrics by Harburg and E. Hartman)

ZIEGFELD FOLLIES (1936)[1]
January 30, 1936 (227)
Music by Vernon Duke
Lyrics by Ira Gershwin

Time Marches On! • He Hasn't a Thing Except Me •

My Red-Letter Day • Island in the West Indies • Words Without Music • The Economic Situation • Fancy, Fancy • Maharanee • The Gazooka • That Moment of Moments • Sentimental Weather • Five a.m. • I Can't Get Started* • Modernistic Moe • Dancing to Our Score (Lyrics by Gershwin and Billy Rose)

[1] The choreography for Vernon Duke's "5 a.m." was by George Balanchine, his Broadway debut. Later in the same season he was to choreograph Rodgers' and Hart's *On Your Toes* and soon afterward their *Babes In Arms*.

ZIEGFELD FOLLIES (1943)
April 14, 1943 (553)
Music by Ray Henderson
Lyrics by Jack Yellen

Thirty-five Summers Ago • This Is It • Love Songs Are Made in the Night • Come Up and Have a Cup of Coffee • The Saga of Carmen • Swing Your Lady, Mr. Hemingway • Back to the Farm (Music and lyrics by Bud Burtson) • Hindu Serenade • The Micromaniac (Music and lyrics by Harold Rome) • Hold That Smile

ZIEGFELD FOLLIES (1957)
March 1, 1957 (123)

Bring On the Girls (Music and lyrics by Richard Myers and Jack Lawrence) • If You Got Music (Music by Colin Romoff; lyrics by David Rogers) • Mangoes (Music and lyrics by Dee Libbey and Sid Wayne) • I Don't Wanna Rock (Music by Colin Romoff; lyrics by David Rogers) • Intoxication (Music by Dean Fuller; lyrics by Marshall Barer) • Music for Madame (Music and lyrics by Jack Lawrence and Richard Myers) • Two a Day on the Milky Way (Music by Dean Fuller; lyrics by Marshall Barer) • Salesmanship (Music by Philip Springer; lyrics by Carolyn Leigh) • Honorable Mambo (Music by Dean Fuller; lyrics by Marshall Barer) • The Lover in Me (Music by Philip Springer; lyrics by Carolyn Leigh) • Miss Follies of 192- (Music and lyrics by Herman Hupfeld) • Make Me (Music and lyrics by Tony Velone, Larry Spier and Uhpio Minucci) • An Element of Doubt (Music by Sammy Fain; lyrics by Howard Dietz) • My Late, Late Lady (Music by Dean Fuller; lyrics by Marshall Barer) • Miss Follies (Music by Colin Romoff; lyrics by David Rogers)

Dropped from production
A Pretty Girl (Is Like a Pretty Girl) (Music by Richard Lewine; lyrics by Arnold B. Horwitt)

ZORBÁ
November 17, 1968 (305)
Music by John Kander
Lyrics by Fred Ebb

Based on the novel *Zorbá the Greek* by Nikos Kazantzakis

Life Is • The First Time • The Top of the Hill • No Boom Boom • Vive la Différence • The Butterfly • Goodbye, Canavaro • Grandpapa • Only Love •

Y'assou • Why Can't I Speak? • The Crow • Happy Birthday • I Am Free

Added to 1983 revival
Mine Song • Woman • That's a Beginning

RA,SEL

THE ZULU AND THE ZAYDA
November 10, 1965 (179)
Music and lyrics by Harold Rome

Based on a story by Dan Jacobson

Tkambuza • Crocodile Wife • Good to Be Alive • The Water Wears Down the Stone • Rivers of Tears • Like the Breeze Blows • Oisgetzaychnet • Some Things • Zulu Love Song • L'Chayim • Cold, Cold Room

RA,SEL

Chronology

Chronology

1911

The Hen Pecks
The Pink Lady
La Belle Paree
Ziegfeld Follies of 1911
The Fascinating Widow
The Little Millionaire
Gypsy Love
The Enchantress
The Quaker Girl

1912

Modest Suzanne
The Whirl of Society
The Count of Luxembourg
Oh! Oh! Delphine
Ziegfeld Follies of 1912
The Lady of the Slipper
The Red Petticoat
The Firefly

1913

The Sunshine Girl
The Honeymoon Express
The American Maid
Ziegfeld Follies of 1913
Sweethearts
Oh, I Say!
The Madcap Duchess
High Jinks

1914

Sari
Ziegfeld Follies of 1914
The Girl From Utah
Chin-Chin
The Only Girl
The Debutante
Watch Your Step

1915

Ninety in the Shade
Nobody Home
Ziegfeld Follies of 1915
The Blue Paradise
‧The Princess Pat
Miss Information

Katinka
Very Good Eddie
Stop! Look! Listen!

1916

See America First
Ziegfeld Follies of 1916

1917

Have a Heart
Love o' Mike
You're in Love
Oh, Boy!
Eileen
Ziegfeld Follies of 1917
Maytime
Leave It to Jane
The Riviera Girl
Jack o' Lantern
Chu Chin Chow
Miss 1917
Going Up

1918

Oh, Lady! Lady!!
Sinbad
Toot-Toot!
The Rainbow Girl
Rock-a-Bye Baby
Ziegfeld Follies of 1918
Yip, Yip, Yaphank
Sometime
Oh, My Dear!
Listen, Lester

1919

She's a Good Fellow
La, La, Lucille
Ziegfeld Follies of 1919
Apple Blossoms
The Little Whopper
Irene
Morris Gest Midnight Whirl

1920

The Night Boat
George White's Scandals

Ziegfeld Follies of 1920
Poor Little Ritz Girl
Mary
Hitchy-Koo
Sally

1921

Two Little Girls in Blue
The Last Waltz
Shuffle Along
Ziegfeld Follies of 1921
George White's Scandals
Tangerine
Music Box Revue (1st edition)
Blossom Time
The O'Brien Girl
Good Morning, Dearie

1922

The Blue Kitten
For Goodness Sake
The Rose of Stamboul
Ziegfeld Follies of 1922
George White's Scandals
The Gingham Girl
Orange Blossoms
The Lady in Ermine
The Yankee Princess
Music Box Revue (2nd edition)
Up She Goes
Little Nellie Kelly
The Bunch and Judy
Our Nell
Rose Briar
The Clinging Vine

1923

Wildflower
George White's Scandals
Helen of Troy, New York
Little Jessie James
Poppy
Music Box Revue (3rd edition)
Battling Buttler
Ziegfeld Follies of 1923
Runnin' Wild
Stepping Stones
The Rise of Rosie O'Reilly

Mary Jane McKane
Kid Boots

1924

Charlot's Revue
Lollipop
Sweet Little Devil
Sitting Pretty
I'll Say She Is
George White's Scandals
The Dream Girl
The Chocolate Dandies
Rose Marie
Be Yourself
Dear Sir
Lady, Be Good!
Music Box Revue (4th edition)
The Student Prince

1925

Big Boy
The Love Song
China Rose
Puzzles of 1925
Natja
Sky High
Louie the 14th
Bringing Up Father
Mercenary Mary
Tell Me More
The Garrick Gaieties (1st edition)
Lucky Sambo
Kosher Kitty Kelly
George White's Scandals
Artists and Models
Earl Carroll's Vanities
June Days
Gay Paree
Captain Jinks
No, No, Nanette
Dearest Enemy
The Vagabond King
Sunny
Merry-Merry
Holka-Polka
When You Smile
The City Chap
Florida Girl
Princess Flavia

Naughty Cinderella
Charlot's Revue
Mayflowers
Oh! Oh! Nurse
The Cocoanuts
The Greenwich Village Follies
By the Way
Tip-Toes
Song of the Flame

1926

A Night in Paris
Hello, Lola
Sweetheart Time
The Matinee Girl
Bunk of 1926
Rainbow Rose
The Girl Friend
Bad Habits of 1926
Kitty's Kisses
The Garrick Gaieties (2nd edition)
The Great Temptations
The Merry World
George White's Scandals
The Grand Street Follies
No Foolin'
My Magnolia
The Blonde Sinner
Bare Facts
Americana
Nic-Nax
Earl Carroll's Vanities
Castles in the Air
Queen High
Naughty Riquette
Countess Maritza
The Ramblers
Honeymoon Lane
Happy Go Lucky
Deep River
Criss-Cross
Katja
The Wild Rose
Oh, Kay!
Gay Paree
Twinkle, Twinkle
The Desert Song
Oh, Please!
Peggy-Ann

Betsy

1927

The Nightingale
The Lace Petticoat
Piggy
Bye Bye, Bonnie
Yours Truly
Rio Rita
Judy
Polly of Hollywood
The New Yorkers
Lucky
Rufus Lemaire's Affairs
Cherry Blossoms
Lady Do
The Circus Princess
Hit the Deck
The Seventh Heart
A Night in Spain
Oh, Ernest!
The Grand Street Follies
Tales of Rigo
Merry-Go-Round
Talk About Girls
Bottomland
Padlocks
Africana
Rang-Tang
Kiss Me
Allez-Oop
The Manhatters
Ziegfeld Follies
A La Carte
Footlights
Good News
Half a Widow
My Maryland
Enchanted Isle
The Merry Malones
Manhattan Mary
Yes, Yes, Yvette
Sidewalks of New York
My Princess
The Five o'Clock Girl
Just Fancy
White Lights
The Love Call
A Connecticut Yankee

Artists and Models
Funny Face
Take the Air
Harry Delmar's Revels
Golden Dawn
Happy
The White Eagle
Show Boat
Lovely Lady

1928

She's My Baby
Rosalie
The Optimists
The Madcap
Sunny Days
Parisiana
Rain or Shine
Keep Shufflin'
The Three Musketeers
The Greenwich Village Follies
Present Arms
Here's Howe
Blackbirds
The Grand Street Follies
Say When
George White's Scandals
Earl Carroll's Vanities
Good Boy
White Lilacs
Luckee Girl
Cross My Heart
The New Moon
Chee-Chee
Billie
Paris
Just a Minute
Ups-a-Daisy
Hold Everything!
Three Cheers
Animal Crackers
Americana
Hello, Yourself!
This Year of Grace
Treasure Girl
Rainbow
Angela
Whoopee
The Red Robe

The Houseboat on the Styx
Hello, Daddy

1929

Deep Harlem
Polly
Follow Thru
Ned Wayburn's Gambols
Boom-Boom
Lady Fingers
Fioretta
Pleasure Bound
Spring Is Here
Music in May
Messin' Around
The Little Show (1st edition)
The Grand Street Follies
Pansy
A Night in Venice
Keep It Clean
Bamboola
Hot Chocolates
Earl Carroll's Sketch Book
Show Girl
Broadway Nights
John Murray Anderson's Almanac
Sweet Adeline
The Street Singer
Cape Cod Follies
George White's Scandals
June Moon
Great Day!
Bitter Sweet
Heads Up!
Sons o' Guns
The Silver Swan
Fifty Million Frenchmen
Top Speed
Woof, Woof
Wake Up and Dream

1930

Strike Up the Band
Ripples
Nine-Fifteen Revue
Simple Simon
Lew Leslie's International Revue
Flying High
Jonica

Three Little Girls
The Garrick Gaieties (3rd edition)
Change Your Luck
Artists and Models
Mystery Moon
Earl Carroll's Vanities
Who Cares?
Hot Rhythm
The Second Little Show
Luana
Nina Rosa
Fine and Dandy
Brown Buddies
Princess Charming
Girl Crazy
Three's a Crowd
Blackbirds
The Vanderbilt Revue
The Well of Romance
Hello, Paris
Sweet and Low
Smiles
The New Yorkers
Ballyhoo
Meet My Sister

1931

You Said It
Private Lives
The Gang's All Here
America's Sweetheart
The Wonder Bar
Rhapsody in Black
Crazy Quilt
The Third Little Show
The Band Wagon
Ziegfeld Follies
Shoot the Works
Earl Carroll's Vanities
Free for All
The Singing Rabbi
George White's Scandals
Fast and Furious
Singin' the Blues
Nikki
Everybody's Welcome
The Cat and the Fiddle
East Wind
The Laugh Parade

Here Goes the Bride
The Social Register
Sugar Hill
Of Thee I Sing

1932

A Little Racketeer
Through the Years
Face the Music
Marching By
Hot-Cha!
Blackberries
There You Are
Yeah Man
Hey Nonny Nonny!
Smiling Faces
Ballyhoo
Flying Colors
Earl Carroll's Vanities
Americana
Tell Her the Truth
Music in the Air
The Dubarry
George White's Music Hall Varieties
Take a Chance
Gay Divorce
The Great Magoo
Walk a Little Faster
Shuffle Along

1933

Pardon My English
Melody
Strike Me Pink
Hummin' Sam
Tattle Tales
Shady Lady
Murder at the Vanities
Hold Your Horses
As Thousands Cheer
Let 'Em Eat Cake
Roberta
She Loves Me Not
Blackbirds

1934

Ziegfeld Follies
Come of Age

All the King's Horses
New Faces
Caviar
Keep Moving
Life Begins at 8:40
Saluta
The Great Waltz
Conversation Piece
Say When
Anything Goes
Revenge With Music
Calling All Stars
Fools Rush In
The O'Flynn
Thumbs Up!
Music Hath Charms

1935

Petticoat Fever
Something Gay
Parade
Earl Carroll's Sketch Book
Smile at Me
At Home Abroad
Porgy and Bess
Jubilee
Provincetown Follies
Jumbo
May Wine
George White's Scandals
Entre-Nous

1936

The Illustrators' Show
Ziegfeld Follies
Murder in the Old Red Barn
On Your Toes
Broadway Sho-window
Summer Wives
New Faces
White Horse Inn
Red, Hot and Blue!
Forbidden Melody
Johnny Johnson
Tonight at 8:30
Black Rhythm
The Show Is On

1937

Naughty-Naught
Frederika
Babes in Arms
Orchids Preferred
Sea Legs
Swing It
Virginia
A Hero Is Born
The Fireman's Flame
I'd Rather Be Right
Pins and Needles
Hooray for What!
Between the Devil
Three Waltzes

1938

The Cradle Will Rock
Right This Way
Who's Who
I Married an Angel
You Never Know
Hellzapoppin
Sing Out the News
Knickerbocker Holiday
The Girl From Wyoming
Leave It to Me
The Boys From Syracuse
Great Lady

1939

Mamba's Daughters
Set to Music
One for the Money
Stars in Your Eyes
Sing for Your Supper
The Streets of Paris
Yokel Boy
George White's Scandals
The Straw Hat Review
The Man Who Came to Dinner
Too Many Girls
Very Warm for May
Swingin' the Dream
Du Barry Was a Lady
Two for Tonight

1940

Earl Carroll's Vanities

Two for the Show
Higher and Higher
American Jubilee
Keep Off the Grass
Louisiana Purchase
Walk With Music
Hold On to Your Hats
Boys and Girls Together
Cabin in the Sky
Tis of Thee
Panama Hattie
Pal Joey!
Meet the People
All in Fun

1941

Night of Love
Crazy With the Heat
Lady in the Dark
Best Foot Forward
Viva O'Brien
Let's Face It!
High Kickers
Sons o' Fun
Sunny River
Banjo Eyes

1942

The Lady Comes Across
Of V We Sing
By Jupiter
Star and Garter
This Is the Army
Count Me In
Beat the Band
Artists and Models
New Faces
You'll See Stars

1943

Something for the Boys
Oklahoma!
Ziegfeld Follies
Early to Bed
My Dear Public
Bright Lights
Hairpin Harmony
One Touch of Venus

What's Up?
Winged Victory
Carmen Jones

1944

Jackpot
Mexican Hayride
Follow the Girls
Allah Be Praised!
Helen Goes to Troy
Dream With Music
Song of Norway
Bloomer Girl
Sadie Thompson
Seven Lively Arts
Laffing Room Only
Sing Out, Sweet Land
On the Town

1945

A Lady Says Yes
Up in Central Park
The Firebrand of Florence
Carousel
Memphis Bound
Marinka
Mr. Strauss Goes to Boston
Carib Song
Polonaise
The Girl From Nantucket
Are You With It?
The Day Before Spring
Billion Dollar Baby

1946

Nellie Bly
Lute Song
The Duchess Misbehaves
Three to Make Ready
St. Louis Woman
Call Me Mister
Annie Get Your Gun
Around the World
Yours Is My Heart
Happy Birthday
Park Avenue
If the Shoe Fits
Toplitzky of Notre Dame

Beggar's Holiday

1947

Street Scene
Finian's Rainbow
Brigadoon
Barefoot Boy With Cheek
The Medium
Louisiana Lady
Music in My Heart
Under the Counter
High Button Shoes
Allegro
Angel in the Wings

1948

Make Mine Manhattan
Look Ma, I'm Dancin'!
Inside U.S.A.
Hold It!
Ballet Ballads
Sleepy Hollow
Small Wonder
Heaven on Earth
Magdalena
Love Life
Where's Charley?
As the Girls Go
My Romance
Lend an Ear
Kiss Me, Kate

1949

Along Fifth Avenue
All for Love
South Pacific
Miss Liberty
Touch and Go
Lost in the Stars
Regina
Texas, Li'l Darlin'
Gentlemen Prefer Blondes

1950

Happy as Larry
Alive and Kicking
Dance Me a Song

Arms and the Girl
The Consul
Great to Be Alive
Peter Pan
Tickets Please
The Liar
Michael Todd's Peep Show
Pardon Our French
Call Me Madam
Guys and Dolls
Bless You All
Out of This World

1951

The King and I
Make a Wish
A Tree Grows in Brooklyn
Flahooley
Courtin' Time
Seventeen
Two on the Aisle
Top Banana
Paint Your Wagon

1952

Paris '90
Three Wishes for Jamie
Shuffle Along
New Faces
Wish You Were Here
Buttrio Square
My Darlin' Aïda
Two's Company

1953

Hazel Flagg
Maggie
Wonderful Town
Can-Can
Me and Juliet
Carnival in Flanders
Kismet
John Murray Anderson's Almanac

1954

The Girl in Pink Tights
The Threepenny Opera

By the Beautiful Sea
The Golden Apple
The Pajama Game
The Boy Friend
I Feel Wonderful
Peter Pan
Fanny
Sandhog
Mrs. Patterson
Hit the Trail
House of Flowers

1955

Plain and Fancy
Silk Stockings
Shoestring Revue
Ankles Aweigh
Phoenix '55
Damn Yankees
Seventh Heaven
Catch a Star!
The Vamp
Pipe Dream

1956

My Fair Lady
Mr. Wonderful
The Most Happy Fella
The Littlest Revue
Shangri-La
New Faces
By Hex
Shoestring '57
Li'l Abner
Girls of Summer
Cranks
Bells Are Ringing
Candide
Happy Hunting

1957

Ziegfeld Follies
Shinbone Alley
Livin' the Life
New Girl in Town
Simply Heavenly
West Side Story
Copper and Brass

Jamaica
Rumple
Time Remembered
The Music Man

1958

The Body Beautiful
Oh Captain!
Portofino
Say, Darling
Goldilocks
Diversions
Salad Days
Flower Drum Song
Of Mice and Men
Whoop-Up

1959

She Shall Have Music
Redhead
Juno
First Impressions
Destry Rides Again
Once Upon a Mattress
The Nervous Set
Fallout
Gypsy
The Billy Barnes Revue
Happy Town
At the Drop of a Hat
Take Me Along
The Girls Against the Boys
The Sound of Music
Little Mary Sunshine
Fiorello!
Saratoga

1960

Parade
Beg, Borrow or Steal
The Crystal Heart
Russell Patterson's Sketch Book
Greenwillow
Miss Emily Adam
Bye Bye Birdie
From A to Z
The Fantasticks
Ernest in Love

Christine
Vintage '60
Greenwich Village U.S.A.
Irma la Douce
Valmouth
Kittiwake Island
The Shoemaker and the Peddler
Tenderloin
The Unsinkable Molly Brown
Camelot
Wildcat
Do Re Mi

1961

Show Girl
The Conquering Hero
The Tiger Rag
Double Entry
13 Daughters
The Happiest Girl in the World
Hobo
The Decameron
Carnival
Smiling, the Boy Fell Dead
Young Abe Lincoln
Donnybrook!
The Billy Barnes People
The Sap of Life
Sail Away
Milk and Honey
Let It Ride!
How to Succeed in Business Without
    Really Trying
Do You Know the Milky Way?
Kwamina
O Marry Me!
Kean
All in Love
The Gay Life
'Toinette
Sing Muse!
All Kinds of Giants
Subways Are for Sleeping
Madame Aphrodite

1962

The Banker's Daughter
A Family Affair
New Faces

Fly Blackbird
No Strings
All American
I Can Get It for You Wholesale
King of the Whole Damn World
A Funny Thing Happened on the Way to
    the Forum
Bravo Giovanni
Sweet Miani
Stop the World—I Want to Get Off
Come On Strong
O Say Can You See!
Mr. President
We're Civilized?
Nowhere to Go But Up
Little Me
Never Too Late
Riverwind

1963

Oliver!
Tovarich
Man in the Moon
Sophie
Hot Spot
She Loves Me
Put It in Writing
The Beast in Me
The Student Gypsy
Here's Love
Morning Sun
The Prince and the Pauper
Ballad for Bimshire
Jennie
110 in the Shade
The Streets of New York
The Girl Who Came to Supper

1964

Hello, Dolly
Rugantino
Jo
Foxy
The Amorous Flea
What Makes Sammy Run?
Cindy
Funny Girl
Anyone Can Whistle
High Spirits

Café Crown
Home Movies
Fade Out—Fade In
Fiddler on the Roof
That 5 A.M. Jazz
Golden Boy
The Secret Life of Walter Mitty
Ben Franklin in Paris
Something More
Bajour
I Had a Ball
Babes in the Wood

1965

Kelly
Baker Street
Do I Hear a Waltz?
Wet Paint
Half a Sixpence
Flora, the Red Menace
The Roar of the Greasepaint—The
    Smell of the Crowd
Pickwick
Mackey of Appalachia
Drat! The Cat!
On a Clear Day You Can See Forever
The Zulu and the Zayda
Great Scot!
Skyscraper
Man of La Mancha
Anya
The Yearling
La Grosse Valise

1966

The Mad Show
Sweet Charity
Jonah
Pousse-Café
It's a Bird, It's a Plane, It's Superman
A Time for Singing
Mame
The Apple Tree
Autumn's Here
Man With a Load of Mischief
Cabaret
Walking Happy
I Do! I Do!
A Joyful Noise

The Penny Friend
At the Drop of Another Hat

1967

The Golden Screw
You're a Good Man, Charlie Brown
Sherry!
Illya Darling
Hallelujah, Baby!
Now Is the Time for All Good Men
Henry, Sweet Henry
Curley McDimple
How Now, Dow Jones
How to Be a Jewish Mother

1968

Love and Let Love
Your Own Thing
The Happy Time
Jacques Brel Is Alive and Well and
    Living in Paris
Darling of the Day
Who's Who, Baby?
Golden Rainbow
Here's Where I Belong
The Education Of H*y*m*a*n
    K*a*p*l*a*n
I'm Solomon
Hair
New Faces
The Believers
Walk Down Mah Street!
The Happy Hypocrite
How to Steal an Election
Her First Roman
Maggie Flynn
Zorba
Promises, Promises
Ballad for a Firing Squad
God Is a (Guess What?)
Dames at Sea

1969

The Fig Leaves Are Falling
Horseman, Pass By
Celebration
Get Thee to Canterbury
Red, White and Maddox

Canterbury Tales
Dear World
Paradise Gardens East
1776
Come Summer
Billy
Promenade
Oh! Calcutta!
Man Better Man
Salvation
Jimmy
Buck White
Sambo
La Strada
Gertrude Stein's First Reader
Coco

1970

Unfair to Goliath
The Last Sweet Days of Isaac
Joy
Gantry
Georgy
Billy Noname
Show Me Where the Good Times Are
Operation Sidewinder
Purlie
Minnie's Boys
Look to the Lilies
Applause
Cry for Us All
Park
Mod Donna
Company
Colette
The Rothschilds
Sensations
The President's Daughter
Touch
Two by Two
The Me Nobody Knows
Lovely Ladies, Kind Gentlemen

1971

Stag Movie
Soon
Ari
Follies
Six

70, Girls, 70
Frank Merriwell, or Honor Challenged
The Ballad of Johnny Pot
Earl of Ruston
Godspell
Leaves of Grass
Jesus Christ Superstar
Ain't Supposed to Die a Natural Death
To Live Another Summer
The Grass Harp
Love Me, Love My Children
Twigs
Two Gentlemen of Verona
Wild and Wonderful
Inner City
Anne of Green Gables

1972

Wanted
Grease
The Selling of the President
Sugar
Don't Bother Me, I Can't Cope
Different Times
Don't Play Us Cheap
Heathen
Joan
Dude
Hurry, Harry
Pippin
Ambassador
Lysistrata
Doctor Selavy's Magic Theatre
The Contrast
Via Galactica
The Bar That Never Closes
Rainbow

1973

Shelter
A Little Night Music
Seesaw
The Karl Marx Play
Cyrano
Smith
The Faggot
Raisin
Molly
Gigi

More Than You Deserve

1974

Let My People Come
Lorelei
Rainbow Jones
Fashion
Sextet
Over Here!
Ride the Winds
The Magic Show
Mack and Mabel
Gay Company

1975

The Wiz
Shenandoah
Diamond Studs
Lovers
Man on the Moon
The Night That Made America Famous
Goodtime Charley
The Rocky Horror Show
The Lieutenant
Doctor Jazz
Be Kind to People Week
Philemon
Chicago
A Chorus Line
Boy Meets Boy
The Robber Bridegroom
Treemonisha
Tuscaloosa's Calling Me But I'm Not
    Going!
Gift of the Magi

1976

Home Sweet Homer
Pacific Overtures
Rockabye Hamlet
Rex
So Long, 174th Street
1600 Pennsylvania Avenue
Something's Afoot
Greenwich Village Follies
Don't Step on My Olive Branch
Music Is

1977

Nightclub Cantata
Starting Here, Starting Now
Movie Buf
On the Lock-In
I Love My Wife
Annie
New York City Street Show
Happy End
Love! Love! Love!
Hot Grog
The Act
Green Pond

1978

On the Twentieth Century
A Bistro Car on the CNR
A History of the American Film
The Best Little Whorehouse in Texas
Angel
Rosa
Runaways
Working
Piano Bar
I'm Getting My Act Together and Taking
    It on the Road
The Coolest Cat in Town
King of Hearts
Platinum
Ballroom
A Broadway Musical

1979

The Grand Tour
My Old Friends
They're Playing Our Song
Sarava
Sweeney Todd
A Day in Hollywood, a Night in the
    Ukraine
Carmelina
Dispatches
The Utter Glory of Morrissey Hall
I Remember Mama
Miss Truth
Sky High
But Never Jam Today
Evita
Sugar Babies
Potholes

God Bless You, Mr. Rosewater
Comin' Uptown

1980

Fourtune
Barnum
Musical Chairs
It's So Nice to Be Civilized
Jazzbo Brown
Charlie and Algernon
Girls, Girls, Girls
Fifth of July
Ka-Boom
Trixie True Teen Detective
Alice in Concert
Onward Victoria

1981

An Evening With Joan Crawford
Real Life Funnies
In Trousers
Bring Back Birdie
Marry Me a Little
Broadway Follies
Maybe I'm Doing It Wrong
    (1st edition)
March of the Falsettos
Woman of the Year
Copperfield
The Moony Shapiro Songbook
Ah, Men
I Can't Keep Running in Place
El Bravo!
Everybody's Gettin' Into the Act
The Life and Times of Nicholas
    Nickleby
Marlowe
Cotton Patch Gospel
Oh, Brother
Merrily We Roll Along
The First
Tomfoolery
Head Over Heels
Dreamgirls

1982

Waltz of the Stork
Francis
Joseph and the Amazing Technicolor
    Dreamcoat
Pump Boys and Dinettes
Lullabye and Goodnight
I Take These Women
Maybe I'm Doing It Wrong
    (2nd edition)
The Evangelist
Bags
Is There Life After High School?
Nine
Little Shop of Horrors
Do Patent Leather Shoes Really Reflect
    Up?
Seven Brides for Seven Brothers
Charlotte Sweet
A Doll's Life
Cats
Upstairs at O'Neal's
Foxfire
Portrait of Jennie
Snoopy

1983

Merlin
Dance a Little Closer
On The Swing Shift
Taking My Turn
Sunday in the Park with George
Preppies
La Cage aux Folles
The Brooklyn Bridge
Up From Paradise
Tallulah
Amen Corner
Blue Plate Special
Marilyn
Doonesbury
Baby
Peg
The Tap Dance Kid
Lenny and the Heartbreakers
The Human Comedy

Index of Films
and Television Productions

Index of Films and Television Productions

ADAM'S RIB (1949) F
Music and lyrics by Cole Porter

Farewell, Amanda*

ALADDIN (1958) TV
Music and lyrics by Cole Porter

Aladdin • Come to the Supermarket • I Adore You • Make Way for the Emperor • No Wonder Taxes Are High • Opportunity Knocks But Once • Trust Your Destiny to a Star • Wouldn't It Be Fun*

ALEXANDER'S RAGTIME BAND (1938) F
Music and lyrics by Irving Berlin

My Walking Stick • Now It Can Be Told

ANDROCLES AND THE LION (1967) TV
Music and lyrics by Richard Rodgers

Don't Be Afraid of an Animal • The Emperor's Thumb • A Fine Young Man • Follow in Our Footsteps • No More Waiting • Strangers • Strength Is My Weakness • Velvet Paws

AROUND THE WORLD IN EIGHTY DAYS (1956) F
Music by Victor Young
Lyrics by Harold Adamson

Around the World in Eighty Days

AT THE CIRCUS (1939) F
Music by Harold Arlen
Lyrics by E.Y. Harburg

Lydia, the Tattooed Lady • Two Blind Loves

THE AWAKENING (1928) F
Music and lyrics by Irving Berlin

Marie

BABES ON BROADWAY (1941) F
Music by Burton Lane
Lyrics by Ralph Freed

How About You

THE BAND WAGON (1953) F
Music by Arthur Schwartz
Lyrics by Howard Dietz

Film version
That's Entertainment

THE BARKLEYS OF BROADWAY (1949) F
Music by Harry Warren
Lyrics by Ira Gershwin

My One and Only Highland Fling • Shoes With Wings On • You'd Be Hard to Replace

THE BATTLE OF PARIS (1929) F
Music and lyrics by Cole Porter

Here Comes the Bandwagon • They All Fall in Love

A BELL FOR ADANO (1956) TV
Music by Arthur Schwartz
Lyrics by Howard Dietz

O.K., Mr. Major • A Bell For Adano • Fish • I'm Part of You • Why Not Surrender?

BLUE SKIES (1946) F
Music and lyrics by Irving Berlin

A Couple of Song and Dance Men • You Keep Coming Back Like a Song

BLUES IN THE NIGHT (1941) F
Music by Harold Arlen
Lyrics by Johnny Mercer

This Time the Dream's on Me • Blues in the Night

BORN TO DANCE (1936) F
Music and lyrics by Cole Porter

Easy to Love* • Entrance of Lucy James • Hey Babe Hey • I've Got You Under My Skin • Love Me, Love My Pekinese • Rap Tap on Wood • Rolling Home • Swingin' the Jinx Away

THE BOYS FROM SYRACUSE (1940) F
Music by Richard Rodgers
Lyrics by Lorenz Hart

Film version
The Greeks Have No Word for It • Who Are You

BROADWAY MELODY OF 1940 (1940) F
Music and lyrics by Cole Porter

Between You and Me • I Concentrate on You •
Please Don't Monkey With Broadway • I've Got My
Eyes on You*

Dropped from film
I Happen to Be in Love • I'm So in Love With You

CABARET (1972) F
Music by John Kander
Lyrics by Fred Ebb

Film version
Maybe This Time • Mein Herr • Money, Money,
Money (Originally titled "The Money Song" in stage
version)

CABIN IN THE SKY (1943) F
Music by Harold Arlen
Lyrics by E.Y. Harburg

Film version
Happiness Is a Thing Called Joe

CAN'T HELP SINGING (1944) F
Music by Jerome Kern
Lyrics by E.Y. Harburg

Any Moment Now • Californi-ay • Can't Help Singing
• Elbow Room • More and More • Swing Your
Sweetheart Round the Fire

Dropped from film
Once in a Million Moons

CAREFREE (1938) F
Music and lyrics by Irving Berlin

Change Partners • I Used to Be Color Blind • The
Night Is Filled With Music • The Yam

CASABLANCA (1942) F
Music and lyrics by Herman Hupfeld

As Time Goes By

Written for the show *Everybody's Welcome* (1931)

CASBAH (1948) F
Music by Harold Arlen
Lyrics by Leo Robin

For Every Man There's a Woman • Hooray for Love
• It Was Written in the Stars • The Monkey Sat in
the Coconut Tree • What's Good About Goodbye?

CAVALCADE (1932) F
Music and lyrics by Noël Coward

Lover of My Dreams (Mirabelle Waltz) • Twentieth
Century Blues

CENTENNIAL SUMMER (1946) F
Music by Jerome Kern
Lyrics by Oscar Hammerstein II

All Through the Day • Cinderella Sue (Lyrics by Leo
Robin) • In Love in Vain • The Right Romance • Two
Hearts Are Better Than One • Up With the Lark

CHECK AND DOUBLE CHECK (1930) F
Music by Bert Kalmar
Lyrics by Harry Ruby

Three Little Words

CHRISTMAS HOLIDAY (1944) F
Music and lyrics by Frank Loesser

Spring Will Be a Little Late This Year

CINDERELLA (1957) TV
Music by Richard Rodgers
Lyrics by Oscar Hammerstein II

Cinderella March (instrumental) • Do I Love You
Because You're Beautiful? • Gavotte • Impossible •
In My Own Little Corner • A Lovely Night • The
Prince Is Giving a Ball • Stepsisters' Lament • Ten
Minutes Ago • Waltz for a Ball • When You're
Driving Through the Moonlight • Your Majesties

THE COUNTRY GIRL (1954) F
Music by Harold Arlen
Lyrics by Ira Gershwin

Dissertation on the State of Bliss • It's Mine, It's
Yours • The Search Is Through

COVER GIRL (1944) F
Music by Jerome Kern
Lyrics by Ira Gershwin

Cover Girl • Long Ago (and Far Away)* • Make Way
for Tomorrow (Lyrics by Ira Gershwin and E.Y.
Harburg) • Poor John • Put Me to the Test* • The
Show Must Go On • Sure Thing • What I Love to
Hear • Who's Complaining?

Dropped from film
That's the Best of All • Time: the Present • Tropical
Night

THE CUCKOOS (1930) F
Music by Harry Ruby
Lyrics by Bert Kalmar

I Love You So Much

DADDY LONG LEGS (1955) F
Music and lyrics by Johnny Mercer

Something's Got to Give

A DAMSEL IN DISTRESS (1937) F
Music by George Gershwin
Lyrics by Ira Gershwin

A Foggy Day (in London Town) • I Can't Be Bothered Now • Jolly Tar and the Milkmaid • Nice Work If You Can Get It* • Sing of Spring • Stiff Upper Lip • Things Are Looking Up

Dropped from film
Pay Some Attention to Me • Put Me to the Test

DANCING LADY (1933) F
Music by Burton Lane
Lyrics by Harold Adamson

Everything I Have Is Yours • My Dancing Lady (Music by Jimmy McHugh; lyrics by Dorothy Fields) • Rhythm of the Day (Music by Richard Rodgers; lyrics by Lorenz Hart)

DANCING PIRATE (1936) F
Music by Richard Rodgers
Lyrics by Lorenz Hart

Are You My Love? • When You're Dancing the Waltz

THE DANGEROUS CHRISTMAS OF RED RIDING HOOD (1965) TV
Music by Jule Styne
Lyrics by Bob Merrill

My Red Riding Hood

A DATE WITH JUDY (1948) F
Music by Jimmy McHugh
Lyrics by Harold Adamson

It's a Most Unusual Day

DELICIOUS (1931) F
Music by George Gershwin
Lyrics by Ira Gershwin

Blah, Blah, Blah* • Delishious • Katinkitschka • Somebody From Somewhere

Dropped from film
You Started It

DESTRY RIDES AGAIN (1939) F
Music by Frederick Hollander
Lyrics by Frank Loesser

The Boys in the Back Room

EASTER PARADE (1948) F
Music and lyrics by Irving Berlin

Better Luck Next Time • A Couple of Swells • A Fella With an Umbrella • Happy Easter • It Only Happens When I Dance With You • Steppin' Out With My Baby

EVENING PRIMROSE (1966) TV
Music and lyrics by Stephen Sondheim

I Remember • I'm Here • Take Me to the World • When

EVERGREEN (1934) F
Music by Richard Rodgers
Lyrics by Lorenz Hart

Dear, Dear • If I Give in to You

EVERY NIGHT AT EIGHT (1935) F
Music by Jimmy McHugh
Lyrics by Dorothy Fields

I Feel a Song Comin' On (Lyrics by Dorothy Fields and George Oppenheimer) • I'm in the Mood for Love

EXCUSE MY DUST (1951) F
Music by Arthur Schwartz
Lyrics by Dorothy Fields

Spring Has Sprung

THE FARMER TAKES A WIFE (1953) F
Music by Harold Arlen
Lyrics by Dorothy Fields

Today I Love Ev'rybody

THE FIREFLY (1937) F
Music by Rudolf Friml
Lyrics by Robert Wright and George Forrest

Film version
The Donkey Serenade* • A Woman's Kiss • He Who Lives and Runs Away (Lyrics by Gus Kahn)

FLYING DOWN TO RIO (1933) F
Music by Vincent Youmans
Lyrics by Edward Eliscu and Gus Kahn

The Carioca • Flying Down to Rio • Music Makes Me • Orchids In the Moonlight

FOLLOW THE BOYS (1944) F
Music by Jule Styne
Lyrics by Sammy Cahn

I'll Walk Alone

FOLLOW THE FLEET (1936) F
Music and lyrics by Irving Berlin

But Where Are You? • Get Thee Behind Me Satan • I'd Rather Lead a Band • I'm Putting All My Eggs in One Basket • Let Yourself Go • Let's Face the Music and Dance • We Saw the Sea

Dropped from film
Moonlight Memories • With a Smile on My Face

FOOLS FOR SCANDAL (1938) F
Music by Richard Rodgers
Lyrics by Lorenz Hart

Food for Scandal • How Can You Forget? • There's a Boy in Harlem

FORTY-SECOND STREET (1933) F
Music by Harry Warren
Lyrics by Al Dubin

Forty-Second Street • Shuffle Off to Buffalo • Young and Healthy • You're Getting to Be a Habit With Me

FUNNY GIRL (1968) F
Music by Jule Styne
Lyrics by Bob Merrill

Film version
The Roller Skate Rag • Funny Girl • The Swan

THE GAY DIVORCEE (1934) F

Film version
The Continental (Music by Con Conrad; lyrics by Herb Magidson)

Original show title: *Gay Divorce* (Music and lyrics by Cole Porter)

GAY PURR-EE (1962) F
Music by Harold Arlen
Lyrics by E.Y. Harburg

Little Drops of Rain • Paris Is a Lonely Town

GIGI (1957) F
Music by Frederick Loewe
Lyrics by Alan Jay Lerner

Film version
A Toujours • Say a Prayer for Me Tonight* • The Parisians

Film and stage version (1973)
I Remember It Well • I'm Glad I'm Not Young Any More • It's a Bore • The Night They Invented Champagne • Thank Heaven for Little Girls • Waltz at Maxim's (She Is Not Thinking of Me) • Gigi*

GIRL CRAZY (1932) F
Music by George Gershwin
Lyrics by Ira Gershwin

Film version
You've Got What Gets Me

GIRL RUSH (1955) F
Music and lyrics by Hugh Martin and Ralph Blane

An Occasional Man

GIVE A GIRL A BREAK (1953) F
Music by Burton Lane
Lyrics by Ira Gershwin

Applause! Applause! • Give a Girl a Break • In Our United State • It Happens Every Time • Nothing Is Impossible

GIVE US THIS NIGHT (1936) F
Music by Erich Wolfgang Korngold
Lyrics by Oscar Hammerstein II

I Mean to Say I Love You • Laughter in the Air • Music in the Night • My Love and I • Sweet Melody of Night

GOLD DIGGERS (1935) F
Music by Harry Warren
Lyrics by Al Dubin

Lullaby of Broadway*

GOLDWYN FOLLIES (1938) F
Music by George Gershwin
Lyrics by Ira Gershwin

I Love to Rhyme • I Was Doing All Right • Love Walked In • Our Love Is Here to Stay* • Spring Again (Music by Vernon Duke)

GOOD NEWS (1947) F

Film version
The French Lesson (Music by Roger Edens; lyrics by Betty Comden and Adolph Green) • Pass That Peace Pipe (Music and lyrics by Roger Edens, Hugh Martin and Ralph Blane)

GUYS AND DOLLS (1955) F
Music and lyrics by Frank Loesser

Film version
Adelaide • Pet Me, Poppa

HALLELUJAH (1929) F
Music and lyrics by Irving Berlin

Waiting at the End of the Road

HALLELUJAH, I'M A BUM (1933) F
Music by Richard Rodgers
Lyrics by Lorenz Hart

Bumper Found a Grand • Dear June (Postcard Song) • Hallelujah, I'm a Bum* • I Gotta Get Back to New York • I'd Do It Again • Kangaroo Court • Laying the Cornerstone • What Do You Want With Money? • You Are Too Beautiful

Dropped from film
Sleeping Beauty

Both Richard Rodgers and Lorenz Hart played bit parts in the film; Rodgers was a photographer's assistant (non-speaking), and Hart played a bank teller (speaking briefly).

HANS CHRISTIAN ANDERSEN (1952) F
Music and lyrics by Frank Loesser

Anywhere I Wander • I'm Hans Christian Andersen • • The King's New Clothes • No Two People • Thumbelina • Wonderful Copenhagen • The Ugly Duckling

THE HARVEY GIRLS (1946) F
Music by Harry Warren
Lyrics by Johnny Mercer

On the Atchison, Topeka and the Santa Fe*

HAVE A HEART (1934) F
Music by Jimmy McHugh
Lyrics by Dorothy Fields

Thank You for a Lovely Evening

HERE COME THE WAVES (1944) F
Music by Harold Arlen
Lyrics by Johnny Mercer

Ac-cent-tchu-ate the Positive • I Promise You • Let's
Take the Long Way Home

HERE IS MY HEART (1934) F
Music by Lewis E. Gensler
Lyrics by Leo Robin

Love Is Just Around the Corner

HIGH SOCIETY (1956) F
Music and lyrics by Cole Porter

High Society Calypso • I Love You, Samantha* •
Little One • Mind If I Make Love to You • Now You
Has Jazz • True Love • Who Wants to Be a
Millionaire? • You're Sensational • Well, Did You
Evah!*

Dropped from film
Caroline • Let's Vocalize • So What?*

HIGH TOR (1956) TV
Music by Arthur Schwartz
Lyrics by Maxwell Anderson

John Barleycorn • A Little Love, a Little While •
Living One Day At a Time • Once Upon a Long Ago
• Sad Is The Life • When You're In Love

HIGH, WIDE AND HANDSOME (1937) F
Music by Jerome Kern
Lyrics by Oscar Hammerstein II

Allegheny Al • Can I Forget You? • The Folks Who
Live on the Hill • He Wore a Star* • High, Wide and
Handsome • The Things I Want • Will You Marry Me
Tomorrow, Maria?

Dropped from film
Grandma's Song

HIGHER AND HIGHER (1943) F
Music by Jimmy McHugh
Lyrics by Harold Adamson

A Lovely Way to Spend an Evening

HIT THE DECK F

Film version (1929)
Keepin' Myself for You (Music by Vincent
Youmans; lyrics by Sidney Clare)

Film version (1955)
The Lady From the Bayou (Music by Vincent
Youmans; lyrics by Leo Robin)

HOLIDAY INN (1942) F
Music and lyrics by Irving Berlin

Abraham • Be Careful, It's My Heart • Happy
Holiday • White Christmas* • You're Easy to Dance
With

HOLLYWOOD CANTEEN (1944) F
Music by Burton Lane
Lyrics by Ted Koehler

What Are You Doing the Rest of Your Life • Don't
Fence Me In (Music and lyrics by Cole Porter)

HOLLYWOOD PARTY (1934) F
Music by Richard Rodgers
Lyrics by Lorenz Hart

Hello • Hollywood Party • Reincarnation (Lyrics by
Lorenz Hart and Jimmy Durante)
Dropped from film
Black Diamond • Burning • Give a Man a Job • I'm a
Queen in My Own Domain • I'm One of the Boys •
Keep Away From the Moonlight • The Mahster's
Coming • My Friend the Night • The Pots • Prayer* •
Yes Me • You Are • You've Got That

HOLLYWOOD REVUE OF 1929 (1929) F
Music by Nacio Herb Brown
Lyrics by Arthur Freed

Singin' in the Rain*

THE HOT HEIRESS (1931) F
Music by Richard Rodgers
Lyrics by Lorenz Hart

Like Ordinary People Do • Nobody Loves a Riveter •
You're the Cats

Dropped from film
He Looks So Good to Me

I COULD GO ON SINGING (1963) F
Music by Harold Arlen
Lyrics by E.Y. Harburg

I Could Go on Singing

I DREAM TOO MUCH (1935) F
Music by Jerome Kern
Lyrics by Dorothy Fields

I Dream Too Much • I Got Love • I'm the Echo
(You're the Song that I Sing) • Jockey on the
Carousel

I'LL TAKE ROMANCE (1937) F
Music by Ben Oakland
Lyrics by Oscar Hammerstein II

I'll Take Romance

THE JOY OF LIVING (1938) F
Music by Jerome Kern
Lyrics by Dorothy Fields

A Heavenly Party • Just Let Me Look at You •
What's Good About Good Night? • You Couldn't Be
Cuter

JUNIOR MISS (1957) TV
Music by Burton Lane
Lyrics by Dorothy Fields

I'll Buy It • Junior Miss • Let's Make It Christmas All Year Round

KISS ME STUPID (1964) F
Music by George Gershwin
Lyrics by Ira Gershwin

All songs, with the exception of "Sophia," were taken from the manuscripts of George Gershwin, who died on July 11, 1937.

Sophia* • All the Livelong Day (and the Livelong Night) • I'm a Poached Egg

LADY, BE GOOD (1941) F
Music by Jerome Kern
Lyrics by Oscar Hammerstein II

The Last Time I Saw Paris*

LADY IN THE DARK (1944) F
Music by Jimmy Van Heusen
Lyrics by Johnny Burke

Film version
Suddenly, It's Spring

THE LADY OBJECTS (1938) F
Music by Ben Oakland
Lyrics by Oscar Hammerstein II

Home in Your Arms • A Mist Is Over the Moon • When You're in the Room • That Week in Paris

LES GIRLS (1957) F
Music and lyrics by Cole Porter

Ca C'est L'Amour • Ladies in Waiting • Les Girls • Why Am I So Gone about That Girl? • You're Just Too, Too

Dropped from film
Drinking Song • High Flyin' Wings on My Shoes • I Could Kick Myself • Is It Joy? • My Darling Never Is Late • My Little Piece o' Pie • Per Favore • What Fun • You're the Prize Guy of Guys

LET'S FALL IN LOVE (1934) F
Music by Harold Arlen
Lyrics by Ted Koehler

Let's Fall in Love • Love is Love Anywhere • This Is Only the Beginning

THE LITTLE PRINCE (1975) F
Music by Frederick Loewe
Lyrics by Alan Jay Lerner

Be Happy • Closer and Closer and Closer • I Need Air • I Never Met a Rose • I'm on Your Side • It's a Hat • Little Prince (From Who Knows Where) • A Snake in the Grass • Why Is the Desert (Lovely to See)? • You're a Child

LOVE AFFAIR (1939) F
Music by Harold Arlen
Lyrics by Ted Koehler

Sing My Heart

LOVE ME TONIGHT (1932) F
Music by Richard Rodgers
Lyrics by Lorenz Hart

Isn't It Romantic? • Love Me Tonight • Lover* • Mimi • The Poor Apache • The Son of a Gun Is Nothing But a Tailor • That's the Song of Paree • A Woman Needs Something Like That

Dropped from film
The Man for Me (The Letter Song)

MAIN STREET TO BROADWAY (1953) F
Music by Richard Rodgers
Lyrics by Oscar Hammerstein II

There's Music in You

MANHATTAN MELODRAMA (1934) F
Music by Richard Rodgers
Lyrics by Lorenz Hart

The Bad in Every Man*

MEET ME IN ST. LOUIS (1944) F
Music and lyrics by Hugh Martin and Ralph Blane

The Boy Next Door • Have Yourself a Merry Little Christmas • The Trolley Song

MEN OF THE SKY (1931) F
Music by Jerome Kern
Lyrics by Otto Harbach

Boys March • Every Little While • Stolen Dreams • You Ought to See Sweet Marguerite

MISSISSIPPI (1935) F
Music by Richard Rodgers
Lyrics by Lorenz Hart

Down by the River • It's Easy to Remember • Roll Mississippi • Soon

Dropped from film
The Notorious Colonel Blake • Pablo, You Are My Heart • The Steely Glint in My Eye

MR. IMPERIUM (1951) F
Music by Harold Arlen
Lyrics by Dorothy Fields

Andiamo • Let Me Look at You • My Love and My Mule

NANA (1934) F
Music by Richard Rodgers
Lyrics by Lorenz Hart

That's Love*

NEPTUNE'S DAUGHTER (1949) F
Music and lyrics by Frank Loesser

Baby, It's Cold Outside*

NEVER GO TO ARGENTINA (1941) F
Music by Richard Rodgers
Lyrics by Lorenz Hart

Never Go to Argentina

NEW YORK, NEW YORK (1977) F
Music by John Kander
Lyrics by Fred Ebb

New York, New York

THE NIGHT IS YOUNG (1935) F
Music by Sigmund Romberg
Lyrics by Oscar Hammerstein II

The Night Is Young • There's a Riot in Havana •
When I Grow Too Old to Dream

THE NORTH STAR (1943) F
Music by Aaron Copland
Lyrics by Ira Gershwin

Younger Generation

ON A CLEAR DAY YOU CAN SEE FOREVER (1969) F
Music by Burton Lane
Lyrics by Alan Jay Lerner

Film version
Go to Sleep • Love With All the Trimmings

ON THE AVENUE (1937) F
Music and lyrics by Irving Berlin

Girl on the Police Gazette • He Ain't Got Rhythm •
I've Got My Love to Keep Me Warm • Slumming on
Park Avenue • This Year's Kisses • You're Laughing
At Me

Dropped from film
On the Avenue

ONE NIGHT IN THE TROPICS (1940) F
Music by Jerome Kern
Lyrics by Dorothy Fields

Back in My Shell • Remind Me* • You and Your
Kiss • Your Dream (Is the Same as My Dream)
(Lyrics by Oscar Hammerstein II and Otto Harbach)

OUT OF THIS WORLD (1945) F
Music by Harold Arlen
Lyrics by Johnny Mercer

Out of This World

PAINT YOUR WAGON (1969) F
Music by André Previn
Lyrics by Alan Jay Lerner

Film version
The Best Things in Life Are Dirty • The First Thing
You Know • Gold Fever • The Gospel of No Name
City • A Million Miles Away Behind the Door

PARIS (1930) F
Music and lyrics by Cole Porter

Film version
Which

THE PETTY GIRL (1950) F
Music by Harold Arlen
Lyrics by Johnny Mercer

Fancy Free

THE PHANTOM PRESIDENT (1932) F
Music by Richard Rodgers
Lyrics by Lorenz Hart

The Convention • The Country Needs a Man • Give
Her a Kiss • Somebody Ought to Wave a Flag

THE PIRATE (1948) F
Music and lyrics by Cole Porter

Be a Clown • Love of My Life • Mack the Black •
Nina • You Can Dance With Any Girl at All

Dropped from film
Manuela • Martinique • Voodoo

PUTTIN' ON THE RITZ (1929) F
Music and lyrics by Irving Berlin

Puttin' on the Ritz • With You

REACHING FOR THE MOON (1930) F
Music and lyrics by Irving Berlin

Reaching for the Moon

RECKLESS (1935) F
Music by Jerome Kern
Lyrics by Oscar Hammerstein II

Reckless

RIO RITA (1942) F
Music by Harold Arlen
Lyrics by E.Y. Harburg

Film version
Long Before You Came Along

ROBERTA (1935) F
Music by Jerome Kern

Film version
I Won't Dance (Lyrics by Otto Harbach, Dorothy
Fields, Oscar Hammerstein II and Jimmy McHugh) •
Lovely to Look At (Lyrics by Dorothy Fields and
Jimmy McHugh)

THE ROGUE SONG (1930) F
Music by Herbert Stothart
Lyrics by Clifford Grey

The Rogue Song • When I'm Looking at You • The
White Dove (Music by Franz Lehar and Herbert
Stothart)

ROMANCE ON THE HIGH SEAS (1948) F
Music by Jule Styne
Lyrics by Sammy Cahn

It's Magic

ROSALIE (1937) F
Music and lyrics by Cole Porter

Close • In the Still of the Night • It's All Over But the Shouting • I've a Strange New Rhythm in My Heart • • Spring Love Is in the Air • Who Knows? • Why Should I Care?

Dropped from film
A Fool There Was • I Know It's Not Meant For Me • To Love or Not to Love

ROSE MARIE F

Film version (1936)
Music by Herbert Stothart
Lyrics by Gus Kahn

Just for you • Pardon Me, Madame

Film version (1954)
Music by Rudolf Friml
Lyrics by Paul Francis Webster

Free To Be Free • I Have The Love • Love and Kisses • The Right Place for a Girl

ROYAL WEDDING (1951) F
Music by Burton Lane
Lyrics by Alan Jay Lerner

Ev'ry Night at Seven • Happiest Day of My Life • How Could You Believe Me When I Said I Love You When You Know I've Been a Liar All My Life • I Left My Hat in Haiti • Open Your Eyes • Too Late Now • What a Lovely Day for a Wedding • You're All the World to Me

SECOND FIDDLE (1939) F
Music and lyrics by Irving Berlin

I Poured My Heart Into a Song

SHALL WE DANCE (1937) F
Music by George Gershwin
Lyrics by Ira Gershwin

Let's Call the Whole Thing Off • Beginner's Luck • Shall We Dance • Slap That Bass • They All Laughed • They Can't Take That Away From Me • Walking the Dog (instrumental)*

Dropped from film
Hi-Ho! • Wake Up, Brother and Dance

THE SHOCKING MISS PILGRIM (1947) F
Music by George Gershwin
Lyrics by Ira Gershwin

Adapted by Kay Swift and Ira Gershwin from manuscripts of George Gershwin.

Aren't You Kind of Glad We Did? • The Back Bay Polka • Changing My Tune • Demon Rum • For You, for Me, for Evermore • One, Two, Three • Stand Up and Fight • Sweet Packard • Waltzing Is Better Sitting Down

Dropped from film
Tour of the Town

SHOW BOAT (1936) F
Music by Jerome Kern
Lyrics by Oscar Hammerstein II

Film version
Ah Still Suits Me • Gallivantin' Around • I Have the Room Above

SILK STOCKINGS (1957) F
Music and lyrics by Cole Porter

Film version
Fated To Be Mated • Ritz Roll and Rock

THE SINGING KID (1935) F
Music by Harold Arlen
Lyrics by E.Y. Harburg

You're the Cure for What Ails Me

THE SKY'S THE LIMIT (1943) F
Music by Harold Arlen
Lyrics by Johnny Mercer

My Shining Hour • One for My Baby (And One More for the Road)

SOME LIKE IT HOT (1939) F
Music by Burton Lane
Lyrics by Frank Loesser

The Lady's in Love With You

SOMETHING TO SHOUT ABOUT (1943) F
Music and lyrics by Cole Porter

Hasta Luego • I Always Knew • Lotus Bloom • Something to Shout About • Through Thick and Thin • You'd Be So Nice to Come Home To

Dropped from film
Couldn't Be • I Can Do Without Tea in My Teapot • It Might Have Been • Let Doctor Schmet Vet Your Pet • Take It Easy

SONG OF RUSSIA (1944) F
Music by Jerome Kern
Lyrics by E.Y. Harburg

And Russia Is Her Name

SONG OF THE WEST (1930) F
Music by Vincent Youmans
Lyrics by J. Russel Robinson

West Wind

Song of the West was the film version of the show *Rainbow* (1928).

THE SOUND OF MUSIC (1965) F
Music and lyrics by Richard Rodgers

Film version
I Have Confidence in Me • Something Good

SOUTH PACIFIC (1958) F
Music by Richard Rodgers
Lyrics by Oscar Hammerstein II

Dropped from production but in film version
My Girl Back Home

A STAR IS BORN (1954) F
Music by Harold Arlen
Lyrics by Ira Gershwin

Gotta Have Me Go With You • Here's What I'm Here For • It's a New World • Lose That Long Face • The Man That Got Away* • Someone at Last

STAR SPANGLED RHYTHM (1942) F
Music by Harold Arlen
Lyrics by Johnny Mercer

Hit the Road to Dreamland • That Old Black Magic

STATE FAIR (1945) F
Music by Richard Rodgers
Lyrics by Oscar Hammerstein II

All I Owe Ioway • Isn't It Kinda Fun? • It Might as Well Be Spring* • It's a Grand Night for Singing • Our State Fair • That's for Me

Re-make, 1962
Music and lyrics by Richard Rodgers

It's the Little Things in Texas • More Than Just a Friend • Never Say No to A Man • This Isn't Heaven • Willing and Eager

Dropped from film
We Will Be Together

SUNNY (1930) F
Music by Jerome Kern
Lyrics by Otto Harbach and Oscar Hammerstein II

Film version
I Was Alone

SUNNY SIDE UP (1929) F
Music and lyrics by B.G. DeSylva, Lew Brown and Ray Henderson

If I Had a Talking Picture of You • I'm a Dreamer (Aren't We All?) • Sunny Side Up (Music by Ray Henderson; lyrics by B.G. DeSylva and Lew Brown) • Turn on the Heat

SWEET ADELINE (1935) F
Music by Jerome Kern
Lyrics by Oscar Hammerstein II

Film version
Lonely Feet • We Were So Young

SWEET CHARITY (1970) F
Music by Cy Coleman
Lyrics by Dorothy Fields

Film version
It's a Nice Face • My Personal Property

SWING TIME (1936) F
Music by Jerome Kern
Lyrics by Dorothy Fields

Bojangles of Harlem • A Fine Romance • Never Gonna Dance • Pick Yourself Up* • Waltz in Swingtime • The Way You Look Tonight*

TAKE A CHANCE (1933) F
Music by Harold Arlen
Lyrics by Billy Rose and E.Y. Harburg

It's Only a Paper Moon

Originally in the show *The Great Magoo* (1932)

THANK YOUR LUCKY STARS (1943) F
Music by Arthur Schwartz
Lyrics by Frank Loesser

Good Night, Good Neighbor • How Sweet You Are • Ice Cold Katy • I'm Ridin' for a Fall • They're Either Too Young or Too Old • Thank Your Lucky Stars

THAT GIRL FROM PARIS (1937) F
Music by Arthur Schwartz
Lyrics by Edward Heyman

Seal It With a Kiss

THEY MET IN ARGENTINA (1941) F
Music by Richard Rodgers
Lyrics by Lorenz Hart

Amarillo • Cutting the Cane • Lolita • Simpatica

THREE COINS IN THE FOUNTAIN (1954) F
Music by Jule Styne
Lyrics by Sammy Cahn

Three Coins in the Fountain*

THE TIME, THE PLACE AND THE GIRL (1946) F
Music by Arthur Schwartz
Lyrics by Leo Robin

A Gal in Calico • Oh But I Do • Rainy Night in Rio • Through a Thousand Dreams

TO HAVE AND HAVE NOT (1944) F
Music by Hoagy Carmichael
Lyrics by Johnny Mercer

How Little We Know

TOGETHER WITH MUSIC (1955) TV
Music and lyrics by Noël Coward

Ninety Minutes Is a Long, Long Time • Together With Music

TOO MANY GIRLS (1940) F
Music by Richard Rodgers
Lyrics by Lorenz Hart

Film version
You're Nearer

TOP HAT (1935) F
Music and lyrics by Irving Berlin

Cheek to Cheek • Isn't This a Lovely Day • No

Strings • The Piccolino • Top Hat, White Tie and Tails

UNDER YOUR SPELL (1936) F
Music by Arthur Schwartz
Lyrics by Howard Dietz

Under Your Spell

UP IN ARMS (1944) F
Music by Harold Arlen
Lyrics by Ted Koehler

All Out for Freedom • Now I Know • Tess's Torch Song

THE VAGABOND KING F

Film version (1930)
Music and lyrics by Newell Chase, Leo Robin and Sam Coslow

If I Were King

Film version (1956)
Music by Rudolf Friml
Lyrics by Johnny Burke

Bon Jour • This Same Heart • Vive la You

VIENNESE NIGHTS (1930) F
Music by Sigmund Romberg
Lyrics by Oscar Hammerstein II

Goodbye, My Love • I Bring a Love Song • I'm Lonely • You Will Remember Vienna

WHAT A WIDOW! (1930) F
Music by Vincent Youmans
Lyrics by J. Russel Robinson and George Waggner

Love is Like a Song • Say "Oui" Chérie

The film *What a Widow!* starred Gloria Swanson and was produced by Joseph P. Kennedy, father of John F. Kennedy.

WHEN YOU'RE IN LOVE (1937) F
Music by Jerome Kern
Lyrics by Dorothy Fields

Our Song • Whistling Boy

WHERE DO WE GO FROM HERE? (1945) F
Music by Kurt Weill
Lyrics by Ira Gershwin

The Nina, the Pinta, the Santa Maria • All at Once

THE WIZARD OF OZ (1939) F
Music by Harold Arlen
Lyrics by E.Y. Harburg

Ding Dong! The Witch Is Dead • Follow the Yellow Brick Road • If I Only Had a Brain (A Heart) (The Nerve) • If I Were the King of the Forest • The Jitterbug • Merry Old Land of Oz • Munchkinland • Over the Rainbow* • We're Off to See the Wizard

YOU WERE NEVER LOVELIER (1942) F
Music by Jerome Kern
Lyrics by Johnny Mercer

Dearly Beloved • I'm Old Fashioned* • On the Beam • The Shorty George • Wedding in the Spring • You Were Never Lovelier

YOU'LL NEVER GET RICH (1941) F
Music and lyrics by Cole Porter

Boogie Bacarolle • Dream Dancing • Shootin' the Works for Uncle Sam • Since I Kissed My Baby Goodbye • So Near and Yet So Far • Wedding Cake-Walk

Dropped from film
A-stairable Rag

ZIEGFELD FOLLIES (1946) F
Music and lyrics by Hugh Martin and Ralph Blane

Love

Index of Composers,
Lyricists and Authors

Index of Composers, Lyricists and Authors